EBERHARD BETHGE

Born in 1909 in Warchau, Eberhard Bethge attended the universities of Königsberg, Berlin, Wien, Tübingen and Halle and obtained the degree of Doctor of Divinity. From 1935 to 1940 he was Assistant to Dietrich Bonhoeffer at the Church College at Finkenwald and other places. In 1953 he came to London as Pastor of the Germans in London where he remained until 1961, apart from a year (1957–1958) which he spent as Visiting Lecturer at Harvard Divinity School. In 1962 he was awarded the Honorary Degree of D.D. at Glasgow University. In 1961 he became Director of the Institute of Continuing Education for Ministers of the Evangelical Church of the Rhineland at Rengsdorf, until his retirement in 1975. In 1966 he went as Visiting Professor to Chicago Theological Seminary and in 1967 as Fosdick Professor to Union Theological Seminary, New York.

A close friend and relative of Dietrich Bonhoeffer's, he is editor of the German edition of Bonhoeffer's *Collected Works*, edited his *Ethics* and *Letters and Papers from Prison*, and is author of *Bonhoeffer: Exile and Martyr*.

Shortly before his death in 1958 Dr. G. K. A. Bell, Bishop of Chichester, came to see us one evening at 14 St. James's Place. He came to talk over the possibility of our publishing his auto-biography, which contained fascinating material about the part he had played during the war, when he was in contact with the underground movement in Germany who were attempting to overthrow Hitler and bring about a negotiated peace. Suddenly Dr. Bell turned to us and said: 'The man who really knows the inside story of the resistance movement that I was in touch with is Eberhard Bethge. He is writing a biography of Dietrich Bonhoeffer.' Dr. Bell then went on to indicate that Dietrich Bonhoeffer was one of the great men of our time.

We knew very little about him, but we asked Dr. Bell who Bethge was and where he lived. He replied that Bethge was pastor of the Lutheran Church in London, the post that Bonhoeffer himself had held before the war. Next morning we telephoned Pastor Bethge and told him of our interest in Bonhoeffer's biography.

After long years of waiting we published this definitive biography, which is a work of great historical importance. It took Pastor Bethge twenty years to collect, sift and verify the vast mass of material available, on which he freely drew.

This translation was published on 9th April 1970 to commemorate the twenty-fifth anniversary of Dietrich Bonhoeffer's death. To meet this deadline, the publishers assembled under the editorship of Edwin Robertson a distinguished panel of translators: Eric Mosbacher, Peter and Betty Ross, Frank Clarke and William Glen-Doepel. Pastor Bethge and Herr Bissinger of Chr. Kaiser Verlag, the original German publishers, and the late Ronald Gregor Smith gave generously of their time, help and advice to ensure that this translation, which has been slightly shortened, should in every way measure up to the original text. To all who have contributed to the translation of this great work, we tender our grateful thanks.

This is the first paperback edition of this definitive work.

DIETRICH
BONHOEFFER

Theologian · Christian · Contemporary

EBERHARD BETHGE

Translated from the German by

ERIC MOSBACHER
PETER AND BETTY ROSS
FRANK CLARKE
WILLIAM GLEN-DOEPEL

Under the Editorship of

EDWIN ROBERTSON

Collins
FOUNT PAPERBACKS

The original edition of this book was published in Germany
under the same title by Chr. Kaiser Verlag München, 1967

First published in the English translation
by William Collins Sons & Co. Ltd, London
and Harper and Row, Publishers Inc., New York, 1970

First issued in Fount and Harper & Row paperback, 1977
Reprinted 1985

Original German edition © 1967 Chr. Kaiser Verlag München
English translation © 1970 William Collins Sons & Co. Ltd, London,
and Harper & Row, Publishers Inc., New York

Made and printed in Great Britain by
William Collins Sons & Co. Ltd, Glasgow

CONTENTS

Contents

ABBREVIATIONS

Works by Dietrich Bonhoeffer

AB   = *Act and Being* (*Akt und Sein*), E.T., Collins, London, and Harper, New York, 1962.

CD   = *The Cost of Discipleship* (*Nachfolge*), E.T., S.C.M. Press, London, and Macmillan, New York, 1959.

CF   = *Creation and Fall* (*Schöpfung und Fall*), E.T., S.C.M. Press, London, and Macmillan, New York, 1959.

E   = *Ethics* (*Ethik*), E.T., Collins, Fontana, London, and Macmillan, New York, 1964.

GS   = *Gesammelte Schriften*, I-V, 2nd edition, Kaiser Verlag, Munich, 1965-9.
(Extracts from these volumes have been translated into English and appear in: *No Rusty Swords*, Collins, London, and Harper & Row, New York, 1965; *The Way to Freedom*, Collins, London, and Harper & Row, New York, 1966; *Christology*, Collins, London, and Harper & Row, New York, 1966.)

LPP   = *Letters and Papers from Prison* (*Widerstand und Ergebung*), E.T., 3rd edition, S.C.M. Press, London, and Macmillan, New York, 1967.

SC   = *Sanctorum Communio* (title in U.S.A.: *The Communion of Saints*), E.T., Collins, London, and Harper & Row, New York, 1963.

Other Works

CW   = *Christliche Welt.*

DEK $^{KAA}_{KK}$ = *Deutsche Evangelische Kirche*: *Kirchliche Aussenamt* / *Kirchliche Korrespondenz*

EvTh   = *Evangelische Theologie.*

IKDB   = *I Knew Dietrich Bonhoeffer* (*Begegnungen mit Dietrich Bonhoeffer: Ein Almanach*), ed. W.-D. Zimmermann and R. Gregor Smith, E.T., Collins, London, and Harper & Row, New York, 1966.

JK   = *Junge Kirche.*

KD   = *Kirchliche Dogmatik*, Karl Barth.

MW   = *Die mündige Welt*, Vols. I-V, 1955-67.

RGG³   = *Religion in Geschichte und Gegenwart*, 3rd ed.

RKZ   = *Reformierte Kirchenzeitung.*

ThBl	= *Theologische Blatt.*
ThEx(h)	= *Theologische Existenz (Heute).*
ThLZ	= *Theologische Literaturzeitung.*
WA	= *Weimarer Ausgabe,* Martin Luther.
ZThK	= *Zeitschrift für Theologie und Kirche.*
ZZ	= *Zwischen den Zeiten.*

PREFACE TO THE ENGLISH EDITION

PLEASING as it is that this biography is now to be presented to the English-speaking world, twenty-five years ago I should have been astonished if anyone had foretold that interest in Bonhoeffer would become so widespread. What has happened?

A man suffered shipwreck in, with, and because of his country. He saw his church and its claims collapse in ruins. The theological writings that he left consisted of barely accessible fragments. In 1945 only a handful of friends and enemies knew who this young man had been. In Christian Germany other names were in the limelight. When his name began to emerge from the anonymity of his death, theological faculties and churches felt uncertain and did little. To the present day there are still inhibitions in Germany about fully integrating him and what he stood for.

But his former theological publisher assumed his heritage, and it is solely due to its inherent weight that it is now so widely known. Bonhoeffer's reputation has spread far beyond the confines of his country and his confession, and indeed he finds readier acceptance beyond these than he does at home. Thus in the German Federal Republic references to and articles about him are innumerable, but only one book about his theology has appeared, and this quite recently, though in other countries a number of studious works have been published.

Meanwhile there has been a Bonhoeffer fashion everywhere. His theology has been taken to be a variant of Karl Barth's dialecticism. For many years he was regarded as a collaborator in Bultmann's demythologizing programme and finally he was acclaimed as one of the patriarchs of the 'God is dead' theology. Did he also have anything of his own to say? Interest in him came from such different camps and seemed to make such disparate use of him that many doubted the substance and continuity of his thought. In the years since his death attention has continually shifted from the later to the earlier Bonhoeffer, and vice versa. In the process the path has led from rather sensationally presented summaries and their eclectic application to special studies less likely to make a public impact. Scholars are now at work on these in many languages, and they will soon be published—with a substantial contribution from the Catholic side.

Why is interest in this man maintained in a world that shifts from topic to topic with ever greater rapidity? Why is it still increasing now, after a superficial fashion has passed?

Is not the explanation the unusual combination of thinker and man of action, martyr and theologian? Is it not the unity of a man who had an admirable understanding of his own cultural and church tradition but nevertheless accepted the shaking of all foundations and at the same time credibly lived and thought a new Christianity of the future? Does not the conviction that he carries derive from the incompleteness of the man and his answers, because he presents us, not with a finished doctrine, but with an active process of learning? And is this not due to the fact that he preserves such a strong identity through all the complexity of his themes, answers and problems? Does his completely unfashionable renunciation of publicity not fascinate us? Has not a man's humanity here triumphed over its betrayal by the means that he used? It is along these lines that we must probably look for the explanation of the fact that such widespread attention is being paid to his theological contentions, Christian testimony and contemporary actions.

My own contribution to making known his ideas and his life story has a history with many vicissitudes and a logic that became discernible in retrospect. I wished to become a minister, and did not aim at the academic work of a systematician or ecclesiastical historian; and it was only the course taken by my life that led me to work on Bonhoeffer's heritage. In other words, my approach to my subject is not that of a scholar approaching it from outside. I am involved. I must try to use this weakness as my strength. But this state of affairs constitutes a challenge to others to make new and more far-reaching studies.

Perhaps the process of becoming his biographer had already begun when Bonhoeffer once remarked to me in jest at the beginning of the war that I should carefully note something that he had just said—I have, of course, now totally forgotten what it was—so that I might one day have something to write about him. But at the time I did not for one moment imagine that the course of things would one day really make me his biographer.

After his death, when I was faced with the task of arranging the unfinished manuscript of his *Ethics*, my only thought was that it was the duty of a friend to make it accessible to others. The result was the publication of the *Ethics* in 1949. Not till the beginning of the fifties did I show my collection of letters to the publisher, and this led to our hesitant publication of parts of them in *Letters and Papers from Prison*. They began to be talked about, first in Germany, then in Britain and America—and finally, after Robinson's *Honest to God*, also in the Catholic world—with all the distortions and exploitations of modern theological formulations. This led me to publish inaccessible and previously widely scattered published material from Bonhoeffer's pen in the *Collected Works* (published in Germany between 1958 and 1961), so that what he said in *Letters and Papers from Prison* might be seen in the light of its theological and historical roots. It was work on these fragments that eventually led to the idea of writing his life.

My qualification for this task derives from my close personal association with him in the last ten years of his life, and the fact that after his death I came into possession of the greater part of the papers.

In 1935 I entered the newly-founded seminary of the Confessing Church at Zingst (later at Finkenwalde). Its head was Dietrich Bonhoeffer, of whom previously I knew nothing. I became a member of the smaller community that arose within the seminary, the so-called House of Brethren, and remained a member until the dissolution of the Finkenwalde fraternity at the end of 1937. Bonhoeffer then made me inspector of studies, a kind of assistant to him, at one of the two 'collective pastorates'—the way in which the previous method of training for candidates for ordination was continued in disguised form until March 1940. Thus I was uninterruptedly associated with Bonhoeffer's work of training for the Confessing Church and with the history of the latter. A close friendship resulted, with the consequence that wherever he lived and worked I went with him. Thus in 1940 I followed him to Berlin, where I often stayed at his parents' house, and in 1943 married Renate Schleicher, the daughter of Bonhoeffer's sister Ursula, who lived next door. Finally there followed the illegal correspondence that began after Bonhoeffer had survived the first dangerous series of interrogations in the military prison of Tegel and that was one day to lead to world-wide discussion. I also saw him several times in Tegel prison, until contact was finally broken off as a result of my own arrest in October 1944. The Gestapo enquired into my relations with the Schleicher family, but omitted to investigate those with Dietrich Bonhoeffer. Thus I survived.

After his death, the family entrusted me with his unpublished theological work in progress, the surviving parts of his library, and most of his papers. From this there eventually arose the obligation to make accessible material that might serve for a more soundly-based interpretation of his life and work. This obligation arose at the point where his life and work overstepped the private sphere and no longer belonged only to those close to him.

E.B.

PORTRAIT

DIETRICH BONHOEFFER was a powerful man. He inherited his tall stature from his mother's side, the Hases and the big, heavy-limbed Kalckreuths, and his supple strength from his Bonhoeffer ancestors. His movements were short and brisk. He didn't like leisurely walks. A successful jumper and sprinter in his schooldays, he still competed with his students even when he was a university lecturer. He was impatient with illnesses and tried to shorten their duration through the copious use of medicines. In periods of stress he did not hesitate to take pills in order to sleep.

He bought good materials for his clothes and wore suits that seemed appropriate to the country and climate in which he lived, though he did not seek to make an impression with his clothes. He liked to eat well and he knew the specialities of many different regions. He was annoyed when the mushrooms or berries he had collected himself were badly prepared.

His head was round rather than long, but it did not look out of proportion on his broad shoulders. His short nose made his forehead and mouth seem prominent. Bonhoeffer's twin sister inherited the dark hair and large brown eyes of his father, and Dietrich the blond hair and blue eyes of his mother. His hair became thin early in life, and, because of his shortsightedness, he wore glasses which he preferred rimless.

He had inherited the sensitive mouth and the full, but sharply curved lips of his father. Dietrich's smile was very friendly and warm, but you could sometimes see that he enjoyed poking fun. He spoke without any dialect, and his conversation was remarkably fast. In preaching, his speech became heavy, almost hesitant. Although his hands seemed delicately shaped, they were very strong. In conversation he generally played with the signet ring on his left hand which bore the Bonhoeffer crest. When he sat down to play the piano he took the ring off and put it in the left-hand corner of the keyboard.

If he was engaged in difficult negotiations or concentrated writing, he smoked a large number of cigarettes. In conversation he listened very attentively and asked questions in a way that gave the person he was talking to confidence and made him say more than he thought he could. It was unthinkable that Bonhoeffer would deal with a person in a cursory way. He preferred a small gathering to a large party because he was used to devoting himself entirely to the person he was with and identifying with him. He kept a certain distance from others out of respect for their privacy, and he saw to it that he was treated likewise. This made many people think he was haughty. His very manner expressed this clearly. If he was angry, he expressed it in a voice that became softer, not louder. In his family anger was not thought wrong, only indolence. They had a marked sense of the right priorities, but they possessed the quality, ascribed to many Englishmen, of treating the daily routine of life very seriously, whereas the really disturbing things, when everything was at stake, were treated as if they were quite ordinary. The stronger the emotions ran the more necessary it was to dress them in insignificant words and gestures.

Dietrich Bonhoeffer was able to work with total concentration and unhesitatingly set about whatever work had to be done. Yet this ability was accompanied by a willingness to be interrupted and even a craving for company when playing music. He loved chess, bridge and guessing games and demanded that those he played with brought to the game the same will to win; he always gave the benefit of the doubt to his opponent. Even in the most hectic periods of his life he never gave up his breaks for recreation. He liked talking to children and took them seriously. He would throw chocolates from his window to his nephews and nieces who were doing their school work in the garden of the house next door.

Bonhoeffer himself was supposed to have been a particularly intense child. He remained intense in the way he set about everything: reading, writing, making decisions, and going into the reasons for them, helping people or warning them—in short, dealing with whatever was presented to, and asked of, him throughout his crowded career.

PART ONE

The Lure of Theology

CHAPTER ONE

CHILDHOOD AND YOUTH

1906 - 1923

THE twins Dietrich and Sabine were born on 4th February 1906, the sixth and seventh children of a family of eight. Their parents, Karl Bonhoeffer, a professor of psychiatry and neurology, and his wife Paula, *née* von Hase, then lived at Breslau. The family tree shows Swabian, Thuringian and Prussian rather than Silesian roots. The Bonhoeffers came to Schwäbisch-Hall from Nijmegen in Holland in 1513, and were active there as goldsmiths, ministers of religion, doctors and councillors until the time of Dietrich Bonhoeffer's grandfather.

The latter, Friedrich E. P. T. Bonhoeffer (1828-1907), a taciturn man with a taste for simplicity and directness, was President of the High Court at Tübingen when he died. His wife, Julie Bonhoeffer, *née* Tafel (1842-1936), came of a family that played a leading part in Swabian democratic circles in the nineteenth century. Some knew the inside of the royal prisons, an uncle emigrated to America, another became a Swedenborgian and, to Friedrich Bonhoeffer's discomfort, one of them actually read Karl Marx. On 1st April 1933, at the age of ninety-one, Julie Bonhoeffer ostentatiously walked through the S.A. cordon in Berlin that was imposing a boycott of Jewish shops.

The other grandfather, Karl Alfred von Hase (1842-1914), a member of the Supreme Church Council and professor of practical theology at Breslau, was at one time court chaplain at Potsdam, but his reputation was overshadowed by that of his more eminent father, Karl August von Hase (1800-90), the ecclesiastical and dogmatic historian, who was once imprisoned in the Hohenasperg by the King of Württemberg, together with a member of the Tafel family, and was appointed to a professorship at Jena by Goethe, who was the responsible Minister at Weimar at the time, and advised the opposition at the first Vatican Council in Rome in 1870. Karl Alfred's wife, Clara von Hase, *née* Countess Kalckreuth (1851-1903), brought music into the family in a big way—she had been a pupil of Klara Schumann and Franz Liszt—as well as painting—her father Stanislaus and her brother Leopold were among the great German painters of the nineteenth century; among the relatives whom they saw frequently were the Yorck von Wartenburgs, the oldest of whom conducted the celebrated correspondence with Wilhelm Dilthey, while his grandson Peter Yorck played an important part in the 1944 plot against Hitler.

The revolutionary elements in the Tafel heritage were compensated for by the traditional loyalism of the Hases, who took their standards from the Mediterranean south rather than the democratic west. Though not blind to defects in the German monarchical system, they did not criticize the existing social order, and led a full life within it. The national ethos was one of the supreme values in the family, and the high humanist standards that its members demanded of themselves and their children came into no apparent conflict with that ethos. Dietrich's mother was the first to experience a painful breach between it and humanism in the fate of her children.

The fullness of his forebears' lives set Dietrich Bonhoeffer the standards of his own. To it he owed an assurance of judgement and of manner that cannot be acquired in a single generation. He grew up in a family that derived its real education, not from school, but from a deeply-rooted sense of being guardians of a great historical heritage and intellectual tradition. To Dietrich Bonhoeffer this meant learning to understand and respect the ideas and actions of earlier generations. It could lead him, when circumstances required, to conclusions that conflicted with tradition—which, nonetheless, he continued to respect. Eventually it led him to an acceptance of the ineluctable judgement on his forebears' world—though he did not allow this to spoil the pleasure he derived from its sympathetic representatives.

I PARENTS' HOME IN BRESLAU

The Suburbs

The Bonhoeffer children grew up in a spacious house next to the newly-built Breslau mental hospital in the Scheitniger Park. The garden was big enough for them to dig caves and put up tents in. Next to it was a hard tennis court, on which their father played in summer and taught them skating in winter. The house was big enough for a school-room with desks, a hobbies room, and another in which—to the servants' alarm—all sorts of pets were kept, such as lizards, snakes, squirrels and pigeons, as well as collections of beetles and butterflies. Opposite the house was a Catholic cemetery, and from the window the children could watch the funeral cortèges with black-draped horses drawing the hearses. A branch of the Oder was close at hand.

In view of the rapid growth of the family, it was decided to buy a house in the country for the summer holidays, and the choice soon fell on Wölfelsgrund, a remote, wooded valley in the Glatzer Bergland. It was right off the beaten track, and almost the only stranger to disturb their privacy there was an obtuse forestry official who makes an appearance as Gelbstiefel in the novel Bonhoeffer tried to write in his prison cell at Tegel in 1943. To the older children the lookout towers and meadows of Wölfelsgrund became the yardstick by which all subsequent holiday places were measured.

Father

Karl Bonhoeffer was not often in the forefront of his children's lives. His study and consulting room were out of bounds to them. But, notwithstanding all the demands on the time of a university teacher and consulting physician, he never missed the family meals. These were rather ceremonial occasions. The children's table manners were strictly supervised, and they were expected to talk only when asked about events of the day. It was generally their mother who decided which situations in their lives should be brought to their father's notice. But on every holiday in the course of the year he devoted himself to them completely; he would, for instance, have himself invited to share in the meals the girls cooked for their dolls in the nursery. When the older children were small he spent the holidays with them at Wölfelsgrund whenever he could, but in Dietrich's time this was rare, because by then their mother usually took her husband to more distant holiday places.

In spite of his retiring nature, their father was a powerful influence. He always spoke quietly, but his eyes gave an impressiveness to what he said that brooked no contradiction. As his daughter, Christine, once wrote, a lecture by him might end with the words: 'In your place I wouldn't say anything else now, but I advise you to think it over. You can come and talk it over with me again this evening, if you like.' But generally, Christine continued, the children realized that this was a good end to the matter and had no desire to reopen it. 'He was not the kind of father whose beard one could stroke or whom one could call by a pet name, but when he was needed he was as firm as a rock. And how he always knew where the shoe pinched is a mystery to me to the present day.'

Dietrich's twin sister Sabine described her father as follows:

His rejection of the hollow phrase may have made us at times tongue-tied and uneasy, but as a result we could not abide any clichés, gossip, platitudes or pomposity when we grew up . . . Sometimes our papa delighted in making us define concepts, or things, and if we managed to do so clearly, without being vague, he was happy . . . Papa was cautious not to restrict us, if possible not to influence us; he was able to watch and wait for things to grow and did not want to tie us too closely to himself and others.[1]

In his memoirs Karl Bonhoeffer was really describing himself when he wrote about his relations with his colleagues: 'I have always believed that the qualifications for a psychiatrist must include, not only a capacity

1. S. Leibholz, 'Childhood and Home', IKDB. pp. 22 f.

for understanding the state of mind of those with whom one differs, but also a high degree of control of the emotions.'

He taught his children to respect the feelings and opinions of others, to recognize their own limitations and see life in proportion.

By present-day standards the Bonhoeffer household was conducted on an inconceivably lavish scale; but, at the same time, the parental dislike of personal boasting or pretension was strong. Money was never discussed in front of the children. The country house at Wölfelsgrund was spacious and airy, but the domestic arrangements were Spartan, and its successor at Friedrichsbrunn, after the family moved to Berlin, was never wired for electricity. If one of the children dropped a toy on the dirty floor of the railway compartment on the way to the country, their mother was capable of dropping it straight out of the window, but suggestions for improving amenities in the country were ignored. There was never any question of fashionable extravagance, either in dress or in the home.

But, in furthering the children's satisfactory and happy development in the world, nothing was spared. After the birth of the eighth child, their father wrote in his New Year notebook on New Year's Eve 1909:

In spite of having eight children, which surprises many people at the present time, we do not have the feeling that it is too many. The house is spacious, the children have developed normally, we parents are not too old, and we try not to spoil them but to give them a happy childhood.

In 1944, after reading the memoirs of his prospective father-in-law Hans von Wedemeyer, Dietrich Bonhoeffer wrote to his fiancée from prison:

This astringency in the relationship between father and son is a sign of great strength and inner security . . . The people of the present day are generally too feeble, they are afraid of losing their children's love, they degrade themselves to being their comrades and friends, and consequently end up by becoming superfluous to them. To me that kind of upbringing, which is not upbringing, is appalling. I think that in our homes similar ideas prevail on the subject.[2]

Mother

The household over which Paula Bonhoeffer presided had a staff of at least five: a governess for the older children, a nurse for the little ones, a housemaid, a parlourmaid and a cook. Before the First World War there was sometimes a French governess, and later there was also a receptionist for her husband and a chauffeur. She managed everything, sometimes causing outsiders to suspect that it was she who wore the trousers. But closer knowledge disclosed a happy relationship in which each partner adroitly supplemented the strength of the other. At their golden wedding

2. Letter of 22.1.1044.

it was said that in their fifty years of marriage they had not spent a total of one month apart, even counting single days.

Their mother herself gave the children their first schooling. In her youth, with a spirit of independence that was shocking at the time, she had fought for and obtained permission to take the qualifying examination for women teachers. She gave lessons at home to her own children, chiefly the bigger ones, together with the children of some of her husband's professor friends, and at the year's end she was always able to enter her pupils successfully for the state examination, in which they did very well. Thanks to the excellent start she gave them, they were able to miss out whole years at school and eventually take the school-leaving examination at a notably early age, as Dietrich did.

This home teaching of course implied some criticisms of the traditional schooling. The Bonhoeffers did not want to hand their children over to others at an early, impressionable age. One of the family sayings was that Germans had their backs broken twice in the course of their lives; first at school, and then during their military service.

Paula Bonhoeffer was a stimulating and indefatigable mother. She managed to make every task interesting and to help the children over stiles. Without the help of textbooks, she taught them a big repertoire of poems, songs and games. When she was a grandmother she still arranged fairy-story plays for the benefit of her grandchildren at Christmas.

She had never learnt dressmaking but, if one of her daughters' dresses did not fit, she unhesitatingly took to needle and scissors. She designed smocks for her children herself, generally in the Reutlingen style. Anything ready-made was too 'ordinary' for her, and it was unthinkable that she should ever buy anything ready-made for herself.

She was used to getting her own way both with children and with adults, and always found ways and means of doing so. When Klaus, the third son, hesitated to jump into the deep pool at the baths, she simply jumped in herself to show him, though she had never learnt to swim. When a salesman in a store tried eloquently to persuade her that a bath she was thinking of buying was big enough, she insisted on his proving the point by lying down in it himself.

During the difficult 1930s her letters and telephone calls opened many closed doors. Before anyone else knew what to do she had done something to help another of her son's pastor friends, who needed protection. Thanks to her intervention, a number of important church matters were brought to a successful conclusion. It was not easy to put her off! She had a disarming way with her that caused the hesitant and nervous to 'get moving', as she put it.

In spite of the obvious imprint that she brought with her from her home, in church and political matters she was undoctrinaire. She was more interested in people than in nature. On their long walks at Wölfelsgrund or Friedrichsbrunn she took little notice of the scenery, but wanted to listen and to talk. When the immediate problem was solved, she would get completely absorbed in thinking out the next step. In spite of all her energy, she never stifled any sign of initiative in others, but fostered it and encouraged it to develop in its own way.

She was a woman of assured judgement, even in medical matters, to her husband's amusement. She permitted herself to have and to express a wealth of feeling, including religious feeling. She sang Beethoven's Gellert *Lieder* with great enthusiasm, and always with her own metrical inaccuracies. But she regarded mistakes as more forgivable than boredom.

We shall meet many of her character traits again in Dietrich Bonhoeffer.

Brothers and Sisters

The eight children were born in the space of ten years. First came the three brothers: Karl-Friedrich (1899-1957), a brilliant physicist who, besides inheriting his father's scientific ability, also adopted his cautious agnosticism; Walter (1899-1918), who became the family expert on the forest and its creatures, distinguished himself early by his linguistic ability, and was killed in the First World War; and Klaus (1901-45), who became a lawyer, and was believed by his father to be the most difficult but also the most amusing and the most intelligent of his children.

Then came the two 'big' sisters: Ursula (born 1902), a girl of unusual beauty, quick in making necessary decisions, with sound practical common sense; and Christine (1903-65), who quickly outpaced her school-fellows and fellow-students and enjoyed doing so.

Then came the three 'little' ones: Dietrich and Sabine; and lastly, the youngest of them all, naturally rather spoilt, Susanne (born 1909). Because of his healthy constitution Dietrich caused his parents little anxiety. The only known serious illness in his childhood was appendicitis, for which he had an operation in 1917, spending several interesting weeks in Professor Hildebrand's nursing home. He consequently plays a smaller part in his father's annual New Year notes than the other children. He got used to being the strongest and most agile of the three youngest children, but he chivalrously helped and protected the two little girls. In such a large family he hardly felt the need of outside friends, and indeed he seems to have had no special friendships until his student years. When he was a small boy he once attacked a neighbour's child weaker than himself, whose mother expressed the significant suspicion that perhaps the Bonhoeffer children had been brought up to be anti-Semitic. Dietrich's mother replied that her son could not have heard of such a thing in her house.

There was no questioning of parental authority in the Bonhoeffer family, yet the children regarded their nursery years as especially happy. Dishonesty and fibbing were severely punished; in comparison broken window-panes or torn clothes hardly counted. Talents were encouraged at an early age. The children knew that it was not impossible for any of their real wishes to be granted, and when others' wishes came true they were expected to share in the pleasure. What their parents told them to do had to be done without hesitation or argument, and complaining about work or unfair treatment was not tolerated. The children's day followed a disciplined pattern; they always knew where they were, and the routine never struck them as restrictive, for they also knew that their parents arranged happy surprises and outings every now and then.

In later years Dietrich Bonhoeffer sometimes became uneasy about his happy and sheltered upbringing, for he felt that it had withheld some of the darker sides of life from him and isolated him from the socially handicapped. True, the latter were the object of generous gifts and sometimes of special invitations. At an early age his sister Ursula spent weeks living in the home of and doing the housekeeping for a sick former maid whose husband was a drinker. Nevertheless Dietrich was aware of the sheltered life he lived. On a walking tour with his youngest sister when he was a student he once said:

I should like to live an unsheltered life for once. We cannot understand the others. We always have our parents to help us over every difficulty and, however far away we may be from them, that gives us such a shameless security.[3]

This sense of uneasiness accompanied him all the way to his cell at Tegel. In a play he wrote in prison he made a young proletarian reproach his opposite number, a doctor's son, for the security he had enjoyed in life. From his earliest childhood Dietrich Bonhoeffer was accustomed to being the privileged and not the underdog.

In relation to his position in the family, this was true only up to a point, however. This position had some significance for his development, and probably also for his choice of a career. His place in the group of the three 'little ones' gave him all the advantages and disadvantages of the youngest child. It was natural that the sturdy and gifted boy should sometimes try to rival or even surpass his big brothers and, indeed, in one field, music, he did surpass them. Against the background of this secret rivalry, theology, which offered him the prospect of achieving something special of his own, certainly later acted as a spur. The distance between the three groups of children was enhanced by the war, which early familiarized the older group with grim reality while the younger children remained at home.

His exclusion from important areas of experience which his older brothers shared was one of Bonhoeffer's early preoccupations. In a

3. Communication from Susanne Dress.

sermon he preached at the beginning of 1929, when he was a curate in Barcelona, he said:

If I am not mistaken, we can distinguish four groups of people in working Germany at the present day who have arrived at different ethical ideologies as the result of historical development. In the first place, there are those whose period of development and maturation took place before the beginning of the war. Then there are those who were matured by the war, and then the generation of revolutionary youth whose awakening and development took place in the years from 1918 until, let us say, 1923. Finally, we must not forget those to whom the future will belong, those who know war and revolution only by hearsay . . . Thus the rapid sequence of events has created four generations in less than twenty years.[4]

The year 1923 that Bonhoeffer mentions in this passage was that in which he took his school-leaving examination. In a radio talk at the beginning of February 1933, on 'The Leader and the Individual in the Younger Generation', he reiterated the same theme with only minor modifications:

An invisible but uncrossable demarcation line runs between those who were in the war and those only slightly younger than they who awakened and reached maturity during the period of the collapse. This is felt by the younger even more acutely than by the older . . .
Thus the younger were impelled by this contrast with their elder brothers to take an independent stand, not so much to take responsibility for and submit to the existing state of affairs as freely to create a full form of life of their own, based on radical criticism.[5]

One senses that Bonhoeffer is here speaking of his older brothers and himself. Their war experience created a barrier between him and them. They had faced perils of which he knew only by hearsay. The feeling of being cut off from them in this way disappeared, interestingly enough, in 1933, when things grew serious for him too, and he never mentioned the subject of the difference in generations again. But even in later years he still betrayed in his theological and ecclesiastical work a certain desire to explain himself to his sceptical and agnostic brother Karl-Friedrich.

II BERLIN

In 1912 the family moved to Berlin, where Dietrich's father was appointed professor of psychiatry and neurology, the leading position in its field in Germany. Here he became the centre of a circle of colleagues and pupils, many of whom became professors of psychiatry in other German universities. Some of his pupils became friends of the family, such as Krückmann, Kramer, Creutzfeld, Kallmann, Jossmann, Zutt and Roggenbau, and later Scheller and Miss Bormann. Many were

4. GS III, pp. 48-58.
5. GS II, pp. 23f.

forced to leave the country by the political catastrophe of the thirties, while others demonstrated their attachment to the family during the resistance period.[6]

From Berlin the reputation of Karl Bonhoeffer spread in the world of academic psychiatry and neurology. True, he turned the city into a bastion against the invasion of Freud's and Jung's psycho-analysis. Not that he had a closed mind to unorthodox theories, or denied on principle the validity of efforts to investigate unexplored areas of the mind; but he never came into personal contact with Freud.

Ernest Jones, in his biography of Freud, mentions only one distant but unhappy link between the two. Soon after Bonhoeffer began working in Berlin, a contribution of Freud's to a medical encyclopedia on the problems of hysteria was rejected by Bonhoeffer's closest associates.[7] Robert Gaupp, who had been a friend of Karl Bonhoeffer's since their student days and was professor of psychiatry at Heidelberg, offers the following explanation:

It may perhaps seem a striking fact that a man who was a sensitive psychiatrist with a remarkable gift for empathy and who did outstanding work on the nature of hysterical symptom-formation never, so far as I know, took up a specific and categorical position in the controversy about the theories of Freud, Adler, Jung and other 'psycho-analysts'. Psycho-analysis means dispassionate analysis of an individual's mental illness with all the resources of intuitive psychology, accompanied by scrupulous observation. In intuitive psychology and scrupulous observation Bonhoeffer had no superior. But he came from the school of Wernicke, which was solely concerned with the brain, and permitted no departure from thinking in terms of cerebral pathology. He practised the psychology of empathy and understanding on the basis of his natural aptitudes and gifts. Theoretical interpretation of unconscious activity taking place *behind* observed phenomena that might project itself into consciousness was foreign to his approach. Intuition was not alien to him, as his whole life's work shows. But he had no urge to advance into the realm of dark, undemonstrable, bold and imaginative interpretation, where so much has to be assumed and so little can be proved . . .

Bonhoeffer, who was by nature so acute and critical, but was cautious and modest in relation to philosophy, remained within the borders of the empirical world that was accessible to him. There are few scientific workers who at the age of eighty, after a career of more than half a century, have had to retract so little of what they once taught. Bonhoeffer, the scientific worker of 1897, could still be compared with the Bonhoeffer of 1948. He adhered to the course that his experiences of life had caused him cautiously but determinedly to follow.[8]

It is not to be overlooked that in Dietrich Bonhoeffer's later work psycho-analysis—even when it was relevant to his own field of the cure

6. Cf. G. Sterz, 'Karl Bonhoeffer 1868-1948', *Grosse Nervenärzte*, ed. K. Kolle, Vol. 1, 1956, pp. 19-26.
7. E. Jones, *Sigmund Freud, Life and Work*, London. 1958, Vol. II, p. 279.
8. Cf. *Deutsche Zeitschrift für Nervenheilkunde*, Vol. 161, pp. 5 f.

of souls—either plays no part or is dismissed with contempt. Underlying this of course are theological prejudices on the lines of Karl Barth, but paternal influence in the matter cannot be denied. Though he possessed a copy of Jung's *Modern Man in Search of a Soul* (1931), as well as E. Spranger's *Psychologie des Jugendalters*, which he carefully studied, he can hardly have been said to have come to grips with Freud, Adler or Jung. Thus in this matter he remained completely within the limits imprinted on him by his father.

Karl Bonhoeffer was the leading Berlin psychiatrist and neurologist from 1912 until his death in 1948. Thus, like his brothers and sisters, Dietrich Bonhoeffer, in spite of all Swabian, Thuringian and Silesian influences, grew up to be a Berliner, and his eventful life cannot be thought of except against the background of Berlin. All the other places that were important to him in the course of his life, such as Breslau, Tübingen, Barcelona, New York, London, or Finkenwalde, certainly influenced him, but the vital influence was the complex multiplicity of Berlin; imperial and then republican Berlin, and the Berlin that slowly succumbed to Nazism; liberal and ecclesiastical, conservative Berlin and the Berlin that opened itself to all the winds of the twentieth century; Berlin with its academic and proletarian districts, its concert halls and museums; the Berlin of street brawls and political plots. 'I believe that it is now perhaps intellectually the liveliest city in the world, and we are beginning to be the right age to enjoy it', the much-travelled Klaus Bonhoeffer wrote in 1928 to his friend and brother-in-law Hans von Dohnanyi. Dietrich Bonhoeffer was neither born in Berlin nor did he die there, but it was the scene of all the important turning-points in his career and in the development of his ideas. In Berlin he enjoyed all the privileges of his sphere of life, and there eventually he had to put everything at stake because of them.

Brückenallee

At about Easter 1912, when Dietrich was six, the Bonhoeffers moved to their first Berlin home in the Brückenallee, near the Bellevue station. Many professors from the Charité clinic then lived in this district north of the Zoo. The country house at Wölfelsgrund was sold, because it was now too remote, and in 1913 the Bonhoeffers bought a former forester's lodge, more accessible from Berlin, lying at the edge of the woods at Friedrichsbrunn, in the eastern Harz Mountains. It would have been hard to imagine a more delightful refuge during the war years, and in the Second World War it was again an ideal shelter for the family, now enlarged by many grandchildren, and their friends. To Dietrich, Friedrichsbrunn became what Wölfelsgrund had been to his elder brothers. In 1944 he wrote from Tegel:

In my imagination I live a good deal in nature, in the glades near Friedrichsbrunn, or on the slopes from which one can look beyond Treseburg to the Brocken. I lie on my back in the grass, watch the clouds sailing in the breeze across the blue sky, and listen to the rustling of the woods. It is remarkable how greatly these memories of childhood affect one's whole outlook; it would seem to me impossible and unnatural for us to have lived either up in the mountains or by the sea. It is the hills of central Germany, the Harz, the Thuringian forest, the Weserberge, that to me represent nature, that belong to me and have fashioned me.[9]

The chief change in the life of the twins brought about by the move to Berlin was that it corresponded with the beginning of their school-days. Their mother no longer did all the teaching herself, and Käthe Horn, the sister of the governess Maria Horn, was the twins' teacher during the first year. In the autumn of 1913 Dietrich, like his brothers, went to the Friedrich Werder grammar school. In spite of their father's and the older boys' scientific bent, all the boys, and Christine too, went to a classical school as a matter of course.

Dietrich had previously shown occasional signs of nervousness and shyness, and at first he was really unhappy on his way to school, but this soon changed. He was put in the eighth form, and found the work child's play. In his 1915 New Year notes his father wrote: 'Dietrich does his work naturally and tidily. He likes fighting, and does a great deal of it.'

Soon there was no doubt that he did not share the scientific inclina-tions of his elder brothers; instead he liked thrilling books, and made unusual progress in music. Not that his brothers and sisters were un-musical; Klaus later played the 'cello with great sensitivity, and none of his brothers or sisters ever wanted to stay away from the family musical evenings. But in Dietrich's case musical and technical progress at the piano were so combined that for a time both he and his parents thought he might become a professional musician.

He was playing Mozart's sonatas at the age of ten, and at the age of eleven he wrote enthusiastically to his grandmother at Tübingen describing how affected he had been by a performance of the Ninth Symphony conducted by Nikisch. Then came a time when he tried composing his own *Lieder*. When he was in the fifth form he composed a trio on Schubert's song, '*Gute Ruh*', to play to his parents with Klaus and Sabine. He wrote a cantata on the sixth verse of Psalm 42, 'My soul is cast down within me', on which he liked preaching so much in later years. On Saturday evenings he skilfully accompanied *Lieder* by Schubert, Schumann, Brahms and Hugo Wolf sung by his mother and his sister Ursula, who had a good voice. After this, no amount of irregularity by any singer could dismay him. He got used at an early age to playing in company without shyness or embarrassment. When

9. LPP, pp. 130 f.

he was seventeen he and his sister still sang at family and other parties to his accompaniment on the lute.

Thus in his boyhood and youth it was music that gave him a special position at school and among his fellow-students. This was granted to him by his brothers and sisters as well. Only when he came home from a school sports meeting with the victor's laurel wreath round his shoulders did he have to put up with ragging by his big brothers.

The War

When the First World War broke out Dietrich was eight and a half. In his reminiscences Karl Bonhoeffer recalled that time as follows:

We did not really believe that there was going to be a war, even though the encirclement by the Triple Entente was felt to be alarming. All the same, I remember having been given the disquieting feeling in the company of some staff officers in the winter of 1913–14 that the possibility of an early armed clash must be taken into account. But on the whole people comforted themselves with the assurance that the Kaiser, in spite of his tendency to magniloquence and his occasional rhetorical deviations about shining armour and that sort of thing, was undoubtedly a lover of peace at heart, and with the superficial hope that international economic interests with their innumerable interconnections would be sufficient to prevent an armed conflict . . . One particular memory of those agitated days that remains in my mind is that of the evening of the day the British declared war, when we and the three boys were on the Unter den Linden. The enthusiasm of the crowds in the streets and in front of the castle and the government buildings of the previous days had yielded to a gloomy silence, which made the scene extraordinarily oppressive.[10]

To the younger children the outbreak of war was a time of great excitement. At the end of July they were hurriedly brought home after a month's holiday in glorious weather at Friedrichsbrunn. When one of the girls dashed into the house shouting: 'Hurrah, there's a war', she had her face slapped. The first German successes filled Dietrich with boyish enthusiasm. When he was nine he wrote to his parents from Friedrichsbrunn asking them to send him all the newspaper cuttings with news from the front; he had been shown by his big brothers and at school how to stick coloured pins into a map showing the advance of the front line.

Then, when food shortages began, his father praised the unexpected skill he developed as 'messenger and food scout'. He knew the black market prices of all the tastier articles of diet, and his familiarity with the queues outside the shops enabled him to direct the servants to the best places. His letters to his grandmother and to his parents when they were away are full of information about such things as the plums he tracked down somewhere in Halensee, the mushrooms he had dried at

10. K. Bonhoeffer, *Lebenserinnerungen, für die Familie vervielfältigt*, 1946-8, pp. 51 f.

Friedrichsbrunn, the goats kept by the family and the difficulty of feeding them on kitchen refuse only, and the gleaning the children did at Uncle Hans von Hase's rectory farm. When the holidays came, the nanny-goat was taken in the luggage van to Friedrichsbrunn to assure the children's milk supply. The great treat on his birthday was to have an egg beaten up in sugar all to himself. He spent all his pocket money on buying himself a hen. His grand attitude to money had already developed at that early age. One day when he found out that his father was sending bills to his patients, he told him indignantly that it was wrong to take money from the sick.

Gradually the war began making its grim impact on the family. News came of cousins killed in action or severely wounded. The war dragged on, the older brothers, who were still at school, approached military age, and in 1917 Karl-Friedrich and Walter were called up. Because of their numerous contacts, the Bonhoeffers might perhaps have been able to some extent to influence the course of their sons' military career, but the boys insisted on enlisting in the infantry, where the need was greatest. Thus they joined the Fifth Regiment of Guards at Spandau, with no intention of obtaining commissions. With a heavy heart their parents let them do so; they did not want 'to try to play Providence'.

After a short period of training, they were sent to the front. Karl-Friedrich, who had been on the point of going to university, took his physics textbook with him in his haversack. Walter had passed his school-leaving examination with special distinction in German. At home on the last evening before his draft left for the front, his eleven-year-old brother Dietrich sang him his own setting of '*Nun zu guter Letzt geben wir dir jetzt auf die Wandrung des Geleite*' ('Now, at the last, we say God speed on your journey'). 'The next day we saw Walter off at the station. When the train started moving, my mother ran alongside, calling out to Walter: "It's only space that separates us", and for a long time these words moved us deeply.'[11]

Walter was wounded in the advance on 23rd April 1918. He dictated his last letter in the field hospital three hours before his death on 28th April:

Today I had the second operation, which was less pleasant, because deeper fragments had to be removed. Also, afterwards I had to be given two camphor injections—at intervals of course—but I hope that that is the end of the matter. My technique of not thinking about pain had to serve here too. But there are more interesting things in the world at present than my wound. Mount Kemmel and its possible consequences, and today's news of the taking of Ypres, gives us great cause for hope. I dare not think about my poor regiment, so severely did it suffer in the last few days. How are things going with the other officer cadets? I think of you all every minute of the long days and nights.

11. S. Leibholz, op. cit., IKDB, p. 30.

His death seemed to break his mother's spirit. She spent weeks in bed at their next-door neighbours', the Schönes'. His father ceased making entries in his New Year notebook.

In the following October news came that Karl-Friedrich had been wounded, only slightly as it turned out. The seventeen-year-old Klaus was also called up and, after a brief period of training, served as an orderly at General Headquarters at Spa. Thus it came about that he was an eye-witness when Hindenburg, 'as rigid as a statue both in countenance and bearing',[12] left the conference room in which he talked to the Kaiser for the last time before the latter's flight.

The death of his brother Walter and his mother's desperate grief left an indelible mark on the child Dietrich Bonhoeffer. This grief and the way in which his brother died came vividly to mind years later, when Dietrich talked to his students about the reverent conduct of services of national sorrow.

Wangenheimstrasse

At this time the family were already living in the big house in the Grunewald district, 14 Wangenheimstrasse, not far from the Halensee station, to which they had moved in March 1916 and where they remained until 1935. Because of the ever-increasing food shortage they grew vegetables in the garden, but the younger children were also able to use it for playing games they had been unable to play except in their Uncle Hans von Hase's rectory garden. Grunewald developed into a regular professors' quarter, and a number of Karl Bonhoeffer's friends and colleagues lived there, including the physician His, Planck, Hildebrand and the anatomist Hertwig, a pupil of Ernst Haeckel.

The historian Hans Delbrück lived only a few doors away, and every Wednesday evening a distinguished company gathered at his house; it included Harnack, Troeltsch, Meinecke and Herkner. Theodor Heuss, the future President of the Federal Republic, also put in an occasional appearance.

The new school to which the children went also resulted in new friendships, as with the von Dohnanyi children, for instance. Confirmation classes resulted in Gerhard Leibholz's joining the group, which at first consisted of Klaus Bonhoeffer, Justus Delbrück and Hans von Dohnanyi. Dietrich was of course at first too young to join this trio, but it was not long before he grew up enough to do so. Notwithstanding his overriding passion for theology, this kept him in lively contact with other intellectual fields.

Revolution

On the morning of 9th November 1918 Karl Bonhoeffer as usual walked

12. K. Bonhoeffer, op. cit., p. 104.

from the Lehrter station down the Invalidenstrasse to the Charité clinic. He described the occasion in his memoirs as follows:

Raggedly marching parties of troops, mingled with civilians carrying posters with the inscription 'Don't shoot'; pale, famished-looking creatures covered with sweat, gesticulating excitedly and pleading with the soldiers and grabbing the rifles from their hands, in so far as they put up any resistance. On the pavement there were other figures, keeping aloof from all this and perhaps hurrying to their places of work more quickly than usual. No shots were fired. At my clinic the porter, wearing a red rosette, stood facing me on the steps, obviously intending to bar the way to my room, or at any rate to discuss the matter. As I took no further notice of him, but walked past him with the usual greeting and went to my room, he took no further action.[13]

Two months later Dietrich, who was by now nearly thirteen years old, wrote to his grandmother at Tübingen about fighting between government troops and Spartakists after the latter had made two night attacks on the Halensee station:

Early today we heard gunfire. There are some more bangs going on now. Karl-Friedrich has at last been discharged from the Charité. He would like to join in, but mama and papa do not yet agree. At present, thank heaven, the government troops are getting the better of it. Our holidays have been extended to 17th January. Either because of the unrest or because of the coal shortage.[14]

Karl-Friedrich Bonhoeffer supported the Social Democratic Government that came into power as a result of the November revolution. He had become a socialist at the front, and this had already brought him into conflict with other branches of the family outside Berlin. His father let him go his own way, but nevertheless his politics made him something of an outsider in the Wangenheimstrasse. Klaus earnestly set about reading Karl Marx's *Das Kapital*, but he and his friends ended up in the German People's Party and the Democratic Party; Stresemann and Brüning embodied their political hopes. Thus Klaus was a more typical representative than Karl-Friedrich of the family's political outlook at that time.

The November revolution and the period that followed corresponded with the awakening of Dietrich Bonhoeffer's interest in politics. On 10th February 1919 he wrote to his grandmother at Tübingen telling her that 'Scheidemann would become Prime Minister and Ebert provisional President'. In 1919 national passions flared up again when the Allied peace terms were published. 'What do you think of the peace terms?' he anxiously enquired of his parents:

I hardly believe they can be accepted in this form. The demonstrations

13. K. Bonhoeffer, op. cit., p. 105.
14. Letter of 11.1.1919.

would develop into a general movement. True, one must take into account the possibility that the enemy might say that we should get no food supplies until we accepted them. Giving up the Saar and Upper Silesia would mean complete economic collapse. But getting no food supplies would have the same effect. I hope Ebert will hold a plebiscite, so that he will not have to bear the whole responsibility himself.[15]

The Constituent Assembly was in a dilemma. On the one hand it was confronted with the task of building a new Germany, while on the other it faced the prospect of having to shoulder a still unknown but certainly very heavy burden when the amount of war debts and reparations was fixed. Large sections of the population were only waiting for the new government to fail. *Putsches* of left-wing and right-wing extremists flared up. But these signs of disintegration strengthened the feeling that existed in some circles that something must be done to establish centres of order. Various regenerative movements arose both at national and international level. The Youth Movement reappeared on the scene, partly with very ambiguous aims and motivations. The thirteen-year-old Dietrich was caught up in this wave. He joined the Boy Scouts.

Youth Movement

This was his only active association with the German Youth Movement, though it is questionable whether the Scouts should be counted as part of it. For the Scout Movement was not led by the young, but by their elders, who were often schoolmasters. This had been rejected by the pre-war leaders of the Youth Movement on the principle of self-determination for the young. The Bonhoeffers had had no contact with this early period of the German Youth Movement.

The second, post-war wave of the movement resulted in the formation of a covenanted organization. The German section of the Scouts, though it occupied a marginal position, in 1918 formally joined this youth covenant within the German Youth Movement and was not immune from its influence and style.

Dietrich Bonhoeffer, with some of his school-fellows, joined the Scouts in the summer of 1919, and at first he rather liked it. 'On Sunday mornings we always drill, have mock battles and that sort of thing. It is always very nice.'[16] It had not yet occurred to him that Sunday morning was the time to go to church. In the winter he was very useful to the Scouts as a musician. He played Schubert and arranged Haydn trios for their concerts.

But during 1920 he gave them up. No very definite reason for this seems discoverable. He may have decided that the marching and drilling

15. Letter of 20.5.1919.
16. To his grandmother, 19.8.1919.

was a waste of time. The current tendencies to radicalization may have affected his group. His older brothers' and sisters' dislike of war games certainly played a part. At all events, the Scouts did not hold him.

Nevertheless the episode represented a first attempt to move outside the sphere of his family and his school and to discover areas of experience of his own, not shared by his brothers and sisters. Many of his school-fellows did the same, and he did not want to cut himself off from them. In later years he showed a knowledge and appreciation of certain aspects of the Youth Movement. 'The aim', he said in an address to his congregation in Barcelona in 1929, 'is to attack a cultural environment that has lost its inner truth, to loosen the shackles of truth. And thus, because the consequence otherwise would be complete scepticism, the deeply moral nature of the movement is assured.'

During his last years at school there is increasing evidence of his opposition to the right-wing radicalism that was becoming more and more obstreperous. When he went off on his last school holidays, he wrote to his parents, he found himself sitting opposite 'a man wearing a swastika' and had to spend the whole time arguing with him. The man, he said, was 'really quite obtusely right-wing'.[17]

A few days before, on 24th June 1922, the assassination of Walther Rathenau had taken place. Bonhoeffer heard the shots in his class-room in the Königsallee. This is what one of his school-fellows has to say on the subject:

I particularly remember Bonhoeffer on the day of Rathenau's murder. The average age of our form in the Grunewald grammar school was seventeen, but he and G.S., who ended by committing suicide in exile, were only sixteen. I remember the shots we heard during the lesson, and then, in the playground during the break, we heard what had happened . . . I still remember my friend Bonhoeffer's passionate indignation, his deep and spon-taneous anger . . . I remember his asking what would become of Germany if its best leaders were killed. I remember it because I was surprised at the time at its being possible to know so exactly where one stood.[18]

The political principles that prevailed in his environment are vividly expressed in a letter from the university written by Klaus to Hans von Dohnanyi in May 1922:

I have now got to know them [i.e. his fellow-students] politically, but when I think about it I feel sick . . . A few days ago there was a meeting at which Professor Goetz of Leipzig spoke on 'The Student in the New Age'. He spoke very well indeed, with complete freedom from personal or party [animosities], but on the basis of democratic principles. The students bawled at him, stamped their feet, and shouted personal insults . . . Haller, the historian here, also failed to distinguish himself when he tactlessly abused

17. Letter of 7.7.1922.
18. Communication from Peter H. Olden, 1946.

his colleague, giving a devastating exhibition of demagogy that caused the student mob to shout with jubilation. My indignation must have been very plain. At all events, I got involved in an argument with a man sitting behind me, an idiotic former lieutenant wearing a monocle . . . It is depressing to see the people on whom one relies for the future . . . arguing only with their eyes perpetually turned back to the 1870–71 period, and even that only in an empty pose . . . Hans, only think of the trouble we shall have later with these people. If only I were a bit older !

III DECISION TO BECOME A THEOLOGIAN

When we turn to the question of the motives and origins of Bonhoeffer's choice of calling, we shall hardly find an answer that does not contain an element of speculation, for he left no biographical clues. But perhaps the very lack of them is significant, a pointer to his belief that the roots of one's innermost vocation should remain a secret; he felt that curiosity in the matter released self-destructive forces. So we must accept a certain amount of uncertainty when we set about searching for some of the determining factors.

Christian Life and the Church

The Bonhoeffers were not a church-going family in the sense of active membership of and participation in the life of a congregation. The children were not sent to church, and the family did not go to church even on the high festivals. For religious events within the family the parish minister was by-passed in favour of relatives, first Dietrich's grandfather and then his maternal uncle, Hans von Hase. Thus one of the children's favourite games was to have a 'home christening'. There was no desire to depart from normal customs, and the children were sent to confirmation class. Their mother tried to make the children understand the seriousness of the enterprise, which was not easy, in view of the strange stories current about confirmation classes among the children.

The family, including their mother, had its own direct relationship with the Bible and the history and traditions of the Church without feeling the need of any ecclesiastical guidance, and thus any direct connection with the Church seemed unnecessary. No church dignitary or minister seems to have played any part in the Bonhoeffers' social relationships at that time, and among Dietrich's early friends there are no names of families having church connections, with the single exception of his cousin Hans-Christoph, with whom he struck up a friendship on his occasional holiday visits to the rectory of his von Hase uncle. The Berlin-Brandenburg Church in whose area Bonhoeffer grew up makes its first appearance in his life during the latter part of his time as a student. The impulse to become a theologian for the sake of the real Church belongs to a later period.

Though the Bonhoeffers could not be described as a church family, it would be entirely wrong to describe them as non-Christian. At all events, Dietrich's mother was the very opposite of a non-Christian. When she was young she had spent months at Herrnhut, and she had adopted the ideals of the Moravian Brethren with youthful enthusiasm. After her marriage, however, these things remained below the surface. She would never have tolerated an oppressively devout atmosphere. When Käthe Horn took over the teaching of the twins Dietrich and Sabine, she kept the religion lessons for herself, telling the children Bible stories from memory and using Schnorr von Carolsfeld's Bible in pictures. Later, when Dietrich began giving religious instruction himself, he simply followed his mother's example in this, and only much later did he see that the over-beautification of these illustrations ran the risk of implanting dangerous preconceptions about the Bible stories in the childish mind. Maria Horn, the beloved family governess from 1906 to 1923, was a real follower of the Moravian Brethren, but she did not have much religious influence over the children. Because of her attractive and imperturbable personality she became practically a member of the family, but it was her personality that was appreciated, while expressions of her piety were merely tolerated. So far as the latter were concerned, she would certainly not have done anything without the parents' knowledge and consent. The children knew exactly where they were with her. Klaus evaded the ban on reading in bed by concealing an exciting book inside the black covers of a Bible, at the sight of which Fräulein Horn silently crept away, leaving the light on.

Domestic religious customs were observed, and were intended to mean something to those who practised them. Grace before meals was generally said by the children. Evening prayers were said in a darkened room, to discourage anyone from posing or watching the behaviour of others. When they were young the children's prayer was '*Müde bin ich, geh zur Ruh*', and later they said the Lord's Prayer and sang a hymn of their own choice; thus they laid in a store of words and music that remained indelibly in their memory. On Christmas Eve their mother read the Christmas story from St. Luke, and New Year's Eve ended with the 90th Psalm and Paul Gerhardt's New Year hymn '*Nun lass: uns gehn und treten*'. Their father was always present on these occasions, as usual setting an example of how the feelings of others should be shared and respected, though everyone knew that this was their mother's affair. There was no conflict in this respect, as there was unanimity in rejecting anything exaggerated or forced in religion, and doubts and scruples were respected when they were expressed without offensive cynicism. When their father said 'I understand nothing of that', he might do so in a tone of condescending humour, but he always betrayed a trace of his awareness of the inadequacy of human reason—and thus revealed a slightly shaming solidarity.

Thus the religious feeling of the household tended to be subterranean or behind the scenes. The dominant atmosphere was that of tolerant empiricism. This was encouraged by the friendships and interests of the older brothers, and their father's critical and matter-of-fact attitude worked in the same direction.

Choice of Profession

Bonhoeffer decided to be a minister and a theologian when he was a boy, and he does not seem seriously to have wavered in this ambition.

At home he made no bones about it. When his brothers and sisters refused to take him seriously, it only made him the more determined. When he was about fourteen, for instance, they tried to persuade him that he was taking the path of least resistance, and that the church to which he proposed to devote himself was a poor, feeble, boring, petty bourgeois institution, but he confidently replied: 'In that case I shall reform it!'

His relatives were already taking his ambitions seriously. Thus on his fourteenth birthday his uncle and godfather Hans von Hase wrote him a letter in which he said: 'If your path should lead you towards theology . . .', and went on to give details of what would be involved. Confirmation lessons with the Rev. H. Priebe at the Grunewald church came later. Bonhoeffer never again referred to these confirmation classes, except that he once mentioned that they were the occasion of his making friends with Hans von Haeften, one of the plotters of 20th July 1944. He found the lessons sometimes interesting, but he was bored by the commonplaces. At the time of his confirmation he had started reading the Bible for himself, and no exciting novel was hidden between the black covers.

Before the final choice was made, his parents wanted to make sure that his true vocation was not music, and they made him play to the pianist Leonid Kreuzer, a virtuoso of the Vienna school, but the result was not unequivocally in favour of music, and in any case Dietrich did not really want to be a musician. At the beginning of his year in the lower first form, he casually announced that he had chosen Hebrew as his optional subject and thus the die was cast. He was fifteen years old at the time. In March 1921, when he and Klaus were invited to a party at their friends the Gilberts, he declined, on the grounds that it was Lent. This made an impression on his friends, who had not previously come across such a reason for refusing an invitation. He now sometimes went to church, occasionally accompanied by his mother.

Once a decision had been made, it was respected in the family. Only many years later did his father reveal what he thought of Dietrich's choice:

At the time when you decided to devote yourself to theology I sometimes thought to myself that a quiet, uneventful, minister's life, as I knew it from that of my Swabian uncles and as Mörike describes it, would really almost be a pity for you. So far as uneventfulness is concerned, I was greatly mistaken. That such a crisis should still be possible in the ecclesiastical field seemed to me with my scientific background out of the question.[19]

Inner Motivations

In trying to track down the motivations of Bonhoeffer's choice of calling, there are some possible ones that can be excluded from the outset. The impulse did not come from the local church or congregation, or from his confirmation lessons. Nor did it come from hero-worship of any great religious personality. It is characteristic of him that—excepting only the occasion of his encounter with Karl Barth, which occurred much later—he developed no enthusiasms for outstanding personalities in the course of his life.

On the contrary, one of the factors that lay at the roots of his choice was a primary urge to independence. This did not exclude an insatiable appetite to take in and absorb things from many different quarters, but it meant that the driving force in his life was the need for unchallengeable self-realization. True, the presence of theologians among his forebears made his choice seem not excessively eccentric, and this no doubt played its part, but it was hardly a decisive factor. Of far greater importance must have been what was in many respects his peculiar position among his brothers and sisters, which must have nourished the urge to outstrip them all. It might be said, with some exaggeration, that because he was lonely he became a theologian and because he became a theologian he was lonely.

The last war years had a deep effect on him. The loss of his brother and his mother's grief gave a new meaning to his early memories of the Breslau cemetery. His childish spirit responded with a fervent longing for the life beyond, and a fervent—though unconfessable—wish to transmit to the others his unqualified faith in eternity. There are two documents relating to this. The first is a recollection by his twin sister:

. . . we heard of the deaths of our grown-up cousins, and the fathers of our school-fellows. So, after the evening prayers and singing . . . we lay awake a long time and tried to imagine what eternal life and being dead were like. We endeavoured every evening to get a little nearer to eternity by concentrating on the word 'eternity' and excluding any other thought. It seemed very long and gruesome, and after some time of intense concentration we often felt dizzy. For a long time we clung to this self-imposed exercise. We were very attached to one another and each wanted to be the last to say good night to the other; this went on endlessly and often we struggled out of our sleep to do so. I believed that this ritual saved Dietrich from being 'devoured' by Satan. We twins kept all this absolutely secret . . .

19. Letter of 2.2.1934.

Of the hymns we learned, Dietrich specially liked: 'Where does the soul find its home, its rest', 'Oh, wait, my soul', 'Jesus, still lead on', and 'Let me go . . ' Dietrich called them 'red' hymns. There were also 'black' hymns like 'Praise to the Lord' and 'Now thank we all our God'. This too was a secret language between us . . . When the lights were extinguished the phosphorescent gleam of our glowing crosses comforted us, though their shape sometimes made us uneasy. When at the age of twelve Dietrich got a room of his own, we arranged that he should drum on the wall at night as a sign that Susi and I should 'think of God'. These monitory bangs happened regularly and became a habit, until Dietrich noticed that they sometimes roused us from our sleep; then he stopped them.[20]

The other document is an unheaded sheet of paper that must be attributed to 1932, the period of upheaval in his theological and inner life. It is impossible to establish on what occasion or for whom he wrote this fragment about the incursion of vanity into more serious self-contemplation, but it is evidence of his life-long preoccupation with whether and how he would face up to death. What he wrote was this:

He liked thinking about death. Even in his boyhood he had liked imagining himself on his death-bed, surrounded by all those who loved him, speaking his last words to them. Secretly he had often thought about what he would say at that moment. To him death was neither grievous nor alien. He would have liked to die young, to die a fine, devout death. He would have liked them all to see and understand that to a believer in God dying was not hard, but was a glorious thing. In the evening, when he went to bed over-tired, he sometimes thought that it was going to happen. A slight sense of dizziness often alarmed him so much that he furiously bit his tongue, to make sure that he was alive and felt pain. Then in his innocence he cried out to God, asking to be granted a deferment. These experiences dismayed him to some extent. For obviously he did not want to die, he was a coward; his theatrical ideas disgusted him. And yet in moments of strength he often prayed that God might after all release him, for he was ready to die, it was only his animal nature that again and again made him contemptible in his own eyes, that led him astray from himself.

Then one day he had a grotesque idea. He believed himself to be suffering from the only incurable illness that existed, namely a crazy and irremediable fear of death. The thought that he would really have to die one day had such a grip on him that he faced the unalterable prospect with speechless fear. And there was no one who could free him from this illness, because in reality it was no illness, but the most natural and obvious thing in the world, because it was the most inevitable. He saw himself going from one person to another, pleading and appealing for help. Doctors shook their heads and could do nothing for him. His illness was that he saw reality for what it was, it was incurable. He could tolerate the thought for only a few moments. From that day on he buried inside himself something about which for a long time he did not speak or think again. His favourite subject for discussion and for his imagination to dwell on had suddenly

20. S. Leibholz, op. cit., IKDB, pp. 23 ff.

acquired a bitter taste. He spoke no more about a fine, devout death, and forgot about it.

Early influences on his theological vocation are touched on here, even though in the Kierkegaard manner they were written down at a much later stage. But the choice itself involved its own special temptations.

Another fragment, dating from practically the same period, sadly describes the theologian's despair at the revelation of the diabolical hollowness of his devoutness that follows from an examination of its origins, and it declares that those things for which others admire him are the most repugnant to himself. The fragment as written certainly does not belong to his youth, but to the period when he was reflecting on religiosity originating from sin, as he did in the 1932 lecture on 'Creation and Fall'. But every line of the fragment betrays its close connection with the period of his life with which we are now dealing. One can imagine the presence of his Greek master, Kranz. He early made the acquaintance of two companions whom he feared, *tristitia* and *accidie*.[21] As a boy, in spite of his reputation for sociability and even-temperedness, he was capable in the midst of a lively conversation of suddenly withdrawing into solitude. This 1932 fragment appears rightly to be an acknowledgment of the big part played by ambition in his early decision to become a theologian. All the greater must have been his eventual discovery that being a Christian consisted in shaking off reflection about one's own beginnings. The 1932 fragment is as follows:

One day in the first form, when the master asked him what he wanted to study, he quietly answered theology, and flushed. The word slipped out so quickly that he did not even stand up. Having the teacher's gaze and that of the whole class directed at him personally and not at his work, and being suddenly called upon to speak out like this, gave him such conflicting feelings of vanity and humility that the shock led to an infringement of ordinary class behaviour, an appropriate expression of the consternation caused by the question and the answer. The master obviously thought so too, for he rested his gaze on him for only a moment longer than usual and then quickly and amiably released him.

He was nearly as disconcerted as his pupil. 'In that case you have more surprises to come', he said, speaking just as quietly. Actually the question 'how long?' had been on his lips, but, as if that would have touched on the secret of his own early and passionately begun and then quickly dropped study of theology—and also because he felt displeased with himself at having nothing better to say to a boy whom he had known and liked for a long time—he grew embarrassed, cleared his throat, and went back to the Greek text which was the subject of the lesson.

The boy absorbed that brief moment deep into himself. Something extra-ordinary had happened, and he enjoyed it and felt ashamed at the same

21. LPP, p. 87.

time. Now they all knew, he had told them. Now he was faced with the riddle of his life. Solemnly he stood there in the presence of his God, in the presence of his class. He was the centre of attention. Did he look as he had wanted to look, serious and determined? He was filled with an unusual sense of well-being at the thought, though he immediately drove it away, realizing the grandeur of his confession and his task. Nor did it escape him at that moment that he had caused the master a certain embarrassment, though at the same time he had looked at him with pleasure and approval. The moment swelled into pleasure, the class-room expanded into the infinite. There he stood in the midst of the world as the herald and teacher of his knowledge and his ideals, they all had now to listen to him in silence, and the blessing of the Eternal rested on his words and on his head. And again he felt ashamed. For he knew about his pitiful vanity.

How often he had tried to master it. But it always crept back again, and it spoilt the pleasure of this moment. Oh, how well he knew himself at the age of seventeen. He knew all about himself and his weaknesses. And he also knew that he knew himself well. And through the corner of that piece of self-knowledge his deep vanity again forced an entry into the house of his soul and made him afraid.

It had made a tremendous impression on him when he had read in Schiller that man needed only to rid himself of a few small weaknesses to be like the gods. Since then he had been on the watch. He would emerge from this struggle like a hero, he said to himself. He had just made a solemn vow to do so. The path that he had known he must follow since the age of fourteen was clearly marked out for him. But supposing he failed? Supposing the struggle proved vain? Supposing he was not strong enough to see it through?

The words 'You have more surprises to come' suddenly rang in his ears. Surprises about what? What did he mean? What was the meaning of the curious, mistrustful, bored, disappointed, mocking eyes of his class-mates? Didn't they credit him? Didn't they believe in his honesty? Did they know something about him that he did not know himself?

Why are you all looking at me like that? Why are you embarrassed, sir? Look away from me, for heaven's sake, denounce me as a mendacious, conceited person who does not believe what he says. Don't keep so considerately silent, as if you understood me. Laugh aloud at me, don't be so abominably dumb—it's intolerable.

There is the throng. He stands in the midst of it and speaks, fervently, passionately. He corrects himself. A leaden silence lies over the throng, a dreadful, silent mockery. No, it cannot be. He is not the man they take him to be. He really is in earnest. They have no right to scorn me. They are doing him wrong, all of them. He prays.

God, say yourself whether I am in earnest about you. Destroy me now if I am lying. Or punish them all; they are my enemies, and yours. They do not believe me. I know myself I am not good. But I know it myself—and you, God, know it too. I do not need the others. I, I. I shall win. Do you see their consternation? I am with you. I am strong. God, I am with you.

Do you hear me? Or do you not? To whom am I speaking? To myself? To you? To those others here?

Who is it that is speaking? My faith or my vanity?

God, I shall study theology. Yes, I have said so, and they all heard it. There is no more retreat. I shall . . . but if . . . ?

And as [illegible] tries to think about something else, all he hears is the form master's voice from a distance, saying. 'Aren't you feeling well? You don't look well.' He pulls himself together, stands up, and as usual begins construing the difficult Greek text . . .

Last Years at School

Bonhoeffer's early determination to become a theologian evidently did not in any way restrict his friendships and interests, as can easily happen to those who choose their career early. 'Everyone who knew him at that time was impressed by his radiant nature; his high spirits knew no bounds.'[22]

He always read a great deal. During his boyhood he wrote a play based on Hauff's tale 'The Cold Heart' that was performed with the aid of his brothers and sisters. Later, with friends, he staged a performance of Hofmannsthal's *The White Fan*. He read his first classics during the holidays at Friedrichsbrunn at the age of thirteen. In the upper forms at school he read the early works of Hermann Hesse. Above all, he discovered Ibsen, whose plays ever again impressed him in later years.

His brother Karl-Friedrich's scepticism, against which he had to defend himself, spurred him into grappling with epistemology at an early age, and he worked hard at philosophy during his last years at school. At a working party in February 1921 he read a paper, based on reading Ranke and his great-grandfather Karl August von Hase, on Plotinus and the Emperor Julian; and in August 1922 he read another on the philosophical aspects of Euripides, based on Eduard Meyer's *History of Antiquity*. He read Schleiermacher's *Talks on Religion* while still at school. Through his brothers, he came across Friedrich Naumann's *Letters on Religion*, which he worked through very carefully. Subsequently he was never able to forget Naumann's dispassionate but nevertheless deeply felt conclusion that Christianity was never more than partial: 'In practice many are traders with their right hand and beneficiaries of the poor with their left . . . All the biddings of the Gospel merely hover like distant, white clouds of aspiration over the real life of our time.'[23] But Dietrich did not want to rest with this discrepancy.

After he had read Tönnies's *Gemeinschaft und Gesellschaft*, his brother Klaus and his friends drew his attention to Max Weber, whose brother Alfred had been a fellow-student of Bonhoeffer's father and had introduced him to Max. The family's friendly relations with Alfred Weber were never interrupted.

The available sources show little in the way of modern theological

22. Communication from Maria Brendel, *née* Weigert, 12.12.1965.
23. F. Naumann, *Briefe über Religion*, 1917, p. 61.

reading during the period before Bonhoeffer's school-leaving examination. Among his books were the first two volumes of Eduard Meyer's *Birth and Origins of Christianity*, published in 1921, in which year he acquired them and, still a schoolboy, wrote his name in them, adding the word 'theol'. He did a great deal of work on these substantial volumes, but many of the annotations, in which he criticizes Meyer as an historian on Harnack's and Heitmüller's lines, may date from his first year at the university. At all events, he went to the university with a considerable grounding in the historical criticism and the religious history of the New Testament. At this time Karl Barth's *Epistle to the Romans*, published in 1919, had not yet attracted wide attention.

During his last days at school his family noted how much he was looking forward to the study of theology. If he had any doubts about his calling, he did not mention them. He was attracted by the prospect of grappling with the still unexplored subject. He was not yet impelled by any love of the Church, by any organized, genuinely theological system of beliefs, or by a discovery of the Scriptures and their exegesis. His interest in the discipline of theology was still coloured by an essentially worldly philosophy of life.

He set out on the path to theology from an essentially worldly base. First of all, there was the 'call' that came to him in his youthful vanity to do something special in life. Then intellectual curiosity plunged him into theology as a branch of knowledge. Only later did the Church come into his field of vision. Unlike theologians who have come from church and theological families and have discovered the existence of the 'world' only later, Bonhoeffer set out on his journey and eventually discovered the Church.

But, however much prematurity and ambition may have lain behind his choice of calling, he made it without any reservations. He did not, for instance, embark on it with the idea of first looking round the broad field of theology and then deciding whether it offered him a satisfactory field of work. His desire to commit himself was always as strong as his desire for knowledge.

The still very vague and unclear idea that there was a kind of 'call' that enjoyed priority over academic study became and remained his objective guiding principle in theological matters; he believed in an indisputable truth underlying everything else. His academic background suggested to him the opposite approach. But he rejected neutrality in advance, and hence always displayed an instinctive dislike of apologetics.

Perhaps, on the eve of going to the university, he wanted to demonstrate his faith to his parents' world and to claim that world for his faith, unorganized as the latter still was. He did not state this secret purpose, but it gave him strength for what was to come.

CHAPTER TWO

STUDY

1923 - 1927

BONHOEFFER left home for the first time when he went to university at the age of seventeen and the world of independent thought and action opened out before him. He greedily absorbed what philosophers and theologians had to offer, and his parents gave him every help and backing.

He remained far more firmly rooted in his home than was usual with his fellow-students. He did little without first consulting his parents. He sometimes had in mind the idea of seeking out the great teachers of the age, but always withdrew when they threatened to take possession of him. Thus we shall see him returning to Grunewald after his first year away. It was there, and not in the outside world, that the beliefs matured that marked him as a theologian.

Family

Notwithstanding his concentration on theology, substantial changes that took place in the family scene contributed to broadening his horizon.

In 1923 Karl-Friedrich became an assistant in the Institute of Physical Chemistry at the Kaiser Wilhelm Society. He succeeded in splitting the hydrogen atom, was invited to visit both the Soviet Union and the United States, and at the age of thirty-one was appointed to the chair of physics in Frankfurt. Klaus, after graduating, worked in the field of international law at the League of Nations in Geneva. Ursula was married in 1923 to the Stuttgart lawyer Dr. Rüdiger Schleicher (1895-1945), who worked in the Transport Ministry in Berlin; in 1925 Christine was married to Hans von Dohnanyi (1902-45), the lawyer son of the Hungarian composer; in 1926 Sabine became the wife of Gerhard Leibholz (born 1901), a constitutional lawyer of Jewish origin; and in 1927 Susanne became engaged to the theologian Walter Dress (born 1904).

Fate was to associate Dietrich with his brothers-in-law far more closely than the diversity of their careers would have led one to expect. In the last resort they are all as much a part of his life-story as he is of theirs.

I TÜBINGEN

It was part of the family tradition that he should first attend the University of Tübingen, his father's Alma Mater. His first two terms there coincided with ominous political and economic events: the French occupation of the Ruhr, unrest in Bavaria and Saxony, the declaration of a state of emergency throughout the Reich, and galloping inflation. In order to economize, at the end of April 1923 Bonhoeffer travelled from Berlin to Tübingen by the cheaper 'local' trains and in the fourth class that still existed at that time. The journey took forty-eight hours. When his parents sent him money it was worth only a fraction of its value by the time it reached Tübingen. In June 1923 he wrote home: 'Müller's History of the Church now costs 70,000 marks instead of 55,000', and on 27th October he told them that 'every meal costs 1,000 million marks'. Students had then arranged to pay 2,500 million marks for fifty meals in advance.

Dietrich's father had a life insurance policy for 100,000 marks, which matured just when the inflation was at its height. He decided to treat himself to a bottle of wine and some strawberries with the money, but by the time it arrived it was enough to pay for a pound of strawberries only—the reward for paying premiums for a life-time. But in spite of this the Bonhoeffers, thanks to the peculiar circumstances prevailing in Berlin, managed to keep four children at the university. Foreigners well-supplied with foreign exchange swarmed to the German capital and were able to buy up property and antiques and modern art objects at minimal cost to themselves; they also took advantage of the opportunity to seek advice and treatment from front-rank psychiatrists. Thus Karl Bonhoeffer acquired priceless dollars or francs. He used to describe how he, his wife and a colleague once spent four days at Jena, paying the fare, the hotel bill and all their meals out of the change from five dollars.

So Dietrich followed his father's and brothers' footsteps to Tübingen, with one franc for emergencies in his pocket for the summer term of 1923. In October Helfferich brought the inflation to an end and restored a stable currency with the introduction of the Rentenmark. Dietrich's first turbulent term was followed by a second at Tübingen.

The 'Igel'

Bonhoeffer's university life was not restricted to the lecture hall. He joined the students' association, the so-called 'Hedgehog' (Igel), to which his father had belonged; incidentally, Rudolph Bultmann had joined it in 1905. The association's quarters were on the hill immediately behind the walls of the so-called 'Twingia' Castle, and it was known to students as the 'beer church'; it looked down on a branch of the Neckar surrounding some beautiful green islands. Dietrich was the only one of Karl

Bonhoeffer's sons to join the 'Hedgehog'; he duly became a 'fox', as first-year members were called.

The 'Hedgehog' was a Swabian fraternity. It was limited to Tübingen, and was not affiliated to any other organization. It was founded in 1871 and was devoted to the patriotic ideas of the new German Reich. It at first deliberately dissociated itself from the behaviour of the duelling and colour-carrying fraternities and, instead of the usual brightly coloured cap and breast-band, its members wore a hedgehog skin and a grey, light grey and dark grey breast-band. With the passing of time and generations it inevitably became one of the many students' associations that eventually adopted disastrous codes of honour and in 1933 accepted the Aryan clause.

Dietrich's elder brothers had not followed their father's example in joining the 'Hedgehog'. After some hesitation, Karl-Friedrich, when he learnt in 1919 that its members were expected to take part in the suppression of risings at Stuttgart and Munich, emphatically refused to do so; he objected to members of the students' association being subjected to nationalist pressure. Karl Vossler, the romance languages scholar, and a friend of Karl Bonhoeffer's, resigned from the 'Hedgehog' at the same time. Karl-Friedrich said later that he had been able to discover no difference between it and other nationalist fraternities. His younger brother Klaus was similarly averse to joining it.

But in 1923 Dietrich had no political reservations about joining it. Not till after 1933 did he, together with his brother-in-law Walter Dress, ostentatiously dissociate himself from it when some of its members exalted as a fulfilment of ancient ideals the *Gleichschaltung*, or 'bringing into line', which was imposed by the Nazis. His resignation is recorded in the senior members' bulletin of March 1936.

During the time of his student membership there were some lively discussions in the fraternity about social questions of the day. A party of his fellow-students went on a study trip to the Ruhr. Friedrich Naumann's influence was very marked, and one of his most enthusiastic disciples was Dietrich's brother-in-law Rüdiger Schleicher.

The fact that Dietrich was the only one of the brothers to join the 'Hedgehog' can again be connected with his position in the family. His elder brothers had had ample experience of the life with their fellows and contemporaries that still lay ahead of him. Here at last was an opportunity of breaking out of what to some extent was his isolation among his brothers and sisters and in his class at school. It was a necessary step in self-discovery.

Here are the opinions of two of his contemporaries about him:

In nearly every field that meant anything to me he was already at home on his own account and stood for something, whether as theologian, musician, philosopher . . . or as a companionable, physically agile and tough young man . . . He already had a sharp nose for essentials and a determination to get to the bottom of things. He was . . . very natural and receptive to new ideas . . . He was capable of subtly teasing people and had a great deal of humour. He was not vain, but tolerated criticism.[1]

In 1923, when Dietrich Bonhoeffer joined the 'Hedgehog' with me, he was seventeen . . . he was already completely a man of the intellectually agitated world . . . I was no match for Dietrich Bonhoeffer's stormy temperament and self-confidence.[2]

After 1933 Bonhoeffer never talked again about his time in the fraternity. For him it had disappeared.

The Black Reichswehr

During the winter term, his second at Tübingen, his membership of the 'Hedgehog' resulted in a singular episode in his life. For two weeks he served with the Ulm Rifles, i.e. he was a member of the so-called Black Reichswehr. An amusing story survives about this episode. On the second day Bonhoeffer is said to have been ordered to clean out the barrack-room with a toothbrush as a punishment for throwing his washing water out of the window, and he is said to have gone back to Tübingen immediately to avoid this ridiculous task. The story tells us something about how hard his contemporaries found it to imagine him subjecting himself to someone else's will, but it is apocryphal or has been transferred to him from someone else—could it have happened to Klaus in 1918? Dietrich Bonhoeffer enjoyed the Ulm exercises at the end of November 1923.

It was an open secret that young men were continually being given military training by the German army, then limited to 100,000 men. Many students received training during term-time, definite days of the week being set aside for the purpose. It was not only the nationalists who welcomed this substitute for the conscription that was forbidden by the Treaty of Versailles. During the crises of 1923 the centre and the left also prepared for possible bloody clashes. In a number of provinces, such as Bavaria, substantial stores of weapons were accumulated by organizations hostile to the constitution. There had been Communist unrest in Saxony, and in Munich Ludendorff's and Hitler's Putsch took place, ending in fiasco at the Feldherrnhalle. After the French occupation of the Ruhr it was feared that similar incursions might take place elsewhere, particularly on Germany's eastern frontiers. Stresemann, who had entered into coalition with the Social Democrats, was denounced by the right because, in spite of the occupation of the Ruhr, he began negotiating with Poincaré and preaching reconciliation instead of resistance. Meanwhile the Reich Government itself made hasty preparations

1. W. Dreier, 2.6.1965.
2. H. U. Esche, 23.3.1965.

in conjunction with the army command. Thus even a man like General Reinhardt, the commander of the Stuttgart military district, encouraged military training by students. The Allied Control Commission, on the other hand, made every effort to put an end to illegal military training.

On 14th November 1923 Bonhoeffer wrote to his parents:

Today I was told that the afternoon military training was off, because here in Tübingen there was a danger of spies. Instead the Tübingen students' associations, as well as many unattached students, are almost without exception going to Ulm early tomorrow morning for a fortnight's training. At first I said it was impossible, but that I would go some time during the vacation. But, when I was told that from 1st December onwards training was to be supervised by the Entente Control Commission, I reconsidered the matter. I discussed it with a few people who are going—the 'Hedgehog' and all the other associations are going in full force—and also with von Rad,[3] and they all said that I should do it as quickly as possible. The fact of the matter is that the Reichswehr, with Reinhardt's personal permission, is training students and other people in Ulm and Constance, and actually for a whole fortnight which, stupidly enough, cannot be arranged during the vacation. One can quit after giving one day's notice, and in serious cases, of course, no compulsion is exercised. The purpose is merely to do as much training as possible before the Control Commission begins operating. In view of the one day's notice, and the fact that all the 'Hedgehogs' up to the seventh term are going, and that it will make difficulties if right at the outset one fewer than the number expected turns up, I said I would go for the first few days, i.e. until about Tuesday, when I should receive your reply, but would come back if you definitely objected. My first feeling was that there was plenty of time, after all, and that it would be better not to interrupt the term, but now I think it better to get it over and done with as quickly as possible, so as to have the assurance of being able to help in the event of critical situations. Grandmother . . . also thinks I should go. Jörg Schleicher [the brother of Bonhoeffer's brother-in-law] is going too.

A letter quickly followed assuring his mother that 'the training of course commits one to nothing else, and in the event of an emergency only Württembergers will be called on to join this regiment'.

Dietrich having presented them with a *fait accompli*, his parents gave him their somewhat anxious consent.

The fortnight at Ulm gave the seventeen-year-old Dietrich a certain satisfaction as he stood up easily to the training. He wrote home that he found the instructors surprisingly decent and 'good-natured'. In his free time he sat down in front of his books. But back in Tübingen he noted that 'it was quite wonderful to eat with a knife and fork at a laid table again and to sleep in a room of one's own, in one's own bed, and above all to be able to wash in warm water'.

Much as this adventure stimulated him, he was greatly concerned by what he noted in the political respect:

3. Gerhard von Rad, later the outstanding Old Testament scholar.

The Reichswehr teams on the whole make a good impression, but nearly all of them are very reactionary . . . They are all awaiting the moment when Ludendorff will do the thing with better, i.e. with Reichswehr, support;[4] the very opposite of the people in the house[5] here, who want to kill Ludendorff.

Bonhoeffer's Ulm interlude was certainly not based on any secret radical right-wing impulses. By nature and family tradition he had as little sympathy with this as he had with the flag-consecrating pastors of whom there were not a few in the Evangelical Church at the time. On the contrary, during the university vacation in the autumn of 1923 he and his brothers ordered Vorwärts, the principal Berlin Social Democratic newspaper, to be sent to them at Friedrichsbrunn. But his letters to his parents show how important to him was the feeling of solidarity with his fellows, from whom he did not wish to cut himself off. He believed he was acting in the service of a state of which he approved, and he was not motivated by a vision of the German people in arms. This military interlude very soon faded from his mind. At Finkenwalde he talked about it with amusement once or twice.

Study

The only teacher at Tübingen who exercised any lasting influence on him was Adolf Schlatter. 'Schlatter interests me most', he wrote.[6] He attended his lectures only during the summer term of 1923, and a more personal contact was not established.

No doubt there was a correspondence between Bonhoeffer's and Schlatter's theological trends, namely the desire to accept the concrete world as fully as possible, and also the distinction that Schlatter made by which he allowed room for the 'good' in the New Testament and for responsibility in relation to the 'natural' and did not merely equate the latter with the 'night of sin' of the Reformation. At times, perhaps, Bonhoeffer practically forgot the latter, but even during The Cost of Discipleship period he never failed to draw his pupils' attention to Schlatter's assessment of the good and the just in the New Testament, that is, that goodness and justice would not be transformed into wickedness and deception.[7] No writer, apart from Luther, was so fully represented in Bonhoeffer's library in later years or was so frequently consulted.

Schlatter's positive attitude to National Socialism in 1933 and his

4. The reference is to the failure of Hitler's Munich Putsch of 9.11.1923.
5. i.e. the 'Hedgehog' quarters.
6. To his parents, 1.12.1923.
7. H. Vogt in his Göttingen thesis on Schlatter compares his Dogmatik, pp. 41 f., with Bonhoeffer's Ethics, pp. 155 f., and concludes that Schlatter's belief that 'denial of the reality of the world means the loss of nature, the self and God' corresponds with Bonhoeffer's contention that the destruction of the natural means the destruction of life.

obstructive attitude towards the Bethel profession of faith roused Bonhoeffer's bitter indignation, but did not diminish his high regard for his Biblical work. He always acknowledged that Schlatter drew attention to *loci classici* usually left to the Catholics, his own concern being to go beyond Schlatter by both setting them free and making them binding again by a close association with Christology.[8]

As he had already learnt Hebrew at school, at Tübingen he immediately attended Volz's lectures on the Psalms and—very prematurely—Rudolph's on Old Testament theology. The 'passion of the prophets' gripped him. During the winter term he attended the lectures of Heitmüller, who had been appointed to Tübingen as one of the leading exegetists of the religious historical school, on the Epistle to the Romans. In these attention was concentrated on questions of the origin and formation of the text; according to Bonhoeffer's lecture notes, Barth's *Epistle to the Romans* was included in the first list of recommended reading, but was not mentioned in the lectures, even as a foil to put the student on his guard. The lectures were concerned, not with grappling with basic theological problems extending beyond the epistle itself, but with the dissection of an ancient text. This could be learnt, and Bonhoeffer took down his lecture notes carefully and conscientiously. He also attended the lectures of the seventy-one-year-old Karl Müller on medieval ecclesiastical history, which was a good preparation for his forthcoming trip to Rome.

In his second term he was no longer to be restrained from dogmatics. He registered for Dogmatics II under Karl Heim. Schlatter had used his influence to secure Heim's appointment to Tübingen because of the latter's emphasis on incorporating science into his thinking. Bonhoeffer was not tempted along this path, but kept his critical distance. But he showed a good knowledge of Heim's theology.[9]

As Heim announced that he was going to concentrate on an introduction to Schleiermacher's and Ritschl's theology, Bonhoeffer took his Schleiermacher with him during the summer holidays at Friedrichsbrunn. 'I am now busy with Schleiermacher's talks on religion, which I am finding much more interesting the second time, when I am working through them systematically, because I am attending a course of lectures on them next term', he wrote.[10] His copy, a critical edition edited by Pünjer (1879), came from the library of his great-grandfather, Karl August von Hase. The number of underlinings and marginal comments show how carefully and critically he read. Opposite the sentence in Schleiermacher's second talk, 'but in the infinite everything finite coexists harmoniously, all is one and all is true', Bonhoeffer wrote: 'This does away with individual determining factors in favour of a general declaration of being.

8. W. Trillhaas, ZThK, 52, 1955, pp. 285-7, 292 f., and also RGG³, IV, p. 1328.
9. Cf. GS III, pp. 138 ff.
10. To his parents, 16.8.1923.

If everything is *true*, the concept of the false is eliminated, and hence that of truth also. In other words, in the infinite all attributes cease to exist, there is only being without choice or any universally valid word.'

Bonhoeffer spent a lot of time at Tübingen on the history of religion and philosophy. The only professor whose lectures Bonhoeffer attended during both his terms there was the philosopher Karl Groos, whose lectures on logic four hours every week in the summer term and on the history of modern philosophy five hours every week in the winter term impressed him. Bonhoeffer also joined his seminar on Kant's *Critique of Pure Reason*, and wrote a paper for it. 'Today Groos's seminar began and I liked it very much', he wrote.[11]

In 1925, when Reinhold Seeberg, after a first encounter with Dietrich, met his colleague Karl Bonhoeffer at a meeting of the Senate of Berlin University, he expressed his surprise and admiration at the solidity of the young man's philosophical preparation and his wide knowledge of contemporary philosophy.

That indeed summed up Bonhoeffer's year at Tübingen. It was marked by a wide range of interest rather than settlement on anything in particular, and by vigorous exploration of the epistemological field.

II ROME

Dietrich Bonhoeffer fell and hurt himself while skating, and his parents came to see him at Tübingen while he was recovering, because they were alarmed at the news that after the fall he had remained unconscious for a long time. Their visit coincided with his eighteenth birthday, and he expressed a wish to spend a term as a student in Rome. On 5th February 1924 he wrote to his twin sister:

Just think, it is not impossible that I may spend next term in Rome. I can hardly imagine how splendid that would be. Papa and Mama are going to make enquiries of Axel Harnack[12] . . . you must all help to talk them into it, and you mustn't be too jealous . . . Papa still thinks it would be better if I went later . . . Talk about it often at home, because that will clinch it.

He went to Rome with Klaus, who had just passed his law examination. The two brothers crossed the Brenner on 4th April. 'Imagination is beginning to turn into reality', he wrote in his diary.

It was to southern and not western Europe that thoughts turned as soon as funds for foreign travel became available again. For some time respectable middle-class Germans had been cutting themselves off from the west, which they regarded as embodying all the evil done to Germany by the Treaty of Versailles. Ecumenical ideas and impulses were still unknown to them. Considering their own political reality by the

11. Letter of May 1923.
12. The librarian son of Adolf von Harnack, then living in Rome.

standards of western democracy, for instance, or looking to the west for theological or ecclesiastical insights, lay beyond the German horizon at the time. But the idea of studying the origins of their own culture in ancient or Catholic Rome was assured of instant approval and every aid, at any rate on the part of Dietrich's mother.

At eighteen he knew far more about ancient Rome than about the city of the Popes. Relations between Catholics and Protestants were still distant and reserved. As a young schoolboy Dietrich was already familiar with the art treasures of classical antiquity in the Berlin museums, but it was not until he was in the upper second form, when he went on a walking tour in the Harz, that it occurred to him to enter a Catholic church at Nordhausen; in a letter to his parents he wrote about its magnificence almost in alarm. Not till the summer term at Tübingen did he learn something about Catholic practices. He readily admitted that the overwhelming impression made upon him by the Corpus Christi procession at Rottenburg had been one of genuine faith. So he went to Italy prepared to receive the impact of Catholicism with as few preconceptions as possible.

A diary concerning this journey has survived. Generally he did not keep a diary, but when travelling abroad he sometimes noted down his chief impressions. According to this diary, he conscientiously prepared himself for the trip and practised Italian conversation. 'By the time the trip began I knew Baedeker by heart.'

The diary makes it clear that Klaus was chiefly fascinated by classical antiquity and Mediterranean colourfulness, as well as by the sense of adventure, while Dietrich succumbed to the spell of Catholic Rome, and found it hard to tear himself away from St. Peter's. Unlike other Protestant pilgrims, he was not angered or revolted by the Eternal City; on the contrary, he fell permanently in love with it. In 1944 he wrote from his cell in Tegel that it was 'the piece of earth that I love so much'.

World of Classical Antiquity and North Africa

The brothers occasionally separated, so that each could follow up his own interests, but Dietrich missed little of the relics of classical antiquity. Like many visitors to Rome, he was disappointed by the first sight of St. Peter's, but the Colosseum overwhelmed him.

Antiquity is not dead [he wrote in his diary], *Pan ho megas tethneken* [The great Pan is dead] is not true, that is obvious after only a few moments. The Colosseum is overgrown with luxuriant vegetation, palms, cypresses, pines, weeds and grasses of all sorts; I sat there for nearly an hour . . . The sight of the Arch of Severus on the Palatine held me in its grip. I went home saying to myself over and over again: the great god Pan is not dead.

In the Vatican he had a special objective:

> I was unable to linger in the first galleries, for curiosity made me go straight
> to the Belvedere. The first sight of the Laocoon was actually a shock, it is
> unbelievable. I spent a long time with it and with Apollo . . .

Whenever he went to Rome, his first visit was to the Laocoon. In
his cell at Tegel he still enquired after this 'classical man of sorrows'.[13]

When Klaus began thirsting for new adventures, he of course did not
oppose them. So the brothers set off for Sicily. There, without informing
their parents, they succumbed to the temptation to cross the Mediterranean and see something of Africa, and they spent ten days in Tripoli
and in the Libyan desert. After a princely reception by a bedouin chief
on the edge of the Atlas Mountains, some complications, not further
described, ensued, which resulted in their being sent packing as 'unwelcome guests'. The diary is silent about this African episode. Only
towards the end of it did Dietrich write home about his first encounter
with the Mohammedan world:

> In Islam everyday life and religion are not kept separate, as they are in
> the whole of the Church, including the Catholic Church. With us one goes
> to church and when one comes back an entirely different kind of life begins
> again . . . Islamic and Jewish piety must be very definitely religions of
> law if national and ritual factors are so intermingled or actually identical.
> Only so are they able to maintain their strict demarcation from others . . .
> It would be interesting to spend more time studying Islam on its own soil,
> but it is very difficult . . . to obtain access. Thus today we entered the Great
> Mosque for the first time, but were admitted only by permission of the
> cadi.[14]

The trip to Africa ended with the young men's funds at a low ebb.
Back in Sicily, Bonhoeffer wrote in his diary on 10th May 1924: 'One
should not spend a longer time in Africa without preparation, the shock
is too great, and increases from day to day, so that one is glad to
return to Europe again.'

The Roman Church

The fascination exercised by Catholic Rome became a permanent influence on Bonhoeffer's thought. It cannot be said to have diminished
his critical awareness, but the universality of the Church and its liturgy
in its Roman guise made a tremendous impact on him, even before his
encounter with Karl Barth's theology helped him to new insights.

Looked at from this angle, his own Evangelical Church at home struck
him as provincial, nationalistic, and narrow-minded. It is significant that
in reference to his own church background he hardly uses the word
'Church' in his letters from Rome and in his diary, but always speaks of

13. LPP, pp. 121, 131.   14. To his parents from Tripoli, 9.5.1924.

'Protestantism', as was usual in his home; in the liberal atmosphere
that prevailed there, that term had more weight and relevance. Devotion
to the 'Church' such as he met here, the sense of universalism of the
ecclesia, was something new to him.

When the two brothers stopped for the night at Bologna on their
outward journey, they made friends with a young priest who was also
bound for Rome. 'I spend a great deal of time with our priest from
Bologna and let him explain a great deal to me.'[15] He acted as Bonhoeffer's guide to the spectacle of Easter week in Rome, and explained the
details of the mass to him.

On Palm Sunday he attended his first mass in St. Peter's, surrounded
by a throng of seminarists, monks and priests of every conceivable shade
of skin. In his diary he wrote down the phrase 'universality of the
Church'. In the evening he attended vespers at Trinità del Monte, the
beauty of which he still remembered in prison.[16] 'I went for a short
walk on the Pincio', he wrote in his diary. 'It had been a magnificent day;
the first on which I gained some real understanding of Catholicism; no
romanticism or anything of the sort, but I believe I am beginning to
understand the concept of the Church.'

Next day, the great day for confession, he spent hours in Santa Maria
Maggiore:

. . . all the confessionals occupied, with worshippers crowding round them
[he noted in his diary]. It is gratifying here to see so many serious faces,
to which all the things that are said against Catholicism do not apply.
Children as well as adults confess with a real ardour which it is very
moving to see. To many of these people confession is not an externally
imposed 'must', but has become an inner need. Confession does not necessarily lead to scrupulous living: often, however, that may occur and always
will with the most serious people. Also it is not mere pedagogy, but to
primitive people it is the only way of talking to God, while to the religiously
more far-seeing it is the realization of the idea of the Church fulfilling itself
in confession and absolution.

On Good Friday he spent four or five hours in the throng in St.
Peter's. Then he attended the early church ceremonial of the Feast of
the Resurrection. Klaus had to leave Rome before him, and he wrote in
his diary: 'St. Peter's; Klaus went for the last time; when I tried to put
myself in his place I grew quite depressed and I quickly started looking
forward to four more marvellous weeks.' The last event of his stay in
the Eternal City was a big Te deum in St. Peter's on 3rd June 1924:

I had always hoped to have one more splendid experience in St. Peter's . . .
I had yet another, last sight of what Catholicism is . . . In the afternoon
I walked through the whole city, then I went by way of the Pantheon

15. To his parents, 19.4.1924.
16. LPP, p. 134.

to throw my coin into the Trevi fountain . . . I must say that leaving was easier than the thought of it; I parted from most of it without sentimentality. When I looked at St. Peter's for the last time there was a feeling of sadness in my heart, and I quickly got into the tram and went away.

For all the tremendous impact that Rome made on him, he did not leave without making some criticisms. A papal audience disappointed him. 'It was very impersonal and coolly ceremonial', according to his diary. 'The Pope made an indifferent impression. He was lacking in everything papal, in all *grandezza*.' Discussions with his mentor from Bologna caused him to draw on the arsenal of his Protestant education:

After church . . . home with P. [he wrote in his diary]. A long discussion, conducted vigorously on both sides. He tried to refute Kant, but in the process involuntarily involved himself in the usual Catholic vicious circle, also he accepts the validity of deducing the existence of God from the purposefulness of the universe, and, of course, in the process continually confuses logical knowledge with knowledge gained by faith, hence the vicious circle. He would very much have liked to convert me, and in his way is very genuinely convinced. But the method he used was the least likely to achieve its purpose—dialectical tricks that he does not use as such. The result of the discussion was a big withdrawal of sympathy on my part. Catholic dogma makes everything ideal dependent upon Catholicism, without realizing it. There is a great difference between confession and the dogma of confession, also, unfortunately, between 'church' and 'church dogmatics'!

The experience nevertheless led him to more and more reflection about his own church at home, which he had hitherto treated in such step-motherly fashion:

Unification with Protestantism, however well it might perhaps become both sides—is, as I see it, out of the question. Catholicism will be able to go on doing without Protestantism for a long time yet, the people are still very attached to it, and, in comparison with the ceremonial here on its tremendous scale, the Protestant Church often looks like a small sect.[17]

A longer entry in the diary contains ideas that remained dominant in Bonhoeffer's life: dissociating the Church from dependence on the State and state privileges; its having the courage and determination to make sacrifices in many fields to achieve concentration; its understanding the essence of the Gospel in confession:

Perhaps Protestantism should never have aimed at becoming an established church, but should have remained a big sect, for which things are always easier—and in that event it would perhaps not be in its present calamitous condition. An established church believes it possesses an expansive capacity that enables it to give something to all. That it was able to do so at the time of its origin was essentially due to the political turn taken by questions which are no longer at issue today; and thus, the more political circum-

17. To his parents, 19.4.1924.

stances have changed, the more it has lost its hold over the many; until finally the term Protestantism has come to conceal a great deal that frankly and honestly can be called nothing but materialism, with the result that the only thing about it that is valued and respected is the possibility of freedom of thought, to which the reformers attached an entirely different meaning. Now, when the official tie between Church and State has been dropped, the Church is confronted with the truth; it has for too long been a home for homeless spirits, a place of refuge for uninformed edification. Had it never become an established church, the state of affairs would be very different; it would still have no small number of enthusiastic supporters, in view of its size it could hardly be described as a sect, and it would present an unusual spectacle of religious life and piety; thus it would be the ideal form of religion for which there is so much search today . . . It would have become the church intended by the reformers which it has ceased to be. Perhaps a way of remedying the terrible plight of the Church presents itself here; it must begin to limit itself and make selections in every respect, particularly in the quality of its spiritual educators and what they teach; and in any event it must completely dissociate itself from the State as soon as possible, perhaps even sacrificing the right to religious instruction . . . Is it a possible solution, or is it not? Or is the whole game up? Will it shortly return to the bosom of the only saving church, i.e. the Roman Church, under the semblance of fraternity? One would like to know.

There is no doubt, then, of Bonhoeffer's open-minded interest in Rome. Not forgetting his Protestant origin, he looked at it without iconoclasm or dogmatic prejudice. His educational background and his desire to expand his own horizon caused him to seek out the different and the unfamiliar and detect the good in it. He did not set out to find confirmation that his own denomination was right in all respects and was *a priori* in possession of the whole truth. The result was critical affection and affectionate criticism. This is still reflected in the advice he sent from his prison cell in 1944 to his friend who was passing through Rome.[18]

Studies

A few short weeks remained in Rome during which he regularly attended lectures. He wrote home that he managed to follow them very well, he had no trouble with the language. 'The lectures are very interesting', he said. 'Unfortunately there is no course on dogmatics, but it is very stimulating to have ecclesiastical history dealt with under a different light.'[19] He systematically inspected the early Christian mosaics and catacombs. 'It would be very interesting to study here for a longer time for that reason alone, for the pictures are marvellous sources of understanding for dogmatics and ecclesiastical history.'[20]

18. LPP, pp. 134 f.
19. To his parents, 21.5.1924.
20. To his parents, 27.5.1924.

Unfortunately the diary gives no details about his studies in Rome. It does not even mention where he worked. Was it in the German College, the Gregorian Library or the State University? He arrived back in Berlin at the last possible moment to register for the summer term there; his student's card is date-stamped 16th June 1924.

For a short time it seemed that he might follow the footsteps of his great-grandfather von Hase and devote himself to the early Christian and medieval memorials of the Church. But his intellectual curiosity and what in Berlin was an entirely unconventional approach deriving from dogmatics soon caused this possibility to be forgotten.

Consequences

The idea of the living Church that made such an impact on him in Rome remained a permanent influence on his thought in the field of dogmatics, and not in that field only. In a sermon he preached when he was a curate in Barcelona on 29th July 1928 on 1 Corinthians 12 : 26 f., he said:

There is a word that when a Catholic hears it kindles all his feelings of love and bliss; that stirs all the depths of his religious sensibility, from dread and awe of the Last Judgement to the sweetness of God's presence; and that certainly awakens in him the feeling of home; the feeling that only a child has in relation to its mother, made up of gratitude, reverence and devoted love; the feeling that overcomes one when, after a long absence, one returns to one's home, the home of one's childhood.

And there is a word that to Protestants has the sound of something infinitely commonplace, more or less indifferent and superfluous, that does not make their heart beat faster; something with which a sense of boredom is so often associated, or which at any rate does not lend wings to our religious feelings—and yet our fate is sealed if we are unable again to attach a new, or perhaps a very old meaning to it. Woe to us if that word does not become important to us soon again, does not become important in our lives.

Yes, the word to which I am referring is 'Church', the meaning of which we have forgotten and the nobility and greatness of which we propose to look at today.

He confessed to an acquaintance in Barcelona that Catholic Rome had been a real temptation to him;[21] and a friend of his Tübingen days, W. Dreier, testifies that after his visit to Rome he 'often defended the value of Catholicism and warned us against spiritual pride'.[22]

In 1927, when Bonhoeffer organized regular discussion evenings for a group of Grunewald schoolboys, every member of which had to present a subject for discussion in turn, he reserved only one of twenty-two subjects for himself, namely the Catholic Church. It did not yet occur to him to devote an evening to the ecumenical movement, for instance.

21. D. Albers to D. Bonhoeffer, 14.4.1929.
22. Communication from W. Dreier, 2.6.1965.

After dealing with the sacraments, the services and the uniqueness of revelation, he outlined the Protestant position to his pupils, illustrated by his Rome experiences, and now with the addition of new notes derived from his encounter with Karl Barth:

The services rendered in the course of its history by the Catholic Church to European culture, to the whole world, can hardly be overrated. It converted barbaric peoples to Christianity and civilized them, and for a long time was the only guardian of learning and art. Its monasteries took the lead in this. It developed unparalleled spiritual force, and to the present day we still marvel at the way in which it combines the principle of catholicity with its claim to be the sole true church, its combination of tolerance and intolerance. It constitutes a world in itself. Infinite diversity has converged in it, and this variegated picture gives it an irresistible fascination (*complexio oppositorum*). Seldom has a country produced such human diversity as has the Catholic Church. With admirable strength it succeeds in preserving unity in all its multiplicity, and in winning the love and reverence of the masses and awakening a strong sense of community.

But it is precisely all this greatness that gives us pause. Has this world really remained the Church of Christ? Instead of being a signpost on the way to God, has it not perhaps instead become an obstacle on the road? Has it not perhaps built over the only road to salvation?

But no one has ever built over the road to God. It still has the Bible, and so long as it still has that we can still believe it to be a holy Christian church. For God's word shall not return to him empty (Isaiah 55 : 11), whether it be preached in our or in the sister church.

We make the same profession of faith, we both use the same Lord's Prayer, and we share a large number of practices. That creates a bond between us and, so far as we are concerned, we shall gladly live in peace side by side with this unequal sister; but we shall allow to be taken from us nothing of what we know to be the word of God. We are not concerned with the terms Catholic or Protestant, but with the word of God.

On the other hand, we shall never try to force the faith of anyone else; God wants no enforced service, and he has given everyone his own conscience. But we can and should pray that our sister church will commune with itself, and know nothing among you except Jesus Christ (1 Corinthians 2 : 2). Until that comes about we must have patience; and if the 'only true Church' in a state of mistaken ignorance about our church pronounces an anathema against it, we must put up with it. It still knows no better, and professes to hate, not the heretic, but his heresy. As long as we let the word be our sole protection, we can look to the future with confidence.

After his excursions into epistemology at Tübingen in 1923, and before the vital encounter with the theology of Karl Barth in 1925, Rome was the first major experience of his student years. It would hardly be an exaggeration to say that the origins of the theological principles of his early period are discernible here. While the Barthians and their master in their early period concentrated on the theme of revelation and related the other articles of faith to it, Bonhoeffer's attention was soon completely absorbed by the phenomenon of the Church. On this ambiguous but concrete structure he erected his basic theological principles, as we shall see. His trip to Rome played a vital part in the formation of his attitude to the subject of the Church. The idea of concreteness, i.e. of not getting lost in metaphysical speculation, was one of the real roots of this approach.

III BERLIN

The Berlin to which Bonhoeffer returned was not that of the *Weltbühne*, nor was it that of great political demonstrations. Rather it was that of the great art exhibitions and concerts—and of course of Max Reinhardt's great productions, which he would not have missed on any account. It was the city in which Werner Jaeger, Oncken, Spranger and Bier taught; also it was the city of the Kaiser Wilhelm Society in which his brother Karl-Friedrich worked under Laue, Nernst, Einstein and Planck. But what really attracted him was theological Berlin.

There was still something of the lone wolf about him. His friends from Tübingen were more interested in seeing him than he was in seeing them. It was hard for any group of people to live up to the standards expected and maintained in the Wangenheimstrasse. Bonhoeffer himself admitted that newcomers to his home were put under the microscope. With that background it was easy for him to create the impression of being superior and stand-offish.

Bonhoeffer was registered at Berlin University from June 1924 to July 1927. He began writing his thesis for Seeberg and this held him in its grip. Thus to the two (half-year) terms he spent at Tübingen there must be added another seven terms (or six working terms) that he spent in Berlin. These equipped him with the armoury for his theology.

When he first went to Berlin University his turbulent thirst for knowledge was still lacking in direction. The broad front of the Berlin liberal and 'positivist' school of theology, embodied in its great teachers, opened out before him. At the end of this period Bonhoeffer could look back on a notable achievement, but the decisive turning-point for his future development took place in the middle of it, when he succumbed to the fascination of dialectical theology, at which he arrived by way of a literary detour. This occurred when he was between the ages of eighteen and nineteen.

The Faculty

Berlin University was just over 100 years old, but its theological faculty could already look back on a history during which it had exercised world-wide influence. Schleiermacher, its founder, was as important in this respect as was its then head, the formerly so controversial figure of Adolf von Harnack. When Bonhoeffer joined it in 1924 its reputation stood high. Of its great teachers only Ernst Troeltsch was no longer living.

1. *Adolf von Harnack's* authority, which had long since overstepped the bounds of the theological faculty, was no longer in dispute. Together with Naumann, he had helped to draft those parts of the Weimar Constitution that were concerned with the Church, education and learning, and to consolidate again the position of the theological faculties in the state universities which were threatened in 1919.[23] He became professor emeritus on his seventieth birthday in 1919, but it was not till 1923 that Hans Lietzmann in fact succeeded him. From 1924 onwards he continued to lecture and hold a seminar on ecclesiastical history for a selected group. As he was a next-door neighbour of the Bonhoeffers, Dietrich often used to walk with him to the Halensee station. Harnack soon began holding his seminar at home, but in 1929 had to give it up for good. Bonhoeffer attended this special seminar for at least three terms, first as a student and then as a graduate, and it was there that he gained his first laurels. The subject was the origins and early history of the Church. Helmut Goes, the brother of the poet Albrecht Goes, has described his meeting with Bonhoeffer in Harnack's house. Bonhoeffer was not only the first to draw his attention to Kierkegaard, but after the seminar also occasionally invited him home to dance in the evening. The evenings he spent at the Bonhoeffers were both gay and stimulating; Dietrich was not only a good dancer, but also played the piano, and was an accomplished conversationalist. Goes writes as follows about Harnack's seminar during the winter of 1925-6, when the subject was St. Augustine's *City of God*:

At the very first sessions I was struck by Dietrich Bonhoeffer, not only because he outdid practically all of us in theological knowledge and ability . . . but because here was someone who thought for himself and already knew what he wanted and also wanted what he knew. I actually had the experience (and to me it was a rather alarming and tremendously novel one) of seeing a blond young student contradicting the revered polyhistorian His Excellency von Harnack, contradicting him politely, but on objective theological grounds.[24]

Another of his fellow-students recalls Bonhoeffer's saying: 'Harnack never goes beyond the *Epistle of St. Clement*. If only he would hold a seminar on the Reformation.'[25]

For the master's seventy-fifth birthday on 7th May 1926 the seminar, at Bonhoeffer's instigation, produced a joint study of the concept of *chara* (joy). Each member dealt with the concept as specifically used by each

23. A. von Zahn-Harnack, *Adolf Harnack*, 1st. ed., 1936, pp. 496 f.
24. Letter of 29.7.1946.
25. Communication from E. Fink, 30.5.1964.

of the New Testament authors or apostolic fathers, as the case may be, in St. John, St. Paul, the Synoptic Gospels, the Epistle to the Hebrews, the Shepherd of Hermas and the Didache. Bonhoeffer corrected each contribution and made substantial cuts and additions of his own, and he wrote the concluding article, entitled 'Joy in Primitive Christianity. An Attempted Survey'. The basic idea and the style reappeared later in Kittel's *Theological Word Book*; it revealed the thoroughness of Bonhoeffer's training in the methods of historical criticism. After his graduation, to express his gratitude to his teachers, Bonhoeffer wrote some phrases of farewell to them on his thesis. The words that he addressed to Harnack were as follows: 'What I have learnt and come to understand in your seminar is too closely associated with my whole personality for me to be able ever to forget it.'[26]

2. Bonhoeffer spent two terms in 1925 in the seminar on ecclesiastical history conducted by *Karl Holl*, the influential interpreter of Luther, who was also a friend of Harnack's. In 1925 Holl was excessively burdened by being also rector of the university, and in May 1926 he died a week after his sixtieth birthday. Harnack delivered the memorial address. Bonhoeffer thought that Harnack 'should have painted a different picture of Holl and concentrated on his strict view of sin'.[27]

Bonhoeffer eagerly immersed himself in Holl's interpretation of Luther's doctrine of justification. Holl irrevocably implanted in him the doctrine of 'by grace alone' as the one *articulus stantis et cadentis ecclesiae*. He convinced him that even the devout are not able really to love God, and henceforward Luther's phrase *cor curvum in se* became a key word to him. He continually applied it also to the epistemological field in order to refute the noetic optimism of idealism and the localization of God in the individual's own mind. But at an early stage he was critical of Holl's interpretation of Luther's faith as a religion of conscience, which seemed to him to threaten the assurance of faith in the *extra me*.[28] As against what had become a vague cultural Protestantism, he liked Holl's epoch-making advance into the centre of Luther's doctrine of justification, though he felt it to be weakly anchored in Luther's Christology. But Holl made a lasting impact on him. In 1943, in Tegel prison, he had sent to him the three volumes of Holl's collected papers.[29] In his student days he seriously considered going on working with Holl, but this was prevented by the latter's death.

Bonhoeffer's first approach to Russian, or Orthodox, Christianity was apparently also due to Holl. It was not only the dialectical theologians, with their predilection for Dostoevsky, who were responsible for promoting a first wave of interest in Orthodoxy in theological circles. Holl did all in his power to encourage it too. He learnt Russian in order to read

26. Cf. also his address at Harnack's memorial service, Ch. IV, p. 102.
27. Communication from H. Goes, 29.7.1946.
28. GS III, pp. 75 f.　　29. LPP, pp. 55, 71.

Tolstoy in particular. Bonhoeffer had eagerly read Tolstoy in his school-days, and he now acquired the volumes of Hans Ehrenberg's *Eastern Christianity*[30] on their successive appearances, especially for the sake of the chapter on Berdiayev[31] and Ehrenberg's postscript.[32] Naturally he also plunged into Dostoevsky. On 13th March 1925 he wrote to his parents:

I have just been reading Dostoevsky's highly interesting speech on Pushkin, in which he represents him as the first man to make a distinction between Russian and European and as the herald of the Russian ideal: 'supra-national pan-humanism', as he calls it. It is remarkable that he should call on what is most specific in a nation to show that nation the way to trans-cending itself, at any rate as a nation. To Dostoevsky this idea, as he continually emphasizes, is necessarily associated with that of Christianity, and the real 'catholicism' of primitive Christianity is thus re-established.

This discovery of east European Christianity also led, among other things, to Deissmann's invitation to Stefan Zankow to give a course of lectures at Berlin University in 1927 on 'The Orthodox Christianity of the East', which were later published in book form by the Furche-Verlag. Thus, when Bonhoeffer later met Zankow, among others, at ecumenical conferences, he was by no means totally unprepared, for Holl as well as the dialectical theologians had roused his interest in the Eastern Church. True, this did not yet lead him to explore Orthodoxy for himself.

3. Bonhoeffer's favourite subject in Berlin was systematic theology, which was taught by *Reinhold Seeberg*, whose seminar he attended without interruption from the summer term of 1925 until he completed his studies in 1927. The fact that Bonhoeffer wrote his thesis for Seeberg created a somewhat delicate situation, for cool relations existed between the latter and Harnack, to whom Bonhoeffer was personally so much closer. Seeberg and Harnack were both of Baltic origin, but they differed politically. During the First World War Seeberg favoured the maximum possible extension of the German frontiers, including the absorption of Livonia and Courland, while Harnack regarded such claims as excessive and dangerous.

But Seeberg was the professor of Bonhoeffer's chosen subject, so he remained with that great middleman between the critical historians and the so-called positivists. He learnt a great deal from him, even though the encounter began with a theological controversy; and Seeberg took an interest in his polite but bristly new pupil.

The five volumes of Seeberg's *History of Dogmatic Theology* are among the earliest in Bonhoeffer's library, and he did a great deal of work on them. His knowledge of St. Augustine, St. Thomas Aquinas, the Scholastics and Melanchthon and Luther came from that source. 'In his

30. H. Ehrenberg, *Östliches Christentum*, 1923-5.
31. Ibid., Vol. II, pp. 246 ff.
32. Ibid., Vol. I, pp. 333 f.

seminars Seeberg in the first place showed his supreme mastery of the history of medieval dogmatics.'[33] Bonhoeffer's favourite quotations from Luther are all underlined in those five volumes.[34] The grounding in Luther that he received from Seeberg and Holl enabled him to maintain his critical independence in meeting the onslaught of Barth's theology. He familiarized himself with Seeberg's great models—Schleiermacher, Hegel and Albrecht Ritschl—and he also acquired from Seeberg the difficult technical jargon of his student years, which is saturated with Seeberg's Hegelian concepts, for example the distinction between 'objective and absolute spirit'. The key to his theology of the following five years, the concept of 'Christ existing as community', was forged here too. Bonhoeffer later shook off this heavy-going jargon, but three important elements in Seeberg's thought remained with him and played a formative part in his development.

a) In the first place it struck him that Seeberg was not content to leave theological tenets in the epistemological field, but always emphasized also their volitional components. To him being always meant will also, and faith awareness of the will created by the primary will. This gave wings to Bonhoeffer's anti-speculative inclinations.

b) Seeberg transmitted to him Ritschl's aversion to metaphysics. This had driven the latter along the road to a far-reaching Christocentrism.

c) Seeberg taught Bonhoeffer to take the social category seriously. To Seeberg the essential mark of man was that he had a history and lived in society. Bonhoeffer made the social field an essential part of all theological concepts.

But, since he had already begun to be fascinated by Barth when he first sat at Seeberg's feet, criticism of his master set in immediately. He rejected out of hand Seeberg's attempt to harmonize the Bible and the modern spirit, Luther and idealism, theology and philosophy. Seeberg attached a great deal of importance to the doctrine of the 'religious *a priori*':[35]

The *a priori* in religion is a purely formal primary characteristic of the created spirit or self that enables and obliges the latter to become directly aware of the absolute spirit. This implies two things, first that the created will is concerned with purposefully acquiring awareness of the primary will, and second that the reason is thereby simultaneously given the capacity to acquire an intuition of it.[36]

For all his respect for the greatness of the nineteenth century and Schleiermacher, the great doctor of the nineteenth-century Church,

33. Communication from E. Fink, 30.5.1964.
34. It can also be shown that he worked thoroughly through large parts of J. Ficker's edition of *Luther's Addresses on the Epistle to the Romans*, 3rd ed., 1925.
35. Cf. L. Richter, 'Reinhold Seeberg's Beitrag zu theologischen Gegenwartsfragen', *Zeichen der Zeit*, 1959, pp. 133-7; G. Koch, 'Reinhold Seeberg und die Bekennende Kirche', *Kirche in der Zeit*, 1959, pp. 208-11.
36. R. Seeberg, *Christliche Dogmatik*, Vol. I, 1924, p. 103.

Bonhoeffer regarded this as an obscuration of the Reformation. Their anthropological and theological optimism made him regard Seeberg and his friends as incapable of understanding the post-war collapse and crisis and interpreting them to his generation. The collapse did not lead them to feel the necessity of a fundamental reappraisal of ideas, and to them the war had been merely an unhappy episode. To Bonhoeffer personally it took the sting out of a burning problem of conscience. He had been wrestling for a long time with the problem of what his own 'religious *a priori*' might be, and he reacted violently against any new attempts to point to a human religious potentiality, no matter how constituted, that led back to investigation of the self.

In the volume of Seeberg's history of dogmatics in which he deals with Luther the passage occurs: 'This enables one to understand the remarkable circumstance that Luther uses religious *experience* as well as the Scriptures as the witness and canon of truth. But in this it is experience that establishes the certainty of the truth of the contents of Scripture.'[37] Bonhoeffer wrote a few words in the margin that throw a flash of light on his basic theological and personal difference with Seeberg. 'No', he wrote. 'On the contrary, it is Scripture that shows the existence of God, and that by way of the Church, the ministry.' This approach was inevitably surprising to the Berlin faculty. In spite of their differences, Seeberg retained Bonhoeffer's loyalty:

So at about the usual time on many Friday evenings I look back with regret to your seminar, and I should very much like to sit down again among your audience and to reflect on the 'meaning of history' with you . . . I think with gratitude of the hours during the past four years which I had the privilege of spending with you.[38]

Bonhoeffer certainly felt that Holl, to whom everything was much gloomier and more difficult, and Harnack, had greater strength of personality, but he never willingly surrendered to strong personalities. The only personalities to whom he granted real authority over him were Karl Barth and Dr. Bell, the Bishop of Chichester—though even then it was very much by himself that he struggled through to the decisions that he believed to be right. Thus in the last resort it was his spirit of independence that caused him to choose Seeberg as his mentor in Berlin, for Seeberg imposed on him the least amount of restriction and obligation.

4. For two terms Bonhoeffer attended the seminar on the New Testament given by *Adolf Deissmann* with the assistance of G. Bertram. Deissmann was the leading German personality in the young ecumenical movement, and in Bonhoeffer's student days he played a prominent part in the world conferences on 'Life and Work' in 1925 in Stockholm and on 'Faith and Order' in 1927 at Lausanne. These conferences and their

37. R. Seeberg, *Lehrbuch der Dogmengeschichte*, Vol. IV, 3rd ed., 1917, p. 340.
38. Letter from Barcelona, 20.7.1928.

subject can hardly have escaped Bonhoeffer's observation, but he failed to notice at the time that this was the field in which exciting innovations were to take place. A student friend—certainly reflecting his own attitude—wrote to him: 'The more one has to do with it,[39] the more dubious it seems; it would not be dubious if its aim was to be no more than an international meeting for the cultivation of ethics—but the aim is to be much more than that. It is to build the Kingdom of God.'[40] It was Deissmann who later helped to open the door of the ecumenical world to Bonhoeffer, and gave him the most flattering recommendations to help him along that road.

He rather belatedly attended *Sellin's* course on the Old Testament, while he was already attending *Mahling's*[41] seminars on practical theology.

Dialectical Theology

The discovery of Barth took place between his stay in Rome and the beginning of his work on his thesis, that is, between the summer of 1924 and that of 1925. It can be attributed to the beginning of the winter of 1924-5.

In the few remaining weeks of the 1924 Berlin summer term he had 'rather to neglect the historical and philological subjects and take up Hebrew again . . . apart from that, every week I meet another theological student and we test each other on ecclesiastical history'.[42] During the vacation he was completely taken up with philosophy, sociology and the history of religion. 'I have a very interesting book, Max Weber's *Sociology of Religion* . . . After Weber I also propose to read Troeltsch's *Social Theories of Christian Ethics* and to finish off Husserl—and, if I have time, to tackle Schleiermacher thoroughly.'[43] In his letters to his friends during the autumn he discussed Max Weber's sociological categories, such as state, people, race, and the characteristics of ethical communities, as well as Kant, Luther, Holl, Husserl, and Hegel's definition of the objective mind. Unfortunately Bonhoeffer's letters have not survived, but only his friends' replies.

But in May and June 1925 the whole tone of these letters suddenly changed. He began discussing Gogarten's *The Religious Decision* with Wilhelm Dreier, and an 'entirely new' note crept in. His mother, who sometimes tried to keep pace with her son's interests, had for his sake read Troeltsch at the beginning of 1925; having finished this in August 1925, she asked him to send her 'the Barth book' in the holidays. This was Barth's first volume of collected lectures, *Das Wort Gottes und die*

39. i.e. the Stockholm conference.
40. R. Widmann, 25.2.1926.
41. Friedrich Mahling, Professor of Practical Theology since 1909.
42. To his parents, 9.8.1924.
43. Letter of 9.8.1924.

Theologie, published in 1924. Dietrich Bonhoeffer now made himself a propagandist for this book, and in the summer of 1925 he presented a copy to his godfather Hans von Hase, who had been sending him occasional letters of advice.

During the winter of 1924-5 Bonhoeffer in fact read more than ever. Several attacks of influenza gave him the leisure. Ibsen's plays, above all *Brand* and *Peer Gynt*, alternated with the works of Barth.

In Berlin he may very well have come across copies of the new journal *Zwischen den Zeiten* and heard that something new had appeared on the horizon. But there were two specific circumstances that drew it to his notice.

In the first place, in the summer of 1924 his cousin Hans-Christoph von Hase, who was close to him, began reading mathematics at Göttingen, where Karl Barth was lecturing, and the impact made on him by Barth was such that he transferred to the school of theology. Bonhoeffer must have heard all about this at the latest during the autumn vacation. Bonhoeffer's papers include some lecture notes—at that time these were laboriously copied out by hand—under the heading 'Karl Barth, dictated notes on "Instruction on the Christian Religion", I and II'. These constitute the principal points of his lectures dictated to his students by Barth in Göttingen during his dogmatics course in the summer of 1924 and the winter of 1924-5, and they are a brief early version of what was to be expanded into the first volume of his *Prologomena to Christian Dogmatics* of 1927. Such dictated notes were passed round by friends from one university to another, and it was from these that Bonhoeffer obtained a first insight into the structure that was to be erected on the foundations of Barth's *Epistle to the Romans*.

Secondly, at the latest at the beginning of the winter term of 1924-5, when he first joined Harnack's seminar at which the apostolic fathers were studied with thoroughness but all the professor's involvements were followed with the greatest interest, Bonhoeffer must have been drawn into a bitter controversy that was the subject of universal comment, namely that between Barth and Harnack in the *Christliche Welt* of 1923;[44] in which neither yielded an inch to the other and each proclaimed a black future for theology if the other were left in command of the field. Each spoke at a level that excluded the other.

Should we theologians [Barth said] not have the courage to let our theology begin with the perhaps fundamentally sceptical but nevertheless clear memory of the certainly 'totally unintelligible', unbelievable and incredible and certainly disturbing testimony that God himself said and did something, actually put something new, that was outside the correlation of all human words and things, into that correlation, and did not just put words and

44. Reprinted in *Anfänge der dialektischen Theologie*, ed. J. Moltmann. Vol. I, 2nd ed., 1966, pp. 323-47.

things side by side with other words and things, but this particular word and this particular thing?[45]

Harnack wrote to his friend Martin Rade:

Our present theology is glad (that itself is a great thing) that it is serious of purpose and aims at the heart of the matter. But how weak it is as a science, how narrow and sectarian its horizon . . . how expressionistic is its logical method and how short-sighted its view of history . . . Ritschl today is scorned, though in my opinion he has a great deal to offer which the Barthians could take up; but the sons are even more hostile to their fathers than to their grandfathers.[46]

In 1929 Harnack was still writing sadly and appealingly to the young Bonhoeffer about the threat to spiritual life represented by 'contempt for scientific theology and the menace to it represented by unscientific theology'. 'Those who hold high the flag of real science must therefore stand by it more steadfastly than ever', he said.[47]

With his discovery of dialectical theology, Bonhoeffer acquired a more positive direction that took the place of his previous rather restless roving. He now took a real joy in his work; it was like a liberation. The mere fact that the new theology came into being with the peculiar task of preaching—the earthly, concrete task of proving the worth of the word of God in human terms—removed him from the field of speculation. This theological experiment at first betrayed no suspicious elegance. Rearguard actions and apologias were scorned, and inconsistencies were left unreconciled; and, when Bonhoeffer discovered that, contrary to the views of many, borrowings from philosophy and anthropology could not be avoided, he nevertheless gladly accepted the determination to establish the right of theology to exist independently and in its own right. Borrowed themes and fields of discussion fell away, and a subject that his elders had so looked down on in his boyhood at last acquired an independence for which it was worth while committing oneself. Much more than intellectual pleasure was to be derived from the brilliant rebel and controversialist Karl Barth.

Barth diverted attention from the facts of humanity as they had been so terribly revealed to that generation. He made the religious experience that Bonhoeffer had long sought with youthful enthusiasm, the religious experience that had caused him such difficulties, seem a matter of no importance. The certainty for which he strove was anchored, not in man, but in the majesty of God, with the result that it was not a theme in itself apart from God. In contrast to many to whom Barth seemed so gloomy, Bonhoeffer ascribed to him true *hilaritas*.[48]

Was it not a feather in the cap of the new theology that it was able

45. A. von Zahn-Harnack, op. cit., pp. 530 f.
46. A. von Zahn-Harnack, op. cit., p. 536.
47. Letter of 22.12.1929, GS III, p. 20.
48. LPP, p. 137.

to win over the young Bonhoeffer? Here was a young man with a thorough philosophical grounding who had also familiarized himself with the latest methods of historical criticism of the time; who, unlike many young Barthians, was not a youthful rebel thrown off the rails by the post-war crisis, and was not a former pietist rebelling against his upbringing. Here was a well-balanced young man from an upper middle-class home who had been objectively convinced; a young man who, thanks to the breadth of horizon of his home environment and his natural gifts, was able to see things as they were without giving way to blind enthusiasm.

Bonhoeffer did not allow his gratitude for the essentials to deprive him of his critical faculty. But he criticized as an ally. On points that he regarded as weak he did not hesitate to put forward alternative suggestions. His first criticism was directed at a point characteristic of his own inner trends. He suspected that Barth's assertion of the inaccessibility and free majesty of God threatened and volatilized the due emphasis on man's concrete, earthly plight. There is a small piece of evidence for this dating from the time of his first acquaintance with Barth's work. A recent book by Max Strauch, intended to be an introduction to and defence of Karl Barth's theology, was being widely read at the time. Strauch describes[49] the eschatological dualism, the infinite qualitative difference, between this world and the next: '. . . in contrast to all the visible is the invisible; in contrast to this world the incommensurable next world; in contrast . . . to all reality and transience is the world of the origin and the goal'.[50] Bonhoeffer underlined the words 'origin' and 'goal', and wrote in the margin: 'Not the faith which is now simply received!' That was where he questioned and criticized: he asked whether the free and inaccessible majesty of God consisted entirely in freedom *from* the world, or whether the truth was not rather that it entered into the world, since the freedom of God had committed itself to the human community.[51]

Bonhoeffer refused to regard Barth's position, as opposed to Harnack's, as a neo-scholastic orthodoxy erected as a bulwark against the corrupting forces of liberalism. There are signs that he feared that the dogmatics being developed by Barth might represent a regression in comparison with the *Epistle to the Romans*, and that he discussed this with his fellow-students critically, as students do. An entry in Richard Widmann's diary confirms the concern they felt at the time. They noted that in the preface to the fifth edition of the *Epistle to the Romans* Barth announced that he would 'say and do, blow upon blow, what must now be said and done—if the whole thing is not to be a will-o'-the-wisp—in order to do justice to the plight and at the same time the hope of the

49. M. Strauch, *Die Theologie Karl Barths*, 1924.
50. M. Strauch, op. cit., p. 15.
51. Cf. Ch. IV, p. 97, and also AB, pp. 80 ff.

Church'. But in the section on Christology, which was the second half of Barth's lectures on dogmatics, he said: 'I prefer erring with the fathers of Chalcedon to painting a portrait of Jesus from the New Testament on my own account.'[52] Bonhoeffer had sent Widmann, who had been a fellow-student of his in Holl's seminar, his copy of some of Barth's lecture-notes. Widmann's letter to Bonhoeffer of 25th February 1926 shows how great must have been Bonhoeffer's fears of 'reactionary gestures' on the part of the new master; these fears were stated anew in the letters from Tegel. Widmann wrote to Bonhoeffer:

You once mentioned that you deplored the servitude into which Barth has relapsed in these dogmatics—that he takes anxious care (yes, just that) to follow in the footsteps of the dogmaticians of ancient times. I do not regard this reactionary gesture as being wrong. The primary purpose, after all, is merely to establish a link with the past, and perhaps not merely a link, but actual reinforcement from the past. Aid, stimulus, fertile ideas—such a dogmatic theology cannot be simply shaken out of one's sleeves, for Barth is cleaning out an Augean stable, and in the process will have cause to be really grateful to his orthodox assistants. But I certainly also think that what we equally need is a dogmatics that manages without these reactionary crutches and looks forward for links. Certainly the *Epistle to the Romans* is much less reactionary in its formulations. In that connection the dogmatics are a step backwards. Perhaps next time, when his dogmatics have fulfilled their 'tactical purpose'—his reliance on the ancients will not have amounted to more than that—he will take two steps forward.

Benkt-Erik Benktson points out[53] that in 1944 Bonhoeffer described Barth as one who had 'started along this line of thought' towards a non-religious interpretation, but had not yet carried it 'to completion'.[54] Where did Barth 'start' to do this? Benktson points to Barth's lecture on 'Biblical Questions, Insights and Prospects', delivered at Aarau in 1920, which Bonhoeffer so eagerly read in his *Das Wort Gottes und die Theologie*, published in 1924-5, which contains assertions in terms astonishingly close to those of *Letters and Papers from Prison*:

There have been . . . definitely non-religious men who . . . [have felt] the whole weight of the question of the existence of God [p. 73]. Biblical piety is not really pietism; it should far rather be described as a well-considered, qualified worldliness . . . [as] worldly objectivity [p. 80]. Thinking and speaking deriving from totality and directed at totality . . . the worldliness of the Biblical line [p. 84]. It is not God's will that he should be transcendent, in separation from this world, [God] does not wish to be a founder of religious history, but to be the Lord of our lives [p. 85]. Biblical history is . . . primarily and above all human history [p. 95].

52. Communication from R. Widmann. 28.9.1965.
53. B. E. Benktson, 'Christus und die mündiggewordene Welt. Eine Studie zur Theologie Dietrich Bonhoeffers', *Svensk teologisk Kvartalskrift*, Year 40, 1964, No. 2.
54. LPP, p. 153.

Perhaps it was these notes that were still ringing in Bonhoeffer's ears when he said that Barth had 'started' but 'had not finished'.

But it was not this trend of the early Barth that influenced him now. He took over Barth's distinction between faith and religion used as human self-justification. He criticized Barth for making revelation and not the Church his point of departure. He asked whether Barth's sequence, his coming to the Church only by way of revelation, did not make salvation too secondary a factor. He did not want to have or conceive of revelation without or apart from its soteriological aspect.

IV DOCTORAL THESIS

Bonhoeffer began working on his doctoral thesis a good year after his return from Rome. Not only was this strikingly early since he was only nineteen; it was also unusual to assume this heavy burden in addition to the normal course of studies without applying for leave, or for an extension, or for special treatment of some kind. Nor was the subject dictated to him; it arose out of his own interests. It crystallized out in several stages—during which he disappointed a number of hopes that he might devote himself to other subjects and other fields.

Preliminary Stages

1. It was Harnack who first persuaded Bonhoeffer to work for his doctorate, and it was for him he wrote his first essay in Berlin in the winter of 1924-5. He submitted no fewer than fifty-seven pages to the old gentleman, and their reception took him aback. Listening to the St. Matthew Passion in his cell in Tegel in 1943 recalled to mind his situation in 1925. 'I was eighteen, and had just come from Harnack's seminar, in which he had discussed my first seminar essay very kindly, and had expressed the hope that some day I should specialize in Church History. I was full of this when I went into the Philharmonic Hall.'[55]

Should he follow the example of his distinguished forebear and devote himself to ecclesiastical history—or disappoint this eminent and friendly neighbour? As a result of his study of Troeltsch he was very much alive to the problems of historicism, but this was a field in which he was merely flexing his muscles. He did not wish to remain in it, but to prepare himself systematically to tackle the really burning questions.

2. He wrote his second essay in Holl's seminar, on 'Luther's Feelings about his Work in the Last Years of his Life, according to his Correspondence of 1540-1546, *Enders-Kawerau*, Vols. 12-18'. He handed it in at the beginning of June 1925. As Harnack had done in the case of his previous effort, Holl marked it with an unqualified 'very good (I)'. Again it was a strictly historical exercise, based on the original sources. But

55. LPP, p. 73.

busying himself with the aged Luther's vivid apocalyptic and eschatological visions had a very disturbing effect. The words *'finis, finis,
finis instat'* haunted him, like a question mark put against his faith.
Luther made an enormous impact on him. Should he choose Holl as his
master?

3.   After these brilliant performances in the historical field, he finally
took the plunge into his favourite subject, dogmatics, but this time the
result was near-failure. The title of his first essay in the seminar on
systematic theology was 'Can a Distinction be drawn between a
Historical and a Pneumatological Interpretation of the Scriptures, and
What is the Attitude to this of Dogmatic Theology?' Underneath
appear the words: 'Satisfactory. Seeberg, 31.7.1925'. To Reinhold
Seeberg the whole thing was a disturbing exercise in Barthianism. The
margin is filled with his queries, critical comments and 'noes', only
rarely interspersed with a 'good'. But it was this clash that led to the
decision about his thesis.

The essay begins as follows:

The Christian religion stands or falls by belief in divine revelation that
became historically real, tangible and visible—that is, to those who have
eyes to see and ears to hear—and thus essentially implies the question that
we are posing today about the relationship between history and spirit, or,
applied to the Bible, between letter and spirit, Scripture and revelation, man's
word and God's.

These are the concluding sentences:

All attempted pneumatological interpretation is prayer, supplication to the
Holy Spirit [here Seeberg with good reason wrote the word 'only?' in the
margin] which alone gives it the hearing and understanding without which
the most highly intellectual exegesis is nothing. Textual understanding and
interpretation, ministry, i.e. the realization of God, is included in the prayer:
Veni creator spiritus.

Bonhoeffer begins by condemning the skill in which he had just
distinguished himself with Harnack and Holl. Textual criticism left
behind nothing but 'dust and ashes', he says. The texts are not just
historical sources, but agents of revelation, not just specimens of writing,
but sacred canon. Proclaiming the significance of that is a task for the
future. Bonhoeffer then turns aside to declare that historical work on
the texts must nevertheless be done, 'for none of us can revert to the
pre-critical age'. The essay shows how well acquainted he was with the
new methods of stylistic criticism, but, since his discovery of the new
perspectives opened up by Barth, not much of them remains. He does
not explain what he means by the impossibility of reverting to the
pre-critical age. He takes the view that in regard to the interpretation
of the Scriptures, textual criticism has little to say, he relativizes it. At
this point he adopts Thurneysen's simile for exegesis, visualizing it, as

he often did in later years, as crossing an ice-bound stream, jumping from one block of ice to another. Revelation is contained in Scripture, because God speaks in it; that is undemonstrable, and is not a conclusion but a premise. Divine revelation enables men to recognize divine revelation, that is, the Holy Spirit. Bonhoeffer adopts as his own for the future Barth's conclusion that things can be known only by their like. 'God can be known only through God. Hence it follows that the idea of revelation must be thought of, not substantially, but functionally, i.e. it is not so much a being as a decision, the will of God expressed in Scripture.' Also he says: 'For history Scripture is only a source, for pneumatology it is testimony.'

Nowadays these conclusions seem restrictive; at that time Bonhoeffer and his friends regarded them as a liberation from the inconsistencies of historicism.

Seeberg was so roused by the 'pneumatological exegesis'—later it came to be known as 'theological exegesis'—that was now rife and was making incursions into his own seminar that soon afterwards he published a paper on it himself.[56]

In the first essay he wrote for him Bonhoeffer boldly disputed the doctrine of the 'religious *a priori*'.

Before the beginning of the summer vacation of 1925 Seeberg spoke to Karl Bonhoeffer at a meeting of the University Senate about his rebellious son, and said that he would like to have a more thorough discussion with him. This duly took place, and on 21st September 1925 Bonhoeffer wrote to his parents:

... in the meantime I had been thinking things over and came to the following conclusion. Doing the work for Holl or Harnack would be pointless, since with a dogmatic-historical subject I should meet with no resistance from Seeberg either, so it makes very little difference whether I go to one or the other, as I think that on the whole Seeberg is also well-disposed towards me. So I decided to remain with Seeberg, to whom I have now suggested a subject that is half historical and half systematic; and he is very pleased with it.

It is connected with the theme of the religious community, which I mentioned to you one evening some time or other as one that would interest me. It involves doing a great deal of historical work, but there is no harm in that. At all events, Seeberg seems to be pretty interested in the subject himself. He said he had been waiting for a long time for someone to work on it; and he was very pleased that I had hit on it by myself.

'Sanctorum Communio'

Bonhoeffer began work on his thesis at the beginning of his sixth term and finished it in eighteen months. His concentration and his ability

56. R. Seeberg, 'Zur Frage nach dem Sinn und Recht einer pneumatischen Schriftauslegung', *Zeitschrift für Systematische Theologie*, 1926, IV, pp. 3-59. Also Seeberg, 'Zum Problem der pneumatischen Exegese', *Sellin-Festschrift*, 1927, pp. 127-37.

to make the best use of his time must have been extraordinary, for during the same period he also handed in at least seven essays and nine draft catechisms and sermons. He also took charge of a children's religious instruction group, with all the consequential obligations, and he was no more willing to sacrifice holidays in northern Italy or at Friedrichsbrunn than he was to give up playing tennis with new friends such as Helmut Rössler, who also introduced him to the works of Franz Werfel. In the Bonhoeffer home it was regarded as bad form to let it be seen that one had a great deal of work, and it may be true that he dealt too cursorily with his sources. At all events, he is criticized nowadays for eclecticism and misrepresentation in his treatment of Hegel, for instance.[57] But superficiality was not one of the criticisms made of him at the university by men such as Seeberg and Titius.

So he sat down and came to grips with his subject, the Church. To him it was both a riddle and an aspiration. Who was it? What was it? Where was it? His sub-title was 'A Dogmatic Enquiry into the Sociology of the Church'.

Was the subject in the air? When Bonhoeffer wrote to his friend Widmann about it, the latter replied:

Your thesis may have all sorts of topical consequences: see Althaus and his 'living community'; see Barth's speech at Duisburg-Meiderich in the latest number of *Zwischen den Zeiten*;[58] see Kierkegaard's *Attack*, see the latest 'movement' in the Youth Movement: everything is crying out for 'association,' 'fellowship', 'community'; see the Bavarian concordat.[59]

Althaus was working on the same subject; his title was 'Communio Sanctorum. The Community in Luther's Idea of the Church'. His contention was that 'the renewal of the doctrine of the Church that is incumbent upon us today must learn something from the history of the idea of the community on Lutheran soil.'[60]

Both are criticized nowadays for a certain romanticism in their concept of the community. But, unlike Althaus, Bonhoeffer found himself falling between too many stools when he tried to reconcile disciplines with such powerful centrifugal tendencies as historicism and sociology on the one hand and the theology of revelation on the other. His cousin Hans-Christoph von Hase, who was a student at Marburg and kept him supplied with news about Heidegger and Bultmann, who were working there, wrote to him: 'There will not be many who really understand it,

57. Thus D. Böhler wrote to the author on 2.7.1964: 'At the time of *Sanctorum Communio* Bonhoeffer had absorbed the bourgeois Hegel renaissance, but hardly Hegel himself.'
58. K. Barth. 'Wünschbarkeit und Möglichkeit eines allgemeinen reformierten Glaubensbekenntnisses', *Die Theologie und die Kirche*, *Gesammelte Vorträge*, Vol. II, 1928, pp. 76 ff.
59. R. Widmann to D. Bonhoeffer, 17.11.1925.
60. P. Althaus, *Communio Sanctorum*, 1929.

the Barthians won't because of the sociology, and the sociologists won't because of Barth.'[61]

Bonhoeffer's aim, however, was no less than that of reuniting his divergent intellectual heritages, bringing sociology and the critical tradition into harmony with the theology of revelation, i.e. reconciling Troeltsch and Barth. Applying the irreconcilable to the concrete Church, he adapted to his purpose a phrase from Hegel's *The Absolute Religion*. Hegel's words were 'God existing as community';[62] in Bonhoeffer they became 'Christ existing as community'. To Hegel the community was the dwelling-place of the Holy Spirit in the form of absolute spirit. To Seeberg it was the dwelling-place of the Holy Spirit in the form of absolute will. Bonhoeffer set out to refashion the whole Christologically, believing he was overcoming the Troeltsch-Barth antithesis by attaining an overriding third position. Later critics regarded this as more bold than successful.

There was a personal impulse behind Bonhoeffer's aim of establishing the word of God in a sociological community. In the living Church, salvation acquired its *pro me* in an *extra me* without either disappearing in favour of the other.

He found the tools for this ecclesiology in the I-Thou personalism prevalent in those years. He apparently discovered Grisebach[63] from his reading of Gogarten. He criticized Grisebach for attempting to make the I-Thou relationship absolute, and tried to assure it against relapsing into a neo-idealism by incorporating it into his Christological ecclesiology. But Seeberg had also introduced him to the idea of man's being characterized by sociality and mutuality, and by these means he thought he could describe both the other-worldliness and the transcendental nature of revelation. He took to these tools the more readily because he was afraid that Barth's emphasis on the diastasis of God threatened the 'humanly involved and yet divinely detached presence of God'. Ferdinand Ebner is often quoted nowadays as the source of this personalism, but there is no evidence that Bonhoeffer was then acquainted with his works.[64]

To Bonhoeffer rigid theological tenets became fluid again when he revealed their thoroughly social character. He already developed here what later was to become current under the concept of fellowship. His argument for the giving of brotherhood paved the way first theologically and then practically for the rediscovery of oral confession. Here lay the roots of the Tegel formula of 'being there for others'. In *Sanctorum Communio*, to judge from the quotations, Barth still played a minor role, but Bonhoeffer wrote with him in the background. His main question to Barth now was whether his concept of revelation did not

---

61. Letter of 13.10.1930.
62. G. W. F. Hegel, *Sämtliche Werke*, ed. G Lasson, Vol. XIV, Part III, p. 198.
63. E. Grisebach, *Die Grenzen des Erziehers und seine Verantwortung*, 1924.
64. Except through a review by Gogarten in 1932-3, see GS V.

neglect the Church. Under the impact of his discovery, in the critics' view, Bonhoeffer caused the difference between Christ and the community to dwindle to the point of identification, and with the critical function of eschatology he also volatilized the provisional character of the Church, or, as one says today, caused it to lose the marks of 'historicity'. Regin Prenter, however, is correct in showing that Bonhoeffer never regarded his formula of 'Christ existing as community' as being true in reverse.[65]

At all events, it was ecclesiology that dominated Bonhoeffer's theology in its early stages, absorbing Christology in itself. Later it was the other way about. For all its immaturely, ambiguously or mistakenly adopted concepts, this preliminary organization of his ideas served him as a bulwark against metaphysical speculation and transcendental volatilization of the idea of God. God, though distant, was close and concrete encounter with one's fellows, faith was tying oneself in with the community, living a human life was possible through fellowship. He held fast to these things through all his changes of theological language.

The Church's cultural significance, and its pride of place in history, for all the respect it inspired in earlier generations and for all the impact it made on him in Rome, were not vital to him. But the place in which revelation manifested itself in preaching, praise, prayer, or service to one's fellows held him by its persisting greatness, even interpreted sociologically.

When, after endless toing and froing, Bonhoeffer's first systematic incursion into theology was at last published, it was ignored.[66] Interest in this immature early work was first roused by the fragmentary contents of *Letters and Papers from Prison* twenty years later. In 1955 a tribute was paid to it by the man whose unknown, critical ally the young writer believed himself to be. In his *Church Dogmatics* Barth wrote:

If there is one thing that justifies Reinhold Seeberg, it may lie in the fact that there emerged from his school this man and this thesis which, with its broad and deep vision, not only rouses the deepest respect when one looks back at the situation at the time, but also is to this very day more instructive, more stimulating, more enlightening and more truly 'edifying' to read than a great deal of the better-known writing that has since been published on the problem of the Church . . . I frankly admit that I find it difficult at least to maintain the level then reached by Bonhoeffer, and from my place and in my own language to say as much and not to express myself more weakly than that young man did then.[67]

65. Cf. *Lutherische Monatshefte*, June 1965, p. 264.
66. See Ch. IV, pp. 95 f.
67. K. Barth, *Kirchliche Dogmatik*, Vol. IV/2, p. 725.

V SEMINAR ESSAYS

Students were required to produce evidence of attendance at seminars on the basic subjects. The essays that Bonhoeffer wrote show many of the roots from which his thought was continually nourished in later years.

For Sellin (Old Testament) he wrote hastily, and not till his eighth term, an essay on 'The Various Answers to the Problem of Suffering in Job' and used the methods of historical criticism to examine the sources and assess the 'writer's achievement'. For Deissmann (New Testament) his subject was 'St. Paul and the Fifteenth Chapter of the Gospel according to St. John', and in dealing with it he discussed Bultmann's and Barth's categories, this in the summer of 1926. For Holl (Ecclesiastical History) he wrote a study of 'Luther's Views of the Holy Spirit after the Disputations of 1535-1545', influenced by Holl's interpretation of justification by faith. In the school of systematic theology he wrote four more papers, all of which Seeberg marked 'excellent'. They were on 'Reason and Revelation in Early Lutheran Dogmatics' (November 1925); 'Church and Eschatology, or the Church and the Kingdom of God' (January 1926), in which Ritschl's influence can be seen in the definition of the Kingdom of God; and 'The Teaching of Early Protestant Dogmatics on Life after Death and the Last Things' (May 1926).

In the course of this work he was three times brought face to face with eschatology, and it should be borne in mind how new—particularly to the Berlin theological school—was the discovery of eschatological tension for the understanding of the New Testament and its dialectics between 'no longer' and 'not yet'. Althaus's *The Last Things* was published in those years, and notable revisions were made between one edition and the next. Also eschatology was personally a very stimulating subject to Bonhoeffer, even though he seems to have approached it only by way of his routine work during his student days. Those who had dealings with him were apt to be astonished at its immediacy to him and the fervour of his attitude to it, particularly in relation to the ministry and catechism. Later it dominated the whole of the *Cost of Discipleship* period. The fact that he obviously allowed it to recede into the background during the last years of his life was evidently due to his sure instinct that no false refuge must be constructed in that desperate situation. He then preferred relating eschatology to Christology to the reverse process.

Finally, in November 1926, he wrote a paper for Seeberg on the Erlangen school of theology, and took as his subject Seeberg's teacher F. H. R. Frank; his title was 'Frank's Views of the Spirit and Grace, as stated in his *System of Christian Certainty* and *System of Christian Truth*'.

Frank, deriving from Hofmann but modifying him, had applied ideas

taken from Schleiermacher to the subjective experience of spiritual rebirth, and he developed his 'system of Christian truth' out of this.
Bonhoeffer's criticism fastened on this independent act of the new self,
which consents after the Holy Spirit has brought about justification.
Frank and the Erlangen school had vigorously opposed Albrecht Ritschl.
Bonhoeffer went part of the way with both Frank and Ritschl. He
criticized Frank for not having escaped from metaphysics, and he also
criticized his doctrine of the immanent Trinity (which Seeberg himself
claimed he detected in Luther). Frank, Bonhoeffer said, taught the
'immanence of the Trinity usual in Catholic dogmatics, which was superseded by Luther, though it was taken up again after his death in early
Protestant scholastics'. But, as against Ritschl, he granted Frank that he
understood the link between spirit and grace personally and ethically
and 'thus at Frank's level of discourse the metaphysical content is superseded'. The Erlangen school remained a permanent stimulus to
Bonhoeffer.[68] He acquired the complete works of Frank and Hofmann,
and he gladly made use of Frank's four-volume *Theology of the Formula
of Concord*[69] when he discovered the 'confessions' during the church
struggle. Then Hofmann's hermeneutics also began to attract him.

These documents from his student days show pretty plainly where
Bonhoeffer's interests did and did not lie. At Berlin University he came
to grips with the historical critical method, with primitive Christianity,
Luther and Lutheranism, and the nineteenth century. In comparison he
did not gain nearly so much from, or come to grips with to anything like
the same extent, the Old Testament, Calvin and his world—this he
almost completely ignored—and the great medieval theologians. On the
other hand, the new world of dialectical theology was completely his
own discovery.

Catechetical Writings

He took part in the practical theological seminars with notable
enthusiasm, and presented more papers than he need have done. His
inherited gift for dealing with people, and children in particular, was
seeking fulfilment. Dialectical theology did something else as well, since
it originated in practical ministry, which is regarded as the crown of
the theological life. Unlike many of his fellow-students, he did not
regard his work with Mahling as merely of secondary importance. He
wrote his catecheses quickly and with pleasure, and was bored only by
the routine of fixed question-and-answer papers. Later he never
required these of his students. He preferred clear and logical trains of
thought, well expressed, to the repetition of set phrases.

The surviving manuscripts show a number of charming characteristics.

68. Cf. Ch. X, pp. 474 f.
69. H. R. von Frank, *Theologie der Concordienformel*, 1858 or 1863.

He had to write his catecheses on the three would-be disciples (Luke 9: 57-62). This was the text with which he began his exciting lecture to his pupils in 1935 on 'The Cost of Discipleship'. But what a difference there is between the two. Here, ten years earlier, he makes a great deal of play with military metaphors. He sums up the first of the three would-be disciples in the phrase 'Look before you leap', while he characterizes the second by 'All or nothing' and the third by 'Up and at 'em'. Mahling was right to praise the 'vividness with which the children were approached, the rich relationship with real life'. He was less concerned with the theological content. Bonhoeffer incidentally preceded the catecheses with a thoroughly professional critical exegesis.[70]

Curiously enough, his lowest examination marks were in the subject for which he had the greatest natural ability, that is to say, for his catechesis on Matthew 8: 5-13. After receiving the results in Barcelona, he said in a letter to his parents: 'Incidentally you recently . . . gave me a pleasureable afternoon because of the Consistory reports.' The report in question said:

From both the didactical and methodical points of view the catechesis shows notable shortcomings . . . The link with similar ideas, already familiar to the children, is meagre . . . The appeal to children's hearts is insufficient. The whole catechesis is really only an elucidation of the text. It is often so excessively doctrinaire that the children would be bored . . . Criticism of the text of St. Luke forms no part of the lesson . . .

It is only having regard to the diligence undeniably displayed by the candidate and in the expectation that he will make serious efforts to improve himself in the catechistic and psychological field that the work can be said to have reached a sufficient standard.

Sermons

To Bonhoeffer his first efforts in the field of homiletics were far more stimulating even than those in that of catechesis, for here he saw plainly the dividing line between failure and success, between dead sermonizing and the life-giving act.

His examiners said of his first draft sermon that 'the writer, to whom eagerness for development can be attributed, will have to discard a good deal and learn a good deal before he is able to write a really finished sermon . . . He is lacking in clarity . . . The writer is advised sedulously to study model sermons, Dryander, Conrad, Althaus, etc., and . . . while seizing on whatever the most important point may be . . . to cultivate a simple and noble simplicity . . .'

His father sent Dietrich the letter, signed by Otto Dibelius, the Superintendent General, enclosing these reports, and added: 'We were delighted with the general tenor of the Consistory's verdict. To learn the

70. June 1926.

tone of the official Church, you will have to read a great many model sermons. In my case things were quite different; Wernicke told me not to read any psychiatrical literature, because it only made one stupid.'[71]

VI FIRST CONNECTION WITH OFFICIAL CHURCH

At the end of 1925, almost at the same time as he began working on his thesis, he began practical work with a children's religious instruction group. That is to say, just when he was embarking on the heavy course of reading required for his *Sanctorum Communio*, he also devoted himself to a group of children who required a considerable amount of his time, for he always prepared his lessons carefully, and the children made clamorous demands on him.

Sunday School in Grunewald

Church regulations required candidates for the first theological examination to produce evidence that they had taken an active part in parish work. The church at Grunewald was in charge of the Rev. H. Priebe, who had prepared him for confirmation, but responsibility for children's services and religious instruction was in the hands of the forty-year-old Rev. Karl Meumann. Bonhoeffer gave religious instruction for the Sunday-school teachers at Meumann's house on Friday evenings, and on Sundays he held a catechism class, for which he prepared his lesson in writing. After a short time he persuaded his younger sister Susanne to join the circle of helpers. When the children's demands grew, he and Susanne invited them to their home for games and took them on outings.

Bonhoeffer gave as many talks to the children as he could. He made Biblical stories as exciting as sagas or as appealing as fairy-tales. He considered no trouble too great to hold the children's attention, and that is why he so carefully wrote out in advance what he proposed to tell them. He told them tales such as that about the king in his castle who sent out heralds who never returned, and about the devil who stole a pot of red paint and painted the humble mushroom, bestowing upon it the poison of pride, and about the old woman caught in a snowstorm outside a locked door—this last as an Advent story; and he gave a dramatic account of the struggle for the people's confidence between the prophets Jeremiah and Hananiah. The liberties he took with the text never caused him any qualms.

He discovered that when children expect something of one it is impossible to give oneself to them only partially. He also realized the part played by psychological and personal factors, and appreciated that these could endanger the real purpose of religious instruction. He was disturbed when children began to flock to his group. He was so worried

71. Letter of 13.3.1928.

by the question of developing personal ties that he wrote for advice to Richard Widmann, who had been a senior fellow-student of his and now had a parish in Württemberg. His letter has not survived, but Widmann replied:

I do not think it dangerous for one to be successful with children, provided that they are still children . . . I would not take children from another group. I believe that for the sake of the cause one must work against one's own personality. Apart from that, it would certainly give rise to terrible unrest among the children, which would be extremely dangerous.[72]

To Bonhoeffer this first step in practical church work meant much more than fulfilling a requirement for admission to an examination. From the outset it raised the very personal problem whether practical work should be the counterpoint to the main theme of theology in his life— or whether it should be the other way about. Since his uncommitted beginnings at Tübingen it had become plain that a gulf lay between the two, but that its existence should at least not be accepted. So he tried passionately to explain to his former fellow-student in Württemberg that the hardest theological pronouncements of Barth were worth nothing if they could not be explained *in toto* to these Grunewald children.

From his village rectory his Barthian former fellow-student complained about the social gulf that divided him as a theologian from his peasant and bourgeois parishioners:

The Church as it is today is tied to the two social strata of the middle-class bourgeoisie and the peasants, and this is true even of its dogmatics and ethics. I myself belong neither to the bourgeoisie nor to the country folk, but to the intellectual world, which does not go to church, and is undenominational out of necessity. However basically insignificant that may be for the problem of the 'Church', to me the sociological condition of the Church is in practice of the greatest importance. I belong to a world different from my congregation's, and different from what it can ever be; for the world to which and from which I speak does not go to church. It would certainly not be the worst thing—though again it would be insignificant in practice—if I denied my past and out of necessity became reactionary like Barth, because of a feeling of not having the strength to say and do, 'blow on blow', what 'should' be said and done to open the doors of the Church to the intellectual world. But I do not want to deny my past.

I have already seen that it is useless to flavour one's preaching with bigger or smaller quantities of psychology in order to make oneself intelligible to one's listeners. They feel that one belongs to a different world, and one is rejected. For an intellectual minister the only alternative is either to renounce his former world or to leave the ministry, unless he can become a university professor.

Preaching is, after all, a dialogue. But a dialogue between an intellectual and

72. Letter from R. Widmann, 13.3.1926.

a bourgeois or peasant is no longer possible. The two no longer understand each other. As an intellectual priest I am condemned to a tragic solitude.

The Barthian psychology of the *Epistle to the Romans* grew on the soil of the modern world, and from the pulpit of the church of the bourgeoisie and the peasantry it is meaningless. Barthian theology has quite definite sociological assumptions, which are not relevant to the present-day Church. The Barth who remained in the Church became a reactionary. That is how I see the problem today. For the time being I am waiting and giving myself time to think. What do you say to taking the Church seriously as a sociological phenomenon and drawing the conclusions?[73]

Bonhoeffer's reply has not survived, but Widmann's notebook showed that he answered immediately.[74] Widmann's next letter, dated 26th April, shows the vigour with which Bonhoeffer rebutted these clever questions. He charged his former fellow-student with drawing 'undialectical conclusions' from Barth, made the distinction between 'ultimate and penultimate' that was later to be important in his ethics, and rebuked him for making the penultimate the decisive criterion, though 'in the last resort it did not matter'. In reply Widmann asked: 'Do you think that only last things, ultimate things, should affect one's decisions?'

Bonhoeffer was of course younger and more inexperienced than the correspondent who plied him with these difficult questions. But at the moment when he was taking his first steps in the concrete life of the Church it was impossible for him to agree with his friend when the latter was considering the possibility of leaving it. He refused to accept the possibility that the newly-discovered gospel might have to stop—and he with it—at the sociological boundaries of the real Church. In his later life he had to admit and take into account the gulf between the two in many different forms, but now he refused to recognize that it was a decisive factor and was to govern his work. So at this stage, when he was first considering whether eventually to take up practical church work instead of the respected, privileged, but uncommitted career of an academic teacher, he did not allow himself to be thwarted. Widmann's letter, so far from making him uncertain, if anything made him more curious about his ability to put into practice what he had learnt.

In Barcelona he again kept a diary for a few days, and the following entry occurs:

What affected me most was saying good-bye to the church work. On 18th January [1928] we Sunday-school helpers had our last meeting with the Rev. K. Meumann. He spoke cordially and well, and I answered briefly. Without realizing it, we had grown closer together than we thought. Then, on 21st January, we had our last children's service. I spoke on the man sick of the palsy, and in particular on the saying: Your sins are forgiven, and tried yet again to reveal the kernel of our gospel to the children. They were attentive

73. Letter from R. Widmann, 13.3.1926.
74. Communication from R. Widmann, 28.9.1965.

and perhaps affected a little . . . Meumann mentioned my name in his general prayer. For a long time prayer by the whole congregation has sent cold shivers down my spine but, when the throng of children with whom I have spent two years prayed for me, the effect was incomparably greater.

The Thursday Group

Meanwhile a very lively youth group had developed out of the Sunday-school classes. Since April 1927 Bonhoeffer had held reading and discussion evenings in the Wangenheimstrasse for youths who had outgrown the classes. The programme he devised for them would have done credit to a young men's college; religious, ethical, denominational, political and cultural subjects were systematically discussed. He read a paper on Catholicism, and short papers to open the discussion were presented by the young people themselves. They went in a group to the opera and to concerts, and before taking them to a performance of *Parsifal* Bonhoeffer gave them an introductory talk on the subject.

They were very mature for their age, and many of them came from Jewish families living in the Grunewald district. They sent him their sentimental, Nietzschean or atheist poems, and later wrote to him in Barcelona or New York. Here are some extracts:

You will remember a conversation in which I argued that divine revelation was manifested in art, while you said that that put too low a rating on the idea of God.

The third act of *Parsifal* was broadcast a few days ago. I followed with the piano arrangement. Do you still remember taking us to a performance and explaining it to us? I'm still grateful to you for having enabled me, I think with Kundry, to grasp one of the essential aspects of Christianity.

Examinations for the Reichswehr. Don't imagine I wanted to become an officer, I am hardly that kind of person, but at my father's strong wish I qualified as a medical officer . . . The prospects for all students being so appallingly slender, one is glad at having the opportunity to work.

I'm glad I saved up enough money before Easter to be able to buy a folding canoe, and now I can't talk about anything else.[75]

In his Barcelona diary Bonhoeffer wrote:

On 18th January [1928] I held the last meeting of my Thursday group. A newcomer, named Peter Rosenbaum, was there, a young man of unusual intelligence and sensitivity—he defended Luther's doctrine of the real presence. The young people brought questions with them, which we discussed. Finally, I asked them what they thought of the fact that Christianity had conquered the world in competition with other religions; and that brought us to the question of the essence of Christianity, and we discussed

75. From letters from members of Bonhoeffer's group, 1929-31.

revelation and religion, and the contrast and connection between them.

Nearly all the members of this group later died in Hitler's war or his concentration camps.

Examinations

Bonhoeffer's student days ended brilliantly with his graduation on 17th December 1927. After examination by Seeberg, Deissmann, Mahling, Sellin and Lietzmann, he publicly defended his theses against his fellow-students Stupperich, Rössler and Dress. Nine months previously he had himself opposed his brother-in-law Dress. He made notes on his copy of his eleven points. Against the fourth, in regard to Bultmann's concept of potentiality, he wrote: 'The cause of the actualization of our potentiality either lies in God alone, in which case the potentiality is superfluous, or in man, which is inconsistent with God's omnipotence'; and against the eleventh point, in which he rejected the idea of a specifically Christian teaching of history: 'A Christian philosophy of history exists, and so do historically edifying lessons. The purpose of the teaching of history is to present the most likely facts in as objective a way as possible, with the relation which links these facts, so that a correct historical assessment may be made. We cannot see the heart, but the person, we are not judges of the world. Thus basically everything in history evades a Christian evaluation.' Then he noted down the chief points for his speech of thanks to the faculty, in which he referred especially to Harnack and Seeberg. He received the very rarely awarded *summa cum laude*.

Four weeks later, his doctoral thesis being taken into account, he passed the first theological examination of the Consistory of Mark Brandenburg with a 'very good'. His course of training for the ministry then began. The choice between a life of activity in the Church and an academic career lay open to him. His family took it for granted that he would choose the latter; so far from there being any obstacles in the way, he could look forward to aid and swift advancement. But his problem was not how to enter the academic world, but how to escape from it. The pulpit appealed to him more than the professor's chair.

At Christmas 1927 the family gathered in full force in the Wangenheimstrasse. During the past year Karl-Friedrich had qualified as a lecturer, Klaus had qualified for the Civil Service, and Dietrich had graduated. For the first time since Walter's death Karl Bonhoeffer again made an entry in his New Year notebook.

This Christmas, when we have all our surviving children together with us again, allows us to reopen the old book and we shall again report . . . In the spring we had a big masked ball in the house . . . This evening the Schleichers and Dohnanyis are with us, and Karl-Friedrich, Klaus and Dietrich. Next year Dietrich will be in Barcelona. . . .

CHAPTER THREE

ASSISTANT PASTOR IN BARCELONA

1928

BONHOEFFER'S year as an assistant pastor took him to a totally new environment. He felt he was 'starting from the beginning', as he put it in the diary he now resumed. Not only did he have no inner links with Spain, such as he felt he had had with Italy when he went there in 1924, but also the people with whom his new position brought him into contact were of a type unfamiliar to him. In the Grunewald district of Berlin he had had practically no contact with the type represented by these Germans living abroad, businessmen with a petty bourgeois outlook. Here there was little reflection of the hectic post-war years in Germany and the thirst for novelty and experiment that prevailed in Berlin. The small Protestant community in Barcelona clung to its old patterns and ways of thought. After a fortnight in Barcelona, Bonhoeffer noted in his diary that visits to his parishioners were 'very pleasant, except that conversation takes a course completely different from what one is used to at home. Since I have been here, I have not had a single conversation in the Berlin-Grunewald style'.

Hitherto Bonhoeffer had lived in an academic world, and every week had been able to pick what he chose from what the theatre, the concert hall and the latest publications had to offer; and daily he had had the benefit at meal-times of well-informed conversation about political or philosophical matters. Now he was suddenly cut off from all this, and was left with barely enough time to maintain contact by correspondence with the environment to which he was used. •

Hitherto he had been able to devote his time to arduous theological discussions in the seminars, and the latest books came his way almost as a matter of course. Now he was continually occupied with local choral or gymnastic societies, committee meetings, and consultations in the German colony. The rest of his time had to be devoted to visiting parishioners or preparing for services.

Hitherto he had been able to discuss every plan and every project in the broad environment of his home, but now he was thrown back entirely on his own resources. This, however, according to his diary, was the 'realization of a wish that had been growing stronger and stronger inside me in recent years and months, namely to stand entirely on my own feet, right outside my previous circle'.

No sacrifice was yet involved of the privileged position into which he was born and that had left its mark on him; this was not yet a step into the unsheltered life which he had once said he would have liked to have had for the 'sake of a sense of solidarity with 'the others'.[1] For the time being he was filled with a great curiosity about the ecclesiastical calling, and for the first time had the sense of something in the nature of professionalism.

It is a very singular experience when one sees work and life really converging—a synthesis that we all sought but hardly found in our student days; when one really lives one life and not two, or rather half of one, it gives value to work and objectivity to the worker, and results in a recognition of one's own limitations such as is to be gained only in concrete living.[2]

For the first time his personality, his time and his gifts were devoted to the concrete work of his Church, and for the first time also he was subject to the authority of one of its average ministers. The aristocratic-bourgeois child of the Wangenheimstrasse, with his high intellectual standards and demanding tastes, his need for harmony between attitude of mind and verbal expression, was now plunged into the sometimes so pseudo-serious and easily satisfied environment of a parish. But the conflict between aspiration and realization, so far from oppressing him, rather acted as a spur.

I CHOICE OF PASTOR

During his year in Barcelona, Bonhoeffer continued to show little interest in the ecumenical movement. His appointment was arranged in the late autumn of 1927 by the superintendent in whose deanery Bonhoeffer lived, the Rev. Max Diestel, with the Rev. Fritz Olbricht, the German minister in Barcelona. 'After that telephone conversation I was pretty certain of the matter', Bonhoeffer noted in his diary. At the beginning of February 1928 he left for France. Paris was cold and wet, and he reached Barcelona, where the almond trees and mimosa were in bloom, on 15th February 1928. He took lodgings with two impoverished German ladies. 'Dietrich is very comfortable there, though everything is terribly primitive. The only place for everyone to wash is the toilet, which is very like a third-class lavatory on a train, except that it doesn't shake.'[3]

II COUNTRY

The year 1928 was one of exceptional political calm in Spain. The royalist military dictatorship of General Primo de Rivera was enjoying

1. Cf. Ch. I, pp. 9 f.
2. To H. Rössler, 7.8.1928, GS I, p. 51.
3. Klaus Bonhoeffer to his grandmother, 16.4.1928.

a pause between waves of unrest both at home and in Morocco. Another three years were to pass before the monarchy was abolished, and five more before the country was plunged into the terrible civil war.

Bonhoeffer was shocked by the flagrant social contrasts that he saw, and was surprised that the signs of revolt were no greater. Instead, he noted in his diary, he saw in the cafés 'prosperous, rich, not so rich, and really poverty-stricken-looking individuals all mingled together, so that it seems to me that the "social question" . . . plays hardly any role. The incredible conditions in the Old Town here testify to this.'

He took a great liking to Barcelona, with its harbour, its old university and, above all, the country round it, though he thought the Old Town 'even dirtier than Naples'. 'The Spanish landscape almost seems to be part of history', he wrote to his parents. 'The surroundings of Barcelona, which I enjoy more and more, are among the finest in Spain.'⁴

On the other hand, he regretted that he was able to establish no real contact with educated Spaniards. When this occasionally occurred, as in the instance of a professor whom he often saw, it soon turned out that they were violently anti-clerical. He came across the same anti-clericalism in the course of his search for good modern Spanish writing.

Barcelona itself is an unusually lively metropolis, caught up in an economic upsurge on the grand scale . . . there are good concerts, a good—though very old-fashioned—theatre, and only one thing is missing, namely intellectual discussion, which one does not find when one looks for it, even in Spanish academic circles. I believe the Spaniards to be unusually gifted, but so indolent that they simply do not train themselves. In their calm, their patience and their indolence they undoubtedly show strong oriental characteristics, and in general one never gets rid of the impression—whether in language, dancing or music, and often in the most ordinary actions—of being close to the East. Whether Spain as a whole will one day wake up I do not dare to say. But a great deal that is unique and traditional is slumbering in this people, and every now and again something breaks through and comes to life. I am at present looking for ancient games in which contests between Arab and Christian theologians are still produced in small provincial towns.⁵

He read *Don Quixote* in the original. During the Second World War he acquired a German edition. The infatuated knight-errant struck him as being a key to the understanding of Christian ethics in the Nazi period and his own situation in Tegel prison.⁶

Bonhoeffer's pleasure in again encountering Catholicism suffered a sharp setback. In comparison with his visit to Rome, it all struck him quite differently:

There are monks and clerics who really remind one of pictures by El Greco,

4. Letter of 17.5.1928.
5. To R. Seeberg, 20.7.1928.
6. Cf. F., pp. 67 f.; fragment of novel, GS III, p. 510; LPP, pp. 72, 133.

but the average have alarmingly uneducated and sensual faces—a remarkable contrast to Rome. I believe that there is really some justification for the foolish saying that religion is the opium of the people.[7]

It is almost impossible to make any contact with the clergy, it was only by chance that I made the acquaintance of one priest or another, but as a result, and from their faces, I have no real desire for closer acquaintance.[8]

On Corpus Christi Day, however, he missed nothing of the strange attractiveness of the processions and popular customs.

He liked the people in spite of their strangeness, and he tried hard to understand them and to get under their skin, though perhaps his diary notes really tell us more about him than about the Spaniards.

Spain is a diametrical opposite of Italy, a country which the influence of ancient culture—in pre-Christian times and in the Renaissance—passed by, and which instead has been subject for 400 years to the domination of Western culture. It is a country which at first is totally strange to one because of one's humanist upbringing, a country for the understanding of which one lacks, so to speak, all clues; and that applies quite as much to contemporary as to historical Spain.

But, aside from this strangeness, there is also a certain sympathy or sense of kinship which one does not have in relation to Italy, and again I can explain this only from the attitude to ancient and humanist culture. To Italy humanism and the classical period represented the solution of all problems, while in Spain there is a resistance to this which, I think, is also to a certain extent discernible in the Germans. Common to both Spaniards and Germans, I think, is the fact that neither completely exposed themselves to the impact of humanism, but always held something back.[9]

Spaniards laugh at no one so much as at the conceited and the *poseur*. Whenever I discuss German strength and weakness with Spaniards, even the simplest of them very tactfully point out that what we call pose is strange to them. I believe that we have thrown away a great deal of goodwill abroad by this . . . [The Spaniard] is neither proud in our sense, nor is he temperamental in the way that we think of temperament . . . where one can see master and servant sitting at the same café table, and a well-dressed individual is not abused when he walks through the slums . . . No one is so humble that he believes himself to be humbler than anyone else, and no one . . . has such a high opinion of himself that he permits himself to look down on anyone else. This situation appears everywhere, in cafés, in trains, in the street. Of course, there is such a thing here as a closed society, but this is not offensive to social feeling but, on the contrary, seems desirable.

To foreigners Spaniards are not servile, as Italians often are, but correct, and often actually cool. Among Catalans one often meets with great unpleasantness, which no doubt arises from political friendship with France.[10]

7. To his parents, 8.6.1928.
8. To R. Seeberg, 20.7.1928.
9. To his parents, 17.5.1928.
10. To R. Seeberg, 20.7.1928.

Bullfighting

Ten years later Bonhoeffer's students, amused, but unable to relate his enthusiasm for bullfighting to the rest of his personality, used continually to get him to describe the ritual of the bullfight. It seemed so unexpected in a man who could see nothing in any boxing match. But he described the subtleness of this Spanish exercise in elegance and brute force with obvious expertise. His twin sister wrote to him that she would not go to a bullfight for anything in the world. 'In comparison a boxing match must be completely innocuous', she wrote.[11]

He began succumbing to the spell when his brother Klaus visited him at Easter 1928. After the Easter sermon he took him to the bull-ring.

I cannot truthfully say that I was as horrified by it as many people think they ought to be because of their Central European civilization. It is, after all, a tremendous thing, savage, uninhibited brute force and blind fury attacking and being defeated by disciplined courage, presence of mind and skill. Horror plays only a small part, particularly as in this series the horses' bellies were protected for the first time, so that the dreadful scenes of my first *corrida* were lacking. But it is interesting to note that there was a long struggle before the horses were given this protection. So the majority of spectators probably want simply to see blood and horror.

In general, a tremendous amount of emotion is aroused among the people, and one is sucked into it. I believe it to be no accident that the bullfight is ineradicably established in the country of the gloomiest and crudest Catholicism. Here is a remnant of unrestricted passionate living, and perhaps it is the bullfight which, just because it stirs up and produces such an ebullition of popular emotion, enables a relatively high standard of morality to prevail in the rest of their lives, because the bullfight kills their passion—with the result that the Sunday *corrida* becomes a necessary appendage to the Sunday mass.[12]

Dietrich even took his parents to a bullfight when they came to see him during the late summer.

Bonhoeffer's minister allowed him a great deal of freedom to travel. Occasionally he sent him in his stead on duty visits to Majorca or Madrid. When Klaus came to see him, he gave him leave, and so the two went to Toledo, Cordoba, Seville, Granada and Algeciras. The North African coast tempted them again, and they attended another caliph's reception, but they decided that Spanish Morocco was more Europeanized than Libya had been. Klaus was again a very stimulating travelling companion.

In Madrid and Toledo Dietrich learnt to appreciate the greatness of El Greco, and later he took advantage of every opportunity to see his paintings in New York or London. He very much wanted to take his

11. Letter of 12.4.1928.
12. To his parents, 11.4.1928.

parents to Granada, but their departure for Spain was continually put off, because there was a prospect in 1928 of his father's becoming rector of the university. Eventually, however, another physician was appointed, and only a few fine autumn days were left for the trip, during which Dietrich showed his parents the shrine of Montserrat and then accompanied them to Arles, Avignon and Nîmes.

Idea of Going to India

A project that fascinated Bonhoeffer for the next eight years originated during his year in Spain. It deserves a place in his biography because it greatly influenced him, although nothing ever came of it. In February 1928 his grandmother wrote: 'In your place I should try some time or other to get to know the contrasting world of the East, I am thinking of India, Buddha and his world.' This bold suggestion, which was completely in the Tafel tradition, stuck.

In Barcelona Bonhoeffer among other things toyed with the idea of a voyage to Tenerife, for which his grandmother sent him some money. But before the chance arose he had to return to Berlin to qualify as a lecturer, and he laid the money aside for the trip to India he hoped to take some day. In February 1929 he wrote to his grandmother that her present had 'brought his Eastern plans a whole lot nearer'. It was still a very vague and general thirst for new experience which impelled him to seek contact with a different spiritual world, though he may perhaps already have felt the attraction of the figure of Gandhi. A fellow-student at Tübingen recalls a night-time conversation in the winter of 1924-5 in which Gandhi's personality and work already played a part.[13]

III PARISH

The Rev. F. Olbricht treated his new curate very magnanimously, and for his part Bonhoeffer regarded him as a kindly and courteous man. He appreciated the modesty and simplicity with which he carried out his duties. Olbricht was at home in the social life which to a considerable extent constitutes the real life of a congregation abroad. Bonhoeffer appreciated that it was right to enter and share these people's lives, so he went quite a long way with his senior in order not to fall short of what this reality required. He noted in his diary on 10th March—the last entry he made in Spain: 'My theology is beginning to become humanist; what is the meaning of this? Did Barth ever live abroad?'

The minister's principal reading 'was nationalistic literature and newspapers'. He called on Dietrich's parents when he returned to Berlin on

13. Communication from H. U. Esche, 25.3.1965.

his annual leave, and Dietrich announced his visit by describing him as 'a man who prefers a good glass of wine and a good cigar to a bad sermon'. He demanded little of his parishioners, and they liked him, and he was disquieted by his assistant's efforts to bring about a more energetic cure of souls. In the winter of 1928-9, when members of the congregation expressed a desire for week-end services, Bonhoeffer wisely declined, in order to avoid possible friction. 'I seem to have as much work here as I make for myself', he wrote to his grandmother. 'I could be tremendously lazy if I wanted to be, I think, but as it is . . . I shall have plenty to do.'[14]

The congregation, which was founded in 1885, called itself Evangelical, but had no denominational awareness. Presumably it was of Reformed origin. The church council was called a 'presbytery', which caused Dietrich's mother, who was brought up in east Germany, to ask what the word meant. The presbyters were worthy businessmen who regularly paid their dues but did not regularly go to church. 'They support the Church just as they do sport or the German National Party, but less actively.'[15] The German colony in Barcelona was 6,000 strong, but the congregation numbered about 300, of whom an average of about 40 attended services. During the summer holiday period, when many people sought refuge from the heat by going north, this number was expected to diminish, but Bonhoeffer, to his great pleasure, nevertheless succeeded in increasing the average attendance. The consequence was that the minister, who, in his announcements circulated to the congregation, had been in the habit of giving in advance the name of the preacher each Sunday, henceforward dropped this practice.

It was obvious at first sight that the congregation was one of the flourishing groups belonging to the German community. The outer picture was of prosperity and a hectic social life. Bonhoeffer looked at these people with understanding:

. . . the war and in particular the revolutionary period simply by-passed these people, but there is also a good side to that, as the current saying is. There is none of the nervousness and strain, the intellectual affectation and mannerisms that are so widespread in Germany today . . . in the human respect, one meets quite admirable character traits, decency, honesty, simplicity, and a lack of self-assertiveness.[16]

To the pleasure of his brothers and sisters, he joined a number of clubs: the German Club, whose first masked ball he prudently refrained from attending; the German tennis club, where he played regularly; and the German choral society, at which he valiantly played the piano accompaniment to all the sentimental songs. The Berlin assistant minister's fashionable round hat was the talk of all the German school-

14. Letter of 23.2.1928.
15. Ibid.
16. To R. Seeberg, 20.7.1928.

children; 'perhaps that is the way to introduce oneself here', was his comment.[17] He found his skill at music and chess a helpful human factor. 'There is only one thing I lack—the ability to play *Skat*.[18] That is something you have to be good at here; perhaps I may yet learn it.'[19] This world in fact amused him more than it bored him. There was only one thing he found it hard to tolerate, namely the gossip that inevitably proliferated in this kind of environment. 'The best thing to do is to know nothing about it and show not the slightest interest.'[20]

But visits to parishioners, which he paid more conscientiously than they had been used to, soon revealed other aspects of the German colony's life. The German commercial community was in a different position, and strong competition from the Western countries drove a number of its members into bankruptcy. While the minister was away on leave, his twenty-two-year-old assistant was faced with his first case of suicide, a respected member of the congregation, a businessman of long-standing reputation. Bonhoeffer came across cases of severe poverty and 'a great deal of unemployment'. In cases of need he unhesitatingly appealed to his parents, not only with requests for medical advice or prescriptions, but also for interest-free loans. He never appealed to his father in vain. At Christmas he secured such a loan for his two landladies.

In cooperation with the German consulate-general, at which he found, in the persons of Dr. Bobrik and his colleagues, individuals of the type to which he was used in his own Berlin environment, he devoted himself to the social work of the German welfare society, whose office he attended every morning.

One has to deal with the strangest persons, with whom one would otherwise scarcely have exchanged a word, bums, vagabonds, criminals on the run, many foreign legionaries, lion and other animal tamers who have run away from the Krone Circus on its Spanish tour, German dancers from the music-halls here, German murderers on the run—all of whom tell one their life-story in detail. It is often very difficult in these cases to give or to refuse at one's own discretion. As it is impossible to establish any principles in the matter, the decisive factor has to be one's personal impression; and that can often and easily be mistaken . . . so in the course of time one finds oneself becoming sharper and sharper in defence of the interests of those who are genuinely in distress and cannot be helped adequately. Twice since I have been here I have seen long-established and prosperous families totally ruined, so that they have been unable to go on buying clothes for their children or paying their school fees . . . Yesterday for the first time I had a man here who behaved so impudently—he claimed that the minister had forged his signature—that I practically shouted at him and threw him out . . . While taking a hurried departure he cursed and swore, and said something that I have

17. To his parents, 20.2.1928.
18. A German card game. *(Translator.)*
19. Letter of 6.3.1928.
20. Letter of 13.3.1928.

now often heard: 'We shall see each other again, just come down to the harbour!' Afterwards I found out at the consulate that he is a well-known swindler who has been hanging about here for a long time, so I was quite pleased that I had dealt with him in the way I had. On the whole, however, I find that kindness and friendliness is the best way of dealing with these people . . . When Olbricht does not like someone, he gives him a dressing down and throws him out, and he thinks that is more effective . . . the pleasure of seeing that one has been really helpful is rare, because in most cases the money runs through their fingers as soon as they get it . . . The real trouble is that we have no employment bureau, and the reason for that is that businesses here are over-staffed already. The Germans are pulling out . . . We are continually concerned with Germans going home, though we know that things are no better there.[21]

In this situation he wrote to his father asking for a copy of his book on vagrancy.[22] 'In view of my present work with such people, I should very much like to read it',[23] he wrote.

Youth Work

Bonhoeffer was struck by the great contrast between the young people of Berlin and those of the German colony in Barcelona.

They know little or nothing of war, revolution and the repercussions of these things, they live well and comfortably, the weather is always fine—what else could you expect? The Youth Movement period in Germany passed them by, leaving no trace behind. [Diary.]

When one asks ten-year-olds here what they want to be when they grow up, the answer very often is: 'I shall run my father's business.' That is so much taken for granted that no other possibility is even considered. The agreeable counterpart to this is that nothing is felt to be so ridiculous as being blasé, and so people do not make themselves out to be what they are not.[24]

Bonhoeffer's first attempt at youth work in the congregation was intended to help all age groups. The first thing he set about was to establish a Sunday school for the little ones. In this he had the minister on his side, though he had less support from him in his plans for the spiritual welfare of those of secondary school age.

The Sunday school got off to a bad start. In response to the first invitation, only one girl put in an appearance. But on the following Sunday the number increased to fifteen. He wrote in his diary:

[They are] admirably bright and lively. I described to them the fine things

21. To K.-F. Bonhoeffer, 7.7.1928.
22. K. Bonhoeffer *Beiträge sur Kenntnis des grossstädtischen Vagabundentums*, 1900.
23. Letter of 14.8.1928.
24. To his grandmother, 5.6.1928.

there are in the children's service, and this caught on. We shall see how things go next time. Since that last lesson I have felt transformed. The slight anxiety that I might not get anywhere with practical work has vanished. I have touched solid ground and shall go further, and I think I already have the children on my side; my next step must be to give religious instruction at the school. But first I must develop the Sunday school, and perhaps a door will open from there.

He promptly paid a visit to the home of each child who attended. Next time thirty turned up, and the attendance never again dropped below that number.

After a short time Bonhoeffer's room was regularly filled with a swarm of schoolboys. He settled their school problems, helped to improve their work, and won over angry teachers to a more considerate opinion of their charges. He gave one boy a bicycle and another a tent. His pupils gave him a tremendous Christmas, the first that he had spent away from home.

But he was unsuccessful in his efforts to arrange regular religious instruction in the secondary school, for here he had to face, not only the opposition of the staff, but also that of the minister, who was not to be won over to the innovation, which might one day, when he was left alone, involve him in additional duties. As a result of this failure Bonhoeffer decided to give a series of talks, intended primarily for the older boys, during the winter of 1928-9, and a discussion group in fact developed out of this. He wrote home that 'it was shaping well'.

[The boys] are very enthusiastic, though very ignorant, because of the incredible lack of preparation at school. At present we are discussing the nature of Christianity, and we shall go on to deal with particular problems, first of all that of immortality. I always give the seniors something to read. One of them writes an introductory essay, and it is then discussed. The boys of this age and even younger are different from those in Germany. There is a remarkable mixture of maturity in regard to forms and questions of making a living and great *naïveté* in other things. Mental boredom or pomposity hardly exist. At all events, intelligence is not overrated. One has the impression of great honesty and clarity, which may be the result of the Spanish influence.[25]

Preaching

These foreign conditions offered only a limited field of experience in church work. By the standards of a live German congregation, Bonhoeffer rightly missed 'Bible lessons, youth work, lecture evenings, religious instruction'.[26] But in regard to practice in writing and delivering sermons, which he regarded as the mainspring of his office, he missed nothing. In this respect the twenty-two-year-old assistant was given more

25. To his parents, 10.12.1928.
26. To the Rev. M. Diestel, 12.7.1928.

to do than was expected even of older pastors according to the training regulations. In 1928 he had to write and deliver nineteen sermons.

He took a great deal of trouble over each of them. 'Writing sermons still takes up a great deal of my time. I work on them the whole week, devoting some time to them every day.'[27] He was therefore glad when the minister was unable to preach and left him the pulpit: 'On the first Sunday in Advent I shall be able to preach again because Olbricht will not be returning until the following week and I am very pleased about that.'[28]

He was not satisfied with analyzing the present or presenting an accurate and straightforward exegesis of Scripture. He wanted to say something important, and he believed he had something important to say, and that his hearers should be shaken out of their complacency and won over. In pursuit of this aim he dealt boldly and, taking into account the German homiletical tradition, not over-accurately with his texts. He was hardly aware of the excessive demands that he made with his highly specialized theological knowledge on the businessmen sitting below his pulpit. Nevertheless he carried a conviction that overcame the artificial and difficult clothing in which he wrapped his meaning. Only later did he realize how little the word affects the hearer independently of him who speaks it. The word makes use of messengers who are nothing but messengers—and yet everyone is inevitably a quite definite messenger and must also wish to be that. Even though the sermons that Bonhoeffer preached so passionately to the Barcelona congregation to a great extent passed far over their heads, he nevertheless spoke to them as one who, during the week, visited them and filled them with a warmth and pastoral concern to which they were unaccustomed.

The definiteness of purpose behind Bonhoeffer's sermons is expressed in his choice of texts. He did not stick to the recommended pericopes, but always chose brief phrases. His Barcelona sermons have great thematic unity. As he did in his talks to the children at Grunewald, he unhesitatingly dramatized scenes, or put himself in the position of the 'psalmist'. To present-day tastes the language he used borders on the flowery, and he made sweeping statements, but he did not use jargon. He did not draw on the language of the Kurfürstendamm or the daily or illustrated press for his vocabulary, but on the world of fable and myth, and also, perhaps, on his love of nature. He picked what suited him from the world of his education—Heraclitus, the giant Antaeus from the world of antiquity, or Goethe's and Nietzsche's anthropological analyses from the nineteenth century. In his first and last sermons at Barcelona—and several in between—he quoted St. Augustine on the heart that is unquiet 'until it resteth in Thee'.[29] Similarly Barth's Tower

27. To his parents, 27.11.1928.
28. Ibid., and see quotation from letter to H. Rössler in German ed., p. 145.
29. Confessions, I. 6.

of Babel often recurs as the key example to show the dangerousness of 'religion'.

These first sermons nevertheless reveal the whole gamut of his theological work and outlook.

1.   He continually reiterates the antithesis between faith and religion, which he discovered anew in every scriptural text:

What is religion for except to make life more tolerable to men, occasionally to give something to the godly that the ungodly do not have? . . . But what a grievous error, what a fearful distortion of the truth . . .

It is certainly dreadful when a day comes on which our life collapses in ruins about us, but there is a reality that is far more dreadful—and it arises actually out of religion, out of morality. Renouncing worldly happiness is not the hardest thing that God imposes on us; what is hardest of all to bear, and casts us down utterly, is having to renounce the good and God himself . . .

Thus it is clear that religion does not give us what the world denies us, that religion is not the creator of earthly happiness; no, with religion unhappiness, unrest, become mighty in the world. The antithesis of everything that happens in the world is the word of grace . . .

[Thus it is] certain that the cross of Christ destroyed the equation religion equals happiness . . .

With that the difference between Christianity and religions is clear; here is grace, there is happiness, here is the cross, there the crown, here God, there man . . .[30]

His first sermon to the Barcelona congregation, in which he systematically proclaimed justification deriving solely from faith, in accordance with Romans 11 : 6 ('But if it is by grace, it is no longer on the basis of works'), led to this interpretation:

Both the most grandiose and the frailest of all attempts by man to achieve the eternal out of the fear and unrest in his heart—is religion . . . The human race could point proudly to this flowering of its spirit, except for one thing, namely that God is God and grace is grace . . . It is not religion that makes us good in the presence of God, but God alone who makes us good . . . Religion and morality are the greatest dangers to the understanding of divine grace . . . and yet, so long as grace exists, they remain necessary as a feeble attempt, an illustration, a sacrifice, to which God can say yes or no at his pleasure. We have gradually learnt to understand that with our morality we cannot achieve this, but that religion is part of human flesh, as Luther said and this our text tells us . . .

2.   Just as strong as his impulse to secure the correct anchorage of faith by the unmasking of religion for the sake of upholding God's majesty was his urge to emphasize the presence of Christ in the Church

30. Sermon of 9.9.1928 on 1 Cor. 12 : 9.

as the Thou that imposes restrictions and commandments. Taking as his text I Corinthians 12: 26, he described the Church as a place of devotional encounter, mutual intercession and personal confession. He referred to the poverty of the Protestant conception of the Church in comparison with the Catholic.[31] And he preached the social and ethical transcendence of his theology from the *Sanctorum Communio* as follows:

Jesus is with us in his word . . . in what he wishes and thinks about us . . . Jesus Christ, God himself, addresses us through every man; the other human being, that puzzling, inscrutable thou, is God's call to us, God himself who comes to meet us . . .[32]

Christ will wander upon earth as long as men exist, as your neighbour, as he through whom God calls you, speaks to you, makes demands on you. That is the great urgency and the great joy of the Advent message, that Christ is at the door, lives among us in human form. Will you close or open the door to him?[33]

3. There are passages in these sermons that point to his insistence on the concrete and the earthly. His urge to make the contemporary present a partner of the eschatological coming never completely died away. He preached on Romans 12 : 11 ('Never flag in zeal, be aglow with the Spirit, serve the Lord'), with his parents sitting among his Barcelona congregation (on 23rd September 1928). Starting from the problem of modernism, he devoted himself to the concept of time:

In the whole of world history there is always only one really significant hour—the present . . . What men do with it is fashion, that can be either good or bad. Time is what God does; and serving not men, but God, means serving time. Thus the Christian is neither fashionable nor unfashionable, but serves his time . . .

There follow some notes of very concrete solidarity with the political, economic and moral present, and he continues:

. . . we must regain understanding of the meaning of solidarity among mankind . . . God wants to see men, not ghosts who shun the world . . . He made the earth our mother . . . If you wish for God, hold fast to the world . . . if you want to find eternity, you must serve time . . .

That did not prevent him, as when preaching on 1 John 2: 17 ('And the world passes away, and the lust of it') on 26th August 1928, from saying 'time and death are the same!' In this sermon he also used the phrase 'ultimate and penultimate things'.

Political references are rarely discernible. True, in his farewell sermon before leaving Barcelona he mentioned the efforts being made for world

31. Cf. Ch. II, pp. 42 f.
32. Sermon of 15.4.1928 on Matt. 28: 20.
33. Sermon on Rev. 3: 20, Advent 1928.

peace, but only as an occasion to speak of the peace that passeth all understanding.

Lectures

For all his predilection for the pulpit, Bonhoeffer could not resist the appeal of the lecturer's platform. In order to make use of the winter, he laid his plans while Olbricht was on leave. 'I am preparing a series of addresses for the winter, which I propose to give in church', he wrote to his parents.[34]

He devoted three evenings to these addresses, the first on the Old Testament, the second on the New, and the last on ethical questions. He worked hard on them, and wrote them out in advance.

He began by telling his hearers that his underlying theme was that they 'should themselves enter into and take part in the struggle and crisis of the modern mind'.

The questions we shall deal with are profoundly contemporary questions, though their outer dress may seem unfashionable and antiquated. Every word is to be spoken out of the present and for the present . . . We should have so much love for this contemporary world of ours . . . that we should declare our solidarity with it in its distress as well as in its hope.

The characteristic feature of the contemporary world, in his view, was that the ground, 'or rather the bourgeois parquet flooring', had been pulled from under its feet, as was shown by the political, educational, ethical and religious uncertainty of the age. Everyone had to examine his foundations. But only a universal process, in which Asia, Europe and America took part, could provide the answer. These were ambitious words, but he believed in them.

1. The subject of his first address, delivered on 13th November 1928, was 'Distress and Hope in the Contemporary Religious Situation. The Tragedy of the Prophets and its Lasting Meaning'. He wanted to use the prophets as a signpost, because to him they had been 'such a favourite subject of study' and because in their time they had marked the collapse of an old and the beginning of a new world. 'Walking with God means walking a hard path, a path on which the heart's blood of the best men flows and has flowed, as the example of the prophets has amply taught us.' Bonhoeffer established only a very slender link between this and the present day, however, and spent most of his time introducing his hearers to the world of the prophets. He projected himself into the minds of the major prophets, identifying himself with them to an almost impermissible extent, lingering particularly on Jeremiah, who was already his favourite. Because he was here dealing with God, he tried to dissociate the chosen instruments of God from any psychological interpretation, but himself indulged in plenty of psychologizing in the process.

34. On 30.7.1928.

In preparation for these addresses he had had Duhm's lectures, *The Prophets of Israel*, sent from home, and he used his translation, though not without some linguistic emendations of his own, and he un-inhibitedly mingled Duhm's and Barth's theological tenets. He also drew on Stefan Zweig's dramatic treatment of Jeremiah. Bonhoeffer's passion can be felt in the description of the prophet who suffers because he is in league with God, whose nationalism the universal God destroys, who cannot bear the concealment of human 'decadence' and cynicism behind a veneer of meticulous religious observance.

2. On the second evening, 11th December 1928, he spoke on 'Jesus Christ and the Essence of Christianity'. Bonhoeffer's only surviving comment on these addresses is on this one. 'On Tuesday I gave the second address, which was even better attended than the first but, I think, was not so successful', he wrote home. The dismissal of humanist and idealist 'religion' in the name of the free and quite different God of dialectical theology was all too new and provocative.

To us, however, this address is more interesting than the first because it contains resonances and insights that had not been so explicitly stated before and were to make a powerful resurgence in Bonhoeffer's last working period.

a) The lecture begins with what was to be the main idea of *Letters and Papers from Prison*, which Bonhoeffer perhaps derived in the first place from Friedrich Naumann, namely the 'provincialism' to which Christ's teaching had succumbed:

. . . that Christ in practice [has been] eliminated from our lives . . . Christ, instead of being the centre of our lives, has become a matter for the Church, or the churchmanship of a group of people. To the nineteenth- and twentieth-century mind religion plays the part of the so-called 'Sunday-room' . . . We do not understand it when we allot it merely a province of our mental life . . . The religion of Christ is not the titbit that follows the bread, but is the bread itself, or it is nothing.

b) To arrive at the real Jesus, Bonhoeffer began by discussing the phenomenon of the New Testament in its historical setting. He said that the figure of Jesus was embedded in the world of Hellenistic myths and ideas of salvation and overgrown with miraculous fable and legend. The result was that *vita Jesu scribi non potest*. The New Testament derived solely from worship and proclamation of the Kyrios, and had no 'interest in the personal or historical' Jesus. Thus Bonhoeffer identified himself with the work of Harnack, at whose feet he had sat, and of Bultmann, whom he had read.

c) Thus he discovered Jesus, whose remarkable mission it was to direct attention away from his own 'personality' and at the same time un-challengeably to demonstrate God's will. Bonhoeffer illustrated the demands involved with the aid of Ibsen's *Brand* and Dostoevsky's *Grand*

Inquisitor. Surprisingly, they also involved turning attention, shocking though this might be, to children, to social outcasts, to the 'fifth estate'. He reconciled the paradox of the absence of prior assumptions and divine injunctions by 'Jesus' idea of God. God, who is simply superior to the world . . . totally different . . . demands nothing of man but sheer undemandingness . . . He wants an empty space in man into which he can move . . .'

d) This brought him back to 'the way of religion', identified with the tower of Babel. 'The germ of hubris is contained in religion and morality . . . thus the Christian message is basically amoral and irreligious, however paradoxical that may sound.' Here he takes a step further than he had gone before. Earlier he had dangerously approximated the Church to Christ, actually almost identified it with him. Everything had depended on the theological components of the visible Church. But now he put greater emphasis on Christology, thus enabling the Church to be seen in contrast to Christ. Thus he said:

With that we have made a basic criticism of the most grandiose of all human attempts to advance towards the divine—by way of the Church. Concealed in Christianity is a germ hostile to the Church . . . But Christianity nevertheless needs the Church . . . Ethics and religion and Church lie in the direction of man to God, but Christ speaks only and exclusively of the direction of God to man.

e) Together with religion, Bonhoeffer adversely criticized humanism, the Greek spirit, mysticism and the Protestant high evaluation of civilization. His audience must have found this hard to take, or it must have been puzzling to them.

f) The whole of this was made intelligible only by the cross, in which love and death were subsumed. 'Thus Jesus' idea of God is summed up in St. Paul's interpretation of the cross; thus the cross becomes the centre and the paradoxical emblem of the Christian message.' The Christian religion as a way to God did not differ from other religions. 'Christ is not the bringer of a new religion, but the bringer of God.' This sentence is already saying what Bonhoeffer was to say almost at the end, in *Letters and Papers from Prison* of 1944: 'Jesus does not call us to a new religion, but to life.' The development was an enrichment. Where he had said 'God', he later, boldly, wrote 'life'. In this 1928 address, Bonhoeffer continued: 'Thus it is not the Christian religion that is the gift of Christ, but grace and the love of God, which reaches its consummation in the cross.'

3. The third address, 'Basic Questions of a Christian Ethic', was given shortly before Bonhoeffer's departure from Barcelona, after he had given his farewell sermon, on 8th February 1929. It is the most concrete, though the most dubious, of the three. Many passages must have appealed to his younger listeners, as when he echoed Nietzsche in speak-

ing of freedom and claimed his phrase 'beyond good and evil' as the inner meaning and mystery of the Christian message concerning 'the good',[35] or simply denied the continuity of ethical action, because 'there are no Christian norms and principles or morality, and can be none'. Was it merely naïve conviction that he should now put all his trust in the ethical moment, the 'unprecedented situation'?

a) Ethics, he said, was not a system of general principles of universal application, but they were historically tied to their age. Also they were different in different places. In Germany they could not be considered in isolation from the experience of war and revolution. Bonhoeffer felt himself to be associated with and responsible in relation to the latter.

b) The commandment to love, he declared, was not specifically Christian; it could be found in Rabbi Hillel or in Seneca.

The meaning of all Jesus' ethical commandments [and of the Sermon on the Mount—author's note] is rather to say to man: You stand in the presence of God, God's grace rules over you; you are faced with others in the world . . . the nature of that will [i.e., God's will] will become plain at the moment of action.[36]

In directly subordinating man to God, newly and differently at every moment, Jesus restores to humanity the most tremendous gift that it had lost, namely freedom.[37]

Thus it is not Nietzsche's superman, but Christ who makes new commandments. But in 1928 the twenty-two-year-old Bonhoeffer still remained loyal to the old earthly principle of the right of the stronger. In condemning general principles and the law he also condemned Tolstoy and conscientious objectors; and, with a certain defiance of a Christian weakness for generalization, he wrote the dreadful phrases:

[The Holy Spirit] does not shine in ideas and principles, but in the necessary decision of the moment . . . Strength and power and victory also come from God, because God creates youth in men and nations, and he loves youth, for God himself is permanently young and strong and victorious . . . God himself will find a way of amply healing the wounds that he inflicts through us, that we inflict for his sake . . .

c) This brought him to the subject of war. What he had to say about this—and also about the Sermon on the Mount—was quite conventionally Lutheran, though decked out with the titanic ethics of the immediate moment. The later pacifist here still proclaimed and defended the relative right of the stronger in the economic competition of the nations and their struggle for life. Better this than a phoney rejection of the world. Better this than relinquishing the world to Nietzsche. It should not be overlooked, however, that he also here described war as 'sinful and wicked', called it 'dreadful, terrible, murder', and said it

35. GS III, pp. 48, 50.   36. GS III, pp. 51 f.   37. GS III, p. 52.

was revolting to the conscience. But he also said: 'For what I have I thank this nation, through this nation I became what I am.' Living in a German community abroad, he inadvertently moved to a position close to that of those who complained of their nation's lack of *Lebensraum*, space to live in.

But Bonhoeffer's position cannot be simply left at that. Neither in his sermons nor in his letters did he ever make any such statement again.[38] Such propositions were soon to become articles of faith among German nationalists in the Evangelical Church but, before they were interpreted anti-Semitically and chauvinistically and became the hall-mark of right-wing extremism, they were also used by democrats and members of Stresemann's Volkspartei. Here Bonhoeffer is not yet talking his own language. The idea of the struggle for life as the natural basis of human existence came from Friedrich Naumann, on whom Bonhoeffer specifically relied in this address.[39] The same principle, though differently justified, is also to be found in Max Weber.

It did not take long for Bonhoeffer to discover the self-deception that lay in this unquestioned loyalty to the world. Ties of quite a different kind lay ahead. On 16th March 1929, the Berlin *Tag* reported the resolution of the German nationalists at Magdeburg denouncing Günther Dehn's sober address of 6th September 1928 on the war problem. This was the beginning of the agitation against the 'red Dehn'. Just at this time Bonhoeffer was drawing closer to Dehn.[40] His later experiences in America and in the World Alliance of Churches helped him to see that the strange link he had made between Barth's systematic theology and the conventional Lutheran ethic was at least in need of revision. In his theological work ethics had hitherto been relatively neglected, and here again he postponed this address until the last moment. Perhaps some uncertainty in the matter is betrayed by the fact that at the very end of the address he again refers to ethics in a different context, calling it a 'demonstration of weak will, arising out of gratitude for what God has done to us', or when he says: 'Men's actions arise from recognition of God's grace bestowed on humanity and on themselves, and these actions look forward to the grace of God, which relieves them of the distress of the time.'[41] Finally he adds one more adjustment to his balancing act on the point of the needle of the ethical moment with an eschatological sigh:

Only he who has tasted to the full the depth and misery of the kingdom

38. But see SC, p. 83.
39. F. Naumann, *Briefe über Religion*, 7th ed., 1917, Letter 19, pp. 61 ff.; similarly p. 75: '. . . so soon as we say we recognize only the principle of love, we shall never be able to take any action in the face of God and the world that creates the impression of hardness. But such action is necessary if we are to live.'
40. Cf. E. Bizer, 'Der Fall Dehn', *Festschrift für Günther Dehn*, ed. W. Schneemelcher, 1957, pp. 239-61.
41. GS III, p. 58.

of the world, the kingdom of the ethical, and longs for release from it, has one wish only, that our world should pass away, and thy kingdom come.

Barely two years later he felt very uncomfortable at having expressed himself in this way about burning ethical questions and the Sermon on the Mount. The *theologia crucis* and a wider view did their work.

IV PLANS FOR THE FUTURE

In November 1928 the presbytery formally invited him to remain in Barcelona but, after briefly considering the matter, he declined. This could not be the churchly commitment to which he aspired. Moreover, he was still uncertain whether to seek a church or an academic appointment. For the time being he wished to keep open both alternatives, postponing the decision until he had his habilitation, i.e. qualification as a university teacher, behind him, as well as his ordination.

So far as a church appointment was concerned, there was an obstacle in the way that at the time he regarded as totally unnecessary, namely the training course for candidates for ordination at the seminary. He felt not the slightest inclination to attend this, though it was required before he could be ordained. But habilitation provided a way out, and for this purpose he sought a post as a university assistant through Seeberg.

He was already actively considering what subject he should choose for his habilitation thesis. Such time as he could spare for theology in Barcelona was at first devoted to preparing his doctoral thesis *Sanctorum Communio*, for publication, and he then concentrated on choosing a subject for his habilitation thesis.

So far as publication of the doctoral thesis was concerned, the situation was not good. He wrote to Seeberg:

I am engaged in cutting and shortening the work, which I should like to send you at the beginning of November, as arranged. I have had to rewrite a great deal and omit long passages. I found ideas on original sin and their social meaning similar to those that I developed in Brunner's *Mediator*, which, incidentally, I found rather disappointing.[42]

So far as revising my doctoral thesis is concerned, I have more or less finished it. I have not been able to abbreviate or cut as much as I had hoped; all the same, a fourth or fifth of it has gone. I recently saw an announcement of a book by Althaus to appear this autumn, called *Communio Sanctorum*.[43] Would you advise me to wait for its appearance or let my work appear independently of it?[44]

Seeberg was not in favour of awaiting the publication of Althaus's book, but 'so far as the publication of your work is concerned, I am afraid that

42. Letter of 20.7.1928.
43. It was in fact published in the spring of 1929.
44. Letter of 10.10.1928.

some time will have to elapse yet. The publishing house now has a new proprietor, and apart from that it works terribly slowly.'[45] The result was that Bonhoeffer's work was involved in the maelstrom of the great economic crisis.

But he was much more interested in planning his new work than in abbreviating and polishing the old.

I already have something else in mind, though again it is not historical but systematic. It is associated with the question of consciousness and conscience in theology and some quotations from Luther from the great commentaries on Galatians ... In your seminar you once broached the question of consciousness, but this is not to be a psychological but a theological enquiry.[46]

This is the first reference to what was to take shape a year later as *Act and Being*. Epistemology still took precedence over ethics. He was fascinated by the prospect of examining theologically the problem of the form assumed by faith in the believer's mind when it necessarily again developed into religion. The problem of religious consciousness had confronted him with the phenomenon of the child, as is shown by his letter to H. Rössler, in which he gives an account of his ministry and children's services.[47]

Once more Bonhoeffer had the bit between his teeth and was galloping away from the confines of history, and Seeberg again tried to keep him within them. Had his experienced mentor detected the weak side of his pupil? On 19th October 1928, he wrote to him:

Perhaps it would be advisable for you now to find some historical or Biblical subject in order to establish yourself independently in the approach and method of this field. For instance, how about going into the question of why ethical problems receded so far into the background in twelfth-century scholasticism, and of how the account in John of Salisbury's *Metalogicus* is to be interpreted? But that is only one example, and if you have anything that appeals to you more, so much the better, of course. But the history of ethics, and still more that of morality, is a field in which a young man might well establish himself at the present time, perhaps with a view to a systematic and historical treatment of ethics from the Sermon on the Mount to the present day.

But Bonhoeffer was too eager to return to his own chosen field for this to have any influence. On 17th February 1929 he was home again in snow-covered Grunewald.

With his return to academic Berlin, Spain by no means vanished from his mind. Teachers and young people from Barcelona visited him in Berlin and during the holidays at Friedrichsbrunn. In spite of examinations ahead and his forthcoming trip to America, in April 1930 he made another trip to Barcelona, where he once more enjoyed good coffee and bad cakes on the Tibidabo, the mountain above the city from the top of which the Devil is said to have shown Jesus the riches of the world, attended a performance of *Carmen* with a magnificent Spanish Don José, and again succumbed to the fascination of the bullfight.

CHAPTER FOUR

ASSISTANT LECTURER IN BERLIN

1929 - 1930

BONHOEFFER was soon to become aware of the ominous political changes that were taking place in the Germany to which he returned.

So far as its international debt was concerned, it was experiencing an alleviation of its position. The reparations problem was passing from the Dawes Plan phase into that of the Young Plan, which came into force on 17th May 1930. With it the Reich regained a degree of economic and financial sovereignty. The Rhineland became free again.

But every advance in foreign relations achieved by Stresemann and Curtius was obscured by right-wing propaganda, which denounced these men as defeatist politicians who accepted the Treaty of Versailles. In the autumn of 1929 the 'Stahlhelm',[1] the nationalists and the Nazis— these last still numerically weak, though highly vociferous—jointly organized a 'national petition for the drafting of a law against the enslavement of the German people' by the Young Plan. Church circles were among those that helped this bloc to secure the 10 per cent representation necessary to make the Reichstag discuss the petition as if it were a parliamentary bill; thus once more they joined in denouncing as unpatriotic the men of the centre and left who opposed it. The Reichstag rejected the petition, however.

Stresemann died on 3rd October 1929, just a few weeks before the Wall Street crash of 24th October 1929. The repercussions of the world economic crisis were grist to the mill of the forces in Germany opposed to democracy, both on the right and on the left. Radicalized masses went out into the streets. It was no coincidence that Dr. Goebbels, the Nazi Gauleiter in Berlin, became his party's national propaganda chief in that same year. Equally ominous was the withdrawal of the Social Democratic Party from the Government a year later, marking the break-up of the coalition that had hitherto shared the responsibility of government. At the end of March 1930 Brüning became Chancellor for the first time, and the period of government by emergency decree began. The only result of this last attempt to rescue the Weimar Republic was its visible wasting away.

The Bonhoeffers expected more of the Brüning Government than was in its power to perform. 'With Brüning as Chancellor the general situa-

1. The largest of the nationalistic ex-servicemen's organizations in Germany, under the leadership of Franz Seldte. (*Translator.*)

tion seemed to offer a guarantee that both in foreign and economic affairs a period of reconciliation and advancement was at hand.'[2] But at the same time the death of two men in their immediate proximity who had helped the Weimar Republic at the cost of sacrificing older loyalties seemed to symbolize the passing away of a great liberal and humani- tarian tradition. Hans Delbrück, the historian and Klaus Bonhoeffer's father-in-law, died in the house next door in the summer of 1929; and only a year was to pass before Adolf von Harnack died too. Both had been much more active politically and had exposed themselves much more than Karl Bonhoeffer, and years before had fought a joint battle to impose bounds on Stoecker's anti-Semitic activity; they had succeeded in checking his attempt to introduce the Jewish question to the Protestant Social Congress and forced him to leave it. During the twenties they watched with concern the political course taken by the Protestant Church, for royalism and anti-Semitism did not die with the disappear- ance of its royal head. In 1928 Erik Peterson wrote to Harnack: 'Sociolo- gically and in outlook the Protestant Church corresponds roughly with the mentality and sociological status of the German National People's Party.'

The values for which Harnack and Delbrück had stood began rapidly succumbing to the defamation and ridicule of the growing forces of irrational nationalism, and were held to be the decadent morality of the 'system State', which was now to be softened up in preparation for the final assault. The Christian bourgeoisie did not feel that there was a great deal about the latter that was worth defending, and anti-liberal publications such as that of the 'Action Group' of Hans Zehrer, Edgar Jung and Ernst Jünger made a bigger impact for that reason. The desire of the right-wing bourgeoisie for an authoritarian order grew. True, the Christian bourgeoisie did not have much use for the vociferous Nazis, but they listened with pleasure to speeches about the 'Western deca- dence' which democracy had introduced to Germany, and liked to think that a 'rebirth of the German national spirit in a German national com- munity' might yet transform the defeat of 1918 into a victory.

At this very time, however, Bonhoeffer's brother and brothers-in- law, Klaus, Gerhard Leibholz and Hans von Dohnanyi, increasingly identified themselves with the Weimar Republic as they increasingly grew into their professional responsibilities.

'Disinterest'

No doubt Dietrich Bonhoeffer followed these developments with no less concern than they, but because of his exclusive commitment to theology he kept much more aloof than his brothers.

2. K. Bonhoeffer, *Lebenserinnerungen*, p. 114.

But in the lively atmosphere of the Wangenheimstrasse he could hardly have been unaffected by the political events of the day, and he was always a very attentive reader of the newspapers. Apart from the democratic *Vossische Zeitung*, which his parents read, his brothers brought home newspapers of all political trends. During the course of this year the Dohnanyis moved from Hamburg to Berlin, and came to live in the Schönes' house opposite. Hans von Dohnanyi took the post of personal assistant to the Reich Minister of Justice which was first offered to Gerhard Leibholz, and through him political events and their background grew closer and more vivid.

The year he had spent abroad had certainly sharpened Dietrich's view of his own country. Excessively nationalist statements such as occur in his Barcelona addresses henceforward never crossed his lips, for he now saw them transformed into nationalistic slogans and bound up with anti-Semitic propaganda. He had nothing to do with the 'national opposition' of 1929 and had no truck with the right-wing popular petition. During these very months, in fact, he established the first close friendship of his life with a young theologian of Jewish origin, Franz Hildebrandt. The development of his conditional pacifism—then unique in German church and theological circles—also dates from this time. When he attended divine service in 1929 and 1930—which he still did not do regularly—he went to Günther Dehn's church in Moabit, and he cannot have been unaware of Dehn's political outlook. His near-Barthian theology increasingly provided him with the tools to resist the apostles of nationalism in theology and the Church who were usurping all that was dear to him, among other things as a scion of the patriotic-minded bourgeoisie.

Nevertheless at this time he had no thought of committing himself politically. Years later we can see more plainly what a tragedy it was that theologians of Bonhoeffer's stamp tried in their way to mark themselves off from humanist 'Westernizing', for their 'crisis theology' was coloured by strong anti-liberal feeling. On top of this there were many Barthians who were prevented by their personal origins from identifying themselves with the forces that were the mainstay of the Weimar Republic. Bonhoeffer would no doubt have associated himself with the words of Karl Barth's confession in 1945 addressed 'to German theologians in prisoner-of-war camps';

I shall therefore openly confess that, if I reproach myself for anything when I look back on the years I spent in Germany, it is that, out of sheer concentration on my churchly and theological task . . . I failed . . . to give a warning, not just implicitly, but explicitly, not merely privately but also publicly . . . against the tendencies . . . in the Church and the world about me.[3]

3. 'Karl Barth zum Kirchenkampf', ThExh, NF 49, 1956, p. 91.

As early as 1932 Bonhoeffer felt ashamed of his 'disinterest', which he called 'really frivolous at this time'.[4]

However, in 1929 he took little interest either in right- or left-wing politics, but devoted himself solely to theology. Indeed after his first practical commitment to Church and society in Barcelona, he returned to his studies with greater zeal.

Nevertheless, for all his sense of purpose, he was still uncertain about his real goal; and this private uncertainty runs like a thread through the years 1929 and 1930. The sources for this period of his life are relatively meagre, but there is no mistaking his hesitation about his true calling. The new subject he had chosen to work on lay on his desk, and he firmly rejected the many distractions that Berlin in general and his home in particular had to offer. But was this work his real purpose in life? What was it all leading to?

I shall soon be handing in my habilitation thesis . . . and soon I shall be going to Barcelona for a fortnight's visit to my congregation, of which I am very fond, and I feel in general that academic work will not hold me for long. On the other hand, I think it very important to have as thorough an academic grounding as possible . . . Fendt and Dehn are almost the only preachers I can really listen to.[5]

I QUALIFICATION AS UNIVERSITY LECTURER

The theological faculty in Berlin was waiting for its highly promising graduate to hand in his habilitation thesis, but the various problems associated with this were not all solved at the first attempt. There were three of them : finding a position for this very young man which would give him status in the university; securing the necessary publication of *Sanctorum Communio*, his doctoral thesis; and finally the subject and theme of his habilitation thesis.

'Voluntary' Assistant Lecturer

The most important change in the faculty with which Bonhoeffer was faced on his return was that Wilhelm Lütgert had succeeded Reinhold Seeberg. Lütgert had been Professor for the New Testament at Halle but had then taken over the chair of systematic theology there, which enjoyed a high reputation as a result of the work of Martin Kähler. Lütgert was a specialist on German idealism, and he found the hard judgements of the dialectical theologians on idealism difficult to accept.

Seeberg nevertheless successfully recommended his pupil to his successor, and at the beginning of the summer term of 1929 Bonhoeffer became a 'voluntary assistant lecturer' in the university seminar in systematic

4. To H. Rössler, 25.12.1932. GS I, p. 65.
5. To H. Rössler, 23.2.1930. GS I, p. 54.

theology, a position that he nominally retained until September 1930.

This involved him in performing duties for the professor for which he was not especially equipped, such as handing out and securing the return of keys, supervising the seminar library, recommending purchases of books, keeping contact with the other chair of systematic theology (Professor Titius) and keeping abreast of the needs of the seminar, handing out work to the rapidly growing number of students, reading it through and detecting plagiarisms. Thus in April 1929 he began his new job, not with discussions of Heidegger, but with rearranging the library and the introduction of new rules for the seminar. Nevertheless his duties gave him the opportunity for work and access to everything he needed. Also he showed his talent for finding people to do things for him. The position gave him a welcome excuse for extricating himself from obligations that he considered a waste of time, e.g. evening meetings of candidates for ordination with his local dean.

The position of 'voluntary' assistant lecturer was not exactly what he had looked forward to when he approached Seeberg in 1928. He had hoped that with Seeberg's retirement the official assistant's post, which was occupied by Arnold Stolzenburg, would fall vacant, but the vacancy occurred only when Stolzenburg was given a seminar on social ethics after Bonhoeffer's return from America.

Lütgert soon learnt to appreciate his new assistant lecturer, though he felt that he would be unable to exercise any influence on his development. To Hans-Christoph von Hase, who took over Bonhoeffer's position after his departure for America, he once remarked: 'I really only just took over your cousin, otherwise I should have wanted to exercise rather more pressure on his philosophy.' This remark arose out of a critical remark by Lütgert about Heidegger, whom he rejected as a neo-Thomist. Hase tried to defend his cousin who, he said, was not a Heidegger man, but at this Lütgert merely shook his head thoughtfully.

Publication Difficulties

The situation in regard to the publication of *Sanctorum Communio* was still very unsatisfactory. No progress had been made, though two years had passed since its completion. The regulations could have been fulfilled by adopting a cheap method of duplication, but Bonhoeffer insisted on his study and criticism of the dialecticians being made available to the latter in book form. In 1926 he had written: 'It would be a good thing, in order to establish clearly the inner logic of the structure of dogmatics, to begin the subject, for once, not with the doctrine of God but with the doctrine of the Church';[6] and now Karl Barth had published the first half-volume of his *Christian Dogmatics* without being aware of the suggestion, let alone accepting it. Also Bonhoeffer's nervousness was

6. SC, p. 97.

increased by the fact that he was losing his start and was about to be overtaken by the publication of Althaus's book with the similar title. He was still looking in vain for a publisher, while Althaus's reputation was already secure. But the growing economic crisis was making publishers warier with every month that passed, even when faced with a recommendation as impressive as that of Seeberg's. For what sales could be expected for a printed doctoral thesis?

In the end the firm of Trowitzsch declared itself willing to accept the work, provided Bonhoeffer met the printing costs of well over 1,000 marks. But meanwhile Althaus's book appeared under the title *Communio Sanctorum*.[7] Bonhoeffer's manuscript was finally delivered to Trowitzsch at the end of March 1930. It contained some amendments compared with the original version, but Bonhoeffer was able to refer to Althaus's book only in some footnotes.[8]

When the first copies were delivered, more than three years had elapsed since Bonhoeffer had finished it, and he was on his way to embarking for America, so he was unable himself to present copies to his friends and patrons. Together with the parcel, the postman delivered the bill for the printing costs, which in the meantime had increased. His parents paid it.

Meanwhile Bonhoeffer had lost real interest in this work, because in the meantime he had completed *Act and Being*, and he was concerned with the publication of the new book. At the beginning of 1931 Trowitzsch complained vigorously at his lack of interest in *Sanctorum Communio*; he had supplied not a line of publicity material and no list of journals that might review the book; also, at eighteen marks it was exceedingly difficult to sell.

As a theological writer Bonhoeffer certainly did not make a successful start. His first work met with only minimal response. The *Theologische Literaturzeitung* published a review by Wobbermin,[9] who misunderstood him, saying that he envisaged establishing common ground in phenomenology for cooperation between theology and knowledge in general. Wilhelm Niesel reviewed the book in the literary supplement of the *Reformierte Kirchenzeitung* of March 1931 and criticized Bonhoeffer's 'sociological tools' as being unsuitable for application to the study of the 'Church'. 'We wished to draw attention to his work', he wrote, 'only because it contains many very good individual observations and shows how much a pupil of Seeberg's has learnt from Gogarten and Barth.'[10] In the *Protestantenblatt* Schubring, rather bewildered by but also drawn to the book, reviewed it because he had been struck by Bonhoeffer's address at Harnack's memorial service,[11] and was now surprised to dis-

7. On the word order *Communio Sanctorum*, cf. SC, p. 220, n. 1.
8. SC, p. 226, n. 45; p. 240, n. 131; p. 241, n. 149.
9. ThLZ, 1931. Sp., pp. 590 f.
10. RKZ, March 1931, p. 4.
11. Cf. Ch. IV, p. 102.

cover a pure systematician in one whom he had assumed to be Harnack's pupil. In 1933 Ernst Wolf referred to the book favourably in an article on 'Man and Church in Catholic Thought' in *Zwischen den Zeiten*.

But, broadly speaking, the book sank unnoticed in the general debate of the time. The dialecticians did not discuss it, as Bonhoeffer hoped they would, and it did not become recommended reading at any university.

Bonhoeffer himself treated it in step-motherly fashion, as he treated most of his books when they had once been published. He disliked protracted arguments and revised editions; he preferred writing something new. His pupils at Finkenwalde who in 1935 were present at the birth pangs of *The Cost of Discipleship* were not told of the existence of his earlier works. They were not displayed, and even Bonhoeffer's earliest pupils in Berlin in 1931-2 did not quote them; he himself seemed to have forgotten them.

'Act and Being'

Bonhoeffer's second book *Act and Being* was written in the summer and winter of 1929. The theme of *Sanctorum Communio*, how revelation becomes concrete, was taken up again, but was brought out more plainly by intervention in the current theological debate of the time. He directed his critical questions to the Barthians more firmly and outspokenly than he ever did again; for soon afterwards there were too many occasions for entering the fray on their side rather than directing questions at them. True, they took almost as little notice of *Act and Being* as they had done of *Sanctorum Communio*. The later vigorous combatant in the church struggle was noted and welcomed, but the earlier theological partner and critic was ignored.

The choice of subject, *Act and Being*, transcendental philosophy and ontology in systematic theology, was not influenced by any promptings from Seeberg or Lütgert. He had written at an early stage from Barcelona: 'I . . . think about my habilitation thesis every now and then',[12] and the subject of his reflections during those hot summer weeks, the 'problem of the child', became the formula for the conclusion and climax of the book, the description under the heading of 'The Child' of the new being in Christ that unites act and being. Here he united by main force the hostile brothers, whether they be called transcendentalists and ontologists, or theologians of action and theologians of being, or Barthians and Lutherans, his understanding of the Church being still dominated by his idea of 'Christ existing as community'.

Thus he plunged into systematic theology, ignoring Seeberg's suggestion that he should deal with an historical or Biblical problem. He wanted to take sides, criticize, press forward into the field where the debate of the late twenties was raging most fiercely, round the ontologies

12. To K.-F. Bonhoeffer, 7.7.1928.

of Barth and Bultmann, their assumptions, and the appropriateness of the tools they used for their purposes. In the *Christliche Welt* the aged Kattenbusch described the scene with the humour of a veteran:

In one way there is something comic in the fact that practically every one of the theologians whom one sees 'pressing into new fields' has his own special philosopher with whom he associates himself. Partly one has the impression that the accident of locality has contributed to the 'community' of approach to the problems of a 'philosophical' nature . . . Practically all the dialectical theologians employ their own philosophers and thus begin the false road to the distinction between God and the world, into which they have all hopelessly relapsed, in order to be able to overcome it.[13]

The phrase 'accident of locality' referred to the Marburg pair of Bultmann and Heidegger and also to the Jena team of Gogarten and Grisebach.

Bonhoeffer now tackled Heidegger, whose *Being and Time* had appeared in 1927, more seriously. In the index to *Act and Being* Heidegger takes second place only to Luther, and fills more space than Barth. Husserl, Scheler, Grisebach and Tillich are also discussed. Bultmann is criticized for his dependence on Heidegger; Bonhoeffer claims that with the introduction of 'potentiality', the concept of possibility in Christian decisions, he destroys the theological basis of the determined, free act of God and thus all certainty in favour of reflection.[14] Barth, however, is criticized for his formalistic interpretation of the freedom of God.[15] Schleiermacher, the founding father of the Berlin school, appears to have sunk below the horizon,[16] but in reality he is the opponent behind all the philosophies and theologies dealt with all the way down to Holl. Rudolf Otto, who in foreign countries was then considered to be the representative *par excellence* of modern German theology, is not mentioned at all.[17]

In *Act and Being* Bonhoeffer is basically addressing philosophers, whom he schematically finds guilty of the original sin of idealism, namely imprisonment in the self. The philosophers, however, did not admit to recognizing themselves in his schematized version.[18] He also argues with Barth, warning him of the dangers of his transcendental philosophy and trying to make him more 'Lutheran'. He wanted to persuade him of his own belief in the *finitum capax infiniti*, that in spite of everything God was accessible. He valued both the philosophers whom he had read and attacked since his schooldays and Barth, who had convinced him of the independence of theology.

The argument for the concreteness of revelation in the form of the

13. CW, 1929, p. 525.
14. AB, pp. 73 f., 98.
15. AB, pp. 90 f.
16. The only reference is AB. p. 176.
17. The 22nd ed. of R. Otto's *Das Heilige* was published in 1929. It had been translated into all the principal languages.
18. Cf., e.g., B. H. Knittermeyer's review, ZZ, 1933, 11th year, pp. 179 ff.

community, which was conducted on theological-sociological lines in the first book, is followed in the second by an argument on theological-epistemological lines—basically for the same concreteness. Thus the classical passage in *Act and Being* reads:

In revelation it is a question less of God's freedom on the far side from us, i.e. his eternal isolation and aseity, than of his forth-proceeding, his *given* Word, his bond in which he has bound himself, of his freedom as it is most strongly attested in his having freely bound himself to historical man, having placed himself at man's disposal. God is not free *of* man but *for* man. Christ is the Word of his freedom. God *is there*, which is to say: not in eternal non-objectivity but (looking ahead for the moment) 'haveable', graspable in his Word within the Church. Here a substantial comes to supplant the formal understanding of God's freedom.[19]

To Bonhoeffer the old extreme Calvinism is in error when it ends by preventing the complete entry into this world of the majesty of God, and he surmises that it is at work when he sees Barth establishing the majesty of God by the methods of Kantian transcendentalism. To state the position in greatly over-simplified terms, while the early Barth, desiring to proclaim God's majesty, begins by removing him to a remote distance, Bonhoeffer, inspired by the same desire to proclaim his majesty, begins by bringing him into close proximity.

Thus Bonhoeffer's path at the theological-epistemological level of *Act and Being* brings him back to ecclesiology, and vice versa; he makes great play with the principal theme of *Sanctorum Communio*, that the Church is the basic givenness of theology. It is the reality of the Church, again conceived of as 'Christ existing as community', that makes fruitful the tension between the respective legitimate interests; of the existentialist theology of Act on the one hand, as developed theocentrically in Barth and anthropocentrically in Bultmann, and on the other of the neo-orthodox theology of Being of the 'pure doctrine'. Thus both requirements, that of contingency and of continuity of revelation, are preserved.

However, behind this highly abstract discourse, which the uninitiated are hardly able to follow, a passionate personal involvement is concealed. Bonhoeffer's deepest feelings were involved in his insistence on the *extra nos* and *pro nobis* of salvation. His own difficulties sharpened his sensitivity to every loophole in the system through which fatal reflection might invade his own ego and establish its secret domination. Thus he criticizes both Barth and Bultmann for introducing into faith a dangerous element of permanent reflection, Barth for making the believing self permanently reflect on its non-self and Bultmann for referring faith, bearing in mind its 'potentiality', to the situation of decision. This, Bonhoeffer objected passionately, kills faith. Faith must not be guided by itself, it must be totally directed to Christ. Reflection was a diversion from him and left one in an ultimate solitude. But faith is experience of

19. AB, pp. 90 f.

the concrete presence of the Christ who was made flesh, crucified and resurrected; it was in all respects dialectical sociality, sociality that was permanently already fulfilled and yet permanently fulfilling itself anew, both vertically and horizontally. This was the point on which Bonhoeffer hung his heart.

For all the one-sidedness and the conceptual over-simplifications for which it has been rightly criticized, what Bonhoeffer was trying to do in *Act and Being* was very acute and up-to-date. He went to the heart of a vital problem that has remained vital in spite of all changes. Some of his criticisms have been accepted as justified, some of his questions are still raised today.

From our biographical point of view, the importance of *Act and Being* is that—taken in conjunction with *Sanctorum Communio*—it contains many of the ideas that were to be applied to the 'non-religious inter-pretation'[20] in the letters from prison fifteen years later. That deprives them of their supposedly fortuitous character and means that they were better prepared than is generally assumed. Ideas of 1930 that seemed to have vanished for a decade and a half suddenly reappeared in 1944. *Act and Being* gave the social and ethical transcendence of one's neigh-bour, which had already been maintained in *Sanctorum Communio* as against philosophical-metaphysical transcendence, the magnificent formulation 'Jesus, the man for others'. Here, of course, its application is still confined to the bounds of the Church, while it ended by being thought of as permanently and essentially freed from all bounds and applied to the world as Christ's own proper dominion.

Bonhoeffer finished the work in February 1930, and duly submitted it for the appraisal of the theological faculty. The formalities took their course, and the habilitation duly took place on 18th July 1930. On 31st July the rector, Erhard Schmidt, invited the newly-qualified twenty-four-year-old teacher to deliver his inaugural lecture on 'The Question of Man in Contemporary Philosophy and Theology'. In this he used the weapons he had just tried out in *Act and Being* to discuss the anthro-pology of the period and defended his view of man's understanding of himself. 'God is nearer to me than my existence is, in as much as it is he who first discloses my existence to me', he said, for 'in reflexive theological thought I have no closer reference to my existence than to God'.[21] His concluding sentence was: 'Thus not only does every in-dividual theological problem lead back to the reality of the Church of Christ, but theological thinking discovers itself in its totality to be of such a nature that it belongs to the Church alone.'[22]

When *Act and Being* was completed, the manuscript of *Sanctorum Communio* had not yet even reached the printer, but Bonhoeffer had

20. Cf. Ch. XIII, pp. 773 ff.
21. AB, pp. 96 f.
22. GS III, p. 84.

to wait only a year to find a publisher for his second book. Lütgert recommended him to Bertelsmann, who wanted a contribution to the printing costs of only 200 marks. Althaus promised a recommendation to enable it to appear in the series 'Contributions to the Advancement of Christian Theology'. Bonhoeffer had to wait five months for this, but when it arrived it was in very warm terms. 'I consider it to be a very important piece of work, which unquestionably must be printed as soon as possible', he wrote to Bonhoeffer's father on 4th March 1931, and the latter forwarded the letter to him in America. 'It will please you, but not make you presumptuous', he wrote.[23] The book was published in the autumn of 1931, after Dietrich's return from America.

By the time Bonhoeffer sent signed copies to his friends—this time one of the recipients was Günther Dehn—his interests had again moved on elsewhere. 'In the meantime the thing has grown rather unsympathetic to me', he wrote on 26th February 1932 to his new friend Erwin Sutz. The 'thing' had been written in 1929, and in between there lay the impact of America, the beginning of his work as teacher and preacher, and the ecumenical commitment.

This time the critical echo was somewhat greater than it had been in the case of *Sanctorum Communio*, but was still relatively meagre. In 1933 Knittermeyer reviewed it very critically in *Zwischen den Zeiten*, and Eisenhuth did the same in the *Theologische Literaturzeitung*.[24] In his attempt to keep the theological epistemology strictly within the doctrine of justification,[25] Bonhoeffer had dealt with philosophy too one-sidedly for his critics, and had over-simplified and thus done violence to the epistemological problem by continually leading it back to idealism.

But in retrospect one remarkable fact is clear. At a time when on the one hand positivist enthusiasm for the Church was at its height while on the other violent criticism of it prevailed, a young voice was raised which theologically rediscovered and accepted the empirical Church without merely retreating again into criticism of it. Thus Bonhoeffer established firm ground from which to stand up to the storms that lay ahead.

II FAMILY AND FRIENDS

The working rhythm of these eighteen months was interrupted by three weddings in the family. On each occasion Dietrich's organizing ability was made use of. A holiday letter from Friedrichsbrunn says: 'We are leading an incredibly lazy life up here . . . We do a great deal of walking. The noise in the house makes collecting for an eve-of-the-wedding play very difficult.'[26] In 1929 his sister Susanne was married to Walter

23. Letter of 6.3.1931.
24. ThLZ, 1933. Sp., pp. 188 ff.
25. Cf. Ch. II, p. 46.
26. To his grandmother, 18.8.1930.

Dress; in 1930 his brother Karl-Friedrich married Grete von Dohnanyi, the sister of Hans von Dohnanyi; and before his departure for America, Klaus married Emmi Delbrück, the sister of his friend Justus Delbrück. Thus Dietrich was the only member of the big family to remain at home.

People He Knew

His friends during this period came from the familiar circle of the Wangenheimstrasse and theologians at the university. Hans-Christoph von Hase was working on his thesis,[27] and consulted his cousin on the subject. Walter Dress had qualified as a lecturer with his work on Gerson,[28] and used to take Bonhoeffer for walks in the Grunewald where, besides discussing theology, they botanized (a matter in which Dress was an expert). Helmut Rössler already had a parish in Mark Brandenburg, and Bonhoeffer visited him in his village. At Harnack's last private seminar in 1929 he renewed acquaintance with Bertha Schulze, who tirelessly tracked down quotations for him for his work and gave him library assistance. His distant cousin Elisabeth Zinn graduated with a thesis for Lütgert on the theology of F. C. Oetinger,[29] the eighteenth-century Württemberg theosophist, and she and Bonhoeffer exchanged their first publications; a quotation from Oetinger that became one of Bonhoeffer's favourites, 'the nature of the body is the end of God's path', came from this source.

His friendship with Franz Hildebrandt was significant for the future and lent a personal urgency to many of Bonhoeffer's later decisions, and it lasted for life. Hildebrandt's father was the Professor of the History of Art in Berlin University, and his mother was of Jewish origin. Hildebrandt, who was Bonhoeffer's junior by three years, was working on a thesis on the Lutheran *est*.[30] The two had first met at Seeberg's seminar on the morning of the day before Bonhoeffer defended his graduation thesis, when they discussed the relationship between the Old Testament and the New, and Hildebrandt took the side of Marcion. Now on Good Friday 1929 they met again by chance at a performance of the St. Matthew Passion at the Berlin Choral Society.

Their friendship was spiced with a life-long private feud; while Hildebrandt tilted at Bonhoeffer for his dubious mixture of Hegelian and Barthian categories, Bonhoeffer counter-attacked by criticizing his excessive devotion to Harnack. But on all practical problems they later saw eye to eye; each always knew how the other would act or react. Hildebrandt influenced Bonhoeffer's imminent conversion to an ever-increasing Biblicism, and from his immense memory often supplied him

27. Hans-Christoph von Hase, *Die Gegenwart Christi in der Kirche*, Gütersloh, 1934.
28. W. Dress, *Die Theologie Gersons. Eine Untersuchung zur Verbindung von Nominalismus und Mystik im Spätmittelalter*, Gütersloh, 1931.
29. E. Zinn, *Die Theologie des Friedrich Christoph Oetinger*, thesis, Gütersloh, 1932.
30. F. Hildebrandt, Est. *Das lutherische Prinzip*, thesis, Göttingen, 1931.

with vital quotations from the Bible or from Luther. On 31st July 1930 he presented him with a small book of Luther quotations on the pericopes with the inscription: 'To "the prince of ill" on the occasion of his habilitation'. Bonhoeffer liked his dry humour and quick grasp of things. He soon became a welcome guest in the Wangenheimstrasse, and deputized worthily for Dietrich at the piano when the latter could not attend the family musical evenings. This was Bonhoeffer's first really close friendship, which survived the painful separation when Hildebrandt was forced to emigrate in 1937.

Harnack's Death

In the summer of 1929 Bonhoeffer and his friends attended the eighty-seven-year-old Adolf von Harnack's last seminar on ecclesiastical history. The farewell ceremony took the form of an outing to an inn in the Grunewald, and Bonhoeffer was the speaker. 'That you were our teacher for many hours was a passing thing; that we can call ourselves your pupils remains.'[31]

While Bonhoeffer was in the midst of preparations for his examination and his trip to America, news arrived that the old gentleman had died at Heidelberg on 10th June 1930, when about to open the annual meeting of the Kaiser Wilhelm Society. The society held a memorial service in the Goethe Hall of the Harnack House in Berlin on 15th June. After Schmidt-Ott, the Minister of State, Professor Hans Lietzmann, Wirth, the Minister of the Interior, Grimme, the Minister of Culture, and Krüss, the director of the state library, had spoken, Dietrich Bonhoeffer spoke in the name of Harnack's former pupils:

. . . He made it plain to us that truth is born only of freedom. We saw in him a champion of the free expression of truth when it has been recognized, who continually revised his free judgement and always plainly expressed it, notwithstanding the anxious restraint of the many. That made him . . . the friend of all young people who freely express their opinions, as he wanted them to do. And if he sometimes spoke anxiously about or issued warnings about recent developments in our department of studies,[32] the reason lay exclusively in his fear that the views of others might perhaps be endangered by the mingling of extraneous matter with the pure search for truth. But, as we knew that with him we were in kindly and solicitous hands, we saw in him a bulwark against all trivialization and destruction, all schematization of the life of the mind.[33]

Bonhoeffer made a great impression by successfully withstanding comparison with the older and eminent speakers who preceded him. As he was now obviously going a different way himself, many were

31. A. von Zahn-Harnack, op. cit., p. 436; GS III, p. 19; quotation from letter of 18.12.1929.
32. See Harnack's letter to Bonhoeffer of 22.12.1929, GS III, p. 20.
33. GS III, p. 60.

astonished at the breadth of vision and sympathy he showed for his former teacher. Schubring, who secured the address for his *Protestantenblatt*, did not realize what other things besides admiration for Harnack existed in Bonhoeffer's mind. for he asked him to criticize the latest attacks on him in his journal.[34]

Bernanos

Throughout his life-time Bonhoeffer's reading was never limited to his subject, to which his explorations of contemporary writing always provided the counterpoint. An encounter that made a lasting impact on him belongs to this period. His interest in the Catholic world led him to Georges Bernanos, German versions of whose first novels *The Star of Satan* and *The Renegade* appeared in 1927 and 1929. He was disconcerted to find his most intimate problems dealt with here—the priest and saint as the chosen target of the tempter, the man barely able to resist the alternative assaults of *desperatio* and *superbia*. Had he not long been familiar with the perils faced by those who accept the call to special service for God and with the longing to know one's own devotion in early years? Was he not aware of the danger of *accidie*, for the failure of which to appear he later expressed such gratitude?[35]

The renegade priest is the intellectual sceptic whose 'independent thinking is the best weapon against grace'; he writes theological books, 'insidious, wilful work, glittering, sterile books with a poisoned heart, masterpieces'.

Bonhoeffer's encounter with these early works of Bernanos was the most intimate event of this period of which we know. The question of what he had devoted his life to was more acute than ever. The discovery of Bernanos was so disturbing to him that he did something that he seldom did, i.e. tried to rouse his father's interest in what he was reading. The latter indeed read the book his son sent him as a slightly treacherous gift, and wrote to him—warmly and yet coolly at the same time—that it had gripped him, but

. . . I am not sure whether I have understood it all; but for the book itself that is a matter of no importance, as intellectual understanding is less important for it than mystical entry into a kind of different state of consciousness. Much of the dialogue is of such a kind that it is hard to understand the trains of thought involved between the lines. But, psychologically, the uncertainty whether the experience is supernatural or dreamlike illusion, the change of affect with its satanic aspects and its human, peasant-like, unintellectual simplicity, is extraordinarily vivid. Is this modern or medieval Catholic mysticism?[36]

Bonhoeffer maintained his interest in Bernanos, and added each new

34. Letter of 19.6.1930.   35. LPP. p. 87.   36. Letter of 18.10.1930.

book that he wrote to his library. At his suggestion, many theological seminarists read *The Diary of a Country Priest* when it appeared in German translation in 1936.

Berlin Church

During these years the Berlin churches did not see very much of their candidate for the ministry. Diestel, his dean, guided his training in such a way that all bureaucratic rocks were avoided. His academic status and his work on the habilitation thesis enabled him to avoid attending the cathedral seminary.

The dates for the second ecclesiastical examination presented a problem of a different kind. The regulations provided for an interval of from eighteen months to four years between the first examination and the second. Thus, had he not had such a long way to go yet before reaching the prescribed minimum age of twenty-five for ordination, the earliest possible date for him was the autumn of 1929. When the plan to go to America in 1930 took shape, everything had to be hurried. He took the second examination before he left, but the authorities rejected Diestel's request that he might be ordained before leaving for America.

Bonhoeffer took little notice of church politics in 1929-30. He joined no group, neither the Christian Socialists nor the evangelically active S.C.M. Hardly anyone yet took seriously the occasional incidents of Nazi arrogance in German provincial churches. In 1929 a minister at Bochum allowed his church to be decorated with swastika flags, while the neighbouring Catholic church refused admission to Nazis in uniform. When the Congregational Council of Heiligkreuz in Berlin put its churches at the disposal of the Stahlhelm for Christmas celebrations but refused a request by the black, red and gold Reichsbanner, the Berlin Consistory expressed its disapproval.[37] Bonhoeffer did not yet see any necessity to adopt any public position on these issues, let alone give up his time to them. He had just arrived in New York when the first great success of the Nazis in the elections of September 1930 created a new situation, but this at first hardly affected him.

III AMERICAN PLANS

The idea of spending a year in America as an exchange student arose in the second half of 1929. Diestel suggested it on ecumenical grounds, but to Bonhoeffer such considerations weighed less at the time than the prospect of fresh fields of study and new experience.

Nevertheless he hesitated before putting in his application. He mistrusted what awaited him in America. The New World in itself did not fascinate him sufficiently. Was he to become a student again and

37. CW. 1929, p. 809.

devote a whole year to whatever place might be allotted him? He was told something about American 'textbook methods'; and he regarded American theology as non-existent.

So he sought information from a previous recipient of an American grant, and what he was told was not exactly encouraging. One indeed had to go as an ordinary student, subject oneself to the 'credit system', and accumulate the required number of points by attending lectures and seminars and receiving satisfactory reports; agreement to this was insisted on by the American consulate before it granted a visa. To prevent him from being excessively disappointed as a result of his German ideas of academic freedom, his informant advised him to imagine the atmosphere of a German secondary school. In his field of systematic theology there was of course nothing to learn. The only place that was worth while was Union Theological Seminary in New York, which had a great many other things to offer, but he might well be allotted a place at Hartford or St. Louis; seventeenth-century orthodoxy still prevailed even at Princeton, so his German informant told him. He was advised to postpone going to America until he could go there as a professor.

He hesitated, but at the beginning of May, when he was assured of a place at Union Theological Seminary, he did so no longer.

It was his habit to prepare himself thoroughly for enterprises of this kind, not only so far as the language of the country was concerned but also in political and theological and ecclesiastical matters. So far as this last was concerned, there was not very much that was illuminating. Diestel provided him with some literature. The youthful W. A. Visser 't Hooft's *The Background of the Social Gospel* had been published in 1929. There was a book by Hermann Sasse, then still a minister of the Church of the Old Prussian Union in Berlin, about theology and church life in America. Theology of Bonhoeffer's kind could not be said yet to have reached the United States. True, E. Brunner, who had himself been an exchange student in 1919-20, had lectured in America, and his lectures were published by Scribners in New York in 1929 under the striking but dubious title *Theology of Crisis*. In 1928 Douglas Horton had published a first translation of Barth, under the more appropriate title *The Word of God and the Word of Man* (Pilgrim Press); the publisher had incidentally insisted that the word 'theology' must on no account appear in the title, on the ground that it was impossible in the book trade. But the title of Brunner's book, unlike that of Horton's, stuck in the American mind, and had the unfortunate consequence of becoming a label in America for Barth's approach.

A notebook in which Bonhoeffer jotted down American idioms also contains some remarkable notes that indicate something in the nature of an effort to prepare himself politically for the trip. It contains arguments on the question of war guilt; the text of the celebrated Article 231 of the Treaty of Versailles that attributed war guilt to Germany alone and

American and French statements rejecting this; and also some dreadful statements made in connection with American war aims in 1917 by Elihu Root (1845-1937), who had been Secretary of State:

The Germans are only half civilized in all that makes for civilization. Germany has the abnormal instincts which characterize her barbarisms and separate her from any civilized people. She has the intolerance, the incapacity to realize the right of existence of others ... This war is a war between the civilization of this country and the semicivilization of the past ... Most of the Germans have become unclean and will have to walk in the world as marked people, avoided, despised, stoned ... We are now in this war to save our country from being overrun by barbarism. We are trying to save infants from being dangled on the bayonet as was done in Belgium.[38]

Should such things ever have been said about the Germans? Bonhoeffer forgot them when he discovered that the war-time mentality had faded away among American Christians to a much greater extent than it had in his own country. But in his talks to young people in America he did not keep silent about the Treaty of Versailles and its effects.[39] In 1929 and 1930 that treaty was still a most painful subject, even in circles associated with the World Alliance for Friendship between the Churches inside Germany. At a meeting of the Alliance at Cassel in 1929 even a man as free of nationalist prejudices as Siegmund-Schultze said: 'This war educated our German people to peace, this peace educated it to war.'[40] Martin Rade, the editor of the *Christliche Welt*, who had no desire to associate himself with the political right, specifically applauded this statement.

In New York Bonhoeffer did not spend much time arguing with the aid of the material he had carefully collected for the purpose at home. On the contrary, he soon saw that the dropping of old prejudices had made much more progress in America than he had previously assumed.

Thus he set out on his first visit to the West. For all his pleasurable expectations, he still felt uncertain about what he wanted. For at the time of his departure he also had hopes of visiting a part of the world not mentioned in his travelling papers—the Far East. In fact the trip marked a turning-point in his life, the beginning of his link with the English-speaking West. Undertaken only hesitantly as it was, and though there was little precedent for it in his family background, it had a more lasting effect on his life than his other youthful travels, and caused him to make friends who permanently affected him and his outlook.

One day he was forced to confess to these new Western friends that Elihu Root's crude and long-forgotten statements about his country had subsequently been horrifyingly confirmed.

38. *The U.S. and the War*, political addresses by Elihu Root, collected and ed. by R. Bacon and J. B. Scott, 1918.
39. Cf. GS I, pp. 69 f.   40. CW, 1929, p. 858.

CHAPTER FIVE

AMERICA

1930 - 1931

My cabin . . . lies deep in the belly of the ship. I have not yet met my travelling companion face to face. I have been trying to form a picture of him from the things he leaves lying about, his hat, walking-stick, and a novel by Seymour have led me to the conclusion that he is an educated young American . . . I have already eaten two huge meals with a good appetite; I shall go on enjoying the ship as long as enjoyment is possible.[1]

Bonhoeffer had brilliantly fulfilled all the requirements for either an academic career or a career in the Church, and never before and never again was he able to feel so free. Did he really want to go to America? At all events, he hoped to return home round the other side of the world, by way of India. His sister Christine encouraged him. 'Perhaps gentle pressure on our parents will do the trick, possibly dressed up in the form of a big loan . . . I have the feeling they are sympathetic in the matter, and that in the end it will come off', she wrote in November 1930.

His travelling companion in the *Columbus* turned out to be a Dr. Lucas, a prosperous American who was president of a college at Lahore. The result was that he was given expert advice about India, and also received an invitation to Lahore, where Dr. Lucas would accompany him to the hills, to Benares, Allahabad, Agra and Delhi. Further enquiries, however, revealed that returning home via the Pacific would be disproportionately expensive. His mother consoled him. 'I think you will always be able to take leave and visit India from here', she wrote, 'and be able to go there better prepared and at a more suitable opportunity.'[2]

This second attempt to visit Asia got further than the first. Some years later a third attempt followed, and this time much more urgently motivated. Bonhoeffer greatly wanted to be brought face to face with Indian answers to the problem of living as a counter-point to his own philosophy and theology.

But life turned out differently. For years he wanted to broaden his horizon by travelling to the East. Instead he did so by going west. The process began with his trip to America.

1. Letter to his grandmother, 6.9.1930.
2. Letter of 23.2.1931.

I COUNTRY

Bonhoeffer was overwhelmed by New York, the giant concrete buildings between the Hudson and the East River. Lower Manhattan still dominated the skyline. Upper Manhattan did not yet have the Rockefeller Center, and the Empire State Building was still being built.

But he also saw the obverse side of the medal. In 1930 unemployment in America was proportionately much higher than in Germany, and this was causing widespread alarm. Since the Wall Street crash of the previous year the depression had been in full swing. Public opinion was agitated by prohibition; the 'wets' agitated for its abolition and the 'dries' for more effective application of the law. 'Unfortunately I cannot even drink your health in a glass of wine, which is forbidden by law, this prohibition in which nobody believes is a dreadful absurdity.'[3] Anxieties were expressed about German hankerings for another war. These struck Bonhoeffer as very curious; he had not sufficiently taken into account the big Nazi gains in the September elections in Germany.[4] A plan for a German-Austrian union roused fears of an *Anschluss* and rumours of an impending *Putsch* crossed the Atlantic. Dietrich was disquieted and wrote home for information, but his father's reply was reassuring.

You say that the news from Germany sounds displeasing in America [he wrote]. It certainly is not pleasing, and the perpetual brawls between Communists and Nazis are an indication of the existing tension. But *Putsches* predicted so long in advance generally tend not to take place. Also I think that the Reichswehr is firm under Groener, so that no party can hope to carry out a successful *Putsch* . . . According to what you write from New York, things are not pleasing in the economic and social respect in America either. At all events, I don't think that any unrest is to be feared between now and your return . . .[5]

Politically we assume that on the customs union question the Austro-German viewpoint will prevail. It is of course absurd to talk about war. Apart from anything else, even the Nazis are not so stupid as to believe that we are in a position to go to war.[6]

Whenever he had to make a speech, Bonhoeffer spoke at length about peace aspirations in Germany and those who backed them.[7] True, what he said hardly amounted to an expression of qualified opinion about the state of affairs in Germany, but was rather a reflection of his own attitude to the peace question, which was changing.

He quickly came into contact with the busy activity of the New York churches, and soon was hardly able to cope with the invitations that come flooding in. 'I am now continually and on the most varied occasions

3. To S. Leibholz, 21.2.1931.
4. Nazi representation in the Reichstag increased from 14 to 107.
5. Letter of 20.3.1931.
6. Letter of 7.4.1931.
7. GS I. pp. 61 ff.

having to make speeches and deliver addresses; the day after tomorrow I have to preach in English, and next week I am going to talk about Germany to more than 1,000 schoolchildren.'[8] A Methodist church printed the following invitation:

. . . Dr. Deitrich Bonhoefier [*sic*], a professor of the University of Berlin, will speak. From the heart of Germany he will bring to us a message on 'WAR'. Did you ever wonder what the German people are thinking about war? This is an unusual opportunity to find out. Don't miss it![9]

He was sought out as a speaker by student associations ranging from Lutheran to Unitarian. 'It is almost incredible that you should want to be in an international association of ninety-seven nations', his father wrote. The organization in question was the Intercollegiate Y.M.C.A.

Bonhoeffer avoided indiscriminately squandering himself, however. He allowed himself to become really involved only in the Negro district of Harlem, which is not far from Union Theological Seminary. He spent nearly every Sunday and many evenings there. He took part in guided visits to the area, including a 'trip to centres of Negro life and culture in Harlem', beginning with a flight over the district in which Negroes lived at a density of 170,000 to the square mile. He collected the publications of the National Association for the Advancement of Coloured People, and gramophone records of Negro spirituals, with which five years later he introduced to his pupils what to them was a practically unknown world. He also read a great deal of Negro writing.

I have again just finished a quite outstanding novel by a quite young Negro. In contrast to the rest of American writing, which is either cynical or sentimental, I find here a very productive strength and warmth, which continually arouses in one the desire to meet the man himself.[10]

In Reinhold Niebuhr's seminar on 'Ethical Viewpoints in Modern Literature' he followed up the long list of recommended Negro books. He wrote an essay on Johnson's *Autobiography of an Ex-Colored Man*. In spite of his admiration for the capacity of American society for integration and change, 'according to the whole mood in present Negro literature', he concluded in English, 'it seems to me, that the race question is arriving at a turning-point. The attempt to overcome the conflict religiously or ethically will turn in a violent political objection.' Bonhoeffer was wrong only in regard to the date; when he found the same situation in 1939, he maintained his opinion unchanged.

Bonhoeffer's fellow-student and friend Frank Fisher, who was himself a Negro,[11] helped him to gain a detailed and intimate knowledge of the realities of Harlem life. Nearly every Sunday he accompanied him to

8. To S. Leibholz, 7.11.1930.
9. Invitation issued by the Memorial Methodist Church, 21 Tuckahoe Rd., 6.11.1930.
10. To his grandmother, 12.4.1931, GS I, p. 80.
11. GS I, pp. 96 f.

the Abyssinian Baptist Church at 128 West 138th Street, in a squalid
and disreputable district. He became a regular worker in the Sunday
school and the various church clubs. Thus he gained an entry into the
people's homes. Fisher also took him to Howard College, the Negro
university in Washington.

He noted with dismay that the so enviable integration of the white
churches into the life of the community was in fact an obstacle to the
solution of the racial problem; and, greatly impressed though he was by
the fervour of Negro services, he was disturbed by the noticeable and
growing estrangement of the younger coloured generation from the faith
of their fathers, who had accepted all this discrimination so patiently.
He wrote about the problem to his brother Karl-Friedrich, who replied
from Frankfurt:

I am delighted you have the opportunity of studying the Negro question
so thoroughly. I had the impression when I was over there that it is really
the problem, at any rate for people with a conscience and, when I was
offered an appointment at Harvard, it was a quite basic reason for my disinclination to go to America for good, because I did not want either to enter
upon that heritage myself or to hand it on to my hypothetical children. It
seems impossible to see the right way to tackle the problem.

Not suspecting the heritage he would have to enter upon in his own
country, Karl-Friedrich continued: 'At all events, our Jewish question
is a joke in comparison; there cannot be many people left who maintain
they are oppressed here. At any rate, not in Frankfurt . . .'[12]

The huge country lured Bonhoeffer beyond the confines of New York.
His first trip was to Philadelphia, the cradle of Quakerdom and of the
American Constitution, where relatives of his grandmother Tafel lived.
On Thanksgiving Day Fisher showed him Washington, and as a guest
from Germany he attended the annual meeting of the Federal Council
of Churches, the predecessor of the present National Council of Churches
of Christ in the U.S.A. He was not able to work up any enthusiasm for
the churchly or theological content of the conference,[13] but was
impressed by the passing of a widely noted resolution on the question
of war guilt, which took the form of a fraternal message to the Christians
of Germany rejecting 'the theory of the sole guilt of Germany for the
war'.[14] This experience strengthened him for his lectures in the United
States, and made him react even more bitterly to the statement by Hirsch
and Althaus in 1931 accusing German supporters of the ecumenical
movement of being unpatriotic internationalists.[15]

At Christmas Bonhoeffer and his Swiss friend and fellow-student
Erwin Sutz accepted an invitation to Cuba, where he again met Käthe
Horn, his childhood governess, who now taught at a German school in

12. Letter of 24.1.1931.   13. GS I, p. 78.   14. CW, 1931, p. 43.   15. Cf. Ch. VI, p. 148.

Havana. He inspected her class and, after a long interval, preached again. At the Christmas service he painted a gloomy picture to the members of the German colony:

. . . because it seems strange to celebrate Christmas with swarms of unemployed before our eyes, millions of children suffering throughout the world, the starving in China, the oppressed in India and in our own unhappy countries . . . Who, thinking of all this, would wish unconcernedly and uncaringly to enter the promised land?

He chose an unusual text for his sermon: the story of Moses condemned to die on Mount Nebo without entering the promised land.[16]

At the end of the academic year he went to Mexico with his French friend Jean Lasserre. Catholic culture and memories of Spain attracted him more than the novelties of California. The trip turned into an adventure. He failed to get a driving licence, and later he enjoyed telling the story of how he twice failed to pass the test because he omitted to bribe the examiner. Then the departure was delayed, because it was decided that Sutz should join them, but he had to sing in the chorus of a performance of the Mass in B minor at the Carnegie Hall. Then his parents sent him a warning not to stay in New Orleans because of the alleged danger of malaria. Finally, on 5th May 1931 Paul Lehmann set out to drive them to Chicago; this was in the days before the turnpikes. Halfway, at St. Louis, Sutz turned back. The venerable Oldsmobile which had been lent to Bonhoeffer by friends he made in the *Columbus* managed to struggle on as far as the Mexican border, but then gave up for good.

Lasserre had friends in Mexico. At the teachers' training college at Victoria he and Bonhoeffer addressed the students on the subject of peace; 'for the people of Victoria it was a tremendous event to listen to a German and a Frenchman together'.[17] They spent over a week in Mexico City, and visited pyramids and the sites of ancient sacrifices.

On the return journey they were refused re-entry at the United States frontier. Before the immigration officials were convinced that they were not going to be a burden on the American labour market, and that the tickets for their return journey to Bremen were already waiting for them in New York, telegrams had to be sent by the German Ambassador in Mexico and by Paul Lehmann. When they finally arrived safe and sound in hot New York on 20th June in time to catch the ship home, they had travelled well over 1,200 miles by train through Mexico and nearly 4,000 in the decrepit Oldsmobile.

II FRIENDS

In the later church struggle Bonhoeffer abruptly broke off some of the

16. Deut. 32: 48-52. For Bonhoeffer's later use of the same text. cf. Ch. XIII, p. 754.
17. Communication from J. Lasserre.

friendships from his student days, but those from his time at Union Theological Seminary remained. Four friends whom he made in America in 1930-1 played an important part in his life; two were American and two European.

In one of the latter he found an ally in the uphill task of explaining the theology of old Europe to New World audiences. Erwin Sutz, a Swiss, understood the source of his friend's discontent and where his arguments were tending. They were also united by their love of the piano, and in New York they helped each other to secure invitations to places where music could be heard. They went together to hear Toscanini, whom the spoilt Berlin concert-goer did not feel to be so unique. Sutz was astonished and amused at the money lavished by Bonhoeffer on keeping up contacts with his family through the post office and the Western Union; there were always messages of congratulations or good wishes to be sent, or worries about illness or other matters in the endless ramifications of this vast clan. Sutz had the credit of at last bringing about a meeting between Bonhoeffer and Karl Barth; he had himself studied under the latter, and under Brunner. Outside the lecture hall they discussed the criticisms of Barth that Bonhoeffer completely withheld from his American fellow-students. Sutz wrote to Barth in Bonn about his new friend, with the result that before settling down again in Berlin in 1931 Bonhoeffer spent a good two weeks in Bonn and for the first time met the man to whom his deepest interest in theology was due. Sutz also introduced him to Emil Brunner. Finally, during the war he was Bonhoeffer's vital and reliable contact with the West from which he was cut off.

His other European friend was Jean Lasserre, whom at first he did not feel to be nearly so much of an ally. This was his first meeting with a contemporary Christian pacifist; also Lasserre was a Frenchman, and in relations with a Frenchman a German could not so quickly shake off all feelings of resentment. But he was also a European theologian who, unlike his American contemporaries, could not be dismissed as being naïvely ignorant of the relevant history of dogmatics. In contrast to the undoubted sincerity and earnestness of many young theologians at Union Theological Seminary, Lasserre confronted him with an acceptance of Jesus' peace commandment that he had never met before. Not that Bonhoeffer immediately became a convinced pacifist—in fact he never did so—but after meeting Lasserre the question of the concrete answer to the Biblical injunction of peace and that of the concrete steps to be taken against warlike impulses never left him again. Jean Lasserre's impact on him was deeper than he suspected at the time. It is to him that he refers in the reference to a 'saint' in his letters from Tegel prison written on the day after the failure of the 20th July *Putsch*;[18] also it was Lasserre who provided the first impulse for his great book *The Cost of Discipleship*.

18. LPP, p. 201.

In Jean Lasserre he found a man who shared his longing for the concretion of divine grace and his alertness to the danger of intellectually rejecting its proximity. His friend confronted him with the question of the relationship of the word of God to him as its bearer, as an individual living in the contemporary world. This soon led Bonhoeffer to a new understanding of the Sermon on the Mount. Also he soon persuaded the reluctant Frenchman to attend ecumenical conferences, so that his voice might be heard. Later Lasserre was present when Bonhoeffer delivered his peace speech at Fanö in 1934. In the addresses he delivered now in New York in 1930-1 Bonhoeffer stated the Biblical arguments for peace and described the embryonic peace movements existing among the German workers and in the German Youth Movement in a fashion that he had not done before.[19] These addresses made it plain that he was aware of the tiny pacifist movements in Germany. His encounter with Lasserre, this first ecumenical confrontation, transformed his academic knowledge of Lutheran ethics into a committed identification with Christ's peace teaching. He based this on the Biblical-ecumenical belief in the one body of Christ, and in succeeding years he added more and more bricks to the structure.

You have brothers and sisters in our people and in every people; do not forget that. Whatever may happen, let us never again forget that the people of God are one Christian people, that no nationalism, no race or class hatred, can strike effective blows if we are one.[20]

Jean Lasserre took the same standpoint in 1953 in his *La Guerre et l'Évangile*:

Nothing in Scripture gives a Christian the right to destroy the body of Christ, no matter what authority he may appeal to. Do we believe in the holy, universal Church, the community of saints? Or do we believe in the eternal mission of France . . . It is impossible to be both a Christian and a nationalist.

This was an unfamiliar idea to Germans in 1930, and those who took it to heart were few indeed.

As we have already mentioned, Bonhoeffer's relationship with the third of these friends, Frank Fisher, extended beyond the lecture room to joint work in Harlem. Fisher was a slenderly-built Negro with strikingly fine features. It was of course natural that this friendship was not established with the same ease as was that with Paul Lehmann, for instance, and it continually had to be reconsolidated. But Dietrich Bonhoeffer was an artist in offering unqualified friendship. In a restaurant on one occasion, for instance, when it was made plain that Fisher was not going to receive the same service as the other customers,

19. GS I, pp. 66-74.
20. GS I, p. 424.

they ostentatiously walked out. In view of the delicacy of personal relationships between black and white in the United States, Bonhoeffer was surprisingly successful in becoming a welcome guest in the homes of the outcasts of Harlem. He had a gift of restoring the pride and self-confidence of the vulnerable and the sensitive.

What was so impressive was the way in which he pursued the understanding of the problem to its minutest detail through books and countless visits to Harlem, through participation in Negro youth work, but even more through a remarkable kind of identity with the Negro community, so that he was received there as though he had never been an outsider at all.[21]

When Bonhoeffer talked about America in later years, the experience for which he was indebted to Frank Fisher played a big part. After he left America they did not meet again. Fisher became a professor at Atlanta, Georgia, and died in 1960.

Finally, Paul and Marion Lehmann's house in New York became a kind of American home from home for Bonhoeffer, and he celebrated his twenty-fifth birthday there. With Lehmann he could talk and argue; Lehmann understood the nuances of European culture and theology. Lehmann came from the Evangelical and Reformed Church, but later joined the Presbyterians. He was working on a thesis at Union Theological Seminary, where he also had a position as assistant in systematic theology. He could understand why theological statements by both professors and students at the seminary were capable of making Bonhoeffer's hair stand on end.

He thought Bonhoeffer very German indeed, not only in the thoroughness of his theological training and his precise methods of tackling problems, but also 'he was German in his passion for perfection, whether of manners, or performance, or of all that is connoted by the word *Kultur*. Here, in short, was an aristocracy of the spirit at its best.'

But he also discovered in him characteristics that did not fit in at all with the current picture of the German:

His aristocracy was unmistakable yet not obtrusive, chiefly, I think, owing to his boundless curiosity about every new environment in which he found himself and to his irresistible and unfailing sense of humour. Thus he could suggest without offence that we should not play tennis together since he commanded a certain expertness at the game which I could not claim . . . This curiosity about the new and different, this unfailing humour . . . always turned the incongruity between human aspiration and human failing away from human hurt to the enrichment of comradeship . . . the capacity to see oneself and the world from a perspective other than one's own. This paradox of birth and nationality in Bonhoeffer has seemed to me increasingly during the years since to have made him an exciting and conspicuous example of the triumph over parochialism of every kind.[22]

21. P. Lehmann, B.B.C. talk, 13.3.1960.
22. Ibid.

Lehmann always hoped that Bonhoeffer would obtain a professorship in the United States and contribute to the shaking up of the American 'theistic scenery' as it was at the time. Thus in 1939 he did everything in his power to prevent him from returning from the United States to Germany. He patiently followed up all Bonhoeffer's whims and suggestions, procured him invitations, only to have subsequently to decline them on his behalf, thus putting himself in an ambiguous position in relation to his colleagues and college presidents, and finally accepted the vanity of all his efforts with the greatest understanding. Thus he was Bonhoeffer's companion and loyal helper at the most important turning-point in his life.[23]

III UNION THEOLOGICAL SEMINARY

In spite of all his other activities, the real purpose of Bonhoeffer's visit to America, i.e. work at Union Theological Seminary in New York, was by no means neglected. The astonishing extent to which he used this period both for open-minded critical exploration and also for vigorous self-examination in fields that had hitherto been remote from him is shown by a surviving report that he wrote with youthful pungency and also with acuteness.[24]

The seminary was then nearly 100 years old, and was thus by American standards an institution steeped in tradition. It had once been a Presbyterian college, but at the turn of the century it had converted itself into an inter-denominational institution, and it had become a centre of attraction for the most advanced liberal minds. In the process it had roused the mistrust of the fundamentalist churches, not a few of whose young scholars, often against the wishes of their seniors, nevertheless attended this attractive place of education, which was a 'both notorious and admired hive of criticism' of political, social and ecclesiastical conservatism.[25]

At this time its reputation was at its height; it already nursed ecumenical ambitions, and was a favourite goal of visitors from Europe. In 1929 Deissmann had just been there. Its head was H. S. Coffin, a 'church statesman' in the best sense of the word and a great preacher at the main Presbyterian church in Madison Avenue. The staff included a number of distinguished men. W. A. Brown, who came of a banking family, was a follower of Ritschl and at the time was undoubtedly the biggest name in the ecumenical movement, was on a sabbatical year, but Bonhoeffer was soon to meet him at ecumenical conferences. Church history was taught by James Moffat of Glasgow. Reinhold Niebuhr had been appointed Professor of Applied Christianity in 1928. In 1930 John

23. Cf. Ch. XI, pp. 560 ff.
24. GS I, pp. 84 ff.
25. GS I, p. 84.

Baillie began his professorship of systematic theology with an inaugural lecture on 'The Logic of Religion'; P. van Dusen was his assistant and John Bennett instructor. The contemporary style of preaching was taught by Fosdick and Sockman, the greatly sought-after preachers of the Riverside Church and the Methodist church on Madison Avenue respectively. J. W. Bewer, who came from the Rhineland, taught Old Testament literary history; Bonhoeffer did not attend his lectures, but made friends with him, and in 1939 found him a good counsellor on the occasion of his great decision.[26]

In 1930 Bonhoeffer was granted a Sloane Fellowship. College life was entirely new to him, and he did not find adaptation to it easy. He suffered because of the never-closed doors, and was astonished at the deliberate renunciation of all privacy. But he also discovered the good sides of this, such as the students' willingness to discuss anything with anybody, not only their fellows but also their teachers, at any time. He obtained the necessary 'credits' by attending the required number of lectures and seminars, and five or six essays he wrote here have survived. But he was granted exemption from the examinations, which he considered unnecessary in view of his Berlin · degree, though his friends Sutz and Lasserre obtained their S.T.M. (Master of Sacred Theology), the latter *summa cum laude*. Bonhoeffer was never a regular attendant at morning chapel.

'The Barthian'

Bonhoeffer found it hard to suppress his feeling of European superiority when he was confronted daily with the American unconcern with what to him were the genuine problems of theology. He regarded what he heard, not as theology, but as religious philosophy, long since out-dated, until it occurred to him that he should study its premises. But when the students burst into loud laughter at quotations from Luther's *De servo arbitrio*, which struck them as funny, he again lost patience.[27] Nevertheless he did not express his indignation, as Lütgert did when he said that 'the Americans are naïve enough to order a theology and philosophy to suit their purpose, just as one orders a car from a factory'.[28] His report on his year in America to the Central Office of his church combines criticism with an overriding concern to emphasize the good side of the phenomenon, with the result that it became possible for him to show his own church and its theology that it might perhaps be a little provincial. In spite of his unchanged interest in Barth, at the end of this period European theological self-confidence no longer predominated in

26. GS I, pp. 304-6.
27. GS I, pp. 87-90.
28. To D. Bonhoeffer, 18.2.1931.

his mind. John Baillie reported his impression of Bonhoeffer in America, when he wrote, more than twenty years later:

When I had been in America for a little more than ten years a new situation began to declare itself—I think about the winter of 1930/31. This was when the impact of what I shall call the Barthian movement was first felt on this side of the Atlantic . . . It was late in reaching America . . . It so happened that, I think in the year 1933, it was my turn to read a paper at a social meeting of the Faculty of Union Seminary, and I called my paper 'A Preface to Barthianism'. I was not indeed anything that could be called a Barthian myself, but there were those among my colleagues who could see no significance at all in the movement, and I was bold enough to think that I understood something of what it portended . . .

Bonhoeffer was my student in this Seminary in 1930/31 and was then the most convinced disciple of Dr. Barth that had appeared among us up to that time, and withal as stout an opponent of liberalism as had ever come my way.[29]

The records of the seminary for the years 1929-30 contain not a single thesis affected by the 'theology of crisis.' Those for 1931-2, however, include for the first time a thesis reflecting the 'new situation'; its title is 'The Theology of Schleiermacher and the Challenge of the Theology of Crisis'. This shows that Union Theological Seminary, and not the training colleges of the various denominations, was still the headquarters of the *avant-garde*.

The new impact first became evident in Baillie's seminar, in which he was helped by van Dusen. It was here that Bonhoeffer, backed by Paul Lehmann, fought his battles. Baillie, who was a follower of Ritschl's great pupil Harnack, could hardly imagine or credit the high praise of the latter in Bonhoeffer's memorial address; and yet he knew nothing of the critical questions that Bonhoeffer had just posed to Barth in *Act and Being*. So completely did Bonhoeffer suppress his criticisms that it can be shown in the essays he wrote for the seminar that his proselyting zeal caused him, no doubt without realizing it, to mingle propositions of his own with Barth's and actually attribute them to him.[30]

Baillie asked Bonhoeffer to give a talk on Barth to his seminar, which he began as follows:

I confess that I do not see any other possible way for you to get into real

29. *Union Seminary Quarterly Review*, Vol. XII, No. 2, 1957, pp. 3 ff.

30. 'Thus the proposition "The revelation of God is executed not in the realm of ideas but in the realm of reality", GS III, p. 112, or the idea that the concept of substance is inappropriate to Christian thought, ibid., pp. 117 f. is attributed to Barth, though Barth's paper "Schicksal und Idee in der Theologie", *Gesammelte Vorträge* III, pp. 72 ff., shows that this absolute antithesis between idea and reality is not what Barth means. Also it is worthy of note that Bonhoeffer does not shrink from putting into Barth's mouth the concept of the boundary as developed by himself . . . In the sentence: "Barth could say: *reflecte fortiter, sed crede fortius*", GS III, p. 124, for instance, Bonhoeffer is quoting himself, see AB, p. 151!' H. Pfeifer, *Das Kirchenverständnis Dietrich Bonhoeffers. Ein Beitrag zur theologischen Prinzipienlehre*, thesis, Heidelberg, 1964, p. 79.

contact with Barth's thinking than by forgetting, at least for this one hour, everything you have learnt before.[31]

Baillie was an alert scholar who kept himself informed about developments. He also asked Bonhoeffer for detailed information about Heidegger, and had Bonhoeffer's essay 'Concerning the Christian Idea of God' published in the *Journal of Religion*.

The seminary lecture list for 1930-1 must have been astonishing to a product of the Berlin theology school. There was an almost complete lack of exegesis or dogmatics, but to make up for it there was a great deal of ethics, and an abundance of material devoted to the analysis and explanation of contemporary American philosophy and writing and the American social environment. It was these things that future ministers were expected to master, and not the formation of the creeds or the history of dogmatics. To a German theological faculty the notion of putting their pupils in a position to form a sound judgement on contemporary problems or join in the process of forming political opinion was a very marginal one indeed, and Bonhoeffer was struck by the fact that the American theology student 'knows much more about the things of daily life'.[32] Nowadays the syllabus of Union Theological Seminary is theologically far more thorough.[33]

His teachers were dismayed when he based his work on the theology of revelation, the doctrine of justification or eschatology instead of on so-called realities. Niebuhr and Baillie in particular took trouble annotating the difficult and demanding essays written by their German guest. Baillie noted the German predilection for impossible associations of ideas such as 'revelation in hiddenness'. 'Is it not a perverse expression?' he wrote. He criticized the gulf that Bonhoeffer drew between thought (in the idealist sense) and reality; that sort of thing inevitably struck him as forced and artificial.

Niebuhr was then thirty-eight. Bonhoeffer noted down as follows the beginning of his course of lectures: 'Religion is the experience of the holy, transcendent experience of Goodness, Beauty, Truth and Holiness', and he did not take down very much more. But he liked the free and lively manner in which the early Niebuhr laid bare the factors on which ethics were dependent, and spoke of the 'ethical resources and limitations of religious authoritarianism', and the dubious consequences of

31. GS III, p. 111.
32. GS I, pp. 349 f.
33. The list of courses attended by Bonhoeffer which enabled him to earn the required number of credits was apparently as follows: Religion and Ethics (Niebuhr); Religious Aspects of Contemporary Philosophy (Lyman); Church and Community, the Cooperation of the Church with Social and Character-building Agencies (Webber); Ethical Interpretations (Ward and Niebuhr); Ethical Viewpoints in Modern Literature (Ward and Niebuhr); Ethical Issues in the Social Order (Ward); Theology I: the Idea of God in his Relations to the World and Man (Baillie); Seminar in Philosophical Theology (Baillie and Lyman); Brief Sermons (Fosdick); the Minister's Work with Individuals (Coffin).

religious institutionalism or individualism ('Luther stood for religious individualism, Calvin stood for ethical individualism'). Niebuhr cheerfully criticized the essays of his seemingly so unpolitical student. He declared himself dissatisfied with the assertion that 'the God of guidance' could be discovered only from the 'God of justification', and asked what God's guidance meant ethically:

. . . in making grace as transcendent as you do, I don't see how you can ascribe any ethical significance to it. Obedience to God's will may be a religious experience, but it is not an ethical one until it issues in actions which can be socially valued. Any other interpretation of 'ethical' than one which measures an action in terms of consequences and judges actions purely in terms of notions empties the ethical of content and makes it purely formal.[34]

The question of what was implied by the ethical concreteness of revelation was already a matter of secret concern to Bonhoeffer,[35] but here he insisted defiantly on the priority of the correct premises which, he asserted, must remain independent of premature interest in their ethical effects.

Literature and Contemporary Questions

Though he showed little willingness to listen to counter-arguments in the theological field, he showed unlimited interest in things from which he hoped to gain new knowledge or discover better methods or vantage-points. In the second half of his year in America in particular he concentrated on three things: the American philosophy that he decided must lie behind all the things that struck him as so surprising, contemporary American writing, and socio-political studies. Soon he was so overwhelmed by the mass of material available and the stimulation of it all that he wrote home that he could hardly cope with the impressions that crowded in on each other's heels, but all the same he was enjoying it. 'If one really tried tasting New York to the full, it would practically be the death of one.'[36]

1. Lyman, the Professor of the Philosophy of Religion, gave him private tutorials in which he introduced him to the background of the terminology current at Union Theological Seminary. Under his guidance he studied 'almost the complete philosophical works of William James, which I found uncommonly fascinating, Dewey, Perry, Russell, and finally also J. B. Watson, and the literature of the behaviourist school. The study of Whitehead, Knudson and Santayana was sometimes not so illuminating to me as these radically empirical thinkers. In them,

---

34. Handwritten annotation by R. Niebuhr on 'The Religious Experience of Grace and the Ethical Life', GS III, pp. 94 f.
35. Cf. the letters to H. Rössler of 18.10.1931 and 25.12.1932, GS I, pp. 61, 63.
36. GS I, p. 81.

and James in particular, I found the key to the understanding of the modern theological language and ways of thought of the liberal, enlightened American . . . Questions such as that of Kantian epistemology are "nonsense", and no problem to them, because they take life no further. Truth is not "valid", but "works", and that is their criterion.'[37]

2. The course on modern literature was given by Reinhold Niebuhr. In accordance with the American practice, Bonhoeffer had to write an essay on each book discussed. These present us with an interesting selection of the writers of those years. Niebuhr dealt with European as well as American literature, and in particular the war books which had recently appeared, the letters of students killed in action, the novels of Remarque and Ludwig Renn, and the Englishman R. C. Sheriff's play *Journey's End*, which Bonhoeffer greatly liked, for 'it does not belittle great idealistic feeling [a matter on which he was highly sensitive], nor does it veil the naked reality'. On the whole, however, he was critical of the literary revival of wartime experiences.

He preferred the Czech Karel Čapek to the German expressionist Ernst Toller, whose plays *Mass Man* and *Machine Man* were discussed, and he took the opportunity of using Ibsen's *Brand*, with which he had long been familiar and continued to appreciate in later years,[38] to fight his battle against compromise and its collapse in the face of the *deus caritatis*. He regarded Bernard Shaw's dry brilliance as regrettably impaired by his cynicism; Shaw had, 'as I see it, never taken up any problem of serious ethical or religious importance'. Curiously enough, the work of Shaw's that he misread was *Androcles and the Lion*, which introduced to world literature the church at Sydenham in London that was later to be his.[39] Ten years later, perhaps, he would have looked with different eyes on the Ferrovius in Shaw's play who at the sound of the drum forgets all his Christian vows and hurries to the arms he had been spurning. But now he could see in it no more than mere relativism.

We have already mentioned his interest in Negro writing. He read Ludwig Lewisohn's *Stephen Escott* and *Midchannel*, which opposed Jewish assimilation in the United States. He liked Theodore Dreiser's *Free and Other Stories* and, though he noted *longueurs*, exaggerations and indiscretions in Sinclair Lewis's *Elmer Gantry*, he thought the description of middle-class pietism and misuse of spiritual values masterly. 'Elmer Gantry could serve to many a pastor as the counterpart of the Catholic mirror of confession', are the words he wrote in English.

37. GS I, p. 91.
38. E, p. 127.
39. According to Shaw's postscript, during the First World War the Anti-German League secured the closing of that small German church, obviously with the agreement of the Anglican bishops, who regarded it as unseemly that God should be worshipped in German. 'As far as I have observed, the only people who gasped were the Freethinkers.' Cf. G. B. Shaw, *Androcles and the Lion*, Penguin, 1957, pp. 156 ff.

3. Social and political studies at the seminary consisted of visits paid to social and political organizations in New York led by C. C. Webber, under the heading of 'Church and Community'; and Harry F. Ward's course on contemporary problems, under the heading of 'Ethical Interpretations'.

a) Webber's subject included labour problems, restriction of profits, civil rights, juvenile crime, and the activity of the churches in these fields. Visits were paid for instance to the National Women's Trade Union League and the Workers' Education Bureau of America, which had developed from the class-conscious Workers' Educational Association.

The impact made upon him by the vigour with which churches and other organizations tackled proletarian problems, and the selflessness with which students of Union Theological Seminary, among others, shared the life of the unemployed[40] led him in 1932 to begin working for the unemployed with his students in Berlin, to issue appeals for funds, and to establish a youth club.[41] Hence, in spite of his theological reservations, Bonhoeffer never referred deprecatingly to the 'social gospel'.

b) Ward's seminar was even more political. Harry F. Ward, Professor of Christian Ethics, had a sharp nose, and his thinking was just as sharp. He was an enthusiastic Nonconformist and socialist, and thirty years later would certainly have fallen victim to McCarthyism.

The pupils at his seminar had to analyze articles in newspapers and periodicals with a view to forming objective opinions on foreign or domestic political questions. Some of the subjects dealt with are the subject of lively discussion in Bonhoeffer's correspondence with his parents.

His father was interested in the prohibition experiment and its criminal consequences, on which Bonhoeffer had to write an essay when the Wickersham report on prohibition appeared.[42] A study of various unemployment insurance systems and of the consequences of the Wall Street crash taught him to see the plight of the unemployed in Germany more realistically in its world-wide context. Subjects dealt with in Ward's seminar that he also discussed in letters home included the question of private or public exploitation of the water-power of the Tennessee valley; a 1930 report on birth-control by the Federal Council of Churches; the London Round-Table Conference where the confrontation between Gandhi and Lord Halifax took place; the world economic crisis, and the negotiations for a customs union between Germany and Austria that roused alarm in all the Western countries.

When his time in America was up, Bonhoeffer had by no means come to terms with all the manifold impressions that stormed in upon him.

40. GS I, p. 101.
41. Cf. Ch. VI, pp. 171 f.
42. See the echo of this in his *Ethics*, p. 356.

Niebuhr and Baillie remembered him as having withdrawn into his orthodox European shell at that time:

He felt that political questions in which our students were so interested were on the whole irrelevant to the life of a Christian. Shortly after his return to Germany he became very much interested in ethical and political issues and for a time considered going to India to study Gandhi's movement . . . Once very unpolitical, he became a very astute political analyst.[43]

In 1932 Bonhoeffer did not like being reminded that he once talked in the anti-political fashion for which Rössler reproached him.

You will, I hope [he wrote], not misunderstand the term 'disinterestedness' I used a long time ago—incidentally I can no longer remember it; today it seems to me to be truly frivolous. All it was meant to indicate was the limits within which I see the problems by reason of the fact of the Church.[44]

The fact of the matter was that the America he saw on the eve of Roosevelt's New Deal, the activity of churches and students in the economic crisis, and the enthusiasm of the 'social gospel', made an ineradicable impression on him. Firmly though he stood by his fundamental theological principles, he was yet strongly motivated by an 'insatiable curiosity for every new reality'.[45] Henceforward a purely desk-bound existence could no longer satisfy him. Previously unquestioned habits of thought and feeling suddenly seemed one-sided and inadequate; they were in need of reappraisal.

As before, the presence of Christ as seen through the eyes of this American theology seemed to him to be distorted or inadequately represented. But was it not inadequately represented on the other side of the Atlantic too? How could the two be reconciled? The later Bonhoeffer of *The Cost of Discipleship* and the church struggle had not forgotten what he learnt in New York. His stay in America reinforced his basic interest in the concrete reality of the word of God. His problem now was how this concreteness was to be developed, not in opposition to the law which he had made his own, but out of it.

My stay in America . . . made one thing plain to me: the absolute necessity of cooperation and at the same time the inexplicable gap that seems to make such cooperation impossible. Looked at from across the Atlantic, our standpoint and our theology look so local, and it seems inconceivable that in the whole of the world just Germany, and in Germany just a few men, have understood what the Gospel is. And yet I see a message nowhere else.[46]

43. R. Niebuhr, *Union Seminary Quarterly Review*, Vol. I, No. 3, 1946, p. 3.
44. Letter of 25.12.1932, GS I, p. 65.
45. Lehmann, op. cit.
46. To H. Rössler, 18.10.1931, GS I, pp. 60 f.

IV HOMELAND

Only a few letters survive of the lively correspondence that Bonhoeffer kept up with his home, but some letters that he received still reveal the intense interest with which, in spite of the distance and all the demands on his time in New York, he followed the news from Berlin, whether political, ecclesiastical or about events at the university.

1. After the first turbulent weeks in New York, when he at last saw the implications of the September elections in Germany and read the news about the further growth in unemployment, he realized with concern how hard it was to form an opinion about the course of events from a distance. For the first time it seemed possible that dangers might be looming ahead for his brother-in-law Leibholz; the latter described how anti-Semitic 'Nazis' were now beginning to make their presence felt among his colleagues at Greifswald University. The drastic economy measures taken by the new Government created anxiety lest his brothers-in-law might lose their jobs or have their appointments postponed. His brother Klaus wrote to him about the political change of scene:

Since the elections X has been in a state of exaltation, as he sees the day of vengeance coming for the 'sinister men of November'. Since your departure the political situation has changed greatly. The success of Nazism has convinced the widest circles that the democratic régime has failed in the past ten years. The consequences of the world economic crisis are explained in purely domestic terms. Fond glances are cast in the direction of Fascism. I am afraid that, if this radical wave captures the educated classes, it will be all up with this nation of poets and thinkers.[47]

The Social Democrats still governed Prussia, but the Stahlhelm promoted a popular petition for new Prussian elections. An attempt to give a new and effective form to the democratic-bourgeois centre in the so-called State Party failed.

Then more reassuring news came from home, but a letter from his friend H. Rössler from rural Priegnitz gave a detailed picture of how far the fanaticization of the German agricultural population had gone. Bonhoeffer was so disturbed by this letter that he read it to and discussed it with his American friends. This was in February 1931.

During the summer of 1931 the tension was only slightly relieved, though more reassuring news came from the family itself. In May Leibholz obtained a professorship at Göttingen University and Dohnanyi was given a post as a public prosecutor at Hamburg, which he held for nine months until he was recalled in January 1933 by the Reich Minister of Justice. Thus both were promoted at an unusually early age.

2. Ecclesiastical events played a more incidental part in the New

47. Letter of 3.11.1930.

York correspondence. Bonhoeffer was more affected by events in the university.

A scandal arose in the winter of 1930-1 as a result of the publication of the memoirs of the former Reich Chancellor Prince Bülow, which showed a whole series of prominent Berlin personalities in such a questionable light that a number of professors such as Erich Seeberg, the son of Reinhold Seeberg, for instance, began their lectures with critical comments and corrections. The Bonhoeffers were involved because Harnack's reputation was impugned. His mother wrote to Dietrich on 9th November 1930: 'Do you know that old Harnack has been so nastily attacked in the Bülow memoirs that have just come out? The family now wants to publish letters from Bülow to Harnack.' Bonhoeffer *père* wrote an article, 'A Psychopathological View of the Recollections of Prince Bülow', which was printed on the front page of the *Deutsche Allgemeine Zeitung* of 24th March, in which he subjected to scrupulous examination signs that 'seem to indicate that these recollections should not be read as fully authoritative, but that in many respects they should be regarded as the result of morbid changes due to age'. Publishing this article was an unusual action on the part of a man so averse to putting himself in the public eye.

After this sensation had died down, another and far more significant one engaged public attention for a long time, arising out of Günther Dehn's appointment at Heidelberg and Halle.[48] While Bonhoeffer was still in New York, he heard that Tillich had declined the chair of practical theology at Halle, and that when Becker, the Minister of Culture, thereupon appointed Dehn to the position the first protest demonstrations were staged by nationalist students. It was only later, of course, that he was able to make modest attempts to help.[49]

Also during his absence Berlin University was the scene of excesses against Jewish students. Nationalist students, shouting 'Death to the Jews', assaulted them in the entrance hall and threw them out of the window into the courtyard. The rector of the university, the theologian A. Deissmann, was in a dilemma, being averse to police intervention on academic soil. The theological faculty however, was even more agitated at the time by the battle of words in the university hall building between Barth and Dibelius. Barth spoke on 31st January 1931 on 'The Plight of the Protestant Church',[50] and Dibelius replied on 6th February from the same platform with an address on 'The Responsibility of the Church'. The affair was discussed at an evening party at Diestel's, and Dietrich's

48. At the end of 1928 Günther Dehn had been violently attacked by the right-wing Press because of a speech he made in Magdeburg about Christ and war. Now he was again denounced as a 'pacifist and slanderer of our dead heroes' without the church authorities lifting a finger to defend him; many professors refused him their recommendation. Cf. E. Bizer, 'Der Fall Dehn', *Festschrift für Günther Dehn*, 1957, pp. 231 ff.
49. Cf. Ch. VI, p. 133.
50. ZZ, 1931, No. 2.

mother wrote to him: 'X, of the Evangelical Church Press, was there and . . . attacked Barth's address very uncouthly. Dibelius rebuked him . . . and said that Barth was not to be disposed of so simply.'[51] Hildebrandt wrote in amusement to his friend that Barth had launched his attack against the German church authorities from Schleiermacher's platform, of all places.

In the midst of all his busy activities in New York, Bonhoeffer's thoughts of the future were given a definite direction. At home a double job, with both academic and church connections, awaited him. His father, concerned about his new academic start, advised him to submit his proposed lecture programme for the winter of 1931-2 to the dean of the faculty in good time, at all events before he disappeared into Mexico.

There was now no more room in his programme for a trip to India. 'After all this I am really looking forward to Germany again', he wrote.[52]

51. Letter of 23.2.1931.
52. GS I, p. 82.

PART TWO

The Cost of Being a Christian

CHAPTER SIX

LECTURER AND PASTOR

1931 - 1932

It is not that I am afraid of disappointing . . . but I sometimes simply cannot see what is the right thing to do . . . in the unprecedented situation of our public life in Germany.[1]

How is one to preach such things to these people? Who still believes them? The invisibility breaks us to pieces . . . This absurd, perpetual being thrown back on the invisible God—no one can stand it any longer.[2]

Bonhoeffer's return to Germany in 1931 certainly represented a sharper break in his development than the momentous political and ecclesiastical upheaval that followed two years later. It was at this time, and not really in 1933, that the second great phase of his career began.

The phase of learning and roaming had come to an end. He now began teaching in a faculty whose theology was not his and preaching in a church whose self-confidence he regarded as unfounded. With eyes wider open than before, he fitted himself into a society which politically, socially and economically was heading for chaos.

When he first began practical church work in Barcelona in 1928, he welcomed it as a 'convergence of work and life', because 'it gave validity to the work and meaning to the worker'.[3] Now he was afflicted by the solitude of one who for the first time accepts public responsibility for his own thoughts and actions. Previously he had deliberately kept a certain distance between himself and his teachers, but now he felt the lack of a qualified adviser, a senior, who 'really would be a teacher' to him; 'I do not know why that was never granted me. Should I not have been able to tolerate it?'[4]

He indeed found it very difficult to subordinate himself to those who did not measure up to his exacting standards. His later submission to the 'brothers' at Finkenwalde is the more striking for that reason; but even then it was difficult to advise him. He was lacking in the simplicity necessary to let others make up his mind for him. Also he had an instinctive fear of being surprised by uncontrolled circumstances without having assured himself of an alternative. In this connection it was very

1. To E. Sutz, 8.10.1931, GS I, p. 23.
2. To H. Rössler, 18.10.1931, GS I, p. 61.
3. GS I, p. 51.
4. GS I, p. 23.

difficult for him simply to 'believe'. 'Belief' of that kind he would certainly have tended to describe as slipshod.

He made the decisions of the next two years without any adviser, while doing the strenuous work that laid the foundations for the two books, *The Cost of Discipleship* and *Life Together*. In contrast to *Sanctorum Communio* and *Act and Being*, which used a conceptual language taken over from others, he now stated in his own terminology the contributions he wished to make to theology and the Church. The period of Bonhoeffer's life in which these fruits ripened really began now.

They are new questions which Bonhoeffer now puts to his church, its theology, its ethics and its attitude to Luther. They are questions which make an obvious departure from the purely academic sphere; they pivot round the key questions of the ethical and pastoral authorization to make binding statements. He analyzes the deficient competence of his church and measures its claims against its credibility; and the analysis extends into the ecumenical sphere. Compared to the previous period, his ecclesiology becomes more concrete, but also more open and more critical of the Church. Christology indeed moves into the centre of the field. His sermons at the beginning of this new period have an undertone of unease that fades away only in 1933.

In his personal life something occurred during these months that it is hard for us to see clearly, though its effects are plain. He himself would never have called it a conversion. But a change took place in him that led to all that was to follow during this phase of his life—*The Cost of Discipleship*, the experiment in community living at Finkenwalde, his attitude to the ecumenical movement and the church struggle. It marked the beginning of a phase in his life which continued right up to 1939.

In the next two years the work done by the now twenty-five-year-old Bonhoeffer lay in three different fields.

1. In the academic sphere, every term he held a number of two-hour lectures and seminars in the theological faculty of Berlin University. The text of the lectures, which would have revealed to us most clearly the problems in Bonhoeffer's mind and his answers to them have unfortunately not survived, and we are therefore thrown back on an approximate reconstruction of his ideas at the time from lecture notes kept by his pupils.[5]

2. In the church and pastoral field, he delivered sermons and addresses as a students' chaplain and instructed a confirmation class at Wedding; and he organized a week-end home for students and confirmation candidates at Biesenthal, opened a youth club room for unemployed in Charlottenburg, and tried to secure a parish in proletarian east Berlin.

3. In the ecumenical sphere, he became a youth secretary in the World

5. This reconstruction is attempted in Appendices A-E in the German edition, pp. 1047-95. (*Editor.*)

Alliance of Churches and in the Ecumenical Council for Practical Christianity ('Life and Work'); he travelled, spoke and organized.

In all this strenuous activity he used his home as a base as a matter of course. 'In the last few months because of all the things I have been doing everything has been rather restless, at home as well . . . I am now greatly looking forward to a quiet summer at home.'[6] But no such thing as a quiet summer was to come his way again.

Before really embarking on this double or triple working life, in the late summer of 1931 he conducted a kind of triple prelude, a reconnaissance of all the three spheres in which he was to work, namely university, church and ecumenical movement. He went to Bonn to meet Karl Barth, helped to write a new catechism, and attended the conference of the World Alliance of Churches at Cambridge. The visit to Bonn, arranged through Erwin Sutz, belatedly fulfilled an ambition of his students days; his work on the catechism was an act of friendship for Franz Hildebrandt, who asked him to help; and the trip to Cambridge marked the beginning of his ecumenical work, the way to which was paved by Diestel.

The church authorities had refused Bonhoeffer an extension of leave, though his work at the university and as a students' chaplain could really begin only with the start of the new term in the late autumn. His ecclesiastical superior, General Superintendent Karow, therefore released him from the residential obligation until October 1931. So half of what Bonhoeffer did was what he wanted to do and half what he was supposed to do.

I BONN

First Meeting with Karl Barth

Bonhoeffer, once home from New York, remained in Berlin long enough only to pay the necessary official calls, and on 10th July left again to spend three weeks in Bonn. In the spring his parents had suggested that after his return from America he should take a holiday at Friedrichsbrunn, but the visit to Bonn was so important to him that he declined this attractive proposal; he wanted to spend as much time as possible at Bonn before the term there ended, and the first meeting for which he had prepared himself between the forty-five-year-old Barth and the twenty-five-year-old Bonhoeffer now took place. He wrote to his parents:

I have now met Barth and got to know him quite well at a discussion evening at his house.[7] I liked him very much indeed, and am also very impressed by his lectures. Everything is so well worked out and has not yet become mechanical to him. I think I shall gain a great deal from the time spent here.[8]

6. To his father, 28.3.1932.
7. It was held for some Benedictines from Maria Laach.
8. Letter of 14.7.1931.

According to the story current among Bonhoeffer's later students, he had quoted at Barth's seminar Luther's saying that the curses of the godless sometimes sound better in God's ear than the hallelujahs of the pious, whereupon the delighted Barth asked who had made this contribution to the discussion, and this was the beginning of their personal acquaintance.[9]

On 23rd July 1931 Barth invited him to dinner and conversation. Now at last the two were together. The younger man put questions, argued, and put more questions, and he found to his surprise that 'Barth was even better than his books.'

> He has a frankness, a willingness to listen to criticism, and at the same time such an intensity of concentration on the subject, which can be discussed proudly or modestly, dogmatically or tentatively, and is certainly not primarily directed to the service of his own theology.[10]

Like so many of Karl Barth's visitors, Bonhoeffer noted the quite unusual interest in his interlocutor shown by a man whom 'it is so hard to pin down in his books'. 'I was even more impressed by his conversation than by his writings and lectures. In his conversation the whole of him is present. I have not met anything like it before.'[11]

The result of this encounter was that henceforward the relations between the two were characterized by complete frankness and, when occasion arose, completely frank disagreement. A sporadic correspondence began in which neither concealed anything from the other. In the younger man's letters there was always a trace of respectful distance, but the older man respected no barriers.

It was harder to gain entry to the inner circle of the Bonn disciples. Bonhoeffer's position as a 'theological illegitimate' among the 'genuine initiates' caused him a great deal of amusement. 'They have a sharp nose for thoroughbreds here', he wrote. 'No Negro is allowed to pass for white, his finger-nails and the soles of his feet are carefully scrutinized. So far I have been both shown hospitality and treated as an unknown stranger.'[12] Hans Fischer, a friend of Erwin Sutz's, looked after him and provided him with notes of Barth's lectures to read in his spare time. He was invited to Helmut Gollwitzer's student club to attend a performance of a play written by Karl Barth at the age of fifteen.

His stay in Bonn led to frequent meetings with Barth, which went on until he left for England in 1933. Through Günther Dehn he made the acquaintance of Gertrud Staewen, with whom Barth used to stay in

9. Communication from W. Maechler. In *Act and Being* Bonhoeffer quotes from Luther the passage: 'cum tales blasphemie, quia sunt violenter a diabolo hominibus invitis extorte, aliquando gratiores sonent in aure Dei quam ipsum Alleluja vel quecunque laudis jubilatio' (AB, p. 183), and he quotes it again in 1932 in the lecture 'Das Wesen der Kirche', see GS V.
10. GS I, p. 19.
11. GS I, p. 20.
12. GS I, p. 19.

Berlin and at whose house a small circle of Berlin Barthians used to meet. In April 1932 he saw Barth with his friend Pestalozzi in Berlin. This time Barth delivered an address on 'Theology and Contemporary Mission',[13] and Otto Dibelius did not reply. But there was a reply by Siegfried Knak, the head of the Berlin Missionary Society and, when this was printed in *Zwischen den Zeiten*, the heated atmosphere of the discussion and the full extent of nationalist animosity against the dialecticians transpired.[14] Bonhoeffer described the evening spent with members of the Berlin faculty and church leaders in hardly respectful terms:

. . . then, when questions were asked for, nothing happened except a long, painful silence, because no one wanted to put his foot in it, and then, when the silence was beginning to grow oppressive, Herr Knak started by asking where, in Barth's view, the difference lay between Swiss and Prussian national feeling. That was about the level of the questions.[15]

These were the months in which the 'Dehn case' at Halle reached its height with demonstrations by right-wing students against Dehn and Becker, the Minister of Culture. Barth and those of his way of thinking in the area took up the case as their own.[16] Bonhoeffer, through his father, tried to interest professors of other faculties in Berlin in the injustice done to Dehn, and provided his father with the extensive files on the subject.[17] This points to the conclusion that his meetings with Barth in 1932 were already strongly influenced by concern about the political future and the future of the Church, and did not leave as much time for theological discussion as he would have liked.

At the beginning of September 1932 he visited Barth on the Bergli, just when the latter had finished the preface to the first volume of *Church Dogmatics*, and he also met Brunner as the result of an introduction from Sutz.

During the following winter, when Titius's chair in Berlin fell vacant, Bonhoeffer used his family connections to bring Barth's name forward as a possible successor. But the year 1933 intervened, and the appointment went to Wobbermin. Meanwhile Barth's position at Bonn had become difficult because of his membership of the Social Democratic Party, and Bonhoeffer tried to use his connections in the Prussian Ministry of Culture on his behalf. Barth wrote to him:

In the age of Reich Chancellor Hitler Wobbermin will certainly fill Schleiermacher's chair in a fashion more true to type than I should have done. I

13. ZZ, 1932, No. 3, pp. 189 ff.
14. Cf. the observation in ZZ, 1932, No. 4, p. 351: 'the defamation of the idea of the Führer practised by more than one representative of dialectical theology'.
15. GS I, p. 30.
16. Cf. E. Bizer, 'Der Fall Dehn', *Festschrift für Günther Dehn*, 1957, pp. 239 ff.
17. To his father, 28.3.1932.

hear that you have exposed yourself on my behalf . . . I should undoubtedly have accepted . . . The world is in bad shape, but we shall not let our pipe go out under any circumstances, shall we?[18]

At this time Barth and Bonhoeffer were on closer terms than ever became possible again.

Stages of Relationship

In the relations between the two men four phases can be distinguished, which can be summarized roughly as follows:

1. The phase of Bonhoeffer's unilateral knowledge of Barth through the latter's writings, beginning in 1925. In 1927 and 1929 Bonhoeffer, excited by and grateful for the Barthian message, while holding fast to the principle of *finitum capax infiniti*, raises a number of theological-epistemological questions directed at Barth. These, however, as formulated in *Sanctorum Communio* and *Act and Being*, do not become fully known to Barth until after Bonhoeffer's death.

2. The phase of eagerly sought meetings between 1931 and 1933. Bonhoeffer hopes for Barth's support in his concern for the concrete ethical commandments of the Church, but does not receive it in the form that he desires.

3. The phase of theological differences, accompanied by a very close alliance in church politics. Bonhoeffer attempts to think through the Articles of Justification and Salvation independently of Barth, but with the continued hope that he might be able to have him as an ally occasionally. Barth has reservations; only after Bonhoeffer's death does his *The Cost of Discipleship* receive Barth's special praise.

4. The period of indirect new questions in the letters from prison of 1944. In these there occurs almost incidentally the ominous term 'revelationary positivism', which Barth could not accept and liked least of all in Bonhoeffer's work.

Whatever the implications of Bonhoeffer's earlier or later criticisms of Barth may be, in all four phases he wanted them to be regarded as coming from inside and not outside the Barthian movement. In the bitter secession of former Barthians from the movement he did not wish to be identified with men like Gogarten or Brunner, and he joined vigorously in attacking them. This is very evident in the second and third phases.

Shift of Interest

On their first meeting, and in the years that immediately followed, the whole complex of Bonhoeffer's early critical questions to Barth dating

18. Letter of 4.2.1933, GS II, p. 41. Cf. also the further correspondence between Barth and Bonhoeffer of 14. and 18.4.1933, GS II, pp. 41 ff., and GS I, p. 37.

from 1927 and 1929 seemed to have been buried and forgotten. That was not completely the case, however, because they recur in the university lectures beginning in 1931; but they took second place to the over-riding purpose of presenting Barth's theological revolution to the Berlin forum in as positive a light as possible. They do not occur at all in the documents relating to the personal meetings between the two in the years from 1931 to 1933. On Bonhoeffer's side the interest had shifted to the field of ethical questions and the problem of the authoritative proclamation of the commandments through the Church of Christ, and it remained obstinately concentrated on these.

In 1931 the two men met at a quite definite point in their respective developments. For all their mutual liking, each was at a different phase.

Barth's Standing

In 1931 Barth had no previous knowledge of the man he met. He had not read *Sanctorum Communio*, and *Act and Being*, which contained more important criticism of him, was still in proof. Bonhoeffer was not the type to send people copies of his books before calling on them, and thus Barth knew nothing of Bonhoeffer's subtle transcendental reserva-tions in regard to his then so negatively described conception of revela-tion, or of his ecclesiological suggestions, or of his antipathy to the *incapax infiniti* concept, or of his passionate protest against allowing room for reflection in the act of faith, which should seek knowledge only of its content, namely Christ, and not of itself.[19] Also Barth knew nothing of the concise summing-up of the theological situation given by Bonhoeffer in the inaugural lecture of 1930:

. . . independently of the reality of revelation [there can be] no talk of its possibility . . the rejection of the doctrine of *finitum incapax infiniti* follows from the emphasis on the transcendental nature of revelation.[20]

With the single exception of Knittermeyer's review of *Act and Being* in 1933, the Barthian journal *Zwischen den Zeiten* did not review Bonhoeffer's books or mention them even in the list of publications—an important detail, incidentally, because, so far as Barth's school was concerned, Bonhoeffer first appeared on the horizon as a writer with the publication of *The Cost of Discipleship*, and it was this that stamped him in their minds. Not knowing his previous background, they regarded the newcomer as being capable of all sorts of theological short-cuts, with which they would perhaps not have credited him if they had known him better.

The first work of Bonhoeffer's that Barth himself read was the critical article on Karl Heim that Bonhoeffer sent him at the end of

19. Cf. SC, pp. 97, 121 f.; AB, pp. 82 f., 89 f., 94 f., 135 ff., 175 f.
20. GS III, pp. 62-84.

1932.[21] But by this time theological positions were increasingly moving from the field of intellectual dispute into that of existential decisions.[22] In this paper Bonhoeffer's epistemological criticism of Barth completely lacks the sharpness of 1929:

Barth admits without hesitation that he too is not 'assured against the sin' of making 'God an object of thought', and that his principles too are subject to the danger of being 'a last defence against God himself and his intervention in our life'. The characteristic feature of his theology is precisely that he believes that he cannot offer a sure defence against this danger, and yet thinks of it continually; his knowing that the ultimately concrete can be spoken only by the Holy Spirit and that every concrete human word remains an abstraction unless it is spoken by the Holy Spirit sets a limit to his theological work.[23]

In the same year Bonhoeffer similarly defended Barth in another context. 'Because Barth knows that there is no such thing as perfect reason and yet cannot do without it, he can talk "rationally" more boldly and uninhibitedly than those who grant it a last remnant of its claims.'[24]

In view of such statements, at the beginning of 1933 Barth could hardly regard himself as being called on to reply critically to this public defender of his position. Not long afterwards *Creation and Fall*, the first and only book of Bonhoeffer's on which Barth publicly expressed an opinion during the former's life-time, was published, and Barth agreed with its doctrine of an *analogia relationis*.[25]

Barth's real discovery of Bonhoeffer's early works did not take place till many years later, when he expressed the highest appreciation of them.[26] But this was preceded by the period during which he had reservations about the course that Bonhoeffer was following in *The Cost of Discipleship* and a period of head-shaking over 'revelational positivism' and the 'non-religious interpretation'.

At all events, in the summer of 1931 Barth regarded Bonhoeffer as a young man from Berlin and a product of the school of the suspect Reinhold Seeberg, on top of which he had just arrived back from America —in short, he saw him as a still blank sheet of paper. The fact that he was so interesting to talk to—his mind was quick, objective, penetrating, well-informed—was the more surprising for that reason. Obviously he was a young man of promise.

21. A shortened version of this appears as an appendix in *No Rusty Swords*. (Editor.)
22. GS II, p. 40.
23. GS III, p. 156. Does not this make intelligible the 1944 observation about 'revelationary positivism' being, so to speak, an object of thought?
24. ThLZ, 1932, pp. 563 f.; GS III, p. 137.
25. Cf. KD III/1, p. 219.
26. KD IV/2. pp. 604 ff., 725.

Bonhoeffer's Standing

What then was the picture from Bonhoeffer's point of view? In the summer of 1931 he noted that the interlocutor whom in imagination he had so often previously questioned 'unfortunately' did not lecture on 'the encyclopedia',[27] but on 'ethics'; i.e. was not concerned with the theological system within which his old questions might have been acute. That shifted the whole basis of the discussion, unless he were to be so presumptuous as to force his host into his own former field.

Unlike Barth, Bonhoeffer was very well acquainted with the works of the man he was talking to. Also he was not unaware that changes in Barth's approach were soon to be made public. His Anselm[28] was at the printers, and the first volume of his Church Dogmatics was nearing completion. In the latter he himself stated that 'in this second version of the book I have as far as possible eliminated everything that in the first version might have looked like existential argument, support or merely justification of theology'.[29] Not that Bonhoeffer regarded all his reservations as having been cleared up. 'Barth's book on Anselm has given me great pleasure . . . objectively nothing has grown less questionable, of course', he wrote,[30] but the questions had lost their previous urgency because others had moved into the foreground. Also Barth in fact had accepted some important criticisms. The Barth whom Bonhoeffer met had now unequivocally accepted the premise of the reality of revelation as an historically given event without extraneous support, based it more plainly on exegesis, and developed everything anew from the a priori fact of the Church. His philosophical assumptions no longer seemed dangerously full of his own ideas.

Thus to a large extent Bonhoeffer saw eye to eye with him. Shortly after their first meeting in Bonn he said in his first Berlin lecture in the winter of 1931-2:

In the whole of modern literature Barth has not been seriously contested . . . Perhaps in his Epistle to the Romans he did not always quite see the danger of this proximity [i.e. to neo-Kantian transcendentalism]. But he begins with the concreteness of revelation; where Natorp and Tillich say 'not God', he finds himself forced to say 'Jesus Christ'.[31]

Bonhoeffer was impressed by Barth's ability 'when necessary to correct his note-books'.[32] Thus the Barth he met in 1931 was no longer the Barth to whom he had so long addressed his questions in absentia. He had changed. But had he changed completely?

Also the meeting was the more stimulating to Bonhoeffer in that he

27. GS I, p. 18.
28. K. Barth, Fides quaerens intellectum, Anselms Beweis der Existenz Gottes, 1931.
29. KD I/1, VIII.
30. GS I, p. 257.
31. According to J. Kanitz's lecture notes, GS V.
32. GS II, p. 289.

himself had changed since 1927 and 1929. His stay in the United States had confronted him with ethical questions as never before. Through Jean Lasserre and Frank Fisher his old interest in the given structure of grace had been renewed and transformed into the problem of acting under the constraint of grace and the duty of simple obedience. Combined with this problem was the fact that his prospective ordination would soon face him with the regular task of proclaiming the message of the Church.

Barth had gone from the pulpit to the academic chair. The questions he asked and the answers he gave from the latter were born of his predicament as a pastor. The preacher had needed the systematician. To save the majesty of God from being cheapened from the pulpit, he talked of God's remoteness and unapproachability. So his problem was how hopelessly confusing concretions were to be avoided.

Bonhoeffer, however, came from a predominantly academic environment and secretly had long aspired to the pulpit. In his case the systematician was looking for the preacher. In direct contrast to Barth, to preserve the majesty of God from being cheapened in the pulpit, he concentrated on the terrifying proximity of an actively intervening God and wanted to proclaim him in the concretion of grace-filled commandment. So the man who faced the master was still half a systematician while the other half was burdened with the problem of the authority and credibility of his approaching ministry. In the face of this, the old questions faded into the background.

The references in Bonhoeffer's letters to this aspect of their meeting are painfully succinct. He says that in Bonn in 1931 they 'very soon come upon the ethical problem'.[33] He had alluded to this in *Act and Being*, but paid it no further attention then. At that time he had believed that because Barth—that is, the early Barth, of course—had regarded no historical moment as being *capax infiniti*, 'the empirical action of man —"belief", "obedience"—becomes at most a pointer to God's activity and can never, in its historicality, be faith and obedience in themselves'.[34] With that Bonhoeffer refused to be satisfied.

In his discussion with Barth in July 1931 Bonhoeffer obviously talked of grace and obedience in such absolute terms, i.e. without regard to Barth's eschatological limitation of obedience, that it was impossible to reconcile the two positions, or even make them mutually more intelligible.[35] To Bonhoeffer this Barth seemed too cautious and to Barth this Bonhoeffer seemed too impatient. Barth, to secure his eschatological base, described ethics as being merely 'pointers' or 'demonstrations', but Bonhoeffer questioned the sufficiency of this as the basis and content for the proclamation of the commandments. He suspected it as being a way

33. To E. Sutz, 24.7.1931, GS I, p. 20.
34. AB, p. 83.
35. To E. Sutz, 24.7.1931, GS I, p. 20.

of escape, as meaning that in the last resort grace was not binding. The more deeply he became involved in the practical work of the Church and the ecumenical movement, the more urgently he asked with every month that passed whether the 'proclamation of concrete commandments through the Church' was possible.

Basically all this depends on the problem of ethics, i.e. the question of the possibility of the proclamation of concrete commandments through the Church . . .

It is the problem of concreteness in our ministry that at present so occupies me . . .[36]

If the problem is acute anywhere, it is here. And it seems to me that it is only from here that one can gain an understanding of Barth. I have discussed these things with him several times this year. This was very fruitful.[37]

But did this pull towards a concrete expression of command not impose demands on the Church and its ministry? On what was it to rely for its authority? This raised the whole weighty problem of its authority and credibility. It was this that Bonhoeffer meant. He admitted 'that our church today cannot utter a concrete commandment. But the question is whether this lies in its essence—its limitation by the ends to which we are moving—or represents decay and loss of substance'.[38] This question that he put to Rössler was in reality directed at Karl Barth and the riddle of the authority of the Church. Because of his anxiety to avoid false authorities, Barth strengthened the eschatological components in ecclesiology and ethics. Bonhoeffer feared this was an evasion, by which eschatological considerations were used neatly to by-pass the question of the Church's real authority to take and to enjoin concrete action. Woe to the Church and its authority if Barth's systematically correct warning in practice prevented it from pronouncing commandments.

[It is] the characteristic of the Church's authority (differing from all other authorities) that it does not begin by possessing authority and acting by reason of it, but possesses authority only by reason of the 'arbitrary' pronouncement of God's bidding in so far as it is accepted as such, and with every one of its words sets its whole authority at stake.[39]

Thus Barth was not confronted with a man who evaded the issue by ascribing the proclamation of the Gospel to the Church's official ministry (as Althaus was suspected of doing) or to the 'orders of creation' (Brunner was suspected of this) in order to establish its authority or validity metaphysically or mystically. But he was ill at ease with Bonhoeffer's directness; he preferred approaching the problem with his limitation through the ends to which we are moving, i.e. the 'Eschata'.

36. To E. Sutz, Aug. 1932, GS I, pp. 33 f.   38. To H. Rössler, 25.12.1932, GS I, p. 63.
37. To H. Rössler, 25.12.1932, GS I, p. 65.   39. GS I, p. 63.

This may have been the point to which Bonhoeffer was referring when, after their meeting in Berlin in April 1932, he wrote:

Thus it is now clear to me that Barth himself does not agree with me on this point, but recently he again asked me whether I still thought in the same way about it, and said plainly enough that he too feels at least uncomfortable about it.[40]

All his anxiety in the matter was summed up in a passage in 2 Chronicles 20: 12, to which Franz Hildebrandt drew his attention: 'We do not know what to do, but our eyes are upon thee'. He used this as the text for his sermon on Exaudi Sunday 1932,[41] and 'unloaded my whole dismay in the matter';[42] and he mentioned the passage again in October 1933 in a letter to Barth from London.[43]

While he was wrestling with the problem of the authority of the Church, it now struck him more and more frequently that the Church might be better served by silence than by the continual comments and marginal observations about God and the world into which it was continually led astray. He had taken an interest at an early stage in the question of 'qualified silence' by the Church.[44] To his students this was a completely alien point of view, but to him the categories of 'authority', 'concrete commandment' and 'qualified silence' of the Church meant the same thing, that is, the whole challenge of its ministry.

Some notes of a lecture of his, delivered during the winter of 1932-3 on the history of the systematic theology of the century, end as follows:

The Barthian view of ethics as 'demonstration' excludes all concrete ethics and ethical principles (these certainly!) . . . Proclaiming the concrete Christ always means proclaiming him in a concrete situation. What is the foundation on which ethics can be constructed? Where is the principle of concretion in the general injunction to obey? The reason why our churchly pronouncements are so lacking in force is that they are half-way between general principles and the concrete situation. The sorry plight of the Church is always also the plight of the theological faculties, but this is little noticed. Luther could write both *De servo arbitrio* and about the tribute money. Why cannot we do that? Who shall show us Luther?

At the turn of the year 1932-3 Bonhoeffer wrote a letter of thanks to Barth, confessing that he was struggling in a theological abyss in which one might perish. But Barth was able to keep him on the right lines:

If I was a burden to you in August because of my perhaps too stubborn and —as you once said—'godless' questioning, I ask for your forgiveness. But

40. To E. Sutz, 17.5.1932, GS I, p. 31.
41. GS I, p. 133.
42. GS I, p. 31.
43. GS II, p. 133.
44. Cf. GS I, pp. 143 f.; SC, p. 174.

please realize that I know no one but you who might be able to free me from
these tenacious questions . . . in talking directly to you I am brought close
to what I have always been only circling round at a distance . . . The brief
hours I spent with you in the past year resulted in directing my thoughts,
which continually tended to relapse into 'godless' questioning, and keeping
them to the heart of the matter.[45]

This letter was written on the threshold between the second and third
phase of the relations between Barth and Bonhoeffer. Bonhoeffer's
questioning became 'godless' when his insistence on concrete proclamation threatened to rob revelation itself of its majesty, because it
concentrated interest upon its own authority and absolutized the
concrete proclamation. Barth may have reminded the younger man of
the basic belief they shared, and Bonhoeffer may later have admitted
that Barth was right, because he said in prison that his road to *The Cost
of Discipleship* had not been without its perils.[46] But now he was not
to be diverted from that road. The 'tenacious questions' about authority
and credibility grew deeper and called for an answer in life. He sought
for it both personally in his private life and ecumenically in his church
life. Without security and without proof decisions had to be made,
sometimes in blind obedience, for the sake of the majesty of revelation.

The church struggle to some extent served again to strengthen the
alliance between Barth and Bonhoeffer against secessionists and
renegades, but in the third phase of their relations it was not only the
spatial distance between them that grew greater. The warmth of
Bonhoeffer's letter of thanks does not conceal the fact that he did not
allow his confidence in the path he was following to be shaken. He
believed he saw things that did not come within Barth's field of vision.
Barth has himself described the feeling of slight unease that the younger
man always gave him, because he was continually surprising him with
new perspectives and was able to see things in a different light. This
weighed more heavily than the imperfect knowledge that Barth still had
in 1931 of an ally who had never been his pupil.

Bonhoeffer showed his gratitude and loyalty, not by repeating what
had already been said, but in courageous and critical new thinking or at
least new foundations. The Sermon on the Mount now moved into the
foreground of his thought, and here he did not yet find anything helpful
in Barth.

. . . the real struggle which will perhaps arise later is bound to be simply a
faithful suffering and then, then, perhaps, God will again make known his
word to his Church, but until then there will have to be much faith, much
prayer and much suffering. Do you know, I believe . . . that the whole thing is
decisively expressed in the Sermon on the Mount. I believe that Barth's

45. GS II, p. 39.
46. LPP, p. 201.

theology is only putting it off . . . but he certainly made it possible for that to be seen.[47]

The second phase, between their meeting in Bonn and Bonhoeffer's departure for London, was the high point in the relationship between the two men. It provided a happy prelude to the coming church struggle and led to unbroken cooperation in questions of the life of the Church. But theologically it came too late. The answers to his questions that Bonhoeffer obtained at this stage from Barth did not take him far enough. When he himself provided an answer in *The Cost of Discipleship*, it was only after his death that Barth expressed the agreement and approval that he so badly wanted.

Nevertheless there is no disputing the fact that there was no contemporary to whom Bonhoeffer opened his heart so completely as he did to Karl Barth. 'I have, I think, seldom regretted anything in my theological past so much as the fact that I did not go to him sooner', he wrote from Bonn in July 1931 to Sutz. The urge to independence on both sides, combined with an intense interest in his differently constituted interlocutor, made the meeting one of the most pleasing events in Bonhoeffer's life. This was again expressed in 1943 when I visited him in his cell at Tegel and brought him Barth's personal greetings from Basle. 'Karl's cigar is on the table in front of me, and that is something really indescribable—it was so kind and thoughtful of him.'[48]

II CATECHISMS

Between the visit to Bonn in July 1931 and the trip to Cambridge in September, Bonhoeffer helped to write 'a Lutheran catechism', entitled 'If you believe, you have'.[49] It is a short document, showing the great freedom with which Bonhoeffer devoted himself to such work half-way between systematic theology and practice. The occasion for it did not arise out of any teaching duties; he still knew nothing of the confirmation class in Wedding that was to claim him a few months later. The suggestion that he do it, and a great deal of cooperation, came from Franz Hildebrandt, who was now the practising churchman.

After acting as assistant to Siegmund-Schultze in east Berlin, Hildebrandt spent the remainder of his training period in the small town of Dobrilugk in Brandenburg. He spent a fortnight's holiday in Berlin working with Bonhoeffer on this revolutionary task. While it was in progress Bonhoeffer gave him one of the first copies of *Act and Being*, writing on the flyleaf 'Is this to become a catechism?' Bonhoeffer enjoyed teaching, and his Sunday-school work in Harlem had encouraged him to make unconventional experiments.

Bonhoeffer was so convinced of the need for new catechisms that two

47. To E. Sutz, 28.4.1934, GS I, p. 40.
48. LPP, p. 98.   49. GS III, pp. 248-57.

written by him have survived. One dates from 1931 and the other from 1936, and they are very different. The first is short and manageable, and is limited to about 40 questions, while the second is too long, consisting as it does of nearly 170 questions. Neither is catechetically simple or practical from the teaching point of view. Bonhoeffer was not so much interested in teaching as in 'formulating what the Lutheran faith says today. Questions and answers are intended for concentrated reading'.[50]

Bonhoeffer's and Hildebrandt's 1931 approach was very Harnackian. Instead of the Apostles' Creed, they took as their basis Luther's statement of faith that Hildebrandt had discovered while working on his thesis.[51] Bonhoeffer liked this so much that for the rest of his life he kept it in his daily prayer and service book and occasionally used it instead of the Apostles' Creed even in the most orthodox confessional services. What appealed to him in it was that Luther immediately connected the ontological and functional affirmations with their ethical implications. The Luther document, as a trinitarian profession of faith, provided the pattern for the division of the catechism into three. Thus the Creed, the oldest part of the Church's teaching to catechumens, remained the basis, but that other relic of the ancient Church, the Lord's Prayer, was left out. True, Luther's arrangement in the *Shorter Catechism* is no longer recognizable. The Ten Commandments no longer appear as such. One is reminded of the Barcelona lecture, in which the Christian is represented as continually creating his own commandments. Instead, everything follows from the first question: 'What is the Gospel?' The answer is: The tidings of salvation and of the Kingdom and will of God, who speaks today. The catechism ends with the refrain from Luther's statement of faith, which Bonhoeffer continually used as 'an antiphon in his sermons, addresses and letters':[52] 'But this is the Christian faith: to know what you should do and what has been given you.' The main questions are not followed by 'thou shalt not' sentences, but, instead of imperatives, by indicative statements of here and now actions. Thus the whole is imbued with the positively commanding tone of a master, rather than the forbidding tone of a policeman; but the catechism also includes questions such as are asked by modern man and require an answer:

How do I know about God? . . . Where is the proof? Does not the story of Creation conflict with science? . . . Can a God who is good permit so much wrong in the world? . . . Is the instinct of self-preservation itself a sin? . . . Does one not have to take life in war? . . . What should a Christian do in politics? . . . Did Jesus really live? . . . Why are there so many churches? . . . Do I need the Church?

50. GS III, p. 248.
51. WA 30, I, 94; GS III, p. 249.
52. J. Glenthoj, 'Dietrich Bonhoeffer und die Ökumene', MW II, p. 128.

It was a complete novelty to introduce the subject of war and peace or the ecumenical question into the elementary teaching of the Church. Bonhoeffer's conventional defence of war in the Barcelona lectures has vanished. At that time he said: 'Love of my people will . . . sanctify war',[53] but he never expressed himself like that again. True, he did not encourage or recommend the individual to refuse war service—nor did he do so in 1936—but he says that the Church as a whole should speak:

. . . therefore the Church knows nothing of any sanctity of war. War is a struggle for life using dehumanized means. The Church that prays to Our Father appeals to God only for peace.[54]

The peace commandment is based on the anti-nationalist principle of the unity of the human family, the arguments that he had heard Lasserre use. This ecumenical argument, and also the idea of the Church's share in the responsibility for the course taken by the political struggle for life between the nations, were here adopted by Bonhoeffer in the autumn of 1931, and he never again departed from them.

In 1936, in far more difficult circumstances, Bonhoeffer again wrestled with the problem of formulating this part of the catechism; not with formulating what he personally should do, but with trying to say what a church catechism could and should say in the matter. In his 1936 draft he first wrote: 'Can a Christian go to war?' but crossed this out and wrote instead: 'What does God say about war?' He then crossed that out too. This, after all, was in 1936, when Bonhoeffer himself was inclining to the principle of the rejection of war service, but was not even able to convert to it his students for ordination in the Confessing Church who were so closely associated with him.

How should the Christian act in war? There is no plain commandment of God on this point. The Church can never bless war or weapons. The Christian can never take part in an unjust war. If a Christian takes to the sword, he will daily pray to God for forgiveness of the sin and pray for peace.[55]

In his second draft catechism of 1936 Bonhoeffer returned to the conservative pattern of catechism-structure. To counter the falsifying modernization of the German Christians, his pupils now were to learn to guide the congregations into the profession of faith of the fathers of their church. So Bonhoeffer again adhered to Luther's pattern in the *Shorter Catechism*. Under the heading 'Of Obedience', he began with an interpretation of the Ten Commandments. The Commandments were there 'so that we may keep them';[56] 'we' meant the community of Christ. The numbering of the Commandments was this time not Luther's but the Bible's, and the affirmations are supported by quotations from

53. GS III, p. 56.
54. GS III, p. 252.
55. GS III, pp. 342 f.
56. GS III, p. 344.

Scripture and not from Luther as in 1931; for the purpose of relating
the new 'Israel' to the present day, the Old Testament is drawn on.
The teaching and passion of Christ occupy a central position. The Barmen declaration has become part of the catechism, and the racial question is touched on: 'in the Church there is neither . . . Jew nor
German'; [57] also included is the question of how to live under an unjust
government which was really a novelty in a Lutheran catechism.[58]
Oral confession, which was not mentioned in 1931, is now given more
space than the passages on baptism and the sacrament together.

In 1936 Bonhoeffer presented this catechism to his pupils as an encouragement to them to carry out their own experiments. It was a reply
to their request for a conference to state what should unquestionably
be said by the Church, and in it, in the dangerous situation of those
years. After the lecture he did not produce the manuscript again or do
any further work on it. He had made a proposal, so he believed, at a
time when the Confessing Church was everywhere encouraging and
actually organizing attempts at formulating things anew.

Nevertheless, the 1931 catechism is perhaps the more important.
Hildebrandt and he actually had it published,[59] and in 1933 reprints
were distributed for discussion at meetings of ministers.[60] But the new
challenge of that year made even the authors themselves lose interest
in the enthusiastic, liberal but nevertheless central experiment, for it
was necessary to make professions of quite a different type.

Apart from its didactic value or lack of it, the 1936 catechism is
interesting because it summarizes what Bonhoeffer would have liked to
have seen stated at that time as the minimum position of the Church.
We possess it only in the form of his original, fragmentary notes, un-
influenced by consultation with anyone and unrevised. He quickly
jotted them down on rough paper, alone with his Bible and concordance;
it is not the work of a compiler, surrounded by the relevant literature,
producing a carefully considered whole.

In his own practical work as a teacher, Bonhoeffer worked in complete freedom from any preconceived ideas of his own, as when he
prepared the Kleist-Retzow children for confirmation in 1938, for
instance.

III CAMBRIDGE

The most momentous of the three events that filled the summer between
his return from America and the beginning of his career was the

57. GS III, p. 362.
58. GS III, p. 363.
59. Because of the date of publication the catechism has been erroneously connected
with Bonhoeffer's teaching a confirmation class at Wedding; cf. *Zeichen der Zeit*, 1957,
No. 6, pp. 213-18, and MW II, p. 128.
60. JK, 1933, p. 122.

ecumenical conference at Cambridge. His interest in the ecumenical movement was at first merely incidental, but it took such a hold on him that it became an integral part of his being. Soon he was engaged in a lively battle concerning its interior alignment and was enthusiastically representing it in its relations with the outside world. The world of the early stages of the evangelical ecumenical movement came to play a vital part in his theology, his part in the church struggle, and finally in his political commitment.

The leaders of the movement in Berlin, primarily Diestel, made him a member of the German youth delegation to the annual conference of the World Alliance of Churches, held at Cambridge on 1st-5th September 1931. There the executive appointed him one of the three European youth secretaries. This happened at a time when the world political crisis, together with its own impulses, was forcing new ideas upon the movement.

Ecumenical Berlin

Berlin had played a prominent part in the ecumenical movement from a relatively early stage; it could, indeed, be described as its German headquarters. The theological faculty of Berlin University took the lead. In contrast to Britain, for instance, in Germany academic rather than church dignitaries first adopted the ecumenical idea, and that was how the position in Germany was regarded from abroad. Later, during the church struggle, this had disadvantageous consequences, because the professors seldom really represented the Church, for as state officials they were disastrously linked with the Third Reich.

World Alliance

Bonhoeffer's ecumenical career began with the World Alliance. This resulted in his association with the Council for Practical Christianity ('Life and Work'). He was never directly associated with the 'Faith and Order' movement.

It was both characteristic and uncharacteristic of him that he should make a start with the World Alliance of Churches. This was the ecumenical organization in which the spirit of liberal and humanist Anglo-Saxon theology was most dominant, but it was also the freest organization, not nearly so ecclesiastical as the others. Also, with its emphasis on work for peace, it was the one most committed to something.

A self-respecting theologian, particularly a Barthian, was bound to have strong reservations about such an organization. Barth himself held out for a long time before finally accepting election to the theological committee of 'Life and Work' in 1932. His attitude attracted a great deal of attention.

'Faith and Order' provided a platform for qualified experts in comparative theology. Since the Stockholm conference, 'Life and Work' had been the official field of the Alliance of German Evangelical Churches. With the World Alliance of Churches, the older organization, the situation was different. It was based on a most varied collection of church, semi-church and non-church groups, which could not be said of the 'Life and Work' conference in Stockholm or the 'Faith and Order' conference in Lausanne. In the *Kirchliche Jahrbuch* of 1931 Sasse wrote: 'The World Alliance is the only ecumenical organization which through its national and local groups reaches right down to the congregations', and it had the important task of promoting among the latter, not only the idea of the churches working for peace, but the ecumenical idea in general. Many influential laymen were members.

In 1931 it had reached the high point of its influence on public opinion in Germany, but at the same time it was faced with a threat that eventually proved fatal. As a result of the economic crisis its financial position became critical. Diestel was compelled to dissolve the secretariat and have the work taken over by his own deanery office, and travelling abroad again became nearly impossible. Above all, however, the ecumenical 'internationalists', and the German supporters of the World Alliance in particular, were henceforward subjected to a deliberate campaign of defamation by the nationalists. That is a matter which will concern us later. Three years afterwards the German branch of the World Alliance was forced to dissolve. Ecumenical work necessarily passed from the free and fruitful form of activity by numerous associations and groups to the institutional level of 'Life and Work' and 'Faith and Order'. It was only on this basis that it was able to survive for a little while longer under the Nazi régime.

That the driving force and dedication of the World Alliance was finally extinguished was no small loss. The prophetic call for reconciliation retreated, and was forced to seek new outlets within more cautious ecclesiastical organizations.

It was of course difficult for a young German theologian of Bonhoeffer's stamp to accept the efflorescence of the liberal, humanitarian type of theology that prevailed in the World Alliance; one of its purposes was actually the promotion of friendship between all religions. Of his own accord Bonhoeffer would hardly have found his way to it at that time, and the credit for rousing his interest in it must be attributed to Diestel's persistence. But that alone would hardly have been sufficient to maintain his interest. It was the peace question, and the new wave of defamation in Germany, that assured his loyalty to the organization, and reconciled him to its slender theological reputation. Besides, he appreciated the opportunities that its conferences gave him of meeting people such as Gandhi's friend C. F. Andrews. Also there was always an element in Bonhoeffer's theology that made him mistrustful of church enterprises that had purely church aims, and in the

World Alliance there could be no question of this. Thus, in spite of all his concern at its theological deficiencies, he wrote from Cambridge, already deeply committed:

But, notwithstanding all criticism, it is plain that the World Alliance . . . is doing work the urgency of which must set everyone's conscience alight, and that so far we know no other way of doing it better or more quickly.[61]

Nationalist Protest

Attending the Cambridge conference involved the German delegates in acute ecclesiastical, political and economic difficulties. It was a prelude to all the future disagreeable concomitant phenomena of ecumenical work.

a) While Bonhoeffer and Lasserre were still in Mexico, looking at pyramids and sending off peace greetings, a kind of ecumenical scandal took place in Germany that re-echoed for a long time in the ecclesiastical and theological press.

In preparation for Cambridge, the German branch of the World Alliance held a conference at Hamburg on 1st-3rd June 1931. So that the German position at the conference might be decided, votes were to be taken on three issues: 1. national and international obligations; 2. disarmament; 3. minority questions. Guests from abroad were expected, in particular Lord Dickinson, the tireless president of the World Alliance, and Bishop Ammundsen from Denmark, who was later to be such a loyal and informed friend of the Confessing Church.

On the morning of the opening day the *Hamburger Nachrichten* published a statement, under the heading 'Protestant Church and International Reconciliation', which among other things said:

In this situation[62] there can in our opinion be no understanding between us Germans and the nations that were victorious in the World War; we can only show them that while they continue the war against us, understanding is impossible . . . This gives full force to the demand that all artificial semblance of cooperation should be broken and that it should be unreservedly recognized that Christian and churchly understanding and cooperation on questions of *rapprochement* between the nations is impossible so long as the others conduct a policy lethal to our nation.

He who believes that understanding can be better served otherwise than by this denies the German destiny and confuses consciences at home and abroad, because in this matter he does not honour the truth.

Professor D. P. Althaus, Erlangen
Professor D. E. Hirsch, Göttingen

61. GS I, p. 117.
62. The statement described it as follows: There had been an open breach of the Allied promise made to Germany at the time of its surrender in 1918; Germany had been robbed of space in which to live and breathe; it was being bled white by payments made under the false description of reparations, and the Allied disarmament obligation undertaken in the peace treaty had been flagrantly broken.

All the right-wing newspapers in Germany immediately reprinted the statement on their front pages.[63] This broadside was effective, and it re-echoed from all directions until well into the following year. Althaus's and Hirsch's statement received the official backing of the German Evangelical Alliance. The *Allgemeine Evangelische Lutherische Kirchenzeitung* opened its columns to Hirsch to air the matter further and reply to those who attacked him. Althaus announced that he was not a member of the Nazi Party—incidentally Hirsch was not a member either —but that he nevertheless supported the movement, which had the backing of the majority of students, and he once more attacked 'superficial talk about international understanding'.[64]

The Hamburg conference came to an understanding with its foreign guests that the German delegates should not intervene in the discussion of disarmament at Cambridge, but leave it to representatives of other nationalities. Bonhoeffer commented: 'On 15th August I am being sent for three weeks to England to attend the Cambridge conference. What shall we say to the Americans about cooperation between the churches? Surely we shall not talk such nonsense as Hirsch did recently . . .'[65]

b) In July 1931 banks, exchanges and other financial institutions were closed for several days, and one emergency decree after the other imposed control of payments and restriction on withdrawals of cash. In the course of a fortnight the discount rate was raised from 7 to 15 per cent. At the end of August all holdings of foreign currency exceeding 1,000 marks in value had to be registered with the authorities. Next, in spite of the danger of renewed political unrest, pay and pension cuts were introduced, the period of entitlement to unemployment pay was reduced, and economy measures were introduced throughout the country.

Thus great obstacles were put in the way of foreign travel, and the German ecumenical leaders found themselves in a humiliating position. Bonhoeffer was unembarrassed, however, and asked insistently for the funds he considered necessary. Since he generously spent money of his own for the purpose, he expected others to make sacrifices too.

The economic crisis also affected the Cambridge conference directly, i.e. in regard to the proposed resolution on disarmament. Others besides Germans pointed out that there was a connection between the economic crisis and the payment of war debts. A successful disarmament conference and a resulting restoration of equal rights to Germany would contribute to relieving the economic situation. Siegmund-Schultze tirelessly emphasized this point in his writings, and it was appreciated by the Americans at Cambridge, since President Hoover had proposed a large-scale remission of debt in the interests of his own country. The French

63. For full text, see e.g., CW, 1931, p. 605.
64. CW, 1931, p. 1034.
65. GS I, p. 18.

showed much less comprehension and could be expected to dispute this at Cambridge.

Bonhoeffer's attention had already been drawn to such problems in New York, and he was now eagerly acquiring new knowledge. He wrote to his friend, E. Sutz, in Switzerland:

Come to Berlin, there are no emergency decrees in your country. I have already written to you that I am going to Cambridge. If only I don't have to talk about things I know nothing about yet. Incidentally, I am eagerly studying political economy—you cannot completely disclaim responsibility for that—and I am reading some really interesting and simple books on the subject.[66]

He plunged into political economy, not only to have facts with which to back his arguments at Cambridge, but also with a view to his forthcoming students' chaplaincy at the Berlin Technical University. The more vigorously he proposed to bring the real theological factors to bear, the more necessary did a sober knowledge of economic causes and effects seem to him to be. Thus what he had learnt at Union Theological Seminary in New York continued to exercise its influence.

c) At Cambridge and subsequent World Alliance conferences there was no one with whom Bonhoeffer reached quicker and better understanding than the French, though for the next two years he regarded the Franco-German problem as the most acute of all. In *Die Eiche* Siegmund-Schultze tried to make up for all the things that had been left undone between Germans and French in previous years by printing a report which the French themselves presented at Cambridge:

[The struggle] would certainly have been less hard if the attitude of the German Evangelical Church had not filled the French Reformed Church with deep concern and painful surprise. When war mania had disappeared, our churches expected from the German churches some gesture of regret about what had happened and a desire to lead their people along the path of justice and fraternity. No act of penance was expected from them, only a word of sympathy for our plundered and destroyed churches. But nothing came. The German churches bewailed only the suffering of their own people, whose complete innocence they proclaimed. Hence one can understand the mistrust and suspicion that filled our churches in view of this attitude of their sisters in Germany.[67]

Conference

Bonhoeffer's visit to England was divided into three parts; first he attended a preliminary student conference at St. Leonards and Westcliff-on-Sea, then a youth conference of the World Alliance, and finally the conference itself. Little is known of the days spent in meeting other delegates at St. Leonards.

66. To E. Sutz, 24.7.1931, GS I, p. 21.   67. Quoted from *Die Eiche*, 1931, p. 481.

In comparison with its predecessors, the Cambridge conference stood out for two reasons. In the first place, this was the first time the conference was held on the soil of a nation which had taken a leading part in the war. It had not seemed possible to risk doing this earlier, but now war-time prejudices, at any rate so far as the World Alliance were concerned, had died away.

In the second place, the conference for the first time granted full and unrestricted participation to its youth delegates. Bishop Ammundsen, the president of the conference, said that the Alliance was running the risk of becoming 'too respectable'. This earned him some criticism,[68] but nevertheless the experiment was carried out. It was agreed that up to half of each national delegation could consist of youth delegates, with the result that the latter were able to take part in the deliberations of the main conference as well as in the committee work. The result was a sudden surge of activity by young people in the World Alliance. This overflowed into 'Life and Work', not without causing some headaches at the Geneva headquarters.

To Bonhoeffer the youth conference of 29th-31st August became a significant event. The youth committee of the World Alliance had been in existence since the Prague conference of 1928, which for the first time issued an appeal to the Allies to keep their promises in relation to the defeated powers. But before 1931 the committee had met only once, at Avignon in 1929. Its members included a number of men who later became well-known, such as Dr. E. A. Burroughs, then Bishop of Ripon, Professor Alivisatos, Captain Etienne Bach, a former officer in a French alpine regiment who had become a pacifist, Sir Stafford Cripps, Hromadka, Visser 't Hooft, Sparring-Petersen from Denmark, and Wilhelm Stählin from Münster. The youth conference now demanded a more active role; as *Die Eiche* put it, they said: 'Make room for us, give us something to do, give us a good organization.'[69] The cooperation of young church people in international tasks was discussed.

The delegates submitted a resolution to the main conference putting forward three concrete proposals, the third of which closely affected Bonhoeffer. These proposals were: 1. That the youth committee should be enlarged; 2. That a secretary should be appointed to assist the chairman, the Bishop of Ripon, and work at the Geneva headquarters; the name of the Swiss, H. L. Henriod, who was already secretary-general of the World Alliance and of 'Life and Work', was put forward for this post; 3. That three international honorary youth secretaries should be appointed to do coordinating work, their travelling expenses to be met by the World Alliance; for the British Empire, the United States and the Far East the name of the Englishman, F. W. T. Craske, was put forward, and for France, Latin America, the Balkans, Poland and Czecho-

68. CW, 1931, pp. 975, 982.
69. *Die Eiche*, 1931, p. 457.

Slovakia that of the Frenchman, P. C. Toureille. Lastly, it was proposed that Dietrich Bonhoeffer should be responsible for the work in Germany, central and northern Europe, Hungary and Austria. On 4th September these proposals were approved by the management committee and accepted by the conference; and the three youth secretaries were also made members of the management committee and of the council itself.

His election to the inner circle of the World Alliance had many consequences for Bonhoeffer. In Sofia in 1933 and at Fanö in 1934 he was an *ex officio* member of the council without the delicate question of German representation at those conferences being affected. Thus the lines he was to follow were laid down.

Apart from the official sessions, there was a special Franco-German youth meeting that went on until late at night and revealed the extent to which the aspirations and criticisms of the younger theologians in both countries coincided.

The opportunity was also taken to hold a meeting of the executive committee of 'Life and Work'. The latter also had its youth committee, the deputy chairman of which was Dr. Erich Stange, the head of the German Y.M.C.A. This meeting is of interest to us because it was decided that the 'Life and Work' youth committee should seek and organize close cooperation with that of the World Alliance. At this period, however, the leadership remained firmly in the hands of the World Alliance.

The Cambridge conference was the principal reason why 1932 was a very restless year for Bonhoeffer. Organizing ecumenical youth work involved him in an endless succession of meetings, and it was only the advent of the church struggle that caused him gradually to loosen his links with the ecumenical youth secretariat. His work for it in 1931-2 was by no means associated only with success and popularity for the ecumenical idea. On the contrary; six months after the Cambridge conference he reported to a meeting of the committee in London:

The results of the Cambridge conference in Germany are meagre, because nationalist professors of theology oppose the work of the World Alliance.[70]

Before they left Cambridge the newly elected youth secretaries discussed and agreed on a programme for 1932. This was based entirely on their own ideas and, apart from practical problems, such as unemployment, was to include consideration of basic theological questions. They refused to be intimidated by the difficult foreign exchange situation, fixed dates, and believed the necessary resources would be available.

The increased activity and status of the youth committee was not pleasing to everyone at Cambridge, however. It put an extra burden of work on the Geneva office of the World Alliance and the Ecumenical Council. The need for coordination was seen at once by the research

70. GS I, p. 118.

department of the Ecumenical Council and its secretary Hans Schönfeld, who was responsible for theological questions. Would the youth secretaries allow themselves to be guided? In fact complaints soon arose from council or committee members that the youth section was invading fields that were already being dealt with and was causing duplication of work at Geneva.[71]

Thus Bonhoeffer's relations with the Geneva headquarters were immediately associated with certain difficulties. If he noticed them at all, he did not take them seriously. But they piled up in the background, and became evident and assumed substantial proportions when the various groups in Germany broke up into deeply hostile camps. Looking back at these tragic developments, it is clear that he did not pay sufficient attention to his relations with the Geneva office. Perhaps he persisted too long in believing that everything was in order.

IV THE THEOLOGIAN BECOMES A CHRISTIAN

Bonhoeffer, reflecting on his past life in Tegel prison in 1944, wrote that his development had been 'really' uninterrupted, though he admitted that there had been one change:

I don't think I have ever changed very much, except perhaps at the time of my first impressions abroad and under the first conscious influence of Father's personality. It was then that I turned from phraseology to reality ... Neither of us has really had a break in our lives. Of course, we have deliberately broken with a good deal ... I sometimes used to long for something of the kind, but today I think differently about it.[72]

When Bonhoeffer wrote this, he was referring to the contrast in the Epistles to Timothy between 'I formerly blasphemed' (1 Timothy 1 : 13) and 'I thank God whom I serve with a clear conscience, as did my fathers' (2 Timothy 1 : 3).

What Bonhoeffer so serenely describes as a 'turning away from phraseology' and as 'longing for a break' turns out on closer examination to refer to a change in him that took place at a definite time and can be attributed to the period when he was beginning work at the university, in the Church and in the ecumenical movement. Apart from outward signs which even his students noted in him, the later enquirer can detect some concealed references in Bonhoeffer's own hand that reveal a momentous change in him.

Those who met him after 1931 were impressed by his breadth of knowledge, concentrated energy, analytical and critical acumen and also by a personal commitment that engaged the whole of his personality and showed itself in innumerable ways of practical behaviour. What these observers saw was the result of the change in him, not the change

71. Cf. letter of H. Schönfeld to Runestam of 6.2.1932, MW V, IV, 1.
72. Letter of 22.4.1944, LPP, pp. 149 f.

itself. Only those who knew him well from earlier days were struck by the difference in him, as, for instance, Paul Lehmann was when he met him again in Berlin in 1933.[73] The impression he made on his students was that he had always been like that. He now went regularly to church, though in New York Lehmann had been struck by how freely he behaved in this matter. Also he engaged in systematic meditation on the Bible that was obviously very different from exegetic or homiletic use of it. In their conferences in 1932 his students were surprised at this unusual practice, and did not fail to make ironic comments on it. He spoke of oral confession no longer merely theologically, but as an act to be carried out in practice. In his Lutheran ecclesiastical and academic environment this was unheard of. He talked more and more often of a community life of obedience and prayer from which the isolated and privileged ministry might perhaps derive renewed credibility; and, so far from doing this in spite of his Protestant theology, he based it on the latter. More and more frequently he quoted the Sermon on the Mount as a word to be acted upon, not merely used as a mirror. He began taking a stand for Christian pacifism among his students and fellow-ministers, though hardly anyone took any notice at that time. To his students his piety sometimes appeared too fervent, and was impressive only because it was accompanied by theological rigour and a broad cultural background. This reminiscence from a student dates from 1932:

There, before the church struggle, he said to us near the Alexanderplatz, with the simplicity that was perhaps used by Tholuck in the old days, that we should not forget that every word of Holy Scripture was a quite personal message of God's love for us, and he asked us whether we loved Jesus.[74]

But incidents of this kind took place only in the inner circle of his students. At all events, the world of *disciplina pietatis* was touched on more than merely incidentally. Only once did he state outright what was now happening inside him and what he meant, for instance, when he wrote to Sutz that 'in the meantime he had taken rather a dislike' to *Act and Being*.[75] This was at the beginning of 1936, in a letter to a girl-friend to whom he was close for a time. Looking back on his past life, he wrote:

I plunged into work in a very unchristian way. An . . . ambition that many noticed in me made my life difficult . . .

Then something happened, something that has changed and transformed my life to the present day. For the first time I discovered the Bible . . . I had often preached, I had seen a great deal of the Church, and talked and preached about it—but I had not yet become a Christian . . .

I know that at that time I turned the doctrine of Jesus Christ into some-

73. Cf. Ch. VII, p. 198.
74. Communication from J. Kanitz, 1955.
75. GS I, p. 26.

thing of personal advantage for myself ... I pray to God that that will never happen again. Also I had never prayed, or prayed only very little. For all my loneliness, I was quite pleased with myself. Then the Bible, and in particular the Sermon on the Mount, freed me from that. Since then everything has changed. I have felt this plainly, and so have other people about me. It was a great liberation. It became clear to me that the life of a servant of Jesus Christ must belong to the Church, and step by step it became plainer to me how far that must go.

Then came the crisis of 1933. This strengthened me in it. Also I now found others who shared that aim with me. The revival of the Church and of the ministry became my supreme concern ...

I suddenly saw as self-evident the Christian pacifism that I had recently passionately opposed—a disputation at which Gerhard [Jacobi] was also present. And so it went on, step by step. I no longer saw or thought anything else ...

My calling is quite clear to me. What God will make of it I do not know ...

I must follow the path. Perhaps it will not be such a long one. Sometimes we wish that it were so (Philippians 1:23). But it is a fine thing to have realized my calling ...

I believe its nobility will become plain to us only in coming times and events. If only we can hold out.[76]

With greater reserve, but nevertheless revealing the whole truth, he wrote to his brother Karl-Friedrich in 1935:

It may be that in many things I may seem to you rather fanatical and crazy. I myself am sometimes afraid of this. But I know that, if I were 'more reasonable', I should in honour bound be compelled to give up the whole of my theology. When I first began, I imagined it quite otherwise—perhaps as a more academic matter. Now something very different has come of it. I now believe that I know at last that I am at least on the right track— for the first time in my life. And that often makes me very glad ... I believe I know that inwardly I shall be really clear and honest with myself only when I have begun to take seriously the Sermon on the Mount. That is the only source of power capable of blowing up the whole phantasmagoria[77] once and for all ...

I still cannot really believe you genuinely believe all these ideas to be so completely crazy. There are things for which an uncompromising stand is worth while. And it seems to me that peace and social justice, or Christ himself, are such things.[78]

To his brother-in-law Rüdiger Schleicher, who, in contrast to the now so 'orthodox' Dietrich, liked to think of himself as a follower of Harnack and Naumann, he wrote in April 1936:

Is it ... intelligible to you if I say I am not at any point willing to sacrifice the Bible as this strange word of God, that on the contrary, I ask with all my strength what God is trying to say to us through it? Everything outside

76. From Finkenwalde, 27.1.1936.
77. i.e. Hitler and his rule. (*Translator.*)
78. GS III, pp. 24 f.

the Bible has grown too uncertain to me. I am afraid of running only into a divine counterpart of myself . . .

Also I want to say to you quite personally that since I have learnt to read the Bible in this way—and that does not date from such a very long time ago—it becomes more marvellous to me every day . . .

You will not believe how glad one is to find one's way back to these elementary things after wandering on a lot of theological side-tracks.[79]

These three documents indicating, one directly and two indirectly, a momentous inner revolution all date from a time when the battle for the new insight, that the theologian must also be a Christian, had been fought and its fruits were ripening. They also seem to point to an almost fixable date. But Bonhoeffer's certainty and joy in his commitment were the fruit of a longer struggle. For, on the one hand, he had written from New York to his young friends at Grunewald of 'new views' that had changed his philosophy and theology, and, on the other, there are those secret, self-tormenting accounts of how he revealed his choice of a career while he was still at school and of how he longed for death, written apparently in the second half of 1932, at a time when in his lecture on 'Creation and Sin' he was working so hard and lecturing on the idea of the 'origins' that one could not and should not know.

Bonhoeffer never revealed the biographical background of these ideas to his students. They knew nothing of any inner revolution that took place at any particular time. Bonhoeffer always greatly disliked stories of conversion told by pietists for purposes of edification. But that did not cause him to shrink back from decisions that had matured in his mind which could become the foundation for a new future, including a new sense of responsibility for the world in his last years.

V UNIVERSITY

Bonhoeffer's connection with Berlin University was now twofold. In the first place, his *venia legendi* of 1930 entitled him to give lectures and hold seminars. He was at liberty to give as few or as many as he liked, and to choose his own subjects; all that was required of him was to announce them in good time and to apply for the necessary accommodation. The other side of this was that as an unsalaried teacher his only reward was the slender fees payable by such students as might be attracted by what a non-examining lecturer had to offer and registered for his courses.

His second link with the university was the post of non-registered assistant in the seminar of systematic theology which, thanks to Lütgert, he took over from Stolzenburg. This did not make him an established official, which he had no ambition to be, but it gave him a fixed contract which—reduced as it was by the various emergency regulations of the

79. GS III, pp. 28 f.

time—assured him of a regular income of 214 marks a month. When the contract, back-dated to 1st August 1931, was finally signed at the beginning of 1932 and the arrears were paid up, he used the money to buy a wooden living hut at Biesenthal, of which we shall hear more later. Extra work did not devolve upon him as a result of this post. Lütgert, the professor, allowed him every freedom to develop his own plans.

Bonhoeffer's Circle

In 1931 conditions were not unfavourable for the beginning of a lecturer's career. Berlin University played a big part in the 'boom' in theology that was then taking place; there were about 1,000 students of theology at the university at that time. Lecture rooms and seminars were overcrowded. Though men like Guardini attracted multitudes of students apart from their routine lectures that winter, there was always something left over for beginners, provided they did not disqualify themselves by being excessively boring. A loyal minority soon crystallized out that was impressed by the interest and novelty of what the newcomer had to say. He obviously met the needs and aspirations of students who were satisfied neither by the elegance and precision of Berlin theology on the one hand nor by crude political propaganda on the other. Here more than purely intellectual demands were made on them.

'I must say that the students were noticeably more interested in theology than the lecturers were',[80] Bonhoeffer wrote to Sutz after holding open evenings at his home for both.

Most theology students were already attracted to Hitler's party; the Nazi *Angriff* had a wider circulation among them than the *Vossische Zeitung*. At the end of 1930 the *Christliche Welt* reported of one university that apparently 'nearly all the theology students are Nazis . . . [and] about ninety per cent of the Protestant theology students wear the Nazi Party emblem at lectures'. The *Christliche Welt* added that complaints came even from the churches' seminaries that 'more than half the candidates for ordination were followers of Hitler'.[81] This was not yet true to the same extent in Berlin, but the political split was already playing a role.

At that time a teacher who maintained his independence in the face of the approaching storm necessarily attracted students who did not react strongly to the new magnetic forces. During his two years' work at the university Bonhoeffer gradually acquired a substantial audience and a firm following in his seminars. The very young lecturer was a minor sensation, and was talked about. His regular followers were self-

80. To E. Sutz, 25.12.1931, GS I, p. 25.
81. CW, 1930, p. 1162.

selected by the intellectual and personal standards required. There were none of the German Christians among them, except perhaps some who believed for a time that politically they could line up with the Nazi Party without their theology being affected.

Seminars, open evenings and excursions led to the formation in 1932 of the so-called Bonhoeffer circle of students, from which there emerged a number of close colleagues in the church struggle and members of the Finkenwalde community, such as Joachim Kanitz, Albrecht Schönherr, Winfried Maechler, Otto Dudzus, Jürgen Winterhager, Wolf-Dieter Zimmermann, Herbert Jehle, Christoph Harhausen, Rudolf Kühn, Reinhard Rütenik, Inge Karding, Helga Zimmermann, Klaus Block and Hans-Herbert Kramm. They all played a substantial part in the formation of the opposition fraternity of young theologians in Berlin-Brandenburg in 1933 and 1934. In 1932 they still engaged in such things as taking potatoes, flour and vegetables on a wheelbarrow to the Stettin station to spend the week-end in the country, first at the Prebelow youth hostel and then in the hut at Biesenthal. They talked theology, hesitantly attempted spiritual exercises, went for long walks, and listened to Bonhoeffer's collection of Negro spirituals on the gramophone. They discussed such things as forming fellowships, committing themselves to organized spiritual life, and possibilities of service in social settlement work. But there was still a long way to go before any of this was put into practice, and everything was on a free and informal basis. Bonhoeffer made no attempt to force the pace. But these were the hesitant beginnings of what later took shape at Finkenwalde and in Bonhoeffer's *Life Together*.

As links with the German S.C.M. arose out of this group and Bonhoeffer became known to a wider circle of students through his chaplaincy, he was more and more frequently invited to give addresses and talks to the Berlin S.C.M. At the request of Martin Fischer, its secretary, he took Bible classes on texts from St. Mark and organized discussions. Some surviving notes by Jürgen Winterhager of an ecumenical evening held at the S.C.M. show that Bonhoeffer was already talking to his students on the lines of his peace speech at Fanö and of *The Cost of Discipleship*. His subject was 'Christ and Peace', and his point of departure, according to the notes, was the failure of the Geneva disarmament conference.[82] Then, on the basis of Matthew 28: 37-8, he went on to make four points, with a sharpness that must have been shocking to his audience at the time. According to the notes, they can be summarized as follows:

Let us base ourselves on the central point of the New Testament and hence

82. This also provides a clue to the date, as in July 1932 Papen announced in the name of his Government that it would take no further part in the Geneva negotiations; cf. *Die Eiche*, 1932, No. 4, pp. 305 ff., in which Siegmund-Schultze expressed his disapproval of Germany's having now assumed the role of saboteur, just at the point when France had manœuvred herself into a position of relative isolation.

consider these questions according to the highest and noblest commandment of all. We shall not tear a single word about worldly authority from the whole context of the New Testament and thus fail to recognize that Christ announced the Kingdom of God, against which the whole world, thus including 'the powers that be', lives in hostility.

Point 1 : Christ does not wish to change things for the sake of our peace and quiet; still less can we do that for ourselves. Discipleship stands entirely on simple faith, and faith is real only in discipleship. The faithful are addressed, but the world is judged through Christ's witness for peace. Faith must be simple, otherwise it breeds reflection, not obedience. There is no such thing as assured peace. The Christian can dare aspire to peace only through faith. Thus there is no such thing as direct brotherhood among men, but there is access to the enemy by way of prayer to the Lord of all nations.

Point 2 : The misunderstood relationship between Law and Gospel, i.e. a forgiveness of sin is taught that does not affect man's earthly, civil life. Men are still told they are sinners, but are not called out from their sinful structures. How are we, who go on sinning in the expectation of grace, to go on taking seriously the forgiveness of sins and prayer to God? We make grace cheap, and with the justification of the sinner through the cross forget the cry of the Lord which never justifies sin. 'You shall not kill', 'love your enemies', is commandment requiring simple obedience. Any form of war service, any preparation for war, is forbidden to the Christian. Faith, which sees freedom from the law as an arbitrary disposition of the law, is human faith and in defiance of God. Simple obedience knows nothing of good and evil, but follows the call of Christ as something self-evident.

Point 3 : Without being ourselves at peace with our brothers and neighbours we cannot preach peace to the nations. When a nation refuses to listen to the peace commandment, Christians are called forth from it to testify. But let us take care that we sinners announce peace in a spirit of love and not out of any zeal for security or any political objectives.

Point 4 : True peace is in and from God; it is inseparably associated with the Gospel. Hence it is not reconciliation with religious philosophies of life. Forgiveness is for sinners; but there can be no reconciliation with sin and false doctrine. The weapons are faith and love, purified by suffering. Pure love, which first seeks out God and his commandments, prefers to see a brother slain without defending himself to seeing his and our souls stained with blood. It is impossible for love to direct the sword against a Christian, for that is aiming it at Christ. 'Can God have commanded us to do such a thing?' is the question of the serpent.

We summarize these notes here because they show plainly that *The Cost of Discipleship* and *Life Together* did not arise out of the circumstances of 1933. *The Cost of Discipleship* arose out of the course of development that Bonhoeffer had been pursuing long before the political upheaval of that year. He was already saying these things to his students, and in the same terms.

He was not concerned with propagating fanatical slogans, but rather perhaps with finding a common answer to the challenge of faith and obedience. He would hardly have spoken so plainly in public sermons, lectures and addresses before these then so startling words of his had been accompanied by concrete steps of his own, and in general he shunned the idea of an individual's undertaking to do exceptional things.[83] Abroad, at ecumenical meetings, he spoke much more openly. There he came into contact with fellow-men who belonged to different traditions but were faced with similar problems. He answered only very indirectly Wilhelm Stählin's attack on 'certain soft pacifist ideas' at the conference of the Berlin Centre in April 1932,[84] but at Ciernohorské Kúpele he spoke openly:

We shall not shrink back here from the word pacifism, the next war must be outlawed, not out of enthusiastic imposition on others of a command-ment—the fifth for instance—but out of obedience towards a command-ment of God that affects us today, namely that there shall be no more war, because it blinds men to revelation.[85]

The S.C.M. invited Bonhoeffer to address a large audience. Johannes Kühne, its director of studies, invited him to speak to a meeting in the Hoffbauerstiftung at Potsdam-Herrmanswerder together with a number of artists and writers during Holy Week in 1932. Bonhoeffer's speech, 'Thy Kingdom Come',[86] shows that the approach indicated in those four points was far from being aimed at a ghetto of perfectionist personal piety. The whole thing, indeed, is an assault on this world. The Church is taken to task for a certain self-satisfied and hypocritical 'other-worldliness'. The universal earthly implication of Christ's message is more firmly emphasized in this address than ever before in Bonhoeffer's theology.

In the Lecture Room

Uncommitted students of course found their way more easily to Bon-hoeffer's approach to theology than many highly specialized and com-mitted teachers of the subject; the latter followed with interest and also with a certain suspicion the course being followed by this product of their own faculty. 'My theological origin is gradually becoming suspect, and the feeling exists that they have nursed a viper in their bosom', Bonhoeffer wrote to his friend Sutz, giving his first impressions of his colleagues.[87] Not only did he dare question their theological assumptions, but also he seemed to be tending towards a different habit of mind. It very quickly struck his students that there was something essential that marked him off from the behaviour and ideals of a professor.

He himself was aware of a certain isolation which, however, he did

83. Cf. his letter to K. Barth of 24.10.1933, GS II, p. 132.
84. GS I, pp. 130 f.
85. GS I, p. 155.
86. GS III, pp. 270 ff.
87. Letter of 25.12.1931, GS I, p. 24.

not wish simply to eliminate. After spending a summer day with Karl Barth on the Bergli, he described it as a 'home for the theologically homeless', to which he 'looked back regretfully in the cold loneliness here'.[88]

Though during the two years when he taught at the university he naturally prepared new lectures and seminars every term, he found delivering monologues a burden. He greatly preferred study groups and seminars, though for his students it was the other way about. He disliked repetition, and was continually searching for fresh ideas. He still felt remote from what he wanted to understand and say, and always remained sceptical about the answers he had established. The further he advanced into the unknown, the more he longed for dialogue and criticism.

The notes and manuscripts of all his lectures and seminars must be considered to have perished.[89] Only the lecture 'Creation and Sin' of the winter of 1932-3 has survived, because he agreed to publish it on the insistence of his students.

'Creation and Fall'

During the summer of 1932 his seminar, in the course of discussing the problem of conscience and marking itself off from the nationalist hubbub about the 'orders of creation', was brought up against the first three chapters of Genesis, and Bonhoeffer had given a brief interpretation of the story of Creation, which he frankly described as a legend. Now, in the winter term of 1932-3, he devoted half his two-hour lecture time to a series on 'Creation and Sin. A Theological Interpretation of Genesis 1-3'.

The doctrine of Creation had hitherto played practically no part in Bonhoeffer's writings. In *Act and Being* there is only an incidental reference to it, though it was written with an eye to the coming danger: 'In theology there are no pre-existing categories of pure creaturehood which are divorced from these concepts [Adam and Christ].'[90] But in the meantime the general debate had entered a stage in which theological arguments for the 'orders of creation' approached the hymnic or, as in the Dehn case, took the form of threats of outlawry backed by physical violence against those who resisted them. It was necessary to prepare defences for the struggles ahead.

Also Bonhoeffer found it stimulating in connection with this classical text to deal with his old themes of conscience and reflection in combination with his new theme of commandment. Moreover, as we have already

---

88. To E. Sutz, 27.10.1932, GS I, p. 36.
89. For an attempted reconstruction see Appendices in German edition, pp. 1047-95. (Editor.)
90. AB, p. 16; similarly p. 174.

indicated, the question of 'origins' in his case had a very personal background; it engaged him again in his meditation on the 119th Psalm, eventually written down in 1940.[91]

He called the work a 'theological interpretation'. The intention was both modest and ambitious. He did not want to invade the field of the fraternity of Old Testament scholars and amend their historical and theological work, but to examine the text as a systematician from the point of view of the Church of whose Bible the book of Genesis forms part. The method he uses is a continuous referral from the text ('which has to be ascertained with all the methods of philological and historical research') to this presupposition that Genesis is part of the Church's Bible. 'That is the objectivity of the method of theological interpretation.'[92] Since the Barthian 'revolution', the idea of interpreting the whole of Scripture as the book of the Church from the point of view of the single idea that it is the word of *Christus praesens* had been in the air. Bonhoeffer set vigorously about drawing conclusions from Barth's Christocentric treatment of the Old Testament and the First Article before Barth himself or others had yet got so far.

The lecture made such an impression that Bonhoeffer's students persuaded him to have it published. How little he himself thought of making a proper book of it is shown by the fact that he did not take the trouble to indicate the Biblical and literary references by means of footnotes, as he had done as a matter of course in his previous books. He did not even provide a table of contents; the fact that it was a lecture was to remain evident, and only the title was changed to avoid confusion with Emanuel Hirsch's *Creation and Sin*, published in 1931, though the remainder of Hirsch's title, '. . . in the natural reality of the human individual', was very different. Thus Bonhoeffer's work was published as *Creation and Fall*.

He wrote a new introduction, however. He had begun the lecture with the words 'In these three chapters God speaks to us as we are today, as sinners who are crucified with him',[93] but he now expatiated somewhat on his method of theological interpretation. When he wrote this introduction, however, the year 1933 was far advanced, and the brief sentences now assumed a note different from that which they had had in the lecture room. What then may have sounded already eschatological, now—particularly in regard to the Creation—sounded truly eschatological:

The Church of Christ bears witness to the end of all things. It lives from the end, it thinks from the end, it acts from the end, it proclaims its message from the end . . . But the Church is naturally in tumult when these children of the world that has passed away lay claim to the Church, to the new,

91. GS IV, pp. 506-10, 523.
92. CF, p. 8; other references to Bonhoeffer's method throughout CF.
93. According to U. Köhler's notes.

for themselves. They want the new and only know the old. And thus they deny Christ the Lord.[94]

The theological advisers of the Christian Kaiser Verlag were far from enthusiastic about the manuscript. The Old Testament interpretation was too unconventional for them, and it was solely due to the insistence of Otto Salomon, the head of the firm, that it was accepted.

The booklet was in fact a first small literary success for Bonhoeffer. 'You will be pleased to hear that the *Kreuzzeitung* gave an excellent review to your *Creation and Fall* last week', his mother wrote to him in London.[95] The method, the language and the ideas all attracted attention. Wilhelm Vischer's *Christuszeugnis des Alten Testamentes* appeared only a year later. What were the critics to make of Bonhoeffer's work?

The *Kirchliche Anzeiger für Württemberg* of November 1934 remarked laconically that 'Bonhoeffer's theological basic principle might almost be described as the well-known *credo quia absurdum*'. Bonhoeffer's incursion into the field of the Old Testament specialists was taken amiss. The *Theologischen Blätter* said: 'At all events, it is no credit to the Old Testament specialists that nowadays non-specialists should be the first to attempt and present us with such an exegesis of Genesis 1-3.'[96] As in *Sanctorum Communio*, Bonhoeffer had again fallen between two stools. The exegetists regarded the work as systematics and the systematicians regarded it as exegesis. The former were indignant and the latter took no notice.[97]

As we have mentioned, *Creation and Fall* was the first book of Bonhoeffer's that Barth read;[98] though his attitude to it was critical, he nevertheless considered that there was sometimes greater fidelity to the text in Bonhoeffer's work than in the parallel passages in Wilhelm Vischer's book.

Bonhoeffer did not give up the idea of further such attempts at 'theological interpretation'. The content of what he said turned out to be more important than the demonstration of any 'theological method'. Today there is hardly anyone who does not have his doubts about the latter, but there can be no ignoring the profundity of his utterances, nor can it be denied that he provided the defences with good armour and equipment to detect and resist the enemy of the day. This eschatological interpretation of Creation represented no retreat from the world. *Creation and Fall* was aimed at the 'centre of life'. Never previously had

94. CF, p. 7.
95. Letter of 17.1.1934.
96. ThBl, 1934, No. 4, pp. 110-12.
97. Thus Eugen Gerstenmaier, for instance, in his *Die Kirche und die Schöpfung*, published in 1938, does not mention Bonhoeffer's book, though one of his chapter headings is 'Creation and Sin' and another is devoted to the problem of 'Act and Being' and is headed accordingly.
98. KD III/I, pp. 218 f.; cf. also Ch. VI, p. 136.

the idea of the centre of life as against its borders and margins played such a part in Bonhoeffer's mind.

It was an ethical uneasiness that led him to devote himself to the subject of this lecture. Ten years later it was again ethical uneasiness that caused him to return to the idea of the centre of life when he said that God was to be sought in the centre and not at the borders of reality.

Christology

In spite of its turbulence, the summer of 1933, in which he gave a course of lectures on Christology, was the high point of Bonhoeffer's academic career.

This he felt to be the hardest task he had yet undertaken; not because interruptions became more frequent, but because he was faced with the task of bringing together, preserving and testing out all he had previously thought, said and attempted.

Christology, which he had once regarded as having been so remarkably neglected in Holl's seminars on Luther, in the last resort lay behind the 'change' which he had referred to already in his 1931 lecture. It had been the magnetic or even the explosive centre of 'The Nature of the Church' of 1932; and it was to be the basis for ethics and serve as a defence against misuse of the concept of 'orders of creation'.

Was it not Christology that must most plainly reveal where liberal demolition of old formulae was right and where it was wrong, where the new theology of revelation laid bare the intentions behind ancient formulae, and from where one's own churchly or religious ties derived their convincing authority?

The students were expecting something. Otto Dudzus reports that during that restless summer an audience of nearly 200 sat through those demanding lectures:

He looked like a student himself when he mounted the platform. But then what he had to say so gripped us all that we were no longer there to listen to this very young man but we were there because of what he had to say —even though it was dreadfully early in the morning. I have never heard a lecture that impressed me nearly so much.

Bonhoeffer's own notes cannot be traced, but a large number of students' notes make possible a reasonably adequate reconstruction. His outline-summary was new and original at the time. In accordance with all that we know about his earlier lectures, he took as his point of departure the Christ who is present in the Word, in the sacrament, and in—what we have now learnt to recognize as a distinguishing feature of his theology—the community. Only then did he go on to deal with the 'historical Christ' and critical Christology in all its vicissitudes in the history of dogmatics, and its oscillation between old concepts of substance and more modern dynamic concepts. Only at the end did he set about attempting to develop a positive Christology, for which he had little time left. But the suggestions and formulations that he made recurred in his mind ten years later when he set about revising his theology.

When Bonhoeffer reached the high point of his academic life in 1933 he brought it to an end. The last thing he published of any serious theological concern was his comment on Heim's book in the December number of *Christentum und Wissenschaft*. From now on he would not enjoy the privileges of an academic position. The aged Titius expressed his regret in 1933: 'It is a great pity that our best hope in the faculty is being wasted on the church struggle.'

VI CHURCH

Ordination

Bonhoeffer, who had been refused ordination a year previously because he had not yet reached the required age of twenty-five, was ordained on 15th November 1931.

No one in his environment at that time discussed the laying on of hands as the real assurance of apostolic succession. A few years later he made the occasion and preparations for it an unforgettable experience for his candidates for ordination, but now it was not yet a matter of consequence that the laying on of hands should be carried out under the valid church auspices, and the importance that the ceremony was later to assume in his eyes did not yet exist for him. He did not seek out the ordinating ministers, none of whom were especially close to him either spiritually or personally, and later he hardly ever mentioned the occasion. That Sunday was not treated as an unusual one in the family, and in the afternoon he went tô see his friend Franz Hildebrandt, who was now assistant minister to Fendt at Heilsbronnen, and to hear his sermon on the centenary of Hegel's death.

He certainly attached importance to the genuineness of the *rite vocatus* in regard to the propagation of the Gospel and to the celebration of the sacrament, and less importance to the 'privileges of clerical status'. He regarded the latter as a danger rather than a prop to the authority of the ministry. It was during these weeks that he was so troubled by the problem of valid authority, when he wrote: 'How is one to preach such things to these people? . . . The invisibility breaks us to pieces.'[99] At the time of his ordination the so-called 'Harzburg front' was being talked about, the nationalist alliance under whose banner Hitler, Hugenberg, Seldte and Schacht presented themselves on 11th October 1931 as

99. To H. Rössler, 18.10.1931, GS I, p. 61.

the saviours of Germany from chaos. Bonhoeffer, however, saw no hope in such guardians of Christian Germany. He wrote:

Will our church survive another catastrophe? Will it not be all up if we do not immediately become quite different? Talk differently, live differently . . . ?[100]

Student Chaplain

An ordained university lecturer in the service of the Church was not free to seek out a ministry at his pleasure. Under the regulations of the General Synod of 1930, he was subject to another year's 'auxiliary service' at the discretion of the church authorities.

The post to which he was appointed was the entirely new one of chaplain to the students of the Technical University at Charlottenburg. According to the *Christliche Welt*,[101] in the winter of 1931-2 there were only twenty Protestant chaplains in all the universities in Germany, though the Catholics had thirty-seven. The ever alert General Superintendent Otto Dibelius had been advocating the appointment of a chaplain to the Technical University since 1930, and his proposal had now been accepted.

Bonhoeffer's work in this post was not successful. He hardly succeeded in making his position and purposes known. The Berlin S.C.M. had its weakest bastion at the Technical University at Berlin-Charlottenburg, and nothing in the nature of a student group developed under Bonhoeffer's influence. Before it did develop there intervened the years of terror during which, among other things, the S.C.M. was compulsorily dissolved; during those years a new understanding of church life grew and developed viable forms. Bonhoeffer's work at the Technical University preceded the upheaval in which the arts faculties were forced out of the Church under totalitarian pressure and the scientists acquired a new relationship with it.

Bonhoeffer procured a notice-board, but in the multitude of other notices displayed it hardly attracted attention. He secured himself a room for two hours weekly in a hut in the student quarters, and somewhere or other he found a room for weekly prayers; four of his short sermons have survived.[102] He tried to make contact with the student associations, and at one of them he held a discussion meeting on Christianity and technology. With Hanns Lilje, the Secretary General of the S.C.M., who had attended the Cambridge conference, he arranged a series of talks at the Technical University in January and February 1932; Lilje spoke on 'Technology, Man and God', Stolzenburg on 'Occultism

100. To E. Sutz, 8.10.1931, GS I, p. 24.
101. CW, 1932, p. 669.
102. GS IV, pp. 137-46.

and Christianity', and Bonhoeffer on 'The Right to Self-Preservation'. He wanted to address himself to a basic feeling existing among the students at that time and discuss the spreading Nazi 'biological' philosophy. He started out from what had become the dispensability of mass man—a phenomenon also prevalent among the academic 'proletariat'—and ended with the assertion of a right to dispose of one's own life in self-sacrifice for others, for the nation and for humanity. The talk shows how greatly Bonhoeffer was still impressed by Indian ideals; he contrasted the 'Indian' answer to the question of life, namely that suffering is better than living by violence, with the 'Western' answer. He actually risked giving a cautious pacifist note to what he said. War and machinery were aspects of the Western solution, he said, but 'the machine has made war impossible, not just through its idea of subjecting nature to man and letting him live like that, but also because of its reality'.[103]

Bonhoeffer succeeded in having these talks announced in the student journal *Die Technische Hochschule*, but only after they were nearly over. The same issue also at last carried a short article about the newly established student chaplaincy.[104] It was a conscientious effort to address the students and communicate to them a sense of the Church's presence.

Bonhoeffer wished to make the Church an interesting place, in which things happened; a place where answers were to be found even when others had ceased to provide them; but the Church was not an institution that weakly ran after everything and everybody. It was only on this basis that he wished to identify himself with it. He also tried at the same time to ascribe to it self-awareness and solidarity.

The sermons he preached as students' chaplain show little sign of being affected by the fact that he was addressing technicians and scientists. In fact, he had no pulpit of his own at the Technical University; his sermons were part of the programme of Bronisch-Holtze, the students' chaplain at Berlin University. The latter had been minister of Trinity Church in the centre of Old Berlin for a considerable time, and Bonhoeffer's congregation also consisted predominantly of students from the University, not from the Technical University which was over on the west side of Berlin.

The Charlottenburg post fulfilled Bonhoeffer's statutory obligations from 1931 to 1933 and enabled him to obtain the pulpit that he desired, though elsewhere. His university lectures and his sermons at Bronisch-Holtze's church led to a student group gathering round him. When he sought helpers for the Charlottenburg settlement two theological students but only one student from the Technical University came forward. Before he left for London in 1933 he made two serious efforts to obtain a ministry in Berlin. His view of the prospects of the students' chaplaincy at the Technical University were so discouraging that there

103. GS III, p. 268.
104. *Die Technische Hochschule*, 1932, No. 99, pp. 200 f.

was no thought of continuing with it for the time being in view of the new political difficulties, and Bonhoeffer left without a successor being appointed. On the basis of his final report, Bishop Karow suggested establishing a teaching post in philosophy at the Technical University to be filled by a theologian, but in 1934 this was no longer feasible.

Confirmation Class at Wedding

While he was working on his first lectures, in addition to his ecumenical and student chaplaincy work, he received instruction to take over a confirmation class in the Zion parish in Wedding which was out of control; the minister responsible was at the end of his tether, and in fact a few weeks later he died. Bonhoeffer wrote to Sutz that he had 'more or less literally been harassed to death'.[105]

According to Bonhoeffer's own account, his first encounter with the fifty boys who were running wild took place that autumn as follows. The aged minister and Bonhoeffer slowly walked up the stairs of the school building, which was several storeys high, while the boys looked over the banisters, making an indescribable din and dropping things on them. When they reached the top, the minister tried to force the throng back into the class-room by shouting and using physical force. He tried to announce that he had brought them a new minister who was going to teach them in future, and that his name was Bonhoeffer, and when they heard the name they started shouting 'Bon! Bon! Bon!' louder and louder. The old man left the scene in despair, leaving Bonhoeffer standing silently against the wall with his hands in his pockets. Minutes passed. The fact that he failed to react gradually made the noise less enjoyable, and he began speaking quietly, so that only the boys in the front row could catch a few words of what he said. Suddenly silence fell. Bonhoeffer merely remarked that they had put up a remarkable initial performance, and went on to tell them a story about Harlem. Next he said that, if they wanted to listen to him, he would tell them more next time. Then he told them they could go, and after that he had no more cause to complain about their lack of attentiveness.

This is practically the most fantastic district in Berlin, with the most difficult social and political conditions [he wrote]. At first the boys behaved as if they were crazy, so that for the first time I had real difficulties with discipline. But one thing helped here, namely that I quite simply told them stories from the Bible wholesale, and described eschatological passages. I also had to fall back on telling them stories about Negroes. Now absolute quiet prevails, the boys see to it themselves . . .[106]

The Wedding experience made a deep impact on Bonhoeffer. When it

105. GS I, p. 25.
106. To E. Sutz, 25.12.1931, GS I, p. 25.

was decided that he should continue with the class and take it to the stage of confirmation, he reduced his other obligations to the minimum, and at New Year 1932 he left his parents' house in Grunewald and rented a room with a master baker called Heide at 61 Oderbergerstrasse, north of the Alexanderplatz, thus living in the same district as his proletarian pupils. When one of them was faced with a serious operation and he wanted to help him, he unconcernedly left his students to wait in the lecture room.[107] 'I devoted the second half of the term almost completely to the boys preparing for confirmation.'[108] He vividly described to Sutz how he set about the task of teaching them:

It is completely new to them to be asked to do anything but learn the catechism. I based all my teaching on the community idea, and the boys, who daily hear talk of political organizations, see very plainly what it is all about.[109]

Henceforward his free evenings were devoted to his confirmation candidates. They were allowed to come and see him uninvited, to play chess or have English lessons. At Christmas each received a present. At week-ends he took them to youth hostels. Such exercises in community living were still unknown in ordinary German parishes.

. . . also they see the boundary lines with incredible clarity, so that, when we talked about the Holy Spirit in the community, over and over again they pointed out that in reality everything was quite different, in all this the congregation lags far behind any political youth club or sports club. Yes, in the club we feel at home, but in church?[110]

The pleasure of teaching and gaining the confidence of difficult or refractory boys was counterbalanced by the difficulties he experienced in pastoral visits. He felt he did not match up to the task, and that his theological training had failed to equip him for it. It cost him a tremendous effort to ring uninvited at a strange door and make himself and his purpose known. True, the son of the house gave him a talking point, but:

How painful are those hours or minutes when another or myself try to begin a pastoral conversation, and how hesitantly and lamely it proceeds . . .
Sometimes I try to console myself with the thought that this kind of pastoral work is something that did not exist in earlier times and is quite unchristian. But perhaps our failure in this respect is really the end of our Christianity. We have learnt to preach again, at any rate a little, but the care of souls?[111]

Five years later Bonhoeffer was able to give his candidates for ordina-

107. IKDB, pp. 58, 65 f.
108. To E. Sutz, 26.2.1932, GS I, p. 27.
109. GS I, pp. 27 f.
110. GS I, p. 28.
111. GS I, p. 29.

tion at Finkenwalde the courage to carry out such pastoral work; and another five years later he discovered the right way to approach and talk to a type of human being that was not so very different from the Wedding type. This was in the situation of human solidarity created by prison.

When the confirmation day approached, Bonhoeffer distributed a big bale of cloth for making confirmation suits. The boys' help was requested in the writing of the sermon by their being asked to say what they expected of it. On the day itself, 13th March 1932, election fever prevailed in the streets; Hitler was standing for the Presidency of the Reich for the first time. In fact Hindenburg obtained 49 per cent of the votes, Hitler 30 per cent, Thälmann, the Communist, 13 per cent and Duesterberg of the Stahlhelm 7 per cent. But the confirmation service proceeded undisturbed. Bonhoeffer preached on Jacob at Jabbok:[112]

No one shall ever deprive you of your faith, that God has in readiness for you a day and a sun and a dawn, that he guides us to this sun which is called Jesus Christ, that he wishes us to see the Promised Land in which justice and peace and love prevail, because Christ prevails.

He rephrased the official vow that he made his candidates take so that it contained nothing false or impossible to fulfil, and subsequently he always did the same; the words that he used for a confirmation in 1938 have survived.[113] At the celebration of communion he invited them to an evening service two days afterwards.

A few days later he took a party of the boys he had confirmed to Friedrichsbrunn at his own expense; he had obtained his parents' permission for this invasion of their country house for Easter. To the boys from Wedding the 150-mile trip was like a journey to the end of the world.

Bonhoeffer wrote his parents a letter of thanks:

I am delighted to be able to be here with the confirmation boys; even though they do not show any special appreciation of the woods and nature, they are very keen on climbing parties in the Bode valley and playing football in the field. It is often by no means easy to keep these mostly very unsocially brought-up boys under control, but the domesticity and inhibitions that this imposes upon them is by itself a great help. Also I think that afterwards you will not notice any after-effects on the house as a result of these occupants. Apart from a broken window-pane, everything is as it was . . . Only Frau S. [the housekeeper] is somewhat indignant at the proletarian invasion. Hans Christoph is here with me, and is a great help. It is only possible to get any work done in the early morning (literally from seven to nine o'clock) and later in the evening, when they have all gone to bed. On Thursday it will all be over. After such an experience one wonders of course what the value of such an enterprise may have been.

112. GS IV, pp. 44-50.
113. GS I, p. 27.

But in things of this sort one has to wait and see . . .[114]

Bonhoeffer's work in Wedding officially came to an end with the confirmation, but his influence and his pastoral work did not. 'The teaching I gave them was such that I cannot just stop.'[115] 'I have rented nine acres of land outside Berlin and am putting a little wooden house on it. I intend to spend my week-ends there with confirmation candidates and students.'[116] The boys from Wedding were allowed to go to Biesenthal whenever they liked. A number of them remained in contact with Bonhoeffer until well into the Second World War, and one of them, Richard Rother, was employed in his brother Klaus's lawyer's office. He published a brief account of how Bonhoeffer taught them.[117]

Youth Club

The Wedding experience was soon supplemented by another: the Charlottenburg youth club experiment. Behind this idea lay his acquaintance with Harry Ward's work in New York, as well as his contact with Siegmund-Schultze and his social work in east Berlin, with which Hildebrandt was associated; Bonhoeffer was also in contact with Siegmund-Schultze in connection with his new ecumenical duties.

Some of the supporters of the project were non-Christians or people without definite connections with the Church. Anneliese Schnurmann, who had been a school-friend of Dietrich's sister Susanne and was of Jewish origin and now a student, wished to use part of her wealth for social and educational purposes. The Charlottenburg project was decided on in the summer of 1932 at a gathering of family and friends in Dietrich's grandmother, Julie Bonhoeffer's room. The latter encouraged the project and took part in the discussion of the first practical steps.

The youth club in the Schlossstrasse in Charlottenburg opened in the autumn of 1932. There were successes, but difficulties were also encountered with trouble-makers and drinkers, and there were lively arguments with young Communists.

There has been some trouble at the club . . . Z., together with A., seems to have made himself very unpopular with the boys. A few days ago, apparently when he was drunk, he gave himself out to be the club leader. I think we shall have to get rid of him as quickly as possible. Otherwise there will be a real row. Apart from that, things are still going well. But we are thinking of moving. The premises are getting too small. What do you think about that? Two theology students are helping in the work. There is also a student from the Technical University who would be glad

114. Letter of 28.3.1932.
115. GS I, p. 27.
116. To E. Sutz, 17.5.1932, GS I, pp. 32 f.
117. R. Rother, 'A Confirmation Class in Wedding', IKDB, p. 57.

to earn 25 marks a month and can spend three evenings a week at the club.[118]

The new premises were made ready at the end of November, the boys worked hard to help, and the move took place on 1st December. On 8th December Bonhoeffer invited Anneliese Schnurmann to the opening party:

There will be sausages, cakes and cigarettes. The boys worked really splendidly during the last few days, and this is a treat that we must give them. The whole thing will cost 20 marks . . . As for the Technical University student, I thought it would be a good idea for him to come three evenings a week, give shorthand lessons and help in other ways, for which he would receive 15 marks from parish funds and 15 marks from you.

The club flourished for only a very short time. As a result of Hitler's accession to power on 30th January 1933, Anneliese Schnurmann had to leave Germany. Communist members of the club were molested in the street and, when it became known that the club was going to be raided, Bonhoeffer spirited them away to his wooden hut at Biesenthal for a short time; they then scattered to different parts of Berlin. When the club was searched in the hope of finding the card index, the organizers had to reconcile themselves to closing it. Concern for the unemployed workers now yielded to concern for another, far more deeply branded, category, the Jews.

New Plans

Harlem, followed by Wedding and the youth club, led Bonhoeffer to aspire to a ministry in the overcrowded slums of east Berlin. The prescribed year's 'auxiliary service' ended in the autumn of 1932, and he could now set about finding himself a parish. The specialized work of a students' chaplain no longer interested him. Seeking a position in west Berlin, to which he belonged, seemed too easy a course, and working in proletarian east Berlin was much more important. Faced with the choice between university and parish work in east Berlin, he was ready to follow a call to the latter.

At present I am faced with a pretty momentous decision, whether to undertake a ministry at Friedrichshain in east Berlin at Easter . . . So perhaps when you next come to Berlin you will be able to come and see me at the rectory at Friedrichshain, but perhaps not . . .[119]

However, in the vote by the parish council on 28th February 1933 Bonhoeffer was defeated by forty-seven to twenty-five.

Thus his first application failed. He was too young, his preaching

118. To A. Schnurmann, 23.11.1932.
119. To K.-F. Bonhoeffer, 12.1.1933, GS III, p. 24.

too severe, and the demands he made on his congregation too strange. His rival was too popular. Subsequently he never talked about this setback. The failure of his next attempt made a bigger impact on him.

He, and Franz Hildebrandt with him, did not drop the idea of an appointment in east Berlin. The prospect of an appointment for both of them arose, again in Superintendent Zimmermann's area, at the Lazarus Church, still deeper in east Berlin, between the Frankfurter Allee and the Warsaw Bridge. But the Aryan clause was about to be extended to the Church, and this made Hildebrandt's appointment doubtful. Bonhoeffer wrote to Barth:

... I knew that I could not accept the ministry I had wanted unless I were willing to give up my attitude of unconditional opposition to this church, unless I were willing to make my ministry unconvincing in advance, and were willing to drop my solidarity with the Jewish Christian ministers— my closest friend is one of them and is now faced with a void. So the alternative of becoming lecturer or minister, and certainly not a minister in Prussia, remained.[120]

Thus Bonhoeffer's wish for closer contact with the working class was frustrated by the political upheaval. In September 1934, when he visited Jean Lasserre's parish in the coal-mining area of northern France, the wish revived again; and ten years later he was reminded of Wedding and the youth club when he again met the proletariat in army uniform in Tegel prison. In a play which he tried to write there, one of the characters is a gifted but mistrustful working-class man named Heinrich.[121] The play is based on the encounter between this under-privileged and rootless individual and the bourgeois Christoph. Both have suffered war wounds, and death has set its mark on them; the theme is the attempt to overcome Heinrich's mistrust by a supreme trust.

Bonhoeffer had little time to concern himself seriously with church politics between 1931 and 1933. Perhaps he was still too aloof in the matter. Nevertheless a wedding was celebrated at Königsberg in 1931 with the bridegroom in a brown shirt, and the Horst Wessel[122] song was sung in church. Also in 1931 Greifswald reported an action for slander against a theology student who had refused an invitation from the republican students' association on the ground that he could not associate with people who had 'betrayed their fatherland for money'.[123] In 1932 Röhm, the S.A. Chief of Staff, appointed chaplains to brown-shirt formations, and Goebbels was married in a Protestant church with a swastika flag on the altar;[124] and at the church elections in November

120. Letter of 24.10.1933, GS II, p. 131.
121. GS III, pp. 478-95.
122. Horst Wessel, the Nazi hero, killed in a brawl, who was later considered a martyr.
123. CW, 1931, pp. 694, 740.
124. CW, 1932, pp. 142, 1103.

1932 in Berlin the 'German Christians' won 2,282 seats on church councils while their opponents won 2,419. Were these developments to be ignored?

It was partly for reasons of taste that Bonhoeffer did not take part in public debate on nationalistic race questions in the Church. Instead, in 1932 he joined a small circle of colleagues that was later to become an important nucleus of Martin Niemöller's Emergency League of Pastors.[125] A study group of theologically active ministers used to meet at the house of Gerhard Jacobi, the minister of the Kaiser Wilhelm Memorial Church, to discuss matters coming under the heading of 'Church and Ministry'. It was here that in April 1933 he presented his first broadsheet attacking the Aryan clause. But his criticism and his unusual approach, though it made him a stimulating member of the group, led him into a certain isolation. His own view was 'that there are a lot of lively people here, but almost no one with whom one can reasonably discuss theology'.[126] 'We are both beings who are somehow on the margin of our church.'[127]

Behind all that he did and did not do there was still the feeling that something lay ahead of him that remained to be discovered and lived through. Every now and then the thought crossed his mind that India had something to offer that he must investigate.

I can hardly think of it [his stay in America] without feeling violently attracted by the idea of going abroad again, this time to the East. I don't yet know when. But it cannot be much longer delayed. There must be other people in the world who know more than we do. And in that case it is simply philistine not to go and learn from them. At all events, those people are not the Nazis, and nor are they our Communists as I got to know them during the past winter. The Germans are hopelessly set in a fixed direction, in which one can see and know more than the Americans do, but that is not much yet.[128]

Preaching

With his self-tormenting search for a personal commitment, Bonhoeffer may not strike us as an attractive figure during this period, and his search for a one-sided church theology may strike us as immature. He was obviously unsure of what he wanted, and kept withdrawing himself or pursuing new ideas. Only as a preacher do we find him fully giving himself; to this role he devoted himself without reservation or qualification. Preaching was the great event in his life; the hard theologizing and all the critical love of his church were all for its

125. Cf. Ch. VII, pp. 240 f.
126. To E. Sutz, 17.5.1932, GS I, p. 32.
127. To E. Sutz, 27.10.1932, GS I, p. 36.
128. To E. Sutz, 17.5.1932, GS I, p. 32.

sake, for in it the message of Christ, the bringer of peace, was proclaimed. To Bonhoeffer nothing in his calling competed in importance
with preaching.

In Barcelona his preaching had still been accompanied by the
pleasure of youthful discovery. In New York he had been shocked to
discover that it was 'degraded to marginal ecclesiastical observations
about events of the day', 'the quoting of edifying instances . . . willing
descriptions of one's own religious experiences, to which of course no
binding character is attributed in practice'.[129] But now, in the Berlin
of 1931-2, his preaching acquired an urgency vibrant with his own
questioning and demanding action. There must be no self-deception, no
use of religion as an opiate, he insisted, for 'the living Jesus wishes
himself to tell the world from the pulpit that in those in whom he
enters fear vanishes'.[130] 'Every sermon must be an event', he said to
Franz Hildebrandt.

The Gospel cannot be preached . . . tangibly enough. A truly evangelical
sermon must be like offering a child a fine red apple or offering a thirsty
man a cool glass of water and saying: Wouldn't you like it?[131]

He always began working on his monthly sermon very early. Then,
when the idea and the form that it should take were fixed in his mind,
he wrote it out word for word in a single draft, and subsequently made
very few corrections. Consequently nearly all his sermons could be
posthumously printed exactly as they were delivered.

Sermons on specific texts were rarer than they had been in Barcelona,
but he still showed independence in his choice of passage; indeed, the
passage selected was a sort of sermon on the situation in itself. He
showed greater fidelity to the text now, and drew just one message
from it and impressed this on his hearers as the theme. Thus, on two
consecutive Sundays when he deputized for Jacobi at the Kaiser Wilhelm
Memorial Church he preached two entirely different sermons on the
same brief text from Colossians.[132] He did not yet preach so exclusively
Christocentrically as he did later at Finkenwalde, or in so ardently an
eschatological way as he did in London.

Though he often took liberties with his text, he avoided modernist
tricks which twisted the meaning to make direct comment on current
events in politics and the Church. Nevertheless the reference to events
of the day, in so far as we can reconstruct them, are unmistakable. The
contemporary hearer was well and convincingly orientated.

His sermon on Harvest Thanksgiving Day 1931 was preached against
the background of coming unemployment and hunger during the

129. GS I, pp. 77, 86.
130. 15.1.1933, GS IV, p. 105.
131. 29.5.1932, GS IV, p. 51.
132. On 12.6.1932 and 19.6.1932, GS IV, pp. 60 ff., 69 ff.

winter. He looked at the situation beyond the narrow confines of Germany. 'We must count on seven million workless in Germany this winter, in other words that from fifteen to twenty million people will go hungry, another twelve million or more in Britain, twenty million or more in America, and sixteen million are now starving in China; and in India the situation is not much better.'[133]

At the beginning of June Brüning finally resigned and Papen became Reich Chancellor. Many Germans expected a restoration of stability from a Christian and conservative government. But on 12th June 1932 Bonhoeffer outspokenly preached against the misuse of the name of God by the Papen Government.

We read that a government has proclaimed that a whole nation is to be saved from collapse—by the Christian attitude to life. So we, both individuals and nation, are escaping from an inconceivable catastrophe. 'In the name of God, amen', is again to be the slogan, religion is again to be cultivated, and the Christian view of life is to be spread. How meagre, weak and pitiful all this sounds. Are we really to be taken in again by this 'In the name of God, amen'? Do we really believe that we shall be governed by it in our actions? That we, rich and poor, Germans and Frenchmen, will allow ourselves to be united by the name of God? Or is there not concealed behind our religious trends our ungovernable urge to . . . power—in the name of God to do what we want, and in the name of the Christian attitude to life to stir up and play off one nationality against another? . . . It is not our irreligiousness that is disobedience to God, but the fact that we are very glad to be religious . . . very relieved when some government proclaims the Christian attitude to life . . . so that the more pious we are the less we have to tell ourselves that God is dangerous, that he is not mocked.[134]

A week later, again in the Kaiser Wilhelm Memorial Church, he attacked the Church for having given a false twist to the words 'seek the things that are above' from the Epistle to the Colossians: the Church, he said, was using what was in reality a stubborn worldly protest as a drug to produce spurious self-satisfaction. He then went on to speak some words the clairvoyance of which, still unrealized by himself, was to become plain only ten years later:

We should not be surprised if times come for our church, too, when the blood of martyrs will be called for. But this blood, if we really have the courage and the fidelity to shed it, will not be so innocent and clear as that of the first who testified. On our blood a great guilt would lie: that of the useless servant.[135]

Bonhoeffer well understood the emotions of those years, but saw through them:

133. GS IV, pp. 20 f.; cf. similar references in letter to E. Sutz, 8.10.1931. GS I, pp. 23 f.
134. GS IV, pp. 65 f.
135. GS IV, p. 71.

It is not difficult at present to talk of freedom, and to do so in such a way that a German's passions are roused and agitate him so completely that he forgets everything else. In present-day Germany there may be many like the Israelites of old in captivity who, deeply absorbed in themselves, were able to dream of nothing but liberty, and saw great visions of it and grasped for it, until they awakened and the vision faded . . .[136]

He spoke these words on 24th July 1932. On 31st July nearly 38 per cent of the German electorate voted for Hitler's party.

When Bonhoeffer mounted the pulpit again after the late summer vacation of 1932 there was another election, and Hitler's share of the vote dropped to about 33 per cent. Bonhoeffer directed his words, not so much at the German people, as at the Church, which was celebrating the anniversary of the Reformation. What he said was more provocative than before:

It should gradually have become clear to us that we are in the eleventh hour of the life of our Evangelical Church, so that not much more time remains before it is decided whether all is up with it or whether a new day is to begin . . .'The fanfares of the Reformation celebrations are the fanfares for a funeral.' The day of the Reformation celebrations is an evil day. The thousand fanfares that today bear witness to the mortal illness of Germany also proclaim the death of the Church in the world . . . The Church of the Reformation . . . does not see that whenever it says 'God', God turns against it. We sing 'Ein feste Burg ist unser Gott', . . . but God says: 'I have this against you'.[137] The church that is celebrating the Reformation does not allow Luther to lie in peace, he has to be dragged in to justify all the evil that is taking place in the Church. The dead man is stood up in our churches, made to stretch out his hands and point to this church, and repeat with self-confident pathos: Here I stand, I can do no other . . . It is simply untrue, or it is unpardonable frivolity and pride, when we entrench ourselves behind that saying. We can do otherwise! . . .[138]

He went on to ask what was the point of all the protests in the churches against secularism and godlessness, against Catholicism, disbelief and immorality, against all those who took no notice of the protest of that day. 'Leave the dead Luther in peace at last and listen to the Gospel.' He ended his sermon to members of the Church of the Reformation, who had learnt their 'by faith alone', as follows:

It may sound almost indecent on Reformation day . . . : Do the first things . . . The story of the destruction of Jerusalem by pagans is beginning to have a terribly close significance for us. How it may come about—we shall prefer today to avoid magniloquence about our heroic deeds in such a catastrophe—the Lord, he is God![139]

136. GS IV, pp. 81 f.
137. Bonhoeffer's text was Rev. 2: 4 ff.
138. GS IV, pp. 93 f.
139. GS IV, p. 100.

Before many weeks passed a new note crept into Bonhoeffer's sermons. They grew more consolatory, more confident of victory, and also more defiant. The first sermon after Hitler's accession to power dealt with Gideon, the champion of God, who attacked and conquered with an absurdly small force.

VII ECUMENISM

1. *Work at Home*

When he returned from Cambridge as a youth secretary of the ecumenical movement, his first task was to gain closer acquaintance with the ecumenical organizations already active in Germany and to associate himself with their activities as quickly as possible. Many welcomed him as a stimulating force, while others regarded him as an ambitious interloper.

The German Centre. While he was still in America the various groups had united to form an umbrella organization called the German Coordination Office for Ecumenical Youth Work. This had three tasks: a) the joint theological study of ecumenical problems, which necessarily tended to overstep the limits of 'youth work'—in fact a number of older and more experienced theologians spoke at the first big conference in April 1932; b) the improvement of propaganda for the ecumenical idea; and c) the organization of information services, conferences and international exchanges.

Thus, when Bonhoeffer returned from Cambridge, an agency was already in existence that provided him with a base from which to work. As an international secretary he soon began to play an important part.

The chief obstacles were financial and political. Soon after the Cambridge conference H. L. Henriod wrote to his impatient and busily planning youth secretary that it had been decided at Cambridge that 'the youth commission should be active and effective to the maximum with a minimum of means'.[140] When Bonhoeffer pointed out that 'at present we cannot expect any German member to be in a position to contribute himself',[141] Henriod sent him the reassuring information that the Geneva budget had been increased.

The political difficulties had to be met at home. The Hirsch-Althaus statement of 1931 made an especial impact in the youth sector. The *Christliche Welt* of 1st February 1932 said:

The national leader of the German Evangelical youth organizations, Dr. Stange, has replied to an invitation to international meetings that the send-

140. Letter of 28.10.1931.
141. Letter of 14.2.1932.

ing of a delegation from Germany is out of the question and that a clear word of protest against wrong and oppression must be expected.[142]

This reply of Stange's was announced even before the Geneva disarmament conference had begun. The German Y.M.C.A. associated itself with Stange's statement. Bonhoeffer found delegates such as Karl G. Steck, Karl Nold, Dietrich von Oppen and Werner Koch, who was recommended to him by Lilje. All these were ready to attend such 'international meetings' in spite of the slanderous attacks that this involved.

a) The centre made a good beginning with a theological conference at the Central Church Office on 29th-30th April 1932. It was typically German, and also completely typical of Dietrich Bonhoeffer. It was typically German in the sense that it was exclusively concerned with the theological basis of ecumenical work; in 1934 Dr. William Temple, then Archbishop of York, wrote rather impatiently to his wife:

The Germans can never discuss what to do tomorrow without showing how their view depends on the divine purpose in creation—the existence of which must therefore be first established.[143]

The 'divine purpose in creation' was indeed a primary purpose of the discussion. How quickly the severest consequences became evident in 1933 depended on one's view of that 'purpose'. The subjects for discussion at the conference were what Bonhoeffer regarded as the two basic questions underlying ecumenical work, namely 'The Church and the Churches' and 'The Church and the Nations', i.e. the confessional question and the peace question, or, to put it differently, the continuum of tradition and the problem of the present day. The chief debate ranged round the question of the nation and its 'creative' dignity. Though profound divisions appeared and Bonhoeffer noted a 'deep bewilderment' that made necessary a continuation of the conference in the autumn, he made preparations for it gladly and with a good conscience, contributed to it vigorously, and finally reported on it at length.[144] The antagonisms that appear in Bonhoeffer's report already show the fronts that crystallized out in the later church struggle: the German Christians and their church committees, the Lutheran Council, the moderate and the radical Confessing churches.

Bonhoeffer was the youngest speaker at the conference, and he was not satisfied with any of the theological arguments that were presented. Supported by Lilje, he opposed the older generation, and maintained that ecumenical work was evading the truth if it did not grapple anew with the concept and fact of 'heresy'. He vigorously attacked the idea of 'orders of creation' introduced into his speeches by Wilhelm Stählin.

142. CW, 1932, p. 142; *Die Eiche*, 1932, pp. 253 f.
143. F. A. Iremonger, *William Temple*, 1948, p. 403.
144. GS I, pp. 121 ff.

Peter, a member of the Nazi Party and later German Christian Bishop of Magdeburg, talked with tireless loquacity about the advance of 'formations ready for the defence' of the State and the nation, and he was the first to hand to Bonhoeffer copies of his excessively long speeches to be printed in the conference proceedings.

b) Bonhoeffer's report of the discussions in *Die Eiche* was intended to be in preparation for the second conference, to be held on 9th and 10th December 1932. The invitation to the latter, signed by him and Stählin, said: 'In connection with our previous discussion, this time both the questions raised will be discussed, i.e. the theological place of the nation and the meaning of confession in connection with the ecumenical movement.' This time the conference was associated with the meeting in Berlin of the German Ecumenical Study Group, on which Stockholm and Lausanne and the World Alliance and their sub-committees—still to some extent peaceably—had a vote.

c) The work was continued at a subsequent conference of the Central Church Office at Dassel on 6th-9th March 1933.

Two speeches on the confessional problem made by Bonhoeffer at the conference have survived. Both are very condensed, and in them he shows himself already to have been the conscious Lutheran that he had always wanted to be in the ecumenical movement and that he later showed himself to be in his 1935 statement of principles. He insists on two things, the necessity of avoiding the danger of confessional relativism on the one hand, and on the other the necessity of loosening up the rigidity of confessional absolutism. One of the subjects of the Dassel conference was 'Confession and Truth', and he tries to show that the truth of the word is double-sided, in that it represents both the word of God and the confessional word of the Christian congregation.

Ecumenical dialogue is achieved in confessional profession of faith and thus exposing oneself to others in human modesty . . . The Lutheran message is this recognition of the Church in atonement.[145]

This theological proposition that he advanced at Dassel we meet again in more developed form in his struggle to secure a place for the Confessing Church in the ecumenical movement in later years.

Local Work. Bonhoeffer could not completely evade the calls on him made by local and national organizations of the World Alliance. The latter had been instrumental in securing him entry into the ecumenical movement, and was in fact his base. A busy study programme was organized for 1932 in Berlin, and as part of this, with his fresh memories of the subject, he reported on the so-called 'social gospel'. He did not rely solely on his own impressions, but devoted a great deal of correspondence to securing a copy of Visser 't Hooft's book on the subject, which was very difficult

145. GS I, p. 180.

to obtain. Bonhoeffer's criticism of the social gospel was less violent than was expected. While he criticized its shortcomings at conferences abroad, at home he regarded it as more important to do justice to its merits. The Kingdom of God 'on earth is truly Biblical and is the opposite of an other-worldly view of the Kingdom'.[146]

At the national level of work for the World Alliance, the wind was blowing more and more strongly against the ecumenical movement, which was denounced for 'internationalism' and for pacifist tendencies. In 1932 the annual conference of the German branch of the movement had to be cancelled; the excuse given was the disastrous financial position. In 1933, after invitations to delegates and guests had been issued to a conference at Herrnhut, they had to be withdrawn, obviously for political reasons. For a time the World Alliance lived on in local but very lively cells in the German provinces, but at the national level it ceased to exist in 1932. In 1933, if local cells wished to cling to the view, so passionately held by Bonhoeffer, that peace on earth was a commandment of the Gospel, and wanted to build anew on the ever more unavoidable basis of a 'confession', they had to renounce all publicity and go down into the catacombs.

The position of the more official church organizations of 'Life and Work' and 'Faith and Order' was rather better.

After the 1932 meetings they began taking an interest in the young theologian who laid such emphasis on theology. Thus in 1933 'Faith and Order' invited him to join the German preparatory committee of the Lausanne movement, and he was invited to a meeting in the autumn.[147] Among the pioneers of this movement were Wilhelm Zoellner, Martin Dibelius, Hermann Sasse, Georg Wobbermin, Heinz Renkewitz and August Lang. Bonhoeffer was to have become a member of a working party that was to prepare for the conference to mark the tenth anniversary of the foundation of 'Faith and Order' in 1937, but his departure for London frustrated this. Bonhoeffer's contacts with 'Faith and Order' were revived through Hodgson, the secretary-general, in 1935. An important correspondence ensued, but did not result in cooperation; on the contrary, deep and perhaps tragic differences were revealed.[148]

2. *International Youth Secretary*

Bonhoeffer's chief ecumenical labours were concerned with relations with churches abroad. In relation to most of his German colleagues, his combination of experience of foreign countries, familiarity with foreign languages, then unusual among German theologians, and theological

146. GS I, p. 110.
147. Letter to Bonhoeffer from Bishop Jensen of the Moravian Brethren, 6.10.1933.
148. Cf. Ch. IX, pp. 398 ff.

training put him in a class by himself. True, to his foreign opposite numbers, particularly those from English-speaking countries, he sometimes seemed only too German with his shackling and unpractical devotion to theological analysis; they nevertheless noted, not just his obstinacy, but his charm and humour and good-fellowship.

He himself felt as if he were in a magnetic field in which attracting and repelling forces violently alternated. Nowhere else did he find so many allies for his continual call for peace as among these foreigners, but they showed little understanding of his theological argument for it.

In October 1931, i.e. soon after his return from Cambridge, he sent the first letters to organizations in his area in preparation for the big youth conference planned for 1932. He wanted preparations to be made in good time, to have facts, figures and ideas ready for discussion of the unemployment problem, for example.

This conference, to be held at Gland, was his first major objective. In accordance with a tradition that had now been established for several years, a number of so-called regional conferences were also planned. The first that Bonhoeffer attended was an Anglo-French conference at Epsom, Surrey, associated with a routine meeting of the youth committee in London.

The conference took place at the beginning of April 1932. As an Anglo-French affair it lay outside the field of Bonhoeffer's responsibilities; it was organized by Craske and Toureille. Bonhoeffer was a critical guest, as his report in *Die Eiche* shows.[149] He believed that a strictly theological basis for such a meeting should have been worked out in advance, and in particular he criticized the excessive prevalence of a 'fine feeling of international friendship'. He was too impatient to be satisfied with mere exchange of information. Thus, in spite of his appreciation of the excellent hospitality provided, in a private letter to Sutz he rather off-handedly dismissed the affair as 'a very superfluous meeting'.

He took a more favourable view of the Franco-German regional conference organized by Toureille and himself at Westerburg in the Westerwald on 12th-14th July. The subject was 'The Unity of Franco-German Protestantism between Catholicism and Bolshevism'. The conference was overshadowed by the old Franco-German tension, which had been acutely revived at that moment, because the unyielding attitude of the French spokesmen had made the Geneva disarmament negotiations hopeless and the German delegation had withdrawn. But the direct confrontation of young people from both countries was very well worth while. Papers for discussion had been 'long since prepared and in part exchanged'. Bonhoeffer spoke first, and was followed by Karl Nold and a Frenchman. In the evening Fritz Söhlmann and August de Haas, the Reformed minister from Dresden who later became an un-

149. GS I, pp. 119 f.

compromising champion of the Confessing Church, dealt with the question from the German viewpoint. He told the French what was to be expected of the Nazi movement. In his report on the discussion in *Die Eiche* Bonhoeffer claimed, as he was to do in his memorandum to the British from Geneva in 1941, that 'the greatest share of responsibility' for the phenomenon of Nazism in its present form 'must be attributed to the policy of foreign countries'.[150] The conference was so successful that a study group was appointed to prepare for a similar conference in 1933. Later in the year Bonhoeffer referred to it in a sermon at the Technical University.

I shall never forget the day on which this text [Daniel 10] first made its impact on me. It was at a meeting of young Frenchmen and Germans; we had met on the common ground of the Church and wished to discuss the things that lay between us, to submit ourselves to the commandment of God in our time under the commandment of 'peace on earth' . . . we were all full of fear and dismay about our task . . . and when we were together, and somewhat alarmed in this way, a young Frenchman read out these words . . . and when he came to the words [spoken to Daniel] 'fear not, peace be with you', we all felt that afterwards we could say, 'Let my Lord speak, for you have strengthened me.'[151]

Ciernohorské Kúpele. Ten days after the Westerburg conference, and while the campaign for the 31st July election in Germany was in full swing, Bonhoeffer was again in the train, this time on the way to Czecho-Slovakia, in the place of Diestel, who was ill, knowing that three weeks later he would again be on his travels to attend yet more meetings. He undertook the trip with understandable reluctance, but the result was one of his most important contributions to the ecumenical movement and the peace question.

He was to take part in a youth conference on peace at Ciernohorské Kúpele in the Carpathians—in the old Austrian days the place had been known as Bad Schwarzenberg. The initiative for the conference came from the young Czecho-Slovak Church under its Patriarch Prochazka. Among subjects such as 'Present-day Youth and its Attitude to Spiritual Ideals' or 'Public Opinion and World Peace', the title of Bonhoeffer's address—'On the Theological Basis of the Work of the World Alliance' —may indeed have seemed unimportant and tedious to some members of his audience, though they were all given summaries in advance.[152]

What he said went far beyond the confines of the conference's subject-matter, for the implications of his introductory statement that 'there is no theology of the ecumenical movement' were incalculable for many of the delegates. Had the World Alliance ever seen itself in the light in which he presented it? Was it capable of seeing itself in that light?

150. GS I, p. 172.
151. GS IV, pp. 144 f.
152. GS I, pp. 159-61.

He realized himself that the stand he took put him in a position of relative isolation. 'I have just returned . . . from a very mediocre conference,' he said, 'which once more makes me doubt the value of all this ecumenical work' and he deplored the lack of discussion of the basic issues involved. He developed his attack on three fronts:

1. He criticized the practice of the older leaders of the ecumenical movement, who refrained from the task of establishing a theological foundation for their work. This made ecumenical committees *ad hoc* bodies, dependent on changes in the political climate. They comforted themselves by referring to the existence of 'Faith and Order' as an organization in which ecumenical theology was being developed, but that was a mistake. The situation was that the lack of an ecumenical theology made the World Alliance in practice defenceless against the latest attacks. 'The ecumenical worker must allow himself to be decried as unpatriotic and insincere, and all attempts to reply are easily shouted down.'[153]

2. He attacked nationalism, which was associated with denominationalism, and quoted the instance of the *Allgemeine Lutherische Kirchenzeitung*, which opened its columns to the propaganda of Hirsch and Althaus; and he delivered a theological onslaught on the concept of the 'orders of creation'.

3. He criticized the Anglo-Saxon Kingdom of God and peace ideals as manifested in the tendency of conferences to pass premature resolutions.

The work of trying to reach understanding as carried out by the World Alliance had no meaning for Bonhoeffer unless it led to a 'great common proclamation'. Meetings that did not search for this 'wasted their time in idle talk'; true and genuine reconciliation and understanding could come about only from truly contemporary proclamation and theology.[154] The World Alliance should therefore take up the almost impossible challenge of becoming a 'church'. Bonhoeffer never aimed at less than that. This implied that the World Alliance must develop beyond the stage of collecting comparative church statistics and must tackle the confessional problem. It could achieve the objective of becoming a 'church' only by delivering the message of peace that it had specifically adopted. It should not justify this message, but deliver it. 'The Church must . . . abandon all attempts to justify God's commandment. It delivers it, and that is all.' But there would be sharp disharmony, for 'the truth is divided. And that must make our word powerless, indeed false';[155] but that would provide the real impulse to attain the ecumenical aim.

Bonhoeffer's view of the ecumenical movement was as ambitious as that. Few followed him. Later, during the church struggle, the majority

153. GS I, p. 141.
154. GS I, p. 157.
155. GS I, p. 158.

regarded it as imprudent to draw the consequences. In 1932 Hermann Sasse was one of the few who obstinately asked the same kind of questions as Bonhoeffer did and were alive to the connection between the confessional problem and peace.

Siegmund-Schultze alone at that time responded to Bonhoeffer's arguments. He also of course noted that the liberal-humanist basis of the World Alliance was crumbling away. In the last leading article in *Die Eiche* in 1932[156] he said that the 'outstanding characteristics' of the ecumenical crisis was the discrediting of internationalism. He agreed with Bonhoeffer that the World Alliance must inevitably perish because of its dependence on the political situation unless the necessary work of laying the foundations of an ecumenical theology were guided into more positive channels.

In his own report on the conference Bonhoeffer sounded a more encouraging note.[157] He said that the way to peace must be opened in spite of everything, and that the 'internationalists' must be given the necessary support. Two years later, when things had grown much more critical, he met many friends he had made at this conference again at Fanö. Though he arrived late at Ciernohorské Kúpele, he left before the conference ended in order to record his vote against Hitler and the German nationalists on 31st July.

Meetings at Geneva. Immediately before the Gland conference, on the occasion of which Bonhoeffer for the first time attended a meeting of the whole executive committee of the World Alliance, the Ecumenical Council of 'Life and Work' met in Geneva (7th-14th August 1932). Bonhoeffer was not present on this occasion, so he did not meet all the leading figures on the council.

But decisions were made the significance of which were only to be revealed by the turbulent history of the next few years. Karl Barth was elected to the theological committee of 'Life and Work'—to Bonhoeffer this was a hopeful sign—and an amalgamation of the youth committees took place as a result of the appointment of Henriod as general secretary both of the World Alliance and of 'Life and Work'. But, above all, Dr. G. K. A. Bell, the Bishop of Chichester, was elected president of the Ecumenical Council, actually against the rules. The Bishop of Winchester had died before his period of office as president expired in 1932, and Cosmo Lang, the Archbishop of Canterbury, had appointed Dr. Bell to take his place. At Kapler's suggestion, his period of office was now extended for two more years, on the ground that the business of putting relations with other ecumenical bodies on a new footing, which was already in train, and the preparations for another world conference (the eventual result of which was the Oxford con-

156. *Die Eiche*, 1932, No. 4, pp. 308 f.
157. GS I, p. 172.

ference of 1937) required the continuation in office of a president of
Dr. Bell's experience. The importance of this decision was to appear in
the years ahead: in 1933 and 1934 the Confessing Church had the
benefit of having in that office a man who threw its status and prestige,
which extended beyond frontiers, into the scales. In 1935 and 1936
there was again a regularly elected president, the Orthodox Archbishop
Germanos, but he would hardly have been in a position to conduct the
dispute with Bishop Ludwig Müller as Dr. Bell did.

In August 1932 Bonhoeffer attended, not the Ecumenical Council,
but the meeting of the executive committee of the World Alliance (19th-
22nd August 1932), at which he made closer contact with men who
interested him, including the Danish Bishop Valdemar Ammundsen, its
chairman. He and Dr. Bell were the two men on whom Bonhoeffer set
great hopes for the future. On this occasion Bonhoeffer also met Gandhi's
friend, C. F. Andrews, whom he would hardly have met in 'Life and
Work'.

A fusion of the World Alliance and the Ecumenical Council was not
envisaged. In reply to an enquiry by Dr. Bell about how the splitting up
of the international Christian organizations was to be prevented,
Ammundsen wrote:

'Life and Work' is the form with the broadest scope and is the most important. But its organization is very heavy and its financial position is rather
precarious. The World Alliance has a more limited object, but its central
organization is more effective, and its financial basis is somewhat better,
owing to grants from the Church Peace Foundation. I am afraid that an
amalgamation now would only tie the World Alliance down to the heavier
body, without helping 'Life and Work' sufficiently.[158]

No amalgamation ever took place. In 1948 the World Alliance was
dissolved, and its objectives were expressed, though in a different
manner, at the Prague conference on peace ten years later.

Not all the subjects of discussion during those hot August days at the
École Nationale in Geneva were of interest to the new member in an
open-necked shirt.

1. A new position had to be adopted in relation to the disarmament
conference in view of the frustration and disappointment the failure of
its last meeting had caused.[159] In a sermon at the opening of the disarmament conference at Geneva, Dr. Temple, the Archbishop of York,
had said:

One clause there is in the existing treaties which offends in principle the
Christian conscience and for the deletion of which by proper authority
the voice of Christendom must be raised. This is the clause which affixes
to one group of belligerents in the Great War the whole guilt for its occur-

158. Letter of 7.5.1932.
159. Thus F. Siegmund-Schultze, *Die Eiche*, 1932, pp. 13 ff., 183, 304 ff.

rence . . . We have to ask not only who dropped the match but who strewed the ground with gunpowder.[160]

2. The Minorities Commission had long been a member-organization of the World Alliance, and Bishop Ammundsen was its chairman. Under his wing in 1933—as we shall see in connection with the conference in Sofia—Bonhoeffer was able to sound the alarm and make suggestions for combating the Aryan clause.

3. It was a great surprise to Bonhoeffer and his French co-secretary Toureille when Wilfred Monod, whom the Germans were accustomed to regarding as an obdurate French nationalist, presented a memorandum suggesting an examination of the principles and task of the World Alliance precisely on the lines indicated by Bonhoeffer at Ciernohorské Kúpele; that is to say, by way of a Biblical and dogmatic enquiry into the principles of Christian unity, peace aims, and definition of the lines of advance. A debate immediately flared up between the veterans, who vigorously opposed taking the plunge into theological questions, and 'others, particularly the younger men', who 'the more vigorously called for an "ecumenical theology"'.[161] As a result of this debate Bonhoeffer was instructed by the working committee in Sofia in 1933 to draft proposals in response to Monod's memorandum.[162] Nothing came of the matter in this form, but a straight line led from Monod's memorandum to Bonhoeffer's peace speech at Fanö.

4. C. F. Andrews argued forcefully that east Asia should be drawn into the organization's work more effectively than previously, but his proposal that a delegation should be sent there was not carried.

5. Finally, it was proposed to form a publications committee, and the name of Bonhoeffer was put forward as its chairman. Its object was to publish a newsletter.

Conference at Gland. About sixty delegates from all over the world met at Gland, on the Lake of Geneva, on 25th-31st August for a joint youth conference of the World Alliance and the Ecumenical Council. Dr. Arthur Burroughs, the Bishop of Ripon, was in the chair, and the conference organizers were the three youth secretaries and Mr. Steele for 'Life and Work'.

After long negotiations, it had been agreed that the main theme of the conference should be 'the call of Christianity in the present crisis'; thus the unemployment problem was relegated to second place. Bonhoeffer had the feeling that he had not succeeded in pushing through his ideas; the programme seemed to him to be too much concerned with the economic and international crisis and too little with the call of Christianity, which—as we see from his speech at Ciernohorské Kúpele—

160. F. A. Iremonger, op. cit., p. 376.
161. Thus J. Richter, *Die Eiche*, 1932, p. 326.
162. Cf. Ch. VII, p. 244.

seemed to him far more appropriate to a Christian gathering. He invited
Sutz to the conference, 'which is only partially under my management.
At all events, I already feel I am not responsible for its course. The British
have now put their fingers in the pie too much for that . . . though in
spite of everything it will perhaps be quite interesting.'[163]

To Bonhoeffer the difficulty lay in the insufficiently discussed and so
very different conception of the Kingdom of God that prevailed on the
European continent and in the Anglo-Saxon countries.

Short opening speeches on the general theme of the conference were
made by Toureille, Zernov and Bonhoeffer. Bonhoeffer's speech has not
survived; all that is available is its reflection in the Bishop of Ripon's
report to the *Yorkshire Post*:

Opening addresses by the French and German youth secretaries of the World
Alliance quickly struck the keynote of these two national approaches. The
Frenchman[164] emphasized that there are no cheap remedies for such a
condition as we have to face. The refrain of the German was the Old
Testament word: 'We know not what we should do, but our eyes are unto
Thee', as the expression of a pessimism that verged on passivism. A young
Russian[165] who followed gave a more constructive picture of an 'organic
society', in which the creative principle is love . . .

Thus Bonhoeffer had followed the lines of his Exaudi Sunday
sermon[166] and his speech at Ciernohorské Kúpele, but had not
sufficiently secured his passionate protest at the over-hastiness of the
British programme against the possibilities of misunderstanding; the
British believed they were listening to an example of German pessimism
and a German tendency to passivity. But battle was joined over a
proposal by the British that a public statement should be issued: 'For
we believe that youth will still listen to a message in spite of its outspoken criticism and apparent indifference to the Church', they stated,
according to the minutes. Bonhoeffer, however, favoured a 'qualified
silence', and opposed this throwing away of religion, and he succeeded.
'With that yet another proposal or resolution or official message put
forward by the Anglo-Saxons was passionately rejected . . . Our quite
young work should not be so unduly burdened right at the outset. We
must learn to wait',[167] he wrote in his reports.

Bonhoeffer gained notably in authority in the course of the conference.
At its conclusion a 'summing-up message' should have been delivered by
Bishop Ammundsen, but he was compelled at the last moment to call
it off, and the task devolved on Bonhoeffer. The speech he made was an

163. Letter of August 1932, GS I, p. 34.
164. Toureille.
165. Dr. Zernov, from Paris.
166. GS I, pp. 133 ff.
167. GS I, p. 174; also p. 177.

impressive one.[168] This time he made himself better understood by the British. He replied to the allegation that his basic attitude was pessimistic; the danger points in the world situation were concretely evaluated, but the claims of the Church and theology were not one whit diminished:

We are not an *ad hoc* organization for church action, but a definite form of the Church itself . . . The World Alliance is the alarmed and anxious Church of Christ that has pricked up its ears . . . and calls upon the Lord.[169]

A call for peace followed. The Bishop of Ripon listened attentively, and this time reported to the *Yorkshire Post*:

At a later session the German leader corrected his first pessimistic emphasis by a passionate proclamation of the Church, and ended: 'Europe has to be conquered a second time by and for Christ. Are we ready?'

But Dr. Burroughs must have changed the wording slightly. Bonhoeffer did not use the phrase 'for Christ'; he never did.

The bishop revealed in his article that among the Germans at the conference 'one was a fully-fledged Nazi and gave us an impassioned and moving statement of that viewpoint'. Among Bonhoeffer's own students there were at first a number who identified their hopes for Germany with those of Hitler's party. Bonhoeffer did not reject such people out of hand, but preferred to hope that when it came to the point he would be able to raise them to a different level, and he succeeded. At Gland he may have wanted his ecumenical friends to see a representative of the type that was coming to the top in Germany, and also to show the Nazi a different dimension at the international level. The presence of the latter at Gland led to Germans and Frenchmen once more spending many hours of discussion together.

Bonhoeffer's energetic weeks in Switzerland ended with his climbing the Rigi with Sutz and visiting Brunner and Barth on the Bergli.

Winter 1932-1933. The autumn and winter of 1932 were devoted to planning the ecumenical programme for 1933, which was to be similar to that for the previous year, with regional and international conferences and committee meetings. But the New Year took a different course.

Bonhoeffer's first acquaintance with Dr. Bell was literary, as Siegmund-Schultze asked him to translate his *A Brief Sketch of the Church of England*; in the end, however, he did no more than check the translation, which he handed over to a friend.

At the end of this period we see that the two opposite poles of Bonhoeffer's thought were more firmly and more broadly anchored—the

168. GS I, pp. 162-70.
169. GS I, pp. 164 f.

eschatological majesty of revelation on the one hand and the relevance of the real world on the other. His knowledge of the real world was now much greater, personally, geographically and politically. Were the two poles to attract or repel each other? Eschatology had undoubtedly gained in intensity, but reality too had put on more flesh and blood.

During the last few weeks of the year Bonhoeffer put more passionate emphasis than ever before on the 'right of Prometheus, which allows him to be near the Kingdom of God, in contrast to the cowardly fugitive into other-worldliness, which makes him love the earth, "the mother of all things" (Ecclesiasticus 40 : 1)'.[170] The Church consists of the 'children of the earth who do not cut themselves off, who have no particular proposals for the improvement of the world, who are not better than the world, but now hold out in the centre, the depths, the ordinariness and subjection of the world'.[171] Such phrases might just as well have been written in the letters from Tegel prison in 1944.

But this Church was to speak and bear witness to the eschatological revelation. A test of strength was imminent:

Out of its knowledge of it the Church must here and now be able concretely to speak the word of God, the word of power, or it will say something else, something different and human, the word of impotence. The Church must announce no eternally valid principles, but merely commandments that are valid today. For what is 'always' true is not true 'today'. To us God is 'always' God 'today'.[172]

That is how Bonhoeffer presents himself to us on the threshold of 1933. A bitter struggle was to begin about the authority and credibility of the earth-bound Church. And thus the two poles entered into a new relationship with each other.

170. GS III, p. 274.
171. GS III, p. 276.
172. Speech at Ciernohorské Kúpele, see GS I, p. 145.

CHAPTER SEVEN

BERLIN

1933

A FOREST of swastika flags surrounded the altar of Magdeburg Cathedral. Similar scenes in other churches were explained from the pulpit in much the same words as those used by Dean Martin at Magdeburg:

In short, it has come to be the symbol of German hope. Whoever reviles this symbol of ours is reviling our Germany. The swastika flags round the altar radiate hope—hope that the day is at last about to dawn.[1]

The first sermon given by Bonhoeffer in the Dreifaltigkeitskirche in Berlin after Hitler's seizure of power used different words:

The Church has only *one* altar, the altar of the Almighty . . . before which all creatures must kneel . . . He who seeks anything other than this must keep away; he cannot join us in the house of God . . . The Church has only *one* pulpit, and from that pulpit faith in God will be preached, and no other faith, and no other will than the will of God, however well-intentioned.[2]

At noon on 30th January, Hitler came to power with the help of Hindenburg. That evening Dietrich's brother-in-law, Rüdiger Schleicher, as he came home said: 'This means war!' All the Bonhoeffers, including Dietrich, thought as he did. When in later years friends taxed Bonhoeffer with the excessive pessimism of that opinion he replied that, while the estimated time of the event might have to be revised, there could be no doubt about its eventual coming. Unlike many people of their class, the Bonhoeffers took a serious view of what had happened on 30th January 1933; they may have continued to underestimate the full extent of Hitler's abilities, but not his unscrupulousness. Looking back, fifteen years later, Bonhoeffer's father reviewed the events of that time:

From the start, the victory of National Socialism in 1933 and Hitler's appointment as Reich Chancellor was in our view a misfortune—the whole family agreed on this. In my own case, I disliked and mistrusted Hitler because of his demagogic propaganda methods, his telegram of condolence after the Potempa murder, his habit of driving about the country carrying a riding crop, his choice of colleagues—with whose qualities, incidentally, we in Berlin were better acquainted than people elsewhere—and finally

1. CW, 1933, p. 45.
2. On 26.2.1933, GS IV, p. 110.

because of what I heard from professional colleagues about his psycho-pathic symptoms.[3]

The political turning-point that came on 30th January 1933 was also to force Bonhoeffer's life on to a different course. He did not have to reorientate his personal convictions however, or his theology. Rather, it was becoming increasingly clear that academic discussion must give way to action and that it was imperative to relinquish the shelter and privilege of the academic rostrum as well as 'the protected rights and duties of the ministry' if the strength of weakness was to be authenticated.

But that turning-point also meant that personal initiative was under constant threat of restraint—a sore trial for a man for whom independent decision was a necessity. Yet it was to be characteristic of his life that by knowing the right moment at which to give way, he was always able to win back his own freedom, and that he plotted his unswerving course within theology, the Church and contemporary history as their disciplines determined.

That turning-point meant, moreover, that the day-to-day struggle made unprecedented calls upon Bonhoeffer. Thus it was four years before he was able to finish his next book. Until 1933 the young lecturer and preacher had not been involved in decisions concerning larger ecclesiastical issues, in which he had no voice. Nor, indeed, had he desired any. But now, at the age of twenty-seven, he found himself among those men whose names had suddenly come to the fore. Customary groupings no longer applied, and new ones were beginning to appear within the structure of the Church. Bonhoeffer's existence, which till now had been private, acquired a public dimension. It happened so quickly that he himself found it uncanny: 'I long terribly sometimes for a quiet parish';[4] and he said that probably one of the most impelling reasons for his accepting the invitation to an obscure church in London was 'that I no longer feel physically capable of coping with the questions and claims that beset me'.[5]

As a result of the upheaval, friendships by which Bonhoeffer set some store came to an abrupt and sometimes harshly discordant end. It was not that he antagonized students who were closely associated with him —some of whom were Party members—by failing to explain matters to them. But he could not and would not remain in relation with men holding ecclesiastical office who had compounded—even unwillingly— with the Nazi Aryan clause.[6] So he wrote his farewell letters to them and would not listen to plausible excuses or professions of good intentions.

He now returned to his former idea of a visit to India, for he wished

3. Karl Bonhoeffer, *Lebenserinnerungen*.
4. To E. Sutz, 14.4.1933, GS I, p. 37.
5. To K. Barth, 24.10.1933, GS II, p. 132.
6. Legislation in the Third Reich, whereby Jews were to be excluded from the Civil Service and/or were forbidden to accept such posts.

to become better acquainted with the ethics and practice of passive resistance.

There is very little source material for 1933, a year which he spent in Berlin, when he had little time and less freedom for letter-writing. 'If I no longer say anything about conditions here it is because, as you know, there is now no privacy of post.'[7]

I FEBRUARY: CONTROLLED CHAOS

During the days in which Hitler was coming to power, Bonhoeffer's schedule was a heavy one: besides his regular lectures at the university and his Bible studies at the German S.C.M., he gave a broadcast talk on the Berlin radio. His time was also taken up with visitors and meetings connected with the ecumenical organizations which had foregathered in Berlin both before and after 30th January.[8]

Concept of Führer

It has not been possible to establish the reason why Bonhoeffer was, on 1st February 1933, at the microphone in the Potsdamerstrasse *Voxhaus* (Broadcasting House). The subject, 'The Younger Generation's Changed View of the Concept of Führer', was much the same type of presentation as that in Söhlmann's *Vormarsch*. But Bonhoeffer's might also quite possibly have been arranged by the university, for Bonhoeffer's father had broadcast not long before, on 17th and 24th January 1933, on the subject of mental disease. It seems more probable, however, that Wolf-Dieter Zimmermann was responsible for putting forward Dietrich Bonhoeffer's name: Zimmermann was working voluntarily at this time with Dr. Kurt Böhme, head of the radio division of the Evangelical Press Union, and was also collaborating with Harald Braun and Jochen Klepper[9] on Berlin Radio. Bonhoeffer had planned the talk on this controversial subject even before Hitler had become Chancellor. Two days after the Führer's enthusiastic acclamation by the crowds in the Wilhelmsplatz, Bonhoeffer broadcast the talk which, however, was cut off before the end.

His talk analyzed the development of the concept of Führer and the changes it had undergone in the post-war Youth Movement. He made no secret of his contempt for the 'unnatural narcissism of . . . youth made vain by old fools'.[10] It would be a misinterpretation, however, were we to pretend that his argument against the leadership cult was based on liberal, democratic ideas; it derived rather from a conservative notion of order, and this in spite of the idea simultaneously evolved of

7. To E. Sutz, 14.4.1933, GS I, p. 38.
8. Cf. Ch. VI, p. 179.
9. The poet who committed suicide in 1942 because of his Jewish wife
10. GS II, p. 19.

the breaking up of the 'penultimate' orders as opposed to the 'ultimate'. Bonhoeffer was concerned with the correct structuring of authority. If recent developments had made the leadership concept historically and psychologically necessary, its authority must, Bonhoeffer felt, be at once well-founded and circumscribed, lest it 'become a form of collectivism turning into intensified individualism'.[11] Bonhoeffer, however, saw this as having already happened in the development of the latest political form taken by the Führer concept inspired by the youth movement. Thus, two days after Hitler came to power and in spite of the prevalent intoxication, his theological insight enabled him to warn his listeners that, should the leader 'allow himself to succumb to the wishes of those he leads, who will always seek to turn him into their idol, then the image of the leader will gradually become the image of the "misleader" . . . This is the leader who makes an idol of himself and his office, and who thus mocks God.'[12]

Before these last sentences could be broadcast, Bonhoeffer's microphone had been switched off. Was it merely because he had overrun his time? Or can it really be assumed that Goebbels's team had gained complete control of the station in the course of barely two days? And to whom were the conclusions in this broadcast so insufferable as to require intervention? The script shows clearly that the syllables had been carefully counted and worked out. Whatever the truth of the matter, the significant fact is that the broadcast was cut short at the crucial point. With his speech thus deprived of its sting, Bonhoeffer was much troubled by the thought that he might actually be suspected of joining in the general acclaim. He therefore had the script duplicated and sent to all available friends and relations with the explanation that its disastrous curtailment 'had distorted the whole effect'. Never again did he have to use this treacherous medium.

He was able to publish his script in full in the conservative *Kreuzzeitung*, and was further asked by Theodor Heuss, then a teacher at the Berlin Political University, to give a longer version as a lecture at the college at the beginning of March.[13]

Ecumenism in Berlin

At this particular time Berlin was offering hospitality to the leading personalities of the World Alliance and the Universal Christian Council for 'Life and Work'. The executive committee of the World Alliance, the Geneva secretaries and the executive committee of 'Life and Work' met one after the other. On the night of 30th January, Bishop Ammundsen accompanied by Henriod mingled with the cheering and singing

11. GS II, p. 32.
12. GS II, pp. 35, 37.
13. GS II, pp. 22-38; also delivered at the Technical University on 23.2.1933.

crowds in Wilhelm-Platz. And the Bishop of Chichester, George Bell, was never to forget his fiftieth birthday amid that great sea of flags in Berlin. The March number of the *News Letter* records:

The coincidence of the election of Adolf Hitler as Chancellor of the Reich and the meeting of the Executive revealed once more to its leaders the great difficulties of the country of which they were the guests and the frailty of the plans which men make.[14]

The theologians of Berlin gave the guests a festive welcome at Harnack House, where Deissman presided and Martin Dibelius delivered the formal address. There was also a reception by Berlin churchmen, presided over by Kapler, at the Church Federation Office. It was the last time that German churchmen and theologians were to meet the ecumenical movement in a relatively free and harmonious atmosphere. From that time on, every conference was to be oppressed by the strain of internal German dissension and embarrassed by the uncertainty of not knowing exactly who truly represented the German churches. It was, too, the last great ecumenical event to be organized by Siegmund-Schultze from his office in the Fruchtstrasse. Six months later he was forced to leave Germany for Switzerland and was not allowed to return until after the Second World War.

Bonhoeffer had already met Henriod on 25th January 1933 for preliminary talks in the theological department of the university, when the latter had gone there to speak to the Berlin students about 'National and Supra-national Church Work'. He spoke in German, seeking to guide the thoughts of his audience into realms that transcended their own immediate crises. Some of the items on the ecumenical agenda were of considerable interest to Bonhoeffer as, for instance, those on the amalgamation of the World Alliance with the 'Life and Work' youth commissions; on negotiations for an informal Franco-German meeting to take place in Basle; and finally the preparations for the World Alliance conference planned to take place in September in Sofia —a conference at which Bonhoeffer was to play an unexpected role.

The ecumenical sessions in Berlin concluded with the committee meetings of the Universal Council for 'Life and Work' on 3rd and 4th February. The impression the visitors took away with them was that they had witnessed a genuine exhibition of popular enthusiasm. The church leaders in Berlin soon wrote to inform them that what they had experienced was in fact the prelude to a revolution effected with unprecedented discipline. They could not have discerned, during so brief a visit, the full extent to which the forces of destruction had been unleashed.

14. *News Letter*, 1933, March, p. 10.

Dangerous Weeks

Hitler, in his proclamation to the German people published in the *Völkischer Beobachter* of 1st February, promised to take Christianity—'the basis of our whole morality'—under his 'firm protection'. What did this really mean?

In February 1933 none of the existing political parties had yet been proscribed and none envisaged voluntary dissolution. Thus, until the election of 5th March, the struggle went on. There was constant fighting in the streets, and the Party newspapers published lists of those who had died in the bloody demonstrations. A reader's letter in the *Christliche Welt* asked whether, in this internecine war, there was such a thing as an unbiased casualty list.[15] Was the chaos genuine, or was it directed?

Politicians such as Stegerwald, of the Catholic Centre Party, were publicly attacked in the streets by the S.A. The state of disorder was laboriously being reduced to the desired new order by one-sided police and emergency decrees issued by Frick for the Reich and by Göring for Prussia. These extraordinary conditions of chaos reached their height with the Reichstag fire, which also marked the beginning of Hitler's radical reign of terror and his correspondingly drastic legislation. A week before the elections, the left-wing Press was proscribed, Ossietzki was arrested, and 4,000 Communists were taken from their homes.

These events did not immediately affect Bonhoeffer's family. However, by 3rd February Rust had already been appointed Prussian Minister for Cultural Affairs, and this was a danger-signal for so completely academic a family. At a demonstration the evening after his appointment, Rust made the following announcement: 'First thing on Monday the Bolshevist cultural invasion will come to an end . . . I shall ask the churches outright whether or not they intend to help us in our fight against Bolshevism'; he had, he said, moved into the ministry bag and baggage and had no intention of leaving until he had completed his task.[16]

Such pronouncements by the minister must have worried Gerhard Leibholz, Bonhoeffer's brother-in-law, because of his Jewish origin, though as yet no legal steps had been taken. All that happened to begin with were brawls, conducted on the very thresholds of churches and universities.

February was a period of relative calm for the higher church authorities, but the churches themselves experienced the invasion of Party demonstrations overflowing from the market-place. Was this merely desire for conquest, or did it mark the beginning of a mass movement into the Church?

15. CW, 1933, p. 240.
16. *Völkischer Beobachter*, 36/37, of 5.6.1933.

Bands of S.A. men went to church services, but in many cases this led to fighting with other political groups outside the doors. Schubring, the minister of the Berlin Marienkirche, therefore asked the national leader of the German Christians, Hossenfelder, to suspend demonstrations outside and inside the churches. The Cathedral chapter refused a request to allow the body of a Nazi police official, the victim of a shooting-incident, to lie in state. In Cassel the local branch of the National Socialist Party asked for a special service of their own on 12th February, and the same thing happened in some other parts of the Reich. In 1932 Hossenfelder's directives to the German Christians had stated that the National Socialist Party did not wish 'to save the fatherland without the cooperation of the vital forces of the Church'. Might this not mean that the hour of revolution was also the hour of revival —an opportunity not to be missed but rather, indeed, welcomed with enthusiasm?

On the day before the Reichstag fire it was Dietrich Bonhoeffer's turn to preach. His sermon on Gideon, taking as its text 'The people with you are too many for me' (Judges 7:2), remained imprinted on the minds of his students:

Do not desire to be strong, powerful, honoured and respected, but let God alone be your strength, your fame and your honour . . . Gideon, who achieved faith in fear and doubt, kneels with us here before the altar of the one and only God, and Gideon prays with us: 'Our Lord on the cross, be thou our one and only Lord. Amen.'[17]

II MARCH: HITLER'S LAWS

Within a short time Hitler had turned the controlled chaos to his own advantage and made the legislature into a tool of his will. On the upsurge of their enthusiasm for the new national era, the people submitted to decree after decree, to law after law, in the belief that they were experiencing a new freedom, whereas in fact they were being deprived of numerous rights.

1. On the night of 27th/28th February, behind an impenetrable police cordon, the Reichstag was burnt to the ground. The following morning Hitler promulgated his most portentous emergency decree, the 'Reich President's Edict for the Protection of People and State'. The edict was to remain in force 'until further notice'—in fact, it lasted until 8th May 1945. It abolished virtually all those personal rights conceded by the constitution, and hence made concentration camps possible. The election of 5th March meant that the majority of the German people accepted *de facto* the terms of paragraph 1 of the edict of 28th February 1933:

Therefore *restriction* of personal freedom, of the right of free speech, includ-
17. GS IV, pp. 115, 117.

ing the freedom of the Press, of the right of association and of public assembly, *intervention* in the privacy of post, telegraph and telephone, *authorization* of search warrants and the confiscation and restriction of property, beyond the hitherto legal limits, will henceforward be admissible.[18]

This instrument provided Hitler with the supreme powers he desired. It remained to be seen whether he would use them by continuing to build upon the foundations that he had already laid, or whether he would fail to exploit them.

Neither the churches nor the universities really felt themselves to be immediately affected by the fire or the edict to which it gave rise. For the most part, they saw the edict as a new desire for order which they could only applaud. The Evangelical Church, moreover, had for centuries enjoyed immunity from the attentions of an omnipotent and ubiquitous police; and there seemed no reason to be suspicious now.

The Bonhoeffers were not yet really in danger and hence did not take measures against possible visits from the police to their home in the Wangenheimstrasse. They were less vulnerable than many active politicians, not a few of whom during these weeks were sleeping in a different place every night in order to avoid the consequences of the edict.

Nevertheless to Dietrich Bonhoeffer, with his many 'internationalist' connections, the censorship of letters and telephone conversations must needs have been irksome, especially after his broadcast.[19] Even in his parents' house politics could not be openly discussed because of the many employees there. When, at the beginning of April, Paul Lehmann arrived in Berlin from New York with his wife to visit his old friend of Union Theological Seminary days, he was forcibly struck by the fact that Klaus Bonhoeffer would get up from time to time—in the course of conversations that admittedly were not wholly innocuous—to see if there was anyone listening outside the door.

Before very long the family was to find itself uncomfortably involved in the affair of the Reichstag fire. Hans von Dohnanyi had been temporarily seconded to the Supreme Court[20] and as an observer for the Ministry of Justice had to attend all stages, first in Berlin, then in Leipzig, then again in Berlin, of the proceedings against van der Lubbe, who was accused of having started the fire. This was not all, however, for when in March van der Lubbe went on hunger-strike in prison, the investigating judge called upon Bonhoeffer's father and his colleague Dr. J. Zutt, subsequently professor in Frankfurt, for expert psychiatric opinion. For a whole year the family was oppressed by their involvement

18. W. Höfer. *Der Nationalsozialismus. Dokumente 1933-1945.* 1957, p. 53.
19. GS I, p. 38.
20. After May 1933 he returned to his post with the Minister of Justice, Gürtner, whom Hitler had retained in his cabinet.

in this emotionally complex, and in many ways enigmatic, case.[21] Karl Bonhoeffer and Zutt saw van der Lubbe three times in March 1933, but not again until September and October, after his return from Leipzig; during November they saw him four times. Outside Germany it had at once been assumed that Göring's henchmen had been responsible for burning down the Reichstag, van der Lubbe being merely an unwitting tool, and it was hoped that this, the most eminent of German psychiatrists, with his reputation for common sense and incorruptibility, would provide the conclusive evidence which others had failed to elicit. Everywhere, then, the expert opinion was awaited with eager anticipation, and disappointment was extreme when the medical and psychiatric findings omitted all mention of guilt or innocence, of van der Lubbe's possibly having been instigated by others, or of indications that drugs had been administered to the prisoner during the period of observation. Indignant letters, and even a scurrilous leaflet, arrived at the Bonhoeffers' house.

In 1933, however, it would have been quite inconceivable for Karl Bonhoeffer to put his name to expert opinion dealing with anything other than purely medical matters. The document, in spite of its wholly factual professional language, betrayed some sympathy for the patient; it appeared in the *Monatschrift für Psychiatrie und Neurologie*.[22] And just as, in this case, medical ethics demanded that Karl Bonhoeffer should conscientiously exclude all political considerations, so seven years later he was to close his mind no less resolutely against those biological theories advocating the elimination of what were described as 'useless lives'. In his memoirs the doctor mentions the van der Lubbe case:

When I was asked to carry out a psychiatric examination of the Reichstag arsonist, Lubbe, and to give expert opinion on the case, I had the opportunity of meeting some of the leading Party members. A large number of them had foregathered to attend the proceedings in the Supreme Court at Leipzig. The characters I saw at this gathering were not altogether prepossessing. During the hearings, the impassiveness and the painstaking objectivity of the President of the Court contrasted pleasantly with the undisciplined manner of the Party members in the witness box. The impression of intellectual superiority given by the other accused, Dimitroff, infuriated beyond bearing Minister President Göring, who had been invited to attend. As for Lubbe he was, humanly speaking, a not unsympathetic young man, a psychopath and a muddle-headed adventurer who, during the proceedings, reacted with a kind of stupefied defiance, in which he persisted till shortly before his execution.[23]

It was under Hitler's 'Reichstag Fire Edict' bearing Hindenburg's signature, that four and a half years later Bonhoeffer's seminary and

---

21. The main proceedings against van der Lubbe did not begin until 21.11.1933; he was executed on 10.1.1934.
22. *Monatschrift für Psychiatrie und Neurologie*, Vol. 89, 1934, pp. 185-213.
23. Karl Bonhoeffer, *Lebenserinnerungen*, p. 115.

community house at Finkenwalde was dissolved and sealed by Himmler's deputies. And in one of the concentration camps which this edict made possible, Dietrich Bonhoeffer was murdered; only a month afterwards the edict was finally rescinded. Bracher has described it as 'the fundamental emergency law upon which the National Socialist dictatorship . . was primarily based', and as more important than the Enabling Act of 24th March.[24]

2. In view of these events, the *Reichstag election of 5th March* can be regarded only in a restricted sense as the last of Germany's free elections. It was preceded by appeals, half voluntary and half extorted, by public bodies such as the Protestant Federation which hastened to canvass for 'the strong national forces . . . seeking in conscious belief in God, to build up a . . . new Germany upon the wreckage left by the unholy November Revolution of 1918. For fourteen years the forces of the [Catholic] Centre, of Communism and of Social Democracy, with their *international* affiliations, have left their stamp on German politics and the cultural life of our people . . . Fight . . . so that the national counter-revolutionary movement may come to power by legal means.'[25] The German Evangelical Church Committee led by Kapler issued a more dignified appeal to recollect the eighth commandment during the election and to show devotion to 'that which transcends all else—to the whole nation, the whole fatherland'.

Dietrich Bonhoeffer accompanied Franz Hildebrandt to the polls before leaving for the Dassel Conference. Hildebrandt voted for the Christian People's Party, but Bonhoeffer believed that there was only one party that gave any promise of stability and independence—precisely because of its 'international' ties—and that was the Catholic Centre Party. For a Protestant minister of his standing this was, at that time, a quite exceptional step.

The National Socialists obtained 44 per cent of the poll and thus were still dependent on the rump German National Conservative Party. There was no doubt, however, that the latter would give its assent to Hitler's legislation.

3. By means of *a display of pomp and ceremony in the Potsdam Garrison Church* on 21st March, Hitler succeeded with great skill in capturing the imagination of the people. Before the ceremony, Hindenburg and the Protestant deputies attended Dibelius's service in the Nikolaikirche, while Hitler and Goebbels made their 'devotions' beside the graves of the Party dead. The crowd looked on the ceremony as marking the end of the 'bloodless, legal revolution'. It is said that a few days before, Bonhoeffer had been invited to tea by Dibelius and had

24. Bracher-Sauer-Schulz, *Die nationalsozialistische Machtergreifung*, 2nd ed., 1962, p. 82.
25. CW, 1933, p. 239.

remarked that acclamation was not the Church's sole duty.[26] And in fact the lavish praise in Dibelius's sermon was followed by the statement: 'Political office must not be combined with personal arbitrariness. Once order has been restored, love and justice must once again hold sway.'[27]

4. On the same day, 21st March, the *Treachery Law* was promulgated, and the net of political judiciary measures was drawn closer. It was applicable to anyone who 'with malice aforethought spreads or puts out an untrue or grossly distorted assertion of a factual nature calculated seriously to impair the welfare of the Reich or of a province or the reputation of the Reich Government or of a regional government or of the parties or associations behind those governments'.[28] Combined with the Emergency Decree of 28th February, the Treachery Law imposed dangerous restrictions on anyone like Bonhoeffer who was unwilling to identify his loyalty to Germany with acceptance of Hitler's administration.

With increasing anti-Semitic and anti-Communist measures, culminating in the boycott of Jewish firms on 1st April and the first non-Aryan law for the 'reconstruction of the professional Civil Service',[29] that danger became acute.

Bonhoeffer's grandmother, then ninety-one years old, calmly walked through the S.A. cordon to the Kaufhaus des Westens.[30] At about this time his parents went to stay with the Leibholz family in Göttingen so as to help them in the event of demonstrations. At home, Dietrich and Klaus Bonhoeffer discussed with their New York visitor, Paul Lehmann, how genuine information about what was afoot might be conveyed to suitable circles in America, among them Rabbi Wise, Chief Rabbi in the U.S.A., whom Bonhoeffer had met during his 1930-1 visit. While Bonhoeffer was thus 'committing treason', certain ecclesiastical dignitaries were showing themselves prepared to perform services of quite a different nature.

Article 10 of a National Socialist directive, with reference to the boycott procedure of 1st April, ran:

Action committees are further responsible for ensuring that every German with connections outside the country makes use of these, by letter, telegram and telephone, to explain and disseminate the truth—that peace and order reign in Germany, that the German people desire with all their hearts peacefully to pursue their occupations and to live at peace with the rest of the world, that their fight against the Jewish conspiracy is only con-

26. Cf. K. Scharf, 'D. Dr. Dibelius im Kampf der Bekennenden Kirche', *Die Stunde der Kirche*, 1950, p. 35.
27. G. van Norden, *Kirche in der Krise*, 1933, 1963, p. 175.
28. W. Hofer, op. cit., p. 56.
29. It appeared under this euphemistic title in a Nazi publication on 7.4.1933.
30. See Ch. I, p. 3.

ducted in self-defence . . . National Socialists! On Saturday, at the stroke of 10, Jewry will know who it is they are fighting.[31]

Highly-placed officials in the territorial and free churches who had ecumenical connections accordingly wrote formal communications on 30th March to their opposite numbers abroad or to their sister churches in England and the United States, requesting them to oppose propaganda against Germany's new order and assuring them that everything was being done in an atmosphere of calm discipline. Kapler wrote in these terms to Bell, Germanos, Cadman and Henriod. Otto Dibelius and the Methodist Bishop Nuelsen broadcast on the German short-wave Overseas Service to America and other countries about the peaceful aspect of Berlin and the good treatment that was being received in prison by those who had been arrested.[32]

The Treachery Law threatened all contacts with countries abroad, and later the Confessing Church was apprehensively to withhold from the ecumenical movement much that in normal circumstances would have been communicated to it as a matter of course.

5. The *Enabling Act* of 24th March was the final blow. Before the concluding session of the Reichstag, Hitler had a number of deputies arrested under the edict of 28th February, ignored all privileges and made the S.A. and S.S. responsible for organizing the next session in the Kroll Opera House. The law was called 'The Law to Relieve the Need of the People and the State'.[33] It conferred legislative power upon the Government, legalized its past and future edicts and released Hitler from any dependence upon the Constitution if it proved embarrassing. Legally he had attained his goal. Six months later even the collaborationist parties had ceased to exist. Hitler no longer had to fear legislative restrictions but only what remained of traditional, politically responsible elements in the law, the administration, the army and education. These could not be coordinated quite so rapidly, or so thoroughly.

In his long conciliatory speech on the eve of the Enabling Act, Hitler told the Churches: '. . . the National Government sees the two Christian confessions as the most important factors safeguarding our national heritage'; he would concede 'to them and assure them the influence that is their due'; and he saw 'in Christianity the unshakeable foundations of our people's ethical and moral life'.[34] The Churches were relieved to hear the word 'influence'—the qualifying phrase 'that is their due' went almost unnoticed. They could hardly have imagined that only a few weeks later the revolution would be knocking at their own doors.

31. W. Hofer, op. cit., pp. 283 f.
32. Cf. the account in the Reichsanzeiger, 82, of 6.4.1933.
33. W. Hofer, op. cit., p. 57.
34. G. van Norden, op. cit., p. 45.

III APRIL: GERMAN CHRISTIANS

The first days of April which had brought the reunion with Paul Lehmann could, in other circumstances, have been delightful for Bonhoeffer. Each found the other changed. In 1931 Lehmann, in saying good-bye to Dietrich, had presented him with the book *Which Way Religion?* by that most liberal socialist, Harry Ward. Now, returning from Bonn where he had heard Karl Barth speaking, he gave Dietrich the recently published work by Reinhold Niebuhr, *Moral Man and Immoral Society*, a reformatory critique proclaiming the end of liberalism. Bonhoeffer was impressed by the way in which it laid bare the position of the moral individual in immoral circumstances, but he was less tolerant of its criticism of pacifism; in 1941 he was to return to what he regarded as an 'abstract' distinction between the individual and society in the 'American philosopher of religion', Reinhold Niebuhr.[35]

For his part, Lehmann found Dietrich, whom he had known in New York as a young man full of fun and games, 'taking life seriously now'. Dietrich and Klaus Bonhoeffer predicted that Hitler would not last long, but that while he remained in power things would be very dangerous. During this time Dietrich was engaged in writing an article on the non-Aryan question.

National Conference

It was not only the Jewish boycott that cast a cloud over Bonhoeffer's time with Paul Lehmann, but also the chauvinistic National Conference of the German Christians on 3rd and 4th April in Berlin. The dynamic of 30th January continued to act within the Church in the shape of the 'Faith Movement of German Christians', organized by the Nazis in 1932. Hitler experienced some difficulty in maintaining the official fiction, as far as other countries were concerned, that the revolution was over.

There were not a few Protestants who envied the Catholics their apparent unity in their conduct of negotiations with the Third Reich—a unity which had secured for them the relatively peaceful terms of the Concordat. That the Catholics were not as closely knit as at first appeared did not become plain to the Protestants until later.[36] A source of weakness among the Protestants, moreover, was the circumstance that National Socialist ideology had infected, not only laymen in the synods, but also a large proportion of the clergy, even those in key positions. In this way they became either the instruments of the Party or else forfeited their freedom to negotiate and were eventually to lose every vestige of independence.

35. E, p. 191.
36. H. Müller, *Katholische Kirche und Nationalsozialismus, Dokumente*, 1963.

The National Conference on 3rd and 4th April brought about a land-slide at all levels of the Church. Some of the proceedings were broadcast. Frick and Göring made an appearance, and the conference was attended, not only by radical, convinced German Christians, but also by expert theologians. Many were eager to apply the Party tenets of the *Führer* principle and of racial conformity without more ado to a unified German church, whilst others—Professor Fezer of Tübingen, for example, and the executive of the Berlin Missionary Society, Weichert—whose inter-pretation of racial conformity was less drastic, were at bottom inspired by a true missionary zeal. Not unnaturally, the first group was the more vociferous and was indeed responsible for introducing into the Church a train of chaotic action and reaction. These people maintained that men of alien blood had no place in the pulpit and should not be allowed to be married before German Evangelical altars.

The slogans of the conference were: coordination, the *Führer* prin-ciple, the Reich Church, and racial conformity. A number of theologians now began to reflect that the 'Reich Church' and 'racial conformity' might perhaps go some way towards effecting the desired growth in the influence of the Church.

On 16th April Hossenfelder demanded that a German Christian representative should attend all sessions of the Supreme Church Council, the Church Senate, the Consistories and the Provincial Church Councils; but President Kapler refused. However on 22nd April the Church of Mecklenburg was temporarily saddled with a State Commissar. And on the 26th of that same month Hitler, hoping to exploit the state of con-fusion thus brought about, appointed as his 'confidential adviser and plenipotentiary in questions concerning the Evangelical Church' a hitherto unknown chaplain to the forces in Königsberg, one Ludwig Müller. The latter was an insignificant character who spoke with a strong regional accent. When, however, the church leaders and authori-ties failed to comply with the demand to adopt the Führer principle and, indeed, at last began to show signs of independent activity, the German Christians, reverting somewhat illogically to democratic pro-cedure, on 30th April asked for new church elections.

So that the ground should not be cut from under their feet, the exist-ing church administrations themselves took up, during the course of this month, the cry for a united Reich Church in place of the twenty-eight independent regional churches. They hastily set machinery in motion to create a new constitution for a single Reich Church. There was a busy interchange of proposals and plans for the reorganization of the German Evangelical Church, hitherto so much divided. Their intense preoccupation with the problem almost led them to believe they could ignore the German Christians. On 14th April Bonhoeffer wrote to Erwin Sutz:

We are about to witness a great reorganization of the churches which, to all appearances, will not be a bad thing. It is to be hoped that it will bring about the automatic withdrawal of the German Christians from the churches of both denominations—however regrettable this may be in other respects —so that, *hominum confusione et dei providentia*, we may once again rescue the Church . . .[37]

A letter from Karl Barth to Bonhoeffer of 18th April 1933 testifies to the difficulty at this time of presaging the future:

Whether and how I shall be able to adapt spiritually to a Germany that has changed so much is a different question altogether. And this applies particularly to Zoellner's 'Evangelical Church of the German Nation'. The name speaks for itself! But for the moment I can only wait and see, with as much patience as I can muster. I am really glad to see so many signs that the Church is more aware of her responsibilities than she was in 1914.[38]

Thus, on their own initiative, the Supreme Church Council and the Church Senate announced their plans for a new constitution. It is true that their declarations were largely taken up with the renewal of people and Reich, but they also said something about the proclamation of the pure gospel. On 25th April a three-man commission was set up, consisting of President Kapler, the Hanoverian Bishop Marahrens and the Elberfeld minister of the Reformed Church, Hermann Hesse. They had been commissioned by the German Evangelical Church Committee to draft the new constitution for the Reich Church. This independent move, however, was to be vitiated by Hitler's appointment of Müller and by the German Christians' insistence on elections.

When the triumvirate met in Loccum on 4th May for its three weeks' deliberations, they discovered that there were now four of them; at the conference table sat Ludwig Müller, awaiting their conclusions with eager anticipation. The discussion could no longer be confined to their common aim, the 'Reich Church', for the 'Führer principle' had become an inevitable ingredient in the talks. The third point, 'racial conformity', was not yet specifically named. Yet this matter, hitherto the province of individual cranks and extremists, now became the subject of serious theological debate. Men asked whether it was worth making an issue of a question such as the Aryan clause—of material concern only to a small and ever dwindling group within the Church—when what was at stake was the status of the Reich Church as an influential, evangelizing body. 'The Church is much concerned with the Jewish question, which has caused the most sensible of men to lose their heads and forget their Bibles.'[39]

37. GS I, p. 37.
38. GS II, p. 43.
39. To E. Sutz, 14.4.1933, GS I, p. 37.

Jewish Question

How did Bonhoeffer arrive at a penetrating assessment of this question so early?

When at the beginning of April it was proposed, in Jacobi's group of ministers, to discuss the Jewish question with an introductory talk by Bonhoeffer, a colleague from Jacobi's church expressed unconcealed opposition to the choice of this particular subject. Indeed as a result L. Fendt, one of the most influential members of the group, whose sermons Bonhoeffer admired, decided to leave. In the Rhineland on 1st April, Lic. Wilhelm Menn confided to the General Superintendent his concern that the Church should applaud the national revolution at a time when part of the population was exposed to mob violence. The General Superintendent's reply was highly characteristic:

To me it is fairly understandable, because of what Jewry, by its control of the Press, finance, the theatre, etc., has done to us . . . that justifiable collective anger, even when the people's frame of mind is not specifically anti-Semitic, should for once vent itself in violence. Never for a second has the black, red and gold flag[40] had any place either in my heart or in my home. I have always been a man of the extreme right.[41]

The main body of the Christian middle class may not altogether have approved of the boycott's methods, but to anti-Semitism itself they hardly objected at all. To resist the Third Reich's intentions regarding the Church by making an issue of the Aryan clause seemed to the clergy not only distasteful but also short-sighted if the Church was to receive protection and regain her influence. Not until August and September, when the German Christians forced the Church to adopt the political Aryan clause, did the clergy begin to show any marked reaction. What happened then, however, fulfilled Bonhoeffer's prediction that one day professors of theology and ministers would seek theological justification for the application of the Aryan clause within the Church.

Bonhoeffer was among the very few who, at the time of the political Aryan legislation on 7th April 1933, really sat down and made an effort to work out its possible consequences, both from the political and the ecclesiastical standpoint. Indeed, he may have been the first to see this matter as the crucial problem in the impending struggle,[42] though other theologians, for instance Heinz Kloppenburg and Heinrich Vogel, had published articles on the race issue.

Bonhoeffer's paper exposed the theological absurdity of a 'purely German' church from which members would be excluded on biological grounds. He had not at that time clearly formulated the concept of 'fatal

---

40. The flag of Germany during the Weimar Republic.
41. Stoltenhoff's letter to Menn, reprinted by G. van Norden, op. cit., p. 60.
42. 'Die Kirche vor der Judenfrage', GS II, pp. 44-53.

privilege', in this instance a privilege inseparable from the creation of an 'Aryan church'. His paper says:

We are in no way concerned with the question whether our members of German stock can continue to share responsibility with Jews for the communion of the Church. Rather, it is the task of the Christian proclamation to say: here, where Jew and German stand together under God's word, is the Church, here it is proven whether or not the Church is still the Church.[43]

By August 1933, Bonhoeffer was to conclude beyond all doubt that there could be no question of remaining with a church which excluded the Jews. In April the idea of repudiating church membership had still been too abstract for real consideration.

While he was engaged in writing the first section of his paper, the Jewish boycott had begun on 1st April. Bonhoeffer heard through Dohnanyi of the legislation for non-Aryan civil servants which the Government intended to promulgate on 7th April. He therefore added an introductory section[44] to the six theses, which in the event proved the most stimulating and important part of the paper, even though it contains much conservative thinking. He asks what must be the Church's opinion of a political action by the State which, on racial grounds, places the Jews on a separate legal basis. Bonhoeffer here tacitly calls in question the very 'criterion of race'—and proceeds to ask by 'what task the Church is confronted in consequence'.[45] Here the subject is the Jewish question as such, not only the church membership of Jewish Christians. To Bonhoeffer's distress, the latter question was ultimately entirely to swamp the former in the struggle by the Confessing Church to assert her claims, but the words 'Open your mouth for the dumb'[46] were constantly on his lips.

As a good Lutheran theologian, Bonhoeffer does not mince his words in this part of the article, when discussing whether and to what extent the Church should intervene in political matters. 'It is not her business either to praise legislation or to condemn it.'[47] We might well ask how that sentence would have sounded in his ears ten years later. But in 1933 Bonhoeffer still spoke a theological language that did not admit of an humanitarian-liberal policy. Yet already he was beginning to sound a new note and one which sometimes had a distinctly democratic ring about it, such as, for instance, his remark that 'a strong state' needs opposition and argument, and that these 'should be fostered by a certain amount of reserved encouragement'.[48]

Yet Bonhoeffer's then theological doctrine of the invasion of history by the Christian witness enabled him to write about the State in such

43. GS II, pp. 52 f.
44. GS II, pp. 45-50.
45. GS II, p. 44.
46. Prov. 31:8.
47. GS II, p. 45.
48. GS II, p. 46.

subversive terms that it is surprising that the edition of *Vormarsch* where this paper was published, escaped Goebbels's censorship. Perhaps the difficult theological argument with which it began was too much for the censor. But this is followed by a perfectly clear exposition of what Bonhoeffer expected of his church in April 1933. He saw the Church's responsibility as having three distinct phases.

1. The Church must ask the State 'whether it could answer for its action as legitimate political action . . . In relation to the Jewish question, the Church must now put that question with the utmost clarity.'[49] But who was to 'put that question with the utmost clarity'? Virtually everyone in those days, even Martin Rade in the *Christliche Welt*,[50] was talking in terms of the relative right to use force in revolution. No appreciable objection to political action was raised by the Church until the 1936 memorandum to Hitler.[51] When, ten years later, Bonhoeffer himself conceded the 'relative right to use force' he was, so far as the Church was concerned, the only man to do so.

2. The Church's second task, as Bonhoeffer saw it, was service on behalf of the victims of political action. 'The Church has an unconditional obligation towards the victims of any social order, even where those victims do not belong to the Christian community.'[52] It was something that needed to be said. As the persecutions initiated in April 1933 began in later years to assume considerable proportions, the Büro Grüber took on this responsibility on behalf of the Confessing Church.

Bonhoeffer sought criteria by which to estimate the moment when the first two tasks for which the Church was responsible would present themselves. These criteria he found to be either 'too much' or 'too little law and order' when 'any one group of political subjects is outlawed'. His answer was neither vague nor evasive: 'In the Jewish question, the first two possibilities for the Church today will be the exigencies of the hour.'[53] But the position he had adopted proved so wholly isolated that a few months after his article appeared, Bonhoeffer's disappointment at the continuing silence of his church nearly led him to turn away from it, and his decision to go to London was not unconnected with those sentiments.

3. What then was the third task? This went to the limit to which Bonhoeffer himself was prepared as a man to go. He declared that if the Church were to see the State unscrupulously meting out either too little or too much law and order, it was her position 'not only to bind up the victims beneath the wheel, but also to put a spoke in that wheel.'[54] Yet who should, indeed who could, assume responsibility for putting a spoke in the wheel? Evidently Bonhoeffer knew what he was saying. In the case of the first two tasks, he envisaged the possibility that individual

49. GS II, pp. 46, 48.   52. GS II, p. 48.
50. 'Neuer Anfang', CW, 1933, pp. 377 f.   53. GS II, p. 49.
51. See Ch. X, p. 440.   54. GS II, p. 48.

Christians might know that they would be called, 'should occasion arise, to accuse the State of offending against morality'.[55] But in the case of the third task, he could venture at this time to express no more than the Utopian hope: 'The necessity for immediate political intervention by the Church, however, must be decided by an Evangelical Council as and when the occasion arises, and hence cannot be casuistically construed beforehand.'[56] It is characteristic that Bonhoeffer should already have been aware of the hazards, if not the impossibility, of setting up in advance binding norms for revolutionary action. Years of growing oppression and of disillusionment both in his own church and in the ecumenical movement—years which he could not at this time have anticipated—would be needed before he could assume responsibility himself instead of placing it upon a 'council'. The young theologian still shied away from trusting to a personal decision where it was a question of endangering the structure of Church and State. But the third stage of responsibility, necessitating action without corporate decision, was to obtrude increasingly and in unsuspected ways into the course of his life. At last, one day, he became aware of it and it was then he renounced his ecclesiastical reputation.

That month of April was indeed disquieting. 'It is impossible to say where it will lead us.'[57] The consequences of the treatment of the Jews by the State were brought home to Bonhoeffer by the case of his brother-in-law Leibholz, their treatment by the Church, by the case of Franz Hildebrandt.

On 11th April Gerhard Leibholz's father died; he had never been baptized. Dietrich's relations would have liked him to conduct the funeral service, but on this occasion he succumbed to persuasion and consulted the General Superintendent. The latter advised him strongly against taking a funeral service for a Jew at this particular time. A few months later, on 23rd November, Dietrich wrote to his brother-in-law:

I am tormented by the thought . . . that I didn't do as you asked me as a matter of course. To be frank, I can't think what made me behave as I did. How could I have been so much afraid at the time? It must have seemed equally incomprehensible to all of you, and yet you said nothing. But it preys on my mind . . . because it's the kind of thing one can never make up for. So all I can do is to ask you to forgive my weakness then. I know now for certain that I ought to have behaved differently . . .

Hence it was the Jewish question upon which Bonhoeffer had from the outset been reluctant, both on personal and theological grounds, to embark on discussion relating to *Weltanschauung* with the National Socialists. The 'missionary spirit' was therefore equally foreign to him

55. GS II, p. 45.
56. GS II, p. 49.
57. To E. Sutz, 14.4.1933, GS I, p. 37.

and he left the evangelizing of the S.A. to the more moderate among the German Christians and to their tracts. His energies were wholly taken up in combating the Aryan clause. For he believed that only if everything were staked upon this one point could the message that was worthy of proclamation perhaps reveal itself.

It was wholly in keeping, both with his theology and his character, that Bonhoeffer's very first utterance in the church struggle should have been provoked by the complex of problems which his superiors in the Church, and even his friends, continued to regard and treat as a secondary issue.

Dismissals

During these weeks the universities were hit by their first severe crises. The Law for the Reconstruction of the Civil Service affected not only the so-called non-Aryan academic teachers but also professors with left-wing sympathies. National Socialist action committees at the universities were instructed on 1st April to bring about resolutions demanding the restriction of Jewish participation in academic disciplines, particularly as regards medicine and the law. The purpose of this was to prepare the ground and to provide the minister with a pretext for the law of 7th April.

As early as March Rust had suspended Emil Fuchs, a religious socialist and Professor of Theology at Kiel. Subsequent agitation by the committees against Paul Tillich at Frankfurt, Günther Dehn at Halle, and Karl Ludwig Schmidt at Bonn, was to lead sooner or later to their dismissal or exile.

Consequently all eyes were directed towards Bonn, wondering what would happen to Karl Barth who was a card-holding member of the Social Democratic Party. In Berlin Bonhoeffer met Georg Merz who told him that Barth was in danger. Bonhoeffer immediately tried to rally friends and colleagues to take up their stand for Barth, and also sent out requests to ecumenical friends asking them to put pressure from outside on the Ministry of Religious Affairs. It was said at this time that he was making use of contacts inside the Ministry to 'avert the fatal mistake'.[58] But soon Barth was able to write and tell him that work for the present 'was going on as usual', although he had informed Rust that he would not resign from the Social Democratic Party, and had reminded him of his intervention on behalf of Günther Dehn.[59]

Bonhoeffer was right in thinking that at that time it was still possible as it were, to fly in the face of the enemy, for agitation about measures taken against respected men was still of some avail. When, for example, E. Spranger in protest demanded his own suspension at the beginning

58. Letter of 14.4.1933, GS II, p. 42.
59. Letter of 18.4.1933, GS II, pp. 42 f.

of the new term, the Ministry was at great pains to get him to withdraw his request. At this juncture the departure of men such as Werner Jäger, Wilhelm Röpke or Paul Hindemith was unwelcome to the State because it impaired its reputation abroad.

Hindenburg, too, intervened in the spate of dismissals that followed 7th April by securing the exemption from the terms of the law of those non-Aryans who had fought in the war. At this stage it had still been possible to stave off the dismissal of Bonhoeffer's brother-in-law, Leibholz, who was not suspended from office until March 1935.

But isolated action could do nothing to alter the overall development. Berlin University had never before been drained of so much academic ability. When Bonhoeffer took up his London pastorate six months later, he shouldered the laborious task of finding means to provide for this first wave of dismissed *émigrés*.[60]

Ecumenism

After such tremendous upheavals, it was not surprising that, during this month, a wide variety of visitors converged upon Berlin in an endeavour to assess the new position at first hand.

The Bishop of Chichester, G. K. A. Bell, Chairman of the Universal Council for 'Life and Work', had received from Kapler the 'official' letter of 30th March.[61] The assurances it contained were, Bell found, contradicted by the disquieting news from Berlin daily published in *The Times*. He therefore initiated the first of a long series of actions on behalf of the German Church. He himself was immobilized throughout April by a throat operation. So half way through the month Henriod was asked to go from Geneva to Berlin to obtain first-hand information. There he met Bonhoeffer who had good reason to fear that his colleagues and superiors might present things to Bell's envoy in too optimistic a light. They might seek to reassure him and would ask him not to upset the apple-cart from the outside when all was still in an initial state of crisis, with the added argument, perhaps, that it was necessary to erect a strong bulwark of order against the atheist East. Bonhoeffer's own views were of quite a different kind.

In his diary Henriod wrote of Berlin in April: 'It is astonishing in Germany to discover that foreigners are expected to be grateful that Germany has raised a bulwark against Bolshevism.' And the annual report of 'Life and Work' does in fact contain the information that the leaders of the German Church:

. . . explained to them the difficulties which the Church was facing, and the steps they were taking to deal with them, and had requested their

60. See Ch. VIII, pp. 258 f., 336 f.; cf. GS I, p. 317; GS II, pp. 158, 195 f.
61. Minutes of Novi Sad., pp. 4, 5.

fellow Christians to have patience and not to press them for action which might be premature.[62]

The annual report of the World Alliance also demonstrates what was, in Bonhoeffer's view, the excessive caution shown in Berlin:

It became increasingly clear in the course of these discussions that, in passing judgement upon the conditions in Germany, there is one thing above all that foreign countries must not overlook; in Germany they are experiencing, not a change of Government, not a reorganization, but a real revolution. It is owing to this fact that so little that is definite, so little that is final and conclusive can be said in regard to ecclesiastical conditions and likewise to the work of the Alliance.[63]

Bonhoeffer believed, however, that the people who were most anxious for reticence were now the National Socialists. This was reason enough to speak out.

IV MAY: YOUNG REFORMERS

Beginning of Term

In the Wangenheimstrasse preparations were being made for the beginning of term. The new policy in education was now making itself felt at the universities. Karl Bonhoeffer recalled with shame those early weeks of the summer term at Berlin University:

Of the official ceremonies at the university, the only one I attended was the address by Rust, the Minister for Cultural Affairs. Unfortunately neither I nor any of the other professors had the courage on this occasion to get up and walk out in protest against the insulting attitude adopted by the Minister towards the academic profession.[64]

Young and hitherto wholly unknown medical trainees came, as Party representatives, to heads of hospitals whom they instructed to dismiss out of hand the Jewish doctors employed in their establishments. Some allowed themselves to be persuaded. Any suggestion that such matters came under the jurisdiction of the Ministry and not under that of the Party was countered by threats. The Dean tried to persuade faculty members to join the Party in a body. His attempt was foiled by individual refusals. Nor did the Ministry at first make any move to meet the demand for the dismissal of Jewish assistant doctors. But doctors in individual hospitals were constantly spied upon to discover their attitude towards the Party . . . So far as my own hospital was concerned, I can say that most of the doctors withstood the pressure. But the hospital was a thorn in the flesh of the *Dozentenführung* [the leadership of the university teachers]. I managed to avoid putting up a portrait of Hitler, and in this my hospital

62. Annual Report, 'Life and Work', Sept. 1933, p. 45.
63. Annual World Alliance Report, 1932-3, pp. 20 f., 33.
64. K. Bonhoeffer, *Lebenserinnerungen*, p. 118.

was probably unique among those of the Charité. My successor after I left in 1938 made up for this by setting up an outsize bust in the entrance hall.[65]

In the theological faculty things were at first rather better. But although they were training future servants of the Church, the teachers were civil servants and as such were subject to the Aryan clause. It was to be a few weeks, however, before the activity of the German Christians was to make itself felt among the students.

As in every other university town in Germany, the new cultural 'will to live' was celebrated on 10th May with a holocaust which took place in the Opernplatz. Beneath the monument to the brothers Humboldt outside the university, students threw hundreds of books into the blazing bonfire, shouting the names of the banned authors as they did so: Albert Einstein and Thomas Mann, Sigmund Freud and Walther Rathenau, Stefan Zweig, Erich Maria Remarque, and Theodor Heuss. Goebbels concluded this anti-intellectual celebration with Ulrich von Hutten's cry: 'Oh century, oh scholarship, it is a joy to be alive!'

But should not some theologians' names also have been numbered among the 'decadent'? The new ecclesiastical journal, *Evangelium im Dritten Reich*, in its nineteenth issue of 7th May, suggested that the faculties were reacting much too sluggishly.

Coordination of the theological faculties . . . At Kiel, Marburg and Bonn, to name only a few, former Democrats and even Marxists occupy the desks where they ply their long-defunct liberalism. When a chair fell vacant in Berlin, the faculty is reliably reported to have put forward names that would grace a museum . . . We demand that chairs now vacant, or becoming so during the next few years, be filled by theologians of our own way of thinking, until the time comes when only German Christians are working in German faculties.[66]

When, on Titius's dismissal, a chair fell vacant at Berlin University it was given to Georg Wobbermin, who proceeded to do all that the Third Reich expected of him. However, there was no immediate public rift in the faculty, even when Siegmund-Schultze was dismissed during the summer as 'politically unacceptable'. As a junior lecturer, Bonhoeffer was not really involved in departmental politics. The only influence he could exert was through go-betweens of whom there were very few. He did his best to concentrate on the most difficult of his lectures, that on Christology.

First Opposition

Not only had the progress of the German Christians during April induced the principal ecclesiastical bodies to fight for the independence of

65. K. Bonhoeffer, op. cit., p. 115.
66. CW, 1933, p. 476.

the Church by tactical and constitutional means; it had also brought into being throughout the country theologically-orientated groups. These early, informal associations looked for suitable ways to express and safeguard the character of the Church in face of the new challenge. They used slogans and wrote articles, which might take the form of anything from defence to reluctant criticism of the oppressed church administrations. At the end of April, Georg Schulz published, on behalf of the Sydow Fraternity, a manifesto, 'Discerning the Spirits'. In May, eleven Westphalian pastors, among them the future martyr Ludwig Steil, issued a declaration in which, just like Bonhoeffer, they rejected the exclusion of Jewish Christians from the Church as heretical and schismatic. This was also the implication of Heinrich Vogel's 'Eight Articles of Evangelical Doctrine'.

Less extreme was the comprehensive opposition in the nucleus of the Young Reformation Movement, amalgamating a number of different groups, which was constituted at the beginning of May. They wanted unabridged Reformed theology, but they also wanted, as was indeed imperative, to influence church politics. The Café am Knie in Berlin-Charlottenburg was the meeting place of Gerhard Jacobi, Walter Künneth, H. M. Schreiner-Rostock and Hans Lilje. Each represented a number of groups of varying complexions. A manifesto appeared on 12th May bearing a list of resounding names, a list impressive enough to cause a considerable stir in Germany. But those in the know were bound to realize that the hopes this aroused rested upon too many unresolved antitheses as embodied, from the standpoint of theology and ecclesiastical history, in these very names. For there, set down peacefully cheek by jowl, were the signatures of many who would soon be only too anxious to part company again. In this instance the desire for reform was to culminate in strongly illiberal tendencies which showed a quite remarkable similarity to the German Christians.

The members responsible in Berlin distributed the manifesto with an appendix which was distinctly sharper in tone and had a 'confessionally conscious' ring about it.[67] This leaflet bore the names of thirty-seven Berlin personalities who were later to move into the forefront of the church struggle. Here Niemöller's name appeared for the first time. Here, too—but not in the manifesto mentioned above—were the signatures of Sasse and Bonhoeffer. The Berlin appendix was a sign of independence; it passed on the 'rallying cry' as 'guiding principles which we regard as a suitable working programme for the restructuring of our Church'. The conclusion contains expressions as strong as 'abuse' and 'leading astray'.

That the Reformed manifesto was one of compromise can hardly have escaped Bonhoeffer. Gertrud Staewen, Barth's hostess in Berlin, wrote him a letter full of misgivings about the Young Reformers, 'as one of

67. Kirchenkampfarchiv, Berlin, File 264A.

whom Bonhoeffer, most distressingly, regards himself'. But in all probability Bonhoeffer took part because he did not yet know for certain whether the movement would uphold the demand for independence in ecclesiastical affairs and for the rejection of the Aryan clause, or whether the dangerous elements of the 'Church of the German Nation' would win the day. We shall see presently what Bonhoeffer was subsequently to make of his Young Reformers' student group.

The fronts were still remarkably fluid. Thus to many Young Reformers it came as a pleasant surprise to discover that their illiberalism and rejection of parliamentary procedure closely resembled that of, say, the East Prussian branch of the German Christians, who also shared a strong revulsion for the old, and desire for a new, Church. But a breach came during the second half of May on the question of the future leadership of the Reich Church as laid down in the Loccum constitution.

During Ascension week the German Christians nominated Ludwig Müller as their candidate, since they maintained that only a man who enjoyed Hitler's trust could now become National Bishop. On 27th May the regional church leaders, on the other hand, those who had agreed to the Loccum constitution in Eisenach, by a small majority elected Bodelschwingh as National Bishop, though Schöffel, Wurm and Rendtorff voted for Müller! The Young Reformers immediately gave their support to Bodelschwingh. The German Christians, however, enlisted the help of publicity media and the Party offices in an attempt to have his election rescinded. Thus the controversy brought the Young Reformers into the limelight sooner than they would have liked. They were hardly aware that this time was to some extent a favourable one, for after his important appeasement speech of 17th May, Hitler wished for a general lowering of temperatures.

V JUNE: STATE COMMISSAR

Basle

In the week after Whitsun, four Frenchmen and four Germans met on 7th-9th June at the house of the Basle pastor, Iselin. Lord Dickinson and Henriod were also there on behalf of the World Alliance. Bonhoeffer, Toureille and Henriod had been full of optimism while arranging the discussions during the previous winter. Wilfred Monod on the French side, and Siegmund-Schultze on the German, had long desired this sort of consultation, unattended by any kind of publicity.

When the meeting finally took place, however, circumstances were very different from what had been anticipated. Controversial matters such as Versailles, disarmament and equality of status still remained unresolved. Both parties were conscious of the tragic omissions of past years. But whereas on the German side the question of allegiance or non-allegiance to the new German State remained unclarified, on the French side the old mistrust had been rekindled and furthermore there had been disturbing statements on the part of the Church. The 1933-4 annual report of the World Alliance contains the words: 'The French delegates expressed the keen uneasiness which some aspects of the aforesaid revolution and the orientation of the German Evangelical Church cause them.'[68]

The meeting was overshadowed by anxiety lest Siegmund-Schultze's days in Germany might now be numbered. His community social work and voluntary service association in Berlin had already been dissolved. In recent weeks he had been devoting himself to the assistance of non-Aryan officials and academics who were being forced to emigrate. And, in fact, three weeks after the Basle meeting, Hitler ordered his expulsion from Germany.[69] As far as church politics were concerned, there was still some hope during these early June days that Bodelschwingh's election might stabilize the situation.

Bodelschwingh

The German Christians alienated a great deal of sympathy by their attacks, at the moment of his nomination as National Bishop, upon a man so patently sincere and moderate as the director of Bethel.[70] The blatant way in which Müller, on the evening after the election, expressed his sentiments in a broadcast would, in more normal times, have disqualified him for good; this man, who had suffered defeat on 27th May, told his fellow-countrymen:

The church authorities have not listened to the call of the hour . . . The solution they have proposed to us in the question of the National Bishop has nothing to do with the belief and hope and love now stirring among the hitherto apathetic millions . . .'[71]

Almost reluctantly, Bodelschwingh came to Berlin and took up his quarters in the Church Federation Office. He brought with him as his assistant the Westphalian pastor, Gerhard Stratenwerth, and also engaged Martin Niemöller, formerly of Westphalia and now of Dahlem, for special duties. From then on, Niemöller was constantly involved in the church troubles. He appeared from time to time in the Jacobi circle where church politics became increasingly the subject of discussion, as they grew ever more turbulent. It was in this circle that Bonhoeffer met Niemöller.

From day to day the German Christian campaign against the 'undesirable' National Bishop was intensified. They prevented his reception

68. Annual World Alliance Report, 1933-4. p. 21.
69. On 24th June 1933.
70. The famous epileptic settlement at Bielefeld, Westphalia. (Editor.)
71. *Gotthardbriefe*, 27th May 1933. p. 80

by Hitler, obtained readily forthcoming expert legal opinion on procedural errors at the Eisenach election, and organized throughout the country demonstrations of 'seething popular emotion'. In this way, the wave of factitious anti-Bodelschwingh pro-Müller agitation at length reached the universities and led to Bonhoeffer's first public appearance in the church troubles.

Very soon after this there occurred the clash for which the German Christians had been waiting. It came about as follows: Towards the end of the month the Minister for Religious Affairs discovered that the Church had exceeded her terms of reference in the question of Kapler's succession, and he was thus able to install a state commissar. But this development was to take a more serious turn than Hitler would have wished at the time.

Stormy Meetings

In June the German Christians succeeded in setting up a 'German Christian Students' Fighting League' at nearly every university. Partly with the support of other student bodies, they organized meetings for the purpose of passing resolutions in favour of Ludwig Müller, and put their plans into operation with chauvinistic ruthlessness.

The *Junge Kirche*, then recently founded by Hanns Lilje and Fritz Söhlmann as the organ of the Young Reformation Movement, contains an account of a students' meeting in Breslau from which we learn that, of the 300 people present, 200 had already left the meeting when a resolution in favour of Müller was proposed.

In Berlin, disputes began at the university during the eventful week that was to end in the installation of an ecclesiastical state commissar. There were two meetings, the first on Monday 19th June, arranged by the German Christians, the other on Thursday 22nd June, organized by the university chaplains and the opposition. The second had been carefully prepared; it was to be a discussion of the conflicting points of view. But for a time it seemed doubtful whether it would take place at all because of the German Christians' action in arranging their own meeting first. During that meeting, Bonhoeffer took a back seat, and left the talking to his students among the audience. At the second, he took a public stand as one of the speakers.

What was stated and done during these days is comprehensible only when it is remembered that the opposition was concerned solely with combating Müller's advancement and the terrorization of the Church; they did not wish to abjure their national allegiance and thus be convicted of 'reaction', nor did those among them who also objected to Hitler on political grounds, desire to incur accusations of treachery on account of their opposition on behalf of the Church.

Bonhoeffer and his circle hastily concocted a plan of action for the

German Christian meeting on the Monday. The opposition party agreed that the signal to leave should be given when the resolution in favour of Müller was moved. It was a dangerous gesture for it might be branded as reactionary and unpatriotic and entail the rustication of the spokesmen and a prohibition of assembly for the opposition, which in turn would endanger the meeting of 22nd June.

Hence, on Saturday 17th June, Bonhoeffer and the university chaplain Bronisch-Holtze sought out Secretary of State Lammers at the Reich Chancellory where a preliminary meeting between them and Counsellor Wienstein was arranged.[72] There Bonhoeffer and Bronisch-Holtze pointed out that the students' meeting on the Monday was liable to be browbeaten into conformity and that this would present a false picture, since in reality most of the students, including those organized by the National Socialists, supported Bodelschwingh and not Ludwig Müller. Wienstein made a note of these objections, but for the sake of form referred his visitors to the Ministry for Religious Affairs.

At one o'clock hundreds of students assembled in the university's *Auditorium Maximum.* The meeting was expected to determine the spontaneous adherence of the students to the German Christian Movement of Faith. But as reported in the *Tägliche Rundschau* of 20th June, 'upon the announcement of the resolution for the episcopal candidature of Chaplain Müller, nine-tenths of the audience left the auditorium'. Immediately following this, the opposition held its own meeting in the courtyard beside Hegel's statue; among those present were men who were recognizably Party and S.A. members. While rejecting the proceedings in the *Auditorium Maximum,* the opposition affirmed their allegiance to the State; according to the *Tägliche Rundschau,* 'at a subsequent meeting they submitted themselves to Adolf Hitler's leadership'

These two demonstrations had aroused considerable tension because of the unplanned nature of much of the proceedings. Now both university chaplains, accompanied by two student supporters of Bodelschwingh in S.A. uniform, visited the office of the Minister for Religious Affairs. As Bonhoeffer was subsequently to relate at Bradford, they did not succeed in speaking to the Minister, Rust, but were received by a counsellor, one Gerullis,[73] to whom they recounted what had happened. As a precaution, however, that same day Bonhoeffer also sent a short account of the proceedings to Wienstein at the Reich Chancellory, and this was put before Lammers.[74] Concluding the description of the students' anti-Müller actions, he remarked: '. . . immediately afterwards there was a brief demonstration . . . during which one student gave a *Heil* for the Reich Chancellor, the rest following suit.'

Three days later, on 22nd June, the second meeting took place in the

72. For a full account see MW V, VI, B.1.
73. GS II, p. 124.
74. MW V, VI, B.1.

university's new hall. Though lively, it was more dignified and academic than the previous meeting, and there were no interruptions.

This time invitations were sent out by a 'Working Committee of Evangelical Students', with the backing of the university chaplain's department. Bronisch-Holtze had founded a loosely-knit association of Protestant students, either members or non-members of students' corps, and had given it the above name. The subject for discussion was described as 'The Struggle for the Church'. Those speaking for the German Christians were Emanuel Hirsch, Lic. Vogelsang—then a colleague of Ludwig Müller's—and Professor Fabricius; speakers for the Catholic Centre Party were the Berlin professors Deissmann, Sellin and Lütgert, and also F. K. Schumann from Halle; and for the Young Reformers, Bonhoeffer. There were heated exchanges between the professors and individual students before a university audience said to have numbered 2,000.

Hirsch and his friends insisted that there should be no attempt at disassociation from the new State, and that advantage must be taken of the great missionary opportunities it offered. Winterhager relates that F. K. Schumann sought to conciliate both sides, thus incurring vehement reproaches from Bonhoeffer after the meeting. The minutes read:

Lic. Bonhoeffer discussed the meaning of the struggle. If God had involved the Church in struggle, it was to humble her. There was therefore no place in this dispute for self-justification. Anyone who simply made accusations without also accusing himself had failed to understand the meaning of the struggle. (The strength of the Church rests in her ability to enter into atonement.)

Once more the difference became apparent which is described in Romans 14 between the strong in faith and the weak in faith. The strong in faith was he who did not expel others, the weak in faith, he who restricted the community. Today the weak in faith had introduced a racial law. The strength of the others would now consist in being open to the petition of the weak. But they must beware, for it was precisely the weak who were the aggressive ones, the reformers. (The substance of the Church is at stake in the tension between the strong and the weak.)

A movement of faith should not underrate the Confession (in answer to Fabricius's statements about the Jewish question). When this happened in early Christian times, a council was called.

And today we should demand a council. Its decisions should be binding. (Everyone must legitimate himself before the Confession.) The last possibility open to Protestantism was separation. Now the Confession was at stake. There were two points of doctrine to be decided: the doctrine of the Church and the doctrine of Creation. While the struggle in the Church was a great gift, the greatest gift was peace.[75]

75. Kirchenkampfarchiv, Berlin. The comments enclosed in brackets are from the notes of the Hungarian student Ferenc Lehel (see IKDB, pp. 68 ff.).

Three points emerge clearly from this report:

1. Bonhoeffer's serious conviction that the struggle was taking place within an undivided church.

2. During the preceding weeks, theologians had been consulting the Bible to see if it presented any opportunity of permitting the acceptance of the Aryan clause. From now on we shall constantly encounter the argument that, for the sake of the weak in faith, it might actually be possible to eliminate the offence of racial non-conformity in certain members of the community by means of a regrouping. This argument was unmasked by Bonhoeffer as a trick of the 'weak' who would like to see their wish become the heretical law of the 'strong', but had not yet succeeded in bringing this about.

3. If the 'weak' were to win, this would inevitably result in separation. This is where Bonhoeffer introduces his idea of the council decision. To most of the audience this must have seemed like routing out ancient halberds from dusty ecclesial armouries. And Schumann, in his contribution to the discussion, emphatically rejected any idea of 'schism'. But more than any other aspect of Bonhoeffer's speech this one was seized upon for discussion. 'I'm told that in your speech you suggested convening a "council"', ran a postcard from Gertrud Staewen.[76] Bonhoeffer displayed a faith in the concreteness of the Church that astounded his audience. Schumann immediately warned against any 'idolization' of the Church. And again, how was a council, willing and able to make decisions, to be brought into being? But Bonhoeffer was aiming high; his own church and the ecumenical churches must be brought to have greater faith in themselves and in their concrete assembly. Was he not thus infringing Protestantism's sacred possessions, tolerance and liberalism?

Indeed Bonhoeffer, thoroughly impregnated as he was with a liberal tradition, was now becoming increasingly illiberal. With sure intuition he sensed that in 1933 respectable political and theological liberalism was digging its own grave because, out of supercilious or merely weak *laissez-faire*, it was leaving decision-making to the tyrant; he could see that the time for compromise was fast disappearing, and that the time for a clear 'yes or no' had almost arrived. Thus in his writings of 1932 and 1933, Bonhoeffer proposed to his own church and to the ecumenical movement that they should rediscover 'council', 'heresy', 'Confession and doctrinal decision'—and this at a time when scepticism was paralyzing the experienced and when his elders looked upon the younger man as a mere visionary.

But these were no idle dreams. What Bonhoeffer had in view was, to his intense joy, to be realized a year later: the Barmen and Dahlem Synods—as a 'council'—acknowledged and arrived at doctrinal decisions, defined the heretic and called upon the Church, in obedience

76. Postcard of 26.6.1933.

to the Gospel, to separate from him. It very soon became apparent, however, that Bonhoeffer's belief in synods was deeper and more concrete than was that of the majority who attended them. For both at home and in the ecumenical movement he was finally to suffer defeat in the unequal struggle against the synod members and their image of themselves as 'fathers of the council'.

As a man, Bonhoeffer's commitment was made possible by his strength of mind, and as a theologian by his faith in the Holy Spirit. He may also have believed that now, once decisions had been taken, it was only by adhering to them that the valuable tradition of liberalism could be preserved through the period of tyranny.

Two days after this Berlin University debate the position had altered drastically. Here, again, Bonhoeffer was to profess very definite ideas, which were beyond his fellows and were regarded by them as illusory.

August Jäger

On that same Thursday, 22nd June, Kapler resigned his office as President of the Evangelical Church Federation (Reich) and of the Supreme Church Council (Prussia). His successor in the latter post, although provisionally appointed only as commissar by the Church Senate, was the Rhineland General Superintendent Stoltenhoff. Although Stoltenhoff's attitude towards the new State was one of impeccable conformity, the Minister for Religious Affairs saw this as a favourable opportunity for intervention. He decreed that there had been an infringement of the state agreement of 1931 in accordance with which the Prussian Government, with Göring at its head, should have had a say in the appointment, and declared a state of emergency in Prussia; then, on Saturday 24th June—Saturday was a favourite day for revolutionary action—he nominated the Wiesbaden magistrate, August Jäger, State Commissar of Prussia, 'to put an end to strife within the Church'. In fact this was to mark the real beginning of that strife. Without delay Jäger appointed state commissars for each of the ecclesiastical provinces in Old Prussia, as also for the larger associations. The commissars, some of them in S.A. uniform, at once took over the consistorial presidents' offices. In a broadcast on 27th June, Jäger declared that resistance was 'betrayal of the people and the State' and would be suppressed 'as revolt and rebellion against the state authority'. The police chiefs were instructed to prevent any sabotage of these dispositions; all representative church bodies were declared dissolved, the employees of the Evangelical Supreme Church Council were dismissed and the General Superintendent was relieved of office. The lawyer, Dr. Friedrich Werner, whose role in later years was to be of some significance, appointed Jäger President of the Supreme Church Council, Hossenfelder Spiritual Vice-President, and Ludwig Müller head of the Old Prussian Union and of the Church

Federation Office. On 28th June at Müller's orders, the latter building was occupied by the S.A.

It was a tremendous shock, and the resulting chaos was indescribable. Nothing of the kind had ever happened before. On 24th June Bodelschwingh resigned immediately from his office as National Bishop in protest against the installation of a state commissar. Dibelius also protested—and his attitude was joyfully applauded throughout the country—'I cannot allow any state commissar to relieve me of the most personal responsibilities of my office.'[77]

On Sunday, 2nd July, there was a series of dramatic crises. As the supreme spiritual authority in Old Prussia, Hossenfelder ordered services of praise and thanksgiving for which the churches were to be decorated with flags, and directed that the following message be read from the pulpit:

All those who are concerned for the safe structure of our Church in the great revolution of these times, must . . . feel deeply thankful that the State should have assumed, in addition to all its tremendous tasks, the great load and burden of reorganizing the Church.[78]

At ten o'clock Ludwig Müller conducted a service in the Cathedral as did Hossenfelder in the Kaiser Wilhelm Memorial Church in the course of which this proclamation was read.

The dismissed general superintendents, on the other hand, had suggested a service of atonement and prayer, and their recommendation was disseminated throughout Berlin by the Young Reformers in every possible way. In Steglitz Pastor Grossmann was arrested by the S.A.—the first arrest in the church struggle. That evening Jacobi conducted the service of atonement in the Kaiser Wilhelm Memorial Church beginning with the announcement of Grossman's arrest and a call for a prayer of intercession. In the Jesus-Christus Church in Dahlem the ministers Fritz Müller, Röhricht and Niemöller, appeared together before the congregation. As they pronounced the second article of the Creed, the congregation joined in spontaneously. Such a thing had never been known before. From then on the practice was to spread until it ultimately found acceptance throughout the German Church.

The unrest assumed the proportions of an avalanche. Protest delegations and teachers travelled to Berlin and converged on the Chancellory. Bonhoeffer composed a 'Declaration of the Ministers of Greater Berlin' which was concluded on 6th July and sent, with 106 signatures, to the Reich Chancellor.[79] Bodelschwingh obtained a hearing from Hindenburg, who protested to Hitler. The latter, who was engaged in conduct-

77. i.e. the spiritual leadership of his diocese which had been invested in him by the Church and which only he could occupy. Letter of 27.6.1933.
78. From G. van Norden, op. cit., p. 74.
79. For the text see MW V, VI, C.2.

ing a policy of appeasement abroad and was also concerned with inducing a more favourable frame of mind in the Catholic Church, promised Hindenburg that he would soon placate the Evangelical Church. Hence the Minister of the Interior, Frick, was told to speed up the work of producing a new constitution for the one Reich Church in cooperation with the twenty-eight regional church authorities. The state commissars were withdrawn and the dismissals of the general superintendents and *Oberkirchenräte* revoked. On 14th July Hitler proclaimed that work on the constitution was complete. Surprisingly soon afterwards, on 23rd July, he announced a general church election. All at once things seemed to be conforming to Hitler's speech of 6th July in which he announced the end of the revolution. Another indication seemed to be the Concordat, which the Holy See concluded with the Third Reich on 20th July.

The battle had been short if hard. Now it remained to be seen if victory had really been won and the attack averted.

Interdict

The struggle was now no longer merely against part of the Church, but against the State and its political measures. Bonhoeffer and his students were energetically involved in a dramatic conflict that lasted barely three weeks. The students not only provided an indispensable news service for those who had been dismissed, they also formulated and disseminated their own protests. One such declaration plainly derives from Bonhoeffer himself. This essay already has the character of a short confession. It states in three theses the Biblical and reforming truth applicable to the contingency. Regeneration was only attainable by a return to the pure proclamation; membership of the Church was irrespective of race, and offices must be filled on an entirely spiritual basis. The whole is written in the first person plural—'we see', 'we want', 'we believe'—and concludes with concrete and real demands: 'We reject . . . we demand . . . no intervention, no Hossenfelder . . .'[80]

All this went off with encouraging smoothness: demonstrations on behalf of the general superintendents, protesting delegations and services of atonement. Then, at the beginning of July, Barth arrived on the scene. But Bonhoeffer was still not satisfied, for he was alarmed by the sluggish reactions of the church assemblies. He felt that the clergy should have displayed greater vigour and efficacy in countering state intervention, and in such a way as to make everyone realize unmistakably that the whole Church as such was involved, and not merely her leading figures.

At the meetings Bonhoeffer and Hildebrandt represented the view that the clergy and general superintendents should proclaim what amounted to an interdict. This would mean that while the government

80. GS II, pp. 56 f., 4.7.1933.

of the state commissars lasted, the clergy would announce and put into effect a boycott on funeral services. But all attempts to get the idea of an interdict accepted proved vain; very few people showed any understanding for the ideas of these two young men. The reaction was either one of indignation over such political intransigence or of failure to recognize the potential of these tactics. Indeed the notion was not so illusory after all, for in 1941 the Norwegian clergy did not hesitate to lay down office in this way, thus securing a lasting victory.[81]

Now, for the first time, the two friends contemplated the possibility of leaving the Evangelical Church. Martin Niemöller also considered a schismatic move.[82] On 18th June, a week before the seizure of power by Jäger, Hossenfelder and Müller, Hildebrandt had been ordained. Now the friends were puzzled by the question as to what ordination signified in a church which allowed herself to be coordinated, and which issued decrees on 'racial conformity' such as would legally exclude from office the man who had just been ordained. They therefore held that this organization should be denied the name 'church', a name that should be contested not by words alone. The boundary of the possible *status confessionis*, which, at the students' demonstration, had been hardly more than an implication hinted at with fear and trembling, seemed to have been reached sooner than might have been expected.

To Bonhoeffer and Hildebrandt the struggle seemed too much like a reactionary attempt to recapture former positions, an attempt which was, indeed, soon to succeed. What they sought, however, was the rebirth out of crisis of a regenerated church. 'I am afraid . . . that the erosion will be gradual and continuous since there is now insufficient strength for united action . . . Then back we go to the conventicles.'[83] By 'united action', he meant interdict.

While the two friends were engaged in these impatient deliberations, a message came from Bonn to clarify the situation. This was Karl Barth's document *Theological Existence Today*. In a very short space of time 30,000 copies had been distributed throughout the country.

VI JULY: CHURCH ELECTION

Although the church election of 1933 was to a large extent rigged and there was little doubt that the German Christians would win, the Young Reformers had to play their part and do the best they could. Bonhoeffer threw himself without reserve into the desperate campaign.

I have been fully taken up with what has been happening in church politics. Now we are on the eve of a decision which is, I believe, of prime import-

81. See Ch. XII, pp. 656 f.
82. See G. Niemöller, *Die erste Bekenntnissynode der Deutschen Evangelishen Kirche zu Barmen*, 1959, p. 42.
83. To E. Sutz, 17.7.1933, GS I, p. 38.

ance in the politics of the Church. I have little doubt that the German Christians will emerge victorious and that concomitantly the outline of the new Church will soon become apparent, but it will be questionable whether we shall be able to recognize it as the Church.[84]

Election Prospects

The decree issued at short notice by the Reich Government was itself of doubtful legality. It unequivocally favoured the German Christians, who had at their disposal the help of Party organizations and publicity media. With hardly a week to go after the election had been announced, there was small hope of success for the opposition which, although discredited and unorganized, was the only voice raised against the State capable of emphasizing the need for justice, impartiality and dignity in the election. There was no longer enough time for the opposition to get organized, which would have meant at least the reinstatement in office of the general superintendents and the members of the Supreme Church Council.

It is true that the Government had appointed Secretary of State Pfundtner 'plenipotentiary of the Minister of the Interior for the supervision of the impartial conduct of the church elections', and declared that the elections were free and that any attempt to swing them by forcible means was inadmissible; but who was going to investigate, or expose the innumerable local cases of coercion? The *Tägliche Rundschau*, the only daily to publish news favourable to the opposition, had now been proscribed; bands of S.A. broke up election meetings and intimidation was the order of the day; it took the form of threats of dismissal or financial sanctions against anyone who, by opposing the German Christians, revealed himself a traitor to the National Socialist State. Indeed Hitler himself wrote in blatant terms to Ludwig Müller on 19th July: 'I wish . . . to thank you and the German Christians, and to assure you of my especial and lasting confidence.'[85] It was almost a miracle that in many places the Young Reformers were able to draft a programme offering an alternative to that of the German Christians.

The traditional parties in church elections, the Positive Union and the Liberals, seemed to have totally disappeared. Both liberals and orthodox suddenly found themselves side by side with the German Christians, or else with the Young Reformers, and many, surprised to find themselves in such company, felt ashamed of their new allies. All, however, hastened to affirm, not once but many times over, that the past was now finished and done with and that everyone was putting his shoulder to the wheel to ensure the success of Hitler's state. Even the Young Reformers excelled themselves in the endeavour not to become politically suspect. And the *Junge Kirche* went so far as to

84. Ibid.
85. G. van Norden, op. cit., p. 82.

declare: 'Thankful and determined, we stand behind Hindenburg and Hitler as the leaders of our state, for by their intervention they have now paved the way to freedom for the Church . . .' There was no place for reaction either within the Church or in her politics . . . 'Our attitude to the State is one of obedience and love. In this election we are concerned *only* with the Church.'[86]

The other side, of course, immediately spotted the different phraseology. They would never have spoken of 'leaders' in the plural, mentioning Hindenburg as one of them, nor would they have placed the names, where both were used, in that order. Their turn of speech was of a somewhat different kind—and not only where Hossenfelder was concerned. Even a churchman as trusted and influential as Erich Stange could bring himself to say:

It is inexcusable that the Church today should remain aloof from a State which is patently and explicitly expiating the fall from grace,[87] instead of welcoming that state with open arms.[88]

Hans Schomerus was actually able to suggest the dissolution of the Church as an independent organization, so that 'a national office of Christian education' might be formed on a denominational basis, under an archbishop appointed by statute 'Supreme Head of national Christian education'.[89]

All these zealous assurances of loyalty to the Third Reich notwithstanding, the electors were perfectly alive to the difference between the German Christian slogan, 'Build the new Church of Christ in the new State of Adolf Hitler', and that of the Young Reformers, 'Gospel and Church'.

Gestapo

Bonhoeffer had not really ever allowed these tumultuous events to interfere with his Christology lectures, but he cancelled the lecture in election week, when he and his students were devoting themselves night and day to feverish preparations for the election. His parents put at his disposal their home and his father's car and chauffeur. During the weekend of 15th and 16th July, leaflets were written and duplicated.[90]

However on Monday 17th July the Gestapo entered the offices of the Young Reformers in Dahlem and by confiscating the leaflets and electoral programmes set all their laborious preparations at nought.[91] The German Christians had succeeded in obtaining a legal injunction

86. JK, 1933, pp. 43, 59.
87. In the nineteenth century the State had maintained a false neutrality towards the Church.
88. W. Niemöller, *Die Evangelische Kirche im Dritten Reich*, 1956, p. 87.
89. *Deutsches Volkstum*, 1933, pp. 918 ff.
90. See for example GS II, pp. 59 ff.
91. JK, 1933, p. 60.

against the use by the Young Reformers of the first name they had chosen for their programme, 'Programme of the Evangelical Church'.

The morning after this set-back, on 18th July, Bonhoeffer and Jacobi drove to Prinz Albrecht Strasse, later so notorious. The Gestapo were not yet pursuing Bonhoeffer and Jacobi; for the time being it was they who were on the tracks of the Gestapo.

Jacobi tells us that the Gestapo headquarters showed every evidence of their recent move. He himself was wearing, as was then customary, the two Iron Crosses he had won in the First World War. They would like to have taken with them (but at the last moment decided to leave behind), a real, flesh and blood, uniformed S.A. member of the Young Reformation Movement. By obstinate insistence Bonhoeffer and Jacobi finally succeeded in making their way to the head of the Gestapo, Rudolf Diels. They reminded him and the official immediately responsible of the State's promise that the election should be free and secret, and pointed out that the action taken on the previous day was a clear case of obstruction and interference. Diels yielded, on condition that the name 'Evangelical Church' should be dropped,[92] and consented to Jacobi's suggestion that the words 'Gospel and Church' be used instead. Some of the confiscated leaflets were returned. Diels made both men responsible for the strict observance of the agreement; if any leaflets were to appear privately with the old or similar slogans or if they were insulting to the German Christians, Bonhoeffer and Jacobi would be liable to arrest.

This visit took place five days before the election. That same afternoon, the two men sent out a circular asking that their agreement with Diels should be honoured, but also urging that irregularities in electoral procedure should be reported promptly and without hesitation.[93] The *Junge Kirche* printed a fresh edition of its 17th July issue, No. 4, which had just left the press, and new leaflets were distributed by the 'national leadership' of the Young Reformers.

The first visit paid by the two pastors to Gestapo headquarters gave rise to rumours which, by the time they reached friends abroad, had acquired a distinctly dramatic character. When the events of September revived the story, Siegmund-Schultze wrote to Bonhoeffer from Switzerland: 'Some very important people in the ecumenical movement have heard wild rumours alleging, for instance, that you are to be sent to a concentration camp and that it is not yet certain that you will be able to avoid this.'[94] Bonhoeffer's reply was: 'I have not actually been in a concentration camp, although, on the occasion of the church election, the prospect of being sent there was held out to me and my colleague by the highest police authority.'[95]

On the eve of the election, during an interval in the Wagner Festival

92. See GS II, pp. 58 f.   94. Letter of 28.10.1933, MW V, IV, E.1.
93. GS II, pp. 58 f.   95. Letter of 6.11.1933, MW V, IV, E.2.

in Bayreuth, Hitler made a broadcast to the German people. He expected, he said, that in support of all he had done, those forces would be elected on the morrow, Sunday, which, 'as exemplified by the German Christians, have deliberately chosen to take their stand within the Nationalist Socialist State.'[96]

The election results were as overwhelming as they were crushing. Seventy per cent, in some places even more, of the votes enabled the German Christians to take possession of key positions in the Church. Their exultation knew no bounds.

On 23rd July Bonhoeffer preached in the Dreifaltigkeitskirche on the rock against which the gates of hell shall not prevail:

... it will not be taken from us—its name is decision, its name is discerning of the spirits ... Come ... you who have been left alone, you who have lost the Church, let us return to Holy Writ, let us go forth and seek the Church together ... For the times, which are times of collapse to the human understanding may well be for her a great time of building ... Church, remain a church! ... confess, confess, confess.[97]

Defeat

'In loyal recognition of the changed situation',[98] some of the members of the Supreme Church Council and the General Superintendent, Otto Dibelius, asked to be released from office on the day after the election. During the fever of election week, the church authorities had given evidence of remarkably 'objective' restraint and neutrality. Now the more moderate German Christians were entrusted with the conduct of affairs in the German Evangelical Church until the meeting of the National Synod under Ludwig Müller, that had been convened for the end of September. These provisional administrators were Professor Karl Fezer (Tübingen), Bishop Schöffel (Hamburg), Professor F. K. Schumann (Halle) and President Koopman. In the Old Prussian Union, Müller became President of the Supreme Church Council with the title of bishop; in accordance with the leadership principle he was also invested with supreme powers enabling him to exercise independently the authority of the Supreme Church Council. Thus the 'leadership principle' and 'racial conformity' were already being enforced, although legally such matters could be formulated and validated only by synods. While there could be no doubt of the majorities that would prevail in the synods there were still some grounds for hope in the unresolved tensions between the moderate, evangelistic German Christians and their more extreme fellows.

96. *Kirchliches Jahrbuch 1933-44*, ed. J. Beckmann, 1948, p. 22.
97. GS IV, pp. 130-6.
98. *Gotthardbriefe* 95.

On the day after the election, the Young Reformers rapidly took stock of their defeat, with the result that they announced their withdrawal from church politics. For by the terms of the movement's foundation, church politics were in any case of secondary importance, and the recent excursion into the tactical sphere had been undertaken only with reluctance. Now that responsibility lay entirely with the newly elected authorities, all the efforts of the Young Reformers were to be devoted to evangelistic work.

This declaration set the key for the future and marked the beginning of a new phase of development. Now it was a question of forcing the German Christians to a decision in what they said from the pulpit: In this year of 1933, what is it that a reforming church must confess?— In other words the intention was to confront the German Christians with a relevant Confession worked out in concentrated detail.[99]

The events of the 23rd July had decided the question of power in the Church but not the question of truth. An appreciable divergence between power and truth could be anticipated. The boundary might soon be reached where a minority, however small, could no longer remain silent, and the future seemed to hold a struggle of a new kind to be fought out on new ground. Who, up till now, had concerned himself with the centre and the boundaries of the Confession? Three years earlier, at the General Synod of the Old Prussian Union, during deliberations on a way of life for the Church, a certain passage had been deleted on the grounds that it contained a 'confession of faith' and 'it cannot conceivably be the task of the General Synod to vote on a confession of faith'.[100]

On 24th and 25th July Niemöller had played a predominant role in determining the new point of departure—namely, the decision to formulate a binding Confession. By their decision they endeavoured to synthesize what had hitherto been sporadic and personal attempts to formulate new confessions. Immediate steps were taken to put this into practice and a date for its commencement was laid down. Bonhoeffer, the youngest of those discussing the question, and Sasse, were instructed to go into retreat at Bethel[101] during August, in order to make an initial draft. Bonhoeffer therefore asked for leave of absence during August to go to Bethel. On 26th July his general superintendent wrote to him: 'I grant you a time of rest. During the past weeks we have all suffered as much from psychological tension as from physical strain.' Karow did not then know that there was any ulterior motive behind this request for leave.

99. JK, 1933, pp. 80 ff.
100. Cf. *Kirchliches Jahrbuch*, 1930, pp. 492 f.
101. This epileptic settlement included a theological seminary, as it still does. (Editor.)

London

Bonhoeffer took a roundabout route to Bethel, via London, leaving on 27th July. On 30th July he preached to two German-speaking congregations, the Reformed congregation of St. Paul's in the East End, and the United congregation in Sydenham. He was also able to inspect the pastorate at Sydenham. This in no way resolved his inner tension, or lessened his uncertainty about which was the best course to pursue:. if anything, it added to his problems.

Small wonder, then, that Bonhoeffer, during these summer weeks, relinquished all his commitments relating to regional and international ecumenical youth conferences.

In the middle of July during the last weeks of the State Commissariat, an invitation to the Sydenham pastorate was transmitted to Bonhoeffer by Heckel of the Church Federation Office; it was accepted during the hectic week of the election.[102] Heckel had met Bonhoeffer frequently since the Mittelstellen conference, and most recently in the spring with the Young Reformers. Heckel was responsible for communities abroad and as such had been pressed by the two[103] London parishes named above to help them find a successor to Pastor Singer. Bonhoeffer was attracted by the possibility of thus finally ridding himself of internal and external problems more especially since, in view of recent developments, Franz Hildebrandt was considering the possibility of a ministry abroad. Tempting though the offer was, however, Bonhoeffer still could not make up his mind and in his search for the right decision tormented those around him almost as much as he tormented himself.

In answer to his request for advice whether or not to go to London, the Bishop of Ripon wrote:

As to the move suggested to you, it is only you who knows how far you would be accepting a narrower sphere of influence by leaving the Student world of Berlin, or on the contrary giving yourself freer scope for development and wider experience. What you say about the disinclination in Germany at present for the goods the World Alliance seeks to supply, is perhaps a sufficient reason for coming to England, where you might be available as an interpreter of Germany at a time when such interpreters are badly needed . . .[104]

Hermann Sasse sought to persuade him: 'I saw in him one of Germany's best theologians and did not want to see him go under in the petty war against the Gestapo and Rosenberg.'[105] London put pressure on the man whom Heckel had so warmly recommended, as one whom 'I personally like very much, and who has proved himself here

102. GS II, p. 120.
103. St. Paul's was attached to Sydenham under the one pastor. (*Editor.*)
104. Letter of 21.7.1933, GS II, p. 122.
105. Communication from H. Sasse, 28.9.1956.

in the most diverse situations'.[106] After his trial sermon, their plea became more urgent. Yet he did not agree at once. It was only the disappointing turn taken by events at Bethel and developments connected with the Berlin Provincial Synod that finally decided him to go to London. His general superintendent wrote to him resignedly:

I am deeply distressed by the fact that theologians of your stamp should believe that there is no more room for them in the German Church. A material factor in your decision will have been your relations already established with other countries through your ecumenical work. Thus in your case the line of development is at least apparent . . . [Your activity abroad] will give you the opportunity of rendering services to the Evangelical Church and to things German, more valuable, perhaps, than would be possible here . . .[107]

VII AUGUST: THE BETHEL CONFESSION

From London, Bonhoeffer went to Bethel where he met Hildebrandt who had arrived there from Hengelo in Holland. Whereas in London all doors had been open to Bonhoeffer, Hildebrandt had met with little success. Bonhoeffer promised his friend that, should the impending synods reach decisions that made a move imperative, he would invite him to London.

Friedrich von Bodelschwingh welcomed the newly appointed confessional experts and himself showed them round the community's institutions. Bonhoeffer had never been to Bethel before. Shaken by the experience he wrote to his grandmother who, after playing a lively part in the events of the previous weeks, was now on holiday at Friedrichsbrunn:

It is said of the Buddha that he was converted by a meeting with a man who was gravely ill. It is sheer madness to believe, as is done today, that the sick can or ought to be legally eliminated. It is virtually the same as building a tower of Babel, and is bound to bring its own revenge.[108]

During his visit, Bonhoeffer also had the chance to meet some of the teachers at the School of Theology such as Schlink, Frick, Wilhelm Vischer and Georg Merz.

Intention

In Berlin, the German Christians' increasing power was demonstrated by Göring's appointment of Ludwig Müller as Prussian Counsellor of State on 4th August, while at Bethel Sasse and Bonhoeffer began work on the

106. To Singer, 19.7.1933, GS II, p. 121.
107. Letter of 21.8.1933, GS II, p. 123.
108. Letter of 20.8.1933, GS II, p. 78.

document that was to confront those same German Christians with the question of truth. The time seemed ripe for such a move. In various parts of the country drafts for confessions were being made. This question of Confession was now beginning to go beyond the frontiers of expert theological circles. It was Bonhoeffer's and Sasse's purpose to produce something serviceable and widely accepted by the time the National Synod met at the beginning of September. They therefore set to work on 15th August.

The first stage of work was, Sasse tells us, '. . . a phase of happy collaboration'. In Bonhoeffer's letter to his grandmother on 20th August delight is tempered by scepticism:

Our work here is very enjoyable but also very hard. We want to try to make the German Christians declare their intentions. Whether we shall succeed I rather doubt. For even if they admit the formulations officially, the pressure behind them is so strong that sooner or later it is bound to sweep away all promises. It is becoming increasingly clear that what we are going to get is a big, popular, national church whose nature cannot be reconciled with Christianity, and that we must be prepared to enter upon entirely new paths which we shall then have to tread. The real question is between Germanism and Christianity, and the sooner the conflict comes out into the open the better. Nothing could be more dangerous than its concealment . . .[109]

Hans Ehrenberg, himself working on a confession, sent Hans Fischer on a visit to Bethel to pass on his ideas.

In an address to German pastors at Bradford, Yorkshire,[110] Bonhoeffer described the nature of the work which, he said, had defined confessional statements from the trinitarian doctrine to eschatology. A number of reformulations had been made: The doctrine of *justification*, for example, in order that Ludwig Müller's trite doctrine of trust in God and of the sufficiency of common human decency could be revealed for what it was—a *simpliste* interpretation of Christianity; the doctrine of the *cross*, so as to pillory the re-interpretation by Wieneke, the tame German Christian theologian, of the cross as symbolizing the Nazi slogan 'public interest before self-interest'; and finally, the doctrine of the *Holy Spirit*, from a Christological standpoint, with renewed emphasis on the *filioque*, so as to guard against the dangerous stress placed on the revelation of the Creation by Hirsch, Althaus and Fezer, and its consequences in Stapel's independent notion of the law of Race. To Bonhoeffer's joy, Wilhelm Vischer produced the first draft for the article on the Jewish question.

The work was concluded in a spirit less happy than that in which it had begun. This may have been because the Bethel Confession was hampered from the start by the compilers' anxiety not to omit anything,

109. GS II, pp. 78 f.
110. On 28.11.1933, from a copy by J. Rieger, see Ch. VIII, pp. 266 f.

or perhaps because it took too Lutheran a turn. Whatever the case, its reception by the experts was unexpectedly disappointing. The path leading from individual and local attempts at confession, by way of the Bethel draft, to the effective Barmen confessional decisions was to be longer and more arduous than Bonhoeffer and Sasse could have at first imagined.

Reactions

On about 25th August the authors of the first draft handed over their work. The period that now began was, in Bonhoeffer's view, one of compromise in the course of which their text was watered down to such an extent that he ultimately refused to collaborate in the final edition.

In any case he had objected to the list of some twenty experts to whom on 26th August Bodelschwingh sent out the Confession for consideration and eventual signature.[111] Amongst the recipients were Martin Niemöller, Künneth, Lilje, Jacobi, Ehrenberg, Asmussen, Barth, Schlatter and Heim. Bonhoeffer immediately sensed that Heim and Schlatter, at any rate, would never pass the whole text, and indeed, Schlatter's sarcastic refutation was not slow in coming: if there was to be a confession at all, he maintained, it must be in the opposite direction from that of Bonn; and that meant against Karl Barth. At Bradford, Bonhoeffer spoke of the 'strange course taken by Bodelschwingh' which 'cancelled out' the progress made in the formulation of the Confession.[112]

In addition, they failed to keep to their programme; in view of the imminence of the synods, the experts had been allowed far too much time. In Berlin Bonhoeffer himself collected the amendments made by Künneth, Niemöller and Jacobi, but to no avail.

He felt, moreover, that the most important points of the Confession had been emasculated. This applied especially to Vischer's article on the Jewish question. To the section on the State, sycophantic riders had been added concerning 'joyful collaboration' in the aims of that State, and again, a paragraph on sharing responsibility for the country's guilt had been changed into participation by the Church 'in her country's glory and guilt'.

Finally, during the argument about signatures, the confessionalists themselves began to have second thoughts, even Sasse and Merz refusing to sign if their names were to appear alongside those of Reformed churchmen.

One day Merz informed Niemöller that Bonhoeffer—who had by then been in London for some time—'has declared himself wholly dissatisfied with the new version and opposed to its publication in its present form'.[113] When Bodelschwingh finally realized that his team of older

111. GS II, pp. 90 f. 112. Copy, J. Rieger. 113. To M. Niemöller, 5.12.1933.

and younger theologians could no longer be kept together, he tired of the whole business. But at the insistence of Lücking, Stratenwerth and Merz, Niemöller eventually brought out the revised form of the Bethel Confession.[114]

Even in this version it went through several editions, but it lacked the pungency which it had promised at the start. Clearly the time was not yet ripe for what Bonhoeffer had in mind. One of the motives he mentioned to Barth for his departure to London was that he saw '. . . a further indication in the almost total lack of understanding shown towards the Bethel Confession'.[115]

Alarm in Berlin

It was at Bethel that Bonhoeffer decided definitely to go to London. He was given leave from the university by the Dean, Erich Seeberg, who added the heart-warming comment that in the discussions as to who should fill Titius's vacant post, Bonhoeffer's name 'had been mentioned and strongly seconded'.[116] But for the time being his eagerness to get away was tempered by the events of the late summer in Berlin. Indeed Bonhoeffer eventually postponed his London début until mid-October. Once again he was wholly taken up with the inevitable aftermath of the German Christians' overwhelming victory in the election.

He returned by way of Friedrichsbrunn; it was eighteen months since he had had a chance to walk through its woods. Meanwhile, on 24th August, Jacobi with a small minority had already fought and lost a battle in the Berlin Provincial Synod. He and his supporters had been unable to prevent the Synod from adopting out of hand the Aryan Civil Service legislation in respect of their own ecclesiastical district of Berlin. This was a storm-warning for the approaching General Synod. Bonhoeffer's place was in Berlin. He himself had already decided what this would mean for him personally—schism. But what would it mean for his colleagues?

VIII SEPTEMBER: ARYAN CLAUSE

September saw the culmination of the crisis, and also its turning-point. This was not the work of the National Synod at the end of August; it was brought about at the beginning of September by the Prussian General Synod, known as the 'Brown Synod'. The Young Reformers were no longer in the van, their place having been taken by the Pastors'

114. *Das Bekenntnis der Väter und die Bekennende Gemeinde*, Chr. Kaiser, Munich. Here is the text of the rider: 'Submitted for consideration by a group of Evangelical theologians and issued in their name by Martin Niemöller.'
115. GS II, p. 132. On the history of the Bethel Confession, cf. my own attempt, GS II, pp. 77-119, and the more comprehensive, amended versions by J. Glenthoj, MW V, VI, F.
116. Letter of 20.8.1933, GS II, p. 124.

Emergency League which was to become the most important connecting link in the formation of the Confessing Church.

Pamphlet

During August it was not yet really known what resolutions the synods would pass on 'racial conformity' within the Church. Would a milder or a stricter form of the Aryan clause be enforced? Would they decide on the radical exclusion of Jewish Christian congregations, or legislate less drastically on fitness for the ministry, ultimately applying the law only to those as yet unordained, and not to men already in the ministry?

Bonhoeffer drafted a pamphlet[117] forecasting what the results of such procedure would be. Under the title 'The Aryan Clause in the Church'[118] it was circulated in good time to Synod members and to the congregations. It was not without effect. Siegfried Knak, the director of the Berlin Mission, wrote to Professor Richter: 'Others within the group,[119] of course, repudiated any differentiation between Jews and Germans within the Church. A short private memorandum by Bonhoeffer helped to confirm many in this opinion.'[120] A few weeks later the Church Federation Office decided that 'in view of this attitude [Bonhoeffer] could not be sent abroad'.[121]

The style of the pamphlet, like that of Hildebrandt's election leaflets,[122] was terse and to the point. 'The German Christians say— We answer!' As compared with the April theses on the Jewish question, new issues were introduced and discussed: the 'national order' which is that of God; the evangelistic opportunities among millions of fellow-citizens afforded by the exclusion of a few hundred Jewish Christians; the *adiaphora*, and the 'weak in faith' to whom Paul submitted.

Three possibilities are considered, only to be rejected:

1. The exclusion of non-Aryans from the Reich Church and their formation into special congregations: this would necessitate an immediate departure from such a church. To do this would be 'my act of solidarity with my Church which I can never serve except in entire truth, with all the consequences of that truth'. This was not, however, the conclusion of the 1933 synods.

2. The application of the State's Civil Service Law to church officials:

117. An early form of this pamphlet is probably C. S. Macfarland's *The New Church and the New Germany*, a book on Church and State in the Germany of 1933, especially pp. 68-71, 'Appeal to the Ministers of the Old Prussian Union'. J. Glenthøj has discovered that during the last days of July Bonhoeffer probably dictated this passage to Jürgen Winterhager, so that the latter could translate it for Macfarland. See J. Glenthøj's account and documentation in MW V, VI, E.
118. GS II, pp. 62-9.
119. The 'Gospel and Church' group.
120. Letter of 13.9.1933.
121. Bonhoeffer to F. Siegmund-Schultze, 6.11.1933.
122. GS II, p. 59.

this would mean resigning from the ministry. At this point we find the characteristically Bonhoefferian argument, of 'fatal privilege'. Thus clergy 'must see that the only service they can still in all truthfulness render their Church is to lay down their pastoral office which has become a privilege'. This became a crucial issue in Berlin on 24th August, and at the General Synod of 5th and 6th September.

3. The Reich Church constitution of 14th July 1933, by its silence on the legislation already in force for the (state) universities (including the theological faculties), had excluded the possibility of a new generation of Jewish-Christian pastors. No one had said a word. Bonhoeffer and Hildebrandt must have felt that they were crying in the wilderness. In his pamphlet, therefore, Bonhoeffer envisages the possibility that the Church might find means other than existing universities to prepare Jewish Christians for the ministry. 'For should she fail to do this, she must accept responsibility for the whole of the Aryan clause.'

With this final point, and from a position that was primarily concerned with the internal affairs of the Church, Bonhoeffer had again raised the problem of the Church's silence on the Jewish question as such. It was a lone stand. He had advanced beyond his colleagues' range, and even among the Young Reformers there were former fellow-combatants who now belonged to the school of Elert and Althaus. And both these were soon to subscribe to the portentous expert opinion from Erlangen[123] which contained the sentence: 'The Church must therefore demand that Jewish Christians hold back from the ministry.'[124]

Even Martin Niemöller found it difficult to decide what attitude to adopt towards the Aryan clause. This indecision is still apparent—although Niemöller was never one to keep silent when and where something needed saying—in his 'Propositions on the Aryan Question in the Church' which he published after repeated requests on 2nd November 1933.[125] He did not disguise the fact that he would greatly have preferred to consider the Aryan clause as adiaphoron. A comparison of Bonhoeffer's and Niemöller's propositions reveals the difference in emphasis in spite of the similarity of their actions at this time. Niemöller admitted the possibility of reconciling the exclusion of the Jewish Christians from church office with 1 Cor. 8 and the concept of the 'weaker brethren'.[126] Bonhoeffer, on the other hand, asked 'whether, precisely in the cause of the Church the acceptance of such a scandal[127] must not be demanded of the congregation . . . Those who remain unaffected by that, and hence privileged, will wish to align themselves with their under-privileged brethren rather than make use of privileges within the Church.'

123. Of 25.9.1933.
124. JK, 1933, p. 273.
125. JK, 1933, pp. 269 f.
126. JK, 1933, p. 270.
127. i.e. the Jewish Christians in a ministry of the community.

Brown Synod

On the final day of the 'victory of faith' Party rally at Nuremberg, the Old Prussian General Synod met in the *Herrenhaus* in Berlin for a two days' session. It fell to Martin Niemöller to take the minutes of this ominous synod.

The dwindling minority of the Young Reformers was led by the Westphalian president Karl Koch. When this group arrived at the scene of action on 5th September a para-military spectacle met their eyes. Most of the men had appeared in brown uniform. Dr. F. Werner was elected president of the Synod; Hossenfelder, Reich leader of the German Christians, and August Jäger were elected his deputies.

From the start the Synod took on the nature of a demonstration rather than of the more customary deliberating assembly. When Jacobi tried to bring the motion which he had already brought two weeks previously 'that guiding principles must be worked out for proclamation to our nation, a proclamation to which the Confession of the Church today pledges the clergy',[128] the presidium dictatorially refused him permission to speak. No committee work on the important new legislation was admitted. Thus the Bishops' Law abolishing the general superintendents in Old Prussia and replacing them with ten bishoprics under the National Bishop, Ludwig Müller, was passed with a minimum of delay—Bonhoeffer's General Superintendent Karow accepted his appointment to the see of Berlin. They also passed the 'Church Law Relating to the Legal Position of Clergy and Church Officers', which laid down that only those could become ministers of the Church who were prepared to give 'unconditional support to the National Socialist State and the German Evangelical Church', and were also of Aryan descent.

It is true that those general superintendents who were present voted against the dismissal from office of non-Aryans, or men married to non-Aryans, who were already employed, yet they voted that such persons should not be eligible for employment in the future. The Pomeranian General Superintendent, Kalmus, spoke for the other general superintendents when he said: 'We understand and appreciate the measures taken by the State and recognize that the Evangelical Church also has cause for vigilance in the preservation of the German race . . .'[129] Karow was delighted that those at least who had already been ordained were to be allowed to remain.

When Präses Koch at last put forward the opposition's objection to the law, he was literally shouted down, whereupon he and his supporters left the hall. Thus no member of the minority was present at the election of the Prussian representatives to the Wittenberg National Synod, and as a result not one Prussian Young Reformer was nominated

128. CW, 1933, p. 912.
129. *Die Deutsche Evangelische Kirche und die Judenfrage*, p. 36.

a delegate. A few of them turned up at Wittenberg, but only to create a disturbance by handing out leaflets in the streets.

Schism

Suddenly the work on the Bethel Confession, Jacobi's motions at the synods, and the hope of being able to hold discussions with moderate German Christians, all seemed relatively unimportant.

On the evening of 6th September, when the General Synod was over, the Synod opposition and other indomitables foregathered at Jacobi's; the following day they reassembled at Niemöller's. Bonhoeffer and Hildebrandt made an impassioned plea for widespread resignations from office. They believed that, with the Aryan clause, their opponents had brought schism to the realm to which they all belonged. Nothing therefore remained but to accord that fact material recognition. The saving clauses, potentially applicable to Hildebrandt, only served in Bonhoeffer's opinion to obscure the issue—namely, that the best service that could be rendered the other side was to take their schismatic decision in earnest.

But neither at Jacobi's in the Achenbachstrasse, nor at Niemöller's in the Cecilienallee[130] were Bonhoeffer and Hildebrandt able to gain support for their view. To this circle the step into separation seemed too grave to be linked merely with the anti-Semitic problem, for there were only eleven pastors in Prussia who would be affected by the Aryan clause. Siegfried Knak rejected the Aryan clause not because it would, in future, debar Jewish Christians from the ministry, but only because of its retrospective unfraternal effect upon those who had already been ordained.[131] Under Knak's leadership, therefore, the circle decided to postpone schismatic action until the National Synod. Bonhoeffer and Hildebrandt continued to insist that to effect an immediate exodus would not only be more logical theologically but would also be more successful in the field of church politics than would a delay. Hildebrandt declared that he would begin by refusing to preach in any German church. Bonhoeffer announced his intention of winning allies for his views in academic circles and in the ecumenical movement. As far as the impending National Synod was concerned, the group proposed to put out a common statement of the dissenting clergy's views to enable the 'intact' South German bishops to put up a more effective opposition. Bonhoeffer was invited to play a leading role in its formulation.

He immediately despatched a telegram to Henriod in the hope that it would reach him before the ecumenical conferences in the Balkans:

130. Niemöller's pastoral diary contains the following entry: '6.9. 11 a.m. J.B. [i.e. Young Reformers Movement] and Evgl. and Church at hostel. Discussion Knak-Bonhoeffer. Stählin, etc. 8 p.m. Bonhoeffer and lots of students, Röhricht, Hildebrandt. 2 1/4 to bed.'
131. Cf. his letter to J. Richter of 13.9.1933.

General Assembly finished. All general superintendents dismissed. Only Teutonic Christians admitted to National Synod. Aryan clause at once. Separation at hand. Further information Sofia.

Next he wrote to Sasse who had meanwhile been installed in his chair at Erlangen, and also to Barth in Bonn, asking them for their opinion.

While Sasse shared Bonhoeffer's view of the gravity of the decision he, too, advised postponement until the National Synod. The intention behind his advice was to place as much responsibility as possible at Wittenberg on the Lutheran Bishop Meiser.[132] Unfortunately the hope that Meiser would precipitate a decision in the National Synod was to prove illusory.

The question addressed to Barth was as follows:

Several of us are now very close to the idea of the Free Church . . . I know . . . that you'd advise us to stay until we're thrown out, but some already have been thrown out . . . What has become of the solidarity among the clergy?[133]

Barth replied by return on 11th September from the Bergli: '. . . I, too, am of the opinion that there is a *status confessionis.*' But to Barth this meant that the church government must be told, in so many words, that in this respect they were no longer the Church of Christ. This protest should be followed by others until such time as silence was imposed and the protesters were expelled. 'If there is to be schism, it must come from the other side.' Bonhoeffer was surprised that even Barth could still advise waiting, until 'there is a clash over an even more central point'. The older man advised the younger to allow the decision to take effect, 'to let the facts, as it were, speak for themselves'.

We shall certainly have no cause later to regret a delay filled with highly active polemic . . . This battle will be won by those who begin by being very economical of their ammunition and later employ it ruthlessly and with unerring aim. One day, believe me, one day all this Hossenfelder business will go up in smoke, and leave a very foul stink behind it.[134]

And, indeed, within three months Hossenfelder had played himself out—unlike the Church which supported him. What point, though, could be more 'central' than the Aryan clause? This time Barth had rather disappointed Bonhoeffer, and more especially Hildebrandt. Nor did the delaying tactics of their other friends bear much resemblance to Barth's 'delay filled with highly active polemic'—quite the contrary, in fact, for the reply to the question respecting Hildebrandt himself had been reserved rather than direct.

132. GS II, pp. 71-3.
133. Letter of 9.9.1933.
134. GS II, p. 129.

Birth of the Pastors' Emergency League

The immediate consequence of 6th and 7th September was an association of pastors which, against all expectations, rapidly gained support all over the country. This, indeed, was a show of solidarity with non-Aryan colleagues. Thus the Brown Synod had led directly to the founding of the Pastors' Emergency League.

The League, with its celebrated four points of commitment, grew out of a protest to the church government, drafted and signed by Bonhoeffer and Niemöller. It was then sent by special messenger to Bodelschwingh on 7th September for transmission to the new masters of the Church. This was the text:

1. According to the Confession of our Church, the teaching office of the Church is bound only to the authorized calling. The Aryan clause of the Church Civil Service Law has given rise to a legal situation which is in direct opposition to the fundamental principle of the Confession. In this way, a situation which must be regarded as unlawful from the point of view of the Confession has been proclaimed as the law of the Church and has violated the Confession.
2. There can be no doubt that the ordained ministers affected by the Civil Service Law, in so far as they have not been deprived by formal procedure of the rights of the clerical profession, should continue to exercise in full the right freely to proclaim the Word and freely to administer the sacraments in the Evangelical Church of the Old Prussian Union, which is based upon the Confessions of the Reformation.
3. Anyone who assents to such a breach of the Confession excludes himself from the communion of the Church. We therefore demand the repeal of the law which separates the Evangelical Church of the Old Prussian Union from the Christian Church.[135]

This brought an immediate invitation on 8th September from Bodelschwingh to some of the brethren, accompanied, however, by the comment that he did not altogether like the first sentence of the third paragraph of the protest. He regarded the threat of exclusion as impossible to implement. But on 11th September Bodelschwingh sent a protest to Ludwig Müller which largely incorporated the above text. He watered down the second sentence of paragraph one:

In the Aryan clause of the new Church Civil Service Law, the clauses on the exclusion of clergy from their ministries (para. 3, section 2) are at best contrary to the basic Confession of our Church.

In this way he left open the discussion about future ordination of non-Aryans. The astringency of the third paragraph was attenuated into a tentative request:

I would earnestly request the immediate withdrawal of those clauses in this

135. GS II, pp. 70 f.

law which would involve the departure of the Evangelical Church of the Old Prussian Union from her confessional basis.[136]

The three paragraphs drawn up by Bonhoeffer and Niemöller on 7th September needed only the addition of the promise of help for those affected by the new law or by compulsory measures, to make up the four points of the 'Pastors' Emergency League' pledge. On 12th September, Niemöller called upon the German clergy to protest and to pledge themselves: 1. To a new allegiance to the Scriptures and Confessions, 2. to resist infringement of these, 3. to afford financial help to those affected by the law or by force, and 4. to reject the Aryan clause. He sent out the document by the hand of trusted Young Reformers to pastors 'for the sake of the many lonely ones, for the sake of our Church and for the sake of those who are threatened by the decisions of the Prussian General Synod which infringe the Confession'.

After this pledge an appeal 'to the German National Synod' was distributed.[137] The main substance of this appeal again took the form of the declaration drafted by Bonhoeffer and Niemöller on 7th September. In his letter to Barth of 9th September, Bonhoeffer wrote on behalf of the Young Reformation pastors of Berlin:

We have begun by drafting a declaration by which we wish to inform the church government that the Evangelical Church of the Old Prussian Union has, by the Aryan clause, separated herself from the Church of Christ.

The response exceeded all expectations. The first twenty-two signatories of the appeal were able to circulate the protest in Wittenberg in the name of 2,000 sympathizing pastors. By the end of the year membership of the Pastors' Emergency League had risen to 6,000. On 20th October it convened a Council of Brethren and so became a distinct organization. Until the end of the Nazi period the Council administered and distributed voluntary contributions in aid of persecuted colleagues. One day Bonhoeffer himself was to be among the persecuted.

The new phase of church resistance was now ushered in by a team more homogeneous than the original band of Young Reformers in May.[138] It could hardly have been expected of those first militants that they should adopt the Aryan clause as their sole platform, since to do so would have involved immediate disintegration.

Sofia

The World Alliance conference at Sofia, from 15th to 30th September, was the only regular ecumenical conference which Bonhoeffer did not refuse

136. Text provided by W. Niemöller, 23.3.1958.
137. GS II, pp. 74-6.
138. Cf. the names in Ch. VII, p. 214.

to attend during those hectic days of 1933. For him the moment was opportune.

As usual, the World Alliance and the 'Life and Work' conferences took place in close conjunction. Although Bonhoeffer took no part in the 'Life and Work' conference at Novi Sad, it is of interest to us because of the subtle differences by which it was distinguished from Sofia, and also because of its consequences for Bonhoeffer.

In Sofia the chief German protagonist was Bonhoeffer, in Novi Sad, Theodor Heckel. The latter had failed to draw conclusions from the Brown Synod with regard to his official position, nor had he had anything more to do with the Young Reformers' deliberations of 6th and 7th September. As the foreign affairs administrator of the German Evangelical Church he was shortly to become Bonhoeffer's superior. Novi Sad and Sofia revealed the extent to which the two men's paths were diverging. For Heckel now pursued a quite different course in his attempt to steer safely into harbour that rudderless ship, the German Church and her congregations abroad. Though he was never to join the German Christians, yet he continued to hazard his reputation throughout the Nazi period and, indeed, was to lose it irretrievably so far as Bonhoeffer and his friends at home and abroad were concerned. In Bonhoeffer's eyes, Heckel's way was tantamount to surrender, for his policy seemed like a betrayal of the Church and the ecumenical movement. To express appreciation of the new State was not necessarily to forfeit Bonhoeffer's friendship, as the example of Niemöller shows, but in Heckel, where such appreciation was combined with practical decision-making, it inevitably appeared suspect.

1. The executive committee of 'Life and Work' met at Novi Sad from 9th to 12th September, with the Bishop of Chichester in the chair. The German Evangelical Church was represented by Heckel, Schreiber, Wahl and Hinderer. Kapler's resignation, also operative in this sphere, meant that Heckel was correspondingly more in the limelight. After Bell's account of the initial steps he had taken during the church conflict in the spring, Heckel made his report. The minutes are as follows:

[Heckel] painted a clear picture of the vast changes and preliminary reconstruction in Nation, State and Church, and sought to clarify the great questions and tasks which hereby assume particular importance for the whole work of the churches in the ecumenical field.[139]

An assignment that obliged a churchman to interpret the domestic scene before an audience of foreigners in a foreign country, just after the General and before the National Synod, was indeed a delicate one. Conflict inevitably ensued.

Wilfred Monod, rejecting Heckel's account, expressed his regret that the German should have passed over in silence, in front of a Christian

139. Minutes of the Meeting, Novi Sad, pp. 2, 15, 37 ff., and *Die Eiche*, 1933, pp. 368 ff.

assembly to which they would have been of particular interest, certain points such as, for instance, the recent resolutions passed by the Brown Synod and the general disabilities imposed upon Jewish Christians. After a heated debate, the conference brought two resolutions with which the German delegation recorded their disagreement—it was the first time this had ever happened at an ecumenical conference. The first of these resolutions, brought at the instance of Bell, was a declaration:

... grave anxieties were expressed by the representatives of different churches in Europe and America in particular with regard to the severe action taken against persons of Jewish origin, and the serious restrictions placed upon freedom of thought and expression in Germany ...

The other was that Bell should undertake the task of writing a letter to the then German church government. This latter resolution led to the now famous correspondence between the Bishop and Ludwig Müller, beginning with a letter from Bell to Müller on 23rd October and culminating in Bell's 1934 Ascension Day message to the member churches of the ecumenical movement.[140] Dietrich Bonhoeffer was to become Bell's chief adviser in this correspondence. Thus Heckel was unable to capture the opposition's influence over men such as Bell, whom they continued to keep informed and who therefore always remained aware of the existence of another leadership. This state of affairs had begun with the telegram to Henriod after the events of 6th September. Yet it must not be thought that the ecumenical movement was unanimous in these matters. Geneva was not to maintain an ideal partnership with Bonhoeffer, and was to establish in the course of time far closer relations with Heckel's office. As we shall discover, it was only a minority in the ecumenical movement that ultimately showed any understanding for Bonhoeffer's point of view. But for the time being he continued to enjoy the support of influential men such as Bishops Bell and Ammundsen.

2. Some of the delegates who came to Sofia from Novi Sad had therefore already been forewarned; one of these was Ammundsen himself, who was to preside over the World Alliance conference. The only Germans present were seventy-one-year-old Julius Richter and twenty-seven-year-old Bonhoeffer. Siegmund-Schultze, ill in Switzerland, was anxious lest the conference should show too much hostility towards conditions in Germany and thus prove fatal to his World Alliance work. And in fact his journal, *Die Eiche*, was suppressed in 1933.

Next on the agenda, after questions of disarmament and problems concerning the amalgamation of the two Youth Commissions, was the forthcoming major conference (at Budapest or Fanö). Monod, who had resigned from the presidency of the French branch of the World Alliance, entrusted his theological memorandum on the peace question, which had been commissioned in 1932, to Jézéquel. Out of this debate arose

140. Cf. Ch. VIII, p. 296.

the programme for the international conference in 1934:

. . . the suggestion was made that Professor Monod should be asked to formulate more precisely the *catechism of peace* for the Budapest meeting, that this should be sent to two or three persons . . . that they should formulate together the memorandum for Budapest; and thirdly, that one member of the Youth Commission should be asked to sit with these members . . . It was ultimately agreed that Dr. Monod should be asked to prepare his memorandum, that Dr. Bonhoeffer should be responsible for another and Professor Zankow for another and the Bishop of Ripon for another.[141]

For the next and most burning question of the day, 'Racial Minorities', Bonhoeffer had made preparations outside the plenary sessions. The previous evening Ammundsen, W. A. Brown, Atkinson, Toureille, Henriod and Bonhoeffer had met in A. Bouvier's hotel room. In his diary Henriod wrote:

At Sofia, Bonhoeffer was able to inform us in a private group . . . about the real situation in Germany and of the brutal and intransigent attitude of the German Christians. We are instructed to tell his friends:
1. that they can count on our sympathy and understanding abroad.
2. that in principle it would be necessary for a delegation to decide whether the churches are able to recognize the new German Church.
We closed with prayer together. Bonhoeffer was very moved.[142]

Bonhoeffer himself described that evening in a letter to Siegmund-Schultze:

On this occasion I spoke very frankly about the Jewish question, the Aryan clause in the Church, and the General Synod, as also about the question of the future of the minority, and met with a great deal of understanding . . . Incidentally, during this little meeting we decided on a plan to send a delegation to the German church government, and this is still under discussion here in London.[143]

Thus, in spite of all his discouraging experiences, Bonhoeffer continued to work along the lines of his earlier proposals of 6th and 7th September, and now suggested that the ecumenical movement should withhold recognition of the new church government and send a delegation. He was to keep to this plan, for on 6th November he wrote to Siegmund-Schultze telling him that the idea of a delegation 'is still under discussion here in London . . . A few days ago I met all the ecumenical people over here.' But Bonhoeffer was never after all to be able to put that idea into practice, though he believed that the world organization, so impotent in other respects, had the whip hand in this particular instance. This view was corroborated by the extreme sensitivity in Berlin to reactions from abroad. Both Ammundsen and Brown, and later also the Bishop of Chichester, seemed inclined to favour the suggestion. From now on it was to be one of Heckel's more disagreeable tasks to ward off 'outside interference' on the grounds that the ecumenical movement was inadmissibly exceeding its terms of reference, and he was gradually to succeed in winning allies for this view within the movement. Indeed, Bonhoeffer postulated too much. He was not the kind of man to be a stickler in the observance of the informal ecumenical organization's terms of reference but was likely rather to spur on the movement by challenging it with the tasks that lay ahead, and to mould it to his demands.

The next question, then, on the agenda of the Sofia plenary sessions was the Jewish problem. Bonhoeffer, who had hitherto shown himself so averse to resolutions, intervened vigorously here. Henriod wrote in his diary:

20 September. A resolution on racial minorities proposed by Atkinson, an amendment to the text proposed by Bonhoeffer which was accepted.

Hence the Sofia conference produced a resolution that was more outspoken than that of Novi Sad:

. . . We especially deplore the fact that the State measures against the Jews in Germany have had such an effect on public opinion that in some circles the Jewish race is considered a race of inferior status. We protest against the resolution of the Prussian General Synod and other Synods which apply the Aryan paragraph of the State to the Church, putting serious disabilities upon ministers and church officers who by chance of birth are non-Aryan, which we believe to be a denial of the explicit teaching and spirit of the Gospel of Jesus Christ . . .[144]

In this judgement of 'a denial of the teaching and the spirit of the Gospel', the theology of the World Alliance came extraordinarily close to the theology of the German Confessing Church. Yet it also brought many of those present to the limits of acceptance. Julius Richter, who knew nothing of the previous evening's discussion,[145] insisted, when the debate on the Jewish question began in the plenary session, on going with Bonhoeffer to the German Embassy in Sofia to assure them that the German Government as such was not the target of their strictures. Later, Richter wrote to Siegmund-Schultze:

Bishop Ammundsen was moved almost to tears by the proceedings in the plenary session . . . Perhaps the finest and deepest religious experience was the occasion when Bonhoeffer conducted morning prayers.[146]

Whereas Heckel's aim at Novi Sad had been to conceal and to inhibit the crystallization of opinion, Bonhoeffer in Sofia sought to achieve the exact opposite.

144. Minutes (duplicated), pp. 12 f.
145. D. Bonhoeffer to F. Siegmund-Schultze, 6.11.1933.
146. Letter of 25.9.1933.

Serious though the situation was, Bonhoeffer and Toureille did not miss the opportunity of exploring the Bulgarian markets where they bought Eastern antiques.

Sequels to Sofia

Even Siegmund-Schultze, in his exile in Switzerland, experienced some misgiving when he heard the news from Sofia and the resolution that had been passed there. In a letter to Bonhoeffer he said that the resolution would have far-reaching consequences for the World Alliance in Germany.[147] In what was to be the very last issue of *Die Eiche*, he wrote about these events, but taking special care not to implicate the protagonists, Richter and Bonhoeffer, who were now back in Germany and hence were in jeopardy.[148] However, the account also revealed that an attempt had been made before Sofia to prevent the conference coming to any public decision, in order not to imperil further what still survived. The presidium and secretariat had accordingly agreed before Sofia that the conference, as a limited executive session, should not be empowered to pass resolutions. But Bonhoeffer's influence, together with the pressure of circumstances, had overridden this arrangement. This is why Bonhoeffer, in his letter to Siegmund-Schultze on 6th November, stressed the fact that the private meeting at the hotel had taken place 'at Henriod's request'—at the request, that is, of the Secretary of the World Alliance.

Thus, understandably enough, the picture given in *Die Eiche*'s account, was not altogether free of deliberate embellishment:

. . . During the Sofia conference, however, the executive committee overrode this agreement, and passed a resolution on the racial question in relation to the position of the German Church. The representatives of the churches of the great powers declared that it would mean the end of the World Alliance's work if one of its bodies, meeting this year, were to fail to declare itself on a question of such import to the whole of Christianity. Thus the German representatives who took part in the session were unable to prevent the passing of a resolution. They took good care, however, that no criticism should be extended to the Government of their country and that the declaration should apply only to those church measures which have also been contested inside Germany. It would not be right were we in Germany to suppress this resolution . . .

The text of the resolution then follows.

On 6th November, Bonhoeffer wrote to Siegmund-Schultze from London, in an attempt to allay his misgivings:

In fact I regard the resolution as it stands as both good and defensible,

147. Letter of 28.10.1933, see MW V, IV, E.
148. *Die Eiche*, 1933, pp. 372-81.

and would not feel able materially to alter its wording . . . It seems to be questionable whether the German Christians will seriously attack the Sofia resolution, since a certain amount of confusion exists within their own ranks about the Aryan clause. I don't know by what means the resolution was officially conveyed to the church government, but I do know that they got it. I really don't think we need be afraid of spreading it about as much as we can. The *Junge Kirche,* too, ought to publish the text.

For Bonhoeffer, Sofia produced no immediate political repercussions but there was some reaction from the Church. For the church government, of course, knew exactly what had taken place. 'There's been a fearful row at the Church Ministry about my mission; apparently it almost toppled Theodor [i.e. Heckel]', wrote Bonhoeffer to Siegmund-Schultze.[149]

After the events of Novi Sad and Sofia, Heckel felt obliged to send his own account with comments to all pastors abroad. Bonhoeffer, by then in London, was automatically sent a copy of the document which ran:

. . . The German delegation frustrated all attempts at a detailed statement of opinion by the executive committee[150] . . . during the course of difficult deliberations. In the event the following comparatively neutral resolution was passed . . . [Pastors abroad must help to avert the threat of deteriorating relationships with other churches, to correct false ideas and to place the development within a wider context.] The need for a theological counter-attack and for theological attacks on the untenable theology, the *Weltanschauung,* and the ideology upon which the attacks from abroad are so largely based, has already been shown. In general, circles abroad are surprisingly well-informed about details, yet are not in a position correctly to assess overall development within the German Church . . . The German Christians, however, can claim the merit for having assumed responsibility for erecting the new structure with exceptional vigour. Beside these broad outlines of development, individual manifestations are of little importance. Especially in regard to the Aryan clause in the Church, there are very considerable difficulties . . . [More recently, the report goes on to say, the unsatisfactory clauses relating to the regional churches had been suspended under the law of 16.11.] Yet we must not fail to point out that this does not finally solve the Aryan problem for the German Evangelical Church. We must reckon with the possibility that within a proposed skeleton law of the German Evangelical Church, corresponding, even if attenuated, clauses will be provided for. We are of the opinion that there are very strong elements among the National Socialists by whom the Church's rejection of the Aryan clause would not be understood, and that the work of the Church among the German people would thereby again be balked or imperilled . . . It is not now the business of other countries to judge, but first they must get to know the facts. Above all, public demonstrations,

149. Letter of 6.11.1933.
150. At Novi Sad.

particularly by church circles abroad, must be avoided in future, as in the present international situation they would have the appearance of being mainly political demonstrations. Special discretion should be observed in voicing such opinions in former enemy countries. For in the eyes of the German people they have to a considerable extent forfeited the moral right to pass judgement on conditions in Germany . . . Signed p.p. Heckel.[151]

By adopting a position from which it was possible for him to credit the German Christians with valuable services, and defend the Aryan clause on the grounds of the evangelistic possibilities it offered, Heckel forfeited a great deal of confidence among Bonhoeffer's colleagues, the Evangelical pastors in England. This attitude was to persist for many years until the financial dependence of the congregations abroad on Berlin began to make itself felt.

National Synod

Bonhoeffer returned from Sofia in time for the National Synod at Wittenberg. Various things had happened during his absence.

Following the Brown Synod and its devastating international repercussions the Foreign Ministry had intervened on political grounds, forbidding the discussion of the Aryan clause at Wittenberg and hence its enactment by the National Synod. Indeed, the Ministry sent an observer to Wittenberg on 27th September, as Bonhoeffer was aware at the time.

We have already mentioned the 2,000 signatures collected for the Emergency League's manifesto, 'To the National Synod'. Within the Church, expert opinion on the Aryan clause had been collected from faculties and individual academics by various bodies. Support came from Marburg, in the form of expert opinion from the faculty, under von Soden's signature; there was another report, equally lucid and authoritative, by twenty-two New Testament professors; and later yet another from Bultmann. But from Erlangen—for even scholarship does not produce unequivocal results—came a report which did not imply outright rejection, and this was signed by Althaus and Elert.[152] Wobbermin declared his explicit opposition to the Marburg theologians and described the opinion of the twenty-two New Testament scholars as 'premature and misleading'. The law passed by the Brown Synod, he believed, was 'practical and justified', and should not admit of any exceptions, 'for in so doing the Church would endanger the unity of German culture which at present it is so imperative to consolidate, above all in the Evangelical Church . . .'[153] When, two years later, Bonhoeffer became involved in an argument with Professor Hodgson, the Secretary of 'Faith and

151. DEK KK III, p. 474, of 30.11.1933.
152. See Ch. VII, p. 236.
153. Expert opinion, cf. *Die Evangelische Kirche in Deutschland und die Judenfrage*, Geneva, 1945, pp. 46 ff.

Order', it was to Wobbermin of all people that the latter turned for support.[154]

Nevertheless, the wave of protest that preceded Wittenberg was impressive enough.

Early on that beautiful autumn morning, Bonhoeffer was driven to Wittenberg by his father's chauffeur. He took Frau Staewen and Hildebrandt with him; the back of the car was filled with parcels containing 'To the National Synod' leaflets. In Wittenberg, 'the first theological teaching platoon of the Augustusburg Leadership College in Saxony,[155] complete with field-grey uniforms and knapsacks, stood on guard beneath the windows of the future National Bishop'.[156] Wurm, the Bishop of Stuttgart, preached the inaugural sermon. Bonhoeffer witnessed the ceremony from a corner in the castle church. Ludwig Müller gave a situation report which included the word 'racial conformity' but he did not yet express an opinion on the law passed by the General Synod on 5th September, nor did he mention either the expert opinion from the faculties or the 2,000 signatures. During the lunch break, therefore, Bonhoeffer and Hildebrandt sent a telegram to Müller demanding that he mention these things during the afternoon, but to no effect. They and their friends then distributed the leaflets in the streets and nailed them to trees. *Evangelium im Dritten Reich* later reported:

Meanwhile the town is full of rumours. Impossible though it may seem, it is true: the enemy is making his presence felt. Appeals without any printer's name, minutes, communiqués, details, etc., are being circulated. But unerringly and surely, our leaders will take steps . . .

The afternoon was not particularly peaceful, however. The election of the National Bishop and the staffing of the Church Ministry aroused heated argument. Lutheran bishops such as Meiser, Wurm and Schöffel quarrelled with Hossenfelder because they felt that appointments to the Ministry should be proportionate to the numbers in each denomination. But Ludwig Müller was unanimously elected its head. Over Luther's tomb in the church of Wittenberg Castle, Hossenfelder declaimed: 'I greet thee, my *Reichsbischof*!' At this, Hildebrandt whispered to Bonhoeffer that now he believed that Luther really would turn over in his grave in the castle church.

Both regarded the outcome of Wittenberg as disastrous—precisely because it had produced nothing that was not predictable. The much-needed protest by the still intact regional churches outside Old Prussia, especially those in South Germany, had not been made. While nothing immediately heretical had been concluded, the most crucial matter had been passed over. Thus the performance at Wittenberg had in practice

154. See Ch. IX, pp. 399 f.
155. The class of the preachers' seminary, suddenly transmogrified into an S.A. unit.
156. *Evangelium im Dritten Reich*, p. 41.

confirmed the Brown Synod, which therefore continued to remain operative. There had been no mention of repealing 'the law that violated the
Confession of the regional churches'. For the sake of preserving their
own dioceses intact, the Lutheran bishops had remained silent.

Bonhoeffer and Hildebrandt now began to reconsider the question of
the need for a free church. On Sunday 1st October they went to the Old
Lutherans in the Nassauische Strasse in Berlin-Wilmersdorf, to assess
the possibilities. Though the façade was swathed in a flowing swastika
flag, they were warmly welcomed. However they were told they must
bring their congregations with them.[157] This did not, of course, present
a solution and the free church remained a burning issue until the situation changed with the Barmen Synod.

The victories at Wittenberg marked the apogee of German Christian
power. Ricarda Huch resigned from the Prussian Academy of the Arts
in protest against the abusive expulsion of Thomas Mann, Fritz von
Unruh and Franz Werfel; by contrast, the new National Bishop and
Theodor Heckel were nominated 'honorary senators' of the Academy of
Sciences. Magdeburg Cathedral, 'the only former arch-episcopal cathedral . . . in Protestant hands', was chosen for Müller's consecration
which would, it was supposed, be succeeded by peace. In the event these
plans proved over-optimistic.

Departure

1. Since his decision in August to go to London, so much had happened
that Bonhoeffer could hardly expect his departure to remain unchal-
lenged. At the beginning of October Heckel informed him that, all
things considered, he could not be allowed to go unconditionally. Bonhoeffer replied that he would retract nothing, nor would he sign any
undertaking not to engage in ecumenical activity. He insisted on speaking to the National Bishop himself. He told Müller that he had no
intention of representing the German Christian cause abroad, and would
speak, as before, for the ecumenical movement. On his suggestion that
they should prohibit his departure altogether, the church leaders asked
him to declare that he had changed his mind because of obligations
within the Church. Bonhoeffer stood his ground, however, causing Heckel
to complain: 'What complex people you all are!'[158] The following day
the National Bishop informed Bonhoeffer that he might leave. This was
the time of attempted appeasement after the Wittenberg victory.

No doubt what finally persuaded them to ask me to go to London was the
fear that the congregations here would break away. I then arranged for
my conversation with the National Bishop and the opinions I had put
forward to be placed on record so that I could literally have an absolutely

157. Communication from F. Hildebrandt.
158. Communication from F. Hildebrandt.

free hand and need in no way regard myself as the emissary of a German Christian church—quite the opposite, in fact.[159]

In his declaration made for the record,[160] Bonhoeffer took care to scotch the dangerous rumours about 'foreign propaganda' by affirming his loyalty to his country. And here he did not say 'National Socialist State', but 'Germany'. He was also careful to mention his family origins and connections, among them one cousin in particular who was a Counsellor of State holding an important official post. For it would have been foolish to ignore the tendency, even within the field of the church struggle, to regard every contact with other countries as tantamount to collaboration in the 'atrocity campaign of the foreign Press' (*vide* the Treachery Law). At the notorious meeting between the Chancellor and the church leaders in January 1934, Göring was able to create a considerable stir with his account of the way the treatment of German church affairs by the foreign Press had seriously interfered with general reconstruction.

Julius Richter, in genial misunderstanding of the situation, remarked to Siegmund-Schultze that, considering Bonhoeffer differed in almost every respect on church matters from Ludwig Müller, the National Bishop had again shown 'astonishing understanding' in sending Bonhoeffer to England, entrusting him, moreover, with the task of 'looking after the new church government's ecumenical interests'.

J. Glenthoj has discovered a letter written on 6th October, from Birger Forell to his archbishop, which gives a lively account of what happened. From this it would appear that Bonhoeffer was not to be allowed to go abroad because he had signed the Wittenberg leaflet, 'since this implied an attack on the unity of the Church'.

B. was sent for by the National Bishop and was asked if he still stood by his signature. He answered in the affirmative, with a reference to *Augustana*, Chapter 7, but when he proceeded to recite the whole of this chapter in Latin, M. got a bit hot under the collar and suggested postponing the conversation until later . . . [Forell further reported that the Foreign Ministry had intimated that] when making appointments of men overseas the effect of these appointments on the Church's image abroad should be taken into account and only those appointed who are trusted by the country concerned.[161]

2. Bonhoeffer was loath to leave his students. As a small parting gift he gave them his fine essay 'What must the Student of Theology do Today?'[162] It is significant that he should expressly forbid them 'to speak contemptuously of theological learning' at a time when he was leaving their academic ambit, and that he should urge them to 'test the

159. To F. Siegmund-Schultze, 6.11.1933.
160. GS II, p. 125.
161. See MW V, VI, H.1.
162. GS III, pp. 243-7.

spirits in the Church' at a time when the appointed representatives of theological science were not doing this. The students must realize, he wrote, that the theologian 'does not live by his superior knowledge or by self-righteousness, but by forgiveness alone'. From the point of view of what he was to say later, in 1944, it is of interest to note that in 1933 Bonhoeffer warned the theologian that 'the air of worldliness which he likes to assume may yet serve him very ill, and it is really quite impossible to see how unmitigated worldliness can be regarded as the decisive criterion of the good theologian'.[163] We may be certain that the man who discovered the 'worldliness' of the Gospel in 1944, would not have wished his 1933 admonition to be abolished for the benefit of a worldliness understood in non-dialectical terms.

This essay was written either at the beginning of August during the short time in Berlin, between the London and Bethel visits, or else during October, just before his departure for England. During that interval at the beginning of August he had once again invited his seminar to go walking in the Mark of Brandenburg. In the autumn, he went out to Prebelow with a group of those students closest to him. They celebrated on bread rolls and cocoa. 'We must now endure in silence, and set the firebrand of truth to all four corners of the proud German Christian edifice so that one day the whole structure may collapse.' Such was Bonhoeffer's farewell, as recorded by Winfried Maechler.[164]

It may have been on this occasion, or perhaps during the outing with the seminary at the beginning of August, that Bonhoeffer thrashed out his 'Theses on Youth Work in the Church'.[165] In August 1933 Baldur von Schirach decreed that no one might belong both to the Hitler Youth and to denominational youth clubs. The prohibition affected a great many young people and congregations and therefore gave rise to considerable uncertainty. In this essay Bonhoeffer called upon the congregations to see themselves in proper perspective and to avoid the godless idolization of youth.[166]

3. On 14th October 1933—two days before Bonhoeffer's departure to London—Hitler announced that Germany had left the League of Nations. This was the Chancellor's reply to the rejection of his demand for 'equality of status', and it was gleefully welcomed by everyone, including the church opposition. In the name of the Pastors' Emergency League Niemöller at once sent a telegram to the 'Führer' expressing gratitude, and swearing loyal allegiance.

This was not at all the view of Bonhoeffer and Hildebrandt. Julius

163. GS III, p. 245.
164. *Bonhoeffer Gedenkheft*, ed. E. Bethge, 1947, p. 26.
165. GS III, pp. 292 f.
166. Besides the undated MS. in Bonhoeffer's writing, there is a copy by W. D. Zimmermann which may have been made in the summer or autumn of 1933, and another by J. Rieger, London, when Bonhoeffer gave this essay as a lecture in April 1934 before the German Y.M.C.A.

Rieger, who happened just then to meet his future colleague in the 'Pilsen' restaurant by the Zoo, noted in his diary a remark of Bonhoeffer's which at the time seemed to him exaggerated: 'This has brought the danger of war very much closer.'[167]

Bonhoeffer and Hildebrandt now went together to Dahlem to hear Pastor Röhricht preach on 'God is Faithful'.[168] Then they said good-bye, and Bonhoeffer assured his friend that he hoped to see him soon in London where they would at first share the stipend between them.

A few days later Franz Hildebrandt refused the offer of a post in the Pastors' Emergency League, and wrote to Niemöller saying he was shortly going to join Bonhoeffer in London; the letter ended thus:

I find it impossible to understand how you can joyfully welcome the political move in Geneva when you yourselves refuse to adopt an unequivocal attitude toward a church which persistently denies us equality of status. As one who is comparatively young and to some extent suspect, I don't want to harm your cause by repeating in public what has been my constant refrain within our own circle ever since the end of June. Anyway, what does 'public' mean here now? It is my part to remain silent and this, you will, I hope, forgive your old friend, Hildebrandt.[169]

167. Communication from J. Rieger, 9.12.1960.
168. 1 Cor. 1:9.
169. Letter of 24.10.1933.

CHAPTER EIGHT

LONDON

1933 - 1935

THE conflicts of the past six months had taken Bonhoeffer far outside his previous sphere of operations. They had also revealed how very greatly his views differed from those of his fellow combatants. In nearly all his suggestions he stood alone.

His notion of an interdict at the beginning of July had seemed quite impracticable to his colleagues. In September, ideas about a free church had come to nothing. When the Aryan clause was adopted into ecclesiastical legislation the schism for which Bonhoeffer had sought to pave the way among the clergy never materialized. The 'Bethel Confession' was emasculated by those bodies whose voice carried authority. A decision in September in favour of mass resignations from the ministry was postponed for an indefinite period by his friends and even like-minded theologians such as Barth and Sasse decided to wait for even 'worse' heresies than the Racial Conformity Law for the Civil Service. Experienced comrades-in-arms feared what they ought to have welcomed—resolutions and delegations from abroad. Unlike Bonhoeffer, the leaders of the church opposition applauded Hitler's withdrawal from the League of Nations. Even the discerning clerical circle in the Achenbachstrasse in Berlin failed to understand his secret hankering after India and his interest in Gandhi's methods of resistance. No one shared his leanings towards pacifism.

Had Bonhoeffer lost confidence? He wrote to Karl Barth:

I feel that in some way I don't understand, I have somehow got up against all my friends; my views about what should be done have seemed to cut me off from them more and more although our personal relations, now as always, continue to be very close. All this has frightened me and shaken my confidence so that I began to fear that dogmatism might be leading me astray—since there seemed no particular reason why my own view in these matters should be any better, any more right, than the views of many really able pastors whom I sincerely respect—and so I thought it was about time to go into the wilderness for a spell . . . It seems to me that at the moment it is more dangerous for me to make a gesture than to retreat into silence.[1]

Bonhoeffer's close friends, during that late summer of 1933, remember that doubts about what was the proper course of action continued to

1. Letter of 24.10.1933, GS II, p. 132.

torment him, even after he had decided to go to London. The decision in favour of a distant parish in a foreign country was not an easy one, but to it we owe the lively exchange of letters between Bonhoeffer and Karl Barth.[2] Bonhoeffer's letters reveal a close connection between his trusting request for advice and his need for independence.

At this time there was no one he would listen to more readily than Barth. Yet he wrote to him only when there was no longer any chance of cancelling his London plans. In his first letter, he remarked that he himself could not understand why he had not asked Barth to decide for him in the first place. In his reply, Barth did not mince his words: 'In no circumstances should you now play Elijah under the juniper tree or Jonah under the gourd, and in fact you ought to return to your post by the next ship.'[3] Bonhoeffer was so impressed by Barth's letter that he sent it to his parents; his father's comment was:

It is striking testimony to a fiery spirit. As regards the case in point I would not venture to comment. But I do think that to be able to look at things from the outside whence, perhaps, some influence can be brought to bear, and particularly to save oneself up for the right moment, can be extremely valuable.[4]

His father's words 'the right moment' exactly expressed Bonhoeffer's doubts, and also explained his final decision. For he neither wished nor would have permitted that anyone else should determine how and when he should act. What, he asked himself, was the crucial hour, and had it struck with the Young Reformation Movement, with the Pastors' Emergency League, or with Karl Barth? When he finally left Germany, it was because the experiences of the summer had only added to the uncertainty. And there was something else he had also come to realize:

. . . although I am working with all my might for the church opposition, it is perfectly clear to me that this particular opposition is only a temporary and transitional phase that will lead on to opposition of a quite different kind, and that only very few of the men in this preliminary skirmish will commit themselves in the next struggle. And I believe that the whole of Christendom should pray with us that it will be a 'resistance unto death', and that people will be found to suffer it. Simply suffering—that is what will be needed then—not parries or blows or thrusts such as may still be possible or admissible in the preliminary fighting; the real struggle which perhaps lies ahead must consist only in suffering belief, and then, then perhaps God will again indicate the Church by his Word . . .[5]

Bonhoeffer's vision of another, quite different opposition does not as yet evince any of the characteristics of a new political ethic. Its commit-

---

2. GS II, pp. 126-37.
3. GS II, p. 135. This situation can be compared with a later one in September 1944 when Bonhoeffer, in circumstances that were wholly different, linked his own fate with that of Jonah (LPP, pp. 222 f.).
4. Letter of 22.12.1933.   5. To E. Sutz, 28.4.1934, GS I, p. 40.

ment is still entirely confined to ideas concerning 'discipleship'. What lends seriousness and depth to the preliminary fighting with its 'blows and thrusts' is this discipleship, not political resistance as such and the proposals for a future programme that go with it. In clearly distinguishing between the political struggle and the church struggle, Bonhoeffer differed little at this time from his theological friends in Berlin. Active responsibility for the production of a political alternative to the Nazi State, or at least for vigilant observance of the democratic constitution, he saw as being incumbent on those who were eligible by reason of their calling and position in the state machine. Yet, unlike most of the opposition, he was in no way embarrassed by the fact that the church opposition naturally represented an eminently political factor; moreover, he showed far greater vision in his desire to study passive resistance under Gandhi and to evolve from this a form of struggle against the National Socialist claim to power that would be in keeping with Christian tenets.

Thus Bonhoeffer left Berlin, partly because of doubts about the course it was his duty to pursue, and partly in order that his thinking and doing might not be forced into one single ecclesial dimension. What he wanted was a period of seeking and probing in a small, quiet congregation.

Yet this attempt at evasion was completely unsuccessful. '. . . one is close enough to want to take part in everything, and too far away for active cooperation. And during the past weeks this has made things exceptionally difficult for me.'[6] Thus, even in the small London parishes, Bonhoeffer could not enjoy so much as a week's respite from the restless Berlin scene. Letters of protest went to and fro; friends and official messengers would arrive, expecting him to state his views; every couple of weeks or so he himself travelled between London and Berlin, although he was not much addicted either to Channel crossings or to flying. At Forest Hill post office the telephone bill was so astronomical that, as Hildebrandt and Rieger remember to this day, the G.P.O. made a substantial deduction from the foreign pastor's bill!

Thus the eighteen months he spent in London were dominated by the church struggle and its indirect effects upon the ecumenical movement. The latter took up a great deal of Bonhoeffer's time. His parish work, although not neglected, became increasingly involved in the struggle. His deepest commitment at this time, however, was to his reflections on the Sermon on the Mount and on 'discipleship'.

Hence from now on there were to be two different sides to Bonhoeffer. On the one hand, the man who was to dare more for the sake of the Church than most of his friends; to whom the German church opposition's plans—from which, before long, the Confessing Church would spring—were to mean just that little bit more than they meant to his fellow militants; the man who behaved as though the ideas of tomorrow were the realities of today and who, when the inevitable setbacks came,

6. To K.-F. Bonhoeffer, Jan. 1934. GS II, p. 157.

was always ready to renew the attack. On the other hand, there was the Bonhoeffer who sometimes seemed so reserved as almost to be a stranger to these struggles, who might suddenly be irritated by the limitations of his Confession; who was driven by quite different visions of the realization of the Gospels.

I PARISH MINISTER

On 17th October 1933 Bonhoeffer moved into the German vicarage in the South London suburb of Forest Hill. This was situated on a southern slope below the well-kept grounds of Horniman Park.

The huge Victorian vicarage was surrounded by a garden in which there were lots of trees. The principal rooms were occupied by a German private school. Bonhoeffer had two of the rooms with windows facing north-east, as incapable of keeping out draughts and fog as the ill-fitting doors, so that in spite of a strong constitution he became subject to influenza and colds. He fought a losing battle against an invasion of mice. However, with furniture imported from home, including of course, the Bechstein piano, he did his best to make both rooms habitable.

It was these rooms that for nearly three months he shared with Franz Hildebrandt. The physicist Herbert Jehle, who was also a pacifist, sometimes came on a visit from Cambridge. Wolf-Dieter Zimmermann and Jürgen Winterhager, members of his student group in Berlin, came to stay with him for several weeks. Other, more exacting visitors, were relations such as his brothers-in-law, Dohnanyi and Dress, with their wives.

It was in these rooms, too, that the community's youth groups or musical circles gathered, to rehearse a nativity play, to play trios or quartets, or sometimes to listen to concerts from his large collection of gramophone records. Bonhoeffer greatly admired the quality of English choral singing and bought himself a recording of an English rendering of the Mass in B Minor. It was through music that he made friends with the Whitburns who were cousins of Lokies, the head of the Berlin Gossner Mission. They taught him English carols. He was invariably a generous host, in spite of his meagre stipend.

Ministry

For the first time Bonhoeffer now had a regular pastorate. Yet this did not mean that he could enjoy fully the 'rights of the clerical profession' —nor, indeed was he ever to do so, since throughout his life the conditions of his employment were never normal. Though in London, the church committee actually fulfilled the letter of the law as though they were a church in Germany and carried out an election in due form on 12th November. In accordance with the agreements obtaining between the London pastorates and the German Evangelical Federation of Churches, the election required the ratification of Heckel's External Affairs Office. At first Bonhoeffer deliberately procrastinated in the matter of the ratification and eventually, after the Ludwig Müller affair in Berlin at the beginning of 1934, allowed the correspondence to lapse. He wanted to avoid all semblance of recognizing the Reich Church Government.[7] By this he was hazarding his right to a pension and provision for his old age.

Bonhoeffer administered two of the six German pastorates in London, whose independence and compactness were reminiscent of free church conditions. At one time each had paid its own pastor and organist and had also financed the maintenance of its buildings. After the First World War some of them, such as St. Paul's and Sydenham had decided, through lack of funds, to amalgamate and to share a pastor between them. They were still able to maintain a relatively independent attitude towards the church authorities in Germany.

One of the parishes, that of Sydenham, possessed a church in South London. Elias Schrenk, the Swabian missionary and evangelist, was responsible for the foundation of this parish in 1875. The congregation consisted mainly of well-to-do businessmen, but in addition there were German diplomats who, before the First World War, used to live in that part of London. Sydenham regarded itself as a congregation of the United Church. Some thirty to forty people attended Bonhoeffer's services.

St. Paul's, the other parish, belonged to the Reformed Confession. Its history went back more than 200 years. In the eighteenth century the church had stood where the north pier of Waterloo Bridge stands today. In Bonhoeffer's time the church was in Whitechapel in the East End, but it was subsequently destroyed in an air raid. Where it once stood, Petticoat Lane market attracts visitors on Sunday mornings today. In church on Sundays more than fifty parishioners used to listen to Bonhoeffer's sermons, after which they remained for a friendly chat. They were tradesmen—butchers, bakers and tailors—and their families, of German origin, mostly from Württemberg, but many of them were fluent only in English. During the First World War they had endured a good deal of hostility, and some had had to close their businesses. But now they listened readily to Bonhoeffer's plea to help German *émigrés*; in this he found an able second in his church-warden, Gottlob Henne, who long continued, even after the Second World War, to help German refugees make a fresh start in life.

Bonhoeffer did not much care for parish meetings and minute-taking when these were only concerned with matters of routine. He induced the officers to authorize a number of innovations. In this way he introduced services for children and founded youth clubs, and helped the

7. See GS I, p. 202.

latter to produce nativity and passion plays. He sanctioned the collections for Dr. Goebbels's *Winterhilfe* (Winter Aid Fund) which by then were becoming the norm in German churches, but at the same time he insisted that there should be collections on behalf of German refugees in England. A German Embassy proposal to collaborate with the German parishes in setting up a 'German House' in London was successfully foiled by Bonhoeffer and his officers.

His main concern was for those who came over with the first wave of refugees from Germany: '. . . in London I spent most of my time with these people and I felt it was a great privilege to do so.'[8]

Bonhoeffer's congregations were apt to find him too exacting. At the very start he attempted to introduce the revised hymnbook for churches abroad, and arranged services on Christmas Eve and New Year's Day which his faithful working families could not attend because they did not coincide with English holidays; what his parishioners found particularly hard to accept was the severe and exigent nature of his sermons. They had received from his predecessor a mild, humdrum, pietistic form of address and by comparison found Bonhoeffer's sermons altogether too oppressive and emphatic. Some, indeed, found that only by staying away could they avoid such exacting demands.

For the first time he had to give a sermon every Sunday, which he found difficult. Each sermon was written out in full and often the manuscript was sent to acquaintances in Germany. Sixteen of these sermons preached in London have survived.[9] Unfortunately they do not include those in which he dealt with the Sermon on the Mount.

Please write and tell me some time what you say when you preach about the Sermon on the Mount. I am working on this now—trying to keep it extremely simple and straightforward, but it always comes back to *keeping* the commandment and not evading it. Discipleship of Christ—I'd like to know what that is—it is not exhausted in our concept of faith.[10]

There is no doubt that the church struggle constantly underlay everything else, yet there are few references to it in his sermons. His own impassioned commitment is most strongly evident in a sermon delivered in January 1934 which was virtually a personal Confession. At this time he was expecting events to take a bad turn. He chose for his model Jeremiah, the prophet who, though mocked by God, is caught up in his mission. The Röhm *Putsch*, and the ensuing massacres of 30th June 1934, led him to give what was an undisguised sermon of atonement.

The predominant note in the London sermons is a strong eschatological fervour; he sought quite simply to awaken a longing for the kingdom

8. GS I, p. 317.
9. Five are in GS IV, pp. 154-82.
10. To E. Sutz, 28.4.1934, GS I, p. 41.

of heaven. When he was preparing his Remembrance Day sermon in 1933, he wrote to his brother-in-law:

Remembrance Day is a particularly moving day this time because, after everything that has happened during the past months, one feels such a tremendous longing for real peace, in which all the misery and injustice, the lying and cowardice will come to an end.[11]

Colleagues

Bonhoeffer's arrival in England meant that the German pastors already living there now acquired a first-class source of information on events which it had been difficult for them to assess from afar. Like most expatriate Germans, they had acclaimed what had happened in the spring as Germany's rebirth and had been at pains to combat the unfavourable public reactions in England. The church troubles of the past months had considerably upset their picture of the new Germany. They still continued to distinguish between Hitler's 'good policy' and the 'excesses' of his more objectionable paladins in church matters. A letter, written on New Year's Eve in 1933 by a pastor who had joined the National Socialist Party gives an exact idea of what well-meaning clergy abroad were thinking at the time:

. . . I spent two years at the front, where I fought and bled for my country. With my own eyes I saw many of my best friends pay with their lives for their service to their fatherland . . . In my youthful enthusiasm I regarded their death as a sacred legacy . . . we had to fight on so that their death for Germany should not have been in vain or even be forgotten. But what had become of Germany? A land of injustice and corruption, subject to the whims of black and red rulers alike. As a pastor it was not my business to take part in politics, let alone party politics . . . Then the National Socialist Party came into power, a party that didn't want to be a party, with a programme having a moral and religious basis. That's why I became a member of the movement. Another reason . . . was the realization that the lower ranks of the Party hierarchy were not permeated with the same deep morality and religion as the Führer and his ideas, that many of them believed they could simply change the colour of their hearts from red to brown, and that not a few agitators—for as such I regard the movement of the 'German Christians'—would seek to use the movement to climb to positions of influence. The proclamation of the Gospel might well be prevented in consequence, so destroying the very fundament upon which the fatherland could be reconstructed . . . For this reason it seems to me absolutely necessary to collaborate for the sake of the Church of Christ and for the sake of the national community in which God has placed us. That this is best done as a Party member is self-evident . . .

And I believe that already there may be opportunity to collaborate in the way I have just mentioned. After the National Bishop's sorry performance,

11. To G. Leibholz, 23.11.1933, see also Ch. VII, p. 209.

the Party is trying to coordinate our youth work. This might perhaps be possible in Germany but not for us here . . . Today I shall make representations to the *Obergruppenleiter* [Nazi group leader] who, I am convinced will listen to me because I am a member. In no circumstances shall I allow any deviation from the clear line we must follow in our work.

The writer of this letter, though much disturbed by Bonhoeffer's commitment to the church opposition, not to speak of his poor opinion of the National Socialist Party, did in fact for a time succumb to his persuasion and joined the struggle for the German Church.

During 1933 the Party, when they were not courting them, made appreciable claims on the London pastors. In Lancaster Gate the local Nazi group organized regular evening discussion groups, to which the pastors and their congregations were invited and plied with beer. The Party regarded the pastors as potential contacts and mediators between the registered passport-holding Germans and the unregistered *Volksdeutsche*.[12] During the summer the Nazis also sent contingents to the lectures organized by the churches.

In this way Hossenfelder himself got in touch with the German Lutheran St. George's Church, proposing that he should come and lecture there. The pastor and his council were able to sidetrack this proposal by saying that the date was unsuitable. When in the late autumn Hossenfelder, again invited by Frank Buchman and supported by the Bishop of Gloucester (A. C. Headlam), next suggested an appearance, the fronts in the church struggle had already become all too clearly demarcated. The church and its pastor, Rieger, successfully evaded the compromise a Hossenfelder demonstration would have involved.

The North London ministries were held by two older men, Pastor Wehrhan, the doyen of the London pastorate, and Schönberger who was an active member in the Party. As long as Bonhoeffer remained in London, both these men supported the cause of the church opposition and the Confessing Church. In the East End there was the young clergyman Dr. J. Rieger who became the close friend of Bonhoeffer and Hildebrandt;[13] later, when Bonhoeffer had returned to Germany Rieger took over his task of helping Bishop Bell whenever information on events in Germany was urgently required. He also assumed responsibility for the *émigrés'* welfare so that his St. George's Church eventually became a place of refuge for Lutherans. One refugee was Hildebrandt, after his precipitate flight in 1937. Besides those in London, there were about five other German pastors elsewhere in Great Britain.

From the start Bonhoeffer was distinguished by his youth and his theological pre-eminence, as well as by his intimate knowledge of ecclesiastical and political circles in Berlin. All but one of his colleagues

12. People of German origin and culture who are nationals of the country in which they live. (*Editor.*)
13. See J. Rieger, *Dietrich Bonhoeffer in England*, 1966.

immediately recognized his authority and, until his departure, continued to adhere to the decisions of the Confessing Church. This did not mean that they all accepted his political views.

The German pastors in London met at frequent and regular intervals, while those from the whole of Great Britain convened at a yearly pastoral conference and at the 'Association of the German Evangelical Congregations of Great Britain and Ireland'. The Association's chairman was the London banker, Baron Bruno Schröder, who supported a number of German charitable foundations in London and, moreover, showed a lively interest in church affairs, siding with Bonhoeffer's opposition in the church troubles. The secretary of this association was Wehrhan.

The clergy further belonged to the 'Foreign Pastoral Society', to which ministers of all countries were admitted. These gatherings listened eagerly to what Bonhoeffer had to say on the German situation, especially after the Fanö episode. In the society's diary his name appears as a speaker on 4th December 1933, 14th May and 1st October 1934. Since members of Bonhoeffer's parish of St. Paul's performed responsible functions connected with the Y.M.C.A., he too offered his services,[14] although he was not altogether happy about the organization's German branch.

It was undoubtedly due to Bonhoeffer's presence in London that, of all the German congregations abroad, only those in England made any real or effective attempt to intervene in the church struggle at home. But since these congregations were the focal point for Germans living abroad, active opposition was not easy. In London, Bonhoeffer, too, experienced considerable difficulty in overcoming occasional manifestations of 'national discipline'. The understandable opinion that it was better to maintain a discreet silence outside Germany was shared even by certain circles within the Confessing Church in their anxiety not to appear in a false light politically. There was, further, quite naturally a certain distaste for anything to do with the distant 'church disputes', a term which those in authority, both in Party and in State, employed in preference to the term 'church struggle'. Astutely, they reckoned on widespread aversion among the population to involvement in ecclesiastical or theological disputes. It could even be assumed that a good and pious Christian would rather keep away from 'church disputes'.

Bonhoeffer had little time for such considerations. Again and again he succeeded in imposing his views upon his colleagues and the church officers as well as upon Baron Schröder.

II FIRST ATTACK AGAINST REICH CHURCH GOVERNMENT, WINTER 1933-34

Two factors received wide publicity during the early part of Bonhoeffer's

14. GS III, p. 292.

time in England and served to increase his influence in both ecumenical and German circles in London.

Firstly, the whole of the English Press, from *The Times* down to local newspapers, had published and discussed in detail the 2,000 pastors' Wittenberg manifesto 'To the National Synod'. By virtue of its initial letter, Bonhoeffer's name was prominent at the head of the list of twenty-two signatories.

Secondly, in November there took place the scandal of the Sports Palace demonstration which shattered the German Christian movement and its church government. Everyone was eager to learn the details of what had happened, why it had happened and what the consequences were likely to be. Bonhoeffer with the added advantage of inside knowledge could not possibly have been in a better situation to demonstrate convincingly the justice of his cause.

The Sports Palace Demonstration

Franz Hildebrandt's pre-arranged visit to London began on 11th November. No sooner had he concluded his account of recent events in Berlin than sensational news began to arrive which seemed to overshadow all that had gone before. On 13th November the German Christians had staged a mammoth demonstration in the Berlin Sports Palace at which the officers of the new Reich Church Government had appeared. Its main feature was the speech by the Berlin *Gauobmann* [the senior Nazi of the district], Dr. Krause. Now that leading ecclesiastical positions had been taken over by 'men of the movement', Krause declared, there must be further dismissals and the immediate implementation of the Arvan clause; above all he called for 'liberation from the Old Testament with its Jewish money morality and from these stories of cattle-dealers and pimps'. The Church Affairs officers and bishops who were present allowed this speech to pass without protest. The following morning the German Press—in which not all criticism had yet been suppressed—carried detailed reports. Indignation spread even into the ranks of the German Christians, who had never dreamed such a thing could happen. The opposition began to hope that the weakness of the Church Affairs officers would lead to the reorganization of the church government. The Emergency League believed it would be possible to compel the National Bishop either to adopt a new line or to resign.

Bonhoeffer himself was not unduly surprised by the events at the Sports Palace demonstration and he put its repercussions to good use in promoting his own fight for enlightenment. He did not delude himself with the belief that the kind of men who in Berlin had needed the crude vituperation of a Krause to rouse them, would be able to hold out for very long once the difference between the two sides in the church struggle became really pronounced.

Anxiety about Berlin Friends

The state of uncertainty that obtained in Berlin both for the German Christians and for the Emergency League, brought anxiety to Bonhoeffer and Hildebrandt, far away in London. The news that reached them was not always unequivocal and they found it difficult to allay their scepticism about the attitude of their own side. Every morning they read the excellent reports in The Times and nearly every evening carried on anguished telephone conversations with Jacobi, Niemöller, or with Bonhoeffer's mother, herself as committed as they were.

Everything the Brown Synod and the Wittenberg Synod had enacted and established seemed, after what had happened at the Sports Palace, to be in jeopardy. On 16th November Ludwig Müller was forced to rescind the Aryan clause; then, after the confiscation of the Emergency League's proclamation from the pulpit on the Sports Palace demonstration and the first suspensions of Emergency League pastors, Frick, the Minister of the Interior, announced that Hitler would not intervene in the church dispute, to which he had no intention of applying police measures; further, Hossenfelder's Church Ministry was obliged to resign, and the National Bishop had to cancel at short notice his solemn consecration scheduled to take place in Berlin Cathedral on 3rd December.

Was a victorious mood justified? In Berlin the regional church bishops were girding up their loins to do battle with the National Bishop for a new church government. What did this mean for the opposition?

On 30th November Bonhoeffer and Hildebrandt heard that the South and North German bishops—that is to say the men who had elected Müller without protest at Wittenberg—were holding discussions with him, discussions in which Niemöller did not feel it was possible responsibly to participate. The friends immediately wrote to Niemöller in Dahlem:

. . . we should really have preferred to telephone you again to put all the force of our youth into a brotherly exhortation not, at this decisive moment, to leave the control of the ship to those who are bound to steer her once again into uncharted seas and who will not relinquish the tiller until it is too late . . . False modesty and timidity brought about our downfall once before—last June . . .[15]

They went on to develop an emergency programme for Niemöller to follow: the synods of the summer of 1933 were to be dissolved; any of their members who wished to enter the new synods about to be formed must submit to a process of doctrinal scrutiny. The Emergency League must set up machinery to limit membership so as to prevent infiltration by the German Christians now they had suffered defeat. In the new church leadership Sasse must represent the Lutherans and

15. GS II, pp. 149 f.

Barth the Reformed Church. To an earlier remark of Niemöller's in a telephone conversation that it was no longer a question of individual personalities and jobs but of the Church and her doctrine, they replied that this was precisely why Niemöller and his friends should not be too diffident.

After sending off their letter, Bonhoeffer and Hildebrandt began to draft forms of repentance for those German Christians wishing or being obliged to resume their functions in the synods or the church administration under the new conditions.

Scarcely had the letter been posted, however, than a disquieting rumour reached the two friends according to which their comrades in the struggle, Niemöller and Jacobi, had been unable to agree on the proper assessment of the situation and the tactical decisions it demanded. And this at the precise moment when Bonhoeffer and Hildebrandt had just persuaded the German pastors in England to join the Pastors' Emergency League. On 4th December the friends despatched an urgent telegram to Niemöller:

Dismayed to hear of breach in Council of Brethren. Jacobi's exclusion from negotiations would compel us to resign immediately and would foil imminent adherence of German pastorate in England ... Stop shameful fence-sitting. Why evade responsibility? Brotherly greetings from Londoners.[16]

Niemöller replied assuring them that 'united action would be taken as regards the Lutheran bishops'. Behind this assurance, however, Bonhoeffer and Hildebrandt sensed the danger that, in concert with the Lutheran bishops, there might be some reluctance to put clear demands regarding the Aryan clause before the National Socialist Government:

This is just the time when we must be radical upon all points, and that includes the Aryan clause, without being afraid of disagreeable consequences to ourselves. If we prove in any way disloyal at this juncture we shall discredit the whole of last summer's struggle. Please, please, do everything you can to keep things clear, courageous and untainted.[17]

Although deeply concerned that events in Berlin should have so clearly shown up the opposition's weaknesses, Bonhoeffer could not but be glad at the unexpected turn of events:

During these past few weeks in which the authoritarian church government has been collapsing, I could not help feeling rather ashamed. Not that I believed that the line we had been following was wrong—on the contrary, it is in fact being proved right; rather, it was because we had been so unbelievably shortsighted in regarding as securely ensconced things which, when the moment came, collapsed into nothingness.[18]

16. GS II, p. 150. See also JK, 1934, p. 25 and M. Niemöller's reply to this protest, with which 'in times that were already difficult enough, you made my life even more difficult!' (GS II, pp. 150 ff.)
17. To M. Niemöller, 15.12.1933, GS II, p. 152.
18. To his grandmother, Christmas 1933, GS II, p. 157.

But he was afraid that it would simply mean a return of the old Church and the premature interruption of the newly-joined struggle for the Confession and the sovereignty of the Church. He had already progressed both in thought and deed to a point not reached by the rest of the opposition until months later, when fresh upheavals had taken place. Five months were to elapse before Barmen, and during that time the forces upon which he was counting began to muster: on 3rd and 4th January, at Barth's instigation, a 'free, reformed synod'[19] convened in the Rhineland. On 14th January a meeting of the Berlin-Brandenburg Emergency League of pastors and laymen was held in Berlin in the form of a church conference with the intention of paving the way for a free synod; the latter was planned for 27th January 1934, but the course of events dictated otherwise; indeed the return of the old Church now began to seem more and more implausible. These conditions re-moulded the opposition into what came to be known, at the time of the Barmen Synod, as the 'Confessing Church'.

The crisis that struck the German Christians and the Emergency League after the Sports Palace scandal was to have personal repercussions for the two friends. By their increasing exhortations, Bonhoeffer and Hildebrandt had so drawn attention to themselves that Niemöller now requested the latter to come and take over the affairs of the Pastors' Emergency League. Niemöller had run into difficulties because the man who had hitherto been his collaborator, his one-time fellow naval officer, Captain Schulze, was having to leave. As there now seemed some hope that the 'opposition' might develop into the 'Confessing Church', Hilde-brandt responded to Niemöller's call for help. A fortnight after his return he was occupying the Dahlem pulpit, from which Niemöller had meanwhile been banned.

Bradford

The annual conference of German pastors resident in England took place at Bradford in Yorkshire from 27th to 30th November, thus coinciding with the period of the collapse of the German Christian movement.

As usual, the pastors worked at their theological assignment. But the real emphasis had now shifted to the heart-searching necessary to discover an appropriate attitude towards events in Berlin and formulate a statement in accordance with it. This enabled Bonhoeffer to put his views for the first time before his assembled colleagues.

The question under discussion was a pertinent one because the pastors in England had been invited to send a delegation to attend the formal consecration of the National Bishop in Berlin Cathedral on 3rd December. It was not yet known in Bradford that the invitation was to be cancelled. What they did know, however, was that during the past

19. GS I, pp. 182 f.

few days several pastors had been suspended from office.

At this point of time Bonhoeffer thought it out of the question for the conference to send a delegation to Berlin. Since he was unable to impose that view, however, he insisted that a document should be sent with the delegation stating in clear terms the extreme difficulty experienced by pastors abroad in continuing to feel any kind of confidence in Ludwig Müller's government. The discussion revolved round this document.

Bonhoeffer described in detail what had happened during and since the summer, including the September synods and the suspension of the Pomeranian pastor, Wilde, who had proclaimed in his church on 19th November:

Before God and this Christian congregation I charge the National Bishop, Hossenfelder, Peter and the other German Christians with having, by their principles of conduct, violated the honour of the Church, and with having enacted ecclesiastical laws that are contrary to the spirit and the teaching of Christ.[20]

The pastors finally agreed upon a declaration 'To the Reich Church Government'.[21] Couched in theological terms, it acknowledges that on 14th November the National Bishop spoke strongly in favour of 'unity of doctrine', but adds the unequivocal threat that 'the close tie between the German Evangelical diaspora in England and the mother Church will be broken' should sections of the church government permit any further infringement of the unity of the Old and New Testaments or of the Reformed belief in justification.

When the pastors learned that Müller's consecration had been postponed they sent the declaration, which was originally to have been presented by the delegation, by post to the Reich Church Government. A copy was sent to the Emergency League. The London pastors suggested to Baron Schröder that he should send a similar document to Berlin in the name of the Association of Congregations. In the event, this was a rather more incisive version of the Bradford text which declared that 'the statutes . . . should give us full liberty to resign from the Church Federation should we so desire'.

Berlin recognized the double threat, and on 20th December Heckel sent the following anodyne reply:

The events which have since occurred[22] testify to the existence of the earnest desire, not only to uphold the full authority of Bible and Confession as the inviolable foundations of the Church, but to bring peace to the Church herself . . . The responsible church authority is fully aware of the special

20. From the minutes of the pastoral conferences, in St. George's parish files, London.
21. For complete text see GS II, pp. 147 f.
22. Heckel means the new Church Ministry without Hossenfelder, but including Lauerer, Beyer, Weber and Werner, as also Ludwig Müller's enforced abandonment of his patronage of the German Christians.

nature and situation of the German Evangelical congregations in Great Britain . . . It therefore derives considerable pleasure and satisfaction from the evidence in this declaration of their complete unanimity in confessing to the fundamentals of the Evangelical Church.

But it was too late for appeasement. To London, the reply seemed implausible, recent events having not only confirmed but exceeded their earlier fears. On the day Heckel's letter was sent off, the National Bishop arbitrarily signed the agreement incorporating the Evangelical Youth into the Hitler Youth. And instead of the promised efforts to restore peace, he enacted the notorious 'muzzling decree' on 4th January 1934, entirely on his own responsibility and unassisted now by a Church Ministry or by the regional church leaders; by this decree he despotically forbade any discussion of church disputes in ecclesiastical premises or in church publications, adding a threat of dismissal should the prohibition be disregarded. As if that were not enough, on 16th November he reimposed the Aryan clause which had been suspended.

In such circumstances the Bradford declaration seemed to the London pastors to be now little more than a mild admonition. The National Bishop was making it exceptionally difficult for Heckel, in charge of foreign relations, to make the pacification and 'inviolability' of the Church sound plausible in London.

Telegrams

Bonhoeffer and his colleagues soon got to know only too well what was happening in the Reich Church Government and in the Pastors' Emergency League; sometimes they also had information about what was happening in Wilhelmstrasse. Since they were able to apply pressure by threatening to break the connection between their own churches and the German Evangelical Church, they determined to impede every fresh move on the part of the church government and to take some of the burden off the shoulders of their brethren in the Emergency League.

They therefore began an onslaught by telegram[23] which eventually compelled Heckel himself to visit London in an effort to quell that source of constant disturbance.

1. When Ludwig Müller on his own responsibility began negotiations for the amalgamation of the Evangelical Youth with the Hitler Youth, the pastors sent a timely cable on 19th December to Bishops Marahrens and Meiser with a somewhat strange text:

Expect Lutheran bishops to preserve Gospel for Christian youth and honour of German Evangelical Church. Congregations here extremely perturbed. German pastors in London. Wehrhan.

The amalgamation was supposed to extend even to the London

23. From the files of St. George's Church, London, and of the Association of Congregations.

parishes. Around the New Year a Party official arrived for the purpose of incorporating the church youth into the Hitler Youth. On British soil the intention was easily foiled.

2. Upon the appearance of the 'muzzling decree' entitled 'The Decree for the Restoration of Orderly Conditions in the German Evangelical Church', which was an attempt to protect the church government and its policies against criticism by threatening with immediate punishment those who failed to comply, they sent a telegram direct to the Reich Church Government:

Following today's *Times* report extremely worried about relations of churches here with mother Church request elucidation facts. German pastors in London. Wehrhan, 6th January.

3. On the day this telegram was sent, the text of the Emergency League proclamation from the pulpit was received in London; this called upon pastors not to obey the decree of 4th January, the 'muzzling decree'. It was the first proclamation of a *status confessionis*. Most pastors did not read out the proclamation until 14th January, though some did so on 7th January, when the London pastors also cabled the Reich Church Government:

For the sake of the Gospel and our conscience we associate ourselves with Emergency League proclamation and withdraw our confidence from National Bishop Müller. German pastors in London. Wehrhan.

They had in fact wished to send the telegram in the name of all the German pastors in the country, but there were complications. Bonhoeffer's draft telegram had declared bluntly: '. . . and no longer recognize the National Bishop', instead of 'withdraw our confidence'. His version was stronger than the Emergency League wording, 'loss of confidence'—too strong, indeed, for his colleagues—and he yielded. Schreiner, the Liverpool pastor, however, rejected the text of this telegram and rather than become involved in prolonged argument, Bonhoeffer and Hildebrandt decided to go ahead, on the principle that a rapid and strong reaction was more important than unanimity reached only at the expense of a delay.

4. The pastors' message was again followed by a cable from Baron Schröder, as chairman of the Association of Congregations, to Müller on 9th January:

. . . rooted in the Biblical Gospel our congregations, much as they love their mother Church, cannot tolerate that the latter's foundation be shaken or that pastors be persecuted by the church government for obeying their consciences in fighting for this foundation. I fear fateful consequences in the shape of secession of German churches abroad from their mother Church which, for the sake of the past community of faith, I would utterly deplore.

Schröder was an independent Englishman whose telegram provided redoubtable support for the pastors' protest.

Bonhoeffer considered that there might be rapid changes that would favour the opposition, and constantly fostered similar hopes in those around him. In a New Year's letter in English to Henriod he wrote:

Since we met last, things have changed very rapidly . . . And it is very satisfactory to me to see that the aims of the opposition become more and more radical and to the point. Müller must be done away with and with him his bishops, and what seems most important of all—the new court theologians (you find their names in the new periodical: *Deutsche Theologie*) must all undergo an '*Irrlehreverfahren*' [heresy trial], '*Lehrzuchtverfahren*' [doctrinal examination]; for they are the real source from which the poison goes out . . . I do not believe that with the settlement of the struggle with the German Christians the dangerous time for the Church is over. On the contrary, it is only the beginning of much more serious and dangerous fights in the near future . . .[24]

Bonhoeffer was not mistaken about the increasing gravity of the situation but his prognosis that changes were imminent proved over-optimistic, for he had failed to anticipate the half-measures which, during the ensuing weeks, threatened once more to impede the course of events.

The Londoners had received no reply to their first four telegrams. In Berlin one event rapidly succeeded another, and Proclamation Sunday, on 7th January, ushered in one of the most turbulent weeks in the church struggle.

The opposition had arranged a service of protest, to take place in Berlin Cathedral on Monday 8th January. Müller asked the police to prohibit this and in consequence a large crowd gathered in front of the cathedral and began singing '*Ein feste Burg ist unser Gott*'. Some of the regional church leaders intimated that they would not enforce Müller's decree of 4th January, and decided to confer in Berlin on 13th January, an occasion they further used to discuss possible secession from the Reich Church. Seventy-two professors and university tutors issued a protest against the National Bishop, whereupon the Minister for Cultural Affairs forbade professors of theology, as civil servants of the Third Reich, to associate themselves with manifestoes concerning the affairs of the church government or to join oppositional organizations such as the Emergency League. On 11th January the Reich President, von Hindenburg, invited Müller to come and see him, in the hope of bringing some influence to bear. On 12th January, the President was visited by Bodelschwingh and the Finance Minister, Graf Schwerin von Krosigk, a member of the Dahlem congregation. Meanwhile all the factions were preparing for a reception initially arranged by Hitler for 17th January. On 13th January the church leaders who were not

24. Letter of 2.1.1934.

German Christians convened and decided to postpone for the time being the threatened secession, even concluding an 'armed truce' with the National Bishop until the time of Hitler's reception. For his part the National Bishop promised a renewal of his pacification policy and on the same day, Saturday 13th January, the church leaders, among them Wurm and Meiser, broadcast a message to their clergy asking them not to read out the Emergency League proclamation from the pulpit on 14th January. The Hitler reception was twice postponed, however, and in fact did not take place until 25th January. This not only increased the already unendurable tension, but obscured the issue still further and led to an intensification of the intrigue behind the scenes.[25]

Influence on Chancellory Reception

Bonhoeffer was now telephoning Berlin almost daily. His mother turned out to be exceedingly well-informed, being herself an active and energetic supporter of his friends in the Emergency League, for whom she was able to establish important contacts. It was not yet certain whether Hitler would get rid of the National Bishop, a decision which everyone expected would be taken at the Chancellory reception. Hindenburg and Frick, it seemed, were advocating Müller's dismissal, whereas Göring and Rust were looking for an opportunity of weakening the opposition. On 17th January Bonhoeffer received a letter from his mother:

Müller's audience with the Reich Chancellor has been postponed from today until tomorrow. At the moment all we can think about is how to make him realize sufficiently before the meeting that the bishops' armed truce is not in fact a peace. I may have found a way of doing this, with Uncle Rudi's[26] help; we hope that our man in Dahlem may get an audience with the old gentleman.[27] So now we can only wait and see, but our man in Dahlem is stout-hearted and abounds in confidence.[28]

Meanwhile, the London pastors had abandoned their onslaught by telegram upon the Reich Church Government, and were now addressing themselves direct to the temporal authorities. On 15th January they sent a letter to the Reich President:

We implore you, Mr. President, now, at the eleventh hour, to avert the terrible danger that threatens the unity of the Church and the Third Reich. For, as long as the National Bishop Müller continues in office, the danger of secession remains imminent.[29]

---

25. For these events, see esp. J. Glenthoj, *Hindenburg, Göring und die evangelischen Kirchenführer*, Vol. 15 of the works on the history of the church struggle, pp. 45 ff.
26. General von der Goltz, Frau P. Bonhoeffer's brother-in-law.
27. Niemöller with Hindenburg.
28. Letter of 17.1.1934.
29. GS II, pp. 159 f.

Copies of this letter were sent to Hitler, to Foreign Minister von Neurath, to Minister of the Interior Frick, to Finance Minister Schwerin-Krosigk and to the National Bishop.

In addition Bonhoeffer persuaded the Bishop of Chichester to approach Hindenburg, since the latter was the *membrum praecipuum* of the German Evangelical Church.[30] In his capacity as Chairman of the Universal Christian Council for 'Life and Work', Bell therefore wrote a letter—translated into German by Bonhoeffer—to Hindenburg and on the same occasion sent a curt enquiry to the National Bishop to whom, after Novi Sad,[31] he had already officially voiced his misgivings.[32]

The London petitions aroused considerable attention in Berlin.[33] On 17th January von Neurath answered from the Ministry of Foreign Affairs:

I too have followed with considerable concern what has been happening in Germany's Evangelical Church . . . In so far as there is any possibility of influencing the course of the disputes in the Evangelical Church I have endeavoured to do so . . . However I would strongly advise the German Evangelical churches in Great Britain to postpone for the time being the drafting of their proposed resolutions.[34]

Secretary of State Meissner confirmed that Hindenburg had received the letter on 19th January '. . . with the comment that the Reich President follows the events in the Evangelical Church with the closest attention.'[35] On the previous day Hindenburg had in fact forwarded the London document to Hitler with the observation that he viewed with strong misgivings the increasing gravity of the situation 'and in particular its repercussions on the German Evangelical churches abroad, and would beg the Reich Chancellor to be kind enough to . . . give the petition his closest attention'. This letter was put before Hitler, but he and Göring had other ideas about handling the 'repercussions abroad' argument, which was to be used, not against Müller, but against those in the opposition who were allegedly disseminating atrocity propaganda.

The important reception by Hitler of all the leading protagonists, from Ludwig Müller and the bishops to Martin Niemöller, finally occurred on 25th January. It took an extremely dramatic turn and failed to bring about Müller's dismissal, thus disappointing the more extravagant hopes of the opposition; the blame for this was laid on a telephone conversation of Niemöller's in which he had spoken disparagingly of the influence exerted by Hindenburg on Hitler. Göring, who

30. GS II, pp. 142 f.
31. Cf. Ch. VII, p. 243.
32. Letter of 23.10.1933, GS I, p. 183.
33. See the really excellent documentation—in all respects—by J. Glenthoj: *Dansk Theologisk Tidsskrift*, Vol. 26, No. 4, pp. 224 ff., and Vol. 15 of the works on the history of the church struggle, pp. 70 ff.
34. To Wehrhan, 17.1.1934.
35. To Wehrhan, 19.1.1934.

had had the line tapped, read out the text of the conversation to the assembled guests at the beginning of the reception.[36]

Ostensibly, the reception had resulted in the complete submission of the regional church leaders to the National Bishop who for his part had emerged stronger than before. On 27th January the church leaders, including Wurm, Meiser and Marahrens, 'under the influence of the great hour when the heads of the German Evangelical Church met the Reich Chancellor', made an astonishing declaration:

. . . The assembled heads of the Church take up a united stand behind the National Bishop and declare themselves willing to enforce his policies and decrees in the sense desired by him, to hinder ecclesio-political opposition to the National Bishop, and to consolidate his authority by all available constitutional means . . .[37]

Only now did Heckel reply to the disturbing petitions and telegrams from London in a general letter to all pastors abroad containing the church leaders' declaration of 27th January. To this Heckel added:

. . . In particular I would impress upon the clergy abroad the necessity for the greatest possible discretion in regard to church politics. Just as the front-line soldier is not in a position to assess the overall plan but must carry out the duties that immediately concern him, so I expect the clergy abroad to distinguish between their own particular task and the task of the church authorities in shaping the German Evangelical Church at home . . .[38]

But for the London pastors, who had succeeded in making so deep an impression on so many people, mere generalities would not be enough. Heckel therefore informed Bonhoeffer and his colleagues, as well as Baron Schröder and the Bishop of Chichester, that he intended to visit England.

In Bonhoeffer's view the Chancellory reception had resulted in a severe reverse. Before it he had written to Geneva: 'with any luck this will clarify matters'.[39] Now he wrote to de Félice: 'My best regards; may your work prosper at this disastrous time.'[40] But in spite of the reverse, his faith in the cause never wavered.

On 21st January, when the outcome was as yet undecided and tension was at its height, he chose as the text for his sermon Jeremiah 20: 7: 'O Lord, thou hast deceived me . . .' His depiction of the refractory yet obedient Jeremiah became as it were a personal confession to the congregation:

. . . as the noose is drawn tighter, Jeremiah is reminded of the fact that

---

36. See works on the dramatic Chancellory reception by W. Niemöller, *Hitler und die evangelischen Kirchenführer. Zum 25. Januar 1934*, 1959; and 'Epilog zum Kanzler-empfang', EvTh, 1960, pp. 107-24; also the new works named above by J. Glenthoj.
37. J. Beckmann, *Kirchliches Jahrbuch, 1933-44*, p. 39.
38. DEK KK III, 334/34, 31.1.1934.
39. To de Félice, undated.   40. Undated.

he is a prisoner. He is a prisoner and he has to follow. His path is prescribed. It is the path of the man whom God will not let go, who will never be rid of God . . .

He was upbraided as a disturber of the peace, an enemy of the people as throughout the ages until the present day all those have been upbraided who have been possessed and seized by God, for whom God had become too strong . . . how gladly would he have shouted peace and hail (Heil) with the rest . . .

The triumphal procession of truth and justice, the triumphal procession of God and his Scriptures through the world, drags in the wake of the chariot of victory a train of prisoners in chains. May he at the last bind us to his triumphal carriage so that, although in bonds and oppressed, we may participate in his victory!

Heckel's Visit

It has frequently been said that British public opinion evinced more sympathy for the travails of the Church in Germany in January 1934 than was shown towards the first refugees in the spring of 1933. Thus, if Ludwig Müller was to consolidate his victory of 25th January, something had to be done to mollify or dissipate unfavourable reactions in the foreign Press. It was essential in Heckel's view to prevent the pastors in London from abusing their freedom by making contacts with ecumenical circles and with the world Press. Eventually, of course, they must come back to their allegiance to the National Bishop and his church government.

Heckel informed the pastors, Baron Schröder and the Bishop of Chichester that he would be in London on 8th and 9th February. He regarded the mission as so important that he took with him the theologian Krummacher and the jurist Wahl from the Church Federation Office. The turn taken by church affairs since 25th January seemed ominous indeed to the pastors in London as they awaited the arrival of the delegation from Berlin, nor were they reassured by what they learned from telephone conversations and letters from home, or read in the daily press.

The most portentous news for those in London was that of Niemöller's suspension from office on 26th January, and the fact that so far he had observed the prohibition. A Morning Post reporter had visited Dahlem church on Sunday 4th February fully expecting to find a member of the 'other side' officiating. From his dramatic report we learn that a slim, dark-haired man entered the pulpit, his first words betraying the surprising fact that 'another Niemöller' was preaching. It was Franz Hildebrandt.

Before the arrival of the delegation the pastors in London also learned that the National Bishop had arrogated to himself the powers both of the Church Senate and of the Old Prussian Union in order to achieve 'unified leadership'. On February 3rd the Prussian church administration had assumed the power to remove clergy 'in the interests of the church', thus infringing one of the most cherished of the pastors rights. At the beginning of February more than fifty pastors were suspended. In view of all this, Heckel could hardly expect a conciliatory atmosphere in London.

So ominous was the news that Bonhoeffer and his colleagues felt impelled to make meticulous preparations for the unwelcome visitation. Together, on 5th February, they worked out a six-point memorandum:

1. It is questionable whether decrees enacted by the National Bishop of the Reich Church Government are binding upon the churches abroad, since the transfer of authority from the German Evangelical Church Federation, or original party to the agreement, to the new German Evangelical Church was effected on 11.6.33 without the prior assent of the other free party to the agreement (churches abroad). Until further clarification of this question, no decree is binding.
2. Compulsory measures taken by the German Evangelical Church must first be rescinded (only last month the National Bishop requested police intervention to assist him in his duties).
3. There can be no confidence so long as a National Bishop remains in power who has been the patron of the German Christians and who, after introducing the Aryan clause into the Church, first rescinds and then reintroduces it.
4. The incorporation of the [Evangelical] Youth into the Hitler Youth is dangerous, and the National Bishop's authority in this matter is questionable.
5. There can be no question of confidence where the highest minister in the Church can insult his clergy with vulgar abuse in the Press.
6. We would support Baron Schröder's proposal that the National Bishop should give a written undertaking to rescind compulsory measures, this to be effective retrospectively, and, further, to guarantee conditions that would enable the churches abroad to remain within the mother Church.[41]

When discussions began on 8th February between the Berlin delegation and seven of the German pastors in England, the atmosphere was already stormy. The pastors thought it out of order that Heckel should have been to see Schröder before themselves. Heckel for his part wanted an explanation of the Bradford declaration on the National Bishop's consecration and criticized the conference's choice of recipients for copies of the letter of 15th January to Hindenburg.

According to the minutes of the meeting,[42] Heckel next outlined an 'overall plan', drafted on 31st January by the Church Commission, of the work to be done by the German Church. This would comprise reorganization to bring German Protestants into line with the centraliza-

41. Files of the Association of Congregations, Schröder's Bank, London.
42. From the files of St. George's Church, London.

tion of the State, administrative centralization of youth work, the home mission, and evangelical social organizations, and finally, a theological survey of topical problems, especially that of the relationship between Law and the Gospel. This plan had been agreed by the bishops and church leaders. 'But', Heckel added, in an allusion to the Chancellory reception, 'I would not venture to say whether agreement in such cases is wholly spontaneous or whether it is influenced by specific circumstances.' Ecclesio-political partisanship, he went on, was incompatible with the continued independence of the congregations abroad and would also invalidate the 1924 Diaspora Law.

He further said that Hitler considered that Protestantism had achieved unity too late and that, having regard to the general situation, it was likely to disintegrate within five months if the squabbles among its leaders deteriorated into a chronic dispute. Unity and orderly conditions must therefore be restored. 'I have been empowered to inform you that there is no cause for further concern in the matter of the Aryan clause.' Heckel then described what had happened after the Sports Palace demonstration as a total failure either to change the climate of opinion or to get Niemöller into the Church Ministry. The opposition, he said, had presented the National Bishop with an ultimatum which he must needs reject, because he could not tie himself down to any one set of proposals. Yet Müller had remained open to suggestions. His agreement with Schirach on the amalgamation of the Evangelical Youth Associations with the Hitler Youth had been sanctioned by the church leaders, and had been described by Hitler as the Christmas present that pleased him most. The fact remained that Müller was the man most highly esteemed by the Party, and in this respect nothing had changed after the Chancellory reception.

Heckel next turned to the disciplinary action taken against the clergy and gave an account of the incriminating evidence against opposition pastors. Influence exerted from abroad, he said, especially by an 'English and a Swedish bishop'—obviously meaning Bell and Ammundsen—was dangerous. It should not be forgotten that to oppose Ludwig Müller was tantamount to opposing the State. The second period of church development was now over, he said; it was time to look at the situation in a realistic light and for the best theological brains to apply themselves to confessional work in the German Evangelical Church. Should Niemöller not conform, he added, there might be a 'terrible ending'. Finally Heckel sought to allay their fears by saying that Müller's emergency decrees would only be applied in extreme cases, and that no one had been dismissed, but only suspended, from office.

When the meeting was thrown open for discussion, Bonhoeffer was the first to speak. The London minutes record him as asking why discussion was almost always confined to tactical matters and ecclesio-political events, and seldom dealt with questions of principle relating to, say, the Old Testament, the Confessions, or freedom of speech.

Could Müller, he said, really be regarded as a responsible representative of the Church in view of his lamentable failure to solve the problem of youth work, his use of dictatorial force and his inability to make up his mind over the Aryan clause? Bonhoeffer then suggested that the most urgent ecclesio-political task was secession from such a church rather than an attempt to achieve unified organization whatever the circumstances.

Heckel replied that the Old Testament presented an unresolved task. As for freedom of speech, he said, they must concede that, in spite of Rust's decree, it was still possible to bring out publications such as the *Junge Kirche* and Künneth's *Nation vor Gott*. The proposal for the eventual repeal of the Aryan clause had not in fact come from the Lutheran, but from the German Christian bishops. 'Relations with the Reich preclude open discussion of the clause which, by the common assent of the bishops, would in any case not be dealt with. Heckel went on to explain that, firstly, the Aryan clause was not applicable to the Reich Church but only to individual regional churches; secondly, it was applicable only to the clerical profession; thirdly, it would not be systematically applied abroad; and fourthly, there was no cause for disquiet about the future. The National Bishop's dictatorial emergency decree (the 'Decree to Establish Unified Leadership in the Evangelical Church of the Old Prussian Union' of 2.1.1934), had been essential if the authorities were to continue their functions; in the Church Senate alone, for instance, there had been five 'parties'. The National Bishop, according to Heckel, had not really wanted the Aryan clause; the incorporation of the Evangelical Youth into the Hitler Youth had taken place without any friction; the language used by the National Bishop amounted to nothing more than what was used in this 'age of soldiers' slang'; Bishop Glondys of Siebenbürg had praised Müller's strategic foresight. And, Heckel concluded, the work abroad was very close to the National Bishop's heart.

Dr. Wahl corroborated Heckel's statement that the German Evangelical Church was the lawful successor to the Church Federation.

At the end of the day the real object of Heckel's visit emerged.

The vote of no confidence in the National Bishop expressed in the telegrams and the letter of 15th January from London was, he said, symptomatic of undesirable radicalism; now he wanted to take back to Berlin a declaration of allegiance by the brethren in which each individual German pastor would affirm his 'regard for the whole'.

Before the next day's meeting and the further widening of the breach, Heckel, Krummacher and Wahl spent two hours with Bishop Bell at the Athenaeum. Here, too, things did not go as smoothly as Heckel had hoped. He had previously consulted Schönfeld who had advised him to keep to questions of principle and not allow himself to be drawn into a discussion of 'concrete' matters; in other words, he should try to make plain that, from the ecclesiastical and theological viewpoint, Lutheranism was seeking to sever itself from the theology of the West determined as this was by political liberalism.[43] But the conversation quickly took a 'concrete' turn. Heckel suggested that the bishop should not concern himself with German problems, since questions of heresy were not under debate. He asked Bell to consider the possibility of refraining from all public comment for a period of six months—virtually until the time of the Fanö conference. Bell refused.

Of this visit to the Athenaeum the German Press noted that the discussion had led to an improvement in the relations between the ecumenical movement and the German Evangelical Church, relations which could now be regarded as unclouded. This was hotly refuted in a letter written by Bishop Bell to *The Times* on 10th March, in which he said that in fact he had put questions before the delegation and that these had not been dealt with, nor could he modify the protest expressed in his letter of 18th January to the National Bishop, indeed, fresh grounds for complaint had unfortunately arisen in the meantime.[44] Obviously the delegation from the Church Federation Office was in something of a dilemma, both as regards Berlin and London.

The second session with the pastors, following this conversation with Bell, was no more successful and came to an abrupt end. The argument revolved round which document should be signed—the declaration put forward by the pastors or Heckel's proposed declaration of allegiance.

Hanging over the dispute was the ominous suggestion that the pastors had unwittingly, if not indeed consciously, submitted to 'foreign influence'. For when, after the Chancellory reception, the church leaders had framed their declaration (from which we have already quoted), it was not without intent that they included the following clause—one which Heckel had been quick to pass on to the pastors abroad:

The church leaders most strongly deprecate any intrigue involving criticism of State, People, or Movement, because such criticism is calculated to imperil the Third Reich. In particular they deprecate the use of the foreign Press to present the false view that the controversy within the Church is a struggle against the State.[45]

It was with reference to this that the pastors now drew Heckel's attention to the fact that the account he had given them on the previous day tallied very largely with the reports carried regularly by *The Times*. Hence there could be no question of the London clergy having been driven into opposition by misrepresentations in the Press.

When the London pastors put forward their declaration which

43. Cf. footnote 132 on p. 311.
44. JK, 1934, p. 346.
45. J. Beckmann, op. cit., p. 39.

followed the lines of their previous memorandum, it was rejected by Heckel on the grounds that the German Evangelical Church had no intention of meddling in the affairs of the churches abroad, and hence the latter should refrain from meddling in the affairs of the German Evangelical Church.

Bonhoeffer at once objected that 'meddling' was not the issue under discussion. What was under discussion was, in fact, a pre-eminently theological concern with a bond, both credible and religiously acceptable, with the German Church, a bond that would remain incumbent upon the clergy abroad. But now the group of pastors began to show signs of wavering. Their Liverpool colleague, Schreiner, declared himself satisfied with Heckel's explanations, and further that he wished to disassociate himself from the earlier declarations of the London brethren, since the latter were on principle in opposition.

After this Heckel read out the declaration he had drafted:

I explained that in regard to the Aryan clause . . . there was no longer any cause for anxiety. In so far as the German Evangelical churches in England showed concern about alterations to the Bible, I denied that the German Evangelical Church had any such intention . . . During the session of 9th February 1934 this declaration was unanimously agreed by all the German Evangelical pastors in England.

Heckel now asked the pastors to sign this declaration for the record, whereupon Schönberger exclaimed: 'I find all this reassurance very far from reassuring!' Bonhoeffer pointed out that the declaration included only what Heckel held to be important while it ignored practically all the critical points raised by the brethren. There was no need, he said, to assure the independence of the churches abroad, since that had never been in question, nor had it ever been the motive for the attacks on the present church government.

Upon this Heckel expressed his deep regret over the course the talks had taken and since he could not 'go home empty-handed' he suggested duplicating his draft so that the pastors could each have a copy and thus have the opportunity to study its wording carefully. He then added infelicitously that in their own interests they should toe the line, else they would inevitably find themselves in the ranks of the 'Prague émigrés'. This was a collective term denoting refugee journalists and left-wing politicians, and to 'ecclesiastically and patriotically minded' men it was in those days a particularly distasteful and insulting epithet. When in addition Heckel proceeded to cite examples of treacherous activity, Bonhoeffer, Rieger and Steiniger got up and left the room in protest.

Schönberger and Wehrhan continued to seek a loophole that would permit further consideration of Heckel's declaration. Heckel left his draft with the remaining pastors and expressed the hope that they might yet sign it. Thus the conference broke up without any final agreement having been reached.

Bonhoeffer's connection with the Reich Church was strained to the utmost, but there had been no final breach; his relations with Heckel, however, had reached a nadir. After their initial interest in one another, each had begun to look upon the other as his antagonist in the ecumenical field, and each saw the other, highly gifted as he was, as dangerous, but also—and this, perhaps, not without undertones of regret—as endangered. But each had so pledged himself to his cause and to his group that there was no longer any hope of return, and certainly no chance of reconciliation.

Sequels

Difficulties soon arose as a result of these London talks with Heckel and his deputation, more especially as regards the interpretation of the proceedings.

Bonhoeffer was to experience the first consequences during the following week, when his church officers in Sydenham rebelled. On the evening of 9th February they had been invited to a reception at the German Embassy, together with the three visitors from Berlin. They had had a long conversation with Heckel who had succeeded in winning them over to his point of view so that suddenly they saw the conflict, not as a 'church struggle', but simply as a regrettable 'church dispute'. Thus Bonhoeffer who, like Rieger, had refused the invitation to the reception, was taken to task by some of his church officers for having so dangerously involved the churches abroad in internal German disputes. Why, they asked, should a parish in England ally itself to a movement such as the confessional front in Germany? The discussion with his church officers went on late into the night; finally they agreed that, after divine service, Bonhoeffer should give the congregation a detailed explanation of what had happened and of his proposed future policy. This he did; the church committee put it to the vote and this resulted in the expression of their complete confidence in their pastor.

The controversy as to which was the correct version of the meeting on 9th February was less easy to settle. Before he left Heckel had again gone to see Schröder and the two men had exchanged generalized assurances that each would do all he could in the cause of peace and would endeavour to keep politics out of the Church and to keep the congregations together.[46]

As soon as Heckel had proposed leaving his declaration behind for their consideration, the pastors had feared that this might be used against them. They therefore drew up minutes recording that this declaration had not been unanimously agreed, that, in fact, objections

46. Schröder to Heckel, 9.2.1934; Heckel to Schröder, 15.2.1934.

had been raised and that no vote had been taken; they further declared that: 'Discussion of the declaration was severely handicapped in that the pastors felt that they might risk incurring political defamation.' Indeed, there was a rumour that the Ministry of Foreign Affairs had been considering the withdrawal of passports.

The suspicion that the Berlin delegation would give too rosy an account of the conference was confirmed by a letter from Heckel to Schröder on 8th May:

During our last conversation in London in February we agreed that, in order finally to clear up the situation induced by your telegram to the National Bishop, and the telegram from the London pastors to the church government, you would lay before the committee of the Association of Congregations the declaration handed over by me to the London pastors, a declaration which had received their unanimous assent. Might I therefore perhaps enquire whether the committee has yet met and what conclusions were reached as a result?

Schröder replied on 25th May:

Dear Bishop, many thanks for your letter of 8th May which I found on my return here. In view of the still very unsettled state of ecclesiastical affairs in Germany the churches here are not at present in a position to make any reply. I hope that the time may soon come when unity will be restored in the Evangelical Church in Germany and we shall then have to reconsider the question of the churches over here. To obviate any misunderstanding I would point out that there was no unanimous assent to the declaration of 9th February. Meanwhile I remain, etc. (signed) Bruno Schröder.

It was becoming increasingly difficult for Heckel to do anything about pacification, for in May, at the time of this correspondence, there took place the first major compulsory amalgamation of the regional churches with the centralized German Evangelical Church, under the aegis of *Rechtswalter* (legal administrator) Jäger. This in turn gave rise to the Ulm and Barmen acts of confession.

Yet another consequence of 9th February was a final effort on the part of the church government to extract a written declaration from Bonhoeffer But this was in a different context, that of Bonhoeffer's ecumenical activity in London which so greatly disturbed the External Affairs Office.

III GEORGE K. A. BELL, BISHOP OF CHICHESTER

The Sports Palace demonstration and its sequel was favourable to Bonhoeffer in as much as it brought him into contact sooner than would otherwise have been the case with circles in England to whom a reliable informant was highly welcome. 'I have been talking to English churchmen and to some very interesting politicians [about] all sorts of plans.'[47] Yet unless it was Bonhoeffer's intention to become a refugee himself, these conversations and plans could not fail to have dangerous repercussions.

English Contacts

Three days before Bonhoeffer's arrival in London, in October 1933, two other Germans had made an appearance there. These were the Bishop of Berlin and the Minister for Religious Affairs, Hossenfelder, and Fezer, the Tübingen professor and author of the German Christian principles —a somewhat ill-matched pair, both tactically and theologically. The two men had come over to try and gain the support of prominent ecumenicals for the consecration of the National Bishop, scheduled to take place in Berlin Cathedral on 3rd December 1933. They had been invited to England not, as they so much desired, by one of the Anglican bishops, but by Frank Buchman's Oxford Group Movement. This provided a platform, both in London and Oxford, from which they were able to make anodyne statements about the Church in Germany and, if the *Deutsche Allgemeine Zeitung* of 21st October is to be believed, to transmit 'in the German language greetings from churchmen in Germany'.

The London Press, while little interested in these 'greetings', carried detailed reports from Berlin of the dubious pronouncements made by Ludwig Müller, the visitors' lord and master, who had been demanding the ruthless implementation of the Aryan clause, regardless of public opinion in other countries. In ecumenical circles, however, there was some anxiety that Hossenfelder and Fezer might succeed in obtaining a hearing. But Bonhoeffer reported to Siegmund-Schultze:

. . . Hossenfelder had no discussion at all with Canterbury. Chichester told me about this in detail the day before yesterday. Canterbury refused because he wished to avoid any misunderstanding about or misrepresentation of, such a reception—eventualities he evidently regarded as not improbable. Hossenfelder saw the Bishop of Gloucester, who was evidently rather taken with him[48] . . He [Hossenfelder] came to London at the invitation of the Oxford Group Movement about which he was very enthusiastic. Apparently the reception was nothing much. He wanted to make a speech in a German parish hall whose trustees included some eminent Jews, but was not allowed to.[49] Instead, after a dinner given by Hoesch,[50] to which parsons and church elders had been invited, he gave a speech that was extremely inept and made little impression . . . Obviously he was also intent on

47. To K.-F. Bonhoeffer, Jan. 1934, GS II, p. 158.
48. i.e. Bishop A. C. Headlam, who played a leading role in 'Faith and Order'. He repeatedly offered his help to the German Christians and later to Heckel, received Ribbentrop and wrote letters to *The Times* in favour of the new Germany. He utterly repudiated the Confessing Church.
49. By Pastor Dr. J. Rieger of St. George's Church.
50. The German Ambassador.

ingratiating himself with the English Church and, as obviously, failed.[51]

Unlike the National Bishop's two envoys, Bonhoeffer was able within a fortnight of his arrival in London, to gain access to a number of leading ecumenicals. Between 2nd and 4th November the executive of the World Alliance was meeting in London for its work session, as was also the Universal Council for 'Life and Work', of which Bishop Bell of Chichester was chairman. On this occasion Bonhoeffer met the Bishop of Ripon, Burroughs, and also Tom Craske with whom he was already well acquainted from his work with the Youth Commission. Siegmund-Schultze had advised him to seek out H. W. Fox, the English general secretary of the British World Alliance League. On one of the days of the session, Bishop Bell invited Dietrich Bonhoeffer to lunch for the first time at his club, the Athenaeum, in Pall Mall.

The Bishop of Chichester

Bonhoeffer had first seen the Bishop of Chichester, George K. A. Bell (1883-1958), at the Geneva conferences in the summer of 1932.[52] Later that year there had been a literary connection when Bonhoeffer had supervised the translation of *A Brief Sketch of the Church of England*.[53]

To the bishop, however, Bonhoeffer had hitherto been only one of the many committee members of the World Alliance and as such had little connection with his own immediate sphere of responsibility. All this was now to be radically changed.

More than Bonhoeffer's introduction from Bell's old friend of the 1925 Stockholm days, Professor Adolf Deissmann, it was a letter from H. L. Henriod on 3rd October 1933 that really aroused the bishop's interest:

I want to report briefly to you, also on that occasion,[54] a conversation some of us had with Bonhoeffer, who is *Privatdozent* in the University of Berlin, and one of the most promising young men in Germany, who spoke freely to us and made a deep impression on all of us at Sofia . . . He promised to write me again from Germany without signature but with a sign on which we had agreed, so that I can forward to you this information. He is one of those who are prepared to accept any sufferings but cannot in conscience remain in the New Church, as finally elaborated at Wittenberg.[55]

After the meeting at the Athenaeum, the bishop recommended the young German to other friends. A few days later he wrote to Canon Peter Green of Manchester, a well-known advocate of the evangelical trend in the Church of England, and a friend of William Temple:

51. Letter of 6.11.1933.
52. See Ch. VI, p. 186.
53. G. K. A. Bell, *A Brief Sketch of the Church of England*, 1928: cf. also Ch. VI, p. 189.
54. An allusion to Sofia, see Ch. VII, p. 244.
55. Ecumenical Archives, Geneva.

If you want to get really first hand information of the situation in the German Church I would recommend your seeing Herr Dietrich Bonhoeffer. He has just come over from Berlin as German Pastor. He was one of those who signed the manifesto of the two thousand Protestant Pastors. He is a pupil of Deissmann and was introduced by Deissmann to me as one of the best younger theologians. He is under 30, unmarried, and speaks English perfectly. He is extraordinarily critical of the present rulers of the German Church. But of course one must be careful not to embarrass him . . .[56]

He went on to say that Bonhoeffer had told him that Hossenfelder was not the 'slum pastor' with the great missionary gift as portrayed by Frank Buchman and the Bishop of Gloucester. On the contrary, Hossenfelder had had quite a small parish in Berlin, which had notably been one of the two not to return a German Christian in the church election of 23rd July 1933.

Bell also recommended the young German to interested politicians, such as Lord Lothian, but Bonhoeffer himself, as will be evident later, felt that this placed him in an ambiguous position.

The rapidity with which Bell and Bonhoeffer established a *rapport* was indeed surprising, but during those early November days they did not come to any agreement about a possible ecumenical initiative. As before in Sofia, Bonhoeffer did not confine himself to purveying information; during the London sessions, too, he continued to advocate his idea of a delegation which, he wrote: 'during these days in London has been further pursued'.[57] As had been decided at Novi Sad, Bell had written to Müller on 23rd October. Now he wished to allow time for the letter to take effect and to give the National Bishop a chance to act. The Geneva secretaries had never really favoured the idea of a delegation in Bonhoeffer's sense. What Schönfeld had in mind at this juncture was probably less a deputation sent to intervene with the National Bishop, than a representative ecumenical delegation such as the latter had requested. Bell, however, wrote on 11th November to the Swedish archbishop, Eidem, to tell him that all had now agreed that a delegation would not then be opportune, but might become necessary should a fresh emergency arise. Hence to Bonhoeffer it did not seem that his plan, because shelved, had been rejected, but rather that it was under consideration and would 'be pursued'. It was a view to which he clung tenaciously during the weeks that followed. However, his plan was never to be put into effect.

A few months later another project for a deputation was in fact realized but it bore little resemblance to what Bonhoeffer had intended. In conjunction with Schönfeld, the Swedish Embassy chaplain in Berlin, Birger Forell, began to press for personal intervention by Eidem and

56. Letter of 15.11.1933.
57. To F. Siegmund-Schultze, 6.11.1933.

Bell with Hitler. Bell—in agreement with Bonhoeffer—would not listen to Forell's and Schönfeld's pleas, for if, at their request, Hitler himself intervened like a *deus ex machina* to settle the church troubles, this would invest him with the highest authority in spiritual matters.[58] Eventually, in May 1934, Eidem went on his own to see Hitler by whom he was outrageously treated. His visit remained without tangible results.

Like Bell, Bonhoeffer did not expect any good to come of such intervention with Hitler in 1934, and when his Swiss friend Erwin Sutz made a similar proposal, he refuted it outright with weighty theological arguments:

From now on, I believe, any discussion between Hitler and Barth would be quite pointless, indeed no longer admissible. Hitler has shown himself quite plainly for what he is and the Church must be aware with whom it is she has to reckon. Isaiah didn't go to Sennacherib either. We have often—all too often—tried to make Hitler realize what's happening. Maybe we've not yet gone about it the right way, but then Barth won't go about it the right way either. Hitler must not and cannot hear. He is obdurate and it is he who must compel us to hear—it's that way round. The Oxford Group Movement has been naïve enough to try to convert Hitler—a ridiculous failure to understand what is going on—it is we who are to be converted, not Hitler . . .

What sort of a person is Brand?[59] I cannot understand how a man can remain in Hitler's entourage unless he is either a Nathan or else an accomplice in the guilt of 30th June[60] and 25th July,[61] of the lie of 19th August,[62] —and also of the next war! Please forgive me, but these things seem to me so terribly serious, and to trifle about them is to me now quite unbearable.[63]

By the time Bonhoeffer wrote this letter, a great deal had happened. He and Bell had grown very close. Bell understood how it was that Bonhoeffer had to keep political and theological judgements apart and yet relate them closely to each other.

The Sports Palace demonstration, which took place on 13th November, after their first meeting at the Athenaeum, had stimulated a lively correspondence between the two men. This culminated in Bonhoeffer paying a visit to the bishop at Chichester, where the younger man assailed his senior with pleas and suggestions.

Bonhoeffer's letter of November[64] shows that he did not subscribe to the renewed hopes engendered by the events that followed the Sports

58. See H. von Koenigswald, *Birger Forell*, 1962, pp. 97 ff.
59. E. Sutz had got to know Hitler's personal physician on a glacier expedition and hoped this contact might prove useful.
60. Blood-bath on the occasion of the Röhm affair.
61. Assassination of Dollfuss, the Austrian Chancellor.
62. Plebiscite to approve the amalgamation of the offices of Reich President and Reich Chancellor under the title of 'Führer'.
63. Letter of 11.9.1934, GS I, pp. 42 f.
64. GS II, p. 138.

Palace demonstration, but rather envisaged the opposition's ultimate secession from the legal-ecclesiastical body of the German Evangelical Church. Such a step, however, would mean that the opposition would become clandestine, which in turn would intensify police surveillance as well as lend plausibility to accusations of political unreliability. He therefore held that the ecumenical movement should at an early date make known precisely which church it regarded as the true Evangelical Church in Germany. He pointed out that this was a matter in which Bell, as chairman of the Universal Council, was deeply concerned, and that he should therefore again demand that the National Bishop declare himself.

There can be no doubt that this letter was a product of Bonhoeffer's own initiative, for it is evident that he is already thinking in terms of two separate phases of development—firstly, that of the actual situation upon which his friends in Berlin were basing their actions, namely, the possibility of detaching Müller from his German Christian advisers, in which case a letter from the bishop would be of assistance; secondly, a future phase and a much later decision—that of separation, a step which, in 1933, those friends were not yet prepared to take, although to Bonhoeffer it already seemed inevitable. In this way he often seized upon the more advanced elements of a situation, exploiting them in order decisively to influence its development. The procedure was not without its dangers for if no one should follow his lead he would find himself in isolation.

Bell replied immediately, but with some reserve.[65] He was, he said, still waiting for Müller's reaction to the letter of 23rd October[66] and had, indeed, been led by Schönfeld, who had seen the National Bishop, to expect an early reply and perhaps even an invitation for an ecumenical delegation to visit Berlin. Since Sofia the opposition had been threatened with this plan, the purpose of which was to steal a march on the ecumenical investigating delegation by issuing an official invitation—a plan too clever to have been thought up by Müller himself. But since Schönfeld had passed on the National Bishop's message to Bell, there had been the Sports Palace scandal which had effectually invalidated any move such as an official invitation to the ecumenical movement.

When the news arrived of the first suspensions following the Emergency League proclamation, Bonhoeffer at once began to urge that Bell's Ecumenical Council should initiate a campaign to help the families of the victims.[67] Unlike many of his friends he was quite undeterred by the risk of compromising the cause by enlisting foreign aid. But nothing came of Bonhoeffer's suggestion this time. It was only

65. GS II, p. 139.
66. Cf. Ch. VII, p. 243.
67. GS II, p. 140.

much later, when non-Aryan pastors were forced to leave Germany, that the diocese of Chichester embarked on any major relief scheme.

On 21st and 22nd November 1933 Bonhoeffer visited Bell for the first time in his fine old apartments at Chichester. The visit resulted in fruitful discussions and introduced an element of personal and theological sympathy into an association which hitherto had been based upon church politics. This gave rise to frequent and close consultations, continuing sometimes from one day to the next. Their understanding was based on mutual interests, but only friendship could render tolerable the demands they made upon each other.

As chairman of the Universal Council, Bell was already in receipt of information through his Council secretaries in Geneva, Henriod and Schönfeld. This was complemented and confirmed by frequent letters from Cragg, the British Embassy chaplain in Berlin, whom he had asked to write to him. He also valued highly the cool precision of judgement shown by Pastor Koechlin in Basle, who was later to be chairman of the Swiss Church Federation. But in Bonhoeffer he now had a source of information and advice which came not from some outside observer, but from one who was intimately involved. He not only tolerated, but to some extent even encouraged, his new partner's theological intransigence and passionate pursuit of a given concept. Yet there can be no doubt that Bell felt a certain anxiety lest the opposition and its young representative, Bonhoeffer, might lack the required circumspection and advocate a theology that was too one-sided. He was obviously relieved when, in the autumn of 1934 and at Bonhoeffer's behest, he finally visited Präses [church president] Karl Koch and was thus able to see for himself that the man who represented the allegedly radical sector of the German Church was in fact a phlegmatic Westphalian and a natural conservative. But Bell's concern in this respect was tempered by his keen realization that, in a critical situation, 'circumspection' might be used as an excuse for irresolution. Whether Bonhoeffer came as the emissary of the leading men in the Confessing Church or, as happened more often, of his own accord, the bishop never called in question either his judgement or the information he supplied, but relied constantly upon both. He possessed the rare gift of being able to accept advice, which he avidly sought, and yet preserve his own objective independence.

Just as Bell had been motivated by practical considerations in seeking out Bonhoeffer as a partner, so the latter had a very real practical interest in establishing contact with the chairman of 'Life and Work'. The bishop had been chairman at Novi Sad and was to preside at Fanö. No one else, Bonhoeffer found, could so rapidly assess a situation that was unprecedented both in the German Church and in ecumenical Christendom. Nearly everyone in the ecumenical movement was naturally outraged by what was happening in Germany and did something to help the refugees. Bonhoeffer demonstrated that this was not enough; what was necessary was to decide between two ecclesiastical bodies. By what standards should one group be recognized and the other rejected when no such qualification was laid down in the statutes of the ecumenical federations and when, in addition, the theological friends and foes of earlier years were now to be found in both camps? He felt that the problem of a confessionally bound church within a federally organized, juridicially powerless ecumenical movement was becoming acute. He therefore did not hesitate to put this problem to Bell as the responsible authority. And here, to his astonishment, he was met with understanding.

There is no doubt that he expected of Bell decisions which were beyond the competence even of so powerful a head of an organization as loose-knit as 'Life and Work'. Yet he hoped—as did, perhaps, the bishop—that the ecumenical movement, as it came to understand itself better, would grow to accept this new challenge. Bonhoeffer believed in any case that the most recent events in the Church had called in question the ecumenical movement's right to exist more because of its excessive neutrality and failure to act than through too overt partisanship. Under these circumstances Bell, too, seemed ready to rehabilitate the movement by the use of bolder measures. He could easily have withdrawn from decision-making on procedural grounds, as had, indeed, been suggested to him; instead he made full use, between conferences, of the freedom conferred on him by his executive powers, yet so adroitly that no one—for instance at the Fanö conference—could accuse him of abusing the authority of his chairman's office. Whenever there was a choice between caution and daring, he would proceed to the limits of the latter. Bonhoeffer knew this and encouraged it, and Bell never begrudged him his demands.

Their relationship, hitherto concerned with practical matters, now became enriched by an element of personal interest. Bell was a high church diocesan bishop, mentally disciplined and highly cultivated. In his youth he had gained a coveted Oxford poetry award, and as Dean of Canterbury had initiated the Festival of Music and Drama for which he secured the collaboration of T. S. Eliot, Christopher Fry and Dorothy Sayers. Not only did he manage to carry out the additional duties arising from his ecumenical work, but he also contrived to write a biography of Archbishop Davidson, 1,400 pages long, which placed him among the foremost English biographers. After the Stockholm conference of 1925, Nathan Söderblom in a letter to Davidson wrote: 'This Bell never rings for nothing.'

Bell liked the well-brought-up young German, who never let himself be carried away into forgetting his good manners, who was a good listener and who realized that excited reiteration can only detract from what has already been said. Their sympathy for each other expressed itself in mutual trust. Later, when Hildebrandt had joined them, Bell would refer to them as 'my two boys'. His birthday, 4th February, was the same date as Bonhoeffer's. Every year they exchanged greetings, and when this was no longer possible, the bishop wrote to Bonhoeffer's twin sister, by then an *émigrée*. When the end came, it was to Bell that Bonhoeffer's last recorded words were addressed.[68]

In 1948, in the introduction to *The Cost of Discipleship*, Bell wrote of him:

I knew him in London in the early days of the evil régime: and from him, more than from any other German, I learned the true character of the conflict, in an intimate friendship. I have no doubt that he did fine work with his German congregation: but he taught many besides his fellow-countrymen while a pastor in England. He was crystal clear in his convictions; and young as he was, and humble-minded as he was, he saw the truth, and spoke it with a complete absence of fear.[69]

Dangers

Bonhoeffer's close connection with the bishop did not go unnoticed by the authorities in Berlin, and there were other factors by which he became increasingly imperilled: there were rumours, for instance, about his contacts with the Press, of his having had a hand in an article in *The Round Table* and in Bell's letter to Hindenburg, and of an invitation to a reception at Lambeth Palace.

1. Round about Christmas time it was being rumoured in Berlin that Dietrich Bonhoeffer was connected with *The Times*' embarrassingly accurate account of the church troubles. Now, unlike many of his fellow-combatants, he saw nothing particularly deleterious about supplying accurate information to the international Press and was, indeed, later to help in this way.[70] But at this time journalists were still in a position to obtain information themselves and consequently it would have seemed foolish to expose himself now to prosecution under the Treachery Law.[71] He therefore deemed it necessary indignantly to deny any such contact with the Press.

2. *The Round Table* was one of the most respectable English monthlies. Lord Lothian, subsequently ambassador in Washington, was closely connected with it. Early in the new year, having decided that the March number should contain an analysis of the crisis in German Protestantism, he turned to Bell who passed the request on to Bonhoeffer. This was the time of the appearance of Müller's 'muzzling

68. LPP, p. 233.
69. D. Bonhoeffer, *The Cost of Discipleship*, London, 1948, p. 7.
70. GS I, pp. 262 f.
71. See Ch. VII, pp. 201 f.

decree', and Bonhoeffer declined. Bell therefore undertook the work himself on condition that Bonhoeffer should look it over. But Lord Lothian still wished to meet him. The meeting took place in St. James's on 16th January, at a most crucial moment in church politics.[72] Quite inexplicably, it soon became known in the Church Federation Office that Bonhoeffer was helping Bell with an article for The Round Table.

3. Bell's intervention with Müller and Hindenburg during the January upheavals in Berlin created more of a stir in the Church Federation Office than either of the two other matters described above. The National Bishop had in fact written to Bell as chairman of the Universal Christian Council on 8th December 1933, replying to his letter of 23rd October with promises of pacification. Now the insincerity of those promises had become clearly apparent. This induced in Bell an unprecedented burst of activity, beginning with a letter to The Times on 17th January—the date initially laid down for the Chancellory reception—a letter intended to draw attention in Berlin to Müller's breach of faith. Secondly, at Bonhoeffer's behest, he wrote two further letters. In the first, addressed personally to Müller, the bishop's tone was sharper than before[73] although he would not go so far as to tell the National Bishop that he was no longer fit to be associated with the ecumenical movement, as Bonhoeffer had urged him to do.[74] His second letter was to President Hindenburg. Finally, during these critical days, Bell and Bonhoeffer once again began to consider the possibility of sending a delegation to Berlin.

When Heckel and his companions arrived in London, they found the bishop surprisingly well informed and little inclined to be mollified by any exchange of mutual assurances; for Bell had taken the precaution of securing the approval of the 'Life and Work' executive committee, which had met at Chichester on 26th and 29th January 1934, for his most recent letter to Müller, written on 18th January.

Hence Berlin now had proof enough of Bonhoeffer's disturbing influence and attempted once again to suppress it. The occasion for this arose shortly after Heckel's return from London.

4. One day the External Affairs Office learned—and this, oddly enough, before even Bonhoeffer himself had heard of it—that the Archbishop of Canterbury wished to speak to the German pastor. The gates of Lambeth Palace had been closed to Hossenfelder and Fezer, and Heckel's delegation had got no further than the Athenaeum. Could it really be true that Bonhoeffer was to be received?

The delay in the transmission of this information was due in Bonhoeffer's case to one of his frequent visits to Germany. On 13th February, shortly after the London meeting with Heckel, he went to

72. See GS II, p. 158.
73. See the text of the minutes of the Council meeting, Fanö, pp. 63 f.
74. GS II, pp. 142 ff.

Hanover to attend a Pastors' Emergency League conference, the question under discussion being whether the opposition should remain within the German Evangelical Church under Müller and there continue the fight for her true constitution, or whether there should be separation, a move for which the first free synods were paving the way.[75] Bonhoeffer left Hanover, disappointed that the conference should yet again have confined itself to theoretical discussion interlarded with jeremiads about the dangers of separation. When he arrived home in Berlin, he went to bed with flu.

Meanwhile, on 19th February, there had been a routine reception at Lambeth Palace for foreign clergy working in London. Archbishop Lang, who had been kept informed about events in Germany by Bell and hence knew of Bonhoeffer, asked after the latter and said he would like to see him when he returned to England. By the following day this little item of news had reached Heckel's office in Berlin.

When it was further learned that the chairman of 'Life and Work' was planning a confidential discussion of the position of the Church in Germany, to which a German delegation was to be invited,[76] and that Bonhoeffer would again be involved, an attempt was made to get hold of him.

Summoned

But Bonhoeffer was already back in London, where Heckel now rang him up,[77] ordering him to return at once by air. He flew back to Berlin on 5th March and remained there until the 10th. This journey was to be his last act of obedience towards the authority which nominally remained his superior.

The discussion took a serious turn. It concerned authority in the ecumenical field and Bonhoeffer's interests there; mention was also made of apprehensions about his safety.

The question of authority had grown more acute since 21st February when the National Bishop had set up the 'Church Office for External Affairs' with Heckel, now a bishop, at its head. He was to combine the responsibility for the Evangelical diaspora with the work of 'nurturing relations between the German Evangelical Church and well-disposed churches abroad' under one administrative unit.[78] Heckel was thus well and truly answerable to the state authorities for the desired improvement in the attitude of other countries towards ecclesiastical affairs in Germany. It was not long before any ecumenical activity that had not received the sanction of the Jebensstrasse was liable to be condemned as

75. See GS II, p. 145.
76. In Paris, April 1934.
77. From J. Rieger's diary under 27.2.1934.
78. DEK Kirchl. Aussenamt K. III, 637, II, of 27.2.1934.

'participation in foreign intervention in German internal affairs'. The National Bishop even went so far as to accuse of 'high treason' any pastor who gave information about German church matters to foreigners.

Heckel now asked whether Bonhoeffer intended to continue his opposition to this dual authority and by so doing manœuvre himself into a position of 'national indiscipline'. He further suggested that the job in London and the regard in which Bonhoeffer was held there might prove dangerous, which would be regrettable in view of the pastor's youth and talents.

In the course of the discussion, Heckel demanded that, in the interests of both sides, Bonhoeffer 'should refrain from now on from all ecumenical activity'.[79] He placed before him a written declaration to that effect and asked him to sign it. Bonhoeffer refused, but he did undertake to think matters over, after which he would write.

In a well-considered letter dated 18th March he stated that he would not sign the document.[80] He said he had nothing to add to his October declaration to the National Bishop[81] and that he intended to continue with his 'purely ecclesiastical, theological, ecumenical work'. He had heard no more about being received by the archbishop and had therefore concluded 'that nothing would come of it, at least for the present'.

But hardly had the letter been posted than Bonhoeffer received an invitation through H. W. Fox to go to Lambeth Palace on Monday 26th March. Of the conversation there, Rieger wrote in his diary:

Lang knew that the prospect of this interview had made trouble for Bonhoeffer in Berlin [with Heckel]. Lang asked for an account of this and wanted to know about a great many other things. Recognition of the existing Church is out of the question so far as Lang is concerned. This would manifest itself in, for example, Lang's refusal to receive Heckel. The conversation lasted three quarters of an hour and ended by the archbishop's saying he hoped he would soon see Bonhoeffer again.

Bonhoeffer was not going to allow the External Affairs Office to decide what was meant by 'purely ecclesiastical, theological, ecumenical work'. To Sutz he wrote: 'They'd give anything to get me away from here and, if only for that reason, I am digging my heels in.'[82]

Preparation for Barmen

It was wholly unrealistic to suppose that anything could stop or silence Bonhoeffer in that spring of 1934. His 'purely ecclesiastical, theological'

79. To F. Sutz, 28.4.1934, GS I, p. 39.
80. See GS II, pp. 160-2.
81. See Ch. VII, p. 243.
82. Letter of 28.4.1934, GS I, p. 39.

frame of mind would have made this impossible, even had developments in Germany not been moving irrevocably towards the crucial events of Barmen and the birth of the 'Confessing Church'. Hence Bonhoeffer's collaboration with Bishop Bell entered its most vital phase, but in his relations with the Geneva secretaries the first cracks were beginning to appear.

With the increased confidence he had derived from Hitler's support, the National Bishop was doing everything that could possibly promote the drift towards schism. In March he appointed as his 'Chief of Staff' the young, energetic Dr. Oberheid who, in his native Rhineland, had been promoted from curate to bishop because he was a National Socialist. He also gave him executive powers. When the police dissolved the Westphalian Synod, Oberheid suspended from office its venerable head, Präses Koch. The National Bishop closed down all the preachers' seminaries in Old Prussia. On 12th April he nominated Dr. Jäger,[83] who had won notoriety as State Commissar during the summer of 1933, to the post of 'legal administrator' *(Rechtswalter)* of the whole of the German Evangelical Church. This inaugurated the chaotic attempts in Berlin to centralize and coordinate the individual regional churches.

The opposition which, after the Chancellory reception, had fallen virtually silent, was now becoming more and more vociferous. By summoning Bonhoeffer to Berlin, Heckel quite unintentionally gave him a chance to take part in the first 'Free Synod' of his own church of Berlin-Brandenburg, which met on 7th March 1934. The Westphalian Synod, following its dissolution by the police, had reconstituted itself as a 'Confessing Synod', and there was a plan to inaugurate a free General Synod for the whole of Germany on 18th April. But because of the confusion caused by the attempts at centralization, a rally of the 'Confessing Front', consisting of interested clergy and laity from all over the country, occurred beforehand on 22nd April, at Ulm. Eventually the first representative German Confessing Synod of Barmen met on 29th May. The Synod was bold enough to condemn as heresy the teaching of the German Christians, thus advancing to the brink of separation.

As was only to be expected, the closer they drew to this decision the more urgent the warnings against it became, both inside Germany and in the ecumenical movement. Even Wilhelm Menn, dispassionate and politically incorruptible as he was, wrote in March to Schönfeld in Geneva declaring that separation would be disastrous for the confessing congregations, for anyone who sought or maintained relations with the opposition, once this had become a 'free church', would expose himself to the suspicion of treason. It would, he thought, mean the end of the opposition if it succeeded in winning the support of the ecumenical movement. Bonhoeffer had, as early as November, been equally aware

83. See Ch. VII, p. 221.

of the dangers of separation,[84] but he drew quite different conclusions. He resolutely seized on every opportunity of urging upon the ecumenical authorities the fact that separation was imminent; they ought, he said, to recognize its necessity and help to bring it about. But there were signs that he would not be able to impose his views upon those in Geneva. Heckel's newly consolidated office was already making its presence felt, at least to the extent that in Geneva no steps were taken that might prejudice the issue one way or the other.

In a letter written on 7th April 1934 he gives eloquent expression to his impatience with the irresolute both inside Germany and elsewhere:

My Dear Henriod . . . I would very much have liked to discuss the situation with you again; the slowness of ecumenical procedure is beginning to look to me like irresponsibility. A decision has got to be taken some time, and it's no good waiting indefinitely for a sign from heaven that will solve the difficulty without further trouble. Even the ecumenical movement has to make up its mind and is therefore subject to error, like everything human. But to procrastinate and prevaricate simply because you're afraid of erring, just when others—I mean our brethren in Germany—are daily having to come to infinitely difficult decisions, seems to me almost to be going counter to love. To delay or fail to make decisions may be more sinful than to make wrong decisions out of faith and love. 'Allow me to go before . . .' says the Gospel—a pretext we use often enough, in all conscience—and in this particular case, it really is now or never. 'Too late' means 'never'. Should the ecumenical movement fail to realize this, and if there are none who are 'violent to take heaven by force', Matt. 11:12, then the ecumenical movement is no longer Church, but a useless association fit only for speechifying. 'If ye believe not, do not stay', but to believe means to decide. And can there still be any doubt as to the nature of that decision? For Germany today it is the Confession, as it is the Confession for the ecumenical movement. We must shake off our fear of the Word—the cause of Christ is at stake, and are we to be found sleeping?

I am writing to you because your last letter seemed to be hinting at much the same thing. And if all the 'wise', the old and the influential are unwilling to act with us and are held back by all kinds of considerations—then it is you who must attack, you who must advance. Don't let yourself be stopped or misled; after all, if we're really honest with ourselves, we do know in this case what is right and what is wrong. Someone has got to show the way, fearlessly, and unflinchingly—why not you? For there's much more at stake than just people or administrative difficulties—Christ is looking down at us and asking whether there is anyone who still confesses him. I think I am right in believing that you and I think alike in such matters. Very sincerely yours, Dietrich Bonhoeffer.

The aims and plans of writer and recipient still appeared so similar as to be almost indistinguishable. There was a kind of brotherly matter-of-factness in the way each demanded of the other what in ordinary circumstances would be considered exorbitant. And indeed their mutual

84. GS II, p. 138.

confidence seemed to be justified by the nature of their intercourse ever since the Berlin conferences and the time of Hitler's seizure of power and, later, their discussions at Sofia. But the more imminent and uncompromisingly real the challenge of schism became, the more shaky their concord showed itself to be. Their understanding of the situation was suddenly revealed as radically different. One of the two saw his executive office as bounded by his organization's statutes, and found himself restricted by questions of procedure, while the other felt impelled to ask whether that organization could, in fact, now begin to justify its existence. The ecumenical secretary maintained contact with the Reich Church, while Bonhoeffer endeavoured to prevent any kind of infiltration of the ecumenical movement by German Christian or neutral representatives of that same Church. Yet these were only first steps in what, during the months that followed, was to become his campaign of persuasion in the ecumenical movement. He was convinced that the latter would forego a significant experience if it failed to come to a decision. At the same time—and he hinted as much to his friends in Berlin—he was under no illusion about the difficulties that would be in store for them should the men in Geneva and in the World Council decide to give them their definitive support.

Pastoral Letter

During these months his efforts were seconded, not so much by the Geneva secretaries as by the chairman of the whole ecumenical movement, Bishop Bell. They collaborated during the weeks that followed to produce a circular letter from the bishop to all members of the World Council on the occasion of Ascension Day 1934. This 'pastoral letter' carefully laid down the lines that it was desired to follow at the Fanö conference.

Bonhoeffer's letters to Bell contain suggestions for an 'ultimatum' to be addressed by the bishop to the Berlin church government as soon as he received the information from himself that the Barmen Synod was about to convene. In November 1933 Bonhoeffer was asking for nothing more than 'a strong demand from the side of the ecumenic churches'.[85] In January he requested 'a most dramatic disapproval of Müller's policy . . . A definite disqualification of Müller by the ecumenical movement'.[86] But in March, on the same day as his letter to Henriod, he wrote: 'I beg to ask you once more to consider the possibility of an ecumenical delegation and *ultimatum*.'[87] Bonhoeffer insisted that in taking such a step the bishop would not lay himself open to the charge of 'intervention', and further that the common cause of European Christianity was at stake: 'Please do not remain silent now!'

85. GS II, p. 138.   86. GS II, p. 143.
87. Letter of 14.3.1934, GS I, p. 184.

Upon hearing the alarming news of August Jäger's return, he wrote on 15th April that the moment had arrived 'to take a definitive attitude, perhaps in the way of an ultimatum or in expressing publicly the sympathy with the oppositional pastors'.[88] He urged the bishop, as chairman of 'Life and Work', to warn all member churches against taking independent steps to recognize the existing church government in Germany; for the latter, in its renewed attempt forcibly to consolidate the German Evangelical Church, would certainly sue for recognition— as, indeed, it had already successfully done in the case of Headlam, the Bishop of Gloucester. For this reason Bell must 'send a letter to all other churches connected with the ecumenic movement warning them. . .'

As far as the 'ultimatum' was concerned, Bell was unable to envisage exactly what this might be, but he agreed to the suggestion of a monitory circular letter to member churches and began to deliberate upon it.

On 27th April, Bell and Bonhoeffer met at the Athenaeum for their initial discussion on the subject. Five days previously the 'Confessing Front' at Ulm had for the first time publicly declared itself to be 'before the whole of Christendom the lawful Church in Germany'.[89] As Bonhoeffer had already heard, Hitler had thereupon angrily declared that he intended to retain Müller. He therefore proposed that Bell should include in the letter a strong expression of solidarity for those in danger.

With characteristic modesty Bell sent Bonhoeffer a draft on 2nd May, requesting amendments, deletions or additions.[90] In his reply, Bonhoeffer advised him to avoid saying anything in his letter that would indicate the possibility of a choice between two groups in Germany. He did not conceal his intention to steer the bishop towards the 'ultimatum' he had in mind and advised him to propose that at Fanö the conference should not just talk but act, for only this could intimidate the National Bishop's faction.[91]

On 10th May the ecumenical chairman's pastoral letter was sent out as 'A message regarding the German Evangelical Church to the representatives of the Churches on the Universal Council for Life and Work from the Bishop of Chichester'. The letter did not contain everything that Bonhoeffer would have wished, nor was it an 'ultimatum' in the exact sense of the word. Yet at this crucial moment of time between the centralization troubles and the Barmen Synod it did at least formulate a comprehensive catalogue of essential grievances couched in unequivocal terms: leadership principle, régime of force, disciplinary measures and racial discrimination 'without precedent in the history

88. GS I, p. 187.
89. H. Hermelink, *Kirche im Kampf*, 1950, p. 87.
90. GS I, p. 189.
91. GS I, p. 190.

of the Church . . . incompatible with the Christian principle'.[92]

No one else would have gone so far, except perhaps Ammundsen who at this time was in a less exposed position than Bell. Bonhoeffer was unreserved in his expression of thanks:

In its conciseness it strikes at the chief points and leaves no escape for misinterpretation . . . your letter . . . is a living document of ecumenic and mutual responsibility. I hope it will help others to speak out as clearly as you did.[93]

Bell received no answer to his pastoral letter either from the National Bishop or from Bishop Heckel. Ludwig Müller was content with a mere allusion to it in an abusive speech he made that summer, when he declared that in Germany there was now no state of emergency for faith. Bell's authority had gained in stature, however, for one day in November he actually received a visit in Chichester from Hitler's envoy extraordinary, von Ribbentrop.

Two weeks after Ascension Day, and fortified by this show of ecumenical solidarity, the oppostion met at Barmen. Bonhoeffer's initiative and assistance in promoting the pastoral letter may be regarded as his contribution to the Barmen Synod. He was not present at this, the most important event of the whole church struggle, and there is no evidence of there having been any suggestion that he should play a part in it. He had attended only preliminary meetings such as the conference at Hanover.

Under the chairmanship of Präses Koch, free and legal representatives of all the German regional churches proclaimed a Confession to the fundamental truths of the Gospel in opposition to the 'false doctrine' of the German Christian Government, and in so doing severed themselves from the teaching and practice of the 'brown Church'. In the famous Barmen Declaration based on a draft by Karl Barth they rejected:

. . . the false doctrine that the Church, as the source of its proclamation, could and should, over and above God's one Word, acknowledge other events, powers, images and truths as divine revelation . . .
. . . the false doctrine that the form of her order and mission can be left to the discretion of the Church or to the ideological and political views that happen to prevail . . . or that she can set up, or allow herself to be given, special leaders with sovereign powers.[94]

Henceforward the opposition was no longer 'opposition' within the Reich Church under the obligation to recognize the latter's governance, but must see itself as the one 'Confessing Church' in Germany. Bonhoeffer felt relief at this justification of his views. The Barmen Synod

92. GS I, pp. 192 f.
93. Letter of 15.5.1934, GS I, p. 194.
94. The six Barmen theses.

had proclaimed and enacted what he had long been putting forward as the criterion of his words and deeds. Like those who attended Barmen, he had generally used the term 'opposition', but always in the cause and with the claim of the Confessing Church, and in this he had met with little understanding or assent. Now the expression 'Confessing Church', though it found more or less general acceptance, was used almost entirely as a synonym for 'opposition'. This was almost incomprehensible to Bonhoeffer whose own analysis and conception met with sympathy and understanding in Bell. The bishop further understood the consequences implicit in Bonhoeffer's claim.

The concern of the western ecumenicals was to a large extent determined by practical—that is to say, political—considerations; consequently, when the struggle became a tedious contest for the Confession, their interest flagged, to flare up again as soon as there was any sensational news of police action in Germany. Holding the political views he did, Bonhoeffer could easily have won over ecumenical sympathy. Instead he began a campaign against 'heresy' and thus found himself in notable isolation. There were very few people—and one of them was Bell—whose minds he had really been able to prepare for this crisis; in the eyes of the rest he merely seemed to have an awkward disposition to orthodoxy.

Bonhoeffer's position was a peculiar one. In spite of his whole-hearted partisanship, his brethren in the German Confessing Church had come to look upon him as an outsider because of his perpetual concern with the Sermon on the Mount. Yet among his ecumenical friends, to whom the Sermon on the Mount was of prime importance, he had become a stranger as a result of his insistence on the Confession and the need to repudiate heresy. He himself believed that the sterility threatening the confessionally based opposition to the usurpers must be offset by the Sermon on the Mount, while the Confession must be used to combat enthusiasm in the opposition which had based itself upon the Sermon.

IV FANÖ

During the summer of 1934, Bonhoeffer was fully taken up with the preparations and disputes that preceded the Fanö conference. Yet these months were momentous chiefly on account of the political events which so materially increased Hitler's power. The deliberations both before and during Fanö were overshadowed by this threatening background in which took place the Schacht crisis, the 'Röhm revolt', the Dollfuss murder, and Hindenburg's death, followed by the creation of the office of 'Führer and Reich Chancellor' combining the two highest offices of state.

Political Pressure

The early summer was not without hopes of a crisis within the cabinet and the leading caucuses of the Party, and people began to ask whether the 1933 forecast that Hitler would 'play himself out' was about to be fulfilled. In May Bonhoeffer learned, through his brother-in-law Hans von Dohnanyi, of the existence of certain tensions—Schacht, then president of the Reichsbank, was thinking of resigning—which might make things difficult for Hitler. On 30th June, news arrived of the suppression of the Röhm revolt. In justifying his action before the Reichstag, Hitler said there had been seventy-seven deaths. This did not tally with the figure given to Bonhoeffer by his brother-in-law, as we learn from Rieger's diary: 'Bonhoeffer has heard from the Ministry of Justice that 207 people were shot on 30th June and 1st July.' During July there was news of attempted *coups* by the Austrian National Socialists, and on 25th July the Federal Chancellor, Dollfuss, was assassinated in Vienna. Italian troops marched on the Tyrolean frontier. On 2nd August Hindenburg died. Though the hopes that had been pinned on him as a moderating influence had scarcely been justified, he had enjoyed the confidence of large numbers of people. But now Hitler combined the two highest offices in the country in his own person and had himself confirmed by plebiscite on 19th August 1934 in his new capacity as 'Führer and Reich Chancellor of the German People'.

At this time of extreme political tension the factions within the Church found themselves in a strange position. There were growing difficulties for the opposition. The Minister of the Interior, Frick, issued a decree on 9th July 'for the protection of the national community' prohibiting all discussion of church disputes in the Press and in places of public assembly. The ecclesiastical Press, which had remained relatively independent, was brought under control on 7th July by a 'Church Law for the Evangelical Press'. On 9th August Ludwig Müller had his measures and laws confirmed by the National Synod. In gratitude for the rescue of Germany from the dangers of revolution and for the creation of the new office of 'Führer', the Synod resolved that pastors should swear a 'service oath', although they had already taken an oath of allegiance to the State on their ordination. The oath ran: 'I . . . swear before God . . . that I . . . will be true and obedient to the Führer of the German people and State, Adolf Hitler, and I pledge myself to every sacrifice and every service on behalf of the German people such as befit an Evangelical German . . .'[95]

Heckel and his faction, who were then busy girding up their loins for the Fanö conference, were party to this resolution which, as a result of Frick's prohibition, could not be publicly challenged or even subjected to critical comment.

95. JK, 1934, p. 673.

But within the Confessing Church there were also many who, during the services on 8th July 1934, asseverated their allegiance. In innumerable sermons and prayers thanks were offered up to the Führer for having saved the nation from the most dire peril. Even the parish magazine of the German communities in London carried an article enthusiastically describing the rescue, not of Germany alone but of the whole world, by Hitler's intervention. Yet it was becoming ever more difficult to substantiate the thesis which the Confessing Church was still striving to uphold, namely that its ranks comprised the 'better National Socialists'. In a letter to E. Sutz at the end of April 1934, Bonhoeffer gave vent to his feelings on this subject:

Ingenuous visionaries like Niemöller still go on thinking they're the true National Socialists—it may indeed be Providence that has fostered their illusion, and this might even be in the interests of the church struggle . . .[96]

The sermon preached by Bonhoeffer before his London congregation on 8th July 1934 was subsequently duplicated for circulation among his students. They were sensible to the contrast between the incisiveness of this sermon of atonement, wholly centred on the congregation, and the general emotionalism and sometimes tormented enthusiasm of the thanksgiving sermons that followed the blood-bath. For his text, Bonhoeffer had taken the story of an ancient report of a murder—the pericope of the tower of Siloam in Luke 13:1-5:

. . . unless you repent, you will all likewise perish . . . Now things are getting dangerous. We are no longer spectators, observers, or judges of what is happening. It is we who are addressed. It has happened for us, God is speaking to us, it is we who are meant . . .

For the proper understanding of this sermon it is necessary to recall a passage from a letter which we have quoted before: 'It is we who are to be converted, not Hitler.'[97] But the form to be taken by that 'conversion' was yet to undergo many changes.

Allotment of Tasks

Thus the Barmen Synod and the increasing gravity of the political situation exercised a determining influence on Bonhoeffer's preparations for Fanö. He had already been given two assignments—a lecture, and the organization of the Youth Conference; now a third task came his way, a task which at times threatened to exclude the other two—the struggle for the participation at Fanö of the newly constituted Confessing Church.

It was Bonhoeffer's intention that his youth sector should uncompromisingly validate the Barmen declaration of heresy, and when the question of the composition of the German delegation to the Youth

96. Letter of 28.4.1934. GS I, p. 40.
97. See Ch. VIII, p. 285.

Conference was raised, both in Germany and in Geneva, he returned vigorously to the attack. There could be no mistaking his threat:

I have, incidentally, already written to tell Herr Schönfeld that the question of our German delegation's collaboration at Fanö is largely dependent on whether representatives of the present Reich Church Government are to take part in the conference. Anyhow the members of our delegation have agreed that they will absent themselves from those Fanö meetings that are attended by representatives of the church government. It would be a good thing if this could be generally and clearly realized. And I hope that you, too, will help us to get the ecumenical movement to state openly, before it is too late, which of the two churches in Germany it is prepared to recognize.[98]

Those preparing to go to Fanö were so alarmed by the steady deterioration of the political climate after the deaths of Röhm, Dollfuss and Hindenburg that they recommended circumspection in the arrangement of the youth programme. On 12th August Bonhoeffer wrote to de Félice:

In view of the extreme seriousness of the situation we are most anxious that you should not lay on a 'social evening' or any other form of light-hearted entertainment. Some of the members of the German youth delegation will have been involved in very difficult ecclesio-political circumstances, and will not know what lies in store for them and all other confessing Protestants after their return from Fanö and during the weeks to follow.

At times his worries about the Youth Conference and about his lecture were completely overshadowed by his passionate involvement in the third task of promoting the participation of the Confessing Church which had come into being at Barmen. Though he felt to some extent directly involved in the first two assignments, he made them conditional upon ecumenical recognition of the Barmen declaration. Yet this task, more than either of the others, brought him into conflict with people and circumstances.

Crisis about Participation

In the days immediately following Barmen (29th-31st May 1934), Bonhoeffer received from Geneva a list of directives and questions, along with other preparatory material for Fanö. Schönfeld requested him to send in suggestions and ideas on the theme 'the Universal Church and the World of Nations', upon which Bonhoeffer was to speak.[99] This at once raised the question as to whether he would be able to carry out the two tasks he had previously undertaken, just as if nothing had happened in the meantime. Whom was he likely to encounter from the Reich Church at the Fanö meetings? Could he share a table with them? Did not even

98. To de Félice, 4.7.1934.
99. Letter of 14.6.1934, see GS I, pp. 195 f.

a modicum of self-respect demand that the ecumenical movement should recognize the Barmen Synod's claim that, as the true German Evangelical Church, it had stated bindingly what must be confessed and what rejected by the present Christian faith? Could this remain entirely without consequence?

Before replying to Schönfeld's letter, therefore, Bonhoeffer went to Berlin on 19th June to discuss the matter with the head of the Confessing Synod, Präses Karl Koch, and with Martin Niemöller. All three agreed that no member of the Confessing Church could collaborate at Fanö unless one of their number was invited specifically as a representative of the Confessing Church. Bonhoeffer proposed that they should confront Geneva with the choice either of inviting such a representative, or of forfeiting his collaboration altogether. He held that, should the invitation not be forthcoming, it would be better to let the External Affairs Office appear alone at the ecumenical gathering, when the silence of the absentees would speak for itself and where there would, moreover, be authoritative spokesmen from other churches. Bonhoeffer was also able to attend a meeting of the Berlin branch of the World Alliance. Here, too, it was debated whether the German World Alliance delegates should keep away from Fanö if Heckel, and he alone, was to represent the Reich Church.

Bonhoeffer returned to London entrusted with the task of clearing up the question of invitations. He began by writing to Geneva, and then initiated a joint action with the Bishop of Chichester.

1. Empowered by Koch and Niemöller, he wrote a comprehensive letter to the Genevans and received an answer from Henriod on 7th July. The latter went to considerable pains to express adequate sympathy for the awkward quandary in which the men of the Confessing Church found themselves; but circumstances being what they were, he was unable to see his way to cancelling the invitation to the Church External Affairs Office as representative of the Evangelical Church at Fanö. Nor could he envisage any possibility of issuing a further invitation to the Confessing Synod to which he passed back the initiative by saying that it must first expressly declare itself to be a second church, alongside the Reich Church, and inform Geneva officially of this step.

Through some other channel Bonhoeffer also heard that his refusal to give the main lecture had already been accepted. In respect of this premature reaction he wrote: 'I am glad you have so quickly found a substitute for me for Fanö.'[100] With this letter he returned the preparatory material to Geneva.

He now strenuously denied the false assumption that the Confessing Church was a separate, free church alongside the Reich Church—an assumption that would have been welcome to many.[101] At Ulm and

100. To Henriod, 12.7.1934, GS I, p. 202.
101. GS I, pp. 200 f.

Barmen, he maintained, the opposition had made it perfectly clear that, unlike the other churches, it was grounded both theologically and legally in the constitution of the German Evangelical Church. Hence the Confessing Synod could never declare that it had founded another church or request the latter's recognition by the ecumenical movement. The responsibility for the Fanö problem did not therefore lie with the Confessing Synod's Council of Brethren, but with the organization in Geneva.

The general secretary of the Ecumenical Federations regarded himself as bound by his statutes, which made no allowance for what the Germans were insistently demanding. Bonhoeffer, for his part, knew that the claim and struggle of his church admitted of no delay, and found it hard to believe that the statutes were so entirely unyielding. In 1934 all he was fighting for was an invitation to the Confessing Church alongside the Reich Church. In 1935, after the Dahlem Synod, he was arguing for a decision that would exclude either one or the other.

2. The second attempt to solve the invitation problem with the help of Bishop Bell was rather more successful.

Since existing circumstances debarred the Confessing Synod from Fanö, Bonhoeffer asked the bishop to consider the possibility of issuing an invitation himself. Bell endeavoured to find a way of doing so at this late stage without infringing his terms of reference. He even took the trouble to study legal expert opinion—for instance that given by Reichsgerichtsrat Dr. Flor [the highest legal authority]—in order to demonstrate that the Confessing Church's claims to legality were in fact justified. For Bell had to be careful to avoid charges of irregularity or abuse of authority. The Church External Affairs Office was obviously nursing its ecumenical connections, as Bonhoeffer had predicted when he and Bell were preparing the Ascensiontide message. Now it was fighting for the recognition of the unimpaired legality of the Reich Church. The Archbishop of Canterbury had received a letter from a previously unknown 'Central Authority for Ecumenical Matters', signed by a Professor Fabricius and asking for an explanation for the assertion that 'the German Evangelical Church is in danger to cease to be fully Christian'.[102] Bell asked Bonhoeffer to draw up a list of arguments and to write an account of Fabricius's position and background for the archbishop.

In considering the matter of the invitation, Bell turned for advice to the man with whom he shared the responsibility for Fanö, Bishop Ammundsen, the chairman of the World Alliance. Like Henriod, Bell was fully aware that, in accordance with the statutes, every country must decide for itself what delegates to send. But he also knew that there could be no negotiations between Koch and Heckel over a German delegation and upon that fact he based his argument. In pointing this

102. GS II, pp. 175 f.

out to Ammundsen, he insinuated that he was very anxious to see the Confessing Church represented at Fanö.[103] On 11th July Ammundsen replied with some reserve but not without encouragement. From this letter it is evident that even Bonhoeffer's well-wishers were sometimes confused by the stormy course of events. He wrote:

As to the question raised in your letter I think:—
1. that it would be premature to take any step involving a formal recognition from our side of the German Free Synods; the position of these Synods inside Germany is not yet clear enough, and it would be wrong for the Presidency to do anything which would prejudicate the opinion of the Ecumenical Council.
2. that it would be most helpful to us to have such representatives and that we are only true to our convictions when we let them feel our sympathy and fellowship.

The conclusion of this is that, in virtue of the power, which an Executive and in emergency cases the President is always regarded as possessing to invite people helpful to clear up the problems, you should invite Präses Koch to send say two representatives to our meeting in no official capacity but so to say as experts for giving us information and adding to our discussions. It then must be for our German friends themselves to decide whether it will be wise to accept the invitation or not. Sincerely yours . . . In fact I think it is a good suggestion to invite such people, only that we do not precipitate matters.

By 12th July Bonhoeffer was already asking Bell with some impatience about the invitation which did, in fact, go off to Koch on 18th July. In a warm-hearted letter requesting the presence of Koch—and if possible of Bodelschwingh—at Fanö, he showed the utmost understanding for the difficulties involved, since the invitation might well place its recipients in a politically awkward position.[104]

Did this mean that Bonhoeffer could now go to Fanö? The matter was still not quite clear. The stipulation that he, Koch and Niemöller had made on 19th June had been fulfilled and there was nothing further that Bell could do. But the form of the invitation and the circumstances in which it had been made had revealed clearly enough that there could as yet be no question of any wider appreciation of the claim put forward by the Confessing Church at Barmen to be the rightful German Evangelical Church. Again, as a result of Bell's Ascensiontide message it was likely that the question of German internal affairs would be raised, in which event two separate German factions would have to adopt opposing positions—and this, in the tense political atmosphere following Röhm's assassination and Hindenburg's death.

Bonhoeffer hesitated, and Koch, too, was in some doubt. On 30th July Siegmund-Schultze arrived in London to urge Bonhoeffer to go, and

103. GS I, p. 203.
104. GS I, p. 204.

Ammundsen wrote to say how much he counted on seeing him at
Fanö.[105] Finally Bonhoeffer made up his mind, only to hear the disappointing news that Koch and Bodelschwingh would not be attending
because of the political situation.

On 1st August Bonhoeffer went on leave, but his holiday had to be
given up to preparations. Some two weeks later he went to stay at
Esbjerg, opposite the island of Fanö. The Youth Conference began on
22nd August and the main Fanö conference two days later.

The Resolution

Of Fanö, A History of the Ecumenical Movement by Rouse and Neill
relates:

The biennial meeting of the Council at Fanö . . . stands out as perhaps the
most critical and decisive meeting in its history. Here the Council solemnly
resolved to throw its weight on the side of the Confessing Church in
Germany against the so-called 'German Christians' and by implication against
the Nazi régime.[106]

It could not be taken for granted that the conference would in fact
arrive at a resolution. There were many, both inside and outside Germany, who believed that a statement on the German question at this
particular point of time would be inopportune and wrong. And whereas
nationalists such as Wilhelm Stapel protested against the 'international,
Western, liberal, democratic' character of the conference,[107] there were
also those in the Confessing Church who, in the strained political situation, feared the unsettling effect of a statement from abroad. 'I am more
afraid of many of our own supporters than I am of the German Christians', Bonhoeffer wrote to Ammundsen.[108] And there were many outside Germany who were ridden with doubt; they were confused by the
fact that men of 'Christian character' were to be found on both sides in
Germany, and wished to eschew 'intervention' as well as any definite
decision.

What was certain, however, was that the Universal Christian Council for 'Life and Work' would be obliged, at this conference, to react
either positively or negatively to the Ascensiontide pastoral letter from
its chairman, Bishop Bell. It remained to be seen whether this occasion
would lead to a joint resolution with the World Alliance.

Bonhoeffer had begun in good time to seek support for a strongly
worded resolution, and had left no stone unturned. He could be certain

105. GS I, pp. 205 f.
106. R. Rouse, S. C. Neill, A History of the Ecumenical Movement 1917-1954, London,
1954, p. 583.
107. W. Stapel, 'Die politisierende ökumenische Weltkonferenz in Fanö', Deutsches
Volkstum, 2.9.1934.
108. Letter of 8.8.1934, GS I, p. 205.

of Bell, and he also found other good allies. On 8th August he turned to Ammundsen:

It's possible that our side may be terribly cautious for fear of seeming unpatriotic—not that fear is the motive, but rather a false sense of honour. A lot of people, even people who have been doing ecumenical work for quite a long time, still seem incapable of realizing or believing that we are really working together purely as *Christians*. They are horribly suspicious and it prevents them from being completely frank. If only, my dear Bishop, you could manage to break the ice so that people became more trusting and completely open with each other! And it is particularly here, *in our attitude towards the State*, that we must speak out with absolute sincerity for the sake of Jesus Christ and for the sake of the ecumenical cause. It must be made quite clear—terrible though this is—that we are immediately faced with the decision: National Socialist or Christian, and that we must advance beyond where we stood a year ago (I know you said so at the time!)[109] However hard and difficult it may be for us all, we have got to face it and go through with it, without trying to be diplomatic, but speaking frankly and as Christians. How to do so we shall discover by praying together. I felt I had to say this.

In my opinion a resolution ought to be taken—no good can come of evasion . . . The only thing that can help us now is *complete truth* and *complete truthfulness*. I know that many of my German friends think otherwise. But I do beg you to consider this thought.[110]

When Hildebrandt arrived, bringing news of the National Synod and of the Council of Brethren's decision that they would not send anyone to Fanö, Bonhoeffer again wrote urgently on 18th August to Ammundsen:

In view of the most recent developments, it now seems to me imperative that not only 'Life and Work', but also the World Alliance, should put forward a resolution, perhaps indeed the same resolution. I know there are strong feelings against this, but I shall do everything I can to counteract them . . . I would like . . . you to advise me what I ought to do about this and, what is much more important, to help me do it. I would so very much appreciate your assistance![111]

Ammundsen arranged a meeting with the Council of Brethren in Hamburg to discuss their decision not to send delegates to Fanö. He recognized the risk of political defamation to which they would be exposed if their presence compelled them to speak on the pro-posed resolution and he promised that, should occasion arise, he would speak for them in their absence. Bonhoeffer's attendance was no longer in question—indeed, it was regarded as desirable that, based as he was in England, he should go to Fanö in the dual role of conference speaker and delegate of the Confessing Church. Bonhoeffer himself, however, considered his colleagues' refusal of the invitation to be wrong: 'I am

109. In Sofia.
110. GS I, pp. 205 f.
111. GS I, pp. 207 f.

wondering how things are going to turn out. I'm the only one of us here, which I think is a bad mistake.'[112]

On the very first day of the proceedings, Saturday 25th August, the conference started to discuss the position of the Church in Germany. The meeting began with a declaration by the German World Alliance members, who were independent both of the Reich Church delegation and of the Confessional Synod:

The peculiar situation in the political and ecclesiastical development in Germany induces the members of the German delegation of the World Alliance to request you, Mr. Chairman, to make the following statement *before* the commencement of the proceedings: The German Delegation of the World Alliance does not wish to take any part in a public discussion on the internal affairs of the German Church.[113]

Bonhoeffer's name is not to be found among the speakers discussing the resolution. There was no longer any need to mention it.

The conference appointed a committee to draft the resolution. The composition of this committee must have more than satisfied Bonhoeffer, for it consisted of Bell, Ammundsen, Marc Boegner (later to be co-chairman of 'Life and Work'), Professor Brun of Norway, Professor Keller of Switzerland, Dr. Leiper of the United States, who took a lively interest in the church struggle and, finally, Henriod. There was an animated plenary discussion but, after a mishap with the Press, all further discussions of this subject were held *in camera*. On Wednesday 29th August, a special emissary—one, Oberkirchenrat [senior church councillor] Birnbaum—sent by the National Bishop and Rechtswalter Jäger arrived in a special aircraft. Birnbaum's request for a hearing was an affront to Heckel even though the latter, as Bonhoeffer later told Rieger, had brushed aside the Jewish question amongst others on the grounds that 'this was not his province'. Birnbaum was allotted a quarter of an hour for his speech and used it, Rieger's diary tells us, 'for an absurd rigmarole about his personal experiences of people who, because National Socialist, became Christians'.

The resolution was carried on 30th August.[114] It confirmed Bell's message as well as the course he had taken, and listed the most recent complaints: autocratic government, the use of force, the service oath, the ban on free discussion. Unequivocally, it spoke out for the absent delegates with the words:

The Council desires to assure its brethren in the Confessional Synod of the German Evangelical Church of its prayers and heartfelt sympathy in their witness to the principles of the gospel, and of its resolve to maintain close fellowship with them.[115]

112. To his grandmother, 19.8.1934, GS II, p. 183.
113. Minutes of the meeting of the Council, Fanö, p. 37.
114. Op. cit., pp. 50-2.
115. Op. cit., pp. 51 f.

That same day the assembly, using its right of cooption, made the gesture of electing Dietrich Bonhoeffer and the absent head of the Confessional Synod, Präses Karl Koch 'consultative and coopted members' of the Universal Christian Council for 'Life and Work'.

Bishop Heckel, placed as he was between the assembly and his masters at home, was in an uncomfortable position. In these circumstances he did three things. First he succeeded in introducing a small clause into the resolution, a clause which at the time no one thought was worth bothering about, but which was to allow the Reich Church to put its foot inside the door and so prevent the Confessing Church from ever fully achieving its aim. The clause stated that the Council wished 'to remain in friendly contact with all groups in the German Evangelical Church'.[116] This meant that the Council's support, though presently effective, could not remain so in future. Secondly, Heckel minuted a protest on behalf of the delegation[117] in which he denied, or put a different interpretation on, the alleged abuses, accused the Council of exceeding its terms of reference, and objected to the 'one-sided stress on a particular group in Germany'. Further, the German delegation repudiated 'the allegation that in the German Reich the free proclamation, either verbal or written, of the Gospel is imperilled . . . On the contrary, it holds that the conditions prevailing in Germany today provide a more favourable opportunity for proclaiming the Gospel than ever before . . .'[118] Thirdly, in express reference to the election of Bonhoeffer and Koch, Heckel recorded an objection to 'the biased attitude towards the internal affairs of the German Evangelical Church'.[119]

The only clauses to make any public impact were, firstly, the rejection of the use of force and, secondly, the decision to support the Confessing Church. The Bishop of Chichester wrote an excellent report on Fanö for *The Times*,[120] giving pride of place to the conference's recognition of the Confessing Church. This viewpoint was substantiated by the complaints of 'foreign interference' that persisted for weeks in the columns of the official Reich Church organ and similar publications. There were also some strange undertones in the reports carried by the *Junge Kirche*[121] for, hampered by Frick's decree of 9th July, the paper could no longer provide full and accurate information. Thus even here we find expressions of approval for Heckel's protest, and disgust at foreign intervention in internal German affairs. In addition the paper constantly reiterated, no doubt in self-protection, that the Confessing Church was not represented at Fanö.[122] It contained nothing about Bonhoeffer's pre-

116. Op. cit., p. 51.
117. Op. cit., pp. 52 f.
118. Op. cit., p. 75.
119. Op. cit., p. 60.
120. *The Times*, 7.9.1934.
121. JK, 1934, pp. 704-5.
122. JK, 1934, pp. 705, 750.

sence, although he gave one of the principal addresses, nor did it mention his election to the Council. Hence even recent historiography has failed to take account of this latter event.[123]

Yet to begin with Fanö was regarded as a major breakthrough both by the Councils of Brethren in Germany and by their ecumenical friends. Bonhoeffer thanked Bell and Ammundsen out of a full heart for all they had done and achieved,[124] and a year later, in his long ecumenical article, he wrote that Fanö represented an incomparable step forward for Christendom.[125]

In fact at Fanö the ecumenical movement had gone as far as it was ever to go in its commitment towards the Confessing Church. To Bonhoeffer, however, it seemed only a beginning and this is why he raised no objection to the dubious clause about 'friendly contact' with all German groups. The Confessing Church must, he thought, learn to take itself in earnest. Everything seemed to have gone smoothly and it had proved possible to initiate ecumenical discussions on the concept and actuality of 'heresy', a question to which leading personalities had agreed to contribute. It was not till later that Bonhoeffer came to realize than Fanö did not in fact represent an initial stage but a short-lived climax. He did not as yet take sufficient account of the divergent forces at work inside the 'Confessing Front', nor did he permit himself to feel any scepticism about possible weaknesses within its ranks.

Lecture: The Universal Church and the World of Nations

To Bonhoeffer the resolution seemed of infinitely greater import than his own contributions, a lecture and a sermon, yet it was these rather than the more dramatic events at the conference that were later to become the focus of attention.

The chairman and speakers for the specialized discussions at Fanö were provided on alternate days by 'Life and Work' and the World Alliance. The first day was devoted to the theme of 'The Church and the State Today', and the second, when Bonhoeffer spoke, to 'The Universal Church and the World of Nations'. This was to comprise a discussion upon whether the Church was empowered to take sides in international disputes, the lengths to which she might go and the means she ought to employ in the solution of such problems. To elucidate this, Bonhoeffer had based his lecture on the debate on Monod's 'Peace Catechism' at Sofia.[126] Not only did a 'peace catechism' interest him personally, but it would also highlight the urgency of the latest events in Europe.

123. For example W. Niemöller, *Kampf und Zeugnis*, pp. 254 ff.
124. GS I, pp. 222 f.
125. GS I, pp. 241 f.
126. See Ch. VII, pp. 243 f.

The theses for the lecture were supposed to reach Geneva by July, for scrutiny and return. But because the matter had been temporarily in abeyance, Bonhoeffer did not begin to draft his lecture until early August at a time when the political barometer was exceptionally low: there had been the advance of the Italian troops on the Austrian border and the breakdown of disarmament talks, followed by the outbreak of the Abyssinian War and the failure to apply sanctions. Bonhoeffer did not regard these occurrences as the birth-pangs of a new age but as sinister confirmation of his prediction that Hitler meant war.

When his succinct text finally arrived in Geneva[127] it was not approved by the Ecumenical Research Department responsible for the preparation of the specialized discussions at Fanö. Certain lines had already been laid down for these in April at a meeting in Paris not attended by Bonhoeffer. To his colleague, Ehrenström, Schönfeld wrote: 'I must confess that I am a little dismayed by Herr Bonhoeffer's material and its narrow concern with the problem of war.'[128] To Bonhoeffer himself he wrote in a critical vein:

I have recently seen the theses for your Denmark address and would beg you to adopt a more comprehensive attitude to the theme 'Universal Church and the World of Nations' or 'Internationalism and Ecumenicalism', especially in your preamble, than is evident here.[129]

The way in which Bonhoeffer had adapted the subject matter of his lecture to 'conform with existing circumstances'[130] is indicative, not only of his own high-handed methods, but also of the fact that he and Schönfeld were thinking in two wholly different theological dimensions. The latter felt that the lecture should comprise matters such as right intentions and the problems raised by the concept *Volk*, the responsibility of the Church for what is intrinsic to a nation and, further, the orders of creation and preservation. These theological perspectives should be presented in such a way as to help the ecumenical assembly to understand the viewpoint they represented. Indeed, Schönfeld had detailed one section of the Ecumenical Research Department to study the question of 'the order of creation and the natural law'.[131] A letter he wrote in December 1933 to Krummacher, the official in Heckel's External Affairs Office, strikingly reveals how different was his attitude. He had been consulted about the best means of protesting against the Archbishop of Canterbury's indictment in *The Times*, relating to Jewish refugees. Schönfeld advised against a protest, suggesting that instead those in Berlin should press 'for a radical theological re-thinking of the racial problem'. He went on to say: 'This is a field in which, more than

127. GS I, pp. 212-15.
128. Letter of 10.8.1934.
129. Letter of 13.8.1934, GS I, p. 207.
130. Letter from Bonhoeffer to de Félice, 12.8.1934.
131. Minutes, p. 31.

in any other, these people [the British] have much to learn.'[132]

Far from complying with Schönfeld's wishes, Bonhoeffer spoke, as Monod had done, of the war threatening the nations. As a German Lutheran theologian, his formulation was, perhaps, rather too Christo-logical for his Western, liberal audience, yet what he said approximated sufficiently to their own views for them to recognize its essentially pacifist premises.

His theses posed much the same question as formerly at Ciernohorské Kúpele in 1932, when he had enquired into the World Alliance's mandate for peace work, and they were based more upon Christological ecclesiology than upon humanitarianism. The pragmatic community of the World Alliance becomes the community of the Church by hearken-ing to the divine Word of Peace, which it freely imposes. Compared with 1932 there is a new forthrightness—from this command and its execu-tion there can be no dispensation. It is a foretaste of the intellectual climate of *The Cost of Discipleship*. His terminology was highly pro-vocative. Never before had he declared that there could be no justifica-tion for war, even where that war was defensive.

He had ignored Schönfeld's appeal to 'adopt a more comprehensive attitude' and had altered nothing; the theses were delivered exactly in the form in which they had been drafted at the beginning of August. There were translations in three languages for the preliminary speakers' conference on 24th August and for the conference day, 28th August. The manuscript of his actual lecture is still missing. From the minutes of the discussion on 28th August, which were edited in Geneva, we only learn that:

The discussion dealt with the attitude of the Churches to concrete inter-national conflicts, and especially to the war problem, which was seen, how-ever, as being only one problem in the whole struggle for the creation of international order. The Churches were recognized as having a unique contribution to make towards the achievement of genuine cooperation between the states and nations.[133]

The working committee resolved that the subordinate groups of the World Alliance should adopt a common attitude to cumulative re-armament and the flourishing arms industry.[134]

Richard Crossman, who was later to hold office under the Labour Government, went to hear Bonhoeffer on Bell's advice. He was highly critical of the lecture and the discussion that followed it, but he was, of course, unfamiliar with the theological premise. The editorial of *The Church in Action News Letter* commented:

Unfortunately the discussions on the 2nd day did not seem to attain the

132. Letter of 12.12.1933, Ecumenical Archives, Geneva, *General Church Struggle*, 1933.
133. Minutes, p. 39.
134. *World Alliance Handbook*, 1935, p. 46.

same level of earnestness and of clarity as those of the first. Stirring statements were made on pacifism, and these never failed to arouse feelings of approval and applause. But feelings are fickle guides; the pressing problem of peace needs the deduction of hard, clear-cut thinking and of decision and will. Mr. Crossman sought to compel the conference to face the full cost of radical pacifism . . .

The resolution of the Youth Conference put in a needed plea for the right of conscientious objectors in peace as in war. Dr. Bonhoeffer made the important point that there is no path to peace by way of security; behind the quest for security there lies the same distrust and defensiveness which is the root cause of war.[135]

Sermon on Peace

The document entitled 'The Universal Church and the World of Nations' which has become known as Bonhoeffer's Fanö 'peace speech',[136] has been wrongly described, even by the present author, as the lecture delivered at the conference meeting on 28th August. It was, in fact, Bonhoeffer's address at morning service on that day as is testified beyond doubt by Otto Dudzus and others who were present.

The text of his sermon was Psalm 85 : 9. It expresses in highly concentrated form the most unequivocal and emphatic of his statements on peace that we possess. While it bears the stamp of those ominous weeks, its impact has lasted far beyond Hitler's time. Since this was a proclamation delivered in the course of divine service, he was able to ignore considerations which the problems of argument and counter-argument would have raised. Here he was concerned, not with a bootless exchange of unanswerable questions, but with a direct challenge to risk decisions.

He had considered on what authority, at the age of twenty-eight, he could appear before this assembly. He was as capable as any other of analyzing the world situation; alternatively he could have sought and passed on advice. He concluded, however, that he could lean on no other authority than that deriving from the commandment for peace itself. So he passionately exhorted this carefully prepared assembly to justify its right to exist by imposing the Gospel of peace in its fullest extent. Once again he used the word 'council' which must have shocked some of his listeners. But he wanted to lead them beyond their idea of themselves as an advisory or opinion-forming body; a council proclaims, binds and releases, and in so doing, binds and releases itself. As in his lectures in 1932 and at the student meeting in 1933, and as in his Christology lectures and his later ecumenical article of 1935, his concern was with the concrete and binding nature of this community, now gathered together in the name of Christ.[137] He believed that the behest of a coun-

135. G. F. Allen (Oxford), The Church in Action News Letter, 6, p. 2.
136. GS I, pp. 216-19.
137. GS III, p. 206; GS I, p. 261; see also Ch. VII, pp. 218 f.; Ch. IX, pp. 400 ff.

cil was more powerful than that of an individual or of an individual church; the latter '. . . is oppressed by the force of hatred';[138] the very fact that this Council had met was an act of peace that would lend authority to what was said.

Yet Bonhoeffer's peace sermon does not place him unequivocally among the supporters of a fundamental and general pacifism. Never before, however, had he stated so distinctly that, for the disciple, the renunciation of force meant the renunciation of defence.[139] Christians 'may not use weapons against one another because they know that in so doing they are aiming those weapons at Christ himself.'[140] This was the strongest argument upon which his 'Christian pacifism' was based.

It should be noted that these statements bear the characteristics of a sermon and hence do not represent a chapter in a book of ethics intended to elucidate and define the nature of valid behaviour. The call that he proclaimed ignored 'ifs and buts'. Peace was not under discussion but, like the assembly gathered together in Christ, was a present reality and hence a commandment.

Those assembled at Fanö on 28th August 1934 were probably the most eminent congregation before whom Bonhoeffer had ever preached. Indeed, he had very seldom preached to large numbers of people, nor did this really appeal to him. He preferred a small, compact congregation which he could carry along with him as he developed his train of thought. Of this morning service Dudzus tells us:

From the first moment the assembly was breathless with tension. Many may have felt that they would never forget what they had just heard . . . Bonhoeffer had charged so far ahead that the conference could not follow him. Did that surprise anybody? But on the other hand: could anybody have a good conscience about it?[141]

Youth Conference

Even the Fanö Youth Conference earned a special mention in Rouse's and Neill's book:

A conference held at the same time by the Ecumenical Youth Commission went even further than its elders in bluntly urging the Churches 'to dissociate themselves from every Church that does not affirm this universalism [of the Word of God], on the ground that it is not Christian'.[142]

More than fifty people attended the Youth Conference. Political developments in Germany, however, were generally unfavourable to participation at Fanö; consequently the German delegation consisted

138. GS I, p. 219.
139. GS I, p. 218.
140. GS I, pp. 217 f.
141. O. Dudzus, 'Arresting the Wheel', IKDB, p. 90.
142. R. Rouse and S. C. Neill, op. cit., p. 583.

almost solely of Bonhoeffer's former Berlin students—and nearly all of these were subsequently to become ordinands at his preachers' seminary at Finkenwalde. Hence this group could not be said to be representative of German youth generally. They were already disenchanted with nationalism in Germany and were seriously considering the question of conscientious objection. They cannot have been particularly surprised by Bonhoeffer's reply when one day 'on the beach a Swede asked, "What would you do, sir, if war broke out?" Reflectively, he allowed the sand to trickle through his fingers, then turned calmly towards the questioner and replied: "I pray that God will give me the strength not to take up arms".'[143]

Bonhoeffer opened the conference with a service and, during the first day, occupied the chair. The group discussions were principally concerned with the universal (which at this time meant anti-nationalist) nature of the Church and with the question of conscientious objection. The fact that ten German students could with impunity play a leading role in the discussion of these dangerous themes would seem to indicate that the National Socialist authorities still possessed only a rudimentary intelligence network and were, moreover, fully engaged elsewhere.

The Youth Conference debated two resolutions.[144] Controversy arose over the first when it was suggested that the superiority of God's commandment over all claims of the State might, for instance, give the foreign Press the inherent right to criticize incidents inside Germany.[145] Bonhoeffer believed that violations of the divine commandment's claim were 'increasingly and rightly incurring general opprobrium in a number of different countries' (Jotting on Bonhoeffer's agenda). This kind of 'right', he hoped, would receive the support of the Fanö Conference, yet when the resolution was put to the vote it found many opponents, among them some of the German students.

The second resolution demanded in even more radical terms that the Church should be independent of national aims and went on to declare that support should be withheld from 'any war whatsoever'. This latter phrase was opposed by the Polish and Hungarian delegates, who proposed to substitute the words 'aggressive war'. The French and English delegates supported Bonhoeffer's version and only after a dramatic break in the discussion and a time of communal meditation and prayer did the conference finally agree to retain the words 'any war whatsoever'.[146]

On the same day that Bonhoeffer gave his sermon and lecture before the main conference, Jean Lasserre on behalf of the Youth Conference presented 'the resolutions that it had adopted on conscientious objection

143. Related by W. Maechler, 'Vom Pazifisten zum Widerstandskämpfer: Bonhoeffers Kampf für die Entrechteten', MW I, p. 92.
144. GS I, pp. 209-11.
145. GS I, p. 209, para. 3.
146. GS I, p. 210, bottom.

and on the universal nature of the Church'.[147]

The Germans who had taken part in the Fanö Youth Conference were to show considerable enterprise in the course of the years that followed. At the meeting of the Youth Commission in January 1935 Bonhoeffer reported:

The German Fanö group has been doing a great deal of propagandistic work in the respective universities. A very encouraging step forward could be taken in Tübingen and in Heidelberg. Some of the speeches delivered at Fanö were mimeographed and spread among the students. There seems to be—mostly perhaps under the influence of the steadily growing military spirit—a readiness to take seriously the Christian message of peace. In Berlin a group of students of various nationalities met under the auspices of the youth commission in the house of the Swedish pastor Forell and had a very satisfactory meeting.[148]

Sequels: Würzburg and Bruay

It was by a very roundabout route that Bonhoeffer returned to his London parishes from Fanö. First he went to Würzburg to attend a session of the Reich Council of Brethren on 3rd September.[149] He informed the assembly that the failure to send delegates to Fanö had given rise both to disappointment and to some confusion, and it had been asked why the Confessing Church should have remained a 'group' within the German Evangelical Church. By emphasizing this and similar points, Bonhoeffer was pointing the way to the conclusions that were ultimately to be drawn by the Dahlem Confessional Synod when it declared itself the only legal church in Germany. In this context he also referred to the Achilles' heel of the Fanö declaration, the 'contacts with all groups' clause, which he declared to have been the inevitable result of the Confessing Church's failure to make its position perfectly clear. Nevertheless, the Council of Brethren should write expressing its gratitude for the declaration, in particular to Bell. Finally he suggested that the situation demanded that the Confessing Church appoint a representative whose sole concern would be ecumenical affairs. This advice, frequently reiterated, was never followed.

The minutes of the Würzburg session notably record two further expressions of concern. The first relates to the consecration of the National Bishop in Berlin Cathedral on 23rd September and the possible attendance of representatives from churches abroad. Bonhoeffer, however, asserted that attempts after Fanö to secure ecumenical guests for the occasion would fail. Here he proved right; for of all the prelates who paid homage to Ludwig Müller that day, Heckel was the only one who

147. Minutes of the Council, Fanö, p. 39.
148. Letter to de Félice, 29.1.1935.
149. Minutes, see GS I, pp. 220 f.

was not a German Christian. On the second point of concern, the possibility of a Lutheran breakaway, he showed himself over-confident in denying significance to the 'Lutheran confessionalists' who, he said, did not at this time 'necessarily mean a breach in the Confessing Front'.[150] This view was going to require painful revision.

From Würzburg Bonhoeffer went to Bruay in Artois, where Jean Lasserre worked among the poorest industrial labourers, to attend the regular Anglo-French-German regional meeting arranged in a last minute decision by the heads of the Youth Commission at Fanö. This time it took a somewhat unconventional turn when the group ventured out to preach in the streets.

Dietrich spoke one or two times . . . I remember his speeches were very direct . . . He gave me the feeling that he was quite at ease in such a work to which he probably was not accustomed . . . He really spoke the Gospel to the people in the street.[151]

On his return to London Bonhoeffer conducted a service on 16th September, taking as his text Matt. 11:28-30, with the phrase those 'who labour and are heavy-laden'. In his sermon he described the profound impression made upon him by the French mining towns. However this renewed confrontation with social questions was soon totally forgotten in the fresh struggles for the Church.

V SECOND ATTACK AGAINST REICH CHURCH GOVERNMENT, WINTER 1934-35

By the autumn of 1934 Bonhoeffer's energies were once again wholly taken up by his disputes with the Reich Church Government. Whereas in the winter of 1933-34 the disputes had concerned withdrawal of confidence from that government, the new phase threatened an actual breach of relations, in other words the transfer of allegiance by the German congregations abroad to the emergency church government of the Confessing Church.

October Storms in Berlin

The logical conclusion of the Barmen Declaration on the German Christian heresy (in May) was the formation by the Dahlem Confessional Synod (in October) of its own emergency church government. This was rendered possible by Ludwig Müller's ham-handed measures which temporarily closed the ranks of the divided opposition.

When the consecration of the National Bishop at length took place on 23rd September in Berlin Cathedral—and, in fact, it was unattended

150. Ibid.
151. Related by J. Lasserre, 17.12.1965.

by representatives of the ecumenical movement—Hildebrandt sent Bonhoeffer a postcard containing only the chapter and verse of that Sunday's text, Luke 14:11: 'For every one who exalts himself . . .' And, indeed, abasement was not long in coming.

At this point Müller's '*Rechtswalter*', Jäger, took it upon himself to extend compulsory centralization to the South German regional churches. Barely two weeks after his consecration, Müller put the refractory Bishop Wurm of Württemberg under house arrest. Six days afterwards, on 12th October, he meted out the same treatment to Bishop Meiser of Bavaria. This led to spontaneous demonstrations in support of the bishops in the streets of Munich and Stuttgart. Once again the church struggle had made world headlines.

Now the Reich Council of Brethren unanimously agreed to convene the Reich Confessional Synod at the end of the month. The Synod was to instruct the congregations, in accordance with the general terms of the Barmen Declaration, that they no longer owed obedience to the Reich Church Government which had violated the constitution, but must pledge themselves to such ecclesiastical emergency organizations as the Synod should appoint.

In the midst of all this Hildebrandt arrived in London on 11th October with instructions for Bonhoeffer. He was to inform Bishop Bell, as chairman of 'Life and Work', of what had happened and ask him to visit the Synod. Bell was not free at the time and therefore rang up the Swiss Church president, Koechlin, to ask him to undertake this mission for the Council. When Hildebrandt arrived in Düsseldorf on his way home he was told by Lic. Beckmann that, under pressure of the events in Bavaria, the Synod had been put forward and would in fact convene on the 19th and 20th October. Koechlin made arrangements to be present in Dahlem on those days. As before, Bonhoeffer did not participate in the Synod.

The general clamour of protest against the National Bishop together with the surprising unanimity shown at Dahlem on 20th October 1934 in the resolutions on emergency organizations and on Müller's alleged violation of the constitution, now reactivated even the Reich Chancellory. Bonhoeffer learned from his brother-in-law that Hitler had summoned the Minister of Justice, Gürtner, to discuss the legal aspect of recent events in the Church. Subsequently the legislation authorized in August 1934 by the National Synod for the centralization of the German Evangelical Church was rescinded, reviving hopes that the Wilhelmstrasse now seriously meant to change its tune. When these hopes were only partially fulfilled, the ensuing disappointment was to bring disintegration. On 26th October August Jäger resigned. Not only were the South German bishops released, but they were actually received by Hitler on 30th October and returned in triumph to their dioceses where they restored the previous *status quo*. Hitler publicly disassociated himself from the Reich Church; indeed, he declared that professions of loyalty to the Third Reich and its Führer could not be identified with commitment to any one of the groups in the Church.

But what was to be done now about the 'destroyed' ecclesiastical regions, such as Old Prussia? And could the emergency church law passed unanimously by the Dahlem Synod still apply? For Ludwig Müller had not been compelled to beat a wholesale retreat. Bell asked Bonhoeffer what was likely to happen should Hitler really allow the conflict to find a satisfactory conclusion. In the hope of helping to achieve this, the bishop accompanied the Archbishop of Canterbury to the German Embassy. Lang saw the Ambassador, von Hoesch, while Bell visited the First Secretary, von Bismarck. The embassy was authorized by the Foreign Ministry in Berlin to tell the two men that changes were imminent, but Bonhoeffer, who had been kept informed by Dohnanyi, gave the bishop his own analysis of the precarious situation, and was soon proved correct.[152] Hitler, he said, would probably postpone any decision, including the possible recognition of the Dahlem emergency organizations, at least until after the Saar plebiscite.[153]

It may be asked whether Hitler was not all too well informed about the 'opposition'. After a few weeks of indecision it was clear to everyone that cracks were appearing in the front which, on 19th and 20th October, had appeared so united. The Confessing Church had taken fright at its own daring and there was growing criticism of the Dahlem resolution. Indeed, the Reich Government could see little reason for any additional effort, beyond a small degree of restraint imposed upon Ludwig Müller, to placate the opposition which in October had been somewhat too rudely provoked.

Resolution to Secede

Naturally this did not deter Bonhoeffer from supporting the Dahlem resolutions and applying them to his own sphere. Amongst other things they declared:

We call upon the Christian congregations, their pastors and elders, to ignore any instructions received from the former Reich Church Government and its authorities and to refrain from cooperating with those who wish to continue to obey that same church government. We call upon them to adhere to the directions of the Confessional Synod of the German Evangelical Church and of its recognized organs.[154]

For the past year Bonhoeffer had been longing to hear this kind of plain speaking. Now he could not bear to wait and see whether and to what extent the emergency church government would be able to impose

152. Letter of 24.10.1934, see GS II, pp. 177 f.
153. On 13.1.1935.
154. J. Beckmann, op. cit., p. 77.

itself and win recognition. He believed it essential to show immediate recognition of the step that had been taken, and to enforce the new order. Furthermore this should be done promptly and unequivocally so as to confirm the Confessional Synod and its organs in the path upon which they had already set forth, and inspire others to follow suit. In this way the Jebensstrasse would have little time or opportunity to adopt counter-measures.

On 5th November 1934 the elders of nearly all the German Evangelical congregations in England met in London in Christ Church. Bonhoeffer spoke about the situation of the Church in Germany and Rieger about the effects of the struggle on opinion abroad. Forty-four church officials from nine congregations[155] resolved that:

The elders assembled here in Christ Church declare that intrinsically they hold the same position as the Confessing Church, and that they will immediately take up with the church authorities (External Affairs Office of the Reich Church, and also the Confessing Church) any necessary matters arising out of this . . . London, 5th November 1934. The Church Vestries.[156]

The resolution was a tremendous achievement on the part of Bonhoeffer and Rieger, for the prevailing mood had seemed to be against it. On 3rd November Wehrhan had written to Baron Schröder: 'In my opinion we ought to wait until we see how things are shaping at home.' On the morning of 5th November the Baron replied: 'I quite agree that the situation as regards the German Evangelical Church is still far too nebulous for us to come to any decision now.' This may account for the inclusion of the word 'intrinsically' which was later to become such a bone of contention. Heckel and those under his influence regarded it as a limiting term, indeed one that might even have the effect of debarring the congregations from leaving the Reich Church *qua* organization, whereas his opponents were insistent that they had intended to express their total agreement with the Confessing Church as constituted at Dahlem. Bonhoeffer wrote to inform Bell that the step towards union with the Confessing Church had now been definitely taken: 'I am very happy about it', he added.[157]

Copies of the resolution taken in Christ Church were despatched with a covering letter to three separate destinations. The first was sent out by Wehrhan and Schröder on 10th November, together with a letter written on the Association of Congregations' notepaper addressed to Heckel's External Affairs Office:

The German Evangelical congregation in Great Britain have heard with the greatest pleasure that, as a result of the Führer's declarations, the conscious

155. St. Paul's, Sydenham, St. Mary's, St. George's, the Hamburg Church (all in London); Hull, Liverpool, South Shields, Newcastle.
156. There follow 44 signatures, 24 of them from Bonhoeffer's and Rieger's parishes; see GS II, p. 186.
157. Letter of 17.11.1934.

profession of loyalty to the Third Reich and its Führer does not involve adherence to any one church group. These congregations have been based, some of them for centuries, upon the Bible and the Confession, and therefore consider the Confessional Church to be the rightful successor of the German Evangelical Church Federation which they joined in 1928 so as to preserve their connections with the Church at home. The representatives of the German Evangelical congregations who met on 5th November in the German Evangelical Christ Church have therefore unanimously resolved to inform the Church External Affairs Office in Berlin of the foregoing, and at the same time to enter into negotiations with the Confessional Church at Oeynhausen . . .[158]

On 13th November the resolution was sent to the Confessional Synod at Bad Oeynhausen, addressed to Präses Koch, and was accompanied by the request that he should receive Bonhoeffer and Pastor Schönberger for the purpose of negotiating the union. The letter also contained the suggestion that an authority analogous to the External Affairs Office should be set up without delay.[159]

Finally, those in London composed a circular letter to be sent out in the name of the ministers' fraternal in Great Britain to other German pastors abroad.[160] The letter contained an account of their resolutions and expressed the hope that this was only a prelude to official action by the Confessional Synod. At the same time they asked their fellow clergy to state their opinion of the London action as soon as possible so that negotiations could be conducted with the Confessional Synod upon 'as broad a basis' as possible.

First Reactions

1. Before the responsible parties in London had sent the communication described above to the Church External Affairs Office, Heckel had already received private information about the 5th November gathering. He at once realized that this represented an extremely serious threat, much more serious than that of the February crisis, and that it could jeopardize his hard-won position. His first action was to ring up the London embassy early on the morning of 13th November. A minute recording this telephone call was sent from London to the Reich Chancellory and was brought to Hitler's attention. The minute read:

Bishop Heckel rang up Prince Bismarck early this morning and told him that he had been informed that the German Evangelical churches, in close collaboration with Baron Schröder, had unanimously resolved to join the German Confessional Church. Because he believed this could be followed by unfavourable international repercussions, Heckel asked Bismarck to contact

158. GS II, pp. 186 f.
159. GS II, p. 187.
160. GS II, pp. 188 f.

Baron Schröder in order temporarily to delay this step which, in view of the fact that the clarification in German internal church affairs was not yet complete, he described as at best premature . . .

Bismarck replied that the ambassador . . . would be unable, without instructions from the Ministry of Foreign Affairs, to undertake on his own initiative what Bishop Heckel had asked . . .

I would request . . . guidance on this point. Hoesch.[161]

Next, Heckel sent for the Liverpool pastor, K. H. Schreiner, with whom as a fellow Bavarian he had a personal link.

Meanwhile the bishop had been calculating on the supposition that the National Bishop would follow Rechtswalter Jäger into disgrace and compulsory retirement. The larger regional churches were working for Müller's overthrow, theological faculties were sending in resolutions signed by the overwhelming majority of their professors requesting his removal, and even moderate German Christians were expressing their dissatisfaction with the National Bishop. Heckel himself joined in this game. In a confidential letter addressed to the pastors abroad on 14th November he intimated:

The resignation from office of the former Rechtswalter was an unmistakable symptom of crisis; it was in no way a solution . . .

I would beg you, my brethren in the ministry, to believe me if I say no more than . . . that I have, in the course of the past days and weeks, discussed openly and frankly with the National Bishop the need for a genuine ecclesiastical decision. With the consent of all my colleagues I made several definite suggestions.

Needless to say, Heckel had no intention of helping to consolidate the Confessional Synod's emergency church government. Indeed, in his letter he asseverated his intention of 'preserving the independence of German church work abroad in the face of the demands of factions and opinions within the Church'; the work abroad, like 'the External Affairs Office, should be above all differences'. Yet it was being rumoured that Heckel, not content with joining in the assault upon the National Bishop —now an easy target—was actually on the point of going over to the Confessing Church. This rumour was also current in London and inspired Wehrhan to write in the name of the London pastors to Präses Koch. The letter, dated 13th November, expresses reserved approbation at the prospect of Heckel's move, but adds that the bishop's tortuous policy in February had, in their view, disqualified him for any ecclesiastical office.

In common with the Liverpool pastor, Schreiner, Heckel now decided that the section of the London resolution which appeared to reflect on the acceptability of the National Bishop should be allowed to stand; the

161. For full text, see MW V, VIII, B.2

other section, however, concerning union with the Confessional Synod, should be temporarily withdrawn and eventually dropped altogether. This would mean stopping the London deputation to Präses Koch. Hence Pastor Schreiner and a number of others called at the Reich Chancellory in Berlin to present the protest of the German congregations in England against Ludwig Müller.[162] He indicated that a widening of the breach with the Reich Church could only be prevented by Müller's resignation. In addition Schreiner wrote on 16th November to Baron Schröder and Pastor Rieger about his Berlin talks, some of which had been 'with leading members of the confessional front'. The latter, too, had assured him that relations between the congregations abroad and the External Affairs Office should not be upset; 'the evidence has only intensified my fears that this secession[163] might well be a premature move'. In his letter to Rieger, Schreiner also criticized Bonhoeffer whose account of things he described as inaccurate and generally too pessimistic. There followed what was then a favourite expression in uncommitted circles, '. . . we don't have to play at being confessing heroes'. The 5th November resolution, he continued, was a good weapon and could do no harm 'provided it has no further repercussions'.

While Bonhoeffer was, of course, open to the charge of inaccuracy, this was only because he stressed and delineated the most forward-looking elements in a situation and would take no account of objections and representations from the uncommitted centre. It all depended who succeeded in gaining whose ear in the broad 'confessional front'. Schreiner, therefore, implored the brethren in London to proceed no farther. After consulting Baron Schröder, however, they refused to be deflected from their proposed plans or, when the Liverpool pastor returned, to have anything more to do with him.

Yet this visitor provided Heckel with proof that the front in England was not wholly united and he had gained detailed knowledge that was to be helpful in framing future policy.

Hence, on 16th November, Heckel wrote his first official reply to the senders of the 5th November London resolution. In it he expressed his regret that so momentous a decision should have been based on insufficient information and made without prior verbal consultations. He contested the Confessing Church's legal status as a church on the grounds that it had not yet been publicly recognized as such by the State. The former Church Federation's rightful successor as a partner to the agreement with the congregations abroad could only be the German Evangelical Church which had been validated by the legislation signed by the Führer on 14th July 1933. Heckel further declared that the Association of German Evangelical Congregations was not empowered to speak for the congregations in questions of secession which would require individual notice in writing from each of the vestries.

162. MW V, VIII, B.3.   163. Separation from the Reich Church.

Indeed, this was a procedural matter which had so far been overlooked in England and from what he had gathered during Schreiner's visit Heckel could be fairly certain that such decisions would not be taken with the same unanimity as the general resolution on 5th November.

Heckel was further able to detract from the effect of the circular letter sent from London to fellow clergy in other parts of Europe. He won over H. Rössler who was pastor of the German community at Heerlen in Holland and who, on 16th November, sent out a message to the West European Pastors' Convention, comprising the German clergy in Holland, Belgium, Luxemburg and France, in which he urged them to refrain from further action in support of the Confessing Church. In his circular letter Rössler wrote:

... The Confessional Synod, citing the Reich Ministry of Justice, proclaims a state of emergency law according to which the legislation enacted by Müller's church government has been invalidated since the implementation of the new church constitution. In total disregard of the existing church government, the Synod proposes to effect a fundamental legal reconstruction on the basis of the church constitution of 11th July 1933. Conversely, Hitler, as the mouthpiece of the State, has declared that profound disappointment in the course taken by the church dispute has led him to adopt a neutral and impartial attitude to the church struggle as such. Although it will have been considerably relieved by this declaration, the Confessional Synod can hardly hope, in view of the statement made last week by Minister of the Interior, Frick, to be accorded corporative rights by the State.

This is a matter for serious anxiety, for if the Third Reich should dissociate itself altogether from church affairs, the church struggle might well end with a drift towards the establishment of free churches, as in America. In that event the tie which has existed since Luther's day between the Evangelical Church and the German State would cease to be, and the foreordained community of German Evangelical Church and Third Reich would be destroyed. Whether we in Germany would then find ourselves with one or more free churches in place of the federation represented by the present German Evangelical Church is of minor importance compared with the certain prospect that state subsidies for all church bodies and activities—the evangelical theological faculties, confessional schools and work among the German communities abroad—would be in jeopardy. It would therefore seem obvious that a present total victory for the confessional front would mean the end of the existence of the National Church and the beginning of the growth of free churches—indeed, perhaps even a definitive ecclesiastical schism in German Protestantism ...

This was followed by an apologia for the Church External Affairs Office:

... it has introduced integrity into church administration. We abroad have in consequence until now largely escaped, thanks be to God, the internal dissensions within the Church ...

I can well understand that many brethren in the ministry should feel themselves spiritually related to the Confessional Church and hence fail to understand why they should not simply give way. But as things are now, they would, in so doing, stab the Church External Affairs Office in the back at a time when that office, fully aware of its responsibility for German Protestantism throughout the world, is struggling to find a solution for the whole Church that does not necessitate the complete disintegration of what now exists . . .

This being the position, individual demonstrations by congregations abroad would do more harm than good, quite apart from the fact that congregations abroad which intervene in internal German church disputes may at any time easily incur, but much less easily repudiate, accusations of treason . . . This would be to achieve the very opposite of what we must fight for today— a unified, German Evangelical National Church both for the Third Reich and for Evangelical German culture throughout the world . . .

In 1935, Bonhoeffer informed Präses Koch that there had been a few victories for the Confessing Church in South-West Africa;[164] there were no others for him to report. The Confessional Synod was not viable, and the strong position it had attained by the end of October was gradually lost during the course of November. The Heerlen pastor was right when he said in his circular letter, 'If one is to believe what one hears, the Confessional Synod is torn by profound differences of opinion regarding the situation in general and the course to be pursued, and this impairs its powers of decision.' Hence a letter from the Association of Pastors in England could have little effect, especially since the German congregations in other countries were financially much more dependent on the Jebensstrasse. It would have required infinitely larger resources than were in fact available to induce that discernment and initiative in the congregations abroad which would have made secession a practicable proposition.

2. On 15th November, Präses Koch wrote on behalf of the Confessional Synod, thanking the London pastors and asking Bonhoeffer and Schönberger to come for negotiations on the union. But it would seem that they were led to postpone their journey by the painful controversies that were raging over the formation of the emergency church administration (the 'Provisional Church Administration' which was ultimately set up on 22nd November under Bishop Marahrens).[165]

On 25th November, the evening of Remembrance Sunday, during which Bonhoeffer had joined with his St. Paul's choir in a performance of Brahms' Requiem, he at last left with his colleagues Wehrhan and Schönberger. Before going to Berlin, they stopped at Oeynhausen, but little is known about this visit except that they held discussions, probably on 28th November, with Präses Koch of the Confessional Synod and

164. GS I, p. 226.
165. These weeks later came to be known as 'the Confessing Church's Battle of the Marne'.

Oberkirchenrat Breit of the Provisional Church Administration.

On his arrival in Berlin, Bonhoeffer went to the Ministry of Foreign Affairs where he saw, amongst others, Hans-Bernd von Haeften, now back from Copenhagen. Through him he got to know Adolf Freudenberg, a councillor in the Cultural Department of the Ministry, who was later compelled to emigrate, became a minister and found employment in 'Life and Work'.[166] The fact that some of the protagonists had recourse to this particular quarter with a view to obtaining its eventual protection for the work of the Confessing Church abroad testifies to their optimism about future plans, though these were never, of course, to materialize.

The files of the London parishes and of the Association of Congregations, from which we drew our sources, show that the exchanges between London and the Jebensstrasse were lively and prompt by comparison with the meagre, and soon almost non-existent, correspondence with the Confessional Synod and the Provisional Church Administration. In the case of the latter the initiative and drive lay entirely with London—in other words with Bonhoeffer. For him, the visit to Berlin was in no way decisive since he and his parishes had already, as it were, crossed the Rubicon.

The comparative absence of source material on the relations between the Confessing Church and the congregations abroad can be ascribed, superficially, simply to a shortage both of manpower and of money. Yet there was another more basic reason, and that was the internal quandary of the Provisional Administration which included among its leaders men who held that the Dahlem resolutions had been too extreme; one of these, indeed, was its own chairman, Bishop Marahrens, who explicitly used the term 'confessional *movement*' rather than 'Confessing *Church*'. Marahrens had been selected in the belief that the Reich Government would in consequence be more inclined to recognize the Provisional Church Administration. When that recognition failed to materialize, the consequences of the Dahlem resolutions were rendered wholly ineffectual. Finally, the Provisional Administration was inhibited from venturing into the dangerous zone of foreign relations by its fear of becoming politically suspect.

Hence the emergency organs of the Confessing Church never comprised an office to take care of the congregations abroad, though later Bonhoeffer was to press for this on several occasions.[167] When later General Superintendent Zoellner and the Church Committees superseded Müller's administration, there was no institutionalized organ to maintain relations between the Provisional Administration and the congregations abroad. Thus the initiative taken by London in November 1934 was no longer operative yet still, astonishingly, a minority among the English

166. Cf. A. Freudenberg, 'Visits to Geneva', IKDB, p. 166.
167. GS I, pp. 225 f.

congregations remained loyal to the Confessing Church. The impetus behind the 5th November resolution on secession had been strong enough to determine their future course, independent of institutionalization. This was immediately evident from the obduracy with which they combated Heckel's counter-attacks.

Confrontation

While the London deputation was in Berlin, Schröder wrote to Heckel as follows:

I greatly regret that in your opinion the congregations and myself have erred in sending out our decision without first consulting you. Previous experience led us to conclude that discussions such as took place earlier this year must necessarily prove unfruitful. This step was taken after long and careful consideration and no discussion could have influenced our decision.[168]

When Heckel, who had received no answer to his letter of 16th November, learned that the three pastors were holding discussions in Berlin, he threatened on 28th November to draw the attention of every pastor and every parish individually to the 'false view of the law'.[169] He hoped by this means to deter any waverers.

Meanwhile the National Bishop, who seemed to have survived the difficult period of public demands for his resignation, declared in the official journal of the German Evangelical Church on 27th November: 'I forbid all pastors and church officials to subordinate themselves to the unconstitutional "Provisional Church Government".'[170]

But London was not going to listen to Heckel, and still less to Ludwig Müller. The next step in the former's counter-offensive, therefore, was to write on 10th December to all pastors and parishes and, in more condensed form, to the Association of Congregations.[171] In repeating the representations he had made in his first letter of 16th November, he was careful to show that he knew 'from reliable sources' what was afoot in London and Berlin:

I am sorry to say that two representatives of the London congregations . . . spent some time in Berlin without deeming it necessary so much as to try to discuss matters with the Church External Affairs Office. I am aware of the proposals which they made in official quarters in Berlin respecting the re-organization of church work abroad, proposals which the said persons are in no way legally qualified to make and which, indeed, represent a plan that is wholly impracticable, both on ecclesiastical and on national grounds.[172]

From what I hear, the proposed plans were rejected by those quarters to

168. Letter of 27.11.1934.
169. GS II, p. 190.
170. *Gesetzblatt* of the German Evangelical Church, No. 70, 1934.
171. See GS II, pp. 191 f.
172. This is in the letter to the Association of Congregations, GS II, p. 191.

which they were submitted. The extent to which the two gentlemen's procedure was authorized by the congregations in England is not altogether clear to this office.[173]

Heckel's main target, however, was the 5th November resolution and the way it had been handled: while the tenor of the resolution had been determined by the word 'intrinsically' it had, so Heckel argued, nevertheless provided for negotiations with the External Affairs Office: the resolution could not be valid without an individual written declaration from each congregation; should they make this, however, the congregations would jeopardize their pastors' pension and retirement schemes. He concluded: 'To the best of my knowledge, the action of the Association of Congregations does not have the approval of the Liverpool, Bradford, South Shields and Newcastle congregations.'

This released two separate reactions in London. In the first place they repudiated the aspersions cast by the External Affairs Office upon their national allegiance as implied in Heckel's warnings on 16th November against 'opposition to the constitution sanctioned by the Reich Chancellor' and, more recently, against plans which 'on national grounds' were wholly impracticable. They protested against 'the repetition of this kind of allusion to possible consequences'.[174] They further rejected the attempt to drive a wedge between pastors, congregations and the Association of Congregations.

Secondly, they called in Herr E. Crüsemann, a lawyer and member of the Sydenham congregation, so that he might take retrospective measures that would render the resolution on secession unimpeachable in relation to the congregations' agreements.[175] Baron Schröder wrote to the Jebensstrasse:

. . . with reference to your communications of 28.11. and 10.12. of this year, it is, of course, axiomatic that, in so far as individual congregations here intend to secede from the German Evangelical Church, this would require an express resolution by the vestry concerned.

On 4th January 1935, when London was engulfed in almost impenetrable fog, Bonhoeffer held an extraordinary meeting of his churchwardens. The following is the text of their unanimous resolution:

The vestries of St. Paul's and Sydenham here assembled unanimously declare that they refuse to recognize the present Reich Church Government now administered by National Bishop L. Müller. The congregation of St. Paul's and Sydenham regards as no longer tolerable a church government whose aims and methods are contrary to the most elementary principles of the Protestant faith. The vestries declare further that the Reich Church Government's unevangelical procedure during the past eighteen months has

---

173. In the more detailed communication to the congregations.
174. Letter of 21.1.1935, GS II, p. 194.
175. GS II, p. 192.

severely impaired the reputation of the German nation abroad. The vestries asseverate that they are prepared to recognize the Reich Church constitution as laid down by the Reich law of 15th July 1933 as a legal basis for union, and feel themselves bound, now as hitherto, to a German Evangelical Church having such a basis.[176]

It seems doubtful whether, without Bonhoeffer's strong backing, the congregations in Britain would have been able to overcome their misgivings in the face of Berlin's threats of financial and legal sanctions— threats which could hardly be ignored. On the other hand, so imbued had those congregations become with the free church ambience around them, that they had acquired a need for independence which now asserted itself in the resolution.

For all that, they had no desire to be thought wanting either patriotically or politically, and it was agreed that, 'out of consideration for the political situation', the resolution should not be sent to Berlin until after the Saar plebiscite, that is, until after 13th January 1935.

Inconclusive Results

This resolution was to be the last, for shortly afterwards Bonhoeffer left London. The legalistic details of the London church struggle could no longer hold his interest. Two years after their resolution, the Church External Affairs Office—still administered by Heckel—made contact with Bonhoeffer's former parishes of Sydenham and St. Paul's through his successor, Pastor Boeckheler. Devotedly loyal to their former pastor, the parishioners were still making collections for his preachers' seminary at Finkenwalde. Now they were informed by Dr. Krummacher of the External Affairs Office that their secession had never been placed definitely on record. In other words, the final legal step had been omitted, which meant that a conclusive union with the Confessing Church had never been legally ratified.

Julius Rieger's parish of St. George's became more and more embroiled in difficulties with the office in the Jebensstrasse. When the church celebrated its 175th anniversary, Rieger invited, not the Bishop for External Affairs, Heckel, but the head of the Confessing Church, Präses Karl Koch. Upon this, the grant he had been promised by the External Affairs Office to build an organ was withdrawn and it was only much later, after strong representations had been made, that he was able to obtain the money. St. George's Church was Franz Hildebrandt's first place of refuge after he had been compelled to flee. Although it had been Bonhoeffer's wish that Hildebrandt should take over from him at Forest Hill, the latter could not bring himself to abandon the work in Dahlem where, at the beginning of 1933, the Confessing Church was still in process of formation. But after Niemöller's arrest in 1937, Hildebrandt had to leave

176. The complete minutes, see GS II, pp. 192-4.

precipitately and it was then he took refuge in St. George's Church which, indeed, was to serve many refugees in the same capacity until the very end of the Hitlerian era. Naturally this contributed in no small measure to Rieger's quarrel with the External Affairs Office.

No sooner had Bonhoeffer disappeared from the London scene than the majority of the German congregations in England began to see the church struggle in a different light. Most fell under the spell of a new slogan, coined during the new era of General Superintendent Zoellner's Church Committees, 'the preservation of the National Church'. The files of the English Pastors' Conference reveal that in Bonhoeffer's time it was the phrase 'Bible and Confession' that predominated. After 1936 this was superseded by the words 'concern for the National Church'. Pastor Schönberger ceased to play any role in the cause, devoting himself instead to work on behalf of the National Socialist Party in London. Pastor Wehrhan visited Zoellner in 1936 as the self-appointed spokesman of National Church interests. The minutes of the Pastors' Conference of June 1936 record the isolated remark of one of the participants: 'You will, I hope, not think too ill of me if, having been subjected for years, whether voluntarily or involuntarily, to Bonhoeffer's influence, . . . we now take our stand with the Confessing Church.'[177]

VI PLANS

The decisions taken by the Confessional Synod at Dahlem established the frontiers by which Bonhoeffer's life was to be bounded during the next five years. They led to the creation of the Confessing Church's preachers' seminaries, and Bonhoeffer was summoned home by the Old Prussian Council of Brethren to take charge of one of them. It was to this task that he finally sacrificed his plan to go to India.

India

It was only reluctantly and with a heavy heart that Bonhoeffer gave up his long-standing idea of going to India. This was the third time he had seriously considered it, and never before had he come so close to realizing his desire. His friends among the clergy and theologians found this incomprehensible, for had he not demonstrated to them the need to throw oneself unreservedly into the church struggle? They failed to realize that Bonhoeffer's spiritual ardour concealed a certain scepticism combined with a thirst for knowledge:

. . . since I am becoming daily more convinced that in the West Christianity is approaching its end—at least in its present form, and its present interpre-

177. On sections II and V see also G. Niemöller, 'Die deutschen evangelischen Gemeinden in London und der Kirchenkampf', EvTh, 3, 1959, pp. 131-46.

tation—I should like to go to the Far East before coming back to Germany.

This was written to his brother, Karl-Friedrich, after barely three months in London.[178] In April 1934 he wrote to Erwin Sutz:

How long I shall remain a pastor, and how long in this church, I don't know. Possibly not very long. This winter I'd like to go to India.[179]

From the time of his arrival in London he missed no opportunity of furthering his plan, nor did he allow himself to be deflected from it even by a major crisis, such as that of Fanö. On 22nd May he wrote to his grandmother:

Before I tie myself down anywhere for good, I'm thinking again of going to India. I've given a good deal of thought lately to Indian questions and believe that there's quite a lot to be learnt there. Sometimes it even seems to me that there's more Christianity in their 'paganism' than in the whole of our Reich Church. Of course, Christianity did come from the East originally, but it has been so Westernized and so permeated by civilized thought that, as we can now see, it is almost lost to us. Unfortunately I have little confidence left in the church opposition. I don't at all like the way they're going about things, and really dread the time when they assume responsibility and we may be compelled yet again to witness the discrediting of Christianity. I'm not yet absolutely sure how the Indian plan is going to work out. There's a possibility—but please don't mention this to students and so on—that I might go to Rabindranath Tagore's university. But I'd much rather go to Gandhi and already have some very good introductions from close friends of his. I might be able to stay there for six months or more as a guest. If this is ever arranged and I can manage it financially, I shall go in the winter.[180]

People in Berlin regarded Bonhoeffer's Indian scheme as thoroughly eccentric. Word of it reached Karl Barth, and in writing to Bonhoeffer in October 1936 about other things, he said:

Do you remember that business of 'the next ship but one'? And yet the only thing I have heard about you in ages is the strange news that you intend to go to India so as to learn some kind of spiritual technique from Gandhi or some other holy man and that you expect great things of its application in the West.[181]

Jacobi did everything in his power to dissuade him from these ideas and to induce him to take up the post at the preachers' seminary without further delay. Even Hildebrandt begrudged him the time that would have been required for this trip.

Yet throughout all these months he was busy improving his Far Eastern connections. His acquaintance with C. F. Andrews of the World Alliance opened many doors to him, and in the summer of 1934 Mira Bai, formerly Madeline Slade, an admiral's daughter, returned to Eng-

178. GS II, p. 158.   180. GS II, pp. 181 f.
179. GS I, p. 41.   181. GS II, p. 288.

land. Since 1925 she had been cooperating closely with Gandhi and had become a disciple in his *ashram*. In order to share fully in the Mahatma's fight for freedom, she had turned herself into an Indian, had taught herself weaving and cattle-rearing, and had given up everything she owned. Like Gandhi, she had taken a spell of imprisonment completely in her stride. Bonhoeffer read accounts of her and heard her speak. He studied the writings of Jack Winslow, an expert on Asiatic exercises, and sought out English pacifists who were in sympathy with Gandhi. One of these gave him Beverley Nichols' book *Cry Havoc!* It was Gandhi's way of life that inspired part of Bonhoeffer's sermon on peace at Fanö 'Are we to be put to shame by heathens in the East? Are we to desert those individuals who have staked their lives on this message?'[182]

Reinhold Niebuhr relates that Bonhoeffer corresponded with him from London about his projected Indian journey. Many an evening was spent with Theodor Lang, First Secretary at the German Embassy, who had spent some time in Singapore and was able to give advice about living conditions in the East. He also gave Bonhoeffer his tropical suits, which Frau Lang altered to fit him. Rieger sometimes took part in these deliberations.[183] His enterprise was given unreserved support by Herbert Jehle, at this time a physicist and mathematician at Cambridge, who shared to the full Bonhoeffer's interest in the Sermon on the Mount, as also his pacifist ideas. Bonhoeffer even went to the Wellcome Institute where he underwent tests to see if he was fit for the tropics.

In the late summer of 1934 Fanö temporarily distracted him from his projected trip. Later, there was renewed pressure on him to take on the preachers' seminary, and although this was an almost inescapable demand and one, indeed, that he was willing to meet, it was a decision he continually postponed, largely on account of the proposed journey to India. Finally the Confessional Synod agreed to wait until the spring of 1935 so that he was able to begin making definite plans. He now wished to obtain a personal introduction to Gandhi, and as soon as Bishop Bell returned from the Continent to Chichester that October, Bonhoeffer asked him if he could help. Bell wrote to Gandhi:

A friend of mine, a young man, at present German Pastor in London, Pastor Bonhoeffer, 23 Manor Mount, London S.E.23, is most anxious that I should give him an introduction to you. I can most heartily commend him. He expects to be in India for the first two or three months of 1935. He is intimately identified with the Church Opposition Movement in Germany. He is a very good theologian, a most earnest man, and is probably to have charge of the training of Ordination candidates for the Ministry in the future Confessional Church of Germany. He wants to study community life as well as methods of training. It would be a very great kindness if you could let him come to you.[184]

182. GS I, p. 219.
183. J. Rieger, 'Contacts with London', IKDB, p. 95.
184. Letter of 22.10.1934, GS II, p. 185.

Soon after this, Herbert Jehle tells us, a very friendly letter of invitation arrived from Gandhi. The two friends were invited to live in the Mahatma's *ashram* and to accompany him on some of his journeys.

The invitation, however, arrived just as the events preceding the secession of the London congregations from the Reich Church were reaching their climax. Bonhoeffer could not possibly have abandoned his colleagues and his congregations at that moment. By the time the quarrel with the Church External Affairs Office had begun to die down, the inauguration of the seminary was already imminent and there was no time left for the journey. For a long time Bonhoeffer had been trying to avoid having to choose between India and the seminary, seeing the first, rather, as a necessary preparation for the second. But now, faced with the alternative, he chose Pomerania, where he would have to form his own '*ashram*'—the seminary—without prior experience in the Far East.

In 1928 it was a desire for a wider experience of the world that led to the first Indian project. In 1931 an additional factor was scepticism regarding the Western form of Christianity. And in 1934 Bonhoeffer was motivated by the desire to witness the experiment along the lines of the Sermon on the Mount as exemplified by Gandhi—namely, the purposive exercises and the Indian methods of resistance to a power that was regarded as tyrannous. At that time it would have seemed unthinkable to Bonhoeffer to take part in a conspiracy against Hitler. What he sought was a prototype for passive resistance that could induce changes without violence. His quest concealed an unacknowledged anxiety that the church struggle might become an end in itself and remain satisfied with reiterated confessions and ceaseless activity. What he was aiming at, therefore, was a means of combating Hitler that went beyond the aims and methods of the church struggle while remaining legitimate from a Christian standpoint. For while he supported the church struggle with all his might, he was inwardly seeking another form of legitimate commitment. Bonhoeffer's third attempt to go to India was determined in part by this factor.

Preachers' Seminary

His pastorate, the church struggle, the ecumenical movement and his Indian scheme accounted for all of Bonhoeffer's time and energy. Yet he remained constantly aware of what, since his university days, he had felt to be, not only his greatest pleasure, but also his vocation—the teaching and writing of theology. When he heard of Barth's struggle to retain his professorial chair at Bonn, he began to wonder what his own real job in life should be:

I have just read about Barth's dismissal in *The Times*. I can hardly believe it's true. But if it is, perhaps I ought to come home, so that there's at least one university teacher who's prepared to say these things.[185]

The initial impetus to return to teaching came from his own university —though the form it took was not altogether reassuring. On 9th May the dean of the Berlin faculty, Erich Seeberg, wrote: 'But I have not given up hope that conditions within the Church will become settled enough for you to feel inwardly able to return.'[186] The reason for this friendly letter was a new regulation concerning sabbatical leave. Rust, the Minister for Cultural Affairs, had decreed that leave of absence for university teachers during the summer of 1934 was to be subject to ministerial reappraisal. In this way Bonhoeffer's name was brought before Rust at a time when his reputation did not stand very high in that particular quarter. So well-connected was his family academically, however, that they were able to muster sufficient support to obtain a further extension of Bonhoeffer's leave from the university. But the incident made him reflect on what his final decision ought to be—either 'this, the university, or something quite different . . .'[187]

[I assume] that I shall then have to decide definitely whether or not I shall return to an academic career. I'm not so tremendously keen on it any more, and there seems no reason to suppose I shall feel any keener by this winter. It's just that I'm concerned about the students. But perhaps other ways will be open to me.[188]

Those 'other ways' were to lead to an independent theological chair in the Confessing Church. This was due initially to the shutting down of the Old Prussian preachers' seminaries in March 1934, by order of the National Bishop. Moreover, theological students were no longer able to take examinations unless they could give proof of their 'Aryan' descent. In this way the Confessing Church was ultimately compelled to take into its own hands responsibility for theological training, for colleges, seminaries and examining boards. A start was made in March by the Reformed seminary at Elberfeld where the National Bishop's order to close down was simply ignored, and the Confessing Church found itself obliged to support this establishment. In the autumn of 1934 the Confessing Church set up the first of its own preachers' seminaries when it reopened the institution at Bielefeld-Sieker.

Bonhoeffer was first approached on 4th June with a view to possible participation in this new type of work, but as yet nothing definite was settled. A fortnight later while he was in Berlin to discuss the Fanö invitation with Koch and Niemöller, he raised the project in talks with friends, asking them to let it be known at the next meeting of the

185. To K.-F. Bonhoeffer, Jan. 1934, GS II, pp. 157 f.
186. GS II, p. 179.
187. To J. Winterhager, May 1934, GS II, p. 180.
188. To his grandmother, 22.5.1934, GS II, p. 182.

Council of Brethren that he would be willing to accept the post. The 4th July session of the Old Prussian Council was concerned with the project for a preachers' seminary. Jacobi recommended Bonhoeffer as a possible director but met with some opposition. His proposals in the field of church politics in 1933 were still too vivid in many minds for him to be regarded as either sufficiently pliable or sufficiently discreet for a teaching post in the Church. His influence upon theological students was known, but there was some doubt as to whether he would really toe the reformatory line. Finally Jacobi prevailed over the objectors and Niemöller closed the session with the statement: 'It is agreed that Bonhoeffer may take up the post of director of the Berlin-Brandenburg preachers' seminary on 1st January 1935.'[189]

Bonhoeffer was greatly tempted by the idea of practising theology under the aegis of the Confessing Church, but did not for all that abandon his Indian scheme. No doubt he was also aware that an early return to Germany under the conditions then prevailing would decisively affect the course of his life. He was still uncertain when Hildebrandt arrived from Denmark with a message from Koch to the effect that the Präses would like Bonhoeffer to stay in London, at least over the winter, so as to maintain contact with the ecumenical movement; he wrote to his grandmother: 'It seems to me that this would mean turning down the seminary, which I would really rather regret.'[190] Yet a letter of 11th September to Sutz which contains the passage about Hitler's obduracy and about complicity in the next war,[191] reveals that he was in a state of mental flux, though his comments on the place of theology in the new Germany are far from equivocal:

I am hopelessly torn between staying here, going to India, and returning to Germany to take charge of a preachers' seminary shortly to be opened there. I no longer believe in the University, and never really have believed in it— a fact which used to rile you. Young theologians ought now to be trained throughout in conventual seminaries where the pure doctrine, the Sermon on the Mount and worship are taken seriously as they never are (and in present circumstances couldn't be) at university. It is high time we threw off a restraint that is grounded in theology—and which is, after all, only fear— towards the conduct of the State. 'Open your mouth for the dumb'—who in the Church today realizes that this is the least of the Bible's demands? And then there's the matter of military service and war, etc. etc. . . .[192]

When Hildebrandt returned to Berlin in mid-September after his spell as a locum tenens in London, he brought a message from Bonhoeffer accepting the post of director of the seminary, on condition that he would not have to take it up until the spring of 1935.

189. Information given by F. Hildebrandt.
190. Letter of 19.8.1934, GS II, p. 183.
191. See Ch. VIII, p. 285.
192. GS I, p. 42.

When he had asked Bell for an introduction to Gandhi, he had also requested recommendations to Anglican seminaries and communities. He desired to gain an impression of other traditions before he himself attempted a *vita communis*. Hence in October the bishop wrote on his behalf to Father Talbot of the Community of the Resurrection at Mirfield, to Father Tribe of the Society of the Sacred Mission at Kelham, to Father O'Brien of the Society of St. John the Evangelist at Cowley, to Canon Tomlin of St. Augustine's College, Canterbury and to the Reverend J. R. S. Taylor of Wycliffe Hall, Oxford, the latter being a low church centre, while the others were high church establishments.

He is very anxious to have some acquaintance with our methods in England, both with regard to training for the ministry and with regard to community life. He expects to leave England at the end of December.[193]

The 'end of December' was in fact the time he hoped to leave for India. Bonhoeffer was eventually to visit nearly all the places named above, though not until March 1935, and then more cursorily than he would have wished. For this, church politics were to blame. He went to Mirfield, where he joined in the horary prayers during which Psalm 119 was recited on every day of the week; this was subsequently to be the Bible passage most frequently quoted by Bonhoeffer. Together with Rieger he went to Kelham,[194] but he also visited seminaries belonging to other denominations. He took note of the way in which, for example, among Presbyterians, Congregationalists or Baptists, both the church in general and his own parish in particular influenced the personal life of the candidate during his time of study. He often spoke of the impression left on him by a visit to the Methodist college in Richmond where he had been introduced by a German exchange student, Rudolf Weckerling. In the entrance hall there were boards with long lists of names, each followed by the date of ordination and the date of death, often both in the same year, indicating that for many decades men from the college had been rapidly sacrificed one after the other in the fatal climate of the mission stations. Bonhoeffer also visited the Quakers at their centre in Selly Oak near Birmingham. 'I liked it very much there.'[195]

During the winter he visited Berlin in connection with the delegation that was to negotiate the union of the congregations with the Confessional Synod. He then stayed on so that, during the first days of December, he could go house-hunting in the province of Brandenburg with some of his friends, including Jacobi, Albertz and Hildebrandt. It was essential, he thought, that the work should be done in a place remote from the distractions of Berlin, but as yet he had not decided exactly where this should be.

193. GS II, p. 184.
194. J. Rieger, op. cit., IKDB, pp. 97 f.
195. A postcard written, but not sent, to one 'Ernst', as yet unidentified.

The approaching task acted as a catalyst for everything that had been preoccupying Bonhoeffer during the past few years: a theology of the Sermon on the Mount, a community in service and spiritual exercises, a witness to passive resistance and ecumenical openness. The mood of optimism about his future project which this train of thought induced is reflected in the memorandum addressed to the session of the Ecumenical Youth Commission in Paris on 29th January 1935, at which he could not himself be present. His main premise was the concept pursued by his Berlin students since the time of Fanö.

... it is also there that a group of young Christians are seriously considering the possibility of starting a small Christian community in the form of a settlement or any other form on the basis of the Sermon on the Mount. It is felt that only by a clear and uncompromising stand can Christianity be a vital force for our people. It is also felt that the developments of the church disputes in Germany are tending more and more towards a sort of conservative Christianity which of course would go very well with the rather conservative spirit which is steadily growing under the present Reichswehr and Industry régime. This group would also make a definite stand for peace by conscientious objection . . .

Finally, would you be willing to help me to find some young students or pastors for the Seminary which I am supposed to start in the near future on behalf of the Confessional Synod. I should like to have the ecumenic aspect of it made clear from the beginning. We are now thinking if we could combine the idea of a Christian community mentioned above with the new Seminary. At any rate the support from the ecumenic movements would be most valuable for the carrying out of plans. I know of similar ideas in England among some student groups . . .

De Félice quoted from the above memorandum in the circular letter he sent out from Geneva at the end of February 1935 to the ecumenical youth groups. Two years later Bonhoeffer was to set another project on foot, that of including the seminaries of the Confessing Church in the ecumenical exchange scheme.[196]

Quasi-political Activity

During Bonhoeffer's final weeks in England, he and Bell again began to make demands upon one another in matters extending beyond the framework of the church struggle.

1. The Saar plebiscite was due to take place in January 1935. Bonhoeffer, realizing that the incorporation of that area into the Reich would bring a fresh wave of refugees, organized accommodation for refugee children among his parishioners—no simple matter, in view of the general patriotic fervour stirred up by the plebiscite. An *émigré*

196. See GS I, pp. 268-70.

lawyer prepared a memorandum for him which exposed Britain's double-faced attitude towards the refugees; one of its pages contained the solemn declaration made before the council of the League of Nations that England was proud to provide asylum for the exiles, the next showed the impasse in which the latter had been placed by the law which denied them the right to work. He first passed this memorandum to Bell, who replied by return without, however, being able to offer any solution to the problem.[197] Bonhoeffer estimated the number of refugees from the Saar at from three to five thousand—a mere trickle compared with what came later when the bishop initiated the great campaign of British churches on behalf of refugees.[198] Hildebrandt tells us that Bell even thought of giving up his diocese in order to become the *émigrés'* bishop, and he might well have been described as such when, after the outbreak of war, he used to visit the German refugees interned on the Isle of Man. Both Jews and Christians would say to Hildebrandt: 'I'm in trouble; will you write to the Bishop of Chichester?'

2. Another plan—which in the event proved fruitless—was connected with the Anglo-German *rapprochement* of the winter of 1934-5. Bell had hoped to be able to exploit this for his own ends, but the leaders of the Confessing Church did not know what to make of his proposal, if they understood it at all.

In 1934 Hitler was very anxious to improve his relations with Britain, while the British Government in its turn seemed ready to acknowledge the *status quo*. Trade agreements were negotiated between the two countries, and in March 1935 Anthony Eden and Lord Simon saw Hitler in Berlin. The talks culminated in the Anglo-German naval treaty of 18th June 1935. Among the advocates of equal rights for Germany, internal abuses notwithstanding, were men such as the Archbishop of Canterbury, Cosmo Gordon Lang. It is symptomatic that the *Junge Kirche* thought proper to publish a selection of such pro-German remarks made by English churchmen.[199]

In accordance with Hitler's policy, his envoy extraordinary, von Ribbentrop, called on Bishop Bell at Chichester on 6th November 1934 as has already been related, and was treated to a detailed inventory of complaints about acts of coercion against the Church in Germany. In 1935 Ribbentrop again met the bishop, this time at the Athenaeum, and proposed that when next Bell visited Berlin he should meet Hitler's deputy, Rudolf Hess, and also Kerrl, the newly appointed Minister of Church Affairs. These meetings did in fact take place in September of the same year. This second encounter between Ribbentrop and Bell received far more publicity than the earlier one. It coincided with the

197. GS II, p. 196.
198. Bell did not take his seat in the House of Lords until 1938, when he became a very active member. (*Translator*.)
199. JK, 1935, pp. 559-62.

first release of Protestant pastors, among them Peter Brunner, who had been interned in a concentration camp.

It would not have been in Bell's nature to let so favourable a political opportunity pass. With several of his friends he planned a meeting between leading figures in public life in Britain and eminent members of the Confessing Church to discuss what contribution the churches might make to improve relations between the two countries. He had even found people who were prepared to give the scheme their financial support. It seemed to the bishop that the Confessing Church could only benefit from the political respectability it would thus acquire. Bonhoeffer, with whom he discussed the matter, endeavoured to win over Präses Koch.

Do you still think of the plan of an official British delegation to the Confessional Church on behalf of world peace? The more I think of this idea, the more it strikes me as most important and helpful.[200]

Unfortunately, however, this project was evolved at a time when Präses Koch was also envisaging a delegation, but one of a quite different kind. For the Council of Brethren were then busy preparing an important declaration against the idolatry of 'Blood, Race and *Volkstum*', which would be followed by a new Confessional Synod at Augsburg. The Council, and Koch in particular, would have liked an ecumenical delegation to be present on both occasions, a project that was incompatible with the London plan.

. . . so Chichester doesn't quite know what to do; he thinks his plan would be of benefit to us and has got all sorts of people interested in it (e.g., Dr. Oldham). Bonhoeffer has promised him that you'll be writing again, when you will clear up what was perhaps only a linguistic misunderstanding and will state your intentions about the peace delegation plan . . .[201]

But it proved impossible to carry out the plan, though Bell and the Archbishop of Canterbury had already held discussions with von Hoesch and von Bismarck at the German Embassy.[202]

This did not, however, exclude the possibility that Bell might comply with Koch's wish that he should visit the synods. When Bonhoeffer took leave of him in April 1935, Bell asked him to take a message to the Präses, '. . . assuring him of my sympathy and my desire to help in case of need.'[203]

Return

Bonhoeffer so arranged his transfer from the pastorate to the seminary as not to preclude a possible return, a precaution he never failed to take as long as circumstances allowed.

200. D. Bonhoeffer to G. Bell, 7.1.1935, GS II, pp. 195 f.
201. F. Hildebrandt to Koch, 12.1.1935, see MW V, X, F.1.
202. According to J. Rieger's diary. 203. GS II, p. 198.

In 1933, after he had taken up his ministry in London, the Foreign Department of the German Evangelical Church had suggested that he resign from his post as lecturer at Berlin University. This caused Bonhoeffer to obtain a resolution from the church-wardens of Sydenham and St. Paul's stating that he should not resign from his teaching post, since the times demanded no post should be left voluntarily but only under compulsion. Now, on 11th February 1935, he asked the vestry to record in their minutes that he was leaving London on sabbatical leave, initially for a period of six months, and that during that time his locum tenens was to be Pastor Boeckheler from Hull. When in 1939 he again proposed to strike out in a new direction, he exercised the same caution, but that was to be the last time, for subsequently he was to burn all his boats.

Such remarkably consistent procedure when changing jobs cannot be ascribed simply to a desire for security, in which case he would have showed more concern for his rights as a member of the clerical profession. He set little store by such privileges, however, and it may be supposed that he was prompted rather by his desire for freedom, his anxiety not to be wholly dependent on one employer, not even the Councils of Brethren. Hence he took steps to keep open any post that he had to leave.

Bonhoeffer preached his farewell sermon before his congregations on 10th March 1935. There were collections in all the churches for the Third Reich's *Winterhilfe*, but it was to the second collection in aid of German refugees in England that Bonhoeffer himself attached particular importance. Before leaving the country he went on his round of communities and colleges, taking in Scotland and a visit to John Baillie, his former teacher at Union Theological Seminary in New York.

Bonhoeffer's return to Germany coincided almost exactly with Karl Barth's departure, which had now become inevitable. Barth's refusal to take the unconditional oath that was incumbent on all civil servants had brought him into conflict with the National Socialist State—a struggle which he had fought unaided by the Confessing Church. Thus at a time when Bonhoeffer was preparing himself for his return, Barth retired to Basle. Both men had been at considerable pains, both inside and outside Germany, to uphold, and indeed to emphasize, the distinction between the church struggle and political resistance to the Nazi régime. In the fifth volume of his *Theological Existence Today*, Barth wrote:

Above all I would like to point out that to interpret the church opposition in Germany as actual resistance to the present State is to misunderstand its character . . . I am not a National Socialist. But that has nothing at all to do with the controversy I am conducting in these pages . . .[204]

204. K. Barth, 'Die Kirche Jesu Christi', ThEx, No. 5, 1933, pp. 7 f.

That passage was written at the end of 1933. Was it an attitude that admitted of no change? When, in May 1934, Bonhoeffer wrote to thank Bell for his Ascensiontide message, he said: '. . . this letter will help the opposition to see that this whole conflict is not only within the Church, but strikes at the very roots of National Socialism.'[205] In July, after Frick had issued the decree forbidding all public controversy over the church struggle, he wrote: 'I hope that the pastors will this time dare to come up against the State.'[206] At this period Bonhoeffer did not expect the Church to provide a new political conception, either in opposition to Hitler, or for the time that would follow his overthrow. Yet he felt that the Church could only justify her existence in so far as she spoke out upon questions of tyranny and on behalf of its victims. Would this in fact take place in Germany?

When Bonhoeffer was back in Berlin during the Easter vacation, the first ordinands began to arrive at Niesel's office. They had been waiting since March to be summoned to the new seminary and were about to be temporarily accommodated in Burckhardt House, when, on 25th April, they were offered the loan of the Rhineland Bible School at Zingst on the Baltic until the beginning of the summer season. The place was still intensely cold, but there was little doubt that it would be deserted. So, on 26th April, the candidates, along with their director, who was little older than themselves, made their way to the cabins among the dunes on the Baltic coast.

205. Letter of 15.5.1934, GS I, p. 194.
206. Letter of 12.7.1934, GS II, p. 177.

CHAPTER NINE

PREACHERS' SEMINARY

1935

'THE summer of 1935 . . . has been the fullest time of my life, both from the professional and from the human point of view',[1] Bonhoeffer wrote in a letter to the members of his first session at the seminary. At last he had embarked on work about which he had no reservations, whereas previously he was ridden by the thought that he had not yet found his true task in life. Now his new calling afforded him the opportunity of doing what he had always longed to do.

The compact, closed circle of students enabled him to devote all his energies to his new theological theme, discipleship. And the work could be carried out under the auspices of the Church. The living community, about which Bonhoeffer had thought so much during the past four years, was now to be realized through a *praxis pietatis*, that provided an ambience favourable to the development of his theological ardour.

A preachers' seminary had once seemed to him a place to be avoided; now it was the place where, for a few years, his doubt and unrest were to make way for the satisfaction of meaningful activity. His search for other and more worthwhile work ceased. It was a delight to him to confirm young theologians in their calling in the hard-pressed Church and to share with them, not only his gifts, but everything he possessed. Those students who were meeting him for the first time were surprised to find that the director of their seminary was always ready to make himself available.

I THE SEMINARIES

Apart from a very few special institutions, preachers' seminaries as a whole were a late (and to many undesirable) invention of the territorial churches which had incorporated them into their general theological training schemes. By tradition, theological training—as opposed to 'education'—was largely in the hands of state-appointed university teachers. The study of theology and the research it involved were held of themselves to constitute an education; consequently theological education was not regarded as an independent activity and was, on the whole, neglected. By the twentieth century, however, the churches had

1. GS II, p. 458.

recognized the need to acquire some influence over young ordinands before they entered the ministry. Yet it proved difficult to set up seminaries in their own right, able to assert themselves and to acquire their own particular imprimatur in the face of existing academic institutions. Their syllabus was dictated by academic tradition and hence the seminaries had to go over the same ground already covered by the universities where the students had enjoyed, not only greater freedom, but probably also a higher level of instruction.

The more ancient and reputable seminaries such as Loccum, Wittenberg or the Berlin Cathedral Seminary were formerly élite establishments for those with the highest results in the university examinations. They provided, as it were, a sinecure for brilliant students to devote themselves to theological research. In some ways they resembled a college of fellows such as All Souls at Oxford and were, no doubt, very useful institutions, yet their very existence confirmed the inadequacy of the Church's own conception of education. At the turn of the century, the number of seminaries increased and attendance at one of them was made compulsory—though not until 1928 in the churches of the Old Prussian Union. Of the two years between first and second examinations, six months—or at the very most twelve—were allocated to this part of the training. And even that was regarded as a waste of time by ordinands such as Bonhoeffer and Hildebrandt.[2]

Now, however, things had changed fundamentally, the stepchild having become the darling of the Church. The severe crisis convulsing the university faculties and the territorial churches compelled the Confessing Church to set up new preachers' seminaries. What happened next was little short of miraculous; under the anonymity conferred upon them by their comparative obscurity, the new seminaries were able to turn themselves into remarkable power centres of theology. They were able to carry on their work unmolested and with fewer interruptions than were the high schools[3] of the churches; these had come into being at the same time as the seminaries, but because they had been set up in open opposition to the state faculties, thus achieving immediate notoriety, and had been banned on the day of their inauguration, 1st November 1935, they were immediately forced underground.

But the seminaries, although they owed their immediate existence to the daily struggle of the churches of the Old Prussian Union, were themselves to remain outside the fray for some considerable time. Indeed, they enjoyed two and a half years of intensive work before the police came to seal their doors. Yet while they were still in their heyday, the State was already taking measures that would one day relegate them

2. Cf. Ch. III, p. 87.
3. Compared with the seminaries which were preparatory institutions for ordinands, the church high schools virtually competed with the faculties up till the first examinations.

into hopeless 'illegality'. Nor was it to be very long before Bonhoeffer, his superiors and his ordinands would be carrying out their work at the seminary in direct contravention of the express injunctions of the State.

Church Politics of the State

In 1935 the Confessing Church had reached the peak of its development as an organization. This was a time when there still seemed to be a reasonable prospect of success for the church opposition, particularly as regards the Dahlem resolutions. The Councils of Brethren were still hoping that the State and the territorial churches would eventually recognize the Dahlem decisions concerning emergency church bodies. The fiasco of the German Christians was evident to all, and Ludwig Müller's fortunes seemed to be definitely on the wane.

On the other hand, 1935 saw the early phase of the legislation that would ultimately bring about the destruction both from within and from without of the newly created Confessing Church. Three laws were passed, the first signed by Göring and the other two by Hitler. To all appearances these were measures taken by a patient arbitrator, the State, to restore order among the squabbling pastors.

1. In March 1935 the Prussian State set up *finance departments* for 'legal aid' to the churches of the Old Prussian Union. Allegedly they were to protect the congregations' property and charities, but in fact their sole endeavour was to bring, little by little, all congregational and provincial church offices under state jurisdiction.

2. In June 1935 the Reich Government created a *legislative authority* for the administration of legal matters in the German Evangelical Church. The Confessing Church had been wholly successful in its appeals to the normal courts, but the legislative authority was to inhibit such procedure. The activities of this body made severe inroads into the Church's own administration of its canon law.

3. In July 1935, Hitler established the Ministry of Church Affairs under the leadership of Hanns Kerrl. Initially this aroused vague hopes that, by bringing to an end the era of Ludwig Müller, Hitler intended to make a new start. But September 1935 brought to light the instrument by means of which Kerrl meant to administer the Church. This was the *Law for the Protection of the German Evangelical Church* which eventually contained seventeen clauses. Its repercussions were to be greater than those of the other decrees, for it brought about the ultimate disintegration of the Confessing Church by creating irreparable schisms within her ranks.

Thus the year which saw the foundation of Bonhoeffer's seminary brought about a fundamental change in the course of the church struggle. What had previously been a tussle with the German Christians and their methods now seemed simple by comparison; indeed, it had not been without its lighter side and had, besides, given a new lease of life to the old concepts of heresy. But now a position must be assumed in direct opposition to the State, involving the contravention of its laws. Did Romans 13, as so far understood, apply to the present situation? And was the insistent emphasis on the need to distinguish between internal church resistance and political resistance now coming home to roost? To attack the Church through the German Christians had been a relatively clumsy device on the part of the National Socialist régime which, however, had since discovered just where its opponent's internal weakness lay; consequently its new offensive was likely to be far more dangerous and insidious. The Protestant Church was not in the habit of opposing state legislation, but from 1935 onwards it was becoming increasingly clear that resistance would have to be offered.

To begin with, however, the seminaries of the Old Prussian Confessing Church felt little anxiety. They had arisen out of the movement of protest against Ludwig Müller and this gave their beginnings a special impetus. The work was not the result of any official decree but ordinands, clergy and presbyteries had themselves urged the 'official' Councils of Brethren finally to open their own seminaries. For the young ministers, the seminaries would provide living proof that the Councils of Brethren were in earnest, both as regards themselves and as regards their claim, and that they were not afraid of incurring risks. The students considered the primitive conditions attendant upon the early stages as a privilege and believed that eventually a clash with the official church or with the state authorities would be unavoidable. All this had a stimulating effect upon the 'young brethren' who helped to build up the seminaries.

Old Prussian Seminaries

Five preachers' seminaries were set up and maintained by the Old Prussian Council of Brethren. The Reformed seminary at Elberfeld under Pastor Hermann Hesse was the first to start work at the behest of the Council of Brethren in 1934. November of that year saw the opening of the seminary at Bielefeld-Sieker under Professor Otto Schmitz. The remainder were set up in 1935; one in East Prussia at Bloestau under Professor H. J. Iwand, another in Silesia at Naumburg on the Queis under Pastor Dr. G. Gloege, and the third in Pomerania under Bonhoeffer. It had originally been planned to have the latter in the Rhineland and for some time the ordinands had been expecting to be summoned to Düsseldorf.

The five directors had been skilfully chosen; they aroused the interest of young theologians, they had earned a reputation for scholarship and had demonstrated their spirit of determination. The placing of ordinands was determined very largely by their home districts, though an attempt was also made to have representatives from as many of the provinces of the Old Prussian Union as possible in each of the houses.

When Bonhoeffer's seminary opened in the summer term, the Old Prussian Council of Brethren had found some hundred ordinands for its five seminaries. The responsible official in the Council of Brethren was Wilhelm Niesel who, incidentally, had been a contemporary of Bonhoeffer's elder brother at the Friedrichswerder School. Upon Niesel's shoulders fell the main burden for equipping, financing and coordinating the seminaries and for the allocation of the ordinands.

By opening these five seminaries, the leadership of the Old Prussian Union Council of Brethren took upon itself a tremendous burden of responsibility. Since the Dahlem Synod's emergency resolution and directive the great majority of ordinands in the churches of the Old Prussian Union had subordinated themselves to the government of the Council of Brethren who, they hoped, would train and ordain them and send them out to work with congregations. They expected that demands should be made on them, but also that their needs should be provided for.

But the opening of the five seminaries also marked a phase in the church struggle which was to bring about a profound estrangement between the so-called 'intact'[4] Lutheran churches and the 'destroyed' churches of Old Prussia. For the financial and legal problems in connection with the 'young brethren' and their training as prescribed by the Dahlem resolutions did not apply to the 'intact' churches where these things were provided for in the traditional way. But the Councils of Brethren in the 'destroyed' churches had to find means where none existed, and to evolve completely new forms in a situation of illegality. Provision had to be made from voluntary gifts as need arose. Yet this fine achievement of the Councils of Brethren only served to isolate them from the churches of other provinces.

In cases where intact churches such as those of Bavaria or Württemberg disassociated themselves step by step, first from the common resolution of Dahlem, then from the notice of disobedience towards the Reich Church Government, and lastly from the declaration of the emergency church measures, their inner structure remained unimpaired. But the Council of Brethren, even had they considered such disassociation, would not have been able to negate the consequences of the Dahlem resolution. They remained responsible for the mass of those who had followed the call of Dahlem and all that was implied by that call.

When, after the Barmen Synod, the Lutheran Council was formed alongside the government of the Confessing Church, thus establishing

4. Regional churches which had retained their old leadership and had thus preserved their inner unity; by contrast, the 'destroyed' churches were those in which the German Christians had disrupted the existing order and the Confessing Church had set up emergency governments alongside official church governments that were subservient to the Nazis.

an advisory body unhampered by emergency church business, there was yet another cause for mutual and embittered disclaimers. The men of the Old Prussian Council of Brethren denied the Lutherans the right to use the name 'Confessing Church', and allowed them instead to use only the term 'confessional *movement*' or 'confessional *front*'. The Lutherans, on the other hand, castigated their opponents as 'Dahlemites', a name which was to become almost synonymous with 'radical fanatic' and was attached more especially to those responsible for the seminaries.

II ZINGST AND FINKENWALDE

Bonhoeffer had had a very precise and comprehensive idea of what the internal structure and the syllabus of the new institution was to be; by comparison its beginnings were but improvised and exiguous in the extreme.

As the director of the institution, he was in the employment of the Old Prussian Council of Brethren and was to remain so until the end of his life although later he would be technically on leave. His stipend was 360 marks a month. The circumstances of his appointment subsequently spared him many of the harassments suffered by pastors officially appointed by the church of the province, as we shall see later, because he was not required to swear the oath of loyalty to Hitler.[5]

The Council of Brethren appointed as his assistant a young Rhineland pastor, Wilhelm Rott (born 1908). A product of the school of Karl Barth, Rott belonged to the Reformed tradition of the Rhineland; by many his appointment was regarded as a sensible step in that he would to some extent counterbalance Bonhoeffer's influence on the ordinands. Rott himself was quite unaware of any such intention. He was able to make his own mark on the seminary's communal life and theological dialogue, thereby constituting an independent and responsible element. This was not easy, for a number of the ordinands had formerly been Bonhoeffer's students in Berlin and had taken part in the Fanö delegation, so that from the first the balance was in favour of the director and his own particular imprimatur. However Rott good-naturedly adhered to the principle that 'of course it could be done another way';[6] both he and Bonhoeffer were, moreover, much too magnanimous to allow themselves to be played off against one another.

The majority of students came from Berlin-Brandenburg. Some of them had heard Bonhoeffer's lectures on 'Creation and Sin' and on Christology or had taken part in the seminar on Hegel; they knew of the Prebelow and Biesenthal experiments in meditation.

Three groups came from Pomerania, East Prussia and the province of Saxony (Halle-Magdeburg), the author of this book being from the

5. See Ch. XI, pp. 503 ff.
6. W. Rott, 'Something Always Occurred to Him', IKDB, p. 132.

latter. These students knew nothing about Bonhoeffer and their anticipation of what lay before them was tinged by their provincial outlook. For the four ordinands from the province of Saxony, Bonhoeffer's seminary represented their second attempt to train at such an establishment. At the time of the Dahlem Synod they had been attending the Wittenberg seminary where in conformity with synodal instructions they had refused obedience to Ludwig Müller's church government. The National Bishop had then telegraphed an order for their expulsion from the seminary.

Zingst

A few days elapsed before all twenty-three candidates had arrived and been housed in the Zingsthof cabins. The place turned out to be an ideal refuge. Little more than a hundred yards from the beach and the dunes lay a timber-framed house surrounded by subsidiary buildings with low thatched roofs; the whole complex extended as far as the heath. No other farmhouse was visible, while the village of Zingst lay a mile or more to the west. From the dunes, in good weather, it was possible to see Hiddensee to the east and beyond it the island of Rügen. The members of the seminary would have been only too glad to spend the whole summer at Zingst. Whenever the May sun shone warm enough, the classes would adjourn to a hollow among the dunes where they would hold a discussion or perhaps sing a setting for four voices by Josquin des Prés. But on the 14th June they had to move out. Hence the early days of the seminary were disturbed by the need to find a fixed place of abode.

After their removal from Zingst and before they settled down in their permanent house, the men spent ten days in youth hostels at Greifswald.[7] Meanwhile an advance party was preparing the new quarters.

Finkenwalde

Out of all the houses that had been considered, from Lake Constance to the Ziethen Castle near Neuruppin, the choice fell upon the former estate of the von Katte family, in the small country town of Finkenwalde. Finkenwalde was the first station on the main railway line from Stettin to the east. To the north and the west were the waters of the Oder estuary and to the south the land rose towards the green of the beechwoods. The estate had been very much spoiled by the inroads of

7. In his endeavour to give the work of the seminary an ecumenical orientation (cf. p. 336), Bonhoeffer made contacts with the Swedish Church with a view to a possible visit in order to make profitable use of this interval (cf. introduction to MW V, IX). This plan was to be realized in a different form and another situation in March 1936 (see p. 420).

commercial undertakings; a further half of the grounds had been turned into a gravel-pit, and the roomy house, which had been used for a private school, had been enlarged by the addition of a jerry-built gymnasium and a number of useful extra rooms. The private school had fallen victim to the disfavour with which the National Socialists viewed such establishments, and a new tenant was wanted for the building. Unattractive as much of it was, its many rooms were perfect for the requirements of a seminary.

By the time Bonhoeffer gave his first lecture in the almost empty house on 26th June, the advance party had already sent out to the confessing congregations letters containing the 'Ordinands' Humble Request', a poem by Winfried Maechler. This evoked a tremendous response not only from congregations, but also from individual patrons. The church struggle was still at the stage when people wanted to give tangible expression to their feelings, and when rich men could still be found to support the opposition. Seldom can any preachers' seminary in Germany have become, as did Finkenwalde, the living concern of congregations.

The gifts continued over the years. At the time of the harvest thanksgiving, boxes of fruit and an enormous joint of meat arrived from the Kleist estates. One March day in 1937 the telephone rang: 'This is the goods yard. A live pig has just arrived for Pastor Bonhoeffer.' The slaughtering and processing of the animal presented something of a problem for in those days a special permit was required. Somehow, that permit was obtained.

Bonhoeffer and many of the ordinands took part in furnishing and decorating the house. The music room already contained two Bechstein grand pianos which were constantly in use. The loose covers on the chairs had all been made by Ewald von Kleist-Schmenzin's mother in person. The sculptor, Wilhelm Gross, helped the students to transform the gymnasium into a chapel by means of whitewash, packing cases and hessian, and Gross himself carved the heavy wooden cover of the altar Bible. On the end wall in shining gold letters stood the strategic word 'HAPAX', from the Epistle to the Hebrews (9: 26-8), 'once and for all'. The Greek word expresses with the utmost concision the first Christocentric principle confessed at Barmen against the German Christians' false doctrine of revelation in contemporary history. Every week a different series of drawings and etchings from Rembrandt's Bible illustrations were hung in the entrance hall. These were out of a large Dutch edition owned by Bonhoeffer. His collection of gramophone records, which for those days was remarkable, was at everyone's disposal and the rooms often rang with then little known Negro spirituals such as 'Swing low, sweet chariot . . .'

To build up a working library from nothing proved more difficult. Bonhoeffer provided the basic stock with his fine collection of reference books, commentaries and histories of dogma from Berlin. He also placed at the library's disposal the Erlangen edition of Luther which he had inherited from his von Hase great-grandfather. His way of making free with his most valuable possessions for the benefit of all and sundry was a tremendous inspiration. When, two and a half years later, the police dissolved the seminary, Bonhoeffer's collection of books became scattered, and he was never again able to reassemble them all in one place.

Curriculum and Methods of Work

The improvisation, the wandering life, the lack of books and the church struggle might well have impeded the success of the training and work of the first Finkenwalde course. But there were two things which prevented these distracting influences from gaining the upper hand. These were the daily time-table laid down by Bonhoeffer and the inspiration provided by his system of work.

The programme for the day began and ended with two long services. In the morning the service was followed by half an hour's meditation, an exercise that was not interrupted by the circumstances of the removal, though packing cases and youth hostel bunks were the only furniture. The services did not take place in church but round the ordinary dinner-table. They invariably began with a Psalm and a hymn specially chosen for the day. There followed a lesson from the Old Testament, a set verse from a hymn (sung daily for several weeks), a New Testament lesson, a period of extempore prayer and the recital of the Lord's Prayer. Each service concluded with another set verse from a hymn. Readings from the Psalms and the Scripture took the form of a *lectio continua*, for preference without any omissions. In structure this very much resembled Anglican evensong. Bonhoeffer believed that this sequence of readings and prayers was the most natural and suitable form of service for theologians. It was only on Saturdays that he also included a sermon, which was usually very direct. The ordinands discovered that he liked to choose hymns such as Tersteegen's '*Kommt, Kinder, lasst uns gehen*', Michael Weisse's '*O ihr alle, die ihr euch im Herrn vereiniget*', and Christian Friedrich Richter's evocative poem, '*Sie wandeln auf Erden und leben im Himmel*'.

Bonhoeffer did not look kindly on attempts to evade this daily routine. To obviate the dangers arising from too much proximity and the restless weeks of the removal, he asked the ordinands to observe only one rule—never to speak about a fellow ordinand in his absence or, if this should happen, to tell him about it afterwards. Almost as much was learnt from the failure to observe this simple rule and from the renewed resolution to keep it as from sermons and exegeses. Bonhoeffer was able to impose this discipline on the seminary because he did not begrudge them time for pleasure or exclude outspoken discussion.

Sometimes in fine weather he might suddenly break off a lesson and go with his students to the woods or the coast. On Sundays he allowed no class work to be done, but would organize every imaginable recreation. When he discovered the inadequacy of his students' literary background he gave them readings from Keller, Stifter and Droste-Hülshoff's *Judenbuche*; the latter was deliberately chosen. However, when he wanted to introduce the practice of reading aloud during meals, voices were raised in protest against such a monkish custom; nevertheless some books were read in this way—C. B. Büchsel's *Erinnerungen aus dem Leben eines Landgeistlichen*, and Agnes von Zahn-Harnack's biography of her father, Adolf von Harnack. But Bonhoeffer's proposal to substitute a light meal for the heavy German lunch, with the principal meal in the evening, met with insurmountable opposition.

What was truly impressive was his love of music-making which manifested itself in his performance, when he could be induced to play for others, as well as in his readiness to explore musical areas hitherto unknown to him. His romantic leanings came strongly to the fore in his playing of Chopin and Brahms, or of excerpts from the delightfully subtle *Rosenkavalier*. But no request that he should join in one of Bach's concertos for two pianos was ever made in vain. While he was at Finkenwalde, he was introduced to what was for him the new world of Schütz, Schein and Scheidt, and he would love to sing one of the voices in Schütz's duets, '*Eins bitte ich vom Herren*', and '*Meister, wir haben die ganze Nacht gearbeitet*'.

Clearly this was all part of the practice of communal and fraternal living, as also of the personal education of the future preachers. The process, however, relied more on indirect intimations than on actual instruction. In England Bonhoeffer had heard of a pledge given by Baptist students before entering a seminary in which they affirmed their intention to become a preacher and undertook to conduct themselves accordingly. As early as the second day at Zingst the opportunity arose for him to demonstrate the lesson of this personally to the brethren. A request arrived from the kitchen for help with the washing-up but there were no immediate volunteers. Without saying a word Bonhoeffer rose from the table, disappeared into the kitchen and refused admission to those who hastened to follow suit. Later, when he rejoined the students on the beach, he made no comment. And in Finkenwalde many a student was to discover with shame that someone else had made his bed in the big dormitory.

His method of work was especially remarkable. What would have seemed to another a normal day's task he would accomplish in two or three hours. Even at the most hectic moments of his career he never forfeited his leisure time. His desk was very far from being a model of tidiness; in any case it was not nearly big enough and had only two small pigeon-holes. Not that he could have done with more, for he had no fondness for card indexes and coloured pencils. He had an excellent memory upon which he could rely. He was also a very fast reader, and his only notes were an occasional line or question mark written in the margin with a blunt pencil. For teaching or discussion, however, he would make notes from what he had read.

While he was at Finkenwalde, exegetic literature took pride of place. However contestable his 'theological exegesis' of that time may seem to us today, there is no reason to suppose that he failed to appreciate the quality of contemporary works, or what was then the comparatively new method of Kittel's *Theological Word Book*, and the results this produced. In fact, he was careful to keep in touch with current theological knowledge. After exegetic literature, he concerned himself chiefly with the fathers of the Reformation and with confessional writings, but showed small interest in church history. While he could absorb an enormous amount, he seldom reproduced what he read undigested. By his own questioning and evaluation he would sift it, and brilliantly exploit it for his own purposes. He had confidence in his own ability to recognize the essential, yet would listen objectively to the argument of a specialist and, should it prove valid, would approach his subject from this new angle.

He never worked during the night and seldom in the evenings. To produce a well-constructed lecture or sermon he needed only to be left undisturbed for a few hours by the end of which he would have written, not just notes, but a completed text. At first sight his manuscripts give the impression of being as untidy as his writing-desk; in fact they contain full texts with no gaps or omissions. Even when Bonhoeffer did not envisage publication, his manuscripts could have been sent to the press virtually as they stood. He was one of those people who write down what they have already thought out, whereas others, by writing something down, are led on to further thought. This does not mean, of course, that he made no preliminary notes, quantities of which, indeed, still exist, but they are in a state of disorder that is very far from pedantic. He never sat down to write, however, until he knew what his goal was going to be. This contributed to the tautness of style in his books. He would never revise them after they had been printed; if he went over a work again it was only as a preliminary to something else. It was as though he was already aware that his days were numbered and too few.

Bonhoeffer's own pace and his ability to interrupt work for play without ever falling behind sometimes made him unjust towards others who were toiling night and day in preparation for some examination. But he was also able to make them discover resources within themselves which they had never previously suspected.

Discussion Evenings

One evening a week was devoted to the discussion of topical questions
for which the politics of the day supplied ample subject-matter. In
spite of its seclusion the community at the seminary was inevitably
involved in the political situation.

The new law relating to military service came into force on 1st May
1935.[8] At Tempelhof, during an unseasonable blizzard, Hitler proclaimed Germany's resurgence as a military power. Excitedly, the
ordinands in Zingst listened to his speech on the wireless and wondered
when their turn would come to put on uniform. It was something most
of them looked forward to, little realizing their director's feelings on the
subject. The number of conscientious objectors in the Protestant Church
at that time could have been counted on the fingers of one hand, nor
did the Confessing Church herself show any great inclination to
challenge the Lutheran view of military service. Hitler's new move to
'extirpate the ignominy of Versailles' met with general approval. Even
those ordinands who had been among the 700 to be arrested on that
well-remembered proclamation Sunday ('Against idolatry') looked upon
the revival of the 'military mentality' as a matter of course; indeed
many of them volunteered for military service soon after this. '. . . all
we can feel towards the State is an unhappy love that does not ask to
be requited or recognized . . . but if all goes well, the 1st November will
see me in uniform . . .'[9] It was widely felt in the Confessing Church
that it was desirable to provide as many commissioned reservists from its
own ranks as possible, a matter upon which sympathizers in the Civil
Service were also agreed. To some extent the motive was a genuine
feeling of participation, but there was also a calculated desire to demonstrate that, despite calumniators in the Party and among the German
Christians, the church opposition was truly patriotic, reliable and
honourable. The status of officer still enjoyed undiminished respect.

A casual question thrown out by Bonhoeffer during Hitler's speech
suddenly brought home to the unsuspecting students that his views on
the subject might be quite different from their own. An animated argument ensued and as a result the evening discussions naturally began
with the subject of pacifism. The majority of the brethren completely
rejected his suggestion that conscientious objection was something a
Christian ought to consider, and cheerfully endorsed the decision
reached by their ethical theologians and church leaders. When Bonhoeffer's friend, Herbert Jehle, came to the seminary on a visit, they
accused him, a scientist, of theological *naïveté* on account of his
pacifism. Gradually, however, the climate of these discussions changed
as the ordinands came to realize that their director was not in the least

8. Conscription had already been introduced on 16.3.1935.
9. B. Riemer to E. Bethge, 27.8.1935.

fanatical about the matter and that the most he required of them, if he could not gain their sympathy for this possible mode of Christian behaviour, was to respect anyone who adopted it in the belief that he was complying with Christ's commandment. Far from seeking to impose a universally valid doctrine of non-violence he merely sought personally to believe and obey Jesus' behest. However, it was bruited about in church circles that Bonhoeffer's opinions in this matter did not conform with those of the generality. This led to the appearance at Finkenwalde of Dr. Hermann Stöhr of Stettin, secretary of the German Fellowship of Reconciliation, who also worked on behalf of the World Alliance for Promoting International Friendship through the Churches. His pacifism was more strongly characterized by the logical principle of total disarmament than was Bonhoeffer's who, however, was far from being worried by this and, indeed, defended it. But they were never really to collaborate because Bonhoeffer considered that, in view of his indifference to questions of the Confessing Church, Stöhr ought not to be in charge of arrangements for ecumenical visitors. Hence he refused to support his ecumenical work in Stettin. But Bonhoeffer was all the more distressed when, in 1939, Stöhr was prosecuted by the military authorities and, despite all the attempts to save him, was executed as a conscientious objector.[10]

The news of Karl Barth's exclusion from Germany gave rise to a heated discussion which centred upon the question of the oath. Barth had declared himself ready to take the Civil Service oath, but only with the rider, 'in so far as I can responsibly do so as a Christian'. This had not been allowed. As the Reich Confessional Synod of Augsburg (4th-6th June 1935) loomed closer, so too the question as to whether the Confessing Church would make the cause of the 'political' Barth her own assumed greater urgency; for in that event she must not hesitate to compromise herself by calling upon him to take up a teaching post at a church seminary. Should she decide against Barth, however, she would have to remain aloof, if not actually manifest satisfaction at his departure. In anticipation of what he believed would happen, Bonhoeffer had vigorously spoken his mind even before he had left London. In a letter to Präses Koch on 1st December 1934 he wrote:

Should the church government [i.e. the emergency bodies formed by the National Synod of Dahlem] fail to make any gesture of sympathy or solidarity with Barth's cause, this would most seriously jeopardize the interest shown hitherto by the ecumenical movement in the Confessing Church. It would give the impression of a deviation from the Confessing Church's original and true course, an attitude which would have a definitely alienating effect. I know that the gaze of the whole of the Protestant world is at

10. See *Du hast mich heimgesucht bei Nacht, Abschiedsbriefe und Aufzeichnungen des Widerstands 1933-1945*, pp. 233 ff.

present focused upon the decision to be taken by the new church government and I feel it my responsibility to let you know this.[11]

In the weeks preceding the National Synod at Augsburg attempts to forestall a compromising gesture of sympathy with Karl Barth gave rise to a considerable amount of intrigue within the 'confessional front'. Many of the seminary's ordinands argued about whether Barth's fight against the oath really constituted a Christian question with which the Church should concern herself, or whether it was 'merely' political and hence not a matter for the Church at all—as many confessional people maintained. Bonhoeffer's students showed themselves more tractable here than on the question of pacifism. When, on 25th June, Barth finally accepted the appointment in Basle, he wrote a farewell letter to Pastor Hermann Hesse a copy of which was sent to Bonhoeffer. The ordinands duplicated the letter which they sent out to all their friends, not in the hope of reversing what had happened, but because the final passage expressed something that had been troubling both Barth and Bonhoeffer for some time, namely the fact that the Confessing Church 'has as yet shown no sympathy for the millions who are suffering injustice. She has not once spoken out on the most simple matters of public integrity. And if and when she does speak, it is always on her own behalf.'[12]

Spiritual Centre

Soon the whole Evangelical Church was buzzing with rumours about the terrible heresies at Finkenwalde—Catholic practices, enthusiastic pacifist goings-on, and radical fanaticism. But Finkenwalde attracted more than it repelled. It drew visitors who knew that they would hear questions discussed there which had too long remained unasked. Bonhoeffer insisted on generous hospitality—indeed, that had been one of the reasons for choosing Finkenwalde with its many rooms.

1. Students from Greifswald, finding their own faculty deficient in following the clear lines laid down by the Dahlem Synod, asked that the seminary should arrange informal study sessions which would give them both stimulation and support in matters of theology and church politics. The Finkenwaldians undertook this work in Greifswald, a step which was regarded by the university faculty as an infringement of its territory. Thus relations had already become considerably strained when Bonhoeffer wrote to the Council of the Old Prussian Union, asking to be entrusted with regular work among the Greifswald students.

2. The Pomeranian Brotherhood of the younger confessional preachers and ministers liked to hold their conferences at Finkenwalde. During their first conference Bonhoeffer gave a three-day Bible-study on

11. See Ch. VIII, pp. 339 f.
12. From a duplicated copy in the possession of the author.

King David[13] which provoked violent disagreement among Old Testament scholars. He spoke regularly at these conferences and as time went on felt impelled to lay increasing stress on the need to observe the decisions and resolutions made at Barmen and Dahlem.

3. Neighbouring parishes would also hold their pastoral conferences in the seminary, but from 1936 onwards the determined line taken by the Finkenwaldians was felt to be a disturbing element and the meetings were held elsewhere. These parish meetings were replaced by voluntary working associations of pastors who wished to hold discussions and to pursue the course they had begun under Bonhoeffer's guidance.

The Finkenwalde experiment aroused much interest, and clearly revealed weak points in German Protestantism. An emissary from the Bielefeld seminary expressed his thanks in the visitors' book for 'the opportunity of seeing the work and the—so very different—way of life of the brotherhood'.

Pomerania

When the preachers' seminary had settled in Finkenwalde, Bonhoeffer found himself translated into surroundings that were quite unknown to him as a city-dweller living in the academic quarter of Grunewald. The church people he found there were confidently and deeply religious, their core consisting largely of independent patrons living on their estates, and he was pleasantly surprised to find that some elements of the Pomeranian revivalist movement still survived. Sometimes, however, when necessary decisions had to be reached in church politics, he found the slow pace of the rural province irritating. In Pomerania, too, he made enduring friendships, and indeed it was here that he met his future fiancée. In the course of the common political struggle these connections were to bring out Bonhoeffer's inherent conservatism.

By the time the seminary opened at Zingst, Pomerania had long since concluded its successful campaign against the inept German Christian bishop, Thom, who had assumed the title of 'Bishop of Cammin'. A provincial Council of Brethren of the Confessing Church had been set up with Reinhold von Thadden at its head. It was difficult to impose the measures required by the Barmen and Dahlem resolutions because the people of Pomerania had always prided themselves on their 'Lutheranism'. Even under the leadership of 'Dahlemite' minded Pomeranians, the Erlangen point of view set forth by Althaus and Elert still found almost universal acceptance. The two theologians' criticism that the Barmen theses had erred in following Barth's rejection of 'original revelation' in creation and history had met with a large measure of agreement here, and this tended to make Bonhoeffer appear isolated and radical.

13. GS IV, pp. 294-320.

He thus immediately found himself among the small minority which did not acquiesce in the general satisfaction over the outcome of the National Confessional Synod at Augsburg (2.-4.6.1935). Although the Synod had achieved the apparent consolidation of the entire Confessing Church and had passed a useful resolution on the question of training, its unanimity seemed suspect to Bonhoeffer. He did not look upon the Barth affair as merely transitory but saw it as symptomatic. He enumerated four omissions of which the Augsburg Synod had been guilty.[14] Firstly, it had failed to say anything positive about the freedom of the Church; secondly, it had not mentioned the lie contained in paragraph 24 of the National Socialist Party programme ('positive Christianity'); thirdly, it had remained silent on the Jewish question (he himself had been receiving advance information on the preparation of the Nuremberg Laws from his brother-in-law, Dohnanyi); lastly, nothing had been said about the military oath which, since the rejection of Barth's declaration of the Civil Service oath, could not be taken unreservedly by Christians. It seemed all too obvious to Bonhoeffer that the Synod had been hamstrung by its anxiety to cling to Dahlem and by its fear of showing any opposition towards the State. He was all the more relieved when Martin Niemöller called for renewed determination, and asked for signatures to his manifesto 'To our Brethren in the Ministry'. The manifesto appeared on 30th July 1935 and contained the names of Pomeranians such as J. Bartelt, E. Baumann and H. Rendtorff. The latter's signature carried especial weight, for in 1933 he had supported the other side. Bonhoeffer wrote to Niemöller:

I am delighted that you have again given the signal for the attack . . . I think the time has come to form an Emergency League within the Emergency League, and we shall have to find a very different interpretation of Matt. 22 : 21[15] from the one that prevails now. I hope we have now got to the stage of speaking out and deciding, and if no one else speaks out, I shall certainly give voice to this important matter. I really believe that you've chosen the right moment, and for this I am most thankful. The whole seminary, myself included, sends you warmest regards . . .[16]

Relations with the State, whose 'decrees for legal aid and order' had only made confusion worse, were now such that Bonhoeffer foresaw a parting of the ways; it was not the decrees of the National Bishop but the laws of the State, that would have to be combated.

Hence it is no matter for surprise that the first encounters between Bonhoeffer's seminary and other centres in Pomerania struck a note of discord. Their difference of approach was underlined by the ordinands'

14. W. Niemöller's diary on a meeting in Dahlem. W. Niemöller, *Aus dem Leben eines Bekenntnispfarrers*, 1961, p. 145.
15. 'Render therefore to Caesar the things that are Caesar's, and to God the things that are God's.'
16. GS II, p. 205.

somewhat off-hand manner combined with their extreme youthfulness. During the ten days' interval between Zingst and Finkenwalde, Bonhoeffer and his seminarists spent some time in Greifswald, a visit that in no way served to restore harmony; from there they moved on to Stettin to attend the third Pomeranian Confessional Synod.

1. The visit to Greifswald had been planned in order to introduce the students to the theological faculty, and to enable them to do some missionary work in the town. For the latter purpose the minister of the town, K. von Scheven, made the cathedral available for them. Von Scheven was then still a member of the Pomeranian Confessional Synod, though six months later he was to become head of the Pomeranian Church Committee (the neutral official governing body).

Hence the time at Greifswald came more to resemble a preliminary skirmish for future disputes than an amicable visit among allies. When, at one of the student gatherings, a member of the seminary shouted, 'We're here to get something done!' he may have coined a slogan for Finkenwalde, but from the faculty he earned more disapprobation than sympathy.

2. The Greifswald visit was immediately followed by a visit to the third Pomeranian Confessional Synod which convened in H. Rendtorff's Wartburg church in Stettin from 20th-22nd June. The legislative authorities and finance departments set up by recent state decrees were confusing innovations, of which the full impact was still unpredictable. J. Beckmann from Düsseldorf gave the keynote address. The appearance of the seminary provided one of the highlights of the Synod. When the Präses announced that it had been decided to take the house at Finkenwalde 'eight of the Synod's church groups spontaneously offered each to furnish a room' (Synod report).

The Synod brought Bonhoeffer into contact for the first time with the Pomeranian Council of Brethren. In this way he met E. Baumann, the Reformed pastor in Stettin, and Frau von Mackensen, wife of the Deputy Chief President of Pomerania and a tireless manager of the Council of Brethren's office. Henceforward he was to collaborate happily with them both. Soon the irruptions of impatient Finkenwaldians, protesting perhaps against some move by the Council of Brethren, or coming to offer their services for work in the confessional communities, became a familiar occurrence in the Council's office in Pölitzer Strasse.

Church contacts were to prove less fruitful to Bonhoeffer than his encounters with the landed aristocracy of Pomerania. These had begun with the begging and thank-you letters on behalf of Finkenwalde, and he often made new friends when, seeking to introduce a protégé into a living against the wishes of the consistory, he had to pay a call on the patron. For while the system of patronage might appear from some points of view to be nothing more than an anachronistic nuisance, it could also prove of enormous use to the Councils of Brethren on occasions when they were able to benefit from the patron's independent right to fill a living. Indeed, there were a number of patrons who considered it quite in order to go over the heads of the consistorial authorities Reinhold von Thadden, in his capacity as President of the Confessional Synod, helped Bonhoeffer to make the contacts he needed.

In this way he made the acquaintance of families with whom he continued to keep contact after the closure of Finkenwalde—the Kleist-Retzows of Kieckow, Ewald von Kleist of Schmenzin, the Bismarcks of Lasbeck, and finally the Wedemeyers of Pätzig. Frau von Wedemeyer and Frau von Bismarck were the sisters of von Kleist-Retzow of Kieckow. Their mother, Ruth von Kleist-Retzow, a widow, had retired to the estate of Klein-Krössin near Kieckow, but still possessed a flat in Stettin at the time the seminary was at Finkenwalde; this enabled her grand-children from Kieckow, Lasbeck and Pätzig to go to school in the provincial capital. She became a resolute champion of the seminary's needs, and when, in the autumn of 1935, regular services began to be held in Finkenwalde's emergency chapel, she made a habit of driving out with some of her grandchildren to attend them.

Ruth von Kleist-Retzow, a daughter of Count Zedlitz of Breslau, was a remarkable woman. Throughout her life she was always sympathetic towards movements that brought fresh life to the Church, and even when she was very old, she read every new book written by Karl Barth. She had a very good feeling for quality and subject-matter, and never hesitated to say exactly what she thought, which often led her to speak with refreshing forthrightness of this or that cleric's insidious lack of backbone, or perhaps his glib suavity. Bon-hoeffer's arrival in the Stettin area introduced a new spiritual stimulus into her life, and she promoted his interests with all the means at her disposal. With feminine candour she would remind patrons of their duties and would keep on at them until they had really done some-thing to help. She was thrilled by the progress of Bonhoeffer's book, *The Cost of Discipleship*, and was insatiable in her thirst for informa-tion. At first Bonhoeffer was almost alarmed by the torrent of questions and wished that his ordinands might share something of her ardour. As time went on, he got into the habit of spending his holidays at Klein-Krössin or with Hans-Jürgen von Kleist-Retzow at Kieckow. Between 1935 and 1937 the Kleist-Retzow grandchildren had frequently attended services at Finkenwalde—afterwards, incidentally, enjoying games of table-tennis in the garden with the ordinands. Hence in 1938 their grandmother—not, perhaps without the ulterior motive of attending some of the classes herself—was able to persuade Dietrich Bonhoeffer to prepare three of the children for confirmation. The dissolution of Finkenwalde interrupted the plan and there were times when Albrecht Schönherr had to stand in for Bonhoeffer, but the latter was able to

conduct the final class at Kieckow, where he also confirmed his pupils.[17]
Amongst those who sometimes came to services at Finkenwalde were
Frau von Kleist's granddaughters, Ruth-Alice and Maria von Wedemeyer, as well as the former's fiancé, Klaus von Bismarck. Years later—
when two of the boys he had confirmed had already been killed on
active service—Bonhoeffer again met Maria von Wedemeyer at Klein-
Krössin.[18] By the time their engagement was announced Bonhoeffer was
in Tegel prison. Ruth von Kleist-Retzow sent him the biography of
her father-in-law, Hans von Kleist-Retzow, once President of the Rhineland and Bismarck's pugnacious opponent (1814-92).[19] On the fly-leaf
she wrote:

... To my dear Dietrich, to whom I owe some of the most important insights
of my life. I am happy to send you this book on the day when you have
definitely become a member of our family. The man who is its subject has
left a tangible blessing behind him, and one in which you are now included.
Klein-Krössin (Kieckow), 24th June 1943.

In these great houses of Pomerania, Bonhoeffer encountered a society
which, while familiar to him, was also in many ways strange. For there
were hardly any close ties between the Grunewald academic circles and
the farming, political and military circles of the landed aristocracy.
Moreover Bonhoeffer himself, a man who did not seek to conceal his
pacifist bent, was an unusual friend for the *Junkers* of Pomerania. That
a close *rapport* quickly established itself between Bonhoeffer and the
Kleists can be attributed to both personal factors and contemporary
history. In Pomerania Bonhoeffer found much the same hospitality,
manners and mode of living to which he had been accustomed at home.
The difference consisted mainly in the extent to which feelings and
inclinations found expression. Where the Kleists were emotional and
direct, the Bonhoeffers were restrained and only the practised eye could
detect the strong feelings behind their ordinary, terse, matter-of-fact
gestures. What really broke down their mutual reserve, however, was
that both parties, when confronted by the demands of the time, were
prepared to risk their inherited privileges, whether in politics or in the
Church. The academic world of Grunewald, like the world of the
Junkers, was divided against itself on the question of the meaning and
application of the right priorities. In this way the minorities of both
worlds discovered each other.

The Province of Saxony

Bonhoeffer's ordinands from the province of Saxony had been able to

17. See the confirmation address, GS IV, pp. 441 ff.
18. See Ch. XII, p. 694.
19. H. von Petersdorff, *Kleist-Retzow. Ein Lebensbild*, 1907.

persuade him to attend the conference of their fellowship in Hauteroda at the end of August 1935, after a last minute cancellation by Hans Asmussen. As yet the Confessing Church of Magdeburg knew nothing at all about the young theologian and felt strong misgivings about him as a 'stand-in'. He was to introduce the subject of 'The Relevance of New Testament Texts'.[20] He made a very successful appearance and as a result he continued to give a helping hand in the province of Saxony as long as circumstances allowed him to do so.

This was where he met Wolfgang Staemmler, the mentor of the young confessional theologians in the province of Saxony. In Staemmler he found a man with a rare faculty for meeting him on his own ground and one who, in addition, possessed Biblical insight and the willingness to translate what he had heard into concrete action. From the very first, the two men agreed that it was their responsibility to demand sacrifice and self-denial of their charges. It was a determination that was to be found remarkably seldom among the leaders of the Confessing Church. When Bonhoeffer was in Tegel he drew up a short list of those whom he would like eventually to conduct his burial service; Staemmler figured among them.[21]

III THE SYLLABUS

On the surface of it there was nothing particularly unusual about Bonhoeffer's syllabus for the seminary. Homiletics and catechetical studies, pastoral care and liturgical studies, lectures on church, ministry and community—such was the stuff of any German preachers' seminary. There was only one theme which distinguished Bonhoeffer's seminary from the rest for the first two and a half years, and that was the series of lectures on discipleship. After only a few hours newcomers would realize that this was the nerve-centre of the whole, and that they were witnessing a theological event which would stimulate every area of their professional life.

Wilhelm Rott was responsible for the catechetical section and the work on the Heidelberg Catechism. Little attention was paid to liturgical studies, though the seminary did make practical experiments in liturgy and tried out Asmussen's suggestions on liturgical singing.[22] From his previous studies of the Psalter, Bonhoeffer had retained a real interest in liturgical problems, but the subject was assessed in accordance with the times. From the point of view of church politics, most liturgiologists, particularly those of the Berneuchen movement, displayed indifference towards church politics, so that they were suspect to the Confessing Church and often subject to judgements that were over-harsh. 'Only he

20. GS III, pp. 303-24.
21. GS II, p. 442.
22. H. Asmussen, *Ordnung des Gottesdienstes*, 1936.

who shouts for the Jews can sing the Gregorian chant', Bonhoeffer once remarked to his ordinands in this connection.[23] Thus there was no special liturgical 'teaching' at Finkenwalde, although Bonhoeffer was able to impart an instinctive feeling for the content of worship. He could spend whole periods of homiletics on the inner reasons for right speech and action in worship,[24] and he made some very definite statements about congregational devotions and about singing and reading in 'communal life'. This was not the result of thorough liturgical research, however, but originated from a genuine theology and the practice of prayer.

Homiletics

Bonhoeffer would sometimes entrust the discussion of sermons to his assistant, but the actual teaching of homiletics he always reserved for himself.

At first, it seemed very strange to his students that their sermons, however hesitant and wanting, were treated in all seriousness as the expression of the true *viva vox Christi*. Nothing, he insisted, is more concrete than the real voice of Christ speaking in the sermon. To this principle he adhered strictly with regard to any sermon preached at divine service which must, he held, be listened to in all humility and must not be analyzed. The only sermons he allowed to be discussed were those that were read aloud, never those that had been delivered before a congregation; about the latter he might, on rare occasions, say a word in private. Once, when Erich Klapproth read out a sermon during tuition, he had no sooner finished than Bonhoeffer dismissed the class because he felt that at that moment a critical analysis would be inopportune. Needless to say he gave due attention to problems of method and form, but nothing exerted so chastening an effect as Bonhoeffer's method of listening to sermons. He himself demonstrated daily what he required in the way of expression, taste and imaginativeness. Thus homiletics began with the most difficult lesson of all—one's own listening to sermons.

In 1932 he had said that a good sermon should be like a lovely red apple which is held out to a child with the question 'Would you like it?',[25] and had continued, 'Thus we should be able to speak about our faith so that hands will be stretched out towards us faster than we can fill them.'[26] But whereas he had then used the conditional 'should', he now no longer did so. Nor did he still yearn for a truly evangelical sermon, or intimidate his ordinands by setting his sights impossibly high. Indeed

23. Bonhoeffer did not himself set down this remark in writing.
24. See GS IV, pp. 278-84.
25. See Ch. VI, p. 175.
26. GS IV, p. 51.

their confidence grew with every lecture because of his insistence that it is the preacher who holds the red apple and who shares it out. Therefore 'Do not try to make the Bible relevant. Its relevance is axiomatic . . . Do not defend God's Word, but testify to it . . . Trust to the Word. It is a ship loaded to the very limits of her capacity.'

Bonhoeffer had difficulty in persuading his ordinands that there was more to preaching than the reasonable, but in fact quite useless arrangement of an *explicatio* followed by an *applicatio*. Indeed, the discussion in the final class developed from the dissent of an ordinand who had once been taught by Karl Heim and was a passionate advocate of the need for concrete 'application'. After getting two of the students to speak, Bonhoeffer, as was his method, put forward his own theses for discussion: God alone is concrete . . . the concrete situation is the substance within which the Word of God speaks; it is the object, not the subject, of concretion.[27]

Bonhoeffer's understanding of the sermon was based on his Lutheran Christology. In the first term of the 1935 course he still saw the sermon as grounded in ecclesiology: the sermon has its 'causality and its finality' in the Church. The Church preaches nothing but the Church. Preaching exists because the Church exists—and men preach in order that the Church shall exist. He did not revoke that argument, but in the second course he omitted the lecture based upon it and replaced it with one in which he put forward the idea that the sermon was grounded in the incarnation: 'The Word of the sermon is Christ accepting and bearing human nature. It is not a new incarnation, but the Incarnate One who bears the sins of the world. The Word of the sermon seeks to accept men, no more.' The Word of the Bible assumes form as a sermon; thus it goes out to the congregation in order to bear it. The preacher must permit this autonomous outgoing of the Word towards the congregation to take place, he must not hinder it.[28] Luther's hypostatization of the 'Word' was taken up by Bonhoeffer as '*sacramentum verbi*' in such a way that to other confessions and denominations it seemed strange and difficult of realization.

Nevertheless, Bonhoeffer's homiletics were extremely practical and replete with advice that was immediately applicable. For instance: write your sermon in daylight; do not write it all at one go; 'in Christ' there is no room for conditional clauses; the first minutes in the pulpit are the most favourable so do not waste them on commonplaces but confront the congregation straight off with the pith of the matter; extempore preaching can be done by anyone who really knows his Bible. These were homiletics such as few ordinands elsewhere had the opportunity of hearing, whether at Berlin or at Halle or at Greifswald. There can have been few of Bonhoeffer's students who did not return changed

27. See GS IV, pp. 253 f., also GS III, pp. 303, 312 ff.
28. GS IV, pp. 241 f.

and happier to their preaching and their congregations. And there can hardly have been one whose confidence and determination did not grow with his knowledge of his ability to do things and demand things of others, or who was not convinced that the freshness of his sermon would depend in large measure upon his view of Scripture as an end in itself and upon his belief in what it presented to him. It was both the strength and the weakness of these homiletics that they were so exactly adapted to the thirties.

Bonhoeffer did not advocate exchanging the pulpit for the academic rostrum for he believed that the former must regain an independence which cannot be exchanged. It is true that he appreciated the academic rostrum in so far as it acted as a corrective to the sermon, but it never made the pulpit superfluous. His own sermons at that time were startlingly direct; they made things clear and they made demands. He did not look for the assistance of new communication media or the refinements of interpretation, for he knew just what he wanted—and, further —he wanted what he knew.

Ministry and Church

The series of lectures on 'The Ministry and the Church' did not provide a clear description defining the existing churches, but dealt with the most burning questions of the time. Each dogmatic article was removed from its context of past controversies and was brought forward as an existential argument against the German Christian solutions of ecclesiological problems. In the second half of term the lectures followed the ecclesio-theological tendency of the day by turning to the study and interpretation of confessional writings. These were largely unfamiliar to the ordinands of 1935, nor had they formed a part of Bonhoeffer's own studies in Berlin.

Thus during the 1935 summer term Bonhoeffer began by considering a few of the general problems that were central to the controversy of that time, going on to demonstrate that the decisions against the German Christians and their uncommitted servants were grounded in the confessional writings. At this distance of time the excitement of those classes cannot easily be conveyed.

a) The series 'The Ministry and the Church' began with a discussion of constitutional and legal problems. Two years of struggle had familiarized the ordinands with their German Christian masters' remarkable thesis which held that constitutional questions did not touch the essential being of the Church; it was upon this respectable premise, put forward by Sohm, that they based their intervention. This meant that the ordinands must learn to deduce an opposite view from their understanding of the visible Church. Regarding the question of the Church's legal authority, Bonhoeffer taught that this could not be exercised externally, but only internally, and then in the form of church discipline over her own members; externally all she could do was to confess and to suffer. In 1934 and 1935 it was quite common for confessional ministers to bring actions against the new church governments before the secular courts; the ministers inevitably won. This used to delight the ordinands but Bonhoeffer was not so sure and was little inclined to attach value to the lawsuits except in so far as a *re publica male informata ad rem publicam melius informandam.*

b) The lecture on church schism and re-unification—the substance of the Confession—proved equally exciting and topical. Bonhoeffer had already been elaborating the theses upon which he based his articles on the ecumenical movement[29] and on church relations[30] when he had been in Zingst. In these he investigated the process by which, in a *status confessionis*, divergencies forming 'schools of opinion' necessarily intensify till they become 'schismatic divergencies', and also the opposite process whereby schismatic divergencies diminish till they are nothing more than divergencies between schools,[31] a process which must have become apparent to all from the common Confession of Lutherans and Reformed at Barmen. He found evidence to support this distinction in *Apologie* Art. VII, according to which the Fathers 'sometimes divided up the ground for straw or hay, but for all that did not seek to destroy the ground'. Thus Bonhoeffer maintained that the Church must leave room for bad theologies and that the better ones must not be allowed to expel the worse. This brought him back to the Articles of Schmalkalden which he discussed in greater detail. In this context he pointed out that the Lutheran Confession was especially open to ecumenical thought because it saw and recognized as the very essence of its teaching the insistence on atonement; this excluded all possibility of its clinging to orthodoxy, for to do so would be to practise in its teaching the very opposite of what was implied in its essence. It seems strange that for so many years ecumenical discussion should have ignored this viewpoint, and that, at a time when the confessional problem was becoming ever more explosive.

c) In his lecture on the relationship between the ministry and the congregation he touched on the question of the apostolic succession. This would appear to be the first and last time he ever did so. In spite of his time in England and his ecumenical experience he had never considered that this Article had any importance in inter-church disputes between continental Protestants. The Anglicans had not yet got to the point of declaiming it loudly in a conditional sense. Hence Bonhoeffer only mentions the apostolic succession incidentally, as one way of under-

29. GS I, pp. 240 ff.
30. GS II, pp. 217 ff.
31. Karl Barth also uses this pair of concepts, 1934; cf. 'Gottes Wille und unsere Wünsche', ThEx, Section 7, 1934, pp. 16-30.

standing the ministry, a way which assures the latter's priority over the congregation and is based on the same premise that Christ created the ministry and the latter created the congregation, as opposed to the collegialist thesis that the congregation appoints the ministry. Bonhoeffer criticized this on the ground that it postulated history, in the sense of uninterrupted continuity, as the mediator of the means of grace and of the latter's efficacy and at the same time turned the true proposition 'no congregation without a ministry' into the false proposition 'the ministry creates the congregation'. Bonhoeffer's own view was that grace derived only from 'conformity to the Scripture' and not from the succession. Significantly the Anglican doctrine and practice of apostolic succession is not mentioned in the section of Barth's *Dogmatics* dealing with the problem of succession.[32]

d)   But nor did Bonhoeffer adhere to the collegialist doctrine which deduces from the true proposition that the ministry exists *for* the congregation, the false proposition that it exists *through* the congregation. His thesis assumed a position in between the Roman, the Orthodox and the Anglican on the one hand and the Congregationalist on the other; the ministry comes neither before nor after, neither above nor beneath the congregation, but within and together with it. One is not the subject of the other—the subject of both is the Holy Spirit—nor is one the object of the other, for that would mean that the ministry was delivered up to the communal spirit or, alternatively, that the congregation was deprived of the right to pronounce on doctrine. By this means Bonhoeffer sought to obviate any conflict between the ministry and the priesthood of all believers.

e)   A discussion of the three classical grounds for unfrocking a priest —doctrine, conduct and gifts—was of immediate topical concern, on the one hand because of the Dahlem declaration and its implications for Ludwig Müller, and on the other hand because of the threat hanging over the non-Aryan clergy. Bonhoeffer declared unfrocking on grounds of false doctrine to be the *duty* of the congregation and unfrocking on grounds of conduct to be the *right* of the congregation; from this he went on to ask the problematical question as to what grounds, if any, applied in the case of 'gifts', a theme upon which he set the seminary a task of immediate topical relevance: 'Can the Aryan clause be justified on the basis of the requirement that a pastor must qualify as a suitable holder of office, not only by doctrine and conduct, but also by having the necessary gifts?' This was the most burning question of the day and one upon which Bonhoeffer had already stated his views publicly and clearly in 1933. The argument he now put forward in the closed circle of his ordinands ran as follows: Where gifts are concerned, the minister is not suspended for the sake of the Gospel, as in the case of false doctrine, nor because of public offence, as in the case of conduct

32. See K. Barth, KD I/I, pp. 105 f.

but, if at all, only 'for the sake of the congregation's weakness'. Where this is the case, it should not be described as 'unfrocking'. The argument based on the weakness of the congregation can apply only to the individual, isolated case where, perhaps, resignation from office but not unfrocking might possibly be envisaged. In other words, exclusion from the ministry should never occur on principle, for then the congregation's shortcomings, its weakness, would become its most vital criterion. Consequently where gifts are concerned there could be no question either of the duty or the right of an assembly to unfrock; at the very most there might be a fraternal *request* that the person concerned should consider the question of resigning. Hence this would completely exclude the regular procedure of suspension. In this way Bonhoeffer succeeded in answering the question in the negative while theoretically leaving the way open for the remote eventuality of a congregation being unable, in regard to the Aryan clause, to achieve complete clarity in its testimony and its faith. Obviously Bonhoeffer did not envisage a situation that could ever permit of such an eventuality. His criticism and admonition were therefore aimed at the congregation which insisted that its 'weakness' was in fact its strength.

Confessional Writings

From July 1933 onwards, study was centred almost wholly on the confessional writings which at that time aroused the same passionate interest as does the hermeneutic question today. With each term more and more time was allocated to these classes than to any other subject. The authenticity of the binding declarations made by the Protestant churches was examined in the light of the concepts of ministry, Church State, adiaphora and scriptural doctrine.

a) A favourite subject of Bonhoeffer's was the Articles of Schmalkalden; in discussing the question of schism in the Church, he would underline the striking fact—one which, indeed, had been responsible for the conflict—that the Reformers alone were restricted to the Article of Justification, and he would further emphasize the affirmation of unity with the Catholics evinced by other of the Articles, such as those concerning the doctrine of the Trinity or of Christology. This impressed the ordinands all the more because it was Bonhoeffer, that consistent and unwavering advocate of Barmen and Dahlem, who propounded it and, in addition, enjoined them to moderation. Their theological education had, of course, shown them that in the old schism a different spirit had been at work as, indeed, was detectable in every one of the Articles. But now the man who showed such a keen awareness of the different spirit informing all present-day pronouncements was teaching them that there was a very marked and noteworthy distinction between the theologies of the Church and the decisions which she reached. Each was deserving of a different kind of respect; there were, he held, as many theologies as there were intellects, they might or they might not convince and must remain subject to discussion; decisions once reached, however, demanded obedience. For, he said, the Church cannot wait for theological unanimity but must decide and must demand respect for the decisions she has made.

It may have been his ecumenical experience that had endowed the Protestant Bonhoeffer with this special insight and perhaps, too, he had a feeling for 'policy', a word for which there is no exact equivalent in Germany, doubtless because what it stands for is found there comparatively seldom. The German tradition gives precedence to theology—above all to its own—whereas the decisions of the Church are relegated to second place and enjoy scant respect, partly because of the habit of scrutinizing them for elements of false or bad theology. But Bonhoeffer, as a theologian, was at pains to avoid this, a fact which gives us a key to his attitude and arguments respecting the synodal decisions of Barmen and Dahlem. When his students came out with the current cliché that the way of a liberal Christian led to the German Christians and that of an orthodox or positive Christian to the Confessing Church, because this was the logical outcome of their theologies, he would object, not only that this was factually untrue, but that the decision which had been or was to be taken did not constitute an element in theology. In 1937 he could, as a Lutheran, condemn as bad theology, and question the basic reasoning of, the Halle Synod's decision on the common celebration of communion, yet acclaim the decision as such with gratitude: 'Much though I approve of the result, I cannot but deplore its theological premise.'[33]

While he himself had a keen nose for theological inconsistency, it was a faculty he mistrusted because it so often offered a pretext to evade decisions or engendered an incapacity to abide by decisions that had already been made. The encouragement of ostensibly honest and considered theological solutions, while it might suggest a sense of responsibility, was in reality nothing but evasion, the indefinite procrastination of what ought to be done. In this, Bonhoeffer discerned an inability to be a church—an inability which, on the one hand, was bringing about the progressive fragmentation of the Church, while on the other it was inducing a greater readiness to accept a unity which had been tyrannically imposed from without.

b) After a heated discussion on the *Augustana* and *Apologic* Articles on the State, Bonhoeffer concluded by telling the class: 'The whole business is extremely problematical.' The very abstractness and diversity of the terminology betrayed, he went on, a certain perplexity and some vacillation between concepts of function ('authority') and concepts of being ('state'). The relationship between the factual positiveness of order

33. GS II, pp. 518, 380 f.

and its binding right had remained unsatisfactorily vague so that clearly previous solutions had been inadequate. In this way Bonhoeffer presented, not only Luther's 'unresolved and contradictory answers', but also—and without explicit censure—the answers of Thomas Münzer, and those of the Scottish Calvinists, as well as those of the Enthusiasts, Melchior Hoffman and Sebastian Franck. From this he went on to discuss the attempts that had been made to distinguish between a man's right to resist in his private and in his official capacities.

Unfortunately we have no written record of those classes. Though his ordinands did not know it at the time, Bonhoeffer was much troubled by another preoccupation; many of his closest friends and relations held responsible posts in the legislature and the administration and were now faced with the possible alternative of fulfilling their official mandate or resisting the régime. This was the time when the Nuremberg Laws were in preparation and Bonhoeffer was kept informed of developments by his brother-in-law Dohnanyi, in Berlin. Hence it was not always easy for his students to follow his train of thought when he criticized the familiar Protestant Lutheran solutions and cast doubt on the traditional rejection of the right to seditious resistance.

c) In his final lectures of this series Bonhoeffer dealt exclusively with the *Formula Concordiae*. He considered the Articles on free will, predestination, the doctrine of original sin, good works, Law and Gospel, *tertius usus legis* and justification. The *Formula Concordiae* had not formed part of his own studies, nor had the ordinands been much concerned with it during their time at university. When Bonhoeffer was a student, interest had centred mainly on Luther and the premises of Troeltsch had been discussed; now it had become necessary to listen to the binding statements of the Church at a time when she was being most violently assailed. Every page of the *Formula Concordiae* in Bonhoeffer's copy of the confessional writings is covered with exclamation marks, scoring and question marks. During later courses at Finkenwalde it was to become the predominant theme in this series of lectures, and his notes, which cover his whole time at the seminary, contain no fewer than eighty-one themes and questions on this subject which he gave as tasks to the ordinands. He loved the *Formula Concordiae* and liked nothing better than to discuss its tendency to express, in the guise of traditional philosophical formulae, the saving truth, and in the doctrines of confessional differentiation, the invitation to salvation.

'The Cost of Discipleship'

The two series of lectures we have just discussed would have been enough to earn for Bonhoeffer the reputation of a hard-working seminary director. They dealt with the usual, obligatory themes. The number of classes and the time needed for their preparation might well have kept him fully occupied. But the reason Finkenwalde was 'the fullest time' of his life was that he was at last enabled to get to work on the theme of his own choice and, by subjecting himself to a regular time-table, to give it shape and form. It was a theme that had steadily been gaining a hold over him ever since the early years of the thirties. Thus *The Cost of Discipleship* was to become Finkenwalde's own badge of distinction. The first classes at Zingst were, for the newcomers, a breath-taking experience. Suddenly the realization burst upon them that they were not there simply to learn new techniques of preaching and instruction, but were to be initiated into something that represented altogether revolutionary prerequisites for those activities.

At Zingst Bonhoeffer did not in fact begin with the phrase now found in the opening pages of the book, 'grace sold on the market like cheap-jack's wares'; instead he began by investigating the nature of 'the call' which alone constitutes the relationship between Jesus and Peter. At the end of the first course, on 14th October 1935, he concluded the series with a postscript (which does not appear in the same form in the book):

The Sermon on the Mount is not a Word to be treated cavalierly—this, that or the other is no good, here we find an inconsistency. Its validity depends on its being obeyed. This is not a Word to be freely evaluated, not a Word that you can take or leave. It is a compelling, dominating Word.

Thus what Bonhoeffer produced at the preachers' seminary was not a manuscript ready for the press, although whole sections of his lectures went straight into the book. He continued to make alterations and deletions and to insert whole new chapters until the very last page of the manuscript had to be delivered. The essence of the exegetic sections had been adumbrated well before the time of Finkenwalde, but the final version of the important systematic theories reached completion at the same time as the book itself. The section that is now found between the 'Sermon on the Mount' and 'The Church of Jesus Christ'—'The Messengers'—was inserted later.

It has been remarked that this part of the book, the *corpus Paulinum*, is not so compact and finished as the first two parts.[34] In fact it is an abridged and rearranged version of what Bonhoeffer wrote for the main series of lectures on the New Testament delivered in all but the first course at Finkenwalde. From the beginning, however, it had been his intention to use this material for *The Cost of Discipleship*. There can be no doubt that the book owes its impetus and pungency to a pre-occupation with the Sermon on the Mount dating back to a time long before 1935. The reconsideration and re-examination of its implications in regard to the *corpus Paulinum* was a new departure.

The third part of *The Cost of Discipleship* derives from the following Finkenwalde lectures: 'The Visible Church' (winter course 1935-6); 'The

34. For instance, K. Barth, KD IV/2, p. 604.

New Life in Paul' (summer course 1936); 'Concrete Ethics in Paul' (winter course 1936-7); 'Discipline and Formation of Congregations in the New Testament' (summer course 1937). The whole of Bonhoeffer's manuscript for *The Cost of Discipleship* has been lost.

Bonhoeffer concluded the book very shortly before the closure of the seminary by the police. In what was to be the last regular circular letter to the brethren from Finkenwalde, on 26th August 1937, we read: 'And now for some good news. In spite of all our many other activities, the book we have been expecting has now been completed and dictated on to the typewriter . . .'

The book appeared in time for Advent 1937. The first copies were sent to the members of the now dissolved community house with the inscription:

. . . 1st Advent 1937. In gratitude for two and a half years' loyal communion at Finkenwalde. May our path become ever more the path of joyous discipleship. *Jesu juva!*

When Bonhoeffer had resumed his work in a new guise he wrote in a circular letter to all Finkenwaldians:

When it appeared, I often dedicated it in spirit to you all. I would have done so on the title page had I not feared to lay the responsibility for my theology and my ideas on your shoulders. Our community is founded upon something else. I would have liked each one of you to receive the book as a Christmas present, but this finances would not allow. In any case, you all know what's in it.[35]

Needless to say, the ordinands would have been only too glad to accept 'the responsibility'. But this was typical of Bonhoeffer's modesty; the more he knew about his subject, the less confident he felt about it. One copy found its way into a prison cell. It was inscribed: 'To Martin Niemöller in brotherly gratitude. A book he himself could have written better than its author.' Another was sent to Franz Hildebrandt, by then an *émigré* in London and at work on the theme 'Gospel and Humanity'. To him it seemed that Bonhoeffer's preoccupation with the Commandment and the Law was in danger of becoming somewhat one-sided. In reply to Hildebrandt's thanks and criticism, Bonhoeffer wrote:

I am delighted both by your approval and your criticism of my book. Admittedly, Asmussen's commentary on Galatians does not agree with my interpretation of Matt. 5:17 ff. But it's a very different matter where Luther's commentary on Galatians is concerned.

As for you, you'll probably end up an antinomian laying down the law for humanity! Your work fascinates me and I follow it with approval and criticism as you do mine.[36]

The completion of the book on top of a full teaching curriculum and

35. GS II, p. 525.   36. Letter of 3.1.1938.

a great deal of travelling, combined with the worry of ever more frequent arrests of pupils and friends, was a tremendous achievement. Up to the very last Bonhoeffer continued to devote his Sundays and evenings to the ordinands, and to write articles, Bible studies and lectures. Yet had he not completed the work before Finkenwalde was dissolved, it seems doubtful whether this would ever have been possible since afterwards he would not even have had a study to work in.

The study of the New Testament during the time of the collective pastorates[37] (1937-40) assumed the form of terminological group work with the seminarists. After a discourse by one of the brethren, Bonhoeffer would put forward his own theses (as yet only two volumes of Kittel's *Theological Word Book* had appeared). Amongst Bonhoeffer's papers there are many notes written by him containing fragmentary classifications of Biblical material and systematic principles. There are also notes under the following headings: sin, the good, work, change and growth, *dokimos*, peace, *hodos*, the Holy Spirit, angels, the anger of God, Law, death, temptation, *pistis*, gratitude, *eucharistia*, *egkrateia*, *diakonia*, *nikan*, catalogue of vices, *tapeinophrosyne*, false doctrine. His treatment of these subjects recalls certain passages in *The Cost of Discipleship*. Some idea of the work he was doing is evident from the fact that in his circular letters to the brethren Bonhoeffer twice informed them of his findings on '*chara*' and on '*long-suffering*'.[38]

The Cost of Discipleship quickly found a relatively wide readership whose attention was caught by the book's handling of the ancient theme of 'sanctification' which, it suggested, must be wrested from the conventicles and handed back to the Church. At the start, however, the circulation of the book was apparent only from its sales, not from any immediate public reaction. That it went beyond the small world of specialists became evident to Bonhoeffer himself when in 1940 he was working on his *Ethics* in the Benedictine monastery at Ettal; at Christmas-time he heard the monks reading aloud passages from *The Cost of Discipleship*. Until 1945 there was no critical reaction of any significance to Bonhoeffer's view of discipleship. Early reviews spoke highly of his use of language—a somewhat unusual standard to apply to a new book on theology. There was one opinion which would have meant far more to Bonhoeffer than all the rest—that of Karl Barth—but this was not to appear until many years later. While still in the throes of writing his book, Bonhoeffer had written to Barth:

At bottom I have all the time been conducting a silent argument with you . . . there is such a very great deal I would like to ask you and could learn from you.[39]

37. A form of group ministry described later, Ch. XI, p. 492.
38. GS II, pp. 546 ff., 541 ff.
39. Letter of 19.9.1936, GS II, p. 284.

At that time Barth had seen no concrete evidence of what Bonhoeffer was doing. He answered that evidently Bonhoeffer was 'dealing with the inexhaustible themes of justification and sanctification' which he found 'a little worrying'. He went on, 'I shall have to watch carefully to see how the cat jumps before I can tell you whether I think your ideas are feasible or not.'[40]

Twenty years later his *Church Dogmatics* contained the words:

I should say that by far the best that has been written on the subject is *The Cost of Discipleship* by Dietrich Bonhoeffer: by this I do not mean the whole book, but some of its passages, in which the matter is handled with such depth and precision that I feel tempted to quote them at some length because I really do not feel capable of saying it better than is done here . . . It pleases me that, in following my own line, I can for once lean as heavily on another as has been possible in this case.[41]

The Thesis of the Book

1. Basically what Bonhoeffer was seeking to do in this book was to reaffirm the elusive concept of 'faith' in all its implications. The tireless search, upon which he had been engaged ever since he wrote *Sanctorum Communio*, for the concrete social nature of the Body of Christ was bound ultimately to lead him to re-examine the Reformers' habitual condemnation of faith as an *'habitus'*, which means that all interest in its dimension of existence is, by definition, rooted in evil. This is what he had been taught himself and what he also taught. But again, Bonhoeffer had always been inclined to add a third *nota*, that of earthly community, to the two classic *notae ecclesiae*, the Word and the Sacrament.

Church is not a community of souls, as is maintained today. Nor is Church merely the proclamation of the Gospel. In other words, Church is not merely pulpit, but Church is the Real Body of Christ on earth.[42]

From this he went on to unite the Reformed Articles of 'Faith', 'Justification' and 'Sanctification', under the one concept 'Discipleship'. Yet with his key formula, 'only he who believes is obedient, and only he who is obedient believes',[43] he did not intend to question the complete validity of Luther's *sola fide* and *sola gratia*, but rather to reassert their validity by restoring to them their concreteness here on earth. He denies emphatically and explicitly that this in any way represents a betrayal or distortion. Justification is an uncontested premise which is complete in itself. Indeed the aim is to divest it of cheap verbalism and to rediscover and restore to it its full value. Discipleship is an interpretation of justi-

40. Letter of 14.10.1936, GS II, pp. 288-90.
41. K. Barth, KD IV/2, p. 604.
42. *Unser Weg nach dem Zeugnis der Schrift*, 1938, GS II, p. 327.
43. CD, p. 54.

fication which sees justification as applying to the sinner rather than to the sin:

Justification is the new creation of the new man, and sanctification his preservation until the day of Jesus Christ.[44]

Yet, by comparison with the age of the Reformation, Bonhoeffer's emphasis in his interpretation of earthly discipleship on the concreteness of faith, and his placing of the disciple within the boundaries of historical and local decisions, fraught as these are with visible inconsistencies, took him on to wholly new ground and into a changed intellectual climate. When he attempted to support his thesis by quotations from confessional writings, he could find little more than allusions.[45] Like Kierkegaard, Bonhoeffer had always believed that 'Luther would say now the opposite of what he said then',[46] whereby he would really be saying the same thing, the vital thing. Once, faith had meant leaving the cloister; faith might come to mean a reopening of the cloister; and faith might also mean taking part in politics.

2. Bonhoeffer's conception of faith as discipleship was strengthened rather than weakened by his early discovery of the social substance of each individual Christian Article:

It is impossible to become a new man as a solitary individual. The new man means more than the individual believer after he has been justified and sanctified, it means the Church, the Body of Christ, in fact it means Christ himself.[47]

It is true that what is stressed in *The Cost of Discipleship* is the fact that social organization takes place as the result of the self-abandonment of the individual. And concomitantly, social concretion takes place in the sphere of the individual. Jesus calls the individual, and he can no longer seek safety in numbers. Discipleship opposes mass credos and 'world movements', because it is personal commitment. The Church is based upon individual disciples and not upon the flock. On the other hand, individual discipleship and 'individualism' are mutually exclusive. When, in his letters from prison, Bonhoeffer described 'religion' as, among other things, 'individualism', he was not gainsaying his emphasis on the individual in *The Cost of Discipleship*.

3. He draws a sharp distinction between discipleship and an ideal. The call of Jesus cannot be turned into a programme or an ideology. This would mean a failure in discipleship. Ideals and programmes lead to a craving for casuistic realization, but this is the opposite of the step into discipleship. For discipleship means breaking away from casuistic and legalistic programmes. To be called, to go and to follow—this is a true

44. CD, p. 250.
45. CD, p. 55.
46. LPP, p. 71.
47. CD, p. 218.

Christology; to be called and not to follow, but instead to work out a programme for use in this or that situation—this is a false Christology. For then Christ is left out in the cold, an occasional help towards salvation. But the call creates a new and full existence, it makes new relations possible and hence breaks its way through legalism. It does not effect constitutions and decrees, but brings human beings into relation with each other.

In this context there is an impressive passage on the 'weakness' of the 'Word'.

The Word is weaker than any ideology, and this means that with only the gospel at their command the witnesses are weaker than the propagandists of an opinion. But although they are weak, they are ready to suffer with the Word, and so are free from that morbid restlessness which is so characteristic of fanaticism.[48]

The Word of Christ must not be mistaken for triumphant, all-pervasive conviction, for it can also respect the impossible, take into account the barriers which it encounters; it esteems the individual—the more so when that individual disagrees. The idea, on the other hand, invades the individual, and nothing is impossible to a programme. But the Word incarnate is content to be despised and rejected.

God's freedom confines itself within the limits of a weak human community of individuals. This had already been the view of the Bonhoeffer who wrote *Act and Being*, whereas 'the weak Christ, the weak Word' here presages the Christology of the final year of his life. The belief in the power of weakness was one of Bonhoeffer's most basic insights, and he was to hold to it throughout his theological life.

4. In the interpretation of the weak Word we are close to the profoundest thought ever expressed by Bonhoeffer: discipleship as participation in Christ's sufferings for others, as communion with the Crucified. Here a wealth of personal experience is apparent between the lines. Yet Bonhoeffer succeeds in avoiding both the painful, self-pitying mood found in many hymns, and he avoids also the exaltation of mysticism. The deputizing element in discipleship prevents it from becoming introverted and an end in itself. Disciples are the kind of people who take upon themselves what others would like to shake off. 'His life on earth is not finished yet, for he continues to live in the lives of his followers.'[49] These words are found at the end of the book. This was how Bonhoeffer developed the premise of *Christus praesens* he had put forward in *Sanctorum Communio*. It is a view which can be found in concentrated form in the short Bible study, 'Temptation', which was delivered at a moment of crisis in 1938, and during the last year of his life it was to remain

48. CD, p. 166.
49. CD, p. 274.

a dominant concept in what has become known as 'Christianity without Religion'.

5. There is a particularly interesting passage in which Bonhoeffer writes of the 'first step' prior to, or towards, faith.[50] This foreshadows the later distinction drawn in *Ethics* between the 'ultimate' and the 'penultimate'. For the ultimate and the penultimate are correlatives, each conditioning, qualifying and validating the other. Even here, in *The Cost of Discipleship* in which he so resolutely turns his face towards the ultimate, his desire for concreteness keeps him close to the penultimate. It should not, of course, be overlooked that, in the 'penultimate', the 'first step' is still of little significance, a mere transitional move without the autonomy that is later attributed to it. Elsewhere Bonhoeffer wrote:

One cannot and must not speak the last word before the last but one . . . In *The Cost of Discipleship* I just hinted at this, but did not follow it up; I must do so later.[51]

Place and Evaluation

Bonhoeffer, as the author of *The Cost of Discipleship*, made a deep impression on the consciousness of the Protestant Church. The book continued to be regarded as characteristic until the publication of his letters from prison substituted another image of him. This gave rise to the suggestion that there had been a constrained period of his existence, a state of affairs for which the church struggle had been responsible—a thesis particularly favoured by Hanfried Müller.[52]

Indeed, the breadth and variety of themes apparent in 1932 dwindled, after 1933, to a mere trickle, only coming into evidence again during the final years of Bonhoeffer's life. Hence the question arises as to the nature and the depth of the change marked by *The Cost of Discipleship*. When did it really come about, what was its crucial moment and what its accidental consequences? Did it represent a sort of intellectual mishap which interrupted for a whole decade a promising development—a development that was resumed only in 1943 for two brief and difficult years? Did Bonhoeffer, without disowning a word of *The Cost of Discipleship*, come to recognize its limitations?[53] And what was the part played by the year 1933?

The answer is self-evident: Both the theme and the underlying thesis of *The Cost of Discipleship* were already fully evolved before 1933, but it is to that year that the book owes its single-minded concentration.

It may be recalled that in 1928, when he was in Barcelona, he had

50. CD, pp. 54 ff.
51. Advent II, 1943, LPP, p. 104.
52. H. Müller, *Von der Kirche zur Welt*, 1961, pp. 20, 38, 197 ff.
53. GS III, p. 54.

still read the Sermon on the Mount in the conventional, harmless rendering of the unemotional, traditional Lutheran, whereby to understand it literally was to make it into a law, and that law was abolished in Christ.[54] While he was in America he had grown less sure of this interpretation, and in his university seminar of 1932 he had dealt with the relationship between faith, commandment and obedience along the lines, and even in the terminology, of *The Cost of Discipleship*, so that at Zingst the ordinands from Berlin were already initiates by comparison with their fellow-students. The preaching from the pulpit of a message of grace that was not binding, and the triviality of ecumenical pronouncements on peace had, since 1931, been posing new questions which were related to crises and decisions of a purely personal kind. Indeed, in taking his departure from the concrete, earthly image of the Body of Christ in *Sanctorum Communio* and from the actuality of revelation in *Act and Being* he was already inevitably committed to the subject of *The Cost of Discipleship*. The theological relevance of the 'Child',[55] the twin concepts 'simplicity and discord',[56] intuition as opposed to reflection —all these at an early stage helped to form his concept of faith: 'Belief is never directed to itself, but only on Christ'.[57] These trains of thought provided crucial insights for his book. 'Obedience is action', he said in a lecture in 1932,[58] and the idea of 'cheap grace' was formulated in a lecture to a branch of the German S.C.M.[59]

Bonhoeffer does not appear to have written anything explicitly relating to New Testament passages about the call or the Sermon on the Mount prior to the London period when, after the stormy summer of 1933 was over, he had settled down as a pastor. In May 1935, in a lecture at Zingst, he dealt at some length with the three disciples in Luke 9, the disciple who offered himself, the disciple who was called and the disciple who turned back. He had handled this theme in 1934 in a New Year's Day article for the parish magazine *Gemeindebote*.[60] Later he gave sermons on separate passages of the Sermon on the Mount, but these have not survived. In April 1934 he wrote to E. Sutz:

Please write and tell me some time what you say when you preach about the Sermon on the Mount. I am working on this now—trying to keep it extremely simple and straightforward, but it always comes back to *keeping the commandment and not evading it*. Discipleship of Christ—I'd like to know what that is—it is not exhausted in our concept of faith. I am setting to work on something I might describe as an essay—this is a first step.[61]

54. GS III, p. 54.
55. In Barcelona, GS I, p. 53; also AB, pp. 180 ff.
56. A recurring theme in CF.
57. AB, p. 95.
58. GS III, pp. 162 ff.
59. See Ch. VI, pp. 158 f.
60. GS IV, pp. 171 ff.
61. GS I, p. 41.

To sum up, it might be said that in 1932 not only were the basic tendency and basic questions underlying *The Cost of Discipleship* already in existence in a complete form, but the answers had also been formulated. The events of 1933 prevented their schematic elaboration. The first notes were made during 1934 in London and the book itself came into being between 1935 and 1937. Thus it owes its origin, not to the single-mindedness induced by the events of 1933, but to the independent theological foundations Bonhoeffer himself had laid. The trains of thought we have discovered here most certainly do not represent an aberration deriving from the circumstances of the day—an aberration which we can therefore safely by-pass in order to proceed as quickly and as directly as possible to the Bonhoeffer of the final period. What we have here, on the contrary, represents the first development of Bonhoeffer's original view of faith and Christology—material which cannot possibly be left out of account.

Yet 1933 was not without influence on *The Cost of Discipleship*. It undoubtedly made Bonhoeffer realize just what it was he wanted to write about and enabled him to devote himself to it with single-minded intensity. This contributed both to the limitation and to the greatness of his exposition and in this light the book might be seen as one of the most pertinent answers to the events of 1933.

Realizing that he was proposing to deal, not just with his own personal theme, but with that of the whole Church, he abandoned subjects in which up till then he had taken a passionate interest. Thus he proceeded no further with a doctrine of the Lordship of Christ over the World, a subject upon which he had just embarked in 1932;[62] there were to be no more of the constructive reflections on the State, such as had then recently appeared in *Thy Kingdom Come*.[63] Nor is the category of 'the orders of preservation' discernible after 1933. He abandoned it at the very time when other Lutherans such as Künneth were adopting it as a basis on which to construct their own concept of the two realms. He further lost all interest during these years in deliberating Brunner's and Gogarten's themes. And the more loudly periodicals and Sunday newspapers clamoured for a new 'theology of creation', the more pregnant Bonhoeffer's silence became. It was not that he claimed any special ability as compared with Gogarten, Althaus, Elert and Hirsch, who had all produced imposing works on this complex aspect of Christian theology, but he felt that the hour for concentration upon it had either passed or been missed. To show an interest, however genuine and earnest, in this particular subject at this particular time was to be dangerously near sacrificing at the altar of Hitler. In his theories of 1932, Bonhoeffer had suggested that it was no longer the time to consider the 'theology of

62. GS III, pp. 279 ff.
63. Winter 1932-3, GS III, pp. 279 ff., but also in the article 'Die Kirche vor der Judenfrage', April 1933, GS II, pp. 46 f.

orders', because the time for the 'theology of break-through' had come.[64] In other words, the emphasis now had to be shifted from the theology of creation to eschatology. He regarded a preoccupation with the theology of creation as anything but concrete. The hour might again come, he thought, when such a preoccupation would be admissible, but not until the hour of the theology of the *eschaton* was past.

Thus since 1933 there had been a change in Bonhoeffer's concept of the role of the 'world'. This explains why those who look back from the 'worldly' Bonhoeffer of *Letters and Papers from Prison* are apt to regard *The Cost of Discipleship* as a temporary deviation.

For the Bonhoeffer of that time saw the world merely as a dangerous jungle which has to be traversed; the world has not disappeared, but is, on the contrary, very much there. Yet it would certainly be a mistake to interpret this as an attempt to escape from the world. The ghetto of *The Cost of Discipleship* is not the peaceful backwater of the Pietists, nor is it the other-worldliness of the Enthusiasts, neither of which remain in touch with reality. It is, rather, the summons to battle, it is concentration and hence also restriction, so that the whole of this earth may be reconquered by the illimitable message. Or, to use Bonhoeffer's later terminology, when the penultimate, in its lust for glory and its thirst for adulation and sacrifice, thrust itself forward upon the pro-scenium—and even in the Church those who bowed the knee were legion—Bonhoeffer turned towards the ultimate, doing so, however, for the sake of the penultimate. He made his own a theme which had hitherto been the prerogative of the Pietists, and this at a time when its ghetto-like character was more inescapable than ever before. But now this was as it should be, for in 1933 the ghetto of Jesus had become *the* theme of the Church.

Thus we can ascertain an intrinsic consistency and continuity in Bonhoeffer's theological development. Its direction, limitation and con-centration were determined by a deep inner need rather than by, say, the requirements of methodology. In 1927 Bonhoeffer was seeking the concrete entity of the Body of Christ in the Church in the form of a sociological structure (*Sanctorum Communio*). In 1929 he reformulated the question to ask whether the earthly continuity of revelation, in its free contingency, could be conceived in terms of the concrete Church (*Act and Being*). In 1932 he examined the relation of the Body of Christ to the world by enquiring into the actual obedience to God's command-ments. In 1933 his exposé of the structure of Christology comprised within it the implication of all his previous thinking. Here we may see how, by interpreting belief in Christ as discipleship, he succeeds in put-ting new life into the sawdust puppet of academic Christology.

At first the ordinands at Finkenwalde felt overwhelmed by Bon-

64. This is most typically expressed in 'Dein Reich komme', GS III, pp. 270 ff.

hoeffer's theology of discipleship and some of them protested courageously against the reversal of the hallowed order which put faith before obedience—a reversal which made of these terms an interchangeable dialectic. But the longer the National Socialist régime remained in power, the more the ordinands—and many others with them—were able to accustom themselves to the Bonhoeffer of *The Cost of Discipleship*. Sermons on the eschatological otherness of the disciples began to multiply, but the final effect of this was that Bonhoeffer's dynamic ghetto increasingly assumed the character of a ghetto that is cut off and has grown sterile. With familiarity, the costly otherness of grace once again grew 'cheap'.

Bonhoeffer may very well have been aware that at some time he must set off in a new direction. From the ethical and political standpoint this soon became patently imperative, but theologically also it was inevitable. Upon completing his work on *The Cost of Discipleship*, Bonhoeffer contemplated making a start on hermeneutics. 'There seems to be quite a large gap here.'[65] But for this there was not to be time. Looking back from the midst of his new preoccupations to *The Cost of Discipleship*, he wrote in 1944: 'Today I can see the dangers of that book, though I still stand by what I wrote.'[66]

IV THE COMMUNITY HOUSE

In 1935 Finkenwalde provided Bonhoeffer with the opportunity, not only of writing the first chapters of *The Cost of Discipleship*, but also of at last realizing a community—later to be known as 'the House of Brethren'—within the preachers' seminary. *The Cost of Discipleship* and the community house are closely related. Anyone with an ear for the language of the book must have realized at once that it meant a departure from the academic sphere. Its subject did not admit of neutral objectivity. Indeed, the Greifswald professor was not altogether wrong when, in another context, he wrote to the Council of Brethren in Stettin: 'I know that Bonhoeffer simply overwhelms the young men by his religious ardour—one might even say passion.'[67]

Bonhoeffer believed that the circumstances of the day and his own theological principles now demanded the creation for Protestants of something which, for centuries, they had known to exist only under Roman Catholic imprimatur. In this he had, of course, had predecessors in the Protestant brotherhood movements of the previous century. Then, after the First World War, there had been, not only the official pastoral conventions, but also free associations such as the Sydow Brotherhood or the St. Michael's Brethren within the Berneuchen Movement. By

65. See Ch. X, p. 474 and GS I, p. 47.
66. LPP, p. 201.
67. Letter from Professor Baumgärtel, GS IV, p. 339; see also Ch. X, pp. 437 f.

comparison with these free experiments involving a certain degree of voluntary commitment, 1934 saw the sudden and seemingly fortuitous emergence, in all the provinces of the Confessing Church, of new pastoral brotherhoods which desired to be of the Church and to evolve ecclesiastically legitimate forms. They deliberately submitted themselves to the government of the Councils of Brethren, from whom they requested spiritual leadership. Later, Bonhoeffer was to make use of this movement in support of his own proposal: 'The existing rudiments of fraternal associations show the need for more definite formations.'[68] Those brotherhoods, however, had not so far attempted any form of *convivium* and it had certainly never occurred to them to abandon the traditional form of parish ministry—in order, perhaps, to revive the classical vows.

But it was the *vita communis* which, for many years, had been exercising Bonhoeffer's mind. The idea of a compact, circumscribed community had come to him as soon as he began to think about discipleship. By the time of the informal study sessions at Prebelow and Biesenthal in 1932, he had thought it out to its conclusion, and it was there, for the first time, that Bonhoeffer included periods of 'quiet' and 'meditation' in the daily routine, though no one except himself knew what to make of these. To his brother, Karl-Friedrich, he wrote:

I think I am right in saying that I would only achieve true inward clarity and sincerity by really starting work on the Sermon on the Mount. Here alone lies the force that can blow all this stuff and nonsense sky-high, in a fireworks display that will leave nothing behind but one or two charred remains. The restoration of the Church must surely depend on a new kind of monasticism, having nothing in common with the old but a life of uncompromising adherence to the Sermon on the Mount in imitation of Christ. I believe the time has come to rally men together for this.[69]

To Sutz, he described his first attempts to write on the subject of 'discipleship', not as exegeses but, typically, as 'spiritual exercises'.[70] He wished training to take place in 'conventional ecclesiastical seminaries where the pure doctrine, the Sermon on the Mount and divine worship are taken seriously . . .'[71] This was one of the reasons for his study of Anglican communities.[72]

Bonhoeffer did not as yet intend to make known his ideas for a community house and it was not until the end of July that he first mentioned it to one or two people. But the prerequisites already existed in the communal life of the seminary, and it is these prerequisites, upon which he was able to build, that we must now consider.

68. GS II, p. 448.
69. Letter of 14.1.1935, GS III, p. 25.
70. GS I, p. 41.
71. GS I, p. 42.
72. See Ch. VIII, pp. 335 f.

Meditation

The daily time-table laid down by Bonhoeffer at Zingst included half an hour's silent meditation every morning after breakfast, before the start of theological work proper. He proposed that meditation should revolve round a few scriptural verses which all would have agreed upon beforehand. These verses were to be quite unconnected with any ulterior purpose such as current theological work, texts for sermons, or the church year. He did not enlarge any further on the subject, leaving the ordinands to their own devices in the execution of what was to them an utterly novel proposal. His suggestions were always made in such a way that those to whom they were addressed felt obliged to comply; in this case, however, so intense were the resentment, the perplexity and general discontent that sooner or later they were bound to find expression. But not at once, for on the one hand the ordinands felt entitled to spend the half-hour as they themselves saw fit, and on the other they were put to shame by their director's evident ability to concentrate upon this exercise. However the period of meditation lapsed at once when, as early as 12th May, Bonhoeffer was summoned by telephone to Berlin (following the Gestapo's first raid on the Dahlem office of the Council of Brethren). From Berlin he was sent by Präses Koch to see Bishop Bell in England and so was away for nearly a fortnight. In his absence W. Rott, who had been no more able than the ordinands to assimilate Bonhoeffer's conception of meditation, could not really force them to adhere to this part of the time-table. No sooner had Bonhoeffer returned, however, bringing with him not only the latest news, but also cheese, eels and a vast ham for the common table, than the students felt ready for another effort to put his proposal into practice.

Eventually an evening was set aside for the discussion of the unpopular period of meditation. Because this discussion was held some time after the introduction of the practice, it could not be restricted to theoretical aspects or to theological preliminaries. Everyone spoke from his own personal experience of trial and error. Bonhoeffer was willing to listen to anything, but from the first he admitted of no doubt that the arrangement was to continue and would not be submitted to a majority decision. Some people said that they went to sleep, others that they spent the half-hour working on sermons, since they had absolutely no idea what else to do; others admitted that half an hour's recollection was too much for them and their minds wandered, so they read commentaries instead. The more advanced complained that some students had been smoking pipes during meditation, but Bonhoeffer thought this a good idea. Criticism was then extended to the services, on the grounds that the lessons and prayers were unendurably long. Other seminaries, it seemed, were already regarding Zingst as a joke—a place, they said, where the ordinands had to meditate while they brushed their teeth, and were compelled to submit to an unevangelical legalism.

Bonhoeffer did his best to advise them and to show them that the enterprise was a vital personal exercise, as prescribed by *Introduction to Daily Meditation*[73] or *Life Together*. One innovation was agreed; once a week they were all to foregather for communal meditation during which, in much the same way as at Quaker meetings, they might speak —provided they stuck to Scripture—or remain silent, as they wished. This practice proved helpful to concentration since what others had said could be reflected upon during solitary meditation. As time went on, fewer and fewer of the brethren tried to get out of the exercise. Some continued to practise it long after leaving Finkenwalde, while to most it did at least bring home the fact that the Scripture was more than just a tool of their trade. Until the time of Bonhoeffer's arrest the circular letter sent out to all Finkenwaldians would contain the weekly texts for meditation and sometimes also an exhortation that they should not abandon so salutary a practice.

There are a number of reasons which explain why Bonhoeffer should have found collaborators in this enterprise and why he should have been able to repudiate allegations that it induced a hot-house atmosphere that was narrow, esoteric and impractical. In the first place, the exercise was more than offset by the daily study of down-to-earth theology. Thus the ordinands learned to distinguish between an intellectual exercise and the care of souls. The times of concentration were further counterbalanced by periods of relaxation and entertainment such as Bonhoeffer, with his wit and imagination, was so well qualified to organize. It was regarded as a gap in a student's education if he showed himself incapable of making the most of his leisure. Apart from all this, Bonhoeffer always made it absolutely clear that the time-table in no way represented a withdrawal from decisions in church politics, but rather a way of preparing to meet them.

Finally, the strongest incentive to the hesitant was Bonhoeffer's own manner of prayer. During the services at the seminary it was nearly always he who was responsible for the prayers which were long and mostly extemporized. Sometimes, however, he also used liturgical prayers. He would begin by expressing detailed thanks for the gift of faith, for the seminary's communal life, for the sun and the sea. Next, he would ask for daily and mutual tolerance within the brotherhood. Much time was devoted to prayer for the Confessing Church, her leaders and her synods, for those in captivity, for those who had fallen by the wayside and for enemies; further, there would be the confession of those sins peculiar to the theologian and minister, and intercession for them. He would give much time and trouble to the preparation of these prayers and their inner order. His language was wholly appropriate to the matter in hand and seemed completely free from all manifestations

73. GS II, p. 478.

of self. Into these prayers he would put his will, his understanding and his heart. Nevertheless, he believed that the language used in prayer should as a rule be modelled on that of the Psalms with which it should in any case harmonize.

He was convinced that prayer had to be taught and must be learnt. But neither faculties nor seminaries included prayer in their curricula. The example daily set by Bonhoeffer, however, gradually began to bear fruit. He deliberately insisted on the observance of outward temporal conditions; sometimes he would give very simple and practical advice on prayer.

[The need to pray] is not obviated, even by the Confessing Church . . . The imputation that these [i.e. periods of meditation and prayer] are legalistic strikes me as totally unreal. How can it possibly be legalistic for a Christian to learn what prayer is, and to spend a fair amount of his time learning it? Recently a leading member of the Confessing Church told me: 'We haven't the time for meditation now; the ordinands must learn to preach and to catechize.' This either shows a total incomprehension of young theologians today, or else a blasphemous ignorance of how preaching and teaching come about. The kind of questions serious young theologians put to us are: How can I learn to pray? How can I learn to read the Bible? Either we can help them to do this, or we can't help them at all. Nothing of all this can be taken for granted.[74]

Confession

The first time the seminary went to communion from Zingst was on the sixth Sunday after Easter. The impending event was mentioned in Bonhoeffer's prayers at evening and morning service for a whole week beforehand. All work was abandoned on the day before communion. He had early made it known that the celebration required mutual reconciliation and had intimated—to the surprise of most of the ordinands—that they might confess privately to one of the brethren or else to the director himself. Hardly anyone was able to make up his mind to take this step and the suggestion aroused a certain amount of embarrassed resentment, for that kind of thing was not usually done in the Protestant Church. The last service on Saturday took place in an atmosphere of seriousness and gloom, in strong contrast to the joyous communion that was celebrated on Sunday morning. Bonhoeffer suspended all work for the rest of the day, suggesting instead that they should go for a walk. The evening was devoted to reading aloud and to general recreation. It was only gradually that the brotherhood was able to accustom itself to this monthly actualization of communion. As the summer wore on, one or another of the ordinands began to go to private confession, but who did so, or how often, was never generally discussed.

74. To K. Barth, 19.9.1936, GS II, pp. 284 f.

However there was an indefinable feeling that things had changed, although the atmosphere did not in any way become inquisitorial. And one day Bonhoeffer himself asked one of the brethren—one who was quite inexperienced in such matters—to hear his confession.

Bonhoeffer did not lay down any liturgical form for this procedure. Just as services were held round the dinner-table and not in the emergency chapel, so private confession at Finkenwalde was conducted without vestments or formal ceremony. Bonhoeffer gave excellent instruction on the subject of confession and its elements; he advised pastors to preach an annual sermon on the blessing of private confession which enabled a person to unload his conscience on to a brother in place of God. For absolution by a brother in the name of God carried more conviction than absolution after general confession, fraught as this was with the danger of self-deception and self-forgiveness. His advice was that there should not be too much insistence on the trustworthiness of the confessor, but rather that he who confessed should humble himself and trust that, in the other, Christ was confronting him and listening to him. And there were some who understood when, in his sermon on forgiveness, Bonhoeffer said:

My dear brethren, anyone who has ever had the experience of being wrested away from grave sin by God and then receiving his forgiveness, anyone to whom God in such an hour has sent a brother to whom he can tell his sin, anyone who knows the resistance put up by his sin to that help because he does not really want to be helped, and has nevertheless found himself absolved from his sin by his brother in the name and at the behest of God—will lose all desire to judge and to apportion blame. All he will ask is a share in his brother's burden, and to serve, to help, to forgive, without measure, without conditions, without end.[75]

The New Proposal

The August holiday for the first intake had not yet begun when Bonhoeffer made up his mind to speak about the 'House of Brethren'. His intention was that a group of brethren should remain in the spacious house at Finkenwalde where they would continue to work with him when, in the late autumn, a new course of ordinands was due to arrive. Towards the end of July the first discussion was held with those who wished to stay on and who, it was suggested, should take time during the holidays to think the matter over and discuss it with their superiors in the Church. When the holidays were over, at the beginning of September, they and Bonhoeffer together drew up an official proposal for a community house, to be sent to the Council of Brethren of the Old Prussian Union. The Council would have to release the young ministers for the purpose and grant them the necessary accommodation. The name

75. 17.11.1935, GS IV, pp. 405 f.

'Evangelical House of Brethren' which figured in the proposal of 6th September 1935[76] was then quite new. The remark that the plans had been under consideration with some of the brethren for several years was a reference to the discussions with the Berlin students which had been going on since the time of Prebelow and Biesenthal. In support of his proposal Bonhoeffer adduced the following reasons:

a) The content and manner of preaching can be sustained with greater objectivity and staunchness by a community than is possible for an individual in isolation. The principal objective, therefore, is not contemplative introversion, but proclamation.

b) The answer to the now general question as to the nature of the Christian life cannot be given in the abstract, but only by a concrete experiment in communal living and communal awareness of Christ's commandments. Thus the second objective is the theological question of discipleship.

c) The renunciation of traditional privileges postulates a group of ministers who are always available and who, in a community, will find that concentration which is necessary for service outside. In other words, the church struggle demands a new form of pastoral office.

d) The community would afford a spiritual refuge to pastors working on their own who, from time to time, would be able to retire there and renew their strength for further service.

The *vita communis* envisaged in the proposal was to take the form of a daily order of prayer, brotherly exhortation, free personal confession, common theological work and a very simple communal life. The brethren would pledge themselves to answer every emergency call from the Church and, should they wish to leave the community, they would be free to do so. Admission would be by common consent of the community.

Bonhoeffer further pointed out that for him, a group of this kind was a personal necessity if he was to assure the seminary's continuity of work and its standards. When, in 1936, he was trying to persuade Staemmler to allow a member of the community from the province of Saxony to stay on there, he wrote:

There are two things the brethren have to learn during their short time in the seminary—first, how to lead a communal life in daily and strict obedience to the will of Christ Jesus, in the exercise of the humblest and highest service one Christian brother can perform for another; they must learn to recognize the strength and liberation to be found in brotherly service and communal life in a Christian community. This is something they are going to need.

Secondly they have to learn to serve the truth alone in the study of the Bible and its interpretation in their sermons and teaching. I personally am responsible for this second duty, but the first I cannot shoulder by myself.

For this there must be a body of brethren who, without fuss, involve the

76. GS II, pp. 448 ff.

others in their communal life. That is what the House of Brethren is.[77]

The proposal for the House of Brethren was signed by Bonhoeffer and the postulants on 6th September 1935. In view of the fact that parishes were in urgent need of young theologians, Bonhoeffer was not at all certain that the proposal would be favourably received, and indeed it met with some reluctance, and with a certain amount of criticism which was never completely silenced. But such was Bonhoeffer's reputation that the Council of Brethren would have hesitated to turn down the proposal altogether.

Six brethren were granted permission to remain at Finkenwalde, where they stayed over the holidays and then on for the second and later courses. From Berlin-Brandenburg there was J. Kanitz who was entrusted with the care of the Reformed congregation of Pasewalk and several confessional congregations in Stettin, as well as taking tutorials in the seminary; also W. Maechler, who took over the confessional congregation and the emergency church in Finkenwalde itself; and A. Schönherr, who was made responsible for correspondence, circular letters, deputations and tutorials. From East Prussia there was H. Lekzsas (killed on active service), who carried out the difficult work with the Greifswald students; from Pomerania, F. Onnasch (later killed by the Russians), who was seconded to near-by Podejuch as assistant preacher to the superintendent, a supporter of the Confessing Church. Finally, from the province of Saxony there was E. Bethge who, at first, was put in charge of accounts, and who also conducted a tutorial.

All these young men were also preparing for their second examination at the university. It was not long before Maechler, Kanitz and Schönherr were called away for normal service with congregations; they also got married. Inevitably the House of Brethren saw a good deal of coming and going, and there were brethren whose stay was little more than a transitory visit, among them W. Brandenburg (killed on active service) and R. Grunow from Brandenburg, K. F. Müller from Pomerania, H. Thurmann from the Rhineland, O. K. Lerche (killed on active service) from the province of Saxony, and P. Wälde (killed on active service) from Hesse.

Board and lodging was paid for by pooling the very unequal stipends of ministers and assistant preachers, who were paid (or not, as the case might be) by their respective Councils of Brethren. The highest contribution invariably came out of Bonhoeffer's own pocket. The House of Brethren kept as closely as possible to the seminary's time-table and it was only at midday, when the ordinands had singing instruction, that the brethren would meet for a short period of discussion and prayer in Bonhoeffer's room.

While the proposal for the House of Brethren and the form of life

77. To W. Staemmler, 27.6.1936.

followed there contained the implication of classical monastic vows, these were never explicitly taken, nor was it envisaged that they should be taken in the immediate future. (It was a step which the Anglican community at Mirfield, founded at the end of the nineteenth century, postponed making for thirty years.)

The rumour that Bonhoeffer insisted on celibacy was quickly scotched by the three brethren from Brandenburg. But although the community was unaware of this, the director had himself meanwhile broken with the girl who, in the twenties and, more recently, since the beginning of the church struggle, had been a close friend of his. In this he was partially motivated by the thought that at that particular time, and while he was experimenting with a *vita communis*, there could not really be any question of marriage. Indeed the fact that Bonhoeffer had no second commitment to a family and could himself make do with only one and a half rooms[78] was an incalculable asset at a time when the seminary and the House of Brethren were in process of development. For him, the plans he had so long nurtured admitted of no alternative. He dedicated himself and all that was his to the House of Brethren.

When in the autumn of 1937 the Gestapo closed down Finkenwalde Seminary, it also brought an end to the House of Brethren after an existence of only two short years. The new, clandestine seminary of the 'Collective Pastorates' precluded any continuation of the House of Brethren's *vita communis*. Bonhoeffer's dearest wish, the object of which was not 'the seclusion of the cloister but the most inward concentration for the service of others',[79] was never to get beyond the first, rudimentary stage.

'Life Together'

The premature dissolution of the community, however, led to the publication of a little booklet entitled *Life Together* (Munich, 1939). During Bonhoeffer's life-time this was the most widely read of all his books. It would never have been written but for the intervention of the police, for Bonhoeffer was reluctant to publicize his experiment too soon, or to have to justify point by point something that had hardly got beyond the stage of trial and error. When in 1936 Finkenwalde and the House of Brethren had become a topic of general interest, he left the brethren to cope with the enquiries that started pouring in; a request from Staemmler resulted in the production of 'Introduction to Daily Meditation'.[80] Bonhoeffer sketched out a rough draft for internal consumption, but never finished it.[81] But when Finkenwalde was no more, he felt he would

78. To the Old Prussian Council of Brethren, GS II, p. 452.
79. GS II, p. 449.
80. GS II, pp. 478 ff.
81. 'Der Morgen', GS IV, pp. 290-3.

like to record what had been done there. Thus the experiments which had been devised especially for Finkenwalde as a theological community were given a new and more generally applicable form.

The publication of *Life Together* caused quite a sensation, for this was something entirely new in Protestant Germany. Though short-lived, Finkenwalde had disclosed one of Protestantism's weaker points and had further attempted to find practical solutions where failure had left others lost and helpless. It seemed as though something had been restored to the Church which had long been confined to conventicles or sects and had been sought by group movements or brotherhoods such as those of St. Michael and Sydow. For here were the outlines of a living Protestant community, a revival neither in opposition to, nor outside, the churches of the Reformation (as once at Herrnhut), but within the Church, having been undertaken and upheld out of a renewed understanding of the Church herself. In the midst of the great crisis and weakness by which the privileged pastoral office of the National Church was beset Finkenwalde, with its new forms of service, had shown the way to a possible alternative. For Bonhoeffer always drew a sharp distinction between the office of the pastor as preacher—an office which could not be relinquished—and the office of the parish minister, which need not be preserved at all costs.[82]

It is true that in the nineteenth century German Protestantism had gone so far as to evolve monastic training for deacons and deaconesses, but it had never formed free communities such as those in England. When the attempt was finally made in the twentieth century by Bonhoeffer, it was in exceptional circumstances, even though the project had been conceived before 1933. It would be interesting to know how his ideas would have evolved in more normal conditions; what we do know, however, is that his experiment began to prove its worth when the great crisis in the privileged National Church came. Similar experiments and reflections are also discernible in the Bonhoeffer of the final years, with his thoughts about the arcane discipline in which Christians surrender their privileges, pray, study and act in ways that are not for the generality, nor intended to make the headlines.[83]

At a time when Finkenwalde and the House of Brethren were becoming known, they were visited by members of the Oxford Group who thought that Bonhoeffer seemed a likely ally. In this they were mistaken, however. The man who, in *The Cost of Discipleship*, had advocated 'the first step', found the Oxford Group's demand for 'change' very disturbing; he held that they had replaced the witness of the Gospel with the witness of personal change. He was incensed by people who allowed themselves to be led full circle into reflecting upon their own beginnings, and was most strongly averse to any interpretation of *The Cost of*

82. See for example GS IV, pp. 247 ff.
83. Cf. Ch. XIII, pp. 784 ff.

Discipleship or *Life Together* as special pleading on behalf of conversion. The strength of the preaching of the Cross was, he believed, lacking in the Oxford Group and in its supporters, and he further censured their indifference to the 'Confession' and their 'unsteadiness' which proved so inhibiting in all that related to church politics.

The Oxford Movement has been naïve enough to try to convert Hitler—a ridiculous failure to understand what is going on . . .[84]

But here the affair's beginning to look very dubious indeed. Uncommitted churchmen are rushing, all agog, to have a look at and to dally with this live, unpolitical phenomenon.[85]

There were other affinities to be repudiated, however, besides those with the Oxford Group. In 1936, when working on his lectures on Zinzendorf's hymns, his partiality for these did not prevent his writing:

By the time I'd finished, I felt really depressed. What a musty cellarful of piety . . . And all this in hymns! Yes, such is man—pious man! I have a horror of the consequences of this *finitum capax infiniti*! We must have the pure and genuine air of the Word around us. And yet we are incapable of getting away from ourselves. But for goodness' sake let's turn our eyes away from ourselves![86]

But there was another area in which he felt it even more essential to define his limits. To the head of the Berneuchen Movement in Pomerania, Dr. Friedrich Schauer, he wrote:

It would seem to you that the Holy Spirit is not only the Reality committed to the true, consistent Word of God by which, in knowledge and life, we are inescapably bound, but is also the formative principle of a Christian ideal of life . . . The Confessing Church would sacrifice the promise that has been given her should any power other than obedience to the truth wrought by the Holy Spirit be brought in to infuse new life into the Church.[87]

Some members of the Berneuchen Movement were also members of the Pomeranian Council of Brethren; it might have been expected that they would be anxious to foster relations with Finkenwalde because they, too, were concerned with the renewal of the ministry and of the laity in the Church. On the contrary, their relations with Finkenwalde became acrimonious to the point of a final breach,[88] while in due course they themselves left the Council of Brethren altogether. Yet with Dr. Baumann, the Reformed member of the Pomeranian Council, Finkenwalde was to establish warm relations in spite of his innate mistrust of pious conventicles and his undisguised theological reservations towards Bonhoeffer as a Lutheran. Nevertheless, Baumann would send

84. To E. Sutz, 11.9.1934, GS I, pp. 42 f.
85. To E. Sutz, 24.10.1936, GS I, p. 46.
86. To E. Bethge, 31.7.1936, GS II, p. 278.
87. GS II, pp. 215 f.
88. Letter of 26.1.1936, GS II, pp. 209, 281.

those young ministers in whose spiritual development he took an especial interest to spend a few weeks at Finkenwalde where, if no pretext could be found for them to attend the seminary regularly, they might, for a time, share in the life of the community.

When, at the end of 1940, Bonhoeffer was working in Ettal, he encountered the monastic wisdom of the Benedictines as one who himself was no stranger to it.[89] Though the time of community life was past for him in appearance, it was not so in practice. In 1943 and 1944, when he was compelled to lead a cruelly lonely existence, the exercises he had practised at Finkenwalde proved an invaluable solace, and also helped to keep him frank and open-minded towards his agnostic fellow-sufferers.

V ECUMENISM

Bonhoeffer's work at Finkenwalde meant his withdrawal from the round of ecumenical conferences. His involvement in the ecumenical movement had reached its peak in 1934 but during the following year he allowed his duties to lapse almost entirely, and it was only when the leaders of the Confessing Church needed him or Präses Koch sought his intervention that he would leave the seminary to manage without him. On the other hand, in his writings and his disputations with senior members of the movement, Bonhoeffer's views of the ecumenical question in 1935 were expressed with a cogency he never matched before or afterwards.

1. *Unavoidable Journeys*

Now that he was again living in Germany, it was difficult for Bonhoeffer to escape the problems of the Confessing Church's representation at future ecumenical conferences, problems which had grown much more acute since the Dahlem Synod. He attended two conferences of ecumenical experts from the Confessing Church representing the whole country, during which he took issue with several experienced men; indeed, this was to precipitate the crisis in his relations with Geneva.

Hanover. A conference was arranged for 13th and 14th May 1935 at Hanover in preparation for the 1937 Oxford Conference. Among those expected was Dr. J. H. Oldham who had the responsibility for preparing the themes for Oxford and was thus cooperating closely with the Research Department in Geneva. From Hanover he would be going to a meeting of the executive committee of 'Life and Work' in Paris where he was to give Bell the news from Germany. Bonhoeffer was summoned to the Hanover meeting by telegram.

He arrived at a time when matters were beginning to look very serious for the Church: Peter Brunner and two other pastors from Rhineland-Hessen had been interned in Dachau concentration camp for more than

89. GS II, pp. 382, 384, 398, 411, 588.

four weeks and the Councils of Brethren had ordered weekly services of intercession on their behalf. On 11th May the Council's office in Dahlem was searched by the Gestapo for the first time. This was the background to the meeting at which Bonhoeffer made it very clear, firstly, that the ecumenical representatives from abroad must no longer expect that they could persuade the Reich Church (Heckel, in other words) and the Confessing Church to carry out joint preparations for Oxford; secondly, that the Confessing Church, in conformity with Barmen and Dahlem, must insist on a less equivocal attitude on the part of the Research Department to the claims of these two Synods. He went on to say that preparations for Oxford could only emanate from a theology supported by a real church; Geneva, however, was evading a decision as to which was then the real Church in Germany.

Six weeks later, at a meeting in Berlin, the first item on the agenda was a paper from Schönfeld defending Geneva's attitude. This gave rise to a heated discussion. Menn, Wendland and, to some extent, Lilje took the side of the Research Department. In reply to Bonhoeffer's allegations, Schönfeld had written that in Geneva the entire work in connection with Oxford sprang from the very 'soil of the Church', but, he went on, 'if what is demanded is a theology held to be absolute, it cannot really be included within the framework of our ecumenical research'.[90] Despite every assurance of Geneva's sympathy for the Confessing Church, Bonhoeffer insisted that they were dealing with the other side on terms of parity. Geneva was advancing 'theological problems' which, he pointed out, 'Heckel is using to confuse the decision. What is demanded is an ecclesiastical decision, not a theological dialogue with the German Christians'.[91] The official minutes of the meeting summed up:

A message transmitted by Dr. Schönfeld (Geneva), under the heading 'An Unspoken Last Word', was submitted (by Dr. Lilje) to those present . . . Discussion of the message: This concerns the attitude of the Ecumenical Research Department in Geneva to the Confessing Church. While some deplored the absence of any clear decision in favour of the Confessing Church and complained about parity of treatment with the German Christians, others called attention to the Department's confessional and ecclesiastical work and its considerable commitments. Views differ . . .[92]

In Hanover Bonhoeffer pressed once more for the establishment of an ecumenical office for the Confessing Church and put forward his proposals in a memorandum,[93] but again without result. It was, however, decided to form a 'Provisional Church Administration Ecumenical Advisory Board'. That Bonhoeffer was then still relatively optimistic is evident from a letter to Präses Koch in which he wrote: 'It seems to me

90. Minutes of 27.6.1935, printed in MW V, X, K. 1.
91. Ibid.
92. GS I, p. 227.
93. To Präses Koch, 4.6.1935, GS I, pp. 224 ff.

that it depends more than ever on the work being properly tackled.'[94] The Advisory Board failed to survive the collapse of the first Provisional Administration in 1936. In the second Provisional Administration, ecumenical affairs were entrusted to Dr. Hans Böhm, between whom and Bonhoeffer a close relationship was to develop, although by then the major battles had been fought and lost. Böhm retained this post for as long as the Confessing Church lasted.

Berlin. On 27th June, the Provisional Church Administration Ecumenical Advisory Board, with Präses Koch in the chair, met for the first time in Berlin in order to discuss their attitude to the impending summer conference. Bonhoeffer, having recently declined peremptorily[95] to take part on equal terms with other German delegates in a 'Faith and Order' conference at Hindsgavl, now voiced the complaint that 'Lausanne says nothing about the German church question.'[96] From the minutes it is apparent that the Advisory Board foresaw a steadily deteriorating situation.

The Confessing Church may well have the right to demand that the Provisional Church Administration be the one lawful representative of the German Evangelical Church. On the other hand, some doubt must be entertained about whether the ecumenical movement is ready for this, or whether it might not attempt to treat the two Evangelical church governments in Germany on equal terms. A literal interpretation of the constitution of 'Life and Work' would make such treatment imperative, should the ecumenical movement not find the courage to refuse recognition to the Reich Church as a church. It is also thought that the fundamental views of the Confessing Church do not permit her to negotiate with the External Affairs Office of the Reich Church on terms of parity.
Conclusion: The general feeling is that an invitation to an ecumenical conference should be declined if Bishop Heckel is to be represented there.[97]

This meeting—no less than the general atmosphere of uncertainty—had convinced Bonhoeffer of the need to speak out so that both the Confessing Church and the ecumenical movement might realize that this was their hour of crisis. The result was his important article: 'The Confessing Church and the Ecumenical Movement'.[98]

London. During the first summer at Finkenwalde, Präses Koch sent Bonhoeffer to see Bell on two occasions.

Having learned at the Paris meeting that there had been some misgivings about his proposed visit to Düsseldorf with Ammundsen, Bell did not want to imperil the Council of Brethren still further by his presence: an additional factor may have been the searching of the Dahlem office by the Gestapo. But Koch had further requests to make

94. Ibid.   95. See Ch. IX, pp. 398 ff.   96. Minutes of 27.6.1935.
97. GS I, pp. 228 f.   98. See Ch. IX, pp. 400 ff., and GS I, p. 240.

to Bell in connection with the major assembly of representatives of the 'destroyed' regional churches arranged for 22nd and 23rd May in Gohlfeld. This event was being kept strictly secret as a precaution against interference by the police, whose custom it had by then become to break up all assemblies. Koch hoped that the chairman of 'Life and Work' would send a message to Gohlfeld and also, if at all possible, make an appearance at the forthcoming Reich Synod of the Confessing Church in Augsburg.

Bonhoeffer, then on his way home from Hanover, was therefore asked by Koch to turn about and proceed to London where, on 18th May, he reported to the Bishop of Chichester. He made arrangements with Bell that, should the situation suddenly deteriorate,[99] the latter, in company with Koechlin, would at once make his way to Berlin, there to meet friends of the Confessing Church for discussions, 'say at the Grand Hotel am Knie'.

In view of his long absence from Zingst, Bonhoeffer wrote in his memorandum for Koch : 'A travelling secretary for the Church whose job would be to keep both sides regularly informed. Very important!'[100]

The second visit to England on Koch's behalf took place during the first two weeks of August. Part of the time was devoted to a final settlement of matters relating to his leave of absence from the London parishes, so making way for his successor, Lic. Boeckheler.

There were two reasons why the Bishop of Chichester needed to be thoroughly briefed : firstly, the Provisional Church Administration had decided not to attend the 1935 Chamby Conference because Heckel would be there; secondly, Bell would be coming to Germany after Chamby as a result of Ribbentrop's visit in June when, in the Athenaeum, the latter had promised to introduce Bell to Rudolf Hess and to Kerrl, the newly appointed Minister for Church Affairs.[101] Prior to these meetings he wanted a report from the Councils of Brethren on the 'finance departments' set up by the State for the Church.

With Niemöller's 30th July manifesto 'To our Brethren in the Ministry' in his pocket,[102] Bonhoeffer paid his call on Bell. This manifesto bore the signatures of forty-nine prominent people in all parts of Germany and Bell was to refer to it at Chamby when he emphasized that the Universal Christian Council 'could not ignore the growth in compactness within the Evangelical Confessional Church' in opposition to the State's 'pacification measures'.[103] Bell now asked that arrangements be made for his visit to Germany.

After Chamby Bell met Koch, Asmussen and Lilje on 12th September.

99. See GS II, p. 199.
100. GS–I, p. 224.
101. See Ch. VIII, pp. 337 f.
102. See Ch. IX, p. 356.
103. Minutes of the Meeting of the Executive Committee, Chamby, 18-22.8.1935, p. 45.

By the time he saw Hitler's deputy (Hess) and the Minister for Church Affairs (Kerrl), the Nuremberg Laws had been promulgated. At their meeting on 20th September Hess mollified Bell by saying that since the laws were henceforth immutable, the treatment of the Jews would in fact be regularized and therefore better. Kerrl spoke with great optimism on 28th September when assuring the bishop that, by his laws for 'the protection of the German Evangelical Church', he was bringing back peace to the Church and to this end was negotiating with reliable people, including members of the Confessing Church.

2. Invitations Not Accepted

Youth Conference. Initially, under the compelling influence of Fanö, Bonhoeffer still took some interest in the Youth Conference. In his memorandum to de Félice dated 29th January 1935[104] he made some very definite proposals (in English) on possible subjects for discussion, which were derived from the Fanö Youth Conference.

. . . The question which it has not yet succeeded to find an answer to, is whether in case of war a service in a sanitary group would be christianly justifiable . . . I am in favour of an international youth conference and I should be glad if the question of conscientious objection would be one of the subjects under discussion. I feel that one of the weaknesses of our cause is the lack of a common and definite attitude in the very crucial question. We should march on whatever the older people think and do . . .

One of the special topics I should like to propose for the youth conference is: the use of coercion, its right and its limitations. Before this fundamental question is given an answer to, the theoretical basis of pacifism is very weak.

Indeed, the theme of conscientious objection was briefly resumed at the 1935 Chamby Youth Conference: 'The presentation by Pasteur Toureille of recent experiences of Christian conscientious objectors in France made a deep impression.'[105] Meanwhile the principal discussions were concerned with the theme of 'Freedom and Authority'.

Shortly after writing this memorandum Bonhoeffer, no longer wishing to enter into serious commitments with the Youth Commission, arranged that Winterhager should deputize for him. Perhaps he no longer hoped for any real solution at these major conferences to the questions which must be raised if the Church was to decide between heresy and truth and further to ask for a determined obedience to the peace commandment. He was also fully aware of the Geneva secretariat's increasing hostility towards him and was not therefore sorry when, at the beginning of August, his mission to England precluded his attendance at the Youth Conference.

104. See Ch. VIII, p. 315.
105. H. L. Henriod, *The Joint Ecumenical Youth Commission; How and Why it came to be*, Geneva, 1936, p. 8.

For their part, too, the World Alliance and the Geneva headquarters had begun to consider a reorganization of the ecumenical youth secretariat. To the people in Geneva the Fanö youth meetings had seemed a little sinister, highly explosive, and much too close to the deliberations of the main conference. For this reason changes were proposed and Henriod, in his progress report, explained: '[It] had met with various objections and difficulties which made it desirable that the Youth Conference in the future should be held separately.'[106]

The executive committee of 'Life and Work' envisaged[107] a full-time youth secretary based on Geneva—a plan for which the World Alliance promised financial support. The American, Edwin Espy, was appointed to the post in the autumn and took up his duties at the beginning of 1936. There was never any intention of disposing of the services of the honorary youth secretaries since Espy's main task was to prepare for a world youth conference, which eventually took place in 1939 in Amsterdam. Nevertheless, it was, of course, hoped that there would henceforth be better supervision of youth work by Geneva. Espy had been acquainted with Bonhoeffer at Union Theological Seminary in 1930-1, although neither had come to know the other well. Subsequently, in accordance with the wishes of the staff at Geneva, he proposed to Bonhoeffer that the latter should assemble a delegation composed of representatives not only from the Confessing Church, but also from other groups, for the impending 1936 youth conference.[108] It would seem that Bonhoeffer never replied to this suggestion. Eventually Espy met him in Berlin in June 1936 but in his report to Henriod, he speaks only of 'Bonhoeffer's downright rejection of Gerstenmaier, and his readiness to admit members of the free churches and the Lutheran Council to the youth delegation, but not the delegates of the Reich Church'.[109]

Schönfeld sent an effusive recommendation to the Church External Affairs Office on the occasion of Espy's visit to Berlin. In his letter introducing the youth secretary and Henriod to the responsible official, Gerstenmaier, he wrote:

Perhaps you have already heard a lot of alarming things about the work of this ecumenical youth commission, and I might say that my feelings would be the same as yours, had not the position with regard to this work changed fundamentally now that we have found the right man for it . . . If that solution had not been available, we in the Research Department would have done all we could to put a stop to the work in the form it has taken in the past . . .

You may be certain that Mr. Espy's work is in complete accord with the

106. Ibid.
107. Minutes, 53 and 72.
108. Espy to Bonhoeffer, 13.4.1936.
109. Information supplied by A. Boyens on the basis of the archives of 'Life and Work' in Geneva, 23.12.1965.

methods of the Research Department and with the problems and tasks we have set ourselves here . . . I am telling you all this so that you will understand that a fundamental change is now under way. Myself, I have long thought it impossible that this part of the work should be determined exclusively—or almost exclusively—by a man like Bonhoeffer. But it is most desirable, particularly when this is about to be changed, that people should be available who will support Mr. Espy in his work.[110]

Thus the exchanges taking place between the Geneva secretariat and Heckel's office were now far more lively than was the correspondence between the secretariat and the Councils of Brethren.

Chamby 1935. On the agenda for the 1935 conference in Chamby, above Montreux, were the endorsement of the Fanö resolution and also preliminary arrangements for the 1937 Oxford Conference. The Provisional Administration of the Confessing Church, however, and Bonhoeffer himself, found themselves unable to accept the invitation since the representatives of the Reich Church led by Heckel were to be present.

In the summer of 1934 the Fanö battle had revolved round the question whether the Barmen 'opposition' should be invited as such, along with the Reich Church. That battle had been won. The resolution passed at the conference represented the greatest success ever scored by the Confessing Church in spite of or even, perhaps, because of, the fact that she was not present.[111] Now, in 1935, it was no longer a question of being invited along with, but as *the*, representative body of the German Evangelical Church. This was consistent with the declaration made by the Dahlem Synod in October 1934—that is, after Fanö—which placed the Reich Church Government outside the Church of Christ in Germany and superseded its institutions with the emergency organs of the Confessing Church. So the situation became one of real tragedy because, on the one hand, Geneva headquarters and its committees felt that to recognize the decision and to act accordingly would be going too far, while on the other the Confessing Church could hardly abandon her claim without also demolishing her own case.

In this impasse it must have come as a relief to outside observers and to those ecumenicals who were incapable of perceiving this correlation, that they were able to deal with German church bodies which did not insist on an immediate decision. One such was the Lutheran Council, the new organ of the 'intact' Lutheran churches, which gradually evolved from the somewhat indeterminate body it had been in 1934 to become a fully established assembly in March 1936. Many of its members were respectable theologians and for some of those 'observers and ecumenicals' it must have been difficult to see the necessity for an exclusive decision such as that of Dahlem. Moreover, confusion was made worse by the

110. Schönfeld to Gerstenmaier, 2.6.1936. For full text see MW V, X, O. 1.
111. See Ch. VIII, pp. 307 ff.

fact that the theologians of the Church External Affairs Office, and more notably Heckel, made use readily and confidently of these Lutherans' theological categories. For this reason the Councils of Brethren of the Confessing Church found themselves falling behind in the contest to enter the ecumenical sphere, so much so that the confusion even began to spread to their own ranks. Either the Councils put forward their claims without being aware of the true circumstances obtaining in the ecumenical field, or else they did so only half-heartedly. To this day their activities remain so obscure that some writers pass over them in silence, while others adopt a purely emotional approach.

The 1935 Chamby Conference was presided over by the Orthodox Archbishop Germanos who, by rotation, now succeeded Bell. On the German side Bishop Heckel had the field to himself. Having, with his External Affairs Office, survived the end of the era of Ludwig Müller and August Jäger so successfully, he was in a decidedly more favourable situation than he had been at Fanö. Heckel gave an optimistic and comforting picture of the development of the German Church, with especial reference to the State's 'legal aid' in the form of finance departments, the legislative authority and the newly established Ministry of Church Affairs.[112] On the subject of the Jewish question he even gave the assurance 'that it was being dealt with much more openly in Germany than a year ago, and that plans that had been put in hand by the Reich Church were on the way to fulfilment'. Thus Heckel, no more than a few days before the announcement of the Nuremberg Laws, was presenting Bell with much the same arguments as those later used by Hess.

Bishop Bell spoke out on behalf of those who were absent and referred to the rejection by the Councils of Brethren of the ostensibly reassuring 'finance departments'. His speech endorsed 'the resolution adopted by the Council at Fanö to maintain close fellowship with the Confessional Synod' and 'to inform the leaders . . . of the Committee's strong desire for their attendance at all future meetings, and to make it plain that the help of the leaders of the Confessional Church Government and of those whom they represented was indispensable to the Ecumenical Movement . . .'[113] Heckel, who was not to be caught napping, pointed out that this 'implied that the reference in the Fanö minutes to a desire to remain in friendly relations with *all* Christian brethren in Germany, still held good. The ecclesiastical officers of the Foreign Department of the German Evangelical Church claimed to represent the whole Church in a legal and equitable manner . . .'[114]

The third invitation refused by Bonhoeffer in the course of this year was of a new and very flattering kind. It came from 'Faith and Order'.

112. Minutes, 45 and 48.
113. Minutes, 56.
114. Ibid.

The ensuing correspondence relating to this provides us with an important background to his considerable paper on the ecumenical movement.

3. *Canon Leonard Hodgson*

On 17th June 1935 Bonhoeffer received an invitation from 'Faith and Order' through its secretary, Canon Leonard Hodgson, asking him to take part in the summer session of the Continuation Committee at Hindsgavl. The proposal to include Bonhoeffer came from the Swede, Dr. Brilioth (Lund), after the wish had been expressed that there should be an infusion of young blood. Brilioth gave Hodgson the names of three potential German participants, all of them men who had already made their mark. They were Lietzmann, Althaus and Bonhoeffer. Replying to an enquiry from Hodgson, Deissmann wrote: 'It would, of course, be a very good thing if our young lecturer, Pastor Dietrich Bonhoeffer, were to take part. He is now 29 and one of the most eminent representatives of the younger generation here.'[115]

Bonhoeffer refused the invitation because Hodgson had failed to give an assurance that the Reich Church—that is Heckel and Krummacher—would not be appearing on equal terms with himself.

. . . we cannot, as a Movement, exclude the representatives of any Church which 'accepts our Lord Jesus Christ as God and Saviour' . . . we cannot arrogate to ourselves the right to discriminate between them.[116]

This was straightforward and only what was to be expected. But Bonhoeffer had hoped for something different and, in a long letter,[117] pointed out that the Reich Church had betrayed Jesus Christ as God and Saviour; his church had made a binding declaration to this effect and was unable to spare the ecumenical movement from drawing the necessary conclusions. He went on to say that he was well aware that, to anyone removed from the arena, all this must sound very pharisaical and, perhaps, deficient in humility. Bonhoeffer fully recognized that he was not making things easy for his British correspondent, far removed from the scene of the crisis, though Hodgson certainly knew enough to appreciate its complexity and to become mistrustful whenever an attempt was made to reduce everything to one common denominator. How then could he accept and endorse the dictum 'The Confessional Church has therefore declared, that the Reich Church Government has dissociated itself from the Church of Christ'?[118] It was neither accepted nor endorsed. But Bonhoeffer did not relent though he was fully aware that by taking this course, he risked exclusion.

115. Letter of 22.6.1935.
116. Hodgson to Bonhoeffer, 9.7.1935, GS I, p. 231.
117. See GS I, pp. 230-9.
118. GS I, p. 233.

[We know] that we are fighting for Christianity not only with regard to the Church in Germany but in the whole world . . . If now the ecumenical movement, and, in particular the Faith and Order Movement were complying with that decisive question and taking the challenge seriously in obedience towards Jesus Christ and His Word, an inward regeneration and a new unification might well be bestowed upon all Christendom . . . On the other hand, if the ecumenical movement were to leave this question out of sight, it might bring in its own verdict and lose the power of speaking and acting in the name of Jesus Christ . . .[119]

Bonhoeffer requested and was given Koch's approval for his decision and the reasons behind it.[120]

Once again the two virtually irreconcilable elements within the ecumenical movement had inevitably clashed—elements which have continued their mutually disruptive if seminal activities up to the present day. Unlike Hodgson, Bonhoeffer was not the general secretary of an organization restricted by rules, nor was it only to a general secretary and his organization that he addressed himself, while Hodgson, for his part, had not been a member of the Barmen and Dahlem Synods but was a cautious and sceptical church historian. Bonhoeffer had reached the point of believing in the Church within the ecumenical movement—indeed now more than ever—whereas Hodgson continued to believe that the ecumenical movement was only a platform for churches.

. . . it is necessary for us to guarantee to every church, when we invite it to send representatives, that it will not find itself in any way compromised by action taken by the conference at which it is represented . . .[121]

Bell thought that there must be compromise when the cause of Christ was irrevocably at stake, a view which Hodgson's position did not permit him to share, although he did concede:

It may be the duty of the Life and Work Movement to run the risk of this— of that I cannot express any opinion. But for Faith and Order to do so would be to be false to its own vocation.[122]

However, there can be no doubt that a careful study of the relations of 'Faith and Order' with the disputing parties in Germany during those years would confirm that it maintained much better and closer contacts with the opponents of the Confessing Church than did 'Life and Work' and, more especially, the World Alliance. Dr. A. C. Headlam, for example, the Bishop of Gloucester and a leading member of 'Faith and Order' was, for a number of years, the German Christians' spokesman in England.[123] When Bonhoeffer read Hodgson's warm-hearted and careful reply to his letter he must have thought it curious that the sole opposing witness produced to present the claims of the Reich Church

119. GS I, pp. 233 f.   122. Ibid.
120. GS I, pp. 234 f.   123. See Ch. VIII, p. 261.
121. GS I, p. 236.

was. of all people. Professor Wobbermin who had so unequivocally defended the Aryan clause![124]

Hodgson thought that 'Faith and Order' might provide a platform for the disputing parties without prejudice to their own cause, but at this moment there could be no neutrality anywhere for the struggling Church in Germany. Thus, while 'Faith and Order' continued to adhere to its correct but narrow concept of a platform for each party and declined the challenge in a manner that was as unequivocal as it was friendly, the Confessing Church refused to be argued out of its awkward and absolute claim, and so excluded itself from the conferences. In view of all this, Bonhoeffer hoped that the well-considered challenge contained in his article might help to shed fresh light on the question. But it evoked no response.

Nearly four years later there was a revival of the correspondence with Hodgson which did not, however, produce any different result.[125]

4. The Article

Bonhoeffer's article. 'The Confessing Church and the Ecumenical Movement',[126] written during the latter part of June and the first half of July 1935 appeared in the seventh issue of *Evangelische Theologie* that year. It is presented in programmatic form. His demands are addressed to both sides—the ecumenical movement as well as the leaders of the Confessing Church.

He begins with an analysis of the events of the two preceding years in the ecumenical movement: '. . . never before has the Protestant ecumenical movement been so much in evidence on the occasion of a church dispute . . .'[127] As a result of Fanö, Bonhoeffer says, '. . . many leading churchmen are faced by the reality of the ecumenical movement for the first time . . .'[128] The movement 'has pledged itself to stand sponsor for the Confessing Church'.

In the first main section Bonhoeffer examines the question inescapably confronting the ecumenical movement as a result of the existence of the Confessing Church. All too clearly. he recognizes how 'enormous' was the claim of the Confessing Church in demanding recognition of her decision. For this would mean that the ecumenical movement would have to accept a breach with the Reich Church Government such as had already been effected by the Confessing Church. But if the Confessing Church were to abandon this demand, it would mean 'that the

124. GS I, p. 237; see also Ch. VII, p. 248 f.
125. Cf. Ch. XI, pp. 545 f.
126. GS I, pp. 240-61.
127. GS I, p. 240.
128. GS I, p. 242.

German church struggle was already decided *against* her, and with it the struggle for Christianity.'[129]

The first question put by the Confessing Church to the ecumenical movement was: Is the ecumenical movement a church? This was a question with which Bonhoeffer had been much preoccupied ever since the start of his work with the movement. He, of course, like any other supporter of the movement, knew that it was not a church and said so. But what then was the movement's point of departure if it did not claim to be a church, and did not seek to become a church? This was a question that had long been successfully evaded, Bonhoeffer declared, 'But now this question has been raised by the Confessing Church and demands an answer.'[130]

In his analysis of the two preceding years, during which uninformed optimism had so auspiciously been compelled to make way for a 'spirit of theological enquiry', Bonhoeffer speaks highly of the achievement of the Research Department in Geneva. But this stage was now past. To persist any longer in 'theological dialogue' was a dangerous, indeed diabolical, piece of camouflage, a respectable façade behind which overdue decisions on theological as well as church matters were neglected or even withheld. In reference to Schönfeld and his Research Department, he says:

The question of the Confessing Church has taken us beyond the stage, necessary in itself, of theological dialogue.[131]

The insistence on 'defining' the Church now became the refusal to 'be' the Church. For Hodgson's benefit, he goes on:

There is still one way out for the ecumenical movement and that is to accept this question courageously in the form in which it has been received and, in obedience, to leave everything else to the Lord of the Church. Who knows that it is not precisely by way of this disruptive task that the ecumenical movement will emerge fom the struggle strengthened and with greater authority?[132]

The second section reverses the question: Is the Confessing Church allowing herself to be called in question by the ecumenical movement? Bonhoeffer answers this in the affirmative as follows:

Firstly, the ecumenical movement existed prior to and independently of the Confessing Church. Considered more profoundly this means: Should the Confessing Church isolate herself in her confessional claim to such an extent that her Confession would leave no further room for ecumenical ideas, the question would then arise in all seriousness whether the Confessing Church herself was still the Church of Christ.[133]

129. GS I, pp. 244 f. 132. GS I, p. 249.
130. GS I, p. 246.   133. GS I, p. 257.
131. GS I, p. 248.

That would be 'orthodoxy in unlimited self-glorification all on its own'. Bonhoeffer sees the limit of the confessional claim and recognizes from the beginning the extent to which the Confessing Church takes part in the ecumenical movement.

Secondly, the Confessing Church, along with the other churches, recognizes the sacrament of baptism and thereby places 'the grace of God above the doctrine of the Church', not to make light of the schism, but in order to become aware of it in all it oppressiveness.[134]

Thirdly, and this was of particular concern to Bonhoeffer, the Confession of a church determined by Lutheran doctrine was essentially the Confession of atonement 'because this Church derives her life not from herself but from without, thus owing her existence to ecumenicity in every word she utters. That is the hidden compulsion which draws her to ecumenical work.'[135] And so the Confessing Church takes part in the ecumenical movement not as a group or as a movement, neither does it do so simply as a serious opposition within the German Evangelical Church, but 'as Church'.

Underlying the confessional problem, so constantly and agonizingly on the brink of becoming an absolute, we find Bonhoeffer's earlier question of the authoritative command addressed to both sides. He concludes the article by demanding an answer, asking the ecumenical council whether it is prepared to 'give guidance on war, racial hatred and social exploitation; whether, through such true ecumenical unity among Protestant Christians of all nations, war itself will not one day become impossible . . . what is demanded is not the independent realization of individual aims but obedience.'[136] And it is only in the light of this conclusion that all previous deductions are shown to be right. It was not confessional legality that would one day legitimate the ecumenical movement, but rather an inward validity which would create or, alternatively, renew, the validity of the ecumenical movement, as Church.

Bonhoeffer was for long much preoccupied with the confessional problem and, indeed, the questions of schism and heresy were becoming ever more immediate. A year later, therefore, he embarked on another paper which was to produce the most violent reactions.[137] Intended for internal German consumption, the wording was more provocative than ever. This time, although Bonhoeffer received a hearing, his views were largely dismissed. Both papers should be considered together.

At the time, the ecumenical movement remained unaware of this article tucked away in a German theological periodical. Hence it was not debated when, during their negotiations with the Confessing

134. GS I, p. 259.
135. GS I, pp. 259 f.
136. GS I, p. 261.
137. See Ch. X, pp. 428-36.

Church, headquarters in Geneva failed to take seriously the claim put forward by her leaders. Geneva was further negotiating with the Reich Church whose leaders' acceptance and tolerance of the National Socialists' 'national evolution' based on blood, race and soil they also failed to take seriously. Was it admissible, as early as 1935, to let that pass? Was it also admissible, on the ecumenical plane, to countenance the use of such jargon as a tactical ploy on the part of the Reich Church to remain in existence? At the time, conduct of this sort at ecumenical level met with Bonhoeffer's sharpest disapproval. Here as always he opposed Gerstenmaier's argument that it was necessary to maintain relations with Heckel as a 'front'.

In *A History of the Ecumenical Movement* by Rouse and Neill there is no mention of the 1935 paper and its dramatic story. Nevertheless, Bonhoeffer's problem has become increasingly a part of the history of the ecumenical movement.[138]

VI RESOLUTIONS AT STEGLITZ

The Mission Tour

Before the beginning of the last term of Finkenwalde's first year, Bonhoeffer and a group of ordinands set out on a bicycle tour which took them through the Pomeranian parishes of Naugard and Daber, eventually ending on the shores of the Baltic where they spent a few days in relaxation. The idea of visiting lonely confessional pastors and holding mission evenings in their parishes sprang from a mutual need. This expedition in August 1935 marked the prelude to the mission work that Finkenwalde was later to carry out on a systematic basis.

Old Prussian Confessional Synod

The seminary's visit to Berlin-Steglitz from 23rd to 26th September 1935, following an urgent telephone call from the parsonage at Dahlem, was a result of Bonhoeffer's capacity for making lightning decisions in an emergency. The seminary was to operate simply as a 'pressure group' in the gallery at the meeting of the Steglitz Confessional Synod. The students began the day in class at Finkenwalde. The morning was taken

---

138. Armin Boyens further points out that W. A. Visser 't Hooft, in a paper written for the Oxford Conference ('The Church as an Ecumenical Community' in *Die Kirche und ihr Dienst in der Welt*, 1937, pp. 79-96), 'plainly draws on the questions raised by Bonhoeffer' even though his understandable reluctance to make mention of German writers in the Confessing Church precluded a personal reference to Bonhoeffer. But at the time even Visser 't Hooft's 'thoughts on the "Church in the Churches" attracted no attention'. They were not taken up until 1948 in Amsterdam when Visser 't Hooft gave the names of the three men on whom he had based his ecclesiological position. Karl Barth, Dietrich Bonhoeffer and William Temple (A. Boyens to E. Bethge, 7.7.1966).

up with 'discipleship'—possessions and concern[139]—and the discussion of confessional writings. But in the evening everyone attended the opening service in Berlin-Steglitz where Rendtorff preached on confessing and denying. On the following morning, after Iwand's address on 'discipleship', the tense proceedings began.

State interference by way of the finance department, the legislative authority, the Ministry for Church Affairs, and the protection laws (promulgated as recently as 24th September) primarily concerned the churches of the Old Prussian Union where its effects had been both drastic and confusing.

To some the 'finance departments' for which, they imagined, level-headed, sensible men were responsible, seemed harmless compared with the German Christian attacks of 1933; others immediately saw in them an infinitely more effective stranglehold on the liberty of the churches. 'A policy of pacification so that the "Church may again be the Church" ' was the formula adopted by Kerrl's new Ministry when it started operations. Would it not be better to play for time and negotiate rather than simply say no? The Councils of Brethren could no longer give a negative answer—one which might involve considerable sacrifices—on their own responsibility; in order to do so, they needed the support of a synodal resolution. But the synod which convened on the morning of 24th September was no longer a united assembly unanimous in its resolve to say no.

Thus there followed the only instance in the history of the church struggle in which a representative of the State appeared at a confessional synod and was given permission to speak. On behalf of his Minister (Kerrl), Dr. Stahn attempted to make palatable the meaning and intentions of the new 'finance departments'.[140] Heckling from the Finkenwaldians in the gallery served to highlight this disagreeable situation, particularly during and immediately after Dr. Stahn's speech.

In the final analysis the Steglitz Synod upheld the independence of spiritual decisions. While it could not, of course, put an end to directives from the State's legal and financial organs, it reserved the right to reconsider them from time to time—whatever this might ultimately mean in practice. It continued to lay claim to its power of disposal over the Church's property and the money received from collections. Indeed, after a heated discussion, it forbade members of the Confessing Church to cooperate with the agencies of the finance departments in the Old Prussian Union.

But the decisions aroused somewhat mixed feelings. The discussions had revealed weak points in the oppositional front; the rift between those who supported and those who rejected the 'finance departments' could not be long delayed.

139. CD, pp. 154 ff.
140. See W. Niemöller, *Kampf und Zeugnis der Bekennenden Kirche*, 1948, p. 289.

It was, however, neither Stahn nor premonitions about the possible acceptance by the Synod of the finance departments that brought the Finkenwalde seminary to Berlin. The impetus had been provided by Franz Hildebrandt who, in that telephone call from Dahlem, had given the alarming news that the committee of the Confessional Synod was drafting for the Synod a resolution on Jewish baptism, which included a clause apparently approving the recently promulgated Nuremberg Laws.

These laws, which had been announced by Hitler on 15th September at the Party rally at Nuremberg to the accompaniment of thunderous applause, introduced a second, 'more ordered' phase of Jewish persecution. The 'Reich Citizens' Law' distinguished Reich citizens 'of German or related blood' from a second class of 'nationals' who were without full political rights. The 'Blood Protection Law' forbade so-called mixed marriages and the employment of female 'Aryans' under forty-five in allegedly Jewish households. Bonhoeffer had learnt a certain amount from Dohnanyi about the various stages in the preparation of these rigid laws and about the stratagems adopted in the endeavour either to modify them or to find suitable compromises which would permit of a more elastic interpretation.

Now, within the province of the Church, the Steglitz Synod wished to reaffirm its outright rejection of the Aryan clause as it affected baptism, but a qualification was envisaged to the effect that the Church expressly conceded to the State the right to legislative settlement of the Jewish question in the political sphere. Coming as it did ten days after their promulgation, this could only be seen as condoning the Nuremberg Laws. That was why Hildebrandt had told Niemöller that he would resign his post in the Pastors' Emergency League and would feel compelled to leave the Confessing Church if the Steglitz resolutions were to endorse the new laws and not, as was imperative, reject them.

Bonhoeffer reacted instantly on receiving Hildebrandt's telephone call. In June 1935, at the Augsburg Synod, he had already accused the Synod of making no pronouncement about the Jewish question (not only the question of Jewish baptism). He did, of course, hope for a statement on Jewish baptism which must not be allowed to be restricted or hampered in its purpose of building up a Christian community. But to his mind such a pronouncement on Jewish baptism would be an embarrassment if it were not accompanied by a clear statement condemning the general persecution of the Jews. Here Bonhoeffer was not alone. After the conclusion of the Augsburg Synod in the summer, Superintendent Albertz in Spandau was already making arrangements for the preparation of an exhaustive memorandum 'On the Position of German Non-Aryans':

Where is Abel your brother? In our case, too, in the case of the Confessing

Church, there can be no answer other than that given by Cain . . . And if the Church, afraid for her own destruction, can in many instances do nothing, why is she not at least conscious of her guilt? Why does she not pray for those who are afflicted by this undeserved suffering and persecution? Why are there no services of intercession as there were for the imprisoned pastors? The Church makes it desperately hard for anyone to defend her . . . But that there can be people in the Confessing Church who dare assume that they are entitled, even called, to preach to the Jews, whose present sufferings are our crime, is a fact that must fill us with icy fear. Since when has the evildoer had the right to pass off his evil deed as the will of God? Let us take care that we do not conceal the horror of our sins in the sanctuary of God's will. Otherwise it could well be that we too will receive the punishment of those who desecrated the temple, that we too must hear the curse of him who made the scourge and drove them out.

Not being a member of the Steglitz Synod, Bonhoeffer himself was unable to speak. But he stood by his friends such as Albertz. The clause favourable to the Nuremberg Laws, which had been mooted initially and had aroused such misgivings, was not adopted. The mission to the Jews and Jewish baptism were defended in a declaration.[141] Vis-à-vis the Jews this was embarrassing, but vis-à-vis the National Socialist State even this assertion could be regarded as a protest even if there had been no actual word of judgement pronounced against the State. Following a resolution by the Synod the unpleasant discussion on the Jewish question in general was referred to the Council of Brethren for further action. The resolution runs:

The present official way of handling the Jewish question is to a large extent bound up with an unresolved conflict between the Gospel and the Christian Church. In view of the confusion thus threatening our congregations, the Reich Council of Brethren intends, at the earliest opportunity, to assume responsibility for an answer in conformity with the Bible and the Confession that will provide a pointer to those deeply concerned on specific issues raised.

The 'assumption of responsibility' became a fact in 1936 with the famous memorandum sent by the Confessing Church to Hitler, for this did at least contain the affirmation that, for Christians, the commandment to love one's neighbour must still prevail over what was an officially inspired hatred of the Jews.[142]

Bonhoeffer was in a depressed state of mind when, on his return to Finkenwalde, he discussed Romans 9-11 with his ordinands. He had expected that his Old Prussian confessional brethren would do better than the Augsburg Reich Synod, and Steglitz could hardly have been convened at a more dramatic moment—ten days after Nuremberg. To

141. See W. Niesel, *Um Verkündigung und Ordnung der Kirche*, p. 20.
142. See Ch. X, pp. 440 f.

Bonhoeffer, the Synod was a vital opportunity that had been thrown away. For he believed that Steglitz had allowed financial autonomy and state recognition to be foisted upon it as its principal theme instead of breaking new ground by insisting on a discussion of how they could become a voice for the voiceless. It had, he felt, shown itself culpably dilatory in restricting its statement to the subject of Jewish baptism while leaving the remainder of the question to be dealt with by the Council.

With its Pyrrhic victory at Steglitz, he maintained, the Old Prussian Confessing Church had assented to a fatal reversal of priorities, and he feared that the same thing might happen in ecumenical discussion. This in fact meant that the inner validity of the Church was excluded from the discussion of her legal status, instead of her validity being used to regain the legal status that was being lost. He felt convinced that validity could not be safeguarded by constitution and law, but could only survive by testifying for the dumb. Hence he saw Steglitz less as a victory than as a defeat.

Hardly a month after the Steglitz Synod the Reich Church Committee set up by Minister Kerrl made its first public appearance. One of the misleading things about it was that it was headed by the respected Lutheran, General Superintendent W. Zoellner. Hence many of the Steglitz Synod members believed that he would be able to save and preserve the National Church—presumably their prime objective—that he would also stand warrant for its confessional conformity, and that he would ensure peace. For this reason they put themselves at his disposal. Yet Zoellner's first major summons to collaborate with the Church Committees, issued on 19th October 1935, contained the words: 'We accept the National Socialist development of our people on the basis of blood, race and soil . . .'

End of the First Course

The seminary was still full of optimism and ready for the fray. It occurred to no one to succumb to the blandishments of the consistories or to return to their fold. The first course at the Finkenwalde seminary celebrated its conclusion on the evening of 16th October 1935, before Zoellner had issued his general summons to rally round Kerrl's Church Committees.

The ordinands went back to their home churches where they were soon ordained thus becoming, however, what were then known as 'illegals'. Hardly any of them could expect to be given an ordinary living with a house and garden. Those who desired this would have to attend, if they were in Pomerania, the preachers' seminary at Kückenmühle on the far bank of the Oder. This seminary had been set up by the Consistory's Church Committee. Wherever possible the uncommitted or German Christian consistories debarred from a normally endowed living anyone who had been trained or ordained under the Councils of Brethren. These particular ordinands could, if the occasion arose, hope for an appointment in their province from one of the independent patrons who had the right to confer a living. They might also, perhaps, be accepted as an assistant preacher by an unintimidated superintendent, in which case their ministry would not be officially confirmed and would hold no prospects of preferment. Again, newly-formed confessional emergency congregations in the towns might, when the situation permitted of an appointment, summon the young theologian, and assist him in his struggle to gain entry to the church and church buildings. Other ordinands, in association with the provincial Councils of Brethren, travelled about seeking to form emergency congregations in private homes—an operation that grew increasingly dangerous.

This, then, was what lay in store for those now leaving Finkenwalde. Bonhoeffer promised to help them, whatever course they might adopt, with letters, visits and informal study conferences.

First, however, he spent a few days of his holiday with his parents. In October 1935 they had moved from his boyhood home in Grunewald to a new house near the Heerstrasse in Charlottenburg. No. 43 Marien-burger Allee had been built to their own design and was surrounded by tall pines. Henceforward the attic room facing west was to be Dietrich's own; from his window he could look over to No. 42, the house belonging to the Schleichers, which had been built at the same time. It was in this room that Dietrich was arrested in 1943. One year later, his brother Klaus was to be arrested in the music-room of No. 42.

CHAPTER TEN

FINKENWALDE

1936 - 1937

DURING its short span of life between 1935 and 1937, the Finkenwalde seminary played a part in all three great phases of the German church struggle—the periods of Ludwig Müller (1933-5), Wilhelm Zoellner (1935-7), and Friedrich Werner (1937-45).

At the time of the seminary's inception Ludwig Müller was still nominally in power; but there was still a vestige of hope that the government of the Church might be transferred from the National Bishop to the Confessing Church; the church struggle was not yet in its death throes.

In its heyday, Finkenwalde was under the shadow of the agonizing controversy over Zoellner's attempts to govern the churches by what was considered a false mandate. This widely respected churchman, who was well versed in theological matters, accepted the mandate from the Church Minister, Kerrl. The classic *notae ecclesiae*, the Word and the Sacrament, were being pushed into the background by a feature that threatened to assume paramount importance in the Church—her recognition by the State. During this period the struggle grew into an arduous tug-of-war between Zoellner's Church Commissions, the Councils of Brethren, the Lutheran Council and the still active German Christians. It became extraordinarily difficult to make plain to the world at large exactly what was at stake. At best only the most dramatic highlights—and these were not lacking—ever got through to the public. Eventually Zoellner had the courage to hand back the State's mandate. Doubtless he was forced to the conclusion that his attempts to establish a spiritual authority must appear absurd, for the mandate bound him to an intolerable state of dependence.

After Finkenwalde's closure in 1937, Dr. Friedrich Werner, a lawyer and president of the Office of Church Affairs, the Finance Department and the Evangelical Supreme Church Council, helped in the establishment of an administration that threatened to stifle all traces of spiritual independence. This obsequious ecclesiastical lawyer unscrupulously connived at the isolation of what still remained of the Confessing Church. The church struggle went beyond that of a genuine 'struggle of the churches'; it turned into an unequal contest with Himmler's police.

The deterioration of the ecumenical movement's relations with the Confessing Church became increasingly evident during the second and third phases of the church struggle. In 1935 the Geneva secretaries could find no answer to the crucial question posed by the Confessing Church: whether or not the Oikumene represented the Church. During 1936, men such as Henriod and Wilhelm Menn expressed their misgivings that the Confessing Church—and Bonhoeffer and Asmussen in particular— might be unable to see ecumenical activities in any light other than that of the church struggle. In 1937 Geneva's dilemma in the matter of invitations was solved, firstly because the Confessing Church withdrew, and secondly because the State withheld the passports of the German delegates to the Oxford Conference.

Bonhoeffer himself was to acquire quite a reputation during the second phase, amongst all factions of the Church. He was branded as a disturbing opponent of Zoellner's policy. Hitherto he had been little known in ecclesiastical circles, for his books *The Cost of Disciple- ship* and *Life Together* had still to appear. But in 1936 everybody was talking of his ominous phrase, 'He who separates himself from the Con- fessing Church separates himself from salvation',[1] a modern rendering of the early church dogma *extra ecclesiam nulla salus*. Thus Bonhoeffer acquired a reputation that was soon to demolish his renown as a theologian, the more so as he had also laid himself open to severe criticism through his Old Testament Bible studies in *Junge Kirche*; it was said that he was incorrigibly radical, that his theological conclusions were over-hasty, that he abused exegesis, that he was reviving legalism and monasticism.

There were, however, plenty of ordinands who asked their provincial Councils of Brethren to send them to the seminary at Finkenwalde if at all possible. Once there, they found Bonhoeffer little troubled by these onslaughts; rather he continued to raise even more incisive questions about the spiritual validity of the Church in the Third Reich. Sometimes, when the ordinands were taxed with the provocative propositions put forward by their director, they themselves were at a loss as to how these should be interpreted. Nevertheless, the fact remains that from the day of its foundation to the day its doors were sealed, Finkenwalde constituted one of the focal points of the Confessing Church—a church to which Barmen and Dahlem had given birth.

I FIFTH IMPLEMENTATION DECREE

The second course at Finkenwalde began in the middle of November 1935 under a dark cloud of church politics. All the portents seemed to indicate a fatal attack on the institutions of the Confessing Church. Bonhoeffer, who had returned to his university duties as a lecturer at the beginning of the winter term and hence travelled frequently to

1. GS II, p. 238.

Berlin, would come back with the latest alarming news gleaned at each of his many talks with Hildebrandt and Niemöller.

As a result, Finkenwalde took a well-informed interest in the meetings that were to take place between Reich Minister Kerrl and each of the main church groups. These meetings were awaited with some anxiety, for upon them depended the Minister's final decision on the centres of the church opposition. All these meetings took place on 27th November 1935, in the following order:

1. The Minister, first interviewed Zoellner and his colleagues, namely the members of the Reich Church Committee who were later to form the Provincial Church Committees.

2. His second interview was with the First Provisional Church Administration led by Marahrens. Kerrl informed them that he did not propose to wait for more than a few days before abolishing the Councils of Brethren.

3. For the Finkenwaldians the third interview was the most significant since it concerned their superior authority, the Old Prussian Council of Brethren. Präses Koch was represented by Fritz Müller of Dahlem. The Minister made a nervous speech: '. . . I shall no longer tolerate any attempts by the Councils of Brethren to intervene in the internal affairs of the Church. The composition of Church Committees provides a guarantee that the Confessing Church's vital interests are looked after . . . I do not wish to hear anything more of false doctrines . . . I have set time-limits. I shall wait until the end of this week . . .' Fritz Müller replied, but after several minutes Kerrl broke in: 'Why talk so much? As far as I'm concerned· it's quite pointless.'[2] Then Müller ended the discussion by replying that if the Minister considered that what they had to say was pointless, there was no point in continuing. Thus the meetings of 27th November presaged a dark future.

Two days later a circular letter went out to former members of Finkenwalde preparing them for the possibility of extensive restrictions:

We are writing to let you know that you will not be left on your own in the days to come. After recent events we must now reckon seriously with the possibility of the Confessing Church being forbidden—camouflaged perhaps as the closing down of our Church Administration. Now as always our Church Administration stands firm by Barmen and Dahlem . . . Even a forbidden Church Administration will remain irrevocably ours . . . Any directives that invalidate, or run counter to, our Church Administration may be complied with only on its express instructions . . .[3]

In its reference to the determination of 'our Church Administration', the above advice contained a premise which, although it might hold true for the administration of the Old Prussian Council of Brethren, could

2. See W. Niemöller, *Kampf und Zeugnis*, pp. 303 f.; G. Niemöller, *Die 1. Bekenntnis-synode der Deutschen Evangelischen Kirche in Barmen*, Vol. 1, 1959, pp. 233 ff.
3. GS II, pp. 459 f.

no longer apply to the other provincial churches. Heinz Brunotte, for example, in Hanover, thought that an impartial attitude should be adopted towards the Reich Church Committee: 'What in fact is left; Is there really anything more than a small circle in Old Prussia which has reached a dead end as a result of Niemöller's tactics?'[4] Bavaria, Hessen-Nassau and Saxony came out in support of the Committees. Marahrens, speaking on behalf of the First Provincial Administration of the Confessing Church, expressed his readiness to cooperate with the Reich Church Committee thus sealing the Administration's fate and conceding a major victory to Wilhelm Zoellner.

2nd December

In the late afternoon of 2nd December, a Monday (at that time there were no Monday morning newspapers in Germany nor were there radios in every room in Finkenwalde), one of the students arrived back from Stettin excitedly brandishing an evening paper in which appeared the 'Fifth Decree for the Implementation of the Law for the Protection of the German Evangelical Church'. He took it at once to Bonhoeffer's room. Did this decree mean the total proscription of the Confessing Church? Not altogether; but the content was clear enough, namely that 'no powers of ecclesiastical government or administration [are] to be vested in associations or groups within the Church'. The decree bore the signature of a Reich Minister. Not only were proclamations, the conferment of offices, and the raising of funds by collections and subscriptions 'in particular' prohibited, but the decree also expressly forbade all examinations and ordinations. Had things really come to such a pass that a National Socialist minister was to decide spiritual questions of church order, examinations and ordination? There could be no doubt that preachers' seminaries came under the powers of ecclesiastical government and administration vested in a 'group', in this case the Old Prussian Council of Brethren.

Finkenwalde, already declared illegal by Ludwig Müller in the sight of the Church, was now confirmed as such by the State. This gave rise to the question whether the ordinands could be asked to stay on at the seminary, for sooner or later it was inevitable that the Church Committees would reorganize the structure of training, examinations and ordination in accordance with the new law. The other question was how the work could be carried on since the ban on ecclesiastical activities would extend to the circular letters from the Councils of Brethren, so materially increasing the isolation of ordinands and assistant preachers. Such immediate and specific interference in the Church's internal activities and organization was unprecedented in the church struggle,

4. H. Brunotte, 'Antwort auf den "Osnabrücker Aufruf" vom. 10.12.35', in G. Niemöller, *Die Erste Bekenntnissynode*, dissertation (manuscript), p. 206.

for the first four decrees had been confined to the creation of national and regional Church Committees. Such were the results of Kerrl's interviews on 27th November.

That Monday evening Bonhoeffer called everyone together to explain to them the situation created by the Fifth Decree. He was anxious that each should be free to make up his own mind and therefore he evaluated dispassionately the consequences of carrying on. He explained why he had himself decided to continue with the work, and assured them that all who remained would be fully provided for. How the Councils of Brethren, for their part, were going to reply and what they would say to their charges, was their own affair; they did, however, badly need the independent cooperation of those on whose behalf they continued to exercise their 'powers'.

Bonhoeffer's frankness made a deep impression. The evening ended with mutual assurances that the daily routine of the course would stay unchanged, each pledging himself to yield to nothing but force. On the following day, Bonhoeffer wrote to Martin Niemöller:

Despite the seriousness of the situation we are very happy and confident. For the rest we act in accordance with Matthias Claudius's wonderful hymn . . .

> I pray that God may grant
> The little that I want;
> For if he doth the sparrows feed,
> Will he not fill my daily need?

One ordinand, in a letter to friends on 8th December, was rather less composed:

. . . everything we do here is now illegal and contrary to the law of the State. First there were the bans on newspapers and circular letters, and now copies run off on duplicating machines are forbidden . . . The Church Committees are merely a screen to mask the destruction of the Church.

But the students were invigorated by the fact that something was really being demanded of them, for in the past they had often lacked a clear lead. This was now provided by Bonhoeffer, as also by Staemmler who asked those in his charge to stand firm and whose appeal, because unemotional, secured a hearing.

The time has now come for you to make your decision . . . We can give no guarantee that you will find employment, that you will receive a stipend, or that you will be recognized by any state authority. We do not wish, nor are we entitled, to conceal this from you. It is likely that your path from now on will be very hard . . .[5]

Curiously enough, some time elapsed before the immediate consequences of the Fifth Decree became evident; only gradually did its

5. Letter of 29.2.1936 from the Provincial Council of Brethren of Saxony to its students.

provisions begin to take effect in some of the fields that had been specifically mentioned.

The entire German confessional movement became torn by bitter strife over the question of conformity or resistance. Here the Finkenwalde seminary and its director did everything in their power to recall any ministers and students who were uncertain or confused and to put before them the case for disobedience to Kerrl's decrees.

The seminary devoted both time and money to the distribution of the pamphlet, *The State Church is Here*, written by Otto Dibelius and edited by Martin Niemöller in prompt protest against the Fifth Decree. The students descended on bookshops over a wide area to buy up stocks, and when the police began to hunt for the pamphlet, they placed their orders by telephone. There was feverish activity at Finkenwalde as consignments were packed and then posted to widely separated addresses. Although the police naturally searched parsonages for stocks, Finkenwalde had not yet occurred to them.

Hermann Ehlers, who visited the seminary, reported that there were 100,000 copies of the pamphlet, and hence it would be absurd for the police to hope to confiscate them all.

Strife in Stettin-Bredow

In Pomerania the struggle came to a head on 27th December 1935 with the appointment of a Provincial Church Committee for the region under Superintendent von Scheven from Greifswald. The bewilderment which followed this appointment even spread to the Council of Brethren. It was felt necessary to obtain an overall picture in order to find out who could still be counted on, whether it would be possible to continue and what attitude to adopt at the Reich Confessional Synod which had been arranged for 17th-22nd February 1936 at Bad Oeynhausen. To this end the clergy were invited to Stettin-Bredow on 10th January. Some two hundred came and passed the entire day in argument; the whole seminary attended.

Bonhoeffer spoke, endeavouring to strike a pastoral note in the expression of his uncompromising opinion; he based his speech on the unfortunate circumstance that worthy people would be misled into accepting a false calling.

The false calling arises out of connivance with the wrong doctrine of the German Christians for the sake of peace. Concern for the survival of the National Church has already virtually replaced concern for the undisguised Word of Truth. Rather than advance, we choose to mark time, asking ourselves what we really are—a church, a movement, or a group? Whoever looks on the Confessing Church as a movement or as the upholder of a cause is lost; all he sees is a wretched crowd of obstinate, despondent people barely worthy of the name of 'a movement'; he sees, in fact, nothing more than an undisciplined crowd without obedience, a non-church in fact. But he must not see us like that! By standing still we destroy the Church which can exist only by going forward. The way ahead is marked by the beacons of the synods: Barmen a tower against subversion of church doctrine, Dahlem against subversion of the ecclesiastical order. Barmen holds the sword forged by the Word. Without Dahlem, however, Barmen would be like a weapon carelessly left in the hands of a foreign power's general staff. A third synod [Oeynhausen] must now provide protection against the subversion of the Church by the world which, in the shape of the National Socialist State, is intervening through its finance departments, legislative authority, and committees, and is now splitting into groups the church of those who uphold the 'Confession'. Here we cannot and must not yield for one moment.[6]

Bonhoeffer's speech elicited some applause; not so, that of a respected pastor who put the opposing point of view. In spite of a plea by the Council of Brethren to avoid emotive statements in an already over-heated atmosphere, there were a number of embarrassing outbursts. Indeed, both sides at the meeting were fighting for their future. As a result, the speeches made by two of Finkenwalde's ordinands after Bonhoeffer had spoken left much to be desired in the way of moderation.

Surprisingly, at the end of this arduous day, three-quarters of those present expressed themselves still willing to recognize the controlling function of the Council of Brethren in church affairs. The remaining quarter of the 'apostates' did not, however, lack weight, for they aligned themselves with Greifswald and its theological faculty.

The meeting at Bredow led to a painful exchange of letters with the Stettin pastor, Dr. Schauer. He was a Berneuchen man, who had been one of the dissenting minority in the Brown Synod in 1933 and had led the Pomeranian Young Reformers; he now sympathized with Greifswald although still a member of the Council of Brethren. To his reproaches that Finkenwalde had shown a 'lack of discipline', Bonhoeffer replied at some length[7] saying that he could 'not get very worked up' about the outbursts of temperament for which the Finkenwaldians had, in this case, only been partly responsible.

But it is much harder to make good the damage when, in her testimony of Christ, the Church strays from the path of faith and truth . . . I do not need to tell you that I agree with you that all indiscipline discredits the truth we proclaim. But the proper testimony to Christ lies not in the act of discipline, but in the assurance of hope for the future.

I do not enter such meetings as would a Quaker who, on principle, must await the directions of the Holy Spirit, but rather as one who arrives on a battlefield where God's Word is in conflict with all manner of human opinions . . . what takes place here is not the presentation of a fragment of Christian life made real, but a battle for the truth.

6. From Bonhoeffer's hand-written index card, headed 'From Barmen to Oeynhausen'.
7. See GS II, pp. 209-16.

Bonhoeffer went on to defend one of his ordinands, Winfried Krause who, in his speech, had accused Marahrens of betraying the Church:

Moreover he did not say that Marahrens was a 'traitor' but that he had betrayed the Church. There is a specific difference. It is a judgement of an objective decision and action, not of an individual. There can be no dispute about the theological justice of this statement. And my only factual objection to it would be that Marahrens could not possibly have betrayed the Confessing Church since he had never belonged to it.

This was harsh, stubborn stuff. In such a situation any hint of accommodation struck him as wholly inopportune. Furthermore, a Church Committees' preachers' seminary had been established on the other side of the Oder at Kückenmühle by the faction supported by Marahrens, thus disputing Finkenwalde's spiritual lead and threatening its intake of students. He spoke as harshly as he did because for his part any exchange of question and answer between the two sides was now plainly impossible.

Proclamation from the Pulpit

The Old Prussian Council of Brethren had fixed the Sunday that followed the Friday meeting at Bredow as the date for an important proclamation on the attitude to be adopted towards the Church Committees. Police supervision was strict so that more and more people were asking themselves who would or would not read out the word from the pulpit. To do so would represent a formal act of disobedience by pastors to political decrees, and there could be no doubt that the authorities would carefully note the names of those who continued to support the Councils of Brethren. Yet to remain silent was inevitably to damage the cause.

Finkenwalde arranged a confessional service in its emergency church for 12th January 1936 and invited the people from the locality and from Stettin.

Bonhoeffer himself preached, choosing an apposite text from the wall-building passages in the Books of Ezra and Nehemiah.

The sermon followed the reading of the Council's proclamation:

[There] can be no possibility of complying with the Minister's request and handing over the leadership of the Church to the State's Church Committees . . . we have to make it quite clear to ourselves that we shall not arbitrarily abandon the claims of the Confessing Church, even if this should lead us along a fresh path of suffering . . .[8]

Many evaded the issues presented by the reading of the proclamation

8. J. Beckmann, *Kirchliches Jahrbuch für die Evangelische Kirche in Deutschland 1933-1944*, pp. 107 f.

on the grounds that it should not have anticipated a pronouncement by the Reich Synod. In fact it required courage and determination for a man to read out the notice of disobedience—alone, on his own responsibility, and often in hostile circumstances. Bonhoeffer therefore set an important example on this day. Almost all of Finkenwalde's former members acted as he did:

I am glad that you read out the proclamation, for otherwise you would have been plagued by a bad conscience later on. Ehlers confirmed yesterday that about 80 per cent had read it out in Berlin-Brandenburg . . . in the Council it is thought that the State is taking the proclamation lying down, firstly because of the Winter Olympics and secondly because it does not wish to disturb the Confessing Church's self-dissolution . . .[9]

But for Finkenwalde this was still not enough. After the service, the congregation which had now been foregathering for three months, was invited to a meeting where it constituted itself a confessional congregation and elected a parish Council of Brethren. Those present, among them Frau von Kleist-Retzow, signed the Confessing Church's card of personal commitment—and all this at a moment when such things had been forbidden. The Finkenwalde confessional congregation constituted on this day maintained its independence until well into the war, long after the seminary had been disbanded.

Divided Household

Finkenwalde, during the days of Bredow and the proclamation from the pulpit, had shown vigour and spirit, but the community also underwent some painful experiences. After the Christmas vacation, one of the quietest and most earnest students approached Bonhoeffer and told him that after discussions with Superintendent von Scheven, he had decided to follow the lead of the Pomeranian Church Committee. During those weeks virtually nothing could have hit Bonhoeffer harder than the news that a brother, with whom he was linked in daily prayer for the Church, was now turning away. There were long talks until the day, an oppressive one for the community, when his departure could no longer be delayed. It was the first time that the tragic rift in the Confessing Church had encroached on Bonhoeffer's own domain in Finkenwalde and it constituted a humiliating reverse for the House and its community. It was for this reason that, on the occasion of the Bredow meeting, the seminary assembled not as a self-confident group but as one aware of a potential weakness. The determination remained, however, that everything possible must be done to check the bursting of the dam.

In the ensuing period there was hardly a course which did not lose a member to the Committees, this being known as 'going over to the

9. E. Bethge to G. Vibrans, 21.1.1936.

Consistory'. In proportion to the whole, however, it was a loss that represented a small percentage. But nothing took a greater toll on Bonhoeffer than the prospect of a departure from his circle. Suddenly, all efforts to prevent it seemed vain. 'Nothing we have been able to say has done any good.'[10]

Now, it seemed, the theological criticism put forward by the Lutherans of Erlangen had prevailed over Barmen's claim of scriptural justification for its synodal declaration; faced by the lure of consistorial legality, the determination to endure the hardships of illegality began to wane; service in the National Church seemed more sensible than in the circumscribed emergency congregations; the members of the state-appointed Church Committees, pious men, well-versed in theology, created a much more reasonable impression than the tough, uncompromising men of Dahlem. The truth of love had turned against the love of truth.

Counter-forces

The remarkable delay in implementing drastic measures against the institutions of the Confessing Church, whose members continued to enjoy, if not always to exploit, a surprising freedom of movement and protest, is attributable to two factors. Firstly there was the purely technical problem of destroying an organization of the size of the Confessing Church by means of administrative and police measures. Furthermore, the Ministry and the Reich Church authorities harboured the not entirely unfounded hope that their best ally would prove to be the internal erosion and disintegration of the groups supporting Barmen and Dahlem. Again, with the approach of the Olympic Games, it was in the State's interest to avoid all hint of persecution of the Church while large numbers of foreigners were visiting the country. Consequently no action was taken to stop the seditious proclamation from the pulpit against the Fifth Decree, although the names of those who read it out were carefully recorded for use at a later date.

Secondly, from the point of view of the Church Committees, it seemed as though matters could be confidently left to take their own course. It was not only in the Lutheran regional churches, such as those of Bavaria, Württemberg and Hanover, but also in the churches of the Old Prussian Union that the change of mood turned in Zoellner's favour. Members of the Union had discovered their Lutheran soul and with it some critical reservations towards the Barmen and Dahlem resolutions: to them these resolutions which once had been a 'claim' by the Confessing Church, now became estimable 'suggestions' which might even admit of inclusion in Zoellner's attempts at pacification.

Hence, to a decidedly Lutheran theologian such as Bonhoeffer, this form of Lutheranism now grew to be the most dangerous enemy of all,

10. GS II, p. 511.

for he believed that it provided ideological justification for those who were confused or had grown weary. 'For me, the greatest anxiety is the Lutheran Council.'[11] Curiously enough, Bonhoeffer's attitude was held to be 'estranged by the influence of the Reformed Brethren'. He, however, believed that this was precisely the attitude which represented the correct interpretation of Lutheran confessional writings, and that the other view was false because it held that the safeguarding of an established Lutheran confessional tradition was possible although what in fact it really desired was to rescue the traditional National Church at too high a cost.

Many believed that Zoellner was valiantly striving to make good the damage suffered by the National Church and her order in 1933, and that he would subsequently seek to clarify questions of theology. To them, Bonhoeffer and his friends must have seemed 'radicals', quite incapable of understanding that these considered and clever tactics could ever be justified.

If, however, ministers like Bonhoeffer felt that their calling was not to rescue what still survived but, in the Germany of the day, to place their only hope for a mission of truth in an unprivileged church, then their harsh judgements became more comprehensible.

Where there is no calling, no good can be expected, for even should 'successes' be achieved, these might well be the successes of Satan. A right calling belongs only to the Councils of Brethren of the Synods of the Confessing Church.[12]

Those who followed the lead of the Fifth Decree and pressed for the reconstruction of the National Church were invalidated in Bonhoeffer's eyes. For to do so was, firstly, to ignore the convocation by Barmen and Dahlem of the Councils of Brethren, secondly, to acknowledge the State's authority to appoint spiritual leaders, and lastly, to consent to the curtailment of the testimony of truth.

The months immediately before and after the turn of 1935 were strenuous ones for Bonhoeffer, for the course required his attention and there were, too, his weekly lectures in Berlin. The then incipient House of Brethren remained at Finkenwalde for Christmas Eve. Those brethren from the first course who were awaiting Bonhoeffer's visit to their pastorates scattered about Brandenburg, Pomerania and Saxony, did not wait in vain. Assemblies and brotherhoods in these provinces looked to him for support in their discussions with ministers who had begun to falter. At home, the Nuremberg Laws threatened to disrupt the peace of the family.

After Christmas, Bonhoeffer's grandmother contracted pneumonia. There followed daily telephone calls between Berlin and Finkenwalde.

11. 10th Finkenwalde Circular Letter of 22.7.1936, GS II, p. 495.
12. A. Schönherr, 4th Finkenwalde Circular Letter of 15.1.1936, GS II, p. 464.

On 15th January 1936, Dietrich gave the address at her funeral service, taking his text from Psalm 90, one always read at home on New Year's Eve. When the address was over, a cousin who was present, a high government official, refused to shake his hand. His grandmother had been the oldest member of the family and she was ninety-three when she died. Of her, Bonhoeffer said:

The inflexibility of what is right, the free word of a free man, the obligation to stand by a promise once it is made, clarity and sobriety of speech, uprightness and simplicity in public and private life—on these she set her whole heart . . . She could not bear to see these aims held in contempt or to see the violation of another's rights. Thus her last years were clouded by the great grief she endured over the fate of the Jews among our people, a fate she bore and suffered in sympathy with them. She was the product of another time, of another spiritual world—and that world does *not* go down with her to the grave.[13]

The second half of the term was a bad time for Bonhoeffer. There were days when he was overcome by what he later called his '*accidie, tristitia*, with all its menacing consequences'.[14] These depressions were not occasioned by feelings of deprivation or by vain desires. Rather, they tended to beset him precisely when he realized how strongly others believed he would succeed in the course he was pursuing and how great was their faith in his leadership. These moods were an effect more of excellence than of weakness. He would tremble before his own powers which enabled him to control and influence others. Then self-contempt would overwhelm him, and a sense of inadequacy so strong that it threatened to rob of all meaning those of his undertakings that were happiest and most successful; intellect had gained an evil ascendancy over faith. Then, by way of private confession, he would seek and find a renewed innocence and sense of vocation.

Eventually he went down with a severe attack of influenza, a circumstance which nearly prevented what was to be a splendid ending to the second term at Finkenwalde—the visit to Sweden.

II JOURNEY TO SWEDEN

Birthday Wish

On Bonhoeffer's thirtieth birthday, at the end of February, the members of the seminary gathered round the open fire in the hall. After he had been prevailed upon to talk yet again about Barcelona, Mexico and London, one of those present suggested that now it was the students' turn to express a birthday wish; they asked that Bonhoeffer, through his

13. GS IV, pp. 458 f.
14. LPP, p. 87, also p. 45.

ecumenical connections, should help them to organize a visit to Sweden before the end of term. He agreed to arrange it for 1st March, saying that he would use his influence as a secretary of the Ecumenical Youth Commission—a post that he still held. Dr. Eugen Rose assumed responsibility for all the preparations and immediately set about learning the rudiments of Swedish.

It was, in fact, contrary to the rules of courtesy not only to ask for an invitation but to do so without having given the Swedish Church proper notice. Furthermore, the seminary would be wholly dependent on Swedish hospitality since a German national was at that time only permitted to take the equivalent of about one pound sterling in foreign exchange out of the country. But a Confessing seminary could only contrive to cross the border by making preparations so quickly that there was no time for interested agencies in the Reich Church and the State to become aware of its plans and take the necessary steps to frustrate them.

On the advice of the chaplain to the Swedish Embassy in Berlin, Birger Forell, Bonhoeffer, on 11th February, requested an invitation from Nils Karlström whom he had met at Geneva and Gland, and who was now the secretary of the Ecumenical Committee in Uppsala.[15] On 22nd February this invitation arrived in Finkenwalde, signed by Karlström on behalf of the Ecumenical Committee of the Swedish Church. The joy over the proposed journey was only clouded by the Oeynhausen Synod (17th-22nd February).

The Provisional Committee had been reformed after Marahrens' withdrawal and now included Superintendent Albertz, who was spiritual director of the Brandenburg ordinands. The seminary felt some confidence that their complaints would be heard and therefore, on the eve of their departure, sent a protest against the Oeynhausen resolutions to the Provisional Committee, which included the following statement:

After the Oeynhausen Synod, we find it difficult to know whether the Council of Brethren accepts these resolutions or stands opposed to them in the name of the Confessing Church. How shall we younger brethren make up our minds about them? Are we to choose between accepting the resolutions or losing our office as ministers? What separates us from those who accept these resolutions, a matter of wise choice or the Word of God? We expect guidance on these matters from the Provisional Committee.[16]

The party sailed from the port of Stettin after Bonhoeffer had urgently admonished them to be discreet in their behaviour, and had strictly pledged them to refrain from sensational stories of resistance and similar matters when speaking to the Press. Nevertheless, the Swedish papers contained references to the 'persecuted', thereby adding to the many

15. See MW V, IX, B.1, a. 1.
16. GS II, p. 469.

worries which Bonhoeffer incurred as a result of this enterprise.

The Journey

Copenhagen was the first stop on the journey prepared so admirably and at such short notice by Karlström. Bonhoeffer saw Bishop Ammundsen and Dr. Görnandt. The ordinands made use of every opportunity to find out whether German Lutherans, should they decide to cooperate with the state Church Committees in Germany, might be justified in pleading the satisfactory functioning of the Lutheran state churches in Scandinavia. Almost everywhere they got the unfavourable answer they had hoped to hear; indeed the verdict on the Oeynhausen Synod was distinctly harsh.

Schönherr's report on the journey in the circular letter reads:

[There was] a splendid evening with Professors Nörregaard and Torm. We were amazed to discover how clearly they saw our situation and understood our attitude; above all to discover how definitely these Lutheran professors rejected the attitude of our Lutheran bishops. This was something we found again and again . . . it is our gain that among these Lutheran churches our attitude is not condemned as un-Lutheran but meets with approval.

In spite of Karl Barth's *Church Dogmatics* it was then still rare for German theologians to make the discovery that theology was determined by the Church, not the Church by theology. The meeting between Bonhoeffer and Björquist was to some extent mutually disappointing for at that time their basic assumptions were too different. Bonhoeffer could hardly bear it that a man like Björquist should listen to German theologians who did not support Barmen and Dahlem.

Bonhoeffer gave a number of lectures, not only on church politics, but also on the Christology of discipleship, like those he delivered at Finkenwalde. His method of question and answer was almost as strange and unusual to the Swedish audiences as it had been to his students. The trend of his lectures may be seen from a report on the visit by G. Lohmann:

How does Christ manifest himself as Christ? Is Christian existence no more than a purified, everyday existence, or does the life of a Christian, as a friend of God, postulate his rejection of the world?

And elsewhere:

It is no longer possible, as it was in the past, to lead a Christian life and at the same time be fully immersed in civic life. Rather, three things are demanded of Christian youth today: confession to Christ and with this the renunciation of all other gods in this world; discipleship of Christ in simple and modest obedience to his Word; communion in the community of Christ which is the Church.

Collaboration with Foreign Office

That the temerity of this journey did not receive the acclaim that was its due is evident only in retrospect when the full scope of the opposition has become apparent. Not only did the Church Office for External Affairs (Heckel), the Foreign Ministry and the Reich Education Office make efforts to sabotage this enterprise by the Confessing Church, but they also sought to damage Bonhoeffer personally.

There can be no doubt that Bonhoeffer had brought this down upon his own head. Wishing to observe the correct procedure, he had written shortly before his departure not only to his superior authority, the Old Prussian Council of Brethren, but also to the Foreign Ministry. There, however, his hopes of obtaining clearance were not fulfilled. Instead, the responsible official, von Twardowski, who later became a friend of Eugen Gerstenmaier, immediately made enquiries with Heckel of the Church Office for External Affairs, after which he warned the German Embassy in Stockholm against Bonhoeffer 'because his influence is not conducive to German interests. Government and church departments have the strongest objections to his visit . . .' Hence it was with marked coolness that Fürst zu Wied the Ambassador, received Bonhoeffer beneath a life-sized portrait of Hitler.

A Finkenwalde report after the visit which had been sent to the Foreign Ministry[17] was passed in turn to Heckel with the query 'whether and with what success the Reich Church Committee [Zoellner, that is] had protested to the leaders of the Swedish Church over the invitation?'[18]

Heckel, as a result of Swedish press reports about the Finkenwaldians' visit in general, and their reception by Archbishop Eidem in particular, had already drafted a letter for Zoellner in which Eidem was asked whether the Swedish Church had, perhaps, by her invitation officially 'taken sides against the responsible church administration of the German Evangelical Church'. (Drafted and despatched on 6th and 14th March respectively.)

Heckel, moreover, sent the following admonition to the Provincial Church Committee on 7th March:

Lecturer and Pastor Lic. Bonhoeffer, the director of a confessional seminary in Finkenwalde near Stettin, received an invitation from the Ecumenical Committee of the Swedish Church to visit Sweden in company with the confessional seminary. So far as foreign policy is concerned, the matter is being dealt with by the appropriate authorities. I feel impelled, however, to draw the attention of the Provincial Church Committee to the fact that the incident has brought Lic. Bonhoeffer very much into the public eye. Since he may incur the reproach of being a pacifist and an enemy of the

17. See GS II, pp. 470 ff.
18. GS II, p. 472.

State, it might well be advisable for the Provincial Church Committee to disassociate itself from him and take steps to ensure that he will no longer train German theologians. (signed) D. Heckel.[19]

Heckel, of course, as the bishop in charge of foreign affairs, once again found himself, vis-à-vis his political and ecclesiastical masters, in the unfortunate position of having been taken unawares by an excursion of Bonhoeffer's into the ecumenical field. He must have felt it as a setback to his efforts to centralize and monopolize German ecumenical relations. Also present in his mind was the knowledge that Bonhoeffer and his friends had been accusing both him and his officials of aiding and abetting heresy since 1933. So he now hit back with weapons which could hardly have been more deadly. Nor, in 1936, could there have been any more extreme form of denunciation directed against a clerical adversary than the description 'pacifist and enemy of the State', especially when this was used officially and in writing, and in conjunction with the urgent recommendation that Bonhoeffer should no longer be permitted to train 'German theologians'. Moreover, by thus shifting the conflict into a highly political dimension, Heckel was placing Bonhoeffer at the mercy of the National Socialist State. Yet Heckel could acquire nothing but kudos in the eyes of the secular authorities from being described as a 'heretic' by such as Bonhoeffer.

Dilemma for Eidem

On 14th March, Archbishop Eidem received a warm letter of thanks from Bonhoeffer, but also the communication from Zoellner containing the passage which seemed to offer a way out: 'I assume that . . . the invitation is to be regarded as a private matter.'

In his reply to Zoellner of 18th March, he wrote that a report on the circumstances was in preparation. He could, however, assure him that the Ecumenical Committee had wished to help the Finkenwaldians; the invitation had been a personal one, and in no way implied an official bias in matters of church politics; 'the young German brethren were very nice and kept away from church politics'.

After seeing Karlström's report, Eidem was, of course, compelled to inform Zoellner on 15th May that the invitation had been 'in fact semi-official'.

Bonhoeffer on the other hand, who was wholly ignorant of these events, wrote to Eidem from Finkenwalde on 13th May, saying how much he was looking forward to the archbishop's visit to Germany—the journey had been mentioned in Uppsala on 4th March: '. . . the brethren and the church leaders would like to meet you here. What days can you make available for us?' To this Eidem replied evasively on 20th May. Those at Finkenwalde still knew nothing of what was going on

19. See MW V, IX, B. II, a. 3.

behind the scenes when they wrote in their circular letter:

Unfortunately a letter arrived today from Archbishop Eidem in which he says that he has unexpectedly been compelled to curtail his visit; he will only be able to spend a few days in Germany and hence cannot fit in anything extra.[20]

Their experience with Bonhoeffer's seminary instilled in the Swedes a cautious attitude towards further visitors from Germany. Thus, when in September 1936 the Berlin Cathedral ordinands went to Sweden with Zoellner's and Heckel's blessing, naturally in deliberate contrast to Bonhoeffer's party, it was as a model Church Committee's seminary. They did not manage to see Eidem, however, who conveyed his regrets to the visitors.

After Eidem's more or less satisfactory answer to Zoellner in May 1936, Heckel was able to inform the state authorities that the Swedish archbishop had acted in the best of faith and had expressed his indignation that the members of Finkenwalde should have given the visit so official a character. Hence 'responsibility for the initiative in the field of church politics must be allotted to the German participants rather than to the Swedish Church'.[21]

Heckel was exaggerating when he maintained that Eidem had 'clearly and consistently emphasized that the affair must not be treated officially', since the archbishop had, after all, invited the twenty-six candidates to a reception at his house where he had made an extremely partial speech, and had raised no objection to its being fully reported in the press. Furthermore, the Swedish committee had arranged not only a welcoming party for the seminary in Stockholm, which was attended by the king's brother, Prince Bernadotte, but also a visit to the private art gallery of a second brother, Prince Eugen.

It was impossible to prevent the seminary's Swedish visit from being drawn into the struggle, even had the Confessing Church desired to do so, which was very far from being the case. The official Reich Church, on the other hand, was anxious to safeguard its rights of sole representation and, moreover, had to comply with the demands of a powerful state. By falling upon the rebels it could protect itself from those above. The preconceived attitudes of both sides to the role of the Church in the Third Reich were irreconcilable.

The annual report of the World Alliance and the minutes of the 'Life and Work' conference at Chamby in 1936 both record Bonhoeffer, who was evidently quite uninhibited by the presence of Heckel and his minions, as saying that the Swedish trip was an activity of his office as youth secretary of the Alliance.[22]

20. Circular letter dated 22.5.1936.
21. GS II, p. 474.
22. Minutes of the Management Committee of the World Alliance, Chamby, 1936. p. 46.

Forbidden to Lecture at the University

The most drastic consequence of the visit to Sweden was the termination of Bonhoeffer's duties as a lecturer at Berlin University by the Reich Ministry of Education. Was this perhaps a sequel to the suggestion made by the Church External Affairs Office that steps should be taken to ensure 'that he will no longer train German theologians'?

There is no doubt that the visit to Sweden provided the Ministry with a welcome opportunity to make a move that had already been long deferred. But Bonhoeffer did not submit without a struggle to an event which he had, indeed, long been anticipating, and once again he did all in his power to stave off the end of his academic career.

On returning from London in 1935, he had notified the university authorities that his sabbatical leave, begun in 1933, was now over. During the 1935-6 winter term he announced and held a series of lectures on 'discipleship'. He also reported that he was taking over a preachers' seminary. In fact, a preliminary decision had been made by the Reich Ministry of Education on 29th November 1935 to the effect that by agreement with the Church Minister (who at the time of Bonhoeffer's notification did not even exist!) the lecturer could not be permitted to direct the seminary in Finkenwalde and at the same time pursue his university activities. This document had, however, been treated in a dilatory fashion, having lain in the faculty's files for many months, so that it was some time before Bonhoeffer had to make the decision that he would not abandon the seminary.

During his Swedish visit he finally sent off to the university authorities the long political questionnaire which all active lecturers, including his father and eldest brother, were obliged to complete. He attested that he had not belonged to communist or socialist associations, that he was not a member of a freemasons' lodge, and that neither his parents nor grandparents were Jewish. He also provided the required 'Aryan certificate' on the advice, curiously enough, of his cousin Leibholz, whose own inability to produce this document had lost him his post. Thus, since 1933, the Confessing Church had gradually been shifting its position and adjusting its views; now it no longer recommended that those affected by the new laws should resign of their own accord from official posts, but rather that they should wait until dismissed. Perhaps it was at this time that Bonhoeffer's thoughts first turned to the possibility of political action. At all events, he thought it worth the effort to hold on to his university post, even if this meant producing an Aryan certificate, and this, not out of timid compromise but because he must not be forced away from his students and out of yet another position in public life.

But it was too late. On returning home he discovered that he had unwittingly contravened an order issued by the Reich Minister of Education in June 1935 concerning the authorization of journeys abroad on the part of university lecturers. On 18th April, in an attempt to retrieve the situation, he requested further leave of absence from his teaching post. The application was unsuccessful. It was not until 5th August 1936 that the definitive withdrawal of his right to teach was conveyed to him in writing on the grounds that he was continuing to direct a seminary which, by the terms of the Fifth Decree ought no longer to exist, and that although the visit to Sweden had been 'at the invitation of the Ecumenical Committee' there, it had not been sanctioned by the Ministry.[23]

Bonhoeffer gave his last lecture at Berlin University on 14th February 1936. At the same time his thirty-four-year-old brother-in-law, Gerhard Leibholz, was compulsorily retired. It was also in the same month, curiously enough, that his father reached retirement age (1.4.1936), although he did in fact continue in his post for a further two years. Thus the family's links with the university were becoming ever more tenuous.

In church politics prospects seemed to be improving. After the convulsions that had been shaking the Confessing Church, the forces were regrouping.

The Oeynhausen Synod was followed on 12th March by the formation of the Second Provisional Administration of the Confessing Church, as distinct from its predecessor, the Provisional Church Administration, or the 'VL' as it was generally called. Consisting of Fritz Müller (Dahlem), Fricke, Albertz, Böhm and Forck, it was nothing like so numerous or so comprehensive as the first administration under Marahrens. On the other hand, its determination to uphold the institutions of Barmen and Dahlem against Kerrl's proscriptions was incomparably greater.

By contrast, the Lutherans' tendency towards independence, strengthened by long-standing tradition, as also by their theological criticism of Barmen and their aloofness from the consequences of Dahlem, had led to the definitive formation of the Lutheran Council on 18th March. Its members were Marahrens, Meiser, Wurm, Breit, Hahn, Lilje and Beste. Hanns Lilje was appointed the Council's secretary with an office in Berlin. This body had no wish to break away from the Reich Council of Brethren of the Confessing Church, but intended to pursue its own policy so far as the 'Dahlemites' were concerned. Consequently its member churches were free to establish positive connections with the Church Committee—the organization with which the Dahlemites were locked in such bitter strife.

Conflict between the Provisional Administration and the Lutheran Council could not therefore be long in coming. In the event the breach was created by a lengthy memorandum to Hitler prepared by the Reich Council of Brethren.

While the seminary was in Sweden, Hitler created a political sensation by marching into the Rhineland, a military reoccupation which was

23. See GS II, pp. 293 f.

totally unopposed by the Allies. He celebrated the victory on 29th March with a plebiscite which was intended to demonstrate to the world yet again the support he enjoyed from ninety-nine per cent of the population.

At this time the seminary was on holiday. Bonhoeffer was glad that he had been able to avoid handing in his ballot paper at home; instead his 'no' was recorded in a village somewhere in Saxony.

When in the province of Saxony during his holiday travels he ordained a number of students at Stendal in company with Staemmler. This was a daring thing to do after Kerrl's decree but one in which the parish actively participated. Then he arrived in the old town of Hildesheim and enjoyed the spring at Friedrichsbrunn.

III THE PAPER ON CHURCH COMMUNITY

During the 1936 summer term, Bonhoeffer was to earn a reputation that caused many to disassociate themselves theologically from the group of which he was a member. On the other hand he now aroused the interest of those who had hitherto been indifferent to him. The reason for this was a paper in *Evangelische Theologie* and a Bible study in *Junge Kirche*. Both pieces had been written originally for his students at Finkenwalde, or rather for the study conferences to which members of earlier courses were invited.[24]

Inspiration for the Article

In April 1936 when the 1935 summer course reassembled for a refresher conference at Finkenwalde they were faced with a very different situation from what they had known in 1935. Then there were no Committees, no Fifth Decree, nor had there yet been an Oeynhausen Synod. In view of the many pressing questions, Bonhoeffer thought it advisable to give the students a report and a survey so that recent developments might

---

24. The details of the five conferences are:

April 1936 (1st Course): Bible Study 'The Reconstruction of Jerusalem according to Ezra and Nehemiah' (GS IV, pp. 321-35); lecture 'On the Question of the Church Community' (GS II, pp. 217-41).

October 1936 (2nd Course): Bible Study 'Timothy, the Servant in the House of God' (GS IV, pp. 344-57); 'Scheme of Instruction for Confirmation Candidates' (GS III, pp. 335-67).

April 1937 (1st Course): Repeat, 'Timothy'; Review of book by H. Sasse, 'What does Lutheran mean?'; 'The Power of the Keys and Community Discipline in the New Testament', lecture (GS III, pp. 369-81).

June 1937 (3rd Course): Repeat, 'The Power of the Keys and Community Discipline'; 'The Confessional Question in the Light of the Halle Resolutions' (no longer extant, see GS II, p. 518).

June 1938 in Zingst (Courses 1-5): Bible Study 'Temptation' (published in book form in 1953).

This syllabus shows that the studies had been thought out to meet the demands of the moment and that, indeed, was their main purpose.

be assessed in the light of theology and the internal affairs of the Church. Who was still in the Church with them and what were the relevant criteria? What was the significance of the separation from those who had previously been good friends? What consequences were to be expected and what conclusions should be drawn? Was the decision on whether a ministry was in good standing or not to be based on the given facts of Barmen and Dahlem, or dependent upon the subjective schemes of individuals in positions of authority? Were they to adhere to the Old Prussian Council of Brethren as the government of the Church because of the excellence of that church, in order to maintain its numbers, or because of its true Confession? A bewildering factor was the high repute of many of the Committees' members. How much significance was to be attached to the demarcations made at Oeynhausen and how much to the inconclusive advice it had proffered?[25]

By cutting a few avenues through this tangle of problems and views Bonhoeffer hoped to bring his students reassurance. There was, as he saw it, nothing actually new in his discourse. For the last six months the Finkenwalde circular letters had been dealing with the *rite vocatus* and the danger that a false calling might induce silence in the face of wrong doctrine.[26] If the question of *rite vocatus* and related data had definitely passed to the Confessing Church, then the question of a true unity must inevitably be dealt with in order to present a united front against those who took a different view of *vocatus*. This should have been, but was not, clarified by the Oeynhausen Synod. Hence the seminary's complaint on the eve of its visit to Sweden: 'The word for which we have been waiting should therefore have produced a fundamental settlement of the question of church community and created the beginnings of doctrinal and church discipline.'[27] By leaving the effective decision to the provincial Councils of Brethren whether or not to cooperate with the Committees, the Synod had thrown open the door to all manner of factions and dissensions and thereby evinced 'the highest measure of unfraternal and uncharitable conduct'.[28]

Bonhoeffer thought it dangerous for an excessive concern to arise about the limits of the Church and to attract so much attention. For this reason he devoted the main body of the article to the principle that the Church did not determine her own boundaries. But he also held that it had become necessary to acknowledge another fact, namely that the Church was now encountering boundaries 'drawn against her from outside'. To what extent were they to be recognized? In a letter to Dr. Schauer on 25th January 1936, Bonhoeffer vividly described the oppressive experience of the boundary when one of the brethren had decided

25. See Ch. X, p. 421.
26. GS II, pp. 460, 463 f.
27. GS II, p. 467.
28. GS II, pp. 468 f.

to withdraw. Commenting that a decision on the boundary could hardly be expected of the individual and that the synod alone must decide, he went on:

I am, of course, of the opinion that anyone who in any way subordinates himself to the Committees is not in the same church with us. What is valid here is not the word of the individual, but the word of the synods or Councils of Brethren for which many are waiting. The lack of decision on this point hitherto strikes me as both ominous and symptomatic . . . My concern in all that is said and done in the Church is solely with the primacy, the unique dignity and truth of God's Word. There is no greater service of love than to place man in the light of the truth of this Word, even when it gives pain. God's Word discerns the spirits. This implies no spirit of judgement but only the humble and truly awed understanding of the ways which God himself desires to go with his Word in his Church. The boundaries of this Word are also our boundaries.[29]

Bonhoeffer's paper was written because the Oeynhausen Synod had failed. He could not, of course, make up for what the Synod had left undone but under the pertinent and controversial title 'On the Question of the Church Community', he could present these questions as incisively as possible:

The intention of these short notes cannot be to anticipate the Church's decision. Their intention must be to remind the government of the Church of the need to make this decision. By doing this step by step, it will be doing alien work in order to carry out more efficiently its proper task. The dissolution of the community is the community's last offer.[30]

Publication

Those taking part in the conferences came to the unanimous conclusion that this controversial dissertation should be published without delay. It was duly put into the June 1936 number of *Evangelische Theologie* by Ernst Wolf. One sentence in the third section of the paper: 'Whoever knowingly separates himself from the Confessing Church in Germany separates himself from salvation'[31] spread like wildfire throughout the German churches. During the course of hundreds of discussions and assemblies it acquired, and was disseminated in, the simplified form: 'Those without a Red Card won't go to heaven!'[32] On 1st July, the sentence appeared on its own in bold type in the *Information Service of the Evangelical Church of the Old Prussian Union*. published by the

29. GS II, pp. 213 f.
30. GS II, p. 238.
31. GS II, p. 238.
32. The 'Red Card' was the declaration of personal commitment by the members in confessional congregations. In some provinces it was a green card.

Church Committee Information Service, an agency headed by General Superintendent Eger. Underneath was the following comment:

No, this sentence is not some sort of malicious invention or imputation by which the 'enemies of Christ' seek to harm the cause of the Confessing Church; it was set down in black and white by a man of the Confessing Church, Lic. Bonhoeffer . . . Poor Protestant Church in which it is possible to achieve notoriety by such trifling conceits . . .[33]

The sentence, in isolation, states the case with such self-confidence and pungency that to read it in context may, perhaps, have appeared superfluous. Professor H. Lietzmann wrote to Archbishop Eidem:

. . . and recently Lic. Bonhoeffer, a highly-gifted but now altogether fanatical teacher, wrote *'extra ecclesiam nulla salus'*, meaning that whoever cooperates with the Reich Church Committee stands outside the Church of Salvation.[34]

Lutheran clergy in Pomerania demanded a theological debate. 'Since then many have refused to pay over any more collections.'[35]

By the middle of July *Evangelische Theologie* was sold out. 'I had hoped to send each of you a separate copy of "Church Community" but it was no longer obtainable.'[36] The uproar took Bonhoeffer somewhat by surprise. He maintained that he had put forward the same demand in 1935 in an ecumenical paper when he wrote: 'But if the Confessing Church were to abandon this demand, it would mean that the German church struggle was already decided against her and with it the struggle for Christianity as well.'[37] It had made no stir at the time. But now the thesis contained in the offending sentence created turmoil among a church public that had grown nervous and was intent on self-justification. Bonhoeffer wrote to Barth: 'People are getting terribly excited about it. And really I thought that what I was writing was axiomatic.'[38] And in a letter to Sutz:

For the rest, my paper has made me the most reviled man of our persuasion. Not so long ago some sort of 'Lutheran' association even proposed that I should be removed from my teaching post in the Confessing Church. The Rhinelanders are standing by me splendidly . . . It is coming to the stage when the beast before which the idolators bow down will bear the caricature of Luther's features. 'They are adorning the graves of the prophets . . .'[39]

Some of the leading bodies and heads of the Church did in fact request the Councils of Brethren to disassociate themselves entirely from Bonhoeffer.

33. See GS II, p. 242.
34. Letter of 17.8.1936.
35. That is to the Council of Brethren; letter from Bonhoeffer to E. Bethge 11.7.1936, GS II, p. 242.
36. To the members of Finkenwalde, 22.7.1936, GS II, p. 496.
37. GS I, p. 244.
38. Letter of 19.9.1936, GS II, p. 286.
39. Letter of 24.10.1936, GS I, p. 47.

Wherever the members of Finkenwalde went, they were hard put to it to defend their master's theses. Initially they themselves had to learn not to be mesmerized by the one passage, but to comprehend that the paper's main emphasis lay in the first section with its denial of the whole legalistic view implying that the Church was to set her own boundaries and determine their extent. They had to grasp that this must not be 'wittingly' suppressed in relation to the sentence. It was only gradually that many began to see that the sentence should never be adopted by the Church as a rigid device for counting heads, or as a 'prerequisite for pious speculation on the saved and lost'. All timid enquiries were patiently answered by Bonhoeffer.[40]

On the Lutheran side much use was now made of labels, those attached to Bonhoeffer being 'legalism', 'enthusiasm' and 'Romanism'. On 9th July Pastor Duensing of Hanover reproached him in *Um Glauben und Kirche* for his legalistic view of the concept of the Protestant Church, and further elaborated this in a letter to H. Gollwitzer on 20th August:

Has not another revelation now been placed alongside Holy Scripture, the sole rule and guiding principle, thus throwing the door wide open to enthusiasm? Or again, the question might be asked: Is not this claim on the part of the 'Confessing Church' an exact repetition of the claim raised by the Pope?

The extent of the rift can be gauged from Künneth's criticism and from an article written by Sasse, who had once been a staunch ally at Bethel:

This Confessing Church shaped according to the wishes of Barth and Asmussen, as distinct from the confessional movement upheld by the Lutheran churches, is a sect, the worst sect in fact ever to have set foot on the soil of German Protestantism. Anyone who doubts this should read the papers by Bonhoeffer and Gollwitzer in the June number of *Evangelische Theologie*. Founded on the miracle of Barmen, held together by Barth's *Theologumenon* on the worthlessness of the remnants of natural theology to which Calvin and Luther adhered, knocked up by the harsh experience of the church struggle, there stands the alleged church . . .[41]

George Merz wrote to Gollwitzer saying that he could only interpret Bonhoeffer's sentence 'as the ecstatic effusion of a hitherto level-headed man which contradicted everything that Luther had found essential'.[42] Finally some correspondence took place at the highest level when the Lutheran Council sent the following enquiry to the Provisional Administration (VL) on 17th July:

What attitude does the VL propose to adopt to the declarations made

---

40. See letter to G. Vibrans, GS II, pp. 243 ff.
41. H. Sasse, 'Wider das Schwärmertum', 1936.
42. Retailed by H. Gollwitzer in a letter to E. Wolf, 21.8.1936.

in the following passages? . . .[43] We should like to have a clear-cut opinion on these passages, since they are not a matter of one enthusiastic individual's false doctrine but represent views which are widely shared and which, on occasion, are logically in keeping with a definite course of action.

The Provisional Administration replied on 28th July 1936:

The important question discussed by Bonhoeffer in his article . . . derives from the ecumenical sphere; he seeeks to introduce a theological debate on the question of the ecclesiastical community. Bonhoeffer's article cannot be dismissed by taking a passage at random and out of context.

In the Rhineland, General Superintendent Stoltenhoff wrote on 1st August to the Rhineland Council of the Confessional Synod for information: 'I am enquiring from the Council whether Dr. Bonhoeffer's sentence . . . is approved or not. To me it is nothing more than an atrocious piece of false doctrine.' The Rhineland Council replied on 23rd September. After an allusion to the general context of Bonhoeffer's sentence, the letter continued:

Bonhoeffer's statements are based on the thesis that the call 'Here is the Church' is synonymous with the call 'Here is the Gospel'. The Rhineland Council sees in this thesis a legitimate interpretation of the reformatory concept of the Church . . .
Anyone who persistently repudiates the call 'Here is the Church, here is the Gospel' raised by the Confessing Church in 1934, and who knowingly breaks with the Confessing Church, has broken with the Gospel as it is preached . . .

In June, before Bonhoeffer himself had incurred the charge of 'false doctrine', now so lightly and generally bandied about, he had drafted a learned memorandum, 'False Doctrine in the Confessing Church?', for the Pomeranian Council.

The Confessing Church is allegedly to be defeated with her own weapons . . . The rejection of the Committees as the lawful government of the Church and the grounds for this rejection are said to be false doctrine. Thus, what is now proclaimed in the name of 'Lutheranism' does an ill service to true Lutheranism. These accusations are accompanied by the pseudo-learned assertion that the Confessing Church has long been infiltrated by an alien 'Reformed' doctrine. But Lutheran pastors and communities are concerned with freeing themselves from servitude to Reformed 'legalism' which ultimately means accepting the oversight of the Committees or, alternatively, the Lutheran Council.[44]

In these circumstances, Wolf asked Gollwitzer to write an article for *Evangelische Theologie* contesting obvious or less obvious misinterpreta-

43. Here follow some sentences from Bonhoeffer's paper asserting that the Confessing Church is the true church in Germany.
44. GS II, pp. 264-75.

tions. To some extent Gollwitzer had already been doing this by individual correspondence without, however, concealing his view that a
number of Bonhoeffer's formulations, notably his identification of the
word of the synod with the Word of God, demanded verification.[45] In
fact Bonhoeffer, when replying to Gollwitzer's 'Comments and Reservations'[46] with his 'Questions',[47] did not seek to defend this passage but
adopted the term 'testimony'.[48] On the other hand, Gollwitzer made it
clear how blind were the assailants to their own particular brand of
'legalism', 'enthusiasm' and 'Romanism'.

Bonhoeffer's latest contribution was wholly characteristic of the man.
His confidence in the cause was evidently quite unshaken, for he did
not allow himself to become enmeshed in the endeavour to justify his
earlier theses, but continued the dialectic with his pugnacious questions
and his criticism of Oeynhausen's deficiency. To those readers who
waited eagerly for a sharp clash with Gollwitzer, Künneth and Sasse over
the confessional question, he gave scant satisfaction. Intrinsically he set
no store by polemical victories, for without doubt he too had been
responsible for misunderstandings; moreover, he was, on occasion, even
prepared to agree with serious critics. To him more important things
were at stake.

The resumption of the controversy in the October number of
Evangelische Theologie did not, however, bring any change. Accusations of all kinds against Bonhoeffer's paper were still the fashion. On
both sides existing preconceptions proved stronger than argument as
did, to an even greater extent, membership of one or another influential
organization. Nevertheless Gollwitzer continued to speak on Bonhoeffer's behalf. He wrote to Oberkirchenrat Pressel:

You have . . . accused Bonhoeffer of enthusiasm. It is unfortunate that
nowhere did you define this word which is currently so popular. The
'identification' you attack is in no sense the enthusiastic one of the organized
congregation with the Church of the Saints but the Lutheran identification
of the Church, visibly gathering around the true Confession, with the true
Church of Christ. Your attack is upon the Lutheran fathers no less than
upon Bonhoeffer. You will surely not wish seriously to maintain that this
enthusiastic identification among our Prussian brethren represents an 'acute
danger' . . . The real dangers of an (enthusiastic) evasion of Word and
Sacrament today seem to me to lie in the theology of the order of Creation
propounded by many alleged Lutheran theologians who, I notice, have
still to be disavowed by the Lutheran Council . . .[49]

Bonhoeffer himself had plainly set out the alternative:

Either the Barmen Declaration was a true confession to the Lord Jesus

45. GS II, pp. 230 f.
46. EvTh, October 1936, pp. 398-405, see GS II, pp. 245-55.
47. Also in EvTh, October 1936, pp. 405-10, see GS II, pp. 255-63.
48. See GS II, p. 259, bottom.
49. Letter of 10.2.1937.

effected through the Holy Spirit, in which case its character is one that shapes and divides the Church, or it was an expression of the opinion, without binding force, of a few theologians, in which case the Confessing Church has been treading a wrong and fateful path ever since.[50]

His emphatic and self-confident style sprang from an intense concern for steadfastness in the prevailing state of instability.

His main anxiety was for the word and the true Church, as a watchman speaking to the need of the times, and he was as little concerned with confessional dogmatism as with a conservative insistence upon the position of the Church. The price of dogmatism was too high and what remained of the Church was not worth defending. But he was prepared to stake his reputation in order to preserve or build up anew the place where the voice for the voiceless might make itself heard. At the time he was all the readier to do this because a memorandum addressed to Hitler had been prepared by the Provisional Administration—undoubtedly a dangerous procedure on the latter's part but one that justified its existence.

Humanly speaking, he also found it almost intolerable that the word put out at Barmen and Dahlem should have been abandoned so quickly and universally.

We are not vagabonds who obey one government one day and another the next. We have no grounds for suddenly breaking faith with one church government when another is presented to us from outside.[51]

That the motives of the Barmen Declaration, as well as the manner of its making, should suddenly have become more crucial than the declaration itself was again, in his view, an ominous confusion of theology with church decisions. As we shall see he still held to this view when he had to draw a distinction between his adverse judgement of Oeynhausen and the actual resolution passed there. When he attended Chamby in 1936 he undoubtedly accepted the practical consequences of the synod's lack of determination in the hope that there might yet be a decision.[52]

Thirdly, it was his concern for a new congregation of the faithful that closed his mind to the worthy attempts to save the National Church. Those who saw Zoellner's attempt as the last chance of preserving the National Church had to stomach the fact that such an attempt could only be made, even by such pious and conservative men as Zoellner and Eger, at the cost of painful tributes to the National Socialist 'national evolution'. Bonhoeffer could never have brought himself to pay such tributes, even had he wished to save the National Church.

50. GS II, pp. 259 f.
51. A. Schönherr in the 4th Finkenwalde Circular Letter, GS II, p. 464.
52. See Ch. X, p. 458.

By contrast with other years he did not, strikingly enough, assail the essential elements, Word and Sacrament, of the *notae ecclesiae*, in his 1936 polemics, for either state recognition had by now virtually acquired the rank of *nota ecclesiae*, or the determining factor was to be the composition of the Committees made up of patently 'Christian personalities'. So he now adhered carefully to the reliable doctrine that only true administration of the Sacrament and right handling of the Word were necessary in order to be the Church of God. When accused of being under Reformed influence, however, he could be more Lutheran than the Lutherans, quoting in his arguments, for instance in 'False Doctrine in the Confessing Church?',[53] statements made by their bishops in 1934 and 1935.

Bonhoeffer's fault was, perhaps, that he underestimated the staying-power of the National Church. Or was he so intransigent because he recognized its toughness only too well? At any rate, it was not in this quarter that his heart lay.

Ezra and Nehemiah

The study conference in April 1936, where the offending paper had its origin, also destroyed Bonhoeffer's reputation as an interpreter of the Old Testament. His exegesis 'The Reconstruction of Jerusalem according to Ezra and Nehemiah'[54] found him in a weaker position professionally than at the time of the article we have discussed. Yet both sprang from the same impulses and both sought to clarify and strengthen the minds of those who had become confused. This made for absorbing lectures even if the principles of exegetic scholarship applied by Bonhoeffer are not entirely defensible.

At the beginning of 1936, a similar Bible study, 'King David',[55] had already appeared in *Junge Kirche*. This aroused little or no scholarly interest but there was a political reaction in the National Socialist paper, *Durchbruch*, where Friedrich Imholz wrote: '. . . there is much that might be called innocuous by comparison with such exponents of an oriental religious doctrine which has the impudence, even now in the year 1936, to represent the world-enemy Judah as the "eternal people", the "true nobility", "the people of God".'[56]

The text for the Bible study on Ezra and Nehemiah had occurred to Bonhoeffer at the time of the proclamation from the pulpit on 12th January 1936,[57] while his confessional sermon on that day, following the Bredow meeting, also determined the tenor of the longer exegesis of 21st April. Thus, while the actual events of 1936 may have influenced

53. GS II, pp. 264 ff.
54. GS IV, pp. 321 ff.
55. JK, 1936, pp. 64-9, 157-61, 197-203; see GS IV, pp. 294-320.
56. GS II, pp. 292 f
57. See Ch. X, pp. 416 f.

the chapters of the Old Testament which he read and the verses he selected, as a scholar he sought as far as possible to exclude contemporary events in order to achieve greater proximity to these literary documents of the late canonical Jewish period. Bonhoeffer did not draw attention to the lapse of time, he eliminated it altogether. This Bible study took the form more of a sermon than a critical examination of the text. As a topical comment it was also sent to *Junge Kirche*.

Junge Kirche, under Hanns Lilje and Fritz Söhlmann as editor and sub-editor respectively, was the vehicle for current disputes. In the skirmishes between Lutherans, the supporters of the Committees and the Dahlemites, the purpose of which was to capture this periodical as a publicity weapon, Bonhoeffer's Bible study now served both as target and ammunition. Söhlmann wrote to Bonhoeffer on 3rd July.

. . . the Bible study gives me particular pleasure. If it were up to me alone I would bring it out at once. I do not anticipate any difficulties from Dr. Lilje. The publishers are pushing him so hard that it seems highly probable he will at last resign his co-editorship, which he has been hesitating to do . . . But I must expect difficulties from the publishers. Generally I don't allow myself to be influenced. But an article by Ehrenberg[58] has just gone through to the accompaniment of terrific arguments . . . I have written to the publishers today telling them that I am considering printing your Bible study in one of the next numbers . . .

Bonhoeffer certainly intended his contribution to embrace both the contemporary struggle in church politics and the question of Old Testament textual exegesis. And this latter question had become particularly controversial since the appearance of Wilhelm Vischer's *Christuszeugnis des Alten Testamentes* in 1934. By its Christological elimination of the historical interval from the text, Vischer's book caused a rift among theologians by incensing the specialists and delighting the members of the school of Karl Barth. Since *Creation and Fall*[59] Bonhoeffer had been numbered among the latter group: he, too, sought in 'theological' exegesis to preach Christ in the Old Testament.

Scarcely had this number of *Junge Kirche* appeared on 18th July than Friedrich Baumgärtel, the Greifswald Old Testament scholar, sent off a letter of protest to Eberhard Baumann, the theological expert of the Stettin Council of Brethren. He also began work on a sharp refutation[60] the preface of which had been completed by 4th August. His criticisms found wide acceptance, for example in *Das Evangelische Westfalen*.[61] 'Baumgärtel's demand for clarification is patently necessary. Bonhoeffer's "Bible study" cannot remain uncontested.' An exhaustive corres-

58. The 'non-Aryan' pastor, Hans Ehrenberg.
59. See Ch. VI, p. 161.
60. F. Baumgärtel, *Die Kirche ist Eine—die alttestamentliche jüdische Kirche und die Kirche Jesu Christi? Eine Verwahrung gegen die Preisgabe des Alten Testaments*, 1936.
61. *Das Evangelische Westfalen*, September 1936, p. 142.

pondence developed with Baumann.[62] After the latter had assured him that articles published in *Junge Kirche* were not the official pronouncements of the Confessing Church and were open to discussion, Baumgärtel wrote:

I know that young pastors and ordinands feel inwardly distressed about the Old Testament since they find themselves defenceless against Bonhoeffer's onslaught. For the sake of these weak ones I have written this booklet, all the more readily because I realize how difficult it now is for students to meet together academically and to get to the roots of a problem. I simply had to help them. My anxiety is not lessened by your writing to me that Bonhoeffer's pronouncements are not to be seen as the pronouncements of the Confessing Church. How can a man from whose theological pronouncements the Confessing Church must explicitly disassociate herself hold such a vital position as a teacher of theology?[63]

In his selection of verses Bonhoeffer had failed to take account of their context so that Baumgärtel was now able to contest his thesis proving that, on the contrary, at the time of Israel's return from Babylon the reconstruction of the 'church' of Ezra and Nehemiah had been undertaken with considerable 'state assistance' and under the protection of the state commissars.

Bonhoeffer ceased to put up a detailed defence against these attacks by the specialists. There is no doubt that he had been over-hasty in the collation of material for his study. Perhaps he also detected the weakness of his exegetical method for not long afterwards he was considering the draft of an article on 'Hermeneutics'.[64] Although he never carried out this plan, we do nevertheless find a noticeable change in his treatment of Old Testament texts in his letters from Tegel prison.

Bonhoeffer did not however allow himself to be deterred from applying his subjective contemporary experience to an eclectic examination of texts. He was even able to inspire his students with such highly questionable theses as that one contestable exegesis on its own does not necessarily result in a false sermon, in the same way that, conversely, the correct use of exegetic material can be no guarantee that a sermon will be true. Again, he would not admit that the wealth of a text is exhausted in its literal meaning. Without an element of risk in the transition from exegesis to sermon, Bonhoeffer's sermons on Judas and on the Psalm of Vengeance as well as his experiment with Psalm 119 would never have come into being.

His Bible study on Ezra is, therefore, at once false and correct. In a Biblical-historical context it does not bear examination, but what it preaches remains valid, namely that the Church does not escape her judgement and that she will be able to find her truth not in restoration,

62. See GS IV, pp. 336-43.
63. Baumgärtel to Baumann, GS IV, p. 339.
64. See Ch. X, p. 474.

however well-intentioned, but only in the independent renewal of her faith.

Greifswald

The background to Greifswald's theological criticism of Bonhoeffer as an exegetist was one of acrimony, even though Baumgärtel set great store by his assertion that, so far as he was concerned, his polemic was a matter of theology and exegesis in no way connected with questions of church politics. The differences with the Greifswald faculty that had begun with the seminary's passing visit in 1935[65] had grown into a deep rift after the formation of the Pomeranian Church Committee. Unaided by the university teachers and, indeed, forced to oppose them, the Finkenwalde Seminary was now working in Greifswald among those students who did not wish to leave the Councils of Brethren. When the members of Finkenwalde actually set up a hostel at Greifswald, the teaching staff were conspicuous by their absence from the dedication service.

Yet the work at Greifswald was not solely the brain-child of Finkenwalde. The Confessing Church as a whole was compelled to look after the students in the theological faculties, for ecclesiastical colleges had been proscribed and forced into illegality. Furthermore, the universities were becoming increasingly Nazified so that it was almost impossible for a state-appointed lecturer to keep his students informed about events in the church struggle, or, for instance, to go into any detail about the Confessing Church's memorandum to Hitler. What is more, the overwhelming majority of lecturers—in Greifswald the entire teaching staff —were advocating the cause of the Committees and the abandonment of all demands put forward by the Confessing Church.

Thus the new theological generation is in great danger of never coming into touch with a well-defined confessional theology. At this moment the preachers' seminaries of the Confessing Church are the only places where the Confessing Church can, with complete independence, show the way to a clear confessional attitude in life and doctrine.[66]

Hence the Provisional Administration set up their own boards for theological students; in Greifswald this took place at the beginning of the 1936 summer term. After he had been compelled to give up his lectures in Berlin, Bonhoeffer went to Greifswald nearly every week during that summer.

At the beginning of the 1936 winter term the work gained a firmer foothold by reason of the fact that Schönherr was able to adapt an old student fraternity house as a hostel modelled along the lines of Finken-

65. See Ch. IX, pp. 356 f.
66. Proclamation in the 10th Finkenwalde Circular Letter of 22.7.1936. GS II, p. 500.

walde. Whenever he could find a church. Bonhoeffer preached. On such occasions congregations of 500 were not unusual.

The conflict attracted sympathy on all sides. Bonhoeffer wrote:

It is a hard struggle in which he [Schönherr] is opposed by the entire faculty, but harder still for the small band of students who have taken it upon themselves to effect the breach with the faculty whose members meant a great deal to them at one time. Now, in fact, it is as if they had been turned out for the sole reason that they had placed themselves firmly behind the Council of Brethren . . . The fronts unfortunately seem to be hardening a little so that it is no longer possible to count on a hearing. In fact the Confessing Church is being torn asunder here in the name of the Confessing Church, a circumstance which in truth cannot long remain tolerable. Everything goes to show that clarification is necessary . . . Unfortunately the situation in Greifswald is fairly typical of the province as a whole.[67]

Repeated attempts were made to enter into fresh discussions but all were unsuccessful. In 1936 it became virtually impossible to remain united when one brother belonged to a theological faculty and another to a confessional seminary. In his last letter to Baumgärtel, Baumann wrote:

. . . the students' confidence is based not only on what the teaching staff say, on the *intellectual* exposition arising from the responsibility of their educational task, but also on the attitude adopted by those same lecturers to the Church's decisions. When the younger generation, itself averse to all forms of schism, suspects a lack of logical consistency when thought is translated into action, confidence is likely to evaporate. This, from the students' point of view, would seem to be the crux of the matter. And this is the source of all the distress which deeply affects both sides.

The foregoing problem completely dwarfs the dread question of how long it will be possible for teachers of Protestant theology, in their capacity as civil servants, to teach both within the meaning and in the service of the Protestant Church to which they belong; of how long there will still continue, here and there in the universities of the Third Reich, such freedom of research and instruction as still remains.[68]

IV MEMORANDUM TO HITLER

The stubborn dispute over the valid calling of a spiritual church administration, in which Bonhoeffer felt himself increasingly involved, took up more of his time and energy than he would have liked. In his view, its justification depended on whether the Church with a valid administration still had something to say. She had. He was passionately involved in the evolution of the memorandum to the Reich Chancellor

67. From the 10th Finkenwalde Circular Letter of 22.7.1936, GS II, p. 490.
68. Baumann to Baumgärtel, 26.10.1936, GS IV, p. 242.

which, he believed, presented these disputes for the first time in their true perspective. After his disappointment over the line taken by the Steglitz Synod he saw a ray of hope when, early in 1936, the new Provisional Church Administration in company with the Reich Council of Brethren set about preparing a written account of legal infringements and encroachments by the secular authorities. Whereas the important proclamations of 1935 and earlier had been concerned essentially with warding off political encroachment on the province of the Church, or had turned in admonition against the new paganism, the Confessing Church now at last raised her voice for the 'voiceless in the land' against the alarming developments outside the Church's own sphere. Initially she addressed herself, not to the general public, but to Hitler alone, so that he might have the opportunity of giving a factual reply.

Each individual complaint was accompanied by numerous comments. Because of Hitler's mentality, an effort was made to present the truth in such a way that the door was left open for discussion. The complaints and questions were put forward in seven main sections: 1. Is the de-Christianization of the people part of the Government's official policy? 2. What is the actual or ostensible meaning of the Party formula 'Positive Christianity'? 3. The recent 'pacification work' muzzles the churches. 4. In breach of existing agreements young people, schools, universities and the Press are being forcibly de-Christianized by the slogan 'deconfessionalization'. 5. With the new ideology people are being forced into anti-Semitism which commits them to *hatred of the Jews*, and which parents have to combat in the education and bringing-up of their children. 6. Cause for anxiety is given by the popular materialistic morality, exalting of the oath, *manipulation* of the Reichstag elections, *concentration camps* which make a mockery of a constitutional state, and the activities, unhampered by legal scrutiny, of the *State Secret Police.* 7. Spying and eavesdropping exert an unhealthy influence . . .[69] Here the Church was still speaking largely on her own behalf, but this was the first and, indeed, the last time that she was to go so far in matters which concerned every German.

The general confusion that must have reigned during discussions of, for instance, the far too mildly worded clause on anti-Semitism, is evident from the March 1936 number of the organ of the Rhineland Confessional Synod. Here we find juxtaposed an excellent analysis of the ecclesiastical position from the point of view of Dahlem and, under 'News in Brief', the following note:

40 to 60 per cent of leading posts serving the bolshevist cause are filled by Jews [this was set out in spaced type]; in important fields such as foreign

69. For text and further details see W. Niemöller, *Die Bekennende Kirche sagt Hitler die Wahrheit*, 1954. Also J. Beckmann, *Kirchliches Jahrbuch*, 1948, pp. 130 ff.

politics, trade with abroad, etc., the proportion of Jews in leading posts is as high as 95 per cent.[70]

The memorandum was written after the appointment of the new Provisional Administration on 12th March 1936. Three committees were set to work on it. The second, which was concerned with individual details in the preliminary work, included Franz Hildebrandt who frequently conferred with Bonhoeffer on problems connected with the form and content of the project. Hildebrandt also took an important part in the final editing of the whole. On 4th June 1936 Wilhelm Jannasch personally handed in the original of the memorandum at the Reich Chancellory.

Among those in the know there was naturally considerable tension over Hitler's possible reaction, However things turned out otherwise than expected and in a way that was to involve Bonhoeffer also.

Premature Publication

From Hitler came neither acknowledgement nor reply. Six weeks went by. Then, on 17th July, the London *Morning Post* produced a report of a challenging memorandum to Hitler. On 23rd July the entire memorandum appeared word for word in the *Basler Nachrichten*. All at once everyone was able to read a text which not even its compilers and signatories themselves possessed. The situation was most embarrassing for the originators of the document, the more so as a reasonably pertinent reply was still expected from Hitler. It was now up to the Provisional Administration to demonstrate that they had acted in all loyalty and seriousness. By 20th July, they had already written to the church administration of the regional churches and to the Provincial Councils of Brethren: 'Publication took place without the knowledge or assistance of the Provisional Administration'—which, on the face of it, was correct. Indeed they even visited the Presidential Chancellory of the Reich Chancellor and called for the unmasking of the perpetrator, since it seemed possible that someone in the Government might have attempted to discredit the Confessing Church by this means. They also provided the Gestapo with a copy of a foreign newspaper and requested them to search for the culprits—a unique case of cooperation between the secret police and the Confessing Church.

Although the memorandum's publication created a deep impression within the ecumenical movement, at home it was to increase still further the estrangement between Dahlemites and Lutherans.

The Lutheran Council publicly disassociated itself from the memorandum after its publication abroad, while Gauleiter Holtz

70. 49th Occasional Letter, exclusively for members of confessional congregations, published by the Rhineland Evangelical Confessional Synod, 2.3.1936, p. 23.

described the authors as 'guilty of high treason'.[71] When it was proposed to make the memorandum the basis for a proclamation from the pulpit, the representatives of the regional churches affiliated to the Lutheran Council absented themselves from the 30th July session of the Reich Council of Brethren, which body was thereafter reduced to impotence. Doubly distressing was the fact that this disassociation coincided with Kerrl's prohibition of the use by the Provisional Administration of the word 'administration' and his instructions to all authorities to sever their connections with it. At the time Bonhoeffer wrote to former members at Finkenwalde:

Dear Brethren, we can all tell that things have once more started moving in our Church. We do not know what the destination will be. The most serious anxiety of all is the Lutheran Council. We are faced with the proclamation of a Lutheran Reich Church. Then we shall have the Confessing Church for which many yearn. Yet incomprehensibly we shall not be able to participate. Then our conscience will be racked with fear and anguish . . . may God build a wall about us so that we can keep together.[72]

And in a letter to Eberhard Bethge:

. . . the unrest in church politics! 'The heart is a stubborn and despondent thing.' Stubbornness and despondency—these can only be overcome in prayer.[73]

The signatories had meant to present Hitler with a sincere plea and an admonition. This made it all the more easy to brand them as the tools of foreign propaganda. For a time they were in genuine ignorance of what could have happened.[74] But Bonhoeffer soon knew. Two of his students, Werner Koch and Ernst Tillich, had been instrumental in the memorandum's publication.

Ernst Tillich had at one time belonged to the Berlin students' group which used to travel out to Prebelow and Biesenthal with Bonhoeffer in 1932. He had also been one of the youth delegates to Fanö but had then quite lost touch with his earlier connections. The Rhinelander, Werner Koch, had been suggested to Bonhoeffer by Hanns Lilje in 1932 as a possible member of the youth delegation to the Gland Conference. He joined the second course at Finkenwalde in the winter of 1935-6 and during the Swedish visit made himself useful by his handling of the Press. He was a fluent and gifted writer and this, together with the fact that he had studied abroad, earned him the recommendation of Karl Barth which led to his becoming a contributor of articles and information to a number of important foreign periodicals.

Since Koch's journalistic activity was a source of some disquiet to

71. W. Niemöller, op. cit., p. 45.
72. From the 10th Finkenwalde Circular Letter of 22.7.1936, GS II, p. 495.
73. Letter of 28.7.1936, GS II, p. 277.
74. Cf. the session of the Reich Council of Brethren of 29.10.1936; W. Niemöller, op. cit., p. 48.

those members of the Councils of Brethren who knew of it, steps were taken to make his contacts with Berlin more difficult by transferring him to a seminary at Barmen. But once there he successfully carried on with his activities as a correspondent with the help of his friend Ernst Tillich in Berlin. Both Koch and Tillich had long been in contact wth Dr. Weissler.

Many years later, on 12th July 1948, Werner Koch gave an account of how the memorandum came to be published:

[Ernst Tillich] was the one who borrowed the memorandum to Hitler for one night from Weissler and who, during the course of that night, secretly copied out the whole text word for word. It was Weissler's tacit, but my explicit, intention that Tillich should do no more than issue a brief communiqué to the foreign Press on the existence and the essential contents of the memorandum. When, however, Hitler continued to maintain an obstinate silence over the document and when the Confessing Church, in spite of her earlier proclamation to the contrary, appeared to acquiesce in this silence, Tillich felt himself bound to give full weight to the memorandum by publishing the complete text.

During the second half of July Bonhoeffer was in Berlin, and it was not long after the appearance of the report in the *Morning Post* that he discovered the details of what had happened.

Ernst Tillich and Friedrich Weissler were both arrested on 6th October, Werner Koch on 13th November. During interrogation by the Gestapo, Koch contrived to keep silent about his most recent contacts with Bonhoeffer, although these details were later discovered.

On 13th February 1937 the three men were moved from their place of detention in Alexanderplatz in Berlin to Sachsenhausen concentration camp. As a Jew *(Volljude)* Weissler was separated from the other two. Six days later he succumbed to the maltreatment he had suffered there. Ernst Tillich was released in 1939. Werner Koch regained his freedom on 2nd December 1938 after a harsh spell in a penal company. No one at Finkenwalde thought of disavowing him.

Declaration from the Pulpit

While the memorandum was under preparation, it had been decided that should Hitler fail to reply, a suitable message should be despatched to the congregations. In the event this provided unmistakable evidence, at a time when confidence had been shaken, that the Church had not completely lost her voice in the face of flagrant injustice even though the power of the State had, in June 1936, become unassailable by the amalgamation under Heinrich Himmler of all the police forces in the Reich. The Gestapo had again appeared in the Berlin office of the Provisional Administration. Could it be expected of every parish minister that, by making a proclamation from the pulpit, he should inculpate himself in something that bore the stigma of having been published abroad? Despite the approaching Olympics, there was no lack of intimidation by Party speakers and the Party Press. In a Berlin bookshop Bonhoeffer came across a card bearing these lines of doggerel:

> After the end of the Olympiade
> We'll beat the CC to marmalade,
> Then we'll chuck out the Jew,
> The CC will end too.[75]

On the other hand it was quite obvious that the influx of foreign visitors was imposing restraint upon the State; so far there had been little interference in 1936. Bonhoeffer believed that the prospects for the proclamation were good, and was in favour of an announcement:

Opinions vary tremendously. For my part I don't think that anything violent will happen. You know about my English friend. The day before yesterday he wrote something that was very good and useful.[76]

Finally it was decided on 3rd August that the proclamation, a modified version of the memorandum, should be read out on 23rd August. In addition it was issued as a pamphlet, about one million copies being printed. Thus, in a year during which everything seemed to have gone right for Hitler—from the occupation of the Rhineland by way of the splendid Olympic Games, by way of the Rome-Berlin axis, the recognition of Franco and the anti-Comintern pact with Japan—the Church was venturing open criticism, which could readily be represented to the majority of the population as outrageous carping at the new Germany and at her Führer whose foreign policy had been crowned with such success.

The decision to publish the proclamation soon became known. The Lutheran regional churches, which had failed to send representatives to the decisive sessions of the Reich Council of Brethren, would have nothing to do with it. Reich Minister Kerrl instructed the Church Committee to take disciplinary action against any who read out the proclamation; the Committee then sent telegrams to its superintendents asking them to warn their clergy.

In this situation the Provisional Administration urged that, come what may, Bonhoeffer must attend the summer conference of 'Life and Work' at Chamby. For should the State take drastic action against the authors of the word from the pulpit and those who proclaimed it, the Provisional Administration wanted to have a spokesman in the ecumenical movement who knew the history of the memorandum and who could advise on measures from without in the shape, perhaps, of a delegation.

So Sunday 23rd August arrived. A number of courageous men read

75. GS II, p. 280.
76. To E. Bethge, 6.8.1936, GS II, pp. 279 f.; also Bishop Bell's letter to *The Times* of 4.8.1936.

out the proclamation from the pulpit, among them, in their lonely villages, the majority of the Finkenwalde pastors. After the service conducted by G. Vibrans, a former ordinand in the first course at Finkenwalde, the local schoolmaster came up to him and, hailing the village policeman who happened to be passing, demanded: 'Arrest this traitor!' To this the policeman replied: 'Can't. No orders.' And indeed such was the case—there were no orders. In fact, as it turned out, the Gestapo had received instructions to avoid violent intervention. Once again all that was done was to register the names of those who had read out the proclamation. There was also a press campaign against the 'fellows without a fatherland'. Nevertheless the state authorities realized that with the Zoellner experiment they had got as far as they could and that eventually some other means would have to be found if they were to proceed further.

On the morning after the Sunday proclamation the Swiss newspapers came out with detailed reports which were examined as anxiously by the other ecumenical delegates in Chamby as they were by the Germans. Some of the delegates already knew what had happened, for Henriod had been in Berlin and had managed to bring out a copy of the memorandum at the beginning of June.[77] Now they congratulated the four members of the Confessing Church on what had been done.[78]

Berlin Olympic Games

Part of all the extravagance and display during the Berlin Olympics was intended to demonstrate to visitors from abroad that the Reich capital was eminently Christian in character. Frank Buchman was received by high Party officials including, it is believed, Heinrich Himmler himself. In an interview with the *New York World Telegram* on his return on 25th August, he said: 'I thank Heaven for a man like Adolf Hitler, who built a front line of defence against the antichrist of Communism.'

The Reich Church erected an enormous tent near the stadium for religious services. For a time it was thought that pastors from the Confessing Church, Bonhoeffer among them, might participate. A series of learned theological lectures by professors from the university was held in Holy Trinity Church. The Berlin Council of Brethren, too, were not idle, for they announced a programme of lectures on the theme 'The Way of the German Evangelical Church in the Present Day' in Pauluskirche, with Jacobi, Asmussen, Dibelius, Niemöller, Iwand and Bonhoeffer as speakers. But once again Bonhoeffer disapproved of the way in which it was proposed to exploit an auspicious occasion:

I would far rather call everything off. I was particularly annoyed when

77. Information provided by A. Boyens, 30.8.1965.
78. See 12th Finkenwalde Circular Letter of 22.9.1936.

we were asked to send a photograph because they wanted to bring out a propaganda booklet with our pictures in it. This I find both ludicrous and degrading, and in any case I shall send nothing. As I see it, it's thoroughly old-fashioned. I shall write and tell them so.[79]

Behind the seductive pomp and the universal jubilation over Hitler's successes Bonhoeffer saw only renewed signs of the war he had earlier prognosticated: 'On the whole things certainly seem to be getting more and more critical. We must keep very calm and pray much more.'[80]

The propaganda booklet appeared, only to be immediately confiscated. Nevertheless every meeting was packed. The *Christliche Welt*,[81] at that time hostile to the Confessing Church, reported that the Church Committees' lectures in Holy Trinity Church, though highly satisfactory from a scholarly point of view, were being poorly attended while those of the Confessing Church, whose theological content was controversial in the extreme, were attracting crowds of listeners: 'a huge reverently attentive congregation. Such a state of affairs must arouse the gravest misgivings over the future of the Evangelical Church.'

On 5th August Bonhoeffer spoke in Pauluskirche as well as at the over-flow meeting in the Church of the Twelve Apostles. This was the last occasion in his life on which he was to stand before such a multitude of people.

Not a bad evening yesterday. The church packed; people were sitting on the altar steps and standing everywhere. I would rather have preached than given my lecture . . . A group of Berlin friends, pastors, etc., met at Rabenau's where I had to continue my talk. I didn't get home until 2 a.m.[82]

Bonhoeffer had chosen as his subject 'The Inner Life of the German Evangelical Church'. Drawing on typical verses from hymns by Luther, Paul Gerhardt, Zinzendorf, Gellert and Spitta he described Protestant modes of prayer and concluded by showing how the spirit of the Reformation was again manifesting itself in prayer in the Confessing Church.[83]

The reporter from the *Christliche Welt* wrote: 'If we consider that this man is a pupil of Harnack's we can only feel deeply sad when con-fronted by such a "view of history".'

V 'SERVICE TO OTHERS'

The phrase 'intensive preparation for service to others' used by Bon-hoeffer in his proposal for a community house[84] was more than just an

79. GS II, p. 276.
80. To E. Bethge, 23.7.1936, GS II, p. 276.
81. CW, 1936, No. 16, also GS II, pp. 278 f.
82. GS II, pp. 280 f.
83. See the postscript to the lecture, GS IV, pp. 385 ff.
84. Cf. Ch. IX, p. 385.

empty phrase. In fact the seminary's 1936 summer course was characterized by concern for matters transcending their own personal life and studies. Supported by the House of Brethen, Bonhoeffer identified the seminary with the cause of persecuted colleagues. Together with the entire House he also embarked on an imporant popular mission in Pomerania, a mission which was henceforth to become a Finkenwalde institution, endowed by Bonhoeffer with his own individual stamp.

The formulation he was to make eight years later, which postulated an indissoluble relation between the *arcanum* of the Christian, understood as compassion, and the reinterpretation of the Gospel, was basically in existence at Finkenwalde even though the 'interpretation' still found expression in conventional terms. But one was already implicit in the other, and all concerned sensed that this was right.

Identification with the Persecuted

Neither Zoellner nor the Olympics could wholly preclude isolated terrorist incidents in 1936 which, by their very isolation, made a deeper impresson than did the much more comprehensive wave of arrests in 1937. The name of every victim was unfailingly mentioned by Bonhoeffer during prayers, devotions and meditation. Everyone at Finkenwalde was to learn to concern himself like a brother with at least one of these cases, and eventually to regard such incidents as nothing really out of the ordinary.

1. At the very beginning of the third course W. Süssbach, a young pastor of Jewish origin, was set upon by a group of S.A. in the province of Brandenburg and badly beaten up. Bonhoeffer immediately brought him to Finkenwalde so that he could recover from his injuries and shock. He later helped him to emigrate.

2. A few days later Pastor Johannes Pecina together with Willi Brandenburg, the minister sent by the Council of Brethren to replace him, was arrested in Seelow, a small town near Frankfurt on the Oder. This happened, firstly because Pecina would not permit himself to be turned out of his church and parsonage by a rival nominated by the Consistory, and secondly because he had failed to comply with a state eviction order. A. Preuss from the first course at Finkenwalde then took over. Bonhoeffer travelled to Frankfurt and tried without success to get into the prison. A lively correspondence subsequently sprang up between prisoners and seminary.[85] One of Bonhoeffer's favourite hymns at this time was Tersteegen's *'Kommt, Kinder, lasst uns gehen'* with its lines, 'Each sets his face with steadfastness towards Jerusalem' and 'Where the weaker brother falleth, the stronger grasps his hand'. Bonhoeffer included a personal message in the circular letter to former Finkenwaldians:

85. See GS II, pp. 478, 484 ff., 494, 496 ff., 503.

I think that we should all prepare ourselves by physical and spiritual discipline for the day when we shall be put to the test. My thoughts are almost continually with our imprisoned brethren. They have much to tell us. Daily loyalty now concerns us all.[86]

Pecina and Brandenburg had already become part of Finkenwalde long before their release at the end of August 1936, when they arrived there to recuperate from the months of detention.[87] Willi Brandenburg then joined the fourth course and eventually became a member of the House of Brethren where he took part in many of Finkenwalde's popular missions. He was killed in the Russian campaign.[88]

3. In Helbra, a mining locality in the province of Saxony, the large confessional congregation was locked in bitter struggle with a German Christian church executive backed by the State and the Consistory. Since the Council of Brethren was urgently in need of a temporary relief, the House of Brethren sent E. Bethge.[89] Although this did not result in any serious confrontation with the police, it did lead to some acrimonious correspondence between Bonhoeffer, on one hand, and Staemmler, whom he esteemed so highly, on the other, about the priorities proper to the House of Brethren. The Councils of Brethren were getting into the habit of drawing on the House of Brethren whenever the need arose. Yet its whole purpose would be lost if its members were kept to occupy permanent appointments. Accordingly Bonhoeffer insisted that in the case of Helbra the term of replacement should not exceed the period that had already been agreed.[90]

4. In the summer of 1936 Wolfgang Büsing, a member of the second course, was compelled to emigrate because his wife was a 'non-Aryan'. Herbert Jehle, an old friend of Berlin and London days, was also seriously thinking of leaving the country since he found no support within the Church for his unwavering pacifism. Both men had been frequent visitors to the seminary. Bonhoeffer made use of his London connections to help Büsing, and advised Jehle to leave as well. He himself often thought that it might be sensible if he and his family were to emigrate, but at that time any more serious consideration of the matter was out of the question.

5. Finally, Bonhoeffer and the seminary, on Werner Koch's arrest and committal to a concentration camp, added his name to Finkenwalde's intercessory list, since the Councils of Brethren were afraid to admit him into the ranks of those who were named openly. Bonhoeffer missed no opportunity of sending him news. At Christmas 1936 he sent greetings to him in the Alexanderplatz from 'Brother Glocke, one of the trustiest

86. Letter of 24.6.1936, GS II, p. 486.
87. GS II, p. 503.
88. GS II, pp. 593, 596.
89. See GS II, p. 494.
90. See Ch. IX, p. 385.

of men. I look forward to seeing him before long'.[91] Koch, who was familiar with the ecumenical movement, knew that 'Glocke' meant Bell, the Bishop of Chichester. Bonhoeffer made himself responsible for Koch's fiancée whom he entrusted to the care of Frau von Kleist-Retzow. 'In these times', he said, 'you belong to us more than ever.' When Koch was finally released Bonhoeffer congratulated him:

Our joy is indescribable. What we have hoped and prayed for from day to day has come true. To me it still seems like a dream. And now you are reunited with your splendid fiancée whom we all admire. It must seem as though you've been given a new life. Now there's only one thing I look forward to and that is to see you again as soon as possible, so as to make quite sure that you are back among us . . . There's a great deal to tell but it all seems trivial compared with the joy of your release. At the moment I can't think of anything more to say. You yourself know better than I do what is most important . . .[92]

The picture would be incomplete, however, if there were no mention of Bonhoeffer's infectious *joie de vivre* just at a time when things were getting more dangerous: his delight in games, music and the summer in the country. He handed out tickets for the Olympics. For the sheer pleasure of it he paid out of his own pocket the air fare to Berlin for two of his ordinands so fulfilling their dearest wish, for they had never been in an aircraft before. The grand piano, far from falling silent, rang out more often than ever before. Bonhoeffer produced his tennis racket. In hot summer weather, instruction was simply abandoned so that everyone could spend a few days on the beach at Misdroy.

But if he suspected that anybody was confusing relaxation with a lapse from order and moderation, he could be harsh to the point of injustice. Once, when he had been deeply upset by one such incident, he wrote:

The five were up against me and against themselves . . . It was more than I could manage. The only thing I could do was to pray against it inwardly without ceasing.[93]

The Finkenwalde Mission

What was at that time called an 'evangelical mission' did not enjoy the best of reputations. A number of its official representatives maintained a middle, neutral course, because they regarded the 'church dispute' as likely to harm and obstruct evangelism. Many expected something of the Oxford Group Movement while others supported the German Christians because they offered 'possibilities for evangelism'.

Nevertheless in 1936 evangelical missions were again ridiculed by the

91. GS II, p. 513.
92. Letter of 9.12.1938, GS II, p. 545.
93. GS II, pp. 501 f.

National Bishop, this time in a publication entitled *Deutsche Gottesworte*. In the foreword he wrote: 'For you, my comrades in the Third Reich, I have not translated the Sermon on the Mount but Germanicized it . . . Your National Bishop.' The beatification of the meek he interpreted as: 'Happy is he who always observes good comradeship. He will get on well in the world'; and the Cross: 'Take pains to maintain a noble, calm attitude, even to one who insults or persecutes you.'[94] This caused Bonhoeffer to ask where, in all this, faith and church were to be found.

The criticism of the Confessing Church among circles committed to evangelical missions was justified in so far as there was a real danger that the Dahlemites might increasingly waste their time and energy on awkward legal disputes. Yet the church struggle and 'evangelization' were completely indissoluble in their view, and more especially in that of Bonhoeffer, who held that no one was entitled to evangelize who had not remained at a respectable distance from the message of the 'German awakening'. If Finkenwalde was to undertake missionary work on an independent basis, it could only be on condition that such work would promote a clearer revelation of the Gospel. 'The missionary sermon must be the whole Word in all circumstances. It must not be doled out. The whole Word alone is its strength.'[95] Bonhoeffer's homiletics concluded with a comment on mission work in which he hints at its true essence:[96] 'The promise holds true that God's Word will always create a congregation for itself, but not that the whole German people will be converted.' From his earliest days right up to the end he never tried to popularize the message by any kind of artifice, nor did he do so now in this missionary undertaking.

In June 1936 the entire seminary made its way to Belgard, a group of parishes in Further Pomerania where four brethren were assigned to each of six parishes. The operating procedure had already been tried out in an Uckermark church by the House of Brethren and by now had been thoroughly rehearsed with the seminary. Bonhoeffer stayed with the Kleist-Retzows in Kieckow from where he went each evening to visit one of the parishes. Each four-man team spent the whole week in one village. During the day they split up to visit houses and attend children's classes and Bible discussions. On four of the days these activities were followed by an evening meeting in the church, where each of them spent ten minutes in the pulpit dealing with one particular aspect of the prepared subject allotted to him. As a result the evening service never lasted longer than an hour. The number of villagers attending was far larger than they had dared to expect.

Wherever they happened to be, the four brethren adopted the same

94. L. Müller, *Deutsche Gottesworte*, 1936, pp. 9, 17.
95. GS IV, p. 275.
96. GS IV, pp. 275-8.

pattern of morning devotions and meditation that was practised at Finkenwalde. In Bonhoeffer's proposal for a House of Brethren he had declared that preaching, both as regards content and actual performance, was in need of brotherly help and fellowship.[97] This phrase had now become a practical experience for the whole seminary. In the conclusion to his homiletics on mission preaching, Bonhoeffer stated:

It bears the promise of sharing the burden of temptation during preaching in brotherly prayer, confession and forgiveness. The congregation is necessary so that its nucleus wherever it may be can be summoned by example to responsibility, a nucleus which must continue with the work . . .

The common testimony of a saviour in a brotherhood helps to correct the psychic through the pneumatic. The exalted joyfulness of the testimony will be disclosed.[98]

Dead Congregations

In considering these activities, one important aspect was whether the people had not 'already heard and rejected the Word'.[99] Bonhoeffer was concerned with the question whether a pastor's parochial work might not be superseded by a more sensible deployment of forces whereby preaching would gain in clarity and dignity. To this the House of Brethren was already contributing in that it did not conform to the customary distribution of those forces.

One of the first Finkenwaldians, G. Vibrans, was sent by his Council of Brethren to a totally moribund parish. There he wrote to Bonhoeffer:

My parish of 600 souls at Schweinitz is a very poor one, on average only one or two people go to church there every Sunday . . . every Sunday, wearing my vestments, I make a pilgrimage through the whole village primarily to bring home to the people that it is Sunday . . . The people try to comfort me by saying that I will get my stipend even though no one goes to church. On Trinity Sunday nobody was there apart from the woman sexton . . . From the point of view of church politics things are quite dead. They don't know who or what a National Bishop is . . .

Bonhoeffer then started writing letters. The first was to the Council of Brethren to say that the deployment of forces must be better ordered: 'If one village will not listen we go to another. There are limits.'[100] In another letter he gave Vibrans some practical suggestions:

Now, to begin with, you must of course carry on . . . You follow our advice with a docility that almost puts me to shame. Don't take it too literally or one day you might get fed up with it.[101]

97. GS II, p. 448.
98. GS IV, pp. 276 f.
99. Ibid.
100. See GS II, p. 487.
101. He means Bible reading, for example during visits to houses.

Bonhoeffer travelled to the village at the earliest opportunity and preached:

In the best parish twelve people, in the others even fewer . . . I have advised Brother Vibrans in due course to inform the whole of his congregation in writing that this is possibly their last chance of receiving the Gospel, and that there are other parishes whose hunger for the Word cannot be assuaged because there are too few workers.[102]

This particular case remained without sequel or practical solution until after the outbreak of war. The entrenched parochialism of the National Church's ministry had resisted every revolutionary attack. Consequently the endeavours to arrive at a true community church through the church struggle were brought to a standstill, although here and there they had proved very effective. While Bonhoeffer realized this, he also thought it might be necessary to evacuate positions which were not worth the trouble and expense, and he had the courage of his convictions. He had always felt that preaching included responsibility for the image of the Church and her office. Thus the view he was to express in 1944 was already becoming apparent, namely that the time was past when the Church could proclaim her cause by words alone.[103]

The experience gained during the mission to Belgard contributed to the further extension of this fraternal enterprise which was to continue until Finkenwalde's closure. By then a total of thirty-six parishes in Pomerania and the provinces of Saxony and Brandenburg had been visited in this way. The 1936-7 winter course visited Kreis Greifenberg in much more difficult circumstances than those encountered by the Belgard party, while the 1937 summer course travelled to Kreis Anklam in Pomerania. Preliminary experiments were carried out by the House of Brethren in urban districts such as Guben and Köslin.

As time went by incidents multiplied, for news of the mission's success had spread. Occasionally the lectern in the church would be confiscated. On a later occasion a Nazi district group leader in the border area forced the local people, under threat of punishment, to evict the members of the House of Brethren who were staying with them. But on that day more than ever attended church. Not all their experiences were so happy. In one village in the Altmark some of the peasants visited by the mission remained aggressively unapproachable. It was found impossible to establish contact with people who were openly hostile or who had, perhaps, been intimidated. In another locality, out of forty-four confirmation candidates, fifteen attended the inaugural class and only three the next—this because mention had been made of Old Testament prophets and these prophets were Jews. In 1937 there were instances of confiscated collections. Moreover the brethren's names were regularly

102. GS II, pp. 489 f.
103. LPP, p. 153.

taken by the police although no mission was ever fully banned until 1937. After the break-up of the House of Brethren, when helpers could no longer be provided, neighbouring Finkenwaldians joined together on occasion to carry out a communal mission on the well-tried pattern:

In October we had a mission week in R. Kühn's parish. Kühn, Lerche, Veckenstedt and I were there. It gave us all great pleasure. The blessing of such a thing is, perhaps, most evident in oneself and one's subsequent work in one's own parish. I have never preached so gladly as after that week.[104]

Fund-raising Campaigns

The first large-scale mission to Kreis Belgard in June 1936 coincided with yet another scheme. The Prussian Council of Brethren had made it known that the premises at Finkenwalde could not be kept up for financial reasons and that other accommodation must be found. Understandably enough Bonhoeffer was not in favour of a move. Hence consideration was given to the establishment of an association of friends of Finkenwalde to supplement a number of begging operations[105] then being conducted by the brethren in their provinces. Hans-Jürgen von Kleist-Retzow was prepared to give the help needed to start the enterprise. So, on Saturday, the last day of the mission in Belgard, friends and patrons of livings in the district were invited to an afternoon meeting in the manor-house at Kieckow. Bonhoeffer, who gave the gathering a report on the state of the church struggle, succeeded in interesting them in an association of friends of Finkenwalde. Not long afterwards food and money began to arrive at the seminary so that thoughts of a move were once more relegated to the distant future.

It was on this occasion that Bonhoeffer came to know Ewald von Kleist-Schmenzin and the two quickly achieved a close *rapport*. Whenever he spent a holiday in Kieckow, Bonhoeffer would be driven over to Schmenzin. There he also met Dr. Fabian von Schlabrendorff who would often discuss politics with Ewald von Kleist. Schlabrendorff married one of Ruth von Kleist-Retzow's grandchildren, a daughter of Herbert von Bismarck of Lasbeck. In the winter of 1944-5 he was among the last friends near Bonhoeffer in the detention cellar at police headquarters. Meanwhile in the Lehrter Strasse prison Ewald von Kleist, like Klaus Bonhoeffer and his brother-in-law Rüdiger Schleicher, was confined in a cell on the landing reserved for prisoners condemned to death.

VI CHAMBY 1936

Contrary to his earlier plans, Bonhoeffer, accompanied by Bethge, set

104. Letter from O. Dudzus to Bonhoeffer, 11.1.1939.
105. See GS II, pp. 498 ff.

off southwards on 18th August 1936 to take part in the ecumenical conference at Chamby, the last to be held by 'Life and Work' prior to the big conference at Oxford.

The antecedents of Chamby 1936, the sessions themselves and their subsequent interpretation were no less complex than those of Chamby 1935, for on the German side Zoellner's Reich Church Committee was demanding insistently that it alone should qualify for representation. Geneva may well have been relieved to find that Heckel was no longer the mouthpiece of the National Bishop but rather a partner representing more serious churchmen. But for those in Berlin this only increased the confusion. Chamby 1936 was the first and last conference attended by official delegates from the Confessing Church. Nevertheless they do not appear in the minutes of the conference.

Dispute over Invitations

At a meeting of the Provisional Administration's advisory board on 20th May, there was a discussion about attendance at Oxford. The minutes cited below show that Bonhoeffer stood by his earlier opinion and that the board was at least equally convinced of the hopelessness of the situation as it then pertained:

Bonhoeffer pointed out that it was no longer admissible that the leading personalities of the Confessing Church should be treated as private individuals by the ecumenical movement. The ecumenical movement should be asked whether it intended to recognize the Confessing Church as the only lawful church. This was the best service that could be rendered to 'Life and Work' for it would protect the latter against the danger of non-committal theologizing.

To this the objection was raised that such a procedure would be hopeless in practice, for 'Life and Work', organized as it now was, would spend years on the subject of recognition. It was unanimously decided, however, that 'Life and Work' must be confronted with this question.[106]

There had been a lack of harmony between the Reich Council of Brethren and the Provisional Administration. Hence the meeting evinced some willingness to hold discussions with Zoellner on the subject of Oxford. Präses Koch undertook to speak to him about the German side of the literary preparations for the Conference of World Churches.

Yet on 16th June 1936 the Provisional Administration informed Geneva, through Albertz, of their earlier standpoint and included a warning against Zoellner's demand:

According to the resolution of the Oeynhausen Synod, the Church is debarred from recognizing the state-appointed Church Committees, even temporarily,

106. GS I, p. 264.

as the leaders and representatives of the Church. For this reason we request you to refuse recognition, should the head of the Reich Church Committee, Herr Dr. Zoellner, convey such a demand to 'Life and Work' . . . We also request 'Life and Work' to invite the Provisional Administration [to the 'Life and Work' conference], as the authorized executive body of the German Evangelical Church . . .[107]

H. L. Henriod sent a detailed reply to this letter on 19th June in accordance with the instructions already issued by Bell and following consultation with the Administrative Committee of 'Life and Work' in Paris on 18th and 19th June. Confining himself strictly to categories such as 'sections', 'parties' and 'personalities' that avoided any specific reference, he wrote to say that: 1. Decisions on the form of representation for Oxford 1937 must be made within the German Church itself. 2. Up to a point the Administrative Committee reserved the right to approve the German nominees in order to ensure equal participation by the 'parties'. Henriod added that this did not mean that they intended to determine spiritual matters—and thus showed how difficult it would be to find any uncommitted way out of the dilemma. 3. In the specific case of Chamby, the national 'sections' would nominate the important 'personalities', additional members being coopted by the Council to ensure that the various 'parties' of the German Evangelical Church should make 'a broad and valuable contribution to the life and thought of the ecumenical movement'. This would be arranged by Bishop Bell. 4. Fanö still held good in so far as it had established that 'Life and Work', 'as a body without ecclesiastical authority . . . [must] refrain from taking sides in questions which concern the constitution of any one church and [must] remain in friendly contact with all groups of the German Evangelical Church. Since its members do not feel either competent or entitled to pass judgement on questions of spiritual authority in any specific country, they think it important to reassert their adherence to the principles of Fanö.' Should the discussions of German joint representation in Chamby be unsuccessful, 'the Bishop of Chichester must be notified so that he can take steps, notwithstanding, to ensure the presence at Chamby of personalities who share in our work.'[108]

The fatal insertion which, in 1934, had made the Fanö Declaration acceptable to Heckel,[109] now carried more weight than the main clause to which it had been appended.

Nor did Bell himself see any possibility of breaking with Zoellner's Reich Church Committee. At this time it was evident from reports on

107. To H. L. Henriod, 16.6.1936; copy in the Church Struggle archives in the Kirchl. Hochschule, Berlin, File No. 260, p. 49.
108. Quoted from a copy of the translation of Henriod's letter from the files of the Provisional Administration, see MW V, X, R.1.
109. Namely that the Council should maintain friendly relations with all groups in the German Evangelical Church, see Ch. VIII, p. 308.

the situation he received from Koechlin that even within the Confessing Church some circles were warning against a breach with the Church Committee. On 8th June Bell had received a copy of the memorandum to Hitler which Henriod had smuggled out to Geneva. Bell wrote to him on 13th June:

1. that it is absolutely vital to maintain the position we adopted at Fanö and not to deviate from those resolutions;
2. that we should not break with Dr. Zoellner and those whom he represents or leads . . . on one thing I am clear and that is that we must not weaken in our connection with the Confessional [*sic*] Church . . .

Since dictating above, I have read the Confessional [*sic*] Church's address to Hitler—a fine document—our support of the Confessional [*sic*] Church is all the more necessary.[110]

Henriod carried out these instructions, but in such a way that to those in the Provisional Administration who received his letter, his impartiality was more evident than was Bell's anxiety that the Confessing Church should attend Chamby whatever the circumstances. From certain aspects, however, even Henriod's letter appeared to show an inadmissible degree of consideration for the Confessing Church.

After Chamby Bell described the situation in a letter to Eidem:

Dr. Zoellner, before coming to Chamby had been very much upset because I had sent an invitation to Praeses Koch, inviting representatives of the Confessional [*sic*] Church to our Council Meeting—asking that in addition to Praeses Koch and Dr. Bonhoeffer (who were coopted at Fanö) a couple of other Confessional representatives might come. Dr. Zoellner was at first inclined to take the line that this would make it impossible for the Reich Church Committee to have anything further to do with the Universal Christian Council. As a result however of telephone and other communications, he was pacified, and not only did the original German official delegation arrive, but they arrived headed by Zoellner.[111]

Thus the invitation sent by Bell to the Provisional Administration contained the description 'representatives of the Confessional [sic] Church' as distinct from Henriod's wording which had spoken of the inclusion of 'personalities'. The members of the Provisional Administration at Chamby wished to be regarded as none other than a 'delegation of the Confessing Church'. No sooner had the conference ended than a fresh dispute broke out over this invitation.

Bonhoeffer, who had in fact been a coopted member since Fanö, was asked by Henriod before the conference to come to Chamby as interpreter. In refusing, he made the pointed remark that he was 'of course' coming 'as a member of the delegation of the Confessing

110. Information supplied by A. Boyens from the archives of 'Life and Work' in Geneva, 30.8.1965.
111. Bishop Bell to Eidem, 8.9.1936.

Church'. At the conference, the members of the Provisional Administration were indeed treated as the delegation of the Confessing Church, a factor which increased the latter's moral weight perceptibly when on 23rd August the pulpit proclamation, based on the memorandum to Hitler, was made.

But the rules of the Geneva office do not appear to have permitted any mention of the delegation in the minutes; these were so worded that two delegates of the Confessing Church were described as 'coopted members' and two as 'invited to the meeting (with the right to speak)'.[112] There are in fact no official minutes whatever in the keeping of the ecumenical movement which mention that the Confessing Church either took part in, or was a member of, any ecumenical conference during the thirties. Either it was not possible to make the journey (Fanö), or there was no desire to attend (Chamby 1935), or, as in the case of Chamby 1936, there was no procedure by which the Church's presence could be officially recorded.

The Provisional Administration, but more especially Bonhoeffer, resented appearing as a delegation alongside that of the Reich Church Committee because they saw this as a deviation from the requisite line. A possibility that had been raised during the negotiations following Zoellner's protest, was that of a united representation under the latter's leadership. But the Provisional Administration had answered that this was out of the question and that the invitation to the two separate delegations must stand, since 'Zoellner cannot represent us'.

Bonhoeffer complied with the Provisional Administration's instructions to travel to Chamby. On the one hand, he felt he should not shirk the dangerous situation arising out of the memorandum and the proclamation; of all the Confessing Church delegates, he was the best equipped to cope with any ugly situation that might arise, since he was an English-speaker and was, moreover, well acquainted personally with Bell and Ammundsen, both of whom trusted him implicitly. On the other hand, as we have already heard, Bonhoeffer drew a distinction between his personal opinion, about which he had left no doubt, and the decisions taken, or rather not taken, by his church during and after Oeynhausen.[113] In 1935 there had as yet been no Church Committee; now it existed and Bonhoeffer's church was still in two minds about it. So he accepted his share of the responsibility for this ambivalence in the ecumenical field. His own view remained unchanged and he intended to express it in unmistakable terms should the occasion arise.

When Fritz Müller (Dahlem) visited Finkenwalde on 12th August to let Bonhoeffer know exactly what was happening, he reported that Niemöller and Asmussen were considering going to Chamby. Bonhoeffer thought this was an excess of zeal towards the ecumenical movement:

112. See Minutes of the Council, pp. 2, 4.
113. See above pp. 434 f.

Firstly, no one will be able to understand why you are there as well as the official representatives. I can almost hear the conjectures on the part of our well-wishers there. You versus Koch,[114] or something of the sort . . . Secondly—and this seems to me the main point—we must at all costs avoid giving the impression that we are in any way running after our foreign friends. If anything, it would be better the other way round. We should not make them feel that they are absolutely essential to us. It will mean that they lose some face and that's not altogether without importance! At bottom they are all so interested in our cause that they will come to us should we wish it. You are, indeed, regarded as an official person in the truest sense. You must therefore either go in an official capacity, or not at all. Lastly the whole thing is an internal committee meeting and too much importance should not be attached to it. Next year [Oxford] is quite a different matter.[115]

Niemöller and Asmussen did not go.

The Conference

When the conference opened on Friday, 21st August, three German delegations took their seats at the table, the Confessing Church being represented by Präses K. Koch, O. Dibelius, H. Böhm and Bonhoeffer, the Lutheran Council by Hanns Lilje, the Reich Church Committee by W. Zoellner, F. Brunstäd, H. Wahl and T. Heckel. The latter was accompanied on this occasion by Eugen Gerstenmaier who appears in the minutes under 'Guests or Friends'. Besides these there were E. Stange, who attended as the secretary of the German section, and A. Deissmann and M. Dibelius on behalf of the Standing Theological Commission.

The Reich Church group round Heckel, to which in effect H. Schönfeld also belonged, and the group from the Confessing Church kept scrupulously apart and never conversed during the period of the conference. On the other hand, Bell's efforts resulted in a measure of contact between Koch, Dibelius and Zoellner. The latter, despite all the measures taken by the Reich Church against the Confessing Church's proclamation, was approachable on this subject, for he himself was planning his own memorandum on de-Christianization. Bell's integrity and patience eventually brought the hostile brethren together when they were able to discuss, not only the situation resulting from the pulpit proclamation in Germany, but more especially plans for possible joint representation at the 1937 Oxford Conference.

Bishop Bell later wrote a detailed letter to Eidem in Uppsala so that other ecumenical friends could do all in their power to come to some satisfactory arrangement for the 1937 conference. Since Eidem had his own contacts with the Church Office for External Affairs he would

114. For months Präses Koch had tried to cooperate with the Committees in Westphalia, but this was now over; cf. GS II, p. 281.
115. To M. Niemöller, 12.8.1936, GS I, p. 266.

need to know what had taken place at Chamby and the possibilities opened up there. Accordingly Bell wrote:

Bishop Heckel might come for private conversations on the German Church question. But we felt that not very much would be likely to come from conversations with Bishop Heckel. But Bishop Ammundsen will tell you when you see him I think of a little bit of new light of a more hopeful kind which did actually appear at Chamby under the aegis of our 'Life and Work' meetings.[116]

Bonhoeffer did not intervene in the official discussions at the plenary sessions; on the other hand he had a great deal to do behind the scenes. On the very first day he and Koch conferred at length with Bell, reviewing the whole situation. Bell was glad to learn that his letter to *The Times* regarding Kerrl's ban on all relations with the Provisional Administration and on its use of this title had been accurate. He also secured their assent to his talking with Zoellner.

Zoellner made a fair impression on Bell, even though the latter remarked that at first Zoellner 'really did all the talking'. This impression was reinforced at the plenary conference when Zoellner, as Bell wrote to Eidem, made a 'very important speech about the duty and witness of the Christian Church' whereas Heckel and Brunstäd, in their speeches at the preceding meeting on 'Church and Community', 'had appeared to leave out some of the most distinctively Christian factors which Zoellner emphasized in a striking way'.

After Zoellner's fine speech, the Confessing Church delegates approached Bell late the same night with the request that he point out to Zoellner how close his speech was 'in essence' to the proclamation of 23rd August and that he ask him whether, on his return, he would be prepared to act in accordance with what he had said. Zoellner explained to Bell on the following day that he felt very close to the Confessing Church on this point. Here it should be noted that the proclamation, as distinct from the memorandum itself, had completely subordinated the complaints about anti-Semitism and concentration camps to those about the de-Christianization of the people. On the latter subject Zoellner was approachable but on the former—as were, indeed, many in the Confessing Church—much less so.

On Tuesday, 25th August, Bell arranged a first meeting between Zoellner on the one hand and Koch and Dibelius on the other. Besides discussions on a future joint synod, the possibility of church elections and the conditions to be attached to them, it was agreed to investigate the feasibility of a joint delegation to Oxford, although no immediate decision about its leadership was contemplated. The meeting obviously afforded relief to Zoellner. Bishop Ammundsen said later that at the end of the conference Zoellner took leave of Böhm with a handshake and

116. Bishop Bell to Eidem, 8.9.1936.

the words 'Until we meet again in a concentration camp'.[117] Concluding his report to Eidem, Bell wrote: 'It is of course the first step, if they can only be led to take it, which will make so great a difference. And one must hope and pray.'

The official discussions resulting from this relaxation of tension had one further effect which was to be discreditably exploited after the conference. Some of those taking part in the conference, among them Leiper, Oldham and Boegner, had moved that there should be a fresh discussion and resolution on the Jewish question. Koch and Dibelius, on the other hand, expressed doubt whether, in view of the memorandum and the proclamation in Germany, a pronouncement from Chamby in the presence of the members of the Confessing Church was now either appropriate or in the interests of the brethren at home. During a further discussion between Bell, Zoellner, Koch and Dibelius it was agreed that on this occasion they should jointly advise against the proposal. Accordingly, in putting the motion at the final plenary session, Bell spoke:

. . . of the great reluctance with which he personally and the Administrative Committee generally had been led to the conclusion that it was not possible to adopt a resolution adequate to the situation and with due justice both to the necessities of the case and to the rights of members of the Council specially concerned.[118]

Bonhoeffer did not contribute to the debate on this occasion although he had his reservations about the above procedure, the more so since Dibelius and Zoellner had again spoken in support of Bell's opposing motion at the plenary session; also Zoellner's speech had expressed everything that Bonhoeffer, since 1933, had held to be false:

. . . I cannot here describe to what depths Germany has been taken, essentially as a result of decades of activities that seemed open and above board yet behind which German Jewry was the driving force . . . These forces, against whom no power could prevail, were the pacemakers and leaders in the struggle to uphold bolshevism in Germany . . .

For my part I should raise no objection if sometime there were to be an opportunity of discussing here the racial problem in an exhaustive, thoroughly prepared debate . . .

In our country we are fighting an honourable battle so that the Protestant Church, founded on the Gospel as interpreted by the Reformation, can have her place even in an authoritarian state . . . Do not destroy by an over-hasty resolution the chances possessed by the Protestant Church in Germany to achieve validity and to succeed within the limits of the Gospel . . .[119]

117. MW II, p. 171.
118. Minutes, p. 67.
119. From Zoellner's speech on 25.8.1936, see MW V, XQ. 3.

The Chamby minutes contain no record of the text of this speech nor of the reaction to its overtones, for the latter can have made little sense to the advocates of a resolution such as that put forward by Leiper and Boegner. The minutes only make a brief mention of 'great disquiet over those who in various parts of the world must suffer because of their faith, nationality, or race' and record the fact that the motion was referred to the Administrative Committee for further action.[120] The solution met with consent although the motives that had led to this unanimous decision were highly contradictory.

While at this time Bonhoeffer was reasonably satisfied with the memorandum and the proclamation at home, he felt little enthusiasm for the Universal Christian Council for 'Life and Work' in the circumstances that obtained in 1936; he no longer saw it as the supreme authority, the 'Council'. A few days later he described his lack of enthusiasm for Chamby in a letter to Henriod:

One day if I have time, I should like to write and tell you what I too would have to say about wholly fundamental things related to present ecumenical activities. It wasn't without reason that I kept silent at Chamby. But more of that later.[121]

He had carried out the duties demanded of him by the Provisional Administration, had shared in the half-hearted resolutions and, by comparison with two years previously, now expected little or nothing from the ecumenical movement. He did not want to trouble the now easier relationship with Zoellner.

Holidays in Italy

After the end of the Chamby Conference on 25th August 1936, Bonhoeffer continued his journey southwards. The alarming reports expected from home following the Sunday of the proclamation had not materialized. A small bank account he had kept since his time abroad helped to overcome the tiresome shortage of exchange for a few days, and so, leaving everything behind him and accompanied by Bethge, he travelled by way of the Simplon Pass to Rome. Once again entranced by St. Peter's, he sought to reveal the beauty of the magnificent building to his companion. A less agreeable impression during these late summer days was created by the hoardings outside every town and village, which were plastered with strident, martial posters declaiming victory in the Abyssinian war: a foretaste of what Bonhoeffer saw coming at home. Dwindling funds necessitated a return northwards, but did not prevent him calling in on Erwin Sutz at Wiesendangen near Zürich and visiting

120. Minutes, p. 69.
121. Letter of 19.9.1936.

Karl Ludwig Schmidt in Basle. Having missed Karl Barth, Bonhoeffer wrote to him about progress on *The Cost of Discipleship* and received a sceptical reply.[122] He was back in the community house by 13th September, just in time to nurse back to health with paternal efficiency a member who was seriously ill. And he was at last able to find time to resume work on *The Cost of Discipleship*.

War of the Reporters

The *rapprochement* at Chamby between Zoellner and Koch was of short duration. Zoellner had other preoccupations and from the administrative aspect, ecumenical affairs were the responsibility of the Church Office for External Affairs. It was Heckel, therefore, who on 28th September sent an official report to all church administrations for onward transmission to their clergy.[123] Three of the points in this report are of interest to us: firstly, the summary of what Heckel and Brunstäd had stood for at Chamby; secondly, the version given of how the resolution on racial discrimination came to be abandoned; and thirdly, the lists of participants.

1. The report states that, in close concert with the views of the Geneva Research Department, it had been found possible to make clear that 'an ecumenical collaborator, one conscious of his responsibilities to the Church', cannot 'disregard the national situation in his own country and in his church'. The German delegates, the report goes on, had managed to have the term 'Volk', previously deleted, restored to the German version of Oxford's theme of 'Church, Community and State' ('Kirche, Volk und Staat'), an achievement made possible by argument based on a detailed knowledge of the numerous learned works submitted to them by the Research Department in Geneva; they had warned against the use 'in ecumenical discussions of certain catchwords such as "the totalitarian state" without profound reflection and a genuine knowledge of the political reality'.

Through Brunstäd and Heckel, Schönfeld was now better able to implement a policy which he had vainly hoped Bonhoeffer would adopt at Fanö. Schönfeld had already expressed his own opinion of it when stating that this is 'a field in which, more than in any other, these people have much to learn'.[124]

In Heckel's office, Eugen Gerstenmaier, a friend of Schönfeld's, was collecting articles for the Oxford Conference from a number of eminent theologians unconnected with the Confessing Church, among them Brunstäd and Schreiner, his teachers at Rostock. These papers appeared in a book edited by Gerstenmaier and published in 1937 by the Furche-

122. GS II, pp. 283 ff.
123. Letter DEK, KAA, 4942/36 of 28.9.1936.
124. See Ch. VIII, pp. 310 f.

Verlag[125] under the title *Kirche, Volk und Staat, Stimmen aus der deutschen evangelischen Kirche zur Oxforder Weltkirchenkonferenz*.

In most of the contributions the terminology and mode of thought were quite different from those of Bonhoeffer and his friends. Bonhoeffer, in his turn, contributed theses on the theme of 'War and Peace' as preparatory material for the Provisional Administration under Hans Böhm.[126] It need hardly be said that Heckel and his friends did not welcome this topic, and indeed thought it dangerous.

2. Heckel described the abandonment of the resolution on Jewish persecution in the following manner:

When they were confronted at the last minute with a portentous resolution in which it was proposed to deal with German domestic political questions, it was . . . significant that General Superintendent Dr. Dibelius and General Superintendent Zoellner maintained emphatically that it was not the concern of those present to revert to earlier methods by placing Germany as it were in the dock.[127]

In one sense this account afforded protection from inquisitive ministries for those Germans, including Dibelius, who had spoken their minds in the Chamby debates. On the other hand, it concealed the true nature of the proceedings from the German clergy, to whom the report was addressed.

3. It is interesting to note the devious manner in which Heckel set

125. In addition to the 'learned works' mentioned by Heckel in his report, there were also Gerstenmaier's own theological studies. Before coming to help in Heckel's office at a time, incidentally, when hostility between the latter and Bonhoeffer was at its height, he had qualified for his licentiate under Brunstäd with his work 'Creation and Revelation, a Systematic Investigation of a Theology of the First Article' in which he examines such questions as creation and people (Volk) in accordance with his teacher's (and, therefore, decidedly anti-Barthian) ideas. He incorporated parts of this dissertation in a comprehensive book, *Die Kirche und die Schöpfung*, which was completed in November 1937 and published by the Furche-Verlag in 1938. In it he quotes approvingly passages from Althaus such as 'The self-contained we-consciousness of a people (Volk) is not the product of the sum of a number of individuals but is an underived primal creation' (Dissertation, 65, note 1, quoted in *Die Kirche und die Schöpfung*, p. 78, note 1); 'We may consider, for example, the plight of German racial groups (Volksgruppen) under a foreign polity, struggling for their existence, the creation they have inherited' (Dissertation, 67, or in *Die Kirche und die Schöpfung*, p. 89). Later we read: 'Wherever there is a struggle for those things created by God, for their existence, the Church must bless the weapons and join in the struggle' and, as a corollary, the observation: 'This holds good particularly with regard to the politico-racial attempts at reintegration which are concerned with the re-establishment of true community . . .' (*Die Kirche und die Schöpfung*, pp. 269 f.). Gerstenmaier's foreword to the book contains information on his sources and sponsors: '. . . The broad perspective, in which is enacted the present struggle on the part of the communal structure of people and Church for the very basis of their existence, has provided the author with impressions, as seen through the eyes of a metropolitan German, of the struggle abroad by German ethnic groups of foreign nationality and by the German Protestant diaspora. Not least, this perspective has provided impressions derived from research work in the ecumenical movement as well as from church affairs abroad.'
126. GS I, pp. 276 f.
127. Cf. minutes, pp. 68 f.

out the list of representatives; he reported that 'in accordance with the constitution of "Life and Work", an official representative body of the German Evangelical Church' had been in attendance, and had consisted of Zoellner, Heckel, Brunstäd, Deissmann, Lilje and Wahl. In addition, 'German members of the Council . . .' such as M. Dibelius, Stange, Koch and Bonhoeffer, 'who had already long exercised official functions', had attended as 'advisory members'. Next, and this provoked an immediate outcry from the Provisional Administration, there appeared the entry 'Guests . . . O. Dibelius and Böhm'. Heckel concluded with the pointed remark: 'The German Evangelical Church was thus represented by only *one* official delegation, composed, as far as possible, of persons with specialized knowledge.'

It is not surprising that following this widely publicized account the Provisional Administration should have issued a disclaimer. On 13th November, Böhm recounted the distressing story of the events leading up to the Provisional Administration's invitation: 'So it came about that despite the limitations inherent in the structure of "Life and Work", the Provisional Administration of the German Evangelical Church . . . received a special invitation to the Chamby Conference . . . from Bishop Bell of Chichester.' Böhm then spoke of Zoellner's impressive contribution at Chamby and the *rapprochement* that followed, before continuing:

At this point it must be said that Dr. Zoellner did the Evangelical Church the worst imaginable service when he delegated the preparatory work for the approaching Oxford Conference to Dr. Heckel . . . Now, as in the past, the Provisional Administration of the German Evangelical Church as the legitimate representative of the German Evangelical Church will carry out its work on the common tasks of the World Church independently of the organs of the Reich Church Committee.[128]

Meeting of the Youth Commission in London

The situation had become even more involved when Bonhoeffer and Böhm flew together to London on 16th February 1937 for a number of group meetings in connection with the Oxford Conference.

Zoellner had resigned in dramatic circumstances. On the day preceding Bonhoeffer's departure, Hitler had made a surprise announcement ordering church elections. There was no end to the questions thus raised: To what extent would the Minister for Religious Affairs exercise sole power? How much influence would the Church Office for External Affairs possess and how would it be exerted? Could Böhm and Bonhoeffer, at this precise moment, allow themselves to be associated with the Reich Church and with those officials in the Jebensstrasse[129] who had

128. Provisional Administration letter II D, 3, 3803/36 of 13.11.1936.
129. The Berlin equivalent to Church House, Westminster. (*Editor.*)

survived Zoellner's fall? Could the vague agreement made at Chamby with Zoellner, but not with Heckel, still hold good? Certainly not for Bonhoeffer who by then had already grown sceptical. In fact there were violent clashes at the London meeting over Bonhoeffer's joint responsibility towards the youth delegation to Oxford.

Despite his intention of resigning his appointment as Youth Secretary, Bonhoeffer once again found himself involved in his former ecumenical work. When, after Chamby, he was again compelled to absent himself from the Ecumenical Youth Conference,[130] he wrote to H. L. Henriod on 19th September:

I realize that things cannot go on this way. It is highly unsatisfactory for you as well as for me. We must make a change for the sake of the cause. I must resign my post . . . I should like to ask you to leave everything as it is until after Oxford. I have definite reasons for this. I shall do all in my power to carry out the necessary work. But afterwards, that will be that.[131]

The 'definite reasons' were that he did not wish to send his deputy, J. Winterhager, who had always been available hitherto, because the latter had, in the meantime, embarked on a course which was to end with his legalization in 1938. Bonhoeffer sought to replace him with Udo Smidt, then a pastor in Wesermünde and secretary of the Schoolchildren's Bible Circles, but this could not be arranged in time for the London meeting.

The minutes of the meeting on 19th February 1937,[132] which also noted the presence of Henriod, Schönfeld and Espy, record Bonhoeffer as saying that in his view 'the differences between the Churches [were] so great that he would be unwilling to secure a German youth delegation in which the Reich Church would be represented'. The Geneva secretaries thought that he should nominate three representatives, one each from the 'Reich Church', the Lutheran Council and the Confessing Church, and they reminded him of the agreement about a joint delegation discussed at Chamby. The Geneva staff continued to regard Heckel as a party to these discussions, whereas this had never been the case so far as Bonhoeffer was concerned. Moreover Zoellner, who had been a party to the Chamby agreement, had announced publicly that he no longer contemplated exercising any responsibility in the Reich Church. Eventually those present relented to the extent of asking Bonhoeffer whether he would at least nominate the other two representatives and whether he would agree to the third being chosen by direct negotiations between Henriod and the 'Reich Church'. Even then Bonhoeffer did not express unqualified approval, but 'agreed to discuss the proposal with his col-

130. At La Borcarderie from 8. to 15.9.1936 on 'Christian Youth and the Way to Peace'.
131. MW V, X, R.1.
132. GS I, pp. 271 f.

leagues in Germany, and to report their decision at an early date'. Having received an answer, Hunter, Espy and Henriod were then to 'act as they find best in the light of developments in Germany'.[133]

Breach with Geneva and Ban on Oxford

Immediately after the meeting Bonhoeffer sought out Bishop Bell in order to talk over the Chamby discussions and their possible interpretation. Bell agreed that it was not now possible to ensure three German delegations with equal rights—'three groups or none', in Henriod's words[134]—if Zoellner's withdrawal meant that of the Reich Church Committee. For his own part Henriod could not simply ignore his relations with the Church Office for External Affairs or exclude the Reich Church which it represented.[135] Bonhoeffer wrote to him: 'There was no question that, should one German group fail to attend, this would preclude the attendance of another.'[136] On 24th March Bonhoeffer again sought to clarify matters:

Your purpose was to have one of Dr. Heckel's delegates at Oxford. My purpose was to frustrate this. I should mention that I am fully aware that your only concern was to be just and to have a comprehensive representation of the German churches at Oxford. But my view is that such an arrangement, although it may appear just in a formal sense, is in fact unjust and spiritually indefensible for reasons which need not be discussed here.

Among the questions with which he concluded his letter to Henriod were the following:

Do you insist, come what may, on having one of Heckel's delegates at the youth conference in Oxford? . . . How can your decision to nominate the German youth delegates personally in association with the church governments be reconciled with the statutes of the Youth Commission and the functions of the youth secretary? To what extent does this differ from autocracy against which I would be compelled to protest most emphatically in matters affecting the Church?' I am afraid that this is where we come into sharp conflict . . .[137]

Eventually, on 17th April, Henriod asked Bonhoeffer to nominate at least the one delegate from the Confessing Church while the remainder would be selected from lists that had been received in Geneva. It was also suggested that he should address any further letters to Espy.[138]

133. GS I, p. 272.
134. GS I, p. 273.
135. GS I, pp. 273-5.
136. GS I, p. 273.
137. This letter dated 24.3.1937 from Bonhoeffer to Henriod was not included in the correspondence GS I, pp. 273-5; it was found by A. Boyens in the Geneva archives; it is reproduced in full in MW V, X, R.3.
138. GS I, p. 275.

This marked not only the fruitless conclusion of the correspondence between Henriod and Bonhoeffer, but also the virtual end of the latter's personal relations with the secretaries in Geneva.

But in fact there was nothing left to argue about since the Minister for Religious Affairs by refusing passports to everyone except the Methodist bishop, had made impossible the sending of any delegations from churches in Germany.

Kerrl had been advised in this matter by members of ecclesiastical and theological circles. Peter Meinhold, for example, produced a report on an ecumenical seminar in Geneva, concluding with the proposal:

For all journeys abroad, an office should be set up in association with the liaison staff of the National Socialist Party or the Reich Ministry of Education from which permission to travel abroad would have to be sought by theologians, clergy and students. This office would be empowered to deny exit if the participation of an individual appeared to be contrary to the interests of German policy.[139]

Professor Ernst Benz referred to Meinhold's report in a letter dated 27th November 1936[140] and, in an allusion to the Thuringian German Christians, proposed that participation of any kind at the Oxford Conference as well as the 'attendance of a German delegation or delegations, at ecumenical conferences' should be forbidden altogether; to this it might perhaps be objected that 'the views of the German Evangelical Church would be represented solely by a group of German _émigrés_ and that an anti-National Socialist resolution could be passed . . . unopposed'. According to a file entry by Erich Ruppel dated 6th January 1937[141] Benz was in contact with the Ministry for Religious Affairs and had been requested by Heckel 'to cooperate in the learned preparations for the ecumenical conferences and to [join] the section engaged in preparatory work on the theme "Church and State"'.

At the London Youth Commission meetings of 16th-24th February 1937 attended by Böhm and Bonhoeffer, the latter made a definite request that Udo Smidt should replace him as Youth Secretary. This was the last occasion on which prominent figures in the Confessing Church appeared at a regular ecumenical meeting, and it marked the close of an unhappy chapter of official relations and disputes over invitations between the 'Dahlem'-orientated Confessing Church and the ecumenical movement organized from Geneva. From now on Heckel's Church External Affairs Office ruled this roost alone, a position it exploited by

139. From the 'Report on the III Ecumenical Seminar in Geneva from 28th July to 14th August 1936' made by 'Herr Dozent Lic. Meinhold from Kiel' to the Reich Ministry of Education; copied from the files of the Ministry for Religious Affairs, No. 2931, IX O6.
140. Copied from the German Evangelical Church archives in Hanover, file C-I-IV, with the entry number of the Reich Ministry of Education registered in the files of the Ministry for Religious Affairs together with the above-mentioned paper by Lic. Meinhold.
141. G I 20043/37.

sending out its representatives as frequently and for as long as possible.

Consequently the Confessing Church was not represented at Utrecht where in 1938 discussions took place on the formation of an ecumenical Provisional Committee and where Dr. W. Visser 't Hooft was invited to become the new General Secretary in the Geneva office.[142] Nor was the Confessing Church present at the important youth conference in Amsterdam. For this reason many members of the ecumenical movement grew accustomed to seeing only the emissaries of the Church External Affairs Office at their meetings and conferences.

The Confessing Church, and Bonhoeffer himself, did not, it is true, now simply disappear from the sight and mind of the ecumenical movement. Relief work and meetings were arranged through different channels, most of them private, particularly after the plight of Confessing Church members had begun to assume new dimensions, for the secretariats of the ecumenical associations were not, indeed, really suited to these tasks.

As was his custom, Bonhoeffer also pursued his own plans during the February 1937 visit to London. He paid a second visit to Bell and introduced Hans Böhm. In doing so he provided the Provisional Administration's ecumenical adviser with a contact that was urgently needed, for the other great friend of the Councils of Brethren, Bishop Ammundsen, had died in Denmark in October, an event Bonhoeffer had felt as a personal loss.[143]

VII LAST YEAR AT FINKENWALDE

During the last two courses at Finkenwalde, no one could have told that everything was to end so soon. Never had the seminary's theological studies been so intensive as during the 1936-7 winter term, while the following summer term was marked primarily by the great wave of arrests that included so many friends and brethren. Although Bonhoeffer's programme of visits was an extended one—he had probably never travelled so much as he did in 1936—the preachers' seminary was to all intents his home, and his holidays were spent at the House of Brethren rather than with his family in Berlin. Finkenwalde's teaching activities and liturgical life did not, of course, remain insulated from bad news on the ecclesio-political front, but it was never to become a breeding ground of rumour, living from one real or factitious item of news to the next. Meditation and evening intercession continued to be the ruling principle. And the closer disaster loomed, the fewer were the restrictions upon the community's recreational life. In the 1936 annual report Bonhoeffer wrote:

We all know the distress, the inner contradiction, the sloth which seek to

142. For further details see Ch. XI, pp. 550 f.
143. GS II, p. 505.

hold us back . . . We are given both time and encouragement. If one should yield, that will mean a visible or invisible weakening of all the others in the communion of prayer. Let us not despise what God has given to us.[144]

The Family

During his time with the House of Brethren Bonhoeffer sought deliberately to shift the emphasis of his private life to Finkenwalde and away from the intimate ties with his relatives in Berlin. But with the progressive spread of Hitler's power, the different branches of the family drew ever closer together,[145] their centre being the two houses in the Marienburger Allee, which acquired a new significance as rendezvous for the exchange of political views and information.

Karl-Friedrich had moved from Frankfurt in 1934 when he was appointed to the chair of physical chemistry at Leipzig, the place 'which, since Ostwald, may be described as the birthplace of this science'.[146] He abandoned his earlier field of research into nuclear hydrogen, para-hydrogen and heavy hydrogen in favour of electro-chemistry and the kinetics of electrode processes in order to clarify the question of biological processes and basic electro-physical principles in nervous stimulation. He made this change so as to avoid having to cooperate in the development of nuclear armaments. Since he was now making frequent trips to Berlin, he saw Dietrich more often.

Klaus had become the legal representative of Lufthansa. Dr. Otto John joined him as an assistant in 1937 and both men quickly realized that they saw eye to eye on political matters.

In 1937 the Dohnanyis moved from Eichkamp to the Kurländer Allee, a street running parallel to the Marienburger Allee; they used to see Dietrich at his parents' home and also visited him at Finkenwalde.

Gerhard Leibholz, by then pensioned off, was wondering half-heartedly whether he should try to find a teaching job abroad. In 1936 and 1937 none of those in the Marienburger Allee could bring themselves to think seriously of separation. After Niemöller's arrest, Walter Dress took over a pastorate in Dahlem.

On the occasion of the sixtieth birthday of Bonhoeffer's mother the grandchildren gave a performance of Haydn's 'Toy' Symphony; Dietrich had to join in the arduous rehearsals which were held next door, at the Schleichers'. He then went down with an attack of influenza which kept him at home with his parents until January 1937, longer than he had expected. During his illness he renewed his acquaintance with the writings of Georges Bernanos.[147] The German edition of *The Diary of a Country Priest* had been published by Hegner in 1936. From then on

144. GS II, p. 508.
145. See Ch. IX, p. 408.
146. *Zeitschrift für Elektrochemie*, Vol. 62, p. 223.
147. Cf. Ch. IV, pp. 103 f.

Bonhoeffer never tired of recommending the book to his Finkenwaldians,[148] since he thought it of fundamental importance on the subject of pastoral care. It had been a long time since a work of contemporary literature had made so deep an impression on him.

You must surely know Bernanos' books? When priests speak in them, their words carry weight. The reason is that they are not the products of some sort of verbalized reflection or observation but quite simply of daily, personal intercourse with the crucified Jesus Christ. These are the depths from which a word must come if it is to carry weight.[149]

In 1937 the Charité celebrated his father's twenty-fifth anniversary as director of the psychiatric clinic. Dr. Bonhoeffer gave an improvised résumé of his academic career. Although placed on pension in accordance with the law of 1st April 1936, he was requested to remain in his post and it was not until the summer of 1938 that he gave his valedictory speech, surrounded by his colleagues. Among those in the audience were his three sons. A great period for the clinic had come to an end, making way for a new approach personified by Professor de Crinis, who was a member of the S.S.[150]

Changes

Tax complications had arisen between the authorities in Oeynhausen (Präses Koch), Berlin-Dahlem (Council of the Old Prussian Union) and Stettin. Moreover a potential buyer had appeared for the valuable Finkenwalde property. It was to settle these matters that Friedrich Justus Perels, in his capacity as legal adviser to the Old Prussian Council temporarily seconded to the Pomeranian Council of Brethren, arrived at the seminary in the winter of 1936-7. From his official contacts with Bonhoeffer there grew up a friendship which lasted until Dietrich's death. Level-headed and objective, Perels was also endowed with a Berliner's dry wit, and he delighted Bonhoeffer by his ability to cope with the official pedantry the latter found so distasteful. Perels understood Bonhoeffer's interests and contrived to turn aside the threats against the House of Brethren. He soon became a familiar guest at Finkenwalde. Bonhoeffer's attitude to church politics was after his own heart. The two were a complete contrast both physically and in their mode of expression but they appealed to one another because each came quickly and without pomposity to the point. When, later, it became necessary to reach mutual understanding in more delicate circumstances, a few words were all that was needed to convey the required meaning. Bonhoeffer introduced his new acquaintance to his brother-in-law, Hans von Dohnanyi, and to his brother, Klaus. By April 1943 Perels had become a member of the inner-

148. As in the 16th Finkenwalde Circular Letter.
149. To a woman, GS II, p. 43.
150. See Ch. XIII, p. 712.

most circle of conspirators; he was a frequent visitor to the family and showed himself most skilful in helping to cover up Bonhoeffer's and Dohnanyi's traces when both men were in prison. Meanwhile Perels was momentarily endangered, the more so because one of his grand-parents was Jewish.

The fourth course saw the end of Wilhelm Rott's term as director of studies. One of Finkenwalde's pioneers, he left for a more important post but continued an active friend. Rott took over Department IV of the Provisional Administration (Training Panel and Reformed) under Superintendent Albertz. With Eugen Rose, whom Bonhoeffer had sent to Hans Böhm, there were now two Finkenwaldians in the Berlin head-quarters. During the turbulent years that followed, Bonhoeffer rarely visited Berlin without discussing ecclesio-political measures with Rott. This assumed greater importance after Hildebrandt was compelled to leave the country in 1937 so depriving Bonhoeffer, after their many years together, of a like-minded and extremely well-informed friend. At the same time, however, he had acquired in Rott and Perels two excellent informants and supporters at headquarters. During the war Bonhoeffer pulled every string he could to obtain Rott's exemption from military service, for the latter was at times compelled to run the Provisional Administration single-handed in the absence of other leading members through arrests, refusal of entry permits, or conscription.

The new director of studies at Finkenwalde was the imperturbable Fritz Onnasch. Bonhoeffer thus acquired a colleague from the House of Brethren who had assimilated the ways and routine of the House from the start. Onnasch's father, no less steadfast, was the superintendent of Köslin in Pomerania whose friendship with the seminary was to prove of particular value after its break-up.

Disputations

The fourth course, that of winter 1936-7, was distinguished by a theological hunger that was truly insatiable. Among its members were Erich Klapproth and Gerhard Ebeling from Berlin, and Gerhard Krause from Pomerania. The last section of Bonhoeffer's lecture on discipleship, 'Law, Commandment and Exhortation in Paul', together with his Chris-tological interpretation of the Old Testament and his custom of incor-porating Psalm 119 and other psalms in praise of the Law into their daily prayers, might have been thought quite sufficient to make the question of law the unofficial theme for the term. But as if this were not enough, pamphlets as well as discussions at pastoral assemblies were replete with accusations that law and legalism held sway in the Confessing Church. On top of everything, the end of 1935 saw the publication of Karl Barth's booklet *Evangelium und Gesetz* which, to the discomfiture of Lutherans, gave the Gospel precedence over Law.

For these reasons the fourth course held a debate lasting several days on the question 'How do we preach Law?' This was preceded by weeks of preparation during which various groups investigated the term in the context of the Old and New Testaments and of confessional writings. The proceedings were conducted by Gerhard Ebeling who also put forward his own concept, consisting of forty-one theses under the four headings, Law—Christ, Law—Scripture, Law—Universe and Law—Church. His fifth thesis went some way towards Karl Barth:

The Law of God's Word is so encompassed by the revelation of God in Jesus Christ that, apart from this revelation, it is impossible to give a satisfactory definition of the term 'Law'.

The actual substance of the debate was less concerned with contemporary controversies than with an enquiry that should be as objective as possible into Biblical findings combined with an attempt to tackle the problem systematically. A concept that is expressed by Bonhoeffer in his *Ethics* may also be found in the following thesis by Ebeling (III, 15):

In the strict sense, the ecclesiastical preaching of Law is directed only at those to whom the ecclesiastical preaching of the Gospel is addressed.

After the winter months spent in Finkenwalde Ebeling was faced with the problem of his doctorate. In view of the fresh wave of arrests in 1937 and the difficult position of the illegal theologian, he felt inhibited from withdrawing to enjoy a year of quiet study. Moreover, the Berlin-Brandenburg Council of Brethren was most reluctant to release anybody. But Bonhoeffer took a different view and would not admit as criteria categories such as desertion or loyalty which were then undoubtedly current in the thinking of the Confessing Church; at that time anyone who withdrew to an academic retreat was suspect. Hence only a small and ever-dwindling number of young theologians in the Confessing Church continued their academic education, a circumstance that made itself felt particularly after the war. Meanwhile Bonhoeffer urged the reluctant Council of Brethren to grant Ebeling leave. He argued that all would be up with the Confessing Church if it were no longer in a position to pull someone out of the fight for the purpose of academic study or to second them for special tasks. For all his criticism of theological training at the universities, Bonhoeffer never abandoned the criterion of realistic responsibility or lost his ability to assess the nature of contemporary theology. Ebeling then left for Zürich to write his doctoral thesis under Fritz Blanke.[151] On returning to the fray, he became the illegal pastor of the church in Berlin-Hermsdorf supported by the Council of Brethren.

151. G. Ebeling, *Evangelische Evangelienauslegung. Eine Untersuchung zu Luthers Hermeneutik*, 1942.

Before this fourth course, of which Ebeling and Krause were members, had properly found its feet, Bonhoeffer wrote to Erwin Sutz:

I hope now . . . to finish my book, and it would then give me the greatest pleasure to return to hermeneutics. There seems to be quite a large gap here.[152]

The term 'hermeneutics' was then little used and few theologians had heard of it. But just at that time Bonhoeffer had acquired a copy of *Biblische Hermeneutik* by J. C. K. Hofmann, published in 1880. No doubt he felt misgivings that his own theological activities had not been sufficiently thought out. In 1925 in Berlin, which, under Seeberg, was the stronghold of historical-critical research, he had presented—in a tutorial study—the problem of historical and 'pneumatic' interpretation after the manner of Karl Barth.[153] He had then made an ally of Wilhelm Vischer who visited Finkenwalde at the beginning of March 1937 and now found himself the object of angry criticism by Old Testament exegetists. This was due to the sudden and unprecedented revival by the church struggle of the use of Scripture as a weapon in the current dispute. Furthermore Bonhoeffer rejected the proposition that correct interpretation was unknown in the days before learned research. This was why he took a particular interest in Ebeling's and Krause's enquiry into Luther's foundation and premise. Hence it is understandable that Bonhoeffer would now have been glad to devote more time to the detail and background of historic and systematic methods of interpretation of the Word—in fact, to his 'quite a large gap'. But—and this again was characteristic of the man—he abandoned his plan despite his awareness of that 'gap', because the combination of circumstances no longer permitted him to give it its due. More pressing questions to do with the substance of ethics presented themselves, questions which he saw at the time as embracing his life's work. In his eyes, methodology belonged to another time and another existence.[154]

The winter course's disputation on the preaching of the Law was followed that summer by a similar debate, albeit one more immediate in theme. Problems of church discipline were becoming of ever greater moment to the confessional communities. The disintegration of the Confessing Church, secessions from the Church at the instance of the Party, ridicule and, especially in the villages, a strong desire to have the same man responsible for all the activities of the pastoral office— all this, following the introduction of the 'Red Card', called for a fresh appraisal. The National Church theologians were unprepared. Some lacked a clear conscience and few dared to expose themselves to the same extent as Paul Schneider in Dickenschied, who had introduced church

152. Letter of 24.10.1936, GS I, p. 47.
153. See Ch. II, p. 56.
154. See also Ch. IX, p. 379; Ch. X, p. 437.

disciplinary measures. Many sought guidance and advice from the Councils of Brethren or complained of the latter's inability to help. Immediately after Whitsuntide 1937, therefore, Bonhoeffer invited to Finkenwalde some of the most resolute pastors from Pomerania and the provinces of Saxony and Brandenburg for a discussion on the law and potentialities of church discipline. It was on this occasion that he gave his lecture 'The Power of the Keys and Church Discipline in the New Testament'.[155]

Congregational discipline presupposes not only an intact teaching ministry but also a right ordering of the offices in the congregation. The ordering of the congregation must help towards the proper use of the keys and all the actions of the congregation which stem from that . . . It is inconceivable, from the point of view of the New Testament, that people should be appointed to offices in the church from outside the congregation.[156]

The impotence of the ministry within the reality of the National Church weighed painfully on the discussion. All of those present had in one way or another sought to impose church discipline, whether through confirmation or through the publishing of secessions from the Church, thereby incurring the wrath of the secular or ecclesiastical authorities. The aim must be a congregation which would one day be sufficiently mature to practise these things as a matter of congregational discipline rather than of civic responsibility, and to interpret them in such a way as to reveal the Gospel in a clearer light.

Confessionalism

Sasse's newly published book *Was heisst lutherisch?*,[157] as also the investigation carried out in May 1937 by the Halle Synod of the Old Prussian Union into the controversy between Lutherans and Reformed over Holy Communion, gave rise to a more robust treatment of the confessional question during the last term. This was something quite separate from the troubles with the Lutheran Council.

Ever since meeting him in Berlin before the church struggle began, Bonhoeffer had read everything published by Sasse with particular attention; even when roused to sharp disagreement and dismayed criticism, he invariably found something that impressed him. For this reason he discussed the book with the ordinands and also during the informal study conferences. By then Bonhoeffer's earlier delight at his discovery that Sasse's resistance and the views he held sprang not from ecclesial conservatism, but from a new relationship to the Confession, had, of course, given way to profound disagreement over the assessment of

155. GS III, pp. 369 ff.
156. GS III, p. 381.
157. H. Sasse, *Was heisst lutherisch?*, 1936.

the function and dignity of historical confessions. Sasse, for his part, had come to see Bonhoeffer as an 'enthusiast' because the latter credited the living event of communal, actual confessing with so much power that antitheses dividing churches dwindled to antitheses dividing schools. Bonhoeffer, on the other hand, saw Sasse as the confessional formalist who, when there was 'dissent on only one score', regarded the antithesis as 'wholly torn asunder' and who for this reason 'went beyond Luther'.[158]

In fact many theologians thought it strange at the time that Bonhoeffer should question individual points of Lutheranism that were held to be inviolable, yet at the same time should choose to base his Christology, for example, on Luther. He asked whether 'we Lutherans' were not preoccupied with too narrow a concept of 'Law' and, as a corollary, of 'Gospel', and again whether in Scripture 'Law' was not attested in at least two ways although it was customarily restricted to one. He further asked whether it was sufficient to regard the whole of Biblical testimony as being comprised in the forgiveness of sins.

These were then contemporary questions but he was to raise them even more urgently in 1944 during his time in Tegel. In the foregoing context he took the view that the controversy between Lutherans and Reformed was wholly unresolved, though it would be worth trying to put it right. In a letter on the subject to Karl Barth he wrote:

I believe it would be of the greatest importance in the present situation if the essential problems existing between Lutherans and Reformed were aired and discussed. In my view there is no one in Germany capable of doing this, since Sasse's arguments are always much too formal—just like our own counter-arguments. There is simply nobody in Germany with the problem sufficiently at his finger-tips.[159]

Bonhoeffer's candour in confessional matters and his testing of what was held to be inviolable for possible weaknesses did not, however, precipitate him into unionism. He noted the way in which the union he had so much welcomed at Barmen was treated by theologians, synods and church government so that decision, which he thought indispensable, and proof, for which he demanded theological exactitude, should be kept apart. Thus, on the subject of Halle, he wrote to the brethren as follows:

However much I agree with the result, I am equally troubled by the theological proof. This, I should say, is simply the Reformed thesis which holds, without further proof, that the confessional dispute over Holy Communion centres round the *modus praesentiae* rather than the real presence. This leads to conflict with the Formula of Concord and a total failure to absorb its message. To me, as regards a synodal decision, this is a great temptation.[160]

158. Quotations from Bonhoeffer's notes on Sasse's work.
159. GS II, p. 286.
160. Circular Letter, 24.6.1937, GS II, p. 518.

His views on Holy Communion were so decidedly Lutheran that he became embroiled in further controversy in 1940 when Baumann, the Reformed member of the Stettin Council of Brethren, attacked him for his words on Holy Communion in the Pastors' Circular Letter.[161] What Bonhoeffer had in mind was a renewed and really comprehensive airing of differences—and this in the invigorating and healthy atmosphere of theological controversy—after which the necessary decisions could be made. Not, however, one of these things without the other.

When he heard that Finkenwalde's brethren were preparing for their ordination on the basis of various confessional writings and making known their selection while being ordained before the congregation, he remarked: 'This hardly seems the right way to solve the confessional problem.'[162] In this he was determined, not by perfectionism, but by the need to avoid deceiving himself and his generation. Hence he did not expect that ultimately these questions could be solved whatever the circumstances but only that people should be clear what they were doing when they made a decision. In the context of the Catholic question he was to return, in November 1940, to the subject of Halle:

How have we Lutherans joined up with the Reformed? Actually in a wholly untheological manner (the Halle theological formulation is indeed more a statement of facts than a theological solution, which it certainly is not!); it came about in two ways: through God's 'guidance' (union, Confessing Church) and through the recognition of the objective actuality of the sacrament, namely that Christ is more important than our thoughts of him and his presence. Both are fundamentally questionable in theology, yet the Church in faith decided in favour of the community of Holy Communion, in other words the community of the Church. She decided in favour of the recognition of the union as 'divine guidance'; she decided to subordinate her concepts or else her doctrine of Christ to the objectivity of the presence of Christ (even in the Reformed view of Holy Communion). But in the theological sense she did not unite (if we disregard Halle) . . . It seems to me that churches became united, not primarily on theological grounds, but through the decision in faith in the sense already mentioned. That is certainly a most dangerous proposition! Anything could be made of it! But is not that virtually what we have been doing in the Confessing Church?[163]

Whether for good or ill, half-measures and boundaries must presumably remain. But they have to be recognized and defined as such, and it must then be established why they persist. Bonhoeffer, as the advocate of union, was not prepared to leave the Lutheran interpretation of the Gospel to his Lutheran contemporaries.

But he was also suspect to the dyed-in-the-wool Reformed on account of his combination of Lutheranism and revisionist ardour in reforma-

161. See GS III, pp. 393-404.
162. Letter of 22.7.1936, GS II, p. 491.
163. GS II, pp. 380 f.

tory matters. Horst Thurmann, in a letter from Finkenwalde to his spiritual mentor, Hesse (Elberfeld), asking to be released in order to enter the House of Brethren, wrote: 'Furthermore, many theological pronouncements are in need of correction and one particular development on Bonhoeffer's part needs "supervision".'[164]

Crisis in Pomerania

Neither classes, nor disputations, nor the completion of *The Cost of Discipleship* could save Bonhoeffer from becoming entangled in the struggles that took place in Pomerania during the last year at Finkenwalde. Indeed, he was faced with fresh tasks, since it was hoped that his theological influence might benefit those who remained loyal.

Some months after the pastors' meeting at Bredow[165] in January 1936, the split between the supporters of the Councils of Brethren and the Committees grew wider. During May and June the Confessing Church of the Old Prussian Union had instituted a far-reaching visitation throughout the area between the Rhine and the Pregel in an effort to induce a greater measure of spiritual resoluteness.

Subsequently the crisis became really acute in Pomerania, somewhat later than it did elsewhere. As a result of Präses Koch's and J. Beckmann's negotiations with the Church Committees, there had been a period of uncertainty in Bielefeld and Düsseldorf. Once this was over and all prospects of union had been abandoned, serious disintegration began to take its course in Stettin. At the beginning of August 1936 Bonhoeffer wrote of the western provinces:

In the Reich the crisis seems to have been overcome. The Präses has regained his senses . . . not long ago Koch began to stand up straight again! The nadir seems to have been passed.[166]

From Pomerania, however, Baumann reported:

At the moment the position in our provincial church is extremely serious. The Confessing Church is on the point of complete collapse, or else of a move by the majority over to the Committees.[167]

Matters then reached the stage when Bonhoeffer was compelled to write:

. . . the news today: Schauer and Faisst have left the Council of Brethren! Treat this as confidential for the present. The Confessing Church [is said to be] pharisaically legalistic. This is a blow. But Pomerania always lags behind a bit.[168]

164. Letter of 4.9.1936, GS II, p. 503.
165. See Ch. X, p. 414.
166. GS II, p. 281.
167. W. Niemöller, *Kampf und Zeugnis der Bekennenden Kirche*, 1948, p. 353.
168. Letter of 10.8.1936, GS II, p. 281.

Schauer and Faisst were two of the most respected members of the Pomeranian Council of Brethren; one of them had been a pioneer of the Confessing Church, the other was a much valued superintendent, and both were untiring in their concern that there should be a renewal in the ministry.

The Pomeranian Council of Brethren was now faced with the alternative either of losing its legitimation altogether or of renewing it fundamentally. However it could no longer convene a full confessional synod such as that of June 1935 in order to effect a renewal. By way of a solution Reinhold von Thadden summoned a 'General Assembly' of the Confessing Church for the middle of October 1936 in Stettin. He proposed that there should be an airing of all points of view prior to deciding whether the Council of Brethren should be regenerated or whether it should be dissolved in favour of the Committees. Thadden was thus confronted with an involved situation, and feelings ran high. Niemöller and Asmussen came hurrying from Berlin. At the meeting Superintendent Riehl from the province of Brandenburg, an early protagonist of the Confessing Church, declared in favour of the Church Committees. He predicted the consequences should the Council of Brethren persist in its claims to leadership:

. . . no longer a body corporate in the eyes of the public law, no more state assistance, no more service among the general public, no more care of souls in the armed forces, no more religious instruction in schools, the congregations thrown back on their own financial resources—what then will become of the Church? A heap of rubble! The question is 'do you want that?' If the answer is no, then you must take the path of the Committees and avoid any offence that might compromise your activities: then. despite all your unfulfilled desires, you must make use of the great opportunity offered by the State to the Church.[169]

When Riehl described Superintendent Albertz and Pastors Pecina and Willi Brandenburg as 'needlessly and aimlessly fanaticized' and Albertz as having been responsible for the two latter and for their arrest, it was only with difficulty that the Finkenwalde contingent could be subdued, since Willi Brandenburg was one of them. When the speaker made use of Bonhoeffer's paper on church community to illustrate the theological-legal threat to the Confessing Church, quoting the phrase, by then current, 'those without a Red Card won't go to heaven', Bonhoeffer jumped to his feet and cried: 'Bonhoeffer here. You're misquoting!' With a reference to the Eighth Commandment, he then protested against the mutilation of passages from his works and their use out of context. Later on in the debate he was again attacked, on this occasion because he had attempted in his 'False Doctrine in the Confessing Church'[170]

169. Report of the Council of Brethren at the General Assembly, enclosure to letter of 17.10.1936.
170. GS II, pp. 264 ff.

in the June circular letter to justify the attitude of the Council of Brethren by reference to the scriptural conformity of the Barmen and Dahlem decision. This, it was now said, represented a 'sin against reality'. Through reality God had shown that he had 'struck off the arm' of the Confessing Church. It was precisely in this sense that the supporters of the Committee laid claim to a 'conformity with Christ' as opposed to Bonhoeffer's scriptural conformity.

The General Assembly decided that everyone should send in a written declaration saying whether or not the Council of Brethren should continue to administer the government of the Church. The result was better than had been expected: 181 of those who attended the assembly voted that the administration should continue, 58 that it should be transferred to the Provincial Church Committee.

Nevertheless the rot had not been stopped. Increasing numbers went over to the Committees while Zoellner's efforts were to reach the climax of their success only a short time before his fall: on 20th November 1936 the Provincial Church Committees and the Lutheran Council issued a joint statement on the subject of their future cooperation. True, the Vice-President of the Church Committee of Hanover, Dr. Fleisch, described this as 'conditional collaboration', but Zoellner might justifiably record it as his greatest success. The joint declaration inevitably contained a passage such as the following: 'With the Reich Church Committee we stand behind the Führer in the German people's struggle for existence against bolshevism.' Among the signatories were Marahrens, Wurm, Meiser and, on behalf of Prussia, General Superintendent Eger.[171]

Only those who were still wholly resolute saw a ray of light when on 16th December 1936 the Confessional Synod of the Old Prussian Union assailed the statutorily entrenched principle of a six-term course of theological studies in a state faculty, on the grounds that the attitude of many of these faculties had become insupportable.[172] Hence the 'Dahlemites' again demanded acts of disobedience against existing laws. However, this increased the temptation among those with illegal status to acquire legitimation through training, examination and ordination under the auspices of the Committees' authorities or else of the consistories, which would open the way to a regular ministry, recognition and a stipend. A report from the Rhineland in October 1936 estimated at 200 the number of ministers and assistants placing themselves at the disposal of the Consistory, while some 200 remained with the Council of Brethren. And even a Finkenwaldian wrote to Bonhoeffer saying that he was unable to 'elude the reasons put forward by Faisst and Schauer'. The Finkenwalde Circular Letter made the comment:

We are painfully afflicted by the fact that Brother X should have taken

171. See G. Niemöller, *Die Erste Bekenntnissynode*, Vol. I, p. 236.
172. W. Niesel, *Um Verkündigung und Ordnung der Kirche*, pp. 23, 27.

this step without having first sought a discussion either with us or with Brother Bonhoeffer ... it was only by ourselves making an enquiry that we learnt the truth of the rumour of his move. As late as the summer term, Brother X had added his signature to the declaration made by our brotherhood, 'Do you wish to consummate it in the flesh?'[173] We commend him and ourselves to our Lord and his grace. Dear brethren, we must make a firm promise that whenever temptation becomes too strong because of the way things are going in the Confessing Church, we should turn either to a brother who stands firmly by the Council of Brethren, or to Finkenwalde. We owe this to our brotherhood.[174]

Zoellner's Resignation and Werner's Rise

During the winter Zoellner, by means of declarations and other measures, went so far as to oppose the more extreme German Christians and the small provincial churches they controlled. When about to preach in the German Christian stronghold of Lübeck on 4th February 1937, he was prevented by the Gestapo from entering the pulpit. He was a man of sufficient character to tender his resignation from the Reich Church Committee on 12th February.

Thus ended the Zoellner era, even though many regional and Provincial Church Committees remained in office during the months to come and Heckel's Office for External Affairs continued to operate unmolested. It was difficult to forecast what would happen next, for the State's actions were highly inconsistent.

To begin with, Kerrl, in an angry speech on 13th February before what remained of the Committees, spoke of the precedence of the National Socialist State over the Church: 'the Church's proclamation must fall into correct relationship with National Socialism';[175] he, the Minister, would take personal charge of the Church Committee.

Then, on 15th February 1937, came the surprise announcement from Hitler ordering church elections through which 'the Church, in full freedom, may now provide herself with a new constitution and thereby a new order as determined by her members.' Minister Kerrl was to make preparations for the election of a General Synod.[176] In fact the election never took place, being formally cancelled in November 1937. It seemed as though the Ludwig Müller and Zoellner periods were to be followed by an era of anonymity.

The day arrived, however, when this third phase of the church struggle became identified with a name, the day when Kerrl, under Decree No. 13 of 20th March 1937—yet another instrument ostensibly designed for the 'protection of the German Evangelical Church'—appointed Dr. Fried-

173. GS II, pp. 483 f; thus the three eastern seminaries protested against the silent transition to the Church Committees.
174. E. Bethge in the 14th Finkenwalde Circular Letter; cf. GS II, p. 511.
175. W. Niemöller, *Kampf und Zeugnis der Bekennenden Kirche*, p. 380.
176. J. Beckmann, *Kirchliches Jahrbuch 1933-1944*, p. 162.

rich Werner 'to revise current activities'. This meant the paralysis of all spiritual decision. The keystone to this edifice was provided by Decree No. 17 which, on 10th December 1937, laid down that henceforth the leadership of the German Evangelical Church would come under the head of the Church Committee, namely Dr. Werner.

There was now no longer a bishop and general superintendent in control, no longer any church ministry or synod. All these functions had in effect been assumed by Dr. Werner, a lawyer with no interest in theology. In the background to help and guide him there was, it is true, Dr. Muhs, the State Secretary in the Ministry of Religious Affairs. The latter, previously district president in Hildesheim, had seceded from the Church just one month before his appointment to the Ministry of Religious Affairs in the autumn of 1936. Having lost no time in rejoining —questions of church discipline were, indeed, of negligible significance! —he was now in charge of the affairs of the Ministry, a task he carried out with growing enthusiasm, particularly after Kerrl's death in 1941 when existing policy was continued without a break. The association of Muhs and Werner was to last until 1945.

In each of the Prussian provinces the real power now lay in the hands of the finance departments, on whose instructions alone the consistories might act. Presiding over the individual consistories were senior officials, versed in law, who passed on to the superintendents and pastors the ordinances and proclamations issued by Werner; referendums, bell-ringing in celebration of Hitler's victories, even prayers, were all prescribed in this way.

The first two periods of the church struggle had not been without a certain grandeur. In the National Bishop's time there had been the liberating emergence of the Confessing Church, and even Müller's supporters were inspired in some measure by a muddle-headed ardour. During the Zoellner period there was, at least, still evidence of a certain tragic confusion, for while, on the one hand, the true objectives of the Confessing Church had almost vanished from sight, on the other, men who had once been united in brotherhood and who had a deep and real concern for the preservation of the National Church, were now enemies. It was, of course, also a time of great illusions.

The third period was to admit of few illusions, for Dr. Werner's time of office was the most cynical of all. As it gradually revealed itself in its true colours during the summer of 1937, even the brethren, who were bitterly at odds, the 'Dahlemites' and the adherents of the Lutheran Council, drew together. A full meeting of the Reich Council of Brethren conferred again in March 1937; at the beginning of July the Provisional Administration and the Lutheran Council joined forces for a while at Cassel (Kasseler Gremium). But then began the great wave of arrests of 1937 whose aim was to subdue the still intransigent remnants of the Confessing Church.

VIII END OF FINKENWALDE

During the first weeks of Finkenwalde's 1937 summer course little happened to give cause for anxiety, since the election decree masked everything else. At Whitsun the Council of Brethren's intercessory list contained only about a dozen names of church members who had either been expelled or prohibited from speaking. A few months later, however, it had become quite usual to find on every list well over a hundred names of those arrested or otherwise disciplined. By the end of 1937, 804 members of the Confessing Church had been imprisoned for longer or shorter periods.

Tightening the Net

The method used to subdue the church of the Council of Brethren consisted mainly in drawing closer the net of intricate ordinances and proscriptions imposed by the Ministry of Religious Affairs in concert with other ministries, particularly the Ministry of the Interior. These applied primarily to the districts of the so-called 'destroyed' churches, in other words the Confessing Church of the Old Prussian Union, whereas the majority of the Lutheran churches remained relatively unaffected.[177] An intercessory list selected at random, such as that of 13th October 1937, names seventy-three pastors all of whom, apart from one Bavarian (Karl Steinbauer), were from 'destroyed' church districts. From this it is clear that the methods adopted involved not a direct proscription of the Confessing Church, but rather a gradual liquidation by means of intimidation and the suppression of individual activities.

Thus, for example, it was forbidden to hold services and church gatherings on 'secular' or emergency church premises, a measure directed at places where, in addition to a church under either neutral or German Christian administration, a separate Confessional congregation had formed and had appointed a so-called 'illegal' to an emergency pastorate. Many of Finkenwalde's brethren were affected in this way. Initially they were ordered to report for questioning at the local police station where they would probably be detained for one or two nights. They continued, however, to carry out their duties despite this prohibition which they saw as a prelude to a trial of strength.

On 18th February 1937 the Ministry of the Interior had forbidden announcements from the pulpit of the names of those leaving the Church, thereby interfering with the ecclesiastical practice of issuing proclamations. Following denunciations, the police sought to put a stop to the proclamation of intercessory lists, whereupon, in June, the Old

---

177. Cf. E. Klügel, *Die lutherische Landeskirche Hannovers und ihr Bischof 1933-1945*, p. 503, Appendix E, 'Acts of Coercion by State and Party . . . towards Pastors of the Church of Hanover'.

Prussian Council of Brethren instructed its clergy to ignore the restrictions on proclamations in so far as these affected their pastoral activities. The Council provided express confirmation of this resolution when, as a result of it, some Council members were arrested on 23rd July in the church in the Friedrichs-Werder market.

At the end of May the passports of Niemöller and Albertz, the delegates to Oxford, were withdrawn. Shortly afterwards those lecturers who had continued to pursue their activities illegally at the theological college in Berlin received a personally-addressed directive prohibiting them from teaching. University students who had attended were rusticated.

On 9th June the Ministry of the Interior declared that collections during services of the Confessing Church were a punishable offence, and that anyone who allegedly infringed the state collection regulations by collecting other than under the scheme laid down by the state-legitimated church authority, would be liable to arrest. Thus every Sunday, every confessional pastor in the districts of the 'destroyed' church was bedevilled by this prohibition which threatened seriously to impair the continued existence of the Confessing Church and her institutions, for both were wholly dependent on voluntary gifts from the members of their congregations.

Finally, on 30th July, the Propaganda Ministry announced that all communications run off on duplicators were subject to the Editorial Law. This jeopardized communications between the Councils of Brethren and their pastors; it also came as a warning to the Finkenwaldians to exercise caution with their circular letters. They took care of this by writing 'Personal Letter' at the beginning of every copy while Bonhoeffer signed each one himself, a method in fact which ensured their freedom from interference up to and beyond the outbreak of war.

So church activities came to a virtual standstill and barely a day went by without either the administration or the pastors of the Confessing Church contravening one law or another, or falling into some form of trap. By now it had become quite impossible to serve the Confessing Church while remaining within the law.

So far as the pastors were concerned, early measures were confined to a summons to the police station where, during an interrogation that varied in thoroughness, note would be taken of an individual's degree of intransigence. Gestapo action was primarily directed against those in positions of responsibility. They searched the Council's offices on frequent occasions. Niesel, arrested in consequence of the instructions to disregard the prohibition on proclamations, was brought before a summary court in company with Jacobi, Ehlers and Arnim-Lützlow. Von Thadden was arrested and accused on several charges, one being that he had encouraged illegal studies. On 16th June in Dickenschied, Paul Schneider had his first experience of arrest when taken away by the police because he had proclaimed church disciplinary measures against Party members. On 23rd June the Gestapo burst into a meeting of the Reich Council of Brethren in the Friedrichs-Werder Church in Berlin, arresting Beckmann, Böhm, Iwand, Lücking, Müller (Heiligenstadt), Perels, von Rabenau and Rendtorff. On 1st July the Gestapo sealed the Provisional Administration's premises and arrested Martin Niemöller.

1st July 1937

When Bonhoeffer heard of Niesel's arrest on 16th June, he travelled to Berlin the same evening. There, after a conference with Hildebrandt and such Council members as could still be reached, it was agreed that no one must cede any ground. Rieger happened to be in Berlin on a visit from London, so Bonhoeffer was able to provide him with authentic information for Bishop Bell. He also discussed the situation with Birger Forell with whom Nils Karlström was then staying. Later, when the alarming news of the events in the Friedrichs-Werder Church penetrated to Finkenwalde and it was learned that the trial of Niesel, Jacobi, Ehlers and Arnim-Lützlow had been fixed for 2nd July, Bonhoeffer and E. Bethge made their way to Berlin without delay, in order to discuss the situation with Niemöller and Hildebrandt in Dahlem. All unsuspecting, they entered No. 61 Cecilienallee on the morning of Thursday, 1st July, to be confronted by Hildebrandt and Eugen Rose[178] with the news that Niemöller had just been taken away by the Gestapo. Nobody imagined at the time that he was not to see his house again for eight years. A hasty consultation between Niemöller's wife, Bonhoeffer, Hildebrandt, Rose and Bethge was broken short when, through the windows, they saw the arrival of an unmistakable procession of black Mercedes saloons. In an attempt to escape through a back door, they fell into the arms of a Gestapo official named Höhle, already familiar to the brethren in Berlin. On being taken back to the room each of them was searched under the supervision of von Scheven, the leader of the operation, and then placed under house arrest. Thus they became the involuntary witnesses of a seven-hour search during which every corner of Niemöller's study was painstakingly examined, and which eventually led to the discovery behind a picture of a safe containing 30,000 marks belonging to the Pastors' Emergency League. All were astounded at the meticulous tidiness of Niemöller's desk which contained records of his sermons, written down verbatim in a clear copperplate hand. Here was something no one had expected of this spirited man. Unaware of what had happened, Assessor Vogel, Heinrich Vogel's brother, now appeared at the front door and he too was placed under house arrest. Although all incoming telephone calls were taken by the Gestapo, Bonhoeffer's parents must have got wind of the operation in some way, for their car kept passing

178. Eugen Rose had been sent for that morning by Niemöller.

the house during the afternoon with his mother peering anxiously out of the window. When the search ended in the evening those under house arrest were permitted to return home after their particulars had been taken. For Bonhoeffer, this was only the second meeting with the Gestapo; by comparison with his first confrontation in July 1933, their team-work had improved beyond all measure.

Eugen Rose sent a message to Bishop Bell, by a special route via Constance and through Karl Barth, telling him of the sealing of the Provisional Administration's office and the confiscation of funds; he asked him to exercise caution with the Press and to refrain from sending letters to the Provisional Administration for the time being. He further intimated that it would be of service to the Administration and those in detention if somebody were to come to Berlin. 'You will learn further details from Rieger.'[179] On 3rd July Bell had written to *The Times*: 'This is a critical hour. It is not only a case of the fate of individual pastors, it is a case of the attitude of the German State to Christianity.' On Bell's behalf the Dean of Chichester, Duncan-Jones, then proceeded to Berlin in order to make representations at the Reich Chancellory and the Ministry of Justice.

After Bonhoeffer had made his way back to Finkenwalde unmolested on 5th July, he sent a delegation from the seminary to Dahlem where an important service of intercession was to take place on 8th August. In the event, this developed into an open demonstration because the police had cordoned off the church. The protest march by the congregation thus shut out was one of the very few instances of 'revolt' against National Socialism during the thirties. That evening, after vain attempts to disperse the crowd, the police made a large number of arrests. About 250 of the demonstrators, among them ordinands from Finkenwalde, were taken in lorries to the prison in Alexanderplatz where they were temporarily detained.

In his thoughts, Bonhoeffer constantly returned to Niemöller's arrest. Every birthday and every Christmas he would send a thoughtfully-worded greeting to Frau Niemöller. In his short letters to Dr. Bell from Switzerland during the war, there would always be some news of how 'Martin' was getting on, for instance on 12th July 1941: 'Martin is sound in health and faith and many of my friends are with him now.'

In his 1939 American diary he wrote:

Again it has been brought home to me how lucky I am always to be in the Community of Brethren. And for the past two years Niemöller has been on his own. Inconceivable. What faith, what discipline and how evident the work of God.[180]

For Bonhoeffer the most drastic consequence of Niemöller's arrest was

179. Information given by E. Rose.
180. GS I, p. 301.

the departure of Franz Hildebrandt. Following the arrest Hildebrandt had taken the 12th and 18th July services in Dahlem and, as instructed by the Council of Brethren, had proclaimed the intercessory lists as well as the confessional collections. He was thereupon taken away by the Gestapo. On the following day *The Times* reported his arrest. Bonhoeffer and other friends thought Hildebrandt's situation highly precarious since he was a 'non-Aryan' and therefore liable to be treated with special odium. However, intensive efforts on the part of the Bonhoeffer family and others were successful in securing his release after four weeks. Luckily his passport had not been found and was still valid, so that the Bonhoeffers were able to arrange his journey to England. Now he was, quite conclusively, an *émigré*. Rieger accepted him as an assistant preacher at St. George's Church.

For Bonhoeffer this was a grievous separation after nine years of the closest intercourse. On the other hand, important ecumenical colleagues would acquire in Hildebrandt someone with a useful knowledge of the church struggle and one who shared Bonhoeffer's views. Apart from this, there was comfort in the hope that a return home to a new political climate might not be long delayed.

Prisoners from Finkenwalde

Bonhoeffer expected his widely-dispersed Finkenwaldians to disobey the prohibitions whenever they impinged on the business of the village or emergency church congregations. But this demanded an increased measure of support from the House of Brethren. On 24th June he wrote in the circular letter:

During these days of trial for our Confessing Church we often think of you all and pray more intensely for you, particularly for those who are very much on their own. It is now, especially, that we should rejoice in our communion and remain loyal to one another in daily intercession. During the period of meditation please have in mind the names of all the brethren who were with you here so that none is excluded from the communal prayer of the brethren. Let us, besides, remember particularly those who have separated from us. These are times, moreover, when we shall learn again to make those pleas with which the Lord's Prayer begins: Hallowed be thy name; Thy kingdom come; Thy will be done. By these we learn to forget ourselves and our personal condition and to hold them as of little account. How are we to remain steadfast so long as we remain so important to ourselves? And nowhere, indeed, could we be better sustained than in the cause of our church, which is the main concern.[181]

In July 1937 the wave of persecution began to engulf former Finkenwaldians. Letters spoke of interrogations, house searches, confiscations and arrests. Among the first to be affected was Erich Klapproth in Berlin.

181. Circular Letter of 24.6.1937, GS II, pp. 516 f.

It now fell to Bonhoeffer to deal with the 'illegal' ones' parents who felt that things had gone too far when consequences such as these attended their sons' disobedience to Church and State. A mother wrote to her son at Finkenwalde, after visiting one of his friends in prison:

I find it awful and am sad that it is so. Has it really got to be? 'Evangelical Pastor' is written in large letters above the cell door. Every day they are allowed half an hour in the fresh air. Bernhard Riemer was wonderful and said that things were really not too bad. But I can't believe him because he somehow looks different and he is suffering . . . When you see your dearest relatives really inside the place, you ask yourself again and again: must it really be so? Isn't there any other way? I am afraid for you. Reality is hard. May God point the way clearly for you . . . I don't know why it is, but in spite of your explanations which at the time seem quite clear to me, I always return to a different point of view.

Riemer's mother saw it otherwise:

I haven't yet come round to 'Father forgive them' . . . He was content and sent his greetings to everyone and said you must not worry on his account. Annemarie [his wife] is brave and not one to be sorry for herself. On Sunday Heider [the neighbouring pastor], too, was arrested and taken away immediately after church, so there are no longer any services in Völpke. Heider was already fully aware that this might happen and in his last sermon again said clearly what needed to be said . . . Heider gave instructions that if no one was available on Sunday, the bells should not be rung, nor should a service be held, nor should there be a reading . . .

Bonhoeffer now began to write detailed letters to relatives whenever a Finkenwaldian was arrested:

. . . it is often difficult for us to grasp God's way with his Church. But we may attain peace in the certainty that your son is suffering for the sake of the Lord and that the Church of Jesus intercedes for him in prayer. The Lord confers great honour on his servants when he brings them suffering . . . G., however, will pray that you place everything in God's hands and that you will give thanks for everything that God may visit on you and on his Church.[182]

He made arrangements with Frau von Kleist-Retzow that she should invite the young wives of the arrested men to her country-house at Klein-Krössin.

While the wave of arrests was at its peak, the Confessing Church of the Old Prussian Union held a Confessional Synod in Lippstadt from 23rd to 27th August 1937. At the time it was feared that the proscription of the entire Confessing Church would be announced at the forthcoming Party rally in Nuremberg.

It was in this atmosphere that the Lippstadt Synod demanded unanimously that there should be no withdrawal from the contested areas:

182. GS II, p. 522.

For the sake of the Gospel we must assert our right to our own teaching office in the Church, we must hold fast to what remains of church discipline by naming those who have left us, we must name individually in intercession those who have been disciplined or arrested, we may not yield one step in the matter of offertories.[183] Lippstadt, to a greater extent than any other synod during the German church struggle, was overshadowed by arrests, yet it was also the most unequivocal of them all. To Bonhoeffer it came as particularly welcome backing for his actions.

At Christmas 1937—his assistant director of studies, Fritz Onnasch, now also numbered among those who had been arrested—Bonhoeffer summed up:

This time the annual balance-sheet pretty well speaks for itself. Twenty-seven of your circle have been in prison, in many cases, for several months. Some are there still, having spent the whole of Advent in prison. Of the others, there cannot be anyone who has not either in his work or in his private life had some sort of experience of the increasingly impatient attacks by the forces of the Antichrist.[184]

Bonhoeffer's own answer was to set up a visiting service for which purpose the House of Brethren circulated the names and addresses of those who had been arrested. He was deeply moved by some of the visits which he undertook himself, for example to Fritz Onnasch, Willi Rott and others. He was concerned lest the brethren should not know how to pass the time when shut up in a cell. 'Horrid if nothing occurs to you', he remarked to Rott in Moabit.[185]

Sealing the Doors

Remarkably, the summer of 1937 still found the seminary uninvolved in the immediate fray. The emergency church at Finkenwalde with its proclamations and collections every Sunday had either escaped attention or else been deliberately overlooked, and in this it was not then unique. There was no definite ministerial prohibition in which preachers' seminaries were expressly mentioned. And even the far from inconspicuous evangelical missions were not entirely banned.

Bonhoeffer, therefore, carried on the work as before, finished his manuscript of *The Cost of Discipleship* as planned, spent a few sunny July days on the Baltic with the fifth student intake and then, on 8th September 1937, brought the term to an end with the customary farewell party. From foreign newspapers he was able to follow at a distance the ecumenical World Conferences in Oxford and Edinburgh and he became convinced that the absence of the Confessing Church and Niemöller's

183. See W. Niesel, op. cit., pp. 51-7.
184. GS II, p. 524.
185. W. Rott, 'Something Always Occurred to Him', IKDB, p. 135.

imprisonment spoke more eloquently than a full-scale delegation could have done.

Bonhoeffer, accompanied by E. Bethge, then went on holiday to the Königssee and Grainau but because of bad weather he returned north to visit his relations in Göttingen.

While he was there—the date would have been 28th September 1937 —he received a surprise telephone call from Stettin: the Gestapo had arrived at the almost empty house; Fritz Onnasch and the housekeeper, Frau Struwe, had been compelled to accept the closure and move out when the seals were attached to the doors. Not until the next day did the newspapers publish the order 'issued by the S.S. National Leader and Chief of the German Police' on whose authority the closure had been carried out. Mysteriously, this document, which bore the date 29th August 1937, had only just been made public:

The conduct of the organs of the so-called Confessing Church as exemplified in their long-standing practice of training and examining through their own organizations young theologians in defiance of the institutions set up by the State implies a deliberate contravention of the Fifth Decree for the Implementation of the Law for the Protection of the German Evangelical Church of 2nd December 1935 and is likely to endanger the authority and welfare of the State. By agreement with the Reich and Prussian Minister for Science, Education and Popular Training and the Reich and Prussian Minister for Religious Affairs, I hereby direct that in accordance with Article 1 of the Reich President's Decree for the Protection of People and State of 28th February 1933 the *ad hoc* academic institutions, the study communities and the teaching, students' and examination boards set up by the so-called Confessing Church be dissolved and all theological courses and study conferences under its administration forbidden.[186]

The closure of the other confessional seminaries followed shortly afterwards. Everywhere there was much sympathy with these last centres of church resistance. The following is from a leaflet put out by the confessional congregation in Neuruppin on 29th September 1937:

We have been informed that the preachers' seminary at Finkenwalde has been sealed by the Gestapo. Since the welfare of the seminary and particularly the fortunes of its ordinands—Seydel and Klapproth were among their number—have been the object of our sympathy through our prayers and offerings, it is now our duty to commend the brethren to God's protection in their hour of need . . . The Council of Brethren.

Was this a blow to be taken lying down? Must an activity that Bonhoeffer held dear beyond all else collapse in such fashion? Must the House of Brethren be relegated to the past? These questions occupied Bonhoeffer's mind as he journeyed from Göttingen to Berlin. On arrival he could barely make his way to the Marienburger Allee because of the

186. W. Niemöller, *Die Evangelische Kirche im Dritten Reich*, p. 343.

crowds and barricades: Heerstrasse station, only five minutes away from his parents' house, had been prepared for the lavish reception ordered by Hitler for Mussolini on his state visit to Berlin.

A great deal of machinery was now set in motion. One result was a petition based on the view that preachers' seminaries could not be affected by the order since they had not been named in it, nor had they taught 'in defiance of the institutions set up by the State'. Perels sent a memorandum to the state police in Stettin suggesting that they had, perhaps, gone too far in what was an isolated, local case; other seminaries were, after all, still in existence. Through Albrecht Schönherr, who had in the meantime become pastor at Brüssow, the Mackensen estate village, old Field-Marshal von Mackensen was prevailed upon to write a personal letter in his own hand to the Minister. On 26th October there was even a joint protest by the Lutheran Council and the Provisional Administration against Himmler's order; the signatures of Marahrens, Breit and Fritz Müller (Dahlem) appeared together once again.

When it had become evident by the middle of November 1937 that neither legal representations, nor petitions, nor personal letters would be successful in bringing about a review, notice was given terminating the lease of the house at Finkenwalde with effect from 1st December 1937.

Aside from the many discussions, however, Berlin had much else to offer and of this Bonhoeffer did not fail to take full advantage. A party to celebrate W. Rott's release from prison included a visit to *Don Giovanni* at the State Opera. At the end of October there was the festival of German church music. Bonhoeffer maintained that this had brought together the most gifted composers who, in a process of spiritual emigration, had turned to church music. On New Year's Eve 1937 Karl Bonhoeffer wrote: 'So far as we are concerned the [Gestapo's] intervention had its good side because we had Dietrich and his friend Bethge with us for a number of weeks.'

CHAPTER ELEVEN

THE COLLECTIVE PASTORATES
1938 - 1940

BONHOEFFER spent the latter part of September 1938 alone with Bethge in the Leibholzes' house in Göttingen. He had helped his twin sister Sabine and her family in their arrangements to emigrate. Now he was working in the study of his brother-in-law Gerhard Leibholz on his little book *Life Together*. But the times were anything but tranquil; the Sudeten crisis was getting more and more acute, and the news on the English and German wireless was getting more and more ominous every day. Was war coming? Would the preparations for a revolution be in time to forestall Hitler? All at once the time had come to interrupt the writing and hurry off to Berlin.

When he returned to Göttingen, Bethge wrote to some friends:

We are quite exhausted after the frantic strain, and many people are still in no condition to enjoy any peace of mind.[1] As things looked so threatening, we went to Berlin, through endless lines of requisitioned cars and lorries, to get more precise information, and to discuss with the leaders of the Confessing Church what our own position would be as ministers in the event of war, and possibly to compel the authorities of the Evangelical Church to recognize us as doing the essential work of the ministry. Indeed, if the worst came to the worst, all the leaders of the Confessing Church might be put out of action . . . We introduced this argument with all possible force. People were all overcome; it was a good thing we could help to get things moving . . . but now we can hope it is no longer necessary . . . In fact, after 24 hours we wanted to go back at once. But then events happened so quickly that we had to put off our departure from hour to hour.[2]

The events that happened so quickly included not only the surprising departure of Chamberlain, Daladier, and Mussolini for Munich, but also the expectation of General von Witzleben's *Putsch*, which was to begin when Hitler ordered the action against Czecho-Slovakia, and was now held up by the course of events. They included, too, Albertz's and Böhm's recommendation of special prayers in the name of the Lutheran Churches, with a penitential prayer for the averting of 'God's judgement', and the menacing reaction of the 'Black Corps' and the Minister for Religious Affairs.

1. Because of Munich.
2. Letter of 1.10.1938.

Life Together and war, Confessing Church and *Putsch*, the ministry and emigration—all these things together determined the period to which we now turn, and led to Bonhoeffer's most momentous decision.

The fact that the change in the training of ordinands from the Finkenwalde seminary to a collective pastorate meant considerable changes for Bonhoeffer personally was at first realized neither by him nor by those in his charge. On the contrary, the educational activities in the villages of Further Pomerania were designed as a direct continuation of the previous work, and the instruction hardly lost any of the former freshness. And yet the points had been switched over, unnoticed, for a change of direction.

Each of the coming years shared in producing the second great turning-point in Bonhoeffer's life.

The year 1938 saw him heavily engaged in ecclesiastical, political, and family affairs; but he still tried with undiminished strength to keep up his former way of life.

In 1939 he tried hard, with the help of English and American friends, to continue his theological existence; with that in view he went to England and America.

In 1940, when he had come back from America, he found himself ready for the tasks that from now on made his existence seem equivocal; but those same tasks brought a new freedom to his theology.

So the themes for the next two and a half years are the collective pastorate, the disappointments of the church struggle, the entanglement of politics, the fate of the family, the attempted 'flight' westward and the return to Germany, in the first winter of the war.

I THE BACKWOODS OF POMERANIA

When in November 1937 Field-Marshal von Mackensen's intervention for Finkenwalde was rejected, and Perel's for the petition of the Council of Brethren[3] was bluntly rebuffed by the superintendent of police in Stettin, the church authorities in Berlin were not clear what to do about it. W. Niesel, F. J. Perels and Bonhoeffer considered whether the work should not be resumed—openly, in the old form of a seminary—at a fresh place. Was not this the right time for the Confessing Church to claim publicly the right to run its own system of instruction? That was the opinion of H. J. Iwand, for example, who tried, on the authority of Superintendent F. Heuner, to reopen his East Prussian seminary on the old lines in Dortmund. But they were all arrested and later expelled from Dortmund; and moreover the police had now dissolved the seminaries in Elberfeld and Bielefeld too, only G. Gloege's seminary in Naumburg-on-Queis remaining till March 1938. So a persistence in the method of work

3. An association formed in 1934 of the elected governing bodies of the congregations of the Confessing Church.

that had served hitherto became more and more questionable, if a system of instruction were really to be maintained. Bonhoeffer hesitated: 'Either we remain in Stettin, even in a different form, or we go right away from Pomerania, as I should not be loath to do in view of the wretched Council of Brethren.'[4]

At last it was decided that work was to be preferred to demonstration, and agreement was reached on the form of the 'collective pastorates'. There had already been arrangements of the kind in minority groups of a church, for example with the West German Reformed Church. The reflections were based on the fact that up to now teaching ministries with clergymen who were legally installed in the office of pastor were nowhere objected to, even where they were known to be uncompromising supporters of the Confessing Church. Thus ordinands could be installed as 'learning ministers' cheek by jowl in church areas where there were enough superintendents who were prepared to let their 'learning ministries' be used for continued education. The ordinands simply had to be registered individually with the police as being with the pastor of the parish, sent out as they were available, and possibly installed as pastors if the occasion arose. Moreover, an attempt could be made to bring them together in a small number of places for continuous training, and even to have them living most of the time in one and the same place.

Thus it was that Bonhoeffer's ordinands lived in two vicarages in Further Pomerania almost as they had lived in Finkenwalde, only in smaller numbers and in more primitive conditions. Both of the collective pastorates included from seven to ten ordinands for each course. It is true that none of them could claim to be enrolled in a preaching seminary; they had consistently to assert that their position was that of a learning minister in a parish whose name they hardly knew. This way of doing things worked smoothly till the rigorous call-up brought all the ordinands of the Confessing Church into the army, and in March 1940 the police came on the scene to shut down the secluded retreat. In those two and a half years Bonhoeffer's collective pastorate had added to the five courses in Finkenwalde five more in Further Pomerania; and up to then the seminars in Elberfeld (under the direction of Hermann Albert Hesse) and Frankfurt-am-Main (supervised by Walter Kreck and Karl Gerhard Steck) were still able to work in a disguised form.

Köslin and Schlawe

It was an offer made by two neighbouring superintendents which turned the scales in favour of seclusion in Further Pomerania; they accepted the risk and began to work out details at once. In the confusion of the so-called committee period they had been able to keep an appreciable

4. To J. Rieger, 4.10.1937, GS II, p. 521.

number of their pastors in the newly formed Confessing Church; and they were used to turning to good account all the possibilities that remained open to them of self-government in local church affairs. So they now managed to house the two groups of ordinands or learning ministers unostentatiously in more or less remote parishes.

One of these was the parish of the Superintendent of Köslin, the father of Fritz Onnasch. Köslin, a country town with at least 30,000 inhabitants, was about 100 miles north-east of Stettin. In its centre there was, as in many North German towns, a massive Marienkirche. Five confessing pastors in the town, and a few in the villages, could accept up to ten learning ministers or seminary ordinands. But all of them lived together in the spacious vicarage of Superintendent Onnasch in the Elisenstrasse. There was room in the house for instruction as well as for the board and lodging that Bonhoeffer needed when he spent a few days in Köslin. But Bonhoeffer did not register with the police there. Fritz Onnasch had charge of the group as Inspector of Studies. His father had installed him in the vacant post of assistant preacher in his parish, thus saving the Council of Brethren of Old Prussia one man's stipend. Thus the collective pastorate of Köslin shared in the life of the local capital in Further Prussia. The vigorous congregation of the Confessing Church took the brethren to its heart. There was regular contact with the well-known doctor August Knorr. In Köslin the work came to an end in the autumn of 1939 when the demands of the war stopped the supply of ordinands.

The other superintendent, Eduard Block, lived in the small town of Schlawe, twenty-five miles further to the east towards Stolp; its population was barely 10,000. Two old town gates and the solid Marienkirche dominated the rows of houses round the cobbled market square. Here both Bonhoeffer and Bethge, the latter as Inspector of Studies, had posts as assistant ministers. When Bonhoeffer registered with the police, he gave as his place of residence that of the superintendent in the Koppelstrasse, so that there was communication here in 1939 with the recruiting station, and in 1940 with the local headquarters of the Gestapo.

Although there was seldom any call for it, Block always kept a bed ready for Bonhoeffer; it relieved him of applications to the authorities and of telephone calls; it was a neat way of avoiding police enquiries, and ensured that if he was wanted, he was there at the right time. He would send his shrewdly worded messages, in his own code, always on a postcard. No one could rattle him, and Bonhoeffer valued his way of doing things as much as he valued his wife's cooking.

The ordinands moved still further eastward, into the extensive, weather-beaten vicarage at Gross-Schlönwitz, at the boundary of the administrative district. The tiny parish was a few miles south of the Reichsstrasse No. 2, Köslin-Stolp. The group could exist there only with adequate motor transport; and so the work began with the hitherto unheard-of purchase of an additional car and a motor-cycle. Bonhoeffer regularly taught in Schlawe in the second half of the week and then stayed over the week-end; but he was always anxious to let the Köslin ordinands have some relaxation elsewhere, possibly a lengthy break by the Baltic. So, whatever the weather was, he covered the forty miles between his two places of work twice a week, besides being obliged to go to Berlin frequently on personal matters or on questions of church politics.

A year and a half later, when the young pastor in charge of the parish of Gross-Schlönwitz married and needed the vicarage, the collective pastorate of Schlawe moved (in April 1939) to nearby Sigurdshof, an empty farmstead which the landowner, von Kleist of Wendisch-Tychow, put at the superintendent's disposal for the group. The small house was two miles south of the estate's village, and it was more secluded than any place they had lived in up till then. In front four very small windows looked out under an overhanging roof and through luxurious climbing plants on to a little-used courtyard. At the back the idyllic Wipper flowed by. The water-pump was there under the nearest trees of the vast forest, which merged southwards with the Varzin woods of the Bismarcks. There was no electricity, and Frau Struwe, the housekeeper, who had remained loyal from the days of Finkenwalde onwards, had to solve problems that did not arise only from the wartime economy that was beginning. Anyone who even now did not find things quiet enough could withdraw into a hunting-lodge further away in the forest. In summer one had the use of the count's fishing-skiff on the pond and the tennis-court at the Tychow manor-house. In the winter of 1939-40 Bonhoeffer and his ordinands would go ski-ing and skating. Difficulties over food and heating alternated with times of special pleasure:

We are anxious about our coal; and besides that, we have no paraffin, so we have to use candles. We all stay in one room, and someone plays or reads aloud.[5]

I got here yesterday . . . Yesterday afternoon I could not stop myself from joining the skiers in the snow-covered wood. It was really lovely, and so peaceful that everyone else seemed like a ghost. Speaking generally, I really feel more and more that life in the country, especially in times like these, has much more human dignity than it has in towns. Crowds and all that they mean are simply not here. I think the contrast between Berlin and this secluded farmstead is particularly marked now.[6]

We are now fairly snowed up and cut off. No post-van can get through, and we can get nothing except now and then by sledge . . . Minus 28 degrees . . . In the circumstances work goes well. The forester has let us have two loads of wood and two cwt. of coal, and that will do for a few

5. E. Bethge, 19.1.1940.
6. Bonhoeffer to his parents, 29.1.1940.

weeks. Of course, the food supply is rather difficult too, but we still have enough. If I had my way, I think I should like to leave town for good.[7]

The smooth ice here is indescribable after a good deal of flooding. Up to within ten yards of the house the meadows have turned into a magnificent skating-rink. But that is catastrophic for the fields, and for the game too . . . We again have enough fuel for a week.[8]

For two days we have been deep in snow with almost uninterrupted snow-storms. Now the thaw will have to start all over again. From the agricultural point of view things seem to be in a bad way. People had been so pleased about the few days' thaw, and now they are quite depressed.[9]

On 15th March, when the thaw had finally set in, they went on holiday. Three days later, on 18th March, the Gestapo ordered Frau Struwe to shut the place down, as had happened at Finkenwalde.

Work and meditation, prayer, instruction in preaching and examination of the ideas underlying the New Testament—all this was carried on in the small undistracted circle of the collective pastorates almost more intensively than in the spacious house at Finkenwalde so close to the big town of Stettin. In the Confessing Church outside in the country people knew that Bonhoeffer was carrying out his work, and they did not ask where and how it was being done. But the rumours of 'legality' and 'monasticism' still circulated in reference to Bonhoeffer's seminaries, especially as new rifts and obstinate clashes about the line that the Confessing Church ought to take favoured such reproaches. After the course, a Berlin ordinand who was later killed in the war wrote to Bonhoeffer:

I did not go to Schlönwitz eagerly or hopefully . . . I shuddered in looking forward to a time of constriction, both physical and mental. I thought of it as a necessary evil that one had to bear with a good grace and go through for the sake of self-discipline . . . It all turned out differently from the way I had feared. Instead of the stuffy atmosphere of theological cant, I found a world that embraced a great deal of what I love and need: straightforward theological work in a friendly community, where no unpleasant notice was taken of one's limitations, but where the work was made a pleasure; brotherhood under the Word irrespective of the person, and with it all, open-mindedness and love for everything that still makes this fallen creation lovable—music, literature, sport, and the beauty of the earth—a grand way of life. . . When I look back today, I have a clear picture before me: the brethren sitting down to their afternoon coffee and their bread and jam. The chief has come back after being away rather a long time . . . Now we get the latest news, and the world breaks into the peacefulness and simplicity of life on a Pomeranian estate . . . Does it dull the objectivity of your theological view, when I write that it was the peripheral things which increased my delight in what is central?[10]

7. To his parents, 14.2.1940, GS II, p. 562.
8. To his parents, 27.2.1940.
9. To his parents, 6.3.1940.
10. G. Lehne to Bonhoeffer, 2.2.1939.

New Style

1. The collective pastorate did not get from the House of Brethren the support that the Finkenwalde seminary had had. The effect of this was external rather than internal; for within both the collective pastorates Bonhoeffer was helped by inspectors of studies who had been familiar with the methods and aims of the daily community life since 1935; and moreover, the groups were rarely as small as a house of brethren. But externally a number of undertakings that the House of Brethren had made possible, as for instance the evangelical mission, failed to survive.

So now the cessation of all help made contact with the former Finkenwalde people very difficult. At first they were not told even the addresses of Bonhoeffer and his collective pastorates, or anything about the organization of the new work. Bonhoeffer then wrote every circular himself; these had in any case to be marked 'Personal letter' because of the press regulations, and so there are more circulars in Bonhoeffer's own handwriting from the period of the collective pastorates than from the previous years.

Increased distances made frequent visits to the brethren impossible, and so Bonhoeffer offered that they should send him their sermons and that he should return them with his suggestions. A number of them availed themselves gratefully of the offer.

Once again Bonhoeffer managed to arrange a holiday for all his former students. At the end of July 1938—it was a time of the most passionate arguments inside the Confessing Church—he brought together forty-five young pastors at Zingst, the original meeting-place. It was then that there began the dogged campaign of the consistories to legalize the 'illegal' ordinands partly with threats and partly with enticements, an attempt to break through the front of those who were standing firm. The struggle over the pastors' oath of allegiance to Hitler was almost lost. In those days of Zingst Bonhoeffer conducted a Biblical study of 'temptation'. Those present undertook to render the 'pastoral service that we owe to the brethren who have gone from us to the consistory. It is intended that each of them shall be visited by two of the brethren in the near future.'[11]

It is to the cessation of the House of Brethren that we owe, not only *Temptation* and *Life Together*, but also the collection of Finkenwalde circulars, which provide a colourful picture of the life of unauthorized pastors of the Confessing Church in a time of prolonged distress.

2. From the time of the collective pastorate Bonhoeffer's mode of life was unsettled, for up to his death he never had a permanent residence. True, his small writing-desk stood for a year and a half in Gross-Schlönwitz, and for another year in Sigurdshof; but he was never with

11. GS II, p. 537.

it for more than three days a week, and his books and manuscripts were never again available together in one place. The university lectures and the rough draft of *The Cost of Discipleship* stayed in the chests that a loyal member of the Finkenwalde community stored in his box-room at Altdamm, where they might still have been, if the house had not been burnt down. Some of his tasteful furniture went to the collective pastorates, some to Berlin with a number of his books. In the war his possessions were again dispersed, when he transferred valuable books, furniture, and diaries of his time in Spain to the estate of his fiancée's parents in Neumark, where they were lost in 1945.

Thus Bonhoeffer taught, formulated, and wrote after 1937 with no settled place of work and without his stock of books which were so valuable for reference and which had always hitherto been to hand. Only for the work on ethics during the war did he try once more in Berlin to collect any considerable number of relevant books. He hardly spoke of this handicap caused by the lack of a fixed address; he could rely on his memory, which generally provided what he needed.

Yet he longed increasingly for settled work, more than he actually admitted, and sometimes he was heard to heave a deep sigh over his gipsy-like existence. Although he himself never acknowledged it, the flight of 1939 was partly a result of this longing to settle down. The unattainable wish for a few quiet months to work in was expressed in a letter to E. Sutz in September 1938, when he wrote: 'It is a pity that you did not get me to Zürich for a year as a locum for Brunner! That would not have come at all amiss.'[12] He said to friends abroad what he would not say in Gross-Schlönwitz and Köslin, especially when they told him of their professional progress out there:

The only strange thing is this existence in which there can be no anxieties, because each day is a gift. If one forgets that, one sometimes gets rather restive, and would prefer to choose a more settled existence with all the 'rights' that normally go with one's 'rank' and age. That would mean abandoning the work, and it will not do at the moment.[13]

Lasserre has got married. That course is not yet open to people like ourselves; life is too nomadic. But we have a great deal of pleasure in our work instead.[14]

My work goes on normally. Only one sometimes gets a bit fed up with the nomadic life, and would like to be more settled and domesticated . . . But it will not do just now, and I am glad to be allowed to work here.[15]

Thus the new status of an assistant minister showed the former university lecturer and seminary director unmistakably the drawbacks of his present work.

12. GS I, p. 48.   14. To P. Lehmann, 14.12.1938, GS II, p. 348.
13. To E. Sutz, 19.9.1938, GS I, pp. 48 f.   15. To J. Rieger, Dec. 1938.

3. Of course, the discontinuance of the House of Brethren and the unsettled way of living gave added significance to the people who now offered him a home.

Since the closing down of Finkenwalde, Bonhoeffer had enjoyed more and more the holiday home that Hans-Jürgen von Kleist-Retzow in Kieckow or his mother in nearby Klein-Krössin made available to him. The old lady had felt it keenly when the 'Finkenwalde people' had to move to a place more than 120 miles from Stettin, especially as she, together with friends from that town, had begun to study the recently published *Cost of Discipleship* and always had some question about it.

Bonhoeffer was now fairly often sending to the Kleist estates people from his own circle who were feeling worn out. Werner Koch's fiancée found rest and friendship there after his arrest, and after his release Koch himself was at once invited to Klein-Krössin. Another ordinand, who was well cared for in a good hospital after an operation at Bonhoeffer's expense,[16] was able to recuperate at the Kleists' home. Their hospitality was unlimited; anyone whom Bonhoeffer recommended was accepted at once.

But Bonhoeffer was once again concerned with his parents and their home. On the one hand, its importance had been increasing as a meeting-place and a source of political information since the formation of cells of the Resistance Movement. On the other hand, since the action of the police at Finkenwalde there had been acute anxiety there. In fact this kind of thing was not talked about, but now Karl-Friedrich, the eldest son, felt it advisable to warn his younger brother not to do anything that would attract unnecessary attention, as this would increase their parents' existing anxiety about the fate of the Leibholz family. Thereupon Bonhoeffer wrote to his brother:

I am sorry if Mother is uneasy and is making others uneasy too. There is really no good reason for it. The fact that I may fare just as hundreds of people have already fared through Himmler's edict really must not worry us any more. To hold out on the church question means sacrifice. You know, you yourselves put a good deal into the war; why should we not do as much for the Church? And why should anyone want to dissuade us? None of us is keen on going to prison; but if it does come to that, then we shall be ready to go—I hope so anyway—as the cause is worth it. We start again at the beginning of next week.[17]

When in 1943 the arrest actually took place in quite different circumstances, there was not even a suspicion of reproach to be heard in the parents' home.

Although the distances were greater, Bonhoeffer now visited his parents' home oftener and for longer periods than when he had been at Finkenwalde. When he returned, eagerly awaited, to Köslin or Gross-

16. H.-W. Jensen, 'Life Together', IKDB, p. 152.
17. Letter of 29.11.1937, GS II, p. 295.

Schlönwitz, he would give them this or that piece of news from the latest that was available. But if the conversation began to encroach on topics that might affect him and his future course of action, he could no longer take the ordinands into his confidence. The newcomers hardly noticed that at this point a slight reserve might be creeping in. But one or other of the older Finkenwalde students could already sense that in the changed times Bonhoeffer was beginning to turn his attention towards other spheres with which they were less familiar.

II DARKEST MOMENT OF THE CHURCH STRUGGLE

The year 1938 was the year when the Confessing Church reached its lowest point.

Dr. Werner's most startling achievements were in 1938 the promise of the pastors' oath of loyalty on Hitler's birthday, and in 1939 the 'Godesberg Declaration'. The question of the oath of loyalty brought the Confessing Church into a state of paralysis that lasted a long time, so that it reacted either not at all or only feebly to Barth's letter to Professor Hromádka of Prague, to the pressing question of special prayers, and to the so-called 'Crystal Night'.[18] Only the indignation over the Godesberg Declaration united the disordered ranks once more. These matters, which were not usually published in the daily papers, were constantly accompanied by the much less spectacular question of the legal status of the 'illegal' pastors. But in the latter part of the German church struggle this became the key question in the claim for the leadership of the Councils of Brethren and it called for more of Bonhoeffer's attention than what was called 'Werner's trump card'.

At the beginning of 1938 there seemed, in fact, to be some easing of the situation. The number of arrested people fell rapidly, and did not seem likely to increase again. People had held their ground well under the heavy-handed police measures of 1937, and a good part of the clergy had stood firm. Thereupon the Nazi State seemed willing at least to avoid a public commotion, and so it evolved new methods, which proved effective.

Communications Paralyzed

The 'intercession lists' (*Fürbittenlisten*) were certainly still long, but their headings for 'those arrested' were fewer, and one had to get used to a range of new expressions for 'restraints'. The headings now read: Prohibitions against Preaching. Expulsions, Banishments, Prohibitions on Exit and Entry, Ministerial Prohibitions. Every measure thus named was deliberately graded so as to make communication between the leading men of the Confessing Church impossible, without their being arrested. It was very largely successful; for instance, an intercession list of Sep-

18. An anti-Jewish pogrom on the night of 9-10.11.1938.

tember 1938 shows only ten arrests including those sent to concentration camps; but to make up for that there are 93 ministerial prohibitions, 97 prohibitions on exit and entry and expulsions. Another, of 30th August 1939, on the eve of war, lists 121 ministerial prohibitions, 150 prohibitions on exit and entry, expulsions and banishments, 44 prohibitions against preaching and only 11 arrests, besides three internments in concentration camps.

An 'expulsion' forbade a person to stay at the place where he normally worked and lived (as, for example, in the case of Pastor Paul Schneider in Dickenschied), but it allowed him to live anywhere else in Germany. A 'banishment' was a police order directing an arrested person to live in a place distant from his home, as when Karl Lücking, and later Superintendent Onnasch were sent from Westphalia and Köslin respectively to Grenzmark. A 'prohibition on entry' kept important people from attending any meetings in Berlin; and this, together with the 'prohibition on exit' prevented them from seeing people from Berlin such as Niesel, Albertz, Böhm, and F. Müller of Dahlem. 'Ministerial prohibitions' prevented pastors of the Confessing Church from entering certain church buildings to which they had rightful access. By this ingenious system the State made discussions about the oath of allegiance, for example, very difficult, and contributed greatly to the widespread perplexity.

Exiled from Berlin

Since January 1938 Bonhoeffer's name had been in the intercession list under the heading 'Prohibition on Entry'. The occasion of this was his first journey from the collective pastorate to the capital of the Reich.

The chief instructors and chairmen of the ordinands' brotherhoods in the Confessing Church of Old Prussia had met under Niesel's presidency on 11th January 1938 in the parish hall at Dahlem. Then there appeared a column of the Gestapo who thought they would be able to disrupt a secret lecture of the prohibited church seminary college. The thirty young men were taken off to Alexander Square. After an interrogation lasting seven hours those who lived in Berlin were given a prohibition on exit; the Gestapo gave those from the provinces a prohibition on entry, and put each of them into the train for his particular destination. Bonhoeffer and Fritz Onnasch, who had been to the meeting as chairman of the ordinands' brotherhood of Pomerania, were put into a train for Stettin by the police.

In Köslin and Gross-Schlönwitz the ordinands, expecting the building to be searched, cleared away from the desks and cupboards all documents relating to the Council of Brethren. They were naturally afraid that the collective pastorates' work that had just been begun would now be subjected to a most unwelcome investigation.

But the action had obviously not been directed at Bonhoeffer personally, nor did it mean that work for the 'assistant minister of Schlawe' was to be stopped. At the same time, this new encounter with the Gestapo was very far from welcome. To be cut off by the prohibition on entry from his information centre in the Marienburger Allee, just at a time when political crises were brewing in Berlin, was very awkward. Schacht's retirement and the beginning of the General Fritsch crisis were arousing hopes. So Bonhoeffer's father intervened with the Gestapo against his son's exclusion from Berlin. His prestige brought success; the authorities conceded that the prohibition applied only to matters connected with work, and that the son was free to visit the family in Berlin. So at the beginning of February the parents met Dietrich at Frau von Kleist-Retzow's home in Stettin to discuss the matter. He went straight back with his parents to Berlin, where meanwhile Hans von Dohnanyi had been concerned in the Fritsch crisis, and in addition Martin Niemöller's trial was beginning. Bonhoeffer lodged a formal complaint with the police,[19] giving his own account of the session of 11th January and asking for the prohibition to be rescinded, but he got no answer.

So the prohibition on entry for Bonhoeffer was never rescinded; but his father was able to modify its effects. Bonhoeffer went to Berlin oftener than before, but he did not appear at conferences. He now dealt with matters of work or church politics at the homes of Niesel, Böhm, or Perels, or he received his friends at his parents' home; and he preferred personal messengers to telephone conversations.

Bonhoeffer had a rooted dislike of ill-considered ventures, whether in small things or in big ones. Otto Dudzus once told how annoyed Bonhoeffer was when his students ran across the lines at the Danish frontier station, instead of using the bridge.[20] However untidy his desk was, there were never any compromising slips of paper or memoranda to be found there. He could be very vexed when things were not thought out beforehand, and he would reckon up the possible issues of an event carefully and in good time. In this his imaginative faculties sometimes caused him more distress than his friends thought necessary.

Oath of Allegiance

That April, Bonhoeffer's holiday journey took him through Thuringian country that was decorated with flags. On the occasion of the Austrian *Anschluss* the cross on the Wartburg had been replaced in Holy Week by an immense floodlit swastika. Sasse, the Bishop of Thuringia, had already on the 15th March ostensibly taken for granted that his pastors

19. GS II, pp. 295 f.
20. O. Dudzus, 'Arresting the Wheel', IKDB, p. 82.

would take an oath of allegiance to Hitler, and he telegraphed to the latter:

My Führer, I report: in a great historic hour all the pastors of the Thuringian Evangelical Church, obeying an inward command, have with joyful hearts taken an oath of loyalty to Führer and Reich . . . One God—one obedience in the faith. Hail, my Führer![21]

Mecklenburg, Saxony, and other regional churches followed the same 'inward command'.

Bonhoeffer soon turned back and sought rest in the Friedrichsbrunn house. From there he wrote to Frau Niemöller, whose husband had been sent to the Sachsenhausen concentration camp after being acquitted by the court: 'God has so disposed that a special blessing shall now go out from your house to the congregation and the whole Church.'[22] Meanwhile Dr. Werner in Berlin was preparing the evangelical pastors' 'spontaneous' birthday present for Hitler.

Dr. Werner was really the man who was to bring the pastors into line with the régime of the Third Reich in matters of law, finance, and government. But beyond that he had set out to tie people to Hitler intellectually and emotionally and to make the Aryan doctrine paramount. What had been attempted in 1933 with a certain spontaneity in this sphere he now carried on by the use of administrative measures. In 1934 the National Bishop would have been only too pleased to present Hitler with an oath of loyalty at the National Synod, but the attempt failed for the time being. Now, making full use of the wave of enthusiasm over the Austrian *Anschluss*, Werner issued an order in the Law Gazette of 20th April 1938 that all the pastors on active duty were to take the oath of allegiance to the Führer. The order, and the accompanying instruction on the oath, testified to a cynical wantonness. But the action was a great success for Werner, as it plunged the Confessing Church into its most shameful affair.

Anyone who pointed out, at that moment of general enthusiasm, that he had already made a vow of allegiance at his ordination, and had said 'Yes' at the plebiscite on 10th April, was already betraying a caution that was suspect to the Nazis. The text of Werner's ordinance in the Law Gazette was strongly worded:

Whereas only those may be office-bearers in the Church who are unswervingly loyal to the Führer, the people, and the Reich, it is hereby decreed:
Anyone who is called to a spiritual office is to affirm his loyal duty with the following oath: 'I swear that I will be faithful and obedient to Adolf Hitler, the Führer of the German Reich and people, that I will conscientiously observe the laws and carry out the duties of my office, so help me God' . . .

21. W. Niemöller, *Kampf und Zeugnis*, p. 437.
22. GS II, 307.

Anyone who was called before this decree came into force . . . is to take the oath of allegiance retrospectively . . .

Anyone who refuses to take the oath of allegiance is to be dismissed. 20th April 1938. Dr. Werner.

That announcement in the Law Gazette also contained a forceful 'address of the Supreme Church Council of the Evangelical Church regarding the oath of allegiance', in which it was stated that that oath was 'more than a mere confirmation of the duty enjoined on Christians by the New Testament to be subject to the authorities'. 'It means the most intimate solidarity with the Third Reich . . . and with the man who has created that community and embodies it.' The oath of allegiance 'means personal commitment to the Führer under the solemn summons of God'. Indeed, the person who takes the oath testifies 'that he is prepared to fulfil in its entirety the commission that he accepted at his ordination, in the steadfast consciousness of his obligation towards Führer, people, and Reich.'

That oath declared more than most of the pastors could then declare with a clear conscience, for it made the ordination vow a farce. As far as the 'Dahlem' people were concerned, the first reaction in the Confessing Church was a general refusal. Bonhoeffer felt that the oath was quite impossible; but in view of the peculiar conditions of his appointment, he was not a pastor on the establishment, but exactly like those 'illegal' pastors who were supported only by the Confessing Church; and so he was in the happy position of not being anywhere on the list of those due to take the oath under Dr. Werner's orders.

In the dilemma of not feeling able to act against one's conscience and yet of wanting to act with propriety in a national matter, the Confessing Church entered into discussions for its pastors who were appointed by the consistory, namely for most of the older ones. Permission was given to take the oath, provided four conditions were fulfilled: 1. There must be a clear demand by the State, since the Church of Christ does not introduce oaths; 2. The statement by the Supreme Church Council interpreting the oath must be withdrawn; 3. The authority demanding the oath must accept an interpretation given by pastors who are advised by the Confessing Church; 4. The ordination vow must be publicly acknowledged, and this oath must thereby be expressly qualified as the introduction of a civil service law into the Church.

When the Confessing Synod of the Old Prussian Union discussed these conditions on 11th-13th June, many of the pastors of that church had already taken the oath; in the Rhineland the percentage was 60, in Brandenburg 70, in Saxony 78, in Pomerania 80, in Silesia 82, and in the Grenzmark 89. The remaining pastors, who took the Dahlem view, looked forward with very mixed feelings to the moment when those four conditions might be regarded as fulfilled, as in fact was the case one day, although not unambiguously and not, in fact, from Dr. Werner's side. A further session of the Confessing Synod of the Old Prussian Union on 31st July 1938 did, indeed, give permission for the oath to be taken, by deciding over the heads of the minority by what criterion—no one ventured to say more—those four conditions could be regarded as fulfilled. No one felt at ease over the distressing deliberations about discretionary judgements, but the responsible people in the Confessing Church would no longer accept responsibility for refusing the oath.

The pastors' conventions of those weeks were almost unendurable. Bonhoeffer went with his ordinands from one session to another; but as his arguments were regarded as those of a person who was not affected, they did not prevail. Finally there remained only a few who obstinately held their ground, such as K. H. Reimer, the pastor of Naseband in Ewald von Kleist's parish. The discussions between minority and majority were burdened by a guilty conscience, which spoilt the relationship between the members of the Stettin Council of Brethren who were in favour of the oath, and the pastors who still refused; and it even led to venomous reproaches.

Then, when the overwhelming majority of the pastors had taken the oath, a letter was published in the middle of August from Bormann (leader of the Nazi office in Munich) to his district leaders (*Gauleiter*): 'The churches have issued this regulation of their own accord', so its importance was to be confined to the Church. Party and State were to make no distinction 'whether a clergyman has taken an oath of loyalty to the Führer or not'. An oath was of importance 'only if it is taken on the Führer's orders by the Party or by the State from the individual'.[23]

That was crushing. 'When I think of the distressed consciences of the individual pastors till they took the oath after all with a violated conscience, my heart almost stops beating . . . Reimer is said to have handed in his resignation with some pretty straight language'; that is how Frau von Kleist-Retzow lamented to Bonhoeffer after learning how things stood with the Council of Brethren in Stettin.

After the oath had been thus assented to on the 31st July 1938, Karl Barth wrote a bitter letter to Berlin. If no one would say 'No' any more, he said, he would have to say it from abroad:

I am most deeply shocked by that decision and the arguments used to support it, after I have read and re-read them . . . Was it possible, permissible, or necessary that this defeat should come about? Was there and is there really no one at all among you to take you back to the simplicity of the straight and narrow way? . . . No one to beg you not to hazard the future credibility of the Confessing Church in this dreadful way?[24]

23. See J. Beckmann, *Kirchliches Jahrbuch 1933-1944*, p. 262.
24. See 'Karl Barth zum Kirchenkampf', ThExh 49, pp. 79-83.

There were some there, but they could hardly get a hearing, either in a technical or, indeed, in a spiritual sense.

At the same time that Barth's letter reached Berlin, one from Bonhoeffer arrived too. His Old Prussian Confessional Synod's treatment of the question of the oath had plunged him, although he had been so solidly behind the synodal authority, into such a crisis in relation to it as had never occurred before and never occurred again. Now he wrote:

It is a hard decision for a Confessing pastor to feel obliged to oppose the ruling of an Old Prussian Confessing Synod, just when he is able to look back with nothing but great thankfulness and respect to the service that that Synod has rendered up to now.[25]

Bonhoeffer denounced the procedure by which the synod had overruled the minority in such a question and had accused the wrong side of 'obscurity'. He saw it risking the claim on the young 'illegal' pastors' spirit of sacrifice. How, he said, could one demand clarity from the young brethren, if a synod accepted the absence of clarity between Dr. Werner and the pastors, and decided about oath-taking on such a basis? He had already been against the very idea of bargaining about conditions for taking an oath. But now the authority 'to speak again to the young brethren' had been relinquished.[26]

For Bonhoeffer the events connected with the oath were more than an episode. The mere demand for the oath, however grotesque and blameworthy it was, did not upset him too much, as everyone knew where it came from. But the Synod's decision—that was a gash in his own flesh, and it was difficult to heal. And now it had been inflicted, not by the separated Lutherans, but by his own people:

Shall we learn from this? Will the Confessing Church be willing to confess publicly its guilt and disunion? Will it give to prayer for forgiveness and a fresh start the place that it now needs? Will it be able in that way to honour the truth, to revive again the disunited brethren's consciences which are simply anxious to reach the truth, and to bind them again to God's Word? . . . Does it see how it has endangered its word through its latest session? Today these are open questions.[27]

Bonhoeffer felt shame for the Confessing Church, just as one feels shame for a scandal in one's own family. For that Confessing Synod decided in favour of the oath to the Führer when it already knew that a regulation was coming by which non-Aryans were compelled to have a large 'J' stamped on their identity cards—an omen of worse things to come, and the occasion of the flight of his twin sister's family. And the threat of war against Czecho-Slovakia grew louder. The possibility of a

25. GS II, p. 308.
26. See GS II, pp. 308-15.
27. GS II, p. 314.

gap between Bonhoeffer and the Confessing Church was becoming real.

Essen III

Events tended increasingly to isolate Bonhoeffer and the few in Old Prussia who thought as he did. Since the hopes for the church election of 1937 and the heavier pressure by Kerrl, many people were again pursuing the ideal of a 'broad front'. But Bonhoeffer feared that it would weaken the chances of speaking out clearly on the burning questions involved in the struggle.

Throughout 1938, attempts were made to bring the leading men of Munich and Düsseldorf, Stuttgart and Bielefeld, Hanover and Berlin round a table again. Lutheran church leaders and the 'Provisional Administration' had already made a mutual approach in the 'Cassel Group', achieved a common declaration against Rosenberg from the pulpit on the Reformation anniversary of 1937, and, indeed, had protested jointly against the Himmler decree. Now Bonhoeffer saw with uneasiness the brethren travelling around—when they could still travel!—and drawing up one plan after another to harness everyone together—Dahlemites with the Neutrals, Lutherans with members of the Church of the Union.

In April 1938 they began to make an approach to tangible aims. Iwand, Koch, and Held from the one side, Meiser and Wurm from the other, together with one of the neutrals such as D. Burghart, met under Koch's chairmanship, firstly, to arrive at a common understanding of 'Barmen'; secondly, to work out transitional regulations to establish peace with the German Evangelical Church; and thirdly, to work out regulations for the appointment of a directing body of the Church of the Old Prussian Union. The draft plans were called 'Essen I' (report on Barmen), 'Essen II' (German Evangelical Church regulations), and 'Essen III' (Old Prussian Union administration).

'Essen III' concerned Bonhoeffer directly as a pastor of the Old Prussian Union. The draft, with a covering note from Koch and Müller of Dahlem to the pastors, was dated 23rd August 1938, but it did not reach Bonhoeffer till he was actually taking his relatives abroad. After that, he defined his attitude to the 'draft regulations for church administration'. He wanted to destroy the hope, which was growing out of the widespread need for pacification, that this draft, designed to promote unity and order, would be assented to by all the brethren:

The denial of all that God revealed to the synods of Barmen and Dahlem has been made obvious here . . . [Barmen and Dahlem are not to be ignored for tactical reasons . . . What is to happen about the 'illegal' pastors?] Please do not say that for all kinds of reasons it is most ill-advised to put up any opposition at this particular time. In this situation none of us knows what is ill-advised and what is not. But that it is not advisable to act against God's clear direction, against the acknowledged truth, and against one's conscience, that is certain. You yourself know what confusion the 6th Synod caused in the Confessing Church.[28] After that defeat we really had expected a different and more spiritual word from our church leaders. What we are advised to do is to give up, of ourselves, the Confessing Church. Here we can no longer follow.[29]

Frau von Kleist-Retzow's verdict was: 'The Essen draft seems to me nothing but plain unvarnished unbelief, even if I only look at the potpourri of signatures.'[30] That was certainly caustic, in view of the difficulty of trying to bring old comrades-in-arms together again; but in the main Bonhoeffer shared her opinion.

It may be possible to reproach Bonhoeffer with not having taken seriously enough, just then, the question of unity and the broadest possible 'Confessing front'. But he was not at that time suffering so much from the picture of the disunity of the Evangelical Church as a whole; he expected nothing else. What really worried him was the question whether a voice would make itself heard for the acknowledged truth. In the understandable demand for appeasement he saw an evil counsellor. How should a newly-formed assembly of those who had hitherto kept a cautious silence in regard to the Nazi pretentions suddenly bring itself to speak clearly with a common voice? Bonhoeffer expected from the Essen negotiations, not that the voices would become clearer, but that they would be muffled, if not completely silent. On the 9th November 1938, the day of the Jewish pogroms, his apprehensions were confirmed, for everyone was silent.

Gerhard Niemöller has described how far the isolation of the 'Dahlemites' had already gone at the Essen negotiations;[31] some people would no longer be seen with them. Being branded as a man of radical temperament did not worry Bonhoeffer. What was now called Dahlem radicalism he regarded as simply the insignificant remains of a testimony that was later to be a cause of shame. The reproaches of 'Dahlemism' and 'self-martyrdom' that were now heard could be brought only by disregarding the really burning questions of the Christian Church in the Nazi State. In 1938 'Dahlemism' was too expensive a business for anyone to indulge in it simply from temperament or inclination. For all his adherence to the original course, Bonhoeffer certainly did not value the merits of the Dahlem side of the Confessing Church too highly. Later, in 1943, he was also quite ready to forget any awkwardness between the 'Confessing Church' and the 'Confessing movement' when Bishop Wurm, a man of that 'Confessing movement' although not of the 'Confessing Church', whom he had once distrusted, raised his voice against the State's injustice

28. In dealing with the question of the oath.
29. See GS II, pp. 315-18.
30. GS II, p. 319.
31. See G. Niemöller, *Die erste Bekenntnissynode der Deutschen Evangelischen Kirche zu Barmen*, Vol. 1, 1959, pp. 247-54.

and at the same time tried to promote unity.[32] But in 1938 Bonhoeffer remained isolated rather than be disloyal to the scanty group which at least made some approach here and there to prophetic office, and obtained some experience in supporting a competent body of young theologians.

Hromádka

Only a few weeks after Essen III something happened which on the one hand gave a marked impetus to the desire for a broadly based happy mean—to the exclusion of the radical Dahlemites of the left and the Thuringian 'German Christians' of the right—but which on the other hand painfully exposed the Confessing Church's commitment to nationalism. Two different things happened, which everyone regarded as connected, but which those concerned were most anxious to keep separate.

Firstly, in late September of 1938, Albertz and Böhm produced a liturgy for the provisional guidance of the Confessing Church. While Hitler's armoured units were parading through Berlin on 27th September, these two men showed what was for that time an uncommonly daring confession of guilt by calling on the congregations to pray that the immediate threat of war might be averted. It was a spiritual action by the church authorities which today does not seem extraordinary or surprising; but judged by the standards of 1914 it was uniquely level-headed and daring in 1938.

Secondly, just at that time a letter became public that Karl Barth had written from Basle to his colleague in Prague, Professor Hromádka, encouraging the Czecho-Slovaks to vigorous military resistance:

Every Czech soldier who fights and suffers will be doing so for us too, and—I say this unreservedly—he will also be doing it for the Church of Jesus, which in the atmosphere of Hitler and Mussolini must become the victim of either ridicule or extermination.[33]

That was too much, and the Albertz-Böhm plus Barth-Hromádka constellation seemed quite unacceptable. Who could protect whom?

The S.S. newspaper *Das Schwarze Korps*, together with Kerrl, accused the authors of the special prayer and the Union of Lutheran Churches (V.L.) of 'treasonable action in clerical garb'. The men of the V.L., however, regarded Barth as guilty of heretically mixing up politics and religion, and they backed away from the dangerous friends. After the question of political resistance had been laboriously kept under the surface during the discussions about the oath, it now suddenly and openly confronted even the Dahlem side of the Confessing Church, which was not equipped to deal with it. The frightened V.L., under attack from

32. See Ch. XII, pp. 592 f.
33. Text according to J. Beckmann, op.cit., p. 265.

the right, from the S.S. to the Lutherans, tried to pass it on to the left. In a circular to all the governing bodies of the provincial churches it assured the provisional leaders: We have nothing to do with this democratically ideologized political theology directed from Switzerland against our fatherland; there is no connection between Barth and the special prayer or the spirit of this liturgy.[34]

But it was no use. 'Cassel group' and 'Essen I-III' were disposed of at one blow. Many friends of the Confessing Church remained perplexed between the two fronts. At the beginning of November the German News Agency announced:

By their unanimous resolve all Christians, including Bishops Marahrens Meiser, Wurm, and Kühlewein, have categorically assured the Reich Minister for Religious Affairs that they disapprove of the circular on religious and national grounds and most strongly condemn the attitude therein expressed, and that they sever themselves from the persons responsible for that declaration.

The Reich Minister for Religious Affairs has taken disciplinary action against the members of the so-called Lutheran Union of the German Evangelical Church by the blocking of stipends, with the object of dismissal from service. This measure has later been further applied to the persons who have signed as being responsible for the so-called Councils of Brethren, and have thereby supported the so-called Lutheran Union in this matter.

After the war, Bishop Wurm had the moral courage to refer publicly to this hour of new triumph for the Minister of Religious Affairs as one in which 'the power of darkness was greater than the power of light'.[35]

The 'Crystal Night'

In this desperate state of the Confessing Church there came the 9th November with all the terrorizing acts against the Jewish population. It found a group of Christians out of step and bereft of speech. In that night of Wednesday to Thursday, when the synagogue in Köslin was burnt, Bonhoeffer had gone straight to Gross-Schlönwitz behind the woods, as he usually did for the second half of the week; so he did not find out till later what had happened throughout the country.[36] He then sent Bethge to Göttingen, so that he could see to his relatives' house. It was still undamaged.

In the Bible that Bonhoeffer used for prayer and meditation he underlined in Psalm 74 'they burned all the meeting places of God in the land', and wrote beside it '9.11.38'; and he underlined the next verse and added an exclamation mark: 'We do not see our signs; there is no longer any prophet, and there is none among us who knows how long.'

34. 20.10.1938. Cf. J. Beckmann, op. cit., pp. 265 f.
35. T. Wurm, *Erinnerungen aus meinem Leben*, 2nd ed., 1953, pp. 147f.
36. G. Maltusch, 'When the Synagogues Burnt', IKDB, p. 150.

In the circular that he sent to the Finkelwaldians a few days later he wrote: 'I have lately been thinking a great deal about Psalm 74, Zech. 2:8 and Rom. 9:4 f. and 11:11-15. That leads us into very earnest prayer.'[37] So he urged the brethren to look the passages up and to heed the words: 'He who touches you touches the apple of his eye.'[38] It may have been at that time that he produced the dictum that he impressed on his students: 'Only he who cries out for the Jews may sing Gregorian chants.'

In that evil year Bonhoeffer began to separate himself from the rear-guard actions of the defeated remnants of the Confessing Church.

III LEGALIZATION

It was the young 'illegal' pastors on whom the consequences of the collapse of the Confessing Church fell most heavily. At any rate, within the Old Prussian Union the difference between the Confessing pastors who held a legal pastoral office and those who were excluded from it, i.e. those ordained according to Dahlem, became increasingly pronounced. To be sure, this affected only a limited circle, whose fate could therefore hardly attract public notice either within or beyond the German frontiers. But those affected were the very ones for whom Bonhoeffer lived and thought more than for anything else. For him that body of men represented all that Barmen and Dahlem had promised. So the conflicts over their status and their steadfastness came home to him more intimately than the actual events of that time or the coming tragedies, so clear to see. It was his own people who were involved here.

The Situation

It is true that in Werner's time the Confessing Church and its administrative bodies were not yet prohibited as such. But if anyone tried to make the system work or to follow it out at all logically, he was entangled in a net of multiple regulations. He could be prosecuted under the law, for malice, or for illegal use of the pulpit or even for the illegal taking up of collections, under the Himmler decree, or the Press Law. In fact, the Confessing pastor could no longer get through his work legally; and he acted in open protest, or in the vague hope—sometimes justified—that his disobedience might be overlooked.

In 1938 the official churches still had buildings, names, and customs, perhaps even sermons as before; but otherwise they had little in common with the provincial churches of former decades.

Werner and his finance departments ruled from Berlin with strict

37. GS II, p. 544.
38. Zech. 2:8.

control over the church authorities, who could no longer oppose them, even if the law were violated.

In the provincial consistories the work was done on the one hand by the old experienced officials who were set in their ways—of course, with no power to make decisions. On the other hand, men resided there whose anti-church actions and language were well known everywhere. The old system of consistories run on the collegial principle was abolished, in accordance with the leadership principle, in favour of the juridical president, so that well disposed consistorial advisers no longer had the right of objection.

But at congregational level, at the beginning of 1939 the pastor lost his traditional independence, because the authorities could compel a removal or transfer from office 'for reasons connected with the performance of his duties'. The congregations were deprived of their control of the church taxes and collections. In some places there were already finance commissars at congregational level, the local church committees being disbanded because they had contravened some regulation or other —possibly because they had not evicted a pastor, or withheld his salary, because he was said not to have toed the line.

Were the young 'illegal' pastors to allow themselves to be forced back or recruited into these churches? Surprisingly, the legal pastorate of the provincial churches still offered a series of attractive privileges—even the manse!—and possibilities of work which were more peaceful than those that the Confessing Church had to offer. It was clear enough that Werner could make life hard for the 'illegal' pastors; he could have their buildings closed, give them notice of eviction, stop payment of their stipends, and take legal action against church committees who supported them. Indeed, he did so. Were the older official pastors to venture to accept the young men, shield them with their own legal position, and hand half the work over to them? It really was difficult.

So far, the 'illegal' pastors made up a group which was smaller than the rest of the Confessing Church's personnel. Now the presidents of the consistories began systematically to woo them; since the end of 1937 they had been enticing or pressing them—whichever seemed likely to lead to conciliation—repeatedly with new 'final' dates for taking over the fully equipped pastoral office that they controlled. Everyone was asked to make individual applications, accompanied by the examination papers and reports in the possession of the Councils of Brethren; they also had to be checked and interviewed by the consistories, and, finally, give a written acknowledgement of the consistories' authority.

The Alternative

The choice between the way of the Councils of Brethren and that of the consistory became agonizing. The time of arrests in 1937 had, indeed, been endured quite gallantly, but now there was hardly any prospect of being able to work independently. Questions that could previously be answered unequivocally now became dubious.

Everything centred on the alternative: preacher or parish minister. Could an office of 'preacher' exist without the parish? The office of pastor, as occupied by pastors inducted before the outbreak of the church struggle, did after all give one a certain freedom of movement. Perhaps it could be had through some trifling compromise; the State had for centuries held certain rights of supervision, which had always been tolerated in return for the status of a legally-recognized public body. And there were the congregations! After all, with the existing lack of pastors every opportunity ought to be seized to fill vacant places, so that the people should not remain uncared-for. In view of the situation that confronted the parishes there was a danger that clinging to the Dahlem position would be mere obstinacy. What could a preaching office mean, even though it had been lawfully conferred by the Confessing Church, if it shut its occupants out from the framework of the people's church and abandoned what existed?

The alternative called in question the *Junktim*[39] of Barmen and Dahlem and its justification, so a good many people now wondered whether one could accept the consistorial legalization and yet keep to Barmen, on which, after all, more depended than on Dahlem. To put it differently: if Dahlem were now given up, it meant the rejection of training, examination, and ordination by the Councils of Brethren, but not the acknowledgement of the theological justification of the 'German Christians' and their claim to exercise control.

This alternative produced widespread uncertainty and weariness, which initiated theological reorientation in many minds. Some leading members of the Councils of Brethren took fright at their responsibility towards the congregations, and at the human and financial consequences of their duty to look after the 'illegal' pastors. Many of the latter either had had or were now to have disillusioning experiences with particular personalities in the Councils of Brethren, whose treatment of the question of the oath and the special prayers was not particularly creditable; and moreover, they saw that a conservative Reformation theology was now being favoured in neutral circles.

In 1938 and 1939 Bonhoeffer's briefcase was filled with letters, laments, and calls for help from his Finkenwalde students:

I am worried about what to do if the Confessing Church is really at the end of its road, at any rate here in Pomerania. I wonder whether I ought to look round for a different kind of job. Or whether I should declare that, against my better judgement and my understanding of the Church I will go over to

39. A collective treatment of several draft laws, which must be accepted or rejected jointly.

the consistory, because otherwise I shall not be able to follow my calling.[40]

We long for full responsibility in our ministry. This, in my opinion, is the real reason for all the sidelong glances at the consistory. After all, while it is more or less true that we have enough work and that we do it gladly, the ministry of the Word demands more from us! I mean the ministry of the Word in contrast to the word of the synods, where it is said that the 'brothers in office' are to share their ministry and house with us. That is just where the difficulty is: we may be able to share the house, but the ministry is simply indivisible, because there is only one responsibility for it.[41]

One of the congregation said to me lately: 'Will the young pastors stand firm?' I answered: 'If the congregation stands firm, yes . . .' According to the reports, about forty brethren have stood firm, even in Westphalia.[42]

I cannot see that it is theologically right to continue on the way followed so far, nor can I answer for it any longer, either for myself or for others. And so I am writing to you now; I have been glad to hear your advice up to now, and I should not like to be without it in the future. My question is: Will the community of brethren which has united me with the Finkenwaldians hitherto be able to survive—no doubt with the frankness that is particularly needed at present—or not? It certainly is not breaking up and shall not break up on my account. But shall you, and all those who in fact accuse us of destroying the Church, and of other faults, still be willing to have us in your heart and in your midst?[43]

Bonhoeffer felt unwilling to give way on any point to pressure from within or without. He tried, on visits and at conferences, with lectures, circulars, and personal letters, to make his theological and pastoral position clear:

We think we are acting with special responsibility if we re-examine every few weeks the question whether the way on which we set out was the right one. It is particularly striking here that any such 'responsible examination' always starts just when serious difficulties are looming up. We then persuade ourselves that we have not the 'right certainty and assurance for this way', or, what is even worse, that God is not now speaking to us as clearly as he did formerly; and with all that, we are really only trying to evade what the New Testament calls 'patience' and 'trial'. At any rate, Paul did begin to wonder whether he was on the right way when opposition and suffering threatened . . . We cannot even now think that God really wants nothing new from us today, but only a faithful continuance in what is old.[44]

He allowed no play to any defeatism in his company; but at the same time he admitted to his brother Karl-Friedrich:

It has in some ways been quite depressing in recent weeks to see how many people look for quietness and safety with all kinds of reasons and pretexts

40. Letter from O. Kistner, Jan. 1939.   42. Letter from O. Kistner, Jan. 1939.
41. Letter from H. Hoffmann, 3.2.1939.   43. Letter from G. Krause, 18.2.1939.
44. Circular about patience, 20.11.1938, GS II, pp. 541 f.

. . . In such times there is always a great deal to do, with visits, lectures, etc. I am quite sure that for the Church what matters supremely is that we hold out now, even if it means great sacrifices. The greatest sacrifices now are small compared with what we should lose by wrongly giving in. I do not know anything that is worth our whole-hearted commitment today, unless it is this cause. The main point is, not how many are in it, but that there are at least some.[45]

Stages of Development

1. For Bonhoeffer the wearisome struggle had already become acute when, in the winter of 1937-8, the Pomeranian consistory demanded of the 'illegal' pastors that they should apply personally, in writing, for their status to be legalized. Demanding a new examination and a request that the ordination be confirmed, it set a time limit which was extended three times during the next year. In January 1938, at a meeting in Stettin of those concerned, under the chairmanship of Fritz Onnasch, forty-six ordinands and young pastors roundly rejected the consistory's demands. Bonhoeffer had sent to each of them a pastoral letter[46] in which he spoke very plainly of obedience and disobedience, saying that the church struggle was to be endured and carried on 'as gospel' and not 'as law'.[47] He tried to refer them to the positive gift of Barmen and Dahlem, which was a support and not a burden. Weariness over the struggle he saw as a consequence of the creeping disobedience towards what had previously been accepted. What other people now described as a 'new situation' he bluntly called a 'smoke-screen'.

2. Anxiety again increased when, on 26th February 1938, Dr. Werner issued from headquarters an 'order concerning the reception of un-officially examined theologians into the service of the provincial churches'.[48] Did that order possibly allow an interpretation by which legalization need not necessarily be tied to the acknowledgement of control in spiritual matters? The implementing regulations of 5th April caused some disappointment, for they did not in the least allow the consistories' requirements to be regarded simply as a 'relief' to help everyone into the office to which he was entitled; on the contrary, they demanded the unreserved acknowledgement of those consistories' para-mount control.

But in spite of that, the discussion began on a broad front as to whether the term 'relief' was not open to interpretation, or whether it might not be achieved in individual negotiations, making possible the right of the Councils of Brethren also to exercise an 'inward guidance' with their undoubted spiritual resources. Provincial churches, and in-dividual groups within them, now began to drive the best bargains they

---

45. Letter of 28.1.1939, GS II, p. 345.
46. To the young brethren in Pomerania, GS II, pp. 297 ff.
47. GS II, p. 301.
48. Law Gazette of the DEK 1938, No. 3.

could for themselves. The Old Prussian Council of Brethren still tried as far as it could to guide things. Taking the line that the pastoral office must recognize the State's right to a certain amount of supervision, it advocated that the examination documents should be handed over *en bloc* to the consistories, but asked that this should not imply a recognition of the latter as the churches' directing bodies. Nevertheless, provincial Councils of Brethren and groups unfortunately proceeded separately, and that meant that their consistories took very varying attitudes with regard to making concessions. Westphalia, under the guidance of Koch, the chairman, went furthest in the direction of special agreements; four fifths of its 'illegal' pastors voted for the chairman's readiness to compromise, and one fifth for standing firm.[49]

Bonhoeffer reacted trenchantly:

In the first place, anyone who looks solely after himself is deluded as to the community of the Church . . .

[And again] to anyone who wants to make us faint-hearted and diffident by telling us that we ought at least to salvage our remaining resources, that we have been battered, questioned, and locked up quite enough, we must reply that we are promising ourselves nothing at all from those resources. What God intends to batter we are quite willing to see battered. We have nothing to salvage. We have not attached our hearts to organizations and institutions, not even to our own. The works (*Werkerei*) that hang on those so-called church resources are just as godless as any others, and are bound to rob us of the prize of victory. But we trust confidently that God will salvage his Word, and us with it, in his miraculous way. That is the only stock of resources on which we intend to take our stand.[50]

3. In Pomerania everything now seemed to be in a state of indecision. The consistory once again gave a positively final date—30th September. On the 1st September Bonhoeffer, together with Fritz Onnasch, struggled for nearly twenty-four hours for those who were still wavering, and who asked: Has not the Confessing Church failed over the oath and surrendered already? Is not the Confessing Church's influence so small that it ought to disband? How can we carry on and finance ourselves for any length of time?[51] After the meeting, the whole body of the brethren handed in their papers to the consistory, in accordance with the proposal of the Old Prussian Council of Brethren.

The Pomeranian Council of Brethren thereupon found itself compelled to invite all the loyal pastors to an extraordinary convention in October, when the council members, von Thadden, Baumann, de Boor, and Bartelt, set out the problems, and Bonhoeffer gave the principal address.

49. The Epiphany Synod of 1939 therefore addressed a special message to the Westphalians; see W. Niesel, *Um Verkündigung und Ordnung der Kirche*, 1949, pp. 72 f.
50. Circular letter of 25.8.1938, GS II, pp. 538 f.
51. Letter from F. Onnasch, 3.9.1938.

Von Thadden outlined a depressingly unvarnished picture: out of 600 Pomeranian incumbents 318 had at some time or other given their written assent to the Confessing Church's self-commitment; of those 318 only 60 pastors in office followed the Council of Brethren. Added to this there were 57 young 'illegal' theologians, of whom only 17 were in regular pastoral office and 22 in positions which were not legal, while for the time being 15 could not be accommodated. The Council of Brethren had to raise 9,000 Reichsmark a month, 6,000 of which were earmarked for the 'illegal' pastors; but at that time the income was only 4,500 Reichsmark.[52]

After that introduction, Bonhoeffer gave a theological lecture to rouse the consciences of those who were ready to compromise.[53] He was concerned about the question of the certainty of Barmen and Dahlem, beside which the question of 'the way since then' could have no priority:

The Bible does not concern itself at all with the pathos and problems of the question about 'our way' . . . That way has no importance of its own, no set of problems of its own, and still less any special quality of tragedy . . . [But people now want] to see the way before they take it . . . The Scripture does not demonstrate any way, but it does demonstrate God's truth. Scriptural evidence does not take from us the need for faith, but leads us right into the adventure of faith and obedience to God's Word.[54]

To those who were in too much of a hurry to go to the consistory independently he suggested:

That we do not leave a brother in distress, that we stand by him who is attacked for the sake of the Gospel, even when we ourselves do not happen to be attacked, that we take each other's part in danger, struggles, and suffering—that is so self-evident that it hardly needed to be mentioned. Any questioning whether the demand is unconditional brings with it a set of problems that can only serve as an evasion.[55]

He rejected the temptation to get rid of the unpleasant dispute over the spiritual authority of the consistories:

Do not let us persuade ourselves that over there, in the ranks of the consistories, we should be free to devote ourselves to really basic matters! We have given up all inward authority there, because we have not remained in the truth.[56]

The text of this address was duplicated for further discussion. It played a part in the Epiphany Synod of 1939, and in many groups and provinces it was worked through, attacked, and discussed in counter-writings.

4. Even now, the collapse did not seem to have reached its culminating

52. From a postscript by E. Bethge.
53. 'Unser Weg nach dem Zeugnis der Schrift', GS II, pp. 320 ff.
54. GS II, pp. 324 f.
55. GS II, p. 332.
56. GS II, p. 344.

point. It grew clearer from day to day that there was still a nucleus of theologians who were not to be persuaded by arguments or by cajoling. The leaders of all the brotherhoods of 'illegal' pastors except Westphalia issued, on 6th January 1939, a call to their members to stand firm:

Is a congregation built up when such authorities[57] frequently test future servants of the Word on matters of flesh and blood,[58] but are neither willing nor able to test the spirits?

Then came the clear message from the Old Prussian Synod of 28th January 1939 in Nikolassee:

We warn the brethren concerned, that they should not allow the measures of the national church authorities relating to the office of preacher to be accepted by them. Otherwise they incur guilt by losing the comfort of ordination, by supporting a false system of church government, by being self-regarding, by abandoning their brethren, and by confusing the congregations, through by-passing the administrative bodies of the Confessing Church.[59]

Bonhoeffer's arguments were taken up in a condensed form. After the terrible year of 1938, he felt that synod as if it were a liberation after long waiting:

The new start that has lately been granted us through God's goodness against all expectation has freed us from a constricting pressure . . . with our cheerless, resigned, and refractory nature we had no longer deserved this [liberation].[60]

Only a few weeks later there appeared the notorious 'Godesberg Declaration',[61] which amounted to an official legitimizing of the cause of the extreme 'German Christians'. Bonhoeffer wrote to the brethren:

Since I last wrote, much has become clearer. In the decisive weeks it has again been shown that at a certain point the possibilities of discussion are over. We were nearly destroyed by the bandying of arguments. From that we have been delivered.[62]

5. After the Epiphany Synod, most provinces received from the consistories, as an answer to the papers that had been sent in, a summons to a 're-examination'. In plain language, that simply meant an examination. Regardless of any objections and discussions, the ordinands must, moreover, be 'prepared duly to obey the laws of Church and State, particularly as regards all that has to do with collection and dismissals.'[63]

57. The consistories that obeyed Dr. Werner.
58. To ensure that they were Aryans.
59. W. Niesel, op. cit., p. 71.
60. Circular letter of 14.2.1939, GS II, pp. 546 f.
61. See Ch. XI, p. 549.
62. GS II, p. 550.
63. Thus, e.g., the demand made by the Magdeburg consistory to E. Bethge on 13.3.1939.

But it now appeared that the winter's efforts were bearing some fruit. The great majority of those summoned to re-examination refused to comply with the demand for legalization :

Together with the other brethren, I am bound to refuse to take part in an affair in which the authorities employ all their resources against the scruples, often stated in detail, of consciences bound firmly to Scripture and creed . . . I greatly regret that, even now, the consistory does not offer to help us to exercise our rightful ministry in the Church with the clear and easy conscience necessary for that office with all its duties and rights.[64]

Staemmler reported, at that time, that in the province of Saxony 'they all, with hardly an exception, wanted to continue in the way of the Confessing Church'; that, in fact, the Council of Brethren had, in the presence of many theological students from Halle—where Julius Schniewind and Ernst Wolf were still teaching !—carried out new ordinations, everyone having been assigned his work and having plenty to do.[65]

Even in Westphalia the expected landslide did not occur. An 'illegal' pastor, who had been in the collective pastorate at Gross-Schlönwitz, wrote to Bonhoeffer :

I should like to tell you that I received the 'Thoughts about our way'[66] on 30th January. This, together with the declarations of this week,[67] has contributed towards my now seeing the whole business quite differently . . . People think of me in these days, and of very many Westphalian brethren.[68]

6. In Bonhoeffer's immediate neighbourhood, however, in Pomerania, the break in the front was at least halted. Respected members of the Council of Brethren had long since given their advice in favour of re-examination, Greifswald professors had repeatedly attacked Bonhoeffer's theology in the essay of 1936 on the question of church community, and had cast doubts on its Reformation basis; in the Stettin consistory there were obviously some gentlemen who favoured conciliation, while among the 'illegal' pastors there were competent spokesmen who could put the case plausibly for their willingness to be re-examined. They proposed to accept the fact of the regrettable 'split', and to proceed from the existence of a group 'Way A' (those who refused on principle, led by Fritz Onnasch) and another 'Way B' (the legalizers, under Gerhard Krause), but to bear with each other in a brotherhood that would continue to exist in spite of everything. That led to tough arguments, in which Bonhoeffer became deeply involved.

Gerhard Sass gave moving expression to his dissatisfaction with the Epiphany Synod's decision in a circular approved by a Stolp colleague,

64. E. Bethge to the consistory of the province of Saxony on 17.3.1939.
65. Circular letter from W. Staemmler, 2.5.1939.
66. 'Unser Weg nach dem Zeugnis der Schrift', GS II, pp. 320 ff.
67. Epiphany Synod.
68. Letter from R. Lynker, 3.2.1939.

Werner de Boor, and addressed to the divided comrades-in-arms of Pomerania: the synod's basic views, namely the appeal to the right *vocatio* and the right church régime, were, he thought, open to question, for the National Church still offered the effective means of access to the congregations, and the consistories sent legitimate preachers—even if they were 'in captivity'.

The struggle on the front sector about the church régime is long since decided—the Confessing Church has lost. But the front of the church struggle is much broader, and the decisive point is no longer the church régime. But the synod wants to go on fighting for that position, and so it ties down the forces that are so needed in other places, and leaves them to the enemy's fire . . . Way A means charging repeatedly, with diminishing forces and reasons, against a locked door.

The brethren of Way B were now, for the sake of the community which was so much more important, to be 'led to the consistory through their spiritual guide, i.e. the Council of Brethren'.[69]

Bonhoeffer found a commentary on Jeremiah 15:19-21 in Zinzendorf's works, and the ordinands took care that it was circulated:

Do you hear that, you servants of the Lord? You may be suspended, removed, you may lose your income, be turned out of house and home, but you will again become preachers—that is the word of promise! And if you are dismissed from a dozen posts and again get a fresh one, then you are a preacher in thirteen parishes, for in all the previous ones our innocence, our cross, and our faith preach more powerfully than if we were there.

From the correspondence which took place between Bonhoeffer and Gerhard Krause, and which openly treated the difficulties over 'Way A' and 'Way B' both theologically and humanly, we have only a fragment from Krause's pen; but that fragment is enough to show what the issue was and how it was contested:

I followed, as far as it was possible, your advice to keep silence till the Church had spoken . . . Meanwhile the Confessing Church has itself gone beyond those sketchy ideas.[70] I have been listened to in many places, but the Confessing Church would not, and, I suppose, could not in the least bring itself to do so. I suppose the ideas of 'B' would have had to be put forward with more substantiation and more readiness to shoulder responsibility than was actually the case. We did not think of our proposals as a good solution for us privately, but as a help to the whole Confessing Church. Where they are now rejected, there yet remains the conflict between the Confessing Church and myself . . .

In preparation for the Prussian Synod I have re-read fairly long sections of your *Cost of Discipleship*, because I wanted to keep open the possibility of reversing my opinion. But you are quite right when you write of the

69. Circular letter from W. de Boor and G. Sass, 13.2.1939.
70. Epiphany Synod.

'bottomless pit of theological dissent' between us. It exists, though I cannot yet formulate it . . . I suspect in the Church's doctrine of justification, and much more in the doctrine of the Church (especially in the 'questions'), errors, that I do not know elsewhere except in Roman Catholic theology.

Perhaps the ethical contrast is even greater than the theological one . . . It is the practical question : how are Christians to behave in relation to a tyrannical government, where do disavowal and necessary resistance begin? Christians today decide this quite differently in their lives. Unfortunately they often turn it into a far-reaching doctrinal contrast, and give it a momentum that leads to a split in the Church . . .

So the question still remains open about what caused me now to change the decision that was indeed made in faith.

1. One may refer here to the above-mentioned theological contrast, which impressed me more deeply from day to day. It is also relevant that the situation has changed through the fact that many former 'German Christians' are today authorized preachers, that the church régime of the consistory is today less heretical than tyrannical, that our political situation is becoming increasingly plain in its essentials, and that in my case the times of storm have been followed by times of reflection.

2. To this there was added the decisive factor of the 'certainty of the others', from whom the Confessing Church separated if it had not already done so. The existence of orthodox 'neutrals' shook me, and I could not understand the need to separate from them.

3. At last I was called to a halt through realizing that I should have to give up the officially instituted Church, because my work was possible only in the circles of the congregations of the Confessing Church—yet, I know that I am called to serve in the Church, for the admonition and edification of the congregations, not simply to serve in Confessing Church circles alone.

4. Finally, I could not help seeing that the way to the consistory would not necessarily have to be a denial and an 'action-without-faith'. That has been confirmed by my personal discussions in recent weeks . . . To be sure, the men there are 'bound', and little qualified theologically to guide a church. But the legalization that they demand includes nothing that I should have to reject as 'against the faith' or 'against the truth'. If that is so, it means that the protest against the consistory loses for me that necessity that it would be bound to have if it meant my renouncing the pastor's office, the official Church, and fellowship with many like-minded brethren, etc., and endure all the sorrows . . .

It is for the Confessing Church to decide whether I remain in it; whether I remain in the Finkenwalde brotherhood is my question to you.[71]

The discussion was not always so clear, nor so carefully argued. How could it be when uncertainty began to prevail inside the Council of Brethren itself?

At present everything is going backwards here. Almost the whole Council of Brethren is of the Westphalian mind . . . Gerhard Krause, Rendtorff, and

71. Letter of 18.2.1939.

von Thadden all favour re-examination . . . So we are writing a letter which should make it clear that we others do not intend to be ignored, and that the 'assent in Pomerania' is not unanimous.[72]

The middle of February saw the East Pomeranian convention in Köslin, where fifty of the clergy and laity, including Dr. Knorr, declared for 'Way A'. Bonhoeffer spoke. Onnasch reported: 'Strangely enough, the laity were more radical than the radicals among the clergy, and are firmly in favour of letting the Confessing Church collapse, rather than cooperate with the B-people.'[73] At the end of February the West Pomeranian convention (also called *Kirchentag*) followed. Rendtorff and Gerhard Krause spoke for Way B, Gelhoff, Baumann, and Bonhoeffer for Way A. Krause attacked the statement that 'the Confessing Church is the Church of Jesus Christ',[74] and put forward the proposal that those whose status had been legalized should be recognized as members of the Confessing Church. Baumann warned against any arrangement with the wrong church régime. Bonhoeffer attacked Rendtorff's exegesis, as the latter had made John 17 and Matthew 9 and 28 refer to the field ripe for harvest, into which the young pastors were now to be sent with all available resources; Bonhoeffer retorted that one must not, by virtue of those particular passages, preach on the strength of one's own impulse; that the Scripture teaches, not self-offering, but the power of the commission. Boeters, a consistory councillor, summoned the obstinate people to come into line, so that the spiritual capital of the Confessing Church could become effective, like that of a free brotherhood of pastors, in the Church as a whole: 'Yes, we rejoice if the Confessing Church is like the spiritual movements of Berneuchen and Sydow.'[75]

A week later the young pastors in Stettin voted: 11 decided for legalization through the consistory, 28 for standing by the Council of Brethren unconditionally, and 6 abstained from voting. They finally adopted the resolution 'that we all wish to try to remain together, in spite of the different ways, though Way A is generally preferred'.[76] Indeed, the 'attempt' to remain together was at once subjected to very great stress. On the one hand, some radicals of Way A declined to pursue the idea of unity, as though what the others did were of no consequence. On the other hand, the brethren of Way B proved to be very active. De Boor and Gerhard Krause drew up for them a theological expression of opinion against Bonhoeffer, 'which greatly upset the radical A-brethren'.[77]

The special problems of Pomerania were not solved, but they came to

72. F. Onnasch on 24. and 28.1.1939.
73. Letter of 16.2.1939.
74. Minute by A. Ohnesorge, 19. and 20.2.1939.
75. Ibid.
76. F. Onnasch on 1.3.1939.
77. Minute by A. Ohnesorge.

an end when Bonhoeffer went to England and America, and men like Gerhard Krause were called up for military service and so could no longer help to advance matters. The war created a new situation. Bonhoeffer had no misgivings about including Krause and his friends in the circle of the Finkenwalde brethren. He even intensified the correspondence with them by the army postal service, without any further mention between them of 'Way A' and 'Way B'.

There is no doubt that the long-drawn-out struggle over legalization in the Old Prussian Union made heavy demands on Bonhoeffer for the sake of the people involved. On the other hand, it had also had the effect that Werner's offensive against the young brethren either slackened or achieved its aim by less uncompromising methods. But it was impossible to shut one's eyes to the fact that deep rifts had been made in the front. Moreover, it had now become usual in the Confessing Church to take individual steps without discussion; the Councils of Brethren did not prevent them, or else they became accustomed to decisions and recommendations which were not unanimous. The authority of the Old Prussian Council of Brethren had weakened appreciably; among the young theologians people looked round for employment in an 'intact' Lutheran provincial church, or interested themselves in a theology that allowed some freedom from turmoil.

In that field Bonhoeffer, like Wilhelm Niesel for instance, did not give way an inch, nor did he show his disappointment. Yet the plane on which he disputed so energetically with the Pomeranian theologians was no longer so exclusively the place where he lived and thought. In view of the steps that he took in 1933 and 1935 to get away from the embarrassing privileges of the National Church, it was bound to seem to him absurd to let the conditions relating to pastoral service in a provincial church be dictated to him by Dr. Werner and the consistories. It was not to gain an appointment to an official post that he had been concerned for the Christian witness in the Nazi State.

IV POLITICAL INVOLVEMENT

Towards the end of our period, in snowbound Sigurdshof, Bonhoeffer began to write down something that he had had in mind for years—a meditation on Psalm 119, that texture of interwoven sayings, with neither beginning nor end, on the theme of the commandment.[78] Here, at the last place where he could practise his theological teaching and a spiritual life in community, and in view of coming political demands, he wrote on verse 19 ('I am a sojourner on earth; hide not thy commandments from me!'):

The earth that nourishes me has a right to my work and my strength. It is

78. See Ch. VIII, p. 335, Ch. XI, p. 571.

not fitting that I should despise the earth on which I have my life; I owe her faithfulness and gratitude. I must not dream away my earthly life by thoughts of heaven, and thereby evade my lot—that I have to be a sojourner and a stranger—and with it God's call into this world of strangers. There is a very godless home-sickness for the other world, and it will certainly not produce any home-coming. I am to be a sojourner, with everything that that involves. I am not to close my heart indifferently to earth's problems, sorrows, and joys; and I am to wait patiently for the redemption of the divine promise—really wait, and not rob myself of it in advance by wishing and dreaming.[79]

For years Bonhoeffer had meditated on the Christian's 'sojourning', and had practised it personally, ecclesiastically, and ecumenically. Now he began to look at the qualifying phrase 'on earth'. How was that to be understood?

Hellmut Traub tells of a very characteristic meeting in Stettin, where in 1938 a theological circle discussed Romans 13. He was disappointed at the first meeting to find Bonhoeffer so unhelpfully silent on the subject of political resistance, while he, Gollwitzer, and the others spoke impatiently and passionately about it. Afterwards he took Bonhoeffer aside:

He assured me emphatically that he had understood me perfectly. 'But then you must be quite logical, quite different, you must go ahead in quite a different way' . . . I at once realized that what I had taken for 'hesitation' belonged to an entirely different category . . .[80]

At that time, Bonhoeffer already found himself so involved in knowledge of details of underground political activity that he was no longer likely to remain in the non-committal area between discussion and practical steps. So he said nothing, because he knew better what was really being talked about there and what it might cost; perhaps, too, because he suspected that new steps of that kind were not to be justified as a programme prepared in advance.

Thus, and for similar reasons, we do not find in Bonhoeffer's writings a single line commenting on Karl Barth's essay *Rechtfertigung und Recht* which caused such a stir. Barth's writing, with its attack on the usual sterile differentiation between the two realms, appeared in 1938, and Bonhoeffer no doubt knew about it. He even comes close to it later in his *Ethics*. But he was already too involved with those who were taking action; and besides, the problem in German theology seemed to him too new and comprehensive to be settled briefly and incidentally with no systematic presentation. Reinhold Niebuhr, who in 1930-1 could find no trace of a political streak in Bonhoeffer, remembered an incident from the spring of 1939, when he expressed appreciation of Bonhoeffer just after the war:

79. GS IV, p. 538.
80. H. Traub, 'Two Recollections', IKDB, p. 157.

I still remember a discussion of theological and political matters I had with him in London in 1939 when he assured me that Barth was right in becoming more political;[81] but he criticized Barth for defining his position in a little pamphlet. 'If', he declared in rather typical German fashion, 'one states an original position in many big volumes, one ought to define the change in one's position in an equally impressive volume and not in a little pamphlet.'[82]

For Bonhoeffer, as a German theologian and a Lutheran Christian, the step into political action, over which he still hesitated, meant going into new and untravelled country. It was certainly a momentous step when one went over from silent opposition to open ideological protest and direct warning, as did individual bishops and that memorandum of the Confessing Church;[83] but it was a further and more critical step into that politically accountable revolutionary planning for the future. But that is what happened in Bonhoeffer's case. For a long time he merely knew and approved of what was going on, till that knowledge and approval developed into cooperation. But that was preceded by far-reaching positive and negative experiences which grew out of the ecclesiastical and political events of 1938 and 1939.

We shall follow out Dietrich Bonhoeffer's participation in the German political resistance movement in five periods. The first is from the Fritsch crisis at the beginning of 1938 to the Munich agreement on 30th September of that year; the second is from then to the beginning of the offensive in France on 10th May 1940. In both those periods Bonhoeffer knew and approved of what was going on. The third period extends from the campaign in France to his arrest on 5th April 1943, the day on which the resistance work in the counter-espionage service was crippled; this third period is that of Bonhoeffer's actual operational participation. The fourth is from then to 20th July 1944, and consists for him of keeping things at bay. The fifth period is the struggle for survival.

We first have to deal with a period in Bonhoeffer's life when the way towards political activity was beginning to appear, but without yet bringing any changes in his occupation or any new theological departures. Any decisions that had to be made by him or near him did not yet change his position vis-à-vis the Church; they mainly, as we shall see, concerned either his family (his sister had to emigrate) or himself personally (he wanted to avoid being called up). But those decisions tended, without his realizing it, to affect his political involvements as a whole.

Information

To be an accessory or to be informed was dangerous in the Third Reich.

81. That referred to *Rechtfertigung und Recht* and the letter to Hromádka.
82. *Christianity and Crisis*, Vol. V, No. 11, p. 6.
83. See Ch. X, pp. 440 ff.

For Freisler in 1944 it meant the death sentence. The earlier curiosity of many people about what was happening gradually changed under Hitler to an instinctive reluctance to know what was going on. That reluctance was fostered by the régime. Any knowledge of the actual situation, especially after the outbreak of war, exposed one to danger. But Bonhoeffer took considerable pains to have access to exclusive information, as he felt that private information was a necessary component of his responsibility for the future.

He insisted on supplementing his knowledge by reading *The Times* and the *Basler Nachrichten* as long as ever it was possible. Nor was he inclined to stop listening to foreign radio. That re-kindled his very underdeveloped interest in technical details. When the venues were settled for the collective pastorates in November 1937, he made sure of the possibilities of wireless reception in Further Pomerania, and when it turned out that there was no electricity in Sigurdshof, he got an engineer to supply him with a portable battery set, which was something rare at that time. For him, the first thing needed for asserting one's independence was information; he would not delegate his judgement to anyone else or allow Hitler's sudden actions to take him by surprise. The most difficult thing for him to bear was to have to be the victim of some unforeseen occurrence; he meant to hold his head high, even when going into custody. He did so in 1943.

Of course, he was also too anxious to hear details of when and where 'the beams were creaking'; that was the expression used at that time by those who were waiting for Hitler to come to grief—in the Röhm affair, on the death of Hindenburg, over the occupation of the Rhineland, or on Schacht's retirement. Forecasts by well-informed people, however, might be valuable to them as a responsibly handled weapon—such, for example, as the warning by the Bonhoeffer family and its friends from 1933 onward: 'Hitler means war'. Of course, every forecast needed to be confirmed by continued access to fresh information and knowledge of the facts. Even Bonhoeffer's sermon in Fanö included a good deal of information and compact prognosis.[84]

The result of that access to political information was both to separate irrevocably and to bring together. It separated him on an essential point from many of his ecclesiastical colleagues; but it brought him into the company of people who neither shared nor later pursued his theological and ecclesiastical ideas, and whose motives were not always his. But he kept less and less at a distance from them, and did not try to approximate their motives to his own. For instance, Ewald von Kleist of Schmenzin certainly followed Harnack's idea of Christianity, but that did not particularly worry Bonhoeffer, and so it was not to talk him round that he went over to Schmenzin from Klein-Krössin—although Frau von Kleist-Retzow would have been delighted to hear him try.

84. See Ch. VIII, p. 312

Hans von Dohnanyi

For a pastor, Bonhoeffer had unusual connections.

His father was on familiar terms with Sauerbach, who was often able to bring along fresh news from the Party hierarchy; his mother cultivated the family relationship with her cousin Paul von Hase (executed after the attempted *coup* of the 20th July) when he was military commander of Berlin. Klaus had contacts with the lawyer Josef Wirmer, the industrialist Walter Bauer, and Nikolaus van Halem (prematurely arrested), and with Otto John and Prince Louis Ferdinand, bitter opponents of the régime, who for their part had important contacts at home and abroad. Klaus and Dietrich often met for a musical evening with the former Social Democratic Government President of Merseburg, Ernst von Harnack. Rüdiger Schleicher got on well with Dr. Karl Sack, the chief of the Army's legal department. Dietrich Bonhoeffer renewed his youthful acquaintance with Hans-Bernd von Haeften in the Foreign Office.

But in those crucial years, no one was nearer to him than his brother-in-law Hans von Dohnanyi. Bonhoeffer received from him information, counsel, and, later, commissions, while Dohnanyi sought from him ethical certainty and enlightening conversation.

After being employed from 1929 onwards as personal information officer to the Ministers of Justice Koch-Weser, Bredt, and Joel, Dohnanyi was taken over by Gürtner in May 1933, although he had never had anything to do with the Party and did not enter any of its organizations, not even the National Socialist Legal Union (*Rechtswahrerbund*) of K. H. Frank. In the early period the Ministry of Justice still had a certain political freedom of movement, and the struggle to maintain a legal system was not equally hopeless everywhere. Because of his position, Dohnanyi was able to give his brother-in-law in the church struggle various useful and timely hints or warnings. He always had, as Christine von Dohnanyi tells us, 'the full backing of Gürtner, that really tragic figure, who was destined to dig the grave of German law'. When in 1935 Dohnanyi was offered a lectureship on criminal and procedural law in the University of Leipzig, he declined the offer at Gürtner's wish.

In those years, Dohnanyi was constantly able to get a close-up view of the Nazis' evil deeds. He began to document their crimes in a 'chronicle of shame', to the continuation of which Beck later attached great importance because of the possible need to refute a new legend about a stab in the back, and which was to be of fatal consequence when certain parts could not be destroyed in time.

Dohnanyi was able to remain behind the scenes for a long time, till the ground threatened to become too hot for him during the first conspiracy on the occasion of the Fritsch crisis. Just then Bormann wrote from the Party chancellory to Gürtner, complaining that the minister was allowing a person like Dohnanyi, who had no connection with

National Socialism, to be in the closest proximity to him. A Party clique in the Ministry, among whom was Roland Freisler, had denounced him. So it came about that, with Gürtner's help, the young man became a supreme court judge (*Reichsgerichtsrat*) in Leipzig in September 1938. Dietrich Bonhoeffer was afraid that the supply of information would now be badly interrupted, whereas Dohnanyi regarded the change, after the failure of the attempted *Putsch*, as a fortunate removal from the dangerous ground of Berlin. Thus, at the beginning of November Dohnanyi's family moved from the Kurländer Allee in Charlottenburg to Leipzig.

But as Dohnanyi had undertaken to give a weekly lecture in Berlin, he still met Oster, Goerdeler, and Hassell regularly. At one of those meetings, after Hitler had, on 21st October, ordered the armed forces to prepare to occupy the rest of Czecho-Slovakia, Canaris, the head of the counter-espionage service, sent a message through Oster to Dohnanyi that in case of war he would like to appoint him, Dohnanyi, at once to his staff. That was the outcome of the meetings between Oster and Dohnanyi over the Fritsch affair, which will be referred to later.

On 25th August 1939 Dohnanyi had, in fact, taken on the duties of 'special leader' (*Sonderführer*) on Admiral Canaris' staff. In Oster's central department he saw to the section dealing with policy, but in a way he acted as a kind of private secretary to Canaris. He was now fairly settled in the centre of information—and the conspiracy!

From August 1939 he lived, as he had during his weekly journeys to Berlin from Leipzig, entirely with Bonhoeffer's parents in the Marienburger Allee; this greatly facilitated the contacts with his brother-in-law Dietrich.

With a cool intelligence Dohnanyi combined a readiness to help that was always quick and effective, even if at times almost too reticent. His close friends sometimes found him boyishly high-spirited, but he was also characterized by an unexpected, simple piety. His extraordinary abilities led to his being given tasks and positions so early in life as to arouse the envy of some colleagues and thereby create awkward situations.

With the Bonhoeffers he was attracted by the large family and its unfailingly high standards. His wife, Christine Bonhoeffer, had once been his school-friend. Earlier, he had been closely associated with Klaus Bonhoeffer, Gerhard Leibholz, and Justus Delbrück; but that association slackened during the church struggle and in subsequent years, so that Dietrich Bonhoeffer now came to be more in touch with him. Perhaps he was annoyed by Klaus Bonhoeffer's slight difficulty in coming to a decision. Klaus, the lawyer, was continually having ideas and visions of the possibilities that a given state of affairs might hold. That was a hindrance rather than a help to Hans von Dohnanyi. But he felt that in Dietrich, even Dietrich the theologian, he found a more sturdy realism.

As a matter of fact, Dietrich possessed in a high degree the capacity to help other people to come to a decision.

So at that time Dohnanyi confided in no one more than in Dietrich Bonhoeffer. Almost everyone else commented on Dohnanyi's abrupt and reserved manner, but Dietrich Bonhoeffer met his brother-in-law every day when he was stopping in Berlin. Thus it came about that Dohnanyi introduced him relatively early to the narrower circle of conspirators. It was also he who one evening asked Bonhoeffer what he thought about the New Testament passage 'all who take the sword will perish by the sword' (Matt. 26:52). Bonhoeffer's reply was that the word was valid for their circle too—we have to accept that we are subject to that judgement, but that there is now need of such men as will accept its validity for themselves.

Sources

The first two periods of revolutionary activity hardly provide us with written sources or memoranda to show that Bonhoeffer knew of plans to overthrow the régime and was in close touch with the conspirators; but there are two pieces of circumstantial evidence:

Bonhoeffer's diaries for 1938 and 1939 have all the pages torn out relating to any of the critical days of those years. Thus, the pages for 10th to 20th February 1938 are missing, i.e. the period in which there was some hope that a protest by Fritsch would set something in motion; and in 1939 the pages for January, the end of April and the beginning of May, and for August and September, all of which were times that he spent in Berlin. Those pages contained Berlin addresses and telephone numbers that were not in Bonhoeffer's diaries of previous years, and initials and numbers of the Zehlendorf and Grunewald district, but especially of the Tirpitzufer, where the counter-espionage department had its headquarters. The Gestapo was not to be able to question him about such entries if his notebooks should fall into their hands in any search instigated into church affairs.

The other piece of evidence is that during that time code words appear more and more frequently in correspondence with relatives and friends —names of people and places whose full importance is now partly forgotten, and which therefore make some passages in Bonhoeffer's letters obscure. For example, 'Uncle Rudi' plays a very important part. There actually was such a person: he was General Rüdiger von der Goltz, a brother-in-law of Frau Bonhoeffer, and a retired general living near the Marienburger Allee. His name was now the code word for Hitler's preparations for war and their state at the moment: 'I hear that we are to expect no change in our work in the near future. I wonder whether that has anything to do with Uncle Rudi.'[85] That meant that

85. Letter from Gross-Schlönwitz, 29.6.1938.

in view of the mobilization, no steps were to be taken against the 'illegal' pastors.

The Fritsch Crisis

The first cut-and-dried conspiracy in which Dohnanyi took part was preceded by every possible attempt to make contact with people close to Hitler or in key positions in the Army. In that way, Dohnanyi had early knowledge of Hitler's preparations for war. It was Captain Wiedemann through whom he learnt of Hitler's considered war speech to the commanders-in-chief of the three branches of the armed forces on 5th November 1937 in the Reich Chancellory.[86]

Captain Wiedemann had been Hitler's company commander in the First World War, and he had been adjutant in the Reich Chancellory since 1935. Dohnanyi, in attendance on Gürtner, had got to know him, and soon gained his confidence; and so there was disclosed to him important information about what was happening in the Reich Chancellory and on the Obersalzberg. According to Wiedemann's information, Hitler had said on 5th November 1937: 'Every generation needs its own war, and I shall take care that this generation gets its war.' Wiedemann said, in reply to Dohnanyi's expression of indignation: 'I admit that nothing but the revolver is any use here, but who is to do it? I cannot murder anyone who has made me his confidant.'[87] That important thread was snapped when Wiedemann fell into Hitler's disfavour and was appointed Consul-General in San Francisco in January 1939. Frau Bonhoeffer wrote to Dietrich: 'Hans is coming tomorrow. He will be very sorry that his friend is being moved; last time, too, he was quite depressed . . . What is happening to Uncle Rudi is very worrying.'[88]

As Fritsch and Blomberg had ventured, after the disclosure on 5th November 1937 in the Reich Chancellory, to raise political and military objections, they were both eliminated at the end of January by infamous methods. On 4th February it became known to a small circle that Blomberg and Fritsch had been dismissed, the latter with the accusation of having indulged in homosexual practices; the witness and evidence were prepared by Heydrich. Hitler now took over the supreme command of the armed forces, and Brauchitsch succeeded Fritsch as commander-in-chief of the Army. Hitler ordered Gürtner to investigate the case of Fritsch: 'You will know for yourself which end of the rope to pull.' With the same words Gürtner handed the documents over to Dohnanyi for him to deal with the matter, and, of course, Dohnanyi understood which end of the rope had to be pulled.[89] For a time he was freed from

86. See the 'Hossbach-Protokoll', in W. Hofer, *Der Nationalsozialismus, Dokumente 1933-1945*, 1957, pp. 193-6.
87. Related by Christine von Dohnanyi, 1945.
88. Letter of 23.1.1939.
89. Related by Christine von Dohnanyi, 1945.

all other duties, so that he could work at the defamation of Fritsch.

While he was so engaged, he got to know more closely Dr. Karl Sack of the army judicature, and Colonel Oster, the head of the central department of the counter-espionage service. Those meetings gave rise to the first clearly defined cell of resistance with specified regulated plans; General Beck, too, belonged to it. They started from the assumption that the Army could not submit to Hitler's defamatory encroachments, and that Fritsch must challenge Himmler. That would launch a *coup d'état*. Dohnanyi drew up a written challenge by Fritsch to Himmler. But Fritsch hesitated. Then, on 12th March 1938, Hitler marched into Austria, and the men who were to take military action by confronting Hitler felt that, in view of the Vienna triumph, the chance had been missed. Nothing happened.

As a matter of interest, Schellenberg, the S.S. brigade commander and later head of the secret service, says in his memoirs that Heydrich was, in fact, afraid that the Army would march against him.[90]

Thus, even though the first attempted *coup* had been unsuccessful, it led to important conclusions: An opposition that took seriously its aim to stop Hitler had to make sure of possessing the instruments of power through which alone he could be restrained. Efforts in the economic or legislative sphere, through international opinion, for instance, became of secondary importance compared with the task of keeping or gaining influence in the Army. If the scattered 'resistances' were to be turned into a constructive conspiracy of 'resistance', the latter would in future have to become a military plot; so much had been clearly proved in February 1938. Dohnanyi and Bonhoeffer first had to find their way to this conclusion by their own conviction.

This radical change in Bonhoeffer's outlook was bound up with another change. Up to now he had been eagerly on the watch for people who could summon up the courage to say No publicly, and were willing to accept dismissal from their posts in consequence. There now came a period when it was of the utmost importance that people of character should remain at the controls in all circumstances and not allow themselves to be displaced. That meant that what had hitherto been a question of character now became a mere bagatelle—a greeting with the Hitler salute, for instance.

Instead of refusing this, one had to see that it meant nothing if by it one could get into key positions. That meant that the use of camouflage became a moral duty. So the uncompromising Bonhoeffer no longer took offence when Oster and Dohnanyi kept in touch with such very shady people as Himmler's Chief of Staff, the S.S. supreme group commander Karl Wolff, the Berlin police president Count Helldorf, or the director of the Reich criminal investigation office Nebe. If there had to be conspiracy, then they had to go into the lions' den and get a foothold

90. W. Schellenberg, *Memoiren*, 1956, pp. 40 f.

there. And if every rank and status in the country had for years been stripped of its authority, if hope of evolutionary change had remained unfulfilled, if the risk of war were now to be consciously taken, other countries ravished, and the Jewish question made almost unbelievably acute, one had to accept the logical conclusions. Bonhoeffer never tried to put Dohnanyi right by dissuading him from his course of action. The position had been plain to him since the spring of 1938: someone had to take on the shady business. And if he, Pastor Bonhoeffer, was not called on to be one of those directly involved, it could at least be his business to set their consciences at rest.

Sudeten Crisis

In the summer of 1938 the conspiracy was given new cause for action in connection with the Sudeten crisis. On 28th May Hitler laid before the heads of the Army, State, and Party the plan to eliminate Czecho-Slovakia. Then followed blow after blow: on 22nd June conscription of civilian labour; on 13th July the law requiring the population to help in national defence; on 17th August the formation of the armed S.S. as an independent auxiliary to the existing armed forces. At the same time it was announced that at the beginning of the next year the Jews' freedom of movement was to be restricted by adding the names 'Israel' and 'Sarah' in their passports.

On 18th August an unusual thing happened: Beck, the chief of the general staff, handed in his resignation. He had previously tried to get the generals to adopt a common attitude against the plans that Hitler had announced on 28th May. On 16th July he had handed Brauchitsch a memorandum for the purpose of preparing a *démarche* to Hitler, and it contained a passage that deserves always to be remembered:

The final decisions for the nation's existence are at stake here; history will charge those leaders[91] with bloodshed if they do not act in accordance with their professional and political knowledge and conscience.

Their obedience as soldiers must have a limit where their knowledge, their conscience, and their responsibility forbid the execution of a command.

It shows a lack of stature and a failure to understand his task, if in such times a soldier in the highest position sees his duties and tasks only in the setting of his military commissions without being conscious that his highest responsibility is to the people as a whole.

Exceptional times demand exceptional actions![92]

But Brauchitsch declined to fall in with Beck's ideas; and meanwhile, at the Berghof on 10th August, Hitler succeeded in arousing the younger generals' enthusiasm for his warlike ideas. In that situation Beck declined

91. Of the different branches of the armed forces.
92. H. Krausnick, in *Die Vollmacht des Gewissens*, 1956, p. 315.

to share any responsibility for starting a world war, and retired. The nation, it is true, did not learn of this crisis till 1st October.

Meanwhile the nation had become a participator in and a victim of Hitler's dramatic tricks: the threats at the Party rally that the country would intervene on behalf of the Sudeten Germans; the demands screwed up higher and higher when Chamberlain made his two appeasement visits to Germany; lastly the mobilization that was called off when Mussolini intervened at the last moment, and on 29th and 30th September the representatives of the Great Powers met on Hitler's ground.

The world, and with it the Germans, breathed again, as if something wonderful had happened. The German-speaking Church of St. George in London wrote to Chamberlain:

The German Lutheran Church of St. George in London, assembled today for divine service, thinks of you with cordiality . . . It therefore welcomes gratefully everything that you, Prime Minister, have done for the maintenance of peace . . . Its church building[93] is the oldest German landmark in Great Britain. It has had to experience on its own body what a world war means. It will do its utmost, through confessing the name of Jesus Christ, to serve the cause of peace between our two countries, and it remembers in its intercession your statesmanlike work which is directed to the same end.[94]

Hildebrandt and Rieger could not suspect the totally different impression that the event had made on Bonhoeffer at home. His hope of a revolution had again come to nothing. Psychologically everything was more favourable for it, and the action itself was better prepared than in the spring; at that moment, if at all, an intervention by the generals against a Hitler who had gone beyond all bounds would have been intelligible. Halder, Beck's successor as chief of the general staff, would have been ready to start the *Putsch* as soon as Hitler gave the order to attack Czecho-Slovakia. General von Witzleben, the military commander of the Berlin-Brandenburg district would have marched on the Reich Chancellory; at that time he had a certain popularity. The hour of action had been palpably at hand; 'Munich' had thwarted it. The day on which the world breathed again was for the conspirators the '*dies ater*'.[95] The internal and external conditions for a revolution changed so completely after 30th September that the underground movement did not recover from the setback for a long time. Hitler had success on his side, and he used it, not only with propagandist allusions to the correctness of his policy, but also to curtail the authority of the general staff. In future, the latter was no longer to take its traditional share of responsibility for the decisions of the commander-in-chief, but was only to draft the plans in a subordinate capacity. Any divergent views Hitler

93. Of the St. George congregation.
94. *Gemeindeprotokoll*, pp. 72 f.
95. H. Krausnick, op. cit., p. 365.

now called 'defeatism'. Witzleben was moved from the key position in Berlin to the western fortifications. His successor, Paul von Hase, was indeed one of those who were in the know, but he could not simply take over Witzleben's role. For a long time the civilians opposed to the régime, like Dohnanyi, and the few stalwart officers without battalions, like Oster, lost that vital close touch with the irresolute military. They looked like pessimists who had made wrong forecasts of the behaviour of the Western Powers. The shock lasted so long that the conspirators could not prepare for a new *Putsch*—on the occasion of Hitler's entry into Prague on 15th March 1939, or at the beginning of the Polish campaign in September of the same year—as they had done in September 1938. The civilians did, in fact, again make some efforts, but there was no response from the army commanders. When at last in the winter of 1939-40 the possibility of a *coup d'état* again came nearer, its conditions had become very much more complicated.

While plans were being discussed in the summer of 1938, some of the conspirators still thought that a spontaneous popular rising was possible, if Hitler were prevented by force from starting a new war. Dohnanyi was more pessimistic, and advocated a tougher programme, including the removal of Hitler. In August 1938, when Ewald von Kleist of Schmenzin visited Churchill and talked to him about ways and means of getting a new German government, Churchill is reported as saying: 'You can have everything, but first bring us Hitler's head.'[96] But at that time people did not go so far as to think that an attempted assassination was either possible or necessary. They were more inclined to favour Hitler's arrest and public arraignment; and the possibility was discussed of having him certified as mentally ill, on the strength of a psychiatric report that Bonhoeffer was to draw up. In 1938 the conspirators were still able to appeal to the generals' expert knowledge and strengthen them in their belief that their resistance to Hitler could not be regarded simply as a 'plot'. Beck had not thought all along of a plot and conspiracy, but had thought at first that it was sure to be possible to regain common sense and freedom by putting the professional point of view direct, and that resolute action with a suitable document might clear up everything. That was becoming doubtful even towards the end of September, and by 1939 it was a complete illusion. In the next phase of the resistance it was clear, even to those who had so far held back, that Hitler could not be eliminated except through a conspiracy, and that the logical inferences would have to be accepted.

Emigration of the Leibholz Family

The two attempts at revolution in 1939 gave the Bonhoeffers some

96. Communication from K. H. Reimer.

slight hope of escaping the domestic consequences of the anti-Aryan legislation, and Dietrich hoped to be relieved of the dilemma of a coming call-up. In the hope that there would be a successful *coup d'état*, they all tried for a long time to find gaps in the web of laws and regulations, so that the Göttingen relatives could slip through them and find some basis for life in their homeland.

In the earlier years, no one in the family ventured to think of what a final separation would mean. There were also practical difficulties about emigration. As to occupation, a lawyer hardly stood as good a chance in an English-speaking foreign country as did, shall we say, a scientist; money and goods could not legally be taken across the frontier. Might it not be better to continue to make shift at home in association with the big family?

It needed only the threat of immediate war in 1938, and the information (from Hans von Dohnanyi) of the coming regulation about first names, to hasten the decision to emigrate, and the preparations for going. Everyone was now convinced that Gerhard Leibholz could no longer be protected in war conditions. Meanwhile a fifth regulation, which was added to the Nuremberg laws, had shut out the 'non-Aryans' from the last professions open to them. *Das Schwarze Korps* wrote that if war broke out, the fate of the Jews would be 'total annihilation'.[97] Was one to believe that, or were there still possibilities of avoiding it, or was one simply to hope for the success of the revolutionary preparations? Dietrich's twin sister Sabine wrote to him on 26th August 1938:

In the last few weeks he[98] has not been able to maintain his usual calm. After all one's nerves become somewhat frayed in time. It is difficult to think out to the end all the decisions that have to be made and that makes one feel on edge . . . So now I have to be more than ever up to the mark, and it is not always an easy matter to keep in one's head such various things as questions of existence and urgent things that have to be provided for, as well as the children's needs and wishes in large and small matters . . . We should so much have liked to see you before we leave.

When the B.B.C. in London announced the first steps towards mobilization in Great Britain—their importance was over-estimated— and there was reason to fear the immediate closing of frontiers, Dietrich Bonhoeffer set off with the Leibholz family and went part of the way with them on 9th September, so that they could cross the frontier near Basle before midnight.

That meant emigration; but they kept up the fiction of a 'journey' before the authorities and officials—just a little in fact, before themselves. The overthrow might come even yet, and perhaps there would again be

97. G. Reitlinger, *Die Endlösung*, 1956, p. 9.
98. G. Leibholz.

a few quieter months that would allow them to live in Göttingen again, as before the September crisis.

But on 5th October all non-Aryans' passports that were not stamped with a 'J' were declared invalid, and the Bonhoeffer parents thereupon telegraphed to the Leibholz family: 'Your coming now unsuitable.'

Dietrich Bonhoeffer tried in every way he could to make things easy for his relatives in London, first by writing to Bishop Bell and Sir Walter Moberley (of Oxford) whom he had got to know in Chamby in 1936. He made use of the old congregations:

Many thanks for your greeting from my former congregation. I am glad you have been well received and have already had your first invitations. When you have settled down a bit there, you like it much better than just at first. For instance, the badly heated rooms are an English infliction that you cannot escape anywhere . . . I hope you will have a good time with really fine weather. That helps very much to cheer you up when you are in London![99]

He soon decided to go to London himself; and, in preparation, he sent more letters than ever before to his old connections at Christmas 1938. On 1st February he wrote his. twin sister a birthday letter with new hopes:

Now, everything has changed. It occurred to me recently that perhaps there really are laws governing the special case of twins—I don't think they always hold good for us—but certain twins often have the same experiences of life, even when they are not living near each other. I must say that seems to be true to a certain extent, in any case when we compare ourselves with the other members of the family. Our recent experiences have at least been different from what we had imagined, although they were not the same in each case. So far we can perhaps understand our ways of life particularly well at present. It is, in fact, really one and the same thing that has so conclusively determined our life and given it the unexpected course. But however that may be, we shall at least think of each other a great deal on the 4th, and we shall promise ourselves less from all kinds of good wishes than from our really standing by one another. I am already very much looking forward to our meeting each other again.

In association with Magdalen College, Oxford, Leibholz finally obtained a grant from the Provisional Ecumenical Council of Churches, his activities including political tutorials and lectures at Oxford.

Gerhard Leibholz's introduction to Bishop Bell happened at a fortunate time, for the latter had been a member of the British House of Lords since July 1938—a fact which gave importance to what he said on political matters just at the time when war was looming up. So it fell out happily that, in relation to events in Germany, Bonhoeffer the theological adviser was now followed by Leibholz the political expert.

99. Letter of 10.11.1938.

During and after the war, Bishop Bell made full use of his analyses and interpretations.[100]

Call-up

The political developments of 1938 seemed to bring nearer a personal decision on the question of military service, a question that for Bonhoeffer had been answered fairly clearly in 1934 and 1935 for the sake of his Christian discipleship. Now the problem was substantially more complicated. In 1938 the threatened summons to the armed forces was the event about which he spoke least. For who in his Church would understand the problems involved? Perhaps if the political development had been more peaceful, he would have been quietly relieved of the need to make a decision, because a few years later he would have been too old for enlistment. But now the preparations for war had begun to move alarmingly fast.

Feeling that he ought to avoid the limelight as far as possible, he gave up plans for a holiday in Italy: 'Our intention not to force ourselves on the attention of the recruiting offices finally kept us away from all plans involving the German frontiers.'[101]

But at that very time, on 3rd November 1938, Bonhoeffer, like everyone else, had to have his place of residence recorded by the police registration authorities in the 'Military Registration Record' (*Wehrstammblatt*). That was not yet a call-up, but he was now obliged to report any change of address and any considerable holiday journeys, and to apply for special permission in case of foreign travel. His mother wrote to him from Berlin on 23rd January 1939:

On our advertising placards there was a notice calling on the 1906 and 1907 classes to register . . . Anyone who has not been called up on or before 15th February has to report. I often wonder whether and how that will affect your journey. We have been with Karl-Friedrich in Leipzig on his fortieth birthday. In the evening we had a very happy time with Heisenberg and his wife.

For his brother's birthday Bonhoeffer wrote to him: 'In some ways I envy you for being forty', referring to the fact that he was not in the classes to be called up.

But in the military sub-district of Schlawe in January things were not moving so fast as in Berlin. The local recruiting station was in the charge of a Major von Kleist, with whom the friends of the same name, and Superintendent Block, could use their influence for Bonhoeffer. So the

---

100. See E. Bethge, 'Gegen den Strom der Zeit'. From a correspondence between the Lord Bishop of Chichester G. K. A. Bell and G. Leibholz during the war years, in *Die moderne Demokratie und ihr Recht. Festschrift für G. Leibholz*, ed. K. D. Bracher, C. Dawson, W. Geiger, R. Smend, 1966, pp. 3 ff.
101. Letter from E. Bethge, 21.8.1938.

possible difficulties over a journey to England were easily obviated, and Bonhoeffer was given official permission to go abroad in March. But a shackle was now attached, and it could not be shaken off.

After his journey to England, Bonhoeffer at once applied for permission to go to America for a year. Instead of that he received, in the middle of May, a summons to report for call-up on 22nd May. But it was a summons that Bonhoeffer had intended to forestall, and so, pressing his application as urgent:

13th April to his parents: 'I may have to go to Niebuhr as early as June. If only it comes off!'

1st May, Niebuhr to Leiper: 'Today I received word from Bonhoeffer saying that time was short. It is necessary to make arrangements, he ought to have a cable as well as a confirming letter.'

5th May to his parents: 'Leave has not yet come through . . . everything is still uncertain.'

11th May, Niebuhr to Lehmann: Bonhoeffer is 'anxious to come to America to evade for the time being a call to the colors . . . There will be some difficulty in getting him out and if he fails he will land in prison.'[102]

In distress, he called on his father to help:

That of itself has nothing to do with my application for leave. The people in the mayor's office work through the call-up business simply according to the lists. For all that, the question of granting the leave is now urgent. As I am not going to Schlawe at all in the next five days, and (after consultation here) I do not want to go there personally unless it is absolutely necessary, I want to ask you, Father, whether you might not be able to enquire of Major von Kleist by letter, or, perhaps more effectively, by telephone, how the matter stands. I have just gone away for the time being, and am waiting urgently for news, as I want to leave as soon as possible. The application for leave was sent off on 23rd April, and contained a request for leave from 1st May 1939 to 1st May 1940. The recommendations were in the form of private letters to v.K., and may not have been sent on to the other authorities . . . I should be very grateful to you if you could find some way or other of pushing the matter forward.[103]

The intervention was successful just in time; the local recruiting station did, in fact, withdraw the order to report, and was prepared to grant formal consent for one year. On 2nd June 1939 Bonhoeffer was able to leave Berlin for the West. His personal decision, and with it a contingent exposure of his church, seemed to be postponed for at least a year.

Otherwise he would have had to decide on 22nd May whether he would allow himself to be posted to an army unit or would appear as a

102. GS I, p. 287, and II. pp. 348 f.
103. Undated letter, 'Saturday' from 'Köslin'.

conscientious objector before a court martial. Hermann Stöhr of the Fellowship of Reconciliation in Stettin had already decided in favour of the former course. A year later Superintendent Block, Major von Kleist, and even his father were no longer of any advantage to him. Having tried to avoid the issue, Bonhoeffer saw his responsibilities in a new light, and availed himself of other helpers.

V ENGLAND, MARCH AND APRIL 1939

Flight

At first, Bonhoeffer had only playfully voiced the idea of staying abroad, as in his question to Sutz about representing Brunner in the professorship at Zürich,[104] and the renewed contact with Paul Lehmann: 'It would be best if you just invited me for one term; that would not be at all bad!'[105] But then came letters from his sister, which could not quite conceal the difficulties of life abroad. Now he at once asked Rieger and Boeckheler, his successor at Sydenham, to invite him to the two London congregations over Christmas and the New Year. Meanwhile, however, it appeared that the parents could meet their emigrant children over the celebrations in Holland, and so the invitations were postponed till March. Finally, Bonhoeffer learnt that Reinhold Niebuhr was to be in Britain just then for the Gifford Lectures, and he wrote to him that he must meet him. He would certainly help him if the English were at a loss to do so.

The practical problems involved in a journey to the West were solved by his sister's letters and by the imminent compulsory registration. When they were settled, he discussed his journey with the ecumenical delegate of the Lutheran Union, Hans Böhm, and asked him for official commissions abroad. Hitherto, whether he was summoned to a conference or sent as a delegate by the Council of Brethren, he had travelled primarily in the service of the ecumenical movement, and only secondarily on his own affairs; now the position was reversed, and it was the official assignments that took second place, though that certainly does not mean that they were unimportant.

On church matters, what disturbed him most were: the question of the oath, the efforts to achieve unity, the treatment of the young 'illegal' pastors, and the reaction to the special prayers and the 'Crystal Night'. In political matters, he was disturbed by the failure to overthrow Hitler, the preparations for war, and the supposed exclusion of Dohnanyi from the Berlin circle. As to personal matters, we have already mentioned the restlessness of life in the collective pastorate, the imminent call-up, and his emigrant sister's fate.

104. GS I, p. 48; cf. Ch. XI, p. 499.
105. GS II, p. 347.

So it is not surprising that Bonhoeffer had on his hands a whole series of pressing and inter-related questions for the future to settle: Must he really wear himself out over those ecclesiastical and national affairs in Germany? To whom, really, were his life's ambitions to be sacrificed? Might he not pursue theology, to which he was particularly devoted, in more wholesome surroundings? Would not the universal Church and its theology benefit more by the free development of his gifts elsewhere? Might there not be a call waiting for him outside, and would one not need just to go out first so as to hear it clearly? Besides that, did not one's own church regard a contingent refusal of military service simply as a perverse and uncooperative line to take? Finally, Bonhoeffer felt more and more that if he remained in Germany, he would be drawn more deeply into the conspiracy against Hitler; and was it right for him as a pastor and theologian to go beyond his position of accessory to the facts and take an active part in such a conspiracy? Ought he not rather to try to avoid the dilemma? Everything suggested that he might be able eventually to arrive at a definite conclusion on these matters more easily outside Germany.

To describe Bonhoeffer's travels of 1939 as 'flight' is to use hindsight. He himself did not use the term, either to his friends—which of them knew the whole tangle of arguments and ought to have told him that to take such a step was an evasion?—or to his relatives, although they would have been delighted if it had been so and he had actually remained abroad. For all that, he himself was by no means entirely clear about the crucial reasons for those journeys.

While he was in England, he came closest to the real facts of the case in his letter (which was something in the nature of a confession) to Bishop Bell; but even here his presentation includes only a part of the whole:

I am thinking of leaving Germany sometime. The main reason is the compulsory military service to which the men of my age (1906) will be called up this year. It seems to me conscientiously impossible to join in a war under the present circumstances. On the other hand the Confessional [sic] Church as such has not taken any definite attitude in this respect and probably cannot take it as things are. So I should cause a tremendous damage to my brethren if I would make a stand on this point which would be regarded by the régime as typical of the hostility of our Church towards the State. Perhaps the worst thing of all is the military oath which I should have to swear. So I am rather puzzled in this situation, and perhaps even more because I feel, it is really only on Christian grounds that I find it difficult to do military service under the present conditions, *and yet there are only very few friends who would approve of my attitude.*[106] In spite of much reading and thinking concerning this matter I have not yet made up my mind what I should do under different circumstances. But actually as things are I should have to do

106. Bonhoeffer's italics.

violence to my Christian conviction, if I would take up arms 'here and now'.[107]

Bonhoeffer, then, was seeking a solution that would not make the Confessing Church suffer through a personal decision which concerned his own conscience. The expedient of going away for a time might well please the brethren after their experiences with Barth's letter to Hromádka. That is how he argued before the Council of Brethren, from which he had to get leave of absence. That is also how he put the case to Niebuhr: 'The *Bruderrat* [Council of Brethren] of the Confessional [sic] Church would like to have him evade the issue.'[108]

A few weeks later Bonhoeffer was able to report to Dr. Leiper with quite a different emphasis; that was in June, when he was already thinking of going back to Germany:

At first they[109] were very reluctant to let me go at all, since they are in need of teachers. It was only when I expressed my hope that I could be of some use to them by establishing contacts with American theologians and churchmen . . . that they gave me leave. So from the point of view of the Confessional [sic] Church my trip to America was meant to be an ecumenic link between our isolated Church in Germany and our friends over here . . . My personal question and difficulty with regard to military service etc. came in only as a second consideration. Of course, my colleagues were glad, that I would be able to postpone my decision for at least one year.[110]

This letter certainly gave a correct account of the Council of Brethren's real views.

Thus for some time Bonhoeffer reversed for himself again and again the order of priorities that were to be decisive, so as to test the strength of each motive. It was only during his stay in America, on this second journey, that he could see for himself plainly why he had gone. Then he committed the facts of the case—not, indeed, using the word 'flight', but the thing was plain enough logically—to his diary. And years afterwards, when he was in prison, he wrote that that return from abroad really meant something different from a return home at the end of a normally planned mission. Then he wrote serenely: 'that I have not for a moment regretted coming back in 1939.'[111]

• Bishop Bell's Advice

On 10th March 1939 Bonhoeffer and E. Bethge took the night train for

---

107. Written in English, 25.3.1939 in London, GS I, pp. 281 f.
108. Niebuhr to Leiper, GS I, p. 287.
109. The Council of Brethren.
110. Letter of 15.6.1939, GS I, p. 316.
111. LPP, pp 115, 149.

Ostend together. He could not sleep till the train had passed the German frontier controls; he already knew that Hitler's attack on Prague was imminent, and what was military leave of absence worth then?

When he reached London, he arranged at once to visit the Bishop of Chichester. This time, in contrast to his former visits, he wanted to approach him about his personal affairs. This course of proceedings has no parallel in Bonhoeffer's life. In 1931 he was regretting never having met the 'elderly man', whose directions he might have felt to be valid. Now he was seeking the man who, while standing in another world, could listen to him calmly and yet realize the force of the alternatives: Confessing Church and family, pacifism and theology, political conspiracy and ecumenity. In his family he could expect no close commitment to ecclesiastical theology, and among his friends of the Council of Brethren no freedom in relation to political matters. Bell understood both. In recent years, indeed, Bonhoeffer had been used to discussing things critically himself with the House of Brethren and to finding commitment there, as well as relief, in personal confession. For years he had suffered no lack of friendship with people of his own age or younger. For the moment that had provided all he needed.

Now he confided in the older man who, as he knew, understood how to pray and how to demand what was necessary. He wanted to hear his advice—possibly even his Yes or No. But he carried out the great decision later, entirely alone.

All that we know about the conversation between the bishop and Bonhoeffer comes from the latter's preliminary letter and the bishop's comment on it in a later lecture.[112] In his letter Bonhoeffer told the bishop that he was planning to leave Germany and to go on a mission 'somewhere where service is really wanted', and yet where he could at the same time—perhaps as an ecumenical secretary?—serve the Confessing Church. Bell probably relieved Bonhoeffer's conscience about a temporary withdrawal from Germany. Bonhoeffer, who of course discussed with him the ticklish problems of the relationship between the Confessing Church and the ecumenical movement and found him sympathetic, was very pleased about the renewed contact:

Before returning to Germany I just wish to thank you once again for the great help you gave me in our talk at Chichester. I do not know what will be the outcome of it all, but it means much to me to realize that you see the great conscientious difficulties with which we are faced.[113]

On 3rd April Bonhoeffer went with Leibholz and Rieger to Bexhill in Sussex, where Reinhold Niebuhr was on holiday.[114] There was plenty to talk about, on theological and personal matters, from the time between

112. GS I, pp. 279-82, 400.
113. Letter of 13.4.1939, GS I, p. 286.
114. J. Rieger, 'Contacts with London', IKDB, p. 100.

1931 and 1939; for since Paul Lehmann had given Bonhoeffer Niebuhr's *Moral Man and Immoral Society* in 1933, Bonhoeffer had seen little from that quarter. Niebuhr was most helpful, and at once got an invitation for Bonhoeffer to visit his friends Henry Smith Leiper at the Federal Council in New York, and Paul Lehmann at Elmhurst College. That at once set the course clearly for deliberations as to how Bonhoeffer was to escape from his dilemma in Germany, and any discussion of other matters was cut short.

Official Tasks

Although the immediate occasion of the journey to England was Bonhoeffer's personal affairs, most of his time on the island was claimed by problems regarding the Confessing Church.

At a conference of German pastors in Rieger's Church of St. George he gave the principal lecture, on 'Law and Gospel in Pastoral Work'. Some of his colleagues of 1934 were not there, as they now had other views; with others Bonhoeffer had an affectionate reunion—with Hildebrandt and W. Büsing, H. H. Kramm and the retired legation councillor Adolf Freudenberg, who had now emigrated too, and become a theologian. Meanwhile Bishop Bell had brought over a great many non-Aryan pastors from the German Evangelical Church—the number of families had now reached forty. After the November pogrom he had already taken care to have the necessary funds ready for them in advance, and he had undertaken to the British Government to be responsible for them. Bonhoeffer had joined them in a reception committee (formed by Dr. Bell) for non-Aryan Christians in Bloomsbury House, with Barbara Murray and Helen Roberts as hostesses. The tone of the meeting was greatly affected by the action of 'taking Bohemia and Moravia into the protection of the German Reich', as Hitler called his occupation of Prague on 15th March. What new refugee problem would that create, and what helplessness on the part of the Allies would it reveal? There was bewilderment, especially among the older members of the German congregations, that Neurath, formerly an active member of the Sydenham congregation, was now to be *'Reichsprotektor'* in the *Hradschin*.

In accordance with his mission from the Berlin Lutheran Union, Bonhoeffer took great pains, in those weeks, to foster the ecumenical contacts about which he had spoken to Böhm before leaving Berlin. He was to explore the possibilities of a more adequate safeguarding of the Confessing Church's interests by the ecumenical associations, discuss proposals for this, and possibly bring in one of the brethren who had emigrated, such as Hildebrandt. Since the failure of the preliminary negotiations for Oxford in 1937—really since Chamby in 1936— precious time had elapsed, during which the Confessing Church as such had remained excluded from conferences and sessions. In the meantime, however, the provisional World Council of Churches had been formed, and important questions of personnel settled. The attendance of representatives of associated organizations, such as M. Diestel of the World Alliance in Larvik, and certain professors at the theologians' commissions, or Hanns Lilje who represented the Lutheran Council, had not been arranged by the governing body of the Confessing Church. The Utrecht Conference of May 1938 had laid down the basis of the Provisional Committee of the World Council of Churches without any official German representation. Schönfeld and Siegmund-Schultze had been present, and Bishop Marahrens should have officially represented the German Evangelical Church, but had not taken part. In view of the difficult situation of the Church in Germany, no other invitations had been sent there. There had been a similar state of affairs at the second session of the Provisional Committee at St. Germain in January 1939, where Schönfeld's research department had held a two-day session of the committee, to which Gerstenmaier and Menn had been invited. Thus, although the Church's External Affairs Office could not just emerge here, there, and everywhere as it liked, its people could at least act and present their points of view as 'visitors' here and there, without being bothered by the claims of the Council of Brethren or the Lutheran Union. Thus, Canon L. Hodgson negotiated with Heckel and Krummacher about filling the German places on the 'Faith and Order' research committee. In 1938 Schönfeld asked Gerstenmaier whether, if need be, he (Schönfeld) should represent the German Evangelical Church on it. Such letters asking for representation were not received by Böhm from Geneva. Since Utrecht it was W. A. Visser 't Hooft, and not H. L. Henriod, who had been working as General Secretary at Geneva, and that impeded Heckel's attempts to get his office for the German Evangelical Church to the conference table with Schönfeld's help. But for the Confessing Church the change was not at first of much consequence.

In that situation Bonhoeffer took action at once, first with Dr. Bell, Canon Hodgson, and Visser 't Hooft. His conversation with Dr. Bell was soon settled. Hodgson visited Bonhoeffer by arrangement, Visser 't Hooft he met by chance. So on the one hand the tiresome problems reappeared, and on the other hand new and hopeful perspectives opened out.

Canon Hodgson

On 29th March Bonhoeffer went to Oxford with the Leibholz family. While Hans Herbert Kramm showed the family over the University, and Gerhard Leibholz met Beveridge the political economist, Dietrich paid a long visit to Canon Leonard Hodgson, the General Secretary of

'Faith and Order'. Bonhoeffer's introductory letter and Hodgson's memorandum of the following day give a detailed picture of that second attempt to make the standpoint of each clear to the other.[115]

Bonhoeffer proposed that the Confessing Church should be permanently represented outside Germany. In his letter to Dr. Bell he had described the inadequacy of the Geneva representation even more bluntly.[116] With Canon Hodgson he stressed that the matter had to be dealt with very quickly, as the political situation might soon make that visit the last. For 'representation' he no doubt had in mind Franz Hildebrandt, who had not yet found any permanent post in England, would have had the advantage of being free from difficulties over passport and foreign currency, and was best-informed about the German Church.

Bonhoeffer's proposals did not fall on fruitful soil; they came to grief, as in 1935, over legalistic regulations, which Hodgson carefully and patiently enumerated. In contrast to 1935, Bonhoeffer now raised no claims to exclusiveness, but made what sounded more like a call for help. Canon Hodgson offered to invite the provisional leaders of the Confessing Church to the summer conference at Clarens as 'visitors', and to give them as friendly a welcome as that given to the Reich Church. Bonhoeffer found this gesture of impartiality difficult to stomach; and it was, in fact, very one-sided, as Heckel and his representatives could be certain of their passports and foreign currency, whereas foreign travel would always be a more difficult problem for representatives of the Lutheran Union. Canon Hodgson knew this quite well, as we shall see later.

Canon Hodgson's memorandum shows with depressing plainness how tragically the situation of the German Church had developed, and how helplessly the ecumenical movement had reacted in face of it. That unhappy church had now received another blow, and the ecumenical organizations were not capable, as such, of relaxing their well-organized restrictions. Hodgson was again being asked to do far too much:

We are advised that at the present time there is no such Church (i.e. a body having full confidence of the whole church, and able to nominate representatives in its name), and that we must not attempt to treat the different groups within that Church independently as if they were separate churches.[117]

In effect, the attempt to be so painfully correct as not to spoil the thing for either side shut the Confessing Church out. Bonhoeffer had to tell the provisional leaders that the appointment of a permanent representative of the Confessing Church to 'Faith and Order' was out of the question, that they could, at most, send a 'visitor' to conferences and sessions, and that 'Faith and Order' was prepared to provide the

115. GS I, pp. 282-6; cf. Ch. IX, pp. 398 f.
116. GS I, pp. 280 f.
117. GS I, p. 284.

foreign currency. That actually meant, however, that the delegates to the conferences would be appointed as before, and that their information would continue to be one-sided.

Consequences

Canon Hodgson reported on his conversation with Bonhoeffer to his chairman and the Geneva headquarters (among others). So it did not escape Schönfeld how Bonhoeffer, after a period of silence, had again crossed his path—this was the last acute crisis between the two before, as the war went on, there was a radical change, and Schönfeld took an interest in Bonhoeffer. How Schönfeld saw things is revealed by his letter[118] of 24th February 1939 to Bachmann, who was a young colleague of Heckel and was staying in Cambridge for a time. Schönfeld urged him to take every opportunity in personal conversations to point out what efforts Gerstenmaier and the other gentlemen in the External Affairs Office, including Bishop Heckel, were making on behalf of the ecumenical work; and he asked him to keep in mind that assertions to the contrary were rife, partly because of inadequate information about what the department was actually accomplishing.

A few weeks later Schönfeld's friends abroad found their support for the work of the External Affairs Office made very difficult when, in view of ecumenical protests, Heckel came out openly in favour of the German Christians' Godesberg Declaration.[119] But Bonhoeffer was thinking of that close association of Schönfeld's office in Geneva with the Church's External Affairs Office, when he wrote to Dr. Bell:

I am afraid we shall very soon be cut off entirely from our brethren abroad . . . Frankly and with all due respect, the German representatives in Geneva simply cannot represent the cause of the Confessional [sic] Church. So there is a real vacancy . . .[120]

Unlike Dr. Bell, William Temple apparently never came into anything like a close relationship to the Confessing Church. He did not meet Dietrich Bonhoeffer, nor did the latter get as far as looking him up in that month of March 1939; the shift of emphasis in the ecumenical movement since Oxford and Edinburgh, and Temple's greatly enhanced prestige, may have escaped him. Since Utrecht, Temple had been chairman of the Provisional Committee for the World Council, with Mott, Germanos, and Boegner as vice-chairmen. Till then Temple had been more closely associated with 'Faith and Order', and so had never really been confronted with Bonhoeffer's ideas and wishes.

As Temple had hardly had anything to do with the German church

118. Preserved in the Geneva archives.
119. See Ch. XI, pp. 549 f.
120. GS I, pp. 280 f.

struggle before the Second World War, his judgements were sometimes strange, as was the case now. He approved, by return of post, Hodgson's memorandum about the negotiations with Bonhoeffer—'Your statement is entirely exact'; but he added: 'I am becoming more than ever eager to raise the question of putting Heckel into the Provisional Committee.'[121] That, indeed, was going too far for Hodgson, who was better informed; he replied that he could quite well understand Temple's opinion, but 'I wish some other method', as Heckel had been brought into the Provisional Committee of the World Council, and he then gives new and interesting glimpses of his conversation with Bonhoeffer:

It was quite clear to me in my conversation with Bonhoeffer last week that any action on our part which gave any kind of official status to Wahl, Heckel, Krummacher or any of that group, would be regarded as a partisan move unless equivalent status were given simultaneously to Boehm or one of his colleagues. I told him something of our discussion last year and of the argument that the appointment of Heckel would be made possible by the attendance at meetings of Marahrens as well, and quite clearly he did not regard Marahrens as being sufficiently 'Confessionalist' to balance Heckel. He felt that on the essential decisive issues they were both on the wrong side. If we had two places open and could put on both Heckel and a Confessionalist it would be another matter. As it is I fear that the proposal to put on Heckel only may both internally divide our ranks and externally produce an impression of partisanship . . . Might it not be possible for the Provisional Committee to issue such an invitation (invited to sit with the Prov. Com. like Dusen, Henriod, Keller) both to Heckel and a Confessionalist leader? Even if only Heckel could get the passport and wherewithal to attend, the Committee would nevertheless have maintained its impartiality . . .[122]

Temple stated again how he had come to make his proposal, without insisting on it:

I am certainly not going to press this matter against your judgement, but Paton, who was lately here, told me that he thought Visser 't Hooft now agrees with Schönfeld that all the groups in Germany do accept Heckel as their channel of communication with the outside world. It was because of this that I raised the question again . . .[123]

Paton's information possibly went back to the lengthy negotiations that emanated from the 'Cassel group' and had as their objective a unified representation of German church circles, Lutherans and members of the Confessing Church—they had suffered new setbacks and had gone to pieces in 1938; Bonhoeffer did not think much of them. We can see once again from this correspondence how neutral Temple and Hodgson, for 'Faith and Order', remained with regard to the problem of who was to sit as representative of the German Evangelical Church in the

121. Letter of 31.3.1939; on the whole of this correspondence see MW V, X, pp. 1-3.
122. Letter of 1.4.1939.
123. Letter of 3.4.1939.

Provisional Council. Marahrens still seemed to them to be Heckel's vis-à-vis, or alternatively the representative of the Confessing Church. It is true that only a few weeks later Temple signed a protest, which had been initiated by Visser 't Hooft, against the Godesberg Declaration. Temple was bound to see that in this Heckel compromised himself heavily as a 'channel of communication', and finally that Marahrens, too, signed a somewhat watered down Godesberg Declaration.

The Godesberg Declaration

Immediately after Bonhoeffer's Oxford conversation and the correspondence between the secretary and chairman, the official journal of the German Evangelical Church published on 4th April 1939 the 'Godesberg Declaration' signed by Dr. Werner. It included the following:

[National Socialism continues] the work of Martin Luther on the ideological and political side, [and thus helps], in its religious aspect, the recovery of a true understanding of the Christian faith . . . The Christian faith is the unbridgeable religious contrast to Judaism . . . Supra-national and international churchism of a Roman Catholic or world-Protestant character is a political degeneration of Christianity. A fruitful development of genuine Christian faith is possible only within the given orders of creation.[124]

These statements, with their bias towards a nationalistic church, appeared in the official journal with the announcement of an 'institute for investigating and eliminating Jewish influence on the church life of the German people'.

The 'Provisional Committee' of the World Council of Churches thereupon issued to its member churches a manifesto signed by Temple, Boegner, Paton, and Visser 't Hooft. Visser 't Hooft told the present writer orally in 1961 that it had been arranged by him, Visser 't Hooft, drafted by Barth, and corrected by Temple. It included the following:

The national structure of the Christian Church is not a necessary element of its life . . . Recognition of spiritual unity . . . without regard to race, nation, or sex, belongs, however, to the nature of the Church. The Gospel of Jesus Christ is the fulfilment of the Jewish hope . . . The Christian Church . . . rejoices in the maintenance of community with those of the Jewish race who have accepted the Gospel . . . The Church [has] to proclaim his [i.e. Christ's] lordship over all spheres of life, including politics and ideology.[125]

On 6th May the Church External Affairs Office sent, with Heckel's signature, a telegram addressed to the 'Provisional Committee' at Geneva:

Expect immediate withdrawal of manifesto to churches, which far exceeds authority, proceeds from wrong judgement of entire situation of Church in

124. J. Beckmann, op. cit., pp. 293 ff.
125. A manifesto to the Christian churches, in the Geneva archives.

Germany and represents an intolerable interference in Germany's internal affairs. German Evangelical Church.

Was that the 'channel of communication with the outside world' accepted by all groups in Germany?

Visser 't Hooft

Whereas the prearranged meeting at Oxford proved to be both hesitant and reserved, the other informal meeting at Paddington station, arranged almost on the spot, was more promising.

So far, Bonhoeffer had never met Visser 't Hooft, although he had known his essay on the 'Social Gospel' since 1930, and the two had often been near each other at neighbouring conferences. At any rate, Bonhoeffer knew that this man heartily rejected, as he himself did, the German creation theology. Now Visser 't Hooft had moved up into a key position, if not *the* key position, of the ecumenical movement. In May 1938 Temple had been able to arrange definitely that the General Secretary of the provisional World Council should be, not the experienced Henriod, but the young Dutchman, with William Paton and Henry Leiper as co-secretaries.

That change brought with it an increasingly marked change of atmosphere at the Geneva headquarters. Visser 't Hooft had a complete mastery of German (among other things), and was acquainted with German theological literature. His Barthian theological ancestry and his extensive visits to Germany made it possible for him to judge the forces in the church struggle from a fresh point of view. That became clear to everyone when he pushed forward the provisional World Council's manifesto of protest about the Godesberg Declaration so energetically.

Bonhoeffer was in London when he heard that the new General Secretary was coming to the country. 'Would you kindly tell Visser 't Hooft that I am very anxious to see him during his stay in London?'[126] He was so sure that he and Visser 't Hooft would see eye to eye that he also wanted to discuss his own affairs with him. So he met him at Paddington a few days after his visit to Canon Hodgson.

The long conversation with a man six years his senior relieved Bonhoeffer of his fears that the Confessing Church was already written off at Geneva. Two years after that first meeting, the confidence that it produced was still to be of great importance; but even now they discussed, not merely the question of his Church's representation in Geneva, but matters of war and peace, and of theological and political ethics. Directly after the war, Visser 't Hooft wrote of the meeting:

We had heard a great deal about each other, but it was surprising how

126. To Bishop Bell, 25.3.1939, GS I, p. 280.

quickly we were able to get beyond the first stage of merely feeling our way, into the more intimate areas of real talks—that, in fact, he was soon treating me as an old friend . . . We walked up and down the platform for a long time. He described the situation of his Church and country. He spoke in a way that was remarkably free from illusions, and sometimes almost clairvoyant, about the coming war, which would start soon, probably in the summer, and which would cause the Confessing Church to be forced into even greater distress . . . Had not the time now come to refuse to serve a government that was heading straight for war and breaking all the Commandments? But what would be the consequences of such an attitude on the Confessing Church? I remember his acute questions better than his answers; but I think I learnt more from his questions than he did from my answers. In the impenetrable world between 'Munich' and 'Warsaw', in which hardly anyone ventured to formulate the actual problems clearly, that questioning voice was a release.[127]

The reason why Visser 't Hooft remembered the questions better than the answers may be that Bonhoeffer was then only seeking answers to questions he had raised. And he tried these out on several people before he began to give his own, really original, answers.

The balance of ecumenical forces was changing considerably, but certain old laws remained effective. In Utrecht in 1938, 'Life and Work' had at once handed over its responsibilities to the provisional World Council and its General Secretaries. Visser 't Hooft, as secretary of the provisional World Council, became responsible at the same time for 'Life and Work' as long as it still existed. On the other hand, when the formation of the provisional World Council was approved, 'Faith and Order' kept its independent organization and executive, with Canon Hodgson remaining its General Secretary. Among the successful campaigners for that independence was the aged Headlam, who had written to Dorothy Buxton during the great wave of arrests in 1937 that it was nonsense to talk about a persecution of Christians in Germany.

Thus Bonhoeffer saw the new General Secretary of 'Life and Work' continue what Bell and Ammundsen had already begun, namely, to support spiritually, however interruptedly, the Confessing Church 'which was felt to represent the whole Church of Christ in its battle for the purity and truth of the Christian message', as Visser 't Hooft put it in the *Geschichte der Ökumene*.[128]

On the other hand, he saw how the policy of strict non-obligation pursued by 'Faith and Order' benefited the Reich Church's representatives. It had again become clear that, in view of German conditions, no one could avoid taking sides, however anxious he might be to do so. If he tried to reserve his judgement, he nevertheless gave support to one side against the other.

After his visits to Dr. Bell and his meeting with Visser 't Hooft, Bon-

127. W. A. Visser 't Hooft, *Zeugnis eines Boten*, pp. 6 f.
128. Rouse-Neill, op. cit., p. 707.

hoeffer was at least more confident that the excluded Confessing Church would keep its echo in the ecumenical world. When he met Visser 't Hooft for the second time—two years later in Geneva—it was as if they had been intimate friends for a long time.

Departure

Bonhoeffer stayed longer in London than he had planned, more than five weeks, although he soon finished what he had intended to do. The reason was that he thought that war might break out at any moment. He was impressed by the complete change of public opinion in London on Hitler's abrupt breach of the Munich agreement on 15th March; everyone approved of the British Government's answer in the form of a guarantee for Poland.

Bonhoeffer wondered whether he ought not to let himself be caught by the war while he was near his sister in England. 'The main question that is rather holding me back is whether I am to wait here for Uncle Rudi', he wrote to his parents on 13th April. But they reassured him, saying that it had not yet got as far as 'Uncle Rudi's' coming.

While he was in London, he saw the film *Queen Victoria* with Adolf Wohlbrück. He confessed that when he saw that continuous history of the country that was now threatened, he could not keep back tears of anger.

He went back to Berlin on 18th April. As he was coming home, Hitler was holding a menacing birthday parade in front of the Technical College in Charlottenburg. In the official journal of the German Evangelical Church there appeared over Dr. Werner's signature

[We celebrate] with exultant joy our Führer's fiftieth birthday. In him God has given the German people a real miracle-worker . . . Let our thanks be the resolute and inflexible will not to disappoint . . . our Führer and the great historic hour.[129]

But the *Junge Kirche*, too, which had formerly been so brave, wrote:

It has today become evident to everyone without exception that the figure of the Führer, powerfully fighting his way through old worlds, seeing with his mind's eye what is new and compelling its realization, is named on the few pages of world history that are reserved for the initiators of a new epoch . . . The figure of the Führer has brought a new obligation for the Church too.[130]

VI AMERICA, JUNE AND JULY 1939

Only a month and a half after coming home from England, Bonhoeffer left Germany again. May was filled with efforts to forestall the military

129. J. Beckmann, op. cit., p. 297.
130. JK 1939, No. 8, p. 309.

authorities' order to report at the recruiting station, and to convince the
Council of Brethren of the Old Prussian Union, which had no wish to
give up one of its few theological teachers, one who held uncompromisingly to Barmen and Dahlem, that it would be right and proper for him
to go to America. But the Council of Brethren had never liked to refuse
Bonhoeffer a wish. This time there were three reasons for thinking that
the journey would be advisable: first, because it might be able to do
something to mitigate the ecumenical isolation of the Confessing Church;
secondly, Bonhoeffer's old maxim that a church was in a bad way if it
could no longer grant people leave for carrying out special missions, as
he had arranged for Ebeling;[131] and thirdly, there was the hope of once
again avoiding a decision to refuse military service if he were called up.

Eventual Departure

Bonhoeffer and his friends might well have been relieved when the
journey began at the Tempelhof airfield on 2nd June. Everything had
turned out well; he would see the Leibholz family in London, and then,
with his brother Karl-Friedrich, who had been invited to lecture in
Chicago, he would begin the journey across the Atlantic on board the
Bremen. In addition, May had brought no worsening of the international
political situation.

But the departure was becoming more difficult than one liked to
admit. For the first time Bonhoeffer handed over a will to Bethge, and
things did not stand so well even with his church tasks in Germany
as he would have liked on leaving.

Up to his leaving, no substitute had been found for taking charge
of the collective pastorate. For the unknown person who would take his
place in Sigurdshof he left a note on the table: 'To my successor. He
will find here: 1. one of the finest tasks in the Confessing Church . . .'
To requests about the subjects of instruction he added: 'He is asked . . .
to go out walking with the brethren as much as possible, or to be with
them in some other way.'[132]

It was not till weeks later that Hellmut Traub, one of Karl Barth's
former students, came to take up a shuttle service of teaching between
Köslin and Sigurdshof. But unfortunately Bonhoeffer did not get news
of this for some weeks, and he was still worrying about it in New York
when his mind ought to have been free to think of other things.

To add to this, just about the time he was leaving, the church struggle
was being intensified: On 1st June Werner stopped the grants towards
the pastors' stipends in parishes whose pastors still did not make and
hand over the collections according to his official plan but dealt with
them according to that of the Confessing Church. On 2nd June he put

131. See Ch. X, p. 473.
132. GS II, pp. 551 f.

Martin Niemöller, who was in a concentration camp, on the retired list. While the small minority within the Confessing Church was thus being further deprived of its rights, the majority was making efforts to accommodate itself to the new language. On 31st May the church leaders' conference endorsed a declaration addressed to Kerrl and signed by Marahrens, Wurm, Meiser, and others, laying down the alterations subject to which it would acquiesce in the Godesberg Declaration. The statement remained that the Evangelical Church directs its members 'to join fully and devotedly in the Führer's national political constructive work . . . In the national sphere of life there must be a serious and responsible racial policy of maintaining the purity of our nation'.[133] So Bonhoeffer was plagued, from the very beginning of the journey, by the thought of the people who were left behind:

My thoughts are split between yourselves and the future . . . Greet all the brethren; they will be at evening prayers now.

So far I am still surprised that everything has turned out like this. I am already looking forward to your coming to see me.[134]

On board ship he wrote, referring to the *Losung*[135] for 8th June ('Judge rightly'):

That I beg of you, brethren at home. I do not want to be spared in your thoughts.

Great programmes always simply lead us to where we are; but we ought to be found only where he [God] is. We can no longer, in fact, be anywhere else than where he is. Whether it is you working over there, or I working in America, we are all only where he is. He takes us with him. Or have I, after all, avoided the place where he is? The place where he is for me? No: God says, thou art my servant.

And on the day before he landed at New York: 'If only the doubts as to one's own way were overcome.'[136]

As he had done on long journeys in previous years, he now kept a diary[137] with short notes on the day's *Losung*. It gives an impressive insight into his inward conflicts about the way that he was required to take.

Uneasy Arrival

Instead of putting him inwardly at ease, the arrival in New York accen-

133. J. Beckmann, op. cit., pp. 300 f.
134. To E. Bethge, 4. and 6.6.1939 from London, GS I, pp. 291 f.; he was thinking of getting Bethge to come over later.
135. *Die täglichen Losungen und Lehrtexte der Brüdergemeinde*, published yearly since 1731.
136. GS I, pp. 293 f.
137. GS I, pp. 292-315.

tuated his disquieting misgivings. There is no doubt that he was received with nothing but generosity, affection, and helpfulness. Leiper, the Executive Secretary of the Federal Council of Churches, who remembered him from Gland, Sofia, and Fanö, and had always been on his and Monod's side there, was looking forward to his coming: 'I know him well and am keen about him. I shall certainly be glad to do anything I can to help him,' he had replied to Niebuhr.[138] And to Cavert he wrote:

Knowing Bonhoeffer very well, I was struck with the peculiar fitness of the man for just the thing we had been discussing and immediately called up Dr. Paul Tillich who had been appointed with me as committee to find a man. Tillich was even more enthusiastic about Bonhoeffer than I and stated his conviction that he was exactly the right person for this delicate and difficult task . . . His skill and aptitude in pastoral work are exceptional.[139]

But the short notice of the invitation to America, and the caution that had to be observed when writing by post, had caused misunderstandings on both sides and mistakes about the basic requirements. Bonhoeffer's own uncertainty, which at first he did not admit to himself, made him want too much; he wanted to go, but he did not want to slam all the doors behind him. How were the New York friends to understand that, after Niebuhr had wired to them that Bonhoeffer was in danger and must be rescued?

It was only gradually that Bonhoeffer realized that the proposals that were meant to help him had come from four different places (and how this had come about), and that the proposed projects were, in part, hardly compatible with his ideas:

The first proposal, to appoint him to attend the summer conferences of the Student Christian Movement from June onwards, soon fell through. The second proposal was made by Union Theological Seminary; its president, Dr. Coffin, invited him to lecture at the traditional summer course in July and August. That invitation had been the first to reach Bonhoeffer, and had created the possibility of his being freed from the army recruiting office. At first, too, it gave substance to the picture of the future that he had imagined, that would 'give me an opportunity of seeing a good deal of the theological schools'.[140] He began to prepare for the task.

Thirdly, Paul Lehmann had promised to arrange for him to give courses of lectures at various colleges and universities. The proposal was brought forward in June, and was given a very promising reception, but by that time Bonhoeffer was already making ready to go back home.

The fourth proposal became the crucial one; it envisaged that the Federal Council should employ Bonhoeffer for the New York refugees

138. GS II, p. 350.
139. Letter of 31.5.1939, GS I, p. 290.
140. GS I, p. 318.

and appoint him to denominational conferences and summer camps. In agreement with van Dusen and S. McCrea Cavert, Leiper planned a sphere of activity that would have definitely engaged Bonhoeffer for three years. That plan reached Bonhoeffer just before he left Berlin, but was not clearly worded and seemed to ratify the second proposal: 'important combination post theological lectureship and church work at summer conferences and universities'.[141] What that really meant, namely work among refugees, could not, of course, be openly telegraphed to Berlin.

It was not till after his arrival that Bonhoeffer learnt that he was to be entrusted with the care of emigrants in New York, on behalf of the 'American Committee for Christian German refugees in the City of New York'. But to accept such a post would have at once ruled out any return to Germany, so on 13th June, after his first meeting with Leiper, he wrote in his diary:

My starting-point for everything is that I intend to go back in one year at the latest. Surprise. But I am quite clear that I must go back.[142]

And with that there began the inward conflict that he fought out in the days following—without consultation, and without news from Germany—in the guests' room of Union Theological Seminary, the so-called 'Prophets' Chamber', during his stay in President Coffin's country house, and on his way in the streets of New York. On the evening of 13th June, at Dr. Coffin's house in the luxuriant landscape of Lakeville, he wrote down:

With all this, there is only Germany lacking, the brethren. The first lonely hours are difficult. I do not know why I am here, whether it is wise, whether the result will be worth while . . . Now almost a fortnight has gone without my knowing what is happening there. It is almost unbearable . . .

On 14th June:

Prayers. The short prayer—the whole family kneels down—in which we remembered the German brethren, almost overwhelmed me.

On 15th June:

My thoughts about Germany have not left me since yesterday evening. I should not have thought it possible for anyone of my age, after so many years abroad, to be so terribly homesick . . . This inactivity, or activity, as the case may be, has really become simply unbearable to us when we think of the brethren and the precious time. The whole weight of self-reproach because of a wrong decision comes back and almost chokes one.[143]

On the same day he wrote Dr. Leiper a long letter to indicate in advance his points of view for the definitive conversation that they were

141. GS II, p. 349.
142. GS I, p. 296.
143. GS I, pp. 297 f.

to have on the 20th about his future. The way back, he said, must remain open. 'I must not for the sake of loyalty to the Confessing Church accept a post which on principle would make my return to Germany impossible'; his question was whether the work could not at least be organized under a name that would omit the 'refugees' in the title; secondly, he said, he had come to get acquainted with theological training centres, and he wanted to keep time for this; moreover, the post in question ought to be filled by a genuine refugee; he (Bonhoeffer) would not on any account stand in the way of any such person who had not the same kind of opportunities for work as he.[144]

Those considerations meant that Bonhoeffer no longer felt indifferent, as he had felt only two months before in England, whether the war came while he was abroad. On 16th June he noted: 'Disquieting political news from Japan. If trouble comes now, I shall go right back to Germany. I cannot stay out here alone; I am quite clear about this, for, after all, over there is where I live.'[145]

The 20th June

Then came the 20th June 1939, the day that decided Bonhoeffer's future. He probably suspected that it would. On the previous evening he walked aimlessly about Times Square; then he wrote down:

No news from Germany all day, by any post; waiting in vain. It is no use getting angry . . . I want to know what is happening to the work over there, whether it is all going well or whether I am needed. I want a sign from over there for tomorrow's decisive talk; perhaps it is just as well it has not come.[146]

The next day he went to see Henry Leiper of the Federal Council of Churches. Leiper had already cleared the first thousand dollars for the new work, but Bonhoeffer declined. Leiper felt that he had been let down. In the evening Bonhoeffer wrote in his diary:

Went to see Leiper, and made my decision; I declined. He was obviously disappointed and perhaps a little upset. It probably means more to me than I can take in at the moment. Only God knows. It is strange that I am never quite clear about the motives that underlie my decisions. Is that a sign of vagueness, of intellectual dishonesty, or a sign that we are led on beyond what we can discern, or is it both? . . . Today's *Losung* is terribly hard about God's incorruptible judgement. He certainly sees how personal a matter today's decision is, and how full of anxiety, however brave it may appear. The reasons that one gives to others and to oneself for an action are certainly inadequate. We can, in fact, justify anything; but in the last resort we are acting from a plane that is hidden from us; and so we can only ask God to judge and forgive us . . . At the end of the day I can only ask that God may

144. GS I, pp. 316-19.
145. GS I, pp. 299 f.
146. GS I, p. 302.

judge this day, and all the decisions, mercifully. It is in his hands now.[147]

Bonhoeffer had to make the great decision of his life entirely alone. Paul Lehmann, who with his warmth and wisdom meant most of all to him in America, was not in New York. The friends at home were too busy; they did not write in time, and probably did not even know what was at stake for him.

Although Bonhoeffer had made up his mind, he was assailed by new objections in the days that followed. Only now could he speak frankly about his questioning and what had been behind one wish or another:

My decision is, of course, followed by further thoughts. One could, in fact, have argued quite differently: after all, this is where I am (perhaps the mis-understanding[148] itself was a leading?); they have told me that it was like an answer to prayer when I was announced; they would be glad to have me; they do not understand why I refuse; it upsets all plans for the future; I have no news from home, and I do not know whether they are getting on just as well without me, etc. Or one might ask whether I have simply backed out of the work because I want to get back to Germany. And is the homesickness, which I can hardly understand and which has hardly ever affected me before, a sign from above, meant to make my refusal easier? Or: is it not irresponsible, having regard to so many other people, simply to say No to one's own future and to that of many others? Shall I regret it? I must not— that is certain. In spite of everything, I have to think first of my promise, secondly of the joy of work at home, and lastly of the person whom I should supplant. Again today's *Losung* has such hard words: 'He will sit as a refiner and purifier of silver' (Mal. 3 : 3). It is necessary, too. I am at my wits' end; but he [God] knows what he is about, and in the end all our doings will be clear and pure.

22nd June: 'The person I am most sorry for about my decision is Sabine.'[149]

He told his parents about the new situation at once:

[Discussions have] shown that just about everything has changed. I was invited to stay as long as ever I liked, but I have declined . . . So I think I shall go back in the autumn. Nothing else is possible, if I am to reconcile the wishes on both sides. And after all, that is quite right. I do not know, either, whether I should have stood the atmosphere here for long; it is all terribly sensational and full of hatred and horribly pharisaical. Personally I had found the friendliest reception everywhere from my former friends, but that is really not enough. Now I am working hard at my lecture courses, and that is giving me a great deal of pleasure.[150]

What had really caused him to decide on 20th June 1939 to go back to Germany is not equally clear in all the letters and conversations of those

147. GS I, pp 303 f.
148. Plan No. 4 by Leiper.
149. GS I, pp. 304 f.
150. Letter of 22.6.1939.

days. It was simply his readiness to recognize that he now was and would have to remain a German in full acceptance of guilt and responsibility. In his diary Germany now comes into the picture beside the Church, as it hardly did before. On 22nd June he wrote:

To be here during a catastrophe is simply unthinkable, unless things are so ordained. But to be guilty of it oneself, and to have to reproach oneself with it, is certainly devastating. We cannot separate ourselves from our destiny, least of all out here . . .

It is so strange how strongly these particular thoughts move me in these days, and *how difficult it is for any thoughts of the Una sancta to make headway.*[151]

Direct access to the *Una sancta*, which he had longed for and sought through flight, was now barred. On the contrary, he had to give up the *Una sancta* in order to share his nation's destiny and guilt in those evil days. Only in that way would he be able to find access once more to a universal Church.

Perhaps he put his case most clearly in a letter to Reinhold Niebuhr, to whom in particular he owed an explanation of his startling decision:

I have made a mistake in coming to America. I must live through this difficult period of our national history with the Christian people of Germany. I will have no right to participate in the reconstruction of Christian life in Germany after the war if I do not share the trials of this time with my people . . . Christians in Germany will face the terrible alternative of either willing the defeat of their nation in order that Christian civilization may survive, or willing the victory of their nation and thereby destroying our civilization. I know which of these alternatives I must choose; but I cannot make that choice in security.[152]

When the summer school in 'Union' began, Professor McNeill, the specialist on Calvin, occupied the 'Prophets' Chamber'. He was surprised at the masses of illegible sheets of paper of his (to him) unknown predecessor, and at the quantities of cigarettes that he had smoked. He thought he must be either a very hard worker or very slipshod. It was not till later that it dawned on him who had lived there before him and there made the most difficult of all his decisions.

Return Date

Scarcely had the decision to return home been taken when all the business about an early departure began.

The problem of paying for the return journey caused no difficulty between Bonhoeffer and his hosts, as the cost was paid out of an account of his brother-in-law Gerhard Leibholz, which had not yet been blocked.

151. GS I, p. 306. Bonhoeffer's italics.
152. GS I, p. 320.

But there remained the obligation of delivering the lectures at the Summer School. So on 23rd June Bonhoeffer fixed the date of departure for 12th August, which was just after the end of the course. On 24th June there came the long and anxiously awaited post from Further Pomerania; now 'I am again convinced that I must go back to the work'. On 26th June the *Losung*, taken from 2 Tim. 4:21, read: 'Do your best to come before winter.'

That follows me around all day. It is as if we were soldiers home on leave, and going back into action regardless of what they were to expect. We cannot be released from it. Not as if we were essential, as if we were needed (by God?), but simply because that is where our life is, and because we abandon, destroy, our life if we are not back in the fight. It is not a matter of piety, but of something more vital. But the feelings through which God acts are not only the pious but also those vital ones. 'Do your best to come before winter'—it is not a misuse of Scripture if I apply that to myself. May God give me grace to do it.[153]

The news grew more and more ominous every day. In Danzig, Goebbels had made a speech with threats that could hardly be outdone. Then Bonhoeffer heard from Chicago that his brother Karl-Friedrich was also going home and had declined the offer of a professorship. On that, he decided to leave on 8th July.

30th June:

I cannot think it is God's will that, if war comes, I am to stay here with no special task. I must go on the earliest possible date . . .

As, in spite of the present situation, I should have gone anyhow in four weeks' time at the latest, I am deciding, in the existing circumstances, to go with Karl-Friedrich on the 8th. I do not want to be here if war comes; one is thought to be objective here, if one knows nothing about the situation. That was a great decision.

All day long the situation in Germany and the Church has been on my mind.[154]

The next day he wrote anxiously to his parents: Can you 'please write Uncle Rudi's birthday to Sabine for me in good time, so that I can, if necessary, send my personal congratulations?' This time he did not want to be caught by the outbreak of war in England, either.

Meanwhile there was one person whom Bonhoeffer, in his gloomy misgivings, would only too gladly have had his mind changed by—Paul Lehmann. Bonhoeffer himself wrote: 'It would be good to stay another four weeks, but the stakes are too high.'[155]

Paul Lehmann

In spite of the long silence, the old friendship had continued with un-

153. GS I, p. 309.   154. GS I, pp. 311 f.   155. GS I, p. 314.

diminished cordiality. When Bonhoeffer decided on the 8th July as the date for leaving, he wrote in his diary: 'This morning there is another letter from Paul, who was so optimistic about my staying here.'[156]

Lehmann said in his letter:

I do know that it is unthinkable that you should return before America shall have had the fullest opportunity to be enriched by your contribution to its theological hour of destiny. At least I like to think of it in this way. The tragic political occasion for these disturbed times may have one great and positive overtone in the widening of the American theological understanding by the cross fertilization with the continental tradition. So that you must see this also as a responsibility as well as the German need for teachers.—And besides, Marion and I need very badly to see you again. Surely you would not deprive us for the hope that we have carried with us since the day when we left the café on Unter den Linden. With your anticipated permission I have already taken steps to bring this about.[157]

Lehmann had written from Elmhurst College to some thirty or forty colleges, not without stressing Niebuhr's interest in Bonhoeffer; and the first positive answers were already coming in. When Bonhoeffer saw the circular, he noticed that it contained a sentence which was hardly diplomatic; it was mentioned, in the personal details, that since the seminary had been closed by the authorities, his teaching activities had been going on privately in Pomerania. Bonhoeffer drew Lehmann's attention to this: 'If such a document were to get into the hands of any German authority, the work that is going on meanwhile would be over';[158] and he asked him to inform the colleges that it was all a misunderstanding, and that Bonhoeffer had already gone back to Germany. Lehmann at once accepted responsibility for the 'mistake', as well as the probability that the people who received his second circular would shake their heads over such 'inefficiency':

Word has just come that the circumstances of Mr. Bonhoeffer's visit to the United States have been entirely misunderstood and that the contemplated opportunity of inviting him cannot materialize owing to his return to Germany. The committee[159] appreciates the courtesy of your interest in its effort and regrets very much the error of its earlier communication.[160]

It is distressing to think what would have happened if Paul Lehmann had been able to receive Bonhoeffer as early as 12th June on the New York pier. Now it was too late: 'I cannot tell you how deeply it troubles both Marion and me. I write now, believe me, with great heaviness of

156. GS I, p. 311.
157. GS II, p. 355.
158. GS II, p. 357.
159. Consisting of R. Niebuhr and P. Lehmann.
160. GS II, pp. 360 f.

spirit.'[161] Now there was only just time to hurry to New York and take his friend to the pier.

6th July:

At half past two I meet Paul Lehmann in my room; he has come from Columbus, Ohio, to see me again. A great pleasure. From now on we shall have the rest of the time together.

7th July:

The last day. Paul is still trying to keep me back. It will not do now . . . I go on board with Paul. Good-bye at half past eleven . . .[162]

'Protestantism Without Reformation'

The decision did not confine his thoughts to the homeward journey, but also produced a pressure of work at the desk, and intense observation. When he left, Bonhoeffer wrote: 'I have perhaps learnt more during this month than in the whole year nine years ago.'[163] Here the 'month', measured by working time, had hardly been a fortnight.

Bonhoeffer had looked at 1939 with different eyes from those of 1930. His American friends seemed to him changed and more frank. A number of university lecturers arrived on 1st July for the beginning of the summer course. Bonhoeffer did not see Reinhold Niebuhr, who was staying in Glasgow, but he saw his brother Richard.[164] In the course of a few days he read through an amazing amount of work. He analyzed the series of articles which the *Christian Century* publishes every ten years with the title 'How my mind has changed',[165] and which in 1939 contained for the first time Barth's aggressive retrospective survey. He thought that the Americans had in part now reached the position for which he had contended—vainly, he thought—ten years before. He wrote down on a slip of paper: 'Barthianism in small doses; here, as everywhere, amazing ignorance.' Criticism of America's religious propensities was no more lacking than it had been in 1931; it was even more forthright since the church struggle and *The Cost of Discipleship*:

The Anglo-Saxons may be more religious than we are, but they are not more Christian if they put up with sermons like these.[166]

In Riverside Church he heard a sermon on the philosopher James's phrase, 'accepting an horizon'. On the evening of the same Sunday, 18th June, feeling desperately in need of direction instead of brilliant analysis,

161. GS II, p. 359.
162. GS I, p. 314.
163. GS I, p. 315.
164. In those days one of Bonhoeffer's interlocutors was the English writer W. H. Auden, who wrote the poem 'Friday's Child' (MW IV, pp. 175 ff.), as he himself told Christoph von Dohnanyi.
165. GS I, p. 300.
166. GS I, p. 300.

he went to the Broadway Presbyterian Church, and found from the arch-fundamentalist Dr. McComb what he was seeking. He preached on 'our likeness with Christ', not suspecting the decision that was shaping in the mind of one of his audience. A few days later Bonhoeffer discussed the two sermons with friends. He did not know that the fundamentalist is totally opposed to any church union, and was told that, in spite of their Biblicism, they could not really be regarded as more reliable than the Riverside people. Bonhoeffer knew as much from his experience with pietistic groups in Germany. On an essay by a fundamentalist in *Christian Century*, where the root of all evil was found to be the existence of 'modernists' and 'unionists', his comment was: 'That does not get at Satan.'

The real reason why Bonhoeffer, in his short stay in America in 1939, thought he could see so much more deeply than in 1930, lies in the experience of his existential insecurity. This time, the refugee and home-comer could appreciate the refugees' country *par excellence*. In 1930 he had reacted to Christian America with European theological arro-gance. In 1939 he respected, with discriminating love, the peculiar his-tory of America as the country of refugees who have escaped the last conflicts and regard tolerance as sacred.

After a few days' studying he began to formulate the essay that lay in his desk till after the war: 'Protestantism Without Reformation'.[167] The greater part of it he wrote in 'Union' and in London, and the rest during the days of mobilization in Berlin. It did not worry him that there was no longer any possibility of having it printed; he wanted his observations to be recorded systematically.

The essay represents a modification of Bonhoeffer's earlier ecumenical reflections. It is true that the ecclesiology is still Christocentric and not anchored in positivism, but the historical fact of denomination is seen as much more differentiated. Judgement is not given hastily from a systematic presentation, but appraises sociological factors. Analytical observations and the power to systematize are not mutually exclusive, but interpenetrate.

The centre-piece of the essay consists of Parts II and III on the 'Chris-tian's Refuge' and 'Freedom'.[168] Both themes are new compared with the America report of 1931 and the ecumenicity essay of 1935. In the latest period of the church struggle, in the discussion on whether an order of expulsion by the Gestapo should be accepted or refused, the alternative choice between 'holding out and fleeing in times of persecu-tion'[169] was put very plainly. Paul Schneider set a magnificent example by his answer; other brethren answered differently. In his *Cost of Dis-cipleship* Bonhoeffer had written about the weakness of the Word, and

167. GS I, pp. 323-54.
168. GS I, pp. 334 ff.
169. GS I, p. 334.

had expressed the opinion that flight might be legitimate for the disciples.[170] Now he had put flight to the test existentially, and he now found it to be a key to a new understanding of the American 'denomination'. He saw in that indefinite self-characterization of the churches, which consciously lags behind the European concept of the Church, a certain dialectic of humility and pretension. That theological phenomenology is full of Bonhoeffer's latest experiences:

To hold out to the last may be commanded, to flee may be allowed, perhaps even demanded. The Christian's fight in persecution does not of itself mean apostasy and disgrace, for God does not call everyone to martyrdom. Not fleeing but denial is sin; that is to say that there may be a situation in which flight amounts to denial, just as on the other hand flight can be an act of martyrdom . . . The Christian refugee has claimed the right to avoid the final suffering, in order to be able to serve God in peace and quietness. But at the place of refuge the continuation of the struggle is no longer justified . . . His demand for a decision for the truth against its falsification is unfulfilled and must remain so. It is finally the truth against one's own church history which is expressed in this unique relativizing of the question of truth in the thought and actions of American Christianity.[171]

On the Americans' pride in the freedom that has been institutionalized by the churches he expressed himself much more critically from his ample German experiences:

The essential freedom of the Church is not a gift from the world to the Church, but is the freedom of the Word of God itself to get a hearing . . . Where thanks for institutional freedom have to be rendered by sacrificing freedom of preaching, the Church is in chains, even if it thinks it is free.[172]

As before in 1931, Bonhoeffer misses Christology:

In American theology, Christianity is essentially religion and ethics. But that means that the person and work of Jesus Christ have to retire into the theological background, and finally remain uncomprehended.[173]

Here he feels obliged to indicate that there is still a substantial distance between him and the American brethren, in spite of a greater understanding of the relevant history.

Bonhoeffer again brings into play his ecumenical passion by critically expressing what disquiets him. For ecumenical community includes the indication of contrasts; and it would not be positively expressed if it dawdled on a non-committal plane and kept silence on the question: 'What is God doing to us and with his Church in America, and what is he doing through it to us, and through us to it?'[174]

170. CD, pp. 165 f., 189.
171. GS I, pp. 355 f.
172. GS I, pp. 337 f.
173. GS I, p. 354.
174. GS I, p. 325.

We therefore ought to pay careful attention to the partner's question: The Reformation churches in Europe want to be questioned on the basis of their Confession in the act of splitting off; but the American denominations, 'Protestantism without Reformation', which have inherited the consequences of the schism but are no longer conscious of the act itself, do not now want to be judged on the basis of a binding confessional statement and its theology.

With that essay, Bonhoeffer turned his very personal American experience into an essential element of ecumenical understanding that would be generally valid.

Journey Home

On the night of 7th-8th July, in the warmth of high summer, the ship glided out of New York harbour; Dietrich and Karl-Friedrich Bonhoeffer were going back to Europe to face war.

The journey is over. I am glad to have been over there, and glad to be on my way home again . . . I have at least had some realization of what is important for all my future personal decisions. This journey will probably help me a good deal to work things out.

Since I have been on board, the inward disharmony about the future has ceased, and I can think without any reproaches about the shortened time in America. *Losung:* 'It is good for me that I was afflicted, that I might learn thy statutes', Psalm 119: 71. One of my favourite passages from my favourite psalm.[175]

Bonhoeffer stayed ten days with his sister in London and met Hildebrandt, but he communicated with Bishop Bell only by letter:

My passport expires next spring; it is therefore uncertain when I shall be in this country again . . . We shall never forget you during the coming events.[176]

Meanwhile Niebuhr had suggested another project to John Baillie, his colleague of 1930: Bonhoeffer received an invitation to deliver the Edinburgh 'Croall Lectures', which then had a £210 endowment. Bonhoeffer accepted from London for the winter; and on 24th August he sent Baillie the theme from Berlin: 'Death in the Christian message'.[177] A few days later the war began, and so he went on at that disastrous moment with a theme from his youthful days;[178] just after the First World War, when he was fourteen, he had taken with him from an exhibition of Max Klinger's work a reproduction of the lithograph *Vom Tode*. Later he could remark, as if incidentally, that he expected an early

175. GS I, p. 315.
176. Letter of 22.7.1939, GS I, pp. 320 ff.
177. GS II, pp. 361 f.
178. See Ch. I, p. 24.

death.[179] Now, at the beginning of the Second World War, he wrote to the Finkenwalde students in a circular, about the death that belongs to us and the death that does not belong to us, about a 'death from without' and a 'death from within'; 'We may pray that death from without does not come to us till we have been made ready for it through this inherent death; then our death is really only the gateway to the perfect love of God.'[180] Bonhoeffer was already beginning, too, to take a literary interest in the theme of death, for example, in the works of Joachim Wach[181] (which August Knorr gave him in Köslin), Fritz Dehn,[182] and Georges Barbarin.[183]

One afternoon during his last few days in London, Bonhoeffer was sitting at the piano, teaching his sister's children some English nursery rhymes. Rieger came in, took him aside, and told him that on 19th July Paul Schneider had been tortured to death in Buchenwald. That was martyrdom pure and simple, which Bonhoeffer had visualized in his sermon on Jeremiah[184] in 1934 in London, and which he had decided *not* to accept as an alternative. On 25th July 1939 his relatives went with him to the station. On his journey home he visited Hermann Hesse in Elberfeld and Hans Iwand in Dortmund, to discuss with them the continuation of the seminary. On 27th July he was back in Berlin.

VII THE WAR

The Old Job

Bonhoeffer's unexpectedly short absence did not in the least bring home to the Councils of Brethren and his friends what had happened meanwhile in his life. No one knew of his correspondence with Leiper and Niebuhr, let alone of its content; everyone was quite busy enough with what was happening in Church and State. At first there was no striking change in Bonhoeffer himself; he went back as a matter of course to the collective pastorates in Further Pomerania, to finish the term in spite of the general preparations for war.

To celebrate his return, each group of ordinands spent a week of high summer on the Baltic coast, not badly incommoded by the daily manœuvres of the *Luftwaffe* squadrons and the eastward movement of tanks and troops along the No. 2 Reichsstrasse. Bonhoeffer had taken with him to the dunes one of Paul Lehmann's students, George Kalb-fleisch, who had attended the Amsterdam Youth Conference.

But when a messenger came from his parents in the Marienburger Allee with the news that 'Uncle Rudi' was doing so badly that there was

179. W.-D. Zimmermann in *Begegnungen* (German ed. of IKDB).
180. GS II, pp. 558 f.
181. J. Wach, *Das Problem des Todes in der Philosophie unserer Zeit*, 1934.
182. F. Dehn, *Das Gespräch vom Tode*, 1938.
183. G. Barbarin, *Der Tod als Freund* (from the French).
184. See Ch. VIII, pp. 259, 273.

now no hope, and when on 23rd August Ribbentrop arrived in Moscow to sign the non-aggression pact, Bonhoeffer broke off the Sigurdshof and Köslin summer course, as it was much too near the front.

On 26th August Bonhoeffer, together with E. Bethge, arrived at his parents' home in the Marienburger Allee, where he spent the last days of peace and the first days of war up to the middle of October.

On 20th June in New York, Bonhoeffer had probably imagined that the impact of the beginning of the war would be different from what it turned out to be. Everything seemed much less complicated; there was no popular crisis, no intensification of revolutionary hopes, no onslaught by the Allied Powers, not even an enlistment order or a halt to secret training. When Bonhoeffer was in Eichkamp with his brother Klaus on 3rd September—Great Britain had declared war after all, against Hitler's and Ribbentrop's calculations—to discuss the position with him, the sirens wailed above the town. Bonhoeffer jumped on to his bicycle, and was with his parents in five minutes; but no bomb fell, no plane was to be seen, no shot was to be heard; nothing happened.

In the early days of September there was no great display of sentiment. Dietrich's father, Karl Bonhoeffer, writes in his memoirs:

The mood in which we entered the war of 1939 was basically different from that of 1914. In that year there was a fairly general conviction that it was a matter of a defensive war in a righteous cause, and the attitude of the Social Democratic Party in the Reichstag was characteristic of this. Hardly anyone who knew the Kaiser doubted that his outlook was that of a peace-lover who feared war. True, it was widely recognized and regretted that the enlargement of the fleet, and his unfortunate penchant for making speeches in which he brandished the sword rather theatrically, were provocative, and that Great Britain's increasing prosperity was disliked and was regarded as upsetting the balance of power; but it is probably true that the German Government did not actively want an armed conflict. In 1939 the people were in no doubt that it was a matter of a war of aggression, prepared and organized by Hitler, for which there was no kind of sympathy in the mass of the population.[185]

Karl Bonhoeffer's view of the events of 1914 may now be open to doubt, but his account does reflect what was certainly widely believed.

In some Christian circles, there prevailed on 1st September 1939 a feeling of grim acceptance of the catastrophe as a necessary judgement. In the first Finkenwalde circular of the war, in which Bonhoeffer had to lament the death of Theodor Maass, the first former seminarist to be killed in action, he expressed that feeling:

I do not know whether the theodicy question will come up again as tormentingly as in the last war . . . As Christians probably know more today about the Biblical judgement on the world and history, they may be less troubled by present events than confirmed in their faith.[186]

185. K. Bonhoeffer, *Lebenserinnerungen*, p. 120.
186. 20.9.1939, GS II, p. 556.

In contrast to the situation in September 1938, there was nothing on which to pin one's hopes of a *Putsch*. At Hitler's *Berghof* on 22nd August there was no opposition by the commanders, although some of them, even the national-socialistically inclined General von Reichenau, had their doubts.[187] Warning memoranda supplied by Canaris or General Thomas, the head of the department of economic defence, did not get beyond Keitel, the commander-in-chief. The generals' position *vis-à-vis* the National Socialist leaders, who were reckoning on a blitzkrieg, was weaker than ever; and so the out-and-out civilians among the would-be opponents could not at that time make any headway with the generals who might share their views. The only reply that they could get was that the situation was different from that of 1938, that Hitler had success on his side, and that now of all times their commitment by oath could not be disregarded. It was not till the war had brought the most bitter experiences that the military people were prepared to consider new revolutionary plots. That time was still a long way off, although Bonhoeffer thought that the beginning of the war would bring about the final catastrophe for Hitler; he did not suppose that the end was still so distant.

As regards the Church, the outbreak of war brought marginal changes. Speaking generally, one may say that after 1st September 1939 the church struggle became less important and received less publicity. In order to provide a more impressive façade for the church administration that he had introduced, Dr. Werner summoned a church working group on 29th August; it consisted of three men: Marahrens, Dr. Hymmen, the clerical vice-president of the EOK, and Bishop Schultz of Mecklenburg, an extreme 'German Christian', who, for instance, allowed the Lord's Supper to be celebrated in his church as a cult of blood and the soil. No one took that 'religious workers' council' very seriously. On 2nd September it issued a public proclamation, which said of the Evangelical Church: 'It has supplied the weapons of steel with the invincible forces out of God's Word . . .'[188]

For the Confessing Church there were certain alleviations. Some consistories, such as that of Saxony, now allowed the 'illegal' pastors to pursue their calling—unless they had already been taken into the Army —and made it possible to pay them out of official funds, though in doing so they expressly declared that this did not imply any recognition of their eligibility. Yet in September 1939 the police were interfering, in one way or another, with 360 pastors of the Confessing Church; fourteen were arrested, and only a few were amnestied. Indeed, when the war broke out it was greatly feared that the war economy might bear hardly on the inmates of the concentration camps, and that the authorities would make short work of some of them.

187. See *Vollmacht des Gewissens*, p. 377.
188. W. Niemöller, *Die Evangelische Kirche im Dritten Reich*, p. 391.

Niemöller's Offer of Service

In the first few days of the war, such fears were also felt for Martin Niemöller, whom Dr. Werner had dispossessed of his official rights. Bonhoeffer was consulted as to whether and how Niemöller could be protected from that peril. Without hesitation, Bonhoeffer supported the advice that the former U-boat captain should volunteer for the Navy. Perhaps such a message from the cell at that moment might cause the newly created Reich Security Head Office (R.S.H.A.) to review former decisions. In any case, Bonhoeffer held it to be a useful instrument for rescuing important people; and besides, he was then already inclined to consider whether it might not be advisable to have reliable men at headquarters and in key positions of the war machine, if an attempt to overthrow the régime were to be made. Of course, that could hardly be understood abroad. Karl Barth, through his friend Ehrhardt in England, put out a solemn and definite denial of rumours that Niemöller had volunteered.[189] And yet it was so. It would never have entered Bonhoeffer's head that he could in any way have betrayed the opposition to Hitler through that piece of advice, and that he and Niemöller had gone over to the other side, as some people have interpreted the matter since 1945. In any case, it was quite a usual thing for loyal Confessing pastors who were in the reserve of officers to volunteer (some did so too quickly for Bonhoeffer's liking!) so as to find a way out of a dangerous situation. Jochen Klepper's diary reveals, as hardly any other document does, the two-track thoughts and feelings of many Christians in those days.

No doubt, Bonhoeffer's theological thinking, and his actions, were not always the same as Niemöller's, in spite of all their close comradeship and friendship. In the thirties Niemöller did not share Bonhoeffer's 'pacifism' when the latter was pondering it; and, as he later acknowledged, he would not have associated himself with Bonhoeffer's engagement in conspiracy, if he had been free. He was then more disposed to separate service in the Church from service to one's country, and that was an idea that had become suspect to Bonhoeffer.

But it would never have occurred to Bonhoeffer that Niemöller's volunteering would shake the confidence of such a man, for instance, as Bishop Bell. One now had to take responsibility for doing things that might seem equivocal, as Bell himself did without compunction. That is shown by the letters that he wrote, as an expression of continued fellowship, to the three men who for him represented the German Church at that moment—Hans Böhm, Martin Niemöller, and Dietrich Bonhoeffer. Bell had heard that Rieger's family would be repatriated and go home (though that did not, in fact, happen), and so he asked Frau Rieger to convey the letters, just at the time when Niemöller was writing his offer to Admiral of the Fleet Raeder. Bell wrote to Bonhoeffer:

189. *Daily Telegraph* of 3.11.1939.

My dear Dietrich, You know how deeply I feel for you and yours in this melancholy time. May God comfort and guide you. I think often of our talk in the summer. May He keep you. Let us pray together often by reading the Beatitudes; *Pax Dei quae superat omnia nos custodiat.* Your affectionate George.[190]

No Military Chaplaincy

Whereas the army call-up secured a respite for some Confessing pastors whose position was precarious, it meant at the same time that they were suddenly cut off from their work. No authority within the official Church lodged claims for exemption, and so the Confessing Church felt at once, and more than any other group in the country, the loss of colleagues. Almost all its young pastors went to the front, and most of them were sooner or later killed in action. But there were a few men in the Army and in the administration who recognized the problem; and here and there they used their chances, as long as they had any, of keeping individual pastors out of the Army.

Although Bonhoeffer could assume that his friends in Schlawe would try to keep him as long as possible from being called up, he could not rely on it for certain. So he hit on the idea of trying to get an appointment as chaplain with the troops and in a military hospital. The proper line of approach was through the consistories, which negotiated with the armed forces regarding chaplains. Bonhoeffer would not consider this.

So his mother got her cousin, the military governor, to invite her and Chief Chaplain Dohrmann to explore suitable ways and means. In September 1939 Bonhoeffer, acting on Dohrmann's advice, applied for employment as army chaplain. The answer did not come till the middle of February 1940, and it was negative. The reason given was that, according to a regulation of the army high command, only people with a record of active service could become chaplains, and accordingly all other applications were to be refused. Bonhoeffer wrote home:

The other side of the matter is that all the pastors who have already served or are army officers are, of course, conscripted as fighting men, and so there is nothing else left for chaplains![191] Besides, the conscription of Confessing pastors, and the application for exemption by the consistory people, and the taking over by consistory people of Confessing Church posts in the absence of Confessing pastors, lead more and more clearly to a destruction of the congregations that still exist.[192]

The Last Term

When the campaign in Poland was over, and conditions in the interior

190. Letter of 6.9.1939.
191. For that pastoral service.
192. Letter from Sigurdshof, 27.2.1940.

of the country had been more or less stabilized, discussions between Niesel, Perels, and Bonhoeffer led to a decision of the Old Prussian Council of Brethren to continue the collective pastorate in Sigurdshof in spite of the war. Surprisingly, there were still a few ordinands who had passed their examinations with the Confessing Church and were waiting for their final training. The domicile in Further Pomerania was now again outside any area of military concentration. In the middle of October eight ordinands were called to Sigurdshof from Berlin, Pomerania, Westphalia, and the Rhineland. They started work with Bonhoeffer in primitive conditions, and relied on their own ingenuity to solve the problems of coal, paraffin, petrol, and food. They succeeded, menaced and at the same time protected by one of the severest winters. Only one ordinand was taken away from the course by the recruiting officials.

Freed from the reflections of the previous winter, Bonhoeffer once more devoted himself with extraordinary concentration to his theological work. Now he was at last able to make some progress with his meditation on Psalm 119.[193] He had learnt at the university that this was the most boring of psalms; now he regarded its interpretation as the climax of his theological life. He had been trying for years to penetrate into the mystery of its verses; on 18th January 1938 he had written to Franz Hildebrandt:

Now I want to try for the third time; Julius[194] might get me with Cromwell's[195] help *The Way of Holiness* by Father Benson, Oxford. I need it for the exposition of Psalm 119. Many thanks for your trouble.

In Sigurdshof he got as far as verse 21.[196]

That winter, he undertook to cooperate in work on Joachim Beckmann's and Georg Eichholz's volumes of sermons and meditations.[197] Eichholz's attempt was one of the first results of the renewal of preaching in the church struggle, and the precursor of today's 'Göttingen Sermon-Meditations'. Although Bonhoeffer was prepared to cooperate at once, he was critical at first, and wrote to Eichholz:

I had admitted openly all along that I had misgivings about your undertaking. What are sermon-meditations? I have never quite understood, and they are still much the same. They seem to be partly exegesis and partly outlines of sermons.[198] With regard to this, I feel that exegesis can be found elsewhere, and that there are enough and better collections of sermons on the gospels than we have often produced. Theological observations, see Vogel,

193. See Ch. VIII, p. 335, Ch. XI, p. 580.
194. Rieger.
195. An emigrant, from Bonhoeffer's church in London.
196. GS IV, pp. 505-43.
197. J. Beckmann and Fr. Linz, *Meine Worte werden nicht vergehen*, 1940, pp. 42-6; G. Eichholz, *Herr tue meine Lippen auf*, 1941, pp. 120 ff., 124 ff., 141 ff., see GS IV, pp. 473-504.
198. Bonhoeffer always offered his probationers short outlines in the homiletic seminar.

or very general marginal notes on the text, see Asmussen, better elsewhere. I include myself under this judgement . . .

I still have doubts about the whole thing. But on the other hand, I must say that, judging by what I hear from the young theologians, they are very grateful for the work; and that applies not only to the less self-reliant people, but to the others as well. So any gap—it may often be simply the gap in the library—is no doubt being filled, and that fully justifies the work given to it . . .

I should certainly think it is much more necessary to deal with the Old Testament readings than with the Epistles.[199] I ought to tell you, too, that that is the wish of several young brethren. Could you not still change that? There is really a lack of help here . . .

Do invite all the colleagues to get together![200]

I am quite ready to cooperate further, especially as my last few months' work as I went about in East Prussia convinced me that the very isolated brethren in particular found the meditations a real help in their preaching. I repeat my request that you will soon go over to the Old Testament texts! There is a great deal of theological, exegetical, and homiletical helplessness here.[201]

Although I agree with you that a treatment of the Old Testament pericopes is far from easy, I would infer from that very fact that just this work must be tackled, as we now expect of any pastor on Sundays that he should preach on those texts, while frankly we assume that in practice he will *not* do so. In my opinion, help is more urgently needed here than anywhere else.[202]

It was inevitable that the Pomeranian Council of Brethren, too, enquired about its old critical colleague. Bonhoeffer undertook to write regularly a theological supplement for the monthly circular to the Pomeranian clergy,[203] although this brought him into another disagreement, this time with Eberhard Baumann of the Reformed Church about the article on the Lord's Supper. Even the theological commission of the Pomeranian Council of Brethren came to life again. 'The theological commission very active with Bonhoeffer!' Frau Ohnesorge wrote in her diary after the Council of Brethren's session of 8th January 1940.

Bonhoeffer did indeed at times feel it irksome, while the newly begun preparations for a *coup d'état* were going on, with Dohnanyi one of the main people involved, not to be able to spend all his time in Berlin. But he was always happy again when he could escape from the hectic atmosphere of Berlin, and go back once more to theology and the 'life together' in the seclusion of the forest.

199. Bonhoeffer was to cooperate on the Epistles in turn, after the Gospels.
200. Letter of 20.5.1940.
201. Letter of 14.9.1940.
202. Letter of 17.2.1941.
203. GS III, pp. 382-425.

Hesitancy Towards Ecumenical Movement

In so far as his professional work left him time for Berlin in the first winter of the war, Bonhoeffer was occupied with political matters, only a little with the church struggle, and not at all with what was happening in the ecumenical sphere. Here a good many things were changing.

In the western and northern countries various church-people were feverishly busy, even in the winter 1939-40, trying to save the 'peace'. In September 1939 Bishop Berggrav went to see the British Foreign Secretary Lord Halifax, in December he visited Bishop Bell, and in January 1940 he went to Göring in Karinhall, and then again to Lord Halifax, and finally, before Hitler invaded Norway, to Berlin again. The provisional World Council of Churches, which met at Apeldoorn, Holland, in January 1940, tried to draft an appeal for peace; but the leaders of the British and Scandinavian churches could not agree whether precedence should be given to peace at all costs, or to the conditions of peace.[204]

The Confessing Church, i.e. Hans Böhm for the Lutheran Union, was excluded from those proceedings. Nor did Berggrav cultivate relations with it when he went to Berlin, but with the Church's External Affairs Office. Bonhoeffer took no notice of those efforts, not because he would have been isolated by the tragic previous history of ecumenical relationships, but rather because he was not now interested in any peace-feelers that allowed for the maintenance, or even the strengthening, of the Hitler régime. But in the first few months of the war there were many ecumenical attempts to get a state of peace restored first by hook or by crook, and only then to see whether, and how, Hitler could be got rid of. Bonhoeffer mistrusted this; for him the only right course was to eliminate Hitler and then negotiate a peace.

Nor did Bonhoeffer see any need to reconsider his attitude to the Geneva research department, i.e. to Schönfeld. It was not till two years later that friendly contacts were re-established between the two.[205]

It was still too early for any such *rapprochement*; there was as yet no abatement of the old antagonism. For Bonhoeffer, Schönfeld was still simply the man at the Church's External Affairs Office, on which he had depended more than ever since the beginning of the war. Since a drastic financial retrenchment of 1938, he had been living in Geneva on the foreign currency that Heckel had managed to secure for him in Berlin; and that was possible only as long as the political results abroad were demonstrated to the Foreign Office. So again, Schönfeld's position in Geneva was suspect to those who shared the theological and political views of Karl Barth. Schönfeld's difficult situation almost overtaxed his

204. See Rouse-Neill, op. cit., pp. 708 f., and A. Johnson, *Eivind Berggrav*, 1960, pp. 110-14.
205. See Ch. XII, pp. 697 f.

strength; on the one hand he had to produce reports that showed the Foreign Office how well suited that ecclesiastical office in Geneva was for observing Allied propaganda, and on the other hand he had to convince the sceptical that he belonged to the Resistance.

Of course, it did not now enter Bonhoeffer's head to change his relationship to the Church's External Affairs Office. Journeyings and the search for contacts were increasing rather than decreasing there. While Bonhoeffer was on his way back from America, Gerstenmaier was commissioned by Heckel to attend an ecumenical study session in Archbishop Temple's see at Bishopsthorpe near York, with J. Baillie, R. Niebuhr, A. Nygren, J. Oldham, N. Soe, Lyman, Green, Schönfeld, and Ehrenström taking part. In October Gerstenmaier, Ehrenström, and Schönfeld went to the three Scandinavian countries; Gerstenmaier had to make a report on this, showing the Foreign Office how the contacts with the neutral Lutheran churches served the German cause and promoted 'the active conflict with the Western ideologies'.[206] In April 1940 the Church's External Affairs Office, together with the Geneva research department, staged an ecumenical working session in Berlin on the theme 'The Church's Responsibility for the International Order'. The later ecumenical relief work has its roots in that conference, and Bonhoeffer himself took an interest in such matters not long afterwards. But in April 1940 his views on the nature of 'international order' hardly coincided with those of the External Affairs Office. Although he was in Berlin at the time, he did not see any of the delegates at the conference.

But since then the two hostile sides, people of the External Affairs Office and Bonhoeffer, began more and more frequently to work with the same friends. The Church's External Affairs Office depended for its journeys and plans on a good understanding with the appropriate departments of the Foreign Office, received from it the extraparochial status and foreign currency, and delivered its reports. Thus there developed Gerstenmaier's contacts with men who took him into the Kreisau circle in 1942. Bonhoeffer, for his part, renewed during that winter his association with Hans-Bernd von Haeften in the Foreign Office; he saw Adam von Trott before the latter left for his journey to America. Bonhoeffer's brothers and sisters, particularly Karl-Friedrich, had known him well for a long time.

But the difficulty of any approach to the Church's External Affairs Office is illustrated by the case of Siegmund-Schultze. He already had associations at that time with the resistance group of Beck and Goerdeler, and had contacts with England;[207] and of course, Bonhoeffer visited him later on his Swiss journeys. But the Church External Affairs Office felt it necessary to prevent this emigrant from going to

206. Cf. F. von Schlabrendorff, *Eugen Gerstenmaier im Dritten Reich*, 1965, p. 26.
207. See G. Ritter, *Karl Goerdeler*, 1954, p. 252.

Sweden when he was invited to lecture there in the spring of 1940, and it wrote to the Foreign Office:

His negative attitude[208] . . . must be expected to stand in the way of any meaningful German work in Scandinavia. I therefore think, in agreement with Swedish circles that are anxious for a systematic consolidation of Swedish-German relations,[209] that I ought confidentially to ask that, without drawing attention to it, you should have steps taken to prevent Professor S. Schultze's journey to Sweden.[210]

Thus, in the first year of the war, Bonhoeffer did not try to get into touch with either foreign churchmen or German people acting for the ecumenical movement. Of course, ecumenical conferences and synods had to declare for peace at all costs before the war broke out in full fury in May 1940. Bonhoeffer, however, had already taken his stand on the one condition of peace which should not be open to discussion in any church body inside Germany—the removal of Hitler.

New Hopes of an Overthrow

In the first winter of the war, the activity of the German conspirators was renewed in two phases, Dohnanyi being one of the driving forces and Bonhoeffer taking only a small part. The latter had not, as yet, any special commission to carry out, or any field of action for which he was responsible within the group. But he became more and more involved in it, and was sometimes present when tactics and principles were discussed. For the conspirators themselves, the opinion of an expert in evangelical and ecumenical questions, though not of decisive importance, was yet worth hearing.

Two events gave the participants fresh hope of a successful *coup d'état*.

1. On 27th September 1939, the day that Warsaw surrendered, Hitler gave the order to prepare to invade Holland and Belgium. Would not the generals now be faced with the alternative—either with Hitler from a threatened to an actual world war, or against Hitler from a threatened world war to a reasonable peace? Could it be assumed that if the German resisters acquiesced in the invasion, the Allies would still distinguish between Hitler and Germany? Everything depended on the timing of the assault on the West. The decisive stroke, the removal of Hitler, had to be successfully carried out before then.

---

208. Referring to Siegmund-Schultze.
209. Inclusive church institute in Sigtuna, to be set up by Dr. Nils Ehrenström, but to 'act in close association with German Protestantism'.
210. Report of the representative of the Church External Affairs Office of the DEK, Dr. Gerstenmaier, to the department of political culture and information of the Foreign Office on the journey from 27th September to 2nd October 1939, p. 8. Cf. also the account in F. von Schlabrendorff's *Eugen Gerstenmaier im Dritten Reich*, p. 26.

2. Information about the S.S. atrocities in Poland began to circulate. Of course, the ordinary citizen assumed that the appalling stories were foreign propaganda; at first he could not, and then he would not, believe them. At that time it was already difficult to keep informed, and to repeat in one's own circle what was being done in Poland in the German name.

Canaris, together with General Blaskowitz the military commander in Poland, gave other generals accounts of the S.S. atrocities. Could the Army put up with those cruelties, which were contrary to international law, against civilians and Jews? Could they allow their authority to be restricted by the S.S. units and the Gestapo? Blaskowitz protested:

What the foreign transmitters have broadcast up to now is only a tiny fraction of what has actually happened . . . The only possibility of warding off this pestilence lies in bringing the guilty parties and their followers under military command and military justice with all possible speed.[211]

Thereupon Hitler recalled Blaskowitz from his post.

The two preparatory phases for a *coup d'état* in the winter of 1939-40 were determined by the dates fixed for the assault on the West: first, the November date, which was repeatedly postponed and then cancelled, and then the April date. During the critical stages in October and March Bonhoeffer was in Berlin.

Of Halder and Brauchitsch it was rumoured that they intended to resist Hitler's aggressive plans, and that they even had in mind the possibility of resigning.

The first phase. Beck urged Dohnanyi to bring his record of Hitler's evil deeds up to date by including in detail the affair of the Gleiwitz transmitter about the launching of the invasion of Poland and the atrocities in the occupied country.[212] The idea was then being considered of arresting Hitler and using such material to show the public what the régime was really like. Dohnanyi obtained through Count Helldorf S.D. reports and S.S. films of the massacres in Poland, incorporated them in his 'chronicle of shame', and submitted the material to generals who were inclined to be sympathetic. He helped to establish contacts with trade unionists. It got as far as a meeting between Beck and Leuschner, and the possibility of a general strike was examined.

The most important thing, however, was the attempt to negotiate, as a precaution, tolerable conditions of peace, so as to deprive the generals of the objection that the Allies would turn to account any *coup d'état* as evidence of weakness. That was the most dangerous as well as the most uncertain task. After the Polish campaign, therefore, Dohnanyi and Oster got into touch with the Munich lawyer Dr. Josef Müller, who was on friendly terms with the Vatican. Beck got so far as to commission

211. L. Poljakov and J. Wulf, *Das Dritte Reich und seine Diener*, 1956, p. 517.
212. See Ch. XI, pp. 575 f.

Müller to establish contact there with the British Government. The Pope gave his word to the Western countries that the efforts were serious and came from circles belonging to the other Germany. It was agreed, as a fundamental condition of the negotiations, that the assurances should hold good only if the revolt were successful *before* an offensive in the West. The British Government's first answer, which was sent in October, expressed its readiness to enter into serious negotiations with the other party about peace on those terms.

At that stage—the attack in the West was now supposed to start on 12th November—General Thomas, on Beck's behalf, delivered to General Halder, the Chief of Staff, a memorandum for Brauchitsch on 4th November. It was drawn up by Dohnanyi, Oster, and Gisevius; Halder seemed prepared to agree to it, but Brauchitsch, whose authority was essential for a *Putsch* to be started, refused. In fact, there seemed to be signs that Hitler had got wind of the plans for a *coup*. Halder destroyed documents. The mysterious attempt on Hitler's life in the Munich Bürgerbräukeller, and the arrest of the Englishmen Stevens and Best at Venlo through Schellenberg, slowed the conspirators down, till it was ascertained that nothing had leaked out, and that the incidents in Munich and Venlo had nothing to do with the planners of opposition. So they resumed their race against the date for the offensive which had repeatedly been postponed in November. But as Brauchitsch refused to give the resistance any active help, the question of a possible authoritative order to go ahead was made extremely difficult. With the offensive finally postponed and the winter coming on, there was less activity among the conspirators for some weeks.[213]

The second phase. Meanwhile Josef Müller continued his conversations in Rome. Canaris had 'installed' him in the counter-espionage organization, and had assigned its Munich office to him; his journeys were thereby removed from control by the Gestapo, and were not subject to any objections or checks from that quarter. After January 1940 he went often to the Dohnanyis in Berlin, and so got to know Dietrich Bonhoeffer. Although they were quite different in temperament and appearance, they took a liking to each other which often brought them together, apart altogether from their common activities in high politics. Bonhoeffer was referring to those first meetings when he wrote optimistically in a letter to his brother Karl-Friedrich: 'Well, the time of uncertainty will not last much longer now.'[214] For one night at the end of January Josef Müller dictated to Christine von Dohnanyi the final report. His name as negotiator was denoted by an 'X', and so that document has been given the name of 'X-report'. The negotiations through the Vatican had shown that Great Britain was prepared, *before* an attack in the West

213. On those proceedings see *Vollmacht des Gewissens*, pp. 408 ff.
214. Letter of 15.1.1940, GS II, p. 562.

and *after* Hitler had been removed, to agree to an armistice. The basis for subsequent peace talks would be an intact Germany within its 1937 frontiers.

In February the final work on this project was unfortunately delayed. One reason was that the American special envoy Sumner Welles's audience with Hitler held things up somewhat, as Hitler suddenly seemed to be capable of negotiating with the West, though the resistance circles had maintained that there was no chance of this.

Bonhoeffer came straight back to Berlin from his collective pastorate in the snow and ice, as Dohnanyi, Oster, Hassell, and Beck were discussing how the 'X-report' was to be implemented. Hassell's diary of 19th March says:

I first found him [Beck] alone, and discussed the situation with him. Then came O. [Oster] and D. [Dohnanyi]; they read me some very interesting papers about conversations between a Roman Catholic confidential agent and the Pope, who had thereupon got into touch through Osborne (British envoy at the Vatican) with Halifax. Apparently the Pope went a surprisingly long way, after that, in sympathy with German interests. Halifax, who spoke expressly for the British Government, is essentially more cautious in his way of putting things, and touches on such things as 'decentralization in Germany' and 'plebiscite in Austria'. On the whole, the wish for a reasonable peace is clearly there, and the Pope impressed strongly on the confidential agent that such things as 'decentralization' and 'plebiscite in Austria' would be no obstacle whatever to peace if agreement were otherwise reached. Of course, a presupposition for the whole thing is a change of régime and a recognition of Christian morality. The object of the discussion with me was: 1. to hear my view of the international situation; 2. to ask me to approach Halder on the matter, because there was no promise of success from other intermediaries.[215]

Dohnanyi now worked the 'X-report' into a memorandum, which, moreover, summarized the arguments for quick action, dealt with objections that might stand in the way, such as the stab-in-the-back legend and the oath of allegiance, and drew attention in detail to the increasing destruction of the Army's independence by the S.S. troops, and to the latter's atrocities. Bonhoeffer took part in a very small group that met in Dohnanyi's house to consider the memorandum. It was not till 4th April—it was unfortunate that it could not be sooner—that General Thomas took the memorandum to Halder, who showed it to Brauchitsch the next day. Both of them were busy at that moment, working out the final details of the imminent invasion of Scandinavia and the West, and so they could hardly give much time and thought to the study of an exhaustive document. On the other hand, ought not Brauchitsch to have been more willing to listen if the whole burden of responsibility might soon be laid on him? Halder reports on Brauchitsch's reaction:

215. U. von Hassell, *Vom Andern Deutschland*, 1964, p. 124.

He handed me back the paper and said: 'You ought not to have submitted that to me! What is happening here is absolute treason.' Then he demanded I should have the man who had delivered the paper to me arrested. I then replied: 'If anyone is to be arrested, arrest me!'[216]

So the most important instrument for carrying out the plans, the commander-in-chief of the Army, was not available for the purpose. The avalanche was on the move. The chance that a still unbeaten Germany might negotiate on terms with the Western Powers went by the board. The opposition's credibility was at stake, and it was to be feared that Josef Müller's negotiations from the West would now be regarded as a sham, as were the meetings of Heydrich's confidant, Schellenberg, with Stevens and Best at Venlo. Was it not a case of saving what there was to be saved, and for the opposition at least to show that it did not identify itself with the coming violation of neutrality? So in April Josef Müller again went to Rome to break the news that no revolution was now possible, and that the feared offensive was to be expected. 'We must be able to establish contacts again some day; and for that the people must know whom they are dealing with, that there is a decent Germany that is capable of negotiating.'[217]

Colonel Oster

Every hour, in those days of despair, there was less and less hope of putting an end to the wrongs that were being committed in Germany's name, and of preventing fresh atrocities. One of the people whom Bonhoeffer met during those weeks was Hans Oster, with whom he went to his death five years later. He knew from Dohnanyi what Oster was about to do, namely inform the Dutch of the date of the coming attack, and thereby stop Hitler's successes which were bringing disaster on Germany.[218]

Bonhoeffer regarded Oster's action on the eve of the Western offensive as a step taken on his own final responsibility. It seemed to him appropriate in a situation into which a presumptuous German had manœuvred his country, and in which all those who were capable of action were suffering from paralysis of the conscience. So the patriot had to perform what in normal times is the action of a scoundrel. 'Treason' had become true patriotism, and what was normally 'patriotism' had become treason. An officer saw the diabolical reversal of all values, and acted entirely alone so as not in any circumstances, after his experience in Poland, to pave the way for new outrages in other countries—and the pastor approved of what he did. He was willing to incur the odium of having

216. *Vollmacht des Gewissens*, p. 473.
217. Report by Christine von Dohnanyi; see *Vollmacht des Gewissens*, p. 487.
218. See F. Bauer, 'Oster und das Widerstandsrecht' in *Politische Studien*, No. 154, pp. 188-94.

his name mentioned only cautiously after the war, rather than not put everything, even his good name, to the hazard.

For men and nations who have never found themselves in that most unhappy state of divided loyalty, it is difficult to realize in retrospect that abnormal situation in which the most conscientious person has to accept disgrace. Anyone who hastily measures the borderline situation of that time by the yardstick of his own principles, or studiously overlooks its peculiar features, distorts its contours and does not see the realities of those months. Germany's name could no longer be saved by ordinary but blind respectability. All the world over, 'treason' is normally thought of as a mean attitude, speculation for one's personal advantage, and the intention to injure one's own country. The opposite holds good for Oster, Dohnanyi, and Bonhoeffer.

It was then that Bonhoeffer began to write his *Ethics*, in which the passage occurs: 'What is worse than doing evil is being evil. It is worse for a liar to tell the truth than for a lover of truth to lie.'[219] And in 1942 he wrote in the reflections called 'After Ten Years', a Christmas present for Oster and Dohnanyi:

Are we still of any use? We have been silent witnesses of evil deeds; we have been drenched by many storms; we have learnt the arts of equivocation and pretence; experience has made us suspicious of others and kept us from being truthful and open; intolerable conflicts have worn us down and even made us cynical. Are we still of any use? . . . Will our inward power of resistance be strong enough, and our honesty with ourselves remorseless enough, for us to find our way back to simplicity and straightforwardness?[220]

VIII THE CONTEMPORARY CHRISTIAN

In the spring of 1940 one could hardly have noticed anything about Bonhoeffer that would distinguish him from other uncompromising Confessing pastors. His theology and his language still resembled what was to be read in his *Cost of Discipleship* and *Life Together*. The sermons and circulars of those months comforted and admonished as before.

It was only later that friends discovered in expositions such as, for example, the meditation on Psalm 119,[221] turns of speech that hinted at what was to come. Afterwards they recalled conversations such as the one on his thirty-third birthday on 4th February 1939 round the tiled stove of the vicarage in Further Pomerania, when he said that it might be worth while, even for a pastor, to risk one's life for political freedom.[222] It became clear subsequently that Bonhoeffer had always, in fact, left the door open a crack for such a step. Even in *The Cost of Discipleship* there was such a sentence tucked away as 'It is important

219. E, pp. 64 f.   220. LPP, p. 40.
221. See Ch. XI, p. 571.
222. H.-W. Jensen, 'Life Together', IKDB, p. 154.

that Jesus gives his blessing not merely to suffering incurred directly for the confession of his name, but to suffering in any just cause.'[223] There were also his comments at the Steglitz Synod, and later his reference to the *Humanum* in the disputation on the Law. But all this was nothing more than a chink, hardly noticeable, and not yet an open door through which he had already gone.

Yet in the period with which we have just dealt, the way was being prepared for a change that showed itself in a new way of life and action, and then gave a new impetus to his theology. We have seen how the beginning of that period was still entirely shaped by a rigid adherence to the kind of pastoral training that was regarded as necessary for a professional minister. At the end we find a readiness for underground activity and a wish to think out ethical questions afresh. The 'boundary situation', with its particular possibilities of cognition, of which Bonhoeffer once spoke in Tegel, was approaching.[224]

The first change, about 1931-2, was when Bonhoeffer the theologian consciously grasped the fact that he was a Christian. At the beginning of 1939 Bonhoeffer the theologian and Christian was entering fully into his contemporary world, his place, and his time. That means into a world which his bourgeois class had helped to bring about, rather than prevent. He accepted the weight of that collective responsibility, and began to identify himself with those who were prepared to answer for guilt and try tentatively to shape something new for the future, instead of merely protesting on ideological grounds, as had hitherto been usual on the ecclesiastical plane. So in 1939 the theologian and Christian became a contemporary.

Theologian—Christian—contemporary; those three, which may at first sight seem to be a matter of course, do not often go together in history. Each of the two steps that Bonhoeffer took from one to the other changed the dimensions of his career.

Both steps, in 1932 and 1939, took place unadvertised. Bonhoeffer never spoke of them directly, or even publicly; on the contrary, he thought his life had gone on continuously with no breaks.[225] But his friends became aware, if not of the changes of direction themselves, at least of their visible results.

In 1932 he found his calling, in 1939 his destiny. In 1932 he found the unmistakable language in which he wrote his characteristic contribution to theology: well-rounded books, *The Cost of Discipleship* and *Life Together*. The development since 1939, too, found expression in two books: *Ethics* and *Letter and Papers from Prison*. But one of these is a fragment, and the other is a book of posthumously selected letters. They have, indeed, been largely responsible for his growing reputation.

223. CD, pp. 102 f.
224. LPP, p. 87.
225. LPP, p. 149.

He once referred jokingly to the above-mentioned change by calling
Life Together his 'swan-song'.[226]

The year 1932 had taken Bonhoeffer into the community of brethren
which was limited to that ecclesiastical group that protested publicly with
him. 1939 took him into an even more restricted circle of like-minded
people. From that time the Finkenwalde brethren felt that there was
always something of the incognito about him, and that they must not
question him on it. For the new companions, on the other hand, his
Christian existence did not often emerge in a simple form. He instinc-
tively kept the other part of his being in the background from the old
friends or the new ones, as the case might be. Anyone who had to do
with him may have felt that there was more there than he saw; but no
one had the impression of any disruption; everything was in order.

The year 1932 had put Bonhoeffer into a world where things were
comparatively clear-cut, where it was a matter of confessing and denying, and therefore in his case of the one Church for the whole world
and against its betrayal to nationalist particularism. The end of such
a road was bound to be a fate like that of Paul Schneider. In 1939 he
entered the difficult world of assessing what was expedient, of success
and failure, of tactics and camouflage. The certainty of his calling in
1932 now changed into the acceptance of the uncertain, the incomplete,
and the provisional. The new call demanded quite a different sacrifice,
the sacrifice even of a Christian reputation.

The year 1932 had opened up the ecumenical movement to Bonhoeffer,
and he became its passionate advocate as Germany increasingly isolated
itself. When in 1939 he could have saved himself within that ecumenical
movement, he shut himself out from it, confining his way deliberately
to the separate and deadly fate of Germany.

The old priorities could be realized after 1939 only by their changing
places. To want to be only a Christian, a disciple who follows time-
lessly—that now became a costly privilege. To become a contemporary
standing in his right place was so much more liable to misinterpretation,
so much duller and more cramped—that alone was what it now meant
to be a Christian.

The possibility of a 'life together' came to an end for good in the spring
of 1940, and one day the discipleship-theology needed to be revised;
its framework was shattered. The priority of ecclesiology receded still
further; the temporal, bourgeois, national future had to be accepted
responsibly.

The traces of that change provide a less compact picture than those
of the first, but they go down into other depths.

226. GS II, p. 398.

PART THREE

Sharing Germany's Destiny

CHAPTER TWELVE

TRAVELLING

1940 - 1943

IT was in Memel on 17th June 1940. In the morning Bonhoeffer had been talking to Dr. Werner Wiesner at a thinly attended conference of pastors; in the evening there was to be a Confessing Church service. That afternoon, he was sitting with me in an open-air café just opposite the town, on the peninsula. We had come by ferry past submarine tenders and mine-sweepers. On the previous day Stalin had delivered an ultimatum to the Baltic States, but the attention of the world was centred on France.

While we were enjoying the sun, there suddenly boomed out from the café's loudspeaker the fanfare signal for a special announcement: the message was that France had surrendered. The people round about at the tables could hardly contain themselves; they jumped up, and some even climbed on the chairs. With outstretched arm they sang 'Deutschland, Deutschland über alles' and the Horst-Wessel song. We had stood up, too. Bonhoeffer raised his arm in the regulation Hitler salute, while I stood there dazed. 'Raise your arm! Are you crazy?' he whispered to me, and later: 'We shall have to run risks for very different things now, but not for that salute!'

A Double Life

It was then that Bonhoeffer's double life began, namely the pastor's engagement in the political underground movement, which, he wrote in 1943, 'may prevent me from taking up my ministry again later on'.[1] That passage in a letter from Tegel was not an expression of secret uncertainty about the way that was then beginning; on the contrary, he was referring to an inward necessity for which his Church had as yet no formulae ready. By normal standards, things were standing on their heads.

That evening, Bonhoeffer preached, as far as I remember, without reference to the day's event. One would not have preached like that twenty-five years previously, at any rate in a German Protestant church. The victory in France had just brought about what the circles to which Bonhoeffer belonged had dreamed of in 1914, and now he was standing there shocked, separated from the jubilant people. His contemporaries

1. LPP, p. 107.

and pupils were helping to win battles that were smashing a world to pieces, while he was holding Bible classes in out-of-the-way places and was taking no part in strengthening the patriotic morale of people at the front or at home. The crowd jumped on to the chairs and forgot, in noisy delight, both the means and the end of the victory. He felt only shame at the success of the crime.

He shared that kind of feeling with a number of Confessing churchmen; but on 17th June he had other hopes dashed of which few people knew. The expectation that the first military stresses would topple the hated régime had turned out to be false, and all dreams of dislodging it had vanished. The victory in France set the seal on an immense miscalculation of Bonhoeffer's informants and friends in the resistance movement; the professionals—Beck, Thomas, Goerdeler, and Canaris— were wrong, and Hitler the amateur was right. Hitler's estimate of the enemy and of his own methods was upheld before the world, and other estimates were branded as defeatism. One first had laboriously to find one's bearings in relation to it. 'Behind everything that we can see there are now in fact other experiences with which we have to settle, even in dreams', Bonhoeffer wrote from Königsberg to his parents on 21st June.[2] In comparison with the First World War, the military situation seemed to be fundamentally changed; and anyone who had not forgotten the stalemate of 1914 was bound to be overwhelmed by this lightning victory in the West. What did it imply?

A few members of the Old Prussian Council of Brethren, like Kurt Scharf, Wilhelm Niesel, and Wilhelm Jannasch, remember especially a session of the council at the beginning of July with Viktor Hasse in Ncwawes.[3] They say that Bonhoeffer appeared there and surprised the friends by indicating that he, like everyone else, capitulated before Hitler's incredible success as before a divine judgement, and recommended a new attitude towards the National Socialist State.[4] But there were also at the session younger representatives of the Lutheran Union, like Pastor Wilhelm Rott and Dr. Herbert Werner, who even then understood Bonhoeffer's views differently:

I think they were all very surprised, as I was, at what he said. If I remember rightly, it was noted in silence. It was a kind of analysis of the situation after the regrettably successful campaign in France . . . Whether in implicit or in explicit reference to the aged Frau von Kleist-Retzow's fallen grandson,[5] Bonhoeffer reminded us that the death in action of young men from families firmly opposed to the régime implied a commitment to the hard facts of the new situation created by Hitler. The belief of many of our circle that the clash of weapons would involve a catastrophe for the régime had been exploded:

2. GS II, p. 373.
3. Now called the Babelsberg; it was frequently used as an out-of-the-way meeting-place for such discussions.
4. W. Niesel, 'From Keelson to Principal of a Seminary', IKDB, p. 147.
5. A son of the Lasbeck Bismarcks.

and we had to adjust ourselves to Hitler's rule, at any rate for a long time. Then on the way home I talked with Brother Werner about the meeting and about Bonhoeffer's speech. We discussed the possibility that it might be taken as an inward capitulation to the new facts of the case, and as a recognition of the 'new reality'. For myself, I then and there rejected any such possibility. It was clear to me that Bonhoeffer, who was always a good psychologist, described the situation (perhaps a dangerous one for the audience) so forcibly only so that we could deliver properly, in the new situation, the old testimony that was required of us. The friend to whom I was then talking agrees with me today, too, that it would be absurd to infer from that speech that Bonhoeffer had changed sides; and this is confirmed by his obvious attitude both before and after the session . . . It would be beyond me to imagine how anyone could turn what was said at Babelsberg into a sudden access of enthusiasm for National Socialism and a confession of loyalty to Hitler.[6]

Besides this, we have the diary of a lady who took part in a session of the Pomeranian Council of Brethren in Stettin immediately after Nowawes; her notes read :

Dr. Bonhoeffer on the situation : Fundamental change in the nation has taken place; historical 'Yes' given to National Socialism; widespread change of opinion; collapse of liberal democratic world, conspicuous success for Party. This puts Church in a very difficult position; many people ask 'Is it worth while . . .?' Many pastors, now officers in the Army ask 'Shall I go back to such a meagre ministry?' Important, (among other things) to bring ourselves to speak of the glory of the Gospel, and of the glory of the ministry![7]

That, then, is the kind of view that Bonhoeffer put forward to people who had responsible positions in the Church. At the same time he said quite different things to other audiences.[8] According to that diary he was speaking of an 'historical Yes', but not of an ethical or even theological Yes, which he regarded as quite a different matter. The historical facts of a case were recognized and acknowledged, without any liability to contamination by the victor's ideology. The audience kept in mind that Bonhoeffer was revising his outlook : and they were right about that, but some obviously did not understand the manner of the 'revision'.

There can be no talk of a surrender by Bonhoeffer to the facts, not even for a moment; something quite different was going on in his mind.

He wanted to grasp the significance of the fact that the régime of unrighteousness was to continue, through its success, for a much longer time than all his friends in the ecclesiastical and political resistance movement had hitherto assumed to be likely. In that context the contrast between the hopes that were still cherished and the consolidation of the

6. Communication from W. Rott, 14.2.1966.
7. Diary of Anna Ohnesorge, Directress of Studies, at that time a member of the Pomeranian Council of Brethren for catechetical questions.
8. See Ch. XII, p. 627.

régime was much sharper for Bonhoeffer than for his less well-informed audiences.

Further, he wanted to impress on himself and others that after 17th June there could no longer be a simple return to things as they had been before then. The relationship to neighbouring countries, the social structure, the political *status quo*—everything from now on would be, and would remain, irrevocably influenced by Hitler's action, so the object of eliminating Hitler could no longer be a restoration of the past. The road to something new would be infinitely more lengthy and costly, and the objective of unknown shape.

Only a few weeks after that session, Bonhoeffer wrote down clearly what he felt that it all amounted to; he was then working on the earlier sections of his *Ethics*. In September 1940 he produced the chapter on 'success':

The successful man presents us with accomplished facts which can never again be reversed. What he destroys cannot be restored. What he constructs will acquire at least a prescriptive right in the next generation. No indictment can make good the guilt which the successful man has left behind him. The indictment falls silent with the passage of time, but the success remains and determines the course of history. The judges of history play a sad rôle in comparison with its protagonists. History rides rough-shod over their heads . . .

If one is engaged in fruitless and pharisaical criticism of what is past, one can oneself never find one's way to the present, to action and to success, and precisely in this one sees yet another proof of the wickedness of the successful man . . .

Jesus is certainly no apologist for the successful men in history, but neither does He head the insurrection of shipwrecked existences against their successful rivals. He is not concerned with success or failure but with the willing acceptance of God's judgement.[9]

That was a bit of pragmatism that Bonhoeffer thought it necessary to learn. For him it had nothing to do with 'appeasement', although that was not always fully realized. He was anxious that the régime's opponents, who were frustrated at the time, should not allow their minds to be deflected by the course of history, nor try to hold on to what was finally gone and done with. With his fellow theologians in the Confessing Church in view, his efforts to find the right way indicate that he had no wish to take an easy course and be pushed back to the 'last things'.

Finally, those remarks in Nowawes were made at the exact time when Bonhoeffer's double life for the Church and a different Germany began in practice. Now, for the first time, it became a really serious thing with him. What the brethren had experienced in the council session was part of the process of reorientation to the future. The political backgrounds

9. E, pp. 75 ff.

and the personal factors, which were decisive for Bonhoeffer, could, of course, not be matters of discussion in a Council of Brethren.

The three years that followed were very unsettled, being determined by the existence side by side, on the one hand of work for the Confessing Church and on ethics, and on the other of the undertaking of various tasks for the conspiracy. Bonhoeffer travelled to and fro between Further Pomerania, Berlin, and Bavaria, and undertook journeys into countries on Germany's northern and southern frontiers. In those three years he managed to remain a civilian, though in the end he was sent to a military prison as a member of the military intelligence service.

He had two places of residence, which had to be reported in accordance with police regulations, though in fact he did not actually stay at either: till the late autumn of 1940 there was still the accommodation with Superintendent Block in Schlawe, and then, till his arrest, in Munich with his aunt Christine, Countess Kalckreuth, a well-known expert in graphics, and daughter of the painter Leopold von Kalckreuth. But his life really centred once more on his parents' home in Berlin. In October 1940 he arranged in his attic there all of his books that he could collect from Finkenwalde, Köslin, and Sigurdshof; and he also found room for the clavichord that he had owned since his visit to Cassel Music Festival in 1938.[10] Apart from his parents' home, there were three places where he could sometimes go for quietness—the Benedictine monastery at Ettal in the south, and the two Kleist estates of Kieckow and Klein-Krössin in the north. He wrote from Further Pomerania: 'It is strange, and really disgraceful, that staying in Berlin takes away from me, so to speak, the spiritual air of life.'[11] For the rest, he often had to struggle for a place in the blacked-out passenger trains. Sometimes, indeed, his two posts in the *Abwehr* (counter-espionage service) in Berlin and Munich gave him the enviable privilege of travelling by the comfortable trains reserved for the services.

In those three years his life alternated between extreme tension and occasional luxurious relaxation, between involvement in conspiracy and absorption in theology. At the end of that time he became engaged to Maria von Wedemeyer, a clear sign that he did not intend to be pushed back into 'apocalyptic opposition'.[12]

The course of events during the period that is dealt with in this chapter can be only approximately reconstructed. The months of the western offensive, April and May 1940, Bonhoeffer spent in Berlin. From June to August he went to East Prussia three times on church business. In September and October he was in Klein-Krössin. From November 1940 to February 1941 he lived in the Ettal monastery. From 24th February to 24th March 1941 he undertook the first journey to Switzer-

---

10. LPP, p. 106.
11. Letter of 26.8.1940, GS II, p. 375.
12. A phrase used to describe those clergy who spoke in terms of the end of the world.

land. Over Easter he came back to Friedrichsbrunn; from May to August he changed about between Klein-Krössin, Berlin, and occasionally Munich. From 28th August to 26th September 1941 there came the second journey to Switzerland. In late October and during November he was kept in his parents' home with pneumonia, and in December he was convalescing in Kieckow. From January to April 1942 he was mainly in Berlin; he spent Easter in Kieckow. From 10th to 18th April 1942 he went to Norway, and from 12th to 23rd May 1942 to Switzerland for the third time. From 30th May to 2nd June 1942 he was in Sweden. In June he visited Klein-Krössin, Munich, and Freiburg, and in between he repeatedly broke his journey in Berlin. From 26th June to 10th July he was in Italy. During the autumn and winter of 1942-3 he left Berlin only for short spells in Munich, Klein-Krössin, Freiburg, Magdeburg, and Pätzig, the last-mentioned being his prospective mother-in-law's estate.

SECTION ONE: CHURCH

I THE CONFESSING CHURCH IN THE WAR

The double life that Bonhoeffer now led made him no less involved in the fate of the Confessing Church. In spite of his obligations with regard to the military authorities, his official relationship to that Church remained intact; and although he had in the meantime sharply criticized the Confessing synods, his conviction of the validity of the decisions of the Barmen and Dahlem Synods did not change in any way. To the last there was no other church that he would rather have supported or where he would have liked to find his home; and the Confessing Church still remained his own Church when it could no longer take his part or identify itself with his cause.

In 1940 Bonhoeffer was again able to have closer contacts than before with the council's Berlin centres, as he was living with his parents more often and for longer periods, and his future occupation was uncertain. In those contacts, of course, precautionary measures had to be observed, because of the official restrictions on his movements and activities in church work and meetings.[13] A little later, he was making the most of his special political and military connections, up to the limit of what was justifiable, to obtain extra-parochial posts for certain of the clergy, so that the remaining authorities of the Confessing Church could continue their work; this became one of the charges against him in 1943.

The Church in 1940

In 1940 the church struggle was not greatly intensified; in fact, when

13. See Ch. XI, p. 502.

the campaign in France was over, Hitler told the higher local authorities, through the Ministry of the Interior, that he wished them 'to avoid all measures that might impair the relationship of the State and Party to the Church, unless such measures were absolutely necessary'.[14] The Intercession List for 1940 was actually shortened.

But there were interferences that could hardly be passed by in silence. Even in April and May, the consistory took disciplinary action against the council members Albertz and Böhm because they had drawn up the special prayers in the autumn of 1938, and deprived them of their rights as pastors. Erich Klapproth, one of the former Finkenwalde students and spokesman of the 'illegals' of Berlin-Brandenburg, informed Bonhoeffer of the protest that he took it upon himself to send as a front-line soldier:

To the Disciplinary Board of the Brandenburg Consistory . . . Belgium, 30.5.1940 . . .
As a front-line soldier who has to risk his life every day and is therefore used to speaking frankly, I must tell you plainly, gentlemen, what anger and disgust I feel at your conduct. Men whose merits and patriotism cannot be seriously doubted are to be hunted down while most of their friends are engaged in the defence of the fatherland and are therefore in no position to make an effective protest . . . Like innumerable front-line soldiers, I am entirely on the side of the condemned pastors in this matter. With the 'judgement' that you, gentlemen, have now delivered from the security of your green baize table, you have, for one thing, included me in your impudent and insulting challenge. You may as well be clear that by your decision you have wantonly injured the morale of countless soldiers. Your régime, gentlemen, I do not regard as being in any way worth defending . . . However helpless it may be, the Confessing Church is more confident and more certain than you in your unspiritual position of power . . . [Albertz and Böhm] have, according to the evidence of Scripture and of the living Church, a right to their spiritual status and a calling to serve the Word; where do you get your right from? I am afraid you are desperately poor. After incidents like this, I do not know whether you call earnestly to God, and whether you can make any earnest intercession. But this much is certain: the prayers that are offered out here, between death and destruction, are earnest, and will bring the fulfilment of the promise. And those prayers are for the people whom you have condemned, and against you and your evil deeds. Erich Klapproth, soldier *pro tem.*

During the year, the Old Prussian Council of Brethren was hardly able to carry on its work. Fritz Müller of Dahlem went into the Army. Niesel, arrested for the eighth time and then expelled from Berlin, had to try to get along in Silesia. In spite of all that, the necessary meetings were held, with substitutes and members who had been expelled meeting outside the town boundaries, as in Nowawes. This increased the

14. Order of 24.7.1940.

importance of Friedrich Justus Perels, who knew all the official procedures and kept up the connections on all sides. The chairmanship was taken over by Provost Staemmler of the province of Saxony, but he had to drop out again in November 1940, when, after expressing himself too boldly, he was sentenced to a year in prison. But he was in office just at the time when decisions that were important for Bonhoeffer had to · be taken.[15]

Kerrl issued a decree forbidding the despatch by 'civil-ecclesiastical agencies' of religious literature, including duplicated field-post letters, to members of the armed forces.[16] That hit the work of every parish priest. Bonhoeffer, too, had to think out again how he could write to the Finkenwalde students on active service without laying himself open to prosecution.

What worried the Church most were the thirteen points laid down in March by the provincial governor Greiser. By this the Church in the newly formed *Warthegau* was given an association status by which it ceased to be a statutory corporation. Everyone saw here a model for a privately financed and atomized church in the Reich after the war had been won. That even made the neutrals and the Church External Affairs Office uneasy.[17]

It was only in whispers that one spoke about the measures of euthanasia that were carried out within the shelter of boundaries closed by the war. In the summer, Bonhoeffer negotiated with his father on behalf of Bodelschwingh of Bethel and Pastor Braune of Lobethal, so that they could obtain and quote authoritative medical grounds for refusing to hand their patients over. It was not till August 1941 that those measures of euthanasia were stopped on Hitler's directions.

The first rumours of the deportation of Jews came from Stettin in 1940. In February, the provincial Party leader had sent a transport of Stettin Jews in goods wagons to Poland. It was not yet known whether that was the beginning of a large-scale operation or an isolated case. Pastor Grüber, who had set up an agency for helping non-Aryans in Berlin, protested. That brought him a warning, and, months later, arrest and internment in a concentration camp.

In view of those occurrences, Bishop Wurm entered a protest in July 1940 about euthanasia, and in 1941 about the Jewish question.[18] That led to a new relationship between the Württemburg bishop and the Dahlem side of the Confessing Church.

Bishop Wurm, who, of course, had known for a long time about the 'radical' Bonhoeffer, had so far not been in personal touch with him. This now came about through Bonhoeffer's having, as mentioned above,

15. See Ch. XII, pp. 603 f.
16. Decree of 12.7.1940; cf. J. Beckmann, *Kirchliches Jahrbuch 1933-44*, p. 460.
17. See W. Niemöller, *Die Evangelische Kirche im Dritten Reich*, pp. 369 f.
18. See J. Beckmann, op cit., pp. 412 ff.

brought Bodelschwingh, who was in close contact with Wurm over the euthanasia question, to his father.[19] It began a correspondence between Wurm and Bonhoeffer, in which the bishop asked him what his attitude was towards his notorious remarks.[20] But at first, any further contact was prevented by Wurm's serious illness and Bonhoeffer's pneumonia and subsequent journeyings. It was not till 1942 that they were in touch again through the Freiburg conversations.[21] When in 1942-3 Wurm brought forward his comprehensive scheme of unification among the hostile groups with the 'thirteen propositions', Bonhoeffer scrutinized them critically to see where they might contradict the decisions of Barmen and Dahlem. But Wurm's action did not now seem to him to be one of cautious deliberation, as the attempts at the time of the Cassel group and the Essen memoranda[22] had been; on the contrary, it expressed openly the duty of a Confessing Church under the conditions of the times. Before Bonhoeffer could put down in writing the opinions that he had expressed in conversation on Wurm's thirteen propositions, he was arrested.

The Church in 1941

In the second year of the war, the church press and publicity organization had to close down because the allocation of paper to it was stopped; this probably spared the Church a good many printed utterances of 'which it would probably later have been ashamed'.[23]

In May 1941 the whole of the examining board of the Old Prussian Council of Brethren was arrested; and two days before Christmas they were sentenced after a large scale prosecution.

In Berlin things have again been quite unsettled lately. Among others, Albertz, Dehn, Asmussen, Böhm, Vogel, Harder, and a few women have been arrested because of examinations. It is almost incomprehensible why the congregations should be so provoked and harassed just now. But it is bound to serve the cause.[24]

As we shall see later, the severe sentences on twenty-three men and women of the board[25] also hit the 'illegal' pastors on active service.

When the 'final solution' of the Jewish question was begun in the autumn of 1941, what was left of the Confessing Church was fully occupied with questions concerning its own existence, and there were only a few brave isolated actions. Thus, the Old Prussian council of a

19. T. Wurm, *Erinnerungen aus meinem Leben*, p. 157.
20. GS II, p. 405.
21. See Ch. XII, pp. 681 ff.
22. See Ch. XI, pp. 508 f.
23. J. Beckmann, op. cit., p. 350.
24. Bonhoeffer to H.-W. Jensen, 14.5.1941. GS II, p. 589.
25. W. Niemöller, op. cit., pp. 247 f.

Confessional synod appointed a committee to consider the current understanding of the fifth commandment; but there was no large-scale protest
anywhere. Bonhoeffer at once set to work with Perels when the night
transportations began; but that is dealt with in connection with the
Resistance Movement.[26]

Further, in the autumn of 1941 he wrote out, in consultation with
Perels, a memorandum to the Army, drawing attention to the fact that
the State's anti-Church measures were injuriously affecting the military
efforts. He recorded in it, from the two years of war, everything that
impeded the Church's public work; the events of Warthegau, those
relating to the Press and to euthanasia, the arrests, and the prohibition
of pastoral work even in the Church's hospitals:

The hope of evangelical Christians that measures hostile to the Church
might be discontinued, at least for the duration of the war, has been bitterly
disappointed . . . We ask the Army to take the following steps: 1. dis-
continue, for the duration of the war, all measures hostile to the Church; 2.
countermand arrests, expulsions, and prohibitions of speech that have been
put into effect for reasons connected with the Church or church politics; 3.
give the Church help and protection for its responsible task at home for the
duration of the war.[27]

Bonhoeffer could not be very confident of the possibilities of influencing the military authorities, but it was at least an attempt.

He tried unwearyingly to use all his connections to keep the Confessing Church from withering away through indiscriminate drafting
into the Army or for compulsory labour; and he was successful here and
there. At the beginning of 1940 he had put Scharf and Niesel in touch
with Groscurth, the liaison officer of the Army Intelligence Corps, to
check the unlimited calling up of 'illegal' pastors. In this matter he even
tried to influence Kerrl, the Minister for Religious Affairs, through intermediaries. Dohnanyi spoke about it to Canaris, and to Olbricht, the
head of the general army office, asking them to make representations to
Kerrl, to offer the same treatment and exemptions to Confessing pastors
as to others. Through Dohnanyi he induced Gürtner, the Minister of
Justice, to point out to Kerrl what proofs of their patriotic loyalty the
Confessing pastors had given. 'The Gürtner-Kerrl conversation seems to
have gone successfully', Bonhoeffer wrote on 8th December 1940.[28] It
was to be continued with further documentary evidence, prepared by
Perels. On a long walk in icy cold weather at Ettal, Bonhoeffer was able
to go through the matter personally with Gürtner, and the latter gave
optimistic hints:

Gürtner came at midday yesterday. We spent the whole day together, and

26. See Ch. XII, pp. 649 ff.
27. GS II, pp. 428, 432.
28. GS II, p. 389.

talked over a good many things. He is quite optimistic as to the K. business, only it is questionable what K. himself is still able to do. The matter needs to be hurried on somewhat, for the conscription of labour is increasing.[29]

A month later, Gürtner was carried to his grave, and the matter could not be revived at ministerial level. On the contrary, the Russian campaign again increased the number of those called up. According to word from E. Klapproth, in the summer of 1941 there were 270 young Rhineland brethren on active military service out of 300, and from Brandenburg 132 out of 154. Out of about 150 Finkenwalde students more than 80 were killed in action.

Although the efforts to secure a general adjustment in the regulations as to the call-up failed, quite astonishing manipulations were possible at the individual level. No net that the recruiting offices could work had meshes quite small enough to keep all the people that it caught. Various superintendents, and occasional well-wishers in consistories or the higher church council, could obtain exemption for one person or another. Dohnanyi's and Oster's help was the most effective. Over the years they brought into their scheme other friends as well as Bonhoeffer. They managed to have the latter officially regarded as indispensable, so that, although the military claimed him, he was able to remain in his civilian occupation. Later on they had considerable difficulty in standing their ground, in view of his non-church activities, against the reproach that they were helping men to evade military service. With their help, Bonhoeffer kept in office a number of people who were in danger of being taken, such as Wilhelm Niesel, Wilhelm Jannasch, and Ernst Wolf, as well as F. J. Perels and Wilhelm Rott, whose Lutheran Union office was one of the few Confessing Church departments that still continued, and myself in my work in the Gossner Mission.

Direct obligations to non-church authorities, for the *Abwehr*, or alternatively for its resistance circle, existed only for Bonhoeffer himself; the others were free from ties. They felt, with a clear conscience, that they were being kept by Mr. X to serve their Church, and that is exactly what was intended. Bonhoeffer persisted in this, because however small the numbers, these were men he could help. Too much was expected from his brother-in-law and his friends in the *Abwehr*. When they succeeded once again in freeing someone for church work, he wrote:

We find that the lesson that we learn from this business is that we know too few people, and that the circle is getting too narrow. Before Wolfgang fell ill[30] I had been talking with him at some length over this very point, and he wanted to initiate something that would have a bearing on it. Now he has probably not been able to do anything more about it.[31]

29. To his parents, 22.12.1940.
30. Staemmler's arrest on 16.11.1940.
31. To E. Bethge, 1.12.1940, GS II, p. 387.

Since the arrest of Dohnanyi and his friends in 1943, they have been reproached on the ground that those protective measures were dangerous and imprudent. But those things took place during the long life-and-death struggle of the Confessing Church at a time when there seemed to be reasonable hope that everything would soon be different anyhow, and that the overthrow of Hitler was coming. They took place, too, in a feeling of responsibility that competent younger people should be preserved for the expected change, whatever the cost might be. Anyone who was working for the conspiracy was bound, unless he was willing to consign the aftermath to chaos, to think about the survival of at least some bearers of the new responsibility. It is to the lasting credit of Canaris that he did not act small-mindedly, but accepted the risks himself, and used the possibilities of his double position to serve good ends.

Continued Legalization

In the second year of the war, the argument about the bravery of the many young pastors of the Confessing Church going on active service lost more and more of its force, and the unpleasant temptation to have one's position legalized reappeared.[32] Pressure and enticement by the consistories again increased. The wholesale prosecution of the examining board of the Council of Brethren in Berlin seemed to cut the ground from under the feet of the 'illegal' pastors, now that all the examinations by the Confessing Church had been legally invalidated by a court. Besides this, a new labour conscription act affecting people unfit for active service threatened to take away from those who were still at home the last possibility of working for the Confessing Church. Bonhoeffer had his hands full, giving advice to his 'illegal' Finkenwalde pastors.

In November 1940 a decree was circulated by the Minister of Labour —in itself a proof that there was still a hard core of people who were standing fast and would not yield to pressure—according to which the 'Evangelical theological ordinands, ministers, assistant preachers, etc., who have been trained in the prohibited sham colleges of the Confessing Party or illegally ordained, and who are exercising a disturbing influence among the people by their slanderous activities' were to be 'directed without delay into a suitable occupation'.[33] That hit the unfit and the women theologians of the Confessing Church, which now, suddenly and unwittingly, had its 'worker-priests'. The woman minister Inge Koch, who was an appointed representative of the 'illegal' pastors in the province of Saxony, and who had to work in the Leuna factories, wrote:

It is strange what temptations suddenly raise their heads in front of the few of us here, how we learn that all available forces are used up in the mobiliza-

32. Cf. Ch. XI, pp. 512-24.
33. J. Beckmann, op. cit., pp. 466 f.

tion of labour, how tired and empty one gets and does not in the least know how one can prepare a Bible lesson or preach a sermon.[34]

The Magdeburg consistory told Johannes Hamel, who was also liable to be sent to work in a factory, that he could be exempted if he would '1. take up all the consistory's collections, 2. read out all the announcements of the official church, and 3. stop interceding for imprisoned and prohibited people by name from the pulpit.'[35]

Now, too, Bonhoeffer did not give way; he did not advise anyone to submit to legalization. But, in contrast to former years, he sent the circulars to 'illegal' and 'legalized' pastors, answered personal letters from the latter without going into differences of opinion, and so to a certain extent accepted 'Way B'.

Some were made more obstinate by the new existence at the front and in the factory, but others were made more uneasy. How could they not want to know that their congregation, their official position, and their family at home were secure? And how were they still to maintain the subtle distinctions of former times? Willy Brandenburg wrote from the eastern front:

You have heard that, after struggles lasting for years, I have seen my way to undergoing the legalizing process with the consistory. I know, too, that you consider that I am on the wrong track. I felt inhibited from telling you personally about it, as I ought to have done; but that was not because I felt objectively uncertain about it—I still think I acted rightly—but because I have caused some grief and stress to you and the brethren by the step that I have taken.[36]

Another, who remained at home, praised his legalized position:

I should never have thought it possible for legalization to make one's work so much easier! And I find that lightening of work most welcome . . . I have been told that the theological work of the Confessing Church is fully recognized, and that it is entirely responsible for preserving the essentials of the Church.[37]

Bonhoeffer's advice was at least to wait and see:

Who could fail to see that this war has faced us with a cleft that our thoughts cannot bridge? So we will wait in good heart.[38]

One of those at the front refused bluntly when he was told in writing that he could have the office of pastor with all its privileges if, when he was on leave, he would submit to a simplified examination by the consistory. But he wrote to Bonhoeffer:

34. Circular letter of 14.2.1941.
35. Ibid.
36. Letter of 5.10.1941.
37. Doebert to Bonhoeffer, 13.1.1942.
38. Letter of 15.8.1941, GS II, p. 578.

But I keep on having doubts whether we young pastors of the Confessing Church are taking a course that is right and necessary. After all, there are indications that after the war, and to some extent even now, we shall be deprived of all possibility of pastoral work. Has not the Confessing Church laid too heavy a burden on our shoulders . . .? Do not we brethren who were examined by the Confessing Church resemble shock-troops cut off from the main body and gradually becoming casualties . . .? That we are just treated as unemployed and assigned work as such? Is the way that we are going still necessary . . .? I no longer feel certain . . . Please advise me. You once wrote: Wait and see; the war will bring changes that we cannot yet foresee . . . We may then be relegated to a completely illegal status as Confessing Church pastors . . . Whom else am I to ask? As far as I can see, the Council of Brethren no longer counts. So, Brother Bonhoeffer, give me the answer that I am waiting for and shall listen to . . .[39]

For the answer to one of such letters, Bonhoeffer jotted down: '1. Never act from a position of uncertainty; 2. Never act alone; 3. Never be hasty or allow yourself to be pushed. God can open what is locked up.' He gave this answer in a circular letter,[40] and it is his last message on legalization. In that letter, he sticks to the rule 'that our present military situation is unfavourable for undertaking a far-reaching change of direction for the Church . . . Any decision that puts the brethren at home in a more favourable position than those at the front is more than ever open to question'. He then admits, for the first time, that after the prosecution of the examining board it might be possible for some to look for new ways, but without thereby acknowledging the consistories as spiritual controllers. But he shows clearly that he thinks the risking of the Church's established pastoral office is still more pregnant for the future:

The willingness to *renounce* a legitimate office, or even any exercising of the spiritual office, and to serve Christ in a different calling rather than submit to wrong spiritual control—for that is what it amounts to in view of the coming generation—remains a legitimate evangelical attitude . . .

The willingness to renounce any church régime—for it is impossible to recognize a wrong church régime—and to accept the official ministry 'maintaining one's personal theological conviction' in order to serve Christ as a pastor, can, indeed, in the present circumstances, no longer be contested on principle as a Christian possibility; but it is fraught with heavy ecclesiastical and personal dangers and responsibilities. That must be recognized.[41]

So Bonhoeffer was still not aiming at patching things up; rather than do so, he would take no office in that church. If the prosecution of the examining board had now finally closed all the possibilities of training and of a road to the pastorate, he did not see in it any reason for giving way. It would rather mean looking out for some other form of service that would make it possible to deliver a credible message. Then one

39. Letter from J. Mickley, 9.1.1942.   40. GS II, p. 594.   41. GS II, pp. 594 f.

would finally discard the old protective coverings. Thus Bonhoeffer still appealed to one's own unfettered choice; and we can feel that this last word on legalization was intended to leave his students' consciences whole and free, without hurting any of those who decided differently.

And when his loyalty to what he had once discerned—even that letter of 1942 contained an urgent reminder of the Dahlem synodal decision![42] —was hopelessly overtaken by the historical development? It really looked like that. Bonhoeffer did not try to visualize the whole thing to the end. But he would not at any point of time, even in the bleakest moment of the war, follow the movement towards that all-approving consistorial makeshift church that he had once left.

The legalization problem flickered up again at the end of 1942 in one province or another, without causing any essential changes. Then it died out in the total war.

After the war, the consistories hastened to grant unconditionally, to those of the 'illegal' pastors who remained, their qualifications for office, their seniority, and everything that belonged to the privileged pastoral office. Hardly anyone thought of asking himself what conception of a preacher's duties there had formerly been at the back of that bitter and wearying struggle, and what it might have meant.

II VOCATIONAL PROBLEMS

There did not at first seem to be any problems about Bonhoeffer's calling after the collective pastorate had been dissolved in March 1940. The Council of Brethren took its time over giving him any further commission, and it suited him quite well to wait during April and May. Things did not become critical till the autumn of 1940; till then there were plenty of possibilities open to him, as there was no prohibition to hamper him outside Berlin; he could still preach, and he liked to do so.

A few months after he had been prohibited from speaking in public, he heard that an aunt who was suffering from cancer, Countess von der Goltz, had only a few months to live; he wrote to me then: 'What should I do, if I knew that the end would come in four to six months? . . . I think I should still try to teach theology as before, and *to preach often*.'[43] When Frau von Kleist-Retzow pressed him to give a daily exposition to her houshold, he was very gratified; and if one of his friends asked him for assistance with a sermon, he was always ready to help with a suggested outline. It was a blow to him that he was not allowed to preach in public after the autumn of 1940.

Church Visitor

In view of the difficulties of communication between the different

42. GS II, p. 595.   43. GS II, p. 405.

ecclesiastical areas, visitations were a necessary element for the life of the Confessing Church; and Bonhoeffer seemed admirably suited for giving information and theological guidance, and for preaching to those who were called up. So he undertook three such journeys for the East Prussian Council of Brethren. Those journeys were the cause of the real complications with regard to the problem of his calling.

First East Prussian Journey. Bonhoeffer delayed his first official journey eastwards because of the dramatic development on the western front. It was not till the day after Dunkirk—he was very anxious for his relatives in England as he followed the B.B.C.'s news of the débâcle on the coast —that he left with me to visit the church circuits round Tilsit and Memel after a convention of clergy at Schlawe. On the Tilsit-Memel visit he found parishes where the services were conducted by a farmer as an elder, pastors' wives who looked after all the religious instruction in extensive circuits, and places where he was not allowed to enter the church, because intercession by name for the imprisoned brethren of the Confessing Church was prohibited. In Tilsit he found the churches fuller than he was used to in the 'Reich'. He visited brethren from the community house like Horst Lekszas in Königsberg or Richard Grunow with his group of students in Danzig. He got to know Willy Kramp, whose novel *Die Fischer von Lissau* was causing something of a stir; on his way back from Köslin he renewed his contact with the versatile Dr. Knorr and his lay convention, and so brought back home proposals for teaching the laity. There were no incidents during this first journey; France's surrender was exciting enough. It was not till the second journey that his position became problematical.

Second East Prussian Journey. In Königsberg Bonhoeffer was fully occupied for several days with pastors who were having a conference. He conducted the Bible study, lectured on 'Preaching Today', 'Baptismal Grace and Discipline', 'Evangelical Oral Confession', and 'the Problem of Death', his theme for the Croall Lectures;[44] besides that, he led the discussions on 'the Church's Prophetic Ministry' and 'Church and Ministry'. That was an ample pastoral course. He also met the East Prussian fellowship leaders of the Dahlem side of the Confessing Church, and groups of soldier-theologians.

At the week-end of 13th-14th July he went out to Bloestau, where Hans Iwand had previously worked. Invitations had been circulated, on duplicated handbills, to a conference of Confessing students. That was incautious. Bonhoeffer was to speak on the situation and conduct a Biblical study on the text about the rich young ruler. Just as he had finished the Sunday morning service and was sitting chatting with a few students, a fairly large group of police appeared on the orders of the

44. Cf. Ch. XI, p. 565: no notes of these lectures are available.

Gestapo. The conference members were told to disperse, and the order was reinforced by a decree that was said to have been issued in June and to include a prohibition of such meetings by Christian youth, as well as 'Confessional organization' of adults. The Gestapo chief took no further interest in what had been going on, and let it be understood that he had expected a much bigger meeting. After personal details had been taken down, everyone dispersed in relief that no one had been interrogated or, indeed, arrested. Bonhoeffer certainly could not help feeling that there was more behind this than simply the breaking up of a conference at Bloestau. The Gestapo did not approve of speakers from other parts of the country, still less of speakers with his record.

But for the time being he continued his journey eastwards, and visited parishes in Stallupönen, Trakehnen, and Eydtkuhnen. The general mood there was one of depression. Soviet troops had, in fact, appeared opposite Eydtkuhnen on the former Lithuanian frontier. While the Germans in the Reich had their minds occupied with the events in France, Stalin had, after an ultimatum, occupied the Baltic territory that Ribbentrop had conceded to be within his sphere of influence; and this action had caused no small anxiety in East Prussia. 'I made myself go round on what is now the Russian frontier just at the time when things were happening. I preached in villages a mile or so away and found the most surprising changes.'[45] He now broke off his journey and gave up the short holiday that he had intended to have in Klein-Krössin. He went home to take counsel with his brother-in-law Dohnanyi in Berlin.

That was in early August 1940. In agreement with Canaris and Oster, Dohnanyi assured him that if there were any interference by the Gestapo, the Abwehr would be quite willing to interest itself in his journeys to the frontier on the ground that they would provide information; he would be given, as a precautionary measure for his next journey to East Prussia, a commission that would give him adequate protection. Eydtkuhnen had been near what might become a combat area since, at the end of July, Hitler had for the first time begun preparations for an offensive against the Soviet Union. So Canaris or Oster had a good case for trying to get information about the situation of the frontier, and could very well ask a Confessing pastor to report to him about it. That, so Dohnanyi supposed, would mean countering any steps that the Gestapo might take, and getting round the problem of a possible call-up. But above all—and this, of course, was the essential point of the discussions—it freed him for the work of conspiracy in Oster's and Dohnanyi's circle. When, one afternoon in August, Oster, Gisevius, Dohnanyi, Bonhoeffer, and I met in the Marienburger Allee, the arrangements were still only provisional. Bonhoeffer's final commitment to the Abwehr was brought about by the measures that the Gestapo took next.

45. E. Bethge to a friend; undated.

Third East Prussian Journey. On 25th August Bonhoeffer went to Königsberg for the third time, again as a visitor on behalf of the Old Prussian Council of Brethren. But he now called, not only on the Council of Brethren, but also on the officer of the Königsberg *Abwehr*, who was to protect him if anything unforeseen happened. This time he insisted that his visits on behalf of the Council of Brethren should not be advertised by handbills, so that the Gestapo's attention should not be drawn to them unnecessarily. In fact, he now ceased to keep his usual diary of his visits to the townships and people and of the meetings arranged. He came back to Eydtkuhnen. Feeling that he had come to a turning-point, he wrote: 'I think with gratitude of the years that have gone, and with confidence of those that are to come.'[46] Then he received an urgent telephone call from Superintendent Block, telling him to go at once to his place of residence at 9 Koppelstrasse, Schlawe.

Restrictions

On 4th September 1940 an official authorized by the state police in Köslin told him that an order had been issued by the Reich Security Office, forbidding him, on the ground of 'subversive activity' to make any public speeches in the Reich; it also provided that from that time on he was to report his movements to the police regularly, at his place of residence. That was an unpleasant combination of restraints. Bonhoeffer was given nothing in writing, and he could only note down the reference number of the order: Reich Security Office IVA 4b 776/40.[47]

The prohibition of public speaking might not matter too much; but the obligation to report was a deadly blow which, like his expulsion from Berlin, had to be parried at all costs. First, however, he wrote a protest to the Reich Security Office, to put the thing on record. In it the defamatory nature of the reason adduced, and the patriotic reputation of his forebears, played a suitable part: 'It is out of the question . . . for me to identify myself with circles that are rightly tainted by such

---

46. To E. Bethge, 26.8.1940; GS II, p. 374.
47. Among the documents in the head office of the state police in Düsseldorf, there was found after the war a copy of the decree that was sent by the Reich Security Office in Berlin with that reference number to all German state police offices, dated 22.8.1940: 'On account of his subversive activity, I issue against Pastor Dietrich Bonhoeffer of Schlawe, Pomerania, a prohibition against speaking in public in the whole of the Reich territory. By order, signed Roth.' Attached is a 'statement' by the Düsseldorf Gestapo of 20.9.1940: 'I request that any necessary action be taken in respect of the undermentioned persons . . . 1. Bonhoeffer, Dietrich . . . is forbidden to speak in public in the Reich. Report if B. moves there or otherwise comes to notice. Any prominent public appearance is to be prevented.' In that statement similar provisions are laid down against seven other Confessing pastors, among them Gollwitzer, Linz, Kreck, and Superintendent Onnasch of Köslin. Bonhoeffer very soon found out in Ettal how effective such Gestapo circulars were: 'There was an enquiry about me here, about what I was doing here and why I was over there [i.e. in the Benedictine monastery] so often' (10.12.1940; GS II, p. 389).

reproaches [of subversive activity].' And then follows a list, which he would otherwise have laughed at, of his forebears, the families Kalckreuth, Hase, Cauer, von der Goltz, and the honourable councillors of Schwäbisch Hall.[48] The protest remained unanswered.

Before any decision was made about plans for his future occupation, Bonhoeffer went to Klein-Krössin—the real reason for this will soon be clear—where he worked hard for four weeks on the first chapters of *Ethics*. In the evenings he listened closely to the B.B.C.'s reports of the battle of Britain. 'While there is a violent autumnal storm stripping the trees of their leaves outside . . . I am sitting here working quietly.'[49]

The Solution

Bonhoeffer's question about his calling had now become really complicated. What chance did there seem to be of further work for the Church? How could the offer of the *Abwehr* be grasped and made effective?

Any teaching activity was out of the question; visiting for the Church was forbidden, as was the exercise of his ministry in Berlin. What could the Old Prussian Council of Brethren do with its pastor-at-large? It was understandable that some of the council members now wanted to send him to take charge of a small parish in some remote district. Would not that be the best way of meeting his wish for theological work? The small town of Bismarck in Altmark was mentioned.

Perels spoke against this in the Old Prussian council; he certainly could not entirely give away his knowledge of Bonhoeffer's wishes. He pleaded that Bonhoeffer could be given a position that left him free for academic work, because he was writing his *Ethics* and was being used by a department of the armed forces in Berlin anyway—that is how we then expressed it. I myself went to Jena, to discuss the problems of Bonhoeffer's future confidentially with the chairman of the council, Staemmler, and especially to eliminate Altmark from the discussions. The decision of the next council session was in accord with Bonhoeffer's efforts.

On 15th November he went himself on the way to Munich to Staemmler (it was the day before the latter was arrested), and he wrote to his parents:

St. tells me that they attach importance to my doing scholarly work now; with regard to a post as pastor he was pessimistic; they would rather have me free to be at their disposal. I told him that I should like soon to get out of my nomadic existence. Anyway, as far as they are concerned I am free till next spring . . . But first I must wait and see how the military affair goes; I cannot decide anything before then. But it is at least a relief to know that I am not

48. GS II, pp. 363 ff.
49. To his parents, 8.10.1940; cf. also GS II, p. 376.

doing my academic work on my own account, but on other people's orders.[50]

He wrote to me:

So they have decided that I shall continue to have charge of the Confessing Church training place and that they will keep me at their disposal, but that in the meantime I can do academic work, as there is a great deal of interest in it . . . So for the time being I am free, with the satisfaction of knowing that that is what they want. What am I to do?[51]

On the military side, it was no difficult problem to have Bonhoeffer declared indispensable for the *Abwehr*. This was put through, and he was told in Oster's headquarters what he duly repeated in later interrogations: 'The *Abwehr* works with everyone, with Communists and with Jews; why not also with people of the Confessing Church?' But even for the *Abwehr* there was difficulty over the Reich Security Office's latest order about reporting to the police. It was therefore found advisable to keep him as far as possible from the Pomeranian state police office that had begun to watch out for him, and not to provoke the Gestapo by taking him too obviously into the Berlin centre.

So Oster and Dohnanyi hit on the idea of putting Bonhoeffer on the staff of the Munich office of the *Abwehr*. A number of reliable people worked there, especially since Dr. Josef Müller had joined the staff in the autumn of 1939. So in October 1940, when he was on an official journey to Italy, Dohnanyi discussed Bonhoeffer's future activity with his Munich colleagues. That was the reason why Bonhoeffer was able to work at theology for four weeks while he was waiting in Klein-Krössin.

After that, in November, Bonhoeffer had to present himself at the Munich office. The first thing he had to do was to register at the town hall as a resident of Munich although he did not intend actually to live there. His aunt Countess Kalckreuth very kindly took it on herself, by giving him nominal accommodation in her home, to make him a citizen of Munich. It was only after the formalities of this registration with a Munich address had been completed that the local *Abwehr* could apply to the recruiting station for Bonhoeffer to have his secular status; that was settled at last on 14th January. Meanwhile, of course, the police were kept on his track through the notice of removal in Schlawe, for the Gestapo's procedure over compulsory regular reporting could be carried out between the Munich *Abwehr* and the Gestapo only after the appointment had been taken up, and the regular reporting was then actually declared to be in suspense for the duration of Bonhoeffer's service in the *Abwehr*. Meanwhile Countess Kalckreuth had to conduct an exciting telephone conversation for the absent Bonhoeffer: 'This is the secret state police. There is a Herr Bonhoeffer living at your house. He is to come here at once!' With some trouble and anxiety she got her

50. To his parents, 6.11.1940.
51. Letter of 6.11.1940; see GS II, p. 379.

nephew out of the Ettal monastery, and learnt that there was good news waiting for him, namely that his duty to report regularly was cancelled for the time being. At last, on 31st January, the lengthy operation was successfully finished.

But there were two things that remained unsettled—the problem of his livelihood, and that of his actual living-quarters.

Strictly speaking, Bonhoeffer still had a right to his salary from the Old Prussian Council of Brethren. His leave of absence was a partial one for the purpose of theological work. Anyone who wanted to know was to be told that he was freed for work with the high command of the *Wehrmacht*; such military requirements were not unusual in war. But of course, the Confessing Church found itself in straitened financial circumstances, and the Pastors' Emergency League had all too many problems of trying to support the pastors who had been disciplined. To ease the burden on the Church, he now began to have recourse to regular allocations which, in spite of existing difficulties, his Leibholz relatives were able to make him from their German account. His very inadequate talents for the essentials of book-keeping caused a good deal of difficulty to the financial experts of the Council of Brethren in their dealings with the tax authorities, and occasionally led to his having to answer further enquiries. But the arrangement gave him a feeling of independence, now that he was devoting so much time to other matters of which he might give no account, and for which he would not make his Church liable. From now on, he saved the Council of Brethren between one third and one half of his salary. To avoid any misunderstanding, it must be added that, of course, he never expected or received any remuneration for his activity in the *Abwehr*—as 'agent' for instance.

To clear up the question of his future domicile, he visited, on his way through Jena on 15th November, his theological colleague Gerhard von Rad, who had been a friend of Bonhoeffer's brothers and sisters in their younger days, and who now offered him his house on the Chiemsee. This is referred to in a passage in one of Bonhoeffer's letters, of which von Rad says: 'I should be glad if this plan materialized.'[52] But then Josef Müller came along with a more attractive solution—the Ettal monastery. Müller introduced his new Protestant friend to the abbot and commended him to the care of Father Johannes. The latter looked after everything necessary, knew of the underlying circumstances—and said nothing.

Thus Bonhoeffer actually remained a civilian, and could continue his theological work in the Church's service. He wrote pertinently to his Finkenwalde students about the 'academic work in the library of the Ettal monastery'.[53]

He had free time, which was a luxury in those years. And yet he was now—it was a grotesque situation for the man of *The Cost of Disciple-*

52. G. von Rad, 'Meetings in Early and Late Years', IKDB, p. 178.
53. To H. W. Jensen, 26.12.1940, GS II, p. 588.

ship and of the ecumenical movement—a confidential agent ('V-Mann') in Germany's war machine. Secret services all over the world use 'confidential agents'. One cannot be quite sure where the camouflage begins and where it ends; for the enemy they are 'agents'. But here the camouflage went one stage further than usual; or was the notorious designation 'confidential agent' appropriate in this case? Those who commissioned Bonhoeffer wanted to make him and his unusual foreign connections serve their political aims for Germany; and he no longer wanted to withdraw from those who were hazarding their own lives to achieve those aims. He was no longer tied to the seminary or to any congregation. The means were now to be tested on the basis of their greatest possible fitness for the end in view, now that the only way that remained open was that of 'conspiracy'.

For his part, Bonhoeffer never deceived himself about the equivocal position in which he was bound to be landed if he now put his ecumenical connections at the disposal of the resistance group in the *Abwehr*, while he was ostensibly putting them at the disposal of the German military secret service. We shall see later how he cleverly argued at his interrogations that the sacrifice that he made in giving away his ecumenical connections showed his loyalty to the Reich. He went his way alone, and was alone responsible for it, but he also knew that he could and must put a strain on the trust that his ecumenical friends had in him. He never disclosed the exact state of affairs to any of his friends in the Church, with a few absolutely necessary exceptions such as Perels. Because of the unlimited trust that they had in Bonhoeffer, they respected that, too.

The first journey that he was commissioned by the *Abwehr* to make did not take place till the end of February 1941. Till then, he went on with his writing about ethics, got to know Roman Catholic life from the inside, and corresponded assiduously with his Finkenwalde students.

The Finkenwalde Students

The chance that the *Abwehr* gave him to continue to live as a civilian set him free at the same time to go on doing what he had felt called to do for the last ten years: to stand by the young theologians even in the existing conditions of war, and to work at theology himself. The new double life did not give him a feeling of disunity; on the contrary, one side of his work supported the other and continually justified it anew. He took pains to keep abreast of the changing field-post numbers of those who were called up, and he included in his correspondence the wives and parents of those who were killed in action. At Christmas 1940 he sent to more than a hundred brethren a personal letter enclosing a copy of Altdorfer's *Holy Family in the Ruined House*; the regulation that Kerrl had issued prevented him from duplicating.

Bonhoeffer strongly sympathized with the exposed and lonely situation of the brethren among the soldiers. In a way, he, too, had been placed in a lonely situation, and saw how privileged and protected had been the existence in the 'life together' at Finkenwalde. It is true that he now understood how to describe once more to the brethren, with particular force, the gift of meditation,[54] but there is now a new note becoming more prominent in the letters, one that does not impose any unrealizable laws on the theologians for their existence in Hitler's war, but sets their consciences free:

But where we so clearly come up against the limit of our service, we must not allow scruples to wear us down . . . I am not sure whether it is quite suitable to be continually saying to you that you are, and must be, 'in the ministry', even out there . . . When one of you writes regretfully that he can only be a soldier among soldiers, and that, being a soldier, he tries to remain a Christian, but that his strength is not enough to do more, I should like to offer a word of cheer to him and to all who feel as he does. I cannot see that he is guilty of any disloyalty to his calling . . . The great difference between your existence and ours . . . may well be that we are allowed to occupy a post that we, by our occupation, have in a way chosen freely for ourselves, whereas you are now sharing the life of millions of people who have never had a free choice, in commitment to life and work in that sense . . . We must not let ourselves be enslaved. God knows your present life, and finds his way to you, even in the busiest and most trying days, when you can no longer find the way to him.[55]

Bonhoeffer felt all the more ashamed when he got answers from those on active service who had once shown dislike of his regulations in Finkenwalde:

I have meditated when I found time, and when that failed, I have learnt texts by heart. In that way they have often opened out at an unexpected depth. One has to live with the texts, and then they unfold. I am very grateful now for your having kept us to it.[56]

You know that I am one of your very grateful pupils; the psalms that I first began to understand in Finkenwalde are with me through the valley of the shadow of these weeks.[57]

Bonhoeffer sent off quantities of reading matter, which he paid for himself. In fact, he was already beginning to store up theological literature, as occasion offered, against the brethren's return to their own occupation.

He was confronted just as plainly with the other side of life at the front, the involvement of these 'illegal' Confessing pastors in Hitler's merciless warfare, which could only press Bonhoeffer on into conspiracy

54. Circular of March 1942, GS II, pp. 584 f.
55. Circular of May 1940, GS II, pp. 565 ff.
56. Letter from F. E. Schröter, 29.9.1940.
57. Letter from E. Klapproth, 5.2.1942.

with more bitter determination. There was a letter from E. Klapproth in the middle of February 1942, shortly before his death:

Our clothes have been sticking to our bodies—we reckon it is minus 45 degrees outside, but we keep them on even in the overheated farmhouse— since the beginning of the year. For days at a stretch we cannot even wash our hands, but go from the dead bodies to a meal and from there back to the rifle. All one's energy has to be summoned up to fight against the danger of freezing, to be on the move even when one is dead tired. Sometimes, when we are away from the cook-house for a long time, we invade the farmhouse after the fighting and slaughter geese, hens, and sheep, get full and overfull of flitches of bacon, honey, and the nice Russian potatoes . . . We often dream of being relieved, but we are now reduced already to 40 instead of 150, still more we dream of Germany—I dream of the 'calm and quiet life in all godliness and integrity'. But we do not any of us know whether we shall be allowed to go home again.

And he heard this, too, not only from cool reports at the desk of the *Abwehr*, but from one of his pupils of whom he had a high opinion, and who was later killed in action:

In the middle of January, a unit of our detachment had to shoot fifty prisoners in one day, because we were on the march and could not take them with us. In districts where there are partisans, women and children who are suspected of supplying partisans with provisions have to be killed by shooting in the back of the neck. Those people have to be got rid of like that, because otherwise it is a question of German soldiers' lives . . . We have had to burn down villages in the last three weeks from military necessity . . .[58]

A few of the Finkenwalde students became officers; others received military decorations. Some were taken prisoner and later sent to compulsory labour camps; others were condemned to death by Soviet courts martial. Most were killed in action.

Death has now reaped a rich harvest of our Finkenwalde brotherhood . . . It would be easier for us to give them up, if we could say that they died *dia christou.*[59]

Bonhoeffer grieved for every one of them, and wrote the kind of letter that he wrote on the death of Gerhard Vibrans:

I think the pain and feeling of emptiness that his death leaves in me could scarcely be different if he had been my own brother . . . The closer we came to each other, the humbler I felt . . . I shall be grateful to him all my life for two things: for the way he observed Sunday, and for teaching me Claudius's hymn '*Ich danke Gott und freue mich*'.[60]

To the whole group he wrote:

58. Letter from E.S., 4.2.1942.
59. Letter from E. Pfisterer, 25.10.1941.
60. GS II, pp. 590 f.; see also the letter to the widow, GS III, pp. 44 f.

God no doubt means to tear specially large gaps in the ranks of our young pastors, and thereby lay a special burden on us.[61]

When the cell door shut behind Bonhoeffer at Tegel in 1943, he had written twenty-five times to the relatives of a fallen brother. He did not live to know that the final total of dead was more than three times that number.

Bonhoeffer's association with the Finkenwalde seminarists was the fulfilment of his calling, and it remained a delight to him, even when it now took quite different forms. But after 1940 he no longer brought the Finkenwalde students into his decisions and hazards.

III THEOLOGY

It was a remarkable life that Bonhoeffer lived during the war. For weeks at a time he worked in the peaceful surroundings of the Kieckow fields or the snow-covered slopes of Ettal. Judged by length of time, his facilities for steady work were probably better now than they had been in the Finkenwalde years. And in Berlin, not every meeting for quartet playing served conspiratorial ends; as in the time of their youth, Dietrich Bonhoeffer was again accompanying his brother-in-law Rüdiger Schleicher in the violin sonatas of Mozart, Beethoven, and Brahms. Anyone who knew nothing of his involvement in the conspiracy could hardly understand his manner of life in those weeks; and even those who knew about it, such as Frau von Kleist-Retzow, sometimes had their own thoughts. When two of her Kieckow grandsons fell in Russia within three days, one of them being Bonhoeffer's confirmation candidate Hans-Friedrich von Kleist-Retzow, she wrote:

I am feeling a new involvement in the terrible events . . . One does not want to be somehow shut out from all that has come upon us as an inexorable fate and guilt. And that, if I may say so, is what makes me for the first time uncertain about the course that you and Dietrich are taking at this time. Are we not all part and parcel of this intricate business, and ought we not, without balancing things too nicely, to take our spiritual forces into action where things are being fought out? Should we not go on our way more purposefully if we did not avoid this last contact?[62]

But immediately afterwards she again supplied Bonhoeffer with scribbling-paper which had become scarce: 'I still have 500 sheets of typing-paper and 200 sheets of foolscap . . . Shall I send the parcel to Berlin?'[63]

Bonhoeffer understood her well. He himself had often tried, when he was young, to adjust himself to the common destiny; and even in Hitler's

61. GS II, p. 578.
62. To E. Bethge, 24.8.1941, GS II, p. 408
63. To Bonhoeffer, 12.12.1941.

war he took the same attitude when his nephew did not want to differ from his classmates:

Well, as it has got so far, as it is no longer a question of possibilities, reflections, free decisions, but of a given fact in respect of which there are no more reflections and possibilities, a great deal looks quite different all at once; and so the first thing that I would like to tell you is that I am really very glad on your account that the time of uncertainty and waiting is over, and that you can now have a peaceful mind through being where your friends of the same age are; I expect that was mainly what burdened your mind, and will probably also be what will help you in different situations. To wish not to separate oneself from other people's destiny and needs, to wish to cooperate with them, is something quite different from simply wishing to go with the crowd. One ought, too, to guard against wanting to 'share the experiences' of war and its horrors, for who, among those who feel that wish with a light heart, knows how he will stand in the hour of crisis? But to be called, to share in common with others, to contribute and to bear as may be needful— that, I think, is fairly firm ground to stand on for living through difficult times.[64]

The only time when he was really worried about his way of existence was for some weeks in the autumn of 1940, when his position was still so obscure. He wrote to me then, when my own church employment had already been settled: 'Anyway, you are now leading a more profitable life than I am, taking everything into account.'[65]

Indeed, Bonhoeffer had not come back from America to separate himself from other people's needs and destiny—on the contrary. That did not mean letting himself be sacrificed prematurely, deliberately, and passively to that destiny. He was prepared to make his full contribution, but as long and as far as possible through his own personal decision.

What surprised him, when his political action was decided, was the extent of the renewal of his freedom for theological work. At times he could concentrate on it completely, after he had once fought his way through the matters relating to the *Abwehr*. But in the intervals of his purely theological work he never allowed his friends to feel that he might still be standing apart from them and shrinking from accepting the consequences of the conspiracy.

The content of Bonhoeffer's new way of life was bound to set him to work still more on ethical problems, and so it strengthened the feeling that his life's work was to be a theological ethic. He therefore acquired the ability to stand the frequent alternations of writing and travelling without any essential sacrifice of concentration; for the one had to do with the other, and so he could break off in the middle of his work when he was told that a visa had arrived, and could continue his theme at once when he had carried out his commission.

64. To H.-W. Schleicher, 10.10.1942, GS II, pp. 422 f.
65. Letter of 9.10.1940, GS II, p. 375.

Of course, his method of work, which had always allowed him a few hours' quietness in the day for carrying on his projects, was still found to be the right one. It did not depend on a particular desk and a filing cabinet that was difficult to move about.

Report on Baptism

Sometimes, however, the Old Prussian Council of Brethren made use of the theologian whom they had made available, and asked for his expert opinion on current questions. Thus, in 1942 he was asked to formulate in detail advice on baptism.

The break-up of the established Church, the beginning of the Confessing Church, and in particular its new efforts to deal with church discipline, had unleashed a discussion on baptism, before the appearance of Karl Barth's *Die kirchliche Lehre von der Taufe*,[66] a work which vigorously attacked the baptism of infants, and which, in fact, Bonhoeffer had never seen. Thus, in 1941 a pamphlet by the Silesian Confessing pastor A. Hitzer, criticizing the practice of infant baptism, caused something of a stir.

Hitzer went further. He produced passages from the New Testament and extracts from the confessions which made belief a precondition of baptism; and he called upon the Confessing Church in no uncertain terms to pull itself together and make a decision at least to allow 'believer's baptism' for adults. The Old Prussian Council of Brethren took the call seriously, and commissioned a few theologians, including Bonhoeffer, to give detailed advice on Hitzer's effort.

Bonhoeffer worked out his statement of the case as well as he could in view of the limited time available and the absence of a library. Perhaps he did not take Hitzer seriously enough. If he had seen Barth's pamphlet on baptism that appeared later, we should probably be in possession of a more detailed statement of Bonhoeffer's views which would have given us some insight into the changing ideas of the two men regarding the sacrament of baptism.

Bonhoeffer took exception to Hitzer's concept of belief as subjective and individualistic. In opposition to it, he defended the right to baptize infants; he preferred to regard it as an act of praising God and of keeping open the boundary between those inside and those outside the Church. But he did not by any means think of advocating indiscriminate baptism of infants; he considered it out of the question for the Church to discipline those pastors and church members who refused on conscientious grounds to have their children baptized: 'in both cases [i.e. church members and pastors] the Church should regard it as a practical

66. Appeared in the summer of 1943 as No. 14 of the *Theologische Studien des Evangelischen Verlags Zollikon.*

indication of the seriousness of baptismal grace.'[67] He even reversed the enquiry about 'the freedom to baptize adults', holding that what is really to be demanded is 'the freedom to baptize infants'. The situation now is that in practice the Church hardly knows adult baptism any longer, so that what should be a matter of course has come to be a rare exception. Bonhoeffer thought that Hitzer was wrong in making the Church's renewal rest on the 'believer's baptism' of adults; renewal can come only through right baptismal discipline. But he agreed with Hitzer in considering the existing custom as such to be hardly acceptable, and to be very largely a mockery of the sacrament.[68]

Bonhoeffer's position here seems to be much the same as it was in *Sanctorum Communio*.[69] There, too, he could set a limit to the baptism of infants 'where the church cannot seriously consider "carrying" the child any longer'.[70] What had then only been hinted at was now clearly expressed. Although this opinion makes Bonhoeffer look very conservative by comparison with Hitzer and Barth, his attitude today seems to the present German churches much too revolutionary.

When we realize how Bonhoeffer's *Cost of Discipleship* was read in those years as a piece of pleading for conversion and a faithful nucleus, it must be stressed in regard to that opinion that he was clearly arguing there against faith and baptism as one's own work. However, 'Cheap grace is . . . baptism without church discipline',[71] and baptism is baptism into Jesus' death[72] and into the unity of the society in all life's concrete relationships.[73]

It was a relief when he wrote to his godchild's father who was on active service in 1944, that infant baptism was certainly not a law in the New Testament; 'regarded purely as a demonstration, infant baptism loses its justification'.[74]

Primus Usus Legis

During the war, the Old Prussian Union held its Confessing synods outside its territory—for example, in Hamburg or Leipzig—so that people who were hampered by expulsion orders or prohibitions against residence could take part in the sessions, which were arranged unobtrusively. Thus, the tenth of these synods was held in Hamburg in November 1941; it appointed a committee to report on 'the meaning of the signs of the time', and it called in Beckmann as chairman, and Iwand, Peter Brunner, Kreyssig, Wilm, and Bonhoeffer as members. At the

67. GS III, p. 453.
68. For the whole, see GS III, pp. 431-54.
69. See SC, pp. 166 f.; also AB, pp. 182 f.
70. SC, p. 167.
71. CD, p. 36 and GS III, pp. 372 ff.
72. CD, pp. 79, 205-11.
73. CD, pp. 225-6 and GS I, pp. 347 f., GS II, p. 64.
74. LPP, p. 143.

turn of the year 1941-2 there appeared a detailed piece of work, prepared mainly by J. Beckmann, on the signs of the dechristianizing of Germany,[75] its main line of approach being similar to that of Bonhoeffer's memorandum to the *Wehrmacht*.[76] At the time of the synod Bonhoeffer was in bed with pneumonia in Berlin, and did not take part in any of the committee's sessions. Perels, who was present part of the time, may possibly have had with him Bonhoeffer's draft of that memorandum.

Meanwhile, the first news of the deportations of the Jews, which had already begun in Berlin and elsewhere, was going round. The pastors, who were under no illusions about those criminal measures, were distressed in their consciences as to what they now ought to preach; so the Council of Brethren, without any direct order from the synod, appointed a committee to prepare a synodal declaration on the fifth commandment. Bonhoeffer took part in this.

The working group, under the chairmanship of Günther Harder, met for the first time in Magdeburg on 10th August 1942; it included Count Peter Yorck, Niesel, Hammelsbeck, Peter Brunner, and Bonhoeffer. For the last named it was again a question, from the theological point of view, of what had been discussed in Finkenwalde: 'How do we preach the Law?'[77] He undertook to give a critical presentation, at the second session, of the doctrine of *primus usus legis* in the confessions as a doctrine of external discipleship and order among the people. That session was held in Magdeburg on 15th March 1943, only a few days before Bonhoeffer's arrest, just when Schlabrendorff's attempted *coup* had failed. Yorck, Harder, Perels, Niesel, and Bonhoeffer worked all through the day on Bonhoeffer's lecture.[78] When Bonhoeffer had been in prison for six months, the committee's preliminary work produced, at the last Old Prussian Confessing synod at Breslau on 16th and 17th October 1943, a message on the fifth commandment, denouncing the solution of the Jewish question by 'eliminating' and 'liquidating'. It was called 'Notes for Pastors and Elders on the Treatment of the Fifth Commandment', and it therefore confined itself to the question of preaching, and was not intended as a public announcement from the pulpit.[79] In the message for the day of repentance in 1943 there was to be read from the pulpits: '. . . Woe to us and our nation if it is held to be justified to kill men because they are regarded as unworthy to live, or because they belong to another race . . .'[80]

Did the audience in Magdeburg on 15th March 1943 realize, from Bonhoeffer's dry expert examination, that he was bringing out a new

75. J. Beckmann, op. cit., pp. 383-8.
76. GS II, p. 428.
77. Cf. Ch. X, p. 473.
78. E, pp. 303-19.
79. See W. Niesel, *Um Verkündigung und Ordnung der Kirche*, pp. 105-10.
80. W. Niesel, op. cit., p. 110.

theological emphasis? In that work, he firmly opposes the division of those who hear the Gospel and those who hear the Law into believers and unbelievers respectively; the Gospel, as well as the Law, is a matter for both. Without expressly entering into a discussion of Barth's pamphlet, Bonhoeffer declines to lay down once and for all the sequence of Gospel and Law, neither distinguishing them nor coordinating them:

God desires the outward order not only because the gospel exists but also in order that it may exist . . . Both sequences are, therefore, theologically justified and necessary; gospel and law as well as law and gospel. In the symbolic writings the second sequence predominates. But in both sequences the gospel is the 'actual' kingdom of God.[81]

As the symbolic writings would have it, and as he himself held in the *Sanctorum Communio*, he will not now regard the kingdom of Christ as related simply and solely to the Church.[82] The *primus usus legis* belongs to the confession of Christ by the Christian who accepts his responsibility to the world:

But even the congregation in the catacombs will never be deprived of the universality of its mission . . . It will learn that the world is in disorder and that the kingdom of Christ is not of this world, but precisely in this it will be reminded of its mission towards the world . . . apocalyptic proclamation may well be a flight from the *primus usus*.
. . . [the *primus usus*] is not concerned with the christianization of worldly institutions or with their incorporation in the Church, but with their genuine worldliness, their 'naturalness' in obedience to God's word.[83]

On that basis he pleads for the necessary collaboration 'between Christians and non-Christians in the clarification of certain questions of fact and in the furthering of certain concrete tasks.'[84] At this juncture, then, Bonhoeffer clearly rejects a one-sided eschatological preaching, and asserts a 'genuine worldliness' as opposed to a Christianizing and churchifying of the worldly order of things. This emphasis also determines the final phase of his *Ethics*.

Against the Isolation of Theology

In February 1940 there was formed the 'Society for Protestant Theology', thanks to Ernst Wolf's initiative. In the disquieting growth of technical and spiritual isolation among the remaining Confessing groups, this innovation offered a new possibility for all the provincial churches and what was left of the theological faculties to meet together again.

Six years previously Bonhoeffer, who was then in London, had

81. E, p. 314.
82. E, p. 314.
83. E, pp. 315 ff.
84. E, p. 317.

congratulated Wolf on his flair and enterprise in founding the monthly periodical *Evangelische Theologie*:

I shall be glad to help, if you can use me; and my wish to you for this great undertaking is that it may help towards the elucidation of what is obscure and the discovery of hitherto untrodden ways.[85]

Bonhoeffer now canvassed again for the new departure: 'You will join the Society of Protestant Theology, won't you? At least, if you have any regard for yourself!'[86] It is true that he hardly got as far as attending the meetings, especially when they were held in Berlin and he was prevented by the expulsion order. But he hoped that the society would offer a platform from which theological thought could break out from the narrowing circle of the Confessing Church's standard theology. It did so more quickly than expected. The meetings soon produced vigorous arguments.

Rudolf Bultmann. At the society's Whitsuntide meeting on 1st June 1941, Rudolf Bultmann gave his lecture, which has become famous, on 'The New Testament and Mythology'. Ernst Fuchs, who wrote the minutes, announced the paper as a treatise in the *Beiträgen zur Evangelischen Theologie*.[87] He also reported, in the 'Communication to Members',[88] on the first discussion of the problem, in which Peter Brunner, Edmund Schlink, Friedrich Delekat, Ernst Bizer, Gerhard Krüger, Ernst Wolf, Hermann Diem, Günther Bornkamm, Ernst Fuchs, Erich Foerster, and Richard Widmann had taken part. Bonhoeffer did not take part, but received Fuchs's minutes and Bultmann's treatise at the end of 1941. In 1942 he urgently recommended the people on leave who visited him, to get the treatise, as well as Bultmann's commentary on John, which had also appeared in 1941; he described those works as 'the most important event among the latest theological publications'.

In 1942 the society's Berlin-Brandenburg section met several times to discuss the demythologizing question that Bultmann had broached. On 17th June Hammelsbeck opened the fifth meeting by reading a letter from Hans Asmussen, 'who refuses the invitation because of "serious misgivings" about the society in general, and in order to remain "unequivocal" in his rejection of Bultmann's lecture'.[89] Besides Hammelsbeck and Günther Harder, Martin Fischer and Volkmar Herntrich, Hans Lokies and Siegfried Knak, young Gerhard Ebeling and others spoke:

Dr. Ebeling regards the double line of approach as problematic, i.e. to proceed in the same way, both on the basis of a contemporary view of existence and

85. Letter of 11.5.1934.
86. Letter of 14.2.1941, GS II, p. 403.
87. Vol. 7: R. Bultmann, *Offenbarung und Heilsgeschehen*, 1941, pp. 27-69.
88. 'Mitteilung an die Mitglieder', 1941, No. 1, pp. 6-10 (duplicated).
89. 'Protokoll der fünften Tagung am 17.6.1942' (duplicated).

on the basis of a New Testament view. Against this, some say that the mythical view of life is nearer to faith than the modern view is, and others say, as Bultmann does, that the modern view is nearer to faith. The comparative question about demythologizing as it is raised by Luther, for example after the Torgau sermon about Christ's descent into hell, is thought to be particularly useful![90]

Bonhoeffer did not take part in those Berlin meetings either, but he had the proceedings reported to him personally and through the minutes. So he reacted angrily when it became known that the Berlin pastors' convention had used expressions suggestive of judgement on a heretic. He wrote to Ernst Wolf:

I am delighted with Bultmann's new booklet. I am continually impressed by the intellectual honesty of his work. I was told that for two pins the convention would have sent a protest to you against Bultmann's theology! And that from the Berliners of all people! I should like to know whether any one of those people has worked through the commentary on John. The arrogance that flourishes here . . . is a real scandal for the Confessing Church.[91]

Bonhoeffer was asked soon afterwards by a Finkenwalde student, Winfried Krause, who wrote from a military hospital in Marburg, what he had to say about Bultmann's thesis which so excited the theologians of the Confessing Church. Bonhoeffer answered:

. . . I am one of those who welcomed this treatise, not because I agree with it; I regret the double line of approach in it (the argument from John 1 : 14 and from the radio ought not to be mixed up; I consider that the second, too, is an argument, only the separation would have to be plainer); so up to this point I may perhaps still be a pupil of Harnack. To put it crudely: B. has let the cat out of the bag, not only for himself, but for a great many people (the Liberal cat out of the Confessional bag), and for that I am glad. He has ventured to say what many people inwardly repress (I include myself) without having overcome it. In that way he has rendered a service in intellectual integrity and honesty. The dogmatic pharisaism that many brethren are now calling up against it I regard as fatal. The questions now have to be answered plainly. I should like to talk to B. about it, and I would willingly expose myself to the draught of fresh air that he brings. But then the window must be shut again, or the susceptible people will catch cold too easily . . . When you see B., please give him my regards, and tell him that I should be glad to see him, and how I look at things . . .[92]

It cannot be denied that, in that brief incidental expression of opinion, Bonhoeffer came down early and vigorously on Bultmann's side; and this supports Gerhard Krause's criticism of those who in the fifties

90. Ibid.
91. Letter of 24.7.1942, GS III, pp. 45 f.
92. Letter of 25. (or 23.?) 7.1942.

wanted to claim Bonhoeffer as being for Barth and against Bultmann.[93] In any case, Bonhoeffer welcomed the fact that the questions had been squarely put, and felt Bultmann's message as a release for himself, too. That, of course, did not mean that he wanted to make Bultmann's view fully and entirely his own; and he therefore held that the hermeneutic question, which he had once regarded as urgent,[94] was as yet by no means answered.

He was more and more inclined to have misgivings when he saw how the Confessing Church's necessary concentration on the Bible led to a dangerous hostility to philosophy, and to being pushed away from the sources of culture and science, so that the questions that had hitherto been acute were wrongly regarded as settled. Eight years previously he had spoken very fervently against theology at the university,[95] and had favoured its transfer to 'church-monastic schools'. But that was just a vote against faculties that had grown sterile and servile, and for the recovery of a free horizon. So he was now capable of seeing that it might come to a new and different kind of narrowing of the horizon in his own circles, 'a real scandal for the Confessing Church'.

Thus he welcomed Bultmann's effort. But although he had touched on important questions, he had not time just then to engage in more intensive work on the problem that he had posed. Other questions, such as that of the *Ethics*, were urgent and had to take precedence. Otherwise he would probably have found it possible to take part personally in one or other of his colleagues' debates during 1942.

Theodor Litt. The need to break through the narrowing horizon had become strong even before these first Bultmann debates. In the winter of 1938-9 Bonhoeffer had got hold of two booklets by the philosopher and pedagogue Theodor Litt: *The German Spirit and Christianity* and *Protestant Sense of History.* He found a surprising correspondence with his own thoughts in those works, and so he felt urged to enter into conversations with him. With Litt it was a question of the relationship of the Christian faith to the world. Bonhoeffer wrote and told him how keenly he felt the question of the Christian's commission or refusal to work within the world. It was a long time since he had put such a pointed question on the subject;[96] but he was now standing on the threshold between *The Cost of Discipleship* and *Ethics.* He did, indeed, feel obliged to supply, by reference to Christ's incarnation, the foundation that was lacking in Litt's acceptance of this world; but he wrote

93. See G. Krause, 'Dietrich Bonhoeffer und Rudolf Bultmann', in *Zeit und Geschichte, Dankesgabe an Rudolf Bultmann zum 80. Geburtstag,* ed. E. Dinkler, 1964, pp. 457 ff. Unfortunately G. Krause does not here discuss what else Bonhoeffer's interpretation might signify. Cf. also Ch. XIII, pp. 761 f.
94. See Ch. X, pp. 474 f.
95. See GS I, p. 42.
96. GS III, pp. 31-3.

above all because Litt's 'loyalty to the earth' pleased him so much, and because he wanted it to be possible to accept with a good theological conscience 'the present earth in its dignity, its glory, and its curse'.[97]

Oskar Hammelsbeck. It is to that time of external and internal regrouping of Bonhoeffer's life that there belongs his new relationship to Oskar Hammelsbeck. The latter had been a pupil of Jasper; in the Weimar period he had given himself to adult education and worked in cooperation with the socialist Adolf Reichwein,[98] and then he had gone off from the secular sphere into the Church. As Bonhoeffer had done in his young days, he discovered the Church, not in its national privileged form, but as it had been shaped by the Barmen and Dahlem Synods during the church struggle. Late in life he had decided that the rest of his life's work should be for that Church. Now he had come to Berlin from the Saarland, and was doing catechetical training work in the Old Prussian Confessing Church. Hammelsbeck was anxious to keep in view the secular sphere of life, which had once been his own, and not simply to leave it to its own devices. Here he found a partner in Bonhoeffer, who had once tried to leave his former sphere of life behind him both inwardly and outwardly, but who was now engaged in reuniting secular existence and the Church.

Bonhoeffer had occasionally met Hammelsbeck since 1937 in the conferences of teachers of the Confessing Church's educational institutions. In 1939 Hammelsbeck had come to help in the collective pastorate when Bonhoeffer had gone to the United States; but only after that did their professional contacts develop into personal meetings. Politics and philosophy were the main subjects of discussion in Bonhoeffer's attic in Berlin. Hammelsbeck also wanted to introduce Bonhoeffer to Jochen Klepper, but before he could do so, Klepper and his family had committed suicide.[99]

Hammelsbeck summarizes their useful exchange of ideas in an autobiographical sketch in connection with an entry in his diary for 1941:

The question whether my way into the Church can be directed back into the world, that worrying question about the Christian's responsibility to the world, the question 'Church for the World', was exactly what Dietrich Bonhoeffer was asking, and so the conversations with him were the most important also for me at that period . . .

What had been common ground, in those other conversations,[100] for a fruitful meeting, namely the question of education and the consciousness of social and cultural responsibility, I came to realize more than ever in a happy exchange of ideas with Bonhoeffer; but for me it was specially thrilling and a

97. GS III, p. 33.
98. Executed after the plot of 20th July 1944.
99. O. Hammelsbeck 'In Discussion with Bonhoeffer', IKDB, p. 181.
100. In the circles with Anna von Gierke, Gertrud Bäumer, Elly Heuss-Knapp, and Eduard Spranger.

great gain, because I found my timid theological ventures taken up, understood, and confirmed as further questions in his mastery of systematic exegesis, and then critically changed and helped on . . . He took a special interest in my preliminary work on the *Festschrift* for Karl Jaspers' sixtieth birthday in February 1943 . . . My own contribution on 'Philosophy as a Theological Problem' was once more to become the subject of a special exchange of views, when all those hopes were dashed by Bonhoeffer's arrest.[101]

Dietrich Bonhoeffer also took me into his confidence about his active participation in the Resistance Movement. We agreed that he should not tell me the names of any of the conspirators, so that I should have nothing on my mind if I were interrogated. I worked out a cultural-political memorandum, of which only three copies existed . . . To ease my mind, Bonhoeffer sent me a message from prison, through Perels, that both had been destroyed by confidants . . .[102]

We endured the time in the strange schizophrenia of happy thankfulness for the experience of the Church, and of suffering through the Church's guilt, in a strange mixture of power and weakness.[103]

The meeting bore fruit in Bonhoeffer's further thoughts. An entry in Hammelsbeck's diary for 24th January 1941 calls to mind Bonhoeffer's later terminology:

We can make no progress here[104] till we radically grasp the idea of our 'godless' existence in the world. That means, till we refuse to entertain any illusion of being able to act 'with God' from day to day in the world. That illusion repeatedly misleads us into throwing away justification and grace, into artificial piety, into making a legalized ethic, and to becoming unfree in a servitude with all the signs changed . . .[105]

Shortly before Bonhoeffer was arrested, he received a postcard from Hammelsbeck dated 4th February 1943, bearing a quotation from Luther: 'A Christian is a strange bird; would to God that most of us were good pagans who keep the natural law—to say nothing of the Christian law.'

'Ethics'

Since 1939, Bonhoeffer had been amassing works on theological and philosophical ethics whenever he could get anything of the kind, new or second-hand, from a bookshop. His books included the four volumes of the *History of Ethics* by O. Dittrich (1926), five volumes of the *Theological Ethics* by Richard Rothe (2nd edition, 1867), Hofmann's Ethics of 1872, the works of Oettingen, Harless, and Otto Piper, as well as Roman Catholic moral theologies and the Ethics of Scheler and Nikolai

101. There was a draft copy among Bonhoeffer's effects.
102. Nothing of this has been kept.
103. O. Hammelsbeck, *Vita, Pädagogische Autobiographie* (duplicated), 1959, p. 42.
104. i.e. in Christ's service in the world.
105. O. Hammelsbeck, op. cit., p. 45.

Hartmann. Other authors whom he consulted were Hermann Nohl with his *Die sittlichen Grunderfahrungen* (1939), Karl Jaspers with *Die geistige Situation der Zeit* and *Nietzsche*, Bauch, Wittmann, Noack, and Prell; in 1940 he read Kamlah's *Christentum und Selbstbehauptung*. He also went to the historians. He was stimulated by the idea of 'historical cicatrization' in Reinhold Schneider's books, and was impressed by F. W. von Oertzen's *Die Junker* (1939), Heuss's *Friedrich Naumann*, Trevelyan's *History of England*, Alfred von Martin's *Nietzsche und Burckhardt* and *Die Religion in Jakob Burckhardts Leben und Denken*. He thought he learnt more from *Don Quixote* than from many books on ethics. He took up Balzac and *Simplizissimus* again, and began to read the German-speaking writers of the nineteenth century: Gottfried Keller, Stifter, Fontane, all of whom enriched him so much in prison. Whereas he had been taken by Montaigne's wisdom, Bernanos went somewhat into the background; to make up for that, Ernest Hello was his discovery of 1938-9.

That list is certainly not complete, and we cannot now be sure that it is reliable; but the books enumerated show his literary inclinations and capacity for absorption. There was not very much existentialist literature in his attic; he preferred writers with historical and humanistic ideas. Although he read a great deal, he hardly compiled any lists of references, and he rarely presented discussions with other authors. He confined himself to a comprehensive orientation, so as to formulate his own outline free from material worked in from outside. In his *Ethics*, in contrast to his *Cost of Discipleship*, he worked entirely on his own; there was no longer any preparation, as had previously been the case, through exchange of ideas in seminars or lectures. Hardly anyone offered any questions suggesting modifications, or any contradictions. It was only quite seldom that he read a few pages to one of his friends, and even these sessions were sometimes cut short all too soon and for a long period. He never heard a real response to his *Ethics*.

Bonhoeffer himself thought that the problem was more complicated than in *The Cost of Discipleship*. Among the theologians who were influenced by Barth, it was for years considered presumptuous to formulate an ethic; Brunner's and Gogarten's attempts in 1932 were subjected to severe criticism. The impulse to new ethical projects, which eventuated in 1945, was as yet hardly perceptible; and thus far Bonhoeffer's new undertaking was not modern. He thought Dilschneider's attempt[106] brave but unsuccessful;[107] he wanted to controvert, in any case, Dilschneider's Christianizing of the worldly order of things in the name of a 'personal ethos'.[108]

106. O. Dilschneider, *Die evangelische Tat*. 1940.
107. E, pp. 321, ff.
108. We ought here to ask J. Moltmann whether, in his criticism (MW III, p. 52) that Bonhoeffer had treated the personal phenomena one-sidedly and disregarded factual phenomena, he paid enough attention to Bonhoeffer's discussion with Dilschneider.

Bonhoeffer often asserted that ethics was his life's task. If, when he wrote *The Cost of Discipleship*, he felt sure that he was tackling a theme that no one else was tackling and that was waiting for him, this was even more the case in his *Ethics*. 'I sometimes feel as if my life were more or less over, and as if all I had to do now were to finish my *Ethics*.'[109] In 1932-3 he had dropped the ethical theme that had held him since Barcelona, and he had taken no further part in the discussion of the orders of creation and of preservation. He had at that time been stirred by the question how the Church could preach the concrete command, and he had pursued the question of Christ's lordship, not only over the Church, but over the world. But then he had concentrated for years on the smaller area of the rules of life of those people who would wish to put into practice that lordship of Christ in the Church. But now what he had put on one side in 1933 came back in force. His ideas of 1932 he now either verified or changed for more appropriate ones.

The idea of 'reality', for instance, applied in *Act and Being* and stressed in his lecture in Czecho-Slovakia, is developed afresh, and now appears firmly anchored in Christology. Reality is always the acceptance of the world by the one who has become man. Here Bonhoeffer seeks to avoid the positivist and idealistic understanding of reality, as he regards both as abstractions.

He would like to by-pass the rocks of an actualistic situation ethic and yet hold to its validity. He would like to surmount the dim remoteness of a norm-ethic and yet accept its interest in continuity.

In Bonhoeffer's idea of the 'world' there is a new development. In *The Cost of Discipleship*[110] he had declined to pay the 'world' the tribute of glorification. But the concentration on the glorification of Christ in an earthly discipleship called for the 'continuous process of establishing the message in view of unoccupied spheres of existence'.[111] In its catastrophe of 1939-40, the world came under judgement and grace into a field of vision in which both man's historical responsibility and the thankful acceptance of his creative possibilities had scope. For a long time the Church had claimed Bonhoeffer's attention, and the world, with its insistence upon creation and history, had—with good reason—remained unheeded, but now it received new attention as the sphere of the *regnum Christi*.

In 1932 Bonhoeffer had tried to establish, as part of his concept of the *regnum Christi*, the critical formula of 'order of preservation' instead of the dangerous one of 'order of creation', because the latter seemed to him to be bound up with an inadmissible revaluation of the world. Now, in thinking of man's relation to the world, he began to replace 'the

109. LPP, p. 197.
110. See Ch. IX, p. 378.
111. H. Bürkle, 'Die Frage nach dem "kosmischen Christus" als Beispiel einer ökumenisch orientierten Theologie' in *Kerygma und Dogma*, 1965, p. 105.

sphere of the *regnum Christi*' with the less static idea of 'mandate'—only 'mandate', so that the *one* claim of Christ may be defended in all the world's gifts and problems; but *mandate*, so that those who bear the responsibility may have full independence while history is allowed to take its course. The Christological basis of the mandate is to hold the balance between the worldly and the eschatological element.

Ethics, as a book, was never finished; what we have are only post-humous fragments consisting of several approaches fitted together. That means that we have no 'ethics' from Bonhoeffer such as he would have thought ripe for publication. What we have is the record of his process of reasoning on that subject, the process breaking off at a certain point. We can detect in four fresh starts, each time a new attempt to tackle the problem.[112]

1. In 1939 or 1940, Bonhoeffer began to write, still using the language of *The Cost of Discipleship*, but he was already stressing the unity of God and the world in Christ. 'The more exclusively we acknowledge and confess Christ as our Lord, the more fully the wide range of His dominion will be disclosed to us.'[113] Exclusiveness of Christ's lordship—that is the message of *The Cost of Discipleship*; the wide range of his lordship—that is the new emphasis of *Ethics*. The exclusiveness, unless it is mis-understood to mean a self-erected ghetto, presses on to freedoms, per-missions, responsibilities, discoveries, and to legitimate secularization.

2. At Klein-Krössin in September 1940, he began for the second time, and now it was in the immediate presence and aspects of the Western world. Bonhoeffer had met Colonel Oster; Hitler had pulled off his grandiose victories—then Bonhoeffer wrote the surprising confession of the Church's guilt.[114] Europe's new master had put himself beyond good and evil, and no one who thought in terms of conventional ethics could set anything against him.

Theologically, Bonhoeffer now took his stand on the incarnation. The keyword of this second attempt is the Christocentric 'conformity' ('*Gleichgestaltung*'). Christ, by shaping himself in conformity with the temporary nature of this world, draws it into conformity with himself. Thus for Bonhoeffer the scenery of the Western world becomes the appointed field for ethical reflection. It cannot be disputed that Bon-hoeffer's concept here again comes dangerously close to a clericalizing of the world. Nevertheless the Church is clearly regarded as a piece of the reconciled world; and that, in any case, provides a much more positive relation of the Church to the world than existed in *The Cost of Disciple-ship*. There the world was merely the place for faith's first step, whereas now Christ's lordship creates historical responsibilities. Thus the En-

112. The sequence and dates of the four approaches are shown in the preface to *Ethics* (pp. 11-14).
113. E, p. 58.
114. E, p. 110.

lightenment can for the first time be appraised positively. In those September days of 1940 the relation between the Church and the world had assumed in *Ethics* the character, as it were, of a surprisingly mutual discovery of each other.[115]

3. The third attempt was the most compact. Bonhoeffer went into the Ettal monastery at the turn of the year 1940-1 for the longest working period of those war years. He now began with justification, and from that he achieved his new and fruitful distinction between the ultimate and the penultimate, to which he repeatedly returned while he was in prison.[116] Without his being conscious of it, that distinction had existed for a long time in his theology. The last word of justification includes the beginning and the end, and, while limiting the last but one, puts it into force. It prepares the way for the end, but has its time and place before it—and yet receives from it its complete and far-reaching autonomy. Christ, representing the structure of the ultimate and the penultimate, 'neither renders the human reality independent nor destroys it, but He allows it to remain as that which is before the last, as a penultimate which requires to be taken seriously in its own way, and yet not to be taken seriously, a penultimate which has become the outer covering of the ultimate.'[117] The cross is the ultimate, and is the judgement and the pardoning of the penultimate. Christian life is 'neither a destruction nor a sanctioning of the penultimate . . . [it] is participation in the encounter of Christ with the world'.[118]

So Bonhoeffer opened the way for a rediscovery (so rare on Protestant soil) of a theology of the 'natural', but one that was derived, not in the Roman Catholic way from the *analogia entis* or from natural right, but from the doctrine of justification and Christology. The subject had always previously been either left to the Roman Catholics or derived, with doubtful results, from the article on Creation. He joyfully formulated that article while he was in Ettal:

I now begin with the section on 'natural life'; you are right, it is a dangerous subject, but fascinating for that very reason.[119]

Right in the period of the tyranny of the unnatural, Bonhoeffer, on the strength of his Christology, puts reason and what is natural into their own right, so that beyond any moralizing 'life is not only a means to an end but is also an end in itself'.[120] Unlike Kant, he begins, not with life's duties, but with its rights. 'God gives before He demands.'[121]

The first journey to Switzerland on *Abwehr* business broke off that

115. E, p. 109.
116. LPP, pp. 104, 111, 154, 178-9, 188.
117. E, p. 131.
118. E, p. 133.
119. To E. Bethge, 10.12.1940, GS II, p. 389.
120. E, p. 149.
121. E, p. 151.

most happy period of work on the *Ethics*; but its concept of the ultimate and the penultimate remained effective.

4. The fourth new line of approach brings us to those of Bonhoeffer's chapters that have the strongest political imprint; they were drafted during his breaks in Krössin or Friedrichsbrunn at the crucial times of conspiratorial actions of 1941 and 1942. The terms 'appropriateness' and 'acceptance of guilt' indicate a new and sober tone:

Ideologies vent their fury on man and then leave him as a bad dream leaves the waking dreamer. The memory of them is bitter. They have not made man stronger or more mature; they have only made him poorer and more mistrustful.[122]

The spatial line of thought, which seemed to him helpful in *The Cost of Discipleship*, is now critically handled, and the unity of reality is presumed:

It is from the real man, whose name is Jesus Christ, that all factual reality derives its ultimate foundation and its ultimate annulment, its justification and its ultimate contradiction, its ultimate affirmation and its ultimate negation.[123]

At that time Bonhoeffer re-read *Don Quixote*, the story of an honourable knight who isolates himself from reality in his fight for his principles. In 1932, Bonhoeffer thought of reality as the field for preaching, and in 1935 rather as simply a place of transit; now for the first time it becomes a partner which is necessary if action is to take shape. There is no longer any reality without God in Christ, and there is no longer a God in Christ without reality. Christ is not absolute reality, like a norm from outside; and reality is not simply material that is to have programmes or ideals forced on it. Christ neither removes reality nor makes it 'Christian'. Reality is no longer devalued (as by idealists) or revalued (as by positivists). 'To be in Christ' means to share in the world. Good, therefore, is not an abstraction but a process, movement, constantly accepting the world and people and taking part in their life; and so ethics is helping people 'to share in life',[124] it is the Christlike in the midst of the human. Christ sets up no foreign rule: the 'commandment of Jesus Christ . . . sets creation free for the fulfilment of the law which is its own'.[125] Christ leads, not beyond, but right into the reality of everyday life. Christian life is no end in itself, but puts one in a position to live as a man before God, not to become a superman, but to exist 'for other men'.[126] The unity of worldly reality existing in Christ is not a synthetic one, as the Roman Catholic idea would have it, nor is it held in *diastase*, as the enthusiasts imagine it. It is real, not in a

122. E, p. 216.   125. E, p. 298.
123. E, p. 228.   126. E, p. 297.
124. E, p. 269.

magical-cosmic way, but because it is dynamically valid by representing Christ.

Bonhoeffer has now reached the place where the letters from prison come in with their surprisingly simple formulations. What begins like *The Cost of Discipleship* ends with the formulation of 'worldliness':

The cross of atonement is the setting free for life before God in the midst of the godless world; it is the setting free for life in genuine worldliness.[127]

That page of manuscript was on a desk in the Marienburger Allee, when Bonhoeffer was arrested in April 1943. Beside it the notes for the chapter 'The "Ethical" and the "Christian" as a Theme' lay strewn about, and on one of them was the heading 'Being There for the World'.

In the essay 'After Ten Years' that he wrote for his fellow conspirators at Christmas 1942, he said:

We are not Christ, but if we want to be Christians, we must have some share in Christ's large-heartedness by acting with responsibility and in freedom when the hour of danger comes, and by showing a real sympathy that springs, not from fear, but from the liberating and redeeming love of Christ for all who suffer. Mere waiting and looking on is not Christian behaviour. The Christian is called to sympathy and action, not in the first place by his own sufferings, but by the sufferings of his brethren, for whose sake Christ suffered.[128]

Thus in his three years' work at his *Ethics*, Bonhoeffer began with the idea of the amplitude of Christ's lordship; then that of conformity with Christ became central; thirdly, he brought the world as the penultimate under justification; and finally, he reasoned from incarnation to historical responsibility. Each line of approach deepened the two aspects —a more resolute Christ-centredness, and a more realistic openness to the world.

Behind the work produced we sometimes see the contours of the surroundings in which he was living at a particular time: the politically conservative world of Kieckow and Klein-Krössin, including Ewald von Kleist's disgust at the vulgarizing of the environment, and the Roman Catholic atmosphere of Ettal. He was influenced in his writing, not only by his study of the relevant books, but also by his own share in current history, by the impression of the ruling and contending powers, and by the influence of friends and acquaintances. So the aim of the most recent chapters was not only to argue logically, but also to free people for action. Yet it is true that anyone who looks in his *Ethics* for a direct justification of a *coup d'état*, and detailed instructions for it, will be disappointed. It is a question of liberation and of awakening responsibility, not of offering ready-made safeguards that could serve as justifica-

127. E, p. 297.
128. LPP, p. 37

tion for timid souls if it came to the push. Historical action is not justified in advance, so far as it may deserve the name. The broader view, with which Bonhoeffer was concerned in his ethics, and which he had never heard discussed till then, was successful only by the rigorous bringing together of the Christological approach and the concrete structure of his world.

In June 1942, while he was in the middle of his work on ethics, and on his journeys for the conspiracy, he once spoke of being possibly on the threshold of new insights. Dimensions that had hitherto remained veiled from him were now revealed, and some lines of approach that he had already perceived showed him where they were really heading. Bonhoeffer was in a troop train on his way to Munich, after the meeting with Bishop Bell in Sweden, when he wrote:

My activities, which have lately been very much in the worldly sector, give me plenty to think about. I am surprised that I live, and can go on living, for days without the Bible; I should feel it to be auto-suggestion, not obedience, if I were to force myself to read it. I understand that such auto-suggestion might be, and is, a great help, but I am afraid that for me it might mean adulterating a genuine experience and not getting genuine help after all. When I open the Bible again, it is ever so new and cheering, and I should like just to preach. I know that I only need to open my own books to hear what there is to be said against all this. And I do not want to justify myself, for I realize that 'spiritually' I have had much richer times. But I feel how my resistance to everything 'religious' grows. Often as far as an instinctive revulsion, which is certainly not good. I am not religious by nature. But I always have to be thinking of God and of Christ, and I set great store by genuineness, life, freedom, and compassion. Only I find the religious trappings so uncomfortable. Do you understand? These ideas and insights are not new at all, but as I think I shall now be able to see my way through them, I am letting things take their course without resistance. That is how I understand my present activity in the worldly sector.[129]

SECTION TWO: CONSPIRACY

In 1945 Bishop Bell, in the first publication about his meeting with Bonhoeffer in Sweden in 1942, gave an account of a scene from the summer of 1940, the beginning of our period:

We know of the despair which seized all those who were engaged in subversive activities in July and August 1940. We know of a meeting held at that time where it was proposed that further action should be postponed so as to avoid giving Hitler the character of a martyr if he should be killed. Bonhoeffer's rejoinder was decisive: 'If we claim to be Christians, there is no

129. To E. Bethge, 25.6.1942, GS II, p. 420.

room for expediency. Hitler is the Antichrist. Therefore we must go on with our work and eliminate him whether he be successful or not.'[130]

The account contains accurate and improbable parts, and amongst the latter must be included Bonhoeffer's description of Hitler as the Antichrist. But that quotation from Bell has led to its inclusion in many speeches and books.[131]

That kind of report that Bell gave was based on the notes in his diary, which he used to make very accurately, and for the most part directly after the event. The above account might well be related to Bonhoeffer's reporting, while he was in Sweden in 1942, on his first meetings with Oster, Gisevius, and Dohnanyi in his parents' home.[132] But the expression about Hitler being Antichrist does not occur anywhere else in anything that Bonhoeffer said or wrote. Even the passage in the memorandum for W. Paton,[133] about the small 'band . . . that recognized just here [i.e. in Hitler as 'the accomplisher of historical justice'] Satan in the guise of an angel of light' differs from language which Bonhoeffer's theological conscience can scarcely have allowed him to use. I remember clearly how we once came to talking about it; we waited eagerly for his answer and had really expected something from the Bible in answer to our question, when he said: 'No, he is not the Antichrist; Hitler is not big enough for that; the Antichrist uses him, but he is not as stupid as that man!'

It is probable, too, that Bishop Bell's account of despondency and determination is too simplified and stylized. How Bonhoeffer himself had been depressed by the reverses in the summer of 1940 is shown not only by the proceedings in the session of the Council of Brethren in Nowawes; even at the end of the year, on 28th December 1940, he wrote to his mother on her birthday:

When we came to the end of last year, I suppose we all thought that this year we should be a stage further on and see more clearly. Now it is at least doubtful whether the hope has been realized . . . It almost seems to me that we shall have to resign ourselves to this for a long time, to live more on the past and the present, and that means more on thankfulness, than on any view of the future.[134]

Bishop Bell's entry, however, is right in indicating that Bonhoeffer joined the conspiracy at the lowest ebb of its fortunes, and associated his fate irrevocably with that of Oster and Dohnanyi. So if that rather crude theological expression could really have encouraged his friends, Bonhoeffer might perhaps have used it verbally; but he would hardly have been in a position to put it down in writing.

130. GS 1, pp. 397 f.
131. Most recently, for example, Frankel-Manvell, *Der 20.Juli*, 1964, p. 65, and T. Prittie, *Germans Against Hitler*, 1964, p. 137.
132. See Ch. XII, p. 601.   133. GS I, p. 358.
134. GS II, p. 591.

We are now in the third main section of the German Resistance Movement,[135] i.e. between the western offensive of 1940 and the attempted assassination by Schlabrendorff in March 1943—or alternatively the arrest of Bonhoeffer on 5th April 1943. It includes Bonhoeffer's actual complicity in the plot against Hitler. The whole period is overshadowed by a dilemma from which clear-sighted people had constantly to be trying to escape: anyone who tried to encompass Hitler's overthrow after the tremendous success in France was thereby conjuring up a new stab-in-the-back legend—so much was quite rightly noted by Bishop Bell. On the other hand, there was a danger that the fact that waiting till the tables had been turned would make the participants in the conspiracy a liquidation commando of the victorious powers. Under this handicap, the decision to go ahead had to be made and new lines of approach towards the régime's overthrow sought, after that section of the conspirators which controlled the force of arms, namely the army high command, had dropped out since the beginning of April 1940.

This period of active resistance again takes its course in three stages. Each begins in an unpromising situation, finds new lines of approach and raises new hopes of success, till it once more ends in disappointment. In each of these three stages, Bonhoeffer's participation and involvement in the events is considerably increased.

The first stage extends from France's surrender on 17th June 1940 to Hitler's so-called commissar order for the Russian campaign in June 1941. During that period Bonhoeffer was proceeding to restore the relations that had been broken off since Müller's journeys to Rome, and to exchange items of information.

The second stage begins with the invasion of the Soviet Union, and ends with the winter crisis leading to the dismissal of Brauchitsch on 19th December 1941. In this period Bonhoeffer's journeys were directed towards finding out and/or influencing the peace aims of Christian circles among the Allies.

In the third stage, the organizational plan for the revolt was modified with a view to the final giving of the order. It ends, after the unsuccessfully attempted *coup* in March 1943, with the smashing of Oster's centre of the Resistance. In this stage, Bonhoeffer was given commissions that were to help by giving preparatory information about the planned *Putsch*.

Thus the course of Bonhoeffer's life is now much more bound up with victory and defeat at the front, with forecasts of politicians and adventurous conspiracies of soldiers, than with details of the church struggle and sessions of councils. Loyalty was required of friends in the Confessing Church, and tense watchfulness on the part of the conspirators in order to carry out the revolt by their joint action.

135. Cf. Ch. XI. p. 526.

IV FIRST STAGE: INFORMATION, SPRING 1941

The stay in Munich had its attractions; it opened to Bonhoeffer a resistance circle of personalities from Bavarian Roman Catholicism which gathered round the *Abwehr* centre there. Josef Müller took his new friend with him wherever he wanted him, as a northern Protestant hostile to the régime, to meet his fellow conspirators. The hospitality in Ettal, where he was given the key to a room in the monastery set aside for total silence and study (he lived in the monastery's hotel), opened up to him theological, liturgical, pastoral, and religio-political insights and experiences.[136] But there also came to Father Johannes men who were politically important to him. At Christmas 1940 they sat up for half the night together: the abbots of Metten and Ettal, Fathers Leiber, Zeiger, and Schönhöfer from the Vatican, Consul Schmidhuber and Captain Ickradt, Josef Müller, Dohnanyi, and Bonhoeffer. Bonhoeffer often went across to the Metten monastery in the Bavarian Forest, whose abbot, Hofmeister, cooperated closely with Josef Müller. Schmidhuber, who represented the Portuguese consulate in Munich and belonged to the *Abwehr*, became Bonhoeffer's mentor in that service, together with Captain Ickradt. Josef Müller also introduced Bonhoeffer in Munich to the prelate Neuhäusler, with whom he conferred several times, before the latter disappeared in a concentration camp in February 1941.[137]

The 'Ten Commandments'

Bonhoeffer depended on the good counsellors and friends in Munich, for he had to learn to move about in the ticklish routine of a provincial *Abwehr* office, which really made him available for the Berlin centre. The *Abwehr* was not occupied solely by resistance people; and so anything that was likely to arouse suspicion had to be not too conspicuous. The set-up with Berlin commissions and visits worked because Oster, as head of the central department, could also intervene and direct matters locally.

With his information from East Prussia in 1940 and the newly expected information from abroad, on which Admiral Canaris based his decision to employ the pastor officially, Bonhoeffer came into the danger zone between the rival secret services: the military *Abwehr*, which had been able to maintain its status as the only secret information organization independent of Himmler's organizations, and the Reich Security Head Office of Reinhard Heydrich, who would not allow areas controlled by the national machine to be withheld from him.

136. On Ettal in general, GS II, pp. 377-406: criticism of Asmussen's *Una sancta-Praktiken*, p. 380; Gürtner's burial, pp. 399 f.; confessional problems, p. 401; reading from his books in the monastery, p. 588.
137. GS II, p. 400.

The claim to be the only person responsible for the political news service had already forced Heydrich into laborious negotiations with Canaris; and vehement arguments had finally led to a precise written statement of the areas of the division of the secret service into political matters on the one hand and military matters on the other, that statement being the 'Ten Commandments'. Since then, Heydrich had been working on as narrow as possible an interpretation of that agreement, namely that Canaris was to enquire into nothing but military matters, whereas all political information was to be reserved for Prinz-Albrecht-Strasse. But Canaris, as before, would not be dictated to as to where the dividing line was to run. Claiming that he had the right to be in the picture when military politics were involved, he opened out any further sources of information, both at home and abroad, that he felt were needed, even when the 'Ten Commandments' were replaced by an agreement still less favourable to the *Abwehr*—an agreement that Canaris and Heydrich signed in Prague in May 1942, only a few days before Heydrich was assassinated.

Of course, Bonhoeffer's commissions for the *Abwehr* were either on or beyond that hard-contested boundary. Canaris protected him—not because he was kind-hearted towards a pastor, but because he was not willing to give way to the other side's inclination to cramp his authority. On the other hand, it was clear that Bonhoeffer, like the others, had to help keep up the fiction of the agreement, if the conspiratorial activity that had gone on hitherto was to be continued within the framework of the *Abwehr*, and the laboriously achieved extra-parochial position was not to break down. Thus, the interrogations of 1943 concentrated for a long time on the question whether Bonhoeffer and some of his friends had been rightly withdrawn from military service. That meant that the friends in Munich and Berlin had so to edit his reports that their secret political content appeared in a military make-up, if they contained anything for the official files. We shall see how Admiral Canaris later accepted and concealed on his own responsibility everything of this kind, where necessary.

First Swiss Journey

On 24th February 1941 Bonhoeffer left Munich for Switzerland on his first commission abroad. The political situation was at last showing signs that gave the opposition hope of new groupings and new prospects. The invasion of England had not taken place, Churchill seemed to be un-yielding, Roosevelt had been re-elected, and Italy had suffered a disas-trous setback in her invasion of Greece. Meanwhile the armed S.S. was being expanded more and more, and this made it easier for the con-spirators to approach the generals who were inclined to be critical. After a conversation that Hassell, Oster, and Dohnanyi had with General von

Falkenhausen, the military commander in Belgium, the latter, with General von Rabenau, again went to Brauchitsch, but could not induce him to make any move at all. Not that the conspiracy was looking for a centre—that was already available in the person of Beck, at least for Oster's circle—but there remained the difficult question of the military centre with power to give and enforce the crucial order. Bonhoeffer's hopes for an overthrow, as he left, were keen though not very definite.

Oster's and Dohnanyi's main idea for Bonhoeffer's journey was that, in view of the new factors, the communications with the other side would have to be taken up again cautiously. Of course, there were other channels, as, for instance, through Hassell and Josef Müller; but one ought to neglect no possible contact that the other side might think trustworthy. There was not much to be expected as yet; on the contrary, it seemed probable that the difficulties for people trying to make contact had increased in proportion as the campaign in the West had roused the bitterest passions, and—a quite incredible thought for Germans in the Germany of that time—the Allies were calculating their first chances of victory. So Bonhoeffer's tasks for that journey were: firstly, to restore communications with the churches; secondly, if possible, to give signs of new activity; and thirdly, to explore ideas about peace aims.

No doubt, Bonhoeffer's previous history made it particularly likely that his name would inspire confidence, through Geneva, among the ecumenical intermediaries and representatives on both sides of the English Channel. Schönfeld in Geneva was not then in touch with the Beck-Oster-Dohnanyi circle. Moreover, Schönfeld was not recommended by Oster's confidential agent in Switzerland, H. B. Gisevius, then vice-consul in Zürich, as the latter, through old connections with the Confessing Church, especially with Niemöller and Asmussen, knew of the past struggles, and of the reserve with which Schönfeld was regarded. On that account Bonhoeffer and Gisevius were rather inclined to warn against using him as an intermediary with the British. Gisevius himself certainly had doubts about the political aspect of Bonhoeffer's errand too, seeing that he was a politically inexperienced pastor acting in his (Gisevius's) own sphere. At the same time, for some important people on the other side Bonhoeffer's name was irreplaceable.

The departure was subject to annoying delays. On the German side, the journey had been authorized by the Munich *Abwehr*, as regards the passport and foreign currency, promptly and without incident. But Berne would not grant the visa. The Berlin central office had to get Schmidhuber to pull strings in Switzerland, and at last he managed to get the visa. But there was another delay at the frontier.

The Swiss frontier police asked Bonhoeffer for a guarantor, whereupon he at once named Karl Barth. The latter recounted afterwards with what mixed feelings and uncertainty he undertook (over the telephone) to stand surety. Could it be right and proper for anyone like Bonhoeffer, a Confessing pastor who was banned by the Gestapo, to cross the Swiss frontier, with valid papers in the middle of the war? How did he come to do that? Could it be that, after all the German victories, even Bonhoeffer had changed his mind? Barth asked him to go and see him, but the visit took place only on the return journey. Bonhoeffer was only too glad to seize the chance of seeing Barth again; he had a confidential and exhaustive conversation with him, and told him the whole truth.[138]

Bonhoeffer spent four weeks in Switzerland, mainly in Zürich and Geneva. First of all he used the possibility of sending letters freely to England. He wrote to his sister Sabine:

You cannot imagine my joy to be able to write to you directly after this period of silence and after all you had to pass through during the last year.[139]

On the same day, he sent a greeting to the Bishop of Chichester:

My thoughts have been with you and with our fellow-Christians in your country almost every day . . . I need not assure you that we shall do everything to maintain that fellowship in faith and prayer . . . When will we meet again? God knows and we have to wait. But I cannot help hoping and praying that it will not last too long . . .[140]

Bonhoeffer stayed a fairly long time in Zürich. He went out to Rapperswil to see Sutz, who had been sending news regularly, since the beginning of the war, between the Leibholz family, who had moved to Oxford, and Bonhoeffer in Berlin. Sutz remembers that, to his surprise, Bonhoeffer said very definitely: 'You can rely on it, we shall overthrow Hitler!'

Bonhoeffer also looked up his old mentor Siegmund-Schultze, with whom Goerdeler was cooperating. Siegmund-Schultze was keeping up his own communications with London, and they had got as far as Chamberlain;[141] but since Churchill had taken over the government Siegmund-Schultze had grown sceptical about the attempts at negotiation, especially as they had never been accompanied by any concrete report about a plot. That weak aspect of the case grew clearer to the most sympathetic supporters as one plan followed another.

In the second week of March Bonhoeffer reached his main objective, Geneva. There he met A. Freudenberg, who had moved there from London,[142] and since the autumn of 1940 had been working for the provisional World Council of Churches, organizing relief for refugees. Bonhoeffer asked about the camp at Gurs in the south of France, where one of Perels' uncles and Herbert Jehle were said to be interned. He met

138. J. Glenthoj, 'Bonhoeffer und die Ökumene', in MW II, p. 198.
139. Letter of 28.2.1941.
140. Letter of 28.2.1941.
141. G. Ritter, *Carl Goerdeler und die deutsche Widerstandsbewegung*, 1954, pp. 252, 316.
142. See Ch. XI, p. 544.

Professor Courvoisier, and now Schönfeld too, both busy organizing ecumenical relief for prisoners of war. In the office of the World Council of Churches he read up two years' ecumenical church history and what he could find in publications from London and New York. His intimations of the political opposition in Germany were met with a good deal of doubt.[143] But there was one person who listened to him frankly and readily—Visser 't Hooft. The latter was the man whom Bonhoeffer had principally wanted to see, and he gave his German visitor a great deal of time for consultation.

At that first meeting in the war, no messages or memoranda were as yet exchanged—only reports showing that the opposition still existed. Visser 't Hooft at once wrote a personal report to Bishop Bell on the surprising fact that people in Germany reacted to the events 'exactly as you and I' would have reacted, and he sent the Western ecumenical leaders, through his co-secretary William Paton, a detailed account of the situation. In a personal letter to Bishop Bell, he wrote:

Bonhoeffer was a week with us and spent most of his time extracting ecumenical information from persons and documents. It is touching to see how hungry people like him are for news about their brothers in other countries, and it is good to know that he can take back so much which will encourage his friends at home.

On the other hand, we learned a lot from him. The picture which he gave is pretty black in respect to the exterior circumstances for the community which he represents.[144] The pressure is greater than ever. But fortunately he could also tell of many signs that their fundamental position has not changed at all and that they are as eager as ever for fellowship. Many of them have really the same reaction to all that has happened and is happening as you or as I have. And this is remarkable after such a long period of isolation. I hope to send soon through Bill some fuller notes on all that we learned through him about the situation.[145]

In those months, rumours were circulating that Niemöller in the concentration camp had gone over to the Roman Catholic Church. So Visser 't Hooft passed on Bonhoeffer's assurance that that was not so. Bonhoeffer had actually enquired, before he left Germany, both from Frau Niemöller and from the episcopal Ordinary in Berlin, whether the rumour was true. I had myself telephoned to him that Bishop Count von Galen had said to Frau Niemöller: 'He will stay where he is.'

Visser 't Hooft's detailed report which Paton ('Bill') took to England contains news about the conflict between State and Church, a conflict that the war had by no means silenced; it enumerates the arrests and the labour conscription, the thirteen points for the Warthegau, the euthanasia measures, the prohibitions against sending periodicals to

143. See A. Freudenberg, 'Visits to Geneva', IKDB, p. 167.
144. i.e. the Confessing Church.
145. Letter of 19.3.1941.

the front, and so on, but not without the assurance that the Confessing Church was going on with its ordinations. Then Visser 't Hooft sympathetically presents the attitude to the political dilemma, as Bonhoeffer, in contrast to other politically minded people, expressed it from now on:

Inside the Confessing Church there is a certain difference of conviction with regard to the stand which the Church should take. There is, on the other hand, a group which believes that the Church should stick to what is called 'the inner line', and concentrate exclusively on the building up of its own spiritual life. This tendency is often combined with a strongly apocalyptic note. There is, however, another group which believes that the Church has also a prophetic and ethical function in relation to the world and that it must prepare for the moment when it can again fulfil that function.

With regard to the attitude to the war, it is generally recognized among believing Christians that a victory of their government will have the most fateful consequences for the Church in their own country as well as in other countries. On the other hand, they consider that a defeat of their country would probably mean its end as a nation. Thus many have come to believe that whatever the outcome of it all will be, it will be an evil thing for them. One hears, however, also voices which say that after all the suffering which their country has brought upon others they almost hope for an opportunity to pay the price by suffering themselves.[146]

Bonhoeffer returned to Germany on 24th March 1941, leaving word in Geneva that he would be back soon. The old basis of confidence in his ecumenical friends was restored, and for the present that was enough. Visser 't Hooft was left in little doubt as to the strength of purpose among those of Bonhoeffer's circle; and he had had a reliable glimpse of the obstacles in their way.

Forbidden to Publish

On his way to Berlin to give his report, Bonhoeffer broke his journey on 25th March to see Ernst Wolf at Halle an der Saale, as he needed his advice about a new complication. On his return to Munich, he had found two communications from the National Office for Literature (*Reichsschrifttumskammer*) dated 17th and 19th March respectively. The first letter stated that as he had neglected to apply, as a writer, for membership of that body, he had to pay a disciplinary fine; the second informed him that his application for admission to the association had been refused, as he was already forbidden, on the ground of 'subversive activities', to make speeches, and that he was now prohibited from 'any activity as a writer'.[147]

It turned out that Bonhoeffer had not been specially aimed at in this case, but that he had been brought in through a general scrutiny by the

146. From a copy given to the author by W. A. Visser 't Hooft.
147. GS II, pp. 367-72.

National Office for Literature, which had reached church publishers and theologians since the autumn of 1940. He had already heard of it, but he had also heard that earlier decisions had provided that specialist writers ('*Fachwissenschaftler*') could be excused membership, though only on special application. He had therefore sent in such an application in November 1940. And now this was the answer.

He protested on the strength of the regulation's distinction between authors and specialists: '. . . I have no right at all to enrol in the *Reichsschrifttumskammer*.'[148] He then pointed to the negligence through which the penalty had been imposed, as his works had been quite incorrectly classified. Thereupon the fine was remitted, but both membership and exemption from membership were refused:

This refusal has the effect of an official occupational prohibition of literary activity . . . Only those theologians are exempted who occupy chairs at state colleges. Moreover, because their dominating commitments are dogmatic, I cannot readily recognize clergymen as specialists in this sense.[149]

Of all the obstacles that had so far been put in Bonhoeffer's way, the prohibition against writing made the smallest impression on him. It was certainly one of his life's needs to find leisure and concentration for writing; but he had for a long time been counting himself as one of those who could no longer print everything that they wrote. In spite of that, he had so far used every available day for his *Ethics*, and he wanted to do so in the future.

That interference hardly interested his employers in the *Abwehr*; the routine nature of the measure was too obvious. For one administrative department in the Reich to act against another was too common an experience for a fuss to be made about it every time. But it is true that in the later interrogations the prohibition against writing did not weigh in the accused's favour.

Optimism

The first Swiss journey was followed by a period of tense expectation, and on that account Bonhoeffer did not wish to go and live in remote Ettal again for the time being. Apart from his time in Friedrichsbrunn at Easter and a few weeks at Klein-Krössin in the high summer, he spent the whole time in Berlin. There were signs of Hitler's coming attack on the Soviet Union. What would be the consequences? Berlin was full of rumours.

Among the Allies, the feeling was spreading that the time had come to strike back. On 11th March 1941 Great Britain and America concluded the Lend-Lease Act, which brought the flow of war material across the Atlantic. A few weeks later, the British landed in Greece

148. GS II, p. 369.   149. GS II, p. 372.

and made Hitler divert some of his forces to the Balkans. On 12th July the Soviet Union and Great Britain concluded a pact of mutual assistance, which naturally again made attempts by the resistance to get into touch with the West more difficult, because each party to the treaty was now to enter into negotiations only in agreement with the other. On 14th August Roosevelt and Churchill signed the Atlantic Charter, which was not much noticed in Germany, while Rommel in North Africa and the German armies in Russia were storming ahead, but which had all the more effect outside: 'The meeting . . . was a thrilling episode and the eight points of the Atlantic Charter can hardly fail to affect opinion throughout the world.'[150]

In the Reich, Hitler's order about commissars and jurisdiction gave the opposition a new occasion for speaking to the commanders about their honour and patriotism. Hitler had called them together on 30th March, and had briefed them on the planned attack on Russia. In doing so, he asserted that it was necessary 'to smash the governing machinery of the Russian empire'; and for that purpose civil and military commissars who fell into German hands were to be summarily liquidated without legal proceedings by the troops. Whereas criminal measures had hitherto been reserved to the S.S. and their special formations, the regular German *Wehrmacht* was now, for the first time, expected to give and carry out orders that were plainly criminal. When Hitler had left the room after his declaration on 30th March, several generals began to press Brauchitsch vehemently. Halder urged him to resign because of the order. But Brauchitsch finally said, in answer to all arguments about international law, that Hitler had made his decision and would never reverse it. So the 'commissar order' was issued over Keitel's signature to the troops concerned. When it was even enlarged by a provision that German soldiers who committed offences against Russian civilians should in practice be freed from the liability to be court-martialled, Brauchitsch did indeed try, by a 'supplementary order on discipline', to counter the outrage; but the stain of the regulations was left on the Army. 'With that submission to Hitler's orders Brauchitsch is sacrificing the honour of the German Army.'[151]

The effect of the orders was divisive; they drove some officers more than ever into Hitler's arms; others they perplexed and made more inclined to serious misgivings and revolt. In the *Abwehr* Oster and Dohnanyi took the initiative vigorously by working out a memorandum[152] to demonstrate the military and political lunacy of the order.

150. *Letters of Herbert Hensley Henson*, London, 1951, p. 130.

151. U. von Hassell, *Vom Anderen Deutschland*; from his diaries of 1938-44. 1946, p. 202, diary notes for 4.5.1941. See also H. Graml, 'Die deutsche Militäropposition vom Sommer 1940 bis zum Frühjahr 1943' in *Aus Politik und Zeitgeschichte, Beilage zur Wochenzeitung 'Das Parlament'*, 16.7.1958, p. 361.

152. Moltke took part in preparing this document; see K. H. Abshagen, *Canaris, Patriot und Weltbürger*, 1959, p. 307.

In other places, as for instance among the staffs of individual army detachments, resentment was either openly or secretly expressed.[153]

With that, the conditions for preparing a revolt took a more favourable turn. There were remarkable incidents and changes of mind. Rudolf Hess, 'the Führer's representative', flew to Great Britain with the idea of being able, before the catastrophe came, to start talks to end the war on terms favourable to Nazi Germany. Former collaborators began to realize how things stood; Hassell wrote in his diary on 13th July 1941:

Bishop Heckel, who formerly joined very complaisantly in all the attempts to build a bridge between the Evangelical Church and Nazism, was with me lately, and now showed that he fully realized the Party's undoubted will to smash the churches . . .[154]

The optimism of the circle to which Bonhoeffer belonged was for weeks concentrated on the possibility that the commanders could and must resist being put on the same footing as the murder squads of the S.S. As late as 16th June, six days before the invasion of Russia, the matter was discussed with Beck.[155] Then the offensive took its course, and the initial successes left no room for any further thought of united action. At the same time, Bonhoeffer's optimism did not now suffer anything like the same setback as at the beginning of the French campaign. Everything was different.

Indeed, the conspiring section of the opposition was now cultivating an optimism that was both cautious and responsible. While sceptics were beginning to admire Hitler's complete absence of restraint and saw his 'fanatical will for the new order' achieving the impossible, the conspirators did not allow themselves to be deluded about his accelerating progress towards self-destruction. They felt that they had to urge themselves and others to go on working to bring the terror to an earlier end. The work had admittedly become more complicated, for at the beginning of the Russian campaign Hitler moved into the *Wolfsschanze*, his headquarters retreat in East Prussia, and so made himself still less approachable because of the numerous prohibited areas.

Of course, the group worked energetically with the factual material that the members were able to get through friends in important positions, perhaps in the High Command or the *Abwehr*. Facts can always be differently interpreted and are soon overtaken, and a great deal depends on how they are treated. So Goerdeler's much discussed optimism and his way of dealing with the facts were of some account in any further action; and he was not alone in his optimism. Some gave a time-limit for Hitler's failures, and when these turned out to be incorrect, they were at once replaced by new ones. There were numerical data that

153. On H. von Tresckow's reactions see H. Graml, op.cit., p. 362.
154. U. von Hassel. op. cit., p. 214.
155. U. von Hassell, op. cit., p. 212.

showed his enterprises to be Utopian; and when the inferences proved to be wrong, the data were revised. Some evenings at the Schleichers' or at Klaus Bonhoeffer's were very much occupied by such forecasts, to which everyone contributed—Klaus Bonhoeffer and Otto John, Justus Delbrück and Baron Guttenberg, Rüdiger Schleicher and Dietrich Bonhoeffer himself. Hans von Dohnanyi was always a little more sceptical about all this, but Dietrich Bonhoeffer unwearyingly defended the mental attitude that would allow itself to make forecasts; he considered this to be, not blindness or seductive fantasies, but a necessary weapon in the unequal struggle. He would not admit the reproaches that were repeatedly made at Goerdeler's new forecasts after every failure, as here confidence had to be set off against a tired bourgeois scepticism; and that confidence needed strengthening. For him, that was part of the everyday work of the resistance, which did not surrender to the 'facts', but tried to create new facts.

In the essay for his friends at Christmas 1942, he wrote a passage specially about 'optimism', a paragraph which, at first sight, was hardly to be expected of a Lutheran theologian and pupil of Karl Barth:

> The essence of optimism is not its view of the present, but the fact that it is the inspiration of life and hope when others give in; it enables a man to hold his head high when everything seems to be going wrong; it gives him strength to sustain reverses and yet to claim the future for himself instead of abandoning it to his opponent . . . the optimism that is will for the future should never be despised, even if it is proved wrong a hundred times.[156]

One person whom Bonhoeffer had in mind when he wrote such passages was Carl Goerdeler; he understood him, and he felt akin to him in that respect. Bonhoeffer called this, very concisely, a responsibility for life's 'health and vitality, and the sick man has no business to impugn it'.[157] The same was the case with Guttenberg and Oster. Because of that basic attitude, not a few of the conspirators were glad of the pastor's support.

V SECOND STAGE: PEACE AIMS, AUTUMN 1941

1. *Second Swiss Journey*

After the war, Visser 't Hooft described how Bonhoeffer greeted him on the second visit in September 1941:

> The German army was forging ahead incredibly in Russia, and one could not see why it should not march right across Asia. He came into my room, and simply said: 'It's all over now, isn't it?' I could not believe my ears. Was

156. LPP, pp. 38 f.
157. LPP, p. 39.

Bonhoeffer greeting me with the announcement of a German victory? He saw my dismay. 'No,' he said, 'I mean that we are at the beginning of the end. Hitler will never get out of this.'[158]

At the end of the visit, Bonhoeffer wrote to Bishop Bell from Zürich:

Personally I am rather optimistic in hope for better days to be not too far off and I do not abandon the hope that in the coming year we may meet again. What a strange day that will be.[159]

That optimism was based on the opposition's most recent activity in Berlin, and certainly not on anything that Bonhoeffer and his friends could expect from the Allies.

When Bonhoeffer crossed the frontier on his way to Basle on 29th August 1941, General Thomas, head of the army supplies department, was setting off, sent by the same organization as Bonhoeffer, to enquire about, and possibly to activate, the readiness for revolt on the part of some of the commanders on the eastern front. Thomas not only kept the group round Beck, Goerdeler, Oster, and Dohnanyi informed of the situation as to raw materials; he also tirelessly undertook missions that might be carried on unnoticed in the course of his official service.

Parallel with the conspiracy, efforts were constantly being made towards peace contacts. The latter were not, as has often been asserted, a condition for the former, but they could play an important part. It would even have shown a lack of responsibility if the conspirators had not made every possible effort to make contact with the Allies. It is true that in 1941 the favourable situation for discussion that had existed at the time of the X-report (1939-40) had now gone, and a negotiated peace was no longer to be had. But backgrounds and perhaps counteracting forces to the war and peace aims of the Atlantic Charter, which made of Germany a special case, had to be explored. It was a question whether the other side's ideas about the future might still be influenced, whether the Allies might have regard to the mistakes and results of the Treaty of Versailles, so that they would consider how the danger of chaos in Central Europe might be averted, even in their own interest.

By comparison with his first journey, Bonhoeffer was able this time to get a much more vivid picture of the discussion on the other side, especially in responsible Christian circles. Officially, of course, the Atlantic Charter had for the time being ended the discussion. The charter identified Germany in general with Hitler, and that was something that the German opposition could not allow to be accepted without protest. Were there circles over there who realized the full consequences of such identification, and if so, could they be strengthened? Was the discussion still going on?

Bonhoeffer did not confine himself this time to reporting his presence

158. W. A. Visser 't Hooft, *Zeugnis eines Boten*, 1945, p. 7.
159. Letter of 25.9.1941.

and to a mere exchange of information as on his first visit; he entered actively into the discussion by leading Western Christians of peace aims.

Bell's Penguin book.   Bishop Bell was never tired of taking the discussion of his country's peace aims away from the sphere of propaganda on to a matter-of-fact plane, although it made him very unpopular. From the beginning of the war he had been in constant touch with Bonhoeffer's brother-in-law Gerhard Leibholz in Oxford, and had asked him for advice and comments when he wanted to express himself publicly, so as to get as accurate an idea as possible of the German side of the case. Bell's speeches, most of which were delivered in the Upper House, and are published in the volume *The Church and Humanity*, show a far-reaching agreement of outlook with Gerhard Leibholz's English publications during the war.[160]

Bonhoeffer first got hold of Bell's Penguin book *Christianity and World Order* of 1940. The tone was so familiar to him that it could easily have led him to misjudge the response in the England of 1940. He wrote to the bishop from Zürich: 'I have had the great pleasure and satisfaction to read your newest book and I am sharing your hope for a strong stand of the churches after the war.'[161]

In that book, which was published for mass circulation, the bishop spoke of Great Britain's and France's share of guilt for the rise of Hitler, but 'the war is not just the protest of the injured German people against the victors of 1918'.[162]

I have no doubt in my own mind that the results of a victory by Hitler would be so disastrous, morally and spiritually, that Christians ought to do their utmost to defeat him.[163]

But the bishop firmly refuses to call the war 'Christian' or 'holy' or a 'crusade'; one should by all means take care 'not to let slip any genuine chance of a negotiated peace which observes the principles of Order and Justice . . .'[164]

Here Bonhoeffer read an answer to everything for which he had been striving at the risk of his life:

Links should be strengthened between the churches in warring countries on

160. *Germany, the West and the possibility of a new international order*, Winter 1939-40, Report on behalf of the Study Department of the Universal Council for 'Life and Work'; 'Christianity, Politics and Power' in *Christian News-Letter Books*, London, 1942, with a preface by L. Hodgson; 'Germany between West and East' in *The Fortnightly*, October 1942, under the pseudonym S. H. Gerhard; 'Ideology in the Post-war Policy of Russia and the Western Powers' in *The Hibbert Journal*, January 1944; 'The opposition movement in Germany' in *The New English Weekly* of 19.10.1944, pp. 5 f. Cf. now G. Leibholz, *Politics and Law*, 1965, pp. 91-132, 154-73, 174 ff., 182 ff., 210 ff.
161. Letter of 25.9.1941.
162. G. Bell, *Christianity and World Order*, London, 1940, p. 83.
163. G. Bell, op. cit., p. 84.
164. G. Bell, op. cit., p. 85.

both sides in any way that is possible through the help of the churches in neutral countries . . .[165]

Here was an outstretched hand from the other side:

It cannot be wrong for Christians in one belligerent country to seek such opportunities as may be open, to discover through neutral channels, in every way possible, from fellow-Christians in another belligerent country, what terms of peace would be likely to create a lasting peace and not lead to a further poisoning of international relationships . . .[166]

What naïve unconcern when groups of readers in England, on the strength of those sentences, publicly demanded in the newspapers that the bishop should say 'whether any steps had actually been taken on the lines of my suggestion . . .'[167]

The most important chapter in the book was the eighth, on 'Christianity and Peace Aims',[168] which deals with Germany's participation in a new order, on condition of a complete renunciation of National Socialism, as a sensible, wise, and Christian measure. Here we have the bishop's constantly repeated demand and distinction, which he later made sorrowfully in all his speeches after the Sigtuna meeting of 1942: 'Germany and National Socialism are *not* the same thing.'[169] The bishop goes into detail to justify this statement with the help of quotations from Visser 't Hooft, and urges that the distinction must be recognized if the future is to be tolerable.

How little that attitude accorded with official allied policy Bonhoeffer could learn from Siegmund-Schultze, whom he visited again in Zürich. The latter had had depressing experiences.[170] The British embassy in Berne had refused to accept from him, as Goerdeler's intermediary, a document with peace proposals, the reason given being that the embassy was forbidden by London 'to receive any suggestions whatever for peace'.[171] Thereupon Siegmund-Schultze had tried to make headway with the help of both Archbishop Temple and Bishop Bell. Bell wrote to G. Leibholz about this on 27th August 1941:

I have been asked by Siegmund-Schultze a few weeks ago whether I could put him on to any statement in British official circles which was at all in line with the sentiment expressed in my Penguin and particularly the contents of my Chapter VIII.

There was no room for doubt that Churchill did not want any discussions about peace. His speeches and Eden's left little doubt that even

---

165. G. Bell, op. cit., p. 87.
166. G. Bell, op. cit., pp. 105 f.
167. Letter from G. Bell to G. Leibholz, 27.8.1941.
168. G. Bell, op. cit., pp. 88-101.
169. G. Bell, op. cit., p. 92.
170. G. Ritter, op. cit., pp. 316 f.
171. G. Ritter, op. cit., p. 318.

an opposition government in Germany would have to surrender unconditionally. They preferred to stick to the statement that they could see nothing that had happened, or was likely to happen, in Germany, that gave promise of any decisive change.

Demonstration at the Stoll Theatre. But just because it seemed that official circles could still think only in terms of victory and unconditional surrender, discussion was stimulated among influential Christians in Great Britain about responsible peace aims and about what was to happen afterwards, and this led to joint demonstrations by the different denominations.

In *The Times* of 21st December 1940 a letter that attracted a good deal of notice had appeared over the signatures of the Archbishops of Canterbury and York, Cardinal Hinsley, and the Moderator of the Free Church Council, taking up again the Pope's famous five peace points of Christmas 1940—equal right to live and independence for all nations, reduction of armaments, the formation of an international commission for a revision of the Treaty of Versailles, and respect for the needs of national minorities—and adding a further five points, according to which a future economic world order (Temple's influence!) ought to be tested:

1. The crying inequality in the standard of life and possessions must be abolished.
2. Every child, of whatever race or colour, is to have the same opportunities for education.
3. The family is to be protected as a social unit.
4. The consciousness of divine calling is to be restored to human work.
5. The natural treasures of the earth are to be safeguarded, with due regard to future generations, as God's gifts to all mankind.

The Pope's five points and that letter to *The Times* came up during 1941 in every utterance of the British churches about peace, and gave the discussion a public importance that the sceptics of the power-politics school could not simply ignore. The discussion can be followed quite well in the issues of the *News Letter* of those months. Important stages in it were Temple's Malvern Conference in January 1941 with the theme 'Christianity and the Social Order', and a big demonstration on 10th May 1941 in the Stoll theatre, with Cardinal Hinsley in the chair; Bishop Bell said:

'The year 1941,' says Hitler, 'will become the historic year of the New Order in Europe' . . . We proclaim no 'Order' at all. We speak only of 'victory' and 'survival' and 'liberation' of the vanquished nations. Our official spokesmen have never yet uttered any statement of British aims which envisages a situation after victory which could be immediately seen by enemies and neutrals alike to be better than that with which the war began, and out of which the war arose . . .

I am sure that there are very many in Germany, silenced now by the Gestapo and the machine-gun, who long for deliverance from a godless Nazi rule, and for the coming of Christian order in which they and we can take our part. Is no trumpet call to come from England, to awaken them from despair? . . . It is right that this meeting, fully representative of Christian opinion throughout the country, should urge the British Government to make them[172] the basis of any future statement of war and peace aims.[173]

Bell concluded with an appeal to Christians of other countries, and especially to those in Germany, to make the ten points the common basis of a just and honourable peace.

Discussion of a Book of High Politics. From Visser 't Hooft in Geneva Bonhoeffer got hold of another book, which had reached Geneva from London, where it had been published by the S.C.M. Press: William Paton's *The Church and the New Order.* It extended the discussion that was being carried on among groups centred on Temple, Oldham, Arnold Toynbee, Zimmern, Owen, and in America on van Dusen. On reading the book, Bonhoeffer and Visser 't Hooft decided to give, from Geneva, the attitude of a German who spoke from the point of view of the resistance itself. So, early in September, Bonhoeffer wrote a memorandum that kept to the sequence of the subjects in Paton's book.[174] Visser 't Hooft prepared the English version and made it known through Hugh Martin in London.

Bonhoeffer liked to look at things theologically; but here, in the form of that literary review, he really wanted something quite different. It upset him to read the academic observation by the general secretary of the provisional World Council of Churches:

It may be urged as conceivable that the totalitarian system might collapse from internal causes, but there seems little hope that the anti-totalitarian forces which exist can become effective except after a major reverse.[175]

Paton looks to the future: 'The conquest of so much of Europe by the German National Socialists has smashed much of the old order beyond repair . . .'[176] In his opinion, there ought to be a considerable interval between the armistice and the conclusion of peace, so that the right people on both sides can find the way to each other. That will be possible, for

I suppose that few who have known the Confessional [sic] Church leaders

172. The ten points in the letter to *The Times*.
173. G. Bell, *The Church and Humanity 1939-1946*, London, 1946, pp. 50, 56.
174. GS I, pp. 356 ff.
175. W. Paton, *The Church and the New Order*, London, 1941, p. 75.
176. W. Paton, op. cit., p. 85.

would doubt that there are no Germans with whom fellowship in the post-war talks will be so quickly resumed . . .[177]

Bonhoeffer found it depressing that any initial draft for future planning, such as was clearly set out here in Paton's book, was totally lacking in his own Church. Ten years previously, he would hardly have been able to endure the secular Anglo-Saxon tone of the resolutions; now he was occupied, in contrast to most of his friends at home, with that very secular future which might soon have to be shaped.

In his second point ('Why peace aims?'), Bonhoeffer goes straight to the conditions for the coming *Putsch*: its preparations are influenced unfavourably as long as Allied propaganda insists upon the unilateral disarming of Germany. He is surprised that the B.B.C. in its broadcasts says nothing 'about the churches' great discussion of the new order', since the little that has been heard of it by important circles of the political opposition in Berlin had left a deep impression (of course, it had been heard of in Berlin through him). Perhaps he did not sufficiently realize how little concern the Government (i.e. Churchill) felt about the discussion, which it saw rather as a pernicious distraction from its efforts to achieve a victory that was still so far off. But for the conspirators, and so for Bonhoeffer, any such sensible planning for the future meant a good deal. Could its political value be raised from outside? His question is put positively in Visser 't Hooft's English version:

A positive statement of peace aims may have a very strong influence in strengthening the hands of this group. It is clear that recent events have created a psychological situation[178] in which they have an opportunity such as they have not had since 1933. There is, therefore, reason to give very great prominence to this aspect of the whole question . . . We understand that the disarmament of Germany will have to be demanded. But it should certainly not be mentioned as the main peace aim, as is being done too often . . .[179]

We have here what Bonhoeffer wanted by all means to put across to the other side—the announcement of the coming revolt in the hope that those who received it would be able through their influence to ensure that the Allies would suspend military action during the revolt.

Bonhoeffer then tries to discourage the expectation that the revolt would make it possible for the other Germany to set up at once the kind of government that would be democratic in the Western sense. The government that would emerge from a military *Putsch* 'might be formed suddenly. A great deal would depend on whether we could then count on the immediate support of the Allies.'[180] That is what was said in the German draft. The English text reads:

177. W. Paton, op. cit., p. 179.
178. The 'Commissar Order'.
179. GS I, pp. 364 f.
180. GS I, p. 360.

. . . the question must be faced whether a German government which makes a complete break with Hitler and all he stands for, can hope to get such terms of peace that it has some chance to survive . . . It is clear that the answering of this question is a matter of urgency, since the attitude of opposition groups in Germany depends upon the answer given . . .[181]

Bonhoeffer's and Visser 't Hooft's documents are indeed in the form of a theological-ethical discussion of an English churchman's book. But it was obvious that, for practical reasons, Bonhoeffer was anxious to provide information about the conspiracy. Visser 't Hooft understood that very well; he wrote to Hugh Martin in his covering letter of 12th September:

These comments on your book have been written by me in close collaboration with a friend who came to us and who is a good friend of George Bell. I hope you will circulate them to all who are interested and also send a copy to Pit van Dusen. You must accept my word for it that all that we say about the next steps and *the urgency of the situation is not based upon wishful thinking on our part*, but on actual developments in discussion with responsible persons in the country concerned. That is also why I hope that *some* of these considerations will be *brought before responsible* people in Britain.[182]

If one looks carefully, it becomes clear that that communication was meant to be of common concern to British government circles and to the organizers of the revolt. It was, indeed, under that practical aspect, and with no theological accompaniment, that Visser 't Hooft added to the above passage: 'We should, of course, appreciate some answer to this statement, and, if possible, in the near future.' Bonhoeffer indulged in the delusive hope that there might be a response to his political ideas, if he waited for a time in Switzerland. He did not leave till 26th September.

Paton Does Not Understand. But the scope and aim of Visser 't Hooft's and Bonhoeffer's communications were hardly understood in London. It is doubtful whether their names signified enough in Great Britain at that time for the recipients to feel it necessary to make any practical approach to the politicians on the ground that the communications were authoritative enough to be taken seriously. They were taken note of, but no specific answer was given; a much more forcible approach was needed for that. It was not till 1942, after Sigtuna,[183] that Bishop Bell tackled the Government and extracted an answer. But we were then much nearer to the 'unconditional surrender' of Casablanca—and the answer was made as negative as possible.

Certainly, Visser 't Hooft's and Bonhoeffer's effort towards clarification did not remain entirely without an echo; but the answer only proved

181. GS I, pp. 369 f.
182. GS I, p. 361; the italics are the author's.
183. See Ch. XII, pp. 662 ff.

that the letter had not been as convincing as had been hoped. The 'Peace Aims Group' in London received copies of the memorandum from Geneva. Van Dusen, who came to England in October 1941, took part; he belonged to a parallel group in America, 'The just and durable peace commission of the Federal Council of Churches'. On 9th October 1941 Paton did, in fact, send Visser 't Hooft a hopeful answer:

Let me say with what immense interest and gratitude I studied the critique of the book which you sent. I am having it copied and sent to a few people and shall be able, I hope, to send you some considerable reply.

But the 'considerable reply' never came. More detailed examination had produced, instead of actions, doubts 'as to whether there really can be a sufficiently strong party on the lines described to be able really to affect the situation, which I share and have shared with very important people'.[184] So conversations had taken place with influential people, but they had broken off because they could not believe that there was, as Bonhoeffer had said, a German opposition that could be taken seriously. Thus the outcome was discouraging.

Bell certainly did not share Paton's opinion; but he knew only too well how widespread it was; and that was why, at Sigtuna in 1942, he had considerably dampened his German visitors' hopes of a positive British answer. He now exchanged the Geneva memorandum of September 1941 with Leibholz, who pointed out to him the important political points in his brother-in-law's discussion of the book. Bell wrote to Leibholz:

I entirely agree with your view on the comments from Geneva on Dr. Paton's book. I am also entirely with you in what you say endorsing the comments, and have written to Paton strongly in that sense myself.[185]

He answered Visser 't Hooft separately on 5th November:

I read your comments on Paton's book with the greatest interest, and find myself very much in accord with your cautionary remarks about Germany itself.

The deliberations of the London 'Peace Aims Group' were again directed towards independent movements in Germany alone when, in May 1942, Visser 't Hooft brought over to London a memorandum from Adam von Trott, and Bell, with some emotion, recounted his experiences in Sigtuna. That revived interest in the views that Bonhoeffer had expressed in that 'review of a book'.

Karl Barth has told us[186] that Bonhoeffer was at that time too naïve in thinking that Germany might, after an overthrow, remain intact

184. Letter of 6.1.1942.
185. Letter of 30.10.1941.
186. See MW II, p. 185.

within her frontiers of 1939. I am sure that Bonhoeffer no longer thought that possible. It may be that he was repeating here the opinion of some people in Beck's circle; for he himself went much further than some of the opposition in his willingness to see that Germany would have to accept sanctions on moral grounds, and for that reason some called him 'unpolitical'. Indeed, in the review of Paton's book he wrote clearly enough that the Allies might expect 'safeguards' against a return of Nazism and 'far-reaching military measures against Germany'. He was now concerned, not with negotiations about frontiers, but about the willingness of the ecumenical movement to help to improve the chances of a successful revolt. Beck, Oster, and Dohnanyi had sent him out for talks with his ecumenical associates in the hope that it would prove to be a political matter. He knew that more competent friends, such as Hassell or Josef Müller, had been commissioned to discuss practical questions of foreign policy. He may have miscalculated the possibility of putting his views across and exercising a certain influence, as he could, after all, furnish no proofs of the existence of an effective *Fronde*. His justification consists of a series of actions, as undertaken by Bishop Bell in an effort to compel the British Government to make certain declarations that might encourage a revolutionary government in Germany. The realism of such actions is less in dispute today than it was then.

Visits to friends. On that second visit to Switzerland, Bonhoeffer saw old friends and new ones. Otto Salomon, the man who had once carried through the printing of *Creation and Fall* and so begun the relationship with the publishing house of Chr. Kaiser, invited Bonhoeffer to stay with him in Zürich.[187] He went with him over to Erwin Sutz at Rapperswil, to congratulate his friend on his marriage—a visit that gave him some anticipatory thoughts:

. . . now, in the midst of demolition, we want to build up; in the midst of life by the day and by the hour, we want a future; in the midst of banishment from the earth, a bit of room; in the midst of the general distress, a bit of happiness. And what overwhelms us is that God says Yes to this strange desire, that God acquiesces in our will, though the reverse should normally be true. So marriage becomes something quite new, mighty, grand, for us who want to be Christians in Germany.[188]

When he wrote those positive words about marriage, at least a year was to pass before he decided to become engaged.

He visited Koechlin, president of the Federation of Swiss Churches, whose help he was soon to want urgently for a Jewish group. He saw Karl Ludwig Schmidt, who introduced him to Eberhard Vischer, the

187. O. Salomon. 'The Guest', IKDB, pp. 170 ff. See also Ch. VI, p. 163.
188. GS I, p. 50.

father of the Old Testament scholar Wilhelm Vischer. The fact that Eberhard Vischer had some association with the English chargé d'affaires was bound to interest Bonhoeffer, but so far no details have come to light of an attempt to make contact with him; it was probably unsuccessful. Bonhoeffer was glad to accept an invitation to relax in Freudenberg's summer-house on Lake Champex in Valais.[189]

Bonhoeffer did not visit Zürich till the second half of his four weeks' stay in freedom. It was probably in the first half when there occurred that conversation which Visser 't Hooft reported immediately after the war,[190] and which produced an unforgettable remark. One evening with Courvoisier, d'Espine, and others, Visser 't Hooft asked: 'What do you really pray for in the present situation?', to which Bonhoeffer is said to have answered: 'If you want to know, I pray for the defeat of my country, for I think that is the only possibility of paying for all the suffering that my country has caused in the world.'

That was a statement that people did not like to hear reproduced in post-war Germany, but whose essential content can hardly be denied, whatever the actual wording may have been. It shows, above all, how absurd and extraordinary the situation was under Hitler, when the true patriot had to speak unpatriotically to show his patriotism. It is a re-action that defies normal feelings in normal times; and it may be a good thing that it is handed down without defence or explanation, so that one comes up against it and relives the incredible happenings of those days. It is abundantly true that the best people of that time had constantly in their minds that they must wish for Germany's defeat to put an end to the injustice.

Before Bonhoeffer returned to Germany, he reported to Bell that Niemöller had been moved from Sachsenhausen to Dachau, where he shared a cell with two Roman Catholic brethren, but that 'there is no reason to worry about his physical and spiritual state of health'.[191]

He left Switzerland on 26th September. He did not allow himself to be influenced by Siegmund-Schultze's disheartening experiences with the Allies, but thought he had got a little further forward in his contact with London through Visser 't Hooft and Paton. He could as yet have known nothing of Paton's disillusioning answer. He was strongly influenced by his confident hope that decisive actions in Germany would soon change the position with regard to talks, and he was pleased with the cooperation that he had found in Geneva. He saw no reason to abandon the optimism that he had expressed before the journey:

I shall . . . think of the common aims that are bound up with these journeys, of European hopes and tasks, of the Church's commission in the future—and all in the hope that you and I, and a great many others who are of one

189. A. Freudenberg, 'Visits to Geneva', IKDB, p. 169.
190. W. A. Visser 't Hooft, *Zeugnis eines Boten*, p. 7.
191. Letter of 25.9.1941.

mind, that we may all, some time, be allowed to cooperate for that future . . .
We cannot reckon at present how things will be in a year's time, but I am
very confident.[192]

And so he took leave of his sister in a letter from Switzerland:

It has been an extremely satisfactory time with my friends here. I am going
home to work with new strength and hope.[193]

2. Deportation of the Jews

But when Bonhoeffer arrived back in Berlin, there was indeed startling
news awaiting him. On 1st September, while he was away, the decree
about the yellow star had been issued: from 19th September all Jews
had to wear the sign, sewn on. On his way back he saw the star for
the first time. To reinterpret it privately as a badge of honour did not
help. Then, between 5th and 12th October, there came the first notifica-
tions to Jewish families in Berlin that their rooms in 'Aryan houses'
were 'scheduled for evacuation'. During the night of 16th-17th October
the people concerned were taken from their homes and collected in
the Levetzowstrasse synagogue to be taken away.

So the action in Stettin had been, not an exception, but a preliminary
test.[194] What had hitherto only been heard of from Poland or from the
occupied areas of Russia was now to be seen at first hand—one's next-
door neighbours being fetched, and people being taken away from the
Siemens factories.

Soon it was the turn of a sixty-eight-year-old friend of the Bonhoeffer
family to be given notice that her home was to be evacuated and that
she was to go to Theresienstadt. Everyone in the Bonhoeffer family tried
zealously to stand by her but could do no more than help her to pack
only what the severe restrictions on luggage would allow her to take.
At the interrogations in 1944 it was brought up against the Bonhoeffers
and Schleichers that their two houses in the Marienburger Allee had
been visited by people wearing the star.

On the very first day, Dietrich Bonhoeffer collected all the facts that
he could ascertain, so as to put them before sympathizers in the army
command; and Perels helped him to get information from other parts of
the Reich. So by 18th October 1941 a report was drawn up, describing
what was happening in Berlin and mentioning similar proceedings in
Cologne, Düsseldorf, and Elberfeld. On 20th October a more complete
report was concluded, containing the warning that further transport
columns were expected on the nights of 23rd-24th and 28th-29th
October:

192. To E. Bethge, 26.8.1941, GS II, p. 411.
193. Letter of 19.9.1941.
194. See Ch. XII, p. 592.

As the families that are now affected know already what these official communications mean, the despair is unprecedented. The natural result is severe attacks of illness in the case of people with weak hearts, gall-bladder trouble, etc., and there is also the danger of suicide and other hasty actions such as pointless flight, and so on.[195]

Perels and Bonhoeffer gave the reports to Dohnanyi to pass on to Oster and Beck, in the hope that the military would either consent to intervene or accelerate the preparations for revolt.

H. G. Adler describes those papers as the first documentary evidence known to him of any action by the German conspiracy movement in connection with the deportation policy.[196] Besides the drafts of the two reports, there exists another report, dating from the same period, on the so-called 'people of mixed blood'. Perels' and Bonhoeffer's reports bear the signs of haste; they were not the product of careful work by a commission, for no such thing would have been possible.

In late October, Bonhoeffer's work on information and persuasion was brought to an end for several weeks—months, in fact—by a severe and prolonged attack of pneumonia. It happened that at that time Berlin was free from night attacks by the British bomber squadrons. Bonhoeffer might well need the rest, and just then the Jews were wishing that bombs would come down on all the post offices and police stations in Berlin.

The churches' isolated actions for the Jews were hardly noticed by the public. The woman minister Katharina Staritz of Breslau published a word on behalf of the bearers of the yellow star, and was at once arrested. In parishes where special intercession was made, everyone knew what it was about when Frau Staritz's name was mentioned. In the Confessing Church, fellow-workers and members gave some help to enable individuals to disappear illegally by cleverly contrived subterfuge; they helped people to get false papers, ration cards, and shelter—as did, for example, Pastor Reimer in Naseband and Frau Staewen in Dahlem. In the winter of 1942-3, Bishop Wurm included the Jews on his list of protests against infringements of rights and acts of violence, and Bishops von Galen and von Preysing did the same on the Roman Catholic side. The Breslau Confessing Synod's message on the fifth commandment has already been mentioned.[197] It did not occur to anyone to be proud of those small acts of bravery; everyone knew how inadequate it all was in relation to what was actually happening, even though figures and methods could be only vaguely suspected. But, as the synod's message shows, the public was soon well acquainted with the words 'eliminate' and 'liquidate'.

195. GS II, pp. 640-3.
196. See H. G. Adler, *Theresienstadt 1941-1945, Das Antlitz einer Zwangsgemeinschaft*, 1955, pp. 18 f., and letter to the author 3.7.1956.
197. See Ch. XII, pp. 613 f.

For those who were already deeply enough involved in deception to be within reach of a lever in the government machine, the deportation was an incentive to haste. They could no longer expose themselves by uttering belated public proclamations (like pastors from the pulpit), and they said nothing. But in the absence of action their dilemma grew more tormenting with every day that passed.

'Operation 7'. Now, however, as the months went on, Bonhoeffer was involved in a bold action initiated by the *Abwehr* for a few Jews; it was to play a serious part in the trials of 1943. Canaris gave the instructions to save a group of about twelve or fifteen Jews by getting them to Switzerland on the pretext that they were being used by the *Abwehr*. The enterprise was called 'U 7', because at first only seven people were concerned. Canaris was anxious to save a few friends (Conzen and Rennefeld and their dependants), and Dohnanyi wanted to help the lawyers Dr. Fliess and Dr. Arnold to get out of the country. 'U 7' involved Dohnanyi in an extraordinary amount of work, camouflage, and subterfuge; it extended for well over a year, till it at last ended, with complete success, in the late summer of 1942; but it was revived six months later with fateful consequences for its initiators.

Shortly after Bonhoeffer returned from his second Swiss journey, Wilhelm Rott visited him to discuss what could be done to save Fräulein Charlotte Friedenthal, who had been a colleague of his for years in the provisional governing body of the Confessing Church, and who was now wearing the yellow star. Dohnanyi took her into the fictitious body of agents for the *Abwehr*. Dr. Arnold became the group's go-between and spokesman. In 1946 he wrote a report of the rescue,[198] describing his surprise and his initial refusal when Dohnanyi disclosed to him that he wanted to take them out, all as *Abwehr* agents, after the admiral had so decided. Dohnanyi had first been able to have Arnold's name struck off the deportation list. 'The deep sympathy of that much younger man was quite unfeigned and unmistakable.' But when he was told how the escape was to be managed, Dr. Arnold answered:

Neither my friend Dr. Fliess nor I would ever be willing to take part in helping that firm's business.

His answer showed that, for the first time since Herr Dohnanyi and I had been in contact with each other, I had completely misunderstood him. He now told me quite frankly that he did not expect either me or any others of the selected people to undertake any action on behalf of the Third Reich, and that his chief, Admiral Canaris, his neighbour, Colonel Oster, and his colleagues Count Moltke, Delbrück, and Freiherr von Guttenberg thought as he did.

There were immense difficulties, both on the German and on the Swiss

198. Typewritten account by Dr. Arnold, 1946.

side. For Jews to be employed by the *Abwehr*, it was not only necessary to get them freed by finance offices, labour offices, and foreign currency offices, where things could be distressingly delayed by the passive resistance of minor officials; there also had to be direct negotiations with the Reich Security Head Office. For the long duration of the whole procedure, Dohnanyi gave each of them the *Abwehr's* safe-conduct, which, however, did not always give them the desired protection. From time to time one or other of the group got on to the deportation list, and had to be taken off it again with difficulty. Only Canaris' personal intervention with the notorious S.S. group-leader Müller managed to get over the last dangerous delays. In the *Abwehr* itself, where a whole series of officers had to have a routine hand in those 'matters of agents', there were friends and foes, and only a very small number of them could suspect what the aim of the whole business really was.

But there were difficulties on the Swiss side, too, for they were now hardly prepared to receive Jews. As the members of the Lutheran Council were all at that time in Moabit prison, awaiting prosecution because of illegal examinations, W. Rott, after consultation with the sick Bonhoeffer and with Perels' help, sent a petition in the form of a letter to Koechlin as president of the Federation of Swiss Churches:

On behalf of the chairman of the provisional governing body of the German Evangelical Church, Herr Superintendent Albertz, I beg to address to you, as President of the Federation of Swiss Churches, and so to the Churches themselves, a request as sincere as it is urgent.

It is a question of the extreme distress in which many of our non-Aryan brothers and sisters have been for some weeks . . . Since about the middle of October, the practice has been started of transporting to the east non-Aryans from Berlin and other towns. The whole matter confronts the Christian churches with questions and needs in the face of which we are almost entirely helpless.

We know that your hands, too, are almost tied. Reception of the directly threatened non-Aryan Christians into Switzerland seems impossible in view of the attitude of the police towards foreigners, and for other reasons; that was confirmed lately by Professor Courvoisier of Geneva . . . What we now ask you is whether, by urgent representations and official action by the Swiss churches, the door might possibly be opened for just a few, or at least for one solitary case for which we specially plead . . .

There follows an account of the Friedenthal case, and Inge Jacobsen and Dr. Emil Zweig are also included in the request:

It would be of great value, and might lessen the danger, if those concerned could soon have word (by telegram) that their immigration into (or transit through) Switzerland is arranged . . . We ask God, the Father of the forsaken, to show us a way out of all this dire distress.[199]

199. Copied from the archives of the World Council of Churches in Geneva. The letter is dated 'Berlin, October 1941'.

Rott took this letter personally, with a second one from Bonhoeffer to Karl Barth, to Consul Schmidhuber in Munich, who with its help made some arrangement with Koechlin in Switzerland, so that the necessary guarantees for the Jewish '*Abwehr* group' were eventually provided. As permission to enter the country did not include the possibility of working and earning money, Dohnanyi had to arrange for the foreign currency needed to support the 'U 7' group.

Then Fräulein Friedenthal was ordered to go to the Gestapo in the Alexanderplatz to receive the completed passport. But with her star she was not allowed to use any transport from Dahlem; so it was decided that she should go with a rolled-up coat to the Alexanderplatz, so as to be able to appear at the 'Alex' with a star as prescribed. After a long wait, she was at last told: 'Jewess Friedenthal, come along!' But how was she to go on now to the Swiss consulate, where the visa had to be stamped? With a star or without it? And how was she to travel? She was told: 'Without a star!' An hour before she left Dahlem, Dohnanyi came to her for the last time: 'With the star after all!' The star, which had already been taken off, had to be sewn on again in a hurry. In the corridor train the carefully rolled-up coat served as a cushion to sit on, as no one wearing the star might travel in the same compartment as 'Aryans'. It was only after the last German station, Weil, that Charlotte Friedenthal put her coat on again—to the horror of her fellow passengers in the compartment. At the frontier station the officials took all her papers from her, but they came back after a few anxious minutes, and handed everything back to her. At last the train came into Basle. She was still quite dazed, and Gisevius had to reassure her, as he pointed to her coat: 'You don't wear the star here!' That was at the beginning of September 1942.

The successful journey was reported to Berlin, and four weeks later the main group met in Basle, where Koechlin at once saw to their immediate wants.

There is no doubt that the Reich security head officials were very suspicious about the whole affair, and it is only too likely that they finally felt that Canaris had caught them napping and tricked them. In 1943 the matter was again investigated during the interrogations of Bonhoeffer and Dohnanyi. An official was sent to Switzerland to look into the financial aspect and find out whether, and if so, how, Dohnanyi and his friends had made anything out of it. Of course, nothing of the kind was found, but the authorities were left suspicious, probably because they could not imagine that other factors had played a decisive part in such a venture.

3. *Fall of Brauchitsch*

In that autumn of 1941, Germany's name seemed to be indelibly branded

with the 'final solution of the Jewish question'. The *Fronde* could now
hardly entertain hopes of an honourable peace. In those months, the
activity of the opposition increased in a degree hitherto unknown. New
participants came in, and those who had grown hesitant showed themselves more responsive. Hans von Dohnanyi hurried from one discussion
to another; there was evidence of this in Hassell's diary.[200] The revival
was certainly hopeful, but it revealed new problems.

Dietrich Bonhoeffer was now having more frequent meetings with his
brother Klaus, who, together with his colleague in the Lufthansa, Dr.
Otto John, was looking after his own contacts, such as Joseph Wirmer
and Jacob Kaiser, Wilhelm Leuschner and Ernst von Harnack. Otto
John had known Prince Louis Ferdinand since 1937, and brought him
into this group. Dohnanyi was interested only in people whom he
absolutely needed, as he regarded more extensive contacts as involving
additional risks.

In those months the existence of a circle of younger people, who were
later known as the 'Kreisau Circle', became noticeable. This was an
intelligent group which expressed some serious criticism of the leading
men in the active resistance movement. Those young people blamed
Goerdeler for including reactionary elements in his plans, and, of course,
rejected the monarchist ideas that had recently emerged. Helmuth Count
Moltke (adviser on international law to the High Command and assigned
to the *Abwehr*), Peter Count Yorck (senior government councillor, and
later in the military economics office), and Adam von Trott (since the
summer of 1940 legation councillor in the politico-cultural department
of the Foreign Office) associated with Hassell, from whom they expected
the most sympathy for their criticism. But the crisis between this and
other resistance groups was so far checked in the winter of 1941-2 that
they all united under, and recognized, Beck's leadership of the political
opposition.

Dohnanyi gave only as much time as was necessary to those smoulder-
ing discussions; in view of his immediate concerns, he kept away from
those circles whose conversations, though certainly not unimportant,
had a theoretical bias. There were, however, personal and official cross-
connections, for example, with Moltke, who himself belonged to the
Abwehr, and with Trott and Yorck through Baron Guttenberg and
Hassell. Nor did Dietrich Bonhoeffer—as we shall see later—seize the
opportunity to make his relation to the Kreisau group more intimate,
although intellectually and personally he would have had good cause
to. The reasons for his not doing so are, on the one hand, that he was
already too deeply involved elsewhere in practical preparations for the
revolt, and on the other hand, that the group's activity developed only
when he was having to accommodate himself to the possibility of being

200. U. von Hassell, op. cit., pp. 228, 231, 238, 248.

arrested; and moreover, the composition of the group still made him cautious.[201]

In October 1941, Oster and Dohnanyi were offered new and interesting lines of approach, when one day Schlabrendorff appeared from the army group in the centre of the eastern front, to ask on behalf of Henning von Tresckow whether new practical steps could be taken, with the Berlin centre, towards ending the Hitler régime. The S.S. task forces in the interior, and Hitler's interference at the front, had, in Tresckow's and Schlabrendorff's opinion, apparently made some officers inclined to join in a *Putsch*. With that, the vital connection now began to be formed between the resistance centre in Berlin and an action group that was able to put regular army units into action. A firm and stable offer had been made.

The expectations of early action rose still further, when Brauchitsch became markedly more approachable. Since, with the coming of winter, the operations in the east were no longer proceeding according to expectations, and Hitler was interfering drastically in their conduct, Brauchitsch sent for Generals Falkenhausen and Thomas, and promised that he would no longer stand in the way of Hitler's removal.[202]

But into the middle of these tense preparations there came like a bombshell, on 19th December 1941, the news that Hitler had dismissed Brauchitsch and made himself commander-in-chief of the Army. Hassell wrote despairingly in his diary: 'The work of many months has been ruined.'[203] The commander with whom they had striven for so long, finally with good prospects of success, had been dropped; and that meant that the army high command, now directly under Hitler himself, was out of the question as the place for setting off the revolt.

At that time, Bonhoeffer was convalescing with the Kleist-Retzow family at Kieckow. A friend with whom he had exchanged confidences about the new expectations wrote to him: 'You can imagine how my heart stood still when we read today of Brauchitsch's retirement.'[204] Frau von Kleist-Retzow told him that the Schmenzin people were 'quite staggered'.

Drastic changes of organization now had to be thought out and carried through. But from that time new ideas began to develop, which, after many variations, were actually put into effect on 20th July 1944—thus, the sequence of events in the *Putsch*: first the assassination, and then the issuing of the order from Berlin under Beck's direction of the High Command; in other words, the *coup d'état* had to begin with the killing of Hitler. In view of the antecedents and the nature of the conspirators, it cost a great deal of effort to make up their minds to that logical

201. See Ch. XII, pp. 659, 682.
202. U. von Hassell, op. cit., p. 235.
203. U. von Hassell, op. cit., p. 246.
204. Letter from W. Krause, 21.12.1941.

conclusion, and they never felt entirely at ease about it. That, perhaps, had something to do with Bonhoeffer's saying at Sakrow, where the Dohnanyis had been living since September 1941 in a house on the Havel, that if it fell to him to carry out the deed, he was ready to do so, but that he must first resign, formally and officially, from his Church, as the Church could not shield him, and he had no wish to claim its protection. That was certainly a theoretical position, for Bonhoeffer knew nothing about how to handle either guns or explosives.

VI THIRD STAGE: INFORMATION ON THE OVERTHROW, 1942

Brauchitsch's fall was a shock; but the result was only delay, and not an actual loss of determination. On his way back from Oslo, Bonhoeffer wrote from Stockholm to his relatives in England:

I went to see friends of mine up there[205] and in spite of all difficulties, I had a very satisfactory time . . . I am travelling a good deal besides I am writing a book . . . When I wrote to you last,[206] I thought Uncle Rudy[207] would not live much longer, but in January and February he recovered a little,[208] though I am quite convinced only for a very short time. He is so weak that I and my people do not believe that he can live longer than a few more months . . .[209]

The plans of action changed and became more detailed as well as broader. The further they progressed, the greater grew the need, first to plan Germany's reconstruction after the revolt, and secondly to strive for safeguards from abroad, in spite of all the sceptical judgements on the chances of Germany being caught in a moment of weakness due to the conspiracy.

Bonhoeffer took part in both those efforts during 1942. The first was helped by statements prepared for the Beck group as to the future ordering of relations between the State and the Church, and the second by additional journeys. The result was that the third stage of Bonhoeffer's activity in the conspiracy was the most unsettled. It became so unsettled because the expectations were taking more definite shape, and towards the end it resolved into a race between assassination and arrest. His urgent private affairs ranged from making a will to deciding to become engaged.

1. Norwegian Journey

When Bonhoeffer set off on a fresh journey in the spring of 1942, both

205. In Oslo.
206. In September 1941 from Zürich.
207. Code word for war.
208. Through the removal of Brauchitsch, disciplinary proceedings against Hoepner, and von Witzleben's illness and dismissal.
209. To the Leibholz family. 17.4.1942.

he and Dohnanyi had had a warning for the first time. Dr. Langbehn, the lawyer,[210] and Captain Gehre, one of Oster's colleagues, told Dohnanyi in the middle of February 1942 that his telephone was being tapped and his correspondence intercepted by the Gestapo. Langbehn thought that Heydrich and Bormann were behind it, and Gehre mentioned a man by the name of Sommer.

So before he left, Bonhoeffer drew up his will in writing, for his new errand had to do fairly directly with the sphere of interest of the Reich Security Office. He jokingly gave me the sheet of paper for safe custody, so as to give no one in his family any cause for anxiety.

The journey was to Norway from 10th to 18th April. It was not for any 'contact with the enemy', but was to strengthen the people round Bishop Berggrav,[211] who were regarded as allies, at a crucial time in their opposition to the Nazis.

The Norwegian church struggle had flared up on 1st February 1942, when Quisling had been made Prime Minister, and on the same day had forbidden Fjellbu, the provost of Trondheim Cathedral, to hold divine service. That at once identified the church struggle with patriotic resistance. When Fjellbu was removed from office on 20th February, the Norwegian bishops laid down their offices in so far as these had the character of a state church. In March, after a decree establishing a kind of Hitler Youth for the young Norwegians, far more than 1,000 teachers resigned. On the first Easter day, 5th April, all the pastors laid down their offices. Berggrav, who had initiated and inspired the pastors' resistance, was put under house-arrest on Maundy Thursday; on the second day of Easter interrogations and house searches began; on 8th April he was imprisoned. It was expected that he would be prosecuted before the 'People's Court' on 13th April on a charge of sedition and associating with the enemy, on account of his journeys to Great Britain in 1940. But nothing happened. Instead, he was moved from prison on 16th April to a mountain chalet near Asker, where he spent three lonely years under house-arrest. Berlin had intervened.

There was at that time in Norway, as transport officer on the staff of the *Wehrmacht* commander von Falkenhorst, the former district president Theodor Steltzer, together with good friends from the Michael fraternity such as F. Schauer and Herbert Krimm. Steltzer belonged, with Moltke and Yorck, to the Kreisau circle. He had agreed with Moltke that a telegram should be sent at once if Berggrav were arrested. That was done, and the *Abwehr* thereupon sent two emissaries post-haste to object on the ground that Germany's military position would be seriously endangered if the National Socialist church policy upset the whole population of Norway by removing Berggrav. So

210. He maintained a relationship with the S.S.; for a time he was on the resistance list of cabinet members as probable Minister of Justice. See also Ch. XIII, p. 711.
211. See Ch. XI, p. 573.

Terboven, the Reich commissar in Oslo, was instructed by telegram to intervene; in fact, on 15th April there came a telegram from Bormann saying that Berggrav was to be released.[212]

The two emissaries were Moltke and Bonhoeffer. Officially, they were sent to examine the church struggle as a danger to the German occupying troops; secretly, the intention was to advise the Norwegian Lutherans not to deviate one step from the way that they had taken. Berggrav told Steltzer fifteen years later:

Alex Johnson thinks the intention was to declare their concern whether the newly revived Norwegian church struggle was damaging the Nazis . . .

Bonhoeffer seems to have made a deep impression . . . Johnson sketches Bonhoeffer's line: here in Norway it would be seen how impossible the Nazis were. Bonhoeffer insisted on resistance à outrance—even as far as martyrdom.[213]

The journey was arranged at short notice and carried out very quickly; Bonhoeffer was really getting ready for another journey to Switzerland, and was hoping to be able to go to Sweden later. Busy with his *Ethics*, he was spending a few quiet days in Kieckow and Klein-Krössin, awaiting the preparations for the Swiss journey. Then, on the Wednesday after Easter. Dohnanyi called him to Berlin, and two days later he was on the way to Oslo with Moltke. In the three days there they could not visit Berggrav in prison, but only send him a message; but they did meet for detailed talks with his colleagues A. Johnson, Pastor C. B. Svendsen, Professor H. Ording, and H. Sørensen, a painter and a friend of Berggrav. On the day that Berggrav was exiled to the forest chalet near Asker and so seemed to have been saved, Moltke and Bonhoeffer left on their return journey.[214]

Of course, Bonhoeffer was very keenly interested in the Norwegian church struggle, because he saw here suddenly accomplished what he himself had proposed, though without response, in 1933[215]—pastors' strike, laying down of office, and church resignations. The advice that he gave was authoritative; he warned the Norwegians from his own experiences not to give way now.

212. A. Johnson, *Eivin Berggrav, Mann der Spannung*, 1960, p. 138.
213. Letter of 29.1.1957.
214. Bonhoeffer's pocketbook of 1942 has only a few entries. For the Norwegian journey they are:
'April, Friday 10th. 10.35 dep. st. [i.e. Stettin Station in Berlin]—Sassnitz Hotel Viktoria.
Saturday 11th. 4 o'clock ferry to Trelleborg. Night at Malmö.
Sunday 12th. dep. 8h. arr. Oslo 24h.
Monday 13th. O.
Tuesday 14th. O.
Wednesday 15th. O.
Thursday 16th. Day to Stockholm.
Friday 17th. Stockh. Evening to Malmö. Plane.
Saturday 18th. Plane 10 min. to Cop. 4 o'clock to B.'
215. See Ch. VII, pp. 223, 238 f.

Without foreseeing how soon he would be in Sweden again, he took advantage of the return journey to write to his relatives in Oxford[216] from Stockholm, where he stayed from 16th to 17th April. He also renewed his acquaintance with Archbishop Eidem,[217] writing to him that he had seen Ehrenström fairly often in Geneva, and that he agreed with his judgement of the situation and of the problems that resulted from it. He was sorry, he said, that Forell was being recalled from Berlin just at that time, but those two would prepare a journey to Sweden for him. But Eidem did not know what to make of the letter's background, and when Bishop Bell asked him some weeks later whether he could tell him where Bonhoeffer was and how he was getting on, he said that Bonhoeffer had probably been through Sweden recently on his way to Norway as a soldier.[218]

Moltke and Bonhoeffer arrived back in Berlin from Copenhagen, and at once went to the *Abwehr* centre on the Tirpitzufer to report. I went to meet Bonhoeffer there.

He was glad to have had the few days with Helmuth von Moltke, who was a year his junior, and who had initiated the Kreisau group. I cannot remember in detail what Bonhoeffer told me about their conversations. We had not then realized the group's special potentialities; in fact, 'Kreisau' did not yet exist as a term. Moltke himself was four weeks away from the first meeting on his Kreisau estate; it was to be concerned with questions of cultural and church politics. I remember, however, that Bonhoeffer remarked to me how stimulating the journey had been, 'but we are not of the same opinion'. Of course, they were at one in the depth of their Christian convictions, as they likewise were in their judgement of Germany's desperate position; and they were certainly at one in setting their hopes on such a man as Ludwig Beck. But Moltke at that very time 'refused . . . for his own part personally to remove Hitler by violence'.[219] And Bonhoeffer, who also knew that God's necessary judgement cannot be restrained, was already pleading the need for assassination. Whether, as is quite likely, Moltke asked Bonhoeffer on that occasion to go to the meeting at Kreisau, I cannot remember. But in any case, the date of the coming Swiss journey did not allow him to take part in it. And neither time nor circumstances allowed a repetition of such an intensive meeting as the one on the Norwegian journey. One could hardly then take part in a conspiracy in many circles at the same time. There was, of course, danger in this pressure to be exclusive.

216. See Ch. XII, p. 656.
217. MW V, XI, A. 1. Add the most recent researches by J. Glenthoj introducing MW V, XI.
218. Reported by G. Bell to G. Leibholz, 20.6.1942.
219. E. Gerstenmaier, 'Graf Moltke und die Kreisauer', in *Christ und Welt* of 21.3.1957.

2. *Third Swiss Journey*

Three weeks later, Bonhoeffer wrote to Oxford again—oddly enough, just at the time when Canaris and Heydrich were at the Castle in Prague, signing their agreement about Canaris' information service:

Uncle Rudy has recovered a little bit,[220] but he is so terribly nervous and full of anxieties with regard of his personal future . . . his illness is so grave that I believe he will not do much longer.[221]

Bonhoeffer was on his third Swiss journey; the visit was cut short.

The dates are not unimportant, as they throw some light on Bonhoeffer's and Schönfeld's twofold commission for their journey to Sweden. Bonhoeffer probably arrived in Switzerland on 11th May, and he was certainly in Zürich on the 12th. On the 14th, Ascension Day, he turned up in Geneva; and 23rd May was his last day in Switzerland (with Sutz in Rapperswil). On the same day he wrote to Bell in England, as if he had no idea of their forthcoming meeting in Stockholm.

When Bonhoeffer arrived in Geneva on 14th May, he was disappointed not to meet Visser 't Hooft, the latter having already left at the end of April to go via Spain to England, where he took, among other things, the memorandum from Trott, and where he saw Sir Stafford Cripps, who for his part showed Trott's memorandum to Churchill.[222] Visser 't Hooft now personally put Bonhoeffer's points of September 1941 before the assembled 'Peace Aims Group', including Zimmern, Lindsay, and Toynbee, and called together by Paton. The argument was weakened on the political side by the fact that another half year had gone without any indication of an upheaval in Germany.[223] But Bonhoeffer in Geneva could now, at best, cherish expectations about this, and rely on Visser 't Hooft to put his circle's case urgently. Trott's enterprise through Visser 't Hooft was hardly known to Bonhoeffer. Trott belonged to the resistance group in the Foreign Office and to the Kreisau group. It was at that time impossible to coordinate all the contacts abroad to the last detail, for the chances came unexpectedly, and the objects were never certain to be attained.

Presumably, Bonhoeffer did not meet Schönfeld and Ehrenström again in Geneva;[224] that could not have happened before 14th May. But on 26th May they had both been in Stockholm several days, having gone there, not direct from Geneva, but from Germany, where, in fact,

220. Referring to the new offensive on the Volga and in the Caucasus, and Rommel's attack on El Alamein.
221. To G. Leibholz, 13.5.1942, from Zürich.
222. H. Rothfels, in *Vierteljahreshefte für Zeitgeschichte*, Oct. 1957, pp. 388-97; GS I, p. 410.
223. Communication from Visser 't Hooft, 30.5.1961.
224. J. Glenthoj, in the introduction to MW V, XI, provides new information here; thus Schönfeld left Geneva on 18th May.

Gerstenmaier had taken leave of Schönfeld in Berlin on the way to Sweden. Indeed, Bishop Bell asserts that neither of his two visitors knew anything of the other's intended journey. When Bonhoeffer arrived back in Berlin from Switzerland—on Whit Monday the 25th at the earliest, if not on the 26th—Schönfeld's first meeting with Bishop Bell was already taking place in Stockholm.

Thus Bonhoeffer did not meet in Geneva the people whom he was most anxious to meet. A pleasant evening with the Freudenbergs brought him together with Frau Visser 't Hooft, Professor Jacques Courvoisier, the church historian and chairman of the ecumenical prisoners-of-war commission, Professor Henri d'Espine, later president of the Federation of Swiss Churches, Alexander von Weymarn of the ecumenical press service, Professor Lenard, Pastor Charles Brütsch, the preacher Johannes Schneider, Roland de Pury, and Pastor Witt who was engaged in relief work for Jews.

It was here that Bonhoeffer heard that Bell was in Sweden, or at least on the way there. On 1st May a telegram from Bell had arrived in Geneva, telling Visser 't Hooft (who had already left): 'Visiting Sweden for three weeks commencing May 11.' Bonhoeffer must at first have been disappointed not to have heard of this sooner, as he was busy with Forell, who was in Berlin, preparing a visit to Sweden. But it then occurred to him that he might, in the circumstances, break off the Swiss journey and put to his friends in Berlin the daring idea of going for a quick meeting with the bishop. So he went back to Zürich, saw Koechlin —as was necessary because of the 'Operation 7'—and on 23rd May wrote from Zürich to Bell in England, not indicating by a single word that he knew that he was in Sweden, or what plans were brewing. A meeting with the prominent Englishman was 'top secret', and above all, it was not debated with anyone in Berlin:

Let me please thank you for your kind letter which I received only now . . . Mrs. Martin[225] has been ill for a few weeks, so we have no news about her husband. But last time I heard from him he was said to be well physically and mentally. Since I know that Wednesday is your special day for intercessions I will meet you in prayers and my friends when I tell them will do the same. Thank you so much for letting me know. It means so much to us. As far as I can see the day is not so far when we might meet again not only in spirit. What a comfort to know that you will be there in that moment! May God give us strength for the days that will come . . .[226]

3. Swedish Journey

The Commission. Bonhoeffer learnt in Geneva that Bell's visit to Sweden

225. Niemöller.
226. Letter of 23.5.1942, probably from Zürich.

was to end officially on 2nd June 1942.[227] So the plan for his journey was proposed, discussed, settled and made technically possible, in three days in Berlin. It had to be made in consultation with Beck, without whose approval Oster and Dohnanyi now took no decisive step.

The commission was basically the same as in September 1941, but the aims were stated more precisely. Bonhoeffer was to give assurances that, in case of a revolt under the leadership of certain persons whose names it was decided to disclose, the attitude behind it was peaceful, 'in whatever way those men might at first have had to mask themselves to the people, before the real clearing-up could be done,' and—particularly for the British Government—'to ask the military commands not to use that moment to attack, but to give the new government time to restore healthy conditions.'[228]

Bonhoeffer entered the Berlin-Stockholm plane on Saturday 30th May, a day that was much too stormy for him, as he was liable to air- and sea-sickness. In his parents' home there was the greatest secrecy about the haste and the errand; that had not been the case before his journeys to Switzerland, because then he had talked of possible contacts with the relatives in Oxford. This time, Canaris's office supplied him with the Foreign Office's courier pass:

Courier Pass No. 474. The bearer of this, Herr Bonhoeffer, is travelling on 30th May 1942 with official documents and luggage of the Foreign Office to Stockholm. It is requested that the person named be afforded all possible facilities and in case of need all necessary protection and support.

The pass was not made out till early on 30th May.

The Riddle of the Two Messengers. It is obvious that at least two groups in the Resistance Movement had the idea of using Bishop Bell's presence in neutral Sweden to obtain safeguards for the overthrow in so far as the attitude of other countries was concerned. Who was responsible for this step, and who decided it? Through whom was the errand authorized? Why were the groups not coordinated? Even now, the riddle has not been solved; and here, too, only a few points of view can be put forward as a contribution.

Bishop Bell said several times that the two emissaries, Schönfeld and Bonhoeffer, visited him independently of each other and not knowing of the other's plans, although their intentions were almost identical. He put forward that fact to his Government as one of the proofs of the authenticity of the concern that they represented. But in the German Resistance Movement itself such duplication seemed less reasonable.

It seems fairly certain that Schönfeld did not know, and could not have known, anything of Bonhoeffer's coming. The reverse is not quite

227. The bishop could not, in fact, fly back to London before 9th June.
228. Account by Christine Dohnanyi, 1945.

so certain, although the bishop assumed it to be so.[229] Presumably Bonhoeffer heard in outline, in Geneva, of Schönfeld's and Ehrenström's journey together; but his own journey was not thought out and decided on in Berlin till Schönfeld was already in Sweden. The latter was not then having personal contact with Oster and Dohnanyi, nor, of course, with Beck, and his Kreisau friends had their reservations about Goerdeler. Schönfeld's friend and adviser Gerstenmaier, and those who cooperated with him in the Church External Affairs Office, were in contact with the opposition sympathizers in the Foreign Office, with Trott, Popitz, and increasingly with Hassell, whom the so-called 'boys' trusted in spite of his closeness to Beck and Goerdeler. So the plan that Schönfeld was to ask the bishop to disclose to the British Government with a request for its cooperation may have been discussed by those circles in Berlin early in May, and they may have encouraged Schönfeld to use the journey for that meeting. He certainly saw Trott in Geneva in April and felt that he had a link with him through Gerstenmaier. He did not need specially prepared passports or visas, as he would be in any case in neutral countries on the way on behalf of the Geneva organizations, and was covered by the Church External Affairs Office and the Foreign Office. So it may be that Beck knew previously, possibly through Hassell, of Schönfeld's journey; but it may equally well be that he did not know of it *before* Bonhoeffer left. Schönfeld's journey to Sweden did not, of itself, mean that he was certain to meet Bell; he did not travel, as Bonhoeffer did, solely to meet Bell.

Even if Oster, Dohnanyi, and Beck knew of Schönfeld's attempt to meet Bell, it is still understandable that Bonhoeffer should be sent. It was at that time considered in the *Abwehr*, under the influence of Bonhoeffer and Gisevius, that Schönfeld's reputation was not so reliable (as it became later), and that Bonhoeffer had the bishop's personal confidence to a degree that no one else had. For Bonhoeffer and those who commissioned him and had been working on the same line continuously since 1938, Schönfeld and his friends were newcomers to conspiracy—an acquisition certainly, but as yet no substitute for the old hands in personal prestige, and not having quite shaken off their past record in church politics. For Beck, Oster, and Dohnanyi it was not Schönfeld, but Bonhoeffer, who was the right man to be commissioned ecumenically for that contact with the English bishop.

It is fairly certain that Bonhoeffer knew of Schönfeld's journey, but he may not have been so clear whether Schönfeld would really meet Bell; I think I remember Bonhoeffer's expressing surprise, when he came home, at having met them together. We can understand that surprise, if we remember the talks between Bell and Bonhoeffer in the spring of

229. Cf. the different methods of expression: 1945 'to the best of my belief' (GS I, p. 393); 1957 'he had known nothing of Schönfeld's visit' (GS I, p. 404).

1939, where the very unsatisfactory representation of the Confessing Church in Geneva played a part.[230]

The Sources. About Bonhoeffer's two days in Sigtuna and Stockholm we have Bell's notes, made at various times, as excellent sources from the British side. The latest presentation (1957) shows a few slight alterations that had seemed to him advisable at a distance of twelve years.

Bell wrote down his experiences in five different stages. The sources are arranged in order of time: 1. Bell's first letter to Anthony Eden, of 18th June 1942, in which he indicated what had happened and asked for an audience. 2. the memorandum of what had happened, with the inclusion of Schönfeld's notes, all of which Bell submitted to Eden on 30th June. 3. the relevant correspondence between Eden and Bell in July and August 1942. 4. the first comprehensive account of the event, based on his diaries, given in *The Contemporary Review* of October 1945, in which the distance between Schönfeld and his circle and Bonhoeffer's still stands out clearly, and in which the 'Confessional Church' is still often mentioned, whereas he later writes 'Evangelical Church'. 5. the second completed account, more specific in many details, in the Göttingen lecture of May 1957; here the severe risk to which Schönfeld, too, exposed himself is adequately noted.[231]

It is hardly to be expected that detailed authentic records or reports of the meetings in Sweden will come to light on the German side to give an equally exhaustive picture.[232] As far as the *Abwehr* was concerned,

230. See Ch. XI, pp. 545 f.   231. These sources are set out in GS I, pp. 372-413.

232. Jørgen Glenthøj, in an introduction to his important publication of the Kaltenbrunner Letter of 4.1.1945 on the interrogation of Bonhoeffer by the Reich Security Head Office (cf. Ch. XIV, pp. 805 f.), has contested my supposition (EvTh 1966, No. 9, pp. 463 f.). I still think that he has at least misread what I wrote, and that what he has discovered does not provide an 'equally exhaustive picture' of the events in Sigtuna, compared with Bell's notes. An 'equally exhaustive picture' would, of course, have to come from someone who was involved in Sigtuna at first hand, not at second hand.

The Kaltenbrunner Letter is an original document from the turn of the year 1944-5, and not from May and June 1942. Bell's reports try to describe the real meaning of the occurrence itself from the point of view of the participant in the events, as far as he can possibly throw light on the truth. What Kaltenbrunner wrote, however, is primarily the indirect report of the Reich Security Head Office with a definite political aim, from the statements of one of those involved in the affair (i.e. Bonhoeffer)—statements which he used in order to screen himself, and in which he certainly does not reveal the true content of the Sigtuna talks. The document is invaluable, because it gives us a glimpse of the circumstances, methods, and possibilities of Bonhoeffer's interrogations in the winter of 1944-5. It tells how Bonhoeffer carried out an enquiry into British conditions on behalf of *Canaris*; at Sigtuna, however, that was not the case at all; it was a question of a commission from *Beck*, at which Bonhoeffer, according to this document, did not even hint, either in substance or in form, at the interrogation. That quite agrees with a few other witnesses at Bonhoeffer's interrogations, whom Glenthøj disregards. Glenthøj has also neglected to give the report of the interrogation its place in relation to the struggle between the Reich Security Head Office and the *Abwehr* over political or military news service (see the Prague agreement, Ch. XII, pp. 629 f., Ch. XIV, p. 807), within which Bonhoeffer's statements in the interrogations of 1943, and obviously again in the winter of 1944-5, were important and damaging, and perhaps also deviating from Beck who commissioned him.

the matter was kept so strictly secret that even Josef Müller, who, because of his British contacts through the Vatican, was interested in

---

Unfortunately, Glenthoj now joins the many interrelated facts to a thesis on the Zossen documents, which helps to obscure still further the facts (which have not been cleared up) about the Zossen safe and the discovery by the criminal commissar Sonderegger, and to falsify the documents' object and nature. (On the Zossen documents, their origin and skilful composition, see Ch. XI, pp. 528 f., 576 f.; Ch. XIV, pp. 799 f., 827; and particularly the notes by Frau Christine von Dohnanyi, Appendix F in German edition). Glenthoj proceeds from the assumption that Bonhoeffer's official report on Sigtuna to *Canaris* was found at Zossen. To find that was for the Reich Security Head Office neither necessary, as it will have had it officially ready to hand in the *Abwehr* documents that were taken over, nor possible, as the Zossen safe was not there for that kind of report; if it were, a report to *Beck* about the journey ought to have been found, but that is unlikely. Nor does Glenthoj produce any proof or documentary evidence that makes this discovery likely. If he appeals to the Huppenkothen prosecution (in the fifties) and the listening to a tape-recording of statements in those proceedings (told to me orally), precise verification is needed of the actual words used. In the prosecution there was indeed talk of the finding of Bonhoeffer's notes in Zossen, but it was never said that it was a question of a Sigtuna report, let alone of the official (screened) one to Canaris. The written judgement over Huppenkothen of 1955, which names discoveries in Zossen, does not mention any such material; and Christine von Dohnanyi, who is particularly well-informed about sources, has never mentioned a Sigtuna report by Bonhoeffer in that connection.

Only on a mistaken view of the nature of the Zossen documents (Glenthoj says summarily and misleadingly: 'The Zossen documents consisted of material from Canaris' office', op. cit., p. 465) is it possible to suppose that the Sigtuna report to Canaris was in Zossen. The official, and of course 'secret', reports of Bonhoeffer's journeys for the *Abwehr* to Sweden, Norway, and Switzerland were naturally prepared as documents for Canaris on the Tirpitzufer, and there was every reason to suppose that they were there. I myself, after a journey to Switzerland in 1943, provided an 'official' report of that kind for the Canaris files, so that it should be on hand, correct, for checking. Bonhoeffer's Sigtuna journey was already dealt with as an *Abwehr* matter for which Canaris was responsible, in the interrogations by Roeder in the summer of 1943, and played a dangerous part only in the context of the exceeding of one's competence in the sense of the Prague agreement, but was then concealed by Canaris (see Ch. XIII, p. 708).

The Zossen safe was never a place for keeping official 'secret' reports to Canaris; if it had been, reports on many similar journeys could have been or ought to have been kept there. It was the place for material that Dohnanyi and Oster kept, outside their official responsibilities in the *Abwehr*—probably with Canaris' knowledge and passive consent; notice the keeping of parts of his diary, which was not an official document!—in Beck's commission for the revolt or for the arguments that would come after a *Putsch*. That was the place, for example, for the X-report (see Ch. XI, p. 578) of Josef Müller's Rome negotiations of 1939-40, containing responsible promises and conditions on the part of the Allies in case of a *Putsch*. Sigtuna in 1942, however, was a first feeler put out by the conspirators, which was doomed, even at the first step, to be ineffective. There was as yet nothing there to be kept in the Zossen safe, and, as far as we can ascertain from the primary and secondary sources, Bonhoeffer in the winter of 1944-5 was not interrogated about *Beck's* Sigtuna errand, nor had he been previously by Roeder. If Sigtuna had led to encouraging results, documents about it might have been far enough advanced for the safe. If the safe had been provided for documentary evidence of contacts that had just been begun, why did it contain nothing about the enemy contacts (often much more important) that had been made through Trott, Moltke, Goerdeler, Hassell, and others? But Dohnanyi and Oster certainly did not use that dangerous hiding-place, where documents dealing with high politics were kept, as a depot for unnecessary things. But Glenthoj's construction is bound to support the impression that that was exactly what they had done, and his assumption is therefore 'unfortunate'. The discovery, and Glenthoj's other clarifications, lose nothing of their importance and further significance without that assumption, and should therefore be relieved of it.

the Stockholm talks, could not induce Dohnanyi to give him a report. Müller then finally asked me to get him a report from Bonhoeffer himself; and so in that way he notified the Vatican of what had happened. New sources of information may be found there.

The above-mentioned reports from Bell do not mention that when he was at home before the journey, he was already wondering whether he could make contact with Bonhoeffer; for on 6th May he wrote to G. Leibholz: 'I wish I could see Dietrich there. But I shall certainly hear his news.'

Indeed, he tried, with Eidem's help, to find out his movements:

I had heard of his passing through Sweden on his way to Norway . . . but Archbishop Eidem thought he had gone as a soldier and I could not find any way of communicating with him in any case. But he heard that I was in Stockholm and so arrived.[223]

Meeting with the Bishop. On Sunday 31st May 1942, Bonhoeffer heard in Stockholm that the bishop was in Sigtuna; so he set off on the way to the famous evangelical academy of Manfred Björquist. When he made his unexpected appearance in the bishop's room—a memorable moment for both of them after being separated since 1939—Schönfeld had done most of the preliminary work, and Bonhoeffer, in the first private conversation, had the important tasks of confirming that what Schönfeld had said could be vouched for also by him, of handing over a list of names of those ready to cooperate in the overthrow and of pointing out the significance of each of those named, and then of stressing what had already been stressed in correspondence with Visser 't Hooft in September 1941: 'A rising by *them* should be taken very seriously.'[234] The communications were more urgent now than in 1941, because the way to the addresses was considerably shortened.

The names given—Beck, Hammerstein, Goerdeler, Leuschner, Kaiser, and, with some caution, Schacht (the 'seismograph of contemporary events', as Bonhoeffer called him)—more or less show the grouping within the leadership of the Resistance Movement at that time. Hassall is not mentioned. Among the generals taking part are Kluge and Beck, and Bonhoeffer himself knew, not only through Oster, but also through Kleist-Schmenzin and Schlabrendorff, that these two men, or their section of the front, could be expected to unleash the *Putsch*. The slightly hesitant mention of Witzleben reminds one that he had then actually withdrawn for a time from the front rank of the conspirators; he was disappointed, and was, moreover, for the time being without a command and ill.

After the private talk between Bonhoeffer and Bell, more general

233. Letter of 20.6.1942.
234. GS I, p. 405.

aspects were discussed with Schönfeld, who had also gone to Sigtuna, and with Swedish friends. In spite of Bell's warning not to hope for encouragement from London, they settled the various codes and the ways of conveying information on the nature of possible further negotiations on neutral ground between London and the Resistance Movement. It was at first decided to include Sigtuna as a possibility; but at the second meeting on the following day in Stockholm that had to be changed, as Björquist had reconsidered the matter in the meantime, and felt that the participation of his colleague Johansson would be incompatible with Sweden's neutrality. This may be connected with the fact that, since the journey to Sweden in 1936, Bonhoeffer had always seemed to Björquist a bit mysterious, and the latter was unwilling to put himself into his hands in such a complex affair as a conspiracy.

One can still gather, from Bell's first report of 1945, how he felt that Schönfeld and Bonhoeffer although they had a common commission and concern, represented two different temperaments and two distinguishable lines of approach. I share Rothfels's view that Schönfeld's memorandum came rather from the Kreisau environment than from that of Goerdeler and Beck.[235]

Schönfeld negotiates, Bonhoeffer informs; Schönfeld seeks a common basis, Bonhoeffer assumes it; Schönfeld threatens, with German strength, so as to get cooperation on the decisive day, Bonhoeffer asks. Schönfeld warns, Bonhoeffer talks of repentance. Schönfeld is tactical, Bonhoeffer fundamental. No doubt Schönfeld is here the more politic, but in this case and at this moment Bonhoeffer is the better and more effective diplomat.[236]

Bell's account contains things that could come only from Schönfeld, and others that only Bonhoeffer could have said; and finally, there were some things that particularly appealed to the bishop because they fell in with his struggle at home. On the one hand, from Schönfeld with his Kreisau connection, could come (as Rothfels rightly points out) the emphasis on the 'truly socialistic lines', on the other Bonhoeffer was rather considering the revival of conservative possibilities at that time. The assertion that the churches' opposition in Germany was successful could come only from the Church External Affairs Office, and is just as unthinkable in Bonhoeffer's mouth as the mention of Superintendent Blau in Posen. Ritter's summary account (in his book on Goerdeler), 'The enduring strength of faith and self-affirmation that is more and more impressive in reports from the Christian churches in Germany gave their words the right background,'[237] does not fit Bonhoeffer; he took a much more critical view of that 'self-affirmation', and he certainly would not have put it forward to Bell. The colonies did not interest Bon-

235. H. Rothfels, op. cit., p. 388.
236. H. Rothfels, op. cit., p. 389.
237. Cf. G. Ritter, op. cit., p. 322.

hoeffer, and he would never have said that a British victory was very unlikely. The mention of a possible S.S. *Putsch* can be attributed to either of them, for Popitz as well as Dohnanyi (the latter through Langbehn) at times seriously considered using it (they finally decided against it). The question of the British attitude to a possible restoration of the monarchy with Prince Louis Ferdinand was probably raised by Bonhoeffer, who at the time knew of such deliberations through his brother Klaus and his connections.

Ritter thinks that Schönfeld's and Bonhoeffer's wish for a *public* declaration by the Allied governments could not possibly have been expressed on the authority of the Beck circle. 'It would be *best* [author's italics] for that declaration [of willingness to negotiate with an opposition government] to be made publicly.'[238] There is here a shifting, if not a confusion, between agreements for serious negotiations and wishes expressed for Western propaganda. For the former, according to the reports, a detailed code and secret method had been expressly considered, but not any public declarations; these latter emerge only in the concluding parts of Schönfeld's or Bell's reports, not in the substance of the talks themselves.[239] But what Schönfeld wrote down at the bishop's request, perhaps not very fortunately, in the hurry of Stockholm,[240] was essentially the same as what Bonhoeffer had previously asked for in his comments on Paton's book, namely that there should be a reasonable statement and advocacy of British peace aims in the Press and on the radio.[241] That was also the point on which Bell himself had been conducting his struggle in London since 1941, as we have already indicated, and in support of which he never tired later, in opposition to Vansittartism,[242] of pointing to Stalin's politically clever public declaration distinguishing between Hitler and the German people, while London maintained an obstinate silence on the subject.

On 2nd June Bonhoeffer was already back in Berlin. The courier had to keep his composure, coming and going again quickly as a courier does. He still found time to report to Oxford again:

238. Thus in G. Ritter, op. cit., pp. 322, 515; H. Rothfels, op. cit., p. 388.
239. GS I, pp. 376, 384 f., 396, 410.
240. GS I, p. 376.
241. GS I, pp. 357, 364 f.
242. On one occasion when asked by a paper about Vansittartism, Bell, after consulting Leibholz, defined it as follows: 'A disease which causes those who suffer from it to identify Nazism with Germany, and to see in Nazism a specific German phenomenon which could never flourish on any other soil. The gravity of the disease varies in different individuals. Those who suffer from it in its extreme form regard all Germans as butcher-birds just as the Nazis regard all Jews as sub-man' (*Illustrated*, London, 11.9.1943, p. 17). Vansittart himself answered the same question: 'The essence of Vansittartism is that the real enemy is German militarism, of which Nazism is the last and worst manifestation. Militarism is nation-wide in Germany. It is, therefore, nonsense to say that we have the end of it when we have rid ourselves of Hitler. We have to rid Germany of the system which brought both wars. No one has yet suggested that Nazism or Fascism bred the last war' (op. cit., p. 16).

What an indescribable joy to have heard from you through George! It still seems to me like a miracle . . . You will have heard, of course, as we have here in Sweden, that all persons of non-Aryan descent who are outside of Germany have been in general expatriated. As far as I can tell the future of your fatherland that is a good thing for you and will make your return only easier on that day for which we are all longing . . . My heart is full of thanks for these last days. George is one of the very great personalities I have met in my life.[243]

He took leave of the bishop:

. . . this spirit of fellowship and of Christian brotherliness will carry me through the darkest hour, and even if things go worse than we hope and expect, the light of these few days will never extinguish in my heart . . . I shall think of you on Wednesday. Please pray for us.[244]

Bell's Struggle for Negotiation. In his later publications, Bishop Bell described too modestly his efforts to get a hearing for the unexpected concern of the German conspirators.[245] In fact, he never resigned himself to accepting any refusal. On 11th July 1942, Leibholz wrote to Sutz, for Bonhoeffer's benefit:

I have seen George recently . . . His journey impressed him very much, and I very much hope that his efforts will be rewarded by some appreciable success, although, unfortunately, many of his friends and ours have not his breadth of judgement, and will have difficulty in freeing themselves from erroneous prejudices.

We have seen how Bell called, passionately but vainly, for a rational formulation of peace aims, and for the proclamation of a future European order in which Germany, freed from National Socialism, should have its place without being subjected to the mistakes of the Treaty of Versailles. He knew the situation only too well when, loyal to his own Government, he warned the two men in Sweden against exaggerated hopes. But he was not prepared to accept Churchill's attitude passively; his experience at Sigtuna was too strong a corroboration of his own efforts. So he did two things: he persisted in following up his secret commission from Sweden to the Government, and he appealed again to the public with the old demand for reasonable peace aims.

a) The Cabinet's Refusal. Bell was no sooner back than he heard of Visser 't Hooft's visit to London and the delivery of Trott's memorandum, which he must have regarded as very welcome help from a third party. He reported on 18th June to Eden, the Foreign Secretary, with a short account of his meeting in Sweden and with reference to

243. To G. Leibholz, 1.6.1942.
244. GS I, p. 382.
245. GS I, p. 383.

Trott's memorandum, and he was received in person on 30th June. He was very pleased that Eden 'was much interested', but he could not quite dissipate the latter's feeling that the pastors might, without knowing it, have been used, or misused, by the Nazis as 'peace-feelers'. Eden promised to study carefully the documents that had been handed to him, and to give his answer. On 10th July Bell wrote to Leibholz:

I have heard nothing from Mr. Eden since my interview with him on 30th June. I hope that he is giving careful consideration to the matters I laid before him. I hope indeed that other members of the cabinet may also have been informed of what I told him . . . I realize that one has to act fairly quickly.

On 13th July, Bishop Bell saw Sir Stafford Cripps, who was a friend of his and who was also a member of the cabinet. The latter reported that he had seen Visser 't Hooft and told him that Trott ought to be given a word of encouragement for his memorandum. He promised to express to Eden his support of Bell's commissions and wishes.

But on 17th July there came a completely negative reply from Eden:

Without casting any reflection on the bona fides of your informants, I am satisfied that it would not be in the national interest for any reply whatever to be sent to them. I realize that this decision may cause you some disappointment, but in view of the delicacy of the issues involved I feel that I must ask you to accept it.[246]

The official checks made by the Government between 30th June and 17th July had not been able to cast any doubt on the reliability of the two German emissaries; but there was also 'delicacy' to be considered. Churchill's government had just been trying to soothe the Soviet annoyance at the absence of a second front on the west specifically promised by the British-Soviet treaty of alliance of 26th May 1942; that treaty expressly confirmed the Atlantic Charter which outlawed Germany. The two partners, the Soviet Union and Britain, had thus undertaken 'not to enter into any negotiations either with the Hitler government or with any other German government that does not clearly renounce all aggressive intentions and not to conclude an armistice or peace treaty without mutual agreement.'[247] London was careful to avoid even the appearance of any breach of the treaty.

Then, on 30th July, Bell took his material to the American ambassador Winant; Leibholz had urged him to do so. Bell wrote to him:

He was clearly attentive, and I thought more alive to the importance of my conversations and their provenance than the two English statesmen.

Winant promised to inform Washington, but no answer came. At about the same time Louis Lochner, who, as an American journalist, had returned from Germany as late as June 1942, had his disappointing experiences with the American Government. He tried to tell what he knew about the resistance circles in Berlin—all of them were people with whom Dietrich Bonhoeffer was in touch, among them being Josef Wirmer, an intimate friend of Klaus Bonhoeffer—to Roosevelt, and to convince him of the seriousness of the opposition. But he was not received; in fact, his written request that he might be authorized to give the opposition in Berlin an answer met with a flat refusal, because it was 'highly embarrassing'.[248] Even the mere recognition of opposition elements was then outside the official line. So it was no wonder that no answer came from Winant either.

Bell, therefore, could do nothing but send a telegram of refusal to Visser 't Hooft in Geneva on 23rd July, not without a gentle attempt not to let the situation seem entirely black after all: 'Interest undoubted, but deeply regret no reply possible. Bell.'[249] Every word of the telegram was pondered.

But with all his loyalty, Bell was not by a long way willing to rest content, as he was quite convinced that the decision was not a wise one. Twice more he wrote to Eden to try to get across to him, in his own way, his opposite conviction. He pressed him at least to make it clear publicly that Vansittart's policy was not (contrary to the general assumption) that of the Government:

If there are men in Germany also ready to wage war against the monstrous tyranny of the Nazis from within, is it right to discourage or ignore them? Can we afford to reject their aid in achieving our end?[250]

The weak side of Bell's case was, as he admitted, that there still seemed to be no visible sign of resistance inside Germany; he could only assert that the movement existed.

Had the Berlin resistance group, and with it Bonhoeffer, gone completely wrong in appraising the forces? Was the British cabinet's opinion really quite as clear-cut all along as it afterwards seemed, when the opinion of so influential a man as Cripps obviously differed from that of his Prime Minister and Foreign Secretary?

b) A Public Campaign. Bell now tried harder than ever, in every way open to him, to exercise pressure on the Government in public, though he made little mention of this in his post-war accounts.

As soon as he was back from Sweden, he wrote for Joe Oldham's *Christian News Letter* a report[251] in which, while avoiding any reference to his stirring experiences, he again expressed his opinion that after Hitler's fall the most important thing would still remain to be done: to

248. H. Rothfels, *Die deutsche Opposition gegen Hitler Eine Würdigung,* 1949, pp. 166 f.
249. GS I, p. 411.
250. GS I, p. 386.
251. *Christian News Letter* of 24.6.1942.

set up a new order in Europe. There was the remark, whose background we now know:

Hitler's system is doomed, and the crash may come *more suddenly and sooner than some expect* . . . The collapse of Hitler will leave a vacuum in Europe. Unless the problem of how that vacuum can be rightly filled is squarely and immediately faced, the last state of Europe may be worse than the first . . . but the problem of securing immediate order has to be prepared for and faced now by the Allied Powers. Unless our statesmen tackle it now, the victory of which we are certain will be turned into ashes . . .[252]

In the House of Bishops of the Canterbury Convocation of the Church of England, he said on 15th October 1942:

I could wish that the British Government would make it very much clearer than they have yet done that this is a war between rival philosophies of life, in which the United Nations welcome all the help they can receive from the anti-Nazis everywhere—in Germany as well as outside—and would assure the anti-Nazis in Germany that they would treat a Germany which effectively repudiated Hitler and Hitlerism in a very different way from the Germany in which Hitler continued to rule.[253]

In November Bell discovered, through a recently published book,[254] that in July 1942 the B.B.C. had broadcast to Germany an item with questions and answers, questions such as the following being answered entirely on the lines of Bell's views: 'Does Hitler's defeat mean Germany's destruction? . . . Does England expect that the German people will take part in the destruction of the Hitler régime?' He now made that broadcast and the publication of the book the occasion for giving notice in the Upper House of a question 'to see whether they are a correct representation of the policy of His Majesty's Government',[255] so that he could have a basis for his challenge in a speech. But he came up against difficulties. The leader of the Upper House, Lord Cranborne, asked Bell to postpone the question till he had talked over the delicate matter. In that conversation the bishop got so far as to learn that his question was down for the Upper House's session on 9th December. But shortly before that date he was again asked to postpone the question, so as to give time for a talk with Eden.

There is great reluctance to give any publicity to these Questions and Answers in this country.[256] This makes me very anxious. The answers seem to me to give a far clearer and more satisfactory description of what our war aims should be than any we have yet heard.[257]

Bell met Eden on 15th December, and listened to the Government's

252. *The Church and Humanity*, pp. 74, 76; the author's italics.
253. Op. cit., p. 84.
254. H. Fraenkel, *The Other Germany*.   256. The B.B.C. broadcast.
255. To S. Leibholz, 4.12.1942.   257. G. Bell to G. Leibholz, 11.12.1942.

urgent wish not to connect his question in the Upper House with that B.B.C. broadcast, which had not been intended for the British public. When Bell remained unyielding and cleverly proposed to Eden, as a way out, that he should connect his question about the distinction between Hitlerism and Germany with Stalin's speech of 6th November 1942, in which he sharply distinguished between Germany and Hitler, Eden finally consented. Now, however, the question and a speech were not possible till after the parliamentary recess. When it was put down for 27th January 1943, the Foreign Office again asked for a postponement, this time till 10th February. Finally there intervened Bell's speech, notified independently of his question, against Vansittart on 11th February, and arguing against the identification of all the cruelties of Hitler and his people with Germany as a whole.[258]

It was not till 10th March, after consultation with Leibholz, who suggested a few improvements, that Bell at last put his question:

Hitler knows that his only hope of appeasing the opposition is to persuade them that they as well as he are threatened by destruction by the Allies, that the Allies make no distinction between Nazis and other Germans, and regard all Germans as black . . . I can only hope that I have given some evidence of the reality of an opposition in Germany, and of the necessity for encouragement and assistance if it is to carry out its own principles and to be of value to the cause. I also hope that I may have given some ground for believing that on drawing this distinction, and making as crystal clear as possible the choice between Fascism and freedom, between tyranny and democracy, the future of Europe depends . . .[259]

The government spokesman replied:

I now say in plain terms, on behalf of His Majesty's Government that we agree with Premier Stalin, first that the Hitlerite State should be destroyed and secondly, that the whole German people is not, as Dr. Goebbels has been trying to persuade them, thereby doomed to destruction.

Bell had the impression that, on that afternoon, the sympathy of the House was on his side:

The clearness of the answer on the precise point which I raised was a real satisfaction . . . I am in touch with the Ministry of Information about the possibilities of getting a few copies of Hansard[260] over to Sweden.[261]

Three days after Bell's speech in London, Hitler's plane from Smolensk to East Prussia had on board the time-bomb which Schlabrendorff, with Tresckow in Kluge's headquarters, had smuggled in; Dohnanyi and Bonhoeffer and their friends were waiting anxiously in Berlin to hear that the plane had crashed. The *coup d'état* was so far prepared that it would

258. G. Bell, *The Church and Humanity*, pp. 95-109; see also GS I, p. 411.
259. Reprinted in *The Church and Humanity*, pp. 95-109.
260. The official record of parliamentary proceedings.
261. G. Bell to G. Leibholz, 16.3.1943.

have been set in motion from Olbricht's office if the attempted assassination had succeeded. But the bomb did not explode. One can well imagine how Bell would have taken the news of the *Putsch* so soon after his predictions, and how it would have changed his position all at once.

Instead of that, he had word on 7th April that Bonhoeffer had been arrested.

c) Anxiety for the German Friends. The bishop must have wondered constantly what effect his negative telegram had had on his German friends, and what he could do to encourage them in spite of it. For a long time he waited in vain for a direct reaction from Bonhoeffer. In his anxiety he enquired of Leibholz whether his telegraphic answer to Geneva had actually reached Bonhoeffer. For a letter that Bell at last received from Bonhoeffer in September was dated 28th August; Dohnanyi had taken it to Switzerland, where he wanted, among other things, to see about the London answer. And that letter showed no sort of reaction to the 'no reply possible'.[262]

But in the meantime the Geneva people knew about it, and sent word through a personal messenger, Tracy Strong, the Y.M.C.A. secretary, to the bishop, who passed it on to Leibholz:

I also hear from an American (Y.M.C.A. secretary) who was over from Geneva . . . that his colleagues in Geneva—in touch with Dietrich—were disappointed that nothing had come of the proposals, and they thought nothing further was likely while Russia was in the foreground.[263]

Bell continued more than ever to use all possible ways, through Sweden and Switzerland, of letting his friends know that, in spite of everything, things in England were not entirely unfavourable to them. In November, Bishop Brilioth went from Sweden to Chichester, and Bell gave him a detailed report. Bell wrote to Johansson, suggesting that he and Ehrenström should be put in touch with his German informants. He sent the speech that he had made at the Canterbury Convocation, and recommended him to read Eden's remark of 21st May 1942, which contained a glimmer of hope. He mentioned the B.B.C. broadcast with the questions and answers, and told him of the coming debate in the House of Lords.[264]

Brilioth did, in fact, meet Schönfeld and Gerstenmaier in Sweden in December 1942 to report to them, and he told Bell about it on 12th January 1943:

After my return I had—about a month ago—a most interesting visit from two Germans well known to you. They wanted to hear of my impressions, above all what might be the attitude of England to a Germany that had

262. GS I, p. 389.
263. To G. Leibholz, 14.10.1942.
264. Bell to Johansson, 3.12.1942.

changed its government and its policy. I don't think that what I had to tell was very reassuring to them. I tried to make them understand how difficult it is for people in England to form a true estimate of the strength and the reliability of an opposition of which so far they knew little. But I also said that public opinion in England probably would be much surprised if something really happened in Germany—although they could hardly hope for much encouragement before some decisive steps were taken. This makes the situation so very complicated. Yet it is much to be wished in my opinion that some sort of encouragement could be given. On the other hand it is very difficult to make them understand that public opinion in England cannot easily exonerate the German people from all responsibility for the acts of its Government—although as we know, there is very little possibility for the German people to influence the policy of its Government—also because they are largely ignorant of much that has happened.[265]

Bell erroneously thought from that letter that the 'two Germans well known to you' were Schönfeld and Bonhoeffer. But it was Gerstenmaier who had visited Sweden with Schönfeld.[266] And the nature of the talks revealed in Brilioth's letter has an accent that did not suggest the contrast that Bonhoeffer would have presented. Meanwhile, Bonhoeffer had no chance to go abroad during the winter of 1942-3.

Bell also tried to communicate with Bonhoeffer through Sutz in Switzerland, although he was afraid that after the Germans' occupation of southern France the threads might snap there, too:

I do not know how much reaches Switzerland about the policy very often connected with the name of Lord Vansittart. While it is true that there are quite a number of private individuals who agree with him in this country, such personal opinions are opposed to this country's official policy towards the German people. I know that Mr. Eden attaches a great deal of importance to a speech which he made on 21st May, in which he distinguishes between the Nazis and the Germans . . .[267]

At the end of March 1943, Bell received an anxious telegram from Siegmund-Schultze in Switzerland, regarding the heavy responsibility of the churches in the allied countries in view of the drastic intensification with the Casablanca Declaration of 24th January 1943 ('unconditional surrender'). Bell discussed it with the Under-Secretary of State in the Foreign Office, and sent Siegmund-Schultze an answer on 7th April 1943:

Official declaration most deliberate and positive yet made on differentiation between Nazi régime and German people stop declaration also reaffirmed refusal negotiate with Hitler or any Nazi representatives stop but should Hitler and Nazis be overthrown within Germany am personally convinced

265. Letter of 12.1.1943.
266. See also U. von Hassell, op. cit., p. 308.
267. There follows the reference to the above-mentioned B.B.C. broadcast; letter for Bonhoeffer of 3.12.1942.

whole situation transformed stop deeply appreciate your communion of spirit and your emphasis on Church's reconciling function stop.

Bell sent a report of the business to Leibholz, remarking about his conversation with the Under-Secretary of State:

I impressed upon him the importance of recognizing the existence of sound forces in the army and of trying to find phrases when talking about disarmament which would make it plain that the whole army was not brought under complete condemnation; I pointed out that it would only be with the help of armed forces that any overthrow from within could take place. He saw and appreciated this point.[268]

That last telegram to Siegmund-Schultze, at the time when Bonhoeffer had already been several days in a Tegel prison cell, shows again how closely Bishop Bell's thoughts agreed with those of the conspirators in Germany. As that was in marked contrast to the officially promulgated opinion in Great Britain, he scarcely got a hearing at the time. But the German Resistance Movement had in Bishop Bell a unique advocate and ally. It is true that that ally had no great influence then in Great Britain, and to that extent to build up too much hope on him was a political mistake—but only in day-to-day politics, not on a long-term view. The well-known English military writer Liddell Hart wrote in the *Daily Telegraph* on 15th June 1959:

For the wisdom and foresight of George Bell's wartime speeches in the House of Lords, although they met much disagreement at the time, have now come to be widely recognized—and especially by military historians of the war. Hardly anyone would now question the truth of his repeated warnings about the folly of the Allies' unconditional surrender policy . . . While the horizon of technical strategy is confined to immediate success in a campaign, grand strategy looks beyond the war to the subsequent state of peace—and thus tends to coincide with morality. In this way George Bell, standing for the principles of his creed, came to achieve a far clearer grasp of grand strategy than did the statesmen. The present situation of the West would be better if more attention had been paid to his temporarily unpalatable warnings and guidance.

4. Italian Journey

On 26th June 1942, Bonhoeffer set off on a journey abroad for the fourth time that year. This time he went with Hans von Dohnanyi to Italy. They spent a few days in Venice, where Schmidhuber had gone from Munich. Dohnanyi was on good terms with the German consul in Florence, who was in touch with Italian resistance groups. In Rome they hoped to have an answer waiting for them from London. Bonhoeffer met Josef Müller's friends, Fathers Leiber, Schönhöfer,[269] and Prelate

268. Letter of 7.4.1943.
269. LPP, p. 108.

Kaas; and he talked in the Vatican to Dr. Zeiger, the head of the Collegium Germanicum, whose help he used once more to send an uncensored letter from the Vatican to his sister in Oxford:

I had a most enjoyable time with George. You will certainly have had a letter from him too. I am still optimistic enough to believe that it will not last long till we meet again.[270]

But when they left Italy on 10th July, they had still had no news from London.

At the end of August, Dohnanyi went to Switzerland without Bonhoeffer, his main purpose being to make the final arrangements for 'Operation 7'. When he was there, he received Bell's disappointing telegram to Visser 't Hooft. Not that he had expected the British Government to be very forthcoming, but it meant one argument less in his efforts to get the cooperation of some of the generals.

Bonhoeffer had interrupted the work on his *Ethics* at Klein-Krössin, so as to say good-bye to Dohnanyi before his journey to Switzerland. Dohnanyi took with him the above-mentioned letter of 28th August to Bell. The letter disquieted the bishop, because it did not mention his telegram, and there was an undertone of slight fatigue about it:

Things are going as I expected them to go. But the length of time is, of course, sometimes a little enervating. Still I am hopeful that the day might not be too far when the bad dream will be over and we shall meet again. The task before us will then be greater than ever before. But I hope we shall be prepared for it. I should be glad to hear from you soon.[271]

That was the last hand-written greeting that the bishop and the relatives in Oxford had from Dietrich Bonhoeffer from free territory. Things continued to be 'a little enervating', because the conspirators' activities were made more difficult by Hitler's new successes in Russia and Africa, and because the ever-lengthening time needed for the preparations increased the danger of crises within the Resistance Movement.

Dohnanyi, for his part, wrote to the Oxford relatives from Switzerland:

What is going on in the invisible sphere you will have to guess; if you proceed from certain unshakeable assumptions, the solution of the riddle is not difficult . . . Our solidarity as brothers and sisters, and with our parents, is as firm as ever; we stand by each other; and so we can be sure of overcoming the difficulties of these violent times.[272]

270. Letter of 9.7.1942.
271. GS I, p. 389.
272. Sent from Vitznau, 30.8.1942.

5. *Structures of the Future: Cooperation*

In 1942 the planners were more active than ever in a resistance movement whose ramifications were increasing. Not only individuals, but
whole study circles, set about considering various fields of public life,
though Bonhoeffer himself did not outline or advocate any special idea
of what form a future government should take.

In July 1942 Otto John arranged for Goerdeler to visit Prince Louis
Ferdinand in Cadinen, and went with him. In Klaus Bonhoeffer's house
there were discussions, in which Jakob Kaiser and Josef Wirmer took
part, on whether the prince should not give the signal for revolt.
Difficulties among the Hohenzollerns themselves soon put an end to any
such plan; but Bonhoeffer had rightly told the bishop in Sigtuna that a
Hohenzollern was then being considered on the grounds of popularity,
stability, and the effective issuing of the order. The Bonhoeffer brothers
assented to those considerations, mainly on pragmatic grounds and without royalist motives. What Bonhoeffer wanted to see brought about by a
revolt was not a 'restoration'; but if a monarchical beginning could offer
advantages when the revolt was launched, it had to be considered as a
possibility. The sympathy that the death in action of the Crown Prince's
eldest son had aroused among the people, and that had caused Hitler to
withdraw the Hohenzollerns from the front, was at least worthy of
note when the necessary popular support for an overthrow was being
considered.

Bonhoeffer's cooperation in planning the programme of immediate
action after the revolt was confined to working, with Perels, at the
questions arising from Goerdeler's draft constitution on the future
relation between State and Church,[273] and in particular on a new
ordering, after the *Putsch*, of the destroyed churches. Dohnanyi was
specially entrusted, in the Beck group, with the coordination of the
measures immediately necessary.

Reorganizing the Churches. A rough outline by Bonhoeffer[274] and some
pencilled notes by Perels have been preserved out of the proposals on the
immediate measures to be taken for the churches.

Bonhoeffer's notes make it clear which of the Confessing Church's
forces ought to carry out the reorganization, so that on the one hand a
'Confessing leadership' will be restored, and on the other hand neither
the special interests of the provincial churches nor traditional 'confessional hindrances' will threaten the new German Evangelical Church.
'The reactionary circles of the one-time general superintendents and of
the bureaucracy of church authorities must not be in a position to reassert
control.' In the proposals for individual measures that are to restore legal

273. G. Ritter, op. cit., p. 295.
274. GS II, pp. 433 ff.

status and credal freedom, it is held to be possible for some 'German Christians' to co-exist as a free religious association. 'The Church External Affairs Office, which has lost the confidence of foreign churches and of most Germans abroad, will be reorganized as to its personnel, in agreement with the council of the German Evangelical Church.' The theological faculties, 'to a great extent destroyed and robbed of their academic prestige', will be reformed with the churches' cooperation. Of course, there will no longer be a Ministry for Religious Affairs. Efforts should be made for a settlement of financial questions, because they 'persistently plague' the relationship between State and Church. Bonhoeffer had in mind the possibility of a Church independent of the State.

Perels' draft is concentrated on certain paragraphs which were in line with Bonhoeffer's ideas. It provides a clue to the date, as it mentions, in the proposals about personnel, Fritz Müller of Dahlem, whose unexplained death occurred in the East on 20th September 1942. The draft contained a regulation concerning the 'competence of the Reich in church affairs', a law about 'the freedom of Christian belief', a 'decree on the law as to freedom of belief in the German Evangelical Church', and a list of the officials' names.

It is no longer possible to ascertain the final form taken by the Beck group's proposals for the churches' reorganization. A copy fell into the hands of Judge Advocate Roeder when Bonhoeffer was arrested. The title of that draft, 'Ending the Church Struggle', enabled Bonhoeffer to conceal the document's real background.

With those preparations of urgent measures, Bonhoeffer also drafted a pulpit proclamation for the Church and a message to the clergy.[275] The declaration contains an emphatic confession of guilt and a call for the liberation of consciences after so much unfaithfulness and disunity. It is important that Bonhoeffer did not feel that there was any contradiction or break involved in his thinking over, and being satisfied with, the Church's 'mandate' while he was deeply involved in the conspiracy. On the contrary, the break for worldly business that he had made freed him for what needed to be done in the Church's spiritual field.

6. Structures of the Future: Initiative

All possible encouragement was being given by those at the centre of the conspiracy at that time to the writing of memoranda about questions concerning the future shaping of society. For instance, in the summer of 1942 Goerdeler asked Hans Asmussen for a written report of the Church's views on economic questions.[276] Bonhoeffer, however, developed on the basis of his ecumenical contacts a line of his own, which, through the cooperation of friends and experts in particular subjects, grew

275. GS II, pp. 438 f.
276. *Luth. Informationsblatt*, I, No. 17, pp. 284 f.

into a kind of monograph (*Denkschrift*) which has been preserved.

What Bonhoeffer was able to read in Switzerland in 1941 from the publications of English Christian groups, and what Bell told him in 1942 of the ideas that his friends entertained for the period of the vacuum between Hitler's fall and the establishment of a new order, impressed him; and still more, it frightened him when he realized how much his ecumenical friends expected from the Confessing Church, and how little it was doing to think out and prepare for society's future needs.

On the other side, prominent laity and clergy were at work: the group round J. Oldham's *Christian News Letter*, the 'Peace Aims Group', Temple's 'Malvern Conference', and the 'P.E.P.' ('Political and Economic Planning Group'). Paton, in his book, took it for granted that, as soon as hostilities were suspended, talks would be started with the leaders of the Confessing Church,[277] and that the '*dictated* peace of Versailles'[278] would have to be avoided, by general consent, as a blunder 'of the first order'; 'there are no Germans with whom fellowship in the post-war tasks will be so quickly resumed'[279] as with the members of the Confessing Church. And Bell referred in his book to the need for Christians behind both fronts to strive to influence the peace terms, at a time when reason was being suppressed by the bitterness and passions of a long war:

Preparation should be made now for the calling of a conference of Christian leaders, Protestant and Catholic, from amongst the belligerent and neutral countries to meet together as soon as possible after the Armistice . . . both the clergy and the laity from the belligerent and neutral countries . . . should meet before the negotiation of the final treaty.[280]

But on the German side all the presuppositions for taking up that line of thought, and for getting ready for any kind of partnership, were lacking. Anyone who planned, discussed, or wrote down any ideas for the future of society risked being accused of subversive activities. But not only that: the Lutheran theological tradition was against it. Paul Althaus wrote quite characteristically in 1940:

Christianity has no political programme, and has no right to exercise control or censorship over political life in the name of Jesus and the Gospel . . . In reality, politics follows its own laws and necessities.[281]

So Bonhoeffer, in his outline for the discussion on Paton's book at Geneva in 1941, lodged a brief preliminary warning with his British partners:

The absolute uncertainty of human existence leads . . . Christians almost

277. See Ch. XII. pp. 643 f.
278. W. Paton, op. cit., p. 76.
279. W. Paton, op. cit., p. 179.
280. G. Bell, *Christianity and World Order*, p. 107.
281. P. Althaus, *Luther in der deutschen Kirche der Gegenwart*, 1940, pp. 24 f.

everywhere to renounce entirely all thought for the future, and that again results in a markedly apocalyptic attitude. As the day of judgement is felt to be at hand, the historical future may easily be no longer seen.[282]

Bonhoeffer discussed those concerns, on occasion, with Hammelsbeck because they were both uneasy about the eschatological theology that was becoming sterile, and about the Confessing Church's growing lack of contact; and he discussed them, too, with Perels with a view to organizing practical work on the problems. He talked to Hans Böhm, the ecumenical representative of the provisional governing body, and to Otto Dibelius.[283] His persistence finally led to a discussion in the provisional governing body of the Confessing Church.

The Freiburg Memorandum. In the session of the provisional governing body they remembered the distinguished experts who were at the disposal of the Freiburg circle of the Confessing Church. They had been meeting there for some time to deal with questions of political ethics, professors such as Eucken, von Dietze, Lampe, Gerhard Ritter, and Erik Wolf; and Bonhoeffer made contact with them. He had several reasons for doing this: because of his own studies of ethics, on the express authorization of the provisional governing body, on the secret authorization of the ecumenical churches, personified by Bell, and lastly on the secret authorization of the conspiracy. Goerdeler himself already maintained many connections with lawyers, historians, and sociologists, and so, too, with the Freiburg group.

Bonhoeffer met the Freiburg group at least twice, the first time being soon after he had come back from meeting Bell at Sigtuna; that was when the working committee was formed for the memorandum. Then, on 17th November 1942, he came on a short visit for a discussion lasting several days, with the factory owner Walter Bauer, Goerdeler, and Helmut Thielicke taking part. We have a note of or for that discussion written by Bonhoeffer on a piece of paper with the date; the headings, as far as they can be deciphered, read:

Economic questions: Eucken, von Dietze, Bauer, Karrenberg.

Law of the State inside decalogue God and State outside Europe . . . [illegible] Ritter Luther.

God and right: fundamental and human rights . . . [illegible] Böhm-Jena natural right, right of punishment, State-Church.

The Jews.

Education.

The Church's preaching to the world. The Word of God and counsel. The basis of right. Existence of the Church in the world. Perels.

282. GS I, p. 356.

283. O. Dibelius said, in a sermon of 20.7.1960, that Bonhoeffer did in fact tell him of his ecumenical meetings, but that he did not disclose to him the fact of the conspiracy till the beginning of 1943—to his dismay: 'I underestimated then the depth of conscience that existed in those circles.'

These notes suggest that Bonhoeffer formulated the chapters 'State and Church' and 'On the Possibility of the Word of the Church to the World',[284] which are now a supplement to the *Ethics*, for the Freiburg plans. The Freiburg memorandum was finished in January 1943. It sets out its views on the future legal régime, church policy, education, social and economic policy, foreign policy, and future peace, in more or less exhaustive and independent enquiries. In July 1945, Gerhard Ritter duplicated the salvaged memorandum, with an introductory account of its origin, under the heading: 'Political Ordering of the Community; an Attempted Stocktaking of the Christian Conscience in the Political Needs of Our Time.'[285] Ritter there attests that the work was a German answer, or preparation for an answer to Paton's and Bell's suggestions.

A contribution that came in later from Perels, about legal questions, was found by the Gestapo, and led to his being tortured in 1944. Most of his colleagues were arrested, but all except Goerdeler, Perels, and Bonhoeffer escaped with their lives.

The memorandum bore fruit by being used as one of the preliminary works for the Amsterdam conference that founded the World Council of Churches in 1948, as it had successfully combined theological principles with practical details.

In the course of his collaboration in the memorandum, Bonhoeffer did not get in touch with the members of the Kreisau group, nor attempt to fit in with their thinking.[286] Apart from the fact that their work reached its climax rather later than that of the Freiburg group, he considered then that those conclusions which related to the period after a revolt belonged to the ecumenical forum which had emerged out of the direct responsibility of the Confessing Church. In spite of his demand that the Confessing Church, which was dangerously constricted, should in many ways open out and expand its horizon, he still found it difficult to cooperate with church-people who had not taken the sacrificial way of the provisional leaders and the Councils of Brethren. And the Confessing Church, in so far as it stood by Barmen and Dahlem, could not regard the evangelical churchmen in the Kreisau group, such as Schönfeld, Gerstenmaier, Poelchau, or even Steltzer, as its own people.

So it is a little tragic that the Kreisau and Freiburg groups did not then seek out and supplement each other. Bonhoeffer did not live to see what doors opened in that direction.

7. *The Assassination That Did Not Take Place*

The period of Bonhoeffer's important journeys was now over. The

---

284. E, pp. 332, 354.
285. See the mention in G. Ritter, op. cit, pp. 511 f.
286. On the documents relating to the Kreisau group's sessions, see T. Steltzer, *Sechzig Jahre Zeitgenosse*, 1966, pp. 307 ff., 317 ff.

autumn and winter of 1942-3 became a relentless race against time; the need to deliver the blow grew more urgent, as Germany's military and political state was getting visibly worse; at the same time, the Reich's chief security office was preparing its blow at Canaris' office. The Gestapo thought that by prosecuting Dohnanyi and his friends it could deal the *Abwehr* a deadly blow; it did not yet know what kind of a centre of conspiracy it was disturbing, if not paralyzing. In that winter, the centre worked so effectively that it had all its preparations ready and seemed to be on the verge of success.

Political State of the Army. The German public did not yet see that the turning-point in Hitler's military situation was approaching. To some, the extension of the fighting may have seemed inauspicious, but during that autumn Hitler achieved his greatest area of conquests. He pushed as far as the Volga and the Caucasus, and almost to the Nile. Vichy France was occupied, and it was an anxious time for the Genevans, who were afraid that they might be cut off from the world.

Only a few people saw the reverse side. In September, Halder was still trying to keep Hitler from advancing on Stalingrad, whereupon Hitler dismissed him and replaced him with General Zeitzler; that meant that the plans for the *Putsch* were again upset. On 24th September, Bonhoeffer wrote to his parents who were on holiday:

Stalingrad seems to be a fearful struggle. It is very depressing for everyone, and gets on one's nerves.[287]

On 23rd October, Montgomery attacked at El Alamein, and after twelve days' fighting he succeeded in breaking through westwards. On 8th November, the Allies landed in Morocco and at Algiers, and advanced towards Tunisia. From 19th November the Soviets attacked at Stalingrad and surrounded twenty-two German divisions. Hitler telegraphed to General Paulus: 'Surrender inconceivable.' Posters were put up in the shop windows before Christmas 1942: 'Think only of victory, and afterwards of presents.' On 24th January 1943, in Casablanca, Churchill and Roosevelt announced the policy of 'unconditional surrender'. On 31st January the survivors of the Stalingrad cauldron trudged away into captivity.

Hassell wrote in his diary on 22nd January 1943, with reference to the generals who were responsible:

If the Josefs[288] had the ambition to delay their intervention till it was quite clear that the corporal[289] is leading us into the abyss, that dream has come true. The worst of it is that we were right in thinking beforehand that it would then be too late, and that any new régime would be a liquidation-commission.[290]

287. GS II, p. 422.
288. Hassell's nickname for the timid generals.
289. Nickname for Hitler.
290. U. von Hassell, op. cit., p. 292.

For the first time in the war, Stalingrad produced a perceptible shock in Germany. This was followed, in the middle of February, by the circulation of the pamphlets of the 'White Rose' and the appearance of the Scholl brother and sister and their friends of the University of Munich before the People's Court—a manifestation that seemed to the mass of the people to be tragically meaningless.

Attempted Putsch in March 1943. At the time when the Munich students went to their death, the conspirators felt that they were nearer to their objective than they had ever been before. The plans for the assassination were given their finishing touches, and it was simply a case of waiting for the moment of their execution.

The cooperation between Oster-Dohnanyi and Tresckow-Schlabrendorff in the middle army group in the east had developed steadily under Beck's guidance since the summer. The last-mentioned pair had succeeded in having increasing numbers of like-minded officers appointed under their commanders, von Bock and later von Kluge. So the plan matured to assassinate Hitler on his anticipated visit to the front held by the middle army group. When Halder was dropped from the army high command in Berlin, the planning was energetically concentrated on that focal point on the eastern front for unleashing the *Putsch*. To help the plans on, Goerdeler went to Smolensk with passes provided by Oster, and visited Kluge and Tresckow. Tresckow tried hard and persistently to get his chief to cooperate. Bonhoeffer in letters to me referred in code to the progress in that part of the preparations: 'Hans-Christoph and his wife are improving gradually but steadily.'[291] 'Hans-Christoph' was his cousin in the east, and was ill.

In Berlin, the responsibility for the further steps to be taken after the revolt had been started lay with General Olbricht, who as chief of the general staff had authority over the central information office of the *Wehrmacht* and the provincial commanders. He could prepare and issue the crucial orders for the measures to be taken after the assassination. He was an old friend of Oster, and he had also helped in the employment in the United Kingdom of Confessing pastors.[292] Bonhoeffer wrote about how things were going with Olbricht on 29th November 1942, using Josef Müller's name to represent the internal situation:

Sepp is again in very good form and cheerful, and hopes to have finished his work in four weeks at the most.[293]

Again, the estimated time was too short by at least one half.

In February 1943 Schlabrendorff made a last journey to Berlin. Hitler's visit to the middle army group was expected to be on Saturday

291. Letter of 27.11.1942, GS II, p. 425.
292. GS II, p. 412.
293. GS II, p. 426.

13th March. Dohnanyi now fled to his friends in Smolensk to make the final arrangements. But that was not all: in his suitcase there was a special English explosive (available to the *Abwehr*) for Tresckow and Schlabrendorff. With no inkling of what was in the suitcase, I drove Dohnanyi, in the car specially permitted to doctors that belonged to Bonhoeffer's father, to the night train that was to take him to East Prussia. There he took the plane to meet Canaris. While Canaris called his intelligence officers of the middle army sector to a meeting, Dohnanyi, Tresckow, and Schlabrendorff settled the code for the intended notification.

The carefully arranged revolutionary plot began for the first time to take its irrevocable course.[294] When Hitler entered his plane for the return flight, after visiting Kluge's headquarters at Smolensk, there was a small parcel containing the fused time-bombs on board. But he landed safely in East Prussia; the ignition had failed. Schlabrendorff himself has told how he managed to save the critical situation undetected.

The preparations for revolt were not given up. Without hesitation the conspirators turned their attention to the new opportunity that would come on 21st March on the occasion of the national ceremony of the 'heroes' remembrance day'. They got hold of the time-table for Hitler's tour of the arsenal, in which the middle army group's trophies were to be inspected. Major von Gersdorff, an *Abwehr* officer of the middle army group, was determined on that occasion to carry two bombs in his coat pocket, and so to deliver the blow at the cost of his own life.

On that Sunday afternoon, the family with all the grandchildren was practising in the Schleichers' house the birthday cantata for the seventy-fifth birthday of Bonhoeffer's father.[295] Dietrich Bonhoeffer was at the piano, Klaus played the 'cello, Rüdiger Schleicher the violin, and Hans von Dohnanyi was in the choir. At the front door, Dohnanyi's car was ready to leave; the others had no idea how anxiously Dohnanyi kept on looking at the clock, waiting for the vital telephone call. Ursula Schleicher did, indeed, notice how excited her sister Christine von Dohnanyi was; there had certainly often been tense moments because of the warning of the watch that the Gestapo kept on her husband. But now she whispered to her sister: 'It must start any moment!' But minute after minute went by, and the telephone did not ring.

What had happened? Hitler had finished his inspection in the arsenal after ten minutes, instead of staying for half an hour as expected; so Gersdorff had not been able either to get into the prearranged position close to him, or to ignite the fuse in time.

A fortnight later Bonhoeffer, Dohnanyi and his wife, and Josef Müller were arrested, and Oster was banned from the *Abwehr* building on the

294. F. von Schlabrendorff, *Offiziere gegen Hitler*, 1946, pp. 69 ff.; E. Zeller, *Geist der Freiheit*, 1952, pp. 139 ff.
295. See LPP, p. 145.

Tirpitzufer. Besides all that, Beck dropped out for several months, as he had to undergo an operation performed by Sauerbruch; Hammerstein died. The participants abruptly realized how serious a break had been caused by the failure of the attempted _coup_ of March 1943.

Schlabrendorff, Justus Delbrück, Gehre, and Klaus Bonhoeffer were certainly right when, at the end of March, they celebrated with Otto John their unexpected good fortune in that nothing had been discovered and no part of the _Putsch_ organization destroyed. But in fact, the most promising period of the German resistance was over, costly work had been done in vain, fresh crimes and suffering heaped up. The matter now stood as Stauffenberg was to say shortly before 20th July 1944: The overthrow cannot now change everything in the hopeless political and military situation.

At that time, the Gestapo itself did not know what it had achieved by the arrests of 5th April—the smashing of the conspiracy's centre of activity. It was many months before everything was covered up and a new organizing centre created for the work needed for the _Putsch_.

With that break, Bonhoeffer was eliminated from the active conspiracy; from now on, his efforts were devoted to putting the bloodhounds off the scent. The conspiracy remained undiscovered, and went on. Bonhoeffer in his prison cell was kept adequately informed by code words, and remained full of hope till 20th July 1944 came.

VII THE ARREST

The tension during the preparations for the _Putsch_ of March 1943 had been made worse for Dohnanyi and Bonhoeffer through their both being involved in an unfortunate affair inside the Munich _Abwehr_. One day in October 1942 Dohnanyi received from Group Commander Nebe of the Reich Security Head Office, who had for a long time secretly collaborated with the resistance, a warning that he and Bonhoeffer had been named and incriminated in proceedings against the consul Schmidhuber. A storm was brewing over the entire _Abwehr_. The warning to Dohnanyi at the beginning of 1942 that his telephone and post were being kept under surveillance had been of a general nature. But the new warning related to an attempt by the Reich Security Head Office to exploit specific irregularities in the _Abwehr_ as starting-points for its final destruction.

Bonhoeffer had been preparing for fresh journeys since the beginning of September 1942; he was to visit ecumenical friends in the Balkans and Switzerland. On 10th September the Munich _Abwehr_ had applied for him to be given new endorsements 'for repeated journeys to and from Hungary, Bulgaria, Greece, Croatia, and Italy for a period of three months'.[296] The granting of the endorsements was delayed by a new

296. Original of the application in _Wehrkreis_, VII, Munich, among Bonhoeffer's effects.

regulation in the passport system. On 2nd October he went to Munich to get the endorsements and begin the journeys; he told his parents that he might be away for six weeks.

Then the crisis in the Munich *Abwehr* came to a head. Instead of visiting the Balkans, Bonhoeffer had to go back to Berlin in the middle of October and wait for matters to be 'clarified'. What had happened? The customs-search office in Prague had uncovered a currency irregularity by a man who alleged that he had been acting for the consul Schmidhuber and in his interest. Thereupon Schmidhuber, and Captain Ickradt of the Munich *Abwehr* office, were subjected to an interrogation which produced, among other things, questions about the currency transactions for the Jews of 'Operation 7', and incriminating answers. Josef Müller was also interrogated. In late October Schmidhuber was arrested; he was imprisoned for months in the Prinz-Albrecht-Strasse. That gave cause for alarm; in two years' cooperation he had learnt a great deal about 'U 7', about Bonhoeffer's position in Britain, and about all the connections abroad.

It was now unavoidable that the investigations should be directed to the activities of the main *Abwehr* office in Berlin. But it was not simply a matter of course that the Gestapo appeared in the Tirpitzufer and began to make enquiries there. All the courts still recognized that the affairs of the *Abwehr* were subject to certain special rules as to secrecy; and it was largely at Canaris' discretion, as far as he had the power, to decide what steps should be taken by his *Abwehr* as being necessary for the services and how far to cover them up. But the final decision about whether the *Abwehr's* actions might be investigated by security officials lay with Keitel, who had to give his consent as chief of the *Wehrmacht* high command. If he gave permission for the disclosure of the *Abwehr's* activities in particular matters, that could put an end to the organization's independence, or at least give the Reich Security Head Office the chance, which it desperately wanted, to turn the spotlight on to Canaris' office.

So for months now it was a question who was to make or prevent a decision in the matter. Where did an individual's currency offences begin to be a matter for prosecution? And how far was the *Abwehr* justified in claiming secrecy for its affairs? There were interested parties everywhere. The Reich Security Head Office hoped that an individual's lapse would enable it to expose Canaris' office as a whole. But the *Luftwaffe*, headed by Göring, was also taking notice; it had previously been shown up by the 'scandal' of the '*Rote Kapelle*' (a group of 'reds') that had occurred inside the *Luftwaffe*, and was only waiting for some scandal that would implicate the Army. Besides, there was no lack of people in the *Abwehr* itself who would feel satisfaction if Dohnanyi got into difficulties, he being a young civilian who had pushed his way too near the top too quickly. Thus, on Schmidhuber's arrest a man from the legal department of the *Abwehr* acted as one of Dohnanyi's opponents; and thus later, the chief investigator, Judge Advocate Roeder, could count on willing support here and there on the Tirpitzufer, the street in which the *Abwehr* office stood.

There was no doubt that Canaris was prepared to cover up the steps that Dohnanyi and Bonhoeffer had taken on behalf of the *Abwehr*. But they had been named in the Prinz-Albrecht-Strasse; and Keitel's approval was sought for their possible arrest and for more comprehensive investigations.

Precautions. In that situation, all possible actions had to be scrutinized as to their validity in relation to the *Abwehr*, and safeguarded from unwelcome disclosure.

First, Dohnanyi went to Switzerland. The Jews who had been saved in 'U 7' were not safe there from possible visits by an emissary of the Reich Security Head Office, after they had been mentioned in the Schmidhuber interrogations. Dohnanyi looked up the German military attaché and met Dr. Arnold in Berne to check that all financial matters relating to the group were in order according to the documents, and to urge the utmost discretion in answering any enquiries. He was back home on 29th November. The accounts had been checked on the Tirpitzufer, and the reliability of the group in Switzerland confirmed as far as humanly possible.

The question of the extra-parochial position was critical, and it became more so as the theatres of war grew more extended and the casualties increased. Here the documents had to show precisely why it was that a man like Bonhoeffer was indispensable for the military organization of the *Abwehr*. So Dohnanyi and Bonhoeffer talked it over and composed a long letter, dated back to 4th November 1940, in which Bonhoeffer told his brother-in-law, from Munich, how interested the *Abwehr* might be in his information on ecumenical matters. For this they had to search for the necessary notepaper, the 'M-K paper', such as was actually used in business in 1939 and 1940. The draft, which had been preserved, reads:

Dear Hans, When we were discussing ecumenical matters recently, you asked me whether I would not be prepared, if need be, to make available my knowledge of foreign countries and my connections with people in public life in Europe and overseas, so as to cooperate in the acquisition of reliable information about foreign countries. I have been thinking the matter over.

The special feature of the ecumenical work in the context of the problems that interest you is, of course, the fact that leading political personalities of the various countries are interested in the movement, in which all the larger churches of the world, except the Church of Rome, have joined together, so that it really might not be difficult to learn the views and judgements of these personalities by way of such ecumenical relationships. Besides that, I think it is quite within the bounds of possibility that one might in that way establish fresh contacts that could perhaps be of use in dealing with specialized questions . . .

It is then pointed out how many laymen could be contacted in that way; a long series of names is suggested, among them Cripps, Lord Lothian (who was still alive in 1940!), Crossman, Noel-Buxton, and Moberley.

I am at present in Munich for some little time, and of course I would be willing to be at your disposal in any way that suits you, possibly from here, or wherever you think best. I do not think it would be difficult, even in the existing circumstances, to take up the great majority of the connections— perhaps from a neutral country—and use them in the German interest.

That apparent handing over of ecumenical church contacts to Hitler's prosecution of the war was necessary in 1942 in order to make quite sure of camouflaging the revolutionary movement when it was at its most promising stage. Help for the Jews, approaches to the enemy, journeys—everything had to appear to be an obvious activity of the *Abwehr* in Canaris' office, so that it could be kept, on the ground of the need for the greatest secrecy, from possible outside investigation.

The extra-parochial appointments of other pastors (by Oster's office) remained a dangerous remnant; we hastened to have a few supporting documents prepared by other exempted pastors. Thus, I myself, on the strength of my activity with the Indian-based Gossner missionary society, wrote reports in which there appeared in a stylized form facts suggestive of military importance coming from that sphere; in fact, a journey to the International Missionary Council in Switzerland was arranged for me. This, it is true, did not take place till July 1943, but I could then convey to Visser 't Hooft and Barth information about what had happened to Dohnanyi and Bonhoeffer in the meantime.[297]

It was necessary, too, that not even the suspicion of guilt should be aroused; on the contrary, the travelling agent had to be above all a travelling agent. So, as the affair grew more and more protracted, more journeys for Bonhoeffer were envisaged, and at the end of January 1943 the plans for the Balkans and Switzerland were renewed. As the date for the *Putsch* was so close at hand, he did not want to be away just then if avoidable. But he left for Munich expecting to make a short trip to Switzerland (which never materialized). From Munich Josef Müller again went to Rome—from similar considerations, but also in connection with the imminent attempted *coup*. But the latest news from Group Commander Nebe was again unfavourable, and so Bonhoeffer returned to Berlin on 12th February, on the ground that he had been 'urgently warned yesterday'.[298] They did not want to risk his being searched by official order as he crossed the frontier.

297. See LPP, pp. 98 f.
298. Letter from E. Bethge to Renate Schleicher.

But now, under the date of 13th March 1943—the day of the attempted assassination by Tresckow and Schlabrendorff—there came from the Munich recruiting station a new order for Bonhoeffer to report for military service. Since Stalingrad, a strict scrutiny of all German administrative departments for physically fit men in extra-parochial positions had been in progress. Bonhoeffer was told to report in the Seidlstrasse in Munich with all his papers on 22nd March. But it was necessary that his extra-parochial position should not on any account be cancelled just then. Oster therefore exercised his authority for one last time by again releasing Bonhoeffer from the obligation to report. At the same time, he worked harder than ever with Dohnanyi—it was the week between the days of Schlabrendorff's and Gersdorff's attempted assassinations of Hitler —to send Bonhoeffer on another journey; in this connection there remained among the documents a note for Beck, which was to play a disastrous part when Dohnanyi was arrested. For the first half of April, it was arranged that Bonhoeffer should visit the Balkans, Italy, and Switzerland.

So for more than six months one moved to and fro between good and bad news from the Prinz-Albrecht-Strasse and from Keitel's office, between bold plans and detailed arrangements in case of arrest.

The Last Week. Torn between disappointment and relief, the whole family celebrated Professor Karl Bonhoeffer's seventy-fifth birthday on 31st March 1943. The children and grandchildren performed Walcha's[299] cantata 'Lobe den Herren' for the grandfather. A telegram of congratulation from the Oxford relatives was forwarded by Erwin Sutz from Switzerland. Klaus made a speech proposing the toast, and thanked his father for an upbringing in understanding and truth. With the well-wishers from the Charité there also came the bearer of a greeting from Hitler:

In the name of the German people I bestow on Professor Emeritus Dr. Karl Bonhoeffer the Goethe medal for art and science, instituted by the late Reich President Hindenburg. The Führer Adolf Hitler.

Only a few days later, the chief of the *Wehrmacht's* legal department, Dr. Lehmann, who was favourably disposed towards Dohnanyi, reassured Admiral Canaris that nothing unpleasant would be happening in the next few days, and that he was anxious for the matter to be taken out of the Gestapo's hands, if it could not be quashed altogether. Canaris passed that information on to Dohnanyi and Bonhoeffer as late as Sunday 4th April.[300]

At midday on Monday 5th April, Bonhoeffer tried to ring up his sister

299. The great blind organist and composer from Frankfurt.
300. This recollection does not tally with the account in K. H. Abshagen, op. cit., p. 351. But it agrees with what Christine von Dohnanyi wrote down as early as 1945.

Christine von Dohnanyi at her Sakrow house, from the Marienburger Allee. But his call was answered by an unknown man's voice. He at once thought: The house is being searched! Without disturbing his parents, he went across to his sister Ursula Schleicher in the next-door house, and got her to give him a good meal, after which he went up to his attic to check the contents of his desk once more. Then he waited next door with the Schleichers and me. About four o'clock his father came across: 'There are two men wanting to speak to you upstairs in your room!' Shortly afterwards, Judge Advocate Roeder and the Gestapo official Sonderegger drove off with him.

That was the third arrest that Roeder and Sonderegger made in person that day, and the fifth that was made on their orders. The others concerned Dohnanyi and Josef Müller and their wives.

Dohnanyi's arrest. Had Keitel now given his consent for Canaris and his office to be done away with? In any case, the military machine carried out its first measures in the presence of an official of the Reich Security Head Office, and later the hearings conducted by Roeder were regularly attended by Gestapo men.

On the Monday morning Roeder had informed Canaris of the investigation that was to take place at once in his office, and then, with Sonderegger, he searched Dohnanyi's office in the presence of Canaris and Oster. In many publications dealing with the Resistance, the proceedings of that Monday morning have been described in the version that Gisevius gave them after 1945 in his book Bis *zum bitteren Ende*, which sides with Oster against Dohnanyi, with whom his relationship had grown difficult as time went on.[301] We give here an account written down by Christine von Dohnanyi as early as 1945, when there was as yet no public account of the proceedings, so that what she wrote could hardly be dictated by polemical considerations.

The affair concerns some of Dohnanyi's slips of paper that were intended for Beck. One note said that Bonhoeffer would go with Josef Müller to Rome on 9th April. There Müller was to explain the failure of the attempted assassination in March. The slip, which was kept on a kind of 'playing card' usual for *Abwehr* commissions, bore an 'O', with which Beck, whose code name was 'Eye of a Needle' ('*Nadelöhr*') and who therefore initialled like that, had given his assent to the commission. Frau von Dohnanyi says that Bonhoeffer was to see Dr. Zeiger, the rector of the Collegium Germanicum, to discuss proposals and wishes from the Protestant side regarding the Pope's peace message.

Those groups of questions were set out in the document referred to, a slip of paper. It was understood all along by the people concerned that drafts of that

301. See K. H. Abshagen, op. cit., pp. 358 f.; G. Ritter, op. cit., p. 346; M. Boveri, *Der Verrat im XX. Jahrhundert*, Vol. II, 1956, p. 54; G. Buchheit, *Der deutsche Geheimdienst, Geschichte der militärischen Abwehr*, 1966, pp. 419 f. and elsewhere.

kind, if they fell into the wrong hands, were to be called 'coded words' ('*Sprachregelung*') by everyone concerned—that is, material that is not to be taken literally as it stands, but simply shows the direction in which the other party is to take his soundings, and is therefore the so-called 'playing card' of the *Abwehr* . . . A talk with Beck was arranged for the afternoon of the day of his arrest. At this talk some points in those proposals were to be discussed, so that Bonhoeffer, whose arrest was not reckoned as probable, could start the journey as soon as possible . . .

When Roeder now searched my husband's safe, there was nothing for my husband to do except put the said slip before the admiral in Roeder's presence and ask that he might still be allowed to finish that urgent business. But now an unhappy misunderstanding led Oster to think that my husband had put down the slip, whose contents he knew quite well, so that Oster could let it disappear quickly. Then my husband, as he told me later, whispered to Oster: 'Send my wife a slip'. He meant that I was to be warned. Obviously, Oster heard the word 'slip'. His loyalty as a comrade was stronger than his caution and when he thought for a moment that he was not being watched, he took the slip to hide it in the back pocket of his coat. Sonderegger of the Gestapo noticed the move, and that meant a worsening of the situation, both for Oster and for the whole business. Oster was told to go home where he would be under house arrest, and was not allowed to enter the High Command again, or to have any further contact with the members of the *Abwehr* . . .

The first interrogations were essentially about that slip of paper, which, unless it could be made to appear as official material, the prosecution would regard as irrefutable proof of highly treasonable activity. My husband at the moment of arrest had tried to take that line by making the slips a matter of open discussion. Oster had misunderstood him, and the situation now became critical through his suddenly denying ever having known its contents—an incredible assertion in view of the fact that he had tried to conceal it. He tried to prove this by the kind of initialling that was on it, and denied that he had himself written the initial, an 'O', under it. Only my husband's urgent request, which he conveyed to me in a secret note, to acknowledge the slip, in the general interest, as official . . . induced Oster—who had certainly acted with the best intentions and, as he himself said, had been advised in the matter by Gisevius—to acknowledge his initialling. After Canaris, in his interrogation, had also acknowledged the slip as being in the context of official activity, the main danger was eliminated, and Roeder now simply took the usual course of looking for any formal infringements in the official channels and in the making up of the slip.

After Frau von Dohnanyi had been released from the women's prison in the Kaiserdamm, Charlottenburg, at the beginning of May, and had secretly got in touch with her husband as well as with Oster and others, the dangerous affair of the slips of paper was so successfully manœuvred out of the danger zone that she played no further part in the whole business of the prosecution. Soon she did not appear further in Bonhoeffer's interrogations.

VIII THE ENGAGEMENT

In the race between revolution and arrest, Bonhoeffer wrote at Christmas 1942 the short essay 'Aften Ten Years'. He gave it to Dohnanyi and Oster, and left me a copy which has been preserved, hidden away under the roof of his parents' house. In it he wrote:

There remains for us only the very narrow way, often extremely difficult to find, of living every day as if it were our last, and yet living in faith and responsibility as though there were to be a great future . . . It may be that the day of judgment will dawn tomorrow; and in that case, though not before, we shall gladly stop working for a better future.[302]

How Bonhoeffer resisted a false apocalyptic interpretation of that time is shown most clearly by the story of his betrothal. During that winter he was so charmed by the naturalness and grace of an eighteen-year-old girl that he began to see her as his future life-partner. She allowed him to take a step that he had not been able to take ten years earlier.

Maria von Wedemeyer embodied for him what he had learnt to value in the Kleist relatives at Kieckow and Klein-Krössin—alert wisdom, freshness, nobility, and a poise that made her more than equal to dealing with life's gifts as well as its burdens. She was the third of the seven children of Hans and Ruth von Wedemeyer, and so a granddaughter of the aged Frau von Kleist-Retzow and an elder sister of Bonhoeffer's former confirmation candidate Max von Wedemeyer. Her father, a landowner of Pätzig in the Neumark, some sixty miles north-east of Berlin, was a man of wide interests, upright and responsive. He was enthusiastic and successful in the management of his farm and lands and had created the finest of hunting-grounds, and he devoted himself with equal vigour to movements for the reinvigoration of the Evangelical Church. He was a foundation member of the Berneuchen brotherhood, whose annual working sessions had taken place in Pätzig since the death of the Berneuchen landowner von Viebahn. Deeply concerned about the rise of National Socialism, he agreed to help his former comrade-in-arms von Papen in the formation of a new cabinet. But when he saw, after Hitler had seized power, how hopeless and compromising any attempt at cooperation would be, he definitely withdrew, and at once felt the consequences of political animosity towards him. Suffering from the inner conflict between conspiracy (his cousin Fabian von Schlabrendorff used to visit Pätzig) and his own military tradition, Hans von Wedemeyer fell as an officer on the eastern front in August 1942. On that occasion Bonhoeffer wrote to his widow on 25th August 1942:

Hochverehrte, gnädige Frau! It was about seven years ago that your husband

302. LPP, pp. 38 f.

sat in my room at Finkenwalde, to talk about the instruction that Max was then to have as a candidate for confirmation. I have never forgotten that meeting. The thought of it was with me during the whole time of the instruction. I knew that Max had already received, and would receive, what was vital from his home; and it was also clear to me what it means today for a boy to have a godly father who lives a full and busy life. When, as the years went by, I got to know nearly all your children, I was often impressed by seeing what a great blessing it is to have a truly Christian father. It is really one and the same impression that I have felt so deeply in meeting your family and relatives, your mother and your brothers and sisters. The blessing is, indeed, not something purely spiritual, but something that goes deep down to affect one's earthly life. Under the real blessing, life becomes sound, firm, confident, active, just because it is lived from the source of life, of strength, joy, and action. The picture of your husband that I have before my eyes today is of one who lived from such a blessing and handed it on in ultimate responsibility; I am thankful for it, and I should like to tell you so, *hochverehrte gnädige Frau*, in these hard days. If a man has handed on to his own people, and to many others, the blessing that he himself received, he has indeed fulfilled the most important duty in life, for he has himself become happy in God, and has made others happy in God. But the blessing in which he lived remains upon him as the light of God's countenance.

The spirit in which he lived will be the spirit in which you and your children are now together. The same earnestness with which he then spoke to me about his son's Christian upbringing will now inspire you to help your children to a Christian mourning for their father; the same love that was given to him for the Word and Sacrament will unite you with each other and with the community in heaven; the same spirit of sacrifice and obedience to the will of God will cause you to accept in quietness and thankfulness what God has sent you. How God can be praised by such Christian mourning of a whole family for the father who has been called home to God! My thoughts go out specially to Max.[303] How he must miss his father now. And I am quite sure that he can never forget or lose what he has received from his father, and that he is safe as his father was and is.

God help you, *hochverehrte gnädige Frau*, through his Word and Sacrament, to be yourself comforted and to comfort others. With kind regards to you and all your people, Yours respectfully and sincerely, Dietrich Bonhoeffer.

Maria had sometimes been, as a child, to her grandmother in Stettin, and had once been with her cousins to Finkenwalde. Now Bonhoeffer saw her again as a grown-up girl, when he spent a few days in Klein-Krössin between his journeys to Sweden and Italy. He remarked afterwards that the renewed meeting occupied him more than he liked at first to admit. But on the way to Rome, he said in a letter to me:

I have *not* written to Maria. As things stand it is impossible now. If no further meeting is possible, the delightful thought of a few minutes of high tension will no doubt melt once again in the realm of unfulfilled fantasies that is already adequately populated in any case. On the other hand, I do not see

303. At that time a soldier at the Russian front.

how a meeting could be contrived that she would find unobtrusive and in-offensive. One cannot expect that of Frau von Kleist either, in any case not as an idea of mine, for I am really not at all clear about it as yet.[304]

Not long after her father's death, Bonhoeffer saw Maria von Wede-meyer again several times in Klein-Krössin and in Berlin. Now he was no longer in doubt. But her mother was not ignorant of how things stood, and of course, she was anxious for her daughter, who was still quite young. Could the girl adequately weigh up the question of marrying a man whose political commitment and many involvements she certainly could not assess? So she decided to ask Bonhoeffer to talk things over with her.

On 24th November 1942 he went to see Frau von Wedemeyer in Pätzig, simply telling his people that he had to go to Pomerania again. The upshot of the conversation was that Maria's mother proposed that they should keep apart for a year. He was rather at a loss, and wrote to me on 27th November:

I think I could get my way if I wanted to; I can argue better than the others, and could probably talk her round; but that would not be natural to me, it seems to me wrong . . . and like exploiting other people's weakness. Frau von Wedemeyer is stronger through the loss of her husband—that is, in her very weakness—than if I had had to deal with him too. I must not allow her to feel defenceless; that would be mean, but it makes my situation more difficult.

Bonhoeffer rebelled. He wrote next day: '. . . everywhere the same out-of-date ideas from past times',[305] and shortly afterwards: 'I have been wondering whether you will just—without my knowing—very nicely and gently and skilfully . . . if you will write to Frau von Wedemeyer as a friend. But it could be later on as well, perhaps that would be even better.'

But no such letter was needed, for on 17th January 1943 Dietrich Bonhoeffer and Maria von Wedemeyer became engaged. He told his parents at the beginning of February. At the request of Maria's guardian, Hans-Jürgen von Kleist-Retzow, and her mother, he assured them that there should be a fairly long interval before the public announcement of their engagement and before their marriage.

The arrest cut through all their arrangements, and thereupon the families decided that the news should be made public. The strange engagement began. Bonhoeffer wrote from his cell in Tegel on 6th June 1943:

I can hardly tell you how very much my mother-in-law's letter moved me. That I had to cause her such an added grief, after all the anguish of the past year, has haunted me since the first day of my detention, and now she has

---

304. Letter of 25.8.1942, GS II, pp. 419 ff.
305. To E. Bethge, who was in a similar situation regarding young Renate Schleicher, having met the opposition created by her parents' anxiety, 28.11.1942.

actually made this distress that has come on us the occasion to abridge the period of waiting, and so made me very happy.

IX THE 'BOUNDARY SITUATION'

Now I want to assure you that I have not for a moment regretted coming back in 1939—nor any of the consequences, either. I knew quite well what I was doing, and I acted with a clear conscience. I have no wish to cross out of my life anything that has happened since.[306]

I became certain that the duty had been laid on me to hold out in this boundary situation with all its problems.[307]

The end of his activity as a free man in the Resistance Movement suggests a few summary thoughts on Bonhoeffer as a conspirator. The logical consequences of his actions, unusual for a Lutheran pastor and theologian, will appear more plainly than ever in the later account of the interrogations, and may shock the susceptibilities of anyone whose standards are those of traditional ethics and normal times. But one has to realize that what went on in those interrogations was only a continuation of what had been thought out and decided long before.

Today, in more orderly times, some people are reluctant to call Bonhoeffer a 'conspirator', and to give primary importance to such an originally degrading term. The further we are from the events, the more we hesitate to use the term. But it seems as if all attempts to tone it down fail to see the exceptional reality that Bonhoeffer faced, and merely cover up what is shown to us here.

Stages of Resistance

Bonhoeffer undoubtedly belongs to the small and vanishing group of churchmen who went over to active political underground involvement —that is, to 'conspiracy'. Besides the numerous people from the middle class and the nobility, from the military and the socialists, the list of victims of 20th July 1944 contains the names of three Roman Catholic churchmen: Father Delp, Prelate Müller, and Chaplain Wehrle; on the Protestant side we must add to Bonhoeffer the Confessing Church's legal adviser Friedrich Justus Perels.[308]

Bonhoeffer's entry into the conspiracy therefore placed him in a 'boundary situation'. A relevant factor was that in 1940 he was not tied to a parish through being its pastor, as most of his brethren were. Perhaps his life would have taken a different course if Bonhoeffer had been the pastor

306. LPP, p. 115.
307. LPP, p. 87.
308. See '20. Juli 1944. Ein Drama des Gewissens und der Geschichte', *Dokumente und Berichte*, 1960, 3rd ed., pp. 214 ff.; A. Leber (Ed.), *Das Gewissen steht auf*, 1954, pp. 187 f.; T. Prittie, *Germans Against Hitler*, 1964, p. 127.

of a parish in that year. As it was, however, the call to a 'conspiracy' against Hitler came to him in peculiar circumstances. He faced that call after he had gone through several stages of the resistance to the Third Reich, and had begun by hesitating at more than one stage of an intensified struggle. For each new stage of his resistance made him perceptibly more isolated.

I have tried elsewhere[309] to distinguish five different stages of the resistance in the National Socialist period, and to describe what it meant in each case to change one's point of view while in opposition. First, there was simple passive resistance; then there was the frankly ideological attitude which enabled the churches, or men like Count Galen, Niemöller, and Wurm, to meet their problems, though without formulating, or striving for, a new concrete structure for a political future. Thirdly, there was the stage of being accessories to the facts of preparation for a revolt, which brought in church officials such as Asmussen,[310] Dibelius, Grüber, or Hanns Lilje; then the fourth stage, that of active preparations for the post-revolt period, the most distinguished representative being Moltke, with Steltzer, Poelchau, and Hammelsbeck included. Finally there was the last stage, that of active conspiracy, in which anyone of the Evangelical Lutheran traditions found it most difficult to participate, as those traditions did not provide for anything of the kind. In that last stage there was no protection by the Church and no apparent justification of something outside all normal contingencies.

Of the church officials on the Protestant side, only four took that final step—Bonhoeffer and his friend Perels, and Gerstenmaier and his friend Schönfeld; each of those two pairs went into the half-light of active political conspiracy in different circumstances, with different presuppositions, and at different times, from the other.

The course of events did not favour the Bonhoeffer-Perels and the Gerstenmaier-Schönfeld pairs joining forces. Gerstenmaier had once gone into Heckel's service when (in 1936) the latter's differences with Bonhoeffer were at their height;[311] thus Bonhoeffer always saw Gerstenmaier as being associated with the Church External Affairs Office which collaborated theologically, ecclesiastically, and politically with the Third Reich, and in which he was still a consistory councillor, even at the time of the conspiracy, although after 1941 Klaus Bonhoeffer met him more frequently in his resistance circles. For his part, Gerstenmaier saw in Dietrich Bonhoeffer a Barthian who belonged to the Dahlemite wing of the orthodox and unpractical Confessing people. The theological thematic interests of the two men had always been in contrast to one

---

309. E. Bethge, *Adam von Trott und der Deutsche Widerstand, Vierteljahreshefte für Zeitgeschichte,* 11th year, 1963, No. 3, pp. 213-23, here pp. 221 f.
310. He says that in 1942 it was a case of his being drawn in rather than joining, *Luth. Informationsblatt,* 1st year, No. 17, pp. 284 f.
311. See Ch. X, pp. 423 ff.

another.[312] So they belonged to two different groups, each of which had at a different time played a leading part in political resistance.

We have already mentioned the not very happy relationship between Gerstenmaier's friend Hans Schönfeld and Bonhoeffer. Here the first years of the war brought about a certain change. Schönfeld had taken an interest in Bonhoeffer from the time that he had known how exceptionally well-informed he was politically; and Bonhoeffer had relied on Schönfeld since the latter had been able to help him to keep in touch with his Oxford relatives. Schönfeld went to the parents' house for the first time in the winter of 1940-1, when Bonhoeffer was staying at Ettal; later, when he went with Courvoisier on the latter's journey for the relief of prisoners of war, he visited, with Courvoisier, the Bonhoeffer brothers, and Justus Delbrück and Otto John in Berlin.[313]

Types of Resistance

The transitions from the first to the fourth stage of the resistance were almost insignificant compared with the transition from the fourth to the fifth and last stage. In open protest, everything was unequivocal—thoughts, actions, and personal integrity. But here it was no longer possible; and so Bonhoeffer and Gerstenmaier took upon themselves the odium of leading a double life, and they had to face the consequences.

Bonhoeffer was, by profession, academically, a theological adviser to the Confessing Church, but he had also become an under-cover man of the *Abwehr*; Gerstenmaier was a consistorial councillor in the Church External Affairs Office, and, in addition, an 'academic auxiliary in the information department of the Foreign Office'. Bonhoeffer had been drawn into the *Abwehr* circle through his family relationship to Dohnanyi; Gerstenmaier, through his work for the Church External Affairs Office, had to do officially with the Foreign Office, which sponsored him for his 'journeys abroad in the interest of the Reich'; with its help he kept Schönfeld in his post at Geneva, cooperated with people like Herr von Twardowski,[314] but also made friends there with Trott and Haeften, and through them with Hassell, and they took him to the Kreisau group. From the *Abwehr* and Foreign Office respectively Bonhoeffer and Gerstenmaier got the extra-parochial position that they so much needed, as well as their passports in the middle of the war. There they handed in their official agents' reports for the files, but more secretly the information needed by the conspirators. Everyone had to assume that those offices contained plenty of ardent Nazis, and might even have disquieting cross-communications with the Reich Security Head

312. See Ch. X, pp. 463 f.
313. J. Courvoisier, 'Theological Existence', IKDB, pp. 174 f.; also O. Hammelsbeck, 'In Discussion with Bonhoeffer', IKDB, p. 179.
314. See Ch. X, p. 423.

Office. Thus they constantly had to play a double part in their ecclesiastical as well as in their secular offices. They were both double agents.

That was because any responsible resistance under the conditions that Hitler had brought about was bound, strictly speaking, to take the form of a conspiracy. A spontaneous rising did not occur and could not be expected to occur; a spontaneous individual action might be brave, but it left out of account one's responsibility for the future; and there were scarcely the homogeneous lines of approach needed for a revolution that had the eruptive force to throw up a new form of social structure.

Bonhoeffer, therefore, did not commit himself either to the desperate action of an individual, or to the turmoil of a rebellion, or to the ideology of a revolution.

He went into a planned 'conspiracy' that answered for the past and was answerable for the future. That meant a conspiracy which was not to announce its existence in advance by premature collisions, but which acted only when there were good prospects of success from within and without. A conspiracy that would carry camouflage and disguise to extreme limits, so that one would lie better than the master liar. That meant that nearly all the conspirators who survived would have had to count on an act of indemnity;[315] the office papers, in which they had to make their efforts to reach top positions, naturally contain documents with which they could vouch for their irreplaceable usefulness for Hitler's war machine. The things that might be necessary were not only party badges and the Hitler salute; one might also have to remain in incriminating command posts, in the Army, in the *Abwehr*, in the Foreign Office, even in the S.S. The price had to be paid. 'We must stay, to preserve us from worse things'; that guilty remark of the early years of the Nazi period now became the order of the day for those who took over responsibility.[316]

That resistance as 'conspiracy' could not be undertaken till late. It was only when all the ways of legal opposition were barred and the people who were called on to bear responsibility in the various branches of public life had grown dumb that the moment for a conspiracy came. And it was only when the worst came to the worst, and Bonhoeffer the theologian had tried other ways to escape from his dilemma, that he took his stand and no longer ruled out that kind of resistance. As soon as tyranny, in the name of those whom it ruled, threatened the lives of its neighbours and degraded its own name, and as soon as the means came to hand, he felt that on moral grounds the hour for conspiracy had come.

After he had become connected with that 'conspiracy', Bonhoeffer assumed that his Church would no longer be able to use him, once the facts came to light. He knew that the Church was not yet in a position

315. After the war this became a reality for many in the hated Denazification Laws.
316. E. Bethge, op. cit., pp. 219 f.

to support him in something for which he could not ask it to accept joint responsibility. And he knew why his Confessing Church refused him a place in the Intercession Lists: not only because it had to be cautious in a matter of some danger, not only, too, because it did not yet know all the details of the conspirators' activity, but also, no doubt, because it could not yet think along the lines on which Bonhoeffer was committing himself, to answer the extraordinary demands of the situation.

Thus the 'boundary situation' led Bonhoeffer to abandon all outward and inward security. By entering into that kind of conspiracy, he forsook command, applause, and commonly held opinion.

He cannot even demonstrate its ethical validity when he must be most certain of it. He takes it on himself to be condemned before everything and everybody. Indeed, however anxious the responsible person is for success, he must not even turn that success into a god who is with him. Only the true God in the beyond knows whether, at the moment of action, that action has really been taken here in the name of life. And if the sacrifice is made and success is denied, there remains something equivocal about the best names. Bonhoeffer said in a sermon as early as 1932, without knowing how prophetic it was, that times would come again when martyrdom would be called for, 'but this blood . . . will not be so innocent and clear as that of the first who testified. On our blood a great guilt would lie: that of the useless servant who is cast into the outer darkness.'[317]

Evaluation

One can regard Bonhoeffer's participation in the German conspiratorial resistance as important, or as of only secondary importance, according to one's point of view.

If we think of his personal commitment, Bonhoeffer is one of the few figures of the political opposition who bore the burden. He gave himself up to sharing the common fate as completely as any did. The fact that he was not with the conspiracy actively from as early as 1938, but only as a confidant, is explained by his occupation. When he joined the political underground movement, opportunist considerations were far from his view. Afterwards, he no longer made reservations, but even sacrificed his professional reputation in the Church and in theology.

Bonhoeffer's position in the Resistance Movement was of no great importance politically, and he himself did not overrate his place and his professional competence in that respect. On the other hand, he tried in his work on ethics to see what, in that dangerous game, depends on the ability to exercise a practised and expert judgement on means, timing, and grouping. Moreover, political ambition was not one of his characteristics. Although he could not help seeing how practised political

317. E. Bethge, op. cit., p. 222; cf. Ch. VI, p. 176.

expertise became a pretext for avoiding vital decisions, he unerringly formed robust judgements in the political sphere, and he used them effectively. In the preparations for revolt, Bonhoeffer was not of the first political importance except through his journey to Sweden; and even then it was evident that he neither could be nor wanted to be merely a politician. He also knew quite well that his attempt to make contacts was only one among others that were often much more expertly handled.

As regards the planning for a future Germany and its constitutional forms, Bonhoeffer's share in the conspiracy was comparatively small, and we have no notes on it from his own hand. He got the Freiburg group down to work, and influenced the choice of subjects and experts, but confined himself personally to theological and ethical cooperation. The exact position to which he had come in the German resistance through his birth, his occupation, and his personal guidance, he saw as an incentive to examine exhaustively the traditions of his Church and its theology, when he should again have time for such work. For under the National Socialist attack, he had found church doctrine to be dangerously sterile. He often said that after he had finished his work in the conspiracy, he would like to go back to his own occupation, though with fresh insights.

From the point of view of the interpretation and the intellectual penetration of revolutionary activity, we can certainly count Bonhoeffer as one of the few of the innermost circle. He at once reflected the dilemma of Oster's notification to the Dutch of the date fixed for attack in the spring of 1940, and gave pragmatic and powerful expression to the outrageous situation, in which one could no longer love and save one's fatherland except with 'treason'. It was then that he wrote the analysis of the breakdown of reasonableness, of the ethical rigorist, of the man of conscience, of duty and private virtuousness.[318] Two years later he wrote for his companions, first of all Oster and Dohnanyi, as a Christmas present, the essay 'After Ten Years',[319] in which he answers for the place of their action, asserts the future fruitfulness of their enterprise, and describes soberly the far-reaching dangers of the way that they have to take:

We have been silent witnesses of evil deeds; we have been drenched by many storms; we have learnt the arts of equivocation and pretence; experience has made us suspicious of others and kept us from being truthful and open; intolerable conflicts have worn us down and even made us cynical. Are we still of any use?[320]

What Bonhoeffer said about 'conspiracy' in that essay was no apology

318. E, pp. 65 ff.
319. LPP, pp. 25-40.
320. LPP, p. 40.

written after the event; on the contrary, it was written during one of the most promising phases of the resistance, in order to strengthen his friends in their course of action.

When the numerous constitutional proposals of the resistance are forgotten—they were soon superseded—this analysis of Bonhoeffer's about a German conspiracy may perhaps still be interesting. In his capacity to express the spirit in which he and his friends were acting, he is still an effective witness to the resistance. But his merit here is that as a Christian theologian of the resistance he did not look on and analyse, aloof and critical, but coined valid formulas as the action went on.

But he formulated, as the common motive of the conspirators, not once more a 'faith in a single ideology regarded as all-conquering . . . but the common responsibility for Germany's shame, in which they knew themselves to be implicated, and for Germany's survival in the family of nations.'[321] At Christmas 1942 Bonhoeffer wrote:

The ultimate question for a responsible man to ask is not how he is to extricate himself heroically from the affair, but how the coming generation is to live. It is only from this question, with its responsibility towards history, that fruitful solutions can come, even if for the time being they are very humiliating.[322]

321. E. Bethge, op. cit., p. 219.
322. LPP, p. 30.

CHAPTER THIRTEEN

TEGEL

1943 - 1944

THE night of 6th April 1943 was cold in the reception cell at Tegel. Bonhoeffer could not bring himself to use the blankets of the plank-bed, as he could not stand the stench that rose from them. There was some-one crying loudly in the next cell. In the morning, dry bread was thrown through a crack in the door. The staff had been instructed not to speak to the new arrival. The warder called him a 'blackguard' ('*Strolch*').[1]

Bonhoeffer was then taken to the section where the solitary confine-ment cells were, where those condemned to death were held, bound hand and foot. A few days later he too was handcuffed when he was taken to town for his first interrogation at the Reich War Court (*Reichs-kriegsgericht*). As a member of the *Abwehr* he came under the jurisdic-tion of a military court, but Colonel Roeder, who conducted the hearing, always had beside him officials from the Reich Security Head Office (*Reichssicherheitshauptamt*).

The old Tegel prison was one of the military interrogation prisons. At first, Bonhoeffer was housed on the third floor, but later in the single cell, No. 92, on the first, because of the increased danger of bombing attacks.[2] He spent eighteen months in Tegel, until, on 8th October 1944, he was transferred to the detention cellar on Prinz-Albrecht-Strasse, the house prison of the Reich Security Head Office, close to the Anhalter railway station.

Bonhoeffer's period at Tegel was taken up with his stubborn—and successful—efforts to conceal or disguise the true facts. His family and friends assisted him in weaving a complex net of camouflage. Sometimes the threads became tangled, but on the whole it held until after the catastrophe of 20th July 1944, when gravely incriminating material was found in an emergency camp of the *Abwehr*. The discovery of these docu-ments at the end of September 1944, at the Zossen headquarters, put an end to Bonhoeffer's period of military confinement at Tegel.

We can understand Bonhoeffer's tactics during his interrogation by the War Court only if they are seen as part of a greater whole. Hans von Dohnanyi, the chief accused in the trial, was in far greater danger. His persecutors sought to strike, through him, at the whole *Abwehr* under Admiral Canaris. The others arrested, Josef Müller and, at the beginning,

1. LPP, p. 81.
2. LPP, p. 65.

the women Christine von Dohnanyi and Anni Müller, were accomplices in the Dohnanyi case. Bonhoeffer's trial, therefore, depended on the state of his brother-in-law's, on its being speeded up, for which he hoped with impatience, or its being delayed, which he was unhappy about. Bonhoeffer had to adapt his own behaviour to whatever Dohnanyi did. Let us, now, consider first the course of the Dohnanyi trial.

Then, after dealing with Bonhoeffer's period at Tegel and the case itself, we shall go on to consider his life in a military prison and the theological work he did there.

I TRIAL OF HANS VON DOHNANYI

Both Dohnanyi and Josef Müller were taken to the *Wehrmacht* prison at No. 64, Lehrter Strasse. This was for prisoners of officer rank.

Although the prison commandant, Lieutenant-Colonel Maass, soon proved a true friend of Dohnanyi and his family, the strain on Dohnanyi, especially in the first weeks, was almost unbearable. On him more than anyone else seemed to depend the fate of the resistance work outside, as well as the fate of the *Abwehr* and of course that of his family. He learned on 12th April that his wife had also been arrested. At first no one could check with Oster on the affair of the 'slips of paper'. On 16th April he was confronted with his wife for the first time, and on the 19th with Bonhoeffer. This was almost a relief; evidently they had not been caught out as contradicting each other.

During the preparations of the previous winter it had been agreed that if any points should come up on which the others could be incriminated, he was to take as much responsibility as possible himself. Being versed in military politics and legal matters, he would be able to make the quickest and most expert decisions concerning what accusations should be considered *Abwehr* secrets, which Canaris alone could make available for, or withhold from, investigation. Thus Dohnanyi did all he could to make his fellow accused seem as unimportant as possible. To this end he even gave up the opportunity of writing an Easter letter to his parents and children and wrote instead a 'personal' letter to Bonhoeffer in Tegel, reckoning of course that Roeder would read it. In it he wrote on Good Friday, 23rd April 1943:

My dear Dietrich, I don't know if I'll be allowed to send you this greeting, but I'll try. The bells are ringing outside for the service . . .
You can't imagine how unhappy I am to be the reason why you, Christel, the children, and my parents should have to suffer like this, and that my dear wife and you should have your freedom taken away. *Socios habuisse malorum* may be a comfort, but the *habere* is a terribly heavy burden . . . If I knew that you all—and you personally—did not think hardly of me, I'd feel so relieved. What wouldn't I give to know that you were all free

again; what wouldn't I take on myself if you could be spared this affliction. It was wonderful to be able to see you. I've been able to speak to Christel also —but what can you say in front of other people . . .

No one can know what it means not to be able to be with her in this time of stress. It certainly does not help in the matter of this trial . . .

The Fighting Positions

Although the reputation of the *Wehrmacht* was formally preserved in the trial, the actual battle was between the *Abwehr* on the Tirpitzufer and the Reich Security Head Office in Prinz-Albrecht-Strasse. Dohnanyi was both the key figure and the victim. The Reich Security Head Office kept discreetly in the background, but it kept itself informed of the course of events through an observer, once Keitel had released the whole affair for investigation by the court.

The hearing was conducted by Dr. Roeder, who, as a military judge belonged to the *Luftwaffe*. He boasted of being a frequent guest of Göring's at Karinhall and had won his spurs in 1942 with the death sentences against Arvid and Mildred Harnack and Schulze-Boysen in the 'Rote Kapelle' trial.[3] Roeder had connections with Müller, the notorious S.S. leader. Rüdiger Schleicher, who had once been offered the job in the Reich War Court and declined it for reasons of conscience, remembered that Roeder had once said to him : 'I stand on the narrow bridge between the Gestapo and the War Court.' Roeder sought and found support in the *Abwehr* itself, for there were of course in the legal division a few ill-disposed people who resented the fact that Canaris had appointed Dohnanyi legal adviser over their heads. Thus Roeder had some success when he questioned members of the legal and financial departments of the *Abwehr*. This also brought on more quickly the measures taken against him, which subsequently resulted in his being removed from the case. In the summer of 1943, Roeder had frequently questioned Canaris, who cleverly maintained the pretence of being anxious that the charges against Dohnanyi should be thoroughly and speedily investigated.

A bitter struggle ensued between Roeder and Dohnanyi. Each of the two lawyers thought he could see the real intentions of the other. As a Nazi, Roeder identified himself even at the interrogation stage with the prosecution. His aim, from the start, was to obtain a verdict of high treason against the State, and he treated the prisoner, detained for inter-rogation, as if he were already a criminal without any rights. He hinted to Dohnanyi in various ways the potential extent of his power and indicated that the case was arousing interest in the highest quarters. In

3. 'Rote Kapelle' was used as a cover name by the Gestapo for a Communist resistance group that had gathered around Harro Schulze-Boysen and Arvid and Mildred Harnack in the autumn of 1942, seventy-five members of which were condemned to death in the subsequent trials (cf. *Das Gewissen entscheidet*, ed. by A. Leber, pp. 111 f.).

fact, in the course of the investigation, apart from Keitel, progress reports were given to Müller, Kaltenbrunner, Bormann, Himmler, and even Hitler himself. But the endurance and skill of his adversary made things difficult for Roeder and put a quick conclusion, as in the 'Rote Kapelle' trial, further and further beyond his reach.

For Dohnanyi was not simply at the mercy of his accuser. Good friends in influential places sprang to his assistance, especially Canaris himself. The latter understood precisely the method of forward defence and covered everything that Dohnanyi's friends did in order to harmonize the statements of the isolated prisoners. In the Abwehr building itself Karl Ludwig Freiherr von Guttenberg, the editor of Weisse Blätter, was particularly active, as well as Emmi Bonhoeffer's brother Justus Delbrück, both of whom Dohnanyi had got into Canaris's department. When, after four weeks, Christine von Dohnanyi was released, through the intervention of various people, including her father, she maintained complete contact with her husband, with friends in the office on the Tirpitzufer, and, in particular, with Hans Oster, who had been dismissed on 5th April. Via this channel Dohnanyi was able to send requests and suggestions concerning the conduct of the investigation to Canaris, and vice versa.

An important factor was also that the head of the legal department of the Wehrmacht, Dr. Lehmann, who on Keitel's instructions had had to place the whole affair in Roeder's hands, was basically well-disposed. For instance, he successfully countered the suggestion that the prisoners should be dismissed from the Wehrmacht, which would have meant that they would have been at the mercy of the Gestapo. The tireless assistance of Dr. Karl Sack,[4] a judge of the general staff and chief of the army's legal department, was of crucial importance. Dohnanyi had come to appreciate the worth of this man at the time of the Fritsch crisis. He helped the prisoners with information wherever he could, even talking with Canaris after his dismissal in 1944. Dr. Schulze zur Wiesche, a lawyer who was close to the Confessing Church and could not at that time act officially for the defence because, as Dr. Sack told him, 'it would soon emerge that he belonged to the same group as the accused',[5] was able through him to make several visits to Dohnanyi in his cell at Moabit and later in the prison hospital at Buch, in the north-east of Berlin. It was a happy chance that Rüdiger Schleicher was able to frequent Sack's office without difficulty, because of his position as a legal colleague and a member of the legal department of the Luftwaffe. In uniform he did not attract attention. Although running far greater risks as a civilian, Friedrich Justus Perels was also an intermediary for

4. Cf. Ch. XI, pp. 528, 532. It is extraordinary that the literature of the resistance has so far taken hardly any account of this remarkable man, except for one small book (H. Bösch, Heeresrichter Dr. Karl Sack im Widerstand, 1967).
5. Reported by Dr. Schulze zur Wiesche on 2.6.1966.

Sack's information, which was then passed on in code in books and food parcels to the inmates of Moabit and Tegel.

Despite their good intentions, it did sometimes happen that Sack and his assistants pursued a different line from the prisoners, and the situation was assessed differently inside from outside. When, for example, the first grave charges were refuted, Dohnanyi and, still more, Bonhoeffer pressed for a quick conclusion to their case. Dohnanyi placed his hopes on Canaris, whose position, despite the dangerous information that the Reich Security Head Office had already acquired concerning the *Abwehr*, was still intact. But Sack was afraid of the political dynamite in the case, which, if the pace were forced, might lead to an unfavourable decision by Hitler himself. He was satisfied, as long as the case was not taken out of Roeder's hands. Sack's strategy was to keep the case out of the political sphere—in which he succeeded—and to manœuvre Roeder out of it and let it just 'run out of steam' as he put it, until the overthrow came. He was proved dramatically right when Josef Müller managed to detach his own trial from the others and was acquitted at the beginning of March 1944. The preliminary work had been successful. But the Gestapo announced that, immediately he was released, they would put Müller in a concentration camp.

With these sort of helpers, Dohnanyi and Bonhoeffer were kept well-informed in their cells about the progress of the preparations for the overthrow. This remained the case even when, after the break-up of Oster's resistance centre in the office of the *Abwehr*, the new centre had to be set up around Stauffenberg in the next building with General Olbricht. Until that point Bonhoeffer and Dohnanyi had had scarcely any connection with Stauffenberg, who was a 'newcomer'. However, Stauffenberg soon knew all about Dohnanyi and his case and, among other things, obtained for the tireless lawyer Schulze zur Wiesche the precious petrol which enabled him to visit Dohnanyi in the prison hospital at Buch at the beginning of 1944.

Three Stages

There were three separate stages in Dohnanyi's case. The first lasted until January 1944, and in it the Reich War Court, in the person of Roeder, acted with the Gestapo present, until Roeder was forced to leave the case. The second came to an end on 20th July 1944, and during it the plan was to let the case run out of steam under Kutzner. The third phase was dominated entirely by the Reich Security Head Office, represented by Walter Huppenkothen.

Roeder's Attack

The fateful slip of paper[6] that Roeder had seized at the time of the arrest

6. Cf. Ch. XII, pp. 691 f.

at the Tirpitzufer was immediately treated by him as proof of Dohnanyi's high treason against his country. Dohnanyi, however, obstinately insisted that this document was part of the ordinary official material of the Abwehr's work. The character of its contents, i.e. a code card used in routine counter-espionage, naturally had to be confirmed by Oster and Canaris. Roeder ordered that Dohnanyi's imprisonment be made as disagreeable as possible, refusing him permission to write, read or smoke, and threatening to 'finish him off', to have him 'tried summarily by the Führer' if he did not give him all essential information.' When finally the secret connection with Oster was established and the latter was questioned by Roeder, he explained that the fateful 'O' was his sign and confirmed the official character of the document as an Abwehr code card. After Canaris also had rejected any suspicious interpretation and acknowledged the document as part of Dohnanyi's ordinary official work, the greatest danger was over. Merely a few shortcomings in matters of official routine were established, a ridiculous anti-climax in comparison with the first sensational charges. But the mistrust and suspicion were not altogether at an end.

Roeder began his second assault with the investigation of 'Operation 7'.[8] With the help of the Reich Security Head Office he had, for example, bank accounts in Switzerland investigated by the lawyer Ruge and found it hard to understand why these researches did not show that Dohnanyi had used that operation to line his own pockets. The slightest indiscretion by those in the know, or even by those who were safe in Switzerland, could have produced serious complications. But no one slipped up, and the escapees in Switzerland kept as quiet as possible. Here again Canaris defended 'Operation 7' as part of the work of his department.

It was a long and wearisome task to answer the charges that men had been withheld from the forces because Oster's and Dohnanyi's department had declared that certain pastors were needed for special duties. But they gradually moved on to a more harmless plane, as it became more and more a question of the fact that certain official quarters had been by-passed.

The fourth area of investigation was Bonhoeffer's official journeys. These were thought to show that Dohnanyi and Oster had infringed the agreement between Canaris and Heydrich, the so-called 'Ten Commandments'.[9] But here again the responsibility was shifted to Canaris.

As well as all these attacks there was Roeder's persistent suspicion of Dohnanyi's official and private financial dealings. Documents were used in an inexact and selective way in order to isolate Dohnanyi morally. To be forced to defend himself on this trivial level was a great nervous

7. Cf. a note in Dohnanyi's diary of 5.5.1943.
8. Cf. Ch. XII, pp. 651 ff.
9. Cf. Ch. XII, pp. 629 f.

strain on him, as he was a very painstaking official, but in view of the far greater danger involved in the political charges, it was a blessing that his enemies became bogged down in this detailed accounting for foreign currency, travel, tax and interest, which took up a disproportionate amount of time without any tangible result being achieved. It is not necessary, in connection with Bonhoeffer's story, to go into this petty war inside the jungle of war regulations concerning book-keeping. It moved into the background as the real charges became more important.

By the end of July 1943, the most dangerous phase of Roeder's attacks was over. It seemed that they had managed to remove Dohnanyi's case from the political danger zone into the sphere of arguable questions of procedure. Dr. Sack had meanwhile convinced Keitel that Roeder was less concerned with Dohnanyi's misdemeanours than with discrediting Keitel's subordinate, Admiral Canaris and his department. Keitel told Dr. Lehmann to study the documents of the case and to report to him. As a result of this report, on 23rd July 1943, Keitel instructed that the grave political charges be dropped and the case no longer be conducted in terms of high treason. This was a considerable achievement, and it was yet another victory for Canaris. Sack passed on the information to the prisoners that the remaining charges concerning the pastors on special duties and the errors in matters of official routine would not amount to very much.

Removal of Roeder

But this did not mean that the danger was entirely past, for the accuser could still always use matters of form and procedure to bring up the political charges again. For this reason Sack did all he could to get rid of the dangerous Roeder and not to press for a speedy conclusion of the case. Roeder could be removed either by complaints concerning the conduct of the case or by his being promoted to a higher post somewhere else. Both things happened, in fact.

As early as May 1943 Dohnanyi had made a complaint concerning the way in which the investigation was being conducted to the War Court Department Chief, Dr. Schrag, a fraternity colleague of Karl Bonhoeffer's. Dohnanyi had to word it carefully, as it passed through Roeder's hands on its way through the official channels:

On 19th April the investigating magistrate informed me that 'the fate of my wife depended on what I said' . . . On 4th May he said that there could be no question of my being allowed to speak with her if I could not say anything more or different from what I had said hitherto . . . I was put in an especially difficult position because, on 13th May, he confiscated the notes that I had made for my defence during my confinement in order to refresh my memory . . . This defence material has not so far been returned to me, and I haven't even been able to look at it in order to supplement the rough draft of the minutes . . . In this connection I should like to mention that, according to something he said on the 9th of this month, it is doubtful whether I shall even be allowed to choose my own defence lawyer . . . It is of great importance to me that what I say should be taken down in the form that I consider correct. Since 13th May, when he refused to have certain statements of mine that I thought important for my defence incorporated in the minutes and broke off the interrogation without ever continuing it again, this has, on the whole, no longer been done in regard to the form of my statements.

Soon after this there was another letter to Schrag and Lehmann, but this one was not censored. In it he said :

. . . In accordance with the aim of the investigating magistrate to make the head of the department himself,[10] his chief of staff,[11] and his closest colleague[12] appear politically unreliable, the charges are presented without any attempt to discover the truth of the matter, without there being the least connection between what is said and the actual charges made, and without actionable consequences being drawn, or being able to be drawn, so that their sole purpose is to destroy my character . . . After the investigating magistrate failed to prove that there had been treasonable activities among the staff of the head of the department, which seemed to be an established fact for him before the enquiry had begun, he thought he could achieve his aim by the roundabout way of a general political disqualification . . . In this interrogation he again dealt with the document concerning 'Operation 7', using a principle of selection that showed clearly at once that his attack was directed less against me than against the head of the department . . . In connection with these cases the investigating magistrate seemed to accuse me—but in reality it was the head of the department—of not having a perfect political attitude and not being ready unhesitatingly to sacrifice myself for others . . .

But there were also complaints from other quarters. A Dr. Duesterberg, a department chief in the Supreme Military Command, whom Canaris had frequently sent to the hearing in the War Court, made first a verbal, and then a written, complaint that during these official discussions Roeder had tried to 'pump' him concerning the personal and political attitudes of members of the *Abwehr*. During a conference with Keitel, in which *Abwehr* personnel included Canaris, Sack, Piekenbrock, Bentivegni, Klamroth and Duesterberg, the majority agreed with a negative judgement concerning Roeder. In his report Duesterberg also mentioned that Roeder had called the troops at the disposal of the *Abwehr*, the 'Brandenburg' division, a 'lot of shirkers'. This came to the ears of their commander, General von Pfuhlstein. In his own written vindication Dohnanyi also stated that he had heard this expression from

10. Canaris.   11. Oster.   12. Dohnanyi.

Roeder. Pfuhlstein had it confirmed to him when Dohnanyi was admitted to the Charité and could have special visitors. He then called on Roeder and boxed his ears. In the meantime, Roeder was promoted to another post. As far as the case was concerned the Roeder era was over, and in February 1944 Kutzner took over.

This brought a total change in the manner of the investigation, but did not alter the threat to Dohnanyi. Keitel's nervousness in regard to the Reich Security Head Office continued undiminished.

This nervousness had led Dr. Langbehn[13] to attempt to obtain a declaration from Himmler and Müller that the Reich Security Head Office had no further political interest in the case. Such a declaration would inevitably have encouraged Keitel to order that the whole affair be dropped. But Langbehn himself had been arrested as he was preparing this step—a critical moment for Christine von Dohnanyi, who hastily had to destroy everything that might point to her connection with Langbehn.

The Clinic

One day Keitel even countermanded the relaxation of the prison rules that had been permitted because of Dohnanyi's illness.

Dohnanyi's health had been seriously affected by the constant strain. In the summer of 1943, unlike Bonhoeffer, he became ill. In June he developed an inflammation of the veins in both legs. The family attempted to get him a consultation with Sauerbruch, the leading German surgeon in Berlin, but at that time Roeder was able to prevent it.

When, on the night of 23rd November 1943, the heavy British bombing attacks began again, the prison received its first direct hit. Dohnanyi's cell was struck by an incendiary bomb. He was found with his speech and vision disturbed; he was suffering from a brain embolism. The next morning Sack got Dr. Lehmann—Roeder's telephone was out of order—to have Dohnanyi transferred on his own responsibility to Sauerbruch's clinic at the Charité hospital. Only two days later, a furious Roeder confronted Sauerbruch at the Charité. The latter, however, declared that Dohnanyi was in danger of his life and refused to let him be moved. Unfortunately for Roeder, important documents of the military court had perished in the flames during the night raid. Roeder now gave orders that apart from his wife and children no one was to visit Dohnanyi. However, Sauerbruch and Dr. Wohlgemuth, his assistant at the time, permitted infringements of this order and concealed them.

Thus eventually all Dohnanyi's chief friends made their way through the blackout to his bedside: Klaus Bonhoeffer and Rüdiger Schleicher, Perels, Delbrück, Guttenberg and Otto John. Dohnanyi learned of the

13. Cf. Ch. XII, p. 657.

progress since October 1943 of plans for the overthrow. Klaus Bonhoeffer and Otto John now belonged to the intimate circle of the conspirators and worked with Josef Wirmer and Jakob Kaiser. John established contacts via Spain and provided Stauffenberg with information.

In those winter days new dates for the overthrow were fixed and then changed. Young officers like Axel von dem Bussche and a son of Kleist of Schmenzin wanted to use the occasion of a display of new uniforms before Hitler. But the uniforms were burned in a bombing raid and the date for displaying them had to be changed. Nevertheless, after so many reversals the news was such as to cheer up Dohnanyi.

A few weeks after Roeder's first visit to Sauerbruch, he sent some men to the Charité with their own ambulance in order to collect Dohnanyi, but Sauerbruch would not let them near his patient and turned them out of the clinic. But now Roeder was able to make Keitel ask Professor de Crinis to give an opinion on Dohnanyi's condition. De Crinis, who had succeeded to Karl Bonhoeffer's chair and was now the head of the nerve clinic in the Charité,[14] was prominent in the S.S. and an intimate of Schellenberg in the Reich Security Head Office. He gave the report desired, and so, on 22nd January 1944, when Sauerbruch was away, a military doctor appeared in Dohnanyi's sickroom and removed him to the prison hospital at Buch. On 10th February 1944, de Crinis told the Reich Security Head Office:

Group leaders . . . as a result of my investigation von Dohnanyi was removed from the Charité Clinic and taken to the special hospital at Buch . . . As you will see from my report, I have stated that Special Officer von Dohnanyi is fit to be tried and I estimate that he will be in eight to ten days . . Heil Hitler! Yours, de Crinis. Please inform District Chief Kaltenbrunner of this communication.

Playing It Down

With this, despite the longed-for removal of Roeder—he was promoted to be a military judge with an air fleet in the Balkans—the case looked less promising. The interest of the Gestapo was increasing.

Moreover, at the same time there was more and more bad news from the circle of Dohnanyi's friends: Moltke and the Solf circle were arrested. But the worst of all was that in February 1944 Canaris fell as the result of a totally unexpected event, a desertion from the *Abwehr* in Turkey. The Reich Security Head Office had now got what it wanted. The whole *Abwehr* organization was forthwith placed under its jurisdic-

14. Cf. Ch. X, p. 471.
15. This led to the grotesque situation that even *Abwehr* soldiers from the Confessing Church such as Pastor Willi Rott, for example, automatically became members of the Reich Security Head Office. Thus at the end of the war Rott disappeared for months without a trace in the 'automatic imprisonment' in the American camp for civil internees at Moosburg.

tion.[15] A more important consequence for Dohnanyi was that now Delbrück and Guttenberg had to leave the *Abwehr* network.

Despite this, Sack's strategy of letting the case run out of steam was still successful. Things did not suddenly change in the *Abwehr*. Colonel Hansen, a fellow-conspirator, continued to direct the military *Abwehr* as head of a department within the Reich Security Head Office until his involvement in the conspiracy became apparent after 20th July.

Dohnanyi was acquainted with the new investigator by the Ministry of Justice and the Supreme Court in Leipzig. Kutzner handled the case without the political zeal of his predecessor. He, too, was under political pressure; but he still said to Sack that nothing could be done, either legally or factually, with Roeder's charges. We may assume—as Frau von Dohnanyi believed—that he suspected the real state of affairs. He was now working towards a trial with the political sting taken out of it. Frau von Dohnanyi was able to visit her husband regularly in Buch. Dr. Schulze zur Wiesche, who was very close to Perels, was working with Dohnanyi in Buch on his written defence. Since Dohnanyi was not yet fit to be interrogated again, Josef Müller's trial was carried through as a separate case and was concluded with the astonishing verdict of acquittal 'because his innocence had been proved'. Throughout, Müller maintained the position of 'ignorance of who was responsible for what in the *Abwehr*' and successfully passed the suspected evidence as counter-espionage by the *Abwehr*. The fact that Kaltenbrunner threatened him with a concentration camp if the verdict were confirmed was regarded for a while by Dohnanyi and Bonhoeffer as a bluff. They pressed for their own cases to be concluded, as they considered the situation at the state military court favoured them. But Sack warned them. Then, in June 1944, Dohnanyi contracted serious scarlet fever with diphtheria and peripheral paralysis. He had to be taken to the prison hospital for contagious diseases at Potsdam. Kutzner could speak with him only through an isolating window.

Because of the daily-awaited *Putsch*, Sack was feverishly active. He obtained the postponement of the execution of Klaus Bonhoeffer's friend, Nikolaus von Halem, condemned to death by the People's Court. At the beginning of July he had the sick Dohnanyi informed that Kutzner had finally asked Keitel to suspend the whole case, and the suggestion was that the trial against Dohnanyi should be postponed until the end of the war and that he should be interned in a sanatorium, thus remaining out of reach of the Gestapo. The process of 'playing it down' was, in fact, working. Then came 20th July 1944.

In the Hands of the Gestapo

On 21st July 1944, Dohnanyi's case fell entirely into the hands of the Gestapo. The defence ring in the legal department of the Army was

smashed, and Sack himself was among those whose life was forfeit. At
7.30 a.m. Sonderegger who had accompanied Roeder on 5th April 1943,
called at the house of Dohnanyi's parents-in-law, the Bonhoeffers, in
the Marienburger Allee and enquired about Dohnanyi. The father passed
him on to his daughter Christine. Sonderegger also asked her about
Oster, but she said she knew nothing about him. Dohnanyi's quarantine
isolation gave even the Gestapo difficulties. Karl Bonhoeffer was allowed
to visit his son-in-law once again in his professional capacity as doctor:

I was able to see Hans last week. He is in a lamentable condition because
of the appalling diphtherial paralysis which is, however, somewhat better
in his face and throat, but still continues in his arms, legs and trunk and
makes him almost incapable of moving. We may certainly expect that he
will recover, but it is a terrible burden and trial of patience for him and for
Christel. Dietrich is in good health, and we hope to see him in the next
few days. No doubt he suffers greatly from being isolated in these eventful
times and finds it hard to concentrate on Dilthey, whom he is now studying
for his *Ethics*.[16]

Only on 22nd August did Sonderegger dare to remove Dohnanyi from
Potsdam in an ambulance and take him to the concentration camp of
Sachsenhausen. For the first time this broke off for a considerable period
the contact between Dohnanyi and his wife. On 5th October 1944,
Huppenkothen entered the sickroom of the concentration camp and
threw a document on Dohnanyi's bed, saying, 'There! At last we've got
the evidence against you we've been looking for for two years.' Dohnanyi
replied, 'Oh, have you? Where did you find that?'[17] Huppenkothen
had been told to examine the material found at Zossen by Sonderegger
on 20th or 22nd September. In Huppenkothen's document on Dohnanyi's
bed there were photocopies of Dohnanyi's memorandum for the generals
from the winter of 1939-40 and a call to the German people written for
Beck.

From this day on, Dohnanyi made his sickness a weapon, the only one
he had left. With superhuman energy he studied and practised its
symptoms in order to prolong them for as long as it might be necessary.
Perhaps in this way he would be able to prevent the destruction of those
whose fate was linked to his until after the moment of the general
collapse. In this he almost succeeded.

II THE ENQUIRY DIRECTED AGAINST BONHOEFFER

Bonhoeffer's share in what had to be concealed or dealt with on one's
own responsibility in the interrogations of this detention period was not
as great as Dohnanyi's. But a lot depended on how exactly Bonhoeffer

16. To E. Bethge, 30.7.1944.
17. As he reported to his wife in their secret correspondence. Cf. also Appendix F in the
German edition.

kept to the agreed rules of procedure. The slightest carelessness or discrepancy in the story could ruin everything. To have pursued one's own way now for reasons of one's profession or one's private integrity, would really have been treachery.

Thus Bonhoeffer accepted his situation, which had long before been decided and gone over a hundred times, and drew the consequences. For this his Lutheran tradition provided no kind of guidance. 'At the beginning I was worried about whether it was really for the sake of Christ that I was causing you all such grief; but I soon dismissed this question as a temptation . . . and accepted it cheerfully [i.e. his border-line situation], and have continued to do so until today.'[18] The fight of the conspirators was to be continued in prison under new conditions, but with the old skill and alertness.

We shall also be dealing with the fears that Bonhoeffer had in regard to his physical and mental sensitivity in the face of possible torture. But the new task brought with it the strength that it required. From the first day on he kept himself physically fit by doing exercises and eating whatever nourishing food his family and friends sent to his cell. At no stage of the long struggle did he give up his conviction that by his endurance he was sharing in a great cause: 'The thing for which I should be condemned is so unexceptionable that I should only be proud of it.'[19]

Up to 20th July 1944, Bonhoeffer calculated again and again that there were good reasons why his case should have a favourable outcome. Sometimes he even thought that his imprisonment would soon come to an end. There were both interior and exterior reasons for this. A political prisoner in natural self-defence continually sets himself new dates for his release in any case. Hundreds of people in the same situation did the same thing at that time. But Bonhoeffer could in fact base his optimism on the favourable course of the investigation, which sometimes, of course, made him, not more hopeful, but more impatient. Moreover, as we saw with Dohnanyi, he was kept constantly informed of the fresh preparations for the overthrow. One day, his uncle, General von Hase, the city commandant of Berlin, made a conspicuous visit to Tegel to see his imprisoned nephew. After this, Bonhoeffer wrote to me, on 30th June 1944: 'I hope we shall be together again early in the autumn!'[20]

Bonhoeffer's period at Tegel can be divided into three sections. The first, from April to July 1943, was taken up with the interrogation by Roeder and ended with a charge being laid. The second, from August 1943 to April 1944, is that of his continually aroused hopes that there would be a trial; dates were fixed and then cancelled. In the third, from

18. Cf. LPP, p. 80, and also Ch. XII, pp. 696 ff.
19. LPP, p. 89.
20. LPP, p. 190.

April to September 1944, he accepted the strategy of 'letting the case run out of steam'. In this period he again concentrated on theology. On the discovery of the material at Zossen, this period came to an end with a plan of escape and his being transferred to the Gestapo prison in Prinz-Albrecht-Strasse.

Fighting Chances

Bonhoeffer's really tough struggle for his case belongs in the first of the three sections mentioned; between April and August 1943.

He was helped over the first weeks of total isolation by keeping in his interrogations to what had previously been carefully agreed on, namely, the strategy of pushing all responsibility for details onto those who gave the orders in the *Abwehr*, namely Canaris, Oster and Dohnanyi. In this way, Bonhoeffer came through without involving himself in any serious contradictions.

Then there began the arranged passing of information from prison to prison through his family and friends. One way in which it was done was by making particular marks on the pages of the reading matter that he was allowed to receive, as a prisoner held for interrogation. For instance, Bonhoeffer asked for a volume by Karl Holl to be sent him from home. If the owner's name, 'D. Bonhoeffer', was underlined in the book, that meant that it contained a message. The message was entered by putting a faint pencil mark under a letter every ten pages, starting from the back. The letters marked in this way made up for instance the sentence: 'O. now officially acknowledges the Rome coding card', so that Bonhoeffer could now argue with confidence about the business of the slips of paper, if necessary. He replied in a similar way when he gave back the book. Thus he once marked the message: 'I'm not certain that the letter with Hans's corrections has been found, but think so.' This referred to the affair of being exempted from military service, especially Bonhoeffer's letter of complaint to the Gestapo of September 1940.[21]

For hours the family sat deciphering the messages, so that they could reach Dohnanyi, or Perels and Sack, or Delbrück and Canaris.

In the prison of Tegel the isolation to which Bonhoeffer was first condemned was eased after a short period. The fact that the prisoner was related to the city commandant of Berlin had become generally known, and the attitude of the warders changed. Bonhoeffer's mother had asked her cousin to telephone Tegel. Suddenly Bonhoeffer became a kind of star prisoner. The prison commandant, Captain Maetz, an official who always tried to do the right thing, gradually extended the permission for his parents and his fiancée to visit him for the maximum period, if it was approved by the investigating magistrate, and also allowed him to

21. Cf. Ch. XII, pp. 602 f.

receive the vital packages. But above all, Bonhoeffer won the hearts of some of the guards, who ended up by doing everything for him, carrying out the most dangerous assignments as go-betweens on his behalf. Thus, for example, in June 1944, it was possible for me to have a whole hour with him in the visitor's cell alone, when he had permission to receive a visitor, so that we were able to discuss many things unhindered. One of the warders shut us in together. Roeder suspected that things were going on behind his back, but he never found anything out. Even the Gestapo was not able to discover anything later. None of the kindly-disposed guards ever betrayed anything, nor was one ever betrayed by the others.

Roeder himself behaved in a far more dignified way with Bonhoeffer, after his initial severity, than with his legal colleague, Dohnanyi. Bonhoeffer appeared to be, formally, far more cooperative than he in fact was. He presented himself as a pastor unfamiliar with military and *Abwehr* matters.

I am the last person to deny that I might have made mistakes in work so strange, so new and so complicated as that of the *Abwehr*. I often find it hard to follow the speed of your questions, probably because I am not used to them.

Bonhoeffer used his inexperience as a weapon of defence. In contrast to the fears of many of those involved, he was not so ignorant that he made any disastrous mistakes. His triumphant remark in a letter to me on 30th November 1943 was justified: 'Roeder was too anxious at first to finish me for good; but he has now to content himself with a most ridiculous charge, which will bring him little glory.'[22]

During the period of the interrogation, Bonhoeffer used up a lot of paper in his cell writing draft letters to Roeder, in which, after a hearing, he supplemented or corrected his statements. Roeder had from time to time encouraged him to make these notes, and he seized the opportunity to gain time and consider thoughtfully how to build up further the edifice of his stories. The notes that have been preserved give a fairly exact picture of what was at stake in this tiny corner of the fight of the Resistance; the way in which Bonhoeffer defended himself and concealed the real facts of the conspiracy; what he produced and what he suppressed. The fragmentary investigation in his *Ethics*, 'What is Meant by "Telling the Truth"?'[23] emerges in these months, and the notes reveal something of the true background of that study. Its confusing content shows unsparingly the consequences of the conspirators' struggle. The fact that Bonhoeffer wrote his essay in those weeks shows how much he was aware of his dilemma, and that he did not seek to pretend to himself or to suppress anything. He did something else. He

22. LPP, p. 102.
23. E, pp. 363 ff.

could have destroyed his drafts, except for a few references to fact; but instead he preserved them carefully and gave them to his father to look after when, after 20th July, he cleared his cell of its accumulated objects.

The notes show how far the enquiries against Bonhoeffer ran parallel to those against Dohnanyi, covering the same four points: 1. his exemption, as a means of escaping observation by the Gestapo, in order to be able to continue his Church work; 2. 'Operation 7', which was to save, among others, Charlotte Friedenthal, who worked for the Confessing Church; 3. the journeys, which were suspected to have had nothing to do with military intelligence; and 4. the flagrant exemption from military service of officials of the Confessing Church. Each one of these points could probably skirt what the investigation assumed from the beginning was 'high treason and treason against one's country'. But it never penetrated to the real facts of the conspiracy.

The Abwehr Exemption

The circumstances and the date of Bonhoeffer's exemption to serve with the *Abwehr* took up most of the time of the interrogation. He was first accused of evading military service in September 1940, with the help of the *Abwehr*, and of seeking to circumvent the ban on his speaking that the Gestapo had imposed on him.

Bonhoeffer argued that the best way for him to escape from the Gestapo, if further interference from it was to be expected, would have been a straightforward army call-up. But, he argued, the Gestapo's action was not directed against him alone, but was part of a routine injunction against six theologians, of whom he was one;[24] moreover, as he said,

in order to avoid all further conflict, I withdrew into the Bavarian mountains in order to write a long work of scholarship. I had informed the Gestapo, as was obligatory, and really had nothing more to fear from this quarter . . . It was my brother-in-law who suggested to me that with my church connections, I should enter the service of the *Abwehr*. Despite considerable inner scruples, I took advantage of his offer because it provided me with the war work that I had wanted ever since the beginning of hostilities, even making use of my ability as a theologian.

He countered the charge that he joined the *Abwehr* immediately after the Gestapo's action by this explanation of a positive desire to serve.

This had meant a great inner release, since I saw it as a welcome opportunity of rehabilitating myself in the eyes of the state authorities, which I was anxious to do in view of the offensive and, to me, completely unjustified charge against me. The knowledge that I was being used by a military department was, therefore, to me personally of great importance. I made a great sacrifice for this chance of rehabilitation and for my work in the service of

24. Cf. Ch. XII, p. 602.

the Reich, namely the offering of all my ecumenical connections for military use. I think that this idea of my rehabilitation played a role with my brother-in-law as well. He knows me well enough to realize that the political charge against me bore no relation to my own inner feelings and to know how much I suffered from it . . . Perhaps I may also add that if I really only wanted a dispensation in order to continue with church work, I could certainly have obtained this in Schlawe at the superintendent's request . . .[25] But in January 1941, I received the dispensation, not for church work, but expressly for work in the *Abwehr* . . . How could it ever occur to me that there was any objection to my being made available for the *Abwehr*, since, as was explicitly confirmed to me, Admiral Canaris had desired and given the order for it. When I asked sometimes whether the fact that I was not regarded as *persona grata* by the Gestapo could not cause difficulties, both for the *Abwehr* and for myself, I was told that these things had nothing to do with my military function and that the *Abwehr* worked with all kinds of men that were useful to it. This completely reassured me.

Next to 'all kinds of men' Bonhoeffer had first written 'we work with enemies, Communists, Jews—why not with the Confessing Church', but he crossed it out.

Roeder attacked from another quarter. It was not only to escape the Gestapo, but also to be able to continue with his church work. Roeder made the point that General Superintendent Dibelius had declared that he had been told this about Bonhoeffer. Bonhoeffer did not find this difficult to answer:

When meeting colleagues that I had largely avoided for this reason during the last years . . . I also found it difficult to talk about my present work. In so far as they knew of my relations to my brother-in-law, as did, for example, General Superintendent Dibelius, and Superintendent Diestel, and asked me, I always told them—as I had arranged with my brother-in-law—that I was working for the Supreme Military Command in Munich and abroad. They were church assignments, as the Supreme Military Command was interested in church and ecumenical questions. Even Dibelius could not know that I was working for military intelligence, but could only deduce it; for, quite intentionally, I never told him. I also had to preserve the fiction that my work was primarily for the Church, which—apart from security reasons—I did for the sake of the other pastors, to whose ears it might have come and done me harm. Hence I took care that my dispensation was understood in this way in church circles. That it threw a rather strange light on me and on the military department concerned couldn't be helped. So Dibelius's evidence will also have been along these lines.

As a matter of fact, Dibelius said to me on 13th October 1961, 'I was never interrogated by the War Court. What I said to Bonhoeffer about

25. He refers to the dispensation of pastors in this ecclesiastical district, which had come about through the good relations between Superintendent Block and Major von Kleist in Schlawe.

his exemption has never, I think, been divulged to anyone.' The
unscrupulous, but also unreal and hence unintelligent way in which
Roeder tried to play off so-called confessions of his victims against one
another emerges from a note that Dohnanyi made in this context for his
defence, probably in August 1943:

In one of my interrogations, Roeder said that Dietrich had 'confessed' that
he had been in constant touch with Dibelius, who had provided him with
news of church politics and that he had passed these on to me. Since the
latter statement is not true, the former isn't either. Alas, one of Roeder's
many bluffs.

Bonhoeffer countered the charges in regard to his exemption from
military service, which arose as a result of statements by Schmidhuber,
the Munich consul in the autumn of 1942, by calling his knowledge
one-sided. He met Schmidhuber as a fellow-prisoner in Tegel and was
able to harmonize his own story with his. Bonhoeffer noted down the
following for Roeder:

I know . . . that he did not want Schmidhuber to know anything about
the military assignments that I received directly from the Admiral . . . I
myself have certainly often expressed my joy at the opportunity they gave
me to cultivate my ecumenical relations. It is no different from when, for
example, a student or a chemist is sent abroad and is able to work where he
finds it interesting and at the same time has particular military assignments
to carry out.

When it became clearer what the charges were going to be, probably
around the end of June 1943, Bonhoeffer returned again explicitly to the
question of his exemption. In his statement he now appealed to the
popular understanding of Romans 13 as expressing faith in authority, a
view which, in fact, he pointedly opposed.

As an argument it certainly may not have any cogency for you—but perhaps
you will believe me personally, and it is with this hope that I say that it is
very difficult for me to see how the earlier conflicts with the Gestapo, which,
as I profoundly believe, emerged from a purely church attitude, led to my
being held capable of such a grave offence against the obvious duties of a
German towards his people and his country. Still I cannot believe that this
is the charge that is really levelled against me. Would I, in that case, have
turned to an old officers' family, all of whose fathers and sons have been in
the field since the beginning of the war, many of them winning the highest
decorations and making the greatest sacrifice of life and limb, to find my
future wife, who has herself lost both her father and her brother at the front?
Would I, in that case, have abandoned all the commitments that I had
undertaken in America and returned to Germany before the outbreak of war,
where I naturally would expect to be called up at once? Would I, in that
case, have volunteered as an army chaplain immediately after the war broke
out? . . . If people want to know my idea of the Christian's duty of obedi-

ence towards authority, they should read my interpretations of Romans 13 in my book, *The Cost of Discipleship*. The call to submit to the will and demands of authority for the sake of Christian conscience has probably seldom been expressed more strongly than there. This is my personal attitude to these questions. I cannot judge how much such personal arguments mean legally, but I cannot think they can be simply ignored.

Operation 7

The interrogations concerning the moving of fourteen Jews to Switzerland[26] were concentrated at the beginning of June 1943. Here Bonhoeffer had to be careful not to do injury to Dohnanyi's and Canaris's defence. He could rightly maintain that his part in the operation was only peripheral. He was responsible for including Charlotte Friedenthal in the group and also, by introducing Schmidhuber to Koechlin, for making it possible for the fourteen to travel to Switzerland. Thus he did not deny that he was concerned on behalf of someone who worked for the Confessing Church and had asked Schmidhuber to help. 'I shall not deny for a moment that in this whole case the charity and caring attitude of the Church played an important part for me.'[27]

There was a tough struggle between Roeder and Bonhoeffer concerning the exact moment at which Schmidhuber had been sent to Koechlin and at which Bonhoeffer had spoken to Fräulein Friedenthal. The reason for this was that the accused members of the *Abwehr* were anxious that the date should be as early as possible, i.e. before the beginning of the deportation of the Jews from Berlin, so as to substantiate their claim that it was a genuine military operation and not a charitable work by the *Abwehr*. But Roeder sought to establish a later date in order to prove that there had been collusion to camouflage what was going on, namely, sabotage of the Jewish policy of the Nazis. First, in his oral interrogation, Bonhoeffer had been led to admit that the event took place on an indefinite date in spring, 1942. This is why he later corrected himself in writing to Roeder and stated definitely that he had sent Schmidhuber very soon after August 1941—and certainly before the deportation began.

Operation 7 soon disappeared from the interrogation because Canaris explicitly covered it. Bonhoeffer could say to Roeder with a clear conscience:

Fräulein Friedenthal . . . visited me once briefly and asked me if I thought that she could legitimately carry out the assignment which she presumed would be given her. At the time I said 'yes' . . . She spoke only of the fact of the assignment, not of its specific nature. I have never known what it was.

26. Cf. Ch. XII, pp. 651 ff.
27. The notes concerning Operation 7 were written around 10. and 12.6.1943.

He could say that quite honestly because the assignment had never had 'a specific nature'.

The Journeys

In Bonhoeffer's notes made at Tegel in 1943 the foreign travels play a remarkably small part. Right up to September 1944, the investigation never came anywhere near the true facts.

Roeder was concerned primarily with why, how often and how long Bonhoeffer had stayed in Berlin between his assignments, a city from which he had actually been banned by the Gestapo. Had he really been there in order to take up church work again? Bonhoeffer noted as follows:

I had to be constantly in Berlin for the following official reasons: 1. before and after every journey; 2. to make preparations for particular journeys which sometimes took a long time; 3. I was expressly told that I would be at the disposal of Admiral Canaris for special assignments, and so I was frequently asked for addresses, introductions and advice.

Bonhoeffer told the investigating magistrate at length of how the long stay in Berlin from April to June 1941 was taken up with vain preparations for a trip to Sweden, because, among other things, the contacts with Forell were not working properly. It was fortunate that Bonhoeffer was able to explain a long stay in Berlin in the winter of 1941-2 by saying he had pneumonia. In the autumn of 1942 Schmidhuber's arrest had forced the central office of the *Abwehr* continually to make fresh plans:

I myself repeatedly asked to be allowed to do some more travelling, as my military inactivity was becoming frustrating. The personal reasons for my liking Berlin—i.e. my books, which I needed for my work, and my elderly parents, whom I didn't want to leave more than necessary, especially in view of the air-raid warnings—I have already given.

The very full treatment in the hearing of Bonhoeffer's exemption from military service is quite disproportionate to these meagre findings concerning his foreign travel. It was only the problem of the exemption, and not of the travel, that became the subject of Roeder's charges. This proves how well they had done in keeping the conspiracy out of the danger zone. But it shows above all that the finding of the document (with a new travel assignment for Bonhoeffer) at Dohnanyi's arrest with Beck's fateful 'O' on it was later much overestimated.[28]

Niesel's Exemption

Bonhoeffer's attempts to use the *Abwehr* to keep officials of the Con-

28. Cf. Ch. XII, p. 691.

fessing Church for the service of the Church—whether by taking them
directly into the *Abwehr*, as with Rott and myself, or by influencing
other departments in the Supreme Command of the Army, as with
Wilhelm Niesel, Ernst Wolf and the son of Wilhelm Jannasch—also
occupied far more of the hearing than Bonhoeffer's contacts abroad.
After the 'combing out' of civil departments, in order to obtain recruits
to replace the men lost at Stalingrad, and after the severer penalties for
the evasion of military service the authorities were especially nervous on
this score.

Among Roeder's finds in the searches of 5th April there was a letter
of Bonhoeffer's to Dohnanyi, in which he anxiously asked help for
Wilhelm Niesel, who was 'threatened' with the call-up. This word
'threatened' was for Roeder a clear argument that Bonhoeffer had
indulged in anti-military activities. At the end of June 1943 Bonhoeffer
wrote to Roeder:

. . . I must admit that [the word 'threaten'] taken by itself does make a
very disagreeable impression. On the other hand, I should like to say the
following: 1. If a man like Niesel had come under an officially recognized
church authority, it would undoubtedly have declared him indispensable for
purely church reasons. 2. Only a Church whose faith has an inner strength
can perform its grave service on behalf of its country during a war. But
whatever one thinks of the Confessing Church, one thing can never be said
of it without completely misunderstanding it, namely that in it the 'call-up'
was ever regarded as a 'threat'. The hundreds of young pastors of the Confessing Church who volunteered and the large proportion of them who laid
down their lives are a sufficiently eloquent testimony to the contrary. Nor
have I ever spoken to a single pastor of the Confessing Church who did not
joyfully embrace his call-up as an inner liberation from the burden of
political suspicion that rested on the Confessing Church, as a long-sought
opportunity of proving his own attitude and readiness for self-sacrifice as a
soldier. The fact that Pastor Niemöller volunteered for military service right
at the beginning of the war had its effect on the Confessing Church . . .
Because on this point we can have a very clear conscience, I thought that in
an urgent particular case such as Niesel's I might, and, indeed, had to, act
to preserve a pastor for the service of his Church and his country, provided
that this could be justified on military grounds. It was not my job to know
about the latter, which is why I consulted my brother-in-law. Many of
my former pupils who have now been killed or are still at the front as soldiers
have said that despite their happiness at serving their country, they have only
one anxiety, namely that during this period the churches at home should not
be completely uncared for . . . Two things influenced my action: I know
that even religious men can have very different opinions concerning the
Church, but, particularly in the war, no one should deny that the motivating
force behind its conviction and its action is love of the German people and
the desire to serve it during the war in the best possible way. Since the
beginning of the war I have had several long discussions with Minister
Gürtner, whom I knew personally, and have asked that the church struggle

be settled and that the various sections of the Evangelical Church should work together. I made suggestions to Dr. Gürtner on this subject, which he then discussed with Kerrl, the Minister for Religious Affairs, who welcomed them with interest. In December 1940 Dr. Gürtner explicitly told me, during a walk together in Ettal which lasted several hours, that he hoped to achieve this and the way in which he proposed doing so. His death a month later, and the illness and death of Minister Kerrl have destroyed this hope. It was an attempt to establish peace within the Church during the war in order to make the maximum energy available for its conduct. Even this unsuccessful attempt means that I may consider that I did whatever I could to achieve the smoothest and greatest possible war effort on the part of the Church.

Thus that very side of the Confessing Church which Bonhoeffer regarded as dubious had to serve here in his defence.

The Charges

The deeper suspicions of both Roeder and the Reich Security Head Office were scarcely wholly dissipated on all four counts, Bonhoeffer's extra-parochial exemption, Operation 7, the travel and the exemption of Niesel from military service; but the initial charges of high treason and treason against his country could not be sustained. Only in autumn, 1944, were there better proofs of this. After Keitel's order not to continue the case on the basis of this suspicion, Roeder stopped interrogating Bonhoeffer. On 30th July he told him that he would now be laying a charge and that he ought to see about someone to defend him. This was in marked contrast to Dohnanyi, whom Roeder threatened a few days later, saying that he would not allow him a lawyer of his own choice. Bonhoeffer immediately wrote to his parents two letters which passed through Roeder's censorship:

30th July 1943. Dear Father and Mother, At our session today in the War Court Dr. Roeder gave me permission to write to you and to Rüdiger Goltz on the subject of my defence. Since I don't know Rüdiger's exact address in Bavaria, I wanted to ask you to contact him. I don't know whether he can do it himself because of the injury to his leg, which I hear has become worse. But he's sure to be able to recommend someone suitable. Dr. Roeder thought the defence lawyer would need one day on the documents, another for consulting with me, and another for the hearing, i.e. three days in all. This is not a lot, but I imagine you too, Father, know many lawyers. And of course you know Dr. Sack[29] from the Lubbe case. But I wonder if such a big man would really take on a case which must seem trivial to him. Also, he's supposed to be terribly expensive. I only wanted to remind you of this and am not very sure about my facts. I'm thinking in terms of a calm, experienced, older man who is not committed in the matter of church politics, someone who can be trusted as a lawyer and a person. I don't know anyone myself,

29. This Dr. Sack is not the same as Dr. Karl Sack; cf. Ch. XIII, p. 706.

but you'll find the right person. It would be nice if you could attend to this soon. By the way, I can write to you every four days now, which is wonderful for me. I think I'll alternate between you and Maria. Thank you for everything and please don't be worried. With love to you and all the family, Your Dietrich.

This was a carefully considered text. Bonhoeffer was hinting to the investigating magistrate who read the letter at his excellent connections. Von der Goltz, who once defended Goebbels, was still regarded highly by Hitler. On the other hand, he was telling his parents that none of the well-known lawyers of the Confessing Church, such as H. Holstein, should be drawn in. In the letter of 3rd August, which also passed through Roeder's hands, he indicated a certain disappointment.

As far as my request for a lawyer is concerned, I hope that you have not been worried, but are awaiting the course of events as calmly as I am. You really mustn't think that I am in any way depressed or worried. Of course it was a disappointment, as no doubt for you also. But in some ways it is also a liberation to know that now the thing for which we have been waiting so long will be finally settled. I'm waiting daily for definite news . . . If Rüdiger Goltz is not free at such short notice, it doesn't matter. Dr. Roeder said explicitly that it's something that any decent lawyer could do, and I'm happy so long as it's a competent, decent and warm-hearted man, and a calm and dignified negotiator who will preserve the polished tone of the hearings—and you are the best judge of that. Personally, I think that it's best to say oneself what one has to say, but a lawyer is necessary for the legal matters, of which I know nothing. [And he added later the following, which was meant sincerely:] . . . it would be good if the man took time over me and wasn't too hasty. I think a lawyer ought to be like a doctor, who should never give the impression that he has too much to do.

The charge was now that the placing of Bonhoeffer and Niesel on the reserve list had been an anti-military act. All the other points were dropped. This emerges clearly from a final letter that Bonhoeffer wrote to Roeder:

Dear *Herr Oberstkriegsgerichtsrat*, You have allowed me to write to you again, and I want to do so today for the last time before the trial. In the three days since you told me that I was going to be charged, I have taken your advice and tried to go over the whole affair in peace and quiet. I won't bother you with personal matters. I don't need to tell you what a charge against me of acting contrary to the war effort means to me professionally, and personally, as far as my family is concerned; you know my professional and personal situation well enough. If the law demands that the charge should be made, then it must; I understand. That I didn't expect it, may be because I was not familiar with the text of the law and because I felt innocent of the charge and, having considered what you told me on Friday, still do . . .

There followed a lengthy defence, saying how he saw the two points of the charge, his own position on the reserve list and the attempt to help Niesel. Canaris knew and could answer for why he was taken on by the *Abwehr*, and Dohnanyi would explain how it was that they wanted to keep Niesel working for the Church. In the meantime, Dohnanyi had been informed what Bonhoeffer had said about this.

Some weeks later Dr. Wergin, an excellent lawyer and a friend of Klaus Bonhoeffer, accepted the brief to defend Bonhoeffer. The War Court, now moved to Torgau, confirmed him as defence lawyer on 16th September, 1943. After that Wergin was able to visit Bonhoeffer regularly in Tegel. Things seemed to be going well.

The Notes

The literary remnants of this cover-up and camouflage are, in the way that Bonhoeffer preserved them, important documents for the complete picture of his share in the conspiracy. Although some of the family and many in the Church would have preferred to suppress these, I am convinced that to do so would be to falsify the true character of the solidarity which Bonhoeffer had undertaken with the conspirators. The political responsibility involved allowed of no 'pious' exception. The exceptional times called for exceptional sacrifices.

Bonhoeffer did not for a moment refuse the sacrifice of his integrity, but he did not make it easily. He thought it possible that his Church, as the guardian of bourgeois morality, never before confronted with this kind of challenge, would hesitate to regard him as one of its own, because to do so would mean to acquire a new perspective. He wrote concerning this on 15th December 1943:

Then[30] I should discuss with you whether you think that this trial, which has associated me with the Security Branch Resistance Movement (I hardly think that has remained a secret), may prevent me from taking up my ministry again later on. At present you are the only person with whom I can discuss this question, and perhaps we shall be able to talk it over together if you are allowed to see me. Please think it over, and give me your candid opinion.[31]

This discussion took place. His correspondent, already too deeply drawn into the reality of that situation, did not argue against it. But he put Bonhoeffer's question to his friend Hans Lokies, the head of the Gossner mission and then gave Bonhoeffer the answer on 2nd January 1944:

He did not see any problem at the time when all disguises would be dropped, and as yet no one in authority or anywhere else could seriously deal with the subject because of lack of knowledge. Nor did he think that there was a definite general mood against you, because the prestige that you enjoy as a theologian is too great and unassailed.

30. i.e. if I had been with him and been able to have a long discussion. 31. LPP, p. 107.

But Bonhoeffer still knew what difficulties there were in the way. He realized that the Old Prussian Council of Brethren would not put him on the list of intercessions. He was all the more delighted when he heard that the Breslau Confessional Synod had remembered him by name in its intercession.

He personally never doubted the course he had chosen and the opening up of new insights. Thus he calmly made 1 Peter 3: 14 his own: 'But even if you do suffer for righteousness' sake, you will be blessed. Have no fear of them, nor be troubled.'[32] And this serenity was combined with what he had said at Christmas, 1942:

Will our inward power of resistance be strong enough, and our honesty with ourselves remorseless enough, for us to find our way back to simplicity and straightforwardness?[33]

It was based on the fact that in his cell he was also able to write:

'Cast me away! My guilt must bear the wrath of God;
the righteous shall not perish with the sinner!'
They trembled. But with hands that knew no weakness
they cast the offender from their midst. The sea was there.[34]

Second Phase: Dates for the Trial

After the charge was made, the tension relaxed, and Roeder lost his keen interest in his victim. But for Bonhoeffer the trial of patience was just beginning.

First he thought that after the last hearing in the War Court the trial would be over by August. But nothing happened to start with, because after the three severe raids on Hamburg Goebbels set in motion a comprehensive evacuation plan for Berlin, and various courts were moved to Torgau, a small old town on the river Elbe sixty miles south of Berlin. This worried his family, for there was for some days the threat that Dohnanyi would be moved to Torgau too, which would have put an end to the vital communication between the prisoners and those helping them. However, the particular department handling the War Court finally remained where it was, only Roeder himself disappearing for long weeks from Berlin.

On 25th September 1943, a regular warrant was made for Bonhoeffer's arrest, and he was officially charged with anti-war activity. This again aroused his hopes for an early date for the trial. From Hassell's diary we can see the interest that the members of the resistance groups took in the 'Dohnanyi case'. In November 1943 Hassell wrote:

A charge has now been made against Dohnanyi. [Oster] has seen it and said to me that there were a few slips on some points, but Goltz, who is to

32. LPP, p. 95.   33. LPP, p. 40.   34. LPP, p. 223.

defend him, is reasonably optimistic. Politically, nothing seems to have been crystallized despite the zealous efforts of the malign prosecutor. [Oster] also is now accused because of two people he exempted. It is all part of an attack against the set-up of Admiral Canaris, which is unpopular with the Party.[35]

The 17th December 1943 was fixed as a possible date for the trial, but when Dohnanyi fell ill this date was abandoned. The idea of getting on with Bonhoeffer's case separately was strongly attacked, because it was desired not to expose Bonhoeffer alone to the imponderables of a trial concerning matters of the *Abwehr*.

Bonhoeffer was very unhappy about this decision and wrote on 18th December:

As far as I could see, I should have been released on 17th December, but the [lawyers] wanted to take the safe course, and now I shall probably be kept here for weeks if not months. The past weeks have been more of a strain than anything before that.[36]

Although Bonhoeffer thought that 'on purely legal grounds my condemnation is out of the question',[37] he was under no illusion concerning the fact that the Gestapo could intervene, with disagreeable consequences.

I can (I hope) bear all things 'in faith', even my condemnation, and even the other consequences that I fear (Ps. 18:29[38]); but to be anxiously looking ahead wears one down. Don't worry about me if something worse happens. Others of the brethren have already been through that.[39]

There were now hopes for a date in February 1944, when Dohnanyi had been declared 'capable of being tried' by de Crinis and taken to Buch, and Müller conducted his own case so well—without, however, effecting any change in his position. Again Bonhoeffer faced two possibilities:

It looks as if something will be decided about me in a week's time. I hope it will. If it turns out that they send me in Martin's direction[40] (though I don't think that is likely), please make your mind easy about it. I am really not at all worried as to what happens to me personally. So please don't you worry either.[41]

His disappointment concerning the fresh postponement was intense, and Bonhoeffer was very dissatisfied with his friends outside:

About myself, I am sorry to have to tell you that I am not likely to be out of

35. U. von Hassell, *Vom Andern Deutschland*, p. 333.
36. LPP, pp. 108 f.
37. LPP, p. 97.
38. 'Yea, by thee I can crush a troop; and by my God I can leap over a wall.'
39. Letter of 22.12.1943, LPP, p. 115.
40. Dachau concentration camp, where Niemöller was.
41. Letter of 14.2.1944, LPP, pp. 132 f.

here before Easter. No change can be made while Hans is sick. I cannot help feeling that there has been a lot of messing about and dreaming while the simplest things have been left undone. I'm sure that everyone concerned has meant well . . . I am simply amazed that for the last six months nothing has actually been done, although people have obviously sacrificed a great deal of time and sleep on my account with their deliberations and their discussions. The only thing that could have taken place automatically, namely that my case be settled before Christmas, has been prevented . . .[42]

The title of the book *Widerstand und Ergebung* [English title: *Letters and Papers from Prison*], taken from this letter, did not, then, originate in the grand context of one special day in the conspiracy, but in the distressing disagreements of his friends concerning the best date for his trial.

Third Phase: Playing It Down

In April 1944, Sack's final message reached Bonhoeffer's cell at Tegel, saying that he should no longer expect any early change to be brought about by a date being set for the trial. This precipitated Bonhoeffer's most important creative period in Tegel. He now firmly set about doing theological work.[43] Only now, on 4th and 5th May, did Bonhoeffer meet Kutzner, the new head of the investigation. But this calmed him rather than produced new tension.

Just lately I have been in the city[44] again a few times; the result has been quite satisfactory. But as the question of the date is still unresolved, I am really losing interest in my case; I often quite forget it for weeks on end.[45]

He now derived excitement from a quite different quarter: from the preparations for the *Putsch*, of which he could now only be a passive observer. His expectations rose still further after the visit of his uncle, General von Hase, to the guard-room at Tegel.[46] A week later Bonhoeffer wrote:

Who knows—it may be that it[47] will not have to be too often now, and that we shall see each other sooner than we expect . . . We shall very soon now have to be thinking a great deal about our journey together in the summer of 1940, and my last sermons.[48]

This hinted at the imminent *coup* in the East Prussian General Head-quarters. Finally, on 16th July, he became even more explicit; his

42. Letter of 21.2.1944. There follows the passage under the phrase 'Resistance and Sub-mission' (*Widerstand und Ergebung*), LPP, p. 133. Cf. also LPP, pp. 78 f.
43. LPP, pp. 148 f.
44. In the War Court.
45. Letter of 7.5.1944, LPP, pp. 158 f.
46. LPP, pp. 188, 189 f.
47. Writing letters.
48. LPP, pp. 190, 193.

reference to his brother Klaus meant simply that the conspiracy had reached its goal.

I am glad that K[laus] is in such good spirits; he was so depressed for some time. I think all his worries will soon be over; I very much hope so for his own and his family's sake.[49]

The Escape Plan

After the débâcle on 20th July, the only church newspaper still with a licence wrote:

The frightful day. While our brave armies, courageous unto death, are struggling manfully to protect their country and to achieve final victory, a handful of infamous officers, driven by their own ambition, ventured on a frightful crime and made an attempt to murder the Führer. The Führer was saved and thus unspeakable disaster averted from our people. For this we give thanks to God with all our hearts and pray, with all our church congregations, for God's assistance [sic!] and help in the grave tasks that the Führer has to perform in these most difficult times.[50]

Thousands in the Church read this, and for many it was not merely editorial comment, but the expression of their own opinion.

On 21st July, Bonhoeffer was sure that his fate was sealed. In the sick bay of the prison he heard the news broadcast from foreign stations, and from his family he heard of Sonderegger's tracking down of Dohnanyi, or, rather, of his quarantine station. A rumour that Oster had committed suicide reached him, and he soon heard that Canaris had been arrested on 23rd July. But nothing happened to him for weeks. He went on writing his theological work.

At the end of August a new danger threatened. On 18th August Hans John was arrested, who, as legal assistant to Rüdiger Schleicher, had been sent by the latter on several journeys within Germany on behalf of the conspiracy. His brother Otto John had been able to escape to Spain in time. On 22nd August, Dohnanyi was taken to the concentration camp of Sachsenhausen. 'Renate will have written to tell you that Hans has been taken to the camp hospital in Brother Scharf's parish.[51] I am so sorry for Christel and for him; but perhaps this will mean that he will be treated more speedily. Please don't ever get anxious or worried about me, but don't forget to pray for me.'[52]

Christine von Dohnanyi asked the people who wrote to Bonhoeffer to stop, for safety's sake, their secret correspondence with him, smuggled

49. LPP, p. 194.
50. *Pfarramt und Theologie*, No. 7/8, p. 35.
51. Sachsenhausen concentration camp.
52. Letter of 23.8.1944, LPP, p. 215.

through the warders. Bonhoeffer himself did not follow this advice for another month.

In the days when the total situation for the family rapidly deteriorated because of the find at Zossen, Bonhoeffer began to consider seriously a plan for escape that had hitherto been only a vague idea. His most faithful guard, Corporal Knobloch, a worker from the north of Berlin, agreed to 'disappear' with him. Other members of the conspiracy tried the same thing, but only a few, such as Jakob Kaiser, succeeded in getting away. Knobloch wanted to go out of the gate with the prisoner Bonhoeffer while he was on duty and then disappear with him. The family obtained a mechanic's uniform for Dietrich. On Sunday, 24th September, Rüdiger and Ursula Schleicher drove to Berlin-Niederschönhausen with their daughter Renate Bethge and handed Knobloch a packet with the clothing, as well as money and food coupons, so that they could be left for the escapees in a summer house amongst allotments where vegetables were grown for the suburbs of Berlin. Everything seemed ready for a flight in the first days of October. But the following Saturday put an end to the plan.

When Klaus Bonhoeffer came home from work on 30th September, he saw a suspicious car standing before his garden gate in Eichkamp. He immediately turned round and went to his sister Ursula Schleicher in the Marienburger Allee. There one event followed another. On this Saturday General von Hase's wife came out of prison, her husband having been hanged. She was branded and had nowhere to stay. Her relatives had refused to take her in. Ursula Schleicher offered her refuge. Almost simultaneously the guard, Dietrich's emissary, arrived from Tegel in order to discuss details concerning false passports and possible contacts with the chaplain to the Swedish Embassy. But there was no time for this at that moment, and they asked him to tell Dietrich of the new turn of events—the impending arrest of Klaus—and to come again soon.

There followed a terrible night, in which Ursula Schleicher wrestled for a solution with her brother Klaus—his wife Emmi happened to be with her evacuated children in Schleswig-Holstein—flight, suicide or arrest. The next day, Sunday, 1st October, the Gestapo car appeared in the Marienburger Allee at the time for going to church. Klaus was taken out of the same house as Dietrich had been eighteen months before, but now under far more disturbing circumstances.

On Monday, 2nd October, the guard from Tegel was at the house again. He said that Dietrich had given up the escape plan so as not to make things more difficult for his brother and not to expose his parents and fiancée to an extra danger. Two days later, on 4th October, Rüdiger Schleicher was arrested at his office. On 5th October the Gestapo also arrested Friedrich Justus Perels. On the same day the poem on Jonah was written.[53]

53. LPP, pp. 222 f. There it is still wrongly described as written in September.

It was Sunday 8th October, when Dietrich Bonhoeffer was taken from Tegel to the underground prison of the Reich Security Head Office in Prinz-Albrecht-Strasse. His companion in distress, Josef Müller, had been there since 27th September. This was the beginning of a period of totally new enquiries.

This treatment of the period at Tegel up to the end of the military arrest has dealt with only one side of it. But Tegel also opened up for Bonhoeffer new areas of his experience of life and his theology. These are the areas that are reflected in the published letters from prison and have made him so well-known.

III THE CELL AT TEGEL

Bonhoeffer had known Tegel, the north-western suburb of Berlin, from his youth because of its beautiful park with Schinkel's little palais for the Humboldt brothers. It was an attractive area, but bounded in the south by the Borsig locomotive factories—an object of allied air attacks —and by a rambling old prison. It was here that he lived in a room seven feet by ten with a plank bed, a bench along the wall, a stool and a bucket, a plank door with an observation hole to look in from the outside and a garret window above his head on the other side.

We have more writings by Bonhoeffer from the eighteen months in this cell than we have from any other period of his life; notes, letters, scholarly and literary writings. They also contain evidence of suffering and anger, but never of self-pity or scruples concerning what he was doing:

> Driven and hunted by men,
> They make us helpless and condemn;
> Bearing the burdens of our abusers,
> It is we who are the accusers . . .[54]

This was the attitude he took with all his visitors. When once I told Frau Kleist-Retzow of the visit I was allowed to make to Bonhoeffer in June 1944, and she replied, 'How moving it must have been for you', I mentioned this in a letter to Bonhoeffer, adding: '. . . of course it was "moving", but emotion was not our first concern, because we went gaily, concentratedly and as quickly as possible *medias in res*. This is because you have no self-pity and do not seek for any acknowledgement of what you are doing.'

Nevertheless, the son of an upper-class family and an aesthete did have to wrestle with certain things in his situation, especially at the beginning of his unaccustomed new life. There was much that he did not speak of.

54. *Auf dem Wege zur Freiheit*, p. 11.

Justice or Responsibility

Concerning life in the cell and the strain of his interrogations Bonhoeffer said, 'I regard my being kept here . . . as being involved in the part that I had resolved to play in Germany's fate. It is with no reproach that I look back on the past and accept the present.'[55] Why all this had to happen and the way in which it had to happen—on this there is surprisingly little to be found in Bonhoeffer's papers from prison. We have mentioned his reflection on what he was doing, in his essay, 'What is Meant by "Telling the Truth"?'[56] There are also formulations in his literary writings on the subject. There everything else that we have can be properly understood only against the background of the conspiracy and its consequences, but it is all already the result of considerable transformation.

There are good reasons for Bonhoeffer's reserve about giving a connected account, whether in the systematic way of an ethical treatise, or in the form of an apologia, of why he continued with the conspiracy during his confinement for interrogation. Externally, it was the danger of providing his enemies with welcome material, which forbade any treatment of the subject in writing; but inwardly it would have contradicted Bonhoeffer's character to accompany his actions with apologias while he was still involved in them. Moreover, why should he justify himself when there was no competent forum to address?

The representatives of the Church could not be at that time a forum for him. They knew too little of the events and of the extent of the extermination of the Jews to be able to estimate the necessary degree of the conspirators' involvement. Even in the Councils of Brethren their voices were almost silent. The professors of theology and ethics had scarcely considered within their intellectual deductions the crisis of all ethics, from which one day new principles were to emerge.

Still less could officials, soldiers, or German public opinion constitute such a forum, for they had long shared, either actively, or silently, in the régime's outrages against justice.

And there were very few even abroad, whether in the ecumenical movement or among the neutral or allied nations, who could have constituted a forum before which any self-justification would have seemed appropriate. In part they were blind to the areas in which they also were involved in guilt, as in the policy against Jewish refugees. Bonhoeffer knew something of this. For the rest they had not so far experienced, as members of the German resistance had, the split in their loyalty to their government and to their country, so were not in a position to judge.

Bonhoeffer did not set about justifying his actions himself, but rather

55. LPP, p. 115.
56. Cf. Ch. XIII, p. 717.

rendering an account of them to himself. He would have accepted the charge that what he had done was not a 'good response' to the challenge of the age, but, rather, a very tardy one. That he wanted to give an account of his extraordinary behaviour and make it possible for it to be interpreted properly is seen in the fact, among other things, that he preserved all his notes. Justification, however, was for him something that only God could do. And for him the responsible attitude was not to take his justification, before, during and after what he did, into his own hands.

Thus in Tegel he spoke only seldom or indirectly concerning his actions. The profoundest reason is that it was part of the nature of what he did that it should take place without explanation and without being approved. Sometimes, however, this became almost intolerable for him. In a dramatic fragment, written in 1943, he made the protagonist say:

. . . Let us learn for a while to do the right thing without talking about it . . . A person who knows that death is near has his mind made up, but he is also silent. Wordlessly, and even, if it must be, misunderstood and alone, he does what is necessary and right, he offers his sacrifice . . .

Why am I using such big words? Why don't I simply say what I mean and know? Or if I don't want to do that, why don't I remain silent entirely? How hard it is, to do what is necessary and right, remaining truly silent and yet not understood.[57]

Shock of the Arrest

The concomitant circumstances of 'wordless action', namely life in his cell, cost Bonhoeffer more, to begin with, than he wanted to admit. There was the meagre food, the dirt, the ruffians with the keys and the humiliation of the handcuffs, but he came to accept these things. His separation from his friends and his family was more difficult to endure; he felt much more strongly that he was now the victim of time, dragging on with no fixed points to be looked forward to. He noted down the fact that his predecessor in the cell had relieved the pressure of his long suffering by scratching on the wall: 'In a hundred years it'll all be over.'

The first thing he did was to set himself a strict régime of his own from which he did not depart: physical exercise, his long-accustomed meditation, the learning by heart and reading of scriptures after he was given back his Bible on the third day.

Then he proceeded to observe in himself, as if in a psychological analysis, the break with his past that this arrest constituted and the experience of time, which had become an enemy. As soon as he was given pencil and paper, he began to collect notes for an extended work. There was little writing material to begin with, and he had to use the most wretched pieces of paper.

57. GS III, pp. 479 f.

Among these was a leaf from a writing pad on which his father had had to write in the guard-room, on 8th May 1943, the exact contents of a food parcel that he had brought to the prison for his son. It has, in his father's hand, a long list comprising tobacco, matches, a tin of pork fat, malt extract, pumpernickel, etc. This scrap became welcome writing paper for Bonhoeffer. In between the names of the foodstuffs he noted ideas and half-sentences that are a moving testimony to the content of his meditations and analyses in the first weeks, ideas that we see emerging again, in a more integrated way, in many of the more ordered writings of the later weeks. Thus we find on this scrap of paper:

Separation from people, from work, the past, the future, from marriage, from God. The various inner attitudes towards the past . . . forgetting . . . the way experiences are cut up—Fulfilled, unfulfilled, according to history—Self-deception, idealization; concerning the past and concerning the present. A sober view of things instead of illusions—The disappearance of memories, 'self-pity' [he uses the English word]; for the one who has overcome: humour. Passing, killing time. Smoking in the emptiness of time.[58] Remembering the possible, although non-concrete. The significance of illusion.

On the back we find, *inter alia*:

The experience of the past, fulfilment, thanks, penitence—the feeling of time—not only the present results . . . Waiting—but, for example, facing death quite calmly—the peasant's time, but no sense of 'time' itself—the experience of time as the experience of separation, engaged couple, from God—past. Why 'In a hundred years all over' and not: when we [illegible] everything will be all right. No possession that outlasts time, no task.—Flight from the experience of time in dreams, the shock of awakening. Also in dreams, the past means the future, dreams are timeless.—Tooth of time, i.e. gnawing time—also healing time, like the healing of a wound.

Thus we can see that the first study that he conceived in his cell at Tegel became a piece on the 'sense of time'. He worked on it until June 1943.[59] Unfortunately it is now lost; only a few notes, such as the preceding, have been preserved on the subject. In this way he resisted the terrible pressure of the first weeks and obviously managed to avoid a continual nervous involvement with his case, which would have exhausted his reserves.

With these efforts to cope with the new situation, the threat to his inner equilibrium came from two directions: he became uncertain whether he should fight for his life or kill himself. He overcame this temptation more quickly than the other one of worrying about how he was to deal with his past and his longing for it.

We know little of his thoughts on how he could overcome his situation

58. Cf. LPP, p. 55, the reference to 'Kant's exposition of "smoking" as a means of entertaining oneself'.
59. LPP, pp. 45 f., 54 f., 56 f., 88.

through suicide. What he said, in December 1943, about his 'grim experiences', which 'often pursue me into the night' and could hardly be overcome, 'in spite of everything that I have so far written',[60] must not necessarily be taken in connection with this temptation to suicide. But his first notes contain a statement that subsequently never recurs: 'Suicide, not from a sense of guilt, but because I am basically already dead, draw a line, add up the balance.' Undoubtedly there were, at the beginning, inner shocks that led him to consider taking his life. And undoubtedly one of the first things that a man involved in political resistance and arrested in the midst of a conspiracy thinks of is serving the cause by killing himself, in order that weakness should not make him a traitor. Bonhoeffer had sometimes spoken of whether he could bear physical torture.

Thus the idea of suicide came to him in two forms: in the shape of his concern for those continuing the struggle and because of his temptation to *tristitia*. The former could be shaken off, as soon as he had a reasonable prospect of averting the attention of his persecutors and of managing to hold out. The fact that he very quickly overcame the latter almost surprised him—but he was helped by the need to concentrate as much as possible on the tactics of the interrogation. The surprising way in which he succeeded in this is seen from the fact that he was able to write —and to his parents—very early on, on 15th May 1943, during the wedding in the Schleicher household, of the temptation that suddenly, for inexplicable reasons, affects one's 'peace and composure . . . to rob one of what is most vital'.[61] Unlike the earlier days of persistent melancholy in Finkenwalde,[62] he assured me right at the beginning of his first letter from Tegel, in November 1943, that in the first weeks he had 'been preserved from any serious spiritual trial' arising from his earlier *accidie*, *tristitia*, which often lay in wait for him, 'with all its menacing consequences'.[63] His fighting spirit won the upper hand. Bonhoeffer persisted in thinking 'that the duty had been laid on me to hold out in this boundary situation with all its problems'.[64]

The brief stage of desperate depression was followed by that of reflection on the fact of being cut off from his own life. He wrote of this experience in letters and studies, as well as submitting his origins to an intense literary enquiry and attempting to approach this theme lyrically also. His fiancée, his family and his friends, even his ethical thinking, were all, for him, part of the 'past', up to the beginning of the great theological letters of 1944. But the blessing of being able to reflect rationally on this subject was threatened once again:

A few times in my life I have come to know what homesickness means. There

60. LPP, p. 106.   63. LPP, p. 87.
61. LPP, p. 45.   64. Ibid.
62. Cf. Ch. X, p. 420.

is nothing more painful, and during these months in prison I have sometimes been terribly homesick.[65]

This was the other side of the remarkable attachment the Bonhoeffers had to their family, and it was the refusal to give it up in favour of a matter-of-fact attitude to life. He was not ashamed of his homesickness. We have some letters on the theme of 'longing' written explicitly out of his abandonment to this suffering.[66]

The first attempt to express his situation in verse (in the early summer of 1944) came after his fiancée had been allowed to see him. When she went away he saw his life moving inexorably away from him. He called the poem 'The Past' ('*Vergangenheit*').[67] It is the most passionate of them all. He sent me the draft because he thought I was in a similar situation because of my separation:

This dialogue with the past, the attempt to hold on to it and recover it, and above all, the fear of losing it, is the almost daily accompaniment of my life here; and sometimes, especially after brief visits, which are always followed by long partings, it becomes a theme with variations. To take leave of others, and to live on past memories, whether it was yesterday or last year (they soon melt into one), is my ever-recurring duty . . . In this attempt of mine the crucial part is the last few lines. I am inclined to think they are too brief . . .[68]

The last verses expressed the way in which he thought he could legitimately recapture his past life: the Christian exercise of repentance and thanksgiving. Even if he seldom succeeded, at least he turned his own experience into a helpful guide for those who ran the risk of letting their painful isolation affect their capacity for living in the present and of becoming 'incapable of loving their neighbour'.[69]

But one thing he refused, even if things were sometimes very bad for him: he refused to let himself be thought of as a 'martyr'. He rebuked correspondents or visitors who spoke as if he were, or else he gave a markedly harmless interpretation of events:

These things must not be dramatized. I doubt very much whether I am 'suffering' any more than you, or most people, are suffering today. Of course, a great deal here is horrible, but where isn't it? Perhaps we have made too much of this question . . . No, suffering must be something quite different, and have a quite different dimension, from what I have so far experienced.[70]

The more serious things became, the less he spoke about them. Self-pity was not permitted in the family. After his first visit, his father wrote to his son—and the censor read it!—:

65. Letter of 18.12.1943, LPP, p. 110.
66. Cf. LPP, pp. 109-11, 116 f., 141 f., 147 f.
67. LPP, pp. 223 ff.
68. Letter of 5.6.1944, LPP, pp. 176 f.
69. LPP, p. 141.
70. Letter of 9.3.1944, LPP, p. 140.

It was a great relief for us to be able to speak to you recently and to see with our own eyes that you are, by and large, physically fit, and are withstanding the evil trial imposed upon you with a calm mind and the confidence of a clear conscience.[71]

On 17th November, Bonhoeffer wrote to his mother:

You, dear Mother, wrote recently that you were 'proud' that your children were behaving so 'decently' in such a terrible situation. In fact we have all learned that from you both, especially when, at times of serious illness in the family, you became so completely calm and did not show anything. So it's probably something we've inherited.

The Engagement

The wider family circle learned of Bonhoeffer's engagement at the moment at which the couple were separated by the gates of Tegel prison. With the sense of humour common to the family, Bonhoeffer described the grotesque situation of receiving congratulary letters in his cell. But it was hard that his fiancée now had to introduce herself to the family at large—in circumstances in which people's minds were on quite different things from an engagement party.

How would the girl from a landed estate in the Neumark fit into the family of a Berlin professor? When his parents visited the estate at Pätzig, Bonhoeffer was relieved and delighted to receive his father's letter:

Yesterday Frau von Wedemeyer read us memoirs by her husband . . . They interested me because, despite the quite different interests, the basic attitude to life and upbringing was nearly the same as that in our Swabian families.[72]

As it was, the few weeks before the arrest seemed very brief and interrupted for the secretly engaged couple. And now Maria von Wedemeyer, unfamiliar with the background of the political conspiracy, and, at first, without any knowledge of all the personal relations with government departments and Berlin acquaintances, had to leave the planning and other thinking to her in-laws and their friends, whom she hardly knew. She was not even able to be the first to make use of a permit to visit Dietrich in prison. It was not until four weeks after his parents that she was able to meet Dietrich under surveillance in the visitor's cell at Tegel. After this visit he wrote, on 24th June 1943:

. . . I have just come back from seeing Maria—an indescribable surprise and joy ! I had heard about it only a minute before. It's still like a dream—it is really an almost incomprehensible situation—how we shall think back to it later ! What one can say at such a moment is so irrelevant, but that is not the main thing. It was so brave of her to come; I should never have dared to

71. Letter of 25.5.1943.
72. Letter of 27.3.1944.

ask it of her, for it is much harder for her than it is for me. I know what I'm doing, but for her it is all unimaginable, bewildering, terrible. What a prospect, when this terrible nightmare is over.

At that time Bonhoeffer had not yet been able to organize his illegal lines of communication, so he could send greetings to his fiancée only in the letter to his parents that was allowed every ten days.

But Bonhoeffer's mother and Maria von Wedemeyer understood each other, for both possessed remarkable energy and inventiveness in discovering and making use of every little possibility of contact via the prison staff. They did not spare the members of the military court, nor the useful military officials in responsible posts. Those who held back were unhesitatingly encouraged until they 'functioned'. Despite his concern for the difficulties of the girl's situation, however, Bonhoeffer was grateful for the fact that people were caring about him:

When pastors were arrested, I sometimes used to think that it must be easiest for those of them who were unmarried. But I did not know then what the warmth that radiates from the love of a wife and family can mean in the cold air of imprisonment, and how in just such times of separation the feeling of belonging together through thick and thin actually grows stronger.[73]

It was only at the end of the interrogations that Roeder allowed Bonhoeffer to write to his fiancée direct. She received her first letter on 30th July 1943. But Bonhoeffer soon hesitated again:

Dear Father and Mother, I am again sending this letter to you and not, as arranged, to Maria. I don't know if it is right to send her letters with my present address on the envelope. There's so much gossip in the village, and there could be someone who knows what No. 39 Seidelstrasse, Tegel, means, and I'd like to spare Maria that. Moreover, she's not even at home now, and I'd like to be careful not to put her in a position which I cannot so easily judge from here. She has to suffer enough already. So I shall wait to hear from her what she thinks.[74]

When he was expecting dates for the trial in the winter, he ventured to think of the wedding and their future arrangements. On 18th November 1943, he wrote to me:

My marriage plans: If I'm free and I'm not called up for at least a few months, I'll get married. If I have only two to three weeks before I am called up, I'll wait until the end of the war. What an engagement we're having!

He was looking forward to the way they would celebrate a wedding in Pätzig, although he knew very little of the customs of the Berneuchen: the nuptial mass in the morning, the wedding in the middle of the day, and the blessing for the journey in the evening, and all in

73. LPP, p. 57.
74. Letter of 7.8.1943.

the beautifully painted village church of Pätzig. On 12th February 1944, he asked his fiancée:

Have you got your trousseau together yet? Where shall we get a radio? Would it be possible for me to exchange my big Bechstein for a baby grand? . . . If you should ever come across a cembalo, then grab it with both hands!

When his hopes for one of the dates were dashed, he wrote in a different tone:

We have been engaged now for nearly a year and have never been alone together for one hour! Isn't it absurd . . . we have to talk and write about things that are not the most important ones for us both; once a month we sit beside each other, like good children at school and are then torn apart. We know practically nothing about each other, have no common experiences yet for even these months we are going through separately. Maria thinks I am a model of virtue, an exemplary Christian and, in order to satisfy her, I have to write letters like an early martyr, and her image of me becomes more and more false. Isn't that an impossible situation for her? And yet she goes through everything with a marvellous naturalness.[75]

At the end of May 1944, when he wrote the poem 'The Past', he heard 'Solveig's Song' by Greig on the radio in the prison sick-bay downstairs and said he had been moved by this 'triumph over the hostility of space, i.e. separation, and over time, i.e. the past'.[76]

I could not, for example, even bear tonight to imagine myself actually sitting with Maria in the garden by the water at your place, and our talking to each other into the night, etc. etc. That is merely self-torture, which hurts physically. So I take flight in thinking, in writing letters, in my joy at your happiness and forbid myself—in self-defence—my own desire.

After 20th July 1944, Bonhoeffer wanted his fiancée to avoid Berlin so as not to be drawn into complications, in case the Gestapo had their attention drawn to her. On 3rd August he wrote to me:

Maria will go to the Red Cross again, I think . . . It is impossible to know where we shall meet again. Sometimes I think I have placed too great a burden on her. But who could have expected what has happened? And if I had been able to manage this case, the situation would have been quite different long ago. But you must not think that I feel bitter about this. I sometimes surprise myself by how 'controlled'—or should I say 'blunted'?— I am.

But now Maria deliberately planned to come to Berlin. In order to avoid a military call-up, she registered as an assistant to Bonhoeffer's

75. To E. Bethge, 17.12.1943.
76. LPP, p. 176.

father, during his consulting hours, as was allowed him for his medical practice.

For another two months the customary communication with Tegel unexpectedly continued to work. Then there came the agonizing waiting for the escape and the possibility of Dietrich disappearing for an indefinite period. But 8th October brought a new situation. The couple were never able to see each other again, and their written correspondence dried up almost entirely. When comparing it with the cellar at Prinz-Albrecht-Strasse, he must have longed for Tegel, as far as his engagement was concerned.

The strain of Tegel did not destroy Bonhoeffer's positive attitude to the needs of the time and the place. 'We can have abundant life, even though many wishes remain unfulfilled.'[77] He sought energetically and then joyfully the tasks that he fulfilled inside and outside the prison walls:

The great thing is to stick to what one still has and can do—there is still plenty left.[78]

But is it not characteristic of a man, in contrast to an immature person, that his centre of gravity is always where he actually is, and that the longing for the fulfilment of his wishes cannot prevent him from being his whole self, wherever he happens to be? . . . the more he has to overcome in order to live fully in the present, the more he will have the respect and confidence of his fellows.[79]

Thus with his newly discovered and self-imposed tasks he established a daily programme that even found him short of time: '. . . Unfortunately I hardly ever entirely complete my day's work.'[80] This day's work consisted, with varying priorities, of his preparations for the interrogations and the trial, of a growing correspondence, of literary and theological projects, of an impressive row of books to be read and finally of requests for chats and help that came to him frequently both from his fellow-prisoners and his warders.

Correspondence

Letters became Bonhoeffer's elixir of life at Tegel. He lived for them and through them, and through them he exercised a compelling influence. For them he gradually set up a whole secret communication system.

Of these letters those to his fiancée still exist. They run from the end of July 1943 to December 1944, and were delivered partly via the censorship and partly in secret via kindly-disposed guards. They have not been published.

77. LPP, p. 141.
78. LPP, p. 45.
79. LPP, p. 141.
80. Letter of 22.10.1943, GS II, p. 443.

Further there are the letters to his parents written from April 1943 till January 1945 which came through the censorship and have been published in excerpts in the first third of *Letters and Papers from Prison*.

Finally there are Bonhoeffer's letters to me, about 200 closely written pages, from November 1943 to August 1944, all smuggled out. Extracts from these letters constitute the other two-thirds of *Letters and Papers from Prison*. I quickly burnt a final set of letters written in September 1944, when, on my own arrest in October 1944, I inevitably assumed that my connection with Bonhoeffer could be fatal.

At first Bonhoeffer's only connection with the outside world was the ten-day cycle of one-page letters to his parents allowed him. The length of time they took to deliver varied according to the bureaucratic situation with the censor, Roeder. If he was away, as in August and September 1943, a letter could wait for weeks, and answers to questions could take a month or longer. This was one of the reasons why Bonhoeffer, as soon as he was able to, used illegal messengers. In his correspondence with me the delivery time soon became longer again, because after January 1944, I could be reached only via the slow field post in Italy, apart from a holiday in early summer, 1944.

When he had a letter to write to his parents Bonhoeffer did something that he never did with other letters and rarely with his other writing: he made careful drafts, so that they were of the right length and content. Some of these drafts have been preserved and sometimes allow us to give rough dates for the material of the interrogations, because he used these papers for the notes on the interrogation that he was writing for Roeder. Of course such a precious letter home could not omit any request or question. But nor should it reveal any uncontrolled emotion which might disturb his family, if it could not be immediately interpreted. Each of these letters presented the writer anew with the task of being both the person that he was in his cell, and yet of helping all others concerned in their attitude to the situation. He was not to deceive himself and others concerning the state of affairs, and yet he had to assure them that he was equal to the strain and was even using it as an area of new experiences for the future.

There is a difference in the way Bonhoeffer writes to his parents and to his friend. The letters to his parents show great intuition about their state of mind and are controlled, whereas the others are much more frank. In accordance with Bonhoeffer's upbringing, feelings were indicated only in the way that you enquired after the wishes and affairs of the other person. One's own needs seemed to be transposed into advice for others. And when things became particularly difficult, one conveyed more than a hint of consciousness that one was passing with other people through a succession, not only of private, but also of exemplary experiences.

The difference in the letters appears clearly when Bonhoeffer expresses his impatience with the delay in assigning a date to the trial. He hints at it only once with his parents,[81] whereas he writes to his friend several times to say what he thinks of the 'manipulation' of his family and how it threatens his peace of mind for his work.[82] He knew only too well what an obstacle the sensitive imagination of his family could be:

. . . all too easily a conversation, a brain-wave, a hope, is already taken for the deed . . .[83] I wonder whether my excessive scrupulousness, about which you often used to shake your head in amusement (I am thinking of our travels), is not a negative side of bourgeois existence—simply part of our lack of faith, a part that remains hidden in times of security, but comes out in times of insecurity in the form of 'dread' (I don't mean 'cowardice', which is something different: 'dread' can show itself in recklessness as well as in cowardice), dread of straightforward, simple actions, dread of having to make necessary decisions. I have often wondered here where we are to draw the line between necessary resistance to 'fate', and equally necessary submission.[84]

Actually Bonhoeffer caused his family anxiety only by this occasional impatience, which was encouraged by the limited perspective of his prison cell. One day it too departed. He was able to write a year later, about what had at first greatly upset him, that he had not only changed, in natural self-defence, but that 'today I can take a calmer view of other people, their predicaments and needs, and so I am better able to help them'.[85]

Literary Work

It is impossible to imagine Bonhoeffer as doing anything other than using his enforced leisure for new creative ends. It was for him the most beneficial self-protection to objectify in writing the experience of imprisonment. Most of what he wrote in 1943 in Tegel was concerned with the explanation or systematization of the phenomenon we have already mentioned, namely that he saw his own world continually retreating from him. At first he remained entirely objective, with that lost study on time. But then he found the courage to reflect on his world in a much more personal way. Around Pentecost, at the end of May, he began writing a play and soon after started a novel. He said later what joy these experiments had given him. The play broke down because of the over-reflective speeches of his characters, so he began again with the 'story of a contemporary middle-class family', which he had 'had in mind for a long time'.[86] The novel fragment describes the meeting of a

81. LPP, pp. 78 f.
82. LPP, pp. 114 f., 133; see also XIII, pp. 727 ff.
83. He is thinking here of his brother, Klaus.
84. Letter of 21.2.1944, partly in LPP, p. 133.
85. LPP, p. 150.
86. LPP, p. 88.

doctor's family from the big city with one from a country-estate background, seen clearly against the experiences of his own family and his
own in England and Pomerania. But this fragment also soon develops
into long soliloquies more suited to a chapter on ethics than a story.[87]
But this account is conditioned by the actual, specific experiences that
the Bonhoeffer family lived through. The way in which he experienced
all this himself and what it meant to him during his separation from it,
has also passed into the sermons that he wrote in his cell on the celebration of our wedding and the baptism of our son.[88]

The combination of the honest and the mean occupied him in these
literary attempts, just as in that parallel study. 'What is Meant by
"Telling the Truth"?'[89] Here it was the lie of the truthful man and
the truth of the liar, the living element of honesty and loyalty in the
world of seduction through power, small and great. Bonhoeffer was very
concerned with what was the real embodiment of Germany, the real
nature of its brilliant and its disastrous qualities, such as the immaturity
in handling power and the apparent acquiescence in letting its good
name be smirched. He reflected the privilege, dearly paid for, of being
one of the responsible embodiments of this country's tradition.

In the drama fragment he makes the chief figure, called Christoph,
write a note in his diary which shows what made him angry when he
considered Germany;[90] the novel also breaks off with questions about
Germany.[91] Whereas Bonhoeffer used to write down his essays in their
final form from slips with shortened notes and not from complete drafts,
two full drafts have been preserved of that section of Christoph's diary
entry which he was obviously very concerned about and which declared
that 'the soiled words, freedom, fraternity, and even the word Germany'
now had to be honoured through silence and the simple doing of what
had to be done,[92] in order to become respected again.

It was not until 1944 that, as we have already said, he treated his
personal theme of 'the past' more subjectively and yet more universally
than ever before, in the poem for his fiancée. But then this theme was
succeeded by another, which carried him through the worst weeks of
the year 1944. The new theme pointed entirely towards the future, and
his own frontier situation became extended to provide an exemplary
vision of future Christianity. Until then he had limited this theme to
Germany because of the narrowing down of his own life, but now he
looked again at the role of Christianity in the world.

How are we to judge Bonhoeffer's attempts at poetry? They are efforts

87. Parts of the drama and novel fragment have been published in GS III, pp. 478 ff.,
496 ff.
88. LPP, pp. 47 ff., 165 ff.
89. Cf. Ch. XIII, p. 717.
90. GS III, pp. 479 f.
91. GS III, p. 512.
92. GS III, pp. 479 f.

to overcome his isolation. In this situation he had begun to write poetry for the first time since his youth. The venture held him fascinated for months on end. The thoughts in these pieces are important, but they are again so densely packed that they burst the forms of poem, novel and drama. Poems such as 'Sorrow and Joy',[93] 'The Friend',[94] and 'Stations on the Road to Freedom',[95] will probably live on because they convey the particular situation in an original statement and in an appropriate form. 'Powers of Good'[96] has already passed into the schoolbooks. But the attempted drama and the fragment of a novel have come out as ponderous. Stifter's style, which Bonhoeffer loved, is an obstacle for him, and the theme so dominates him that he does not grant either the reader or himself any respite.

The letter, the essay—this is the literary form, apart from his theological style, in which Bonhoeffer makes a direct appeal to us and is convincing. Summer evenings over the prison walls, Karl Barth's cigar, memories of Berlin concert halls, the rhythm of the church year or the surprise at holding a knife and fork in his hands again, the privileges of mothers-in-law, Berlin beer, the anger at shabby cowardice—all this, without intending to be so, makes fascinating reading. It is serious, has touches of humour and conveys the joy in earthly things that surprised the friends of the earlier Bonhoeffer, the theologian, who wrongly imagined him to be a fierce and radical teacher of eschatology. Instead, he praised 'a beauty that is neither classical nor demonic, but simply earthly, though it has its own proper place. For myself, I must say that that is the only kind of beauty that really appeals to me'.[97]

Studies, Reading

As the interrogations moved into the background, he extended his daily work programme with the intensive reading of works of theology, but even more of philosophy, history and literature. Doing this he was able to forget all about his surroundings and the danger he was in and was disturbed only when there was a hitch in the supply of books by his family or if people failed to track down a particular work that he wanted. Thus he felt 'as if I had been given an extra university term with a series of good public lectures. It was certainly beneficial in many ways for my own writing'.[98]

The list of books we know he read is impressive. The real list was probably even longer. He got his books from three sources. His parents provided him with most of them, and by no means all of them were

93. LPP, pp. 183 f.
94. LPP, pp. 216 ff
95. LPP, pp. 202 f.
96. LPP, p. 221.
97. LPP, p. 145.
98. To his parents, 22.10.1943, GS II, p. 443.

used for code purposes. On the other hand the prison library was available to him, which, after the expurgation, ordered by Goebbels for all libraries in Germany, of the 'filth' of the twenties, still had many surprises from Prussian times to offer. He later exchanged books with other prisoners or received the occasional one from the prison chaplains, such as Karl Kindt's *Klopstock* from Pastor Dannenbaum. From the source material it is possible to make a list of his reading, with dates.[99]

a) There were not too many theological works. Unlike the literature of the nineteenth century, they do not seem to have offered him any particular comfort or light in his situation. He read some things from the prison library that he would normally never have come across, such as the three-volume treatment of Christian social work, *Geschichte der christlichen Liebestätigkeit*, written in 1896 by the Hanoverian Lutheran Uhlhorn, which he read in May and June 1943. He enjoyed the travel letters from Palestine, published in 1901 by Hermann Freiherr von Soden, the father of the Marburg Professor von Soden. Above all he delighted in the early Fathers of the Church, whom he tracked down in the library at Tegel. They seemed more 'contemporary' to him than the reformers, since they did their thinking in a non-privileged period of the Church. Their ethical conflicts in a non-Christian environment seemed here incomparably more exciting than the problems of, say, the Augsburg National Synod of 1530.

Later Bonhoeffer asked to be allowed to see the latest volume of Barth's *Dogmatik*; this was the *Kirchliche Dogmatik* II, 2. A few copies had reached Germany from Switzerland, bound in different covers, and were circulating in the Confessing Church. Bonhoeffer did actually receive and read the volume '*Die Lehre von Gottes Gnadenwahl und Gottes Gebot*' (The Doctrine of God's Election and God's Commandment). This is to say that he knew of Barth's doctrine of predestination, but not of his doctrine of Creation and his special ethics. Unfortunately there is no record of Bonhoeffer's reaction to Barth's doctrine of predestination. In general we can probably say that Barth's account of the positive kerygmatic value of this controversial teaching, developed through a critique of Luther and Calvin, was close to what Bonhoeffer had set out in his seminar, when treating the article on predestination in the Lutheran Book of Concord: namely that the significance of this dangerous doctrine should be sought in its proclamation of certainty and not in its threats.

Bonhoeffer's theological work in Tegel was done without the aid of theological classics and compendia, which, even when he had easier access to them, he used less than most theologians in Germany. He had his Luther Bible, a Greek New Testament and a concordance, but no commentary and no dictionary. With this apparatus he read, as he always had, book after book of scripture, asking questions and meditat-

99. See Appendix G in the German edition.

ing. The new position that emerged in 1944 came less from theological publications than from the experiences that he had with the War Court, among his fellow-prisoners, and in reading secular literature.

b) The list of the philosophical, historical and aesthetic books is more impressive than the theological. But it too reveals, especially in regard to the literary selection, a certain limitation. Bonhoeffer's reading in these last two years of his life shared in the isolation that National Socialism had brought to Germany. The library at Tegel had undoubtedly been restricted, through the measures of Goebbels, to the classics of the previous century and the latest approved lists. But Bonhoeffer could hardly have filled this gap from other sources. It was unthinkable that his family, for instance, could have brought to him in his cell books by Thomas Mann, Franz Werfel or more modern foreign authors. Thus Bonhoeffer also shared the fate of the Germans in being excluded from the mainstream of literary development in the world at large.

Bonhoeffer was not, however, greatly concerned about this lack. The restriction in the literary field was in accordance with his own inclinations. He wanted to become better acquainted with particular aspects of nineteenth-century literature and to rehabilitate the tradition of his fathers, from Keller to Harnack, and from Pestalozzi to Dilthey, as against more modern existentialist tendencies. Hence for example he conceived the idea of making a selection from Jeremias Gotthelf. With these writers his cell was opened to that familiar world from which he had been shut out. That is why they have such a dominant place on his Tegel reading list.

On the other hand, he did not greatly care for many contemporary authors, such as Wiechert and Bergengruen, who were generally highly regarded in Germany. Even before his arrest he had scarcely wanted to read them. From his cell he wrote to his fiancée the reasons for this. In a letter to me of 28th November 1943, he used strong language in his description of 'Rilke, Bergengruen, Binding, Wiechert, the latter three of which I regard as not up to our level, and the first as downright unhealthy'.

Maria's generation has unfortunately grown up with very bad contemporary literature, and they find it much more difficult to approach earlier writing than we do. The more we have known of the really good things, the more insipid does the thin lemonade of later literature become, sometimes almost to the point of making us sick. Do you know a work of literature written in the last, say, fifteen years that you think has any lasting quality? I don't. It is partly idle chatter, partly propaganda, partly self-pitying sentimentality, but there is no insight, no ideas, no clarity, no substance and almost always the language is bad and restricted. On this subject I am quite consciously a *laudator temporis acti*.

He asks his fiancée what she is reading, giving her friendly guidance:

Can't you get hold of Rilke's *Malte Laurids Brigge* somewhere? Recently I have been reading only learned stuff, but occasionally I relaxed with your Scheffel. Do you read Fontane?[100]

I think it's very nice that you are reading Schütz![101] But forgive me for laughing a little at it. For I have criticized few books recently—among theologians, and only among them!—as much as this one. But I think that it's only dangerous for theologians—it's not easy to say why in a nutshell—but not for you. But I would be pleased if you would take, as antidote, a strong dose of Kierkegaard (*Fear and Trembling, Practice in Christianity, Sickness unto Death*). Have you read the *Berner Geist* by Jeremias Gotthelf? You ought to, at this stage. I wonder if *Don Quixote*, which I love so much, would mean much to you? And *Wilhelm Meister*? It's much more important even than Fontane, who can wait a little. Do you know Stifter's *Aus der Mappe meines Urgrossvaters*?[102]

The delightful discovery of Tegel was Adalbert Stifter. Bonhoeffer shared here in a way the experience of others of the imprisoned conspirators of 20th July, whose oppressive prison life was heartened by nothing as much as by Stifter's style, which in the normal pressure of everyday life seemed almost unreadable. Bonhoeffer's brother-in-law Rüdiger Schleicher also experienced this intensely. The power and breadth, the dwelling on the obvious events of a walk through the garden, had a uniquely transforming and restorative effect in prison.

The intimate life of his characters—of course it is old-fashioned of him to describe only likeable people—is very pleasant in this atmosphere here, and makes one think of the things that really matter in life.[103]

It was one of Bonhoeffer's great moments in Tegel when, after his family at home had hunted for it for a long time without success, he unexpectedly came upon Stifter's *Witiko* in the prison library:

For me it is one of the finest books I know. The purity of its style and character-drawing gives one a quite rare and peculiar feeling of happiness.[104]

Here it was not only, of course, the literary quality that fascinated him, but the theme, which placed his own life, in a surprisingly comforting and purifying way, within the most universal context of the wide sweep of history. He discovered for himself what Hermann Bahr had already drawn attention to in *Witiko* in 1922:

This old book seems to have waited just for us, to have been written specially for us . . . only now do we comprehend . . . the aim, of depicting 'the

---

100. Letter of 15.2.1944.
101. P. Schütz, *Warum ich noch Christ bin*, 1938; *Das Evangelium, dem Menschen unserer Zeit dargestellt*, 1940.
102. Letter of 18.2.1944.
103. LPP, p. 55.
104. LPP, p. 72.

terrible majesty of the moral law, which destroys . . . the great criminals and bends in two their violent schemes like straws, in such a powerful and brilliant way that men, seeing the terror of it . . . submit in trembling and wonder to the power that forbids evil . . .'

. . . then Witiko starts performing good injustices and helps to bring out of this a new justice . . . Where there has been a lasting victory for revolution it has always been the victory of legitimacy, the victory of illegal justice over a law that had become unjust . . .

New justice must always first expiate its defects through profound suffering; it must first be purified through fire, with the wrongdoing burnt away. Only then, through penance, will justice finally emerge from good injustice.[105]

Bonhoeffer's preference for nineteenth-century literature was the result of an inner disposition. He had an aversion to an unclear style, and he was against rapt reflection on oneself and strained extravagance. He was averse to penetrating into hidden areas. He enjoyed the indication of inner events in all their nuances through outer actions:

In my reading I am now concentrating entirely on the nineteenth century. During recent months I have read Gotthelf, Stifter, Immermann, Fontane, and Keller with sheer admiration. A period in which people could write such clear and simple German must have had quite a healthy core. They treat the most delicate matters without sentimentality, the most serious without flippancy, and they express their convictions without pathos; there is no exaggerated simplifying or complicating of language or subject matter; in short, it is all very much to my liking, and seems to me very sound. But it must have meant plenty of hard work at expressing themselves in good German, and therefore plenty of opportunity for quiet.[106]

Thus he was able to affirm this fruit of both his own personal isolation and that of his country.

Of course the degree to which the philosophical questions of the period had remained uninvestigated did not escape him. And the fact that he had so little knowledge of the sciences and technology that emerged in the same century he simply had to accept with regret.[107]

Prison Life

In the course of time Tegel had provided Bonhoeffer with a mobility that one does not expect from the prisons of the Third Reich and that the majority of Hitler's victims did not enjoy. This was due partly to the nature of a military prison, but partly also to Bonhoeffer's way of treating his warders.

Although there was a palpable attempt to carry out the severe punish-

105. In his essay 'Stifter', reprinted in *Der goldene Schnitt*, 1960, pp. 199, 214.
106. Letter of 25.7.1943, LPP, p. 60.
107. LPP, pp. 173, 174.

ments in Hitler's military forces, even in the military interrogation prison of Tegel—called 'WUG'—there still existed alongside these innovations the long-established military code. Certain rights of a prisoner held for interrogation could be preserved if only they were energetically and skilfully sought.

Among the older staff of the Tegel prison Bonhoeffer came to know a number of warders who were strongly opposed to the régime. Others proved willing and helpful when the 'politicals' or their highly-placed relations showed them kindnesses or gave them gifts. Also, Bonhoeffer's energetic protests against the customary rough behaviour of the warders were successful and they desisted. The staff consisted of long-service privates and corporals, hard-boiled men unfit for fighting in the field.

To these men Bonhoeffer appeared an extraordinarily interesting prisoner: a pastor who is admitted under the greatest secrecy, then turns out to be the nephew of the city commandant and is soon taken for a walk by Captain Maetz personally. Thus this prisoner gradually became an influential inmate of the house. When the effects of the heavy air raids in the winter of 1943-4 affected the order of the prison, many discovered that to be close to Bonhoeffer gave them a feeling of safety which they were happy to enjoy, especially as Bonhoeffer never asked for more than could be reasonably expected of them. Many were glad that he was there.

On 26th November 1943 there was the first severe night raid on Borsig, and the prison also received several hits. Bonhoeffer clearly proved himself during this ordeal by his particular circumspection. For this reason the captain encouraged him to make a report concerning new protective measures. After the summer raids on Hamburg there had already been special drill for the self-protection of the prison, in the course of which Bonhoeffer had, by the late summer of 1943 at the latest, been regularly brought from his cell for practices and when there were alarms. He was appointed the medical orderly for his section. Maetz had learnt sufficient of Bonhoeffer's medical talent and liked to talk to him concerning improvements to the air-raid precautions. As early as 3rd July 1943, Bonhoeffer wrote to his parents concerning suggestions, both foolish and useful, for their air-raid shelter in the Marienburger Allee: 'I've spoken to the captain here about it.' In this way there developed contacts in the house that Bonhoeffer used in every way for the benefit of both the warders and his fellow-prisoners, in order to improve conditions or stem corruption. He gained a deep insight into the persecutions, toadying and favouritism that emanate from the front office and the kitchen staff in such a place.

His experience of the corruption there so haunted him that he wrote —probably in the summer of 1943—a little story with the title '*Leb wohl, Kamerad*' ('Farewell, Comrade'), in which he described this side of military life: a young, seriously wounded guard cannot maintain himself among his comrades because he does not join in the brutal treatment of the prisoners and the self-enrichment of the guard-room. Every feature of the sketch reveals an exact knowledge of the customs of a 'WUG'.[108]

a) *The Guards.* We have to thank the humanity of a few guards that so much material has been preserved from Bonhoeffer's period at Tegel. One day one of them brought him scribbling paper from the guard-room for his work. Many of them tried to arrange the rota of duties so that they were allotted that section of the corridor where Bonhoeffer's cell was. He was so good to have a conversation with, and one always got a piece of sound advice in dealing with one's own little troubles. Sometimes they took up too much of his working time. There were several requests, even from a sergeant-major, to be allowed to be photographed with this prisoner in the courtyard. On 4th February 1944 a warder placed in his cell a birthday bouquet of early spring flowers from the prison greenhouse. Another offered to ask his country relations to send food parcels to Bonhoeffer's relatives. When the sirens howled and the bomber squadrons seemed to take their course directly over Tegel, those in the section got as close as possible to Bonhoeffer, who seemed to remain so calm. A corporal who had to take Bonhoeffer back from the section to his cell asked him surreptitiously to pray for a quiet night.[109] One night when their own quarters were damaged by the explosions nearby, they came to him 'for a bit of comfort'.[110] A warder who had to lock him in again after his exercise in the yard suddenly asked his pardon.

With some of the warders a relationship of firm trust developed. When I married Bonhoeffer's niece in the middle of May 1943 he was able to send a Corporal Linke with a wedding speech written out,[111] greetings and presents. The same thing happened when his godson was baptized.[112] Of course it occasionally happened that Bonhoeffer was cheated of money or gifts by someone he had asked to do something for him, but it was very seldom. It was Linke again who locked me in for a whole hour with Bonhoeffer in the visitor's cell and left us to talk alone. Corporal Holzendorf, among others, did the same sort of thing for Maria von Wedemeyer and the family, until he was killed in an air raid in 1944.[113] And finally it was Corporal Knobloch—he has disappeared—who acted as go-between for a whole year in the illegal correspondence between Bonhoeffer and myself. It was with this trustworthy man that Bonhoeffer had prepared his escape plan.[114]

Such warders found plenty of pretexts to take Bonhoeffer to the 'private section', the sick-bay of the prison, even if there was no drill

---

108. The manuscript has been preserved, but it has not yet been published.
109. LPP, p. 104.   110. LPP, p. 124.
111 LPP, p. 47.   112. LPP, p. 165.
113. S. Dress, 'Meetings in Tegel', IKDB, pp. 215 ff.
114. Cf. Ch. XIII, pp. 730 ff.

or alarm to make his presence necessary. Here there was a radio so that the air-raid warnings could be heard, and Bonhoeffer was able to listen, with other music-lovers, to the *Missa Solemnis* or Pfitzner's *Palestrina*.[115] Except for the angelic choir he did not much enjoy the latter, much to the disappointment of a Pfitzner enthusiast. In this room he began to play chess with other prisoners and warders, so that he again, as in his youth, occupied his mind with the theory of chess. On one of these occasions he came back to his old love of graphology and soon provided a number of clients with analyses of their professional future.[116]

I . . . am enjoying it very much; I am now working through Ludwig Klages' book. But I am not going to try it on my friends and relatives; there are enough people here who are interested in it. But I am convinced of the thing's reliability.

Among the papers from Bonhoeffer's cell there are a few notes on analyses of handwriting that he made.

b) *The Fellow-prisoners.* At first Bonhoeffer was pursued even in his dreams by thoughts of those prisoners who were waiting for death to the left and right of his cell without his being able to reach them. In time, however, he was able to establish relationships with some of those condemned to death and, even more so, with prisoners held for interrogation. He then tried to do something for them or to bring some pleasure into their lives.

The first chance for this was offered by a fellow-prisoner who was sent to him in the first weeks in order to clean his cell. He learned from him the details of events in the house, and when a packet arrived he shared its contents with him. In the early summer of 1943 he first refused the offer of taking a cooler cell on the second floor because of the heat, since then another prisoner would have had to move into his cell.[117] Later, prisoners working somewhere together told one another when Bonhoeffer could be found in the sick-bay, and then tried to arrange things so that they had something to do there, because 'it is so nice to have a chat with me', as Bonhoeffer wrote.[118] Through these conversations Bonhoeffer learned of young prisoners accused of having left their company without leave, of anti-war activities, or sabotage, and who were left in this situation without expert advice or even money for a defence lawyer. He then tried, for example, to get the relatives of these accused to visit his father in his consulting hours on the chance that they could obtain a psychiatric report on the person concerned which would be useful in his trial. Or he asked his own defence lawyer, Dr. Wergin, the

115. LPP, pp. 151, 158.
116. LPP, pp. 146 f., 149.
117. LPP, pp. 61, 65.
118. LPP, p. 114.

friend of Klaus, his brother, to take on the case. He even made money available from his own or his parents' account to get the necessary legal help for some young man. Bonhoeffer actually managed to save several prisoners at Tegel from the worst, among them an Italian called Lanfredi, who had already been condemned to death at the first hearing, as Professor Latmiral attested in a letter of 2nd April 1946. Others he was able to help on their last journey only through his prayers:

> I hear outside a hasty, muffled tread,
> Near my cell it suddenly stops dead.
> I go all cold and hot,
> I know, oh, I know what . . .
> I go with you, brother, to that place
> And hear your last words, face to face:
> 'Brother, when I cease to be,
> Pray for me.'[119]

In order to alleviate the lot of his fellow-prisoners where he could, he used his privileged position with the captain and wrote a 'Report on Prison Life'[120] in the hope that it would reach his uncle, the city commandant, who would set things in order. From his ample personal experience he described the degrading punishments, food and living conditions of men held for interrogation, men who were generally intended to return to the front as combatants. For this report he got warders he could trust to check the weight of the food rations and compare it with what was laid down in the regulations. He worked out a system of punishments of his own.

In the other report after the severe raid on the Borsig works he mercilessly exposed the inadequate protection and preventative measures in the prison and suggested that in view of the shortage of materials there should be far more shelters for protection against shrapnel, and that the prisoners should have their cells unlocked during raids. From the sick-bay shelter he had heard too clearly the screams of those locked in and seen the over-tardy help for the wounded. Here his mother's heritage proved itself; she was always able to act precisely with swift imagination when a disaster paralyzed those around her.

Though he was so ready to help, he could sometimes make exceptions. A district leader of the Party who had been sent to Tegel because of some transgression and had completely collapsed attached himself to Bonhoeffer, who was in a position to obtain the odd favour for him. But when this man let fall an anti-Semitic remark, Bonhoeffer immediately withdrew from him 'the few benefits' he had enjoyed and cut him contemptuously.[121]

119. From 'Nächtliche Stimmen', in *Auf dem Wege zur Freiheit*, p. 7.
120. LPP, pp. 81 ff., 96, 113 f.
121. See LPP, pp. 104, 114, 121 f., 126 f.

For the Christmas of 1943 he wrote prayers for the prisoners.[122] They stemmed from his own prayer, his daily use of the Psalter and the chorales. He cut nothing, neither in the Trinitarian address nor in the Biblical language. The prison chaplains, Dannenbaum and Poelchau, who had obtained illegal entry to Bonhoeffer's cell, distributed the prayers between the cells.

Among the prisoners there were a number of educated men, including foreigners. Bonhoeffer thought that his friendship with some of them could be lifelong and was deeply affected when the one to whom he had grown closest, a Mr. Engel, was killed in a raid.[123] He became friendly with an English officer (?) called Dick Jones and exchanged books with him. In this way he obtained, in the summer of 1944, the thick volume of *The Herries Chronicle* by Hugh Walpole. The book already had in it notes written by English prisoners-of-war in 'Stalag LB 2', from where Jones had probably brought it to Tegel. In the first days of October 1944, Bonhoeffer sent it home, when, fearing the worst, he was again clearing his cell of illegal objects. His book-mark, a piece of the *Völkischer Beobachter* from the end of September 1944, was placed at page 1308 of the book. This novel, which traces the story of a family through many centuries, had clearly given him welcome distraction at the end.

Bonhoeffer became close to some Italian officers who were arrested in Germany after the Badoglio *Putsch* as bearers of 'technical secrets' and on 11th November 1943 had been brought to Tegel. He was especially attached to Professor Gaetano Latmiral and his friend Curcio. After the war Latmiral described his relationship with Bonhoeffer during the Tegel period:

Only a minority of the guards were fanatic or ill-disposed. Most of them were decent or even good. I think that Dietrich's long stay among them had had an influence on them . . . He had received small concessions, for example, he was often allowed to go down to the sick-bay, where he met many friends, or he was able to visit prisoners who sought his spiritual help . . . When we had our walk together, half an hour or longer every day, we talked of political, religious and scientific problems. He lent me the Weizsäcker book . . . He explained to me the meaning of many passages in the Gospel and told me that he was writing a poem on the death of Moses, when Moses climbed Mount Nebo and God showed him, before he died, the land that would one day belong to his people, but that he would never enter. He loved this theme . . .[124] He also spoke of the tragic fate of the German people, whose qualities and shortcomings he knew. He told me that it was very difficult for him to desire its defeat, but that it was necessary. He said he had little hope that a German government could save Germany from the worst consequences of defeat by making a sensible capitulation. The Nazis had a fanatically tragic will to involve everyone in the catastrophe. He observed that Wagner's

122. LPP, pp. 90 ff.
123. LPP, p. 123.
124. GS IV, pp. 613-20.

music was, for him, an expression of this barbarous pagan psychology. He stated that, as a pastor, it was his duty, not only to comfort the victims of the man who drove in a busy street like a maniac, but also to try to stop him. The leading German families had in part expiated their guilt by trying to remove Hitler, though far too late. He said that he was not sure that he would see the end, for he feared that he would then be taken to a concentration camp, where he would be killed along with other political prisoners. In that case he hoped that he would be able to accept death without fear, in the belief that it was in a just cause . . . He was always so interesting and good-humoured. He was the best and the most gifted man I have ever met.[125]

The Church in Prison

The Council of Brethren of the Confessing Church in Berlin was not able, of course, to offer any help to Bonhoeffer. Moreover, it had to be careful not to become too involved with a man who was connected with 'purely' political operations. But men such as Niesel, Asmussen, Böhm, Lokies and others kept themselves informed of what was happening, either via Perels or myself. And undoubtedly the members of the Breslau Synod thought the same as these men when they included Bonhoeffer in their intercessions,[126] since they no longer maintained as formerly the strict distinction between church profession and political action.

At first things were as Bonhoeffer wrote in his first illegal letter to me: 'I have not even been allowed to have a clergyman to see me here'.[127] But after the relaxation that followed the hearings he frequently received visits from two pastors of the Berlin Church. Pastor Dannenbaum of the Berlin city mission, because he was a garrison pastor with the armed forces, had permission to visit the military prison. He used this as soon as he dared, despite the special ban in the case of Bonhoeffer. After 1945 Dannenbaum described Bonhoeffer's cell as 'an almost cosy retreat'. Bonhoeffer, he said, even 'liked to play the host in his cell', but also accepted it gratefully when Dannenbaum concluded his visits with a reading from the Bible and prayer of intercession, just as he himself had done earlier and expected his Finkenwalde seminarians to do when they made pastoral visits.

The second was Pastor Dr. Harald Poelchau, a regular prison pastor in the Civil Service, and thus in charge only of the civil part of the Tegel building. But because of his precise knowledge of the place and the staff he ventured to visit Bonhoeffer's cell illegally more and more from the end of 1943. Like Dannenbaum, he realized what an 'assistant chaplain' they unexpectedly had in the prison.

For himself, Bonhoeffer kept to the daily routine of Bible reading, prayer and meditation. He was now glad that he knew so many of Paul

125. G. Latmiral to G. Leibholz, 6.3. and 2.4.1946.
126. Cf. Ch. XIII, p. 727.
127. LPP, p. 87.

Gerhardt's hymns by heart. An isolated man's need for certainty through a sign led him to cross himself, according to Luther's instruction. But in this environment he carefully observed the distinction between calling on the name of God—and speaking this name before other people. The seriousness in the one excluded the careless use of the name in the other.

After the spring of 1943 there had been no further religious services for Bonhoeffer. Once he said that he hardly missed them and was rather surprised.[128] Was this connected with the fact that such a 'public' function could not be more than a solemn distraction for his fellow-prisoners, with whom he lived at such close quarters? The public spiritual word had, therefore, to wait for its appropriate hour and the 'liturgical' to remain in the realm of the 'arcane', as Bonhoeffer called it in his theological letters.

Who knows if Bonhoeffer would have attempted to organize services if he had had the responsibility and the freedom to do so? He lived the life of hundreds around him and shared their anxieties, their privations and little joys. Here spiritual contacts sprang up naturally. Special functions would probably have hindered rather than helped these contacts. Bonhoeffer was sometimes surprised at how he reacted to this situation without, however, seeking to make a programme out of it. But sometimes he was overcome by longing for the services that he had once had in Finkenwalde amid the brethren. This longing, however, now belonged also to the theme of the 'past' which he wrestled with.

However limited life was in the Tegel cell, in retrospect, compared with what people had to undergo elsewhere, it appeared in an almost rosy light. During this period Bonhoeffer did not have to go hungry, and when after an air raid the cold November air came unhindered through the smashed window of the cell, he did not have to freeze:

A case with tinned food and the fur coat has just been delivered. I got them to take me down immediately and hoped to catch just a sight of you . . . Many, many thanks . . . It is really wonderful, the way you all immediately think of everything and also put it into action.[129]

The influenza, rheumatism and stomach troubles, which came upon him in August and December 1943, and February 1944, were immediately fought with all the necessary medicines. Bonhoeffer had a lawyer for his trial, who visited him. And amid the general danger of life around him he wrote well-ordered wills. But above all he had imposed on himself a precise daily routine, 'so that sometimes, comically enough, I even feel that I have "no time" here for this or that less important matter !'[130] And then there was the most important thing for him, his large correspondence.

128. LPP, p. 108.
129. To E. Bethge, 29.11.1943.
130. LPP, p. 69.

And yet Bonhoeffer could not ignore what was happening outside: the progress of the conspiracy for another Germany, the pointless loss of life at the fronts, which included so many brothers from Finkenwalde, and the fate of the Jews. This remained a hidden, but real burden behind everything that made life at Tegel bearable. Concerning this no more could be said than this: 'As I see it, I am here for some purpose, and I only hope I may fulfil it.'[131]

IV THE NEW THEOLOGY, AN ESSAY

'The non-religious interpretation of Biblical terms in a world come of age' is Bonhoeffer's designation for a task that is just beginning to be understood and that has been both welcomed and attacked since the appearance of the selection from his letters from prison (1951-2). In 1960 the *Encyclopaedia Britannica*, in its article on Bonhoeffer, categorically rejected as 'nonsense' the adjective 'non-religious' as applied to him. Since Bishop Robinson's *Honest to God*, however, it has become common currency even among Anglicans in the debate concerning the future of Christianity and the Church. Even the Archbishop of Canterbury has preached and written on 'non-religious Christianity'.[132] In the debate in Germany there arose an argument as to whether the phrase has its origin in the theology of Barth or of Bultmann and many have thought that it was more characteristic of the former than the latter, whereas others again assigned it to the sphere of atheistic ideas.

The phrase was first used by Bonhoeffer when, in the last year of his life, he was moved by a new impulse to re-examine his theology. This new approach breathed the optimism of a break-through that was entirely in contrast to the situation in which he found himself at that time. He was clearly delighted to be making a new start on theological work; but at the same time he guessed that the task might be beyond his capacities and, as was always the case, called for an intense personal involvement:

But even if we are prevented from clarifying our minds by talking things over, we can still pray, and it is only in the spirit of prayer that any such work can be begun and carried through.[133]

Thus there can be no question of Bonhoeffer's intending his new attempt at constructing a theology of God's solidarity with the world to be the proclamation of a plain intellectual lack of involvement in religious practices. On the contrary, he commended himself to the Holy Spirit precisely at the point where he set about taking the '*etsi deus non daretur*' seriously. Thus the autonomy of 'the world come of age', of

131. LPP, p. 159.
132. A. M. Ramsay, *Sacred and Secular*, London, 1965, Ch. IV.
133. Letter of 3.8.1944, LPP, p. 208.

which he now begins to speak, is not to be understood as the freedom of a Titan, but rather a freedom born of humility. The inevitable theological consequence—as inevitable as it was difficult—was Bonhoeffer's attempt to preserve a place in his new thinking for the 'arcane discipline'.

In the following, we shall consider first the conditions and questions surrounding Bonhoeffer's fresh theological start in Tegel. We shall then attempt to examine, under the heading of his main question 'Who is Christ for us today?' the three chief phrases 'world come of age', 'nonreligious interpretation' and 'arcane discipline'. Lastly, they can also be illuminated by considering the surprised reaction to his letters by his friends and pupils. Hence we shall consider, in three successive sections, the inspiration, the key words, and the reception of the theological letters.

1. *The New Impulse*

April 1944 was clearly a milestone in Bonhoeffer's life in prison. We can see this from the change in his reading, his new manner of working, and the different tone of his letters. This change proved so long-lasting that even the shock of the failure of the attempt of 20th July 1944 did not interrupt it. His new work carried him over those weeks almost without any adverse effect.

The first letter of any length on the new theme was written on 30th April. As we have seen, there had been a preliminary decision concerning whether a date should be sought for the trial or not. Josef Müller's attempt in March to get off with an acquittal had failed; Dohnanyi's health offered no prospect for a hearing. Sack had told Bonhoeffer that he 'had better not, for the time being, expect any change in my present position'.[134]

Thus the time passed in waiting continually for new dates, which was especially detrimental to any continuous work. The acceptance of a truce period was easier and brought increase of energy: 'After a rather long unproductive period, I feel in better form for work now that spring is coming.'[135] Hence the introduction of the letter containing the first formulation of the new theme, written on 30th April, is as positive as can be:

You have no need to worry about me at all, for I am getting on uncommonly well—you would be surprised, if you came to see me. People here keep on telling me (as you can see, I feel very flattered by it) that I am 'radiating so much peace around me', and that I am 'always so cheerful' . . . You would be surprised, and perhaps even worried, by my theological thoughts and the conclusions that they lead to.[136]

134. Letter of 11.4.1944, LPP, p. 148.
135. Letter of 22.4.1944, LPP, p. 151.
136. LPP, p. 152.

There was now a remarkable change in Bonhoeffer's choice of reading material. Hitherto Stifter, Gotthelf, Fontane, C. F. Meyer and Gottfried Keller had confirmed and corrected the ideas that he evolved in the summer and winter of 1943. Now he asked for books by Dilthey, C. F. von Weizsäcker and Ortega y Gasset, for Harnack's *History of the Prussian Academy* and W. F. Otto's *The Gods of Greece*. He was strongly drawn to source books of this kind and could become very impatient: 'Unfortunately the one thing I cannot do is to get hold of the right books.'[137]

Bonhoeffer's writing from his first year at Tegel (1943), for example the drama and novel fragments, still belongs to the sphere of the *Ethics*. They are largely variations on the subject of 'the past'. Now, in spring 1944, Bonhoeffer complained that these writings had become bogged down and that he had lost his real interest in them. In fact it never returned—although the theme of 'the past' was expressed in the form of poems in the summer of 1944 (especially in 'The Past' and 'Death of Moses'). Now Bonhoeffer no longer complained that his writing did not progress because of lack of concentration. It is true that the invasion by the Allies on 6th June aroused many private wishes, just as 20th July destroyed great hopes, but the new theme remained dominant: 'It is as you say: "knowing" is the most thrilling thing in the world, and that is why I am finding the work so fascinating', he wrote on 10th August 1944.[138] I needed only to make the slightest enquiry concerning the development of his new theme in my letters from Italy for him to reply immediately at length with further elaborations of it. And even despite the interruption of air raids he was generally able to continue where he had broken off.

The various writings of his first year in Tegel, which had attempted to return to the spirit of the nineteenth century, prepared the way for the return to long forgotten theological themes of the period, so that, contrary to his attitude in the thirties, he was now concerned with the connecting link with the questions and fruits of this period: 'It would be very useful to draw up a good genealogy here.'[139] He said this in a letter of 9th March 1944, when he first took up again the idea of 'the worldliness' of 'anticlerical secularism', which was 'Christian', not just 'emancipated', a theme at which he had stopped in his *Ethics*.

After his active 'acceptance of guilt' in joining the conspiracy and after his *Ethics* Bonhoeffer became possessed by a new passion for theology. Even before the political task had been completed, it had made a new theological start possible, opening the eye of the lonely man to the conditions and the possible form of Christian belief in the future. He already began to go beyond what politically had not yet been thoroughly experienced.

137. LPP, p. 126. 138. LPP, p. 212. 139. LPP, p. 138.

Preparation. The specific roots of Bonhoeffer's new theology go back to particular ideas of his early period that he had, in part, retained and had, in part, given new emphasis. Moreover, the experiences of his own life had given a new impulse to them. He said that he would 'now be able to see my way through here'.[140]

a) Theologically the 'non-religious interpretation' is clearly prepared for in the Christology that Bonhoeffer had followed since his early days. Ebeling has rightly pointed out that this 'interpretation' is first and last a Christological one.[141] Our chief interest is in the fact that one does observe here a certain continuity. How does this come about? It is the same with elements of his ecclesiology, although the latter caused him great difficulty.

b) Even during his work on the *Ethics* his theological perspective changed from that of *The Cost of Discipleship*. Although his early Christology had to lead Bonhoeffer eventually to *The Cost of Discipleship*, the exclusive claim of Christ he had asserted there had involved the risk of narrowness, and so the onesided cry of 'the world for Christ' had to be counterbalanced by 'Christ for the world'. But this changed the view of the world and of Christ. The universal dimension and the Gospel's provincial interests in life were incompatible with each other.

'Ethics' must not be confined to a limited 'Christian' sphere, left to it after capitulation to the secularism of Western civilization. Thus even in the first chapters of the *Ethics* Bonhoeffer is speaking a new language, in that there is—as, for example, in the section on the relevance of success[142]—a new rationality.

c) In biographical terms the chief influences were Bonhoeffer's experience with the Confessing Church and the political conspiracy, both of which required him to develop new concepts.

We have already spoken of the measure of separation between Bonhoeffer and his Church because it no longer clearly pointed to the shame of the present situation and because its proclamation remained related only to itself. Of course he regarded it as an important task that this Church should preserve the great Christian terms throughout a period in which it failed to understand itself properly. But he could not resign himself to the weakness and irrelevance of the ancient articles to the realities of the day. 'The Confessing Church has now largely forgotten all about the Barthian approach, and has lapsed from positivism into conservative restoration.' The great articles remain 'undeveloped and remote, because there is no interpretation of them'.[143]

His return from America and its consequences—what we have called the process of becoming a 'contemporary'[144]—played a very important

140. See Ch. XII, p. 626.
141. MW II, pp. 19 ff.
142. E, pp. 75 ff.
143. LPP, p. 181.
144. Cf. Ch. XI, pp. 580 ff.

part in this new development. The conspiracy had brought together in a way that went far beyond mere friendly contacts, men from many camps remote from the Church, who were ready to accept responsibility. With these men the remnant, if any, of sentimental piety could not be revived; very few could be brought back into the old 'halls of religion'. So far Bonhoeffer had thought his way through the ethics of the conspiracy on behalf of his friends. Now the time had come at which he sought to discover the faith of the Church in his relationship to this secular world. What did the universal Christ and his name mean where there was real living, carrying responsibility for others? This question made Bonhoeffer's desire for a new encounter with contemporary philosophical and scientific literature all the greater.

d) In the elaboration of his new conception, Bonhoeffer's attempt to get down to the theological literature of the same period seems astonishingly small.

It was years before Bonhoeffer took any account of the influence of Gogarten. It was in fact only after the war that Gogarten's account of the positive share of faith in this process of secularization came to light. Despite his visit to America in 1939, all Bonhoeffer knew of Tillich was what had appeared before the Nazi period. It was this that he had in his mind when he argued for or against him.[145]

But even Bultmann, whom Bonhoeffer had not forgotten, but whose *Commentary on St. John* and essay on demythologizing he had responded to,[146] he did not consider in his preparatory work in the specific way that one might have expected. It is questionable whether Bonhoeffer realized then the permanent disquiet that over the years would penetrate every quarter as a result of that essay by Bultmann. Nevertheless, in his second theological letter[147] he related his new attempted formulations to Bultmann's demythologizing, but at the same time set his own view in contrast to the latter's by saying, surprisingly, that Bultmann did not 'go far enough'. When on leave in 1944 I had spoken to Friedrich Justus Perels concerning conversations in the Council of Brethren on Bultmann, I wrote to Tegel:

When I told Justus in the evening that you were very involved with the problem of Bultmann, he said that that was all old hat and that Bultmann was quite impossible . . . a philosopher, perhaps, but someone who should never have been allowed to be a theology teacher. It is remarkable that the problem does not disturb them.[148]

Bonhoeffer took this up immediately,[149] claiming Bultmann as an

145. LPP, p. 180. Bonhoeffer's critique of Tillich is confirmed by H. Cox's *The Secular City*, 1965, pp. 79-84.
146. Cf. Ch. XII, pp. 615 ff.
147. Letter of 5.5.1944, LPP, p. 155.
148. Letter of 3.6.1944.
149. Letter of 8.6.1944, LPP, p. 177.

ally against Barth's 'defined limits', but again distinguishing his own view from Bultmann's. Bultmann is named three times in the prison letters. Bonhoeffer quotes him each time rather casually in connection with something that he wants to say himself, showing both that he is close to him and that he knows their views do not entirely coincide. He thought that he had absorbed certain elements of Bultmann in his new approach, while he did not find that Bultmann's essay expressed his own opinions. Bonhoeffer's thought has a different foundation, and hence a different terminology. Also, he meant something different from Bultmann by 'interpretation'. Despite all the sympathy he expressed for his views he regarded himself as different from Bultmann.

In 1944 Bonhoeffer would perhaps have said, in regard to his motives, that he had gone back to his own early theological period, rather than to his contemporaries. And thus it was that he set about his work in Tegel without being able to make use of any modern theological library, depending almost completely on his memory. And thus also the stimulus for his new writing did not proceed from that desire to contradict that he might have felt on reading Bultmann and Barth. His attitudes to these contemporary figures emerged, as it were, incidentally in the course of his own reflections on what seemed to present itself immediately to him. Bonhoeffer regarded both the direction and the radical nature of his thinking as something quite new within the Confessing Church and considered that his contemporaries would be shocked by both. And, at that time, they were.

The Problem of the New Start. In 1943 Bonhoeffer made many remarks that were conservative in spirit. Faced with the air raids and the destruction they caused, he spoke again of a new beginning on a 'Christian basis':

The fact that the horrors of war are now coming home to us with such force will no doubt, if we survive, provide us with the necessary basis for making it possible to reconstruct the life of the nations, both spiritually and materially, on Christian principles.[150]

This is the language of the *Ethics*; by the summer of 1944 this tone has vanished. Now we read:

It will be the task of our generation, not to 'seek great things', but to save and preserve our souls out of the chaos, and to realize that it is the only thing we can carry as a 'prize' from the burning building . . . We shall have to keep our lives rather than shape them, to hope rather than plan, to hold out rather than march forward . . . It will not be difficult for us to renounce our privileges, recognizing the justice of history . . .[151]

In regard to the 'basis of Christianity' we are ourselves 'being driven right back to the beginnings of our understanding'.

150. Letter of 27.11.1943, LPP, p. 100.   151. Letter of 21.5.1944, LPP, pp. 169, 171.

In the *Ethics* Bonhoeffer said that Christianity means that man is 'entitled and obliged to live as man before God.'[152] This seems to sound rather conventionally formulated compared with the statement of 1944: 'Before God and with God we live without God.'[153]

Such observations as these have subsequently caused people to ask what the new start in Bonhoeffer's development was. Many placed the change before the *Ethics*, others between the *Ethics* and the letters from prison of 1944, as, for example, R. Gregor Smith, Hanfried Müller, J. A. T. Robinson and H. J. Schultz. They saw the real progress as having been made after the new start of April 1944, and described what had gone before more or less as a preparative phase, if not indeed as orthodoxy, with even its share of 'wrong tacks'.[154] Others also regarded April 1944 as a main turning-point, among them Karl Barth, but for them it was what had gone before, chiefly *The Cost of Discipleship*, that was worth reading, while the theology of *Letters and Papers from Prison* they considered as not having matured and not worth passing on.

It is not altogether easy to decide the question of the turning-point, if only because so many elements of continuity with the past can be traced, even with *The Cost of Discipleship*. Both the latter and *Letters and Papers from Prison* end in a remarkably similar way with the motif of *imitatio*. Moreover, many ideas of 1944 can be found already in the *Ethics* and letters of 1943, such as the love of the richness of the Old Testament and the warning against too direct an approach to the New Testament,[155] the rejection of religious blackmail in acute distress,[156] or the attempt to give a 'non-religious interpretation' of Easter.[157]

And yet there is much evidence that there was a decisive new start in April 1944, which does not mean, of course, that this division into periods makes what had gone before unimportant. On the contrary, it is part of the origin of the new. The bricks are there and are used. But the old arrangement of the bricks has been altered and there is, quite clearly, an extension of the theme that is equivalent to a change of theme. Bonhoeffer himself thought he was pursuing a completely new path. In the collapse of the 'Christian West' he was seized by a belief in a changed face of Christianity that would be viable. The manner of his theology had made his most recent political steps possible, and these steps now influenced the new manner of his theology.

Bonhoeffer's own view. The theological statements in Bonhoeffer's letters of 1944 are often interpreted in a negative way by ascribing them to the particular situation of being in prison, which had certainly shattered

152. E, p. 297.
153. LPP, p. 196.
154. H. Müller, *Von der Kirche zur Welt*, p. 20.
155. Letter of 5.12.1943, LPP, pp. 103 f.
156. LPP, pp. 122 f.
157. LPP, p. 146.

his inner equilibrium. We do have, in fact, written evidence of this.[158] It comes, however, from the first year at Tegel, whereas just at the time of the new theological departure, this kind of shock situation could no longer have any adverse affect on the calm of his thinking. The first theological letter of 30th April 1944, as we saw, had begun with the double assurance of how well he was again, but also of what anxiety his new ideas and their consequences could cause me.[159]

Bonhoeffer certainly felt that he had to undertake an unavoidable task that could overthrow much traditional thinking. 'I feel obliged to tackle these questions as one who, although a "modern" theologian, is still aware of the debt that he owes to liberal theology.'[160]

When the first two great theological letters, of 30th April and 5th May,[161] reached the Italian front after a long journey through the post, I asked in return: 'Would you, I wonder, allow these sections to be given to people like Albrecht Schönherr, Winfried Maechler, and Dieter Zimmermann?' Bonhoeffer's reply of 8th July was still reserved, although these men were not distant figures, but familiar comrades from Finkenwalde. 'If you want of your own accord to send Albrecht Schönherr and others extracts from my letters, you can, of course, do so. I would not do it myself as yet, because you are the only person with whom I venture to think aloud, as it were, in the hope of clarifying my thoughts.'[162] The question of the significance of his ideas pursued him, however, and thus he added at the end of this long letter of 8th July the following:

Incidentally, it would be nice if you didn't throw away my theological letters, but sent them from time to time to Renate, as they must surely be a burden for you there. I might like to read them again later for my work, perhaps. In a letter you can put many things in a more natural and lively way than in a book, and in letters I often have better ideas than when I'm writing for myself. But it's not important.

This passage, which contains an important judgement concerning himself, was years later the authority, in a sense, for me to publish what had been preserved in the form of letters only and thus to see that his writing was handed on.

Finally, Bonhoeffer himself said again how much he regarded himself as being involved in a reshaping of theology; this was when he emerged from the stage of letters into that of actually writing the draft of a manuscript. It is in the last letter to me that has been preserved, that of 23rd August 1944:

I am now working at the chapter on 'A Stocktaking of Christianity' . . . Sometimes I am quite shocked at what I say, especially in the first part,

158. See Ch. XIII, pp. 734 f.
159. LPP, p. 152.
160. Letter of 3.8.1944, LPP, p. 208
161. LPP, pp. 151 ff., 155 ff.
162. LPP, p. 193.

which is mainly critical; and so I am looking forward to getting to the more constructive part. But the whole thing has been so little discussed that it often sounds too clumsy. In any case, it can't be printed yet.[163]

The Manner of Working and its Consequences. The volume *Letters and Papers from Prison* that has been assembled out of Bonhoeffer's prison letters is nothing like the book that he would have published on his new subject. We do not even possess any headings for the book he planned, only a few pages with a sketch under the formal heading, 'Outline for a Book' and three suggested chapter headings: 1. A Stocktaking of Christianity. 2. The Real Meaning of Christian Faith? 3. Conclusions.[164] The posthumous volume *Letters and Papers from Prison* contains, both before and after this sketch, the account in letters of the first stage of his thinking.

The period of work that we know about comprises only four months: first, three months of discussion in letters alone, and then one month's work on the outline, with the beginning of work on the actual writing of the manuscript. Of the latter, which probably made considerable progress, we do not possess a single page.

Bonhoeffer began the theological dialogue by mail at the end of April. In one week he was able to write several letters solely in order to 'tell what is the constant concern of my mind'. But here he frequently passed from letter-writing to manuscript-writing, a transition which was expressed also by his change from Latin script to his almost unreadable Gothic.[165]

In August he began to write the work, side by side with the letters. In this second stage he sent me that 'Outline for a Book', in order that the sketch should be preserved along with other documents from the cell. In August and September Bonhoeffer worked only on his future book. There were interruptions because of the bad news from his family, the escape plan, and finally his being taken to the Reich Security Head Office. During these weeks he had removed everything from his cell that he thought unnecessary—but not the manuscript of the work he was writing. We may safely assume that he took it with him to the cellar in Prinz-Albrecht-Strasse in order to continue writing it.

Apart from the four months of theological letters from the end of April to the end of August 1944, there was another month of theological writing in those letters that had not yet been sent off for safe-keeping, but had to be destroyed.[166]

In spite of his initial complaints that he missed discussing this work, he did find people from time to time to whom he was able to speak at least a little concerning the things that were occupying his mind. Thus the prison chaplains, Poelchau and Dannenbaum, before anyone else learned of much that was being written in Bonhoeffer's cell. Even years

163. LPP, p. 215.   164. LPP, pp. 208-11.   165. LPP, p. 157.   166. See Ch. XIII, p. 742.

later Gaetano Latmiral knew of his ideas from what Bonhoeffer had told him during the prisoners' exercise in the prison.[167]

Given these, the only available sources, the question was inevitably asked—and has been often repeated since—whether these were not fragments of a mass of first immature ideas (conceived, moreover, under the probable effects of shock which we have already mentioned), not to be taken seriously, or whether a vision is presented that is recognizable and is, rightly, growing in influence. It seems to me that what we have is not, indeed, the mature fruit of a new branch in Bonhoeffer's work, but nor, without doubt, is it merely a vague, random stab at something. It is ultimately only the content of the brief fragments and their reception that can decide this. But there are observations concerning Bonhoeffer's style of working that confirm the validity of these statements in the first stage. In the case of Bonhoeffer's earlier books there was generally a period of three or four years between his first ideas and the completion of the manuscript. Thus, for example, as early as 1932 he presented the first formulations of the ideas of *The Cost of Discipleship*, in seminars, Bible-study groups and sermons, and these already contained some of the key words. In 1935 and 1936 the book reached its final form with precisely these key words. In the case of the *Ethics* Bonhoeffer developed, in 1939, the kernel of his Christological concept of reality and began in 1942 for the last time to arrive at the final version of his *Ethics*. Here he made more changes than in the case of *The Cost of Discipleship*, though still holding fast to a certain fundamental conception.

Thus we find generally very early in Bonhoeffer the basic ideas for what is to come, and they retain fairly consistently the form in which they were first expressed. Hence, given his way of working, we may well imagine that the sketches of 1944 were preserved in the final form, having already remained constant from the first stage of the letters, from April on, to the second in the outline in August. His first visions were always very clear-cut. Later he would substantiate further his basic theses, but without smoothing away their sharp edges. For Bonhoeffer something was always ready to be published far more when it presented a challenge that was supported by argument than when all possible objections to it had been painstakingly answered.

There are also examples in Bonhoeffer's life of his taking on themes alongside a major work in order to relinquish them again soon to the experts in the field, as, for example, his Christocentric interpretations of the Old Testament. We cannot, however, ascribe to the work of 1944 this subsidiary character, because this is contradicted by Bonhoeffer's own words.

Thus what we have here is undoubtedly the essential basic ideas of Bonhoeffer. His new starting point is quite clearly defined. Further work

167. See Ch. XIII, pp. 754 f.

on it would inevitably have considered consequences and given examples. But the basic ideas can be recognized in the letter form, in which Bonhoeffer speaks in a carefree and abbreviated way, as one does with an interlocutor with whom one shares common ideas and theological presuppositions.

2. The New Formulae

After April 1944 Bonhoeffer's new theme was not simply the 'non-religious interpretation of Biblical terms in a world come of age'. As we said to begin with, this key phrase is part of an explicitly stated larger theme that Bonhoeffer has expressed many times in the form of a question or suggestive idea.

The Main Question. With Bonhoeffer's fourfold declaration of what his purpose really was, he places his ideas concerning non-religious interpretation in the perspective within which he wishes them to be seen.

1. The theme is stated straightaway on 30th April, before Bonhoeffer begins his new discussions: 'What is bothering me incessantly is the question . . . who Christ really is, for us today.'[168] The chief question, then, is not *what* parts of the creed are still acceptable today, but *who* is HE for us today. Bonhoeffer does not consider from a distance how much of tradition can be retained, but, as in *Act and Being* and the *Christology*, enquires into the person of Christ and into the way in which he encounters and defines us today.[169]

2. In the same letter Bonhoeffer again states his question from the standpoint of the same attitude, when discussing the coming of age of the world:

. . . if our final judgement must be that the western form of Christianity, too, was only a preliminary stage to a complete absence of religion, what kind of situation emerges for us, for the Church? How can Christ become the Lord of the religionless as well? . . . How do we speak of God—without religion, i.e. without the temporally conditioned presuppositions of metaphysics, inwardness, and so on? How do we speak (or perhaps we cannot now even 'speak' as we used to) in a 'secular' way about 'God'? In what way are we 'religionless—secular' Christians, in what way are we the ἐκκλησία those who are called forth, not regarding ourselves from a religious point of view as specially favoured, but rather as belonging wholly to the world? In that case Christ is no longer an object of religion, but something quite different, really the Lord of the world. But what does that mean?[170]

Thus Bonhoeffer is enquiring into the way in which Christ is Lord, and not into a method whereby he can be presented today. With this

168. LPP, p. 152.
169. AB, pp. 138 f. and GS III, pp. 170 ff.
170. LPP, pp. 153 f.

kind of enquiry he took up again what he had said as early as 1932, namely that it is not a question of how we ought to proclaim the Gospels today but, in view of the historical development of the Western world, of who is its content. Given the presupposition of the presence of Christ, Bonhoeffer seeks to understand his presence today.

3. On 8th June he expressed the theme in its most succinct form: 'Christ and the world that has come of age'.[171] Here Bonhoeffer criticizes the liberals, but also Heim and Althaus, for ultimately dispensing—if for different reasons—with Christ's antecedent and comprehensive claim to lordship. But that was the last thing that Bonhoeffer was attempting now.

4. Soon afterwards, on 30th June, he presented another variation on the theme: 'Let me just summarize briefly what I am concerned about— how to claim through Jesus Christ a world that has come of age.'[172] Christ was, is, and will be the Lord. This lordship of Christ that Bonhoeffer is concerned with in all four formulations of his theme is saved by him from clericalization and hierarchic tendencies because this Lord exercises his lordship always and solely through powerlessness, service and the Cross. But this lordship is undoubted. Bonhoeffer is not defending a lost lordship and certainly not any lost positions. Indeed, he wants to give up 'positions' in order that he can learn to understand anew how the suffering and powerless Christ becomes the defining, liberating and creative centre of this world.

After again so clearly stating the fundamental character of his enquiry into the presence of Christ, Bonhoeffer is able to define his task in another quite different and apparently contradictory way, but in fact liberated through that fixed centre, so that he has to defend the world against 'the last of the knights': 'I therefore want to start from the premise . . . that we should frankly recognize that the world, and people, have come of age, that we should not run man down in his worldliness, but confront him with God at his strongest point.'[173] This aim of acknowledging the coming of age so fascinated later readers that many forgot that Bonhoeffer had framed his call to maturity within the theme of the presence of Christ and had not isolated it precisely at this point. His phrase here is: 'confront him with God'. This passage in the letter says something also concerning the majesty of the Word of God: 'it reigns'. Bonhoeffer jotted down on one of my letters, with its anxious questions,[174] notes for his reply, one of which is 'Aristocratic Christianity'.

If this is the character of Bonhoeffer's Tegel theme, then all his

171. LPP, p. 180.
172. LPP, p. 189. The American theologian T. Altizer (*The Gospel of Christian Atheism*, Philadelphia, 1966) could not put it like this, but, at most, speaks of a 'claim on Christ by a world become secular'.
173. LPP, pp. 192 f.
174. Letter of 3.6.1944.

elaborations of it are, from the start, entirely removed from the sphere of apologetics. The question of what can be demanded of a believer today is not the most important thing. There can be genuine doubt about the power of the Church or of a generation to proclaim Christ, but no half-hearted doubt that faith will find what it is seeking. Bonhoeffer's consideration of 'time', which is more frequent now than in previous years, given his main theme, never acquires the pessimistic overtones and undertones that are so characteristic of Heim and Gogarten. Bonhoeffer can threaten, especially the Church and its lack of faith, but never prophesy dark despair. With this theme, declaring oneself for Jesus of Nazareth and his presence is in no way diminished or done away with, however difficult it might be to spell out. The 'interpretation' that Bonhoeffer sets in motion cannot remain within the sphere of contemplative, intellectual questions of understanding, where investigations are undertaken without any regard for what they might yield. His venture is, as it were, part of a journey out of a past commitment into a new one. Bonhoeffer's theme involves a setting out in order to discover the presence of Christ in the world of today: not a discovery of the modern world, not the discovery of him outside this modern world, but discovering HIM in this world. Bonhoeffer asks the simplest of questions, from which it is impossible to emerge unchanged: 'Who are YOU?', and that is why he also mentions prayer right at the beginning of his essay.[175]

Hence this question governs Bonhoeffer's dialogue, and it must preserve the explosive formulae of the world come of age, non-religious interpretation, and arcane discipline, in the right relation and proportion. Without the overriding theme they would fall apart, become stunted or superficial. As isolated intellectual phenomena they have but little to do with Bonhoeffer's thought, but in the Christological perspective of his main theme they achieve their full and independent justification. Thus the question 'Who are YOU today?' involves two things: one, the fact that Bonhoeffer is concerned for the full Christological answer in continuity with the past, and two, the fact that in losing the freshness of past answers, we are concerned with the adventure of a new Christological answer.

The material of the prison letters can now be arranged, commented on, and interrelated in a way parallel to the three chapters 'Outline for a Book',[176] in three groups of ideas under the headings: world come of age (Ch. 1: Stocktaking), non-religious interpretation (Ch. 2: Worldly Faith) and arcane discipline (Ch. 3: Consequences for the Structure of the Church).

a) World Come of Age. Statements concerning the world come of age

175. And not questions as to who and what, see GS III, pp. 170-5. In the first German editions of *Letters and Papers from Prison* there was a disastrous misprint: p. 259, 14th line from the bottom, it must clearly read 'Who is God?', not 'What is God?'
176. LPP, pp. 208 ff.

take up a great deal of space in the letters. This complex of ideas roused the greatest surprise and found the strongest echo with its first readers because of its refreshing analyses.

Bonhoeffer seems to be referring to the stage of a particular historical development to which our eyes must one day be opened if we want to remain in the present. He speaks of 'a world grown of age', of the coming of age', and more rarely of the 'world of age'.[177] This avoids the misunderstanding of seeming to speak as if it were a moral evolution, in the sense of 'grown better'. It is a growing up, with the concomitant responsibilities from which there is now no retreat. Even in a world again enslaved this coming of age remains an ideal by which it measures its condition and of which it dreams. Even the modern tyrant must present his tyranny to his victim as a true liberation and granting of independence.

The concept of 'coming of age' does not appear at once in Bonhoeffer's theological letters, not until 8th June. Until then he uses the concept of 'autonomy' when describing the evolution of the various areas of life towards self-responsibility. On 8th June, however, he speaks of our freeing ourselves from the 'tutelage of "God"'.[178] 'God' here is in inverted commas! The moment the word 'coming of age' appears, it dominates the scene from then on, almost alone. In using the phrase Bonhoeffer is thinking of Kant's formula: 'The Enlightenment is the emergence of man from immaturity that he is himself responsible for. Immaturity is the incapacity to use one's own intelligence without the guidance of another person.'[179] This definition has lain for a century on the Church like a great burden. This is why Richard Rothe bravely transformed faith in the last century into an ethics and defined the process of Christian evolution as a transformation of Christianity into the continually growing ethical autonomy of man coming of age. But Bonhoeffer now takes Kant's irrevocable description of maturity as an essential element of his *theologia crucis*.

Bonhoeffer was not the first theologian who welcomed the evolution of secularization into a coming of age instead of condemning it. If Bonhoeffer had been able to examine the material more thoroughly, he would have seen that L. Ragaz and Paul Tillich had made similar earlier breakthroughs. The others, however, had been concerned with a turning away from the Christology of the Reformation, whereas Bonhoeffer proclaimed the coming of age in the name of the crucified and risen Christ and saw it as a necessary part of his Christology. It was the crucified Christ who, for him, makes possible 'true worldliness', 'genuine this-worldliness' and 'coming of age', judging and renewing it. But this gives a theological quality to the category of coming of age.

---

177. LPP, pp. 178, 179, 182, 188, 189, 192, 196, 200, 208.
178. LPP, p. 178.
179. The introductory statement of Immanuel Kant's *Was ist Aufklärung?* (1784).

Theological Judgement. In connection with a critique of Bultmann, Bonhoeffer pointed out that he sought to 'think theologically'.[180] The recognition of the world's coming of age is, with Bonhoeffer, neither philosophy nor phenomenology, but the knowledge of God, i.e. 'theology', and that is a knowledge that seeks to follow God where he has already preceded us. That is why Bonhoeffer's statement about the world come of age is first and last a theological statement. It is, moreover, the same with his statement concerning 'unconscious Christianity'.[181]

A theological statement is not a statistical operation, but preserves a proclamation of God concerning a piece of history. Its importance consists in the fact that it has its time and it is expressed in a committed and committing way. As a 'theological statement' it possesses critical protesting and liberating elements. It became clear to Bonhoeffer that it was high time to declare, for the sake of God, that the world, Hitler's image of which he was not prepared to accept, had come of age. In this he was concerned not only with the knowledge of its maturity, but also with the unequivocal proclamation of it. In this theological statement, seeing and recognizing are inseparably bound up with the judgement itself, namely the prediction of maturity.

The objection that Bonhoeffer, or the Church is only restating what the world had already done long ago by itself misses the heart of the problem. It is quite legitimate for the Church's blessing to be extended to *faits accomplis*. It always blesses 'after the event', in order to give expression to God's faithful love and involvement in a particular past piece of the history of individuals or communities. A curse or a blessing is always pronounced over something that has come into being, determining its future progress. In the case of the 'world come of age' it was hitherto the case that the Church not only did not bless the autonomously evolving world, but condemned it and called it 'Godless'. But if there is no declaration that it has come of age, then the world itself must pronounce it.

It is only at this point in his theological development that Bonhoeffer came upon this idea, but he then accorded to it an almost polemically important place in his discussions. It is true that he had long since dropped the word 'secularization', so commonly used by the Church, to describe the modern development of the world.[182] And even before this it occurred only seldom. Bonhoeffer disliked its condemnatory, negative tone. This was not the word for what he was referring to. Thus he used the word that emphasized the positive element of the relationship between Christ and the modern world.

180. LPP, p. 156.
181. LPP, p. 205.
182. The last time he used it was in an early part of the *Ethics*, E, p. 105.

Thus the world's coming of age is no longer an occasion for polemics and apologetics, but is now really better understood than it understands itself, namely on the basis of the gospel and in the light of Christ.[183]

Because Bonhoeffer never ceases to think dialectically, what he says about the world's coming of age has two levels and there can be no positivistic levelling out. The Gospel of the *theologia crucis* has room for the world come of age and even accepts that such a world may deny the Gospel, but the acceptance includes assisting it at the same time to become truly itself. The unity and paradox of the *theologia crucis* and the world come of age found its most succinct expression in the passage he wrote on 16th July 1944, which has become famous:

. . . that we have to live in the world *etsi deus non daretur*. And this is just what we do recognize—before God! God himself compels us to recognize it. So our coming of age leads us to a true recognition of our situation before God. God would have us know that we must live as men who manage our lives without him. The God who is with us is the God who forsakes us (Mark 15 : 34). The God who lets us live in the world without the working hypothesis of God is the God before whom we stand continually. Before God and with God we live without God. God lets himself be pushed out of the world on to the cross. He is weak and powerless in the world, and that is precisely the way, the only way, in which he is with us and helps us.[184]

Given this chance of exploring in both directions the knowledge of the theology of the Cross and the knowledge of the world's having come of age, Bonhoeffer is even able to venture to state the contrary proposition, namely that the knowledge of the world's coming of age can help us to a better understanding of the Gospel:

To that extent we may say that the development towards the world's coming of age outlined above, which has done away with a false conception of God, opens up a way of seeing the God of the Bible, who wins power and space in the world by his weakness.[185]

Or, putting it in an even more daring way: 'The world that has come of age is more godless, and perhaps for that very reason nearer to God, than the world before its coming of age.'[186] True, Bonhoeffer was far too alert a theologian not to know that every new piece of knowledge could succumb to isolation, and hence the freedom of the world to become of age could succumb to positivistic misuse. That is why he said one day, 21st July 1944, when he may well have thought that he would not much longer have the opportunity of communicating his ideas:

I don't mean the shallow and banal this-worldliness of the enlightened, the busy, the comfortable, or the lascivious, but the profound this-worldliness,

183. LPP, p. 182.
184. LPP, p. 196.
185. LPP, p. 197.
186. LPP, p. 200.

characterized by discipline and the constant knowledge of death and resurrection.[187]

But it was precisely because the coming of age of this world was so clearly related to the Gospel of the Cross that he was able to affirm it so resolutely. And in fact it was this new affirmation that occupied his mind at first more than anything else and caused him to re-examine his intellectual structures. Now, in different accents from four years previously in the chapter 'Inheritance and Decay' of the *Ethics* he presented the way of liberation of the Western mind, law, philosophy and secular life. The pleasure he had in continually testing this was clear. Now modern 'secularization', or preferably 'worldliness', is seen as a necessary and specific heritage of Christianity and is no longer denounced by the latter. Secularization is no longer an evil falling away, but the free responsible attitude of Christianity; and the secularizers are no longer powerful seducers, but the protagonists and midwives of humanity. It is important to realize the process that one day causes the Church to fall into error if it continues to regard 'worldliness' as of the devil instead of helping to make human beings realize their true humanity. For it suddenly becomes clear that humanity and the world's coming of age are inescapably interconnected.

Now a liberating movement begins to spread in which the Christian listens to Feuerbach and Nietzsche—with a good conscience—and allows them their share in humanity's progress, in that they, for example, warn the Church against becoming a chemist's shop to minister to heavenly needs, leaving the world to its own devices. As against this, the *theologia crucis* of the Church may serve the inheritance of the Enlightenment as a protection against its own tendency towards the unrealistic. It corrects the unquenchable urge of mankind to glorify, deify or demonize its progress, and, today perhaps even more necessarily in the other direction, protects the rationalist from his unfortunate tendency to the sterile fragmentation of himself and his work into pessimistic resignation and sceptical agnosticism.

The effect of what Bonhoeffer says about coming of age was heightened by the fact that he made these astonishing statements at a time when he himself had become the helpless victim of the dumb executive organs of power, and, like Boethius, the philosopher of late antiquity imprisoned for high treason, he strongly relativized what lay closest to him. It seemed that we had never heard things expressed quite like this before: that the lordship of Christ corresponds to worldliness, and discipleship to a sharing in this world; that the natural, the profane, the rational and the humane had its place, not against, but with this Christ.

b) *Non-religious Interpretation.* It is now a characteristic of the world

187. LPP, p. 201.

come of age that the period of 'religion' has passed. Bonhoeffer refers to the end of religion even before he uses the phrase concerning the world coming of age. First he defines religion as 'metaphysics and inwardness', but then it seems to be chiefly its tutelary character that is done away with.

Hence the presence of Christ must be experienced in this 'non-religious interpretation'. Bonhoeffer often approached this task, but without carrying it through to a conclusion.[188] Here he felt the greatest practical difficulties. On 3rd June I asked him about Bultmann, about the abandonment by the Protestants of any special space of their own, about the role of the liturgical and prophetic spheres and the place of tradition in this 'interpretation'. His answer was as follows:

You now ask so many important questions on the subjects that have been occupying me lately, that I should be happy if I could answer them myself. But it is all very much in the early stages; and, as usual, I am being led on more by an instinctive feeling for questions that will arise later than by any conclusions that I have already reached about them.[189]

But he was quite certain that the tasks of the future lay in this direction, i.e. that the Gospel should be freed from its traditional trammels and be understood and passed on, that it should, in other words, continue to live on in a 'non-religious' way.

In the course of his discussions Bonhoeffer varied the term he used and also called it 'worldly interpretation', 'worldly re-interpretation',[190] or 'the new, non-religious language'.[191] For the most part he speaks of religionless 'interpretation', once using the phrase religionless 'Christianity', and, another time, 'religionless Christians', or 'living without religion'. It is notable that in German-speaking countries the only discussion has been concerning the expression 'non-religious interpretation', whereas in the English world the key phrase has been 'religionless Christianity'. There are, in fact, two different things involved: in the one case it is the problems of preaching, and in the other the problems of prayer and the institutional Church. But Bonhoeffer is speaking about both of these.

He does not find the expression 'non-religious interpretation' as 'enigmatic' as Barth does.[192] At any rate, he was so sure of what he was saying that he had no hesitation in giving his book the working title of 'Non-religious Interpretation in a World come of Age', and devoted the work he proposed writing to this programmatic aim.

'*Religion*'. What could Bonhoeffer have meant by 'religion' and hence by 'non-religious interpretation'?

188. Cf. LPP, pp. 151 ff., 155 ff., 165 ff., 190 ff., 198 ff.
189. LPP, pp. 177 f.   190. LPP, p. 157.
191. LPP, p. 172.   192. MW I, p. 121.

His use of the term 'religion' has, on closer examination, given rise to many questions. But Bonhoeffer at Tegel never intended for a moment to write an historical or systematic monograph concerning the phenomenon of religion, as he had done, at much greater length in, for example, *Act and Being*. He would scarcely have allowed himself to become involved in an argument as to whether he had completely clarified the term 'religion', but would have admitted that what he was talking about, considered as an independent phenomenon detached from its connections with Christology, was not clearly defined and, if considered from other aspects, would present a different appearance. The fact that he was not entirely unaware of this is proved, for example, by the books he read which included Orelli's *General History of Religion* and Simmel's *Religion*, on both of which he worked. More recently he had also acquired G. van der Leeuw's *Phenomenology of Religion* and *Man and Religion*, as well as the comprehensive history of religion by Chantepie de la Saussaye.

Although he would always dismiss the phenomenon of religion, he assumed within the framework of his overall theme of the presence of Christ in a world come of age that some things now belonged to the past —he called these, according to his own tradition, 'religion'. They not only obscured one's view of the present world and Christ, but distorted it. It was one of his fundamental experiences as a student to make a diametrically opposite distinction between faith and religion. Every sermon he gave in Barcelona indicated what he had learnt from Karl Barth and what he had seen in the Bible, through Barth's eyes, of opposition to religion.[193] Since then this view of faith and religion had become common currency between a large number of theologians in the Confessing Church. Thus Bonhoeffer in prison explicitly again praised what Barth had done: 'Barth was the first theologian to begin the criticism of religion, and that remains his really great merit',[194] religion meaning that human activity that seeks to reach the beyond, to postulate a divinity, to invoke help and protection, in short: religion as self-justification.

Bonhoeffer emphasized that Barth was the first person 'to have started along this line' of thinking in terms of a religionless Christianity, although he 'did not carry it to completion',[195] nor had he given any 'concrete guidance' 'in the non-religious interpretation of theological concepts'.[196] What Bonhoeffer was probably thinking of in speaking of Barth's beginning, but not thinking through, is explained by Benkt-Erik Benktson's reference to the early essays by Barth, in which some of the latter's formulations bear an extraordinary resemblance to many that Bonhoeffer made in 1944.[197]

193. See Ch. III, pp. 79 f.   196. LPP, p. 181.
194. LPP, p. 156.   197. See Ch. II, p. 54.
195. LPP, p. 153.

Bonhoeffer's treatment of the term 'religion' differs, however, from that of Barth. Barth regarded religion as an unavoidable characteristic of the believer—just as Bonhoeffer had done in his early period, for example in *Act and Being*. But now the phenomenon of religion does not seem for Bonhoeffer, to be an eternal concomitant characteristic of man, but a transitory historical one, and therefore perhaps a unique 'Western'[198] phenomenon that would not return. In this Bonhoeffer certainly went beyond Barth. But Bonhoeffer had not sufficiently considered how disturbing all this was, so that his statements reveal at this point an unguarded weakness.

The Characteristics of the Concept of Religion for Bonhoeffer. Despite the fragmentary character of his utterances, we do have statements that give sharp outlines to what Bonhoeffer describes in his letters as religion. Bonhoeffer himself gives an incidental definition of two of these qualities and thus reminds us explicitly of earlier material: the metaphysical and the individualistic elements. Other characteristics suggest themselves out of the totality of his thought and action: the privileged character of religion, its partiality, its concept of the *deus ex machina*, its tendency to keep people in tutelage, and so on.

We may ask whether such characteristics must necessarily be features of 'religion', but Bonhoeffer considers them to be actually present and believes that religion, with these characteristics, has become a Western phenomenon, thus limiting the challenge and the nature of Jesus to a quite specific direction. But this direction leads us into dead ends and should be abandoned. Dwelling here on terminological objections could prevent us seeing Bonhoeffer's real aim.

Metaphysics.

To 'interpret in a religious sense' . . . I think it means to speak on the one hand metaphysically, and on the other individualistically[199] . . . the temporally conditioned presuppositions of metaphysics . . .[200] God . . . in the conceptual forms of the absolute, metaphysical, infinite . . .[201]

These are Bonhoeffer's own references to religion as a metaphysically determined entity. He is not thinking in terms of 'immanence—transcendence', in order then to eliminate transcendence in favour of immanence. On the contrary, he is concerned here in particular to regain a genuine transcendence, in contrast to a now valueless metaphysics, as an 'extended world' and as a necessary prerequisite to any faith.[202]

Already as a student, in the Berlin of Ritschl, Bonhoeffer had seen the imprisonment of Biblical faith in the philosophical metaphysics of the

198. LPP, pp. 152 f.   201. LPP, p. 210.
199. LPP, p. 156.   202. LPP, pp. 209 f.
200. LPP, p. 153.

West, which the theology of Barth had then further borne in on him. The former overwhelming transcendence of faith appears for Bonhoeffer in the long history of its metaphysical build-up, which is then reduced to something that is painlessly distant. Supernatural and mythological formulations obscure the direct immediacy of the Gospel, and the exotic nature of the context in which it is presented has nothing to do with the message itself. Instead of this, however, the metaphysical Christian religion provided the world with the kind of transcendence that it longed for. God became necessary as the superstructure of existence, and religious longing found its goal in a heavenly domain. Thus metaphysics seduces the Christian religion into thinking statically in terms of two spheres and has forced it to put another worldly emphasis on its redemptive character.

Perhaps Bonhoeffer's use of the concept 'metaphysics' needs some slight correcting by Tillich;[203] but certainly Bonhoeffer's non-religious interpretation is close to Tillich and Bultmann in what it rejects here together with the 'metaphysical' misunderstanding of religion of the Gospel of Jesus. Just as Tillich wants to get rid of the 'supernatural' and Bultmann, the 'mythological', so·Bonhoeffer wants to get rid, for the sake of God, of the 'religious' trappings, i.e. an objectification of God that is conditioned by a particular age. Bonhoeffer is also anxious to break up the traditional structure of dogmas and ideas of them, to discuss 'theism' and begin a new dialogue with the 'a-theists'. And yet, already here, side by side with Bonhoeffer's epistemologically orientated enquiry, other elements that are voluntaristic and related to existence also play a strong part. Let us recall his early interest in 'ethical transcendence'.[204]

It is not with the beyond that we are concerned, but with this world as created and preserved, subjected to laws, reconciled, and restored. What is above this world is, in the gospel, intended to exist for this world.[205]

According to the relevant sections in *Sanctorum Communio* and *Act and Being*, there is a close connection between the metaphysical and the subsequent individualistic element, because—as he never tired of showing—in the epistemological transcendence of the metaphysical everything is ultimately 'drawn' into the subject, the latter alone ultimately remaining. Thus here also in the letters he always speaks of both together.

Individualism.

To 'interpret in a religious sense' . . . means to speak . . . on the other

203. See P. Tillich, *Systematische Theologie*, Vol. I, p. 28; 'Die Frage nach dem Unbedingten', in *Gesammelte Werke*, Vol. V, pp. 141 f.
204. SC, p. 33.
205. LPP, p. 156.

hand individualistically.[206] [The period of religion was, in fact,] the time of inwardness and conscience;[207] the temporally conditioned presuppositions of . . . inwardness;[208] [the attempt to keep God's] place secure at least in the sphere of the 'personal', the 'inner', and the 'private';[209] Pietism as a last attempt to maintain evangelical Christianity as a religion . . .[210]

These phrases point to religion as an individualistic entity.

As early as *Sanctorum Communio* Bonhoeffer had expounded the social element in all Christian concepts. Of course he was always speaking very directly of individual acceptance of faith; but he never lost sight of the social, anti-individualistic direction of faith and the kingdom of righteousness. He never became so rigorous that he rejected the intense personal declarations of faith of the hymns of Paul Gerhardt; but he was sensitive to the tendency to direct one's gaze to the private sphere of man and cultivate the 'salvation of one's own soul' at the cost of the world and the *familia Dei*. This sensitivity had become so keen that the last thing he sought was to lead back men who had 'come of age' into the limitations of this kind of individualistic inwardness.

Non-religious interpretation and existential interpretation may have seemed to be the same thing when viewed in terms of the metaphysical objectification of God, but this does not seem to be the case when we come to the second characteristic. The interest of the existential interpretation lies clearly with the individual, which favours sterility in regard to questions that transcend the individual. Hence it has often been pointed out that there is a connection between the theology of Bultmann and the pietistic world, which Bonhoeffer calls 'religious'. Bonhoeffer probably thought the same when he extended (to existential philosophy as well) his dislike of the practice of a pietistic or 'methodist' pastoral care dwelling on the intimate sphere of human life or on the 'inwardness' of human existence. Thus he would probably have asked whether the modern existential interpretation was not subject to his verdict that the 'secrets known to a man's valet' were 'the hunting-ground of modern pastoral workers',[211] and hence was part of the sphere of 'religious interpretation', where 'in those secret human places . . . God is to have his domain'.[212]

Partiality. We can now add a few important characteristics to these definitions of 'religion' quoted by Bonhoeffer himself, characteristics that emerge from Bonhoeffer's life and theological convictions, or are clearly stated in the paraphrased form of the letters, thus giving an even more exact image of 'non-religious interpretation'.

Bonhoeffer had become disturbed in his youth by Friedrich Naumann's

206. LPP, p. 156.   210. LPP, p. 209.
207. LPP, p. 152.   211. LPP, p. 191.
208. LPP, p. 153.   212. LPP, p. 192.
209. LPP, pp. 190 f.

question as to how far the Christian religion had become a separate area among the other areas of life, a mere section of the whole. God is assigned a more or less respectable sphere within the totality of life. This can be said of the subtle view of a 'religious *a priori*' of his teacher Reinhold Seeberg, which is assigned its own domain alongside other *a priori* elements of life. The same thing is true of the quasi-religious areas that can be discussed in sociological or psychological terms; perhaps, one could go on, it is true of remnants of the past, relics of various kinds that can still be life-giving or that come into the province of the department of education. In the continual process of secularization these areas that are still religiously alive are removed one by one from the number of relevant areas. Thus the Christian God also seems condemned to preside over only those areas of life that remain, as yet, unexplored. Bonhoeffer never tires of describing this fate of the Christian religion of being 'continually in retreat'.[213] 'The "religious act" is always something partial; "faith" is something whole, involving the whole of one's life.'[214]

The fatal thing is that here religion directs all interest towards its frontiers and, institutionalized, keeps watch over them. 'The decisive factor: the Church on the defensive. No taking risks for others.'[215]

Deus ex machina. Bonhoeffer describes the common religious conception of God as a *deus ex machina* most vividly in the first verse of his poem 'Christians and Pagans'.[216] All religion depends on this concept. There must be a supreme being, 'omnipotence, omniscience, omnipresence',[217] so that we can be rescued from dangers, our mysteries solved and our questions answered. This makes the Christian religion a spiritual chemist's shop. The preacher points out to his listeners their need of help in order then to dispense to them the necessary remedies.

Bonhoeffer is concerned here to show that it is precisely religiosity and even pietism that can dangerously conceal man's real godlessness. Christ must not be made the 'answer', the 'solution', or the 'medicine'. Religion depends on the power of God, but 'the Bible directs man to God's powerlessness and suffering'.[218]

This idea again makes religion an escape from real life and from mature responsibility for it. It accustoms us to artificial satisfactions. Perhaps we ought to mention in this connection what Bonhoeffer says concerning 'longing', namely that God is not there to fill the gaps. This is stated with especial clarity in the letter of Christmas Eve, 1943.[219]

Privilege. The idea behind this characteristic of religion is mentioned only once by name in the letters: 'those who are called forth',[220] but

213. LPP, p. 174.   217. LPP, p. 210.
214. LPP, p. 199.   218. LPP, p. 197.
215. LPP, p. 209.   219. LPP, pp. 116 f., but also 109 ff.
216. LPP, p. 200.   220. LPP, p. 153.

it is there in fact all the time and is almost the most important of all. Bonhoeffer's life consists of a constant fight to overcome the dangerously privileged character of the Christian religion: by his decision to take up theology, his move from lecturing to pastoral work, and from that to 'becoming a man of his own time' in the conspiracy against Hitler.

Throughout its history, the Christian religion has been continually perverted into a form of privilege.[221] It was unable to prevent itself being understood, in the most varied ways, as a gift to specially favoured people. This happened in every conceivable area of individual and social life and thought: materially, financially, legally, as a physical or psychic, inborn or acquired gift. Faith becomes a possession that is deserved or undeserved, as the case may be. It appears as something thrust upon people unrelated to anything else and propagated in terms of a restorative 'positivism of revelation'.[222] Its practice becomes the luxury, hedged around with convention, of certain classes of society, who have the time to afford it, or else are compelled by their circumstances to do so. Religion had become, in fact, the strongest guarantor of the safety and continuation of the existing order, power structure and ways of thought.

There belongs here also what Bonhoeffer says concerning religion as 'law', as the condition of salvation—one must belong to it.[223] Religion has become essentially a way of distinguishing people. A victim of its divisive privileged character, it has presided over a vast number of acts of violence throughout history: Christians against non-Christians, theists against atheists, or whites against coloured people.

Tutelage. Closely connected with the privileged character of religion is the role that it plays as the 'guardian' of man, who is regarded, at least in this respect, as not having come of age. This characteristic must again be especially emphasized because the institutions, but also the monarchical, patriarchal character of the thought categories of the Christian religion, seem so ineradicable, and also because the two things are essentially linked in Bonhoeffer and interpret each other: 'the non-religious interpretation' and 'in a world come of age', or, vice versa, 'religious interpretation in a world that is treated as if it were not of age.'

'Religious interpretation' is an interpretation of the Gospel of the powerlessness of Christ that establishes priests (as the givers of life) or theologians (as the custodians of truth) as the guardians and the rulers of the people of the Church, creating and perpetuating a situation of dependence. Nothing will be as difficult as overcoming the monarchical and patriarchal structures of hierarchies, theologies and, indeed, dogmas,

221. See also Appendix B in the German edition.
222. LPP, pp. 153, 157, 181, 182.
223. LPP, pp. 153 f., 171.

for coming of age has an element about it that is alarmingly un-reassuring.

Thus Bonhoeffer is able to speak of 'orthodoxy' as the 'attempt to rescue the Church as an institution for salvation',[224] and of 'false religious obligations and inhibitions',[225] but can also urge us to accept responsibility for others and make possible the mature cooperation and partnership of the world. 'The Church must share in the secular problems of ordinary human life, not dominating, but helping and serving.'[226] Incidentally, is not the reason for Bonhoeffer's personal influence his mysterious capacity to help men on the way to maturity?

Dispensability. We have mentioned above that characteristic of Bon-hoeffer's concept of religion as it emerges in the letters from prison, namely that religion is passing away; it must be considered once more in this list, although Bonhoeffer has left us in the dark as to the relation of Barth's systematic concept of religion to this historical one. Can faith ever escape becoming a religion, whether Western, Eastern or African? But precisely in order to make faith possible, Bonhoeffer explains 'religion' in its 'Western form' as something we can do without and as a relic of past ages. His judgement here is so sure because he regards the age of Jesus as something different from the age of religion.

Bonhoeffer regards the characteristics of religion we have mentioned as failing to recognize not only the presence, but also the person of Jesus. The basic thing is always simply him and the way he is present to us: 1. he, Jesus, does not call for any acceptance of preliminary systems of thought and behaviour; 2. he is anti-individualist, and, in a totally exposed and unprotected way, the man for others; 3. he does not pray as if he made part payment by instalments, but with his life; 4. he turns away from the temptation of the *deus ex machina*; 5. he turns away from the privileged classes and sits down with the outcasts; and 6. he liberates men to find their own responsible answer to life through his own powerlessness, which is both shaming and utterly convincing.

Bonhoeffer finds that Christians daily corroborate his analysis, since their Christian activity has, in fact, become a separate Sunday-like area within their total life. Pestalozzi expressed what had happened to religion in the language of his day, in an individualistic, but still valid way—as pointed out by Hammelsbeck.

I swung back and forth between feelings that drew me to religion and judge-ments that drew me away from it, the dead path of my age. I felt the essence of religion grow cold within me, without ever actually making a decision against religion . . .

In the unspeakable misery I underwent, the strength of the few isolated religious feelings of my younger years disappeared . . .

224. LPP, p. 209.   225. LPP, p. 198.   226. LPP, p. 211.

.I do not believe, not because I regard non-belief as truth, but because the sum of my impressions of life has largely removed the blessing of faith from my innermost self . . . Thus I am a long way from the fulfilment of myself and do not know the heights that I suspect that perfect truth is able to ascend.[227]

Shortly before his execution, after the 20th July plot in 1944, Adam von Trott described the situation in a more urgent way, as might be expected: 'Can our childlike Christian faith . . . grow and adapt to the whole weight and intensity of our problems today?' 'Childlike Christian faith' is here exactly the same as Bonhoeffer's 'religion', and its 'growth' corresponds to Bonhoeffer's search for the totality of faith in relation to mature responsibility in man's contemporary involvement with the world, and the word 'adapt' resembles his comprehensive term 'interpretation'. Just before his death Trott asks, half in hope, half in doubt, Bonhoeffer's question.

Summing up: if 'religion' has a tendency to the 'partial', we can speak of 'non-partial' interpretation instead of 'non-religious', or, when Bonhoeffer says 'worldly', we can speak of the 'totality of interpretation, with all its relevance and claims'. We see here the reason for Bonhoeffer's love of *Witiko*: 'The "religious act" is always something partial, "faith" is something whole, involving the whole of one's life. Jesus calls men not to a new religion, but to life . . . young Witiko . . . set out into the world "to do the whole thing".'[228] The 'whole thing' is other people, is the revelation of one's own godlessness, the acceptance of the common guilt and the sharing of God's powerlessness in the world. Bonhoeffer's non-religious interpretation is, in a full sense, Christological interpretation

More than a Programme of Interpretation. Bonhoeffer's 'non-religious interpretation' makes available to the preaching of the Church and the living body of the congregation solid and dependable criteria. Can it be carried out, as a programme of interpretation, with the interpretative tools of the study and practised as, say, a variation on 'existential interpretation'? G. Krause suggests the latter when, commenting on our attempts to present Bonhoeffer's ideas so far, he warns, with a certain justification, against placing him so far away from Bultmann.[229] Is it an interpretation without the supernatural dogmatic structure, such as J. A. T. Robinson presents, drawing out the parallels with Tillich? Yes and no.

We have already suggested that Bultmann, Tillich and Bonhoeffer resemble one another in certain respects.[230] All three were able to say: 'We are once again being driven right back to the beginnings of our

227. J. H. Pestalozzi, letter to Nikolovius, 1793.
228. LPP, pp. 124, 199.
229. G. Krause, op. cit., pp. 439 ff.
230. See Ch. XIII, p. 777.

understanding.'[231] Bonhoeffer is very much concerned with the hermeneutical question and realized even earlier how urgent it was. But he reacts differently: he gets to grips more with the Church. Moreover, it must mean something that the three men who formulated their views in total independence of one another, each came, on the basis of his different approach, to a different terminology for what he wanted to say, the first on the basis of his philological work of translation and his pondering of its philosophical presuppositions; the second out of his philosophical interest in a reconciliatory universalism; and the third?

Ebeling has warned us against making Bonhoeffer the defender of a new 'form' as against a new language.[232] There is no doubt that Bonhoeffer too is passionately concerned with the contemporary relevance of the kerygma, with the way in which the Gospel can be expressed. And yet he strongly emphasizes the area where philosophical, conceptual and translation questions are transcended. His two chapters 'A Stocktaking of Christianity' and 'The Real Meaning of Christian Faith' are followed by a third: 'Conclusions'. These 'conclusions' raise questions that are wholly concerned with the 'form' of Christianity and that cannot be ignored. Hence non-religious interpretation is more an ethical than a hermeneutical category and also a direct call to penitence directed at the Church and its present form—for the sake of, if one likes, the kerygma, the language.

The starting-point of his thinking is characteristically linked with his interest in an 'arcane discipline', i.e. in the constant relationship between the interpreter and the Lord, whose power lies in his very powerlessness. This approach has not, on the whole, been accepted in theological discussion, but it raises immediately the problem of the identity of the Christian as soon as he begins to see the extent of his identification with the world. If, then, non-religious interpretation means identification, then arcane discipline is the guarantee of an identity.

Bonhoeffer's 'programme of interpretation' is familiar with the advice to the Church to practise particular forms of silence,[233] for 'it is not abstract argument, but example, that gives its word emphasis and power'.[234] Thus honest intellectual effort is combined with ethical decisions. Bonhoeffer also discusses questions of understanding and method, but always comes very soon to 'conclusions' that are both vulnerable and damaging and readily open to criticism, as, for example, the giving away of the Church's possessions. It is difficult to argue about what he says, for he soon reaches points that must be either accepted as prophetic or rejected. For Bonhoeffer, questions of method that postpone the act of 'interpretation', in the false expectation that they can be solved intellectually, cause our present encounter with the past and future Jesus Christ to disappear from view and lead us into false involvements.

231. LPP, p. 172.   233. LPP, p. 172.
232. G. Ebeling, MW II, pp. 34 f.   234. LPP, p. 211.

'We have spent too much time in thinking, supposing that if we weigh in advance the possibilities of any action, it will happen automatically . . . your thinking will be confined to your responsibilities in action.'[235]

c) Arcane Discipline. Everything presses now towards those passages in which Bonhoeffer speaks of the mystery of a 'participation in the suffering of God on this earth', within which there takes place a 'new fusion' that will make available again one day 'the word of reconciliation and redemption' in terms of which 'the world will be changed and renewed'.[236] Bonhoeffer describes this central mystery by the term 'arcane discipline', referring to that part of the sharing, in the closer and wider sense, that is concerned with the 'worship of God'. In the general discussion of Bonhoeffer's ideas this arcane discipline has generally been considered least, for on this subject there has been the greatest uncertainty and also the greatest danger of one-sidedness. And yet here the validity of the main theme is again immediately obvious, namely the actual relationship to Christ as present, which can never be separated from the question: Who is Christ for us today? This is where we have statements about silence and invisibility, about the way in which the just man prays and acts, and about the difference between the ultimate and the penultimate.[237]

The actual phrase occurs only twice in the prison letters,[238] but it does occur in the very first account of his new theological work. Bonhoeffer was undoubtedly at once aware of the possibilities of a one-sided approach, once the inner balance of things was lost. Moreover, the question of arcane discipline was not as peripheral for him as the infrequency of the phrase might suggest. His whole personality led him to put a protective screen around the central events of life, and it was to be expected that he would be interested in the early Christian practice of excluding the uninitiated, the unbaptized catechumens, from the second part of the liturgy, in which the communion was celebrated and the Nicene Creed sung. This was the origin of the 'arcane discipline'. When we were students at Finkenwalde we were surprised when Bonhoeffer sought to revive this piece of early church history of which we had never taken any notice.[239]

While Bonhoeffer developed his ideas on non-religious interpretation

235. LPP, p. 169.
236. LPP, p. 172.
237. Letters of 30.4., 5.5., 18.7., the baptismal address, the poem 'Christians and Pagans', as well as GS III. pp. 41 ff. and IV, pp. 607 f. Gisela Meuss has traced the element of arcane discipline through all Bonhoeffer's work: 'Arkandisziplin und Weltlichkeit bei Dietrich Bonhoeffer', MW III, pp. 68-115. There is, in addition, the model of his own prayer discipline and his own uninterpreted actions.
238. LPP, pp. 154, 157. The word 'secret' is used.
239. GS IV, p. 239; see also his remarkable reference to the arcane element of the 'Confession' in his 1932 lecture: 'The first confession before the world is that action that immediately interprets itself'; cf. Appendix B in the German edition.

of Christianity in a world come of age, he never considered abandoning for himself his connection with the traditional words and customs of the Church. In the same letter in which he mentions the difference between himself and the *homo religiosus* and also the problematical aspects of his *Cost of Discipleship*—this was in the isolation of 21st July 1944—he said:

These theological thoughts are, in fact, always occupying my mind; but there are times when I am just content to live the life of faith without worrying about its problems. At those times I simply take pleasure in the day's *Losungen* —in particular those of yesterday and today[240] and I am always glad to go back to Paul Gerhardt's beautiful hymns.[241]

There is no doubt that Bonhoeffer regarded an arcane discipline as the essential counterpoint of non-religious interpretation. He is not yet, of course, able to achieve a satisfactory theological solution of this problem, much to his own annoyance. Thus, when he developed his new perspective, he immediately raised the question of what was going to happen to the worship service. This was not in any spirit of breaking it up or, indeed, simply getting rid of it. On the contrary, he was concerned to preserve—as he explicitly states—a 'genuine worship'.[242] This means that he has no intention of simply including the religionless world within the Church or making the Church and the world the same thing. It would be a total misunderstanding of Bonhoeffer to imagine that in the realization of his worldly interpretation there would no longer be any community gathered for worship, so that the Word, the Sacrament and the community could be simply replaced by *caritas*. The self-sacrifice of the Church in his non-religious interpretation, which Bonhoeffer was thinking of, both for it and for himself, is not, then, to be at all associated with the loss of its identity. It is precisely this that is to be re-won.

The discipline of prayer, meditation, worship and coming together (in 'genuine worship') is as essential—though of course, reformable—as daily food and drink. But it is also as much an 'arcane' affair as the central events of life, which are not amenable to a missionary demonstration. The degree to which—and the centre from which—those who interpret Christianity in a non-religious way are maintained, led on and 'spiritually nourished', cannot be outwardly propagated or demonstrated. And certainly not when circumstances have evolved that have destroyed the automatic relation of the names of these events of life to the world of those around us.

Hence the Church will not simply jettison such great names and ideas as 'creation', 'fall', 'atonement', 'the last things', 'penance', 'resurrection', but continue to live in them. But if it can no longer relate them to the

240. 'Some boast of chariots, and some of horses . . .', 'The Lord is my shepherd . . .'
241. LPP, p. 201.
242. LPP, p. 181.

world come of age, in such a way that their essence and life become eloquent and effective within this present world,[243] then it should remain silent until there is again a call for them and the precious content of its words becomes again a compelling thing. Bonhoeffer's desire for an 'arcane tact' and a possible silence is, of course, more than can be reasonably asked of a 'Church of the Word' that is continually speaking. But what he means is clearly that when the Gospel is preached the relationship between God's Word and his world is not an obvious thing and cannot be established artificially or by a trick. The invention of new words achieves nothing. This relationship is something Pentecostal. Banging on the recruiting drum destroys any Pentecostal beginnings. To force something on people is to abandon any hope of its really making a mark on them.

That is why Bonhoeffer seeks to re-establish an arcane discipline 'whereby the *mysteries* of the Christian faith are protected against profanation'.[244] These 'mysteries' are creative events of the Holy Spirit, but they become 'religious' objects, a 'positivism of revelation', if they are offered without reason, forced on people and given away cheap. Bonhoeffer also speaks of the Church's obligation to choose both the time and the persons it is addressing, by taking account of 'degrees of significance'. It can also be argued from the other side that the arcane discipline equally protects the world from violation by religion. Thus the arcane discipline acquires the important function of protecting the non-religious interpretation of Christianity from relapsing into religion.

The Problems of the Frontiers. But is not this an abandonment of all the ground that has been won?

Does not the arcane discipline again raise the frontiers that were supposed to have been removed at last? No one can deny that *'arcanum'*, 'mystery', separates and *'disciplina'* distinguishes.

Bonhoeffer spoke firmly of the impossibility of thinking of two spheres and said that this was a static concept that established a law[245] because 'there is no real possibility of being a Christian outside the reality of the world and . . . there is no real worldly existence outside the reality of Jesus Christ. There is no place to which the Christian can withdraw from the world, whether it be outwardly or in the sphere of the inner life.'[246] This means that to understand arcane discipline as a 'place of retreat' would be to deny all that Bonhoeffer intended. And yet it must be a worldliness—the one reality—as the reality of Christ and a Christianity within this world reality. Jörg Martin Meier expresses very well this

243. See also R. Prenter, 'Dietrich Bonhoeffer and Karl Barth's Offenbarungs-positivismus', MW III, pp. 15, 19.
244. LPP, p. 157.
245. E, pp. 196 ff.
246. E, p. 200.

unity in Bonhoeffer in a recently published work,[247] saying that by worldliness Bonhoeffer testifies to Christ as the real one, and by arcane discipline as the present one; worldliness and arcane discipline 'are correlated attitudes of the Christian resulting from the presence of the real one.'[248]

Now there is probably no way of constructing a safeguard against a new frontier, except when the safeguard comes from the real and present Christ himself who alone is our concern in dealing with the *arcanum*. But it proceeds from him in such a way that no new privilege and no place of retreat can be set up with impunity. In the *arcanum* Christ takes everyone who really encounters him by the shoulder and turns him round to face his fellow-men and the world. There is no other safeguard against the assertion of two static spheres and the law of a barrier that confers privilege.

Thus the paradox remains that there is a 'barrier' of the arcane, in order ultimately that barriers of privilege should be removed; and also that the 'barrier' of the arcane in fact distracts us from having a false interest in the barrier between the Church and the world.

If one wishes to speak, then, of the space or sphere of the Church, one must bear in mind that the confines of this space are at every moment being over-run and broken down by the testimony of the Church to Jesus Christ. And this means that all mistaken [sic] thinking in terms of spheres must be excluded, since it is deleterious to the proper understanding of the Church . . .

Whoever sets eyes on the body of Jesus Christ in faith can never again speak of the world as though it were lost, as though it were separated from Christ; he can never again with clerical arrogance set himself apart from the world.[249]

But precisely because this is the case, it must be perceived in the sphere of the arcane. We enter the 'sphere' of the arcane in order that there should be an end to spatial barriers. In other words, the 'ultimate' is praised with the initiates gathered together, so that in the 'pen-ultimate' stage there can be a share in godlessness. Christ prays a cultic psalm and dies a profane death. Hammelsbeck has put it like this:

Our bond with Christ is arcane, in that, as chosen and preferred men, we do not make this a matter of privilege and a special religious life. It is part of this *arcanum* that I set store by preaching, baptism and the eucharist, that I worship, confess and give praise within the congregation.[250]

This means that worldliness and non-religious interpretation in the world come of age are bound up with the arcane discipline and vice versa.

247. J. M. Meier, 'Weltlichkeit und Arkandisziplin bei Dietrich Bonhoeffer', ThExh 136, 1966.
248. J. M. Meier, op. cit., p. 79.
249. E, pp. 203, 205.
250. O. Hammelsbeck, 'Zu Bonhoeffers Gedanken über die mündig gewordene Welt', MW I, pp. 55 f.

If they do not mutually correct each other they become meaningless and banal. Arcane discipline without worldliness is a ghetto, and worldliness without arcane discipline is no more than the streets. Arcane discipline in isolation becomes liturgical monkery, and non-religious interpretation an intellectual game. Although Bonhoeffer remained unsatisfied with his own formulations on this subject, he never considered the dissolution of one in favour of the other.

We might imagine it as follows: in the *arcanum* there takes place the life events of faith, praise, thanksgiving and the fellowship of the communion table, and these are not interpreted outwardly.

Christ, the centre of this arcane discipline, continually sends out the 'initiated' into their participation in the life of the world, promising them that he encounters and questions them there. They stand shoulder to shoulder with those in their sphere of work and 'are there for others'.[251] Thus they are waiting for the day when they also will 'interpret', not by throwing a religious veil over what already exists, but by creating new life. They can make the sacrifice of being silent and incognito because they trust the Holy Spirit, who knows and brings on the time of the proclamation.

In the case of Bonhoeffer's non-religious interpretation, grace has remained 'dear'. Perhaps it costs even more than had been realized at the time of *The Cost of Discipleship*.

An Answer to the Main Question. Almost every time that Bonhoeffer set about outlining the theological and rational part of the non-religious interpretation of scriptural ideas, he was interrupted by bombing raids. What he wrote down later on the subject has been lost. Thus we are left behind in new territory without his ordinance map to guide us. Or has he perhaps shown us part of the way after all?

Let us first recall that, with the structural elements of religious language listed, Bonhoeffer has provided pretty decisive categories for evaluating preaching. As the proclamation of Jesus in our world it must avoid the approach of the 'God of the gaps', an individualistic narrowing-down, the spiritual salon and the *Deus ex machina*. It must seek knowledge of the world and let the children of the world help to bring it about. It is able to be braver, and clearer in its revelation of religious and philosophical fancy dress. It accepts limitations where it has lost, through its own failures and the hangover of privileges, its power over a group of men. It will not be able to separate the preached word from the life of the preacher because this very life speaks more loudly than any words. Only the life of 'participation in the powerlessness of God in the

251. Ernst Lange has convincingly described this situation in the duality of an ecclesia and a diaspora phase of the community in his 'Der Pfarrer in der Gemeinde heute', MPTh. 1966, Vol. 6, pp. 199-229.

world'[252] will speak a word of renewal. That is why the congregation must beware of preaching that can be imagined as taking place everywhere, in all circumstances, by anyone to anyone and at any time. For its proclamation as non-religious interpretation is far more than an objective process of translation.

But in the letters from prison there are some sections that can stand as instances of a non-religious interpretation, although they cannot be simply copied out as such: the letters on the gap kept open, the words on Easter of 27th March,[253] the letter on the Old Testament,[254] the interpretation of blessing,[255] the interpretation of messianic suffering,[256] and then the poem 'Christians and Pagans',[257] with its switch from the religious to the non-religious Christian attitude, and finally the title of Christ, 'the man for others'.[258]

A comparison of Bonhoeffer's last sermons and interpretations with his earlier ones does not reveal any special differences that offer evidence of the new 'method'. The exegesis of the first three commandments of June to July 1944,[259] like the Pentecost services of 1944 on the texts for the day,[260] speak a language that is no different from before. But that confirms how little Bonhoeffer saw his task as suddenly finding other words. If this were what it was about, Barth's caricature would indeed have been correct:

A little non-religious language from the street, from the newspaper, literature, for the demanding mind from philosophy, is sometimes quite a good thing too for communication . . . even revelation positivism . . . it is understood even by the most remarkable outsiders.[261]

But if we examine the exegeses and sermons to see to what extent the seven elements of Bonhoeffer's view of religion we have mentioned are avoided—what life is the basis of the preaching and to what degree the crucified Christ is interpreted in his being turned towards the world—we arrive at a more convincing conclusion and see that being turned towards the world and renouncing 'religious' language had influenced Bonhoeffer's way of preaching even before.

But these observations still remain on the surface of Bonhoeffer's thinking. The main thing is not the Sunday-morning sermons, but how Bonhoeffer interpreted his own life by means of this last theological plan of his—perhaps without even claiming it for himself in this way: as the giving up of a special Christian life, and as the acceptance, once and for all, of an incognito existence, just as, independently of him but in the

252. LPP, p. 200.   257. LPP, p. 200.
253. LPP, p. 146.   258. LPP, p. 210.
254. LPP, p. 185.   259. GS IV, pp. 597 ff.
255. LPP, p. 205.   260. GS IV, pp. 588 ff.
256. LPP, pp. 198 f., 213.   261. K. Barth, *Die Menschlichkeit Gottes*, p. 55.

same year of 1944, in another milieu and another language, Simone Weil and Henry Perrin did in an equally exemplary way for the Christendom of the future. Thus the basic point is how Bonhoeffer's life in the Resistance Movement and his non-religious interpretation mutually interpret each other.

With this theology of his last months Bonhoeffer—whether consciously or unconsciously—prevented his career of solidarity (in his case with members of the political resistance), which began as a 'border-line case', from remaining such, so that one can easily distance oneself from it. This 'borderline case' is suddenly made visible and validly interpreted as an example of being Christian today, in both its task and its destiny. This theology and this life have made a breakthrough in which the nature of this exceptional way reveals itself as the future normality: 'being for others' as sharing in the suffering of Jesus. And thus Bonhoeffer, as we have already said, added a new title to the old ones of Jesus, one that is both intelligible and at the same time profound: 'The man for others'. This is for him a strictly theological statement that reveals truth, both shaming us, and raising us up; and it is a statement about existence, whose relation to reality is obvious. It contains an ethical impulse, prevents both the religious flight from the world and ecclesiastical domination, and finally praises Jesus with words that are soaked in experience. This Christological title of honour, 'the man for others', is confession, hymn, prayer and interpretation.

An Unfinished Ecclesiology. It is a disturbing thing for the Church that at the end of his theological activity Bonhoeffer gives us no completed ecclesiology that we can get hold of, but leaves this, of all things, entirely open. The theologians of the Church feel the lack of this, and canon lawyers are immediately aware of the suggestions that are impossible in terms of a national church. This is a difficulty due not only to the fact that Bonhoeffer did not write more than a tiny fragment on the subject. He saw himself that it would be an arduous undertaking to give a theological account of the nature of the Church, its liturgy and communal life, on the basis of his new ideas. He saw his suggestions on 'arcane discipline' and the 'consequences' only as pointing in a certain direction.

Nevertheless he had a fairly clear idea that the Church would get rid of many things after the catastrophe of 1945 and find new structures. He was probably too optimistic concerning the possibilities of the zero point of 1945. He hoped for a new financial basis, new forms of training, ministry and confessional structure. He scarcely believed that the National Church, which had been so exposed in the Nazi period, could simply survive, and so he made all kinds of 'frivolous' suggestions.[262] He did not imagine that the financial and organizational structures would

262. LPP, p. 211.

emerge scarcely changed; that the ministry would have to revise its structure in only one part of Germany; that it would prove so difficult to effect change in matters of training and confession; that his question of the 'model' could become so much less important than that of terminology. On the basis of the renewal he had lived through—undoubtedly brought about by force—he hoped: '. . . to say simply and clearly things that we so often like to shirk. Whether I shall succeed is another matter, especially if I cannot discuss it with you. I hope it may be of some help for the Church's future.'[263]

But Bonhoeffer failed not only in terms of practical ecclesiology, i.e. in regard to the structure of the Church after 1945, but also in his theological treatise on the doctrine of the Church, with which he once began his theological career so passionately, and which ends with unsettled questions. At the end Bonhoeffer arrived at a stage that was highly critical of the Church. His ecclesiology seems entirely absorbed within the *theologia crucis*. His thinking had begun once ecclesiologically. Then ecclesiology yielded to Christology, but then again in the period of *The Cost of Discipleship* and the church struggle it roused quite distinct connotations. Now we are in a phase where it has again been called into question by Christology. It would be wrong, however, to conclude from this situation that Bonhoeffer was not interested in ecclesiology. For him everything depends on the *theologia crucis*, but the only form in which he knows this is in its urging us towards the concrete fellowship of those who share Christ's sufferings in the world.

It is impossible for us to complete the fragment. This is perhaps also a reflection of the situation, in that there can be no systematically complete conclusion in the movement between Christology and ecclesiology.

In fact everything was left very open at the end. In one of my last letters to Bonhoeffer, of 30th September 1944, I thanked him for the poem 'The Death of Moses'. At the end of these verses there come the lines:

> To punish sin and to forgiveness you are moved,
> God, this people I have loved.
> That I bore its shame and sacrifices
> And saw its salvation—that suffices.

By 'its shame' he did not mean Christ and by 'his people' he did not mean the Church, but Germany.

In the last of his letters to me that have been preserved, Bonhoeffer wrote, on 23rd August 1944:

So you are taking the trouble to copy out extracts of my thoughts, which are still far from being fully formed. I'm sure you'll consider everything that has to be considered if you pass them on to someone else . . . By the way, you can imagine how delighted I am that you are busying yourself with

263. LPP, p. 211.

them. How essential it would be to me now to be able to discuss and clarify
all these problems. It will be one of the great days of my life when we are
able to do that.

Luther says of the true theologian: 'Vivendo, immo moriendo et
damnando fit theologus, non intelligendo, legendo aut speculando.'
('Living, but no, rather dying and being damned, constitutes the
theologian, but not understanding, reading and speculating.') (WA 5,
163, 28, Comm. in Psalmos, 1519.)

3. Reactions

Only after much hesitation and doubt concerning whether the incomplete meditations of Bonhoeffer's letters could be published, and
consideration of how this could be done, did they appear in the winter
of 1951-2. The reaction to them was one of surprise.

Up to that time Bonhoeffer's image was so stamped by The Cost of
Discipleship and his apparently radical orthodoxy in the struggle of the
Confessing Church that no one had expected that he, of all people, would
again take up vehemently liberal questions. Even to his 'Finkenwaldians'
Bonhoeffer appeared in an unexpected light. Gerhard Ebeling was the
first to react, and he described the posthumous work as having
'practically the quality of a breviary':

I should like to state explicitly that I am especially interested in the theological perspectives. Not, indeed, because I find them strange, but because
they are a surprisingly major confirmation to me that I am a pupil of Bonhoeffer, precisely in those matters in which I have developed beyond the
theological level of the Finkenwalde period and which have guided me
towards a path which I only now know was his also.[264]

The second reaction came from Helmut Thielicke:

[Letters and Papers from Prison] has . . . entirely taken up my last week,
accompanying me with an intensity and influencing my life in a way that
nothing has for years . . .[265]

Others reacted in a shocked way. Thus Karl Barth warned against this
late Bonhoeffer. Barth replied to P. W. Herrenbrück's question about
what he thought of Bonhoeffer's ideas altogether and, in particular, of
the attacks on him, by saying that the lonely prisoner might possibly
have 'peeped around some corner' and seen something that was true, but
that it was too 'enigmatic' and that it was better to stick to the early
Bonhoeffer.[266]

People's surprise led them to get out again the early works of Bonhoeffer that had not received much attention hitherto and to discover

264. Letter of 30.9.1951.
265. Letter of 11.10.1951.
266. MW I, pp. 121 f.

with astonishment that there was a broad continuity between the Berlin beginnings and the Tegel period. Formulations and theological hints in *Letters and Papers from Prison* that people found shocking proved not to be as new as had been thought and were to be found, even literally, in *Sanctorum Communio* or *Act and Being*, as well as in various other writings. The Christology was already there in *Act and Being* as Lutheran kenotic Christology (the whole fullness precisely in the total condescension, Phil. 2), and had been the real stimulus for his critique of Barth at the time. Bonhoeffer had preserved this Christology for fifteen years, continually making it more profound, in order to ground the present power of Christ even more clearly in the weakness of the human suffering of Jesus. The phrase 'life for others' had occurred already in *Act and Being* and in the Christology lecture. Faith as being drawn into the vicarious being of Christ in *The Cost of Discipleship*, only that now, instead of the judging element, is the world-preserving one that comes out much more encouragingly. The change of direction from the metaphysical elements of Christology to its place in the 'centre of life', as well as the reference to Christ, who refuses to be relegated to the psychological or moral boundaries of life, but is at the centre and the 'strongest places' of man, all this we have read before in *Creation and Fall*. The antimetaphysical transference of transcendence to one's neighbour, which seemed especially surprising to most people, is to be found, in almost exactly the same form, as social transcendence, in the *Sanctorum Communio*: 'Whoever happens to be one's neighbour and reachable is the transcendent'.[267] As early as 1932 Bonhoeffer severely criticized religious 'otherworldliness'. During his Berlin period he had dealt at length with the religious *a priori* as a key concept of his teacher R. Seeberg.

The continuity seemed to go a surprisingly long way. But despite the same terminology and individual ideas it was not just the same thing that he had said in 1932 that he was now saying in 1944. The passionate theologian of 1932 had handled these terminological tools with the capacities of a young critical intellect; that of 1944 used them with the capacities of an experience full to the brim. In 1932 Bonhoeffer was attacking the existing structures of the Church and of thinking; in 1944 he considered that he was helping to liberate man for a new future.

But, apart from a few exceptions, Bonhoeffer's voice did not find any wide welcome among academic theologians. Not long ago W. Hamilton declared that, in contrast to the general prestige and influence:

Bonhoeffer has not been used very much by the professor, which is why there is such an astonishingly short list of books and articles on him, and an even shorter list of good books and articles.[268]

267. Cf. LPP, pp. 154, 210 with SC, pp. 33-5
268. 'Bonhoeffer, Christology and Ethic United', in *Christianity and Crisis*, Vol. XXIV, No. 17, 1964, p. 195.

In Germany, when the *Letters and Papers from Prison* appeared, the second round of the excited Bultmann debate was in full spate; the voice of Gogarten had made itself heard; Tillich, who had disappeared from the German scene had reappeared; and Barth's doctrine of Creation, ethics and anthropology had shown the old master in a new breadth. The questions of liberal theology had again made themselves powerfully felt in 1952 after the great proving of dialectical theology and the period of a new confessional awareness. In this situation Bonhoeffer's brief notes came too late for the academic discussion. Thus all they could do was constitute secondary weapons for an armoury that was already equipped with fixed types. When one was tired of Barth, one could go to Bonhoeffer's 'revelation positivism' for one's ammunition. A defender of the existential interpretation felt confirmed by Bonhoeffer's 'non-religious interpretation' and was little interested in the differences. If one despaired of the Church, one could discover 'the world come of age' and see the opportunity of atheism in the name of Bonhoeffer's *theologia crucis*. Some of Bonhoeffer's pupils, educated in the spirit of Barth, sought to preserve Bonhoeffer from the Marburg influence (i.e. the Bultmann school).

In other words, the time was not favourable for Bonhoeffer's fragments to speak in their own right. But they had the greatest effect wherever there was experimentation in groups and cells, wherever new community structures were being tried out and forms of political solidarity ventured, where national church and socially privileged bastions were abandoned, and questions of atheism and cooperation with non-Christians accepted within the general process of the humanization of life together. Here Bonhoeffer has proved himself to be someone who encourages men to sail quickly out of harbours that have silted up.

The first wave of sporadic serious writing on his work[269] is now, it seems, being followed by a second more comprehensive one. People thought at first either that Bonhoeffer could be very quickly placed, or else that there was nothing that one could really learn from him. The use of Bonhoeffer's ideas by John A. T. Robinson,[270] if eclectically chosen for his own purposes (though all the more influential on that account), has now unleashed a new search for the specific quality of Bonhoeffer's contribution beyond the frontiers of continents, in the English and American world, and, above all, beyond denominational barriers also, among Roman Catholics.[271] Bonhoeffer regarded the cause of Christ

269. R. Gregor Smith, *The New Man*, London, 1956; G. Ebeling, 'Die nichtreligiöse Interpretation biblischer Begriffe', MW II, 1956, pp. 12-73; J. D. Godsey, *The Theology of Dietrich Bonhoeffer*, 1960; H. Müller, *Von der Kirche zur Welt*, 1960; M. Marty, *The Place of Bonhoeffer*, London, 1963.

270. J. A. T. Robinson, *Honest to God*, 1963.

271. G. Krause, 'Dietrich Bonhoeffer und Rudolf Bultmann', in *Zeit und Geschichte, Dankesgabe an Rudolf Bultmann zum 80. Geburtstag*, 1964, pp. 439-60; H. Ott, *Wirklichkeit und Glaube*, Vol. I; *Zum theologischen Erbe Dietrich Bonhoeffers*; J. A. Phillips, *The Form of Christ in the World, a Study of Bonhoeffer's Christology*, London, 1967.

with optimism and serenity. About anxiety concerning stray and possibly lost papers for his *Ethics* he wrote: '. . . even if you had forgotten it, it would probably emerge again indirectly somehow. Besides, my ideas were still incomplete.'[272]

272. Letter of 28.12.1943, LPP, p. 88.

CHAPTER FOURTEEN

IN CUSTODY OF THE STATE
1944 - 1945

BONHOEFFER's transfer from the Military Detention Centre to close custody at the Reich Security Head Office on 8th October 1944 made a fundamental difference to the conditions of his existence. From this time on the treatment he received was of the kind usually associated in people's minds with that accorded to those imprisoned by the Gestapo during the Third Reich.

In Tegel the interrogations into Bonhoeffer's activities had been confined to the more or less marginal aspects but now the most important ones became the subject of direct enquiry. In Tegel, too, all hope for the cause had not yet been abandoned: on the contrary, the trial itself almost seemed to have become part of the fight for Hitler's overthrow which was being conducted outside the prison. It was this hope which had enabled Bonhoeffer to hold out in his relative isolation. He had known that those outside—his family, Perels, the indefatigable Dr. Sack, and his fellow conspirators—were all working for the cause. His particular task was to divert the attention of the enemy from their activities. As a result he was not yet fully aware of how powerless his situation really was. The tenuous connection he had been able to maintain with his friends had acted as a life-line up to this point.

But now there was little point in maintaining the old masquerade before the enemy, since there was no one left at liberty to bring about a political change. Sack and Perels, Canaris and Oster, Klaus Bonhoeffer and Rüdiger Schleicher had themselves been arrested and committed to solitary confinement and were being subjected to gruelling cross-examination.

Nevertheless, there were still occasional periods which offered a ray of hope or the possibility of some friendly human contact. In the winter of 1944-5 some of the commissars who were interrogating Bonhoeffer were so concerned at the seriousness of the situation in Germany that even they were not above consulting him personally. At times both Bonhoeffer and Dohnanyi seem to have believed they could still outwit the forces that were bent on their destruction.

October 1944 and February 1945 were bad months for Bonhoeffer's family. In the October the means of communication which had been built up between the prisoners in their cells, or between them and the parental home, were disrupted. There had been three further arrests, so that five members of the family were now in the hands of the Gestapo. Hans von Dohnanyi was in the concentration camp at Sachsenhausen, Dietrich Bonhoeffer was in Prinz-Albrecht-Strasse, and Klaus Bonhoeffer. Rüdiger Schleicher and I myself were in the wing of the prison at No. 3, Lehrter Strasse, which the Gestapo had taken over. The only advantage was that all of us were still in Berlin or its environs, and families could at least still send us parcels, which the guards received on our behalf.

Then in February 1945 the death sentence was passed on Klaus Bonhoeffer and Rüdiger Schleicher, and Dietrich was secretly moved from Berlin. It was not until months later that his friends and family learned where he had been taken and what had finally happened to him.

The last six months of Bonhoeffer's life can be divided into three different stages. He spent the first four months in the basement at Prinz-Albrecht-Strasse where he was subjected to a whole series of cross-examinations. During the next seven weeks he lived in an air-raid shelter in the concentration camp at Buchenwald. After this he spent seven days travelling through southern Germany in prison transport *en route* for Flossenbürg, where the end finally came.

I PRINZ-ALBRECHT-STRASSE

Concern in England

It was in the October of 1944 that the first article appeared on the other side of the Channel which had the courage to inform the British public that the people who had been involved in the plot of the 20th July were not just another military clique intent on removing Hitler for their own selfish ends. Gerhard Leibholz, who was the author of this article, presented their attempt in positive terms by referring to the list of conspirators who had been executed:

It is obvious that such a conspiracy had to be built up carefully and must have been prepared for many years . . . In fact, it can be revealed today that the existence of a vast opposition movement, under the leadership of Beck, Goerdeler and Leuschner, had been known in this country for some time. There is even evidence available that the execution of the plot was planned before the cumulative effect of military defeats had added its weight to the decision of the plotters to overthrow the present régime . . . The loss of their battle will certainly not ease the task the Allies will have to perform later on in Germany.[1]

Leibholz was well acquainted with the earlier history of the conspiracy, both from Bonhoeffer's visits in 1939 and from the reports given

1. *The New English Weekly*, Vol. XXVI, No. 1, p. 6.

by Bishop Bell in 1942. He dared not reveal all he knew, however, and was forced to confine his remarks to whatever was made known of the trial through the garbled accounts of the German radio or the neutral Press. So far in these accounts Leibholz had made no mention of his own relatives in Berlin. However, even the little that he said in support of the conspirators seemed to be too much for the British public. Churchill had given the cue for this reaction when on 2nd August he spoke in the House of Commons of the 'conspiracy of militarists, simply a case of the highest personalities in the German Reich murdering one another.'[2] When Leibholz, with Bell's help, tried to publish a word against this statement in one of the big daily newspapers, he met with a refusal both from *The Times* and the *Manchester Guardian.* 'I agree with you in the miserable playing-down of the significance of the Hitler plot,' Bell wrote to Leibholz in the middle of September. Finally, *The New English Weekly*, which numbered T. S. Eliot amongst its editors, had the courage to publish Leibholz's article.[3] It appeared on 19th October, and immediately provoked a negative response from one of its readers: 'Sir, I regret that you should have thought fit to find space for the article.' The only positive response came from an *émigré.* Several months were to elapse before the true facts of the case were publicly acknowledged.

Immediately after Churchill's speech in the Commons Bell had written to Leibholz expressing his great concern for the conspirators. Not everything he said was realistic, but it was all the sign of an ecumenical spirit. On 3rd August he wrote to Leibholz at Oxford:

I heard Churchill yesterday—it was all 'battle', and its reference to ideology and 'internal disease' most depressing. I get more and more worried about the official attitude. I have written to Eden reminding him of the information I gave him two years ago from Stockholm and that the attempt of July 20 was made in far worse circumstances than ever possible in 1942 after the same two men were leaders Beck and Goerdeler—the same plan and organization, etc.: if only he had acted then! I have asked him at least to do what is possible to help those who can escape to escape; for I suppose we have ways and means of assisting prisoners of war to escape. And I then also asked him to say a word encouraging those in Germany who are seeking to destroy the régime.

Two days later Bell wrote another letter, setting out in precise terms what he had done. It shows all the characteristic tenacity with which he pursued an aim he had once set himself:

I had drafted a letter to Cranborne[4] setting out a series of considerations for 'political warfare'; but on the publication of Goerdeler's name as the prime

2. G. Bell, *The Church and Humanity*, London, 1946, p. 174.
3. G. Leibholz, *Politics and Law*, Leyden, 1965, pp. 210 f.
4. Leader of the House of Lords.

mover and actor by Himmler I decided to write direct to Eden pointing out
how closely the information I brought from Stockholm in 1942 fitted in with
the facts of 20th July 1944, reminding him of other names besides Beck and
Goerdeler and including Witzleben (before of course the new denunciation
option in today's press). I asked Eden whether he could not 1. take steps to
help escape any other leaders of the Revolt not yet killed—by such steps
(formidable as the task is) as might be taken to help our prisoners of war
escape; and 2. even at this late hour make a strong public appeal over the
heads of Hitler and Himmler to anti-Nazis in Germany and give them hope
of a life of security for a Germany which has overthrown the Nazis. By the
same post I wrote to Cranborne telling him what I had done and why.
I had already written to Eden last week asking him whether he would care
to do anything (via Stockholm e.g.) to help the clergy in Germany now in
still greater peril, through the areas opened up in the summer of 1942. I have
had no reply to this letter . . . I heard Churchill . . . but he is living in
a world of battles only, and seeing time with the mind of a child with regard
to deep policy—for Home Affairs as well as the far graver matters of Europe.
And disaster gets nearer and nearer. One feels so powerless . . .
I cannot tell you how deeply I share you and your wife's anxieties for
Dietrich. May God spare him for the survival of the Church and Germany
and the world . . . I am writing to Winant to remind him of what I brought
from Stockholm in 1942.[5]

Bell and the Leibholz family were astonished when week after week
passed by without any of the Bonhoeffers being named in the press reports. They tried to obtain information via Geneva. On 14th November
Bell wrote to Leibholz:

He[6] has no reason to think he[7] has come to any harm, and believes him to
be safe, so far as he knows. The fact that he had been in prison for so long
before 20th July was very much to his advantage, for he could not well be
incriminated.

Bonhoeffer was certainly no longer 'safe' at this time, as Visser 't
Hooft imagined him to be, but there were certain delays which undoubtedly afforded him some respite. It is true that at the beginning
Bonhoeffer's involvement in the conspiracy was kept secret for a long
time. Later on, as we shall see, his sentence was delayed because he
became a subject of special interest to his interrogators. Even towards the
end the chaos attendant upon the closing stages of the war delayed once
again the final passing of his sentence.

New Enquiries

The discovery of the Zossen files, which had made the situation so much
worse for the resistance group, had already caused a delay in the pro-

5. Letter of 5.8.1944.
6. Visser 't Hooft.
7. Bonhoeffer.

ceedings against Bonhoeffer. According to the information given by Huppenkothen when he was on trial in the fifties the file contained among other items the following:

Notes for the planning of a *coup d'état*, written in 1938, partly in the hand of Oster;

A record of the results of discussions with the British Government via the Vatican;

A summary of the situation after the campaign in Poland, written by General Beck;

A plan drawn up by General Oster for the carrying-out of a *coup d'état*;

Excerpts from the diary of Admiral Canaris, containing notes concerning the affairs of the Resistance Movement, also remarks about journeys to the front-line addressed to various commanders, for the purpose of winning their support for a revolution;

Correspondence concerning the aforementioned activities of Bonhoeffer, and similar matters.[8]

These discoveries by the criminal investigator Sonderegger provided a sudden increase in the Reich Security Head Office's knowledge of the early history of the conspiracy. Its activities were now known to date back to 1938, to have ranged as far afield as the Vatican and England, and to have involved a wide circle of people (on 20th July Hitler had simply spoken of 'a tiny clique . . . of stupid officers'). When Hitler received this additional information, he rescinded his original command for the prompt 'liquidation' of the conspirators and ordered extensive enquiries into their activities.[9] Contrary to earlier practice, the carrying-out of the death-sentence on those who had already been convicted by the People's Court was postponed for weeks or even months.

Several information groups of the Reich Security Head Office had already been working for two months since 20th July preparing dossiers for the trials to be held in the People's Court under Freisler. The results of these investigations, summarized in the 'Kaltenbrunner Reports', reached Hitler at regular intervals via Bormann. After the discovery of the Zossen file, however, an additional information group was formed under the command of the S.S. Section Leader Walter Huppenkothen, with special instructions to sift its contents and use them as the basis for further investigations. According to Huppenkothen's own statement, made during his subsequent trials, he was given the task of producing his own report independently of the Kaltenbrunner Reports.[10] This document, drawn up specially for the Führer, consisted of about 160 pages, and had a two-volume appendix which included photocopies and

8. Verdict in the trial of Huppenkothen on 15.10.1955, 1 KS 21/50 (LG. Munich) AK Schw. 4/55 (LG Augsburg). Huppenkothen's statements agree in part with those of Christine von Dohnanyi concerning parts of the documents.

9. Statement by Huppenkothen, op. cit., p. 18.

10. Op. cit., p. 41.

original documents. Its contents are said to have been treated as highly confidential, and to have existed in only three copies, one for Hitler, one for Himmler, and one for Kaltenbrunner and S.S. Group-leader Müller. It was a summary of the incriminating evidence collected against Canaris, Oster, Dohnanyi, Sack, Josef Müller and Dietrich Bonhoeffer. Huppenkothen maintains that all copies were destroyed. Certainly, none has so far been discovered.

This special treatment would explain the surprisingly short space allotted to the cases of Dohnanyi and Dietrich Bonhoeffer in the otherwise extensive Kaltenbrunner Reports, compared with the relatively large amount devoted to those of Klaus Bonhoeffer and Rüdiger Schleicher.[11] Neither of the latter became really intimately involved in the planning of the *coup* until Dietrich Bonhoeffer and Hans von Dohnanyi had been arrested. Both of them, in particular Klaus, had had their own private connections with resistance groups. But it was only after the dissolution of Oster's department and the need to restructure the movement that they had a more significant part to play in it. From then on some of the meetings of people who belonged to the Goerdeler and Stauffenberg circle were held in Klaus Bonhoeffer's or Rüdiger Schleicher's apartment. At these meetings the future of the Lufthansa, of which Klaus was an official, was discussed and plans were made for the taking-over of certain offices by him or Schleicher if the *coup* were to be successful. The discovery of these activities was the reason for their both being mentioned in the Kaltenbrunner Reports, which, incidentally, could sometimes be extraordinarily inaccurate. Klaus Bonhoeffer, Rüdiger Schleicher and I myself (who was cross-examined only because I was the latter's son-in-law and never because I was a friend of Dietrich Bonhoeffer) were victims of the Günther and Baumer interrogation group. This was dissolved as early as December, and Günther and Baumer, it was said, joined the fighting forces. On the basis of their preliminary investigations (in which they used torture) the Public Prosecutor of the People's Court drew up an indictment against Klaus Bonhoeffer and Rüdiger Schleicher on 20th December.

In contrast, Dietrich Bonhoeffer's and Dohnanyi's cases never reached the People's Court. Dietrich Bonhoeffer only receives passing mention in the Kaltenbrunner Reports, and even this is accompanied by factual inaccuracies.[12] The Kaltenbrunner Reports had ceased altogether by the Christmas of 1944, but Huppenkothen's information group worked on energetically.

Thus it was that Dietrich Bonhoeffer's case received separate treatment. Of course, this was also due to the fact that it had come rather

11. *Spiegelbild einer Verschwörung. Die Kaltenbrunner-Berichte an Bormann und Hitler über das Attentat vom 20. Juli 1944*, ed. K. H. Peter, 1961.
12. For instance, it speaks of more than one journey undertaken with Moltke. For further information see thesis put forward by J. Glenthoj in 'Dietrich Bonhoeffer vor Kaltenbrunner', EvTh, 1966, No. 9. pp. 480 ff.

late into the enquiries of the Reich Security Head Office about the events of 20th July. The contents of the Kaltenbrunner Reports would suggest that Hitler attached little importance to it, but the reverse is in fact the case. As a result, Bonhoeffer and his closest friends were spared longer than some of the other conspirators, but for the same reasons he became the subject of a meeting held on 5th April 1945, in which Hitler made his final decision concerning the fate of his group.

Huppenkothen

The period of renewed interrogations lasted for Bonhoeffer from October 1944 to January 1945. Huppenkothen and Sonderegger were in charge of the cross-examinations, and they used these additionally, as we shall see, to pursue other lines of investigation within their own spheres of office.

Walter Huppenkothen, a talented lawyer from the Rhineland, had begun his career in the Gestapo in 1935. Since 1941 he had been in charge of counter-espionage (Group E) in Branch IV of the Reich Security Head Office ('Investigation and Combating of Enemy Activities'). When in spring of 1944 Canaris's office was incorporated into the Reich Security Head Office, Branch IV was correspondingly reorganized within the structure of the Head Office. While retaining his previous posts Huppenkothen was also put in charge of the newly created Department Three of Group A, to which now belonged the range of duties formerly assigned to Canaris, and which was concerned with military counter-espionage.

Soon after 20th July he had been put in charge of an interrogation group which was only part of the whole commission set up to investigate the organization of the conspiracy. Huppenkothen's particular task was to prove what could as yet only be surmised—the parts played by Canaris, Oster and Dohnanyi in the planning of the *coup*. He was to be assisted by Sonderegger, who along with Roeder had first arrested Dohnanyi and Bonhoeffer, had then been present at the court martial at which Roeder had produced his evidence, and finally had discovered the Zossen file on 20th September.

Huppenkothen was therefore the right man for this special commission. It is true, of course, that he found himself in the position of having to play different roles at the same time. On the one hand he had to pursue the charges of high treason against his victims; on the other hand he had to make it his business to investigate the connections which these victims, unbeknown to the Head Office, might have had and possibly even still had, with the resistance group which planned the revolt. The Secret Service, now finally concentrated in the Reich Security Head Office, was to have a special striking power. This was one of the main reasons why no one intended to hand over to the People's Court such important figures as Dohnanyi and Bonhoeffer, and why the victims in their turn were able to hope that, in spite of the appalling interrogations they were subjected to, the pronouncement of their sentences might be delayed until events overtook them.

In his biography of Canaris Abshagen describes Huppenkothen as a man who was able to give 'the impression of being an educated official of the governmental service or police force'.[13] It is true that he never became openly aggressive. After threats of torture, which he naturally left others to carry out if they were ordered to, he was quite capable of offering his prisoners a cigarette and encouraging them to discuss matters, the clarification of which would be of advantage to both sides. Although he had every means of power in his hands, he usually pretended to sympathize with his prisoners. Sonderegger, on the other hand, was of humble origins. 'It pleases him if one addresses him as "Sir", and he is not altogether without a heart; but he's crafty.'[14] He did in fact help to ease conditions for Bonhoeffer and Dohnanyi in small ways.

The Interrogations

Klaus Bonhoeffer was tortured, and Dohnanyi was shamefully treated by the notorious Commissar Stawitzky. It seems almost certain, however, that Dietrich Bonhoeffer was never subjected to torture; though his sufferings were great enough without this. Schlabrendorff reports that on the occasion when he encountered Bonhoeffer in the cellar of the Reich Security Head Office Bonhoeffer described the interrogations as 'frankly repulsive'. He added that at first he had been threatened with torture and told that the fate of his fiancée, his parents and the rest of his family depended on his readiness to confess. But afterwards there had been a change of tone. It is possible that Bonhoeffer's own personality may have had a salutary effect on his examiners. Captain Payne Best, who later encountered Bonhoeffer in Buchenwald, was impressed by his composure.

He had always been afraid that he would not be strong enough to stand such a test but now he knew there was nothing in life of which one need ever be afraid.

Bonhoeffer realized quite early on that apart from his own case the authorities were interested in what they could learn from him about others, and he exploited this situation to get some room for manoeuvre. In Bonhoeffer's last letter of 17th January 1945, which is concerned with participating in a 'sacrifice for the nation', and which Sonderegger read and forwarded, he says:

If there is anything you need to know perhaps you would 'phone Herr Commissar Sonderegger . . . Herr Commissar Sonderegger would now and then

13. K. H. Abshagen, op. cit., p. 378.
14. H. von Dohnanyi in a smuggled note of 25.2.1945.

accept [books] for me. if Maria were to bring them along . . . Please also leave some writing-paper with the Herr Commissar.

So far, it has been impossible to reconstruct the contents and course of these interrogations without considerable gaps. Huppenkothen maintains that he destroyed all the records in his possession before the arrival of the American army. The recollections of those who were involved in some way are often vague or coloured by their own view of the situation, and the reports contradict each other in many respects. Only one official document to do with the case has so far been found (though this is admittedly a very important one). We must nevertheless attempt to gain some idea of the contents and course of the interrogations from these sources of unequal value, and the best way of doing this is to discuss them in chronological order. We possess nothing from Bonhoeffer's own hand which could help in this matter unless the two letters written after Christmas 1944[15] confirm our suppositions as to the stage the interrogations had reached by that time.

a) Fabian von Schlabrendorff, who had already been committed to the prison in the Prinz-Albrecht-Strasse by the end of August 1944, was probably the first of the friends who still remained alive to meet Bonhoeffer there. At this time, of course, he still knew very little in detail about Bonhoeffer's activities in the resistance group and even less about the defensive arguments and subterfuges Bonhoeffer had had to employ at Tegel to disguise the real facts of the situation from the enemy. During all this time Schlabrendorff had been at the front and had only occasionally got home to visit Berlin. In 1945 he wrote a report for Bonhoeffer's family which probably reflects the stage which the interrogations had reached between October and December 1944. It was a surprisingly optimistic description of the situation, as may be seen from the following:

He repeatedly told me the Gestapo had no clue to his real activities. He had been able to trivialize his acquaintance with Goerdeler. His connection with Perels . . . was not of sufficient importance to serve as an indictment. And as for his foreign travels and meetings with English Church dignitaries, the Gestapo did not grasp their purpose and point. If the investigations were to carry on at the present pace, years might pass before they reached their conclusions. He was full of hope . . . He also thought he had represented his relation to his brother-in-law . . . von Dohnanyi in a plausible way to his interlocutors, so that this was not a heavy charge against him.[16]

At the end of 1944 Schlabrendorff saw the possible chances of being released himself. In the event of this taking place Bonhoeffer asked him to visit his father and encourage him to seek a personal interview with

15. 28.12.1944, LPP, p. 220; 17.1.1945, LPP. p. 222
16. F. von Schlabrendorff, 'In Prison with Dietrich Bonhoeffer', IKDB, p. 228

Himmler.[17] Up to this time, therefore, he seems to have envisaged the possibility of still getting off without legal proceedings being taken against him. We shall see later what grounds there were for such a hope.

b) In November 1944 the interrogations that I myself was undergoing in the branch of the Head Office situated in the Kurfürstenstrasse brought me dangerously close to Bonhoeffer's case. Strange though it may seem, Commissar Baumer had concerned himself throughout my examination almost exclusively with my connections with Rüdiger Schleicher, but one afternoon he laid a thick typewritten file in front of me and showed me Bonhoeffer's signature on the last page. He said the file contained Bonhoeffer's confessions, and read out to me several passages from it. Among them I recognized parts of the Freiburg discussions of 1942 which dealt with the possibilities of contact between German and English churches in the event of a long armistice being arranged.[18] All this information was not unfamiliar to me. I later learned that Günther and Baumer placed the same file before Perels and Walter Bauer during similar interrogations. I denied all knowledge of the contents of this file. I knew that Bonhoeffer had been able to hide the fact of our close association in the past, and I assumed that he would not, in any case, have made such a detailed confession. I also knew from my own experience of the interrogations that minutes were kept and signed in seven copies. I therefore came to the conclusion that the whole file had been put together by the Gestapo from pieces of evidence obtained in various ways and that one of Bonhoeffer's signatures had then been added to it. Baumer soon returned to the subject of my frequent presence in the Schleicher household, which could be explained away convincingly enough by my engagement and marriage to Rüdiger Schleicher's daughter. He never again brought up the question of my relations with Dietrich Bonhoeffer.

This incident showed quite clearly, however, that by October or November 1944 the Head Office was well enough informed about the sphere and extent of Bonhoeffer's activities as to give serious cause for alarm. They were now not only able to interpret the information extracted during the interrogations at Tegel much more accurately, but had also brought to light some facts which were quite new to them. And yet the optimism evinced by Schlabrendorff was not wholly unfounded.

c) Quite recently Jørgen Glenthoj discovered and published the only document so far found which deals directly with the interrogations by the Head Office.[19] On 4th January 1945 Kaltenbrunner wrote a letter to the German Foreign Office, which was also laid before Ribbentrop. It consists entirely of information obtained from Bonhoeffer during his

17. F. von Schlabrendorff, op. cit., p. 228.
18. See Ch. XII, pp. 681 ff.
19. J. Glenthoj, 'Bonhoeffer vor Kaltenbrunner', in EvTh, 1966, No. 9, pp. 462-99, cf. pp. 853 ff. Reprinted in MW V, XI, G.

interrogations concerning his meeting with Bishop Bell and the conditions in England. There is no mention at all of treasonable activities on the part of the prisoner. The letter suggests that Bonhoeffer succeeded in giving the impression that his visits abroad were made 'in the national interest'—it being no longer possible to hide the fact that they had taken place. He also seems to have been trying to make his presentation of the facts fit in with what he had said at the earlier interrogations conducted by Roeder, and above all, to make himself and his knowledge an object of continued interest to the Head Office. In the letter Kaltenbrunner writes:

The Protestant minister Dietrich Bonhoeffer, formerly chaplain to the German Evangelical Congregation in London, who was arrested in connection with the conspiracy of 20.7.1944, went to Sweden and had meetings with Lord Bishop Bell of Chichester during May and June 1942 by order of the former Admiral Canaris. Bonhoeffer has given the following information concerning the nature of his discussions with Bell:

Lord Bishop Bell, the most respected and best-known of the Lord Bishops of the Church of England, and influential in the ecumenical movement, is considered to be a man who favours mutual understanding and the peaceful settlement of differences, as well as being an outspoken friend of the Germans. For this reason, and because of his attitude to the conduct of the war, he had not become successor to Archbishop Lang of Canterbury as had been expected. He is said to have visited Germany often and to have been on familiar terms with Rudolf Hess. At the beginning he evidently endeavoured to come to an understanding with the German Evangelical Church under Müller but then turned his attention to the Confessing Church and established connections with Niemöller, Dibelius and Koch.

The purpose of Bishop Bell's visit to Sweden was, according to Bonhoeffer, to enquire into the relations between Sweden and the Soviet Union and study the movements in the Scandinavian churches. Bell explained that he had spoken at length with Eden before leaving England and had asked him what he should do if peace-feelers were extended from any particular direction in Sweden. Eden had told him quite bluntly that there was no question of England discussing peace terms before it had won the war. In this matter Eden was totally in agreement with Churchill.

The attitude of Sir Stafford Cripps to these problems was quite different from that of Eden. It was quite wrong to say that Sir Stafford was a Bolshevik. It would be more accurate to describe him as a Christian Socialist. Sir Stafford evidently spoke with great concern about the power of Russia, which almost everyone in England underestimated. He had good relations with sources of information in Moscow and feared that no other power, not even England, would be in a position to stop the Russians from advancing as far as the Brandenburg Gate. He thought the consequences of a Russian victory were unforeseeable, as far as England was concerned. Bell had explained that church circles in England were more in agreement with this view of the situation than with Eden's.

When Lord Bishop Bell was asked whether the U.S.A. might intend to destroy England or absorb it into the federation, he replied that this was totally out of the question. America needed a strong bulwark in Europe, and England without its empire would not be strong. On the subject of a possible union between the U.S.A. and England Bell did not wish to go into details.

During the course of the interview Bell had commented on the visit which Lord Beaverbrook had evidently recently made to Switzerland. Beaverbrook had had meetings with German industrialists and had discussed with them the possibilities of negotiating peace terms with a view to forming a common front between the Western powers and Germany against Russia.

Interrogations concerning these contacts with England took place around Christmas-time at the latest. If Kaltenbrunner's letter can be taken as reliable evidence of the account which Bonhoeffer gave of his activities in Sweden, then it is clear that Bonhoeffer had not only found a way of telling the truth without its harming anybody, but had also managed to give it a particular emphasis that would make it not only plausible to the people in the Head Office, but under certain circumstances worthy of commendation. It could not but be of interest to them if they had given any consideration to what would happen in the event of the war coming to an end or of there being a shift of alliances between East and West. Even apart from this Bonhoeffer had said enough about Beaverbrook to make further enquiries desirable if not imperative, and this in itself could slow down the interrogations and be a means of gaining time. Above all, Bonhoeffer's conviction, reported by Schlabrendorff, that the Gestapo had no clue about the really essential matters, would seem to be borne out by the contents of Kaltenbrunner's letter. The visit to Sweden is clearly presented as taking place in the service of the country's defence, 'by order of the former Admiral Canaris', and not by order of Beck. It is true that Bonhoeffer afterwards admitted to having played a part in the admiral's political information service which, strictly speaking, was against the 'Ten Commandments',[20] but the actual nature of his commission—the establishing of connections between the conspirators and the English Government for the eventuality of a *coup*—remained undiscovered, even though Bonhoeffer had gone so far as to mention that it was concerned with 'peace-feelers'—but of course in a different context. The real reason for Bonhoeffer's journey seems, therefore, to have been kept in the dark to the very end.

In the early part of 1945 serious efforts were made in and by the Reich Security Head Office to discover what opinions the conspirators and their associates held about the outcome of the war and to work out the part they might play in any action to bring about a shift of alliances. I myself was a witness to the fact that in the prison at No. 3 Lehrter Strasse Albrecht Haushofer suddenly received every possible kind of concession in the way of books, food and tobacco, to persuade him to write down his views of the political situation for Himmler and

20. See Ch. XII, pp. 629 f.

make the necessary suggestions for a solution. Dohnanyi was similarly encouraged to 'describe what would have been the follow-up to the conspiracy of 20th July, as he saw it',[21] and to assess the prospects for Germany's future. Nothing is directly known of any such approach to Bonhoeffer, but the whole tenor of the Kaltenbrunner letter is in accordance with the attitude adopted for a while by the Head Office towards Haushofer and Dohnanyi.

Dohnanyi told his wife in a letter smuggled out on 25th February 1945 that the commandant at the prison had 'a soft spot for his prisoners and is sounding out the possibilities for a safe anchorage from future storms . . . to gain time is the only solution . . . there is also the music of the sirens which gives cause for hope'.

d) In the earlier days of February, just after Dohnanyi had been moved from Sachsenhausen to the Head Office and before Bonhoeffer has disappeared from Berlin, the two brothers-in-law were able to see each other secretly and have a brief conversation, when Bonhoeffer took advantage of the confusion caused by an air-raid alarm to get into Dohnanyi's cell for a few moments.[22] On this occasion Bonhoeffer told Dohnanyi that he had confessed to having played a part in Canaris's political information service, and Dohnanyi passed this information on to his wife when she saw him for the last time at the beginning of April in the state hospital. Josef Müller reported having heard the same from Bonhoeffer during the journey from Weiden to Buchenwald on 3rd and 4th April.

e) In the later Huppenkothen trials S.S. Judge Dr. Thorbeck gave a summary opinion concerning the examination of Bonhoeffer which he, as presiding judge of the court martial, held in Flossenbürg on the night of 8th-9th April. Thorbeck said that on that night Bonhoeffer had not attempted to deny 'anything'. Thorbeck's knowledge of the actual facts of the case, however, could only have been superficial.

The last smuggled letter written by Dohnanyi on 8th March 1945 does not give the impression that the Gestapo were still on the wrong track with their questions. Part of the letter reads:

They've discovered everything, absolutely everything. I cannot think who has betrayed us . . . and when all is said and done I don't care . . . P., by the way, seems to have handled things badly when he was asked about Dietrich, and as a result Dietrich in his turn quoted me as his source—a vicious circle of statements, which the Gestapo cleverly play off against each of us to their own advantage. I don't think there is very much more I can do to help.

f) In contrast to the view expressed in Dohnanyi's statement that

21. According to Christine von Dohnanyi.
22. Reported by F. von Schlabrendorff, op. cit., pp. 228 f. as well as by Christine von Dohnanyi and Josef Müller.

they knew 'everything', Huppenkothen's interrogation group in the Head Office seem to have been far from satisfied with the results of their investigations, according to the detailed account given by Huppenkothen himself at his trial in 1955. The reason for this was due partly to the difficulty in cooperating with other departments through the network of a complex organization and partly to the disruptive effects of the increasing number of air raids.

Sometimes the anxiety of the people in the Head Office to obtain more information about the organization of the resistance group and its channels of communication seemed to overcome their desire to pass a hasty sentence on their prisoners and have done with them. For instance, in Bonhoeffer's case new investigations were made into the connections existing between the churches as a result of the ecumenical movement. Although Group B in Department IV of the Head Office, which dealt with the 'Churches and the Freemasons', had for years kept careful watch over all church connections with the outside world, including the activities of the Church External Affairs Office, it was now felt necessary to examine those channels of the Confessing Church which up till then had existed secretly under the protection of Admiral Canaris, and which might be of use again under changed circumstances. It is probable that Huppenkothen sought information from other departments, in an attempt to check the reliability of Bonhoeffer's statements about his Swiss and English connections. If this was so, then further official documents concerning Bonhoeffer's interrogations in the Head Office may well one day come to light in the records preserved in the Ministry for Religious Affairs or even in the Foreign Office, if all the Head Office's own files relating to this complex matter have indeed been destroyed. The papers, if they exist, are in Potsdam and are not open for general research.

Huppenkothen has categorically stated that such investigations were indeed made, both in Germany and abroad, but that their progress was retarded or rendered partially impossible from the end of 1944 onwards as a result of the allied air bombardments.[23] In January 1945 things seem to have become somewhat easier for Bonhoeffer on account of these difficulties and the interest which his case aroused in the Head Office. This is confirmed by the two letters which he was able to write home during this period.[24]

In a summing-up of the situation, the following main points emerge. 1. The facts of the case known to the Head Office since the Tegel period had now been augmented by new discoveries and the statements of third parties to include a knowledge of the Freiburg discussions, the meeting in Sigtuna and the Memoranda. 2. Friends who were implicated in the proceedings or who had implicated others were now in the custody of

23. *Urteil im Prozess gegen Huppenkothen*, 1955, p. 19.
24. LPP, pp. 220, 222.

the Head Office. These included, apart from his brothers and brothers-in-law, the Freiburg professors von Dietze, Lampe and Ritter, as well as Walter Bauer, Hans John and Friedrich Justus Perels. The last-named three were subjected from time to time to severe tortures, so that Dr. Bauer, for instance, who was in the cell next to mine, pleaded with me to get him some poison from Bonhoeffer's father if ever the chance arose, because he did not think he could remain firm under the pain much longer. Bonhoeffer was no longer able to get in touch with any of these so that they could agree on the story they should tell their interrogators. 3. Bonhoeffer had not yet given up trying to save the situation. When he was unable to deny the facts he gave them a slanted meaning or introduced other facts which obscured or complicated the issue. For, as he said, 'the only fight which is lost is that which we give up'.[25]

Life in the Cellar

The time which Bonhoeffer passed in the cellar of the Head Office was spent first in Cell 19 and then in Cell 25. In a neighbouring cell was Schlabrendorff. These cells were smaller than those in Tegel, being barely five feet wide by eight feet long. They contained nothing more than a table, a stool and a bed that could be folded up during the day. At the beginning of February 1945 the heating-system stopped working. Surprisingly enough, however, most of the prisoners suffered less on this account than might have been expected.

For breakfast and supper there was a mug of imitation coffee and two slices of bread and jam; at midday some soup. Even though food parcels were no longer accepted so frequently by the guards, it seems likely that Bonhoeffer did actually receive what Maria von Wedemeyer, or his parents or sisters, brought to him on the Wednesday of each week. Payne Best's description of Bonhoeffer, whom he got to know towards the end of February in Buchenwald, has the ring of truth about it; '[He did] not look in the least like a man who had spent months in prison and who went in fear of his life.'[26]

There was a wash-room and lavatory at the end of the corridor, with a cold-water shower which was welcome to the prisoners in spite of the winter because it gave them the opportunity for many a whispered conversation. Exercise in the prison-yard, which is a common feature of life in most prisons, did not exist at Prinz-Albrecht-Strasse. But during the frequent air raids the prisoners were taken to a concrete air-raid shelter in the yard. This was the so-called 'Himmler Bunker'. On these occasions it was not always possible to enforce the strict discipline that was normally the rule, and as a result the prisoners were often able to

25. F. von Schlabrendorff, op. cit., p. 228.
26. P. Best to S. Leibholz, 2.3.1951.

establish some kind of contact with one another. Schlabrendorff has described what happened in the air-raid shelter during the night of 3rd February 1945, when Berlin suffered its worst air raid:

Tightly squeezed together we were standing in our air-raid shelter when a bomb hit it with an enormous explosion. For a second it seemed as if the shelter were bursting and the ceiling crashing down on top of us. It rocked like a ship tossing in the storm, but it held. At that moment Dietrich Bonhoeffer showed his mettle. He remained quite calm, he did not move a muscle . . . as if nothing had happened.[27]

The behaviour of the guards, who were now all S.S. men, towards their one-time high-ranking prisoners varied from downright sadism to the most formal politeness. Many of them complained about the conditions in general without necessarily being *agents provocateurs*. It frequently happened that the prisoners had no choice but to humble themselves before some brute in order to avoid being brutally treated. It is said of Bonhoeffer that even under these conditions he was able to command respect from the guards, 'so that to my surprise, within a short time, he had won over his warders, who were not always kindly disposed'.[28] Without the least embarrassment he would make modest requests, or enquire at the right moment about the personal circumstances or worries of his guards. He never demanded the impossible of them, since he could see that they too were in a nervous state. Dohnanyi wrote to his wife in a smuggled note of 25th February: 'I have seen Dietrich; he looks cheerful . . . Runge has a soft spot for Maria . . . He thought Dietrich was a "decent fellow"'.

The most encouraging aspect of the period Bonhoeffer spent at Prinz-Albrecht-Strasse was the chance it gave him of meeting friends he had not seen for a long time. There was Schlabrendorff, who was in the neighbouring cell, and whom he had not seen since he had become engaged to his cousin, Maria von Wedemeyer. Then there was Josef Müller, and Canaris and Oster, both of whom had thought they were in a far worse plight. There was also Goerdeler who until his execution on 2nd February was only a few cells away from Bonhoeffer, and of whom he was later able to give a report to the family in Regensburg. There was also Hans Böhm, the pastor and ecumenical officer of the Confessing Church, who had been arrested for helping Gisevius and Nebe to escape. Finally, but only for a few days, there was Hans von Dohnanyi. Many of these enjoyed with Bonhoeffer the contents of the food parcels which were sent to him, and occasionally a strong smell of tobacco smoke emanated from one or other of the cells.[29]

The means of communication with his family in the Marienburger

27. F. von Schlabrendorff, op. cit., pp. 229 f.
28. F. von Schlabrendorff, op. cit., p. 228.
29. F. von Schlabrendorff, op. cit., p. 229.

Allee had been almost completely disrupted. Occasionally Sonderegger passed on a greeting or a message when he handed over the weekly parcel on Wednesdays, or allowed a note to accompany it. Bonhoeffer's parents received only two more letters from him, one written in haste for his mother's birthday on 28th December 1944[30] and enclosing the poem 'New Year', and another written on 17th January 1945,[31] during the time when the Head Office was becoming interested in his knowledge of England. Bonhoeffer's parents never again obtained a permit to visit him.

Maria von Wedemeyer was in Berlin most of the time during these months. 'It is a great comfort for me to know that Maria is with you', Bonhoeffer wrote in the letter to his parents of 28th December 1944. The last letter which Maria herself received from her fiancé dates from 19th December 1944. On one occasion she succeeded in getting a personal interview with Sonderegger, but she failed to obtain permission to visit Dietrich. The officers of the Head Office never made any serious attempt to extort information from her.

Theological Work

We assumed in an earlier chapter[32] that Bonhoeffer had continued to work on his 'Non-religious Interpretation of Biblical Concepts in a World Come of Age' and had brought it a stage considerably nearer to completion. There is admittedly no actual proof in support of this assumption, and his scanty letters make no direct reference to his work. The new series of interrogations to which he was now subjected may have slowed him down. There are, however, various indications that he continued with his writing.

We know that he worked on his manuscript up to the very last moment of his time in Tegel and that this already covered many sheets of paper. We also know that it was among the belongings which he took with him to Prinz-Albrecht-Strasse. During his time at the Head Office he was in possession of writing materials—paper and a pencil—and in his last letter of 17th January he again asked for more paper to be sent to him along with the weekly food-parcel. Schlabrendorff confirms that, unlike himself, Bonhoeffer was able to write in his cell and had the wherewithal for doing so. There were other prominent prisoners of the Head Office who also wrote whole memorandas. Many of these were handcuffed, tightly at night but loosely during the day. This was not the case with Bonhoeffer.

We also know that while in the Head Office he received and read quite a number of books. In his letter of 17th January he complains that he has received no books with the weekly parcel, but that the matter

30. LPP, pp. 220 f.   31. LPP, p. 222.   32. See Ch. XIII, p. 765.

can be rectified by speaking to Sonderegger. He then asks to be sent a whole series of new works—Pestalozzi, Natorp, Plutarch. The volume of Plutarch, which Bonhoeffer did actually receive along with the works of other authors just before he was moved from Berlin, accompanied him as far as Schönberg and even found its way back to his family at a subsequent date. Dr. Hermann Pünder reported in the summer of 1945 that he had exchanged books with Bonhoeffer in Buchenwald. He gave him the biography of Julian the Apostate by the Geneva historian Bidez and received in return Kurt Leese's *Protestantism in Modern Times*.

Kurt Leese's book had appeared in 1941. The official view of the Confessing Church was that its author was an 'outsider', from the theological standpoint. Bonhoeffer was now naturally very interested in a man who had attempted to understand and come to terms with the work of the previous generation of theologians, with Ritschl and Troeltsch, and the whole of the modern tradition, including humanism and scientific discoveries.

It was in Buchenwald that Bonhoeffer shared a cell with General von Rabenau, also a Doctor of Theology, and was able to have long discussions with him over a period of many weeks.

We know with what determination Bonhoeffer attempted to keep strictly to the work-schedule he had drawn up for himself in order to combat the strain of difficult days and weeks of interrogations. It is therefore barely conceivable that during the whole of the four months which he spent in Prinz-Albrecht-Strasse he was not engaged on some kind of theological work. He may just possibly have chosen some other subject than that of the 'Non-religious Interpretation of Biblical Concepts', but if he did we know nothing about it.

Somewhere on the last stages of his journey a sheaf of manuscript notes must have been left behind with the rest of his belongings. But who would have been interested in preserving the illegible jottings of a prisoner, either while he was in transit or when the camp at Flossenbürg was being dismantled? Even those friends of his who managed to escape with their lives had other, more pressing matters to occupy their thoughts when the end came.

The last theologically shaped testimony formulated by Bonhoeffer is really contained in his poem 'New Year'.[33] Written in the form of a prayer its thought-content is inspired by a spirit similar to that of 'Christians and Pagans'. But it has left behind the didactic tone of the latter. He offered the poem to his mother and his fiancée.

Grim February

In the first days of February 1945 so many tragic things happened to the family that the demands placed on everyone, both at home and

33. LPP, p. 221.

away from it, were almost too great to bear. For now events precipitated themselves: the destruction of Pätzig, Hans von Dohnanyi's removal to the cellar of the Reich Security Head Office and his infection of himself with disease, the death sentence passed on Rüdiger Schleicher and Klaus Bonhoeffer by the People's Court, and the unexplained disappearance of Dietrich Bonhoeffer from Berlin.

1. In the last days of January Maria von Wedemeyer returned home to Pätzig, beyond the Oder. The Russian front was moving closer. Maria's mother wrote to Frau Bonhoeffer on 30th January 1945.

Dear Frau Bonhoeffer, I have had to do something very unkind. Please forgive me. In twelve degrees of frost and an icy east wind I sent Maria with my three children, Frau Döpke and her two children, Fräulein Rath, who was sick with a fever, and the very delicate Frau Dienel in a covered wagon to the west, towards Celle, where Döpke's relatives live in a village.

I needed her help now desperately. It is a task far beyond her strength. Her driver is a Pole, and she has the best three farm horses. Pray with me that she will be equal to this hard task.

If all goes well, the journey will take fourteen days. But there has been a lot of snow and the winds are very strong.

People have advised me strongly against Berlin. We are deeply grateful for your offer to take the children. Herr Döpke wanted at all costs to get his family to the west to his parents. I couldn't let them go away in two wagons because there were not enough of the necessary spare parts and we would have needed another driver. We couldn't have afforded it.

Perhaps we shall soon get the order here for general evacuation. We have prepared everything in secret. I hope that I can help to save human lives and prevent panic. When she has delivered the children, Maria hopes to be able to reach you again. But it will take a long time.

May God have mercy and protect you and yours and spare you from suffering too long. Whether we shall see each other in this life or the next rests with HIM. In any case we can look forward to that with great happiness.

Thank you so much for all the motherly and fatherly love that you have shown and are showing my child. Yours, Ruth Wedemeyer.

Two days after this letter Pätzig was destroyed by cannon fire.[34]

Maria von Wedemeyer's trek across the Oder and Elbe was successful. When she reached Berlin two weeks after the successful trek, she found everything changed. Unable to get exact information from the Reich Security Head Office, she set out with a case of warm clothing for the south, in order to find Dietrich Bonhoeffer. She reached Dachau and went the last four and a half miles on foot, carrying her case, to Flossenbürg, only to be turned away at both places without any information. She finally got back to Berlin amid the general disintegration—it was now March—hoping that people were better informed there, but no

34. Part of Bonhoeffer's library was stored there also, including the Erlangen Luther edition and a little casket.

one knew anything, and Prinz-Albrecht-Strasse would give no information.

2. At the end of January Huppenkothen's special group made a new attempt to speed up the enquiry, which was now dragging on. So Dohnanyi, the key figure, was brought from Sachsenhausen to the Reich Security Head Office on 1st February, his illness now being disregarded. 'So far they've left me almost entirely alone.'[35] Now a brutal commissar called Stawitzky took charge of him. He abandoned Dohnanyi to his presumed helplessness and, for example, never had him taken to the bathroom or the lavatory. But Dohnanyi held out until Stawitzky was relieved after three weeks and replaced again by Sonderegger. A doctor who was held in the Lehrter Strasse as a political prisoner was ordered to look after him. Now Dohnanyi was able to smuggle out a long note to his wife in the laundry parcel. He said:

Three days ago a practising doctor . . . who is also a prisoner here, Dr. Eugen Ense . . . was asked to look after me. Until three days ago I was in the hands of a man who was simply a brute. He thought he could break my spirit by leaving me entirely uncared for. That went on for three weeks. I really began to stink. That helped. Now Sonderegger and Ense have come. Ense can visit me as he pleases—my cell door is open—and the worst is past. It was actually very funny, and I often laughed at how I looked . . .

I am using my illness as a weapon. It helps me that people think I'm sicker than I am . . . In fact I feel quite well, and I am well fed, thanks to you. At night I secretly teach myself to walk again. It's going quite well. I must become independent. In the daytime I'm the helpless invalid . . .

The only thing to do is gain time. I must make sure that I'm unfit to be tried. The best thing would be for me to get a solid attack of dysentery. A culture must be available for medical purposes in the Koch Institute. If you wrap up some food in a red cloth, and also put an ink-mark on the glass, then I'll know that it contains a decent infection that'll get me to the hospital . . .

They want to finish things off now by force, and that must be prevented . . .

Think about providing me with some infectious germs. Perhaps Zutt can prepare some such food for you. It musn't be too long in coming, because I might be moved from Berlin. Wrap up the infected food in a red cloth . . . If the whole thing's impossible, put a green paper around something. If I go to hospital, the only possibility is a state hospital . . . It would help with Huppenkothen if some doctor (father . . . ?) were to make a stupid enquiry whether nursing and treatment, invalid transport, massage, and injections, were possible here. But don't you intervene! . . . And avoid a commissar called Stawitzky!

On 8th March the exchange of parcels brought the next note:

You can scarcely imagine the excitement when I saw a glass covered with red in the case. And then the book and the thermos flask. At last, at last a few lines from you—after over six months—a present . . . The hearings

35. Hans von Dohnanyi in a smuggled note of 25.2.1945.

continue, and it is clear what I have to expect unless a miracle happens. The misery around me is so great that I would throw away the little life I have if you were not there . . .

That is why I'm not frightened of any infectious illness. I know very well that I would lie down with the feeling that it would not only save my life, but that of many others also, whose situation is bound up with mine, certainly Dietrich's. Naturally I put the diphtheria culture in my mouth immediately and chewed thoroughly, but for practical reasons it wasn't possible to do it until half past seven at night . . . And it seemed to me that the cotton wool had become quite dry. Now I'm eating the sweets as quickly as possible, I've heard that diphtheria bacilli are not very volatile, but can't stand dryness, needing moisture to keep alive. Incubation period is three to to eight days. I'm afraid I may be immune and won't get anything. But it would always be possible to have a repeat.

I must get out of here into a hospital so that I can't be interrogated any longer. Fainting fits, heart attacks make no impression, and if I go to a hospital without a new illness it could even be dangerous, because they could cure me quickly. Sonderegger said today: 'It lies in your own interest for the hearing to come to an end soon. The *Reichsführer* [Himmler] does not want to keep you here. He wants you to get well.' Shall I translate that? 'Himmler wants to finish the hearing as quickly as possible. During the period in which the charges are being prepared you are to go to a hospital—perhaps in Central Germany or Bavaria, depending on the war situation[36]—there we'll soon get you fit to be tried In the state you're in we can hardly put you in front of a court, but in three or four weeks we'll have you ready.' This is their game, and I'd so like to ruin it for them ! Believe me-- I have seen things correctly so far, unfortunately—there is no other solution than a serious new illness. Have no fear for me. I'll get over it, but even if I don't, much would be gained for the others and nothing lost for myself in the event, for I have nothing more to lose . . . I heard today from Sonderegger that Eberhard has also been arrested . . . Incidentally, he's not been linked with me in any way. Sonderegger just asked how it happened that he had lived with us . . .

We must act as long as we can. The war or the S.S. can spoil things for us at any time, and I'm afraid of being moved from Berlin. I want to stay here in Berlin at all costs, as close as possible to you. As long as that is the case I am not at their mercy. It all comes back to the one solution : a new illness. It's terribly hard for your parents. I want so much to help. Can I do so in any other way?

The concerted effort came off. Medical enquiries by his father-in-law Karl Bonhoeffer and Professor Zutt at the Reich Security Head Office resulted in Dr. Tietze, the head of the neurological division of the police state hospital, being consulted. About two weeks after Dohnanyi had written the note, he was moved to the prison division in Scharnhorst-strasse under Dr. Tietze, who allowed Christine von Dohnanyi to have another secret meeting with her husband.

3. On the afternoon of 2nd February at the People's Court, not far

36. Buchenwald or Dachau.

from the Potsdamer Platz, Freisler pronounced the death sentence on Klaus Bonhoeffer and Rüdiger Schleicher, as well as on Friedrich Justus Perels and Hans John. That evening they were moved from the cells of prison wing B in Lehrter Strasse—I could see their cells from my own, opposite—to wing D, where a corridor was reserved for those condemned to death.

The next morning, early on the Saturday, Ursula Schleicher with her daughter Dorothee set out to see the *Oberreichsanwalt* E. Lautz about the death sentence. At the same time her husband's brother, Dr. Rolf Schleicher from Stuttgart, at that time a senior staff doctor, who had come to Berlin for the end of his brother's trial, went to town in order to make an immediate appeal for mercy. When he arrived at the Potsdamer Platz underground station, no one was allowed up. The heaviest allied daylight attack on the centre of Berlin was just beginning. For two hours squadron succeeded squadron in the bright blue winter sky and transformed the area east of the Tiergarten into a wilderness of smoke and ash. All services were cut off.

After the attack Rolf Schleicher walked across to the nearby building of the People's Court, which was burning. Recognized by his doctor's uniform, he was called into the courtyard. He had to attend to some important person who had run too late across the courtyard and had been hit by a piece of shrapnel. But all Rolf Schleicher was able to do was establish that the man was dead. It was Roland Freisler, whose last death sentences the day before had been passed on Rolf's brother Rüdiger, Klaus Bonhoeffer, Perels and Hans John. He refused to write out a death certificate until he had been taken to Thierack, the Minister of Justice. The latter was very affected by the strange coincidence and promised that there would be a delay in the execution of the death sentence and that the verdict would be reconsidered after a plea for mercy had been submitted. Hours later Rolf Schleicher was able to get back to the Marienburger Allee. He entered the room announcing: 'The scoundrel is dead!' Meanwhile, Ursula Schleicher and her daughter had been able to achieve nothing. They went on foot to Lehrter Strasse and found that the prison had remained unharmed. She was first able to see her husband only a few days later. Prisoners condemned to death were supposed to wear handcuffs all the time, but the warders at Lehrter Strasse did not pay much attention to this rule. They too had observed that after the sentence these men were much calmer than during the period in which they were still being tried.

4. On the same 3rd February Bonhoeffer's parents, accompanied by their daughter-in-law, Emmi Bonhoeffer, had left to deliver a parcel early to Dietrich in Prinz-Albrecht-Strasse for his birthday. Apart from the usual food there were books and a letter, in which his father had written: 'The memory of so many lovely things that you have experienced, and the hope for a speedy end to your time of trial will help you

to get through your birthday.' He intended this time to press on the spot for permission to see his son.

After changing twice they reached the Anhalter underground station, but they too could not leave it because of the alarm. When the three of them were eventually able to leave the by now suffocating atmosphere of the station it was impossible to get through the ruins to the Reich Security Head Office. No one was admitted to the building, which had been badly hit. Full of anxiety, they turned back and started to walk home until, further out, they were able to get a train. Emmi Bonhoeffer enquired for her husband in Lehrter Strasse. They all arrived home covered with soot and ash. Only the next day did they learn that nothing had happened to the prisoners despite the direct hit on the basement of the Reich Security Head Office.

Then his parents tried again, on the usual parcels' day, Wednesday 7th February, to get into the Head Office. Their parcel, which also contained the Plutarch, was accepted this time, but they were not allowed to see their son. The accompanying letter read:

7.2.1945. Dear Dietrich, Your birthday letter for the 4th, which we wanted to bring on Saturday, did not reach you because of the raid. We were in the Anhalter underground station during the raid, and it wasn't particularly pleasant. Apart from looking like chimney-sweeps afterwards nothing happened to us. But later, when we tried to get to you, we were very anxious, as we weren't allowed to go in because of unexploded bombs.

The next day we learned that nothing had happened to the prisoners. I hope that is true . . . Maria is taking her brothers and sisters to the west . . . Unfortunately I had no luck at the library.[37] Pestalozzi is lent out only for the reading room. Natorp was out. Karl Friedrich has chosen the Plutarch for your birthday. I hope that this letter reaches you. We are looking forward to being allowed to see you soon. There are many things to be sorted out at our age, things that have to be discussed with one's children. I'm typing this so that it can be more easily read. Our hearty greetings, Your Father.

This was the last word that Dietrich Bonhoeffer received from his family.

On the afternoon of this 7th February Bonhoeffer was taken from Berlin to an unknown destination. Only on the next parcels' day, 14th February, did Maria von Wedemeyer and his parents discover that there was no longer anyone at Prinz-Albrecht-Strasse to receive their gifts.

On 4th February, the 'common birthday', Maria's grandmother, Frau von Kleist-Retzow, also celebrated hers in the remote village of Klein-Krössin. Although she was frail, she had lost none of her energy and judgement. But she was preparing for the Russian invasion: she intended to stay. In the autumn of 1945 Maria's mother had again managed to reach Klein-Krössin by a long trek on foot through what had

37. Cf. LPP, p. 222.

now become Polish territory. Dietrich Bonhoeffer's old patroness was dying, but she lived long enough to learn what had happened. A few hours later she died.

On 2nd February, Bishop Bell wrote from Chichester to Dietrich's twin sister in Oxford on the occasion of the common birthday:

My dear Mrs. Leibholz, I cannot help thinking very much of Dietrich and you in these days of momentous happenings in Germany. And I take the oppor-tunity of our common birthday to express once again with all the sincerity I possess my affection for and deep trust in Dietrich, as well as my ardent hopes and prayers for his deliverance. I can judge how anxious you must be as the war in all its violence approaches Berlin. Would God that the whole Hitler castle might be brought down in ruin, even now, and so the means granted for the surrender of the German forces and the saving of that true German soul which is yet so precious a care to those silent, suppressed and persecuted multitudes of true patriots like Dietrich, for the gradual if costly rebuilding of the nation. We must pray that God may bring the war to an end, with the breaking of Hitler's spell, and save Europe from even more pitiless destruc-tion. And may the lives of those most needed, as we humans see it, for recovery and illumination be saved. And may God of His mercy guide the three Allied Leaders to seek a common policy as may give hope for unity and charity in Europe, and space and freedom for the European family of nations to breathe again the spirit of the Christian tradition and faith.

We are now at the climax—God grant wisdom, mercy and peace. With love to you all, and especially words of love to Dietrich. Yours affectionately, George Cicestr.

Emergency Quarters

The raid of 3rd February had lasting consequences. After it Bonhoeffer was never again brought before Huppenkothen's group of investigators, although—as was shown clearly by Dohnanyi's removal on 1st February —a new approach was being taken towards the affairs of the 'Zossen men'.

In 1955 Huppenkothen related how far the Reich Security Head Office was affected by the events of 3rd February. Many offices had to be set up in emergency escape quarters in that area of the Reich not yet occupied, with all the unimaginable difficulties of communication. Sach-senhausen was cleared because of the approaching front. The 'house prison' in Prinz-Albrecht-Strasse was now usable only to a very limited extent. Only those prisoners whose trial was about to come up were to remain there. All the others had to be housed elsewhere. Payne Best, who had been imprisoned for a few days in the Reich Security Head Office after Sachsenhausen was moved south, has given a savagely humorous account of the indescribable apprehensiveness of those February days in Prinz-Albrecht-Strasse in his book *The Venlo Incident*.

At midday on 7th February twenty prisoners were summoned to be removed elsewhere. Twelve men had to stand and wait, with their baggage, next to a prison van that had, at the most, eight seats; among them were the former governor of Belgium and Northern France, General von Falkenhausen, Gottfried Count Bismarck, Werner von Alvensleben, Dr. Josef Müller, Dr. Hermann Pünder, who was later in the cell next to Bonhoeffer, the corvette captain Franz Liedig, a resistance man who had been involved as early as 1938 in plans for a *Putsch*, Ludwig Gehre, a colleague of Oster and friend of Otto John, and Dietrich Bonhoeffer. In front of a second van waited Canaris, Oster and the military judge Sack, General Thomas, Major General Halder, Dr. Hjalmar Schacht, Oster's colleague Dr. Theodor Strünck, and the former Austrian chancellor von Schuschnigg. It later emerged that the first van was bound for the Thuringian concentration camp, Buchenwald, and the second for Flossenbürg in the Upper Palatinate.

It is hard to see the principle behind the selection of these two groups. Were they chosen according to the prominence of the members, or was there already the element of the possible exchange value of some of them with the Allies? Was the deciding factor the importance of still unrevealed information possessed by the prisoners? No such criterion, however, could be applied to all the members of the two groups.

Certainly the general confusion, of which the prisoners could not fail to be aware, encouraged many a hope, and the sudden encounter with old friends gladdened their hearts. But when they were loaded into the vans, Josef Müller and Dietrich Bonhoeffer were handcuffed. Dietrich protested but to no avail. Josef Müller says that he then exhorted him: 'Let us go calmly to the gallows as Christians.' Only in Buchenwald were the handcuffs removed.

II BUCHENWALD

We have an excellent chronicler of the period in Buchenwald. Payne Best, an officer of the British Secret Service who was captured in 1939 at Venlo has given a graphic account, vividly observed, of the situation in this camp in his book *The Venlo Incident*.[38] He arrived at Buchenwald on 24th February with the English officer Hugh Falconer, the air force officer Kokorin, a nephew of Molotov, and General von Rabenau.

The Place

The air-raid shelter cells in Buchenwald, which had been promoted to receive prominent prisoners, were damp, cold and without daylight. They lay beneath houses outside the actual area of the camp, which had been built at one time for camp officials, but after air raids had again been converted into command headquarters and barracks. The cells in the

38. P. Best, *The Venlo Incident*, pp. 171 ff.

basement were at first intended for S.S. members who had incurred punishment. In August 1944 the Allies had bombed buildings outside the camp, on which occasion, it was reported, Thälmann, Breitscheid and Princess Mafalda of Hesse had been killed. As a result, after this whenever there was an alarm the sentries went quickly to trenches some distance away, and the prisoners were locked in until it was over. It was said that there was also munition stored in the cellars.

The wide central corridor of the cellar was divided lengthways by two walls into three parallel corridors with gaps in them. On the left there was first the wash-room. Then came the cells: next to the damp wash-room was No. 1, with Bonhoeffer and von Rabenau, who joined him after a fortnight; No. 2, with Dr. Pünder and Liedig; No. 3, with Dr. Heberlein, the former ambassador in Spain, and his wife; No. 4, with von Alvensleben and von Petersdorff; No. 5, a more comfortable cell, with von Falkenhausen; No. 6, with Hugh Falconer; No. 7, with Wassili Kokorin; No. 8, with Josef Müller and Captain Gehre. On the right there were the larger cells; opposite No. 8, the guard room; then No. 9, with a Fräulein Heidl; No. 10, with Dr. Sigmund Rascher; No. 11, with Payne Best; No. 12, with Dr. Hoepner, a brother of the executed general. Payne Best's cell, No. 11, was directly opposite Bonhoeffer's, but not directly visible because of the dividing wall.

The allotting of the cells was undertaken by the camp commandant himself on the night of 7th-8th February. Then there followed the petty sufferings inflicted by the subaltern guards. The food consisted of a soup at midday and some bread, fat and marmalade in the evening. According to the instructions of the Reich Security Head Office the prisoners were to be kept in a condition in which they could be interrogated. Since the camp was getting closer and closer to the front in the west and refugees were flooding into Thuringia from east and west, victualling became a serious problem.

There were no walks in the fresh air because there was no way of ensuring proper surveillance here outside the camp area. Instead the prisoners managed to get permission to use the central corridor of the cellar, divided into three, for their 'walks'. It was too arduous a task for the sentries to take each of the seventeen prisoners separately under guard around the corridors, so it came about that exercise was taken by all of them at the same time. In this way the prisoners made one another's acquaintance. Best tells us that there were even little black-market deals with tobacco, undertaken by service-prisoners who had access to these things for the prominent prisoners in the camp.[39] Best apparently managed to brighten the mood among the prisoners in the cells, and Bonhoeffer helped him: 'He was cheerful, ready to respond to a joke.'[40]

39. P. Best, op. cit., pp. 178 ff.
40. P. Best to S. Leibholz, 2.3.1951.

The Companions in Suffering

Bonhoeffer became friendly with Dr. Hermann Pünder in the next cell, a Catholic politician from the Rheinland and one of the survivors. As we have already heard, they exchanged books;[41] their conversations were about culture and politics and the future relations between Catholics and Protestants.

After a good two weeks Friedrich von Rabenau arrived to join Bonhoeffer in his cell. Making a somewhat critical comparison with the other people in the cellar Falconer said: 'I think they were the only pair of prisoners sharing a cell who got on really well together and enjoyed each other's company.'[42] General von Rabenau had not had a command, but had been the head of the military archives. He was the author of the long book, *Seeckt, Aus seinem Leben* 1918-1936, that had appeared in 1940. Bonhoeffer owned a copy and undoubtedly knew the passages that alone had made it possible for the book to be printed in 1940.

Rabenau had early on been an intermediary between Beck's resistance centre and some of the leading generals who were trying in 1940 to influence Brauchitsch.[43] In March 1941, Hassell and Goerdeler discussed with Rabenau whether and when one could again approach Brauchitsch. Before 20th July Goerdeler sent Rabenau to individual generals as one of his intimates.[44] Retired from the active service in 1942, the old general had taken a degree at the theological faculty of Berlin University and added the licentiate to his doctor *honoris causa*. But then the Reich Security Head Office had tracked down Rabenau as a friend of Goerdeler's.[45]

The life and milieu of Friedrich von Rabenau, general and theologian, were not very close to Bonhoeffer's. And yet the five weeks they spent together seem to have been full of interest. According to Pünder, Rabenau was still writing his memoirs in Buchenwald. He cannot remember whether Bonhoeffer also did any writing, but only that he and Rabenau had in their cell 'enthusiastic dogmatic discussions that I was sometimes able to listen to with great interest'.[46] Payne Best even gave the theologian a chess set, so that Bonhoeffer could again follow his old passion. Rabenau, who had arrived from Berlin with Payne Best, at the first opportunity introduced to him in the wash-room his friend Bonhoeffer. Bonhoeffer was happy to have the chance to speak English again.

41. Payne Best's remark that the prisoners had nothing apart from their clothes is probably not quite true.
42. H. Falconer to S. Leibholz, 1.10.1945.
43. Cf. Ch. XII, p. 631.
44. G. Ritter, *Carl Goerdeler und die deutsche Widerstandsbewegung*, p. 383.
45. He was executed in Flossenbürg after Bonhoeffer.
46. H. Pünder in an address on the opening of the Dietrich Bonhoeffer school in Pulheim near Cologne on 19.9.1960.

This Englishman knew nothing of Bonhoeffer's past, his background or his importance. Among his later descriptions of his fellow-prisoners, sometimes spiteful, sometimes humorous, Best gave the following account of the immediate impression Bonhoeffer made on him:

Bonhoeffer was all humility and sweetness; he always seemed to diffuse an atmosphere of happiness, of joy in every smallest event in life, and of deep gratitude for the mere fact that he was alive. There was something dog-like in the look of fidelity in his eyes and his gladness if you showed that you liked him. He was one of the very few men I have ever met to whom his God was real and ever close to him.

And in a personal letter later to his family he wrote:

In fact my feeling was far stronger than these words imply He was, without exception, the finest and most lovable man I have ever met.

In this letter he tells how most of the prisoners complained:

. . . with the exception of Falkenhausen and Bonhoeffer . . . Bonhoeffer was different; just quite calm and normal, seemingly perfectly at his ease . . . his soul really shone in the dark desperation of our prison . . . [we were] in complete agreement that our warders and guards needed pity far more than we and that it was absurd to blame them for their actions.[47]

Hopes for Liberation

As Easter Sunday of 1945, April 1st, approached, the thunder of the American cannons from the Werra could be heard in the basement. Who could now imagine that there would be a resumption of the interrogations and a session of the People's Court? Escape plans were again considered—without practical results. The sentry Sippach gave orders to keep at the ready to leave at a moment's notice. One guard told the prisoners that they would be going on foot. Did that mean execution in the wood? Another knew that there was a lorry available.

In Berlin Bonhoeffer's parents had tried again to trace him via Prinz-Albrecht-Strasse. They wrote to him:

Since you left Berlin we have heard nothing of you, and presumably you have heard nothing from us . . . We would like to send you the laundry and those little things we were able to send in the past, but so far there has been no way of doing so. I hope that Christel will discover something today at Prinz-Albrecht-Strasse . . . Permission to write to elderly people such as we should be more frequent. With love, Father.

My thoughts are with you day and night, worrying about how you are getting on. I hope you are able to do some work and reading and are managing to keep in reasonable health. God help you and us through this difficult period. We are staying in Berlin whatever happens. Your old mother.

47. P. Best to S. Leibholz, 2.3.1951.

The letter was returned. At Prinz-Albrecht-Strasse nothing more was accepted, and no one would give any information.

III TO FLOSSENBÜRG

We know of the last week of Bonhoeffer's life from the detailed account by Payne Best, which continues as far as Schönberg (3rd-8th April 1945). There are, as well, the accounts of survivors, Hermann Pünder, Josef Müller, Frau Goerdeler, Fabian von Schlabrendorff, etc. And finally there are details from the records of the trials of Huppenkothen and Dr. Thorbeck, conducted in South Germany from 1951 to 1955.

The Move to Schönberg

It was probably on instructions from Berlin that the prisoners were moved from Buchenwald. Otherwise, the camp command would have carried out the general instruction to kill special prisoners in the event of the enemy approaching, and not make a lorry available for them, in the disastrous transport and food situation. In fact there were apparently instructions to the transport organizers to take some prisoners to Flossenbürg and others further south.

Thus in the late evening of Easter Tuesday, 3rd April 1945, a vast closed lorry rolled out of Buchenwald into the night. It used wood for fuel, and there was a great pile of it in the lorry for the generator. Behind this the special prisoners from the basement had to make do, for themselves and what luggage they had left, with a space that was intended for eight people at the most. The vehicle never went faster than twenty miles an hour and stopped every hour. The air filters had to be cleaned, the generator filled and the motor got going again with fifteen minutes' stoking. Each time the air in the stoking area became intolerable. There was no light and nothing to eat or drink. But as the wood diminished the prisoners could take it in turns to go to the back door, two by two, and get some fresh air from the opening. Bonhoeffer, who sat next to Payne Best, found the remnants of his stock of tobacco and shared it out; he 'insisted on contributing it to the common store . . . he was a good and saintly man'.[48] In the grey dawn someone saw a village. The direction was south-easterly. The inmates of the lorry guessed that they were going to Flossenbürg; it was for them an ominous name. Yet they had breakfast, the guards producing unexpected food.

Towards noon, on the Wednesday of Easter week, they reached Weiden. Here they would find out whether or not they were to turn left into the valley up to Flossenbürg. The lorry stopped. There was some conversation outside: 'Drive on, we can't take you . . . too full!' And the lorry set off again—straight ahead, to the south. So it was not going

48. P. Best, The Venlo Incident, p. 180.

to the annihilation camp. But a few miles further on two police motor-cyclists signalled to it to stop. Müller and Liedig were called out and their things pulled out of the pile of luggage at the back. Dietrich Bonhoeffer leaned back so as not to be seen. But the unfortunate Gehre jumped out after them. He had shared a cell with Müller and wanted to stay with him.

Were orders given and then changed again in the general chaos? Were three men from the lorry to be sent to Flossenbürg? The final events at Flossenbürg suggest that Bonhoeffer was supposed to be the third, but now seemed to have been replaced by Gehre. Or had the whole transport, in fact, been intended for Flossenbürg and only here had it been decided, in view of the situation, that the transport leader himself should find a new place to take all but a few selected people.

At last the lorry moved on again. Now that Flossenbürg lay behind them again, the guards became more friendly. They let the prisoners get out at a farmer's house. They were allowed to go to a pump in the yard, and a peasant woman brought a jug of milk and rye bread. It was a bright afternoon down in the beautiful Nab valley.

In the dusk the van drove into Regensburg. Every lodging seemed full. At last a door opened, and the men were ordered to go into the prison attached to the court-house. When the tone was too brusque they objected. 'Aristocrats again!' said one of the guards. 'Get up with the others on the second floor!' In the corridors there lay the relatives of Goerdeler, Stauffenberg, Halder, Hammerstein, Hassell, old and young. The new arrivals had to go five into a single cell, but everyone was able to choose those he was to be locked up with. In Bonhoeffer's cell there were Rabenau, Pünder, von Falkenhausen and Dr. Hoepner. The kitchens were closed, but the prisoners made so much noise that an intimidated guard found some vegetable soup and distributed it with some bread.

On Thursday morning when the doors opened for the prisoners to wash, there were great reunions in the corridors, introductions and exchanges of information. Best relates that the scene was more like a great reception than a morning in prison. The guards tried helplessly to get the men back into their cells. At last food was brought to the cells, and eventually the 'cases' were again sitting behind locked doors. Bonhoeffer spent most of his time at the little opening in the cell door and told the various relatives what he knew of his fellow-prisoners in Prinz-Albrecht-Strasse. He was able to tell Frau Goerdeler about the last weeks of her husband's life. Bonhoeffer may well have thought that he had now escaped the worst danger. An air-raid alarm interrupted their conversations. While the shunting yard outside lay in ruins, they were all safe in the basement. Then, when they were let upstairs again there was the same scene as in the morning.

Towards evening it became quieter and tiredness overtook them. But one of the Buchenwald guards appeared again and got the men down to the familiar van in the rainy night outside. They set off in a good mood, alongside the Danube. But after a few miles the van skidded and stopped. Falconer, as the expert, had to confirm that the steering was broken. Passers-by were asked to order a replacement van from the police in Regensburg. Despite their pistols the guards did not feel very comfortable among the burnt-out cars beside the road. The rain drummed on the roof.

At last, in the morning light of 6th April, the guards let their prisoners out to stretch their legs and warm themselves. Towards midday a bus appeared from Regensburg with all its windows intact. The prisoners' possessions were loaded into it; Bonhoeffer still had some books with him. The Buchenwald guard, who had now become quite human had to stay behind with the wreck and ten new men with automatic pistols took over the transport. But it was still a pleasure to drive through the lovely valley in the more comfortable bus, up from the Danube, past the monastery of Metten into the Bavarian wood celebrated by Stifter. The driver told the village girls who wanted to have a lift that the party in the elegant bus was a film group making a propaganda film. The guards fetched a cap full of eggs from a farmer's house, but only for their own consumption.

By the early afternoon they had arrived: Schönberg below Zwiesel, twenty-five miles north of Passau. The unloading began outside the school. The other prisoners were there already. The group of 'special cases' was taken to the first floor, a school-room, from the windows of which one could see, on three sides, the green mountain valley. Here there were proper beds with coloured blankets. The door was locked, but it was bright and warm. Bonhoeffer sat for a long time at the open window sunning himself, chatting with Pünder and learning Russian with Kokorin. His bed was next to the latter's.

He did a great deal to keep some of the weaker brethren from depression and anxiety. He spent a good deal of time with Wasily Wasiliew Kokorin, Molotov's nephew, who was a delightful young man although an atheist. I think your brother divided his time with him between instilling the foundations of Christianity and learning Russian.[49]

Everyone was animated; they laughed and wrote their name over their bed. Only the food problem was not solved. Their complaints were met by the statement, which was certainly not incorrect, that the place was overflowing with refugees and no vehicle, let alone petrol, could be found to be requisitioned. Later, of course, there were petrol and vehicles enough for other purposes. At last, however, the other prisoners, who had more freedom, made contact with some compassionate inhabitants of the village. Then there was even on one occasion a great dish with

49. H. Falconer to S. Leibholz, 1.10.1945.

steaming potatoes for the hungry prisoners, and the next day potato salad.

The Saturday was a quiet, beautiful day. It began with Payne Best taking an electric razor out of his luggage and each of the men being able to shave with the precious instrument which was connected to the classroom plug. The large room even made it possible for them to take a little exercise. Everyone assumed that, with the general confusion in the country, there would be no more trials.

In the meantime, however, the apparatus of the Reich Security Head Office was continuing to function elsewhere with unexpected efficiency. It was even able to correct mistakes that had already been made.

The Death Sentence

It was apparently in the midday discussion with Hitler on 5th April that decisions were taken which, amongst other things, ordained that Bonhoeffer and Dohnanyi were not to survive.[50] On the afternoon of this day orders were given by the Reich Security Office for the carrying out of the measures of the last days.

On Thursday, 5th April 1945, Kaltenbrunner issued the appropriate instructions. He was certainly advised by Group Leader Müller, and Hitler's approval at least was obtained. It is possible that Hitler gave the orders. Whether Himmler was involved is doubtful.[51]

On the evening of 5th April Dr. Tietze received a message at the state hospital that Dohnanyi was to be 'moved' the next morning to Sachsenhausen. Tietze quickly got hold of Christine von Dohnanyi so that she could see her husband once more, but it was not possible overnight to arrange an escape plan. Dr. Tietze gave Dohnanyi heavy drugs to make him incapable of being tried. Sonderegger collected him very early on

---

50. E. Zeller, in his *Geist der Freiheit*, p. 466, says: 'It was only in the last month of the war, when Canaris's whole diary was discovered, that an enraged Hitler had all the people who had not yet been tried condemned by a swiftly set-up field court of the S.S. and executed on 9th April (Canaris, Oster, Dohnanyi, Bonhoeffer, Gehre, Strünck, Sack).' The source of this version seems to be a statement by the criminal commissar Sonderegger in the Huppenkothen trial. However this is rather thin evidence for the events, which were probably more complicated than that. G. Ritter writes: 'The immediate reason for the execution of all the conspirators still alive in Flossenbürg was (according to Sonderegger) the discovery of Canaris's complete diary in April 1945, which aroused Hitler's special anger' (op. cit., p. 546). And now G. Buchheit: 'Only at the beginning of 1945 did General Buhle, who happened to be quartered in Zossen, find the diaries I-V and six books of "travel reports" in a metal cupboard and give them to the chief officer guarding the Führer, S.S. District Leader Rattenhuber. The latter gave them to Kaltenbrunner on 6th April. After Rattenhuber returned to Munich from captivity in Russia, he called on Dr. Josef Müller, whom he had known before, and told him that, on Hitler's instructions, Kaltenbrunner had ordered the immediate "execution of the conspirators"' (*Der deutsche Geheimdienst. Geschichte der militärischen Abwehr*, 1966, p. 445).

51. According to Huppenkothen, cf. *Urteil im Prozess gegen Huppenkothen*, 1955, p. 21.

6th April. Dr. Tietze has described what happened on 6th April as follows:

Sonderegger stood in front of the hospital waiting for a car that was to come from Prinz-Albrecht-Strasse. I wanted to go to Dohnanyi, but Sonderegger wouldn't let me and engaged me in a conversation that went more or less as follows:

T: Do you want to start the trial now?
S: The matter is settled.
T: Does that mean the finish of Dohnanyi?
S: It's his own fault. He has worked against the Führer and had every opportunity. How could he work against the Führer, who gave him such a well-paid job. Dohnanyi's behaviour was ungrateful.
T: Do you want to kill him?
S: Evasive answer . . . then: We know that he was the mastermind behind the 20th July plot.
T: Where are you taking him?
S: I don't know yet.
T: Do you already have a charge laid against him and will there still be a trial?
S: We already have all the evidence against him, we don't need anything else.
T: Does that mean death?
S: Shrugged his shoulders.

On the morning of 6th April Huppenkothen also went to Sachsenhausen and set up a hasty court martial together with the commandant of the concentration camp, in which they condemned Dohnanyi, who was lying half unconscious on a stretcher, to death.

In the meantime in the Reich Security Head Office, the governor of the house prison, Gogalla, was ordered to prepare a journey for Saturday, 7th April, to Flossenbürg and from there to Schönberg and Dachau. Gogalla was given several 'secret state papers' that he had to deliver in Flossenbürg, Schönberg and Dachau and that apparently contained instructions concerning who was to be killed and who moved further south. Payne Best, of all people, happened to discover the original of one of these 'secret state papers' in Dachau. It played a part in the trial of Huppenkothen and contained orders concerning the moving on of certain important prisoners, their courteous treatment, and the 'liquidation' of Elser, imprisoned in Dachau, the man who attempted the Bürgerbräu assassination in 1939.[52] The secret state paper with orders concerning Bonhoeffer has not been found. It was probably destroyed, according to instructions.

On Saturday, 7th April, Huppenkothen and his wife were in Gogalla's convoy of cars on the way south with petrol, a large number of cases and important documents, including, apparently, the diary of Admiral

52. Op. cit., pp. 23 f.

Canaris. He arrived on the same day at Flossenbürg concentration camp and immediately began to set up a summary court martial. The S.S. judge Dr. Otto Thorbeck had been summoned from Nuremberg on the evening of 5th April. He travelled on the Sunday morning with a goods train as far as Weiden and cycled the remaining twelve miles up to Flossenbürg. At the camp itself everything was prepared to try Canaris, Oster, Sack, Strünck, Gehre and Bonhoeffer. But the list of people in the camp did not tally. Where was Bonhoeffer? During the Saturday night the inmates of many of the cells were asked if they were not Bonhoeffer, sent over from Buchenwald. Schlabrendorff was shouted at twice: 'But you're Bonhoeffer!'[53] It was the same with Josef Müller and Liedig. He was not there. Then he must have remained with the transport to the south, but it was not too late for the mistake on the night of 3rd-4th in Weiden to be rectified. This organization still had a car park and petrol enough to send a transport command up hill and down dale a distance of at least a hundred miles to Schönberg and back.

The End

In the school at Schönberg they even celebrated Low Sunday. Pünder had the idea of asking Bonhoeffer to hold a morning service, according to his own account and those of Best and Falconer. But Bonhoeffer had no wish to. The majority of his comrades were Catholic. And there was the young Kokorin. Bonhoeffer had given him his Berlin address in return for Kokorin's Moscow one, but he didn't want to ambush him with a church service. But then Kokorin expressed himself in favour of it, and so Bonhoeffer, at the general request, held the service. He read the texts for Quasimodo Sunday, said prayers and explained to his comrades the text of the day: 'With his stripes we are healed' (Isa. 53:5) and 'Blessed be the God and Father of our Lord Jesus Christ! By his great mercy we have been born anew to a living hope through the resurrection of Jesus Christ from the dead' (1 Pet. 1:3). He spoke of the thoughts and decisions that this captivity had produced in everyone. After this service the other prisoners wanted to smuggle Bonhoeffer over to their room so that he could hold a service there also. But it was not long before the door was opened and two civilians called out: 'Prisoner Bonhoeffer, get ready and come with us!'

He was able to get his things together. He wrote his name and address in large letters with a blunt pencil in his Plutarch, in the front, the back and the middle. He left the book behind so that it might reveal a trail in the subsequent chaos. One of Goerdeler's sons took the book and gave it to Bonhoeffer's family years later as the last extant evidence of his life. It was the same book that he had asked for on 17th January and had received in the Reich Security Head Office on 7th February.

53. F. von Schlabrendorff, op. cit., p. 230.

He asked Payne Best to remember him to the Bishop of Chichester if he should ever reach his home. 'This is the end—for me the beginning of life' were the last words of his that Best records.[54] He ran quickly down the stairs and received a farewell greeting from Frau Goerdeler.

The journey this Sunday must have lasted until late evening. The summary court, with Thorbeck as chairman, Huppenkothen as prosecutor, and the camp commandant Kögl as assistant, declares that it sat for a long time. It examined—its officers claimed later—each prisoner individually and confronted them with one another: Canaris and Oster, Sack, Strünck and Gehre, and finally Dietrich Bonhoeffer as well. After midnight Canaris returned to his cell after an absence of some time and signalled by knocking signs to the man in the next cell, the Danish colonel Lunding, that it was all up with him.[55]

Before dawn the first transport of those who were joining the mysterious caravan into the Alps left Flossenbürg: Schacht, Halder, von Bonin, the Schuschnigg family, General Thomas. Gogalla was in charge of this transport. On the way the van stopped in Schönberg and took on Falkenhausen, Kokorin, Best and Falconer, amongst others. In Dachau Martin Niemöller was also one of this select group.

In Flossenbürg the execution took place in the grey dawn of the Monday. The camp doctor saw Bonhoeffer without knowing at the time who he was. Ten years later he wrote:

On the morning of that day between five and six o'clock the prisoners, among them Admiral Canaris, General Oster . . . and *Reichsgerichtsrat* Sack were taken from their cells, and the verdicts of the court martial read out to them. Through the half-open door in one room of the huts I saw Pastor Bonhoeffer, before taking off his prison garb, kneeling on the floor praying fervently to his God. I was most deeply moved by the way this lovable man prayed, so devout and so certain that God heard his prayer. At the place of execution, he again said a short prayer and then climbed the steps to the gallows, brave

54. In P. Best, op. cit., p. 200, we read: 'We bade him goodbye. He drew me aside. "This is the end" he said, "for me the beginning of life", and then he gave me a message to give, if I could, to the Bishop of Chichester, a friend to all evangelical pastors in Germany.' Bishop Bell himself has given a fuller account of these last words. According to the notes that he made straightaway in 1945 when Best told him, they were: 'Tell him (he said) that for me this is the end but also the beginning. With him I believe in the principle of our Universal Christian brotherhood which rises above all national interests, and that our victory is certain—tell him too that I have never forgotten his words at our last meeting' (recounted in the bishop's Göttingen lecture of May 1957, cf. GS I, p. 412). This fuller version is recorded at an earlier point than the one in Payne Best's book. Best was not sufficiently aware of the shared earlier history of Bell and Bonhoeffer to attach much importance to the second part of his message when writing his book. But Bell particularly cherished this reminder of their conversations together in Sweden in 1942, and so he put it down in his notes in 1945.

There is, incidentally, a passage in the letters from Tegel prison that closely resembles Bonhoeffer's last words. When, on 21st August 1944, he spoke of immersing oneself in the life, words, actions, sufferings and death of Jesus, he went on: '. . . it is certain that our joy is hidden in suffering, and our life in death' (LPP, p. 214).

55. A statement by H.-M. Lunding in the Huppenkothen trial, cf. *Urteil*, 1955, pp. 50 f.

and composed. His death ensued after a few seconds. In the almost fifty years that I worked as a doctor, I have hardly ever seen a man die so entirely submissive to the will of God.[56]

Prince Philip of Hesse, for years a prisoner in Flossenbürg, took two books out of a pile of effects in the guard-room on that Monday morning. He discovered in one of them, Kantorowicz's *Friedrich II, von Hohenstaufen*, the name Wilhelm Canaris; in the other, a volume of Goethe illustrated with etchings, Bonhoeffer's name. The books were taken from him. All remaining possessions were burned, like the corpses.

IV THE LAST BLOW

All communication with Hans von Dohnanyi had broken off after the nocturnal visit of his wife to the police hospital on 5th April. According to Sonderegger—and there is no reason to doubt him here—Dohnanyi was executed the same day as Bonhoeffer, 9th April, in Sachsenhausen.

The family's efforts to save the lives of Rüdiger Schleicher and Klaus Bonhoeffer continued in Berlin through the whole of March and again in April.

Rüdiger Schleicher's former chief, Dr. Brandenburg, the head of the air division in the Ministry of Public Transport before 1933, gave a fine portrait of him in his plea for mercy:

His frankness and his love of truth in every situation were clearly unbounded. It seemed as if he really did not see the intrigue and dirty side of life. Despite this his work was always successful. I used to call him jokingly 'our Parsifal'. Lies and deception were quite foreign to his nature. His trust in, and fearlessness before men derived, in him, from the same source: it was the rock-like conviction, which penetrated his whole being, of the reality and truth of 'justice'. The word had for him the gravest religious content. Perhaps there lies here the key to another quality. He always had scruples concerning whether his own ideas really were in tune with justice, whether someone was suffering an injustice, whether the inner meaning of an idea had been really expressed or presented in an entirely truthful way . . . Not that the sureness of his work would have suffered from this ! But he sometimes surprised us by suddenly speaking against his own point of view. His inner thinking was in a state of continual dialogue.

Such a man must have suffered almost beyond the limits of endurance during the period of the interrogations and confrontations. But after the death sentence he radiated an irresistible serenity, cheering up his fellow prisoners with a friendly look during his exercise round the prison yard. He did not say one word about himself in his last letters. When his wife came to see him, she would not accept the farewell letters he had written. She did not want to show him that the fight to obtain a pardon was or might have to be abandoned. Hence these letters are lost.

56. H. Fischer-Hüllstrung, 'A Report from Flossenbürg', IKDB, p. 232.

Klaus Bonhoeffer feared a resumption of the trial almost more than the waiting for execution of the sentence. On a piece of paper, written before the announcement of the death sentence, we read:

I am not afraid of being hanged, but I don't want to see those faces again . . . so much depravity . . . I'd rather die than see those faces again. I have seen the Devil, and I can't forget it.

When Karl-Friedrich Bonhoeffer visited his brother in the visitors' cell at Lehrter Strasse, after the sentence, Klaus told him he had the St. Matthew Passion beside him on his folding table. Karl-Friedrich said that it was nice that he could hear the music in his imagination as he read the score. Klaus answered, 'Yes, but the words also! The words!' The farewell letters that he wrote his parents, his wife and children, have been preserved. In these he writes:

The hope that the family might miraculously emerge quite unscathed from the great disaster I scarcely dare utter. For a long time it has been like a natural catastrophe that men have been undergoing, and nature is extravagant. But I think that the storm will soon pass over our house. There will be an end to the persecutions, and it will seem to the survivors that they have been dreaming . . .

I don't just want to live, but to do the most I can with my life. Since this must now happen through my death, I have made friends with it also. On this ride beweeen death and the Devil, death is a noble companion. The Devil adapts himself to the times and has even worn the cavalier's sword. This is how the Enlightenment idealized him. The Middle Ages, which have talked also of his bad smell, knew him better.

It is, at any rate, a much clearer obligation to die than to live in disordered times, which is why those to whom death was assigned as a task were always called fortunate.[57]

Probably after a quick decision by S.S. Group Leader Müller an execution detachment from the Reich Security Head Office collected sixteen prisoners from the Gestapo section of the prison in Lehrter Strasse on the night of 22nd to 23rd April on the pretext they were being transferred to another place in order to be released. After a hundred yards the S.S. men shot the group in the 'Ulap area' near Lehrter station, among them Klaus Bonhoeffer, Rüdiger Schleicher, Hans John, Friedrich Justus Perels and Albrecht Haushofer.

One of the group, H. Kosney, was able to escape. It was through him that on 31st May the family learned for certain what had happened to Klaus and Rüdiger. They are buried with Friedrich Justus Perels, Hans John and many other unknown victims in a bomb crater in the cemetery of Dorotheenstadt.[58] A memorial service was held for them

---

57. Dietrich and Klaus Bonhoeffer, *Auf dem Wege zur Freiheit. Gedichte und Briefe aus der Haft*, 1946.
58. Cf. the report in the *Frankfurter Allgemeine Zeitung* of 18.7.1962, p. 11.

on 11th June 1945 by their families and survivors from prison.

Meanwhile Josef Müller and Fabian von Schlabrendorff had long before been removed from Flossenbürg and escaped with other survivors over the Alps to Italy and into American custody. There they met Martin Niemöller also. Through them, in the absence of any communication with Berlin, the news of Dietrich Bonhoeffer's fate, reached first Visser 't Hooft in Geneva, and then, via him, Bishop Bell and his sister's family in Oxford. Freudenberg telegraphed to Rieger on 30th May from Geneva:

Just received sad news that Dietrich Bonhoeffer and his Klaus have been murdered in Concentration Camp Clossburg near Neustadt about 15 April short time before liberation region by American Army Stop. Please inform family Leibholz and his friends Stop We are united in deep sorrow and fellowship—Freudenberg.[59]

Maria von Wedemeyer, who at the end of the war was looking for Bonhoeffer in the west of Germany, learned the incredible news in June. His parents were the last to know what had happened. It was when H. B. Gisevius came to Berlin in July and the B.B.C. broadcast a memorial service for Bonhoeffer from London.

Bishop Bell, Franz Hildebrandt and Julius Rieger held this memorial service on 27th July 1945 in Holy Trinity Church, Kingsway, London.[60] The announcement of this public remembrance of a German and the broadcast by the B.B.C. of the function was an unusual event in those months. For the reports of the appalling discoveries in the Bergen-Belsen concentration camp had reached the British public only after the cessation of hostilities and made it very difficult not to make a sweeping judgement concerning the conquered country.

The church was packed to the doors with English people and *emigré* Germans, theologians and laymen, including Bonhoeffer's twin sister and her family.

The bishop described in his sermon what Bonhoeffer had meant for ecumenism, from the first moment of his martyrdom:

His death is a death for Germany—indeed for Europe too . . . his death, like his life, marks a fact of the deepest value in the witness of the Confessional [sic] Church. As one of a noble company of martyrs of differing traditions, he represents both the resistance of the believing soul, in the name of God, to the assault of evil, and also the moral and political revolt of the human conscience against injustice and cruelty. He and his fellows are indeed built upon the foundation of the Apostles and the Prophets. And it was this passion for justice that brought him, and so many others . . . into such close partnership with other resisters, who, though outside the Church, shared the same humanitarian and liberal ideals . . .

59. Cf. J. Rieger, 'Contacts with London', IKDB, p. 103.
60. Cf. *Bonhoeffer Gedenkheft*, 1946.

For him and Klaus . . . there is the resurrection from the dead; for Germany redemption and resurrection, if God pleases to lead the nation through men animated by his spirit, holy and humble and brave like him; for the Church, not only in that Germany which he loved, but the Church Universal which was greater to him than nations, the hope of a new life.[61]

Bonhoeffer's own church, that of Berlin-Brandenburg, was a long way from this attitude when it made such a strict distinction between Christian martyrdom and political resistance. In those same weeks, in a pastoral instruction on the first anniversary of 20th July, it presented Paul Schneider to its congregations as 'a martyr in the full sense of the word' and did not mention Bonhoeffer's name, but said that it could never approve the conspiracy of 20th July 1944, 'whatever the intention behind it might have been. But among those who were forced to suffer there were innumerable people who had never wanted such a conspiracy.'[62]

A similar view was taken by those Bielefeld pastors who appealed to the Bonhoeffer family to protest against the naming of streets after Paul Schneider and Dietrich Bonhoeffer in the midst of members of the resistance, 'because we don't want the names of our colleagues, who were killed for their faith, lumped together with political martyrs.'

Karl Bonhoeffer's answer was:

My son certainly would not have wanted streets to be named after him. On the other hand, I am sure that it would not have been his desire to cut himself off from those who had perished for political reasons, with whom he had lived for years in prison and concentration camps. I should, therefore, prefer to decline making any protest against the decision of the town council, all the more so as the choice of the two ministers seems to indicate that the council has made its selection irrespective of the men's political attitudes.[63]

In those summer months the last surviving brother, Karl-Friedrich Bonhoeffer tried to set up once again his physics institute in Leipzig. Leipzig was about to be handed over to the Russians by the Americans. Cut off from all news, he thought that possibly he might not survive the coming weeks. Thus he wrote the story of the last months for his children who were evacuated to the Harz Mountains:

. . . I want to tell you about all that. Why? Because my thoughts are now there, there in the ruins from where no news reaches us, where three months ago I visited Uncle Klaus in prison after he had been condemned to death. Those Berlin prisons! How little I knew about them a few years ago, and with what different eyes I've come to see them since. The Charlottenburg interrogation prison where Aunt Christel was held for a time, the Tegel military interrogation prison, where Uncle Dietrich was for eighteen months, the military prison at Moabit where Uncle Hans was, the S.S. prison in

61. Op. cit., p. 9.
62. Duplicated copy of the instruction, in the author's possession.
63. Letter of 11.2.1948.

Prinz-Albrecht-Strasse, where Uncle Dietrich was kept behind bars in the basement for six months, and the prison in Lehrter Strasse where Uncle Klaus was tortured and Uncle Rüdiger suffered, and where they were kept for two months after their death sentences.

I waited in front of the heavy iron gates of all these prisons when I was in Berlin during the last years and had things to do there in the way of business. I took Aunt Ursel and Christel, Aunt Emmi and Maria there; they often went every day taking things or collecting them. Often they went for nothing, often they were insulted by contemptible officials, but sometimes they also found a friendly guard who was a human being and delivered greetings, took something outside the prescribed hours or gave food to the prisoners despite the ban.

Ah, the taking of food! It wasn't altogether easy in those last years, and Aunt Ursel in particular couldn't do enough. She became as thin as a skeleton. Those were tragic scenes when Uncle Rüdiger sent out the food again with the message that he had enough. Who believed him? Aunt Ursel sent it in again and it came back again. Uncle Klaus was different! He always consumed everything sent to him. It was not so bad for Uncle Dietrich while he was in Tegel. He got on well there with the prison staff, and the prison commandant was a humane man. It wasn't too bad for Uncle Hans either, to begin with. His prison commandant was almost like a friend to him. But then he became ill and was taken to the Charité Surgical Clinic under Sauerbruch, where I saw him for the last time. After he was taken to prison again he got scarlet fever and diphtheria and was in bed for nearly six months with post-diphtheria paralysis, ending up at the Oranienburg concentration camp and the state hospital of Berlin.

And now! The last time I was in Berlin was at the end of March. I had to go back shortly before grandfather's seventy-seventh birthday. Uncle Klaus and Uncle Rüdiger were still alive; Uncle Hans gave us news via the doctor that did not seem quite without hope. Of Uncle Dietrich, who had been removed from Berlin by the S.S. at the beginning of February, there was no trace. It was probably on 8th April, shortly before my leaving for Friedrichsbrunn to come to you, that I telephoned from Leipzig for the last time to speak to your grandparents. At that time everything was just the same. That is now more than two months ago. What happened before Berlin was occupied by the Russians? Someone who came from there said that 4,000 political prisoners had been killed first. And what happened during the occupation, and afterwards? Are they all still alive? Did grandfather and grandmother survive those difficult days? Both were already exhausted. In the last years grandmother had many attacks of weakness, with loss of memory, a consequence of overwork, excitement and malnutrition over recent years. They had no proper help in the house. Uncle Dietrich spoke at some length to someone on 5th April, near Passau.[64] From there he was supposed to have been taken to the Flossenbürg concentration camp near Weiden.

Why isn't he here yet? . . .

When the family had learnt everything, Karl Bonhoeffer wrote to an *emigré* colleague:[65]

64. That was the day in Regensburg. 65. Professor Jossman in Boston.

I hear you know that we have been through a lot and lost two sons and two sons-in-law through the Gestapo. You can imagine that that has not been without its effect on us old folk. For years we had the tension caused by anxiety for those arrested and for those not yet arrested but in danger. But since we were all agreed on the need to act, and my sons were also fully aware of what they had to expect if the plot miscarried and had resolved if necessary to lay down their lives, we are sad, but also proud of their attitude, which has been consistent. We have fine memories of both sons from prison . . . that are deeply touching to both of us and their friends.

ACKNOWLEDGEMENTS

The editor, translators and publishers gratefully acknowledge their indebtedness to SCM Press, London, and The Macmillan Company, New York, for permission to reprint material from the following books: *The Cost of Discipleship* by Dietrich Bonhoeffer, © SCM Press Ltd. 1959; *Creation and Fall* by Dietrich Bonhoeffer, Copyright © SCM Press Ltd. 1959; *Ethics* by Dietrich Bonhoeffer, Copyright © 1955 by The Macmillan Company, © in the English translation by SCM Press Ltd. 1955; *Letters and Papers from Prison* by Dietrich Bonhoeffer (revised edition), Copyright by The Macmillan Company 1953, © SCM Press Ltd. 1967.

ACKNOWLEDGMENTS

CHRONOLOGICAL TABLE

1906   4th February, Dietrich Bonhoeffer born in Breslau

1912   Father appointed to Berlin University; family move to Berlin

1923   Theological studies in Tübingen

1924   Further theological studies in Berlin

1927   Qualifies for licentiate under R. Seeberg with *Sanctorum Communio*

1928   17th January, first theological examination; 15th February, assistant pastor in Barcelona

1929   Assistant to W. Lütgert in Berlin (until 1930)

1930   18th July, qualifies for university teaching with *Act and Being*; 5th September, leaves for New York to study at Union Theological Seminary

1931   In July first meeting with Karl Barth in Bonn; from 1st August onwards lecturer in the theological faculty at Berlin; 1st-5th September, attends World Alliance Conference at Cambridge where he is appointed Youth Secretary; 15th November, ordination; winter 1931-2, lecture course on 'The History of Systematic Theology in the Twentieth Century', and seminar on 'The Concept of Philosophy and Protestant Theology'; from November (until March 1932), in charge of a confirmation class in Berlin-Wedding

1932   In the summer term, lecture course on 'The Nature of the Church', and seminar, 'Is there a Christian Ethic?'; buys a hut at Biesenthal; July and August, at ecumenical meetings in the Westerburg, in Ciernohorské Kúpele, Geneva and Gland; winter term, lecture course on 'Creation and Sin' (published in 1933 as *Creation and Fall*) and 'Recent Theology', also seminar on 'Problems of a Theological Anthropology'

1933   1st March, radio talk on 'Changes in the Concept of Führer'; April, article on 'The Church and the Jewish Question'; summer term, lecture course on 'Christology'; August, pamphlet on 'The Aryan Clause in the Church'; September, preliminary work with Niemöller on Pastors' Emergency League pledge; 17th October, takes up London pastorate

1934   22nd-30th August, ecumenical conference at Fanö; 28th August, co-opted as member of Universal Christian Council for 'Life and Work'; 4th-8th September, with Jean Lasserre in Bruay; 5th November, London parishes repudiate the Reich Church Government

1935   March, visits Anglican communities; 15th April, farewell visit to Bishop Bell in Chichester; 26th April, preachers' seminary opens at Zingsthof (by the Baltic); 24th June, removal to Finkenwalde; July, article on 'The Confessing Church and the Ecumenical Movement';

6th September, proposal to establish a House of Brethren made to Church Administration

1936   February, last lecture in the Berlin faculty on 'Discipleship'; 29th February - 10th March, preachers' seminary visits Denmark and Sweden; 22nd April, lecture in Finkenwalde, 'On the Question of the Church Community'; 5th August, authorization to teach at university withdrawn; 20th August, 'Life and Work' at Chamby

1937   February, last participation in an ecumenical conference in London; 1st July, Niemöller arrested; end of September, seminary closed by police; November, 27 former Finkenwalde seminarists under arrest, *Cost of Discipleship* published; 5th December, beginning of collective pastorates in Köslin and Gross-Schlönwitz (later Sigurdshof)

1938   11th January, expulsion from Berlin; February, first contacts with Sack, Oster, Canaris and Beck; 20th June, meeting of former Finkenwaldians at Zingst, Bible study 'Temptation'; September, *Life Together* written in Göttingen; 26th October, lecture on 'Our Way in accordance with the Testimony of the Bible'

1939   10th March, journey to London for talks with Bishop Bell, Visser 't Hooft, Reinhold Niebuhr and Gerhard Leibholz; 2nd June, leaves for U.S.A.; 20th June, letter of refusal to Leiper; 27th July, back in Berlin

1940   15th March, end of term in Köslin and Sigurdshof; two days later Gestapo orders closure; June and July, visitations in East Prussia; 14th July, dissolution of study conference in Blöstau; August, talks with Oster and Dohnanyi on extra-parochial status in regard to work for the *Abwehr*; 4th September, forbidden to speak in public and required to report regularly to the police; September and October, working on *Ethics* at Klein-Krössin; 30th October, seconded to *Abwehr* office in Munich; from 17th November, visits the Benedictine abbey in Ettal

1941   24th February - 24th March, first journey to Switzerland; 27th March, forbidden to print or publish; 29th August - 26th September, second journey to Switzerland, with Visser 't Hooft writes to W. Paton on *The Church and the New Order*; October, first deportations of Jews from Berlin, Operation 7

1942   10th-18th April, journey with Helmuth von Moltke to Norway and Stockholm; May, third journey to Switzerland; 30th May - 2nd June, flies to Stockholm to meet Bishop Bell

1943   17th January, engagement to Maria von Wedemeyer; 13th March and 21st March, attempted assassinations of Hitler; 5th April, house search and arrest, placed in Tegel prison; at the same time, Hans von Dohnanyi and Dr. Josef Müller arrested with their wives; 29th April, warrant of arrest drawn up, charged with 'subversion of the armed forces'

1944   January, chief interrogator Roeder dismissed; February, Canaris dismissed and the *Abwehr* incorporated into the Reich Security Head Office; 6th March, first big daylight raid on Tegel; 30th April, first theological letter; May, charge indefinitely postponed; 20th July, von Stauffenberg's attempt on Hitler's life; 22nd September, Gestapo Commissar Sonderegger discovers files in the *Abwehr* bunker at Zossen; early October, escape plan; 5th October, plan abandoned because of arrest of Klaus Bonhoeffer (brother), Rüdiger Schleicher (brother-in-law) and F. J. Perels and consequent fear of reprisals; 8th October, removed to the Gestapo cellars in the Prinz-Albrecht-Strasse

1945   7th February, in Buchenwald concentration camp; 3rd April, removed from Buchenwald to Regensburg; 5th April, annihilation order announced at Hitler's midday conference; 6th April, moved to Schönberg (Bayerischer Wald); 8th April, to Flossenbürg; during the night, summary court martial; 9th April, executed together with Oster, Sack, Canaris, Strünck and Gehre; von Dohnanyi killed in Sachsenhausen; 23rd April, Klaus Bonhoeffer, Rüdiger Schleicher and F. J. Perels killed in Berlin

INDEX